# Grades K–2

Aardema, Verna. *Borreguita and the Coyote.* Illustrated by Petra Mathers. Knopf, 1991.

Anno, Mitsumasa. *Anno's Counting Book.* Crowell, 1977.

Bang, Molly. *When Sophie Gets Angry-Really, Really Angry.* Scholastic, 1999.

Best, Cari. *Three Cheers for Catherine the Great.* Illustrated by Giselle Potter. DK Ink, 1999.

Curlee, Lunn. *Rushmore.* Scholastic, 1999.

Daly, Niki. *Jamela's Dress.* Farrar Straus Giroux, 1999.

Diakité, Baba Wagué. *The Hatseller and the Monkeys A West African Folktale.* Scholastic, 1999.

Cooney, Barbara. *Miss Rumphius.* Viking, 1982.

de Paola, Tomie. *Strega Nona.* Prentice Hall, 1975.

Gibbons, Gail. *Bats.* Holiday House, 1999.

Gray, Libba Moore. *Small Green Snake.* Illustrated by Holly Meade. Orchard, 1994.

Henkes, Kevin. *Lilly's Purple Plastic Purse.* Greenwillow, 1996.

Hesse, Karen. *Come On Rain*! Illustrated by Jon J Muth. Scholastic, 1999.

Huck, Charlotte. *Princess Furball.* Illustrated by Anita Lobel. Greenwillow, 1989.

Hutchins, Pat. *The Doorbell Rang.* Greenwillow, 1986.

Hyman, Trina Schart. *Little Red Riding Hood.* Holiday House, 1983.

Lillegard, Dee. *Wake up House: Rooms Full of Poems.* Illustrated by Don Carter. Knopf, 2000.

Lobel, Arnold. *Frog and Toad Are Friends.* Harper & Row, 1970.

Pomerantz, Charlotte. *Here Comes H...* Nancy Winslow Parker. ...

Prelutsky, Jack. Ed. *The Ra... Poetry for Children.* Illus... by Arnold Lobel. Random House, 1983.

Sandburg, Carl. *The Huckabuck Family and How They Raised Popcorn in Nebraska and Quit and Came Back.* Illustrated by David Small. Farrar Straus Giroux.

Sendak, Maurice. *Where the Wild Things Are.* Harper & Row, 1963.

Silverman, Erica. *Don't Fidget a Feather.* Illustrated by S. D. Schindler. Macmillan, 1994.

Sierra, Judy. *Tasty Baby Belly Buttons.* Illustrated by Meilo So. Knopf, 1999.

Steig, William. *Doctor De Soto.* Farrar, Straus & Giroux, 1982.

Steptoe, John. *Mufaro's Beautiful Daughter: An African Tale.* Lothrop, Lee & Shepard, 1987.

Stevens, Janet. *Tops and Bottoms.* Harcourt Brace, 1995.

Wilder, Laura Ingalls. *The Little House in the Big Woods.* Illustrated by Garth Williams. Harper & Row, 1953.

Williams, Vera. *A Chair for My Mother.* Greenwillow, 1982.

Yolen, Jane. *Owl Moon.* Illustrated by John Schoenherr. Philomel, 1987.

# Grades 2–4

Aardema, Verna. *Misoso: Once Upon a Time Tales from Africa.* Illustrated by Reynolds Ruffins. Applesoup, 1994.

Ahlberg, Alan. *The Giant Baby.* Illustrated by Fritz Wegner. Viking, 1995.

Arnosky, Jim. *All About Turtles.* Scholastic, 2000.

Burnett, Francis Hodgson. *The Secret Garden.* Illustrated by Tasha Tudor. Harper & Row, 1987.

Cameron, Ann. *The Most Beautiful Place in the World.* Illustrated by Thomas B. Allen. Knopf, 1988.

Cleary, Beverly. *Ramona Quimby, Age 8.* Illustrated by Alan Tiegreen. Morrow, 1981.

Cole, Joanna. *The Magic School Bus Explores the Senses.* Illustrated by Bruce Degen. Scholastic, 1999.

de Regniers, Beatrice Schenk, ed. *Sing a Song of Popcorn.* Scholastic, 1988.

English, Karen. *Francie.* Farrar Straus Giroux, 1999.

Erdrich, Louise. *The Birchbark House.* Hyperion, 1999.

Fleischman, Paul. *Weslandia.* Illustrated by Kevin Hawkes. Candlewick, 1999.

Fleischman, Sid. *The Whipping Boy.* Illustrated by Peter Sis. Greenwillow, 1986.

Fritz, Jean. *Where Do You think You're Going, Christopher Columbus?* Illustrated by Margot Tomes. Putnam, 1980.

George, Kristine O'Connell. *Little Dog Poems.* Clarion, 1999.

Giblin, James Cross. *The Mystery of the Mammoth Bones: And How it Was Solved.* HarperCollins, 1999.

Greenfield, Eloise. *Honey I Love and Other Poems.* Illustrated by Leo and Diane Dillon. Crowell, 1978.

Grimm, Jacob, and Wilhelm Grimm. *Snow White and the Seven Dwarfs.* Illustrated by Nancy Ekhom Burkert. Farrar, Straus & Giroux, 1972.

Hesse, Karen. *Just Juice.* Scholastic, 1998.

Horvath, Polly. *Trolls.* Farrar, Straus, Giroux, 1999.

Lester, Julius. *The Tales of Uncle Remus: The Adventures of Brer Rabbit.* Illustrated by Jerry Pinkney. Dial, 1987.

Lewis, C.S. *The Lion, the Witch, and the Wardrobe.* Illustrated by Pauline Baynes. Macmillan, 1961.

Lisle, Janet Taylor. *The Lost Flower Children.* Philomel, 1999.

MacLachlan, Patricia. *Sarah, Plain and Tall.* Harper & Row, 1985.

McKay, Hilary. *Dog Friday.* McElderry, 1995.

Philip, Neal. *Stockings of Buttermilk: American Folktales.* Illustrated by Jacqueline Marr. Clarion, 1999.

Pullman, Philip. *I Was a Rat.* Knopf, 2000.

Rathman, Peggy. *Officer Buckle and Gloria.* Putnam, 1995.

... d Alligators.
HarperCollins, 1999.
Swinburne, Stephen R. *Once a Wolf: How Wildlife Biologists Fought to Bring Back the Gray Wolf.*

Photographs by Jim Brandenburg. Houghton Mifflin, 1999.
Stanley, Diane. *Joan of Arc.* Morrow, 1998.

## Grades 4–6

Alexander, Lloyd. *Gypsy Rizka.* Dutton, 1999.

Armstrong, Jennifer. *Shipwreck at the Bottom of the Worlds: the Extraordinary True Story of Shakleton and the Endurance.* Crown, 1998.

Bartoletti, Susan. *Kids On Strike.* Houghton Mifflin, 1999.

Babbitt, Natalie. *Tuck Everlasting.* Farrar, Straus & Giroux, 1975.

Collier, James Lincoln, and Christopher Collier. *My Brother Sam Is Dead.* Four Winds, 1974.

Curtis, Christopher Paul. *Bud, Not Buddy.* Delacorte, 1999.

Dorris, Michael. *Morning Girl.* Hyperion, 1992.

Fleischman, Paul. *Joyful Noise: Poems for Two Voices.* Illustrated by Eric Beddows. Harper & Row, 1988.

Freedman, Russell. *Lincoln: A Photobiography.* Clarion, 1987.

George, Jean Craighead. *Julie of the Wolves.* Harper & Row, 1972.

Hamilton, Virginia. *Bluish.* Scholastic, 1999.

Howard, Ellen. *The Gate in the Wall.* Atheneum, 1999.

Hughes, Langston. *The Dream Keeper and Other Poems.* Illustrated by Brian Pinkney. Knopf, 1994.

Janeczko, Paul B., ed. *The Place My Words Are Looking For.* Bradbury, 1990.

L'Engle, Madeleine. *A Wrinkle in Time.* Farrar, Straus & Giroux, 1972.

Levine, Gail Carson. *Dave at Night.* HarperCollins, 1999.

Lewin, Ted and Betsy. *Gorilla Walk.* Lothrop Lee & Shepard, 1999.

Lowry, Lois. *Number the Stars.* Houghton Mifflin, 1989.

Mayne, William. *Hob and the Goblins.* Illustrated by Norman Messenger. Dorling Kindersley, 1994.

Myers, Walter Dean. *Scorpions.* Harper & Row, 1988.

Naylor, Phyllis Reynolds. *Shiloh.* Atheneum, 1991.

Paterson, Katherine. *Bridge to Terabithia.* Illustrated by Donna Diamond. Harper & Row, 1977.

Polacco, Patricia. *Pink and Say.* Philomel, 1994.

Rylant, Cynthia. *Missing May.* Orchard, 1992.

Schertle, Alice. *I am the Cat.* Illustrated by Mark Buehner. Lothrop, Lee & Shepard, 1999.

Scieszka, Jon. *The True Story of the Three Little Pigs by A. Wolf.* Illustrated by Lane Smith. Viking, 1989.

Spinelli, Jerry. *Maniac McGee.* Little, Brown, 1990.

Taylor, Mildred. *The Well.* Dial, 1995.

Warren, Andrea. *Orphan Train Rider: One Boy's Story.* Houghton Mifflin, 1996.

White, Ruth. *Belle Prater's Boy.* Farrar, Straus & Giroux, 1996.

## Grades 6–8

Almond, David. *Skellig.* Delacorte, 1999.

Billingsley, Frannie. *The Folk Keeper.* Atheneum, 1999.

Calabro, Marian. *Perilous Journey of the Donner Party.* Clarion, 1999.

Cart, Michael. *Tomorrowland: Ten Stories About the Future.* Scholastic, 1999.

Choi, Sook Nyul. *Year of Impossible Goodbyes.* Houghton Mifflin, 1991.

Cofer, Judith Ortiz. *An Island Like You: Stories from the Barrio.* Orchard, 1995.

Colman, Penny. *Girls: A History of Growing Up Female in America.* Scholastic, 2000.

Cooper, Susan. *King of Shadows,* Simon & Schuster, 1999.

Cooper, Susan. *The Dark Is Rising.* Atheneum, 1973.

Cormier, Robert. *Frenchtown Summer.* Delacorte, 1999.

Crossley-Holland, Kevin. *The World of King Arthur and His Court: People, Places, Legends and Lore.* Illustrated by Peter Malone. Dutton, 1999.

Cushman, Karen. *The Midwife's Apprentice.* Clarion, 1995.

Dunbar, Paul Laurence. *Jump Back Honey.* Hyperion, 1999.

Fletcher, Ralph. *I Am Wings: Poems About Love.* Bradbury, 1995.

Holt, Kimberly Willis. *When Zachary Beaver Came to Town.* Holt, 1999.

Hickam, Homer H. *Rocket Boys: A Memoir.* Delacorte, 1999.

Jiang, Ji-Li. *Red Scarf Girl: Memoir of the Cultural Revolution.* HarperCollins, 1997.

Lowry, Lois. *The Giver.* Houghton Mifflin, 1993.

Lunge-Larson, Lise. *The Troll with No Heart in His Body and Other Tales of Trolls from Norway.* Betsy Bowen, Houghton Mifflin, 1999.

Kindl, Patricia. *Owl in Love.* Houghton Mifflin, 1993.

L'Engle, Madeleine. *Ring of Endless Light.* Farrar, Straus & Giroux, 1980.

Le Guin, Ursula. *A Wizard of Earthsea.* Illustrated by Ruth Robbins. Houghton Mifflin, 1968.

Nye, Naomi Shihab. *What Have You Lost?* Greenwillow, 1999.

Paterson, Katherine. *Lyddie.* Dutton, 1991.

Taylor, Mildred. *Roll of Thunder Hear My Cry.* Dial, 1976.

*G*reg Couch, *the talented illustrator of such books as* Moon Ball *by* Jane Yolen, Wild Child *by* Lynn Plourde, *and* The Cello of Mr. O *by Jane Cutler is a superb colorist with a unique vision. His cover for this seventh edition of* Children's Literature in the Elementary School *seems to glow with a special light, a glow that recalls Louise Rosenblatt's "live circuit" that exists between a reader and a book. The child who holds the book holds a wonderful key to the multi-verse that can be found in reading. Her own delight in books is attracting a community of readers, the community that brightens classrooms, libraries, and homes when children find true joy in reading.*

# Children's Literature
# in the Elementary School

Seventh Edition
Revised by Barbara Z. Kiefer

**Charlotte S. Huck**
*Professor Emeritus*
*The Ohio State University*

**Susan Hepler**
*Children's Literature Specialist*
*Alexandria, Virginia*

**Janet Hickman**
*The Ohio State University*

**Barbara Z. Kiefer**
*Teacher's College, Columbia University*

Boston   Burr Ridge, IL   Dubuque, IA   Madison, WI   New York   San Francisco   St. Louis
Bangkok   Bogotá   Caracas   Lisbon   London   Madrid
Mexico City   Milan   New Delhi   Seoul   Singapore   Sydney   Taipei   Toronto

*McGraw-Hill Higher Education*
*A Division of The McGraw-Hill Companies*

CHILDREN'S LITERATURE IN THE ELEMENTARY SCHOOL
SEVENTH EDITION

Published by McGraw-Hill, an imprint of The McGraw-Hill Companies, Inc., 1221 Avenue
of the Americas, New York, NY 10020. Copyright © 2001, 1997 by The McGraw-Hill
Companies, Inc. All rights reserved. No part of this publication may be reproduced or
distributed in any form or by any means, or stored in a database or retrieval system, without
the prior written consent of The McGraw-Hill Companies, Inc., including, but not limited to
in any network or other electronic storage or transmission, or broadcast for distance learning.

Some ancillaries, including electronic and print components, may not be available to customers outside
the United States.

This book is printed on acid-free paper.

1 2 3 4 5 6 7 8 9 0 VNH/VNH 0 9 8 7 6 5 4 3 2 1 0

ISBN 0–07–232228–4

Vice president and editor-in-chief: *Thalia Dorwick*
Editorial director: *Jane E. Vaicunas*
Sponsoring editor: *Beth Kaufman*
Developmental editor: *Cara Harvey*
Marketing manager: *Daniel M. Loch*
Senior project manager: *Kay J. Brimeyer*
Media producer: *Lance Gerhart*
Senior production supervisor: *Sandra Hahn*
Coordinator of freelance design: *Rick D. Noel*
Cover/interior designer: *Maureen McCutcheon*
Cover illustration: *Greg Couch*
Senior photo research coordinator: *Lori Hancock*
Supplement coordinator: *Tammy Juran*
Compositor: *Shepherd, Inc.*
Typeface: *10/12 Sabon*
Printer: *Von Hoffman Press, Inc.*

**Library of Congress Cataloging-in-Publication Data**

Children's literature in the elementary school / Charlotte S. Huck . . . [et al.].—7th ed.
    p.    cm.
    Includes bibliographical references and index.
    ISBN 0–07–232228–4 (acid-free paper)
    1. Literature—Study and teaching (Elementary)—United States.   2. Children's
literature—Study and teaching (Elementary)—United States.   I. Huck, Charlotte S.

LB1575.5.U5  H79   2001
372.64—dc21                                                    00–035492
                                                               CIP

www.mhhe.com

To all those students and
teachers whom we have
taught and from whom we
have learned . . .

# Brief Contents

# Contents

*Chapter 3*

The Changing World
of Children's Books  66

*Part Two*        *Exploring Children's Literature*        115

*Chapter 4*

Books to Begin On  116

*Chapter 5*

Picture Books 166

*Chapter 6*

Traditional Literature 229

# Chapter 7

Modern Fantasy   300

# Chapter 8

Poetry   349

# Chapter 9

# Chapter 10

# Chapter 11

# *Part Three  Developing a Literature Program*   567

# Features Guide

# Guidelines

# Webs of Possibilities

# Into the Classroom

# Preface

In 1978 I had returned to college to obtain a master's degree in Reading. A course in children's literature was required and my instructor had ordered Charlotte Huck's *Children's Literature in the Elementary School,* the third edition, as the course text. It had a silver cover, black and white photographs, and was 781 pages long. That book opened up a new world to me. I had always been an enthusiastic reader and teacher who loved reading to my first, fourth and fifth graders, but I had no idea of the thousands of wonderful books that were written for children. Nor had I known how to choose the right book for the right child, nor how to develop a reading program that placed real books in the center.

When I completed my degree and received my certification as a reading specialist, I returned to the classroom and a wonderful group of second graders. The silver edition of Charlotte's book became my "bible," as I struggled to implement a book-centered program in the face of my school's required mastery learning curriculum, an approach called ECRI (similar to the DISTAR program). Concerned with the rigidity of this approach, I began looking for a doctoral program that would provide a child-centered alternative and that would value my love of books and my background in art. Knowing that Charlotte Huck would be speaking at a regional IRA conference, I wrote to her and asked if she could spare a few minutes to speak with me about Ohio State's doctoral program. She not only replied with a lovely note, but she invited me to lunch. We talked for two hours and at the end I knew I had found a mentor in Charlotte and an intellectual home at Ohio State's doctoral program in Language, Literature and Reading. Charlotte became my advisor and I spent three wonderful years of study. It was an exciting time to be a doctoral student as research in psycholinguistics and socio-linguistics and in reading and writing processes was beginning to change the way we saw the teaching of literacy. Moreover, Charlotte played a major role in the field as one of the first and foremost scholars to understand that children's literature was central to children's literacy.

Also at Ohio State at the time were two women who became wonderful friends. Janet Hickman had just finished her own doctoral work and taught several of my classes. Susan Hepler, then a fellow doctoral student, provided me with critical understandings about literature and introduced me to classrooms where teachers were doing all that I had wanted to do with literature-based teaching. Charlotte, Janet, and Susan continued to guide me personally as I finished my degree and moved on to my own professional work. Their voices were also present in each subsequent edition of *Children's Literature in the Elementary School.* When they each decided to "retire" from active involvement with the book, I was thrilled to be asked to take it over. Their profound ideas and their passion for books and children have continued to resonate for me in this seventh edition of the text, and which I hope will continue to guide me in the future.

## Audience

The seventh edition of *Children's Literature in the Elementary School* is written, as it has always been, for all adults with an interest in providing good literature for children. It also provides a rationale and suggestions to teachers for planning and evaluating a literature-based curriculum. The text is designed for classes in children's literature at the pre-service and graduate levels in education or English departments and in library schools in colleges and universities. It is also meant to serve as a resource for classroom teachers and librarians.

## Purposes

The primary purpose in writing this textbook is the same as in the previous six editions—to share knowledge and enthusiasm for the literature of childhood with students, teachers, and librarians in the hope that they, in turn, will communicate their excitement about books to the children they teach.

As a nation, we have become so concerned with teaching the skills of reading that we have often neglected to help children discover the joys of reading. We have always recognized the importance of story and real books in developing readers who not only know how to read but do read. I believe that children become readers only by reading many books of their own choosing and by hearing high-quality literature read aloud with obvious delight and enthusiasm. It is my hope that the students, teachers, and librarians who own this book will have the information and the resources to be able to create in children a love of good books and a joy in reading them.

The growth of the field of children's literature has been phenomenal since the first edition of this text was published in 1961. With more than ninety thousand children's books in print, prospective and in-service teachers and librarians need a guide, based on a knowledge of book-selection criteria and an understanding of children's responses to literature, for selecting the best ones. In addition, educators are using children's literature across the curriculum. They need a book that will enable them to plan and develop programs for their classrooms and libraries.

## Organization

The three-part organization of *Children's Literature in the Elementary School* emphasizes the triple focus of this text: the reader, the book, and teaching. Part One focuses on the values and criteria for choosing and using literature with children at various stages in their development. It also includes a historical overview of the ways in which children's literature has changed over the years. Part Two provides an in-depth look at the various genres of children's literature and establishes evaluative criteria for each genre. Each of these chapters has been written with children at the center and includes references and resources for involving children in exploring books across the curriculum. Part Three explores this curricular strand in depth by focusing on the teaching, planning, and evaluating of literature-based programs.

## New To This Edition

For this edition I have considered the changes that have occurred in approaches to teaching and in the publishing and marketing of children's books over the last forty years. During this time, the research base supporting the centrality of good literature has grown, more teachers have been putting this research into practice in literature-based classrooms, and more and more books have been published for children. At the same time, as a result of state requirements in teacher preparation and licensing, courses in children's literature have often been merged into courses in Language Arts or are offered only as electives. I

continue to believe, therefore, that there is a critical need for an in-depth text on children's literature, one that will provide support for teachers and librarians beyond the confines of a single college course. In the seventh edition I have carefully considered what has always been the central purpose of this text—the sharing of knowledge and enthusiasm for the literature of childhood—and I have attempted to streamline the seventh edition in keeping with that goal. I am pleased that the widespread use of the Internet makes it possible to provide additional supporting materials and information, including an extended database and a website.

The text has been updated to reflect new trends in children's literature. The book lists and examples have been revised to include children's literature that has been printed since the sixth edition was published. I would particularly like to call your attention to the following new features and content included in this new edition:

**Expanded and Highlighted Multicultural Coverage:**  In this textbook, I have discussed multicultural literature as a part of each genre or subject area. Students are introduced to picture storybooks, poetry, novels, informational books, and biographies about people of all races and all cultural backgrounds. A section on evaluating multicultural literature has been added to Chapter 1, and Chapters 5, 8, 9, and 10 each have subsections on multicultural literature. Watch for the multicultural icon in the headings that highlight this content and look at the Features Guide (p. xiv) for a listing of multicultural topics. I believe that this approach assures that the literature and accomplishments of all groups will be a part of every subject taught instead of separated out from the heart of the curriculum.

**Chapters Reorganized:**

- Chapter 5, formerly titled "Picture Storybooks" has been re-titled "Picture Books" and reorganized to clarify understandings about the aesthetic qualities of all picture books.
- The chapter formerly titled "Informational Books" has been re-titled "Nonfiction" to reflect new understandings about this genre.
- In keeping with my attempt to streamline the text, Chapters 13 and 14 have been combined and condensed. I have provided an introduction to literacy programs and shown how children's literature can form the foundation for these programs. I have included an overview of the types of activities that can help children to explore books more fully and to understand them more deeply. Finally, I have also considered the importance of school and community relationships in planning literature programs and made suggestions for assessment and evaluation.

**Expanded WEBs:** In the seventh edition each genre chapter now includes a "WEB" that pictures the possibilities for exploring "Wonderfully Exciting Books." These Webs are especially designed to provide students with a picture of classroom literature exploration. The Webs present suggestions for discussion and activities that are meant to lead children back into books in order to increase their understanding and appreciation of literature and the wider world. New Webs for this edition include *Learning to Read Naturally* in Chapter 4, Lois Lowry's *The Giver* in Chapter 7, *Growing Up Is Hard to Do* in Chapter 9, *The World Beneath Your Feet* in Chapter 11, and *Life Stories* in Chapter 12. Special features such as "Resources for Teaching," "Guidelines," and "Teaching Features" have been updated and added to. New to this edition are an "Into the Classroom" feature that provides additional suggestions for classroom activities and a "Personal Explorations" feature that suggests activities for professionals in college classes.

**"Into the Classroom":** This new feature, located at the end of each chapter, provides additional suggestions for classroom activities.

**"Personal Explorations":** Each chapter includes these suggested activities for the reader to reflect upon and apply what he or she learned in the chapter.

**Beautiful New Design:** The text's interior has been redesigned to be as much a piece of art as the children's literature illustrations it holds. The design is meant to engage students as they journey through the world of children's literature.

**Cover Illustration by Greg Couch:** The seventh edition's cover was created specifically for this text by children's book illustrator Greg Couch. For more information about the cover illustration, see page i.

**Updated Research and Children's Books:** Although the title of this book is *Children's Literature in the Elementary School,* throughout the book I have attempted to include titles that reflect the interests and developmental needs of children from birth through middle school. Careful attention was given to identifying out-of-print books and most of these were removed from the discussion. Each chapter has been rewritten to include the latest research and latest books. Over nine hundred new titles have been added to this edition, and new color pictures have been used throughout the text.

**Children's Literature CD-Rom Database:** This manipulable database—including more than 4,000 children's literature titles—is included with each new copy of this text. In addition, the database is available online at www.mhhe.com/huck and www.mhhe.com/childlit.

**Online Learning Center Website:** *Children's Literature* is accompanied by a comprehensive website that includes learning extensions and resources for both the instructor and student including quizzing, web links, and much more!

As children's literature becomes more central to the curriculum, teachers and librarians need a book that will serve for many years as a reference as well as provide thorough coverage of the issues and genres in children's literature. I have hoped to produce, from endpaper to endpaper, a practical textbook that will serve as a resource both for students who are just beginning their teaching and for teachers and librarians already in the field. I believe teachers and librarians are professional people who want a book of substance, documented with pertinent research and based on real practice in the classroom. This is the kind of book I have tried to write.

## Special Features

*Children's Literature in the Elementary School* has long been regarded as the source for comprehensive information about children's literature and how to use children's literature in the classroom. The text's special features exemplify why this text holds an important spot on teachers' bookshelves:

- **Teaching Features** focus on ways teachers have actually used literature as the heart curriculum.
- The text is full of samples of children's work, photographs, and examples of **classroom applications** of children's literature.
- **Guidelines** provide criteria for evaluating books within each genre, as well as suggestions and criteria for evaluating children's responses to literature and literature-based programs.
- **Resources for Teaching** present a wide variety of useful information regarding children, book titles, and curriculum concerns in a compact, easily accessible format.
- While historically praised as reading like a novel itself, the text also has a strong scholarly foundation. Footnotes in each chapter and Related Readings provide **an impeccable and current research base.**
- **Related Readings** at the end of each chapter present annotated selections of books, articles, and research relevant to the chapter discussion.
- Each chapter concludes with an **extensive listing of children's literature** related to the chapter. Colored tabs make these easy to reference.
- The text includes almost **300 color children's book illustrations** chosen especially to match and augment the text's coverage.
- Three appendices—**Children's Book Awards, Book Selection Aids** (including selected professional websites) and **Publisher's Addresses** (including book club addresses)—provide invaluable resources.

- Endpapers serve as an introductory core to the field of children's literature by providing an **updated list of 170 books to read aloud** to six overlapping age groups.
- The *Features Guide* following the table of contents lists all the text's multicultural topics and features for easy reference.

## Teaching and Learning Resources

This edition of *Children's Literature* is accompanied by an expanded number of supplemental resources and learning aids for instructors and students.

### For the Instructor:

**Instructor's Manual:** Revised for this edition based on feedback by professors who have used it, the instructor's manual is a valuable resource for teaching and evaluating students' understanding of literature.

**Create your own course website using PageOut:** Simply plug the course information into a template and click one of 16 designs. The process takes no time at all and leaves instructors with a professionally designed website. Powerful features include an interactive course syllabus that lets you post content and links, an online gradebook, lecture notes, bookmarks, and even a discussion board where students can discuss course-related topics. For an example, please visit www.mhhe.com/pageout.

### CD-Rom and Website Resources for the Instructor and Student:

*Children's Literature* **CD-Rom Database:** This manipulable database—including more than 4,000 children's literature titles—is included with each new copy of this text. In addition, the database is available online at www.mhhe.com/childlit.

**Online Learning Center Website (www.mhhe.com/huck):** *Children's Literature* is accompanied by a comprehensive website that includes learning extensions and resources for both the instructor and student including quizzing, web links, and much more! Watch for the icon at the end of each chapter that reminds you to visit this site!

*ChildLit* **(www.mhhe.com/childlit):** *ChildLit* invites you to explore the world of children's literature through the Internet. This comprehensive resource includes a manipulative database of children's literature titles; and links to authors' and illustrators' sites (and those written about them), publishers' sites, other children's literature websites, book reviews, book lists, book award information and winners, curriculum ideas, and many other resources. Each month an author and book is highlighted. This is an interactive site—share your thoughts about children's literature and your teaching ideas. Visit frequently to see the currently highlighted author and book, expanded content, and contributions by others. Whenever you are researching children's literature topics on the web, start your voyage here!

## Acknowledgments

No one writes a book of this magnitude without the help of friends. I am deeply indebted to many people: the teachers, librarians, and children in the schools where I have always been welcomed; to students at The Ohio State University, Teachers College, and elsewhere, both undergraduates and graduate students, who have shared their insights into children's responses and interpretations of literature; and those teachers who have sent pictures of, and allowed me to take pictures in, their classrooms. I thank them all and hope they continue to share their classroom experiences and enthusiasm for children's literature.

Specifically, I wish to express our appreciation to the following teachers and schools who shared their teaching ideas, children's work, and classroom photos with us in this and past editions: Carmen Gordillo, The Beginning with Children School in Brooklyn, NY; Mary Sullivan Gallivan, PS 124 and Ilana Dubin-Spiegel, PS 116 in New York City; Faye Freeman of William B. Ward Elementary School in New Rochelle, New York; Jean M. Norman of Anna Maria College, Paxton, Massachusetts; Marlene Harbert and other faculty members at Barrington Road School, Upper Arlington, Ohio; Diane Driessen, librarian, and Jean Sperling, Peggy Harrison, Sheryl Reed, and other faculty members at Wickliffe Alternative School, Upper Arlington, Ohio; Kristen Kerstetter and the staff at Highland Park School, Grove City, Ohio; Marilyn Parker at Columbus School for Girls; Arleen Stuck, Richard Roth, and Melissa Wilson at Columbus Public Schools; Lisa Dapoz and Joan Fusco at Emerson Elementary School, Westerville, Ohio; Linda Woolard at Miller Elementary School, Newark, Ohio; Rebecca Thomas, Shaker Heights Public Schools, Ohio; Barbara Friedberg and other faculty members at the Martin Luther King, Jr., Laboratory School, Evanston Public Schools, Illinois; Joan Manzione, librarian, and Susan Steinberg, Marci El-Baba, and other staff members at George Mason Elementary School, Alexandria City Public Schools, Virginia; Shirley Bealor at Fairfax County Public Schools, Virginia; Nancy Anderson and Joan Schleicher at Mission School, Redlands Public Schools, California; Sharon Schmidt and other faculty members at Idyllwind Elementary School, Idyllwind, California; Janine Batzle at Esther L. Watson

*Exploring Children's Literature*

School, Anaheim, California; Joan Nassam and other faculty members at Mt. Eden Normal School in Auckland, New Zealand; Colleen Fleming at Mangere Bridge School, Auckland, New Zealand; and Roy Wilson, formerly at Dhahran Hills Elementary School, Dhahran, Saudi Arabia. I am also grateful to Valerie and Lars Bang-Jensen and their daughter Bree, Dawn Person-Hampton, Harold Hampton, and their son Bryson, and Lisa Wright and Joe Luciani and their twins Alexandra and Matthew for their contributions. I am grateful to The Ohio State University photography department, to photographers Linda Rozenfeld, of Images Marmor Rozenfeld, and Larry Rose, of Redlands, California, for their careful work in creating many of the photographs used in this edition. I also wish to thank Connie Compton and Regina Weilbacher for special photographs.

I express gratitude to the following reviewers whose comments and suggestions were most helpful:

Carla Aykroyd, *Southwestern Michigan College*
Sandie Baade, *University of Northern Iowa*
Leo W. Berg, *California Polytechnic University*
Julia Beyeler, *The University of Akron, Wayne*
Dawna Lisa Buchanan, *Central Missouri State University*
Rebecca P. Butler, *Northern Illinois University*
Mingshui Cai, *University of Northern Iowa*
John J. Carney, *University of New Hampshire*
Susan Craig, *Marshalltown Community College*
Martha B. Dargie, *Crichton College*
Margaret A. Donovan, *Chaminade University of Honolulu*
Mildred Dougherty, *William Paterson University*
Shirley B. Ernst, *Eastern Connecticut State University*
Jennifer L. Evans Kinsley, *The Ohio State University at Newark*
Angela M. Ferree, *Western Illinois University*
Dan Glynn, *Highland Community College*
Laura Ann Grady, *Paine College*
Steven Grubaugh, *University of Nevada, Las Vegas*
Joyce Hamon, *University of Southern Indiana*
Virginia Harris, *Wayland Baptist University*
Patricia M. Hart, *University of Dayton*
Jan Hayes, *Middle Tennessee State University*
Linda Inman, *St. Louis Community College*
Deidre Johnson, *West Chester University*
Marian Johnson, *Labette Community College*
Beth Jones, *Arizona State University*
Shirley Kaltenbach, *University of Alaska, Fairbanks*
Andrea Karlin, *Lamar University*
Patricia K. Kennemer, *University of Colorado, Boulder*

David Landis, *University of Northern Iowa*
Bonnie Lass, *Boston University*
Linda L. LeBert, *McNeese State University*
Carolyn Lehman, *Humbolt State University*
Carolyn Lott, *University of Montana*
Amy McClure, *Ohio Wesleyan University*
Sheila Macrine, *St. Joseph's University*
Susan R. Merrifield, *Lesley College*
Margaret R. Morris, *Mercer University*
Carolyn Nave, *Mars Hill College*
Ann Neely, *Vanderbilt University*
Judith M. Olsen, *Burlington County College*
Sheryl O'Sullivan, *University of Redlands*
Lenore D. Parker, *Lesley College*
Linda M. Pavonetti, *Oakland University*
Donna Peters, *The Ohio State University*
Barbara Phillips, *North Park University*
Nancy Polette, *Lindenwood University*
Frances Gates Rhodes, *Texas A & M University*
Anne Roberts, *State University of New York, Albany*
Elinor P. Ross, *Tennessee Technological University*
Patricia L. Scharer, *The Ohio State University*
Martha Poole Simmons, *Alabama State University*
Charlotte A. Skinner, *Arkansas State University*
Louise Stearns, *Southern Illinois University*
Stanley Steiner, *Boise State University*
Camilla C. Tinnell, *Longwood College*
Linda Todd, *The Ohio State University*
Joan Trainor, *Anna Maria College*
Nancy Upchurch, *The University of North Alabama*
Mary Jane Urbanowicz, *Shippensburg University*
Mary Ellen Van Camp, *Ball State University*
Nancy A. Verhoek-Miller, *Mississippi State University*
Susan Vodehnal, *Regis University*
Betty Ann Watson, *Harding University*
Kenneth Weiss, *Nazareth College of Rochester*
Beverly B. Youree, *Montana State University*

I give special thanks to our friends at McGraw-Hill, including Beth Kaufman, Cara Harvey, and Kay Brimeyer.

Finally, I want to thank Charlotte, Janet, and Susan for their faith and trust in me. There is no adequate way to thank these three and my other friends and family except to wonder at the glory of having had their company and support in creating this text.

Barbara Z. Kiefer
*Teachers College, Columbia University*

# Part One

## Learning About Books and Children

1

# Chapter One

# Knowing Children's Literature

*W*as there ever a baby who didn't giggle with delight when her toes were touched to the accompaniment of "This little pig went to market"? Children's introduction to literature comes in the crib as babies listen to Mother Goose rhymes and nursery songs. It continues with

the toddler's discovery of Eric Carle's *The Very Hungry Caterpillar* or David Shannon's *No David!* Later, children beg to hear Margaret Wise Brown's *Goodnight Moon* or Beatrix Potter's *The Tale of Peter Rabbit* just one more time.

If he is fortunate in his teachers, the primary-age child will hear stories two and three times a day. He will see his own reaction to a new baby in the family mirrored in *Julius, Baby of the World* by Kevin Henkes. He will identify with the feelings of Max, who, when scolded, takes off in his imagination in *Where the Wild Things Are* by Maurice Sendak. And somewhere in those early years he will discover that he can read, and the magical world of literature will open before him.

The growing child experiences loneliness and fear as she imagines what it would be like to survive alone on an island for eighteen years as Karana did in *Island of the Blue Dolphins* by Scott O'Dell. She encounters personal toughness and resiliency as she lives the life of Gilly in Katherine Paterson's *The Great Gilly Hopkins*, the story of a foster child. She can taste the bitterness of racial prejudice in Karen English's *Francie*, and she can share in the courage and determination of young people who helped others escape the Holocaust in *Number the Stars* by Lois Lowry.

A vast treasure of thoughts, deeds, and dreams lies waiting to be discovered in books. Literature begins with Mother Goose. It includes Sendak as well as Shakespeare, Milne as much as Milton, and Carroll before Camus. Children's literature is a part of the mainstream of all literature, whose source is life itself.

## *Children's Literature Defined*

In the introduction to his book *The Call of Stories*, noted child psychiatrist Robert Coles tells how, during his childhood, his mother and father would read aloud to each other every evening. They were convinced that the great novels of Dickens, Tolstoy, and others held "reservoirs of wisdom." "Your mother and I feel rescued by these books," his father told him. "We read them gratefully."[1]

What is it about literature that can inspire such passionate attention? What is literature? And with more than ninety thousand titles for girls and boys now in print, how can we choose the books that will bring the full rewards and pleasures of literature to children?

There are many ways of defining literature. Our ideas about what should be included have changed over time; definitions vary a bit from culture to culture, from critic to critic, and from reader to reader. In this book we think of literature as the imaginative shaping of life and thought into the forms and structures of language. Where appropriate, we consider fiction as well as nonfiction, pictures as well as words, asking how different genres or sets of symbols work to produce an aesthetic experience. How do they help the reader perceive pattern, relationships, and feelings that produce an inner experience of art? This aesthetic experience might be a vivid reconstruction of past experience, an extension of experience, or the creation of a new experience.

We all have, in our experience, memories of certain books that changed us in some way—by disturbing us, or by gloriously affirming some emotion we knew but could never shape in words, or by revealing to us something about human nature. Virginia Woolf calls such times "moments of being," and James Joyce titles them "epiphanies."[2]

The province of literature is the human condition. Literature illuminates life by shaping our insights.

[1]Robert Coles, *The Call of Stories: Teaching and the Moral Imagination* (Boston: Houghton Mifflin, 1989), p. xii.

[2]Frances Clarke Sayers, *Summoned by Books* (New York: Viking, 1965), p. 16.

W. H. Auden differentiated between first-rate literature and second-rate literature, writing that the reader responds to second-rate literature by saying, "That's just the way I always felt." But first-rate literature makes one say: "Until now, I never knew how I felt. Thanks to this experience, I shall never feel the same way again."[3]

The experience of literature always involves both the book and the reader. Try as we might to set objective criteria, judgments about the quality of literature must always be tempered by an awareness of its audience. Some critics consider Lewis Carroll's *Alice in Wonderland* the greatest book ever written for children. However, if the child has no background in fantasy, cannot comprehend the complexity of the plot, nor tolerate the logic of its illogic, *Alice in Wonderland* will not be the greatest book for that child.

## What Is Children's Literature?

It might be said that a child's book is a book a child is reading, and an adult book is a book occupying the attention of an adult. Before the nineteenth century only a few books were written specifically for the enjoyment of children. Children read books written for adults, taking from them what they could understand. Today, children continue to read some books intended for adults, such as the works of Stephen King and Mary Higgins Clark. And yet some books first written for children—such as Margery Williams's *The Velveteen Rabbit,* A. A. Milne's *Winnie the Pooh,* J. R. R. Tolkien's *The Hobbit,* and J. K. Rowling's *Harry Potter* stories—have been claimed as their own by adults.

Books about children might not necessarily be for them. Richard Hughes's adult classic *A High Wind in Jamaica* shows the "innocent" depravity of children in contrast to the group of pirates who had captured them. Yet in Harper Lee's novel *To Kill a Mockingbird,* also written for adults, 8-year-old Scout Finch reveals a more finely developed conscience than is common in the small southern town in which she is raised. The presence of a child protagonist, then, does not assure that the book is for children. Obviously, the line between children's literature and adult literature is blurred.

Children today appear to be more sophisticated and knowledgeable about certain life experiences than children of any previous generation were. They spend a great deal of time within view of an operating television. According to Nielsen Media Research, actual time spent watching television for children ages 2 to 11 averages almost 23 hours per week.[4] The evening news shows them actual views of war while they eat

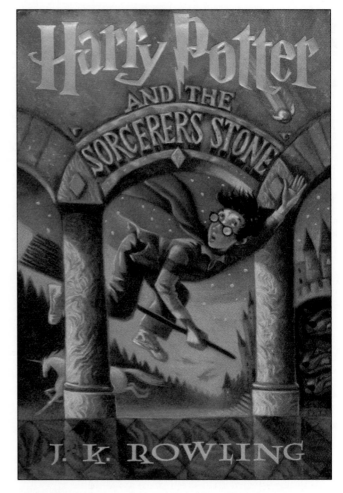

*The enthusiasm of adults and children alike for J. K. Rowling's* Harry Potter *books reflects the universal need for story.*

Illustration by Mary GrandPré from *Harry Potter and the Sorcerer's Stone* by J. K. Rowling. Published by Arthur Levine Books, an imprint of Scholastic Press, a division of Scholastic, Inc. Illustration copyright © 1998 by Mary GrandPré. Reprinted by permission.

their dinners. They have witnessed air strikes, assassinations, and starvation. Though most modern children are separated from firsthand knowledge of birth, death, and senility, the mass media bring vicarious and daily experiences of crime, poverty, war, death, and depravity into the living rooms of virtually all American homes. In addition, today's children are exposed to violence purely in the name of entertainment.

Such exposure has forced adults to reconsider what seems appropriate for children's literature. It seems unbelievable that Madeleine L'Engle's *Meet the Austins* was rejected by several publishers because it began with a death; or that some reviewers were shocked by a mild "damn" in *Harriet the Spy* by Louise Fitzhugh. Such publishing taboos have long

---

[3]W. H. Auden, as quoted by Robert B. Heilman in "Literature and Growing Up," *English Journal* 45 (September 1956): 307.

[4]Nielsen Media Report, 1998.

since disappeared. Children's books are generally less frank than adult books, but contemporary children's literature does reflect the problems of today, the ones children read about in the newspapers, see on television and in the movies, and experience at home.

However, the content of children's literature is limited by children's experience and understanding. Certain emotional and psychological responses seem outside the realms of childhood. For example, nostalgia is an adult emotion that is foreign to most boys and girls. Children seldom look back on their childhood, but always forward. Stories that portray children as "sweet" or that romanticize childhood, like the Holly Hobbie books that go with cards and gift products, have more appeal for adults than for children. Likewise, a sentimental book like *Love You Forever* by Robert Munsch, despite its popularity with teachers, is really not for children. Its themes of the passing of childhood and the assumption of responsibility for an aging parent both reflect adult experiences. The late Dr. Seuss (Theodor S. Geisel) also took an adult perspective in his later books such as *Oh, the Places You'll Go*. His enduring place in children's literature rests on earlier titles such as *And to Think That I Saw It on Mulberry Street* and *The Cat in the Hat*, books that are filled with childlike imagination and joyful exuberance.

Cynicism and despair are not childlike emotions and should not figure prominently in a child's book. Even though children are quick to pick up a veneer of sophistication, of disillusionment with adults and authority, they still expect good things to happen in life. And although many children do live in desperate circumstances, few react to these with real despair. They may have endured pain, sorrow, or horror; they may be in what we would consider hopeless situations; but they are not without hope. The truth of the Russian folktale by Becky Reyher, *My Mother Is the Most Beautiful Woman in the World*, shines clear. Children see beauty where there is ugliness; they are hopeful when adults have given up. This is not to suggest that all stories for children must have happy endings; many today do not. It is only to say that when you close the door on hope, you have left the realm of childhood. The only limitations, then, that seem binding on literature for children are those that appropriately reflect the emotions and experiences of children today. Children's books are books that have the child's eye at the center.

## Writing for Children

Editor William Zinsser says:

> No kind of writing lodges itself so deeply in our memory, echoing there for the rest of our lives, as the books that we met in our childhood. . . . To enter and

hold the mind of a child or a young person is one of the hardest of all writers' tasks.[5]

The skilled author does not write differently or less carefully for children just because she thinks they will not be aware of style or language. E. B. White asserts:

> Anyone who writes down to children is simply wasting his time. You have to write up, not down. . . . Some writers for children deliberately avoid using words they think a child doesn't know. This emasculates the prose and . . . bores the reader. . . . Children love words that give them a hard time, provided they are in a context that absorbs their attention.[6]

Authors of children's literature and those who write for adults should receive equal approbation. C. S. Lewis maintained that he wrote a children's story because a children's story was the best art form for what he had to say.[7] Lewis wrote for both adults and children, as have Rumer Godden, Madeleine L'Engle, Paula Fox, E. B. White, Isaac Bashevis Singer, Jill Patton Walsh, and many other well-known authors.

The uniqueness of children's literature, then, lies in the audience that it addresses. Authors of children's books are circumscribed only by the experiences of childhood, but these are vast and complex. Children think and feel; they wonder and they dream. Much is known, but little is explained.

Children are curious about life and adult activities. They live in the midst of tensions, of balances of love and hate within the family and the neighborhood. The author who can bring these experiences imagination and insight, give them literary shape and structure, and communicate them to children is writing children's literature.

## Valuing Literature for Children

Because children naturally take such delight in books, we sometimes need to remind ourselves that books can do more for children than entertain them. Values inherent in sharing literature with children include personal qualities that might be difficult to measure as well as qualities that result in important educational understandings.

[5]William Zinsser, ed., *Worlds of Childhood: The Art and Craft of Writing for Children* (Boston: Houghton Mifflin, 1990), p. 3.

[6]E. B. White, "On Writing for Children," quoted in *Children and Literature: Views and Reviews*, ed. Virginia Haviland (Glenview, Ill.: Scott, Foresman, 1973), p. 140.

[7]C. S. Lewis, "On Three Ways of Writing for Children," *Horn Book Magazine* 39 (October 1963): 460.

## Personal Values

Literature should be valued in our homes and schools for the enrichment it gives to the personal lives of children, as well as for its proven educational contributions. We will consider these affective values of literature before we discuss the more obvious educational ones.

### Enjoyment

First and foremost, literature provides delight and enjoyment. Much of what is taught in school is not particularly enjoyable. Our Puritan backgrounds have made literature somewhat suspect. If children enjoy it, we reason, it can't be very good for them. Yet literature can educate at the same time as it entertains.

Children need to discover delight in books before they are asked to master the skills of reading. Then learning to read makes as much sense as learning to ride a bike; they know that eventually it will be fun. Four- and 5-year-olds who have laughed out loud at Jules Feiffer's *Bark, George!* can hardly wait to read it themselves. After hearing the ugly troll's cry of "Who's that tripping over my bridge?" children are eager to take parts in playing out *The Three Billy Goats Gruff* by P. C. Asbjørnsen and Jorgen Moe. They respond to the distinctive rhythm of the poem or to the sound of David McCord's "The Pickety Fence." Six- and 7-year-olds giggle at the silly antics in Arnold Lobel's *Frog and Toad* books, and they laugh uproariously when Ramona, in Beverly Cleary's *Ramona Quimby, Age 8,* mistakenly cracks a raw egg on her head thinking it is hard-boiled. Later they empathize with her when she overhears her teacher calling her a nuisance and a show-off.

Jack Henry, a funny and genuine adolescent who inhabits Jack Gantos's *Jack on the Tracks,* is popular with middle graders. This age group also identifies with Amber in Paula Danzinger's *Amber Brown Is Feeling Blue.* Sad books also bring a kind of enjoyment, as the children who have read *Bridge to Terabithia* by Katherine Paterson or *Stone Fox* by John Gardiner will tell you. Most children love being frightened by a story. Watch 6- and 7-year-olds respond to a scary sharing of Joanna Galdone's *The Tailypo* or Charlotte Huck's *A Creepy Countdown* and you will have no doubt of their shivery delight. Many older children revel in tales of suspense such as Cynthia DeFelice's *The Ghost of Fossil Glen,* Philip Pullman's *Clockwork,* or David Almond's *Kit's Wilderness.*

The list of books that children enjoy can go on and on. There are so many fine ones—and so many that children won't find unless teachers, librarians, and parents share them with children. A love of reading and a taste for literature are the finest gifts we can

*Middle-grade readers find delight in reading about characters like Jack in Jack Gantos's* Jack on the Tracks.

Jacket design by Beata Szpura from *Jack on the Tracks: Four Seasons of Fifth Grade* by Jack Gantos. Jacket art copyright © 1999 by Beata Szpura. Reprinted by permission of Farrar, Straus and Giroux, LLC.

give to our children, for we will have started them on the path of a lifetime of pleasure with books.

### Narrative as a Way of Thinking

Storytelling is as old as human history and as new as today's gossip. Ask any of your friends about their weekends or last vacations, and they will organize their remarks in narratives about when their car stalled in the middle of a freeway or their child broke his leg or the marvelous places they stayed at by the ocean. Barbara Hardy of the University of London suggests that all our constructs of reality are in fact stories we tell ourselves about how the world works. She maintains that the narrative is the most common and effective way of ordering our world today:

> We dream in narrative, day-dream in narrative, remember, anticipate, hope, despair, believe, doubt, plan, revise, criticize, construct, gossip, learn, hate, love by narrative. In order really to live, we make up stories

*David Weisner's* Sector 7 *both illustrates and celebrates the power of the imagination that can be found in books for children.*

Illustration from *Sector 7* by David Wiesner. Copyright © 1999 by David Wierner. Reprinted by permission of Clarion Books/Houghton Mifflin Company. All rights reserved.

about ourselves and others, about the personal as well as the social past and future.[8]

If thinking in narrative form is characteristic of adult thought, it is even more typical of children's thinking. Watch young children and observe all the stories they are playing out in their lives. When they are naughty and sent to their rooms, they tell themselves a story about how they will run away—and then won't their parents be sorry? Does this plot sound familiar? Of course, for it is the basis for Maurice Sendak's modern classic *Where the Wild Things Are.* Part of this book's tremendous popularity no doubt rests on the fact that it taps the wellsprings of the stories children have been telling themselves for years. Because it is literature, however, this story brings order and structure to the imagined events. Max returns to his room after his fantastic dream, "where he finds his supper waiting for him—and it was still hot."[9] Ask 5- or 6-year-olds who brought Max his supper and they will reply, "His mother." Then ask them what this ending means, and they will answer, "That she's not mad at him anymore." Critics will call the hot meal a symbol of love and reconciliation, but children are simply satisfied that all is well. The book narrative has provided a reassuring ending for the inner story that they have told themselves.

---

[8]Barbara Hardy, "Narrative as a Primary Act of the Mind," in *The Cool Web: The Pattern of Children's Reading,* eds. Margaret Meek, Aidan Warlow, and Griselda Barton (New York: Atheneum, 1978) p. 13.

[9]Maurice Sendak, *Where the Wild Things Are* (New York: Harper & Row, 1963), unpaged.

## Imagination

Literature develops children's imagination and helps them consider people, experiences, or ideas in new ways. David Weisner's wordless picture storybooks present unique and surprising views of the world and invite children to participate by constructing their own stories. Books like Paul Fleischman's *Weslandia* or Elisa Kleven's *The Puddle Pail* celebrate characters who see the world differently and make the most of their imagination. Children love to discover secrets hidden in certain illustrations: the many visual stories in Kathy Jakobsen's illustrations for Woody Guthrie's *This Land Is Your Land* or the subplots and other small details in the borders of Jan Brett's *The Mitten.*

Good writing can pique the child's curiosity just as much as intriguing art can. Literature helps children entertain ideas they never considered before—"to dwell in possibility," as one of Emily Dickinson's poems suggests. Literature frequently asks "What if?" questions. What if an Arab American girl returned to live with her father's family in Palestine and became friends with a Jewish boy? Naomi Shihab Nye explores that possibility in *Habibi* and helps us to imagine how two young people might begin to overcome hatreds of the past. Madeleine L'Engle explores the idea of changing the past in *A Swiftly Tilting Planet.* What if we could enter history? Could we change certain major decisions? Charles Wallace has to find that out, and so does the reader. Literature explores possibility.

One of the values of fairy tales and myths is that they stretch the child's imagination. How many children would imagine creating a coach out of a pumpkin, horses from mice, and coachmen from lizards? Yet they readily accept it all in the well-loved tale of Cinderella. Bettelheim maintains: "Fairy tales have unequaled value, because they offer new dimensions to the child's imagination which would be impossible for him to discover as truly on his own."[10]

Today television has made everything so explicit that children are not developing their power to visualize. Teachers need to help them see with their inner eye to develop a country of the mind. Mollie Hunter, whose books such as *A Stranger Came Ashore* and *Mermaid Summer* have this power to create the visual image in the mind of the reader and to stretch the imagination, says that the whole reward of reading is

> to have one's imagination carried soaring on the wings of another's imagination, to be made more aware of the possibilities of one's mind . . . ; to be thrilled, amazed, amused, awed, enchanted in worlds unknown until discovered through the medium of language, and to find in those worlds one's own petty horizons growing ever wider, ever higher.[11]

### Vicarious Experience

Their experiences with literature give children new perspectives on the world. Good writing can transport readers to other places and other times and expand their life space. Readers feel connected to the lives of others as they enter an imagined situation with their emotions tuned to those of the story. One 10-year-old boy, sharing his love of Jean George's survival story *My Side of the Mountain,* said, "You know, I've always secretly felt I could do it myself." This boy had vicariously shared Sam Gribley's adventure of "living off the land" in his tree home in the Catskill Mountains. Sam's experiment in self-sufficiency had strengthened the conviction of a 10-year-old that he, too, could take care of himself. James Britton points out that "we never cease to long for more lives than the one we have . . . [and a reader can] participate in an infinite number."[12]

How better can we feel and experience history than through a well-told story of the lives of its people and times? Readers of Lois Lowry's *Number the Stars* hold their breath as Nazi soldiers ask questions about 10-year-old Annemarie's dark-haired "sister." The girl is really Annemarie's Jewish friend Ellen, whose Star of David necklace is at that moment hidden in Annemarie's hand. Fear and courage become very real to the reader in this story of the Danish Re-

sistance in World War II. A social studies textbook might simply list dates and facts related to this episode in history; a quality piece of imaginative writing has the power to make the reader feel, to transport her to Ellen's hiding place and allow her to feel the terror of Nazi persecution.

Literature provides vicarious experiences of adventure, excitement, and sometimes struggle. In fantasy, Will Stanton, seventh son of a seventh son, must do battle against the forces of evil, the power of the dark, and the unbelievably intense cold before he can complete his quest. The strength of this fantasy, *The Dark Is Rising* by Susan Cooper, is the degree to which the author involves the reader in Will's struggle.

### Insight into Human Behavior

Literature reflects life, yet no book can contain all of living. By its very organizing properties, literature has the power to shape and give coherence to human experience. It might focus on one aspect of life, one period of time in an individual's life, and so enable a reader to see and understand relationships that he had never considered. In *The Friends* by Kazumi Yumoto, three boys feed their morbid curiosity by spying on an old man, hoping to see him die. As the boys begin to know the old man, they become more and more involved in his life and put aside their misconception of the aged to find a real, vital human being. Eventually, through their intergenerational friendship, the boys discover important qualities in themselves as well as in the old man.

So much of what we teach in school is concerned with facts. Literature is concerned with feelings, the quality of life. It can educate the heart as well as the mind. Chukovsky, the Russian poet, says:

> The goal of every storyteller consists of fostering in the child, at whatever cost, compassion and humanness, this miraculous ability of man to be disturbed by another being's misfortune, to feel joy about another being's happiness, to experience another's fate as your own.[13]

Literature can show children how others have lived and "become," no matter what the time or place. As children gain increased awareness of the lives of others, as they vicariously try out other roles, they may develop a better understanding of themselves and those around them. Through wide reading as well as living, they acquire their perceptions of literature and life.

### Universality of Experience

Literature continues to ask universal questions about the meaning of life and our relationships with nature and other people. Every story provides a point of comparison for our own lives. Are we as courageous as the tiny mouse who must take responsibility for her family

[10]Bruno Bettelheim, *The Uses of Enchantment: The Meaning and Importance of Fairy Tales* (New York: Knopf, 1976), p. 7.

[11]Mollie Hunter, *The Pied Piper Syndrome* (New York: HarperCollins, 1992), p. 92.

[12]James Britton, *The Dartmouth Seminar Papers: Response to Literature,* ed. James R. Squire (Champaign, Ill.: National Council of Teachers of English, 1968) p. 10.

[13]Kornei Chukovsky, *From Two to Five,* trans. Miriam Morton (Berkeley: University of California Press, 1963), p. 138.

in Avi's *Poppy?* as conflicted by peer pressure as Palmer in Jerry Spinelli's *Wringer?* Are we as careless of the effects our actions have on others as Brent in Paul Fleischman's *Whirligig?* Are we willing to go as far as Brent in facing the consequences that arise?

We also learn to understand the common bonds of humanity by comparing one story with another. Pride of accomplishment is strong for Ahmed when he learns to write his name in *The Day of Ahmed's Secret* by Florence Parry Heide and Judith Gilliland, just as it is for the Haitian children who travel miles to get to school in Denize Lauture's *Running the Road to ABC.*

The story of Max leaving home to go to the island in Sendak's *Where the Wild Things Are* follows the ancient pattern of Homer's *Iliad* and *Odyssey*. This pattern is repeated again and again in myth and legend and seen in such widely divergent stories as *Goose* by Molly Bang, *Homecoming* by Cynthia Voigt, *A Wrinkle in Time* by Madeleine L'Engle, and *Holes* by Louis Sachar. These are all stories of a journey through trials and hardship and the eventual return home. The pattern reflects everyone's journey through life.

War stories frequently portray acts of compassion in the midst of inhumanity. *Number the Stars* by Lois Lowry and *Greater than Angels* by Carol Matas both tell of the uncommon bravery of common people to do what they can to right a wrong. Children's literature is replete with stories of true friendships, as seen in Katherine Paterson's *Bridge to Terabithia* and E. B. White's *Charlotte's Web,* and picture books such as James Marshall's *George and Martha* and Jean Van Leeuwen's *Amanda Pig and Her Best Friend Lollipop.* Other stories reflect the terrible renunciation of friendship, as found in *Friedrich* by Hans Richter or *The Friendship* by Mildred Taylor. Literature illumines all of life; it casts its light on all that is good, but it can also spotlight what is dark and debasing in the human experience. Literature enables us to live many lives, good and bad, and to begin to see the universality of human experience.

## Educational Values

The intrinsic values of literature should be sufficient to give it a major place in the curriculum. Unfortunately, our society assigns a low priority to such aesthetic experiences. Only when literature is shown to be basic to the development of measurable skills does it receive attention in the elementary schools. Fortunately, research has proven the essential value of literature in helping children learn to read and write. There is a wide body of evidence that supports the importance of literary experiences both before and after children come to school.

*Literature in the Home*

Characteristic of the development of all children is the phenomenal growth of language during the preschool years. Kornei Chukovsky, the Russian poet, refers to the tremendous "speech-giftedness of the pre-school child" and maintains that "beginning with the age of two, every child becomes for a short period of time a linguistic genius."[14]

Literature clearly plays an important role in all aspects of oral language development. Reading aloud in the home has also been shown to be powerfully connected to later success in learning to read and in attitude toward reading. In study after study, researchers have confirmed the value of being read aloud to at an early age. Moreover, children in these studies did not necessarily come from wealthy homes, but they all came from homes that valued books. The families made good use of the local library, and valued storytelling.[15]

Gordon Wells's longitudinal study of language and literacy development serves as a touchstone of these research studies. Wells showed that the amount of experience 5-year-old children in this study had had with books was directly related to their reading comprehension at age 7 and, even later, at age 11. Wells concluded, "Of all the activities that had been considered as possibly helpful preparation for the acquisition of literacy only one was significantly

[14]Ibid., pp. 7, 9.

[15]See Margaret Clark, *Young Fluent Readers* (London: Heinemann Educational Books, 1976).

*Reading aloud to older children gives the teacher a chance to introduce and discuss more complex stories than the ones they choose themselves.*

associated with later test scores. . . . That activity was listening to stories."[16]

### Literature in the School

It is clear that experiences with literature at an early age can benefit children in many ways. Once children enter school, they also benefit when literature is placed at the center of the curriculum.

**Reading Aloud and Learning to Read**   The powerful influence of books on children's language and literacy continues once they enter school. Studies with school-age children show that reading to children and giving them a chance to work with real books helps them learn to read. Reading aloud can also result in significant increases in their own reading achievement.[17] Accounts published in professional journals and books are replete with stories of teachers' successes with using children's trade books in their reading programs. These reports confirm the research that links literature with success in learning to read. They also stress that increased enjoyment and interest in reading are important outcomes of regularly reading aloud to children.[18]

**Developing a Sense of Book Language**   Hearing books read aloud is a powerful motivation for the child to begin to learn to read. Children learn that reading provides enjoyment, and they want to learn to read themselves. They also see someone important in their lives valuing books. Too frequently we tell children that reading is important, but we show by our actions that we really value other activities more.

Listening to stories introduces children to patterns of language and extends vocabulary and meaning. Young children love to repeat such refrains as "Not by the hair on my chinny chin chin" from Paul Galdone's *The Three Little Pigs* or the well-loved rhyme from Wanda Gág's *Millions of Cats*:

> Cats here, cats there,
> Cats and kittens everywhere,
> Hundreds of cats,
> Thousands of cats,
> Millions and billions and trillions of cats.[19]

Knowing the structure of a story and being able to anticipate what a particular character will do helps young children predict the action and determine the meaning of the story they are reading. For example, children quickly learn the rule of three that prevails in most folktales. They know that if the first Billy Goat Gruff goes trip-trapping over the bridge, the second Billy Goat Gruff will go trip-trapping after him, and so will the third. In reading or listening to the story of the Gingerbread Boy, the child who has had a rich exposure to literature can anticipate the ending on the basis of what he knows about the character of foxes in stories. As one little boy said, "Foxes are clever. He won't be able to get away from him!"

This understanding of literary patterns extends to expository text as well as to narrative. In her studies of kindergartners' pretend reading of nonfiction books and storybooks, Christine Pappas found that young children are equally successful in taking on textual properties of both narrative and expository texts.[20] Furthermore, she found that the kindergartners often preferred nonfiction books to storybooks. She suggests that

> to become literate the young child has to come to terms with certain important characteristics of written language that are different from spoken language—its sustained organization, its disembedded quality. And children need to understand that different conventions, rhythms, and structures are expressed in different written genres to meet various social purposes in our culture.[21]

The more experience children have with literature—with fiction, folktales, poetry, biography, and nonfiction books—the greater their ability will be to grasp the meaning of the text and understand the way the author tells it. This helps them become successful readers.

**Developing Fluency and Understanding**   The reading of many books is essential to the development of expert readers. This was the kind of reading, even rereading, of favorite stories that Margaret Clark found to be characteristic of avid readers.[22] Such reading is characteristic of middle-grade students who get "hooked" on a particular author or series of books. Frequently, a sign of a good reader is the rereading of favorite books.

In a year-long study of children's reading behavior in a literature-based program in a fifth- and sixth-grade

[16]Gordon Wells, *The Meaning Makers* (Portsmouth, N.H.: Heinemann, 1986), p. 151.

[17]See, for example, Elizabeth Sulzby, "The Development of the Young Child and the Emergence of Literacy," in *Handbook of Research on Teaching the English Language Arts*, ed. J. Flood, J. Jensen, D. Lapp, and J. Squire (New York: Macmillan, 1991), pp. 273–285

[18]See, for example, Susan I. McMahon and Taffy E. Raphael, *The Book Club Connections: Literacy and Learning and Classroom Talk* (New York: Teachers College Press, 1997).

[19]Wanda Gág, *Millions of Cats* (New York: Coward-McCann, 1928), unpaged.

[20]Christine C. Pappas, "Is Narrative 'Primary'? Some Insights from Kindergartners' Pretend Readings of Stories and Information Books," *Journal of Reading Behavior* 25 (1993): 97–129.

[21]Ibid., p. 126.

[22]Margaret Clark, *Young Fluent Readers* (London: Heinemann Educational Books, 1976), p. 103.

class, Susan Hepler found that these children read an average of 45 books apiece for the year, with the range being 25 to 122 books.[23] Compare this record with the usual two basal texts read in a year by children in the typical basal reading programs. Only wide reading will develop fluency.

Such assumptions are supported by studies that link diverse reading experiences to reading proficiency and comprehension.[24] Many researchers have concluded that the extent to which children read is a significant contributor to their developed reading ability. The National Assessment of Educational Progress (NAEP) found a clear relationship between wide reading experiences and reading ability, and suggested that reading self-selected books in school and reading outside of school for enjoyment—including information books as well as stories—were important to growth in reading.[25]

With all the many demands on their time outside of school, we cannot always be sure that children will read at home. It is even more important, then, for teachers at every grade level—from preschool on up—to enable children to spend time with books every day. If they do not have the opportunity to read widely at school, children probably will not become fluent readers.

***Literature and Writing*** Teachers have always believed that there is a relationship between reading and writing—that the good writers are avid readers, and that good readers often are the best writers. Walter Loban conducted one of the most extensive studies of the relationship between reading achievement as measured by reading scores and the ratings of writing quality. He discovered a high correlation, particularly in the upper elementary grades, and concluded: "Those who read well also write well; those who read poorly also write poorly."[26]

If reading provides models for children's writing, then the kinds of reading children are exposed to become even more important. Exposure to much good literature appears to make a difference in children's writing abilities, just as it does in their linguistic abilities. Fox and Allen maintain: "The language children

use in writing is unlikely to be more sophisticated in either vocabulary or syntax than the language they read or have had someone else read to them."[27]

The content of children's writing also reflects the literature they have heard. Whether consciously or unconsciously, children pick up words, phrases, textual structure, even intonation patterns from books they know.

A second grader wrote the following when a researcher asked him to "write a story." No other directions were given. Notice the number of stories that he "borrows" from in telling his own. The titles of his probable sources are given at right.

### The Lonesome Egg

| | |
|---|---|
| Once there lived a Lonesome Egg | *The Golden Egg Book* (Brown) |
| And nobody liked him because he was ugly. And there was an Ugly duck too but they didn't know each other. | *The Ugly Duckling* (Andersen) |
| One day while the Lonesome Egg was walking, he met the Ugly duck. And the Egg said to the Duck, | *Do You Want to Be My Friend?* (Carle) |
| "Will you be my friend?" "Well, O.K." "Oh, thank you." | |
| "Now let's go to your house, Duck." | Dialogue from the *Frog and Toad* series |
| "No, let's go to your house." "No, we'll go to your house first and my house too." "O.K." And while they were walking they met a Panda Bear and they picked it up and took it to Duck's house. And then the baby Panda Bear said: "I'm tired of walking." So they rested. | |
| And soon came a tiger. And the tiger ate them up except for Duck. And right as he saw that he ran as fast as he could until he saw a woodcutter and he told the woodcutter to come very quickly. And when they got there the tiger was asleep. So the woodcutter cut open the tiger and out came Egg and Baby Panda Bear. And they ate the tiger and lived happily ever after.[28] | *The Fat Cat* (Kent) *The Gingerbread Boy* (Galdone) *Little Red Riding Hood* (Grimm brothers) |

[23]Susan Hepler, "Patterns of Response to Literature: A One-Year Study of a Fifth- and Sixth-Grade Classroom" (Ph.D. dissertation, Ohio State University, 1982).

[24]Jim Cipielewski and Keith E. Stanovich, "Predicting Growth in Reading Ability from Children's Exposure to Print," *Journal of Experimental Child Psychology* 54 (1992): 74–89.

[25]Patricia L. Donahue, Kristin Voelkl, Jay R. Campbell, and John Mazzeo, *NAEP 1998 Reading Report Card for the Nation and States* (U.S. Dept. of Education, 1999).

[26]Walter Loban, *The Language of Elementary School Children*, Research Report No. 1 (Urbana, Ill.: National Council of Teachers of English, 1963) p. 75.

[27]Sharon Fox and Virginia Allen, *The Language Arts: An Integrated Approach* (New York: Holt, Rinehart & Winston, 1983), p. 206.

[28]"Study of Cohesion Elements on Three Modes of Discourse," NIE Research project, Martha L. King and Victor Rentel, co-researchers, Ohio State University, 1983.

Not only the content of this writing, but also certain conventions of the text, reflect previous exposure to literature. The conventional beginning, "Once there lived," and the traditional ending, "lived happily ever after," are obvious examples. Phrases such as "and soon came a tiger" and "out came Egg and Baby Panda Bear" have a literary ring to them. Discussion of whose house they will go to echoes the many conversations in the *Frog and Toad* series by Arnold Lobel. There can be little doubt about the influence of other stories on the shape and content of this 7-year-old's writing. The role of literature, then, is significant to the development of writing. For as Frank Smith wrote,

> the development of composition in writing cannot reside in writing alone, but requires reading and being read to. Only from the written language of others can children observe and understand convention and idea together.[29]

### Literature and Critical Thinking

Calls for reform in education have stressed the need for children to become better critical thinkers and problem solvers. Many schools have set goals for developing these abilities, which has resulted in the publication of special practice materials and packaged programs as well as tests to measure specific skills. One of the benefits of using literature in the elementary school is that it encourages critical and creative thinking in a more natural way than worksheet exercises in logic do.

Making inferences, comparing, summarizing, and finding the main idea are generally recognized as components of critical thinking. These are also built-in features of good book discussions and other literature activities. Young children, for instance, will have many opportunities to make predictions as they follow Joseph's rapidly diminishing wardrobe through the pages of Simms Taback's *Joseph Had a Little Overcoat*. As they compare many variants of the Cinderella story children will identify similarities and differences and weigh the comparative merits of each. Talking about the moral of a fable, or the theme of a story, such as what lesson the animals learned in the tale "The Little Red Hen," is a way of exploring a story's main idea. Children might also consider which of two biographies of Christopher Columbus presents the more balanced view of the famous explorer, or which of several books about the Civil War presents the most complete picture of the issues behind the conflict. Because of its variety in content and the availability of many books on one topic, literature provides great opportunity for thinking critically and making judgments.

### Literature Across the Curriculum

The widely read person is usually the well-informed person. The content of literature educates while it entertains. Fiction includes a great deal of information about the real world, present and past.

A 10-year-old reading *Julie of the Wolves, Julie,* or *Julie's Wolf Pack* by Jean George learns much that is authentic and true about wolf behavior. Written by a naturalist who has studied animal behavior, these stories include information about wolf communication, the hierarchy of the pack, and the division of labor within the pack. More important than the factual information, however, is each story's theme of the significance of choice and growing up.

*My Brother Sam Is Dead* by the Colliers gives authentic information about one part of the American Revolution while it contrasts different points of view held by the various characters toward the war itself. This story helps the reader imagine what it was like to live in a family torn apart by divided loyalties. And it raises the larger political question concerning the role of neutrality in a revolution.

Nonfiction books can also add both facts and human perspective to the curriculum. In *Breaking Ground, Breaking Silence,* Joyce Hansen and Gary McGowan tell the story of the recent discovery of an African American burial ground in New York City. They skillfully weave together information about several periods in American history with accounts of the activities and contributions of African Americans.

Picture books, too, offer important understandings across subject areas and grade levels. Children can benefit from the questions and concepts raised in Jon Scieszka's *Math Curse* or Thomas Locker's *Water Dance.* They can find inspiration in the biographies such as *A Picture Book of Amelia Earhart* by David Adler or *Home Run: The Story of Babe Ruth* by Robert Burleigh. They can study American history through Woodie Guthrie's *This Land Is Your Land,* or cement understandings about geography with Laurie Keller's *The Scrambled States of America.*

All areas of the curriculum can be enriched through literature. Children might start with a story and research the facts; or they might start with the facts and find the true meanings in the stories surrounding those facts. Literature has the power to educate both the heart and the mind.

### Introducing Our Literary Heritage

In general, the educational values of literature described here center on learning through literature. We must never forget, however, that as children have experiences with books, they are also learning about literature. As they enjoy nursery rhymes, traditional literature, and well-loved

---

[29]Frank Smith, *Writing and the Writer* (New York: Holt, Rinehart & Winston, 1982).

*Kathy Jakobsen's illustrations in Woodie Guthrie's* This Land is Your Land *provide a wonderful glimpse of United States geography and social history.*
Cover from *This Land Is Your Land* by Woody Guthrie/Janelle Yates, paintings by Kathy Jakobsen. © 1998 Little Brown and Company.

classics, they build a background for understanding genre, story structure, and many literary allusions.

Through in-depth discussions of such books as *The View from Saturday* by E. L. Konigsburg, *Out of the Dust* by Karen Hesse, and *Tuck Everlasting* by Natalie Babbitt, children become aware of what constitutes fine writing. Though children usually will focus on plot or story, teachers can help them see the layers of interconnections among characters in Konigsburg's complex book. They can learn to appreciate the author's skill with language as they follow Billie Jo's story in *Out of the Dust*. Children can be led to discover the recurring references to the wheel, the toad, and the music box in *Tuck Everlasting* as a way of shedding light on their understanding of this lovely fantasy. Children's appreciation for literature and knowledge of their literary heritage should be developed gradually in the elementary school as a way to add to the enjoyment of literature rather than as an end in itself.

## Evaluating Children's Fiction

What makes a good children's book? Who will read it? Why? Whose purposes will it serve? All of these are important considerations to be taken up in later sections of this chapter and throughout the book. The primary concern of evaluation, however, is a book's literary and aesthetic qualities. Children show what they think of books through their responses, but they are not born critics in the conventional sense. Teachers and librarians need to value children's own interpretations and judgments. At the same time, they need to help children discover what practiced readers look for in a well-written book.

The traditional criteria by which we evaluate a work of fiction look at such elements as plot, setting, theme, characterization, style, point of view, and format. Special criteria need to be applied to different types of literature, such as picture storybooks, biographies, and nonfiction books. For example, in picture books it is important that the verbal text and illustrations interact harmoniously. Modern fantasy has to establish believability in a way that realistic fiction does not. Historical fiction requires added criteria for authenticity of setting. Nonfiction books should be accurate and unbiased. Perhaps the most important task for critics of any age is to identify the kind of book they are reading in order to apply the appropriate criteria for evaluation. In general, though, the following elements are crucial to good works of fiction. The Guidelines "Evaluating Children's Fiction" on page 14 summarize the criteria discussed below and may help the reader look at a book more carefully. However, not all questions will be appropriate for each book.

## Plot

Of prime importance in any work of fiction for children is the plot. Children ask first, "What happens? Is it a good story?" The plot is the plan of action; it tells what the characters do and what happens to them. It is the thread that holds the fabric of the story together and makes the reader want to continue reading.

A well-constructed plot is organic and interrelated. It grows logically and naturally from the action and the decisions of the characters in given situations. The plot should be credible and ring true rather than depend on coincidence and contrivance. It should be original and fresh rather than trite, tired, and predictable.

In books that have substance, obstacles are not quickly overcome and choices are not always clear-cut. In Kimberly Willis Holt's *My Louisiana Sky*, 12-year-old Tiger struggles to reconcile her desire for the glamorous lifestyle of her Aunt Dorie with the needs of her mentally disabled mother and her simple father. The eventual acceptance of her role as her parents' caretaker represents a new, more mature perspective that is won at the cost of much anguish.

## GUIDELINES

# *Evaluating Children's Fiction*

### BEFORE READING

What kind of book is this?
What does the reader anticipate from the
   Title?
   Dust jacket illustration?
   Size of print?
   Illustrations?
   Chapter headings?
   Opening page?
For what age range is this book intended?

### PLOT

Does the book tell a good story?
Will children enjoy it?
Is there action? Does the story move?
Is the plot original and fresh?
Is it plausible and credible?
   Is there preparation for the events?
   Is there a logical series of happenings?
Is there a basis of cause and effect in the happenings?
Is there an identifiable climax?
How do events build to a climax?
Is the plot well constructed?

### SETTING

Where does the story take place?
How does the author indicate the time?
How does the setting affect the action, characters, or
   theme?
Does the story transcend the setting and have
   universal implications?

### THEME

Does the story have a theme?
Is the theme worth imparting to children?
Does the theme emerge naturally from the story, or is
   it stated too obviously?
Does the theme overpower the story?
Does it avoid moralizing?
How does the author use motifs or symbols to
   intensify meaning?

### CHARACTERIZATION

How does the author reveal characters?
   Through narration?
   In conversation?
   By thoughts of others?
   By thoughts of the character?
   Through action?
Are the characters convincing and credible?
Do we see their strengths and their weaknesses?
Does the author avoid stereotyping?
Is the behavior of the characters consistent with their
   ages and background?
Is there any character development or growth?
Has the author shown the causes of character behavior
   or development?

### STYLE

Is the style of writing appropriate to the subject?
Is the style straightforward or figurative?
Is the dialogue natural and suited to the characters?
How did the author create a mood? Is the overall
   impression one of mystery? gloom? evil? joy?
   security?

### POINT OF VIEW

Is the point of view from which the story is told
   appropriate to the purpose of the book?
Does the point of view change?
Does the point of view limit the reader's horizon, or
   enlarge it?
Why did the author choose this particular point of
   view?

### ADDITIONAL CONSIDERATIONS

Do the illustrations enhance or extend the story?
Are the pictures aesthetically satisfying?
How well designed is the book?
Is the format of the book related to the text?
What is the quality of the paper?
How sturdy is the binding?
How does the book compare with other books on the
   same subject?
How does the book compare with other books written
   by the same author?
How have other reviewers evaluated this book?
What age range would most appreciate this story?

Plot is the chief element of appeal in stories of mystery and suspense. In series mysteries, the action is frequently predictable—Nancy Drew never fails, and the Hardy Boys move smoothly from one major feat to the next. The action is usually beyond the capabilities of the characters and becomes contrived and sensational. In contrast, Geraldine McCaughrean's *The Pirate's Son* is a tautly constructed adventure story. The action begins sedately but then moves at breakneck speed to the climax as a well-bred English brother and sister befriend the son of a pirate and follow him home to Madagascar. As in other

*Sharon Creech's* Walk Two Moons *involves children in several levels of plot structure.*

Copyright © 1994 by Sharon Creech. Used by permission of HarperCollins Publishers, New York, NY.

well-plotted books, the climax develops naturally from the interaction of characters and events. Children prefer a swift conclusion following the climax. The purpose of this brief denouement is to knot together the loose ends of the story.

Most plots in children's literature are presented in linear fashion. Frequently children find it confusing to follow several plot lines or to deal with flashbacks in time and place. However, several excellent books for middle graders do make use of these devices. Multiple stories are interwoven in the Newbery Medal book *Walk Two Moons* by Sharon Creech. On a cross-country trip with her grandparents, Salamanca Tree Hiddle regales them with the somewhat wacky adventures of her friend Phoebe. As the narrative moves back and forth between the car journey and Phoebe's adventures, however, Sal's own story is revealed. These different plots represent the layers of self-understanding that Salamanca must uncover in order to accept the major changes that have occurred in her life.

In *Cousins,* Virginia Hamilton dramatically portrays the grief and guilt young Cammy feels when her cousin, spoiled Patty Ann, is drowned on a day-camp excursion. Although the book is short, it has multiple plot lines. The reader's attention is also drawn to Cammy's concern over the time her brother spends with troublesome cousin Richie and to her own attempts to brighten the life of Gram Tut, who is in the Care Home. The author uses remembered and imagined events, making part of the "action" take place in Cammy's head. This gives the story a wonderfully rich texture but makes it more challenging. The effectiveness of structure in stories like these depends on the clarity of the author's presentation and the child's ability to comprehend complexity.

Plot is but one element of good writing. If a book does not have a substantial plot, it will not hold children's interest long. But well-loved books are memorable for more than plot alone.

## Setting

The structure of a story includes both the construction of the plot and its setting. The setting may be in the past, the present, or the future. The story may take place in a specific locale, or the setting may be deliberately vague to convey the universal feeling of all suburbs, all large cities, or all rural communities.

The setting for Karen Hesse's *Out of the Dust* is so well developed that readers can almost feel the grit of dirt between their teeth. Hesse's use of free verse conveys the essence of Billie's Jo's terrible experiences during the Oklahoma dustbowl.

> On Sunday winds came,
> Bringing a red dust
> Like prairie fire,
> Hot and peppery,
> searing the inside of my nose,
> and the whites of my eyes.[30]

Just as the wind tore away layers of sod to lay bare the land, Hesse dispenses with flowery rhetoric for words and rhythms that reveal the depths of human courage and the heart of human love.

Both the time and the place of the story should affect the action, the characters, and the theme. Place, time, and people are inextricably bound together in Elisa Carbonne's *Stealing Freedom*. The setting that the author constructs includes geography, weather, and the details of everyday life that surrounded Ann Maria Weems, a young girl born into slavery in 1840s Maryland. Carbonne drew exhaustively from primary sources to follow Ann's journey on the Underground Railroad to Canada.

Stories of the present often seem to occur in homogenized settings that have little impact on character and action. There are notable exceptions, of course.

---

[30]Karen Hesse, *Out of the Dust* (New York: Scholastic, 1997), p. 46.

When Brian's plane crashes at the edge of a wilderness lake in Gary Paulsen's *Hatchet*, the rigors of that setting dictate the terms of the tense survival story that follows. Jazmin and her sister CeCe in *Jazmin's Notebook* by Nikki Grimes lead lives circumscribed by their urban ghetto environment, but the physical presence of New York City provides Jazmin with metaphors for her inner strength. As she writes in her notebook, "though six-storied buildings crowd this sky, The sun scissors through and shines—and so will I" (p. 8). Books that provide a unique sense of place are more memorable than those that do not.

The imaginary settings of fantasy must be carefully detailed in order to create a believable story. In *Charlotte's Web*, E. B. White has made us see and smell Wilbur's barnyard home so clearly that it takes little stretch of the imagination to listen in on the animals' conversations. In *A Wizard of Earthsea*, a more serious fantasy by Ursula Le Guin, the tale of wizards, dragons, and shadows is played out in an archipelago of imagined islands. Ruth Robbins has provided a map of Earthsea, for its geography is as exact as the laws and limits of magic used by the wizards of the isles. The setting of a story, then, is important in creating mood, authenticity, and credibility. The accident of place and time in a person's life might be as significant as the accident of birth, for places can have tremendous significance in our life stories.

## Theme

A third point in the evaluation of any story is its overarching theme, or themes, the larger meanings that lie beneath the story's surface. Most well-written books can be read for several layers of meaning—plot, theme, or metaphor. On one level the story of *Charlotte's Web* by E. B. White is simply an absurd but amusing tale of how a spider saves the life of a pig; on another level, it reveals the meaning of loneliness and the obligations of friendship. A third layer of significance can be seen in the acceptance of death as a natural part of the cycle of life. Finally, E. B. White himself wrote that it was "an appreciative story. . . . It celebrates life, the seasons, the goodness of the barn, the beauty of the world, the glory of everything."[31]

The theme of a book reveals something of the author's purpose in writing the story. Katherine Paterson eloquently states how authors and readers are partners in calling up true meaning:

> We are trying to communicate that which lies in our deepest heart, which has no words, which can only be hinted at through the means of a story. And somehow,

miraculously, a story that comes from deep in my heart calls from a reader that which is deepest in his or her heart, and together from our secret hidden selves we create a story that neither of us could have told alone.[32]

Theme provides a dimension to the story that goes beyond the action of the plot. The theme of a book might be the acceptance of self or others, growing up, the overcoming of fear or prejudice. This theme should be worth imparting to young people and be based on justice and integrity. Sound moral and ethical principles should prevail. However, one danger in writing books for children is that the theme will override the plot. Authors might be so intent on conveying a message that they neglect story or characterization. Didacticism is still alive and well in the twentieth century. It might hide behind the facade of ecology, drug abuse, or alienation, but it destroys fine writing.

Well-written books can make their themes fairly explicit without becoming preachy. In Natalie Babbitt's *Tuck Everlasting*, three motifs provide meaningful threads that keep reappearing: a toad, a music box, and the concept of a wheel. The wheel represents the theme of this gentle fantasy, the cycle of life and death that the Tuck family can never experience because they have drunk by accident from a spring that has frozen them in time, to live forever. As Angus Tuck tries to persuade young Winnie Foster not to drink from this water, he uses the example of a wheel to carry his message about life:

> It's a wheel, Winnie. Everything is a wheel, turning and turning, never stopping. The frog is part of it, and the bugs, and the fish and the wood thrush, too. And people. But never the same ones. Always coming in new, always growing and changing, and always moving on. That's the way it's supposed to be. That's the way it is.[33]

Children in the middle grades can comprehend symbolic meaning and recurring motifs that are woven so beautifully into the fabric of the theme.

## Characterization

True characterization is another hallmark of fine writing. The people portrayed in children's books should be as convincingly real and lifelike as our next-door neighbors. Many of the animal characters in modern fantasy also have human personalities. The credibility of characters depends on the author's ability to show their true natures, their strengths, and their weaknesses.

[31]Dorothy L. Guth, ed., *Letters of E. B. White* (New York: Harper & Row, 1976), p. 613.

[32]Katherine Paterson, "Hearts in Hiding," in *Worlds of Childhood: The Art and Craft of Writing for Children*, ed. William Zinsser (Boston: Houghton Mifflin, 1990), p. 153.

[33]Natalie Babbitt, *Tuck Everlasting* (New York: Farrar, Straus & Giroux, 1975), p. 62.

*Arnold Lobel created two memorable animal characters in the* Frog and Toad *series.*

Copyright © 1970 by Arnold Lobel. Used by permission of HarperCollins Publishers, New York, NY.

Just as it takes time to know a new friend in all her various dimensions, so, too, does an author try to present many facets of a character bit by bit. In revealing character, an author might tell about the person through narration, record the character's conversation with others, describe the thoughts of the character, show the thoughts of others about the character, or show the character in action. A character who is revealed in only one way is apt to lack depth. If a single dimension of character is presented, or one trait overemphasized, the result is likely to be stereotyped and wooden. One-dimensional characters are the norm in folk and fairy tales, where witches are prototypes of evil and youngest children are deserving and good. However, modern fiction requires multidimensional characters whose actions and feelings grow out of the circumstances of the story. Books are usually more satisfying when readers feel they are discovering the character through the story rather than relying on authors' labels, like *jealous, troublesome,* or *shy.* Children do not need to be told that Leon Tillage is courageous for having survived years of segregation and humiliation. His own words in *Leon's Story* reveal his resilience, his bravery, and his human dignity.

In *A View from Saturday,* E. L. Konigsburg constructs personalities for her five characters that are as complex as the pieces of jigsaw puzzle they assemble at their Saturday teas at Sillington House. Even more delightful for the reader, these characters are revealed slowly as Mrs. Olinski, Noah, Julian, Nadia, and Ethan present their views of events. Ethan reflects on discoveries he has made about himself as a result of his friendships.

> Something in Sillington House gave me permission to do things I had never done before. . . . Something there had triggered the unfolding of those parts that had been incubating. Things that had lain inside me, curled up like the turtle hatchlings newly emerged from their eggs, taking time in the dark of their nest to unfurl themselves.[34]

Konigsburg unfolds her characters in just such a way, adding subtle details and connections among the five that invite the reader to take part in a contest of wits similar to the one that serves as the centerpiece of the plot.

In addition to depth in characterization, there should be consistency in character portrayal. Everything characters do, think, and say should seem natural and inevitable. We can expect them to act and speak in accordance with their age, culture, and educational background. Stanley Yelnats, the unprepossessing delinquent of Louis Sachar's *Holes,* is so credible an antihero that he lends believability to a plot that is filled with quirks and coincidences.

Another aspect of sound characterization is growth and development. Do the characters change in the course of the story, or are they untouched by the events in which they have a part? In picture books and short tales, we might expect characters to be fully described but not to change much. In longer fiction, however, characters have time to learn and grow. Many characters are best remembered for the turnarounds they have made or the way they have matured. Readers do not quickly forget the struggle of headstrong, self-centered Jo of Louisa May Alcott's *Little Women* in taming her rebellious ways. Another character who grows before the reader's eyes in a gradual and convincing manner is the title character of Katherine Paterson's *Lyddie.* A nineteenth-century New England girl who becomes a mill worker in an effort to save the family farm, Lyddie is courageous and determined throughout the story. The change

---

[34]Konigsburg, E. L. *A View from Saturday* (New York: Atheneum, 1996), p. 93.

*Beverly Cleary's Ramona has come alive for millions of children in books like* Ramona and Her Father.

Illustration from *Ramona and Her Father* by Beverly Cleary, illustrated by Alan Tiegreen. Illustration copyright © 1975, 1977. Used by permission of Morrow Junior Books, an imprint of HarperCollins Publishers.

comes in her ability to see the options of her life realistically and in her growing sense of the possibilities of her future as she sets off to attend the first women's college in the nation.

Not all characters change, though. A character might be well developed, multidimensional, and interesting and yet seem to remain frozen in that particular time of her or his life. Such characters are common in humorous stories. In Robert McCloskey's *Homer Price* and Astrid Lindgren's *Pippi Longstocking*, the title characters remain consistent in nature through all their adventures. Some stories, then, might be notable for character delineation rather than character development.

Long after we have forgotten their stories, we can recall some of the personalities of children's literature. We recognize them as they turn the corner of our memories, and we are glad for their friendship. The line is long; it includes animals and people. It is hard to tell where it begins, and we are happy that it has no end. In our mind's eye we see the three loyal friends Mole, Toad, and Rat returning from their adventures on the open road; Mary Poppins flies by holding tightly to her large black umbrella with one hand and carrying her carpetbag in the other; she passes right over those comic friends Frog and Toad, who are out looking for the corner that spring is just around. In the barnyard Wilbur has just discovered a wonderful new friend, Charlotte A. Cavatica, much to the amusement of the wise geese and the sly rat,

Templeton. If we look closely, we can see tiny Arrietty and Pod, out for a Borrower's holiday; Stuart Little paddles his souvenir canoe along the drainage ditch; and our favorite Hobbit, Bilbo Baggins, outwits the terrifying Gollum. Gathered in the schoolyard are the Great Gilly Hopkins and her tag-along friend, Agnes Stokes; Meg Murry is consulting with the principal, Mr. Jenkins, about her little brother, Charles Wallace. Ramona comes by wearing the crown of burrs she had made so she can star in a TV commercial; Harriet, with flashlight and notebook, is just beginning her spy route; and Jeffrey "Maniac" Magee comes loping along with his sneaker soles slapping.

The line is long in this procession of real personages in children's literature. It reaches back in our memories to include Beth, Jo, Amy, and Meg; it stands outside the Secret Garden and listens to the laughing voices of Mary, Colin, and Dickon; and, with Laura, it delights in the warm coziness of the fire and the sound of Pa's fiddling in Laura Ingalls Wilder's *Little House in the Big Woods*. We know all these characters well because their authors blew the breath of life into each one of them. They have come alive in the pages of books, and they will live forever in our memories.

## Style

An author's style of writing is simply selection and arrangement of words in presenting the story. Good writing style is appropriate to the plot, theme, and characters, both creating and reflecting the mood of the story. Although some authors develop a style so distinctive that it is easily recognizable, their work might show variation from book to book. Gary Paulsen's *Hatchet* is a survival story told as a continuous record of the thoughts and actions of Brian, the survivor. The brief sentences arranged as individual paragraphs are choppy, breathless, tense:

> I was flying to visit my father and the plane crashed and sank in a lake.
>     There, keep it that way. Short thoughts.
>     I do not know where I am.
>     Which doesn't mean much. More to the point, they do not know where I am.[35]

Paulsen's *The Winter Room* is a more lyrical story that takes as its backdrop the changing seasons of a northern Minnesota farm. Carefully placed sentence fragments punctuate this narrative also, but here they are contrasted to long chains of sensory details. The following is only a part of a sentence:

> . . . [when] Rex moves into the barn to sleep and Father drains all the water out of all the radiators in the tractors and the old town truck and sometimes you suck

[35]Gary Paulsen, *Hatchet* (New York: Bradbury, 1987), p. 47.

a quick breath in the early morning that is so cold it makes your front teeth ache; when the chickens are walking around all fluffed up like white balls and the pigs burrow into the straw to sleep in the corner of their pen, and Mother goes to Hemings for the quilting bee they do each year that lasts a full day—when all that happens, fall is over.

But it still isn't winter.[36]

Most children do not enjoy a story that is too descriptive, but they can appreciate figurative language, especially when the comparisons are within their background of understanding. Natalie Babbitt's vivid prologue to *Tuck Everlasting* invites children to visualize the intense images by describing the month of August as curiously silent "with blank white dawns and glaring noons and sunsets smeared with too much color."[37]

Patricia MacLachlan's style effectively mirrors the setting of the story and the background of its characters in *Sarah, Plain and Tall.* The writing reflects the prairie setting and the straightforward manner of Sarah, a mail-order bride from Maine. The tension of the story lies in its themes of longing and belonging—Sarah's understated longing for the sea and the children's longing for a mother. The beauty of the sea is contrasted with that of the prairie; the light after a prairie storm reminds Sarah of a sea squall. At the end of the story, when Sarah has decided to stay, the child-narrator, Anna, reflects on the future:

> Autumn will come, then winter, cold with a wind that blows like the wind off the sea in Maine. . . . There will be Sarah's sea, blue and gray and green, hanging on the wall. And songs old and new. And Seal with yellow eyes. And there will be Sarah, plain and tall.[38]

The repeated phrases in this passage have a rhythm like music, a cadence that is very satisfying, especially when the book is read aloud.

There is no one style or set of language patterns that is more appropriate than others for a children's book. Yet children's tastes do place some demands on the writer. Because young readers tend to prefer action over description or introspection, those elements must be handled with special skill. Children crave dialogue, like readers of all ages. They feel as Alice in Wonderland did when she looked into her sister's book and said, "What's the use of a book without pictures or conversation?" Masters at writing dialogue that sounds natural and amusing include Rose-mary Wells in her picture books such as *Yoko* and Cynthia Rylant in *Henry and Mudge and the Sneaky Crackers.* Writing the dialogue for a book of contemporary realistic fiction is particularly difficult because slang and popular expressions are quickly dated. Paula Danzinger is one writer who skillfully captures the sound of today's idiom in her stories. Ralph Fletcher's sixth graders in *Flying Solo* sound convincingly real, and Walter Dean Myers captures the sound of urban street language in books like *Scorpions.*

The best test of an author's style is probably oral reading. Does the story read smoothly? Does the conversation flow naturally? Does the author provide variety in sentence patterns, vocabulary, and use of stylistic devices?

Although it is difficult for children to analyze a particular author's style, they do react to it. Children are quick to detect the patronizing air of an author who talks down to them in little asides, for example. They dislike a story that is too sentimental; and they see through the disguise of the too-moralistic tales of the past. Adults are more responsive than children to the clever, the slyly written, and the sarcastic. Frequently children are better able to identify what they dislike about an author's style than to identify what they like. Obviously, the matter of style is important when adults evaluate books for children.

## Point of View

The term *point of view* is often used to indicate the author's choice of narrator(s) and the way the narrator reveals the story. Whose story is it? Who tells it? In folk and fairy tales, for instance, the storyteller tells the tale, and the storyteller knows the thoughts and actions of all the characters. The storyteller's voice is also used in modern fiction, for books in which the author reports the comings and goings, the conversations, and the feelings of all the characters, villains as well as heroes. We say that such stories have an omniscient, or all-knowing, narrator. C. S. Lewis presents his Narnia series in this way. In *The Lion, the Witch, and the Wardrobe,* we are sometimes with Lucy, sometimes with Edmund, sometimes with all four of the adventuring children, and occasionally in places where they can never go. With the use of the third person, the omniscient point of view allows the author complete freedom to crawl inside the skins of each of the characters, thinking their thoughts, speaking their words, and observing the action of the story. It also allows the author to speak directly to the reader, if she or he chooses, just as a storyteller would in a face-to-face situation. C. S. Lewis comments to his readers in parentheses, a practice that some children and adults find detracts from their enjoyment of the story.

---

[36]Gary Paulsen, *The Winter Room* (New York: Orchard, 1989), p. 62.

[37]Natalie Babbitt, *Tuck Everlasting* (New York: Farrar, Straus & Giroux, 1985), p. 3.

[38]Patricia MacLachlan, *Sarah, Plain and Tall* (New York: Harper & Row, 1985), p. 58.

Many children's books take a point of view that also uses the third person but gives the author less freedom. This limited-omniscient, or concealed, narrator view does, however, provide closer identification with a single character. The author chooses to stand behind one character, so to speak, and tell the story from over his or her shoulder. The story is then limited to what that character can see, hear, believe, feel, and understand. Katherine Paterson has told the story *The Great Gilly Hopkins* from this perspective. Gilly is "on stage" throughout, and we see the world as Gilly sees it. We know what others think about her through their reactions to her and her interpretations of their thoughts. For example, Gilly is having her first dinner at the home of Trotter, her latest foster mother:

> The meal proceeded without incident. Gilly was hungry but thought it better not to seem to enjoy her supper too much. William Ernest ate silently and steadily with only an occasional glance at Gilly. She could tell that the child was scared silly of her. It was about the only thing in the last two hours that had given her any real satisfaction. Power over the boy was sure to be power over Trotter in the long run.[39]

William Mayne, a British writer, helps the reader see the world from the limited point of view of a magical being in *Hob and the Goblins* and thus makes the fantasy more believable. Hob, a brownie-like creature, suddenly finds himself in the modern-day London and does not understand that the world has changed from horse-and-buggy days. When a "noisy red house" appears, he climbs "up the big steps," thinking he has found a new home.

> Hob went straight for the staircase, all among the feet of people, and up to see the bedrooms. There were narrow beds, with people sitting on them, looking out of windows. "What a lot live here," said Hob. "Hob will stay downstairs until I know them better."[40]

While it might take children a few pages to catch on to Hob's unusual way of looking at the world of humans, Mayne's consistent point of view adds to the delight of the story.

The more direct narrative voice of the first person, once considered unusual in children's books, is quite common today. In contemporary realism it is almost the norm. Judy Blume helped popularize this kind of storytelling with books like *Are You There God? It's Me, Margaret* and *Blubber*. Blume's stories are not known for strong characterization, but

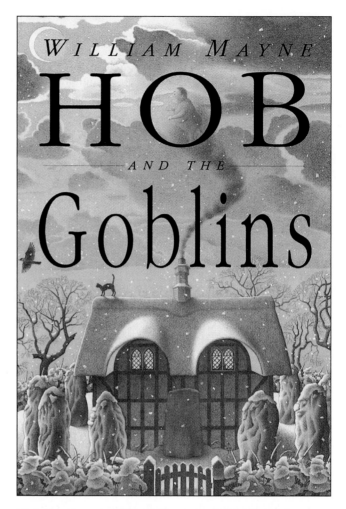

*Hob's unique worldview adds a sense of the fantastic to William Mayne's* Hob and the Goblins.

From *Hob and the Goblins*, by William Mayne. Copyright © 1994 by Dorling Kindersley, Inc., New York, NY. Reprinted by permission of the publisher.

they do reveal the author's ability to recreate the everyday language of children.

The advantage of using first-person narrative is that it can make for easy reading. It attempts to invite its audience by taking a stance that says, "Look—we speak the same language." In many cases this sort of writing does not stretch the reader's vocabulary or imagination. The short, choppy sentences simply reflect a 10-year-old's idiom's and grammatical errors. Moreover, children's perspectives on the world are limited by their lack of experience, just as their vocabulary is. This is an added challenge for an author writing in the first person; for although it might be easy to present the narrator's thoughts and feelings in an appealing way, it will be more difficult to show that the narrator's view might be narrow, misguided, or simply immature when seen from a broader perspective.

[39]Katherine Paterson, *The Great Gilly Hopkins* (New York: Harper & Row, 1978), p. 14.

[40]William Mayne, *Hob and the Goblins* (New York: Darling Kindersley, 1994), p. 9.

Stories told by older characters, or those who are especially intelligent or sensitive, usually do a better job of dealing with complex issues. In books such as *Missing May* by Cynthia Rylant or David Almond's *Skellig,* the authors have created believable characters and lent power to the story through the use of first-person narration.

Almond's young protagonist, Michael, begins his deeply moving story with this description of Skellig:

> I found him in the garage on a Sunday afternoon. . . . He was lying there in the darkness behind the tea chests, in the dust and dirt. It was as if he'd been there forever. He was filthy and pale and dried out and I thought he was dead. I couldn't have been more wrong. I'd soon begin to see the truth about him, that there'd never been another creature like him in the world.[41]

Without the immediacy of Michael's narration, the reader might dismiss this book as make believe and Skellig as a magical creature such as a unicorn or hobbit. The book's strength derives from our irrational hope that creatures like Skellig do exist. Michael's voice helps us accept the events that take place and heightens the emotional power of the story.

At times authors counter the limitations of a single point of view by alternating the presentation of several views within the same story or changing points of view. Konigsburg's multiple narratives in *The View from Saturday* add great richness to the textual tapestry. *Morning Girl,* by Michael Dorris, alternates the stories of a young girl and her brother, who describe their life in an island culture at an unnamed time. Their voices represent typical sibling relationships at the same time that they add depth to the strong family bonds that shape this community. At the end of the story, however, Morning Girl sees an unusual "canoe" approaching her island.

> All the fat people in the canoe began pointing at me and talking at once. In their excitement they almost turned themselves over, and I allowed my body to sink beneath the waves for a moment in order to hide my smile. One must always treat guests with respect I reminded She Who Listens, even when they are as brainless as gulls.[42]

The book ends with a third and chilling voice, that of Christopher Columbus, in a journal entry dated 11 October, 1492. In it he suggests that the people of the island he has "discovered" will make good servants because they "say very quickly everything that is said to them." By adding this third viewpoint

*Karen Cushman's* Catherine, Called Birdy *speaks from the Middle Ages to today's middle grader.*

From *Catherine, Called Birdy* by Karen Cushman, Trina Schart Hyman, illustrator, © 1994. Reprinted by permission of Clarion Books/Houghton Mifflin Company.

at the close of *Morning Girl,* Dorris forces us to reconsider the tales told in our history books and to understand the perspective of peoples who have had no voice for centuries.

Style, structure, and revelation of character necessarily are influenced by the author's choice of point of view (or points of view). In evaluating books, we need to ask not just who is telling the story, but how this influences the story. What perspective does the narrator bring to events, and what vision of the world does that offer to children?

## Evaluating Literature Through a Multicultural Lens

 We consider the author's *choice* of point of view as one of the important literary criteria we apply to children's books. To fully evaluate works of literature for children,

---

[41]David Almond, *Skellig* (New York, Delacorte, 1999), p. 1.

[42]Michael Dorris, *Morning Girl* (New York: Hyperion, 1992), p. 70.

we must also consider the cultural perspective of the writer, her or his *personal* point of view. This approach to criticism is often considered part of the field of multicultural literature. Mingshui Cai and Rudine Sims Bishop suggest that *multicultural literature* is an umbrella term that includes at least three kinds of literature: world literature (literature from nonwestern countries outside the United States), cross-cultural literature (literature about relations between cultural groups or by authors writing about a cultural group other than their own), and minority literature or literature from parallel cultures (literature written by members of a parallel culture that represents their unique experiences as members of that culture).[43] In the 1950s, multicultural books focused on integration (see Chapter 3). These books tended to emphasize similarity of groups rather than unique racial, cultural, or ethnic identities. Increasing activism in the 1960s further encouraged the publication of books that featured Native Americans, Hispanic Americans, and African Americans, although they were often written by caucasian authors. Many of these titles went out of print rapidly when federal funds for schools and libraries diminished. As the century ended, however, the number of multicultural titles written by minorities had increased, although that number still did not reflect actual population figures. In addition, the representation of individual cultures was uneven.[44] We continue to need high-quality literature that reflects many cultures and the changing population of our schools. All readers should be able to find their own cultural heritage reflected in the literature they read.

It is still necessary, then, to evaluate literature about all our diverse cultures according to not only its general literary value but also the image of the group presented by the text and illustrations, and we have attempted to do so throughout this book. The Guidelines "Evaluating Multicultural Literature" introduce some of the general criteria that teachers and librarians should keep in mind when reading literature written about other cultures. More-detailed guidelines can be found in Augusta Baker, *The Black Experience in Children's Books* (New York: New York Public Library, 1984), and Rudine Sims, *Shadow and Substance: Afro-American Experience in Contemporary Children's Fiction* (Urbana, Ill.: National Council of Teachers of English, 1982). Other sources useful in evaluating literature about diverse cultures can be found in Appendix B.

## Additional Considerations

The books we think of as truly excellent have significant content, and, if illustrated, fine illustrations. Their total design, from the front cover to the final end paper, creates a unified look that seems in character with the content and invites the reader to proceed. Today we have so many picture storybooks and so many beautifully illustrated books of poetry, nonfiction, and other genres that any attempt to evaluate children's literature should consider both the role of illustration and the format of the book. We will discuss these criteria in greater depth in Chapters 5, 8, and 11. In general, however, we should consider what function the art in a book is intended to have. Are the pictures meant to be decorations? Were they designed to complement or clarify the text? Are they so much a part of the story that you cannot imagine the book without them?

The format of a book includes its size, shape, page design, illustrations, typography, paper quality, and binding. Frequently, some small aspect of the format, such as the book jacket, will be an important factor in a child's decision to read a story.

All types of books—novels, picture books, poetry, biography, informational books—should be well designed and well made. Many factors other than illustration are important. The type should be large enough for easy reading by children at the age level for which the book is intended. At the same time, if the type is too large, children might see the book as "babyish." Space between the lines (leading) should be sufficient to make the text clear. The paper should be of high quality, heavy enough to prevent any penetration of ink. Off-white with a dull finish prevents glare, although other surfaces are used for special purposes. The binding should be durable and practical, able to withstand hard use. Publishers produce many books in alternate bindings, one for the trade (bookstore sales) and an extra-sturdy version for library use. However, a book should never be selected on the basis of format alone. No book is better than its content.

Bonnie and Art Geisert have created a series of illustrated books that focus on life in the farms and small towns of the Midwest, as illustrated on page 24. This setting is beautifully represented by the wide horizontal shape of the books, the hand colored

[43]Mingshui Cai and Rudine Sims Bishop, "Multicultural Literature for Children: Towards a Clarification of the Concept," in *The Need for Story: Cultural Diversity in Classroom and Community*, eds. Anne Haas Dyson and Celia Genishi (Urbana, Ill.: National Council of Teachers of English, 1994), p. 62.

[44]Ginny Moore Kruse, Kathleen Horning, and Megan Schiesman, *Multicultural Literature for Children and Young Adults*, vol. 2 (Madison, Wisc.: Cooperative Children's Book Center, 1997), p. 1.

# GUIDELINES

## Evaluating Multicultural Literature

Although the emphasis should be placed on selecting high-quality literature, the following guidelines may be useful in evaluating literature that depicts minorities or other cultures.

1. *Diversity and range of representation.* In the portrayal of any minority group, a collection of books should show a wide range of representation of that particular race or ethnic group. Some African Americans live in city ghettos or rural settings; some live in upper-class areas, middle-class suburbs, or small towns. Some Hispanic Americans make a living in migrant camps; most hold jobs that have nothing to do with seasonal crops. Only when a collection of books about a particular group offers a wide spectrum of occupations, educational backgrounds, living conditions, and lifestyles will we honestly be moving away from stereotyping in books and offering positive images about minorities.

2. *Avoidance of stereotyping.* Literature must depict the varieties of a particular culture or ethnic group. Illustrations should portray the distinctive yet varied characteristics of a group or race so that readers know they are looking at a people of, for example, Sioux, Jamaican, or Vietnamese descent. The portrayal of stereotypical articles should be avoided, such as the sombrero and poncho, a feathered headdress and moccasins, or the "pickaninny with a watermelon" so often pictured in children's books from earlier decades. Literature should avoid implying that specific occupations (such as computer expert), recreational pastimes (such as soccer), family organizational structure, or values are descriptive of any particular race or ethnic group. (For further discussion of stereotypes, see the sections in Chapter 5: "Picture Books," Chapter 9: "Contemporary Realistic Fiction," and Chapter 11: "Nonfiction.")

3. *Language considerations.* Derogatory terms for particular racial groups should not be used in stories about minorities unless these are essential to a conflict or used in historical context. Even then, it should be made clear that the use of these unacceptable terms casts aspersion on the speaker, not on the one spoken about or to. Another consideration is the use of dialect or "broken English." Some recent books about African Americans make a conscious effort to reproduce the cadence and syntax of certain language patterns without resorting to phonetically written spellings or stereotypical dialect. Books that incorporate the language of a minority group, such as Spanish, do not need to translate a word if context defines it. Children need to understand that all languages adequately serve their speakers and that no one language is better than another.

4. *The perspective of the book.* In evaluating a book about a minority group, we need to ask if it truly represents that minority's experience. This is a difficult guideline to define because we don't want to suggest there is only one sort of African American experience, for example. Who solves the problems in stories? Do minority characters take the initiative in problem solving, or are solutions provided by paternalistic whites? Are racial pride and positive self-image apparent in the story? Do the details of the story authentically portray the experience of the represented minority?

No one is free from his or her own particular bias or background. Teachers or librarians in specific school settings might want to add other criteria to this list as they select books for children. It is essential to provide books about minorities for *all* children and to choose variety, not merely reflect the minority population served by the specific school. Books can help develop children's appreciation for our ever-changing pluralistic society.

---

etchings used to create the illustrations, and the overall design of the books. Another book that features careful attention to format throughout is Diana Applebaum's *Giants in the Land,* with scratchboard illustrations by Michael McCurdy. The tall, slender shape of the book evokes the giant pine trees of the title that once covered all of New England and that were cut down to make the masts for British warships in the eighteenth century. The book's cloth cover, embossed with a single gold pine tree, the deep red end papers, the black-and-white illustrations, and the careful page design all lend a sense of quiet majesty to this environmental history and invite children to linger over Appelbaum's poetic text.

# RIVER TOWN
BONNIE and ARTHUR GEISERT

*The design, trim size, and layout of* River Town *by Bonnie and Art Geisert all evoke the long meandering river and the broad expanse of prairie that are central to the book's setting.*
From *River Town* by Bonnie and Arthur Geisert, © 1999. Reprinted by permission of Houghton Mifflin Company.

## Comparison with Other Books

A book should be considered not in isolation but as a part of the larger body of literature. Individual books need to be compared with others on the same subject or theme. Is this just another horse story, or like Jessie Haas's *Unbroken* does it make a contribution to our understanding about human motives and desires? Every teacher and librarian should know some books well enough to develop a personal list of books of excellence that can serve as models for comparison. How does this adventure story compare with Armstrong Sperry's *Call It Courage,* or this fantasy with *A Wrinkle in Time* by Madeleine L'Engle, or this historical fiction with Mildred Taylor's *Roll of Thunder, Hear My Cry?* These reference points of outstanding books help to sharpen evaluations.

An author's new book should be compared with her or his previous works. Contributions by the same author might be inconsistent in quality. What is the best book Jean George has written? Is *On the Far Side of the Mountain* as good as *My Side of the Mountain?* How does *Water Sky* compare with *Julie of the Wolves?* Too frequently, books are evaluated on the basis of the author's reputation rather than for their inherent worth.

Many informational and biographical series are written by different authors. The quality of the book varies with the ability of the writer, despite similarities in approach and format. Rather than condemn-

ing or approving an entire series, evaluate a book on its own merits.

A book needs to be compared with outstanding prototypes, with other books written by the same author, and with other books in the same series. It can also be helpful to become familiar with some of the review journals in the field of children's literature and to compare reviews of a given book. What have reputable reviewers said about this book? Where have they placed it in relation to others of its type? Have they singled it out for special notice by starring it or providing a special focus? A comparison of reviews of one book usually reveals more similarities than differences, although reviewers have personal preferences just as other readers do. Appendixes A and B provide sources that will be helpful in evaluating and selecting children's books.

In summary, the basic considerations for the evaluation of fiction for children are a well-constructed and well-paced plot, a significant theme, an authentic setting, a credible point of view, convincing characterization, appropriate style, and an attractive format. Not all books achieve excellence in each of these areas. Some books are remembered for their fine characterizations, others for their exciting plots, and others for the evocation of the setting.

## Classics in Children's Literature

Knowledge of children's classics—those books that have stood the test of time—can provide further guidance for evaluating children's books. What makes a book endure from one generation to another? Alice Jordan states: "Until a book has weathered at least one generation and is accepted in the next, it can hardly be given the rank of a classic."[45]

Many books and poems have achieved an honored position in children's literature through a combination of adult adoration, parent perpetuation, and teacher assignments. Most adults remember with nostalgia the books they read as children. They tend to think that what they read was best and ignore the possibility that any better books might be produced. It is easy to forget that every "classic" was once a new book, that some of today's new books will be to-

---

[45]Alice M. Jordan, *Children's Classics* (Boston: Horn Book, 1974), p. 4.

morrow's classics. Teachers and librarians should begin with modern children and their interests, not adults' interests when they were children.

Certain books became classics when there were very few books from which children could choose. In fact, many classics were not children's books at all, but were written for adults. In their desire to read, children claimed these adult books, struggled through the difficult parts, and disregarded what they did not understand. They had no other choice. Today's children are not so persevering, because they see no reason to be. The introductory sentence of Robinson Crusoe runs the length of the entire first page and contains difficult vocabulary and syntax. Defoe wrote the story in 1719 for adult readers, but children quickly discovered this story of shipwreck and adventure and plunged into it. However, they can find the same tingling excitement and more readable prose in modern survival stories like Iain Lawrence's *The Wreckers* or Cynthia DeFelice's *Nowhere to Call Home*.

The classics should not be exempted from reevaluation by virtue of their past veneration. They should be able to compete favorably with contemporary books. Unimpressed by vintage or lineage, children seldom read a book because they think they should. They read more for enjoyment than for edification. Some books have been kept alive from one generation to the next by the common consent of critics and children; these are the true classics of children's literature. No teacher or parent has to cajole a child into enjoying the adventure and suspense in Robert Louis Stevenson's *Treasure Island*, the mystery and excitement of *The Secret Garden* by Frances Hodgson Burnett, or the memorable characters in Alcott's *Little Women* or A. A. Milne's *Winnie the Pooh*. These books can hold their own amid today's ever-increasing number of new and beautiful books.

# The Book Awards

Teachers and librarians will find it helpful to be familiar with books that have won awards.[46] These awards, which have been established for various purposes, provide criteria for what experts consider to be the best in children's literature. Such awards have helped counteract the judgment of the marketplace by focusing attention on beautiful and worthwhile books. In an age of mass production, they have stimulated artists, authors, and publishers to produce books of distinction and have helped children's literature achieve a worthy status.

---

[46]See Appendix A for various book awards, criteria, and winners. Information also appears in *Children's Books in Print* (New York: R. R. Bowker).

The award books are not always popular with children. However, most of the awards are based not on popularity but on recognized excellence. They were never intended to rubber-stamp the tastes of children; they were intended to raise them. Children's reactions to books are significant, and many awards, particularly state awards, are voted on by children. However, popularity of a book, whether for children or for adults, is not necessarily a mark of distinctive writing or artistic achievement. How many best-sellers win a Pulitzer Prize for literature? Because there are now so many awards in so many categories of children's literature, only the best-known ones will be discussed here.

## The Newbery and Caldecott Medals

Two of the most coveted awards in children's literature are the Newbery and Caldecott Medals. Winners are chosen every year by two committees of the Association for Library Service to Children, a division of the American Library Association. A candidate for either of the awards must be a citizen or resident of the United States.

The John Newbery Medal, established in 1922, is the oldest award for children's books. It is named for John Newbery, a British publisher and bookseller of the eighteenth century. Appropriately called the "father of children's literature," he was the first to publish books expressly for children. The Newbery Medal is awarded to the author of the most distinguished contribution to American literature for children published in the preceding year. Although the award is occasionally given to a book with outstanding illustrations, such as Nancy Willard's *A Visit to William Blake's Inn*, with pictures by Alice and Martin Provensen, the Newbery Medal honors the quality of the writing. Many age ranges are represented, but most of the Newbery Medal books are for able, mature readers. Frequently children need to hear these books read aloud and discuss them with an adult before they develop a taste for their excellence.

The Randolph J. Caldecott Medal is named in honor of a great English illustrator of the nineteenth century, Randolph Caldecott. Caldecott was well known for his sprightly picture books depicting the country life of England. The Caldecott Medal, established in 1938, is awarded to the most distinguished American picture book for children chosen from those first published in the United States during the previous year. The text should be worthy of the illustrations, but the award is made primarily for the artwork.

Students of children's literature would do well to acquaint themselves with some of these medal-winning books and their authors and illustrators. The Honor Books for each award are also worth knowing. Because the selection for the awards must be limited to

*In this Caldecott Medal-winning book,* Ox-Cart Man *by Donald Hall, the father loads up his ox-cart with the many things his family has been making and growing all year to take to market. Barbara Cooney's paintings accurately reflect the New England landscapes and Early American primitive art.*

books published during one year, the quality of the award books varies; certain years produce a richer harvest than others. The passage of time has shown most choices to have been wise ones, but there have been a few surprises. In 1953, for instance, the highly praised *Charlotte's Web* was a Newbery Honor Book, edged out in the medal competition by Ann Nolan Clark's *Secret of the Andes,* a beautifully written but far less popular story. Books by Laura Ingalls Wilder were in the Honor Book category five different years, but never received the medal. Final restitution was made, perhaps, by the establishment of the Laura Ingalls Wilder Award, which serves a different purpose.

The list of Caldecott Medal winners shows great variety as to type of artwork, media used, age appeal, and subject matter. The range of artwork includes the lovely winterscapes by Mary Azarian for Jacqueline Briggs Martin's *Snowflake Bentley;* the comic, almost cartoon, style of William Steig's *Sylvester and the Magic Pebble;* the surrealism of Chris Van Allsburg's *Jumanji;* and the expressionistic collages of David Diaz in *Smoky Night* by Eve Bunting. Various media are represented among the medal winners, including woodcut, watercolor, opaque paint, collage, and various combinations of pen and ink and paint. Marcia Brown has won the Caldecott Medal three times; Chris Van Allsburg, Robert McCloskey, Nonny Hogrogian, Leo and Diane Dillon, and Barbara Cooney have been honored twice. Joseph Krumgold, Elizabeth Speare, Katherine Paterson, and Lois Lowry have each received two Newbery Medals; Robert Lawson continues to be the only person who has won both a Newbery and a Caldecott Medal.

## International Book Awards

The Hans Christian Andersen Medal was established in 1956 as the first international children's book award. It is given by the International Board on Books for Young People every two years to a living author and (since 1966) an illustrator, in recognition of his or her entire body of work. Meindert DeJong, Maurice Sendak, Scott O'Dell, Paula Fox, Virginia Hamilton, and Katherine Paterson are the only Americans to have received this medal so far.

The Mildred L. Batchelder Award was established to honor the U.S. publication of the year's most outstanding translated book for children. Like the Newbery and Caldecott Medals, this award is given by the Association for Library Service to Children of the American Library Association. Appropriately, it is always presented on International Children's Book Day, 2 April, which was Hans Christian Andersen's birthday.

## Lifetime Contribution Awards

The Laura Ingalls Wilder Award honors an author or illustrator for a substantial and lasting contribution to children's literature. It was established in 1954 by the Association for Library Service to Children and was presented first to Laura Ingalls Wilder herself, for her *Little House* books. First presented every five years, and now every three, the award makes no requirement concerning the number of books that must be produced, but a body of work is implied and the books must be published in the United States. The recipients of the award, including Beverly Cleary, Theodor S. Geisel (Dr. Seuss), Maurice Sendak, Jean Fritz, Virginia Hamilton, Marcia Brown, and Russell Freedman, all are creators who have made an indelible mark on American children's literature.

Some of the other awards presented for a body of work are the Catholic Library Association's Regina Medal and the University of Mississippi's Children's Collection Medallion. The Kerlan Award, which honors "singular attainments" in children's literature, also recognizes the donation of original manuscripts, as resource material, to the Kerlan Collection at the University of Minnesota.

There was no major award for children's poetry until 1977, when the National Council of Teachers of English established the Award for Excellence in Poetry for Children, to be given to a living American poet. This award recognizes the writer's entire body of work. Octogenarian David McCord was the first recipient; others have included Aileen Fisher, Karla Kuskin, Myra Cohn Livingston, Eve Merriam, John Ciardi, Lilian Moore, Arnold Adoff, Valerie Worth, Barbara Esbensen, Eloise Greenfield, and X. J. Kennedy.

Several other awards, like the Scott O'Dell Award for Historical Fiction and the Edgar Allen Poe Award of the Mystery Writers of America, honor particular kinds of writing. These prizes are given for individual books rather than for a body of work, however.

No one but the most interested follower of children's literature would want to remember all the awards that are given for children's books. And certainly no one should assume that the award winners are the only children's books worth reading. Like the coveted Oscars of the motion picture industry and the Emmys of television, the awards in children's literature focus attention not only on the winners of the year but also on the entire field of endeavor. They recognize and honor excellence and also point the way to improved writing, illustrating, and producing of worthwhile and attractive books for children.

# INTO THE CLASSROOM

## *Knowing Children's Literature*

**Room 201**

1. Form a mock Newbery award committee and review the medal winners and Honor Books for one year. Do the children agree with the opinions of the actual judges? Have them state their reasons for the choices they have made.

2. Ask children to interview two or three classmates or family members about the influence of literature in their lives. In what ways have books been important to them? What titles are most memorable? Why?

# Personal Explorations

1. Can you think of any one book you read and reread as a child? What particular qualities of the story appealed to you? Reread it now and evaluate it according to the criteria established in this chapter. Would you still recommend it for children?

2. Read one of the series books: for instance, one from the Baby-Sitters Club, Sweet Valley High, Boxcar Children, or Nancy Drew series. Look closely at the literary craftsmanship of the book. How many contrived incidents can you find? Do the characters have real strengths and weaknesses? If you were to read this book aloud, how would it sound?

3. Read a recently published children's book and write a brief reaction to it. Then find two or more published reviews of that book. List the criteria that seem important to the reviewers. How are their criteria like or different from yours?

4. Write your reading autobiography. What memories do you have of your early reading? Did either of your parents read to you? Do you recall any of the books they read? Did any teachers or librarians read aloud to you? What were some of your favorite books? Do you recall any that you did not like? Do you know why you did not like them?

# Related Readings

Bishop, Rudine Sims. *Shadow and Substance: Afro-American Experience in Contemporary Children's Fiction.* Urbana, Ill.: National Council of Teachers of English, 1982.

The author surveys 150 books published between 1965 and 1979 that portray contemporary African American experience. She categorizes images portrayed in three sections: fiction with a social conscience, "melting pot" fiction that essentially assumes a cultural homogeneity, and "culturally conscious fiction." Five African American authors are discussed against a backdrop of other contemporary authors.

Cameron, Eleanor. *The Seed and the Vision: On the Writing and Appreciation of Children's Books.* New York: Dutton, 1993.

This collection of essays by a noted children's author and scholar looks at writing for children, aiming a critical lens at many classic works.

Coles, Robert. *The Call of Stories: Teaching and the Moral Imagination.* Boston: Houghton Mifflin, 1989.

A noted child psychiatrist describes the influence of literature in his own life and its impact on the young adults he has taught at Harvard University and elsewhere.

Egoff, Sheila, Gordon Stubbs, Ralph Ashley, and Wendy Sutton. *Only Connect: Readings on Children's Literature.* 3rd ed. New York: Oxford University Press, 1996.

An excellent collection of essays on children's literature, encompassing literary criticism, standards, changing tastes, children's responses to books, and writing and illustrating books. Many of the contributors are well known, including Katherine Paterson, Natalie Babbitt, C. S. Lewis, and John Rowe Townsend.

Harris, Violet J., ed. *Using Multicultural Literature in the K–8 Classroom.* Norwood, Mass.: Christopher Gordon, 1997.

This book is an indispensable guide to the issues surrounding the teaching of multicultural literature. Various chapters provide criteria and titles for choosing African American, Asian Pacific, Native American, Puerto Rican, Mexican American, and Caribbean children's books.

Harrison, Barbara, and Gregory Maguire. *Origins of Story: On Writing for Children.* New York: McElderry Books, 1999.

A collection of essays by such noted authors as Virginia Hamilton, Ursula Le Guin, Maurice Sendak, and Jill Paton Walsh. In these lectures, originally presented under the auspices of Children's Literature New England, the authors focus on the critical ways in which their own moral and intellectual lives are served by writing for children.

Horning, Kathleen T. *From Cover to Cover: Evaluating and Reviewing Children's Books.* New York: HarperCollins, 1997.

Horning, librarian and coordinator of Special Collections at the Cooperative Children's Book Center at the University of Wisconsin, has written a straightforward and readable guide to evaluating children's books. She provides a thoughtful discussion of criteria for six genres of children's books and concludes with a chapter on writing book reviews.

Hunt, Peter. *Criticism, Theory, and Children's Literature.* Cambridge, Mass.: Basil Blackwell, 1991.

A fresh examination of important questions and issues, such as what children's literature is, the nature of reading, and the role of style and narrative in children's books. Much attention goes to the underlying assumptions of critics and other adults regarding children and their reading, with emphasis on the relationship between ideology and literature. These complex ideas are presented in generally readable terms and will spark discussion and debate.

Kingman, Lee, ed. *Newbery and Caldecott Medal Books 1976–1985*. Boston: Horn Book, 1985.

The acceptance speeches of the medal winners are included, along with biographical sketches, photographs, and illustrations or quotes from their work. In addition there are critical essays by Barbara Bader, Ethel Heins, and Zena Sutherland. Speeches of recent medal winners are published each year in the July/August issue of *Horn Book Magazine*.

Lukens, Rebecca J. *A Critical Handbook of Children's Literature*. 6th ed. New York: Addison-Wesley, 1999.

A careful examination of literary elements in children's books. Lukens concentrates on E. B. White's *Charlotte's Web* to show how elements like characterization, style, and point of view are developed in good children's books.

Manguel, Alberto. *A History of Reading*. New York: Viking 1997.

Manguel places the facts about such wide-ranging topics as the traditions of reading aloud, book design, censorship, and forbidden reading within the context of his own eloquent passion for books, and gives us a very personal view of the history of reading, writing, and books.

Trelease, Jim. *The New Read-Aloud Handbook*. 4th rev. ed. New York: Penguin Books, 1995.

Written for a popular audience by a father who discovered what fun it was to share books with his family, this book is a delight to read and a good gift for parents. The selection is highly personal.

Zinsser, William, ed. *Worlds of Childhood: The Art and Craft of Writing for Children*. Boston: Houghton Mifflin, 1998.

Essays by six gifted writers for children—Jean Fritz, Jill Krementz, Maurice Sendak, Jack Prelutsky, Rosemary Wells, and Katherine Paterson—reveal individual personality and a common concern for the needs of their audience. A special bibliography lists books that were childhood favorites of each author or ones that have influenced their adult lives and work.

# *Children's Literature*

Books listed at the end of each chapter are recommended, subject to qualifications noted in the text. See Appendix C for publishers' complete addresses. In the case of new editions, the original publication date appears in square brackets.

Adler, David. *A Picture Book of Amelia Earhart*. Holiday House, 1998.

Alcott, Louisa May. *Little Women*. Dell Yearling, 1987 [1868].

Almond, David. *Kit's Wilderness*. Delacorte, 2000.

———. *Skellig*. Delacorte, 1999.

Andersen, Hans Christian. *The Ugly Duckling*. Retold and illustrated by Troy Howell. Putnam, 1990.

Appelbaum, Diana. *Giants in the Land*. Illustrated by Michael McCurdy. Houghton Mifflin, 1993.

Asbjørnsen, P. C., and Jorgen E. Moe. *The Three Billy Goats Gruff*. Illustrated by Marcia Brown. Harcourt Brace, 1957.

Avi. *Poppy*. Illustrated by Brian Floca. Orchard, 1995.

Babbitt, Natalie. *Tuck Everlasting*. Farrar, Straus & Giroux, 1985.

Bang, Molly. *Goose*. Scholastic, 1996.

Baylor, Byrd. *I'm in Charge of Celebrations*. Illustrated by Peter Parnall. Scribner's, 1986.

Blume, Judy. *Are You There, God? It's Me, Margaret*. Bradbury, 1970.

———. *Blubber*. Bradbury, 1974.

Brett, Jan. *The Mitten*. Putnam, 1989.

Brown, Margaret Wise. *The Golden Egg Book*. Illustrated by Leonard Weisgard. Golden Press, 1976.

———. *Goodnight Moon*. Illustrated by Clement Hurd. Harper & Row, 1947.

Bunting, Eve. *Smoky Night*. Illustrated by David Diaz. Harcourt Brace, 1994.

Burleigh, Robert. *Home Run: The Story of Babe Ruth*. Illustrated by Mike Wimmer. Harcourt Brace, 1999.

Burnett, Frances Hodgson. *The Secret Garden*. Illustrated by Shirley Hughes. Viking, 1989 [1910].

Carbonne, Elisa. *Stealing Freedom*. Knopf, 1998.

Carle, Eric. *Do You Want to Be My Friend?* Crowell, 1971.

———. *The Very Hungry Caterpillar*. Philomel, 1969.

Carroll, Lewis. *Alice's Adventures in Wonderland* and *Through the Looking Glass*. Illustrated by John Tenniel. Macmillan, 1963 [First published separately, 1866 and 1872].

Clark, Ann Nolan. *Secret of the Andes*. Illustrated by Jean Charlot. Viking, 1952.

Cleary, Beverly. *Ramona Quimby, Age 8*. Illustrated by Alan Tiegreen. Morrow, 1981.

Collier, James Lincoln, and Christopher Collier. *My Brother Sam Is Dead*. Four Winds, 1974.

Cooper, Susan. *The Dark Is Rising*. Illustrated by Alan Cober. Macmillan, 1973.

Creech, Sharon. *Walk Two Moons*. HarperCollins, 1994.

Danzinger, Paula. *Amber Brown Is Feeling Blue*. Putnam, 1998.

DeFelice, Cynthia. *The Ghost of Fossil Glen*. Farrar, Straus & Giroux, 1998.

———. *Nowhere to Call Home*. Farrar, Straus & Giroux, 1999.

Defoe, Daniel. *Robinson Crusoe*. Houghton Mifflin, 1972 [1719].

Dorris, Michael. *Morning Girl*. Hyperion, 1992.

English, Karen. *Francie.* Farrar Straus & Giroux, 1999.

Feiffer, Jules. *Bark, George.* HarperCollins, 1999.

Fitzhugh, Louise. *Harriet the Spy.* Harper & Row, 1964.

Fleischman, Paul. *Weslandia.* Illustrated by Kevin Hawkes. Candlewick, 1999.

———. *Whirligig.* Holt, 1998.

Fletcher, Ralph. *Flying Solo.* Clarion, 1998.

Gàg, Wanda. *Millions of Cats.* Putnam, 1977 [1928].

Galdone, Joanna. *The Tailypo.* Clarion, 1984.

Galdone, Paul. *The Gingerbread Boy.* Clarion, 1983.

———. *The Three Little Pigs.* Clarion, 1979.

Gantos, Jack. *Jack on the Tracks: Four Seasons of Fifth Grade.* Farrar, Straus & Giroux, 1999.

Gardiner, John. *Stone Fox.* Illustrated by Marcia Sewall. Crowell, 1980.

Geisert, Bonnie, and Art Geisert. *Rivertown.* Houghton Mifflin, 1999.

George, Jean. *Julie.* Illustrated by Wendell Minor. Harper-Collins, 1994.

———. *Julie of the Wolves.* Illustrated by John Schoenherr. Harper & Row, 1972.

———. *Julie's Wolf Pack.* Illustrated by Wendell Minor. HarperCollins, 1997.

———. *My Side of the Mountain.* Dutton, 1988 [1959].

———. *On the Far Side of the Mountain.* Dutton, 1990.

———. *Water Sky.* Harper & Row, 1987.

Grimes, Nikki. *Jazmin's Notebook.* Dial, 1998.

Grimm, Jacob, and Wilhelm Grimm. *Little Red Riding Hood.* Illustrated by Trina Schart Hyman. Holiday House, 1983.

Guthrie, Woody. *This Land Is Your Land.* Illustrated by Kathy Jakobsen. Little, Brown, 1998.

Haas, Jessie. *Unbroken.* Greenwillow, 1999.

Hall, Donald. *Ox-Cart Man.* Illustrated by Barbara Cooney. Viking, 1979.

Hamilton, Virginia. *Cousins.* Philomel, 1990.

Hansen, Joyce, and Gary McGowan. *Breaking Ground, Breaking Silence.* Holt, 1998.

Heide, Florence Parry, and Judith Heide Gilliland. *The Day of Ahmed's Secret.* Illustrated by Ted Lewin. Lothrop, Lee & Shepard, 1990.

Henkes, Kevin. *Julius, the Baby of the World.* Greenwillow, 1990.

Hesse, Karen. *Out of the Dust.* Scholastic, 1997.

Holt, Kimberly Willis. *My Louisiana Sky.* Holt, 1998.

Huck, Charlotte. *A Creepy Countdown.* Illustrated by Jos. A. Smith. Greenwillow, 1998.

Hughes, Richard. *A High Wind in Jamaica.* Harper & Row, 1989 [1929].

Hunter, Mollie. *Mermaid Summer.* Harper & Row, 1988.

———. *A Stranger Came Ashore.* Harper & Row, 1974.

Keller, Laurie. *The Scrambled States of America.* Holt, 1998.

Kent, Jack. *The Fat Cat: A Danish Folktale.* Parents Magazine Press, 1971.

Kleven, Elisa. *The Puddle Pail.* Dutton, 1997.

Konigsburg, E. L. *The View from Saturday.* Atheneum, 1996.

Lauture, Denize. *Running the Road to ABC.* Illustrated by Reynold Ruffins. Simon & Schuster, 1996.

Lawrence, Iain. *The Wreckers.* Delacorte, 1998.

Lee, Harper. *To Kill a Mockingbird.* HarperCollins, 1995 [1960].

Le Guin, Ursula. *A Wizard of Earthsea.* Illustrated by Ruth Robbins. Parnassus, 1968.

L'Engle, Madeleine. *Meet the Austins.* Vanguard, 1960.

———. *A Swiftly Tilting Planet.* Farrar, Straus & Giroux, 1978.

———. *A Wrinkle in Time.* Farrar, Straus & Giroux, 1962.

Lewis, C. S. *The Lion, the Witch, and the Wardrobe.* Illustrated by Pauline Baynes. Macmillan, 1986 [1961].

Lindgren, Astrid. *Pippi Longstocking.* Translated by Florence Lamborn. Illustrated by Louis Glanzman. Viking Penguin, 1950.

Lobel, Arnold. *Days with Frog and Toad.* Harper & Row, 1976.

———. *Frog and Toad All Year.* Harper & Row, 1976.

———. *Frog and Toad Are Friends.* Harper & Row, 1972.

———. *Frog and Toad Together.* Harper & Row, 1972.

Locker, Thomas. *Water Dance.* Harcourt Brace, 1997.

Lowry, Lois. *Number the Stars.* Houghton Mifflin, 1989.

MacLachlan, Patricia. *Sarah, Plain and Tall.* Harper & Row, 1985.

Marshall, James. *George and Martha: The Complete Stories of Two Best Friends.* Houghton Mifflin, 1997 [1972].

Martin, Jacqueline Briggs. *Snowflake Bentley.* Illustrated by Mary Azarian. Houghton Mifflin, 1998.

Matas, Carol. *Greater Than Angels.* Simon & Schuster, 1998.

Mayne, William. *Hob and the Goblins.* Illustrated by Norman Messenger. Dorling Kindersley, 1994.

McCaughrean, Geraldine. *The Pirate's Son.* Scholastic, 1998.

McCloskey, Robert. *Homer Price.* Viking, 1943.

McCord, David. "The Pickety Fence." In *One at a Time.* Illustrated by Henry B. Kane. Little, Brown, 1977.

Milne, A. A. *Winnie the Pooh.* Illustrated by Ernest H. Shepard. Dutton, 1988 [1926].

Munsch, Robert. *Love You Forever.* Illustrated by Sheila McGraw. Firefly Books, 1986.

Myers, Walter Dean. *Scorpions.* Harper & Row, 1988.

Nye, Naomi Shihab. *Habibi.* Simon & Schuster, 1997.

O'Dell, Scott. *Island of the Blue Dolphins.* Illustrated by Ted Lewin. Houghton Mifflin, 1990 [1960].

Paterson, Katherine. *Bridge to Terabithia.* Illustrated by Donna Diamond. Crowell, 1977.

———. *The Great Gilly Hopkins.* Crowell, 1978.

———. *Lyddie.* Lodestar, 1991.

Paulsen, Gary. *Hatchet.* Bradbury, 1987.

———. *The Winter Room.* Orchard, 1989.

Potter, Beatrix. *The Tale of Peter Rabbit.* Warne, 1902.

Pullman, Philip. *Clockwork.* Scholastic, 1998.

Reyher, Becky. *My Mother Is the Most Beautiful Woman in the World.* Illustrated by Ruth Gannett. Lothrop, Lee & Shepard, 1945.

Richter, Hans Peter. *Friedrich.* Penguin, 1987.

Rowling, J. K. *Harry Potter and the Chamber of Secrets.* Scholastic, 1999.

———. *Harry Potter and the Sorcerer's Stone.* Scholastic, 1998.

Rylant, Cynthia. *Henry and Mudge and the Sneaky Crackers.* Illustrated by Sucie Stevenson. Simon & Schuster, 1999.

————. *Missing May*. Orchard, 1992.

Sachar, Louis. *Holes*. Farrar, Straus & Giroux, 1998.

Sciezska, Jon. *Math Curse*. Illustrated by Lane Smith. Viking, 1995.

Sendak, Maurice. *Where the Wild Things Are*. Harper & Row, 1988 [1963].

Seuss, Dr. [Theodor S. Geisel]. *And to Think That I Saw It on Mulberry Street*. Random House, 1989 [1937].

————. *The Cat in the Hat*. Random House, 1966 [1957].

————. *Oh, the Places You'll Go*. Random House, 1990.

Shannon, David. *No David!* Scholastic, 1998.

Speare, Elizabeth George. *The Sign of the Beaver*. Houghton Mifflin, 1983.

Sperry, Armstrong. *Call It Courage*. Macmillan, 1940.

Spinelli, Jerry. *Wringer*. HarperCollins, 1997.

Steig, William. *Sylvester and the Magic Pebble*. Simon & Schuster, 1969.

Stevenson, Robert Louis. *Treasure Island*. Illustrated by N. C. Wyeth. Scribner's, 1981 [1883].

Taback, Simms, *Joseph had a Little Overcoat*. Viking, 1999.

Taylor, Mildred. *The Friendship*. Illustrated by Max Ginsburg. Dial, 1987.

————. *Roll of Thunder, Hear My Cry*. Illustrated by Jerry Pinkney. Dial, 1976.

Tillage, Leon Walter. *Leon's Story*. Illustrated by Susan L. Roth. Farrar, Straus & Giroux, 1997.

Tolkien, J. R. R. *The Hobbit*. Houghton Mifflin, 1938.

Van Allsburg, Chris. *Jumanji*. Houghton Mifflin, 1981.

Van Leeuwen, Jean. *Amanda Pig and Her Best Friend Lollipop*. Illustrated by Ann Schweninger. Dial, 1998.

Voigt, Cynthia. *Homecoming*. Atheneum, 1981.

Weisner, David. *Sector 7*. Clarion, 1999.

Wells, Rosemary. *Yoko*. Hyperion, 1998.

White, E. B. *Charlotte's Web*. Illustrated by Garth Williams. Harper & Row, 1952.

Willard, Nancy. *A Visit to William Blake's Inn*. Illustrated by Alice and Martin Provensen. Harcourt Brace, 1981.

Williams, Margery. *The Velveteen Rabbit*. Illustrated by William Nicholson. Doubleday, 1969 [1922].

Yumoto, Kazumi. *The Friends*. Translated by Cathy Hirano. Farrar, Straus & Giroux, 1996.

# Chapter Two

# Understanding Children's Responses to Literature

*F*ive-year-old Michael hurried to the block corner from the story circle, where his teacher had just told "Little Red Riding Hood." He whispered parts of the story under his breath as he worked to build a low enclosure around himself. When an aide walked by, Michael stood

and made a growling noise. "I'm the big bad wolf!" he announced.

One rainy noon hour Sean and Dan, both 7, found a quiet corner of the bookcase and read to each other from Shel Silverstein's book of verse *Where the Sidewalk Ends.* "Listen to this one!" (Giggles.) "I can read this one!" (More giggles.) Two other children discovered the fun and joined them. All four were soon arguing heatedly about which poem was "the best one."

A small group of 9- and 10-year-olds searched the well-stocked library corner of their own classroom for something to read at sustained silent-reading time. Jason picked a book, glanced at the cover, and quickly reshelved it. "Who would want to read a book like *that?*" he muttered. Emily whispered to Julie that she had found another Lois Lowry book about Anastasia Krupnik. "I get it next," the friend said, and went on looking for a book about horses.

At regular silent-reading time, 10-year-old Evie curled up in her class's reading-and-rocking chair to finish Katherine Paterson's book *The Great Gilly Hopkins.* "The way it ended wasn't fair," Evie later protested to her teacher. "Gilly should have gone back to Trotter. This way just isn't right!"

A teacher asked her sixth graders to explain why they thought Jean George had written *Cry of the Crow.* Katie wrote: "I think what the author was trying to tell you is that once something has lived in the wild, it should stay there even if it's just like your brother or sister. . . . When you catch a bird and try to make it do something, it is like being in prison for the bird."

These glimpses of children responding to literature show some of the many different ways in which they might express their preferences, thoughts, and feelings. Although each of these responses is personal and unique, each also reflects the child's age and experience. Young children like Michael are often so totally involved in a story that they relive it through dramatic play. Those like Dan and Sean, who are developing independent reading skills, seem particularly eager to demonstrate that ability and to share newly discovered favorites. Middle graders choosing books, like Jason, Emily, and Julie, show definite preferences. Both Evie's expectation of a happy ending and her concern with injustice in a character's life are typical of middle childhood. Katie's success in generalizing a theme about all wild things from the story of one crow and her fluency in discussing the author's purpose are representative of older children's growing ability to deal with abstract ideas about a story.

To have a successful literature program, teachers and librarians must know books well, but that is only half the task. It is also necessary to understand children and the changing patterns of their responses to literature.

## *Reading Interests & Preferences*

The phrase *response to literature* is used in a variety of ways. Theoretically, *response* refers to any outward sign of that inner activity, something said or done that reveals a reader's thoughts and feelings about literature. A 6-year-old's drawing of a favorite character and a book review in the *New York Times* are both responses in this sense. Teachers or librarians who predict that a book will bring "a good response" use the term in a different way, focusing on the likelihood that children will find a book appealing and will be eager to read and talk about it.

Most of the early research on children and literature focused on this third area of response to discover what reading material children like or dislike. Children's interests and preferences are still a major concern for teachers, librarians, parents, publishers, and booksellers. Everyone who selects children's books can make better choices by knowing which books are likely to have immediate appeal for many children and which ones might require introduction or encouragement along the way.

Studies of reading interests over the years have consistently identified certain topics and elements of content that have wide appeal.[1] Researchers have found that *animals* and *humor,* for instance, are generally popular across age levels. Among other elements that are frequently mentioned for reader appeal are *action, suspense,* and *surprise.* Sales figures, too, can reflect children's reading interests. A recent survey by *Publisher's Weekly* magazine showed that tie-ins to popular movies or television shows and series books, particularly those with supernatural or horror themes, were among the best-selling children's books. The survey showed that teenagers (12- to 17-year-olds) buy fiction slightly more often than nonfiction, a figure that did not vary much with gender. Favorite topics include mysteries, science fiction/ fantasy, books about celebrities and athletes, and how-to-books.[2]

Even though we can identify commonly chosen topics and story features that have wide general appeal, it is still impossible to concoct a formula for books that would have unfailing popularity with *all* children. Teachers and librarians need to be sensitive to children's individual tastes, which often are unique and very particular. Nevertheless, the variations in interests among different *groups* of children seem to be linked to age, gender, and certain other influences.

## Age and Gender Differences

The most obvious change in children's interest patterns occurs with age, as children take on more complex material and new areas of concern. Good book choices for first and sixth graders seldom overlap, even when the general topic is the same. Robert McCloskey's picture book *Make Way for Ducklings* is a favorite ani-

mal story among 4- and 5-year-olds; 12-year-olds prefer their animal characters to be part of something more dramatic, as in Wilson Rawls's story about two coon dogs, *Where the Red Fern Grows.* Seven-year-olds laugh at Peggy Parish's *Amelia Bedelia* and her literal interpretation of instructions like "Draw the drapes" and "Dress the chicken." Eleven-year-olds like "funny" books, too, but prefer a different brand of humor—the comic situations in Roald Dahl's *The BFG* or the deadpan humor of Louis Sachar's *Holes.* Older adolescents prefer the irreverent tone and the wisecracking dialogue in *Extreme Elvin* by Chris Lynch.

Some of the broader shifts in preference that mark the elementary school years include a move away from a preference for fairy tales toward more interest in realistic subject matter. According to many studies, adventure becomes more important through the middle grades. Research continues to confirm older children's liking for adventure, mystery, and contemporary realistic stories. All of these studies also show that upper-grade students begin to show marked content preferences according to their sex.[3]

The influence of gender differences on reading interests is not entirely clear. Previous studies found that interests of children vary according to age and grade level and that girls read more than boys, but that boys had a wider interest range and read a greater variety. Girls showed an earlier interest in adult romantic fiction than boys, while boys tended to prefer nonfiction from an early age. Boys seldom showed preference for a "girl's" book, but girls read a "boy's" book more often.[4] A more recent study done in England with close to eight thousand 10-, 12-, and 14-year-olds found a swing away from book reading as children grow older, particularly among 14-year-old boys. The survey found that although "boys' predilection for non-narrative remains, . . . its significance in boys' reading diet is somewhat overstated." There was strong evidence of the "overwhelming importance of narrative in children's reading choices" but the authors rejoiced in the enormous diversity of types of literature chosen by both sexes.[5]

[1]Angela M. Broening, "Factors Influencing Pupils' Reading of Library Books," *Elementary English Review* 11 (1934): 155–158; Fannie Wyche Dunn, *Interest Factors in Reading Materials* (New York: Teachers College, Columbia University, 1921); Jeanie Goodhope, "Into the Eighties: BAYA's Fourth Reading Interest Survey," *School Library Journal* 29 (December 1982): 33; Mary-Jo Fresch, "Self-Selection Strategies of Early Literacy Learners," *Reading Teacher,* 49 (November, 1995): 220–227; Alan Purves and Richard Beach, *Literature and the Reader: Research in Response to Literature, Reading Interests, and the Teaching of Literature* (Urbana, Ill.: National Council of Teachers of English, 1972), pp. 69–71.

[2]Amanda Ferguson, "Reading Is Cool," *Publishers Weekly,* 245 (October 12, 1998): 28–31.

[3]J. W. Coomer and K. M. Tessmer, "1986 Books for Young Adults Poll," *English Journal* 75 (November 1986): 58–66; M. A. Harkrader and R. Moore, "Literature Preferences of Fourth Graders," *Reading Research and Instruction* 36 (1997): 325–339.

[4]Glenda Childress, "Gender Gap in the Library: Different Choices for Boys and Girls," *Top of the News* 42 (fall 1985): 69–73; Helen Huus, "Interpreting Research in Children's Literature," in *Children, Books and Reading* (Newark, Del.: International Association, 1964), p. 125.

[5]Christine Hall and Martin Coles, *Children's Reading Choices* (London: Routledge, 1999), p. 136.

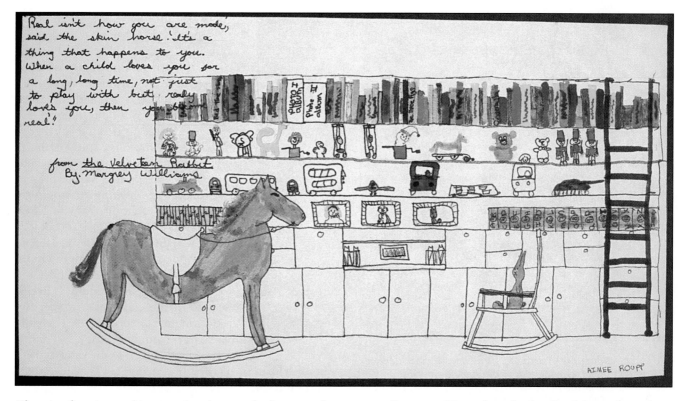

Real isn't how you are made,
said the skin horse. 'It's a
thing that happens to you.
When a child loves you for
a long, long time, not just
to play with but, really
loves you, then you become
real.'

from the Velveteen Rabbit
By. Margery Williams

AIMEE ROUPP

*Choosing favorites and interpreting them are both a part of response to literature. Notice how the details of the modern playroom setting in this child's illustration* The Velveteen Rabbit *provide a glimpse of her unique personal perspective on the book.*
Martin Luther King, Jr., Laboratory School, Evanston, Illinois, Public Schools.

What we do not know about gender differences in children's choices is whether they reflect a "natural" interest or conformity to cultural expectations. Research that updates these preference studies in our postmodern age is certainly important. We can assume, however, that in school and home settings where traditional sexual stereotypes are downplayed, boys and girls share enthusiasm for many common favorites. It is important to give children many options for book choice so that girls and boys can have a chance to explore each other's perspectives. It is just as unfortunate for girls to miss the excellent nonfiction being published today as it is for boys to turn away from fine fiction that offers insight into human relationships.

## Other Determinants of Interest

 Many factors other than age and gender have been investigated in relation to children's reading interests. At one time the influence of mental age as measured by standardized tests received considerable attention. Now, however, we believe that children of varying academic abilities still are more alike than different in the character of their reading interests. It is more likely that

the quantity of books involved and the rate at which interests develop will vary widely.

Illustrations, color, format, length, and type of print can also influence children's choices. It would be unwise, however, to oversimplify the effect of these factors on children's book choices, especially because so much of the research has been done outside the context of normal reading and choosing situations. When children choose and use books in their own classrooms, their reactions to books are more complex than controlled experiments or surveys could reveal.[6]

Social and environmental influences also affect children's book choices and reading interests. Many teachers and librarians feel that cultural and ethnic factors are related to reading interests. One of the arguments for providing culturally authentic picture books and novels about Asian, Hispanic, African American, and Native American children is that readers from a particular culture will find material drawn from their own culture more interesting. One study of African American and Hispanic American fifth

---

[6]Barbara Z. Kiefer, *The Potential of Picture Books from Visual Literacy to Aesthetic Understanding* (Columbus, Ohio: Merrill/Prentice Hall, 1995).

*Although reading preferences are influenced by age, gender, and many other factors, children often make specific choices based on the book itself, its length, format, cover, or the appeal of a sample paragraph.*
Beginning with Children School, Brooklyn, NY.

graders found that African American children preferred to read culturally conscious literature, and they rated books about mainstream characters among their favorites. Hispanic American children were less enthusiastic about multicultural titles.[7] The relationship between interests and culture does not seem to be simple, and unfortunately there is not yet much research to clarify this point.

Although interests do not seem to vary greatly according to geographical location, the impact of the immediate environment—particularly the availability and accessibility of reading materials in the home, classroom, and public and school libraries—can be very strong. Children in classrooms where books are regularly discussed, enjoyed, and given high value tend to show livelier interest in a wider range of literature than do children from situations where books are given less attention. It is hard to tell how much of this effect is due to contact with the books and how much is social. Teachers' favorite books are often mentioned by children as their own favorites, perhaps because these are the stories closest at hand, or perhaps because of positive associations with the teacher.

Children frequently influence each other in their choice of books. In the culture of the classroom, a

title or an author or a topic may rise to celebrity status for a time. Shel Silverstein's *Falling Up* might be "the book" to read in one group of third graders, or children might make their own sign-up sheets to read the classroom's only copy of the latest *Dear America* book. Younger children might spend time on a study of bears and long afterward point out "bear stories" to each other. Media presentations like the *Reading Rainbow* series from the Public Broadcasting System create demand for specific books.

Peer recommendations are especially important to middle graders in choosing what to read. Some fifth and sixth graders are very candid: "'Everyone else in the class read it, so I figured I ought to, too.' . . . 'I usually read what Tammy reads.' '. . . most of my friends just like the same type of book I like. So, if they find a book, I'll believe them and I'll try it.'"[8]

## Explaining Children's Choices

How can children influence each other's book choices so readily? Part of the answer may be simply that agemates are likely to enjoy the same kinds of stories because they share many developmental characteristics. As children grow and learn, their levels of understanding change, and so do their favorites in literature. A few thought-provoking studies have suggested that children prefer those stories that best represent their own way of looking at the world—stories that mirror their experiences, needs, fears and desires at a given age.[9]

There are many things to consider in explaining children's book choices. One of the most important is prior experiences with literature. Some children have heard many stories read aloud at home or have been introduced by their teachers to many different authors and genres. These children are likely to have tastes and preferences that seem advanced compared to those of children their age who have had less exposure to books. Children's personal experiences influence their interests in ways that teachers and librarians might

[7]Gail Singleton Taylor, "Multicultural Literature Preferences of Low-Ability African American and Hispanic American Fifth-Graders," *Reading Improvement* 34 (spring, 1997): 37–48.

[8]Susan I. Hepler and Janet Hickman, " 'The Book Was Okay. I Love You'—Social Aspects of Response to Literature," *Theory into Practice* 21 (autumn 1982): 279.

[9]See Andre Favat, *Child and Tale: The Origins of Interest* (Urbana, Ill.: National Council of Teachers of English, 1977), and Norma Marian Schlager, "Developmental Factors Influencing Children's Responses to Literature" (Ph.D. dissertation, Claremont Graduate School, 1974).

## Asking Children to Tell About Themselves as Readers

**Teaching Feature**

Fourth-grade teacher Roberto Sbordone asks his students to write a "Reader's Portrait" each year to help them reflect on themselves as readers. As Bree, one of his students, reveals her journey to becoming a book lover, she shows how personal each child's responses to books can be.

### A READER'S PORTRAIT BY BREE BANG-JENSEN

I guess I've always loved stories because long before I knew how to read I would listen to a story tape over and over and over again for hours.

My parents used to read to me from a very early age. When I was three my parents read Laura Ingalls books to me.

Years passed, and I had no desire to learn to read. I hated those books called "Easy Readers," because to me they had no point.

In first grade it made no sense to me that I had to learn this bizarre system called reading. Then, in the Thanksgiving vacation of second grade, suddenly it all clicked in place. I was reading the first Boxcar Children Book. I was IN the book! From then on, I spent all my time reading.

For a while, my mother had to make me go outside for half an hour everyday.

My favorite book author is Jean Little, and my favorite book is *Mine for Keeps*. My ninth birthday party was a "Book Party" where we had a book obstacle course, played charades from books, made bookmarks and used books with "treasure" in the title for a treasure hunt. There were even books in the goody bags.

You know what I like about reading? You can take a vacation almost anywhere for a dollar or two—you buy a book and read it. In reading you can be anyone, anywhere, in any situation!

*Bree Bang-Jensen*, Age 9
*Roberto Cecere Sbordone*, Teacher
Springhurst School, Dobbs Ferry, New York

---

never be able to discover. And sometimes apparent interests are only the product of which books are available and which are not. The Teaching Feature: Asking Children to Tell About Themselves as Readers shows how one teacher managed to survey his student's feelings about books.

We must be careful not to oversimplify the reasons for children's book choices. Even so, it is important not to underestimate a developmental perspective that takes into account both experience and growth. This is a powerful tool for predicting reading interests and for understanding other ways in which children respond.

## Growth Patterns that Influence Response

The child-development point of view begins with recognizing and accepting the uniqueness of childhood. Children are not miniature adults but individuals with their own needs, interests, and capabilities—all of which change over time and at varying rates.

In the early decades of child study, emphasis was placed on discovery of so-called normal behavior patterns for each age. Growth studies revealed similarities in patterns of physical, mental, and emotional growth. Later, longitudinal studies showed wide vari-

ations in individual rates of growth. One child's growth might be uneven, and a spurt in one aspect of development might precede a spurt in another. Age trends continue to be useful in understanding the child, but by the 1960s research began to be concerned with the interaction of biological, cultural, and life-experience forces. Researchers recognized that development is not simply the result of the maturation of neural cells but evolves as new experience reshapes existing structures. The interaction of the individual with his or her environment, especially the social and cultural aspects of that environment, has become increasingly important to researchers. This experience affects the age at which development appears.

Studies in children's cognitive and language growth, as well as in other areas of human development, can be very helpful in the choice of appropriate books and the understanding of children's responses. Although this text can highlight only a few recent findings, it can serve to alert the student of children's literature to the importance of such information.

### Physical Development

Children's experiences with literature can begin at a very early age. Studies of infant perception show that even tiny babies hear and see better than was thought possible a few decades ago. For instance, newborns show more response to patterned, rhythmic sounds

*Sturdy books like Tana Hoban's* Red, Blue, Yellow Shoe *are just right for little ones' hands (and teeth).*

Cover from *Red, Blue, Yellow Shoe* by Tana Hoban. Copyright © 1986 by Tana Hoban. Used by permission of Greenwillow Books, an imprint of HarperCollins Publishers.

than to continuous tones. They also show preferences for the sound frequencies of the human voice.[10] This supports the intuition of parents who chant nursery rhymes or sing lullabies that the sound of songs and rhymes provides satisfaction even for the youngest.

Infants gain visual perception very rapidly within their range of focus. Babies in their first months of life see lines, angles, and adjacent areas of high contrast and prefer black and white to muted colors up to about 2 months of age.[11] They progress to seeing simple dimensions such as forms or colors, and before 6 months are perceiving more complex patterns (faces or colored shapes) as whole units. Books designed for babies and toddlers, like Tana Hoban's *Red, Blue, Yellow Shoe,* often acknowledge this developmental pattern by featuring simple, clearly defined pictures with firm outlines, uncluttered backgrounds, and bright colors.

As visual perception develops, children begin to show fascination with details and often enjoy searching for specific objects in illustrations. One 18-month-old boy spotted a clock in Margaret Wise Brown's *Goodnight Moon* and subsequently pointed out

clocks in other books when he discovered them. Older preschoolers make a game of finding "hidden" things in pictures, like the Mother Goose and fairy tale characters tucked into each illustration of Janet and Allan Ahlberg's *Each Peach Pear Plum.*

Children's attention spans generally increase with age as well as interest. In their first school experiences, some young children have trouble sitting quietly for even a 20-minute story. It is better to have several short story times for these children than to demand their attention for longer periods and so lose their interest. Some kindergarten and primary teachers provide many opportunities for children to listen to stories in small groups of two or three by using the listening center or asking parent aides or student teachers to read to as few as one or two children.

Physical development influences children's interests as well as their attention span. Growth in size, muscularity, and coordination is often reflected in children's choice of a book in which characters share their own newly acquired traits or abilities. *Whistle for Willie* by Ezra Jack Keats, for example, seems most rewarding for young children who have just learned to whistle. The demand for sports books increases as girls and boys gain the skills necessary for successful participation.

American children are growing up faster, both physically and psychologically, than they ever have before. By sixth grade almost all girls have reached puberty, although very few boys have.[12] The age of onset of puberty figures prominently in early adolescents' self-concept and influences book choices. Girls are still reading Judy Blume's *Are You There God? It's Me, Margaret* (1970) because it reflects their own concerns about menstruation. Margaret has frequent chats with God, which include pleas like this: "Are you there God? It's me, Margaret. I just told my mother I want a bra. Please help me grow God. You know where."[13]

Both physical maturity and social forces have led to the development of sexual interests at a younger age. Sophisticated 7-year-olds are teased about their "boyfriends" or "girlfriends." According to 1998 data, 52 percent of girls and 76 percent of boys ages 15 to 19 have had sexual intercourse.[14] It is somehow as if childhood were something to be transcended rather than enjoyed. One result of this shortened childhood is

[10]Aidan Macfarlane, *The Psychology of Childbirth* (Cambridge, Mass.: Harvard University Press, 1977).

[11]Leslie B. Cohen, "Our Developing Knowledge of Infant Perception and Cognition," *American Psychologist* 34 (1979): 894–899.

[12]Frederick C. Howe, "The Child in the Elementary School: Developmental Trends," *Child Study Journal* 23 (1993): 327–346.

[13]Judy Blume, *Are You There God? It's Me, Margaret* (Englewood Cliffs, N.J.: Bradbury Press, 1970), p. 37.

[14]L. Kann, *Youth Risk Behavior Surveillance System,* "Morbidity and Mortality Weekly Reports" (Atlanta: Centers for Disease Control and Prevention, 1998).

a decrease in the length of time in which boys and girls are interested in reading children's literature. Many of them turn to reading teenage novels or adult fiction before they have read such fine books as *The Friends* by Kazumi Yumoto, *When Zachary Beaver Came to Town* by Kimberly Willis Holt, or *The Other Shepards* by Adele Griffin, all well-written, complex stories about young adolescents.

## Cognitive Development

The work of the great Swiss psychologist Jean Piaget has had a great influence on educators' understanding of children's intellectual development.[15] Piaget proposed that intelligence develops as a result of the interaction of environment and the maturation of the child. In his view, children are active participants in their own learning.

Piaget's observations led him to conclude that there are distinct stages in the development of logical thinking. According to his theory, all children go through these stages in the same progression, but not necessarily at the same age. He identified these stages as the *sensory-motor period,* from infancy to about 2 years of age; the *preoperational period,* from approximately 2 to 7 years; the *concrete operational period,* from about 7 to 11; and a two-phase development of *formal operations,* which begins around age 11 and continues throughout adult life.

In recent years the validity of this stage theory has been called into question by many researchers who express many concerns about the interpretation of Piaget's theory. Researchers have suggested that children's social and cultural backgrounds and their familiarity with a task or situation might influence their thinking.[16] The whole idea of stages, in fact, suggests a progression of development that might be far more orderly than what occurs in real life. Some psychologists feel that stage theory fails to describe the intricacy and complexity of children's thinking and might lead adults to focus on what children are supposedly not able to do, thus falsely lowering expectations. We need to keep these cautions in mind if we look to Piagetian theory for guidance in selecting books for children and planning literature experiences.

Piaget's main contribution to our understanding of cognitive development was his recognition of the child as a meaning maker, "his rediscovery of the child's mind."[17] Piaget's work and the work of cognitive psychologists since mid century have helped us view children as individuals. We can expect them to think about their experiences differently as they develop, and we can expect that thinking to change as they move toward adulthood. Thus, it is still useful for us to look at some of the characteristics of children's thinking described by Piaget and to compare it to the children we work with. Then we can consider how children's thinking patterns are related to the books they like and to their responses to literature.

In the first several years of life, infants and toddlers learn through coordinating their sensory perceptions and their motor activity. By the end of their first year, most children enjoy the action or game rhymes of Mother Goose. They delight in the rhythm of "Pat-a-Cake, Pat-a-Cake" and anticipate the pinching and patting that accompanies the rhyme. Tactile books such as *Pat the Bunny* by Dorothy Kunhardt appeal to their sensory perceptions by encouraging them to touch special materials pasted on the page. Such an introduction to books incorporates what the young child responds to best—sensory-motor play and participation with a loving adult.

During the preschool and kindergarten years, children learn to represent the world symbolically through language, play, and drawing. Thinking seems to be based on direct experience and perception of the present moment. Many of the particular features ascribed to this stage of thought seem to be reflected in young children's response to literature. During these years children have a hard time holding an image in mind as it changes form or shape. They enjoy cumulative stories like "The Gingerbread Boy" or *Clickety Clack* by Rob and Amy Spence. The built-in repetition in these stories carries the sequence of the action along from page to page. Older children who are able to follow the more complex logic of stories can remember the events without aid and often say that the repetitious language is boring.

Most children of elementary-school age would be described as being in the concrete operational stage according to Piaget's theory. Classifying and arranging objects in series are important abilities within children's command during this period, making them more systematic and orderly thinkers. Their thought also becomes flexible and reversible, allowing them to unravel and rearrange a sequence of events. It is no surprise, then, that elementary-age children begin to like mysteries and to understand stories with more complex plot features such as flashbacks or a story within a story. Older elementary-age children also

[15]Barbel Inhelder and Jean Piaget, *The Growth of Logical Thinking* (New York: Basic Books, 1962); Barry J. Wadsworth, *Piaget's Theory of Cognitive and Affective Development* (Reading, Mass.: Addison-Wesley, 1996).

[16]Margaret Donaldson, *Children's Minds* (New York: Norton, 1979), chap. 2.

[17]Deanna Kuhn, "Cognitive Development," in *Developmental Psychology: An Advanced Textbook,* 3rd ed. (Hillsdale, N.J.: Erlbaum, 1992).

*The repeated phrases in stories like* Clickety Clack *by Rob and Amy Spence help young children gain control of story patterns.*

From *Clickity Clack* by Rob and Amy Spence, Illustrated by Margaret Spengler, copyright © 1999 by Margaret Spengler. Used by permission of Viking Penguin, a division of Penguin Putnam Inc.

seem to identify more spontaneously with different points of view. A book like *The True Story of the Three Little Pigs* by Jon Scieszka suits this developmental level well because readers understand what the author has done with the structure of a familiar tale and can also begin to see the events through the eyes of a new narrator, in this case the wolf.

One interesting aspect of concrete operational children's thinking is described by psychologist David Elkind as "cognitive conceit."[18] As children begin to have some success in reasoning and problem solving, they tend to get the idea that they must be as able as adults, or even smarter. They enjoy besting an older child, parent, or teacher. Although children's visions of superiority may seldom come true in real experience, books for middle graders often feature young protagonists on their own who manage just as well as, or better than, their elders. In E. L. Konigsburg's *From the Mixed-Up Files of Mrs. Basil E. Frankweiler,* for instance, young Claudia is clever enough to outwit adults by living undetected in New York's Metropolitan Museum of Art and shrewd enough to make an important discovery about one of the statues there.

As students begin the transitional period that corresponds roughly to the middle school years, they begin

to develop abstract theoretical thought; they are no longer dependent on concrete evidence but can reason from hypotheses to logical conclusions. This allows them to think of possibilities for their lives that are contrary to their prior experience and enables them to see the future in new ways. Complex novels and science fiction in particular begin to have appeal for students at this level. Also, students gain understanding of the use of symbols for symbols, such as letters for numbers in algebra or symbolic meanings in literature. While they have understood the use of obvious symbols like the broom in *Hurry Home, Candy* by Meindert DeJong, they can now deal with the layers of meaning found in some poetry and complex stories like Lois Lowry's *The Giver.*

This would appear to be the time, then, when literary criticism would be most appropriately introduced. Although teachers at every grade level would have been steadily building some knowledge and appreciation of literature, detailed analysis of a work would probably not be undertaken before this period of intellectual development. Even then, teachers would want such a discussion to arise from the child's personal response to the book.

It is important to remember that not all young people entering middle schools or junior high schools have reached the level of formal operations.[19] At the same time, some young children demonstrate considerable analytical competence as they talk about books that are familiar and meaningful to them.

Other views of cognitive development can help us broaden our base for understanding children and their response to literature. Russian psychologist Lev Semenovich Vygotsky, for instance, stresses the ties between development of thought and language, the social aspect of learning, and the importance of adult-child interaction.[20] One crucial idea is that children grow in their thinking abilities within a "zone of proximal development," an area in which they are asked to stretch their ability, but not too far. For example, if students can identify the similarities in two

---

[18]David Elkind, *Children and Adolescents: Interpretive Essays on Jean Piaget,* 3rd ed. (New York: Oxford University Press, 1981).

[19]David Elkind, "Investigating Intelligence in Early Adolescence," in *Toward Adolescence: The Middle School Years,* ed. Mauritz Johnson and Kenneth J. Rehage, Seventy-Ninth Yearbook of the National Society for the Study of Education (Chicago: University of Chicago Press, 1985), pp. 282–294.

[20]L. S. Vygotsky, *Thought and Language* (Cambridge, Mass.: MIT Press, 1962); Vygotsky, *Mind in Society: The Development of Higher Psychological Processes* (Cambridge, Mass.: Harvard University Press, 1978).

versions of a familiar folktale like "Little Red Riding Hood," they might also be able to see how these stories are related to Ed Young's *Lon Po Po: A Red Riding Hood Tale from China.* However, they might not yet be ready to connect these tales to the modern spoof *Ruby,* by Michael Emberley, which draws its humor from sly references to "Little Red Riding Hood" and an altered urban setting.

American psychologist Howard Gardner has proposed that there is no single "intelligence," but a cluster of at least eight intellectual abilities, or "multiple intelligences": linguistic, musical, spatial, natural, logical-mathematical, bodily, knowledge of self, and understanding of others.[21] The stages of development he sees for each of these are different. Appreciation of literature falls into the category of linguistic intelligence. Increasing sensitivity to balance, composition, style, and sound of language characterize growth within this domain. The idea of multiple intelligences would help to explain why some children breeze through math but blank out during discussions of literature, and vice versa.

However we look at cognitive development, we need to remember that it is only one part of a much larger picture of growth patterns that influence interests and responses.

## Language Development

The pattern of early language learning moves from infant babbling and cooing to the use of single words, frequently ones that name familiar people or things, like *Mama* or *kitty.* Next, somewhere around 2 years, children begin to use two-word utterances. They develop the ability to change inflection, intonation, or word order to expand their range of meaning ("Daddy go?" "*Bad* kitty!"). Theorists disagree on just how children are able to acquire a functional command of such a complex system as language so early in life. There is strong evidence, however, that the child is more than just an imitator. Children seem to construct on their own the system for making themselves understood; M. A. K. Halliday calls this "learning how to mean."[22] To do so they must *use* language—talk as well as listen.

Verbal participation with an adult is an important element in young children's experience with literature. ABC or picture identification books like Margaret Miller's *Guess Who?* provide special opportunities if they are "talked through" rather than simply read as a string of nouns. Toddlers learn more than vocabulary

from such encounters. Very early experiences with books encourage many aspects of language development. (See Chapters 1 and 4 for more on this point.)

Language development proceeds at a phenomenal pace during the preschool years. By the end of that time, children will have learned to express their thoughts in longer sentences that combine ideas or embed one idea within another. In short, they will have gained access to the basic structure of grammar—all this by about age 4, whatever their native language.[23]

Children improvise and explore words as they learn, chanting and playing with language as they gain confidence.[24] Rhythmic rhymes and nonsense verses are natural choices for preschoolers because they fit this pattern so well. However, children's fun in playing with language as various forms are mastered is not limited to the very young. Middle-grade children, with their wider range of language competence, are fascinated by the variety of jokes, riddles, tongue twisters, and folklore miscellany offered by Alvin Schwartz in collections like *Tomfoolery: Trickery and Foolery with Words.* They are also intrigued by ingenious uses of language in a story context, as in Pamela Edward's *Some Smug Slug,* Norton Juster's *The Phantom Tollbooth,* or Ellen Raskin's *The Westing Game.*

We know that children's language growth continues through the elementary grades and beyond, although the rate is never again as dramatic as during the preschool years. The average length and complexity of their statements, both oral and written, increase as children progress through school.[25] We also know, however, that children's capacity to produce language consistently lags behind their ability to understand it. This suggests that we owe students of all ages the opportunity to read and hear good writing that is beyond the level of their own conversation. Seven-year-olds, for instance, cannot speak with the eloquence and humor that characterize William Steig's picture books, such as *Zeke Pippin* or *Doctor De Soto.* Still, they can understand the language in its story context, and hearing it will add to their knowledge of how language sounds and works. Books by Virginia Hamilton or Natalie Babbitt might serve the same function for older students. Unlike novels that do little more than mirror contemporary speech, the work of these and other fine writers can give children a chance to consider the power of language used with precision and imagination.

[21]Howard Gardner, *Intelligence Reframed: Multiple Intelligences for the 21st Century* (New York: Basic Books, 1999).

[22]M. A. K. Halliday, *Learning How to Mean: Explorations in the Functions of Language* (New York: Elsevier, 1974).

[23]Dan I. Sobin, "Children and Language: They Learn the Same Way All Around the World," in *Contemporary Readings in Child Psychology,* 2nd ed., ed. E. Mavis Hetherington and Ross D. Parke (New York: McGraw-Hill, 1981), pp. 122–126.

[24]Ruth Weir, *Language in the Crib* (The Hague: Mouton, 1970).

[25]Walter Loban, *Language Development: Kindergarten Through Grade Twelve* (Urbana, Ill.: National Council of Teachers of English, 1976).

## Moral Development

Piaget's extensive studies of children included special attention to their developing ideas about fairness and justice. According to Piaget, the difference between younger and older children's concepts is so pronounced that there are really "two moralities" in childhood.[26] Other researchers such as Lawrence Kohlberg[27] and Carol Gilligan have contributed to our understanding of moral development in children.

According to both Piaget's and Kohlberg's descriptions of the general direction of elementary children's development, as children grow in intellect and experience, they move away from ideas of morality based on authority and adult constraint and toward morality based on the influence of group cooperation and independent thinking. To the later stages of this development Carol Gilligan adds a dimension based on gender.[28] She suggests that as girls mature, their sense of their identity is influenced by interconnections with others to a greater degree than for boys. Consequently, their moral judgment develops along lines of an enhanced sense of responsibility and caring for others. Girls might seem less decisive than boys in discussing moral dilemmas because they are trying to take into account a whole network of people who could be affected by a choice. This concern for others is present in boys' thinking as well, but seldom takes precedence over their ideas about what is "fair."

Some of the contrasts between the moral judgment of younger and older children are as follows:

- Young children judge the goodness or badness of an act according to its likelihood of bringing punishment or reward from adults; in other words, they are constrained by the rules that adults have made. Older elementary-age children usually understand that there are group standards for judging what is good or bad and by then are very conscious of situations where they can make their own rules.

- In a young child's eyes, behavior is totally right or totally wrong, with no allowance for an alternate point of view. More-mature children are willing to consider the possibility that circumstances and situations make for legitimate differences of opinion.

- Young children tend to judge an act by its consequences, regardless of the actor's intent. By third or fourth grade, most children have switched to considering motivation rather than consequences alone in deciding what degree of guilt is appropriate.

- Young children believe that bad behavior and punishment go together; the more serious the deed, the more severe the punishment they would prescribe. Its form would not necessarily be related to the offense, but it would automatically erase the offender's guilt. Older children are not so quick to suggest all-purpose pain. They are more interested in finding a "fair" punishment, one that somehow fits the crime and will help bring the wrongdoer back within the rules of the group.

These developmental differences are apparent in the responses of two groups of children to Taro Yashima's *Crow Boy*. When asked what the teacher in the story should do about shy Chibi, who hid under the schoolhouse on the first day, many first graders said "Spank him!" Nine- and 10-year-olds, however, suggested explaining to him that there was nothing to be afraid of or introducing him to classmates so he wouldn't be shy.

Many stories for children present different levels of moral complexity that have the potential for stimulating rich discussions among children. Erica Silverman's picturebook *Don't Fidget a Feather* provides younger

*The characters in Erica Silverman's* Don't Fidget a Feather *face a moral dilemma that will be familiar to many children.*

From *Don't Fidget a Feather* by Erica Silverman, illustrated by S. D. Schindler, illustrations copyright © 1994 S. D. Schindler. Reprinted with permission of Simon & Schuster Books for Young Readers, an imprint of Simon & Schuster Children's Publishing Division.

[26]Jean Piaget, *The Moral Judgment of the Child*, trans. M. Gabain (New York: Free Press, 1965).

[27]Lawrence Kohlberg, *The Meaning and Measurement of Moral Development* (Worcester, MA: Clark University Heinz Wemer Institute, 1981).

[28]Carol Gilligan, *In a Different Voice: Psychological Theory and Women's Development* (Cambridge, Mass.: Harvard University Press, 1982).

Something was rustling along the riverbank. Daisy could hear it getting closer . . .

*Daisy reflects the toddler's ambiguous feelings about exploring the world on her own in* Come Along Daisy! *by Jane Simmons.*
From *Come On Daisy!* by Jane Simmons, first published in the UK by Orchard Books in 1998, a division of The Watts Publishing Group Limited, 96 Leonard Street, London EC2A 4XD.

children with a chance to consider the impulse to help another over the need to compete to be the best. *On My Honor* by Marion Dane Bauer and *Whirligig* by Paul Fleischman provide older readers with a chance to discuss the complexities of a tragic personal experience.

Working through dilemmas, the experts suggest, allows us to move from one level of moral judgment toward another. Literature provides a means by which children can rehearse and negotiate situations of conflict without risk, trying out alternative stances to problems as they step into the lives and thoughts of different characters.

## Personality Development

Every aspect of a child's growth is intertwined with every other. All learning is a meshing of cognitive dimensions, affective or emotional responses, social relationships, and value orientation. This is the matrix in which personality develops. The process of "becoming" is a highly complex one indeed. For children to become "fully functioning" persons, their basic needs must be met. They need to feel they are loved and understood; they must feel they are members of a group significant to them; they must feel they are achieving and growing toward independence. Psychologist Abraham Maslow's research suggests that a person develops through a "hierarchy of needs" from basic animal-survival necessities to the "higher" needs that are more uniquely human and spiritual.[29]

Self-actualization might take a lifetime, or it might never be achieved. But the concept that the individual is continually "becoming" is a more positive view than the notion that little change can take place in personality. Literature can provide opportunities for people of all ages to satisfy higher-level needs, but it is important to remember that books alone cannot meet children's basic needs.

Psychologist Erik Erikson sees human emotional and social development as a passage through a series of stages.[30] Each stage centers around the individual's meeting a particular goal or concern associated with that stage. Erikson theorized that accomplishments at later stages depend on how well the individual was able to meet the goals of preceding stages. According to this theory, a sense of *trust* must be gained during the first year; a sense of *autonomy* should be realized by age 3; between 3 and 6 years the sense of *initiative* is developed; and a sense of duty and *accomplishment* or *industry* occupies the period of childhood from 6 to 12 years. In adolescence a sense of *identity* is built; while a sense of *intimacy,* a parental sense of *productivity,* and a sense of *integrity* are among the tasks of adulthood.

The audience for children's books can be grouped according to their orientations toward achieving *initiative, accomplishment,* and *identity*. Preschool and early primary children can be described as preoccupied with first ventures outside the circle of familiar authority. Most elementary children are caught up in

---

[29]Abraham H. Maslow, *Motivation and Personality,* rev. ed. (Reading, Mass.: Addison-Wesley, 1987).

[30]Erik H. Erikson, *Childhood and Society,* rev. ed. (New York: W. W. Norton, 1993).

the period of industry, or "task orientation," proud of their ability to use skills and tools, to plan projects, and to work toward finished products. Middle school students are more concerned with defining values and personal roles.

Writers of children's books sometimes suggest a natural audience for their work by bringing one of these orientations into the foreground. In Beatrix Potter's *The Tale of Peter Rabbit,* Peter's adventures demonstrate a developing sense of initiative like that of the preschoolers listening to the story. The fearsome aspects of taking those first steps away from Mother are reflected in Jane Simmons's *Come Along Daisy. Jackson Jones and the Puddle of Thorns,* by Mary Quattlebaum, focuses on the industriousness of its middle-childhood protagonist. Diane Matcheck's *The Sacrifice* speaks directly to the adolescent's struggle for identity.

In considering any theory of development, we need to remember that children's prior experiences with

books and their individual backgrounds can have an impact in their responses to literature. For instance, a child who has read stories of King Arthur and Lloyd Alexander's *Prydain* series will have a different understanding of what constitutes a hero in literature than someone who has not read beyond the Hardy Boys. Every child brings to literature a different lifetime of experiences and a set of constructs that is not quite the same as any other's. Whenever we consider the broad outlines of similarity that mark developmental levels, we have to remember that each reader is also one of a kind.

## Guides for Ages and Stages

Adults who are responsible for children's reading need to be aware of child development and learning theory and of children's interests. They must keep in mind characteristics and needs of children at different ages and stages of development. At the same time, it is important to remember that each child has a unique pattern of growth. Resources for Teaching, "Books for Ages and Stages," on pages 45–53, summarizes some characteristic growth patterns, suggests implications for selection and use of books, and provides examples of suitable books for a particular state of development. Remember that the age levels indicated are only approximate. Also, books suggested as appropriate for one category might fit several other categories as well.

## *Response in the Classroom*

Understanding children's responses to literature would be much easier if it were possible to peer inside children's heads. Then we might see firsthand what concept of story guides progress through a book or just what children are thinking as a story unfolds. Instead, teachers must be satisfied with secondary evidence. Children's perceptions and understandings are revealed in many different ways—as the children choose and talk about books, and as they write, paint, play, or take part in other classroom activities.

Classroom responses can be obvious and direct (primary children have been known to kiss a favorite book) or hidden within a situation that appears to have little to do with literature (such as block corner play). Many responses are verbal, many come without words. Some are spontaneous, bubbling up out of children too delighted to be still, or shyly offered in confidence. Other responses would not be expressed at all without the direct invitation of teachers who plan extension activities or discussions (see Chapter 13) to generate thoughtful reaction to literature. To understand any of these observed responses, it is helpful to be acquainted with a few basic theoretical perspectives.

*Jackson assumes responsibility for organizing a community garden in Mary Quattlebaum's* Jackson Jones and the Puddle of Thorns.

From *Jackson Jones and the Puddle of Thorns* by Mary Quattlebaum. Illustration copyright © 1994 by Melodye Rosales. Reprinted by permission of Random House Children's Books, a division of Random House, Inc.

# RESOURCES FOR TEACHING

## Books for Ages and Stages

### BEFORE SCHOOL—INFANCY

| Characteristics | Implications | Examples |
|---|---|---|
| Rapid development of senses. Responds to sound of human voice, especially rhythmic patterns. Vision stimulated by areas of color and sharp contrast; increasingly able to see detail. | Enjoys rhymes, songs, and lullabies. Likes simple, bright illustrations. Looks for familiar objects. | *My Very First Mother Goose* (Opie) *A Lot of Otters* (Berger) *Time for Bed* (M. Fox) *And If the Moon Could Talk* (Banks) *Sleepytime Rhyme* (Charlip) |
| Uses all senses to explore the world immediately at hand; learns through activity and participation. | Gets maximum use from sturdy books with washable pages. Needs to participate by touching, pointing, peeking, moving. | *Baby Dance* (A. Taylor) *Where's Spot?* (Hill) *Pat the Bunny* (Kunhardt) *What's on My Head?* (Miller) |
| Very limited attention span; averts eyes or turns away when bored. | Needs books that can be shared a few pages at a time or in a brief sitting; many short story times are better than one long one. | *Mrs. McNosh Hangs Up Her Wash* (Weeks) *Max's Ride* (Wells) *Dear Zoo* (Campbell) *1, 2, 3* (T. Hoban) |
| Building foundations of language; plays with sounds, learns basic vocabulary along with concepts, begins to learn implicit "rules" that govern speech and conversation. | Needs to hear many rhymes and simple stories. Needs encouragement to use language in labeling pictures and in sharing dialogue with adults as they read aloud. | *I Swapped My Dog* (Zeifert) *Little Clam* (Reiser) *Cow Moo Me* (Losordo) *The Baby's Word Book* (S. Williams) |
| Building basic trust in human relationships. | Needs love and affection from caregivers, in stories as well as in life. Thrives on dependable routines and rituals such as bedtime stories. | *Goodnight Moon* (M. W. Brown) *You Are My Perfect Baby* (Thomas)) *Tom & Pippo's Day* (Oxenbury) *Asleep, Asleep* (Ginsburg) |
| Limited mobility and experience; interests centered in self and the familiar. | Needs books that reflect self and people and activities in the immediate environment. | *Baby High, Baby Low* (Blackstone) *The Cupboard* (Burningham) *How Many?* (MacKinnon) *When Will Sarah Come?* (Howard) |
| Learning autonomy in basic self-help skills. | Enjoys stories of typical toddler accomplishments such as feeding self or getting dressed. | *On My Own* (Ford) *Daisy and the Egg* (Simmons) *I Can* (Oxenbury) *Going to the Potty* (F. Rogers) |

### PRESCHOOL AND KINDERGARTEN—AGES 3, 4, AND 5

| Characteristics | Implications | Examples |
|---|---|---|
| Rapid development of language. | Interest in words, enjoyment of rhymes, nonsense, and repetition and cumulative tales. Enjoys retelling simple folktale and "reading" stories from books without words. | *Talking Like the Rain* (Kennedy) *What in the World?* (Merriam) *Millions of Cats* (Gág) *The Three Bears* (Rockwell) *Magpie Magic* (Wilson) |

*continued*

# RESOURCES FOR TEACHING

## Books for Ages and Stages con't

### PRESCHOOL AND KINDERGARTEN—AGES 3, 4, AND 5 con't

| Characteristics | Implications | Examples |
| --- | --- | --- |
| Very active, short attention span. | Requires books that can be completed in one sitting. Enjoys participation such as naming, pointing, singing, and identifying hidden pictures. Should have a chance to hear stories several times each day. | *The Very Hungry Caterpillar* (Carle) <br> *Each Peach Pear Plum* (Ahlberg and Ahlberg) <br> *Wheels on the Bus* (Raffi) <br> *Mama Cat Has 3 Kittens* (D. Fleming) <br> *Hush Little Baby* (Frazee) <br> *Trashy Town* (Zimmerman) |
| Child is center of own world. Interest, behavior, and thinking are egocentric. | Likes characters that are easy to identify with. Normally sees only one point of view. | *Bunny Cakes* (Wells) <br> *Fix-It* (McPhail) <br> *A Baby Sister for Frances* (R. Hoban) <br> *No David!* (Shannon) |
| Curious about own world. | Enjoys stories about everyday experiences, pets, playthings, home, people in the immediate environment. | *The Snowy Day* (Keats) <br> *What Baby Wants* (Root) <br> *Feast for Ten* (Falwell) <br> *Cowboy Baby* (Heap) |
| Beginning interest in how things work and the wider world. | Books feed curiosity and introduce new topics. | *My Visit to the Dinosaurs* (Aliki) <br> *What Is a Scientist?* (Lehn) <br> *Bashi, Elephant Baby* (Radcliffe) <br> *Mom and Me* (Ford) |
| Building concepts through many firsthand experiences. | Books extend and reinforce child's developing concepts. | *Eating the Alphabet* (Ehlert) <br> *Freight Train* (Crews) <br> *Let's Count* (T. Hoban) <br> *Trucks Trucks Trucks* (Sis) |
| Has little sense of time. Time is "before now," "now," and "not yet." | Books can help children begin to understand the sequence of time. | *Telling Time with Mama Cat* (Harper) <br> *A Year of Beasts* (Wolff) <br> *The Little House* (Burton) <br> *When You Were a Baby* (Jonas) <br> *Clocks and More Clocks* (Hutchins) |
| Learns through imaginative play; make-believe world of talking animals and magic seems very real. | Enjoys stories that involve imaginative play. Likes personification of toys and animals. | *10 Minutes Till Bedtime* (Rathman) <br> *May I Bring a Friend?* (DeRegniers) <br> *We're Going on a Bear Hunt* (Rosen) <br> *Corduroy* (Freeman) <br> *Bark, George* (Feiffer) |
| Seeks warmth and security in relationships with family and others. | Likes to hear stories that provide reassurance. Bedtime stories and other read-aloud rituals provide positive literature experiences. | *The Runaway Bunny* (M. W. Brown) <br> *How Do Dinosaurs Say Goodnight?* (Yolen) <br> *Like Likes Like* (Raschka) <br> *Little Bear* (Minarik) <br> *Ten, Nine, Eight* (Bang) <br> *Edward, Unready for School* (Wells) <br> *The Grannyman* (Schachner) |

# RESOURCES FOR TEACHING

## Books for Ages and Stages con't

### PRESCHOOL AND KINDERGARTEN—AGES 3, 4, AND 5 con't

| Characteristics | Implications | Examples |
|---|---|---|
| Makes absolute judgments about right and wrong. | Expects bad behavior to be punished and good behavior to be rewarded. Requires poetic justice and happy endings. | *The Three Billy Goats Gruff* (Asbjørnsen and Moe)<br>*The Little Red Hen* (Barton)<br>*The Tale of Peter Rabbit* (Potter)<br>*The Gingerbread Man* (Aylesworth) |

### PRIMARY—AGES 6 AND 7

| Characteristics | Implications | Examples |
|---|---|---|
| Continued development and expansion of language. | Frequent story times during the day provide opportunity to hear the rich and varied language of literature. Wordless books and simple tales encourage storytelling. | *Sylvester and the Magic Pebble* (Steig)<br>*When Agnes Caws* (C. Fleming)<br>*Chicka Chicka Boom Boom* (B. Martin and Archambault)<br>*The Clown* (Blake) |
| Attention span increasing. | Prefers short stories; may enjoy a continued story, provided each chapter is a complete episode. | *Frog and Toad Together* (Lobel)<br>*The Stories Julian Tells* (Cameron)<br>*Mary on Horseback* (Wells)<br>*My Brother Ant* (Byars)<br>*It's My Birthday, Too!* (Jonell) |
| Striving to accomplish skills expected by adults. | Proud of accomplishments in reading and writing. Needs reassurance that everyone progresses at own rate. First reading experiences should be enjoyable, using familiar or predictable stories. | *The Day of Ahmed's Secret* (Heide and Gilliland)<br>*The Bee Tree* (Polacco)<br>*Brown Bear, Brown Bear, What Do You See?* (B. Martin)<br>*The Beastly Feast* (Goldstone) |
| Learning still based on immediate perception and direct experiences. | Uses information books to verify as well as extend experience. Much value in watching guinea pigs or tadpoles before reading a book about them. | *My Puppy Is Born* (J. Cole)<br>*I Took a Walk* (H. Cole)<br>*What Do You Do With Something That Wants to Eat You?* (Jenkins)<br>*A Log's Life* (Pfeffer) |
| Continued interest in own world; more curious about a wider range of things. Still sees world from an egocentric point of view. | Needs wide variety of books. TV has expanded interests beyond home and neighborhood. | *Fish Is Fish* (Lionni)<br>*How My Parents Learned to Eat* (Friedman)<br>*Here Is the Coral Reef* (Dunphy)<br>*Red-Eyed Tree Frog* (Cowley) |
| Vague concepts of time. | Needs to learn basics of telling time and the calendar. Simple biographies and historical fiction may give a feeling for the past, but accurate understanding of chronology is beyond this age group. | *The Grouchy Ladybug* (Carle)<br>*Ox-Cart Man* (D. Hall)<br>*The House on Maple Street* (Pryor)<br>*Grandmother Bryant's Pocket* (J. B. Martin)<br>*When I Was Young in the Mountains* (Rylant) |

*continued*

# RESOURCES FOR TEACHING

## Books for Ages and Stages con't

### PRIMARY—AGES 6 AND 7 con't

| Characteristics | Implications | Examples |
| --- | --- | --- |
| More able to separate fantasy from reality; more aware of own imagination. | Enjoys fantasy. Likes to dramatize simple stories or use feltboard, puppets. | *Where the Wild Things Are* (Sendak)<br>*Tops and Bottoms* (Stevens)<br>*Pete's a Pizza* (Steig)<br>*I Know an Old Lady* (Taback) |
| Beginning to develop empathy for others. | Adults can ask such questions as "What would you have done?" "How would you have felt?" | *Fly Away Home* (Bunting)<br>*Crow Boy* (Yashima)<br>*Running the Road to ABC* (Lauture)<br>*The Wild Boy* (Gerstein)<br>*Don't Fidget a Feather* (Silverman) |
| Has a growing sense of justice. Demands application of rules, regardless of circumstances. | Expects poetic justice in books. | *Flossie and the Fox* (McKissack)<br>*Once a Mouse* (M. Brown)<br>*Too Many Tamales* (Soto)<br>*Zelda and Ivy and the Boy Next Door* (Kvasnosky) |
| Humor is developing. | Needs to hear many books read aloud for pure fun. Enjoys books and poems that have surprise endings, plays on words, incongruous situations, and slapstick comedy. Likes to be in on the joke. | *The Seven Silly Eaters* (Hoberman)<br>*The Stupids Have a Ball* (Allard)<br>*Horace and Morris But Mostly Dolores* (Howe)<br>*Dragon's Fat Cat* (Pilkey)<br>*Insectlopedia* (Florian) |
| Shows curiosity about gender differences and reproduction. | Teachers need to accept and be ready to answer children's questions about sex. | *How I Was Born* (Wabbes)<br>*How You Were Born* (J. Cole)<br>*The New Baby at Our House* (J. Cole) |
| Physical contour of the body is changing; permanent teeth appear; learning to whistle and developing other fine motor skills. | Books can help the child accept physical changes in self and differences in others. | *You'll Soon Grow into Them, Titch* (Hutchins)<br>*One Morning in Maine* (McCloskey)<br>*Whistle for Willie* (Keats)<br>*Hue Boy* (Phillips) |
| Continues to seek independence from adults and to develop initiative. | Needs opportunities to select own books and activities. Enjoys stories of responsibility and successful ventures. | *Galimoto* (K. Williams)<br>*Ira Sleeps Over* (Waber)<br>*The Adventures of Sparrowboy* (Pinkney)<br>*Once Upon a Company* (Halperin)<br>*My Rows and Piles of Coins* (Mollel) |
| Continues to need warmth and security in family relationships. | Books may emphasize universal human characteristics in a variety of lifestyles. | *A Bear for Miguel* (Alphin)<br>*A Chair for My Mother* (V. Williams)<br>*Elizabeti's Doll* (Stuve-Bodeen) |
| Beginning to assert independence. Takes delight in own accomplishments. | Books can reflect emotions. Enjoys stories where small characters show initiative. | *Will I Have a Friend?* (M. Cohen)<br>*Lottie's New Friend* (Mathers)<br>*Alfie Gets in First* (Hughes)<br>*Julius* (Johnson)<br>*When Sophie Gets Angry—Really, Really Angry* (Bang) |

# RESOURCES FOR TEACHING

## Books for Ages and Stages con't

### MIDDLE ELEMENTARY—AGES 8 AND 9

| Characteristics | Implications | Examples |
| --- | --- | --- |
| Attaining independence in reading skill. Might read with complete absorption; or might still be having difficulty learning to read. Wide variation in ability and interest. | Discovers reading as an enjoyable activity. Prefers an uninterrupted block of time for independent reading. During this period, many children become avid readers. | *Suitcase* (M. P. Walter) <br> *Ramona's World* (Cleary) <br> *Lizzie Logan, Second Banana* (E. Spinelli) <br> *Finding Out About Whales* (Kelsey) <br> *Ant Plays Bear* (Byars) |
| Reading level might still be below appreciation level. | Essential to read aloud to children each day in order to extend interests, develop appreciation, and provide balance. | *Aneesa and the Weaver's Gift* (Grimes) <br> *Sarah, Plain and Tall* (MacLachlan) <br> *Bubber Goes to Heaven* (Bontemps) <br> *The Secret of Platform 13* (Ibbotson) <br> *Old Elm Speaks: Tree Poems* (K. George) |
| Peer group acceptance becomes increasingly important. | Children need opportunities to recommend and discuss books. Sharing favorites builds sense that reading is fun, has group approval. Popular books may provide status, be much in demand. | *Ever-Clever Elisa* (Hurwitz) <br> *Owen Foote, Soccer Star* (Greene) <br> *Third Grade Bullies* (Levy) <br> *Ghost Trap: A Wild Willie Mystery* (Josse) <br> *Albertina the Practically Perfect* (Fowler) <br> *Spotlight on Cody* (Duffey) |
| Developing standards of right and wrong. Begins to see viewpoints of others. | Books provide opportunities to relate to several points of view. | *Guests* (Dorris) <br> *Molly's Pilgrim* (B. Cohen) <br> *Danny, the Champion of the World* (Dahl) <br> *Ola Shakes It Up* (Hyppolite) <br> *Through My Eyes* (Bridges) |
| Less egocentric, developing empathy for others. Questioning death. | Accepts some books with a less than happy ending. Discussion helps children explore their feelings for others. | *Flip-Flop Girl* (Paterson) <br> *Just Juice* (Hesse) <br> *Stone Fox* (Gardiner) <br> *The War with Grandpa* (R. Smith) <br> *The Quicksand Pony* (Lester) |
| Time concepts and spatial relationships developing. This age level is characterized by thought that is flexible and reversible. | Interested in biographies, life in the past, in other lands, and the future. Prefers fast-moving, exciting stories. | *When the Soldiers Were Gone* (Propp) <br> *Stone Girl, Bone Girl: The Story of Mary Anning* (Anholt) <br> *The Green Book* (Walsh) |

*continued*

# RESOURCES FOR TEACHING

## Books for Ages and Stages con't

### MIDDLE ELEMENTARY—AGES 8 AND 9 con't

| Characteristics | Implications | Examples |
|---|---|---|
| Enjoys tall tales, slapstick humor in everyday situations. Appreciates imaginary adventure. | Teachers need to recognize the importance of literature for laughter, releasing tension, and providing enjoyment. | *Summer Reading Is Killing Me* (Scieszka)<br>*Skinnybones* (Park)<br>*Some Smug Slug* (Edwards)<br>*Get Well, Gators!* (Calmenson and J. Cole)<br>*I Was a Rat* (Pullman) |
| Cognitive growth and language development increase capacity for problem solving and word play. | Likes the challenge of solving puzzles and mysteries. High interest in twists of plot, secret codes, riddles, and other language play. | *The Amber Cat* (McKay)<br>*Cam Jansen and the Catnapping Mystery* (Adler)<br>*I Spy Gold Challenger* (Marzollo)<br>*A Ghost in the Family* (Wright)<br>*The Lost Flower Children* (Lisle) |
| Improved coordination makes proficiency in sports and games possible and encourages interest in crafts and hobbies. | Interest in sports books; wants specific knowledge about sports. Enjoys how-to-do-it books. | *The Young Baseball Player* (Smyth)<br>*Shaquille O'Neal* (Stewart)<br>*In the Paint* (Ewing and Louis)<br>*The Little House Cookbook* (B. Walker) |
| Sees categories and classifications with new clarity; interest in collecting is high. | Likes to collect and trade paperback books. Begins to look for books of one author, series books. | *Ramona Forever* (Cleary)<br>*The Dog Called the Action* (M. Christopher)<br>*Horrible Harry Moves Up to Third Grade* (Kline)<br>*Meet Addy* (the American Girl Collection) (Porter) |
| Seeks specific information to answer questions; might go to books beyond own reading ability to search out answers. | Enjoys books that collect facts, informational identification books. Requires guidance in locating information within a book and in using the library. | *The Magic Schoolbus Explores the Senses* (J. Cole)<br>*Destination Rain Forest* (Grupper)<br>*Snowflake Bentley* (J. B. Martin)<br>*George Washington's Breakfast* (Fritz) |

### LATER ELEMENTARY—AGES 10 AND 11

| Characteristics | Implications | Examples |
|---|---|---|
| Rate of physical development varies widely. Rapid growth precedes beginning of puberty. Girls are about two years ahead of boys in development; both increasingly curious about all aspects of sex. | Guide understanding of growth process and help children meet personal problems. Continued differentiation in reading preferences of boys and girls. | *Asking About Sex and Growing Up* (J. Cole)<br>*Are You There God? It's Me, Margaret* (Blume)<br>*Llama in the Library* (Hurwitz)<br>*It's So Amazing* (Harris) |
| Understanding of sex role is developing; boys and girls form ideas about their own and each other's identity. | Books can provide identification with gender roles and impetus for discussion of stereotypes. | *Belle Prater's Boy* (White)<br>*Reaching Dustin* (Grove)<br>*Flour Babies* (Fine)<br>*When Zachary Beaver Came to Town* (Holt) |

# RESOURCES FOR TEACHING

## Books for Ages and Stages con't

LATER ELEMENTARY—AGES 10 AND 11 con't

| Characteristics | Implications | Examples |
|---|---|---|
| Increased emphasis on peer group and sense of belonging. | Book choices often influenced by peer group; books can highlight problems with peer pressure. | *Wringers* (J. Spinelli)<br>*The Tulip Touch* (Fine)<br>*My Louisiana Sky* (Holt)<br>*Getting Him* (Haseley)<br>*All Alone in the Universe* (Perkins) |
| Deliberate exclusion of others; some expressions of prejudice. | Books can emphasize unique contributions of all. Discussion can be used to clarify values. | *Leon's Story* (Tillage)<br>*Bat 6* (Wolfe)<br>*Roll of Thunder, Hear My Cry* (M. Taylor)<br>*Bluish* (Hamilton)<br>*Petey* (Mikaelson) |
| Family patterns changing; might challenge parents' authority. Highly critical of siblings. | Books can provide some insight into these changing relationships. | *Heaven* (Johnson)<br>*The Other Shepards* (Griffin)<br>*The Birthday Room* (Henkes)<br>*Dicey's Song* (Voigt)<br>*Junebug and the Reverend* (Mead) |
| Begins to have models other than parents drawn from TV, movies, sports figures, books. Beginning interest in future vocation. | Biographies can provide models. Career books broaden interests and provide useful information. | *Knots in My Yo-yo String: The Autobiography of a Kid* (J. Spinelli)<br>*Restless Spirit: The Life and Work of Dorothea Lange* (Partridge)<br>*Firefighting: Behind the Scenes* (Mudd) |
| Sustained, intense interest in specific activities. | Seeks book about hobbies and other interests. | *The Mystery of the Mammoth Bones: And How it Was Solved* (Giblin)<br>*Leonardo da Vinci for Kids: His Life and Ideas: 21 Activities* (Herbert) |
| A peak time for voluntary reading. | Avid readers welcome challenges, repeated contact with authors, genres. | *Harry Potter and The Doomspell Tournament* (Rowling)<br>*The Legend of Luke* (Jacques)<br>*Julie's Wolf Pack* (J. George)<br>*Darnell Rock Reporting* (Myers)<br>*Our Only May Amelia* (Holm) |
| Seeks to test own skills and abilities; looks ahead to a time of complete independence. | Enjoys stories of survival and "going it alone." | *Hatchet* (Paulsen)<br>*Monkey Island* (P. Fox)<br>*The Exiles* (McKay)<br>*Noli's Story* (Dickinson)<br>*A Blizzard Year* (Ehrlich) |
| Increased cognitive skill can be used to serve the imagination. | Tackles complex and puzzling plots in mysteries, science fiction, fantasy. Can appreciate more subtlety in humor. | *The Golden Compass* (Pullman)<br>*The Westing Game* (Raskin)<br>*The Dark Is Rising* (Cooper)<br>*Holes* (Sachar)<br>*The Folk Keeper* (Billingsley) |

*continued*

# RESOURCES FOR TEACHING

## Books for Ages and Stages con't

LATER ELEMENTARY—AGES 10 AND 11 con't

| Characteristics | Implications | Examples |
| --- | --- | --- |
| Increased understanding of the chronology of past events; developing sense of own place in time. Begins to see many dimensions of a problem. | Literature provides opportunities to examine issues from different viewpoints. Guidance needed for recognizing biased presentations. | *Shades of Gray* (Reeder)<br>*Morning Girl* (Dorris)<br>*Now Is Your Time!* (Myers)<br>*Jip: His Story* (Paterson)<br>*The Heart of a Chief* (Bruchac)<br>*The Friends* (Yumoto)<br>*Shadowspinner* (S. Fletcher) |
| Highly developed sense of justice and concern for others. | Willing to discuss many aspects of right and wrong; likes "sad stories," shows empathy for victims of suffering and injustice. | *Out of the Dust* (Hesse)<br>*Bud, not Buddy* (Curtis)<br>*Shiloh* (Naylor)<br>*Missing May* (Rylant)<br>*Flying Solo* (R. Fletcher)<br>*Number the Stars* (Lowry) |
| Searching for values; interested in problems of the world. Can deal with abstract relationships; becoming more analytical. | Valuable discussions can grow out of teacher's reading aloud prose and poetry to this age group. Questions can help students gain insight into both the content and the literary structure of a book. | *The View from Saturday* (Konigsburg)<br>*The Moorchild* (McGraw)<br>*Tuck Everlasting* (Babbitt)<br>*The Great Gilly Hopkins* (Paterson)<br>*Skellig* (Almond)<br>*I, Too, Sing America* (Clinton) |

MIDDLE SCHOOL—AGES 12, 13, AND 14

| Characteristics | Implications | Examples |
| --- | --- | --- |
| Wide variation in physical development; both boys and girls reach puberty by age 14. Developing sex drive; intense interest in sexuality and world of older teens. | Books provide insight into feelings, concerns. Guidance needed to balance students' desire for frank content with lack of life experience. | *It's Perfectly Normal* (Harris)<br>*The Facts Speak for Themselves* (B. Cole)<br>*Human Interaction with Ms. Gladys B. Furley, RN: Expecting the Unexpected* (Jukes)<br>*Achingly Alice* (Naylor)<br>*Extreme Elvin* (Lynch) |
| Self-concept continues to grow. Developing a sense of identity is important. | Books help students explore roles, rehearse journey to identity. Many stories based on myth of the hero. | *The Sacrifice* (Matcheck)<br>*Bearstone* (Hobbs)<br>*The Only Outcast* (Johnston)<br>*A Wizard of Earthsea* (Le Guin)<br>*The Hero and the Crown* (McKinley)<br>*A Girl Named Disaster* (Farmer) |
| Peer group becomes increasingly influential; relationships with family are changing. | Concerns about friends and families reflected in books. School should provide chance to share books and responses with peer group. | *Scorpions* (Myers)<br>*Baseball in April* (Soto)<br>*Maniac Magee* (J. Spinelli)<br>*Walk Two Moons* (Creech)<br>*Parrot in the Oven* (Martinez) |

# RESOURCES FOR TEACHING

## Books for Ages and Stages con't

### MIDDLE SCHOOL—AGES 12, 13, AND 14 con't

| Characteristics | Implications | Examples |
|---|---|---|
| New aspects of egocentrism lead to imagining self as center of others' attention and feeling one's own problems are unique. | Students begin to enjoy introspection; might identify with characters who are intense or self-absorbed. | *Dancing on the Edge* (Nolan)<br>*Jazmin's Notebook* (Grimes)<br>*Jacob Have I Loved* (Paterson)<br>*Stephen Fair* (Wynne-Jones)<br>*Habibi* (Nye)<br>*Rules of the Road* (J. Bauer) |
| Cognitive abilities are increasingly abstract and flexible, but not consistently so. New capacity to reason from imaginary premises, manipulate symbolic language, and make hypothetical judgments. | Students read more complex stories, mysteries, and high fantasy that call for complex logic; enjoy science fiction and high adventure. Metaphor, symbols, and imagery are understood at a different level. | *A Killing Frost* (Marsden)<br>*Sword Song* (Sutcliff)<br>*The Ear, the Eye and the Arm* (Farmer)<br>*A Swiftly Tilting Planet* (L'Engle)<br>*The Pirate's Son* (McCaughrean)<br>*Shade's Children* (Nix)<br>*Kit's Wilderness* (Almond) |
| Able to apply ideas of relativity to questions of values; girls might see moral issues differently than boys do. | Students need discussion time to negotiate meanings in stories that pose moral dilemmas. | *Whirligig* (Fleischman)<br>*Shabanu* (Staples)<br>*Taste of Salt* (Temple)<br>*The Giver* (Lowry)<br>*Making Up Megaboy* (Walter)<br>*Homeless Bird* (Whelan) |
| Sensitive to great complexity in human feelings and relationships. | Students seek richer and more complex stories. | *The Glory Field* (Myers)<br>*Jericho* (Hickman)<br>*Like Sisters on the Home Front* (Williams-Garcia)<br>*Toning the Sweep* (Johnson)<br>*Go and Come Back* (Abelove) |
| Cumulative effects of development and life experience produce wide variation among individuals in abilities and interests. | Reading ability and interests in one class could range from early elementary to adult. | *Thunderwoman* (Wood)<br>*The Hobbit* (Tolkien)<br>*What Have You Lost?* (Nye)<br>*Captain Underpants and the Attack of the Talking Toilets* (Pilkey) |

## Theories of Response

What really goes on between a reader and a story or poem is a complex question with many answers. Theories about reader response draw from many disciplines, including psychology, linguistics, aesthetics, and, of course, literature and education.

Some theories focus on what is read; others focus on the reader. For instance, some researchers have examined in careful detail the structure of stories, noting the precise arrangement of words and sequence of ideas. These patterns are called "story grammars," and studies indicate that they can affect the way readers understand and recall a story.[31] Other theorists are more concerned with individual readers and how their personalities can influence their ideas about what they read.[32] Still other researchers emphasize the cultural or social aspects of response. According to Richard Beach, "While all these theoretical perspectives rest on different assumptions about meaning, they ultimately intersect and overlap. The local—the focus on reader's textual knowledge and experience—is embedded within the global, larger social and cultural contexts." All categories of reader response research focus on the reader's textual knowledge and experience, but they are embedded within larger social and cultural contexts.[33]

One important point on which scholars agree is that the process of reading and responding is active rather than passive. The words and ideas in the book are not transferred automatically from the page to the reader. Rather, as Louise Rosenblatt has argued,

> The literary work exists in the live circuit set up between reader and text: the reader infuses intellectual and emotional meanings into the pattern of verbal symbols, and those symbols channel his thoughts and feelings.[34]

Response is dynamic and open to continuous change as readers anticipate, infer, remember, reflect, interpret, and connect. The "meaning" and significance of a story like David Almond's *Skellig* will vary from reader to reader, depending on age and personal experience as well as experience with literature. However, each reader's response will also change, given time for reflection, discussion, or repeated readings.

Reader response theory also points out that readers approach works of literature in special ways. James Britton proposes that in all our uses of language we can be either *participants* or *spectators*.[35] In the participant role we read in order to accomplish something in the real world, as in following a recipe. In the spectator role we focus on what the language says as

an end in itself, attending to its forms and patterns, as we do in enjoying poetry.

Rosenblatt suggests that reading usually involves two roles, or stances, and that we shift our emphasis from one to the other according to the material and our purposes for reading it.[36] In the *efferent* stance we are most concerned with what information can be learned from the reading. In the *aesthetic* stance our concern is for the experience of the reading itself, the feelings and images that come and go with the flow of the words. Most readers, of course, find themselves switching back and forth from one of these stances to the other as they read. One thing teachers can do to help children share the world the author has created is to help them find an appropriate stance as they begin to read.

## Types of Response

Teachers who are familiar with reader response theories and who study children's responses to literature will discover that they provide a basis for deepening children's satisfaction with books and for supporting children's growth in interpretation.

The most common expressions of response to literature are statements, oral or written. In their most polished form such responses are known as literary criticism, and for many years research in literature involved measuring young people's statements against a standard of mature critical ability.

Where children are concerned, it is important to remember that direct comment is only one of many ways of revealing what goes on between the book and its audience. Language used in other ways—to tell or write stories based on other stories, for instance—often provides good clues about a child's feelings and understandings about the original. Parents and teachers of young children also recognize nonverbal behaviors as signs of response. For instance, young listeners almost always show their involvement, or lack of it, in body postures and facial expressions. Children's artwork, informal drama, and other book extension activities (see Chapter 13) also provide windows on response.

## Interpreting Children's Responses

Previous research in response to literature provides teachers and librarians with a framework for interpreting their students' reactions to books. This classroom-based research can give us a deeper understanding of children's responses.

[31]Dorothy S. Strickland and Joan Feeley, "Development in the Elementary School Years," *Handbook of Research on Teaching the English Language Arts*, eds. James Flood, Julie Jensen, Diane Lapp, and James Squire (New York: Macmillan, 1991), pp. 386–402.

[32]Norman H. Holland, *Five Readers Reading* (New Haven, Conn.: Yale University Press, 1975).

[33]Richard Beach, *A Teacher's Introduction to Reader-Response Theories* (Urbana, Ill.: National Council of Teachers of English, 1993), p. 9.

[34]Louise M. Rosenblatt, *Literature as Exploration*, 5th ed. (New York: Modern Language Association, 1996), p. 25.

[35]James Britton et al., *The Development of Writing Abilities (11–18)*, Schools Council Research Studies (London: Macmillan Education Limited, 1975).

[36]Louise M. Rosenblatt, *The Reader, the Text, the Poem: The Transactional Theory of the Literary Work* (Carbondale: Southern Illinois University Press, 1994).

"Will'am Ernest lay a bolster pillow behind Mrs Trotter's back like

*Children's pictures or other classroom work can furnish important evidence about their understanding of literature.*
Martin Luther King, Jr., Laboratory School, Evanston, Illinois, Public Schools. Ellen Esrick, teacher.

## Recognizing Patterns of Change

Teachers and researchers alike have observed that when children at different grade levels read and respond in ways that are comfortable for them, their responses will be alike in some ways and different in others. What might teachers expect to see in a fourth-grade classroom? What are typical first-grade responses? No one can answer these questions with exactness, for every child is a unique reader and every classroom represents a different composite of experiences with literature and with the world. Even so, it is helpful to know what researchers and teachers have discovered about the responses of their students at various grade levels. This section outlines some of these findings to provide information on the patterns of change in responses that usually take place as children have experiences with literature in the elementary school.[37] Although these findings are presented in an age-level sequence, keep in mind that any of these characteristics can be seen at other ages, depending on the child, the situation, and the challenge presented by the material. Like the Resources for Teaching chart (pp. 45–53), this guide is more useful

for making predictions about a class than for making predictions about an individual child.

### Younger Children (Preschool to Primary)

Younger children are *motor-oriented.* As listeners, they respond with their whole selves, chiming in on refrains or talking back to the story. They lean closer to the book, point at pictures, clap their hands. They use body movements to try out some of the story's action, "hammering" along with *John Henry* by Ezra Jack Keats or making wild faces to match the illustrations in Maurice Sendak's *Where the Wild Things Are.* Actions to demonstrate meaning ("Like this") might be given as answers to a teacher's questions. These easily observable responses go undercover as children mature; older children reveal feelings through subtle changes of expression and posture.

At this age, children spontaneously act out stories or bits of stories using actions, roles, and conventions of literature in their *dramatic play.* Witches, kings, "wild things," and other well-defined character types appear naturally, showing how well children have assimilated elements of favorite tales. Examples of story language ("We lived happily ever after") are sometimes incorporated. Spontaneous dramatic play disappears from the classroom early in the primary years (although it persists out of school with some children) and is replaced by more structured drama of various kinds. Older children are usually much more conscious of their own references to literature.

These children respond to stories piecemeal. Their responses deal with *parts rather than wholes.* A detail of text or illustration might prompt more comment than the story itself, as children make quick associations with their own experience: "I saw a bird like that once" or "My sister has bunk beds just like those." This part-by-part organization can also be seen in very young children's art, where the pictures show individual story items without any indication of relationship ("This is the baby bear's chair, and this is Goldilocks, and this is the house the bears lived in, and here is the bed . . ."). This is the same sort of itemization or cataloging of characters, objects, and events that children sometimes use when asked to tell something about a story. Young children are more likely to respond to the story as a whole if they have heard it many times or if an adult provides that focus by asking good questions.

---

[37]This section is based on observations with reference to the work of Arthur Applebee, *The Child's Concept of Story* (Chicago, IL: University of Chicago Press, 1978), pp. 123–125; Janet Hickman, "A New Perspective on Response to Literature," *Research in the Teaching of English* 15 (1981): 343–354; and others.

*Teachers need to listen carefully to children's responses to literature in order to discover their thinking strategies.*
Mission School, Redlands Public Schools, Redlands, California. Joan Schleicher, teacher. Photo by Larry Rose.

Children at this age use *embedded language* in answering direct questions about stories. Because young children see the world in literal, concrete terms, their answers are likely to be couched in terms of the characters, events, and objects found in the story. One first grader made a good attempt to generalize the lesson of "The Little Red Hen," but couldn't manage without some reference to the tale: "When someone already baked the cake and you haven't helped, they're probably just gonna say 'No'!" A teacher or other adult who shares the child's context—who knows the story, has heard or read it with the child, and knows what other comments have been made—will understand the intent of such a statement more readily than a casual observer will.

*Children in Transition (Primary to Middle Grades)*
Children in transition from the primary to the middle grades develop from being listeners to becoming readers. They go through a period of focus on the *accomplishment of independent reading*. They make many comments about quantity—number of pages read, the length of a book, or the number of books read. Conventions of print and of bookmaking might draw

their attention. One third grader refused to read any of the poems from Shel Silverstein's *Where the Sidewalk Ends* without locating them in the index first; a classmate was fascinated with the book's variety of word and line arrangements for poetry. Another child studied the front matter of a picture book and pronounced it "a dedicated book." So-called independent reading may be more sociable than it sounds, since many children like to have a listener or reading partner and begin to rely on peers as sounding boards for their response.

At this age, children become more adept at *summarizing* in place of straight retelling when asked to talk about stories. This is a skill that facilitates discussion and becomes more useful as it is developed. Summarizing is one of the techniques that undergirds critical commentary, but adults use it more deliberately and precisely than children do.

These children classify or *categorize* stories in some of the same ways that adults do. Middle graders who are asked to sort out a random pile of books use categories like "mysteries," "humorous books," "make-believe," and "fantasy." If you ask kindergartners to do the same, they are more likely to classify the books by their physical properties ("fat books," "books with pretty covers," "red books") than by content.

Children at this age *attribute personal reactions to the story* itself. A book that bores an 8-year-old will be thought of as a "boring book," as if "boring" were as much a property of the story as its number of pages or its first-person point of view. Children judge a story on the basis of their response to it, regardless of its qualities as literature or its appeal to anyone else. This is a very persistent element in response; it affects the judgment of students of children's literature and of professional book reviewers as well as children in elementary school. Personal response can never be totally eliminated from critical evaluation; but with experience, readers can develop more objectivity in separating a book's literary characteristics from its personal appeal.

These children also *use borrowed characters, events, themes, and patterns from literature in their writing,* just as younger children do in dramatic play. In the earliest stages, much of this is unconscious and spontaneous. One example is a 7-year-old who was convinced that her story about a fish with paint-splashed insides was "made up out of my own head," even when reminded that the class had just heard Robert McCloskey's *Burt Dow, Deep Water Man.* A 9-year-old spontaneously combined a favorite character with a field-trip experience in his story "Paddington Bear Goes to Franklin Park Conservatory," but he was aware of his idea sources. Other children produce their own examples of patterns, forms, or genres. The direction of growth is toward more conscious realization of the uses of literature in writing (see Chapter 13).

### Older Children (Middle Grades to Middle School)

Older children express *stronger preferences,* especially for personal reading. Younger children seem to enjoy almost everything that is reasonably appropriate, but older ones do not hesitate to reject books they do not like. Some children show particular devotion to certain authors or genres or series at this time. Some children also become more intense and protective about some of their reactions, and they should not be pressed to share those feelings that demand privacy.

At this age, children are more skillful with language and more able to deal with abstractions. They can *dis-embed ideas* from a story and put them in more generalized terms, as in stating a universal moral for a particular fable.

These children also begin to *see* (but not consistently) *that their feelings about a book are related to identifiable aspects of the writing.* Responses like "I love this book because it's great" develop into "I love this book because the characters say such funny things" or "*Strider* [by Cleary] is my favorite because Leigh is a lot like me."

Older children go beyond categorizing stories *toward a more analytical perception* of why characters behave as they do, how the story is put together, or what the author is trying to say. They begin to test fiction against real life and understand it better through the comparison. They use some critical terminology, although their understanding of terms may be incomplete. In talk and writing, children who are encouraged to express ideas freely begin to stand back from their own involvement and take an evaluative look at literature. One sixth grader had this to say about *A Taste of Blackberries* by Doris Buchanan Smith:

> I thought the author could have put more into it. I really didn't know much about the kid who died. I mean, it really happened fast in the book. It started out pretty soon and told about how sad he was and what they used to do. All the fun things they used to do together. I wished at the beginning they would have had all the things that he talked about and then have him thinking about what a good friend he is and then all of a sudden he dies—a little closer to the end. Because when he died, you didn't much care 'cause you didn't really know him. But I guess the author wanted to talk about how it would be, or how people feel, or maybe what happened to her—how it felt when one of her friends died like that.[38]

In general, children's responses move toward this sort of conscious comment. Young children sometimes make stunningly perceptive observations about stories, but they are not usually able to step back and see the importance of what they have said. Older children begin to know what they know, and can then take command of it. This allows them to layer mature appreciation on top of the beginner's natural delight.

However, older children's increasing capacity for abstraction, generalization, and analysis should *not* be interpreted as a need for programs of formal literary analysis or highly structured study procedures. Opportunities to read, hear, and talk about well-chosen books under the guidance of an interested and informed teacher will allow elementary school children to develop their responses to their full potential.

Children, no matter what their age, will respond to a story on their own terms of understanding. It does little good (and can be destructive to the enjoyment of literature) if younger children are pushed to try to formulate the abstractions achieved by more mature children. However, James Britton maintains that teachers may refine and develop the responses that children are already making by gradually exposing them to stories with increasingly complex patterns of events.[39]

## Collecting Children's Responses

Finding out how children understand literature and which books they like is such basic information for elementary teachers and librarians that it should not be left to chance. Techniques for discovering responses that are simple and fit naturally into the ongoing business of classrooms and library media centers are discussed in the context of planning the school literature program in Chapter 13. Some suggestions for observing and studying responses are presented in the Into the Classroom box.

As elementary teachers become aware of the way they can tune in to children's responses to literature, they will see the value of examining the nature of children's thinking about it. We all believe that literature is important for children, but we do not truly know what difference it makes in a child's life, if any. An indepth study of children's responses to books is just as important as, if not more important than, the studies of children's interests in books. We should explore the developmental nature of response and conduct longitudinal studies of a child's responses over the years. As teachers and librarians, we need to be still and listen to what the children are telling us about their involvement with books and what it means to them.

[38]Recorded in the classroom of Lois Monaghan, teacher, Barrington School, Upper Arlington, Ohio.

[39]James Britton, in *Response to Literature*, ed. James R. Squire (Champaign, Ill.: National Council of Teachers of English, 1968), p. 4.

*When asked to replicate Leo Lionni's story of* The Biggest House in the World *using a new main character, these two children demonstrated different levels in their understanding of the theme. The 8-year-old (top picture) showed a bird growing more elaborate; the 10-year-old (bottom picture) portrayed a change leading to the bird's self-destruction.*

Tremont Elementary School, Upper Arlington, Ohio, Public Schools. Jill Boyd, teacher.

## INTO THE CLASSROOM

### Understanding Children's Responses to Literature

**Room 201**

1. Ask children to make a gameboard that traces the adventures of characters in a book like Sheila Burnford's *The Incredible Journey*. Make note of which events are important enough to represent. Do the children remember the sequence of events or refer back to the book to check?

2. Ask children to translate meaning from a story like *The Biggest House in the World* by Leo Lionni through artwork. Ask children to choose any animal and grant it the same wish as the little snail had—namely, that it could change itself in any way.

3. After older students have read *Tuck Everlasting* by Natalie Babbitt, ask them to chart out, with words and pictures, the cycle of their own lives, including what they know of their past and what they predict for the future. Make note of the children who transfer the ideas about life and death from the book to their own speculations and those that might reveal a deeper connection with the book. Use these charts to begin a discussion relating the book to the students' own lives.

4. Ask a middle grader to write an updated folktale or a story based on the information in Neil Waldman's nonfiction book *Masada*. What does the writing show about the child's knowledge of genre and the general concept of story?

5. Conduct a case study of one child's response to literature, keeping track of a broad range of data like the child's contacts with literature, responses, and developing skills in reading and writing.

6. Ask three children of various ages (e.g., 5, 7, 9) to retell the story "Goldilocks and the Three Bears" from the point of view of Baby Bear. Who is able to begin the story as Baby Bear? Who can maintain the role change? What problems do 5-year-olds have with language that 9-year-olds seem to solve easily?

7. In a middle-grade classroom, assemble twenty to thirty books that are mostly familiar to the children. Ask a small group to categorize and label these for a tabletop display. Tape their comments as they work. What do you notice about their categories? About the process? If possible, repeat the activity with younger children and books that they have heard read aloud. What differences do you notice?

8. Set up a play corner in a primary classroom, including props from stories such as a magic wand, a witch's hat, a cardboard crown. What happens over time? What seem to be the sources for the children's imaginative play?

## Personal Explorations

1. If there is a young child in your household, keep a log for four to five weeks of her or his interaction with literature. What do the child's choices, reactions, comments, and questions reveal about cognitive skills or moral judgment? Do you see any changes that reflect experiences with books?

2. Observe young children as a parent or teacher reads to them. Note as many behaviors (verbal, nonverbal, or artistic/creative) as you can. What clues do you get about the value of reading aloud and about means of effective presentation?

3. If you can meet with a class of children, ask them to submit the names of their ten favorite books. How do their choices seem to reflect their particular ages and stages of development?

4. Visit the children's room of a public or school library or the children's section of a bookstore to watch children in the process of choosing books. Keep a list, if you can, of the books examined and rejected, as well as those finally chosen. What factors seem to influence the children's choices?

5. With a small group of fellow students or teachers, read and discuss an award-winning children's book. Working together, plan two sets of questions that could be used with children, one to discover children's initial response to the story, the other to direct their thinking toward the characters' motivations and decisions, the author's effective use of language, or other noteworthy features of the writing.

6. Arrange to talk or visit a chat room with one or more readers in the 11-to-13 age range about a book that you and the child or children have read individually—for example, Jerry Spinelli's *Maniac Magee*. Plan questions and comments that will encourage the students to share their own interpretations of characters and events. How are their ideas about the book similar to or different from your own? How could you use this information in planning for teaching?

# *Related Readings*

Applebee, Arthur. *The Child's Concept of Story: Ages Two to Seventeen.* Chicago: University of Chicago Press, 1978.

A report of systematic research on children's developing perceptions of stories. Applebee provides fresh insight on the child's sense of story and response to literature. Among the contributions of this important work are a description of organization and complexity in the structure of stories children tell and a model of developmental stages in the formulation of children's responses.

Elkind, David. *The Hurried Child: Growing Up Too Fast Too Soon.* Reading, Mass.: Addison-Wesley, 1989.

In a book addressed mainly to parents, a noted psychologist argues that contemporary children are under too much pressure. They are rushed toward adulthood both at home and at school without regard for normal patterns of development or individual differences. Chapters 5 and 6 present a very readable overview of intellectual, emotional, and social development, with particular reference to Piaget. Chapter 4, which deals with the influence of books and media in "hurrying" children, provides good discussion material for adults considering selection policies.

Holland, Kathleen E., Rachael A. Hungerford, and Shirley B. Ernst., eds. *Journeying: Children Responding to Literature.* Portsmouth, N.H.: Heinemann, 1993.

This collection provides a comprehensive view of recent research in children's response to literature. Chapters in four sections deal with responses of children in grades K through 8 in a variety of settings. Authors describe children's responses to different literary genres, and show how variables such as age, culture, and mode shape children's understanding.

Lehr, Susan. *The Child's Developing Sense of Theme: Responses to Literature.* New York: Teachers College Press, 1991.

The author provides a background of discussion and research as well as a report of her own work in discovering the interpretations of story meaning held by preschool and elementary children. Her findings suggest that adults need to be very good listeners when talking to children about literature. Many examples of children's talk and an engaging, conversational tone make this scholarly work particularly readable.

Martinez, Miriam, and Nancy Roser. "Children's Responses to Literature." In *Handbook of Research on Teaching the English Language Arts,* ed. James Flood et al. New York: Macmillan, 1991.

This comprehensive review of research since the 1960s is organized around three major categories of factors that affect children's response—characteristics of the reader, context factors, and the nature of the text. Included among the many other sections of this reference volume are the essays "Response to Literature" by Robert Probst and "Reading Preferences" by Dianne Monson and Sam Sebesta, and articles on child development in the preschool, elementary, and middle school years.

Paley, Vivian Gussin. *The Girl with the Brown Crayon.* Cambridge, Mass.: Harvard University Press, 1997.

A well-known kindergarten teacher and recipient of a MacArthur award, Paley chronicles the school year that centered upon the works of author-illustrator Leo Lionni. The children's responses to Lionni's books illustrate the power of literature in children's lives. Paley's willingness to learn from and reflect upon their explorations provides a model for a response-centered classroom.

Purves, Alan C., Theresa Rogers, and Anna O. Soter. *How Porcupines Make Love III: Teaching a Response-Centered Literature Curriculum.* New York: Longman, 1995.

This lively book for teachers is designed to explain the implications of reader response theory for literature instruction. Although this book deals with the adolescent years, teachers of older elementary students find many of the ideas and principles discussed here to be useful.

Rosenblatt, Louise M. *The Reader, the Text, the Poem: The Transactional Theory of the Literary Work.* Carbondale: Southern Illinois University Press, 1994.

A scholarly discussion of the reader's role in evoking a literary work from an author's text. The distinction between aesthetic and efferent reading stances is clearly explained. Although elementary children are seldom mentioned, the book gives a valuable basis for understanding the responses of readers at any age.

# Children's Literature

Abelove, Joan. *Go and Come Back*. DK. 1998.

Adler, David A. *Cam Jansen and the Catnapping Mystery*. Viking, 1998.

Ahlberg, Janet, and Allan Ahlberg. *Each Peach Pear Plum*. Viking, 1978.

Aliki. *My Visit to the Dinosaurs*. 2nd ed. Harper & Row, 1987.

Allard, Harry. *The Stupids Have a Ball*. Illustrated by James Marshall. Houghton Mifflin, 1978.

Almond, David. *Kit's Wilderness*. Delacorte, 2000.

———. *Skellig*. Delacorte, 1999.

Alphin, Elaine Marie. *A Bear for Miguel*. Illustrated by Joan Sanders. HarperCollins, 1996.

Anholt, Laurence. *Stone Girl, Bone Girl: The Story of Mary Anning*. Illustrated by Sheila Moxley. Orchard, 1999.

Asbjørnsen P. C., and Jorgen E. Moe. *The Three Billy Goats Gruff*. Illustrated by Marcia Brown. Harcourt Brace, 1957.

Aylesworth, Jim. *The Gingerbread Man*. Illustrated by Barbara McClintock. Scholastic, 1998.

Babbitt, Natalie. *Tuck Everlasting*. Farrar, Straus & Giroux, 1975.

Bang, Molly. *Ten, Nine, Eight*. Greenwillow, 1983.

———. *When Sophie Gets Angry-Really Angry*. Scholastic, 1999.

Banks, Kate. *And If the Moon Could Talk*. Illustrated by Georg Hallensleben. Farrar, Straus & Giroux, 1998.

Barton, Byron. *The Little Red Hen*. HarperCollins, 1993.

Bauer, Joan. *Rules of the Road*. Putnam, 1998.

Bauer, Marion Dane. *On My Honor*. Clarion, 1986.

Berger, Barbara. *A Lot of Otters*. Philomel, 1997.

Billingsley, Franny. *The Folk Keeper*. Atheneum, 1999.

Blackstone, Stella. *Baby High, Baby Low*. Illustrated by Denise Fraifield and Fernando Azevedo. Holiday House, 1997.

Blake, Quentin. *Clown*. Holt, 1996.

Blume, Judy. *Are You There, God? It's Me, Margaret*. Bradbury, 1970.

Bontemps, Arna. *Bubber Goes to Heaven*. Illustrated by Daniel Minter. Oxford, 1998.

Bridges, Ruby. *Through My Eyes*. Scholastic, 1999.

Brown, Marcia. *Once a Mouse*. Scribner's, 1961.

Brown, Margaret Wise. *Goodnight Moon*. Illustrated by Clement Hurd. Harper & Row, 1947.

———. *The Runaway Bunny*. Illustrated by Clement Hurd. Harper & Row, 1942.

Bruchac, Joseph. *The Heart of a Chief*. Dial, 1998.

Bunting, Eve. *Fly Away Home*. Illustrated by Ron Himler. Clarion, 1991.

Burnford, Sheila. *The Incredible Journey*. Illustrated by Carl Burger. Bantam, 1990.

Burningham, John. *The Cupboard*. Crowell, 1975.

Burton, Virginia Lee. *The Little House*. Houghton Mifflin, 1942.

Byars, Betsy. *Ant Plays Bear*. Illustrated by Marc Simont. Viking, 1997.

———. *My Brother Ant*. Illustrated by Marc Simont. Viking, 1996.

Calmenson, Stephanie, and Joanna Cole. *Get Well, Gators!* Illustrated by Lynn Munsinger. Morrow, 1998.

Cameron, Ann. *The Stories Julian Tells*. Illustrated by Ann Strugnell. Knopf, 1987.

Campbell, Rod. *Dear Zoo*. Four Winds, 1983.

Carle, Eric. *The Grouchy Ladybug*. Crowell, 1977.

———. *The Very Hungry Caterpillar*. Philomel, 1969.

Charlip, Remy. *Sleepytime Rhyme*. Greenwillow, 1999.

Christopher, Matt. *The Dog Called the Action*. Little, Brown, 1998.

Cleary, Beverly. *Ramona Forever*. Illustrated by Alan Tiegreen. Morrow, 1984.

———. *Ramona's World*. Illustrated by Alan Tiegreen. Morrow, 1999.

———. *Strider*. Illustrated by Paul O. Zelinsky. Morrow, 1991.

Clinton, Catherine. *I, Too, Sing America: Three Centuries of African American Poetry*. Houghton Mifflin, 1998.

Cohen, Barbara. *Molly's Pilgrim*. Illustrated by Michael Deraney. Lothrop, Lee & Shepard, 1983.

Cohen, Miriam. *Will I Have a Friend?* Illustrated by Lillian Hoban. Macmillan, 1971.

Cole, Brock. *The Facts Speak for Themselves*. Front Street, 1997.

Cole, Henry. *I Took a Walk*. Greenwillow, 1998.

Cole, Joanna. *Asking About Sex and Growing Up: A Question and Answer Book for Boys and Girls*. Illustrated by Alan Tiegreen. Morrow, 1988.

———. *How You Were Born*. Morrow, 1984.

———. *The Magic School Bus Explores the Senses*. Illustrated by Bruce Degen. Scholastic, 1999.

———. *My Puppy Is Born*. Photographs by Margaret Miller. Morrow, 1990.

———. *The New Baby at Our House*. Photographs by Margaret Miller. Mulberry, 1998.

Cooper, Susan. *The Dark Is Rising*. Illustrated by Alan Cober. Atheneum, 1973.

Cowley, Joy. *Red-Eyed Tree Frog*. Photographs by Nic Bishop. Scholastic, 1999.

Creech, Sharon. *Walk Two Moons*. HarperCollins, 1994.

Crews, Donald. *Freight Train*. Greenwillow, 1978.

Curtis, Christopher Paul. *Bud, Not Buddy*. Delacorte, 1999.

Dahl, Roald. *The BFG*. Illustrated by Quentin Blake. Farrar, Straus & Giroux, 1982.

———. *Danny, the Champion of the World*. Illustrated by Jill Bennett. Knopf, 1975.

DeJong, Meindert. *Hurry Home, Candy*. Illustrated by Maurice Sendak. Harper & Row, 1953.

DeRegniers, Beatrice Schenk. *May I Bring a Friend?* Illustrated by Beni Montesor. Atheneum, 1964.

Dickinson, Peter. *Noli's Story*. Putnam, 1998.

Dorris, Michael. *Guests*. Hyperion, 1994.

———. *Morning Girl*. Hyperion, 1992.

Duffey, Betsey. *Spotlight on Cody*. Illustrated by Ellen Thompson. Viking, 1998.

Dunphy, Madeline. *Here is the Coral Reef*. Illustrated by Tom Leonard. Hyperion, 1998.

Edwards, Pamela Duncan. *Some Smug Slug*. Illustrated by Henry Cole. HarperCollins, 1996.

Ehlert, Lois. *Eating the Alphabet*. Harper & Row, 1989.

Ehrlich, Gretel. *A Blizzard Year: Timmy's Almanac of the Seasons*. Hyperion, 2000.

Emberley, Michael. *Ruby*. Little, Brown, 1990.

English, Karen. *Francie*. Farrar, Straus & Giroux, 1999.

Ewing, Patrick, and Linda L. Louis. *In the Paint*. Abbeville, 1999.

Falwell, Cathryn. *Feast for Ten*. Clarion, 1993.

Farmer, Nancy. *The Ear, the Eye and the Arm*. Orchard/Jackson, 1994.

———. *A Girl Named Disaster*. Orchard, 1997.

Feiffer, Jules. *Bark, George*. HarperCollins, 1999.

Fine, Anne. *Flour Babies*. Little, Brown, 1994.

———. *The Tulip Touch*. Little, Brown, 1997.

Fleischman, Paul. *Whirligig*. Holt, 1998.

Fleischman, Sid. *Bandit's Moon*. Greenwillow, 1998.

Fleming, Candace. *When Agnes Caws*. Illustrated by Giselle Potter. Simon & Schuster, 1999.

Fleming, Denise. *Mama Cat Has Three Kittens*. Holt, 1998.

Fletcher, Ralph. *Flying Solo*. Clarion, 1998.

Fletcher, Susan. *Shadow Spinner*. Atheneum, 1998.

Florian, Douglas, *Insectlopedia*. Harcourt Brace, 1998.

Ford, Meila. *Mom and Me*. Greenwillow, 1998.

———. *On My Own*. Greenwillow, 1999.

Fowler, Susi Gregg. *Albertina the Practically Perfect*. Greenwillow, 1998.

Fox, Mem. *Time for Bed*. Illustrated by Jane Dyer. Gulliver, 1993.

Fox, Paula. *Monkey Island*. Orchard, 1991.

Frasee, Marla. *Hush Little Baby*. Browndeer, 1999.

Freeman, Don. *Corduroy*. Viking, 1968.

Friedman, Ina. *How My Parents Learned to Eat*. Illustrated by Allen Say. Houghton Mifflin, 1984.

Fritz, Jean. *George Washington's Breakfast*. Illustrated by Paul Galdone. Putnam, 1984.

Gág, Wanda. *Millions of Cats*. Coward, 1956 [1928].

Gantos, Jack. *Joey Pigza Swallowed the Key*. Farrar, Straus & Giroux, 1998.

Gardiner, John. *Stone Fox*. Illustrated by Marcia Sewall. Harper & Row, 1980.

George, Jean. *Cry of the Crow*. HarperCollins, 1980.

———. *Julie's Wolfpack*. Illustrated by Wendell Minor. HarperCollins, 1997.

George, Kristin O'Connell. *Old Elm Speaks*. Illustrated by Kate Kiesler. Clarion, 1998.

Gerstein, Mordecai. *Wild Boy*. Farrar, Straus & Giroux, 1998.

Giblin, James Cross. *The Mystery of the Mammoth Bones: And How It Was Solved*. HarperCollins, 1999.

Ginsburg, Mirra. *Asleep, Asleep*. Illustrated by Nancy Tafuri. Greenwillow, 1992.

Goldstone, Bruce. *The Beastly Feast*. Illustrated by Blair Lent. Holt, 1998.

Greene, Stephanie. *Owen Foote, Soccer Star*. Clarion, 1998.

Griffin, Adele. *The Other Shepards*. Hyperion, 1998.

Grimes, Nikki. *Aneesa Lee and the Weaver's Gift*. Ashley Bryant. Lothrop, Lee & Shepard, 1999.

———. *Jazmin's Notebook*. Dial, 1998.

Grove, Vicki. *Reaching Dustin*. Putnam, 1998.

Grupper, Jonathon. *Destination Rainforest*. National Geographic, 1997.

Hall, Donald. *Ox-Cart Man*. Illustrated by Barbara Cooney. Viking, 1979.

Halperin, Wendy Anderson. *Once Upon a Company: A True Story*. Orchard, 1998.

Hamilton, Virginia. *Cousins*. Philomel, 1990.

Harper, Dan. *Telling Time with Mama Cat*. Harcourt Brace, 1998.

Harris, Robie H. *It's Perfectly Normal: A Book About Changing Bodies, Growing Up, Sex, and Sexual Health*. Illustrated by Michael Emberley. Candlewick, 1994.

———. *It's So Amazing: A Book About Eggs, Sperm, Birth, Babies and Families*. Illustrated by Michael Emberley. Candlewick, 1999.

Haseley, Dennis. *Getting Him*. Farrar, Straus & Giroux, 1994.

Heap, Sue. *Cowboy Baby*. Candlewick, 1998.

Heide, Florence Parry, and Judith Heide Gilliland. *The Day of Ahmed's Secret*. Illustrated by Ted Lewin. Lothrop, Lee & Shepard, 1990.

Henkes, Kevin. *The Birthday Room*. Greenwillow, 1999.

Herbert, Janis. *Leonardo da Vinci for Kids: His Life and Ideas: 21 Activities*. Chicago Review, 1999.

Hesse, Karen. *Just Juice*. Scholastic, 1998.

———. *Out of the Dust*. Scholastic, 1997.

Hickman, Janet. *Jericho*. Greenwillow, 1994.

Hill, Eric. *Where's Spot?* Putnam, 1980.

Hoban, Russell. *A Baby Sister for Frances*. Illustrated by Lillian Hoban. Harper & Row, 1964.

Hoban, Tana. *1, 2, 3*. Greenwillow, 1985.

———. *Let's Count*. Greenwillow, 1999.

———. *Red, Blue, Yellow Shoe*. Greenwillow, 1986.

Hobbs, Will. *Bearstone*. Atheneum, 1989.

Hoberman, MaryAnn. *The Seven Silly Eaters*. Illustrated by Marla Frazee. Browndeer, 1997.

Holm, Jennifer L. *Our Only May Amelia*. HarperCollins, 1999.

Holt, Kimberly. *My Louisiana Sky*. Holt, 1998.

Howard, Elizabeth Fitzgerald. *When Will Sarah Come?* Illustrated by Nina Crews. Greenwillow, 1999.

Howe, James. *Horace and Morris But Mostly Dolores*. Illustrated by Amy Walrod. Simon & Schuster, 1999.

Hughes, Shirley. *Alfie Gets in First*. Lothrop, Lee & Shepard, 1981.

Hurwitz, Joanna. *Ever-Clever Elisa*. Morrow, 1997.

———. *Llama in the Library*. Morrow, 1999.

Hutchins, Pat. *Clocks and More Clocks*. Macmillan, 1994 [1970].

———. *You'll Soon Grow into Them, Titch*. Greenwillow, 1983.

Hyppolite, Joanne. *Ola Shakes It Up*. Delacorte, 1998.

Ibbotson, Eva. *The Secret of Platform 13*. Dutton, 1998.

Jacques, Brian. *The Legend of Luke*. Philomel, 2000.

Jenkins, Steve. *What Do You Do with Something That Wants to Eat You?* Houghton Mifflin, 1997.

Johnson, Angela. *Heaven*. Simon & Schuster, 1998.

———. *Julius.* Illustrated by Dave Pilkey. Orchard, 1993.

———. *Toning the Sweep.* Orchard/Jackson, 1993.

Johnston, Julie. *The Only Outcast.* Tundra, 1998.

Jonas, Ann. *When You Were a Baby.* Greenwillow, 1982.

Jonell, Lynne. *It's My Birthday Too!* Illustrated by Petra Mathers. Putnam, 1999.

Josse, Barbara. *Ghost Trap: A Wild Willie Mystery.* Clarion, 1998.

Jukes, Mavis. *Human Interaction with Ms. Gladys B. Furley, RN: Expecting the Unexpected.* Delacorte, 1996.

Juster, Norton. *The Phantom Tollbooth.* Random House, 1961.

Karr, Kathleen. *Man of the Family.* Farrar, Straus & Giroux, 1999.

Keats, Ezra Jack. *John Henry: An American Legend.* Pantheon, 1965.

———. *The Snowy Day.* Viking, 1962.

———. *Whistle for Willie.* Viking, 1964.

Kelsey, Elin. *Finding Out About Whales.* Owl, 1999.

Kennedy, X. J. *Talking Like the Rain.* Illustrated by Jane Dyer. Little, Brown, 1992.

Kline, Suzy. *Horrible Harry Moves Up to Third Grade.* Viking, 1998.

Konigsburg, E. L. *From the Mixed-Up Files of Mrs. Basil E. Frankweiler.* Atheneum, 1967.

———. *The View from Saturday.* Atheneum, 1996.

Kunhardt, Dorothy. *Pat the Bunny.* Golden Press, 1962 [1940].

Kvasnovsky, Laura McGee. *Zelda and Ivy and the Boy Next Door.* Candlewick, 1999.

Lauture, Denize. *Running the Road to ABC.* Illustrated by Reynold Ruffins. Simon & Schuster, 1996.

Le Guin, Ursula. *A Wizard of Earthsea.* Illustrated by Ruth Robbins. Parnassus, 1968.

Lehn, Barbara. *What Is a Scientist?* Illustrated by Carol Krauss. Millbrook. 1998.

L'Engle, Madeleine. *A Swiftly Tilting Planet.* Farrar, Straus & Giroux, 1978.

Lester, Allison. *The Quicksand Pony.* Houghton Mifflin, 1998.

Levy, Elizabeth. *Third Grade Bullies.* Hyperion, 1998.

Lionni, Leo. *The Biggest House in the World.* Pantheon, 1968.

———. *Fish Is Fish.* Pantheon, 1970.

Lisle, Janet Taylor. *The Lost Flower Children.* Philomel, 1999.

Lobel, Arnold. *Frog and Toad Together.* Harper & Row, 1972.

Losordo, Stephen. *Cow Moo Me.* Illustrated by Jan Conteh-Morgan. HarperCollins, 1998.

Lowry, Lois. *Anastasia Krupnik.* Houghton Mifflin, 1979.

———. *The Giver.* Houghton Mifflin, 1993.

———. *Number the Stars.* Houghton Mifflin, 1989.

Lynch, Chris. *Extreme Elvin.* HarperCollins, 1999.

MacKinnon, Debbie. *How Many?* Photographs by Anthea Sieveking. Dial, 1993.

MacLachlan, Patricia. *Sarah, Plain and Tall.* Harper & Row, 1985.

Marsden, John. *A Killing Frost.* Houghton Mifflin, 1998.

Martin, Bill, Jr. *Brown Bear, Brown Bear, What Do You See?* Illustrated by Eric Carle. Holt, 1983.

Martin, Bill, Jr., and John Archambault. *Chicka Chicka Boom Boom.* Illustrated by Lois Ehlert. Simon & Schuster, 1989.

Martin, Jacqueline Briggs. *Grandmother Bryant's Pocket.* Houghton Mifflin, 1996.

———. *Snowflake Bentley.* Illustrated by Mary Azarian. Houghton Mifflin, 1998.

Martinez, Victor. *Parrot in the Oven, Mi Vida.* HarperCollins, 1996.

Marzollo, Jean. *I. Spy Gold Challenger! A Book of Picture Riddles.* Scholastic, 1998.

Matcheck, Diane. *The Sacrifice.* Farrar, Straus & Giroux, 1998.

Mathers, Petra. *Lottie's New Friend.* Atheneum, 1999.

McCaughrean, Geraldine. *The Pirate's Son.* Scholastic, 1998.

McCloskey, Robert. *Burt Dow, Deep Water Man.* Viking, 1963.

———. *Make Way for Ducklings.* Viking, 1941.

———. *One Morning in Maine.* Viking, 1952.

McGraw, Eloise. *The Moorchild.* McElderry, 1997.

McKay, Hillary. *The Amber Cat.* McElderry, 1997.

———. *The Exiles.* McElderry, 1992.

McKinley, Robin. *The Hero and the Crown.* Greenwillow, 1984.

McKissack, Patricia C. *Flossie and the Fox.* Illustrated by Rachel Isadora. Dial, 1986.

McPhail, David. *Fix-It.* Dutton, 1984.

Mead, Alice. *Junebug and the Reverend.* Farrar, Straus & Giroux, 1998.

Merriam, Eve. *What in the World?* Illustrated by Barbara J. Phillips-Duke. HarperCollins, 1998.

Miller, Margaret. *Guess Who?* Greenwillow, 1994.

———. *What's on My Head?* Little Simon, 1999.

Mikaelson, Ben. *Petey.* Hyperion, 1998.

Minarik, Else Holmelund. *Little Bear.* Illustrated by Maurice Sendak. Harper & Row, 1957.

Mollel, Tolowa. *My Rows and Piles of Coins.* Illustrated by E. B. Lewis. Clarion, 1999.

Mudd, Ruth. *Firefighting: Behind the Scenes.* Illustrated by Scott Sroka. Houghton Mifflin, 1998.

Myers, Walter Dean. *Darnell Rock Reporting.* HarperCollins, 1994.

———. *The Glory Field.* Scholastic, 1994.

———. *Now Is Your Time! The African-American Struggle for Freedom.* HarperCollins, 1991.

———. *Scorpions.* Harper & Row, 1988.

Naylor, Phyllis Reynolds. *Achingly Alice.* Atheneum, 1999.

———. *Shiloh.* Atheneum, 1991.

Nix, Garth. *Shade's Children.* HarperCollins, 1997.

Nolan, Han. *Dancing on the Edge.* Harcourt, 1997.

Nye, Naomi Shihab. *Habibi.* Simon & Schuster, 1997.

———. *What Have You Lost?* Photographs Michael Nye. Greenwillow, 1999.

Opie, Iona. *My Very First Mother Goose.* Illustrated by Rosemary Wells. Candlewick, 1996.

Orlev, Uri. *The Man from the Other Side.* Houghton Mifflin, 1991.

Oxenbury, Helen. *I Can.* Candlewick, 1995.

———. *Tom & Pippo's Day.* Macmillan, 1989.

Parish, Peggy. *Amelia Bedelia.* Illustrated by Fritz Siebel. Harper & Row, 1963.

Park, Barbara. *Skinnybones*. Knopf, 1982.

Park, Ruth. *When the Wind Changed*. Illustrated by Deborah Niland. Coward-McCann, 1981.

Partridge, Elizabeth. *Restless Spirit: The Life of Dorothea Lange*. Viking, 1998.

Paterson, Katherine. *Flip-Flop Girl*. Lodestar, 1994.

———. *The Great Gilly Hopkins*. Crowell, 1978.

———. *Jacob Have I Loved*. Crowell, 1980.

———. *Jip: His Story*. Lodestar, 1996.

Paulsen, Gary. *Hatchet*. Bradbury, 1987.

Perkins, Lynne Rae. *All Alone in the Universe*. Greenwillow, 1999.

Pfeffer, Wendy. *A Log's Life*. Illustrated by Robin Brickman. Simon & Schuster, 1997.

Phillips, Rita Mitchell. *Hue Boy*. Illustrated by Caroline Binch. Dial, 1993.

Pilkey, Dav. *Captain Underpants and the Attack of the Talking Toilets*. Scholastic, 1999.

———. *Dragon's Fat Cat*. Orchard, 1992.

Pinkney, Brian. *The Adventures of Sparrowboy*. Simon & Schuster, 1997.

Polacco, Patricia. *The Bee Tree*. Philomel, 1993.

Porter, Connie. *Meet Addy* (the American Girl collection). Illustrated by Nancy Niles. Pleasant, 1990.

Potter, Beatrix. *The Tale of Peter Rabbit*. Warne, 1902.

Propp, Vera W. *When the Soldiers Were Gone*. Putnam, 1999.

Pryor, Bonnie. *The House on Maple Street*. Illustrated by Beth Peck. Morrow, 1987.

Pullman, Philip. *The Golden Compass*. Knopf, 1996.

———. *I was a Rat*. Knopf, 2000.

Quattlebaum, Mary. *Jackson Jones and the Puddle of Thorns*. Delacorte, 1994.

Radcliffe, Theresa. *Bashi, Baby Elephant*. Illustrated by John Butler. Viking, 1998.

Raffi. *Wheels on the Bus*. Random House, 1998.

Raschka, Chris. *Like Likes Like*. Dorling Kindersley, 1999.

Raskin, Ellen. *The Westing Game*. Dutton, 1978.

Rathman, Peggy. *10 Minutes Till Bedtime*. Putnam, 1998.

Rawls, Wilson. *Where the Red Fern Grows*. Doubleday, 1961.

Reeder, Carolyn. *Shades of Gray*. Macmillan, 1989.

Reiser, Lynn. *Little Clam*. Greenwillow, 1998.

Rockwell, Anne. *The Three Bears and Fifteen Other Stories*. Crowell, 1975.

Rogers, Fred. *Going to the Potty*. Illustrated by Jim Judkis. Putnam, 1986.

Root, Phyllis. *What Baby Wants*. Illustrated by Jill Barton. Candlewick, 1998.

Rosen, Michael. *We're Going on a Bear Hunt*. Illustrated by Helen Oxenbury. McElderry, 1989.

Rowling, J. K. *Harry Potter and the Doomspell Tournament*. Scholastic, 2000.

Rylant, Cynthia. *Missing May*. Orchard, 1992.

———. *When I Was Young in the Mountains*. Illustrated by Diane Goode. Dutton, 1982.

Sachar, Louis. *Holes*. Farrar, Straus & Giroux, 1998.

Schachner, Judith Byron. *The Grannyman*. Dutton, 1999

Schwartz, Alvin. *Tomfoolery: Trickery and Foolery with Words*. Illustrated by Glen Rounds. Harper & Row, 1973.

Scieszka, John. *Summer Reading Is Killing Me*. Viking, 1998.

———. *The True Story of the Three Little Pigs*. Illustrated by Lane Smith. Viking, 1989.

Sendak, Maurice. *Where the Wild Things Are*. Harper & Row, 1963.

Shannon, David. *No David!* Scholastic, 1998.

Silverman, Erica. *Don't Fidget a Feather*. Illustrated by S. D. Schindler. Macmillan, 1994.

Silverstein, Shel. *Falling Up*. Harper & Row, 1996.

———. *Where the Sidewalk Ends*. Harper & Row, 1963.

Simmons, Jane. *Come Along Daisy*. Little, Brown, 1998.

———. *Daisy and the Egg*. Little, Brown, 1999.

Sis, Peter. *Trucks Trucks Trucks*. Greenwillow, 1999.

Smith, Doris Buchanan. *A Taste of Blackberries*. Illustrated by Charles Robinson. Crowell, 1973.

Smith, Robert. *The War with Grandpa*. Illustrated by Richard Lauter. Delacorte, 1984.

Smyth, Ian. *The Young Baseball Player*. Dorling Kindersley, 1998.

Soto, Gary. *Baseball in April and Other Stories*. Harcourt Brace, 1990.

———. *Too Many Tamales*. Illustrated by Ed Martinez. Putnam, 1993.

Spence, Rob, and Amy Spence. *Clickety Clack*. Illustrated by Margaret Spengler. Viking, 1999.

Spinelli, Eileen. *Lizzie Logan, Second Banana*. Simon & Schuster, 1998.

Spinelli, Jerry. *Knots in a Yo-Yo String: The Autobiography of a Kid*. Knopf, 1998.

———. *Maniac Magee*. Little, Brown, 1990.

———. *Wringers*. HarperCollins, 1997.

Staples, Suzanne. *Shabanu: Daughter of the Wind*. Knopf, 1989.

Steig, William. *Doctor De Soto*. Farrar, Straus & Giroux, 1982.

———. *Pete's a Pizza*. HarperCollins, 1998.

———. *Sylvester and the Magic Pebble*. Simon & Schuster, 1969.

———. *Zeke Pippin*. HarperCollins, 1994.

Stevens, Janet. *Tops and Bottoms*. Harcourt Brace, 1995.

Stewart, Mark. *Shaquille O'Neal: Big Man, Big Dreams*. Millbrook, 1998.

Stuve-Bodeen, Stephanie. *Elizabeti's Doll*. Illustrated by Christy Hale. Lee & Low, 1998.

Sutcliff, Rosemary. *Sword Song*. Farrar, Straus & Giroux, 1998.

Taback, Sims. *I Know an Old Lady*. Dial, 1997.

Taylor, Ann. *Baby Dance*. Illustrated by Marjorie Van Heerden. HarperCollins, 1999.

Taylor, Mildred. *Roll of Thunder, Hear My Cry*. Dial, 1976.

Temple, Frances. *Taste of Salt: A Story of Modern Haiti*. Orchard/Jackson, 1992.

Thomas, Joyce Carol. *You Are My Perfect Baby*. Illustrated by Nneka Bennett. HarperCollins, 1999.

Tillage, Leon. *Leon's Story*. Illustrated by Barbara Roth. Farrar, Straus & Giroux, 1997.

Tolkien, J. R. R. *The Hobbit*. Illustrated by Michael Hague. Houghton Mifflin, 1989 [1938].

Voigt, Cynthia. *Dicey's Song*. Atheneum, 1982.

Wabbes, Marie. *How I Was Born*. Tambourine, 1991.

Waber, Bernard. *Ira Sleeps Over*. Houghton Mifflin, 1973.

Waldman, Neil. *Masada*. Morrow, 1998.

Walker, Barbara. *The Little House Cookbook: Frontier Foods from Laura Ingalls Wilder's Classic Stories*. Illustrated by Garth Williams. Harper & Row, 1979.

Walsh, Jill Paton. *The Green Book*. Illustrated by Lloyd Bloom. Farrar, Straus & Giroux, 1982.

Walter, Mildred Pitts. *Suitcase*. Illustrated by Theresa Flavin. Lothrop, Lee & Shepard, 1999.

Walter, Virginia. *Making Up Megaboy*. Illustrated by M. Katrina Roeckelein. Dorling Kindersley, 1998.

Weeks, Sarah. *Mrs. McNosh Hangs Up Her Wash*. Illustrated by Nadine Bernard Westcott. HarperCollins, 1998.

Wells, Rosemary. *Bunny Cakes*. Dial, 1998.

———. *Edward, Unready for School*. Dial, 1995.

———. *Mary on Horseback: Three Mountain Stories*. Dial, 1998.

———. *Max's Ride*. Dial, 1979.

———. *Noisy Nora*. Dial, 1973.

Whelan, Gloria. *Homeless Bird*. HarperCollins, 2000.

White, Ruth. *Belle Prater's Boy*. Farrar, Straus & Giroux, 1996.

Williams, Karen. *Galimoto*. Illustrated by Catherine Stock. Lothrop, Lee & Shepard, 1990.

Williams, Sam. *The Baby's Word Book*. Greenwillow, 1999.

Williams, Vera B. *A Chair for My Mother*. Greenwillow, 1982.

Williams-Garcia, Rita. *Like Sisters on the Home Front*. Lodestar, 1995.

Wilson, April. *Magpie Magic: A Tale of Colorful Mischief*. Dial, 1999.

Wolfe, Virginia Euwer. *Bat 6*. Holt, 1998.

Wolff, Ashley. *A Year of Beasts*. Dutton, 1986.

Wood, Nancy. *Thunderwoman: A Mythical Novel of the Pueblos*. Dutton, 1999.

Wright, Betty Ren. *A Ghost in the Family*. Scholastic, 1998.

Wynne-Jones, Tim. *Stephen Fair*. Dorling Kindersley, 1998.

Yashima, Taro. *Crow Boy*. Viking, 1955.

Yolen, Jane. *How Do Dinosaurs Say Goodnight?* Illustrated by Mark Teague. Scholastic, 2000.

Young, Ed. *Lon Po Po: A Red Riding Hood Story from China*. Philomel, 1989.

Yumoto, Kazumi. *The Friends*. Illustrated by Cathy Hirano. Farrar, Straus & Giroux, 1996.

Zeifert, Harriet. *I Swapped My Dog*. Illustrated by Emily Bolam. Houghton Mifflin, 1998.

Zimmerman, Andrea, and David Clemesha. *Trashy Town*. Illustrated by Dan Yaccarino. HarperCollins, 1999.

# The Changing World of Children's Books

**S**tories have probably been told for as long as humans have had language. But as we study the changing history of children's literature we find that social, cultural, and political norms have had an impact on the content of those stories. What seems to have remained constant

over the years are broad themes of the stories and the enjoyment of the audience. Themes center around human relationships, love, and conflicts. The three illustrations on page 68 show how one of these themes, has been treated differently just in the last two hundred years.

"Cruel Boys" is taken from *Sunnybank Stories: My Teacher's Gem,* a collection of moralistic stories printed in 1863. It tells of two friends who have wickedly robbed several birds' nests, hurting the fledglings in the process. The purpose of the story, however, was not to tell about the adventures of two friends but to instruct the young by first describing a horrible example of misbehavior and then warning of its dire consequences. It is told in the third person from the point of view of an adult admonishing all children. The moral of the story is explicitly stated.

> And this isn't the whole story about these wicked boys. Don't you see they are in a *quarrel,* how they shall divide what they have so cruelly stolen from the birds? Ah, that is the way in doing wrong—one wrong step leads on to another; and robbing birds' nests does not usually go alone—a quarrel, or some other wickedness, usually follows it. Beware, then, of the *beginnings* of cruelty and wickedness.[1]

*Let's Be Enemies,* published in 1961, also centers on the relationship of two friends. In this case John is angry at his friend James's behavior and decides to pick a quarrel. Janice Udry's text directly captures the experience, the feelings, and the language of the young child:

> "I came to tell you that I'm not your friend any more."
> "Well then, I'm not *your* friend either."
> "We're enemies."
> "All right!"
> "GOOD-BYE!"
> "GOOD-BYE!"[2]

The story is told in the first person from the point of view of the child protagonist, which makes it easier for the reader to identify with John's growing anger at the offenses committed by his friend. But 5-year-olds' quarrels are as fleeting as the brief showers that Maurice Sendak includes in his childlike illustrations. In this story the sun soon comes out; and true to the nature of young children, John and James are fast friends by the end of the story.

*Yo! Yes?* by Chris Raschka was published in 1993. It also centers on the developing friendship between two boys, one black, one white. As the story unfolds they engage in a terse conversation:

> Yo?
> Yes?
> Hey!
> Who?
> You!
> Me?[3]

Raschka makes clear through this minimalist dialogue and the lively illustrations that the boys' developing friendship moves from distrust to trust and from wariness to openness. By the end of the book the two move off together, presumably to the basketball court to shoot a few hoops.

The contrast in these three stories mirrors the changes in literature for children. When we compare the language, the content, and the illustrations in the books, the ways in which society has changed its cultural values and its attitude toward children become strikingly apparent.

"Cruel Boys" lectures to its child audience, and the boys' friendship is seen almost as a deterrent to moral behavior. The animal protection movement in vogue at the time has also got in the way of good storytelling. A wringingly soppy plea for the poor birds all but buries any possibility of an entertaining story: "How unhappy

---

[1] Asa Bullard, *Sunnybank Stories: My Teacher's Gem* (Boston: Lee & Shepard, 1863), pp. 22–24.

[2] Janice May Udry, *Let's Be Enemies,* illus. Maurice Sendak (New York: Harper & Row, 1961).

[3] Chris Raschka, *Yo! Yes?* (New York: Orchard, 1993), unpaged.

*"Cruel Boys" from* Sunnybank Stories: My Teacher's Gem. *Boston, Mass.: Lee & Shepard, 1863.*

"Cruel Boys" from *Sunnybank Stories: My Teacher's Gem* by Asa Bullard. Boston: Lee & Shepard, 1863.
©James L. Shaffer

Let's Be Enemies *centers on the relationship of two friends.*

Yo! Yes? *By Chris Raschka.*

must all these birds now be! and how wicked it is to give needless pain to any of God's creatures!"

The book contains only one print, black and white, the one pictured here. This same illustration was used in many different books at that time. The "pirating" of pictures and stories from other books was a common practice.

In *Let's Be Enemies,* children are allowed their childhood; they can be their 5-year-old selves. Their private feelings, thoughts, and language are considered worthy of attention. As much care has gone into conveying the meaning of the story through the pictures as through the text.

*Yo! Yes?* is also respectful of its child audience as it explores the uncertainty of the unknown as well as the need for friendship. But now the almost all white world of children's books that we find in the first half of the twentieth century has disappeared. We finally see children as they exist in the world of today with all its cultural differences. The concise dialogue celebrates linguistic differences in the manner of rap and the African American call-and-response style. The full-color illustrations carry the burden of the storytelling, just as visual images predominate in the

child's world. They are also indicative of the changed methods of reproduction over the centuries.

It has taken a very long time for children's books to move from the didactic and moralistic to the delightful and entertaining. Literature intended for children always reflects society's changing attitude toward childhood and the family. Philippe Ariès contends that the idea of childhood itself was a seventeenth-century invention that has been transformed and reconstituted in every subsequent historical period.[4] Books for children provide a fascinating record of society and the values it has wished to inculcate in its youth.

Children's literature has a relatively brief history. Nevertheless, it has evolved from a rich and interesting background. Literature reflects not only the values of society but also the books that have preceded it—the literature of one generation builds on the literature of the past generation. An understanding of family stories of today is enriched by an acquaintance with the family stories of the past. How, for example, do the Beverly Cleary stories of the Quimby family (such as *Ramona and Her Father,* 1977) or Cynthia Voigt's descriptions of the Tillermans in *Homecoming* (1981) or the relations in Virginia Hamilton's *Cousins* compare with *The*

*Moffats* (1941) by Eleanor Estes or Edith Nesbit's Bastable children in *The Story of the Treasure-Seekers* (1899) or even that earliest of well-loved family stories, *Little Women* (1868), by Louisa May Alcott?

One danger in evaluating stories of the past is the tendency to use contemporary criteria rather than to recognize the prevailing values of the period in which a book was published. Some modern-day critics see *Little Women* as being antifeminist, but at the time of its publication in 1868 its main character was considered much too independent and tomboyish. Obvious as this might seem, books for children are products of their times. They need to be evaluated in relationship to the other books of the day and against the social and political values of the period. Only then is it possible to identify the books that were real breakthroughs in the changing literature of childhood.

# Early Beginnings: The Middle Ages

Today's literature for children has grown out of oral traditions that exist in every society. Stories and poems that were passed on by bards and retold by the common people were eventually recorded in manuscripts for a wide audience of adults and children.

## The Oral Tradition

Before there were books, there were stories. In the medieval days—from the fifth to the fifteenth century—stories were told around the fires in cottages or sung in the great halls of castles. Young and old alike listened, with no distinction made between stories for children and stories for adults, just as there was little difference in the work they did, the food they ate, or the clothes they wore. All gathered to listen, to be entertained after a hard day's labor.

In the Middle Ages, there were differences between the kinds of stories told in the cottages and the kinds told in the castles, and in the ways they were told. In the castles and great manor houses, wandering minstrels or bards told the heroic tales of Beowulf or King Arthur or the ballad of Fair Isabella, whose stepmother had her cooked and served in a pie. By contrast, the tales told around the peat fires in the cottages or at the medieval fairs were about simple

folk—farmers, woodcutters, and millers—or beast tales about wolves, foxes, and hens. Frequently, the stories portrayed the poor peasant outwitting the lord of the manor or winning the hand of the princess by a daring deed. These tales were told over and over for generations until they were finally collected by scholars and thus passed into recorded literature.

## The Earliest Manuscripts

Before the invention of movable type, the first books that European children might have read were lesson books or picture Bibles illustrated and handwritten in Latin by monks. Mostly religious or instructional, these were intended only for the wealthy or for use by teachers in monastery schools. Such handwritten books were extremely valuable; houses and lands were often exchanged for a single volume.[5]

Most early lesson books followed one of two forms, which continued in popularity up to the early twentieth century: (1) a dialogue between the pupil and teacher, usually in the form of questions and answers, or (2) rhymed couplets, which made for easy memorization. Aldhelm, abbot of Malmesbury during the seventh century, is credited with introducing the question-and-answer approach. Also during this century, the Venerable Bede translated and wrote some forty-five books for his students at the monastery at Jarrow in England.

---

[4]Philippe Ariès, *Centuries of Childhood: A Social History of Family Life,* trans. Robert Baldick (New York: Knopf, 1962).

[5]Louise Frances Story Field [Mrs. E. M. Field], *The Child and His Book,* 2nd ed. (London: Wells Gardner, 1892; reprint: Detroit: Singing Tree Press, 1968), p. 13.

*The layout of this picture bible or* Biblia Pauperum *is strikingly similar to today's picture book. It may have been used for religious instruction of the illiterate poor, or for instruction of the young children of the nobility.*
Kings 5 manuscript, British Library
"Moses and the Burning Bush," King's 5 fol 2 (1010335.011). By permission of the British Library, Special Collections.

Another type of book, the Elucidarium, or book of general information for young students, was developed by Anselm, archbishop of Canterbury during the twelfth century. This type of book, a forerunner of the encyclopedia, treated such topics as manners, children's duties, the properties of animals and plants, and religious precepts.

Early lesson books are important to the history of children's literature only in that they represent some concession to developing specific books for the *instruction* of children. Another six centuries would pass before John Newbery would add the word *amusement* to the word *instruction*.

The *Gesta Romanorum* (Deeds of the Romans), compiled in Latin in the early fourteenth century, served as a sourcebook of stories for the clergy for instruction and for enlivening sermons. This compilation of stories included many myths, fables, and tales from as far away as India. Both Chaucer and Shakespeare drew incidents and stories from the *Gesta*. For example, it contained anecdotes of the three caskets and the pound of flesh found in *The Merchant of Venice* and a synopsis of the medieval romance in *Guy of Warwick*. These tales were often dressed up with suitable morals and then told to children.

Only one well-known work remains from medieval manuscripts, Chaucer's *Canterbury Tales*. Although written for adults in 1387, the tales are full of legendary stories and folktales that were known to children as well as adults of the period.

## Caxton Begins English Printing

Some historians maintain that Western printing first began in Holland sometime between 1380 and 1420.[6] However, in the 1450s, Gutenberg in Germany devised a practical method for using movable metal type, far superior in quality to the early Dutch type. William Caxton, an English businessman, went to Cologne, Germany, to learn the printing trade. Returning to England, he set up a printing press in Westminster about 1476. Among the first books he published were *A Book of Curteseye* (1477), *The Historye of Reynart the Foxe* (1481), and *Aesop's Fables* (1484). Malory's *Le Morte d'Arthur* first appeared in printed form in 1485. Caxton is credited with publishing some 106 books, including traditional romance literature, ballads, texts, and religious books. His books were of high quality and expensive, which made them available only to wealthy adults, not children. The impact of the printing press can be seen, however, in the number of books owned by some individuals. Before its invention in the 1450s, even scholars and physicians possessed only a few books. A century later, to give one example, Columbus of Seville (the son of Christopher Columbus) owned a library of more than fifteen thousand titles.

---

[6]Elva S. Smith, *Elva S. Smith's History of Children's Literature*, rev. by Margaret Hodges and Susan Steinfirst (Chicago: American Library Association, 1980), p. 38.

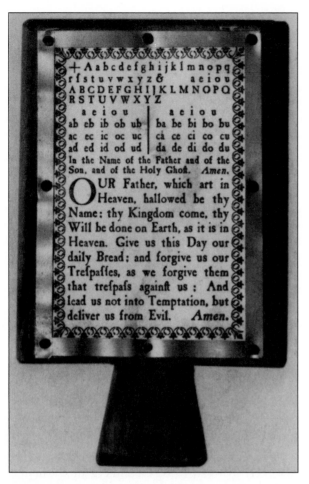

*This facsimile of a colonial hornbook was ordered from The Horn Book, Inc., 11 Beacon Street, Boston, MA 02108.*

The Horn Book Replica, reprinted by permission of The Horn Book, Inc. 56 Roland St., Suite 200, Boston MA 02129, 617–625–0225.

## Hornbooks, ABCs, and Primers

The first children's books to be influenced by the invention of printing were then the only children's books: lesson books or textbooks. Young children learned to read from "hornbooks." A hornbook was really a little wooden paddle to which was pasted a sheet of parchment printed with the alphabet, the vowels, and the Lord's Prayer. A thin sheet of transparent protective horn bound with strips of brass covered the text. Most hornbooks were tiny, measuring two by five inches. Sometimes a hole in the handle made it possible for the child to carry the book on a cord around his or her neck or waist. This also lent them their nickname *battledore*, for they were often used to bat around a shuttlecock in a game of badminton. What made these little "books" unique was that now the child could handle them and see the print close up, rather than merely look at a manuscript held by the teacher.

Children advanced from the hornbooks to ABC books and primers. These had more text than horn-

books but were still of a religious nature. The first primers developed from the books of hours, which were intended as private devotionals for laypeople, with prayers for eight specified times of the day. In 1514 an alphabet was added to a book of hours for use by children. When Henry VIII came to the throne, he authorized printing a set of English primers for children that presented his religious beliefs. These little books, appropriately called King Henry's Primers, appeared about 1548.

## Lasting Contributions of the Period

Children were not much better off after the invention of printing than before. They still derived their enjoyment from the told story. True, some concession had been made to their youth in devising special books of instruction for them. But only crudely written and printed chapbooks provided a kind of underground literature of enjoyment for both adults and children. The two lasting books of this period are Chaucer's *Canterbury Tales* and Thomas Malory's collection of Arthurian legends, later published in 1485 by Caxton under the title *Le Morte d'Arthur*. Neither of these books was written for children, but children probably knew the stories from hearing them told by bards and minstrels.

What strikes a twentieth-century reader as remarkable about this period is how few books there were and how long they stayed in print. Many of the books published by Caxton in the 1440s were still in print in the late 1600s, more than two hundred years later. This seems almost unbelievable when compared with today's publishing world, where some books go out of print in less than a year.

# *Children's Books: The Seventeenth & Eighteenth Centuries*

In the seventeenth and eighteenth centuries, many books for children were meant to be educational rather than entertaining. Over time, however, authors, illustrators, and publishers began to present children with books that were meant to delight as well as to inform.

## The "Goodly Godly" Books of the Puritans

Books of the seventeenth century were dominated by the stern spiritual beliefs of Puritanism. Children were considered to be miniature adults by the Puritans, and they were thus equally subject to sin and eternal damnation. Concern for the salvation of their souls became the central goal of their parents and teachers. Given the high mortality rate of infants and young children (more than half did not live to reach the age of 10), instruction in the fear of God began early.

Children were expected to memorize John Cotton's catechism, *Spiritual Milk for Boston Babes in Either England, Drawn from the Breasts of Both Testaments for Their Souls' Nourishment.* Originally published in England in 1646, it was revised for American children in 1656, the first book written and printed for children in the American colonies. Later books followed its question-and-answer approach. For example, there was the question "How did God make you?" The child had to memorize the accompanying answer: "I was conceived in sin and born in iniquity." Even alphabet rhymes for the youngest emphasized the sinful nature of humans. *The New England Primer*, first advertised in 1683, includes "In Adam's fall/We sinned all." This primer also provided a catechism, the Ten Commandments, verses about death, and a woodcut of Martyr John Foxe burning at the stake, watched by his wife and nine children. This primer was in print for more than a century and sold about three million copies.

In England in 1671, James Janeway published his book of gloomy joy titled *A Token for Children, Being an Exact Account of the Conversions, Holy and Exemplary Lives and Joyful Deaths of Several Young Children.* In his preface to Part 1, he reminds his readers that they are "by Nature, Children of Wrath." Cotton Mather added the life histories of several New England children and published an American edition of Janeway's book in Boston in 1700 under the title *A Token for Children of New England, or Some Examples of Children in Whom the Fear of God Was Remarkably Budding Before They Died.* Virginia Haviland describes the American edition: "An account of youthful piety, in tune with the doctrine of original sin, this is the first of the few narratives that were available to eighteenth century children in America and undoubtedly the most widely read children's book in the Puritan age."[7]

Religious leaders also could give approval to the moral and spiritual instruction in John Bunyan's *Pilgrim's Progress*, first printed in 1678. No doubt children skipped the long theological dialogues as they found adventure by traveling with the clearly defined characters.

Primers and instructional books continued to be popular during this time. Edward Topsell's *Historie of Four-Footed Beasts*, published in 1607, was perhaps the first work of nonfiction written for chil-

dren.[8] Many of these educational books were emblem books. They followed a pictorial format developed in Germany and the Netherlands in which each verse or couplet was illustrated with a small picture. Johann Amos Comenius's *Orbis Pictus* (The World in Pictures) was influenced by this style. It was translated into English in 1659 and published with many woodcuts illustrating everyday objects. *Orbis Pictus* is often referred to as the first picture book for children.

## Chapbooks: Forerunners of Comics

Luckily, there was some relief from the doom and gloom of the religion-oriented books of the Puritans. Chapbooks—small, inexpensive, folded-paper booklets sold by peddlers, or chapmen—first appeared in the late 1500s, but they achieved real popularity in the seventeenth and eighteenth centuries. Sold for a

[8]Mary V. Jackson, *Engines of Instruction, Mischief, and Magic: Children's Literature in England from Its Beginnings to 1839* (Lincoln: University of Nebraska Press, 1990), p. 36.

*This woodcut from a seventeenth-century chapbook has two episodes, "Tom Thumb running a tilt" and "how Tom Thumb did take his sickness, and of his death and burial."* c. 1650–1660.

The Walter Havighurst Special Collections, Miami University Libraries, Oxford, Ohio.

[7]Virginia Haviland and Margaret N. Coughlan, *Yankee Doodle's Literary Sampler of Prose, Poetry and Pictures* (New York: Crowell, 1974), p. 11.

few pennies, these crudely printed little books brought excitement and pleasure into the lives of both children and adults with tales about Dick Whittington, Sir Guy of Warwick, Robin Hood, and other heroes. A ballad of a "most strange wedding of the froggee and the mouse" was licensed as early as 1580. The earliest known edition of "Jack the Giant Killer" seems to have been in a chapbook of 1711. Other chapbooks gave accounts of crimes and executions, descriptions of the art of making love, and riddles.

While these books were decried by the Puritans, they were read and reread by the common people of England and America. Their popularity with children is said to have influenced John Newbery's decision to publish a book solely for children. The chapbooks' greatly abbreviated texts and crude woodcut illustrations suggest that they were forerunners of today's comic strips, still read by both adults and children.

## Fairy Tales and Adventure

Another source of enjoyment for children came in the form of fairy tales; the first was printed in France in 1697 by Charles Perrault. Titled *Histoires ou contes du temps passé, avec des moralités* (Stories or Tales of Times Past, with Morals), the collection included "The Sleeping Beauty," "Cinderella or the Glass Slipper," "Red Riding Hood," "Puss-in-Boots," and "Blue Beard." These tales were in fashion at the French court of the Sun King, Louis XIV, where they were told to adults. The frontispiece of Perrault's book, however, showed an old woman spinning and telling stories to children. The caption read *Contes de ma Mère l'Oye* (Tales of Mother Goose); this was the first reference to Mother Goose in children's literature. Translated into English in 1729, these fairy tales have remained France's gift to the children of the world.

Following the success of Perrault, other French authors, including Mme. d'Aulnoy, created original fairy tales. Only one remains well known today and that is "Beauty and the Beast," rewritten from a longer version by Mme. de Beaumont.

*The Arabian Nights* is a collection of old tales from India, Persia, and North Africa. Galland published these tales in French in 1558, but not until about 1706 were they available in English. Intended for adults, such stories as "Aladdin," "Ali Baba," and "Sinbad the Sailor" were appropriated by children.

Defoe did not write his account of the eighteenth-century hero Robinson Crusoe for them, but children made his story part of their literature. *The Life and Strange and Surprising Adventures of Robinson Crusoe* (1719) was later printed in an abridged and pocket-size volume that became a "classic" of children's literature. This book was so popular that it spawned many imitations—so many, in fact, that a word, *Robinsonades,* was coined for them.

Children, no doubt, did not understand the scathing satire about high society in Swift's *Gulliver's Travels,* but they did find enjoyment in the hero's adventures with the huge and tiny folk and the talking horses. Thus young and old alike enjoyed this tale of adventure, first published in 1726.

## Nursery Rhymes or Mother Goose

No one knows for sure the exact origin of nursery rhymes. Apparently, the rhymes we know as Mother Goose, including counting-out rhymes, finger plays, and alphabet verses, originated in the spoken language of both common folk and royalty. Some have been traced as far back as the pre-Christian era. It is believed that many of the verses were written as political satires or told of tragedy. "Ring Around the Rosie" may have referred to the pink ringlike rash that marked the early signs of bubonic plague. People carried "posies" of herbs for protection, and "We all fall down," of course, would refer to the final demise of the victims. Katherine Thomas cites the account of a deed in the possession of a Horner family signed by Henry VIII that was a "plum" pulled out of the pie— the King's collection of deeds.[9] However, other scholars have found little evidence of these relationships.[10]

Shakespeare evidently knew these nursery rhymes, for they are referred to in *King Lear* and other of his plays. Yet the oldest *surviving* nursery rhyme book was published by Mary Cooper in 1744 in two or perhaps three little volumes under the title *Tommy Thumb's Pretty Song Book;* a single copy of volume 2 is a treasured possession of the British Museum. John Newbery is supposed to have published *Mother Goose's Melody or Sonnets for the Cradle* about 1765, although the book was not advertised until 1780, which is the more likely date of its publication. No copy of this edition exists. However, Isaiah Thomas of Worcester, Massachusetts, produced a second edition of *Mother Goose's Melody* in 1794. Many of his books were pirated from Newbery, and it is assumed that his first edition of about 1786 was a copy of the lost Newbery book.

The legend that Dame Goose is buried in Boston is kept alive for tourists and children who visit the Boston burying grounds, but it has created confusion regarding the origin of the verses. Even the publication of *Songs for the Nursery, or Mother Goose's Melodies* by the son-in-law of Dame Goose is itself a legend. According to the story, Thomas Fleet tired of

---

[9]Katherine Elwes Thomas, *The Real Personages of Mother Goose* (New York: Lothrop, 1930).

[10]Iona Opie and Peter Opie, *The Oxford Nursery Rhyme Book* (London: Oxford University Press, 1952). William S. Baring-Gould and Ceil Baring-Gould, *The Annotated Mother Goose* (New York: Charles N. Potter, 1962).

the good woman's frequent renditions of the ditties as she cared for his children, so he decided to collect and publish them in 1719. No actual evidence of this edition has been found.

Other verses and rhymes were later added to collections of Mother Goose after their publication as small separate books. *The Comic Adventures of Old Mother Hubbard and Her Dog* by Sarah Martin first appeared in 1805. During the same year *Songs from the Nursery Collected by the Most Renowned Poets* was published. For the first time, "Little Miss Muffett" and "One, Two Buckle My Shoe" were included in a Mother Goose book. *The History of Sixteen Wonderful Old Women,* issued by J. Harris and Son in 1820, contains the earliest examples of what we now call the limerick.

Uncertain of her origin as they are, historians do recognize that the venerable Mother Goose became a welcome part of the nursery on both sides of the Atlantic during the eighteenth century. Since then she has never left her post.

## Newbery Publishes for Children

The concept of a literature for children usually dates from 1744, the year the English publisher John Newbery printed *A Little Pretty Pocket-Book.* The title page is shown here. Newbery included John Locke's advice that children should enjoy reading. The book itself attempted to teach the alphabet "by Way of Diversion," including games, fables, and little rhymes about the letters of the alphabet. What was significant about the book was that Newbery deliberately and openly set out to provide amusement for children, something no other publisher had had the courage or insight to do.

Newbery is also responsible for "the first piece of original English fiction deliberately written for children."[11] No documentary evidence is available to determine whether John Newbery or Oliver Goldsmith wrote *The History of Little Goody Two Shoes,* published by Newbery in 1765. London records do show that Newbery gave Goldsmith lodging above his shop, called "The Bible and the Sun." It is probable that Goldsmith was the author of some of the two hundred books published by Newbery. In *Little Goody Two Shoes,* Margery Meanwell and her brother are turned out of their home after the death of her parents, for "Her father had succumbed to a fever, in a place where Dr. James' Powder was not to be had." (Newbery also sold Dr. James' Powder and other medicines in his store.) At first the children are taken in by a kind parson, who properly clothes

---

[11]F. J. Harvey Darton, *Children's Books in England,* 3rd ed., rev. by Brian Alderson (Cambridge: Cambridge University Press, 1932, 1982), p. 128.

---

A Little Pretty
## POCKET-BOOK,
Intended for the
INSTRUCTION and AMUSEMENT
OF
LITTLE MASTER *TOMMY,*
AND
PRETTY MISS *POLLY.*
With Two Letters from
JACK the GIANT-KILLER;
AS ALSO
A BALL and PINCUSHION;
The Use of which will infallibly make *Tommy*
a good Boy, and *Polly* a good Girl.

To which is added,
A LITTLE SONG-BOOK,
BEING
A *New Attempt* to teach Children the Use of
the *English Alphabet,* by Way of Diversion.

LONDON:
Printed for J. NEWBERY, at the *Bible and Sun*
in St. *Paul's Church-Yard.* 1767.
[Price Six-pence bound.]

*Title page of* A Little Pretty Pocket-Book *published by John Newbery in 1744.*

A Little Pretty Pocket-Book . . . Worcester, Mass., printed for John Newbery, London, 1767, title page. Rare Books Division, The New York Public Library, Astor, Lenox and Tilden Foundations.

Tommy and sends him off to sea and provides Margery with two shoes instead of the poor one left to her after their eviction. Eventually Margery becomes a tutor who moralizes as she teaches her young pupils to read. She marries a wealthy squire and continues to carry on her good works. *Little Goody Two Shoes* was read for well over a century. A modern eight-page version of it was sold to be read in air-raid shelters in England in the 1940s.

Newbery was obviously impressed with the advice given by the famous English philosopher John Locke in his *Thoughts Concerning Education* (1693). Locke maintained that as soon as children know their alphabet they should be led to read for pleasure. He advocated the use of pictures in books and deplored the lack of easy, pleasant books for children to read, except for *Aesop's Fables* and *Reynard the Fox,* both dating back to Caxton's times.

Newbery's books were all illustrated with pictures based on the text, rather than just any woodcuts available as was the custom of other printers of the day. Many of his books were bound with Dutch gilt paper covers, which made for a gay appearance. Even

*The title character of* Little Goody Two Shoes *points to her two shoes in a facsimile reprint of John Newbery's best-known publication.*
Little Goody Two Shoes *by John Newbery [Liverpool?, 1878?], title character. Rare Books Division, The New York Public Library, Astor, Lenox and Tilden Foundations.*

though moral lessons were clearly there for young readers, his stories did emphasize love and play rather than the wrath and punishment of God. Except for *Little Goody Two Shoes,* none of his work has lasted, but we honor the man who was the first to recognize that children deserve a literature of their own.

## Didactic Tales

During the last half of the eighteenth century, women writers entered the field of juvenile literature determined to influence the moral development of children. In 1749, Mrs. Sarah Fielding published *The Governess,* which included character-building stories about Mrs. Teachum's School for Girls. *Easy Lessons for Children,* published in 1760 by Mrs. Barbauld, contained moral stories supposedly written for children as young as 2 to 3 years old. Mrs. Sarah Trim-

mer published a magazine titled *Guardian of Education,* which contained articles on moral subjects and book reviews. Mrs. Trimmer did not approve of fairy tales or Mother Goose. "All Mother Goose tales . . . were only fit to fill the heads of children with confused notions of wonderful and supernatural events brought about by the agency of imaginary beings."[12] She saw no inconsistency, however, in writing a story in which a family of robins could talk about day-to-day problems in their lives. First titled *Fabulous Histories* (1786), it was published for many years afterward under the title *The Robins.* The conversation between the parent robins and their offspring (Flapsy, Pecksy, Dicky, and Robin) is stilted and lofty, indeed. Robin, the eldest, is portrayed as a conceited young bird who will take no advice. His parents discuss his behavior in this way:

> "You have been absent a long time, my love," said her mate, "but I perceive that you were indulging your tenderness towards that disobedient nestling, who has rendered himself unworthy of it; however, I do not condemn you for giving him assistance, for had not you undertaken the task, I would myself have flown to him instead of returning home; how is he, likely to live and reward your kindness?"
>
> "Yes," said she, "he will, I flatter myself, soon perfectly recover, for his hurt is not very considerable, and I have the pleasure to tell you he is extremely sensible of his late folly, and I dare say will endeavor to repair his fault with future good behaviour."[13]

Poor Mrs. Trimmer justified the use of this anthropomorphized bird family by calling the stories "fables" and stating that she was following the advice of John Locke, who had advocated the use of *Aesop's Fables* with children. No wonder Beatrix Potter recalled hating this book and refusing to learn to read from it.[14] Some memory of it must have lingered with her, however, for there is a strong resemblance in sound between the names of the young robins and those of her famous rabbit family, Flopsy, Mopsy, Cottontail, and Peter.

Other didactic writers of this period maintained that they followed Rousseau's theory of education by accompanying children in their natural search for knowledge. These stories frequently contained lengthy "conversations" that tried to conceal moral lessons under the guise of an exciting adventure. The priggish children found in these books served as models of behavior for nearly a hundred years.

---

[12]Ibid., p. 97.

[13]Mrs. Trimmer, *The Robins, or Domestic Life Among the Birds,* rev. ed. (New York: C. S. Francis, 1851), p. 93.

[14]Janet Crowell Morse, ed., *Beatrix Potter's Americans: Selected Letters* (Boston: Horn Book, 1982).

## Poetry and Pictures

In this period, poetry for children also emphasized religion and instruction. However, John Newbery printed *Pretty Poems for Children Three Feet High* and added this inscription: "To all those who are good this book is dedicated by their best friend."

Although Isaac Watts spent most of his time writing hymns, he did write some poetry for children. In the preface to *Divine and Moral Songs Attempted in Easy Language for Use of Children* (1715), Watts wrote that his songs were to be memorized, which was how children were to be given "a relish for virtue and religion." Though written by a Puritan, these hymns were kind and loving, and the collection made up a real child's book. Altogether Watts wrote about seven hundred hymns, some of which are still sung today, notably "Joy to the World," "O God Our Help in Ages Past," and the lovely "Cradle Hymn," which begins "Hush, my dear, lie still and slumber."

The engraver and artist William Blake wrote poetry that children enjoyed, but the poems constituting *Songs of Innocence* (1789) were not specifically written for children. Blake's poetry was filled with imagination and joy and made the reader aware of beauty without preaching. Children still respond to his happy poem that begins "Piping down the valleys wild,/ Piping songs of pleasant glee." His desire to open the "doors of perception" is reflected in his well-known poem "To see a World in a Grain of Sand."

One British artist, Thomas Bewick, emerged during this period as an illustrator of books for boys and girls. He perfected the white-line method of engraving on the end grain of a block of wood to achieve a delicacy of line not found in usual carved wood block designs. Bewick's *The New Lottery Book of Birds and Beasts* (1771) was one of the first instances of a master illustrator's putting his name on a book for children.

As the century neared its end, most of the stories for children were about how to live the "good life." Information about the natural world was peddled in didactic lectures sugarcoated with conversational style. Little prigs were models for young people to follow. However, there was now a literature for children. Authors and publishers were aware of a new market for books. Parents and teachers were beginning to recognize the importance of literature for children.

# Children's Literature: The Nineteenth Century

In the nineteenth century, children could choose to read about a wide variety of topics. Books and magazines sought to present children with works of literature that celebrated their unique enthusiasms and explored their special worlds.

A white-line woodcut of "The Fox and the Crow" from Select Fables, *designed and engraved by Thomas and John Bewick, c. 1784.*

Designed and engraved by Thomas and John Bewick, c. 1784. Walter Havighurst Special Collections, Miami University Libraries, Oxford, OH.

## Books of Instruction and Information

During the period immediately following the American Revolution, there was a rush to publish textbooks that reflected the changing social purposes and interests of the new nation. A picture of George Washington was substituted for the woodcut of George III in *The New England Primer*. The alphabet no longer intoned "In Adam's fall/We sinned all" but started with a less pious rhyme: "A was an Angler and fished with a hook./ B was a Blockhead and ne'er learned his book."

Noah Webster's *Blue Backed Speller, Simplified and Standardized*, first published in 1783, was widely used. Revised many times, the third part of the series contained stories and became America's first secular reader. It sold more than eighty million copies during the nineteenth century. Reading for patriotism, good citizenship, and industry was the purpose of the well-loved *Eclectic Readers* by William H. McGuffey. They were used so widely from 1834 to 1900, one could almost say these readers constituted the elementary curriculum in literature. A glance at the *Fifth Reader* reflects the type of material included: speeches by Daniel Webster; essays by Washington Irving; selections from Shakespeare (although the play is often not identified); narrative, sentimental, and patriotic poetry; and many didactic essays with titles like "Advantages of a Well-educated Mind," "Impeachment of Warren Hastings as reported in the *Edinburgh Review*," and "Eulogy on Candlelight."

In the early nineteenth century Samuel Goodrich was responsible for eliminating the British background in books for American children. Influenced by both the English and the American Sunday school movements, which produced moral tales for the uneducated masses of children who could attend school only on Sunday, Goodrich wrote more than a hundred books for children. He created the venerable Peter Parley, an elderly gentleman who told stories to children based on his travels and personal experiences. History, geography, and science were included in his *Tales of Peter Parley About America* (1827). Nearly a million copies of *Peter Parley's Method of Telling About Geography to Children* (1829) were published. This series became so popular that Goodrich employed a writing staff to help him; his staff included Nathaniel Hawthorne and his sister, Elizabeth. Peter Parley books sold over seven million copies, and they were frequently pirated and issued abroad.

The Little Rollo series by Jacob Abbott became as popular as the Peter Parley books. Abbott wrote about Little Rollo learning to talk, Rollo learning to read, and Rollo's travels to Europe. In the first books of the series, published in 1834, Rollo was a natural little boy, but as he became older and traveled about the world he became something of a prig.

Only a few writers and publishers seemed to realize that children want to learn about their world. Children had to plod through pages of tiresome conversations with moralistic overtones to gain the information they sought. It was not until much later that nonfiction books on almost every subject were placed on bookshelves for boys and girls.

## Folktale Collections

Early in the nineteenth century two German brothers went about asking servants and peasants to recall stories they had heard. In 1812 Jacob and Wilhelm Grimm published the first volume of *Kinder und Hausmärchen* (Household Stories). These serious scholars tried to preserve the form as well as the content of the old tales that were translated and published in England by Edgar Taylor from 1823 to 1826. "The Elves and the Shoemaker," "Rumpelstiltskin," and "Snow White," in addition to many others, became part of the literature of childhood.

In America, Washington Irving included "Rip Van Winkle" and "The Legend of Sleepy Hollow" in his 1819 *Sketch Book*. These tales, written mainly for adults, were also enjoyed by older children.

The origin of the story "The Three Bears" has been questioned by various authorities. It was first credited to the poet Robert Southey, who published it in *The Doctor* (1837). Later, Edgar Osborne, the famous English collector of children's books, found the story handwritten in verse by Eleanor Mure in 1831. Both these early versions portray a wicked old woman who comes to visit the bears, which are described as wee, middle-sized, and huge. Through various retellings, the story changed to the more familiar fair-haired Goldilocks visiting a family of bears.

In 1846 Mary Howitt translated Hans Christian Andersen's tales under the title *Wonderful Stories for Children.* Now both English and American children could enjoy "The Princess and the Pea," "Thumbelina," and "The Emperor's New Clothes." In these stories, inanimate objects and animals like the heroic Tin Soldier and the Ugly Duckling come to life. The values and foibles of human life are presented in the stories with action and rich language.

Not until the last half of the nineteenth century were folktales and fairy tales completely accepted for children. John Ruskin was influenced by the Grimm tales as he wrote his *King of the Golden River* (1851). Charles Dickens's *The Magic Fishbone* appeared first as a serial in 1868. *The Wonder Book for Boys and Girls* was published by Nathaniel Hawthorne in 1852, followed by *Tanglewood Tales* in 1853. Now children had the Greek myths written especially for them. Sir George Dasent translated *Popular Tales from the North* in 1859, making it possible for children to enjoy more tales from Scandinavia. Joel Chandler Harris collected stories from the South for *Uncle Remus, His Songs and Sayings.*

Andrew Lang's famous series of collections of folktales began with *The Blue Fairy Book.* The Red, Green, and Yellow fairy books followed the 1889 publication of the first volume of folklore. Joseph Jacobs was also interested in retelling folktales especially for children. *English Fairy Tales, Volumes I and II* were published between 1890 and 1894. All these tales were important contributions to the realm of folklore. As the merits of folklore were recognized everywhere, there was increasing interest in such volumes as Howard Pyle's collections of original stories titled *Pepper and Salt* (1886) and *The Wonder Clock* (1888).

## Family Stories

In the first half of the nineteenth century the didactic school of writing continued to flourish, with perhaps one exception. In 1839, Catherine Sinclair, whose many other books were highly moral and sedate, published *Holiday House,* "certainly the best original children's book written up to that time and one of the jolliest and most hilarious of any period."[15] Her characters were children who got into mischief and they were sometimes aided in this by an adult—their irreverent and fun-loving Uncle David.

[15]Darton, *Children's Books in England,* p. 220.

Children would have to wait several more decades for such fun and nonsense to be totally acceptable. For the most part, women writers in the early nineteenth century wielded influential pens, condemned fairy stories, and relentlessly dispensed information in lengthy dialogues between parent and child. Mrs. Martha Sherwood, a prolific writer, produced over 350 moralizing books and religious tracts. Sherwood is remembered best for a series of stories including *The Fairchild Family*, the first part of which was published in 1818, the third and last in 1847. Considered one of the first "family" stories, it contained some frighteningly realistic passages. In one scene, to teach his quarreling children a lesson, Mr. Fairchild takes them to see something "very dreadful, . . . a gibbet on which the decomposed body of a man still hangs in irons. The face of the corpse was so shocking the children could not look at it." Later revisions of this story omitted the grim scene. However, even without this passage. *The Fairchild Family* was a dramatic, vital story, and it was known on both sides of the Atlantic.

In contrast to the religious severity of *The Fairchild Family*, Charlotte Yonge described the milder Victorian experiences of the eleven motherless children of the May family in *The Daisy Chain* (1856). Women were always portrayed in the Victorian novel as inferior to men. This attitude is reflected in *The Daisy Chain* when Ethel May is advised not to try to keep up with her brother Norman in his university studies because "a woman cannot hope to equal a man in scholarship." Yonge had an ear for dialogue and frequently recorded her friends' conversations. She was a superb storyteller and wrote over 120 books.

American children wept pools of tears over the pious, sentimental *Elsie Dinsmore*. Writing under her maiden name, Martha Farquharson, Martha Finley initiated the Elsie Dinsmore series in 1867. The best-known scene is the one in which Elsie's father demands that she play the piano and sing for a group of his friends. Because it is the Sabbath, Elsie refuses. Her father will not have his authority questioned and makes her sit on the piano stool for hours until she finally faints and cuts her head in the fall. Filled with remorse, her father gently carries her upstairs, only to have her insist that she be allowed to pray before going to bed. Elsie at all times is righteous and good. The series contains eighteen books, published from 1867 to 1905, that follow Elsie from girlhood through motherhood and widowhood and into grandmotherhood. Unbelievable as the stories seem to us today, the Elsie Dinsmore books were tremendously popular.

The next year saw the publication of *Little Women* (1868) by Louisa May Alcott. This story must have blown like a fresh breeze through the stifling atmosphere of pious religiosity created by

*Jessie Wilcox Smith created eight full-color illustrations painted in oils for the popular 1915 edition of* Little Women.

Alcott, Louisa May, *Little Women* with illustrations by Jessie Wilcox Smith, Boston, 1922. Special Collections, The New York Public Library.

books like *Elsie Dinsmore*. As described by the irrepressible Jo (who was Louisa May Alcott herself), the March family were real people who faced genteel poverty with humor and fortitude. Louisa May Alcott didn't preach moral platitudes, but described the joys, the trials, and the fun of growing up in a loving family. Jo, one of the first tomboys in children's literature, hates the false Victorian standards of the day. When her older sister Meg tells her that she should remember she is a young lady, this follows:

> "I'm not! and if turning up my hair makes me one, I'll wear it in two tails till I'm twenty," cried Jo, pulling off her net and shaking down a chestnut mane. "I hate to think I've got to grow up and be Miss March, and wear long gowns and look prim as a China-aster. It's bad enough to be a girl, anyway, when I like boys' games and work and manners!"[16]

The first edition of volume 1 of *Little Women* (which ended before Beth's death) was sold out

---

[16]Louisa May Alcott, *Little Women* (Boston: Little, Brown, 1922, [1868]), p. 3.

within two months of printing. The publisher asked for a second volume, which was ready the next year. Later the two books were combined into one. *Little Men* and *Jo's Boys* were sequels to this American family classic. Still loved today, *Little Women* has been translated into many languages, including Russian, Arabic, Bengali, and Urdu.

Another vivacious heroine appeared in the celebrated Katy stories written by Susan Coolidge (pseudonym of Sarah Chauncey Woolsey). This series included such titles as *What Katy Did* (1872), *What Katy Did at School* (1873), and *What Katy Did Next* (1886). Susan Coolidge also wrote many other stories. Harriet Lathrop, under the pseudonym Margaret Sidney, presented a lively family story about a widowed mother and her five children in a series starting in 1881 with *Five Little Peppers* and concluding in 1916 with *Our Davie Pepper*.

Other authors wrote dramatic family stories with foreign settings. In *Hans Brinker, or the Silver Skates,* Mary Mapes Dodge gave accurate glimpses of Dutch life in 1865. The skating race is actually less important than the daring brain surgery performed on Father Brinker, who had been mentally incompetent for several years after an accident. The bravery and courage of Hans and his sister in facing poverty, scorn, and their father's illness provided further examples for child behavior.

Johanna Spyri's well-loved *Heidi* was translated from the German by Louise Brooks and published in this country in 1884. Not only did readers share the joys and sorrows of Heidi's life with her grandfather, they "breathed" the clear mountain air and "lived" in Switzerland.

Frances Hodgson Burnett described family conflict within the English aristocracy in *Little Lord Fauntleroy* (1886). Although born in England, Mrs. Burnett was an American citizen. Burnett's second book, *Sara Crewe* (1888), told of the pitiful plight of a wealthy pupil who is orphaned and reduced to servitude in a boarding school. Its Cinderella ending delights children and adults, and it was made into a very successful play. Mrs. Burnett then expanded the play into a longer novel under the title *The Little Princess* (1905). Mrs. Burnett's best-written and most popular book is *The Secret Garden* (1910), which presents an exciting plot in a mysterious setting. This story depicts the gradual change wrought in two lonely and selfish children by a hidden garden and the wholesome influence of the boy Dickon. It is still read and loved by children today.

## Tales of Adventure

The rise of family stories and series books for girls prompted more attention to tales of adventures and

the development of so-called boys' series. The best known of the Robinsonades, *The Swiss Family Robinson,* was written by Johann David Wyss, a Swiss pastor, and translated into English in 1814. Inaccurate in its description of flora and fauna (almost everything grew on that tropical island), it still delighted children's imaginations. Sir Walter Scott's novels *Rob Roy* (1818) and *Ivanhoe* (1820), while intended for adults, were frequently appropriated by young people. James Fenimore Cooper's Leatherstocking novels of exciting tales of Indians and pioneers in North America were avidly read by young and old alike. The bloody incidents and tragedy of *The Last of the Mohicans* (1826) brought a sense of tingling adventure to readers. Richard Henry Dana's *Two Years Before the Mast* (1840) describes the author's own adventures as a young seaman sailing around Cape Horn to California. Also written for adults, it provided adventure for children.

British writers such as Captain Frederick Marryat and George A. Henty wrote books based on military histories and adventures that were read with enthusiasm by American children. At the same time the American names Horatio Alger, Jr., Oliver Optic, and Harry Castlemon were well known to English readers. The emphasis in American series was more on individual achievement, usually against unbelievable odds. The stories by Horatio Alger epitomized this rags-to-riches theme. In fact, because his first successful novel, *Ragged Dick* (1868), was based on this formula, he saw no reason to change it in the more than a hundred books that followed.

Though most of these series books did provide plenty of adventure, the characters and plots tended to be superficial and predictable. However, there was one superb adventure story written during the last half of the nineteenth century that included not only a bloody, exciting, and tightly drawn plot but also well-depicted characters. Serialized in an English magazine called *Young Folks* in 1881 and 1882, Robert Louis Stevenson's *Treasure Island* was published in book form in 1883. For the first time adults were drawn to a children's book for adventure, a reverse of the pattern of children reading adults' books. *Treasure Island* was an immediate success.

Gradually books written for boys changed in their portrayal of childhood, and little prigs became real live boys. Thomas Bailey Aldrich's *The Story of a Bad Boy* (1870) was based on his own life in Portsmouth, New Hampshire. The tale of this Tom's pranks and good times paved the way for another story of a real boy's adventures in Hannibal, Missouri. *The Adventures of Tom Sawyer* was published in 1876 by Mark Twain (pseudonym of Samuel Clemens). This book was soon followed by an American classic, *The Adventures of Huckleberry Finn* (1884). Mark Twain combined realism, humor, and adventure in these real-istic portrayals of growing up in a small town near the end of the nineteenth century. Although *Huckleberry Finn* has won literary acclaim, children prefer *The Adventures of Tom Sawyer*. This seems only natural, since Tom's adventures involve children their age.

The beginnings of science-fiction adventure stories came to us from France in the translations of Jules Verne's *Journey to the Center of the Earth* (1864), *Twenty Thousand Leagues Under the Sea* (1869), and *Around the World in Eighty Days* (1872). Modern readers might be surprised to note the early dates of these books.

## Animal Stories

In *A Dog of Flanders and Other Stories* (1872), Louise de la Ramée presented a collection of stories that included the sad tale of a Belgian work dog and his friend, a boy artist. It has been considered the first modern dog story. Anna Sewall's *Black Beauty* appeared in 1877 as a protest against cruel treatment of horses. Children skipped the lectures calling for more humane treatment of animals and read the compelling first-person story of the life of Black Beauty. Some children today continue to enjoy Anna Sewell's rather overdrawn and sentimental tale. Rudyard Kipling's *The Jungle Books* (1894–1895) were exciting animal stories. Many children today know the story of Mowgli, a child raised by a wolf family, a bear, and a panther, although they might be more familiar with the animated movie than with the original book.

## The Rise of Fantasy and Humor

Even though many of the early books for children included the word *amusing* in their titles, their main purpose was to instruct or moralize. Undoubtedly, children enjoyed the broad humor in some of the folktales and the nonsense in Mother Goose, but few books used humor or nonsense before the middle of the nineteenth century.

The first stirrings of modern fantasy can be seen in a tale written by an English clergyman and scientist in 1863. *The Water Babies* by Charles Kingsley is a strange mixture of the fanciful overladen with heavy doses of morality. It is the story of a chimney sweep who has become a water baby with gills. Hidden within this little tale was Kingsley's social concern for the plight of the chimney sweeps, plus his attempt to reconcile the new science (Darwin's *The Origin of Species* had been published in 1859) with his religious belief that salvation can be obtained through love and compassion as easily as through punishment.

On a summer day in 1862 an Oxford professor of mathematics, Charles Dodgson, told a story to three little girls on a picnic. The tale that was told was

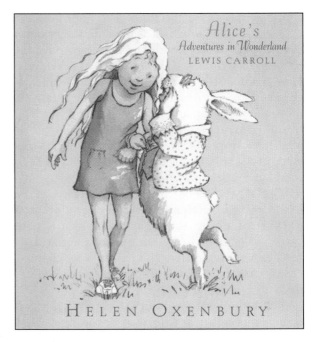

*Helen Oxenbury is one of many artists (including Lewis Carroll himself) who have illustrated* Alice's Adventures in Wonderland.

From *Alice in Wonderland* by Lewis Carroll. Illustrations © 1999 by Helen Oxenbury. Reproduced by permission of Walker Books Ltd., London. Published in the U.S. and Canada by Candlewick Press, Inc., Cambridge, MA.

about Alice, who followed a white rabbit down a rabbit hole and found herself a part of a remarkable adventure. At the children's request, Dodgson wrote down that story (as *Alice's Adventures Underground*) and presented it to his young friends as a Christmas gift in 1864. At the insistence of others, he decided to have it published. By 1865 the artist John Tenniel had completed the drawings, and *Alice's Adventures in Wonderland,* published under the pseudonym Lewis Carroll, was ready for the host of readers to come. What made this story absolutely unique for its time was that it contained not a trace of a lesson or a moral. It was really made purely for enjoyment, and it has delighted both children and adults ever since. Allusions to this book and its companion title, *Through the Looking-Glass* (1871), have become a part of our everyday speech: "curiouser and curiouser"; "much of a muchness"; "begin at the beginning, then go on until you've come to the end: then stop"; "I've believed as many as six impossible things before breakfast"; "O frabjous day"; and many more.

Other well-known fantasies were published near the end of the century. George MacDonald was a friend of Lewis Carroll's; in fact he was one of the persons who had urged the publication of Alice. However, his own "invented fairy-tale" *At the Back of the North Wind* (1871) has much more of the sad spiritual quality found in many of Hans Christian Andersen's fairy tales than the mad inconsistencies of the world of Lewis Carroll.

*Ernest Nister's bicycling bears are on their way to* The Animals' Picnic *in one of today's numerous reissues of Victorian pop-up books.*

From *The Animals' Picnic*, by Ernest Nester. Copyright © 1988 by The Putnam & Grosset Group, New York, NY. Reprinted by permission.

*The Adventures of Pinocchio* by Carlo Collodi first appeared in a children's newspaper in Rome in 1881. Translated into many languages, it was issued in English in 1891 under the title *The Story of a Puppet,* but the title was soon changed back to the original *Pinocchio.* Children still enjoy this story of the mischievous puppet whose nose grew longer with each lie he told the Blue Fairy. Collodi's real name was Carlos Lorenzini.

The prototype for Mary Poppins, Amelia Bedelia, Miss Pickerell, and all the other eccentric women characters in children's literature can be found in the nonsensical antics of Mrs. Peterkin and her family. Published in 1880 by Lucretia Hale, *The Peterkin Papers* provided children with real humor. One of the most amusing stories, "The Lady Who Put Salt in Her Coffee," appeared in a juvenile magazine as early as 1868. Mrs. Peterkin mistakenly substitutes salt for sugar in her coffee. The whole family troops to the chemist and the herb lady to find out what to do. Finally "the lady from Philadelphia" provides the answer—make another cup of coffee!

Also in the category of books for fun may be included the many books with movable parts. Harle-quinades, or turn-ups, first appeared in 1766. They consisted of pages of pictures that could be raised or lowered to create other scenes. Later (from the 1840s through the 1890s), pictures were made like Venetian blinds to create another scene. Circular wheels could be turned to provide more action, and whole pop-up scenes created miniature stages.

## Poetry

Poetry for children began to flourish in the nineteenth century. In the first part of the century, poetry, like prose, still reflected the influence of religion and moral didacticism. The Taylor sisters, Ann and Jane, emphasized polite behavior, morals, and death in the poetry for their first book, *Original Poems for Infant Minds* (1804). While Jane Taylor wrote the often parodied "Twinkle Twinkle Little Star" for this collection and Ann provided the lovely "Welcome, welcome little stranger, to this busy world of care," the book also included some fairly morbid poems.

However, William Roscoe's *The Butterfly's Ball and the Grasshopper's Feast* (1807) provided pure nonsense, rhyme, and rhythm that delighted children.

There were no moral lessons here, just an invitation: "Come take up your hats and away let us haste/ To the Butterfly's Ball and the Grasshopper's Feast." The arrival of each guest was illustrated by copper engravings (a "snail person," a "bumble bee child") by William Mulready. Roscoe, a historian and botanist, wrote the book for the pleasure of his own child. It was so fresh and different that it generated many imitations.

Clement Moore, a professor who also wrote to please his own children, gave the world the Christmas classic *A Visit from St. Nicholas*. One of the first American contributions to a joyous literature for children, it was published with this title in 1823, but it is now known by the title *The Night Before Christmas*. *Mary Had a Little Lamb*, first written by Sarah Josepha Hale in 1830, was included in McGuffey's reader in 1837 and has since been recited by generations of American schoolchildren.

Dr. Heinrich Hoffman's *Struwwelpeter* (Shock-Headed Peter) was translated from the German in about 1848. His subjects included "Shock-Headed Peter," who wouldn't comb his hair or cut his nails; Harriet, who played with fire; and Augustus, who would not eat his nasty soup and became as "thin as a thread/and the fifth day was dead." These cautionary tales in verse were meant to frighten children into good behavior. Instead, children loved the pictures and gruesome verse. Surely these poems are the forerunners of some of the modern verse by Shel Silverstein and Jack Prelutsky.

The century's greatest contribution to lasting children's poetry was the nonsense verse of Edward Lear, a poet who, like Lewis Carroll, wrote only to entertain. Lear was by profession a landscape painter and

There was an Old Man on whose nose, most birds
of the air could repose;
But they all flew away at the closing of day,
Which relieved that Old Man and his nose.

*Edward Lear's laughable limericks and humorous illustrations in* A Book of Nonsense *are over a hundred years old, but they are still enjoyed today.*

From Lear, Edward, *A Book of Nonsense*, London [1862]. Illustration ("There was an old man on whose nose . . ."). Special Collections, The New York Public Library.

illustrator. He wrote his first book, *A Book of Nonsense*, in 1846 for his child friends; *More Nonsense* (1877) appeared twenty-six years later. Generations have delighted in the elderly "Quangle Wangle" and "The Owl and the Pussycat." Lear did not invent the limerick, but he certainly became master of the form. His black-line illustrations are as clever as his poetry.

Some of Christina Rossetti's poetry is reminiscent of Mother Goose, such as the well-loved "Mix a pancake/Stir a pancake/Pop it in the pan;/Fry the pancake/Toss the pancake/Catch it if you can." Others such as "Who has seen the wind?" gave children vivid descriptions of the world around them. Many poems from her book *Sing Song* (1872) are found in anthologies today.

The century ended with a unique volume of poetry that celebrated the everyday life and thought of the child. *A Child's Garden of Verses* (1885) by Robert Louis Stevenson was first published under the title *Penny Whistles*. Stevenson was a poet who could discover joy in child's play and enter the child's imaginings in such well-loved poems as "My Shadow," "Bed in Summer," "The Swing," "Windy Nights," and "My Bed Is a Boat."

Two notable American poets were writing for children at the close of the nineteenth century. Eugene Field's *Poems of Childhood* (1896) included "The Sugar Plum Tree" and "The Duel." James Whitcomb Riley employed dialect as he described local incidents and Indiana farm life. This Hoosier dialect has made most of his poems seem obsolete, except for "Little Orphant Annie" and "The Raggedy Man," which continue to give children pleasure.

## Magazines

Magazines formed a significant part of the literature for children in the last half of the nineteenth century. The first magazines, which grew out of the Sunday school movement, were pious in their outlook. The first true children's magazine for English children appeared in 1853 under the title *Charm*. Stating that there would always be room for stories of the little people or fairies on its pages, it was ahead of its time and lasted only two years. Charlotte Yonge's own stories appeared in her magazine *The Monthly Packet*. In 1866, Mrs. Gatty started *Aunt Judy's Magazine*, which began the policy of reviewing children's books, reporting enthusiastically on *Alice's Adventures in Wonderland* and Hans Christian Andersen's stories.

The first magazine planned for children in America was published in 1826. *The Juvenile Miscellany* was edited by Lydia Maria Child, a former teacher who wanted to provide enjoyable material for children to read. The magazine was very successful until Child, an ardent abolitionist, spoke out against slavery. Sales dropped immediately, and the magazine stopped publication in 1834. *The Youth's Companion* survived the longest of all the children's magazines in America, beginning in 1827 and merging with *The American Boy* in 1929, which in turn ceased publication in 1941. It published such well-known writers as Kipling, Oliver Wendell Holmes, Jack London, Mark Twain, and Theodore Roosevelt, among others. *The Youth's Companion* had a definite editorial policy. It proposed to "exile death from its pages"; tobacco and alcohol were not to be mentioned, and love figured in some of the stories only after 1890. Part of the popularity of this magazine can be attributed to the inviting prizes that were offered each week.

In 1873 Mary Mapes Dodge, author of *Hans Brinker, or the Silver Skates,* became editor of the most famous magazine for children, *St. Nicholas Magazine.* The publisher announced that in this magazine "there must be entertainment, no less than information; the spirit of laughter would be evoked; there would be 'no sermonizing, no wearisome spinning out of facts, no rattling of dry bones of history,' while all priggishness was condemned."[17] The magazine attracted well-known artists and writers such as Arthur Rackham, Reginald Birch, Howard Pyle, Frances Hodgson Burnett, Rudyard Kipling, Robert Louis Stevenson, and Louisa May Alcott. Many of the novels that were first serialized in *St. Nicholas Magazine* were published as books and became classics of their day. These included Louisa May Alcott's *An Old-Fashioned Girl* (1870) and *Jo's Boys* (1873) and Frances Hodgson Burnett's *Little Lord Fauntleroy* (1886) and *Sara Crewe* (1888). This magazine guided children's reading for over three-quarters of a century and set standards of excellence for the whole publishing field.

## Illustrators of the Nineteenth Century

During the nineteenth century, the illustrators of children's books began to achieve as much recognition as the authors. In the early part of the century, crude woodcuts were still being used, illustrators were not identified, and pictures were frequently interchanged among books. This was due in great part to the lack of sophisticated color reproduction techniques. As engraving processes were refined and lithographic techniques developed, the quality of illustrations improved and the great book artists actually preferred to work in black and white. Several outstanding artists emerged as illustrators of children's books during this time. The engraver George Cruikshank illustrated the English edition of *Grimm's Fairy Tales* in 1823. His tiny detailed etchings portrayed much action and humor, real characters, and spritely elves and fairies. His interpretations were so appropriate and seemed

so much a part of these tales that they were republished in Germany with the original text. Other important contributors to book illustration included Alfred Crowquill (pseudonym of Alfred H. Forrestier) and Richard Doyle, whose border illustrations for John Ruskin's *King of the Golden River* influenced subsequent books in mid century.[18]

Charles Bennett, a caricaturist for *Punch* magazine, lent his talents to some surprisingly lively illustrations in books for children from 1857 until his death in 1867. His *Nine Lives of a Cat* has a quality of page design and playfulness that are common in picture books of today. Moreover, Bennett's illustrations took the viewer beyond the literal meaning of the text and deepened the interaction between word and image in a way that is remarkably modern. Had he lived longer, it is possible that he would have rivaled Randolph Caldecott in his works for children. Caldecott was likely familiar with his work, as they shared the services of Edmund Evans—who engraved several of Bennett's books, among them *The Frog Who Would a Wooing Go* and *The Faithless Parrot.*

Evans's extraordinary talent as an engraver and his important improvements in color printing techniques were responsible for dramatic changes in picture books for children in the last half of the nineteenth century. He recruited the three best known illustrators of the nineteenth century—Walter Crane,

---

[18]Joyce Irene Whalley and Tessa Rose Chester, *A History of Children's Book Illustration* (London: John Murray with the Victoria and Albert Museum, 1988), p. 68.

*Walter Crane's decorative borders and fine sense of design are seen in this frontispiece for* The Baby's Own Aesop.

Crane, Walter, *The Baby's Own Aesop,* Frederick Warne, London, 1887, frontispiece. Wallach Division of Arts, Prints, and Photographs, The New York Public Library, Astor, Lenox and Tilden Foundations.

---

[17]Alice M. Jordan, *From Rollo to Tom Sawyer* (Boston: Horn Book, 1948), p. 134.

*Randolph Caldecott was one of the first illustrators for children to show action in his pictures. The design for the Caldecott Medal is taken from this scene in* The Diverting History of John Gilpin.

Cowper, William, *The Diverting History of John Gilpin* with drawings by Randolph Caldecott, London, 1878, illustration (Caldecott medal scene).

Randolph Caldecott, and Kate Greenaway. Walter Crane, the son of a portrait painter, knew that Evans wanted to print some quality illustrated books for children, something that interested Crane also. Crane created beautifully designed pictures for four nursery-rhyme books: *Sing a Song of Sixpence, The House That Jack Built, Dame Trot and Her Comical Cat,* and *The History of Cock Robin and Jenny Wren.* Evans and Crane convinced Warne to publish these high-quality "toy books" during the years 1865 and 1866. They were very successful, and Crane went on to design some thirty-five other picture books, including two well-known nursery-rhyme collections with music and illustrations, *The Baby's Opera* (1877) and *The Baby's Bouquet* (1878). Crane had a strong sense of design and paid particular attention to the total format of the book, including the placement of the text, the quality of the paper, and even the design at the beginning and end of the chapters. He characteristically used flat colors with a firm black outline, and his pages usually were decorated with elaborate borders.

The picture books by Randolph Caldecott established new standards of illustration for children's books. Caldecott filled his drawings with action, the joy of living, and good fun. His love of animals and the English countryside is reflected in his illustrations, which seem to convey much meaning through a few lines. Although Caldecott, like Crane, illustrated many books, he is best remembered for his series of picture books, also called toy books. These included *The House That Jack Built* (1878), *The Diverting History of John Gilpin* (1878), *Sing a Song of Sixpence* (1880), and *Hey Diddle Diddle Picture Book* (1883). On the Caldecott Medal for distinguished illustrations there is a reproduction of one of his pictures showing John Gilpin's ride, a reminder of this famous illustrator of the nineteenth century.

Kate Greenaway's name brings visions of English gardens, delicate prim figures, and the special style of costume worn by her rather fragile children. Her art defined the fanciful world of Victorian sentimentality. After the publication of her first book, *Under the Window* (1878), it became the fashion to dress children in Greenaway costumes with large floppy hats. Greeting cards, wallpaper, and even china were made with designs copied after Greenaway. Her best-known works include *Marigold Garden* (1885), *A Apple Pie* (1886), and *The Pied Piper of Hamelin* (1888). The Kate Greenaway Medal, similar to our Caldecott Medal, is given each year to the most distinguished British picture book.

From France came the remarkable work of Maurice Boutet de Monvel, best remembered for his superb pictures for *Jeanne d'Arc* (Joan of Arc), which he wrote and illustrated in 1896. The power of

**W**ithout alerting Joan, the French had attacked the English bastion of Saint-Loup. The attack failed; the French were retreating in disorder. Joan rushed up, rallied them, and led them once more to the very foot of the bastion. The English, under their commander Talbot, fought back desperately for three hours, but despite their resistance the French overcame them and captured the bastion.

*The extraordinary illustrations by Maurice Boutet de Monvel for the picture book* Jeanne d'Arc *(Joan of Arc) created in 1896 had a pervasive influence on the children's books that followed.*
Boutet de Monvel, Louis Maurice, *Jeanne d'Arc*, Paris, 1896. The New York Public Library, Astor, Lenox and Tilden Foundations.

these paintings—the massed groupings of men and horses and the mob scenes in which every person is an individual yet the focus is always on the Maid of Orleans—made this a distinctive book for young and old alike.

In America, Howard Pyle was writing and illustrating his versions of *The Merry Adventures of Robin Hood of Great Renown* (1883), *Pepper and Salt* (1886), and *The Wonder Clock* (1888). He created *real* people in his illustrations for these collections of folktales and legends. His characters from the Middle Ages were strong; the life of the times was portrayed with interesting, clear detail. In 1903, Pyle published the first of four volumes of *The Story of King Arthur and His Knights,* which was reissued by Scribner's in 1984. He also illustrated and wrote for *Scribner's Monthly Magazine* and *St. Nicholas Magazine.* Another of his important contributions was establishing classes for illustrators of children's books. His stu-

dents included N. C. Wyeth, Maxfield Parrish, and Jessie Wilcox Smith, all of whom became well-known illustrators in the twentieth century.

By the close of the nineteenth century, children's literature was alive and flourishing. Pious, moralistic, didactic books were no longer being written. Gone were the make-believe accounts of impossible children. In their place were real live persons living in fun-loving families. Pure nonsense and the fanciful were welcomed in both poetry and fantasy. The old folktales and the fairies were accepted once again. Children's books were more beautiful, with illustrations by recognized artists and pictures playing an increasingly important role. A few magazines had given consideration to the place of literary criticism. Much would need to be done to bring books to all children in the next century, but a literature for children, designed to bring them joy and happiness, was now firmly in place.

# Children's Literature: The Twentieth Century

The nineteenth century saw the firm establishment of a literature for children; the twentieth has been characterized by the recognition of literary and artistic quality in children's books, the growth of children's book departments in publishing houses, and the expansion of both public and school library service to all children. Technological improvements made it possible to create beautifully illustrated, well-bound books for children and just as easy to mass-produce shoddy, cheap editions. The picture book as we know it today was created early in the twentieth century, as were fine nonfiction books for all ages.

## Recognition of Children's Literature

Disturbed by the influence of the cheaply produced fifty-cent books for juveniles, Franklin K. Mathiews, chief librarian for the Boy Scouts, sought to raise the level of reading for children. His suggestion to establish Children's Book Week was promoted in 1919 by Frederick Melcher as a project of the American Booksellers Association. Schools, libraries, newspapers, and bookstores supported the event, which became a significant stimulant to the development of children's literature. In 1945 the Children's Book Council was established to promote Children's Book Week and to distribute information on children's books throughout the year.

Melcher also promoted another event that has encouraged the development of children's literature: He proposed the presentation of an annual award for the most distinguished book for children. Initiated in 1922, the Newbery Medal was the first award in the world to be given for "distinguished contribution to literature for children." The Caldecott Medal for the most distinguished illustration of the year was first given in 1938. Both these awards have had great influence in raising the standards of writing and illustrating in children's books. They also gave prestige to the idea of creating books for children.

The addition of children's departments to publishing firms indicated the growing importance of literature for the young. In 1919 Macmillan made Louise Seaman its children's editor, and other companies were quick to follow this innovation. May Massee became editor of children's books at Doubleday in 1922. The first critical reviews of children's books appeared in *The Bookman* in 1918. Anne Carroll Moore continued this influential work in her *New York Herald Tribune* column, "The Three Owls." *The Horn Book Magazine,* a publication devoted solely to children's literature, was first published in 1924 under the editorship of Bertha Mahony.

Public libraries instituted children's rooms, and many elementary schools had libraries. By 1915 the American Library Association had established a School Library division. The enactment of the Elementary and Secondary Education Act of 1965 made the concept of school library media centers for *every* elementary school a viable possibility.

The Junior Literary Guild was established in 1929 and was the first organization to send children selected books each month. In the late 1950s, paperback book clubs made it possible for more children to own books and increased their enthusiasm for reading. Currently, many book clubs offer selections of children's literature.

## The Rise of the Picture Storybook

One of the best-loved stories for children is Beatrix Potter's tale of Peter Rabbit, who appeared in Mr. MacGregor's garden at the turn of the century. After writing a short version of the tale in a letter to the ill son of a former governess, Potter expanded the story and submitted it to Warne Publishers. When they rejected it, she had it published privately in 1901. Warne finally accepted and published *The Tale of Peter Rabbit* with the author's own watercolor illustrations in 1902. Potter later introduced stories of many other animals, such as Jemima Puddleduck, Benjamin Bunny, and Mrs. Tittlemouse, but the Cottontail family is the best known and best loved.

*A trusting fowl listens to a "foxy-whiskered gentleman" in this scene from* Jemima Puddle-Duck. *Beatrix Potter created real personalities in both the text and the pictures of her many books.*

Potter, Beatrix, *The Tale of Jemima Puddle-Duck,* New York, 1910. The New York Public Library, Astor, Lenox and Tilden Foundations.

At the same time as Potter was writing and illustrating, Leslie Brooke was creating wonderfully humorous pictures for his nursery-rhyme picture books. No one could draw such expressive faces on pigs as Brooke did in "This Little Pig Went to Market," which first appeared in *The Golden Goose Book* (1905). Brooke added whimsical details to his illustrations, like a picture of "Home Sweet Home" hanging inside the pigs' house showing a mother pig and her little ones. Leslie Brooke's animals in the popular *Johnny Crow's Garden* (1903) were costumed and personified. They included the lion with a "green and yellow tie on" and the bear in his striped pants and tailcoat.

The other well-known English illustrator of this period was Arthur Rackham. He is recognized for the imaginative detail of his pictures, which frequently portrayed grotesque people and humanlike trees, evoking an eerie atmosphere. His illustrations for *Mother Goose* (1913) show imaginative elves and gnomes hiding under mushrooms and in the roots of trees. He illustrated many other books, including Hans Christian Andersen's *Fairy Tales, Cinderella, Peter Pan in Kensington Gardens,* and *Aesop's Fables.*

For many years these English books, along with those of Caldecott, Crane, and Greenaway, supplied the American picture book market. So there was much rejoicing when, in 1923, C. B. Falls's *ABC Book* with its boldly colored woodcuts was published in this country. Only a few persons knew that it was a rather poor copy of William Nicholson's *Alphabet* (1898) and his *Square Book of Animals,* both published in England.[19] William Nicholson is credited with creating the first true picture storybook, *Clever Bill,* published in England in 1926 and in New York

in 1927. Farrar, Straus reissued this book in 1972, including the following statement by Maurice Sendak on the jacket flap: "*Clever Bill,* I have long felt, is among the few perfect picture books ever created for children." At most, the text of this book is only two long run-on sentences. The illustrations carry the

*Arthur Rackham became known for his imaginative worlds of gnomes and anthropomorphized trees. His illustrations appeared in magazines as well as books.*

Rackham, Arthur, *The Arthur Rackham Fairy Book,* London, 1933. The New York Public Library, Astor, Lenox and Tilden Foundations.

---

[19]See discussion and illustrations in Barbara Bader's *American Picturebooks from Noah's Ark to the Beast Within* (New York: Macmillan, 1976), p. 24.

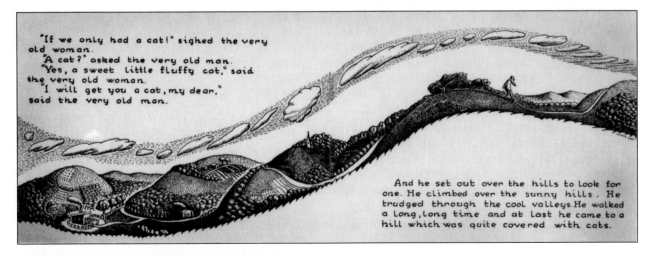

*Wanda Gág's delightful tale* Millions of Cats, *published in 1928, has been called the first American picture storybook.*

From *Millions of Cats* by Wanda Gag, copyright © 1928 by Wanda Gag, renewed © 1956 by Robert Janssen. Used by permission of Coward-McCann, Inc., a division of Penguin Putnam Inc.

story of a little girl who goes to visit her aunt and leaves her favorite toy soldier at home. The toy runs after her and is "just in time to meet her train at Dover." Wanda Gág's delightful tale *Millions of Cats*, published in 1928, has been called the first American picture storybook. This is an outstanding example of how text and pictures work together. In the unfolding drama a very old man goes in search of the most beautiful cat in the world. The long horizontal format enabled Gág to spread the journey over both pages. Like a folktale with its repetition and refrain of "hundreds of cats, thousands of cats, millions and billions and trillions of cats," the story is still popular with children today. It opened the door to what was to become a treasure house of beauty and enjoyment for children, the modern picture storybook.

Progressive education and the growth of the nursery school movement made an impact on the development of books for the preschool child. Lucy Sprague Mitchell of the Bank Street School published her *Here and Now Story Book* in 1921. She pointed out the young child's preoccupation with self and interest in daily experiences. Her collection of stories provided simple little tales of the small child's everyday activities. None of them have lasted, but Mitchell did conduct classes on writing for children, which Margaret Wise Brown attended. When William Scott and his partner decided to start a new firm to publish books just for the very young child, Mrs. Mitchell recommended Margaret Wise Brown. Their first success and breakthrough book for young children was Brown's *The Noisy Book* (1939). In this story a little dog has bandaged eyes and must guess at the noises he hears, as must the child listening to the story. These books (there are seven in the series) invited participation by the child reader-listener.

Writing under her own name and three pseudonyms, Margaret Wise Brown created nearly a hundred books. Her most frequent illustrator was Leonard Weisgard, who won the Caldecott Medal for their book *The Little Island* (1946). Many of her books are still popular today, including *Goodnight Moon* (1947), the most favorite bedtime story of all, and *The Runaway Bunny* (1942) and *The Little Fur Family* (1946). After Brown's untimely death at age 42, William Scott wrote: "All her books have an elusive quality that was Margaret Wise Brown. . . . [They have] simplicity, directness, humor, unexpectedness, respect for the reader and a sense of the importance of living."[20]

Other author-illustrators of this period include Marjorie Flack, who, like Margaret Wise Brown, knew how to tell a good story for preschoolers. Her *Angus and the Ducks* (1930) and *Ask Mr. Bear* (1952) are still shared with youngsters. Kurt Wiese illustrated her popular *The Story About Ping* (1933), the tale of a little runaway duck on the Yangtze River. Lois Lenski began creating her picture storybooks *The Little Family* (1932) and *The Little Auto* (1934) at about this time. These pictured 5-year-olds as little adults doing what young children wished they could do, such as drive a car, sail a boat, or be a fireman.

Machines became popular characters in such books as Watty Piper's *The Little Engine That Could* (1929), Hardie Gramatky's *Little Toot* (1930), and Virginia Lee Burton's *Mike Mulligan and His Steam Shovel* (1939). In *The Little House* (1942), Burton personified a house, which was first built in the country, then engulfed by the city, and finally rescued and returned to the country again. This story, which won the Caldecott Medal, has been called a child's first sociology book.

Dr. Seuss wrote and illustrated the first of many hilarious rhymed stories for children, *And to Think That I Saw It on Mulberry Street*, in 1937. That delightful daredevil Madeline appeared on the Paris streets in 1939. Though *Madeline* was not Ludwig Bemelmans's first book, it is certainly his best known. Robert McCloskey's ducklings made their difficult journey across Boston streets in 1941. *Make Way for Ducklings* richly deserved the Caldecott Medal it received. In the same year H. A. Rey introduced the antics of everyone's favorite monkey in *Curious George*.

During the late 1930s and early 1940s the United States benefited from the influx of many fine European artists seeking political refuge in this country. These artists found a legitimate outlet for their creative talents in the field of children's literature. Picture storybooks were greatly enriched through their unique contributions. A glance at a roster of some of the names of well-known illustrators indicates the international flavor of their backgrounds: d'Aulaire, Duvoisin, Eichenberg, Mordvinoff, Petersham, Rojankovsky, Simont, Shulevitz, Slobodkin, and many more. Certainly the variety of their national backgrounds has added a flavor to our picture books that is unprecedented in both time and place. American children have become the beneficiaries of an inheritance from the whole artistic world.

## The Growth of Nonfiction Books

Increased understanding of human development brought the recognition that the child was naturally curious and actively sought information. No longer did a discussion of nature have to be disguised as "an exciting walk with Uncle Fred," who lectured on the flowers and trees. Children enjoy facts, and they eagerly accept information given to them in a straightforward manner.

[20]Louise Seaman Bechtel, "Margaret Wise Brown, 'Laureate of the Nursery,'" *Horn Book Magazine*, June 1958, p. 184.

E. Boyd Smith created some of the earliest nonfiction picture books—*Chicken World* (1910), *The Seashore Book* (1912), and *The Railroad Book* (1913). The illustrations for these books were large, colored, double-page spreads filled with fascinating detail. His *Chicken World* tells the life story of a chick, ending with a roast bird on a platter. *The Railroad Book* helps its readers visualize all the details of a train trip, whether they have had that experience or not.

From Sweden came a translation of *Pelle's New Suit* (1929) by Elsa Beskow. Large colored pictures illustrate the process of making clothes, beginning with the shearing of Pelle's lamb, carding the wool, spinning it, dyeing it, weaving the cloth, and making the suit, and ending with a bright Sunday morning when Pelle wears his new suit. It is interesting for children to compare this book, which can still be found in libraries today, with Tomie de Paola's *"Charlie Needs a Cloak"* (1974). Maud and Miska Petersham used rich vivid colors on every page of their nonfiction books, which frequently described processes. Their books *The Story Book of Things We Use* (1933), *The Story Book of Wheels, Trains, Aircraft* (1935), *The Story Book of Foods from the Field* (1936), and *The Story Book of Things We Wear* (1939) spawned some fifteen smaller books and were the predecessors of Holling C. Holling's beautifully illustrated story of the travels of a little carved canoe, *Paddle to the Sea* (1941), which gave rich geographical information on the Great Lakes region, and *Tree in the Trail* (1942), which provided much information of historical interest about the Southwest.

W. Maxwell Reed, a former professor at Harvard, started to answer his nephew's questions in a series of letters that resulted in two books, *The Earth for Sam* (1932) and the popular *Stars for Sam* (1931). These books exemplify the beginnings of accurate nonfiction books written by recognized authorities in the field.

As a result of the preschool movement with its emphasis on the "here and now," very young children also had their nonfiction or concept books. Mary Steichen Martin produced *The First Picture Book: Everyday Things for Babies* (1930) and *The Second Picture Book* (1931), while her photographer father, Edward Steichen, provided the pictures of such common objects as a cup of milk with a slice of bread and butter, a faucet with a bar of soap, a glass

*E. Boyd Smith was one of the first Americans to produce artistic and accurate informational picture books.* The Railroad Book *was first published in 1913.*
Smith, E. Boyd, *The Railroad Book*, 1913. The New York Public Library, Astor, Lenox and Tilden Foundations.

holding a toothbrush, and a brush and comb set. No text accompanied these pictures, which were clear enough to provoke recognition and discussion for the child. Their books paved the way for other photographic information books, such as Lewis W. Hine's *Men at Work* (1932), which pictured train engineers, workers on a skyscraper, and cowboys. Harriet Huntington's book *Let's Go Outdoors* (1939) portrayed close-up pictures of bugs and flowers just as a child might discover them on a nature walk. Her style of contrasting a primary object in sharp focus against a blurred background is similar to the contemporary work of Tana Hoban. Henry Kane's fine close-ups of a mouse and frog in his *Tale of the Whitefoot Mouse* (1940) and *The Tale of a Bullfrog* (1941) started the trend to create photographic stories of individual animals.

New books for social studies included *America: Adventures in Eyewitness History* (1962) and *Africa: Adventures in Eyewitness History* (1963), both by Rhoda Hoff. These books, based on original sources, recognized children's ability to read complex materials and draw their own conclusions about history. Alex Bealer's *Only the Names Remain: The Cherokees and the Trail of Tears* (1972) was representative of a new emphasis on readable, carefully documented history. It also attempted to balance recorded history by presenting a Native American point of view.

Biographies appeared to satisfy children's interest in national heroes. Ingri and Edgar Parin d'Aulaire, who had lived in Norway and in many other parts of Europe, were fascinated with the heroes of the New World. They presented somewhat idealized images in their large picture-book biographies *George Washington* (1930), *Abraham Lincoln* (1939), *Leif the Lucky* (1941), *Pocahontas* (1949), and many more. These stories were new to them, so they were perhaps freer to interpret the lives afresh, seeing them as a child discovers them for the first time. James Daugherty portrayed many American pioneers with strong vibrant pictures and ringing epic prose. His *Daniel Boone* (1939) was awarded the Newbery Medal.

The Childhood of Famous Americans series initiated the trend of publishing biographies for girls and boys in series form. By the 1960s, biographies gave less emphasis to the early years of great men and women. More biographies for young children became available, including such lively and authentic books as Jean Fritz's *And Then What Happened, Paul Revere?* (1973) and *Poor Richard in France* (1973) by F. N. Monjo. Biographies of civil rights leaders honored Martin Luther King, Jr., and Rosa Parks. There was more concern to publish biographies about women, and Crowell began their Women in America series.

There is no accurate accounting of the number of nonfiction children's titles that are published, in contrast to fiction titles, but a survey of the new titles would suggest that most of the children's books published today could be classified as nonfiction.

## The Proliferation of Series Books

The dime novel was initiated in the nineteenth century, and the series books of George Henry, Oliver Optic, and Horatio Alger introduced the repetitive incident plot and stereotyped characters. In the twentieth century, "fiction factories" were developed by Edward Stratemeyer, who manufactured the plots for literally hundreds of books, including *The Rover Boys* (1899–1926), *The Bobbsey Twins* (1904– ), the Tom Swift series (1910–1941), and *The Hardy Boys* (1927– ), to name just a few. Using a variety of pseudonyms, Stratemeyer would give hack writers a three-page outline of characters and plot to complete. His daughter, Harriet Stratemeyer Adams, continued his work after his death, writing nearly two hundred children's books, including the well-known *Nancy Drew* series (1930– ), until her death at 89 in 1982. In all her books, Mrs. Adams portrayed an innocent, affluent, and secure world. The original Nancy Drew could be kidnapped, knocked unconscious, and locked in a room with no way to escape, but she always solved the crime and survived to spend another day chasing villains in her blue roadster. Although modern versions of the series books deal with nuclear war, space flights, and submarines, the plots and characters are much the same. The hero or heroine is always a child or adolescent acting with adult wisdom and triumphing over all obstacles—unaided, undaunted, undefeated. The books have found their modern-day counterparts in Ann Martin's *Baby-Sitters Club* series, R. L. Stine's *Goosebump* series, and other popular series.

Books that met with literary approval were also sold in series. The Lucy Fitch Perkins *Twins* series, beginning in 1911 with *The Dutch Twins*, provided authentic information on children of other lands in the form of an interesting realistic story. The series included books at various levels of difficulty; the story of *The Scotch Twins* (1919) was more complex, for example, than that of *The Dutch Twins*. The author also wrote stories of twins living in various historical periods, such as *The Puritan Twins* (1921) and *The Pioneer Twins* (1927).

## Folktales of the World

 The publication of Grimm's *Household Tales* in the early part of the nineteenth century represented only the beginning of interest in recording the told tale. Not until the twentieth century would children have access to the folktales of almost the entire world. A famous storyteller, Gudrun Thorne-Thomsen, recorded stories from Norway in *East o' the Sun and West o' the Moon* in 1912. Kate Douglas Wiggin edited tales from the *Arabian Nights* in 1909, and Ellen Babbitt brought forth *Jataka Tales,* a collection of tales from India, in 1912. Constance Smedley provided children with stories from Africa and Asia in her *Tales from Timbuktu* (1923). The next year, Charles Finger published stories that he had collected from Indians in South America in his Newbery Medal book *Tales from Silver Lands* (1924).

Pura Belpré grew up in Puerto Rico in a family of storytellers and later told these stories to American children in library story hours. Finally they were published in a collection called *The Tiger and the Rabbit* (1946). Philip Sherlock, vice principal of the University College of the West Indies in Jamaica, told stories of his homeland at a meeting of the American Library Association. A children's book editor heard him and persuaded him to write them down; they were published as *Anansi: The Spider Man* in 1954. Harold Courlander, a folklorist and musicologist, gathered many fine collections of stories in West Africa, Ethiopia, Indonesia, Asia, and the islands of the Pacific. His first collection of tales for children was *Uncle Bouqui of Haiti* (1942). Courlander worked like the Grimm brothers, collecting his stories from the native storytellers of the country. The tales in *The Terrapin's Pot of Sense* (1957) were collected from African American storytellers in Alabama, New Jer-

*Noted collector Harold Courlander traveled the world to compile stories such as those from Ethiopia and Eritrea found in* The Fire on the Mountain.

From *The Fire on the Mountain and Other Stories from Ethiopia and Eritrea* by Harold Courlander and Wolf Lesla, illustrations by Robert Kane. Illustrations copyright © 1950, 1978 by Robert Kane. Reprinted by permission of Henry Holt and Company, LLC.

sey, and Michigan. Courlander related these stories to their origins in Africa in his interesting notes at the back of the book.

Lim Sian-Tek, a Chinese writer, spent ten years gathering many different Chinese myths, legends, and folktales from her country. These were introduced to American children in *Folk Tales from China* (1944). Frances Carpenter made "Grandmother" collections, such as her *Tales of a Chinese Grandmother* (1949). *The Dancing Kettle and Other Japanese Folk Tales* (1949) contains the favorite stories from Yoshiko Uchida's childhood. She also adapted old Japanese tales for American children in her popular *Magic Listening Cap* (1955) and *The Sea of Gold* ([1965] 1985). Alice Geer Kelsey introduced American children to the humorous tales of the Hodja of Turkey and the Mullah of Persia in *Once the Hodja* (1943) and *Once the Mullah* (1954).

Many other collections continue to be published each year, presenting American children with the folklore of the world. They also serve as source material for the many individual folktale picture storybooks that became so popular in the second half of the century.

Marcia Brown developed this trend of illustrating single folktales in a picture-book format with her publication of the French tale of trickery *Stone Soup* (1947). Her *Cinderella* (1954) and *Once a Mouse* (1961) won Caldecott Medals; her other fairy tales, *Puss in Boots* and *Dick Whittington and His Cat,* were Caldecott Honor Books. Other illustrators who have brought children richly illustrated picture-book fairy tales include Felix Hoffman, Adrienne Adams, Paul Galdone, Errol LeCain, Nonny Hogrogian, Margot Zemach, and Steven Kellogg.

Greater emphasis was placed on individual African folktales, Jewish folktales, and legends of Native Americans during the decades of the 1960s and 1970s. Gail Haley won the Caldecott Medal in 1971 for *A Story, a Story,* an African tale of Anansi; *Anansi the Spider* by Gerald McDermott won an Honor Medal in 1973. Leo and Diane Dillon were Caldecott Medal winners for *Why Mosquitoes Buzz in People's Ears* (1975), an African tale retold by Verna Aardema. Two Jewish tales, *The Golem* (1976) by Beverly Brodsky McDermott and *It Could Always Be Worse* (1977) by Margot Zemach, were Honor Books. Folktales from around the world are not only an established part of children's literature but a frequently honored genre.

## Fantasy

Fantasy for children in the first half of the twentieth century seemed to come mainly from the pens of English writers. Kipling stimulated the child's imagination with his *Just So Stories* (1902), humorous accounts of the origins of animal characteristics—how the elephant got a trunk or the camel a hump. Much of the delight of these stories is in Kipling's use of rich language like "great grey-green, greasy Limpopo River all set about with fever-trees."

Another English storyteller, Kenneth Grahame, brought to life for his son the adventures of a water rat, a mole, a toad, and a badger. *The Wind in the Willows* was published in 1908 with pictures by Ernest Shepard. This story of four loyal friends became a children's classic and has been reissued in a variety of editions. Individual chapters have also been published as picture books. Obviously *The Wind in the Willows* continues to delight new generations of children.

The boy who refused to grow up and lose the beauties of Never Never Land, Peter Pan, first appeared in a London play by J. M. Barrie in 1904. Later the play was made into a book titled *Peter Pan in Kensington Gardens* (1906), with elaborate illustrations by Arthur Rackham.

*The Wizard of Oz,* by L. Frank Baum, has been called the first American fantasy. Published in 1900, this highly inventive story of the Cowardly Lion, the Tin Woodsman, the Scarecrow, and Dorothy in the Land of Oz has been enjoyed by countless children. Several publishers felt *The Wizard of Oz* was too radical a departure from the literature of the day and refused to publish it. Baum and the illustrator W. W. Denslow finally agreed to pay all the expenses if one small Chicago firm would print it. Within two months of publication, the book had been reprinted twice.

Talking animals have always appealed to children. Hugh Lofting created the eccentric Dr. Dolittle, who could talk to animals as well as understand their languages. In *The Story of Dr. Dolittle* (1920), Lofting describes the way Dolittle learns the animals' languages with the help of the parrot Polynesia and begins his animal therapy. There were ten books in this series; the second one, *The Voyages of Doctor Dolittle* (1922), won the Newbery Medal. Later readings would reveal racial stereotypes in these books, but readers in the 1920s were not alert to such flaws in writing.

Remembering her love of toys, Margery Williams wrote *The Velveteen Rabbit* (1922) while living in England. This story, with its moving description of what it means to be real, has delighted children and adults. It was first illustrated by William Nicholson. More recent editions display the work of Michael Hague (1983), David Jorgensen (1985), and Ilse Plume (1987).

One of the most delightful stories of well-loved toys is A. A. Milne's *Winnie the Pooh,* which he wrote for his son in 1926. Eeyore, Piglet, and Pooh may be stuffed animals, but they have real, believable personalities. Their many adventures in the "100 Aker Wood" with Christopher Robin have provided hours of amusement for both children and the parents and teachers fortunate enough to have shared these stories with boys and girls. Ernest Shepard created unsurpassed illustrations of these lovable toys.

Many American children found the books by Walter Brooks about Freddy the Pig highly entertaining. Starting with *To and Again* (1927), Brooks created some twenty-five novels about high jinks on Mr. Bean's farm. Some of these books were reissued in 1986. Robert Lawson's *Rabbit Hill* (1944) and *The Tough Winter* (1954) captured the feelings and thoughts of the little wild animals that lived in the Connecticut meadows, farms, and woods near his house.

All these stories paved the way for the most loved animal fantasy to be written by an American, E. B. White's *Charlotte's Web* (1952). This book, with its multiple themes of friendship, loyalty, and the celebration of life, is now delighting new generations of children.

Other significant fantasy appearing in the twentieth century certainly must include J. R. R. Tolkien's *The Hobbit* (1937), first discovered by college students and only recently shared with children, and *The Little Prince* by Antoine de Saint-Exupéry, which also appealed primarily to adults. Translated in 1943 from the French, this tale of a pilot's encounter with a Little Prince, who lived alone on a tiny planet no larger than a house, is really a story of the importance of uniqueness and love.

Fantasy in the third quarter of the century emphasized serious themes. C. S. Lewis's *The Lion, the Witch, and the Wardrobe* (1950) was the first of seven books about the imaginary kingdom of Narnia. These popular fantasy adventure tales reflect the author's background as a theologian and carry strong messages about right and wrong. The term *high fantasy* came into use during the 1960s to describe books that took as their themes the battle between good and evil and other cosmic issues. The most memorable works of high fantasy in the United States were written by Madeleine L'Engle, Lloyd Alexander, Susan Cooper, and Ursula Le Guin (see Chapter 7 for further discussion of their work).

As the twenty-first century begins, fantasy has maintained a strong hold on children's imaginations. Teachers do not find it difficult to tempt ten- and eleven-year-olds into reading Brian Jacques's *Redwall* series, even though the books have upwards of three hundred pages. Philip Pullman's *The Golden Compass* inspired websites and other powerful reactions in older children. New author J. K. Rowling surprised and delighted children and adults alike with her *Harry Potter* series, which regularly appear on the New York Times *adult* best-sellers list.

## Poetry

The turn of the last century saw the publication of the first work by a rare children's poet, Walter de la Mare's *Songs of Childhood* (1902). This was a poet who understood the importance and meaning of early childhood experiences. His poems can be mysterious, humorous, or delightfully realistic. De la Mare was also a master of lyric imagery; his often anthologized "Silver" paints a picture of the beauty of a moonlit night. Eleanor Farjeon, also English, was writing merry imaginative verse for children at the same time as Walter de la Mare was creating his poetry. Her first published work was *Nursery Rhymes of London Town* (1916). Many of her poems later appeared in a collection titled *Eleanor Farjeon's Poems for Children* ([1931, 1951] 1984). We remember her for such poems as "Mrs. Peck Pigeon," "Tippetty Witchet," and "The Night Will Never Stay." Still another Englishman brought joy and fun into the nursery with *When We Were Very Young* (1924) and *Now We Are Six* (1927). A. A. Milne could tell a rollicking story, as in "Bold Sir Brian" or "The King's Breakfast" or "Sneezles," or he could capture a child's imaginative play, as in "Lines or Squares" and "Binker."

In the United States, Rachel Field, Dorothy Aldis, and Aileen Fisher were interpreting the delight of the child's everyday world. Frances Frost and Elizabeth Coatsworth were writing lyrical poems about nature. The transition in children's poetry from the didactic to the descriptive, from moralizing to poems of fun and nonsense, had at last been achieved. No longer were poems *about* children; they were *for* children.

The 1930s and 1940s saw many collections of poetry selected especially for children from the works of well-known contemporary poets. These included Edna St. Vincent Millay's *Poems Selected for Young People* (1917), Vachel Lindsay's *Johnny Appleseed and Other Poems* (1928), Carl Sandburg's *Early Moon* (1930), Sara Teasdale's *Stars Tonight* (1930), Emily Dickinson's *Poems for Youth* (1934), Robert Frost's *Come In and Other Poems* (1943) and later his *You Come Too* (1959), and Countee Cullen's *The Lost Zoo* (1940).

Hildegarde Hoyt Swift gave a poetic interpretation of African American experience in her book *North Star Shining* (1947), illustrated with powerful pictures by Lynd Ward. The Pulitzer Prize–winning African American poet Gwendolyn Brooks presented the poignant poems of *Bronzeville Boys and Girls* in 1956. Each of these poems carries a child's name as the title and is written as the voice of that child. Selected works by noted African American poet Langston Hughes were published for young readers in *The Dream Keeper* (1932).

Two fine poets for children, Harry Behn and David McCord, emerged during the early 1950s. Harry Behn's books—among them, *The Little Hill* (1949)—ranged from pure nonsense to childhood memories to lyrical poems about nature. David McCord's poetry is more playful and humorous. McCord's verse includes poems about nature and everyday experiences and an interest in language and the various forms of poetry.

His first book of poetry was *Far and Few: Rhymes of Never Was and Always Is* (1952).

In the 1960s, the publication of several collections of poems written by children reflected new interest in poetry. In 1966 the poignant poetry and drawings of the children imprisoned at the Theresienstadt concentration camp between 1942 and 1944 were published under the title . . . *I Never Saw Another Butterfly*. The strident voices of the protest of the 1960s were heard in *Young Voices* (1971), an anthology of poems written by fourth-, fifth-, and sixth-grade children. Nancy Larrick published a collection of poems written by American youth titled *I Heard a Scream in the Street* (1970).

Specialized collections of poetry celebrating the uniqueness of African Americans, Native Americans, Eskimos, and others were published in the 1960s and 1970s. These included Arnold Adoff's collection *I Am the Darker Brother: An Anthology of Modern Poems by Negro Americans*; Hettie Jones's *The Trees Stand Shining* (1971), a collection of Papago Indian poems; and Knud Rasmussen's recordings of virile Eskimo poetry in his *Beyond the High Hills: A Book of Eskimo Poems* in 1961. Two books about the uniqueness of girls marked a new awareness of feminist perspectives. *Girls Can Too* (1972) was edited by Lee Bennett Hopkins; *Amelia Mixed the Mustard and Other Poems* (1975) was selected and edited by Evaline Ness.

With such increased interest in poetry for children, it seems particularly fitting that the National Council of Teachers of English established the Excellence in Poetry for Children Award in 1977.

## Realistic Fiction

 Early in the twentieth century, authors employed the genre of historical fiction to give children details about the past. Laura Richards quoted from diaries and letters as she wrote *Abigail Adams and Her Times* (1909). A historical overview was provided in Hendrik Van Loon's *The Story of Mankind* (1921), the first Newbery Medal winner. Starting with *Little House in the Big Woods* (1932), Laura Ingalls Wilder gave children detailed descriptions of life on the midwestern frontier in her remarkable series of *Little House* books. Elizabeth Coatsworth began her *Away Goes Sally* series in 1934. Carol Ryrie Brink wrote of a vivacious tomboy in *Caddie Woodlawn* the following year. Forty years later, most historical fiction was more concerned with social conscience than with personal issues. The Newbery Medal winner for 1974, *The Slave Dancer* by Paula Fox, realistically faced up to the wrongs of the past. The publication in 1999 of *The Birchbark House*, Louise Erdrich's Ojibwa view of times and places depicted in Wilder's *Little House* books, seems an appropriate way to bring a century of historical fiction to a close.

In the beginning of the twentieth century, children continued to derive pleasure from works written in a contemporary setting. *Little Women* (1868) and the other Alcott books, Dodge's *Hans Brinker, or the Silver Skates* (1865), Spyri's *Heidi* (1884), and all the Frances Hodgson Burnett books, including *Little Lord Fauntleroy* (1886), *The Little Princess* (1905), and *The Secret Garden* (1910), continue to bring pleasure to children today—although they read them as historical fiction rather than contemporary realistic fiction.

Perhaps the success of the orphaned *Little Princess* accounted for the number of realistic stories about orphans. L. M. Montgomery wrote the very popular story *Anne of Green Gables* (1908) about a young orphan girl living on Prince Edward Island in Canada. Seven sequels covered Anne's growing up, her adulthood, and her children. *Pollyanna* (1913) by Eleanor H. Porter was another popular story of an orphan, in this case one who must learn to live with two disagreeable spinster aunts. Her unfailingly optimistic way of coping made her name last longer than her story. The child in Dorothy Canfield's *Understood Betsy* (1917) was not an orphan, she was a sickly city child sent to live with relatives on a Vermont farm in order to regain her health. Lucinda of Ruth Sawyer's *Roller Skates* (1936) was not an orphan either but was left with her teacher and sister while her father and mother went abroad for a year in the late 1890s. Lucinda was an unforgettable character who loved life and people. Sawyer won the Newbery Medal for this book in 1937.

Kate Douglas Wiggin's *Rebecca of Sunnybrook Farm* (1903) epitomizes the happy family stories that were characteristic of the first half of the century. Carolyn Haywood began her many Betsy and Eddie stories, for younger children, in 1939 with *B is for Betsy;* these stories tell of simple everyday doings of children at school and home. In *Thimble Summer* (1938) Elizabeth Enright told an entertaining family story set on a Wisconsin farm. Enright's *The Saturdays* (1941) was the first of several stories capturing the joyous life of the four children of the Melendy family. In three books, *The Moffats* (1941), *The Middle Moffats* (1942), and *Rufus M* (1943), Eleanor Estes detailed the delights of growing up in West Haven, Connecticut. The four children, Jane, Rufus, Sylvie, and Joey, are clearly realized as individuals and grow up in ways consistent with their characters. Sydney Taylor's *All-of-a-Kind Family* (1951) and its sequels presented the adventures of five Jewish girls growing up on New York's Lower East Side.

Two humorous stories appeared at this time: Robert McCloskey's classic tale *Homer Price* (1943) about Homer's amusing adventures in Centerburg, and Beverly Cleary's *Henry Huggins* (1950). Both centered around all-American boys growing up in small towns, and they have remained popular with children for half a century.

Not all realistic fiction told happy or humorous tales of growing up in mainstream America. Realistic fiction often reflected war, depression, and contemporary social problems. As authors began to write more about the various ethnic and regional groups in our nation, children's books also reflected this interest. Lois Lenski pioneered in presenting authentic, detailed descriptions of life in specific regions of the United States. By living in the communities, observing the customs of the people, and listening to their stories, she was able to produce a significant record of American life from the 1940s into the 1960s. *Strawberry Girl* (1945), which won the Newbery Medal, told of life among the Florida Crackers. *Judy's Journey* (1947), Lenski's most forceful book, concerned the plight of migratory workers. Doris Gates also dramatized the problems of migratory workers in her classic story *Blue Willow* (1940), named after the family's one prized possession, a blue willow plate. Eleanor Estes was one of the first to write about poverty and children's interrelationships in their closed society. Her book *The Hundred Dresses* (1944) enabled teachers to undertake and guide frank discussions of the problem of being "different."

Until the 1950s and 1960s very few books portrayed African Americans or other racial minorities. Books that did portray blacks showed stereotypes—the bandanna-wearing fat mammy and the kinky-haired, thick-lipped "funny" boy. Such stereotypes were epitomized in the *Nicodemus* series written by Inez Hogan in the late 1930s with such titles as *Nicodemus and the Gang* (1939). African American poet Arna Bontemps drew on authentic language patterns of the rural South in *You Can't Pet a Possum* (1934) and *Sad-Faced Boy* (1937). His work, largely forgotten for many years,[21] has seen renewed interest with the publication of *Popo and Fifina* (1993) and *Bubber Goes to Heaven* (1998).

The segregation of blacks was clearly shown in *Araminta* (1935) by Eva Knox Evans and the photographic essay *Tobe* (1939) by Stella Sharpe. It was nearly ten years later that blacks and whites were shown participating in activities together. The theme of *Two Is a Team* (1945) by the Beims is revealed in both the title and the action as a black boy and a white boy play together. Prejudice was openly discussed for the first time in Jesse Jackson's *Call Me Charley* (1945) and Marguerite de Angeli's *Bright April* (1946).

*Mary Jane* (1959) by Dorothy Sterling, *The Empty Schoolhouse* (1965) by Natalie Carlson, and *Patricia Crosses Town* (1965) by Betty Baum discussed the new social problems caused by school integration. By the mid 1960s, a few books showed African American characters in the illustrations, but they did not men-

---

[21]See Violet J. Harris, "From Little Black Sambo to Popo and Fifina: Arna Bontemps and the Creation of African-American Children's Literature," *The Lion and the Unicorn* 14 (June 1990): 108–127.

## *Studying Books of the Past*

**Teaching Feature**

Children in the fourth grade at the Martin Luther King, Jr., Laboratory School in Evanston, Illinois, were studying the past through the history of their families. Their teacher, Barbara Friedberg, shared with them books like *Miss Rumphius* by Barbara Cooney, *When I Was Young in the Mountains* by Cynthia Rylant, *Three Names* and *Sarah, Plain and Tall*, both by Patricia MacLachlan, and *The Night Journey* by Kathryn Lasky.

Together the teacher and children developed questions they could ask their parents or grandparents in an interview or letter. Here are some of the questions they included on their lists:

What were their favorite foods as children?

What did they do on their birthdays or special days?

What did they remember about their schools?

What were their favorite books to read?

What historic days do they remember?

The students made graphs and charts to depict what they found out. Some children, remembering the story of the samovar that the family saved in *The Night Journey,* asked their parents what was the oldest thing they had in their homes that had belonged to the family.

Frequently, the oldest things were books. Several children brought in the favorite children's books of both their parents and their grandparents. They were excited to find out that their grandparents had read and enjoyed *The Secret Garden* by Frances Hodgson Burnett and *Little Women* by Louisa May Alcott. The children made a display of the old editions compared with their new editions. They also exhibited some of the textbooks that were used for reading instruction, including an old McGuffey Reader belonging to a great-grandparent, several Elson Readers that a grandmother had in her basement, and their parents' *Dick and Jane* readers.

Dating and labeling these books for display helped the students see how books had changed over the years. They became aware of how many more books they had than their grandparents had had, for example. But probably the greatest value of this focus unit lay in the discussions that took place between family members recounting the traditions and excitement of the "olden days."

*Barbara Friedberg*
Martin Luther King, Jr., Laboratory School, Evanston, Illinois

---

tion race in the text. Examples include *The Snowy Day* (1962) by Ezra Jack Keats, *Mississippi Possum* (1965) by Miska Miles, and Louisa Shotwell's *Roosevelt Grady* (1963). In the 1970s such books were criticized for "whitewashing" African Americans and attempting to make everyone the same. Books such as *Zeely* (1967) by Virginia Hamilton and *Stevie* (1969) by John Steptoe, both written by African American authors, captured something of the special pride of the African American experience in children's literature.

*M. C. Higgins the Great* by Virginia Hamilton, an African American author, won the Newbery Medal for distinguished writing in 1975. Two years later, *Roll of Thunder, Hear My Cry* by Mildred D. Taylor, another fine African American author, won the Medal. Books by and about African Americans had at long last received recognition. However, even today the number of African American authors is small when compared to the African American population of this country.

The "new freedoms" of the 1960s were reflected in both adult and children's books. The so-called new realism in children's literature can probably be dated from the publication of *Harriet the Spy* (1964) by Louise Fitzhugh. Harriet is an 11-year-old antiheroine who keeps a notebook in which she records with bru-

tal honesty her impressions of her family and friends and characters in her New York neighborhood. Unlike Lucinda, who made friends with the people she met in *Roller Skates*, Harriet spies on them. Harriet's parents are psychologically absent, being too engrossed in their own affairs to be overly concerned about their daughter's activities. Children readily identified with Harriet, for she had the courage to think *and* say the things they didn't dare to say, including swearing. Following the breakthrough made by *Harriet the Spy*, many long-standing taboos in children's literature came tumbling down.

Vera and Bill Cleaver wrote about death and suicide in *Where the Lilies Bloom* (1969) and *Grover* (1970); alcoholism and homosexuality are described in *I'll Get There, It Better Be Worth the Trip* (1969) by John Donovan; and *George* (1970) by E. L. Konigsburg includes divorced parents, a psychologically disturbed child, and LSD. In Judy Blume's popular novel *Are You There God? It's Me, Margaret* (1970), Margaret's vague interest in religion is overshadowed by the more immediate concern of when she will start menstruating. Blume's *Deenie* (1973) is primarily the story of a beautiful girl who discovers she must wear a back brace for four years. This story

*John Steptoe's* Stevie *was one of the first picture books to present an African American family through an insider's eyes. It was published before this gifted author/illustrator was 20 years old.*

Copyright © 1969 by John L. Steptoe. Used by permission of HarperCollins Publishers, New York, NY.

contains several references to masturbation. Even picture books reflected the impact of this new freedom. Mickey falls out of bed and out of his clothes in Maurice Sendak's *In the Night Kitchen* (1970). In *My Special Best Words* (1974) by John Steptoe, bodily functions are discussed naturally, as a slightly older sister tries to toilet train her younger brother.

The literature published for the child's expanding world reflected the changes and challenges of life in the mid twentieth century. Just as adult literature mirrored the disillusionment of depression, wars, and materialism by becoming more sordid, sensationalist, and psychological, children's literature became more frank and honest, portraying situations like war, drugs, divorce, abortion, sex, and homosexuality. No longer were children protected by stories of happy families. Rather, it was felt that children would develop coping behaviors as they read about others who had survived similar problems.

All these problems are legitimate concerns of childhood. They have always existed, but only in the last forty years have they been openly and honestly written about in books for children. Further discussion of realism in children's literature will be found in Chapters 9 and 10.

## An International Literature for Children

An exciting development in children's literature was the rise of international interest in children's books during the years after World War II. This was indicated by an increased flow of children's books between countries. In 1950 *Pippi Longstocking,* by the Swedish author Astrid Lindgren, arrived in our country and was an immediate success. This was the beginning of many such exchanges.

The Mildred L. Batchelder Award, for the most outstanding translated children's book originally published abroad and then published in the United States, was established in 1966 by the Association for Library Service to Children of the American Library Association. It honored their retiring executive secretary, who had worked tirelessly for the exchange of books. This award has served as an impetus in promoting the translation of fine children's books from abroad. Such excellent books as *Friedrich* (1970) by Hans Richter of Germany and *Hiroshima No Pika (The Flash of Hiroshima)* (1980) by Toshi Maruki of Japan have been the recipients of this award.

Another indicator of the growing internationalism of children's literature during the 1950s was the number of congresses, book fairs, and exhibitions of children's books that were held around the world. The first general assembly of the International Board on Books for Young People (IBBY) was held in 1953. Jella Lepman, founder of the IBBY, maintained that the organization should serve as a world conscience for international children's books and call attention to the best in the field by awarding international prizes. Consequently, the IBBY awarded its first Hans Christian Andersen Medal to Eleanor Farjeon in 1956. In 1966 the IBBY decided to extend the award to include a medal for the most outstanding artist as well as author of children's books. Alois Carigiet was the first artist to receive this award. Then, in 1967, Jella Lepman created the annual International Children's Book Day, which was appropriately established on 2 April, Hans Christian Andersen's birthday.

In 1967 the Biennale of Illustrations in Bratislava, Czechoslovakia, (BIB) held its first exhibition. It is now scheduled to meet in the odd-numbered years, alternating with the IBBY congress. Other international displays include the annual Frankfurt Book Fair in September of each year and the Bologna Children's Book Fair in April.

Almost 250 years from the time Newbery first conceived of it, literature especially for children's enjoyment had achieved worldwide recognition. Literature for children has indeed come of age. Resources for Teaching, "Landmarks in the Development of Books for Children," lists significant books and other events in the development of children's literature.

# RESOURCES FOR TEACHING

## Landmarks in the Development of Books for Children

### BEFORE 1700

Oral stories told by minstrels—Beowulf, King Arthur, ballads, etc.

| | |
|---|---|
| c. 700 | Question-and-answer form of instruction—Aldhelm |
| c. 1200 | *Elucidarium*, Anselm |
| c. 1290 | *Gesta Romanorum* (Deeds of the Romans) |
| 1387 | *Canterbury Tales*, Geoffrey Chaucer |
| c. 1440 | Hornbooks developed |
| 1447 | *A Book of Curteseye*, published by Caxton |
| 1481 | *Historye of Reynart the Foxe*, published by Caxton |
| 1484 | *The Fables of Aesop*, published by Caxton |
| 1485 | *Le Morte d'Arthur* (The Death of King Arthur), Malory |
| 1548 | *King Henry's Primer* |
| c. 1580s | Beginnings of chapbooks |

### SEVENTEENTH CENTURY

| | |
|---|---|
| 1646 | *Spiritual Milk for Boston Babes . . .* , John Cotton |
| 1659 | *Orbis Pictus* (The World Illustrated), Johann Amos Comenius |
| 1678 | *The Pilgrim's Progress*, John Bunyan |
| c. 1686 | *The New England Primer* |
| 1697 | *Histoires ou Contes du Temps Passé* (Stories of Times Past), Charles Perrault |

### EIGHTEENTH CENTURY

| | |
|---|---|
| c. 1706 | *The Arabian Nights*, translated into English |
| 1715 | *Divine and Moral Songs*, Isaac Watts |
| 1719 | *Robinson Crusoe*, Daniel Defoe |
| 1726 | *Gulliver's Travels*, Jonathan Swift |
| 1729 | Perrault's *Fairy Tales*, translated into English |
| 1744 | *A Little Pretty Pocket-Book*, John Newbery |
| 1765 | *The History of Little Goody Two Shoes*, published by John Newbery |
| 1771 | *The New Lottery Book of Birds and Beasts*, Thomas Bewick |
| c. 1780 | *Mother Goose's Melody* (may have been Newbery) |
| c. 1786 | *Mother Goose's Melodies*, Isaiah Thomas, American publisher |
| 1789 | *Songs of Innocence*, William Blake |

### NINETEENTH CENTURY

| | |
|---|---|
| 1804 | *Original Poems for Infant Minds*, Ann and Jane Taylor |
| 1807 | *The Butterfly's Ball*, William Roscoe |
| 1823 | *A Visit from St. Nicholas*, Clement C. Moore |
| 1823 | *Grimm's Popular Stories*, translated by Edgar Taylor, illustrated by George Cruikshank |
| 1846 | *Book of Nonsense*, Edward Lear |
| 1846 | *Fairy Tales of Hans Christian Andersen*, translated by Mary Howitt |
| 1848 | *Struwwelpeter* (Shock-Headed Peter), Heinrich Hoffman (English translation) |

*continued*

# RESOURCES FOR TEACHING

## Landmarks in the Development of Books for Children con't

### NINETEENTH CENTURY con't

| | |
|---|---|
| 1861 | *Seven Little Sisters Who Live on the Big Round Ball That Floats in the Air*, Jane Andrews |
| 1865 | *The House That Jack Built*, *Sing a Song of Sixpence*, illustrated by Walter Crane |
| 1865 | *Alice's Adventures in Wonderland*, Lewis Carroll, illustrated by John Tenniel |
| 1865 | *Hans Brinker, or the Silver Skates*, Mary Mapes Dodge |
| 1868 | *Little Women*, Louisa May Alcott |
| 1869 | *Twenty Thousand Leagues Under the Sea*, Jules Verne |
| 1871 | *At the Back of the North Wind*, George MacDonald |
| 1872 | *Sing Song*, Christina Rossetti |
| 1873 | *St. Nicholas Magazine* begun, Mary Mapes Dodge, editor |
| 1876 | *The Adventures of Tom Sawyer*, Mark Twain |
| 1878 | *Under the Window*, Kate Greenaway |
| 1878 | *The Diverting History of John Gilpin*, illustrated by Randolph Caldecott |
| 1880 | *The Peterkin Papers*, Lucretia Hale |
| 1881 | *Uncle Remus Stories*, Joel Chandler Harris |
| 1883 | *The Merry Adventures of Robin Hood*, adapted and illustrated by Howard Pyle |
| 1883 | *Treasure Island*, Robert Louis Stevenson |
| 1884 | *Heidi*, Johanna Spyri, translated by Louise Brooks |
| 1884 | *The Adventures of Huckleberry Finn*, Mark Twain |
| 1885 | *A Child's Garden of Verses*, Robert Louis Stevenson |
| 1889 | *The Blue Fairy Book*, Andrew Lang |
| 1892 | *The Adventures of Pinocchio*, Carlo Collodi |
| 1894 | *The Jungle Book*, Rudyard Kipling |
| 1897 | *Jeanne d'Arc (Joan of Arc)*, Maurice Boutet de Monvel (English translation) |
| 1898 | *Wild Animals I Have Known*, Ernest Thompson Seton |

### FIRST HALF OF THE TWENTIETH CENTURY

| | |
|---|---|
| 1900 | *The Wizard of Oz*, L. Frank Baum |
| 1902 | *The Tale of Peter Rabbit*, Beatrix Potter |
| 1902 | *Songs of Childhood*, Walter de la Mare |
| 1902 | *Just So Stories*, Rudyard Kipling |
| 1903 | *Johnny Crow's Garden*, L. Leslie Brooke |
| 1903 | *The Call of the Wild*, Jack London |
| 1903 | *Rebecca of Sunnybrook Farm*, Kate Douglas Wiggin |
| 1906 | *Peter Pan in Kensington Gardens*, J. M. Barrie, illustrated by Arthur Rackham |
| 1908 | *The Wind in the Willows*, Kenneth Grahame, illustrated by Ernest H. Shepard |
| 1910 | *The Secret Garden*, Frances Hodgson Burnett |
| 1910 | *The Farm Book* and *Chicken World*, E. Boyd Smith |
| 1921 | *Here and Now Story Book*, Lucy Sprague Mitchell |
| 1922 | Newbery Medal established for most distinguished book for children |
| 1924 | *When We Were Very Young*, A. A. Milne, illustrated by Ernest H. Shepard |
| 1926 | *Winnie the Pooh*, A. A. Milne, illustrated by Ernest H. Shepard |

# RESOURCES FOR TEACHING

## Landmarks in the Development of Books for Children con't

### FIRST HALF OF THE TWENTIETH CENTURY con't

| | |
|---|---|
| 1926 | *Clever Bill*, William Nicholson |
| 1928 | *Millions of Cats*, Wanda Gág |
| 1932 | *What Whiskers Did*, Ruth Carroll |
| 1932 | *Little House in the Big Woods*, Laura Ingalls Wilder |
| 1934 | *The Little Auto*, Lois Lenski |
| 1934 | *Mary Poppins*, Pamela Travers |
| 1935 | *Caddie Woodlawn*, Carol Ryrie Brink |
| 1936 | *The Story of Ferdinand*, Munro Leaf, illustrated by Robert Lawson |
| 1936 | *Roller Skates*, Ruth Sawyer |
| 1937 | *And to Think That I Saw It on Mulberry Street*, Dr. Seuss |
| 1937 | *The Hobbit*, J. R. R. Tolkien |
| 1938 | Caldecott Medal established for most distinguished picture book for children |
| 1939 | *Madeline*, Ludwig Bemelmans |
| 1939 | *The Noisy Book*, Margaret Wise Brown, illustrated by Leonard Weisgard |
| 1939 | *Mike Mulligan and His Steam Shovel*, Virginia Lee Burton |
| 1940 | *Blue Willow*, Doris Gates |
| 1941 | *The Moffats*, Eleanor Estes |
| 1941 | *Make Way for Ducklings*, Robert McCloskey |
| 1941 | *Paddle to the Sea*, Holling C. Holling |
| 1941 | *In My Mother's House*, Ann Nolan Clark |
| 1941 | *Curious George*, H. A. Rey |
| 1942 | *The Little House*, Virginia Lee Burton |
| 1943 | *Johnny Tremain*, Esther Forbes |
| 1943 | *Homer Price*, Robert McCloskey |
| 1944 | *The Hundred Dresses*, Eleanor Estes, illustrated by Louis Slobodkin |
| 1945 | *Call Me Charley*, Jesse Jackson |
| 1946 | *Bright April*, Marguerite de Angeli |
| 1947 | *Stone Soup*, Marcia Brown |
| 1947 | *White Snow, Bright Snow*, Alvin Tresselt, illustrated by Roger Duvoisin |
| 1947 | *Judy's Journey*, Lois Lenski |

### SECOND HALF OF THE TWENTIETH CENTURY

| | |
|---|---|
| 1952 | *Charlotte's Web*, E. B. White, illustrated by Garth Williams |
| 1952 | *Anne Frank: The Diary of a Young Girl*, Anne Frank |
| 1956 | *Bronzeville Boys and Girls*, Gwendolyn Brooks |
| 1957 | *The Cat in the Hat*, Dr. Seuss |
| 1959 | *Tom's Midnight Garden*, Philippa Pearce |
| 1962 | *A Wrinkle in Time*, Madeleine L'Engle |
| 1962 | *The Snowy Day*, Ezra Jack Keats |
| 1963 | *Where the Wild Things Are*, Maurice Sendak |

*continued*

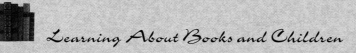

# RESOURCES FOR TEACHING

## Landmarks in the Development of Books for Children con't

### SECOND HALF OF THE TWENTIETH CENTURY con't

1964    *Harriet the Spy*, Louise Fitzhugh

1966    Mildred L. Batchelder Award established for most outstanding translated book

1969    Coretta Scott King Award established for best African American children's literature

1969    *Stevie*, John Steptoe

1969    *Where the Lilies Bloom*, Vera and Bill Cleaver

1970    *Are You There God? It's Me, Margaret*, Judy Blume

1970    *In the Night Kitchen*, Maurice Sendak

1971    *Journey to Topaz*, Yoshiko Uchida, illustrated by Donald Carrick

1974    *Where the Sidewalk Ends*, Shel Silverstein

1974    *My Brother Sam Is Dead*, James and Christopher Collier

1974    *M. C. Higgins the Great*, Virginia Hamilton

1975    *Why Mosquitoes Buzz in People's Ears*, retold by Verna Aardema, illustrated by Leo and Diane Dillon

1977    Excellence in Poetry for Children Award established by the National Council of Teachers of English

1980    *Hiroshima No Pika* (The Flash of Hiroshima), Toshi Maruki

1981    *A Visit to William Blake's Inn*, Nancy Willard, illustrated by Alice and Martin Provensen

1986    *The Magic School Bus at the Waterworks*, Joanna Cole, illustrated by Bruce Degan

1987    *Lincoln: A Photobiography*, Russell Freedman

1987    *Mufaro's Beautiful Daughters: An African Tale*, John Steptoe

1990    *Baseball in April and Other Stories*, Gary Soto

1990    Orbis Pictus Award for outstanding children's nonfiction established by the National Council of Teachers of English

1990    *Black and White*, David Macaulay

1991    *Maniac Magee*, Jerry Spinelli

1994    *Earthshine*, Theresa Nelson

1994    *Christmas in the Big House, Christmas in the Quarters*, Patricia and Frederick McKissack

1995    *Catherine Called Birdy*, Karen Cushman

1996    *The Friends*, Kazumi Yumoto

1996    Pura Belpré Award established for excellence in Latino literature

1997    *Out of the Dust*, Karen Hesse

1997    *Forged by Fire*, Sharon Draper

1998    *Harry Potter and the Sorcerer's Stone*, J. K. Rowling

1999    *The Birchbark House*, Louise Erdrich

2000    The Robert F. Sibert Informational Book Award for a distinguished work of nonfiction for children

# Recent Trends in Children's Books

As the twentieth century ended, several trends seem to be affecting the future direction of children's books. Changes in the ways books are marketed, produced, and used by children are likely to affect the types of literature that children will enjoy in the twenty-first century.

## Children's Books: Big Business

The publication and distribution of children's books is now big business. Enormous growth in children's book publishing occurred in the late 1980s; children's book sales skyrocketed to a billion dollars in 1990. The number of juveniles published in 1993 was more than twenty times the number published in 1880.

The following statistics on the number of juveniles published in the given years shows the increased rate of growth in the publication of juveniles for over a century:[22]

| Year | Amount of books published | Year | Amount of books published |
|------|---------------------------|------|---------------------------|
| 1880 | 270   | 1960 | 1,725 |
| 1890 | 408   | 1970 | 2,640 |
| 1900 | 527   | 1980 | 2,895 |
| 1910 | 1,010 | 1990 | 5,000 |
| 1920 | 477   | 1993 | 5,469 |
| 1930 | 933   | 1995 | 5,678 |
| 1940 | 984   | 1997 | 5,353 |
| 1950 | 1,059 |      |       |

Recent years have also seen a dramatic increase in both high-quality and inferior paperbacks for children. Individual publishing houses are selecting some of the best of their previously published titles for reissue in paperback form. Increasingly, publishers are bringing out new titles in hardcover and paperback simultaneously. Some have instituted new divisions devoted exclusively to paperbacks. In addition, many paperback houses have started commissioning their own original books to be published directly in paperback. Some of these originals qualify as imaginative writing, but many of them are written to formula. Reminiscent of the many series churned out by the Stratemeyer Syndicate beginning in 1885, these books promise to be almost as popular. In 1994 one title of Ann Martin's *Baby-Sitters Club* series, *The*

*Baby-Sitters Remember,* sold 228,000 copies. Interest in ghost and horror stories, particularly R. L. Stine's *Goosebump* series waned in the late 1990s to be replaced by the fantasy/adventure series, *Animorphs.* Of the top twenty-five best-selling paperbacks in 1998, ten were *Animorph* titles.[23]

Another factor hidden in the statistics is the large number of titles that go out of print each year. Although it appears that many more books are being published, title turnover is far greater today. The life of a modern book is seldom more than 5 years, in contrast to the 10- to 20-year life span of books in the mid twentieth century, or, in the case of the very early books, a 200-year life span. However, certain books do stay in print and continue to sell and sell. Judy Blume's publishers report that all her books have sold over 25 million copies. Shel Silverstein's poetry books have also sold over 25 million copies. The *Bowker Annual* listed nearly fifty hardcover children's books that had sold over 750,000 copies by 1985.[24] Heading the list was Beatrix Potter's *Tale of Peter Rabbit* with 8 million copies, E. B. White's *Charlotte's Web* with 1.5 million copies, and *Where the Wild Things Are* by Maurice Sendak with 1 million. Books by Dr. Seuss, Marguerite Henry, and Laura Ingalls Wilder are among the other titles in that rarefied company.

The health of children's literature can also be seen in the large number of children's bookstores and children's book fairs that exist today. Unfortunately, the increasing market share captured by large chain stores has put some of the smaller independent children's stores out of business in the last decade. Chain stores can also buy the cheaper books produced for mass marketing. This also applies to the jobbers whose entire business is supplying book fairs. Generally, book fairs sponsored by independent stores are more responsive to the schools' needs and provide better-quality books.

Another trend in publishing is the increased number of mergers between publishing houses and large conglomerates. Few independently owned publishing companies are left today. A publishing company owned by a large conglomerate must show a profit; it is measured against the success of other companies in the corporation, most of which have nothing to do with publishing. Many of these changes began in the late 1970s, when the cutback in federal assistance to education was felt in schools throughout the United States. To counteract the loss of school sales, publishers put more emphasis on the trade book market than ever before. In spite of the additional mergers and

---

[22]*The Bowker Annual of Library and Book Trade Information* (New York: Bowker, 1983, 1989, 1995, 1998).

[23]Diane Roback, "Licensed Tie-Ins Make the Cash Registers Ring," *Publisher's Weekly* 24 (March 29, 1999): 46–52.

[24]*Bowker Annual* (1995).

*Engineering techniques allow artists such as Robert Sabuda to experiment with three dimensional forms in* The Movable Mother Goose.

From *The Christmas Alphabet* by Robert Sabuda. Copyright © 1994 by Robert Sabuda. Reprinted by permission of Orchard Books, New York. All rights reserved.

company changes needed to meet the economic pressures of recent years, children's book publishing was close to a $2 billion business in 1994.[25]

## New Books for New Markets

As publishers have sought continued profits, they have searched for new markets. In the 1980s, as a result of the many research studies showing the value of reading aloud to young children and the interest of baby boomers in their new offspring, publishers discovered the infant market. Many companies are producing their own line of books for babies and toddlers. Helen Oxenbury's series of board books titled *Friends, Working, Playing, Dressing,* and *Family,* all published in 1981, were the first to portray the infant with her or his concerns and accomplishments. The creation of these new books for the very young, plus the publication of such popular titles as Jim Trelease's *The Read-Aloud Handbook* (1995), contributed to a new awareness among conscientious parents of the value of reading aloud to youngsters.

Wordless books (many of them do contain some print in the introduction or afterword) first made their appearance in 1932 with *What Whiskers Did* by Ruth Carroll. This story of the adventures of a little Scottie dog was reprinted in 1965, when there was a greater emphasis on the importance of "reading pictures" in preparation for learning to read. Wordless books are no longer only for beginning readers—watch adults and older children pore over *Anno's*

*Journey* (1978) by Mitsumasa Anno or David Wiesner's Caldecott Medal winner, *Tuesday* (1991).

Some of today's "new" books are old books revisited. Toy books, including pop-up books and books with revolving pictures, are once again delighting children. Modern pop-ups tell a continuous story like David McKee's *I Can Too!* (1997) or they allow an artist to explore paper engineering through such books as Robert Sabuda's exquisite *The Christmas Alphabet* (1994) and *The Movable Mother Goose* (1999). Unless very well designed and sturdy, these manipulative books are more appropriate for the entertainment of one child than for library use.

In general, reissues and new editions of old favorites appeal to adult book buyers because they are familiar. Today's editions of classic stories often have the added attraction of appearing with illustrations that benefit from improved technology; for instance, in the 1980s Warne reprinted twenty-three of Beatrix Potter's books with new reproductions photographed from Potter's original watercolor paintings. Many of these classics, such as Rachel Field's *Prayer for a Child* (1944), have been reissued in board book form.

Walt Disney was the first to establish movie-related books, rewriting old classics to suit himself and giving them titles like *Walt Disney's Cinderella.* In 1998, books connected to the Disney film *A Bug's Life* sold close to a million copies.[26]

Another trend is the publication of the print book as a secondary form—a book based on a popular television show, film, or even video game. The television show *Blues Clues* accounted for five of the top fifteen best sellers in 1998, with *Barney* and

---

[25]M. P. Dunleavey, "The Squeeze is On," *Publishers Weekly,* 9 January 1995, pp. 44–46.

[26]Roback, "Licensed Tie-Ins Make the Cash Registers Ring."

*Teletubbies* books running close behind in popularity.[27] Frequently the result of this market-oriented approach to publishing is the packaging of cheaply produced books with other items such as plush toys, T-shirts, or greeting cards. Quality writing is seldom part of such a package. More and more often, however, even well-written books seem to have toys or games packaged with them.

## Shifts in Publishing Emphases

One of the most notable trends in children's books today is the dominance of picture storybooks and picture-book formats. Many publishers' catalogs show that a majority of their new titles are picture storybooks or profusely illustrated books. Also, editors report that it is typical to print many more copies of a new picture book than of a novel because picture storybooks are in far greater demand.

This emphasis on the visual is also evident in the tremendous increase in the number of nonfiction books published. It seems likely that the eye appeal of books like David Macaulay's *The Way Things Work* (1988) or the *Eyewitness* series from Dorling Kindersley Publishers has a lot to do with their success. Along with the increase in the number of high-quality nonfiction books has come increased recognition of their place as literature. Russell Freedman's *Lincoln: A Photobiography* (1987) was a Newbery Medal winner, and many other nonfiction titles are earning critical acclaim.

Poetry books also enjoyed a publication growth spurt in recent years. Like nonfiction books, most of these new titles, both collections and single poems in book form, feature attractive illustrations that claim as much attention as the words. The production of new editions of folk and fairy tales has expanded to include many more multicultural and global folktales. At the same time, myths, tall tales, and other lesser-known forms of traditional literature seem to be gaining ground. The success of Jon Scieszka's *The True Story of the Three Little Pigs* (1989) has spawned a number of modern retellings or takeoffs on traditional tales. The year 1999 saw the publication of *Leola and the Honeybears*, an African American retelling of Goldilocks and the Three Bears written and illustrated by Melodye Bensen Rosales.

In books for middle-grade readers, recent years have seen greater emphasis on contemporary realistic fiction. Many publishers have targeted children who have just begun fluent reading with easy chapter books such as the *Best Enemies* series by Kathleen Leverich or Johanna Hurwitz's *Russell* series. The immensely popular series books, such as *Baby-Sitters Club* and even *Kids of Polk Street School*, are marketed directly to their audiences through paperback book clubs and bookstores. Hardcover titles cater to this "more of the same" impulse in middle-grade readers by providing many sequels such as Gary Paulsen's *Brian's Return* (1999) and Phyllis Reynolds Naylor's *Alice* and *Shiloh* series. In general the content of realistic fiction has moved away from the narrowly focused "problem novel" of the 1960s and 1970s. The lighter fiction for elementary school readers today seems more innocent, and the serious fiction more realistically balanced, with characters less prone to despair than in the books of a decade or two ago.[28] Many sober themes remain, of course. Published in the 1990s, Theresa Nelson's *Earthshine* (1994) and Barbara Ann Porte's *Something Terrible Happened* (1994) dealt with parents with AIDS, and Sharon Draper's *Forged by Fire* (1997) focused on sexual abuse. Historical fiction has regained new vigor with the publication, beginning in 1996, of Scholastic's Dear America series—fictionalized journals of girls at different times in America's past. Written by well regarded authors such as Kathryn Lasky and Joyce Hansen, these books have won awards *and* gained best-seller status. The four hardcover titles published in 1998 sold more than half a million copies.[29] In 1998, Scholastic also began the My Name Is America series. Here authors such as Walter Dean Myers and Jim Murphy provide boys' views of history.

Barbara Elleman suggests that the rise in historical fiction offerings in the 1990s is also a result of the increased interest in multicultural literature.[30] Titles like Patricia and Frederick McKissack's *Christmas in the Big House, Christmas in the Quarters* (1994), Walter Dean Myers's *The Glory Field* (1994), Laurence Yep's *Dragon's Gate* (1993), and Louise Erdrich's *The Birchbark House* (1999) are examples of books by minority writers who are examining the stories of their own families and their ancestors, no matter how painful. In addition, authors are looking at other time periods as a way of examining concerns like gender issues. Karen Cushman's *The Midwife's Apprentice* (1995) and *Catherine Called Birdy* (1994) and Patricia Curtis Pritsch's *Keeper of the Light* (1997) focus attention on women's roles in other centuries without sacrificing strength of character.

The return of many classic titles such as *Treasure Island* and *Robinson Crusoe* reflected the shift of the 1980s toward conservative values as well as a concern

---

[27]Ibid.

[28]See Liz Rosenberg, "It's All Right to Be Innocent Again," *New York Times Book Review*, 21 May 1989, p. 46.

[29]Roback, "Licensed Tie-Ins Make the Cash Registers Ring."

[30]Barbara Elleman, "Toward the 21st Century—Where Are Children's Books Going?" *New Advocate* 8 (summer 1995): 151–165.

that children should not miss out on their literary heritage. Publishers also issued classics such as Alcott's *Little Women* (1997) with visual aids, maps, diagrams, photographs and illustrations. These visual additions might be appealing to today's video-oriented youth, but they can also distract readers from a good story. Most of these classic titles are available in libraries, and costly new editions might mean that new authors and artists are not being published. How many different editions of *The Secret Garden* do we need?

## Changes in Writing and Illustration

Today writers and illustrators have great freedom to experiment with style and format. For years it was assumed that all books for children should be told in the third person, past tense; children were not supposed to like introspective first-person accounts. The recognition and popularity of such books as *Meet the Austins* (1960) by Madeleine L'Engle and Judy Blume's *Are You There God? It's Me, Margaret* (1970) certainly put an end to this myth. Even historical fiction and biography have assumed this point of view in such books as *My Brother Sam Is Dead* (1974). Patricia MacLachlan's *The Facts and Fictions of Minna Pratt* (1988) and Adam Rapp's *The Buffalo Tree* (1998) demonstrate how this device gives a sense of immediacy and intimate participation in the character's experience.

Another trend in writing can be seen in the books told from various points of view. Mary Stolz wrote two books about the same events but told from the different protagonists' points of view: *A Dog on Barkham Street* ([1960] 1985) and *The Bully of*

*Barkham Street* ([1963] 1985). The use of shifting points of view, which can heighten the suspense of a story, serves the same purposes as flashbacks, cut-ins, and other devices on TV and in films. Paul Fleischman's *Seedfolks* (1997) and Avi's *Nothing but the Truth* (1991) use these techniques.

Karen Hesse has further experimented with language styles in *Music of Dolphins* (1996), the story of a ferral child raised by dolphins. The book opens with Mila's thoughts as she swims her tropical paradise. Her grammatical structure is quite sophisticated and printed in italic type. After she is "rescued" by humans, her words are printed in large type and mirror the sentence structure of a very young child, one who has just been reintroduced to spoken language. Hesse's Newbery Award–winning *Out of the Dust* (1997) is told in the first person, present tense, but in free verse rather than prose. Other variations in writing styles include the telling of stories through letters and journals. Beverly Cleary won the Newbery Medal in 1984 for her story *Dear Mr. Henshaw*, which consists mostly of a boy's letters to his favorite author and later of entries in his own journal. Karen Cushman's *Catherine Called Birdy*, the journal of a 14-year-old in the year 1290, received a Newbery Honor Medal in 1994.

As authors tell stories in intriguing new ways, they can create books that are hard to classify according to traditional definitions of genre. For instance, books such as *The Root Cellar* (1983) by Janet Lunn and *The Devil's Arithmetic* (1988) by Jane Yolen have combined fantasy with historical fiction. These books use an element of fantasy to unite the past with the present and to capture contemporary children's interest in an earlier

*In Ifeoma Onyefulu's* Emeka's Gift: An African Counting Story, *photographs convey detailed information and provide children with a pleasing visual experience.*

time. As the twentieth century ends, we find more children's authors exploring the genre of magic realism, influenced perhaps by noted South American writers such as Gabriel Garcia Marquez. This point of view accepts the presence of magic in the real world. Writers like David Almond in *Skellig* (1999) and Adele Griffin in *The Other Shepards* (1998) ask their readers to accept (or at least consider) the possibility of alternative, even fantastic, explanations for real events. These books are difficult to classify as traditional fantasy.

Current books cross conventional genre lines in other ways as well. For instance, the boundaries between fact and fiction are crossed and recrossed by Joanna Cole and illustrator Bruce Degen in the *Magic School Bus* series. In these best-selling nonfiction books, Ms. Frizzle takes her young students on a fantasy field trip and then brings them home again to an everyday world of group projects and science reports. Blends of story and information for younger children are offered in Lois Ehlert's *Feathers for Lunch* (1990) and other concept books. Books like this use a playful approach to draw readers into a content topic.

Illustrators have also departed from old notions about what is appropriate for a children's book. Earlier in this century, for instance, experts advised against photography in children's books, claiming that photos were not clear enough or appealing enough for a young audience. Now, thanks to improved quality of reproduction and rising standards of artistry, non-

fiction books like Ifeoma Onyefulu's beautifully designed *Emeka's Gift* (1995) offer photos that are clear and aesthetically satisfying. Technological advances have also lifted restrictions and encouraged experimentation with new tools for picture making. Daniel Pinkwater illustrated his story *The Muffin Fiend* (1986) on his Macintosh computer. Marcus Pfister's illustrations for *The Rainbow Fish* (1992) make use of holography. Barbara Reid is able to use plastecine to build her pictures in such books as *The Party* (1999) because cameras, scanners, and other equipment, which can now efficiently reproduce illustrations created in any medium, have replaced the laborious hand preparation of color separations for the printer.

Although new uses of media might be the most noticeable change in illustrations, artists have also established a more important role for the visual element in books. In picture storybooks, some artists are creating more and more complex interactions between pictures and print, as David Macaulay does with the four intertwined, separately illustrated threads of story in his Caldecott Medal winner, *Black and White* (1990). Steve Jenkins's beautiful collage illustrations for the nonfiction *The Top of the World: Climbing Mt. Everest* are as well designed and artistically pleasing as any good picture storybook. In *City of Light, City of Dark: A Comic Book Novel* (1990) Avi teams with illustrator Brian Floca to stretch our ideas of what constitutes a novel and now the comic book novel is more common. In *Making Up Megaboy* (1998) Virginia Walter and Katrina Roeckelein combine computer generated graphics with first person accounts of the murder of a local store owner. In *Monster* (1999) Walter Dean Myers interweaves handwritten journal entries, a film script, and black and white photographs to relate the story of a sixteen year old on trial for murder. Although these books can be classified as nonfiction or realistic fiction, they are also picture books in their own ways.

## Increased Use in Schools

The last several decades saw the growing use of children's trade books in classrooms—for reading instruction, integrated language arts programs, and a variety of uses across the curriculum. The whole language movement and new understandings about children's literacy learning brought the use of real literature to the classrooms of many schools. Unlike the 1960s, this is not a trend nurtured by government funds (which are largely unavailable now); it is nurtured by the grassroots interest of teachers and the encouragement of professional associations.

The actual extent of the use of children's books in instructional programs across the country is difficult to estimate, however, because many teachers use trade books on an individual basis rather than as part

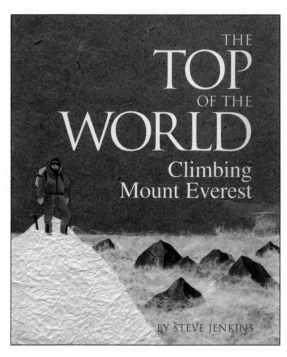

*Illustration and design have been carefully considered in Steve Jenkins's nonfiction book,* To the Top of the World. Climbing Mt. Everest.

From *Top of the World* by Steve Jenkin, © 1999. Reprinted by permission of Houghton Mifflin Company.

of a recognized program. A renewed emphasis on the systematic teaching of phonics might have a negative impact on the trend to use real literature rather than textbooks. Another complicating factor is that teachers and supervisors often use the same terminology to describe widely different practices.

The disturbing side of this trend is that some instructional programs use literature without regard for its imaginative and aesthetic characteristics. In other instances, students read "real" books, but still use the same skill-and-drill activities that teachers were trying to avoid by switching away from the basal textbooks. Uses of literature that ruin children's enjoyment of good books are a real disservice to children and to literature.

Children's books are now also part of many community literacy programs. During the 1980s, problems of illiteracy in the United States were widely acknowledged. Government agencies with an eye to tight budgets worked to involve corporations and private foundations in assisting community and school efforts, particularly among the poor. The National Children's Book and Literacy Alliance was founded in 1997 by such children's book authors as Natalie Babbitt, Lois Lowry and Katherine Paterson to raise the profile of children's literacy issues.[31] First Lady Hilary Rodham Clinton announced the National Partnership to Prescribe Reading to Infants and Toddlers in 1997. This important initiative includes such diverse partners as the American Academy of Pediatrics, National Association of Community Health Centers, American Library Association, and American Booksellers Association.

## Increased Censorship

An account of trends from the 1960s to the present would be incomplete without mention of the increase in censorship of books in schools and libraries. The number of book challenges has increased every decade since the 1950s. According to the American Library Association, about half of the censorship attempts in the United States succeed. It should be emphasized that censorship refers to an attempt to have a book removed from a library, not simply a complaint or challenge.

Most book challenges are directed at young adult books. However, as the new freedoms of the 1960s were reflected in children's books, censorship and book bannings became more common. Books can be objected to for almost any reason. Edward B. Jenkinson lists 116 targets of the censors, including profanity, conflicts with parents, drug use and abuse, homosexuality, violence, depressing stories of the ghetto, realistic dialogue, secular humanism, values clarification—and

the list goes on.[32] Dictionaries, textbooks, trade books, and nursery rhymes have all come under attack.

Judy Blume has long been at the top of the list of children's authors who have come under attack, but it seems the list is growing to include some of the most critically acclaimed children's authors. The American Library Association lists Robert Cormier's *The Chocolate War* (1974), Judy Blume's *Blubber* (1974), and J. K. Rowlings's *Harry Potter* series among the most frequently banned books of 1999. Authors who most frequently came under attack were Robert Cormier, Lois Lowry, Walter Dean Myers, and Phyllis Reynolds Naylor.[33]

There is no doubt that censorship has been on the rise in American elementary schools during the last forty years. The censors represent both conservatives and liberals. Many of them are administrators, teachers, and librarians themselves![34] For a further discussion of censorship and what you can do about it, see "Dealing with Censorship" in Chapter 13.

## The Multicultural World of Children's Books

At the beginning of the twentieth century, publishers, authors, and book buyers clearly recognized children's need for a body of good literature that spoke to their interests and enthusiasm, but the children for whom they wrote, published, and bought were largely white.[35]

During the 1960s and early 1970s, the changing social climate and federal support for children's libraries encouraged publishers to produce books about many ethnic groups. In the wake of the civil rights movement, the influential Council on Interracial Books for Children encouraged minority authors to write about their own cultures. When federal funds were drastically cut and bookstore sales began to play a bigger part in a book's success, publishers found that so-called ethnic books, which were selling poorly in the stores, were not profitable, and publication figures for these books dropped. By the late 1970s almost no new authors of color were being published.

Some changes for the better began in the 1980s. Predictions about the changing demographics of the school population and renewed demand by schools and libraries for multicultural books led to more-active recruitment of authors from a variety of eth-

---

[31]See www.ncbla.org.

[32]Edward B. Jenkinson, *Censors in the Classroom: The Mind Benders* (New York: Avon, 1982).

[33]See www.ala.org/bbooks.

[34]Lee Burress, "Appendix B," in *Battle of the Books* (Metuchen, N.J.: Scarecrow Press, 1989).

[35]See Nancy Larrick, "The All White World of Children's Books," *Saturday Review*, 11 September 1965, pp. 63–65.

nic backgrounds and to better recognition of high-quality titles.[36] There is still a lack of cultural diversity among editors and other publishing professionals who make decisions about what books will be published and how they will be marketed. However, that too may be gradually changing. Hyperion Books, under the leadership of editor Andrea Davis Pinkney, has added Jump at the Sun, an imprint meant to spotlight African American writers and illustrators and to encourage new talent. In 1999 author Sharon Flake won a Corretta Scott King/ John Steptoe award for her first book, *The Skin I'm In.* Small presses, such as Carolrhoda, Children's Book Press, and Lee & Low, that have a commitment to multicultural publishing have also made an impact, particularly in the realm of picture storybooks.

By the end of the twentieth century, publishers, authors, and book buyers finally recognized that the child has many faces, races and cultures. Even though the number of books published about various cultures is still not representative of the population breakdown, there is reason to hope that we are moving in that direction.

The continuing debate about multicultural literature within the children's literature community has been a healthy one. Although we have not settled the definition of "multicultural literature" or agreed upon who should be able to write literature about nonmainstream cultures, the dialogue has forced us all to clarify our understanding of what constitutes a work of literature, what the author's role is in creating that work, and what role multicultural literature must play in our society. Hade argues that we must read all literature from *a multicultural stance,* "one that seeks to understand how race, class, and gender mean in a story."[37] Cai adds that we must also read *multicultural literature* that concentrates on oppressed groups, especially ethnic groups. She argues that "to see the commonality among cultures is important, but to study the differences is equally important."[38]

The recognition of need in the United States for literature that reflects cultural diversity extends to books from and about other countries. Global education is a curriculum concept that has made itself felt

in the world of children's books. One result is a renewed interest in international literature, particularly in books like Beverley Naidoo's South African story *Journey to Jo'burg* (1986), Nina Ring Aamundsen's *Two Short and One Long* (1991), and Kazumi Yumoto's *The Friends* (1996).

## The Development of a Multiliterate Society

Dire predictions have been made about the death of the book as we know it today; our society has been called a postliterate society. Modern technology has certainly affected literature and the arts, with developments like interactive fiction, where the "reader" responds to and actually creates plot variations for the story that appears on her computer screen. Computers can be programmed to generate poetry, pictures, and music. Some of these works meet high standards of artistry and receive appropriate critical recognition. With the rise of CD-ROMs, more publishers are putting popular books on disks. At this point, however, many of these programs represent glorified games rather than literary or artistic encounters.

The Internet and the World Wide Web have had an incredible impact on the world of children's books in the last few years. Children can now find many authors on websites, and some authors will interact with their readers. Even more exciting are the chat rooms where children can discuss books with other readers from around the world. Online bookstores welcome reader reviews, and a book search will reveal that children are responding with enthusiastic and often insightful reviews.

It seems likely, then, that today's youth will become multiliterate, using the new technologies for the rapid retrieval of information of all kinds, for writing and editing their thoughts, for communicating about books with children in distant places, and for creating original programs of their own. Just as many youth today are multilingual, so the youth of the future will become multiliterate, reading a wide variety of formats. They will still need reading for a wide range of skills, and they will need books for pleasure. Perhaps, most importantly, they will still need to touch the pages of books, and be able to hug books close to their hearts.

As we move into a new century, the future of the book is uncertain. Computers, videotapes, cassettes, films, cable TV—all have the potential to give us instant information in many forms. Will the book be as important in the twenty-first century as it was in the twentieth? Those of us who love literature and have witnessed its positive influence on children's lives can only hope that it will be—that it will continue to live and flourish.

---

[36]See titles such as Rosalinda Benavides Barrera and Verlinda D. Thompson, eds., *Kaleidoscope: A Multicultural Booklist,* Vol. 2 (Urbana, Ill.: National Council of Teachers of English, 1997) and other books listed in Appendix B.

[37]Daniel Hade, "Reading Multiculturally," in *Using Multicultural Literature in the K–8 Classroom,* ed. Violet Harris (Norwood, Mass.: Christopher Gordon, 1997), p. 245.

[38]Mingshui Cai, "Multiple Definitions of Multicultural Literature," *New Advocate* 11 (fall 1998), p. 322.

## INTO THE CLASSROOM

# The Changing World of Children's Books

**Room 201**

1. Ask children to compare Caldecott Medal books over the last fifty years. How have the illustrations changed? What changes do they notice in the stories?
2. Conduct a classroom study on the history of books. What factors have caused changes in books' appearance? How has the audience for books changed?
3. Create a timeline showing important milestones in the history of books.
4. Study the history of writing and printing. How has this factor affected the history of books?
5. Visit websites of important libraries and museums, such as the British Library at www.portico.bl.uk/index.html or the Getty Museum at www.getty.edu/museum/main/Manuscripts.htm, to see more about the history of books.

# Personal Explorations

1. Interview five adults of different ages and ask about their favorite childhood books and reading interests. How similar are their responses? How much overlapping of titles is there?
2. Conduct a survey of your literature class to find out how many students have read *Little Women, Alice's Adventures in Wonderland, The Wind in the Willows, Charlotte's Web,* or one of Judy Blume's books. Make a chart of your findings.
3. Prepare a display of early children's books; note the printing and binding, the illustrations, the subject matter. Display a varied selection of recent books as well. What contrasts do you see, and what similarities?
4. Read one of the new original paperbacks produced for a series. Compare it with a Nancy Drew book or a Sue Barton book. What similarities and differences do you see? Another person could compare it with a modern realistic story for children like those by Cynthia Voigt or Katherine Paterson. Again, how do they compare?
5. Plan a panel discussion on the role of the book in the future. What would you lose if you didn't have books?

# Related Readings

Ariès, Philippe. *Centuries of Childhood: A Social History of Family Life.* Translated from the French by Robert Baldick. New York: Knopf, 1962.

A definitive study of the development of the concept of childhood. Ariès maintained that childhood was not discovered until the seventeenth century. While some have disputed this claim, Ariès's book has formed the basis of most historical studies of childhood.

Bader, Barbara. *American Picturebooks from Noah's Arc to the Beast Within.* Delray Beach, FL: Winslow Press, 2000 [1976].

A new edition of a classic work on American picture books, this comprehensive history of the genre includes the influence of foreign artists, the impact of motion pictures and comic books, and the social scene. Over 700 illustrations enable the author to discuss various styles of many illustrators.

Bingham, Jane, and Grayce Scholt. *Fifteen Centuries of Children's Literature.* Westport, Conn.: Greenwood Press, 1980.

An indispensable reference book for the historical scholar of children's literature, providing an annotated chronology of both British and American books from A.D. 523 through

1945. The chronology is divided into six time segments. Historical background, the development of books, and general attitudes toward children are presented for each time period. Information is included on series books as well as those that became classics.

Carpenter, Humphrey, and Mari Prichard. *The Oxford Companion to Children's Literature.* Oxford: Oxford University Press, 1984.

An excellent reference source on many aspects of children's literature, including authors, illustrators, titles, and characters. The historical span stretches from early chapbooks through books published in the 1980s. Nearly two thousand entries are included in this one-volume reference source to children's literature.

Darton, F. J. Harvey. *Children's Books in England: Five Centuries of Social Life.* 3rd ed. Revised by Brian Alderson. Cambridge: Cambridge University Press, 1982 [1932].

This updated version of a well-recognized text on the history of children's literature in England makes fascinating reading. Darton had great respect for children's books, seeing their relationship to the history of children, the socioeconomic situation of the times, the cultural-religious beliefs of the period, and the history of publishing. Alderson added detailed notes to each chapter, but he did not revise the text. Therefore the reader does need to remember that the text's "now" and "today" refer to Darton's time, 1932.

Jackson, Mary V. *Engines of Instruction, Mischief, and Magic: Children's Literature in England from Its Beginnings to 1839.* Lincoln: University of Nebraska Press, 1990.

This readable scholarly work focuses on the economic, sociopolitical, and religious forces that helped shape early children's books. Jackson's attention to issues of class distinction and debates about education provides a useful way to look at recent trends as well as titles of the eighteenth and nineteenth centuries.

Lurie, Alison. *Don't Tell the Grown-Ups: Subversive Children's Literature.* Boston: Little, Brown, 1990.

In a collection of essays from the 1980s, this well-known scholar and novelist demonstrates that the enduring works of children's literature did not conform to the ideal values of their own time. She points to characters who are disobedient and who mock adult hypocrisy from folklore and fairy tales to the middle of the twentieth century.

Marcus, Leonard S., ed. *Dear Genius: The Letters of Ursula Nordstrom.* New York: HarperCollins, 1998.

Nordstrom was one of the legendary children's book editors of the twentieth century, and this collection of her letters to such authors and illustrators as Laura Ingalls Wilder, Maurice Sendak, E. B. White, and John Steptoe reveals a witty, wise, and very independent woman. Marcus's introduction provides a context for understanding children's book publishing during what has been called its golden age.

Marcus, Leonard S. *Margaret Wise Brown: Awakened by the Moon.* Boston: Morrow, 1999 [1992].

Marcus's exhaustive, well-written, and engaging biography has detailed not only a writer's life but also a much broader portrait—of the progressive education movement and the major figures who created, influenced, and guided children's books during a most fertile period.

Silvey, Anita, ed. *Children's Books and Their Creators.* New York: Houghton Mifflin, 1995.

This beautiful book focuses on twentieth-century American children's books. It includes overviews of the types of books written for various ages; essays on issues, history, and genres; biographical information on important authors and illustrators; and essays by creators of children's books.

Townsend, John Rowe, ed. *John Newbery and His Books.* Metuchen, N.J.: Scarecrow Press, 1994.

This collection of essays includes background and commentary on John Newbery by Townsend, edited chapters of Charles Welsh's 1885 biography of Newbery, and selections by Newbery contemporaries Samuel Johnson and George Coleman that give glimpses of this important figure in children's literature.

Townsend, John Rowe. *Written for Children: An Outline of English Children's Literature.* 4th ed., rev. New York: HarperCollins, 1990.

Townsend supplies a readable overview of the development of children's books in England and America, with a brief nod at Canada and Australia. His critical comments add interest to the text and help put the books in perspective. The survey ranges from before 1840 into the 1980s.

# *Children's Literature*

The references for this chapter are limited to books still in print as the 1990s ended. The dates in square brackets refer to the original publication of the text portion of the book.

Aamundsen, Nina Ring. *Two Short and One Long.* Houghton Mifflin, 1990.

Aardema, Verna. *Why Mosquitoes Buzz in People's Ears.* Illustrated by Leo and Diane Dillon. Dial, 1975.

Adoff, Arnold. *I Am the Darker Brother: An Anthology of Modern Poems by Negro Americans.* Macmillan, 1968.

Alcott, Louisa May. *An Old-Fashioned Girl.* Dell Yearling, 1987 [1870].

————. *Jo's Boys*. Penguin, 1984 [1873].

————. *Little Men*. Scholastic, 1987.

————. *Little Women*. Illustrated by Jessie Wilcox Smith. Little, 1968 [1868].

————. *Little Women*. Illustrated by James Prunier. Viking, 1997 [1868].

Alger, Horatio, Jr. *Struggling Upward*. Galloway, 1971 [n.d.].

Almond, David. *Skellig*. Delacorte, 1999.

Anno, Mitsumasa. *Anno's Journey*. Putnam, 1981 [1978].

Applegate, K. A. *The Threat (Animorphs #21)*. Scholastic, 1998.

Avi. *City of Light, City of Dark: A Comic Book Novel*. Illustrated by Brian Floca. Orchard, 1993.

————. *Nothing but the Truth*. Orchard, 1991.

Barrie, J. M. *Peter Pan in Kensington Gardens*. Illustrated by Arthur Rackham. Buccaneer Books, 1980 [1906].

Baum, L. Frank. *The Wizard of Oz*. Illustrated by Michael Hague. Holt, 1982 [1900].

Bealer, Alex. *Only the Names Remain: The Cherokees and the Trail of Tears*. Illustrated by William S. Bock. Little, Brown, 1972.

Belpré, Pura. *Perez and Martina: A Puerto Rican Folk Tale*. Illustrated by Carlos Sanchez. Viking, 1991 [1932].

Bemelmans, Ludwig. *Madeline*. Viking Penguin, 1958 [1939].

Beskow, Elsa. *Pelle's New Suit*. Harper & Row, 1929.

Blume, Judy. *Are You There God? It's Me, Margaret*. Bradbury Press, 1970.

————. *Blubber*. Bradbury Press, 1974.

————. *Deenie*. Bradbury Press, 1973.

Bontemps, Arna. *Bubber Goes to Heaven*. Illustrated by Daniel Minter. Oxford University Press, 1998.

Bontemps, Arna, and Langston Hughes. *The Pasteboard Bandit*. Illustrated by Peggy Turley. Oxford University Press, 1997.

————. *Popo and Fifina*. Illustrated by E. Simms Campbell. Oxford University Press, 1993 [1932].

Briggs, Raymond. *The Snowman*. Random House, 1978.

Brink, Carol Ryrie. *Caddie Woodlawn*. Macmillan, 1970 [1935].

Brooke, Leslie. *Johnny Crow's Garden*. Warne, 1986 [1903].

Brooks, Gwendolyn. *Bronzeville Boys and Girls*. Illustrated by Ronni Solbert. Harper & Row, 1956.

Brooks, Walter. *Freddy and the Perilous Adventure*. Illustrated by Leslie Morrill and Kurt Wiese. Knopf, 1986.

Brown, Marcia. *Cinderella*. Macmillan, 1954.

————. *Dick Whittington and His Cat*. Macmillan, 1988 [1950].

————. *Once a Mouse*. Macmillan, 1961.

————. *Stone Soup*. Macmillan, 1947.

Brown, Margaret Wise. *Goodnight Moon*. Illustrated by Clement Hurd. Harper & Row, 1947.

————. *The Little Fur Family*. Illustrated by Garth Williams. Harper & Row, 1985 [1946].

————. *The Noisy Book*. Illustrated by Leonard Weisgard. Harper & Row, 1939.

————. *The Runaway Bunny*. Illustrated by Clement Hurd. Harper & Row, 1942.

Bullard, Asa. *Sunnybank Stories: My Teacher's Gem*. Lee & Shepard, 1863.

Burnett, Frances Hodgson. *Little Lord Fauntleroy*. Godine, 1993 [1886].

————. *The Little Princess*. Illustrated by Jamichael Henterly. Grossett, 1995 [1905].

————. *Sara Crewe*. Scholastic, 1986 [1888].

————. *The Secret Garden*. Illustrated by Tasha Tudor. Harper & Row, 1987.

Burton, Virginia Lee. *The Little House*. Houghton Mifflin, 1978 [1942].

————. *Mike Mulligan and His Steam Shovel*. Houghton Mifflin, 1939.

Caldecott, Randolph. *Sing a Song of Sixpence*. Barron, 1988 [1880].

Canfield, Dorothy. *Understood Betsy*. Buccaneer, 1981 [1917].

Carlson, Natalie. *The Empty Schoolhouse*. Illustrated by John Kaufman. Harper & Row, 1965.

Carroll, Lewis [Charles Dodgson]. *Alice's Adventures in Wonderland*. Illustrated by Anthony Browne. Knopf, 1988 [1865].

————. *Alice's Adventure in Wonderland*. Illustrated by Helen Oxenbury. Candlewick, 1999 [1865].

————. *Through the Looking-Glass*. Illustrated by John Tenniel. St. Martin's Press, 1977 [1871].

Cleary, Beverly. *Dear Mr. Henshaw*. Illustrated by Paul O. Zelinsky. Morrow, 1983.

————. *Henry Huggins*. Illustrated by Louis Darling. Morrow, 1950.

————. *Ramona and Her Father*. Illustrated by Alan Tiergreen. Morrow, 1977.

Cleaver, Vera, and Bill Cleaver. *Grover*. Illustrated by Frederic Marvin. Harper & Row, 1970.

————. *Where the Lilies Bloom*. Lippincott, 1970.

Cole, Joanna. *The Magic School Bus Explores the Senses*. Illustrated by Bruce Degen. Scholastic, 1999.

Collier, James L., and Christopher Collier. *My Brother Sam Is Dead*. Macmillan, 1974.

Collodi, Carlo. *The Adventures of Pinocchio*. Illustrated by Roberto Innocenti. Knopf, 1988 [1891].

Conly, Jane Leslie. *Crazy Lady*. HarperCollins, 1993.

Cooney, Barbara. *Miss Rumphius*. Viking, 1982.

Cooper, James Fenimore. *The Last of the Mohicans*. Illustrated by N. C. Wyeth. Scribner's, 1986 [1826].

Cormier, Robert. *The Chocolate War*. Knopf, 1994 [1974].

Courlander, Harold, and Wolf Leslau. *The Fire on the Mountain: Stories from Ethiopia and Eritrea*. Illustrated by Robert Kane. Holt, 1995 [1950].

Cushman, Karen. *Catherine Called Birdy*. Clarion, 1995.

————. *The Midwife's Apprentice*. Clarion, 1995.

Dana, Richard Henry. *Two Years Before the Mast*. Airmont, 1985 [1840].

D'Aulaire, Ingri, and Edgar Parin d'Aulaire. *Abraham Lincoln*. Doubleday, 1957 [1939].

de la Mare, Walter. *Peacock Pie*. Illustrated by Edward Ardizzone. Faber & Faber, 1988 [1913].

————. *Songs of Childhood*. Dover, n.d. [1902].

de Paola, Tomie. *"Charlie Needs a Cloak."* Simon & Schuster, 1974.

de Saint-Exupéry, Antoine. *The Little Prince*. Harcourt Brace, 1943.

Dickinson, Emily. *Poems for Youth.* Illustrated by Doris Hauman and George Hauman. Little, 1934.

Disney, Walt (production staff). *Walt Disney's Cinderella.* Random House, 1974.

Dixon, Franklin W. *Absolute Zero (The Hardy Boy Casefiles, No 121).* Archway, 1997.

Dodge, Mary M. *Hans Brinker, or the Silver Skates.* Scholastic, 1988 [1865].

Donovan, John. *I'll Get There, It Better Be Worth the Trip.* Harper & Row, 1969.

Dorris, Michael. *Guests.* Hyperion, 1994.

Draper, Sharon. *Forged by Fire.* Simon & Schuster, 1997.

Ehlert, Lois. *Feathers for Lunch.* Harcourt Brace, 1990.

Enright, Elizabeth. *The Saturdays.* Holt, 1988.

———. *Thimble Summer.* Holt, 1938.

Erdrich, Louise. *The Birchbark House.* Hyperion, 1999.

Estes, Eleanor. *The Hundred Dresses.* Illustrated by Louis Slobodkin. Harcourt Brace, 1974 [1944].

———. *The Middle Moffats.* Dell, 1989 [1942].

———. *The Moffats.* Illustrated by Louis Slobodkin. Harcourt Brace, 1941.

———. *Rufus M.* Illustrated by Louis Slobodkin. Harcourt Brace, 1943.

Falls, C. B. *ABC Book.* Morrow, 1998 [1923].

Farjeon, Eleanor. *Eleanor Farjeon's Poems for Children.* Harper & Row, 1984 [1931, 1951].

Field, Eugene. *Poems of Childhood.* Armont, 1969 [1896].

Field, Rachel. *Prayer for a Child.* Illustrated by Elizabeth Orton Jones. Simon & Schuster, 1997 [1940].

Finger, Charles. *Tales from Silver Lands.* Illustrated by Paul Honore. Doubleday, 1965 [1924].

Fitzhugh, Louise. *Harriet the Spy.* Harper & Row, 1964.

Flack, Marjorie. *Angus and the Ducks.* Macmillan, 1989 [1930].

———. *Ask Mr. Bear.* Macmillan, 1986 [1932].

———. *The Story About Ping.* Illustrated by Kurt Wiese. Viking Penguin, 1933.

Flake, Sharon. *The Skin I'm In.* Hyperion, 1998.

Fleischman, Paul. *Seedfolks.* HarperCollins, 1997.

Forbes, Esther. *Johnny Tremain.* Illustrated by Lynd Ward. Houghton, 1943.

Fox, Paula. *The Slave Dancer.* Illustrated by Eros Keith. Bradbury, 1973.

Frank, Anne. *Anne Frank: The Diary of a Young Girl.* Rev. ed. Doubleday, 1967 [1952].

Freedman, Russell. *Lincoln: A Photobiography.* Clarion, 1987.

Fritz, Jean. *And Then What Happened, Paul Revere?* Illustrated by Margot Tomes. Putnam, 1973.

Frost, Robert. *You Come Too.* Illustrated by Thomas W. Nason. Holt, 1959.

Gág, Wanda. *Millions of Cats.* Putnam, 1928.

Gates, Doris. *Blue Willow.* Viking Penguin, 1940.

Giff, Patricia Reilly. *Kids of Polk Street School.* Delacorte, 1988.

Grahame, Kenneth. *The Wind in the Willows.* Illustrated by Ernest H. Shepard. Scribner's, 1983 [1908].

Gramatky, Hardie. *Little Toot.* Putnam, 1978 [1930].

Griffin, Adele. *The Other Shepards.* Hyperion, 1998.

Grimm, Jacob, and Wilhelm Grimm. *Grimm's Fairy Tales.* Illustrated by George Cruikshank. Dover, n.d. [1823].

Hale, Lucretia P. *The Peterkin Papers.* Sharon, 1981 [1880].

Hale, Sarah Josepha. *Mary Had a Little Lamb.* Illustrated by Tomie de Paola. Holiday House, 1984 [1830].

Haley, Gail. *A Story, a Story.* Atheneum, 1970.

Hamilton, Virginia. *M. C. Higgins the Great.* Macmillan, 1974.

———. *Zeely.* Illustrated by Simeon Shimin. Macmillan, 1967.

Hansen, Joyce. *I Thought My Soul Would Rise and Fly: The Diary of Patsy, a Freed Girl.* Scholastic, 1997.

Harris, Joel Chandler. *Uncle Remus.* Illustrated by A. B. Frost. Schocken, 1987 [1881].

Hawthorne, Nathaniel. *Tanglewood Tales.* Sharon, 1981 [1853].

———. *The Wonder Book for Boys and Girls.* White Rose, 1987 [1852].

Haywood, Carolyn. *B Is for Betsy.* Harcourt Brace, 1987 [1939].

Hesse, Karen. *The Music of Dolphins.* Scholastic, 1996.

———. *Out of the Dust.* Scholastic, 1997.

Hindley, Judy. *A Piece of String Is a Wonderful Thing.* Illustrated by Margaret Chamberlain. Candlewick, 1993.

Holling, C. *Paddle to the Sea.* Houghton Mifflin, 1980 [1941].

———. *Tree in the Trail.* Houghton Mifflin, 1990 [1942].

Hope, Laura L. *The Bobbsey Twins.* Simon & Schuster, 1990.

Hughes, Langston. *The Dream Keeper and Other Poems.* Illustrated by Brian Pinkney. Knopf, 1994 [1932].

Hurwitz, Johanna. *Russell Sprouts.* Illustrated by Lillian Hoban. Morrow, 1987.

Irving, Washington. *Sketch Book.* New American Library, 1961 [1819].

Isaacs, Anne. *Swamp Angel.* Illustrated by Paul O. Zelinsky. Dutton, 1994.

Jackson, Jesse. *Call Me Charley.* Illustrated by Doris Speigel. Harper & Row, 1945.

Jacobs, Joseph, ed. *Indian Fairy Tales.* Illustrated by John D. Batten. Roth, 1976 [1892].

Jacques, Brian. *Marlfox.* Putnam, 1999.

Jenkins, Steve. *The Top of the World: Climbing Mount Everest.* Houghton Mifflin, 1999.

Jones, Hettie. *The Trees Stand Shining: Poetry of the North American Indians.* Illustrated by Robert A. Parker. Dial, 1993 [1971].

Keats, Ezra Jack. *The Snowy Day.* Viking Penguin, 1962.

Kingsley, Charles. *The Water Babies.* Penguin, 1986 [1863].

Kipling, Rudyard. *The Jungle Books.* Illustrated by Fritz Eichenberg. Grossert, 1950 [1894–1895].

———. *Just So Stories.* Woodcuts by David Frampton. HarperCollins, 1991 [1902].

Konigsburg, E. L. *George.* Dell, 1985 [1970].

Lang, Andrew, ed. *The Blue Fairy Book.* Airmont, 1969 [1889].

Lasky, Katherine. *Dreams in a Golden Country: The Diary of Zipporah Feldman, a Jewish Immigrant Girl.* Scholastic, 1998.

———. *The Night Journey.* Illustrated by Trina Schart Hyman. Viking, 1986.

Lawson, Robert. *Rabbit Hill.* Viking Penguin, 1944.

————. *The Tough Winter.* Viking Penguin, 1979 [1954].

Leaf, Munro. *The Story of Ferdinand.* Illustrated by Robert Lawson. Viking, 1936.

Lear, Edward. *Nonsense Poems of Edward Lear.* Illustrated by Leslie Brook. Clarion, 1991.

L'Engle, Madeleine. *Meet the Austins.* Dell, 1981 [1960].

————. *A Wrinkle in Time.* Farrar, Straus & Giroux, 1962.

Lenski, Lois. *Judy's Journey.* Harper & Row, 1947.

————. *The Little Auto.* McKay, 1980 [1934].

————. *Strawberry Girl.* Harper & Row, 1988 [1945].

Leslie, Brooke. *A Nursery Rhyme Book.* Clarion, 1992 [1922].

Lester, Julius. *Iron John.* Illustrated by Jerry Pinkney. Dial, 1994.

Leverich, Kathleen. *Best Enemies.* Illustrated by Walter Lorraine. Morrow, 1989.

Lewis, C. S. *The Lion, the Witch, and the Wardrobe.* Illustrated by Pauline Baynes. Macmillan, 1988 [1950].

Lindgren, Astrid. *Pippi Longstocking.* Illustrated by Louis S. Glanzman. Translated by Florence Lambron. Viking Penguin, 1950.

Lindsay, Vachel. *Johnny Appleseed and Other Poems.* Buccaneer, 1981 [1928].

Lofting, Hugh. *The Story of Dr. Dolittle.* Delacorte, 1988 [1920].

————. *The Voyages of Dr. Dolittle.* Delacorte, 1988 [1922].

London, Jack. *The Call of the Wild.* Macmillan, 1963 [1903].

Lowry, Lois. *The Giver.* Houghton Mifflin, 1993.

Lunn, Janet. *The Root Cellar.* Macmillan, 1983.

Macaulay, David. *Black and White.* Houghton Mifflin, 1990.

————. *The Way Things Work.* Houghton Mifflin, 1988.

MacDonald, George. *At the Back of the North Wind.* Illustrated by Lauren Mills. Godine, 1988 [1871].

MacLachan, Patricia. *The Facts and Fictions of Minna Pratt.* Harper & Row, 1988.

————. *Sarah, Plain and Tall.* Harper & Row, 1985.

————. *Three Names.* Illustrated by Alexander Pertzoff. HarperCollins, 1991.

Martin, Ann. *The Baby-Sitters Remember.* Scholastic, 1994.

Maruki, Toshi. *Hiroshima No Pika* (The Flash of Hiroshima). Lothrop, Lee & Shepard, 1980.

McCloskey, Robert. *Homer Price.* Viking Penguin, 1943.

————. *Make Way for Ducklings.* Viking Penguin, 1941.

McDermott, Beverly Brodsky. *The Golem.* Lippincott, 1976.

McDermott, Gerald. *Anansi the Spider.* Holt, 1972.

McKee, David, *I Can Too.* Lothrop, Lee & Shepard, 1997.

McKissack, Patricia C., and Frederick L. McKissack. *Christmas in the Big House, Christmas in the Quarters.* Illustrated by John Thompson. Scholastic, 1994.

Millay, Edna St. Vincent. *Edna St. Vincent Millay's Poems Selected for Young People.* Illustrated by Ronald Keller. Harper & Row, 1979 [1917].

Milne, A. A. *Now We Are Six.* Illustrated by Ernest H. Shepard. Dutton, 1988 [1927].

————. *When We Were Very Young.* Illustrated by Ernest H. Shepard. Dutton, 1988 [1924].

————. *Winnie the Pooh.* Illustrated by Ernest H. Shepard. Dutton, 1988 [1926].

Monjo, F. N. *Poor Richard in France.* Dell, 1990 [1973].

Montgomery, L. M. *Anne of Green Gables.* Bantam, 1976 [1908].

Moore, Clement. *The Night Before Christmas.* Illustrated by Jan Brett. Putnam, 1998 [1823].

Murphy, Jim. *My Name Is America: The Journal of James Edmund Pease, a Civil War Union Soldier.* Scholastic, 1998.

Myers, Walter Dean. *The Glory Field.* Scholastic, 1994.

————. *Monster.* Illustrated by Christopher Myers. Scholastic, 1999.

————. *My Name Is America: The Journal of Joshua Loper, a Black Cowboy.* Scholastic, 1998.

Naidoo, Beverley. *Journey to Jo'burg.* Illustrated by Eric Velasquez. Harper & Row, 1986.

Naylor Phyllis Reynolds. *Achingly Alice.* Atheneum, 1999.

————. *Shiloh.* Atheneum, 1991.

Nelson, Theresa. *Earthshine.* Orchard, 1994.

Nesbit, E. *The Enchanted Castle.* Illustrated by Paul O. Zelinsky. Morrow, 1992 [1907].

Nister, Ernest. *The Animals' Picnic.* Putnam, 1988 [reissue].

Onyefulu, Ifeoma. *Emeka's Gift: An African Counting Story.* Cobblehill, 1995.

Oxenbury, Helen. *Dressing.* Simon & Schuster, 1981.

————. *Family.* Simon & Schuster, 1981.

————. *Friends.* Simon & Schuster, 1981.

————. *Playing.* Simon & Schuster, 1981.

————. *Working.* Simon & Schuster, 1981.

Paulsen, Gary. *Brian's Return.* Delacorte, 1999.

Pearce, Philippa. *Tom's Midnight Garden.* Harper & Row, 1984 [1959].

Pfister, Marcus. *The Rainbow Fish.* North-South, 1992.

Pinkwater, Daniel. *The Muffin Fiend.* Lothrop, Lee & Shepard, 1986.

Piper, Watty. *The Little Engine That Could.* Putnam, 1990 [1929].

Porte, Barbara Ann. *Something Terrible Happened.* Orchard, 1994.

Porter, Eleanor H. *Pollyanna.* Yearling Classics, 1987 [1913].

Potter, Beatrix. *Jemima Puddle-Duck.* Warne, 1994 [1908].

————. *The Tale of Peter Rabbit.* Warne, 1972 [1902].

Pritsch, Patricia Curtis. *Keeper of the Light.* Simon & Schuster, 1997.

Pullman, Philip. *The Golden Compass.* Knopf, 1996.

Pyle, Howard. *The Merry Adventures of Robin Hood of Great Renown.* Dover, 1968 [1883].

————. *The Story of King Arthur and His Knights.* Scribner's, 1984 [1903].

————. *The Wonder Clock.* Dover, n.d. [1888].

Rapp, Adam. *The Buffalo Tree.* Front Street, 1997.

Raschka, Chris. *Yo! Yes?* Orchard, 1993.

Reid, Barbara. *The Party.* Scholastic, 1999.

Rey, H. A. *Curious George.* Houghton Mifflin, 1973 [1941].

Richter, Hans. *Friedrich.* Penguin, 1987 [1970].

Rosales, Melodye Benson. *Leola and the Honeybears.* Scholastic, 1999.

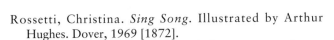

Rossetti, Christina. *Sing Song*. Illustrated by Arthur Hughes. Dover, 1969 [1872].

Rowling, J. K. *Harry Potter and the Sorcerer's Stone*. Scholastic, 1998.

Ruskin, John. *King of the Golden River*. Illustrated by Richard Doyle. Dover, 1974 [1851].

Rylant, Cynthia. *When I Was Young in the Mountains*. Illustrated by Diane Goode. Dutton, 1982.

Sabuda, Robert. *The Movable Mother Goose*. Simon & Schuster, 1999.

Sandburg, Carl. *Early Moon*. Illustrated by James Daughterty. Harcourt Brace, 1978 [1930].

Sawyer, Ruth. *Roller Skates*. Illustrated by Valenti Angelo. Penguin, 1986 [1936].

Scieszka, Jon. *The True Story of the 3 Little Pigs as Told by A. Wolf*. Illustrated by Lane Smith. Viking, 1989.

Scott, Walter. *Ivanhoe*. Airmont, 1964 [1820].

Sendak, Maurice. *In The Night Kitchen*. Harper & Row, 1970.

———. *Where the Wild Things Are*. Harper & Row, 1988 [1963].

Seton, Ernest Thompson. *Wild Animals I Have Known*. Creative Arts, 1987 [1898].

Seuss, Dr. [Theodor S. Geisel]. *And to Think That I Saw It on Mulberry Street*. Random House, 1989 [1937].

———. *The Cat in the Hat*. Random House, 1957.

Sewell, Anna. *Black Beauty*. Grosset, 1945 [1877].

Sherlock, Philip. *Anansi: The Spider Man*. Illustrated by Marcia Brown. Harper & Row, 1954.

Sidney, Margaret. *Five Little Peppers and How They Grew*. Puffin, 1990 [1881].

Silverstein, Shel. *Where the Sidewalk Ends*. Harper & Row, 1974.

Smith, E. Boyd. *The Railroad Book*. Houghton Mifflin, 1983 [1913].

———. *The Seashore Book*. Houghton Mifflin, 1985 [1912].

Spyri, Johanna. *Heidi*. Illustrated by Troy Howell. Messner, 1982 [1884].

Steptoe, John. *Stevie*. Harper & Row, 1969.

Stevenson, Robert Louis. *A Child's Garden of Verses*. Illustrated by Michael Foreman. Delacorte, 1985 [1885].

———. *Treasure Island*. Illustrated by N. C. Wyeth. Scribner's, 1981 [1883].

Stolz, Mary. *The Bully of Barkham Street*. Illustrated by Leonard Shortall. Harper & Row, 1985 [1963].

———. *A Dog on Barkham Street*. Illustrated by Leonard Shortall. Harper & Row, 1985 [1960].

Taylor, Mildred. *Roll of Thunder, Hear My Cry*. Illustrated by Jerry Pinkney. Dell, 1976.

Taylor, Sydney. *All-of-a-Kind Family*. Illustrated by John Helen. Dell, 1980 [1951].

Thurber, James. *Many Moons*. Illustrated by L. Slobodkin. Harcourt Brace, 1943.

———. *Many Moons*. Illustrated by Marc Simont. Harcourt Brace, 1990 [1943].

Tolkien, J. R. R. *The Hobbit*. Illustrated by Michael Hague. Houghton Mifflin, 1989 [1937].

Travers, P. L. *Mary Poppins*. Harcourt, 1934.

Trelease, Jim. *The Read-Aloud Handbook*. Penguin, 1995.

Tresselt, Alvin. *White Snow, Bright Snow*. Illustrated by Roger Duvoisin. Lothrop, Lee & Shepard, 1989 [1947].

Twain, Mark [Samuel Clemens]. *The Adventures of Huckleberry Finn*. Scholastic, 1982 [1884].

———. *The Adventures of Tom Sawyer*. Illustrated by Barry Moser. Morrow, 1989 [1876].

Uchida, Yoshiko. *The Dancing Kettle and Other Japanese Folk Tales*. Creative Arts, 1986 [1949].

———. *Journey to Topaz*. Illustrated by Donald Carrick. Scribner's, 1971.

———. *The Magic Listening Cap*. Creative Arts, 1987 [1955].

Udry, Janice May. *Let's Be Enemies*. Illustrated by Maurice Sendak. Harper & Row, 1961.

Van Loon, Hendrik. *The Story of Mankind*. Updated in a new version for the 1980s. Liveright, 1985 [1921].

Verne, Jules. *Around the World in Eighty Days*. Illustrated by Barry Moser. Morrow, 1988 [1872].

———. *Journey to the Center of the Earth*. Penguin, 1986 [1864].

———. *Twenty Thousand Leagues Under the Sea*. Airmont, 1964 [1869].

Voigt, Cynthia. *Homecoming*. Atheneum, 1981.

Walter, Virginia and Katrina Roeckelein. *Making Up Megaboy*. Delacorte, 1998.

White, E. B. *Charlotte's Web*. Illustrated by Garth Williams. Harper & Row, 1952.

Wiesner, David. *Tuesday*. Clarion, 1991.

Wiggin, Kate Douglas. *Rebecca of Sunnybrook Farm*. Penguin, 1986 [1903].

Wilder, Laura Ingalls. *Little House in the Big Woods*. Illustrated by Garth Williams. Harper & Row, 1953 [1932].

Willard, Nancy. *A Visit to William Blake's Inn*. Illustrated by Alice and Martin Provensen. Harcourt Brace, 1981.

Williams, Margery. *The Velveteen Rabbit*. Illustrated by David Jorgensen. Knopf, 1985 [1922].

———. *The Velveteen Rabbit*. Illustrated by Ilse Plume. Harcourt Brace, 1987 [1922].

———. *The Velveteen Rabbit*. Illustrated by Michael Hague. Holt, 1983 [1922].

———. *The Velveteen Rabbit*. Illustrated by William Nicholson. Doubleday, 1969 [1922].

Wyss, Johann. *The Swiss Family Robinson*. Sharon, 1981 [1814].

Yep, Laurence. *Dragon's Gate*. HarperCollins, 1993.

Yolen, Jane. *The Devil's Arithmetic*. Viking, 1988.

Yumoto, Kazumi. *The Friends*. Illustrated by Cathy Hirano. Farrar, Straus & Giroux, 1996.

Zemach, Margot. *It Could Always Be Worse*. Farrar, Straus & Giroux, 1990 [1977].

# Part Two

## Exploring Children's Literature

# Chapter Four

# Books to Begin On

*One of our colleagues is a proud new grandfather. Every time we meet him, he regales us with tales of his granddaughter's progress in "reading"—Laura is 18 months old. However, he is determined that Laura will grow into reading as naturally as she is learning to speak.*

So he floods her house with books; he mixes books with her blocks so she will think of them as toys; he built her a special bookshelf for her books; he bought a miniature supermarket basket that he filled with books so she can have books available in every room in the house; he takes her to the library frequently. Of course, whenever he visits he is greeted with the welcome words, "Grandpapa, read!" And he always does. Laura's mother and father read to her also, so it is not unusual for Laura to hear six to ten stories a day.

Laura has favorite books, which she can readily find, and she asks to hear them over and over again. She relates books to her own life. Each night when she hears *Goodnight Moon* by Margaret Wise Brown, she softly whispers, "Night night, chair, night night, Bear." Laura's grandfather is achieving his purpose. Laura is learning to love books and learning to read naturally in the process.

## Developing Initial Literacy

What a lot Laura already knows about books and reading at 18 months! First, she knows books are enjoyable, and she even has particular favorites. She also knows that adults hold the key to reading and can give meaning to the text. She herself knows how to hold a book and that it has to be right-side-up to read the print. She is beginning to relate books to her own life. If at 18 months she knows this much about how to read a book, think what she will know when she enters school.

At a year and a half, Laura already has entered the world of literature. She is learning to love books, as she has many opportunities to snuggle up close to her mother, father, and grandfather for story time. She is also increasing her vocabulary as she points to pictures and names them or hears new words used in the context of the story. The language development of children at this age is phenomenal; preoccupation with words and the sounds of language is characteristic of the very young child. Books help to fulfill this insatiable desire to hear and learn new words. Hearing literature of good quality helps children to develop to their full language potential.

Children cannot be introduced to books too soon. The human baby is attuned to various sound patterns almost from the moment of birth. She will be startled by a cross word or a loud noise, soothed by a gentle loving voice or a softly sung lullaby. Gradually the baby begins to develop comprehension skills as she attaches meaning to the sounds around her. Talk is essential at this time, and the special language of books is especially important. One parent read a best-selling novel to her infant son just so he could hear the sound of her voice. Primarily, however, the very young child listens for the "quack quack" of a duck in a picture book or the "roar" of a lion. Singing simple nursery

*Research suggests that one of the most important gifts a family can give to children is an early love of books.*
Photo by Larry Rose.

*Two toddlers share the joys of reading.*
Photo by Lisa Wright.

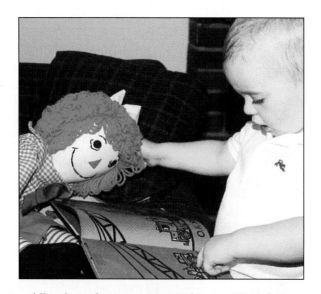

*A toddler shares his interest in* Machines at Work *by Byron Barton with his Raggedy Andy.*
Photo by Susan Fertig.

rhymes or playing such finger rhymes as "This little pig went to market" will make the baby giggle with delight. Increasingly, publishers are producing books for babies' enjoyment, for, in Dorothy Butler's words, "Babies need books."[1]

The young child who has the opportunity to hear and enjoy many stories is also beginning to learn to read. No one taught Laura how to hold a book or where to begin to read the text. Through constant exposure to stories, Laura is learning about book handling and developing some beginning concepts about the print.[2] She is spontaneously learning some of the attitudes, concepts, and skills needed to become literate, including a positive attitude toward books, an understanding about the sense-making aspect of stories, the stability of print to tell the same story each time, and the form and structure of written language itself. All of this learning occurs at the pre-reading stage and seems to be essential for later success in reading.[3]

We have previously discussed, in Chapter 1, the research that shows the importance of books in the young child's life. It is clear that hearing many stories in the preschool years can have lasting benefit for children. Boys and girls who enter school having had many experiences with books are well prepared to acquire literacy,[4] and these children are more likely to remain active readers well into late elementary and middle school.

During the times in which they share books with their young children, parents appear to use consistent language patterns when labeling objects in a picture book. Even before the baby can talk, the child and mother (or father) take turns engaging in a dialogue and collaboratively make meaning out of the text. As they read Margaret Wise Brown's *Goodnight Moon* over the course of many bedtimes, the mother points to a picture and says, "Can you find the red balloon? Where's the mouse?" and the baby delightedly points to these tiny objects. As the child acquires a simple vocabulary, the parent might ask, "What's this?" or respond to the same query from the child with the name of the object. This book-reading context is unique because the attention of both participants is focused on pictures and words that stay the same for each rereading. Thus the child can predict the story and build up vocabulary over numerous readings.

Early exposure to books and plenty of time for talk and enjoyment of the story appear, then, to be

---

[1]Dorothy Butler, *Babies Need Books* (New York: Atheneum, 1980).

[2]See Marie Clay, *An Observation Survey of Early Literacy* (Portsmouth, N.H.: Heinemann, 1993) for a description of her Concepts About Print test.

[3]Don Holdaway, *The Foundations of Literacy* (Sydney: Ashton Scholastic, 1979).

[4]Gordon Wells, *The Meaning Makers: Children Learning Language and Using Language to Learn* (Portsmouth, N.H.: Heinemann Educational Books, 1986), p. 151 (emphasis added).

key factors in the child's acquisition of literacy.[5] One father whose child has been exposed to books from infancy said, "You know, I haven't the slightest doubt that David will learn to read, any more than I was concerned that he would talk." The Web, "Learning to Read Naturally" provides a picture of the types of experiences with books that can naturally lead young children to literacy.

## Babies' First Books

First books for young children are frequently identification books, "naming books," or books with simple narrative lines that allow a child to point to one picture after another, demanding to know "wha dat?" It is probably this give-and-take of language between the adult and the child that makes sharing books at this age so important. Recognizing the need for the young child to identify and name objects, publishers have produced many of these simple, sturdy "first books." The growth of good books for babies and toddlers was a publishing phenomenon of the 1980s and 1990s. As part of the interest in books for babies, publishers reissued well-known nursery classics or enlisted well-known illustrators or writers in creating series of baby books. In addition, publishers have enlisted well-known authors and illustrators of many cultures to create books for preschoolers. Eloise Greenfield's *Water Water* illustrated by Jan Spivey Gilchrist and Pat Cummings's *Purrrr* are among the well-written texts with lively illustrations created for ages birth to 3 by HarperCollins. Books for this age group need to be well constructed with heavy laminated cardboard or plastic pages that will withstand teeth or sticky fingers. Illustrations should be simple, uncluttered, and easily identifiable.

Tana Hoban's photographic concept books such as *What Is It?* and *Red, Blue, Yellow Shoe* present clear, colored photographs of familiar objects like a sock, a shoe, a bib, a cup, and a spoon. Only one object is pictured on a page, shown against a plain white background, in these sturdy first books. Hoban's *Black on White* and *White on Black* picture everyday objects in high contrast and are aimed at very young infants.

Helen Oxenbury has a series of Baby Board Books titled *Playing, Dressing, Working, Friends,* and *Family.* These books feature a delightfully droll roundheaded infant doing what toddlers do, such as banging on pots, messily eating food, or sitting on the potty. A single noun such as *bowl, potty,* or *dog* represents the action

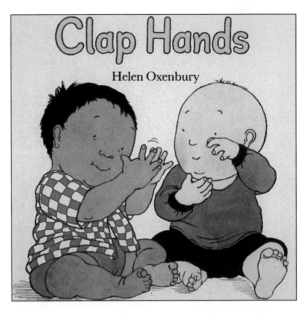

*Delightful babies of different racial backgrounds play together happily in* Clap Hands *by Helen Oxenbury.*

From *Clap Hands* by Helen Oxenbury, copyright © 1987 Helen Oxenbury. Reprinted with permission of Little Simon, an imprint of Simon & Schuster Children's Publishing Division. Reprinted with permission of Walker Books Ltd., London.

on the page in much the same way that the young child uses a single word to carry the force of a sentence. The simplicity of the illustrations is just right for the audience—plain white backgrounds, clearly outlined figures, single-focus composition, attractive but not distracting color. In *Tickle Tickle, Clap Hands* and *Say Goodnight,* the author-artist portrays wonderful babies of several races playing together. Oxenbury continues the exploration of the toddler's world in her Baby Board series with *I Can, I Hear, I See,* and *I Touch.*

Brian and Andrea Davis Pinkney have collaborated on four board books that celebrate African American families and culture: *I Smell Honey, Pretty Brown Face, Shake Shake Shake,* and *Watch Me Dance.* Angela Johnson's four Joshua books—*Joshua by the Sea, Joshua's Night Whispers, Rain Feet,* and *Mama Bird, Baby Birds*—also feature an African American boy. With their poetic text and satisfying emotional vignettes, these are sure to keep parents and toddlers interested through repeated readings.

Rosemary Wells's little board books about Max, a lovable rabbity creature, are labeled "Very First Books." However, the humor is for slightly older toddlers. In *Max's First Word,* Max's sister tries to get him to talk. She names everything she shows him, and Max always responds with "Bang." Giving him an apple, Ruby suggests he say "Yum, yum," but Max surprises her with "Delicious." Other stories continue big sister Ruby's struggle to get Max to eat an egg for breakfast, take a bath, and go to bed. Max manages to outsmart her at every move.

[5]See Susan B. Newman. "Books Make a Difference: A Study of Access to Literacy," *Reading Research Quarterly* 34, no. 3 (July–September, 1999): 286–311.

# LEARNING TO READ NATURALLY: A WEB OF POSSIBILITIES

## PLAYING WITH PATTERNS

Beginning readers need support from predictable patterns in texts.

**Refrains and Repetition**
Teeny Tiny (Bennett)
Chicken Soup with Rice (Sendak)
A Dark, Dark Tale (Brown)
Snow on Snow on Snow (Chapman)

**Cumulative Tales**
One Fine Day (Hogrogian)
The Napping House (Wood)
The Cake That Mack Ate (Robart)

**ABC's and 1,2,3's**
Chicka Chicka Boom Boom (Martin)
Alligator Arrived with Apples (Dragonwagon)
On Market Street (Lobel)
Feast for Ten (Falwell)
Big Fat Hen (Baker)

## CALLING ATTENTION TO PRINT

Beginning readers need to develop concepts about letters, letter sounds and words.

**Look at Letters and Words**
A, B, See (Hoban)
Alphabet City (Johnson)
Small Green Snake (Gray)
Meow! (Arnold)

**Use labels and signs**
I Read Signs (Hoban)
I Read Symbols (Hoban)

**Add your own labels in your classroom.**

**Collect Words on a Word Wall**
Scary words
Noisy words
Holiday words

**Sort words that look alike**

## MAKING BOOKS

Beginning readers need many opportunities to write.

Make Big Books from favorite class books.
Draw pictures to match the printed words.
Collaborate on the writing of a book about a class trip or a special holiday.
Collect a personal library of photo-copied books of favorite nursery rhymes.
Collect wallpaper and make books for dictated writing.
Create shape books for special writing (trucks, giraffes).

## PLAYING WITH SOUNDS

Beginning readers need many opportunities to play with the sounds of language.

Buzz, Buzz, Buzz (Barton)
The Cow That Went Oink (Most)
The Piggy in the Puddle (Pomerantz)
Here Comes Henny (Pomerantz)

## LINKING EXPERIENCES TO BOOKS

Beginning readers need books that match their own experiences.

**Being Little**
Titch (Hutchins)
The Biggest Boy (Henkes)

**New Babies**
When The New Baby Comes I'm Moving Out (Alexander)
She Come Bring Me That Little Baby Girl (Greenfield)

**Changes**
Will I Have a Friend? (Cohen)
Pablo's Tree (Mora)

**Losing Control**
When Sophie Gets Angry—Really, Really Angry (Bang)
No David! (Shannon)

## CELEBRATE BEING A READER

Beginning readers need to be part of a reading and writing community.

Share a favorite book with a reading partner. Have a book character parade. Prepare a literary lunch.

Stone Soup (Brown)
Chicken Soup With Rice (Sendak)
Pancakes, Pancakes! (Carle)
The Little Red Hen (Makes A Pizza) (Struges)

## HAVING FUN WITH PICTURES

Beginning readers can apply reading strategies to pictures before they are able to read words.

Find the hidden clues that artists include in their pictures.

We Hide You Seek (Aruego)
Each Peach, Pear, Plum (Ahlberg)
The Alphabet Tale (Garten)

Read stories in wordless books.
Dictate or rewrite the story in your own words.

Truck (Crews)
Pancakes For Breakfast (dePaola)
School (McCully)
A Boy A Dog and A Frog (Meyer)
Magpie Magic (Wilson)

## READING TO FIND OUT

Beginning readers need experiences with nonfiction.

Flash, Crash, Rumble And Roll (Branley)
All Pigs Are Beautiful (King-Smith)
Zipping, Zapping, Zooming Bats (Earle)
My Five Senses (Aliki)

## BOOKS TO BEGIN READING

Beginning readers can practice reading in books with limited vocabulary.

Freight Train (Crews)
Titch (Hutchins)
Brown Bear, Brown Bear, What Do You See? (Martin)
Sheep in a Jeep (Shaw)

## "READING" FAMILIAR TEXTS

Beginning readers can gain confidence by reading books that they already know well.

**Favorite Songs**
The Wheels on the Bus (Zelinsky)
Over in the Meadow (Langstaff)
I Know an Old Lady Who Swallowed a Fly (Taback)
The Farmer in the Dell (Wallner)

**Memorable Stories**
The Very Hungry Caterpillar (Carle)
Good Night Moon (Brown)
Where the Wild Things Are (Sendak)
Owl Babies (Waddell)

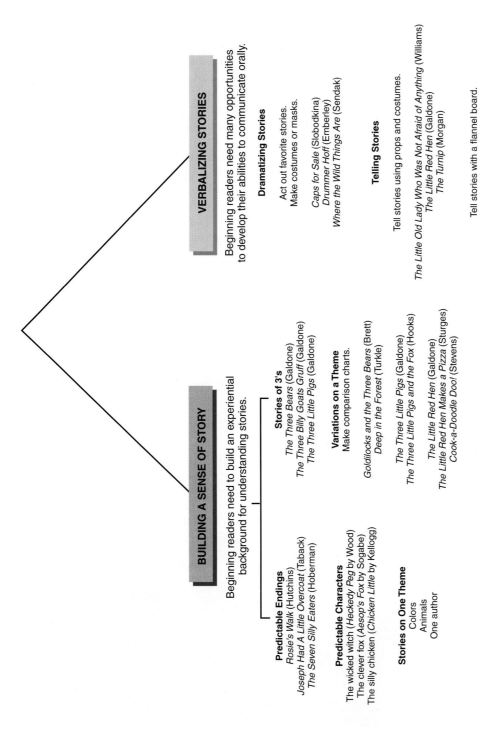

**BUILDING A SENSE OF STORY**

Beginning readers need to build an experiential background for understanding stories.

**Predictable Endings**
*Rosie's Walk* (Hutchins)
*Joseph Had A Little Overcoat* (Taback)
*The Seven Silly Eaters* (Hoberman)

**Predictable Characters**
The wicked witch (*Heckedy Peg* by Wood)
The clever fox (*Aesop's Fox* by Sogabe)
The silly chicken (*Chicken Little* by Kellogg)

**Stories on One Theme**
Colors
Animals
One author

**Stories of 3's**
*The Three Bears* (Galdone)
*The Three Billy Goats Gruff* (Galdone)
*The Three Little Pigs* (Galdone)

**Variations on a Theme**
Make comparison charts.

*Goldilocks and the Three Bears* (Brett)
*Deep in the Forest* (Turkle)

*The Three Little Pigs* (Galdone)
*The Three Little Pigs and the Fox* (Hooks)

*The Little Red Hen* (Galdone)
*The Little Red Hen Makes a Pizza* (Sturges)
*Cook-a-Doodle Doo!* (Stevens)

**VERBALIZING STORIES**

Beginning readers need many opportunities to develop their abilities to communicate orally.

**Dramatizing Stories**

Act out favorite stories.
Make costumes or masks.

*Caps for Sale* (Slobodkina)
*Drummer Hoff* (Emberley)
*Where the Wild Things Are* (Sendak)

**Telling Stories**

Tell stories using props and costumes.

*The Little Old Lady Who Was Not Afraid of Anything* (Williams)
*The Little Red Hen* (Galdone)
*The Turnip* (Morgan)

Tell stories with a flannel board.

*The Gingerbread Baby* (Brett)
*It Could Always Be Worse* (Zemach)
*The Mitten* (Brett)

There are many fine picture books that appeal to babies and toddlers and that introduce them to the rhythms and forms of literature from an early age. These are often the books that, like Margaret Wise Brown's *Goodnight Moon*, become bedtime classics although they don't have to be about going to sleep. Favorites with toddlers include Robert Kraus's *Whose Mouse Are You?*, Vera Williams's *"More More More," Said the Baby*, Trish Cooke's *So Much*, illustrated by Helen Oxenbury, and Eve Merriam's *What in the World?* illustrated by Barbara J. Phillips-Duke. These are books that often invite babies' participation in the form of finding hidden objects in the pictures, repeating simple refrains like "more, more, more" or "so much," or getting tummy tickles and hugs and kisses.

## Toy Books

Young children can respond to a book by pointing or labeling, but some books have a kind of "built-in participation" as part of their design. These books have flaps to lift up and peek under, soft flannel to touch, or holes to poke fingers through. Such books can serve as the transition between toys and real books. *Pat the Bunny* by Dorothy Kunhardt has been a bestseller for very young children for more than fifty years. In this little book the child is invited to use senses other than sight and sound. A "pattable" bunny made of flannel is on one page, and Daddy's unshaven face, represented by rough sandpaper, is on another. Young children literally wear out this tactile

book. Kunhardt's daughter Edith has created a sequel to this classic called *Pat the Puppy*.

An increasing number of sophisticated cutout books and lift-the-flap stories are appearing on the market. Lucy Cousins's Maisy is the appealing mouse heroine in many books. In *Maisy Goes to Bed*, Maisy goes to a potty that "flushes," puts on her pajamas, and ends up in bed reading a bedtime book. Eric Hill's lift-the-flap stories about the dog Spot never fail to intrigue young children. In *Where's Spot?* Spot's mother, Sally, searches for her puppy behind a door, inside a clock, under the stairs, in the piano, and under the rug. As the child opens doors and lifts up flaps to join in the search, highly unlikely creatures such as monkeys, snakes, and lions answer no to the question "Is he in here?" Since *no* is one of 2-year-olds' favorite words, they love to chime in on the refrain. These books are sturdily made, the pictures are bright and clear, and the stories are imaginative. Other titles in the series include *Goodnight Spot* and *Spot Goes to School*. These books are also available in Spanish editions.

Eric Carle's story *The Very Hungry Caterpillar* is a favorite with children ages 3 through 6. This imaginative tale describes the life cycle of a ravenous caterpillar who leaves behind a trail of holes in all the food that he eats. Children love to stick their fingers through the holes and count them. In Carle's multisensory story *The Very Busy Spider*, children are invited to feel the pictures as well as see them. Brilliant collages depict familiar animals whose questions are never answered by the spider, who is too busy spinning her tactile web. Carle's *The Very Quiet Cricket*, *The Very Clumsy Click Beetle*, and *The Very Lonely*

*Lucy Cousins recreates familiar bedtime scenes in* Maisy Goes to Bed.

From *Maisy Goes to Bed* by Lucy Cousins. Copyright © 1990 by Lucy Cousins. By permission of Little, Brown & Company, (Inc).

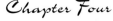

## GUIDELINES

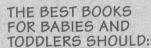

# *Evaluating Books for the Very Young Child*

**THE BEST BOOKS FOR BABIES AND TODDLERS SHOULD:**

Relate to familiar life experiences
Provide clear uncluttered illustrations with little or no
  distracting background
Be well constructed with sturdy, durable pages

Use clear, natural language
Have predictable stories
Provide some humor, especially so the child will feel
  superior
Offer opportunities for participation and interaction
Hold the child's attention

---

*Firefly* have technological support that brings each tale to its conclusion. The sound of the cricket and the click beetle coming from a computer chip imbedded in the pages of the cricket and beetle books and tiny blinking lights in the fireflies' bodies surprise and delight children in these multisensory books.

Books that describe different kinds of sounds invite their own special kind of noisy participation. *Early Morning in the Barn* by Nancy Tafuri begins with a large double-page spread picturing a rooster waking the barnyard with his "cock-a-doodle-doo," which awakens his brother and sister. All three run out of the hen house into the barnyard, where they are greeted by an array of animals each making their familiar noise. Kevin Lewis's *Chugga-Chugga Choo-Choo,* illustrated by Daniel Kirk, incorporates the rhythm and pacing of an exciting train ride with plenty of opportunity for toddlers to join in on the "Whoo-whoo" of the whistle. Bright sunny pictures add to the fun of these noisy books.

If a book does not provide for participation, the adult reader can stimulate it by the kinds of questions he or she asks. For example, when sharing the old favorite *Caps for Sale* by Esphyr Slobodkina, the parent might say to the child, "Find the monkey—not the one in the red hat, not the one in the blue hat, but the one in the green hat!" Such participation will help children develop visual discrimination and introduce the child to important aspects of conversational patterns. More importantly, it will add to the fun of the story time. The Guidelines box "Evaluating Books for the Very Young Child" lists criteria for the best books for infants and toddlers.

# *Finger Rhymes & Nursery Songs*

Finger rhymes are one traditional way to provide for young children's participation as they play "Five Lit-tle Pigs" or sing "Where Is Thumbkin?" and the ever popular "Eensy, Weensy Spider." Finger plays date back to the time of Friedrich Froebel, the so-called father of the kindergarten movement, who collected the finger plays and games that the peasant mothers in the German countryside were using with their children. Priscilla Lamont's *Playtime Rhymes* has amusing illustrations to accompany the twenty-two finger plays and includes photos of children of different ages and races engaged in the action.

Babies and young toddlers often first respond to the sounds of music and singing. Aliki's spirited song *Go Tell Aunt Rhody* is a bit of authentic Americana that will be familiar to many parents. Starting with brilliant endpapers of quilt blocks, this illustrated songbook tells the familiar tale of the death of the old gray goose. The gander and the goslings mourn the death of the old gray goose, but Aunt Rhody is pleased indeed with her new feather bed. Marla Frazee has created a highly imaginative realization of a familiar Appalachia lullaby in *Hush Little Baby.* Pencil and ink illustrations evoke a pioneer setting and spirit as two frantic parents try to calm a squalling baby. An older sister, who is at first jealous of the attention, grows into a caring sister as she enlists an old peddler in finding just the right object to quiet the child. The printed text and background color alternate to highlight the repeated refrain, a nice touch for drawing the young child's attention to words. Jakki Wood and Melissa Sweet have both illustrated *Fiddle-I-Fee,* another American folksong with a cumulative pattern that children enjoy. Sweet's version shows a little boy trying to feed the animals on his farm. As each animal is fed, it joins an ever longer parade through the countryside. When the boy's bucket is empty, his parents appear on a tractor and drive everyone back to the farm house for a final feast. Wood's version has less narrative and focuses on close-ups of a blonde-haired child and the animals. It also ends with an owl rather than a cow.

Children love to make up additional verses to the rollicking old folksong adapted by John Langstaff in *Oh, A-Hunting We Will Go*. Nancy Winslow Parker's childlike illustrations are carefully arranged so as not to give away the last lines of each verse. Once children have determined the pattern of the song, they can guess what will be seen in the next picture. They easily predict the goat will end up "in a boat," but they laugh at the bear who gets put "in underwear."

Counting rhymes have also been made into individual songbooks. *Roll Over!* by Merle Peek shows a little boy in bed with nine animals. Each time they roll over, one animal falls out of bed. As the number of animals in the bed dwindles, children can look to see where they have found resting places in the room. Finally, when only the boy is asleep in his bed, a lion in a picture in his room appears to be winking and all the other animals are seen on a wall frieze that rings the ceiling. The music accompanies this tale of a young child's imaginary game.

Ezra Jack Keats illustrated an old counting song in *Over in the Meadow* with collage pictures in jewel-like colors. The fine recording by Marvin Hayes increases children's enjoyment of the lilt and rhythm of this favorite nursery song. Other versions have been retold by John Langstaff and Paul Galdone.

Christopher Manson used an 1898 book of nursery rhymes and songs as the source for his version of *The Tree in the Wood*, "the finest tree that you ever did see, and the green grass grew all around." In this cumulative song, each new addition to the verse is highlighted and framed on the right-hand page and the words are framed to the left. Manson's hand-painted woodcuts add a lovely antique feel to this familiar song.

In *The Fox Went Out on a Chilly Night*, Peter Spier's setting for the nursery rhyme song portrays the colorful autumn countryside outside of a New England village. Shimmering moonlit pictures won this book a Caldecott Honor Award. The complete text of the song is provided at the end of the book. Youngsters can sing along with a second sharing of the story or join in while viewing the excellent filmstrip from Weston Woods.

Children have their choice of many editions of *Old MacDonald Had a Farm*. Rosemary Wells has created a board-book version for younger readers that invites toddlers to suggest more animal noises to put in the song. By way of contrast, Glen Rounds uses bold primitive drawings to depict his bowlegged farmer and angular animals, including a skunk! Amy Schwartz has a modern-day, young farmer MacDonald and his extended family with animal sounds written in colors to call attention to the print. Carol Jones creates a peephole on each page of her engaging version. The first peephole view shows just a part of a chicken. Turn the page and you see the whole chicken in the hen house.

In *I Know an Old Lady Who Swallowed a Fly*, Nadine Westcott illustrates the traditional version of the popular song. After using seven cans of bug spray to kill the fly she swallowed, the old lady reels from one Epicurean delight to another. Devouring the horse, she dies of course! Colin and Jacqui Hawkins have the old lady sneeze after swallowing the horse and up come all the animals. By lifting up the old lady's apron, the reader can see all the animals in her stomach. This would make an excellent model for an enlarged old lady that children could then insert their drawn animals into. A sealed sandwich bag stapled behind her apron would make a good imitation stomach. Open the bag and you could remove the animals. Also, the speech balloons in the Hawkinses' tale encourage children's own original writing. Simms Taback's hilarious *There Was an Old Lady Who Swallowed a Fly* has die-cut holes in the old lady's stomach. These grow increasingly larger as each animal is swallowed. His Caldecott Medal-winning *Joseph had a Little Overcoat* is a retelling of an old folksong that evokes the lively dances and patterns of an old-world Yiddish village. In both books Taback's amusing visual asides encourage children to look carefully at the illustrations so as not to miss the fun.

*Simms Taback's Caldecott Medal-winning* Joseph had a Little Overcoat *invites young children to participate in "reading" a folksong.*

From *Joseph Had a Little Overcoat* by Simms Taback, copyright © 1999 by Simms Taback, illustrations. First published 1977 by Random House, Inc. Used by permission of Viking Penguin, a division of Penguin Putnam Inc.

One of primary children's favorite songs is "The Wheels on the Bus." In *The Wheels on the Bus,* Maryann Kovalski provides a London setting for her picture story of Jenny and Joanna and their grandma, who sing this song as they wait for their bus. They become so involved with their actions and singing, they miss their bus and have to take a taxi. Paul Zelinsky's interpretation of this song features paper engineering—wheels spin, the windshield wipers go "swish, swish, swish," and flaps and pullouts provide other items to manipulate. Well constructed, this movable version captivates children.

In *We're Going on a Bear Hunt,* Michael Rosen recounts a popular action rhyme as an exciting adventure tale. Pictures by Helen Oxenbury portray a father and his four children (including the baby) crossing a field of waving grass ("Swishy, swashy"), wading in the mud ("Squelch, squerch"), and braving a snowstorm ("Hoooo, woooo") until they reach a gloomy cave and see a bear! Oxenbury alternates black-and-white pictures with sweeping landscapes in full color. Children will relish the sound effects, the humor, and the drama of this tale.

All children need to hear songs, from the time they are babies right through school. Many emergent readers' first books are shared nursery rhymes and songs or chants. Children "read" the familiar words as they sing the songs. Just as families have favorite songs that they sing in the bath or in the car, classes should have favorite songs to start the day or to sing while they are waiting to go to lunch or outside to play. A class without favorite songs is as sad as a class without favorite books.

## Mother Goose

For many children, Mother Goose is their first introduction to the world of literature. These folk rhymes are passed down from generation to generation and are found across many cultures. The character of Mother Goose, discussed in Chapter 3, has come to represent this type of speech play.

Even a 1-year-old child will respond with delight to the language games of "Pat-a-Cake! Pat-a-Cake!" or "This Little Pig Went to Market." Many of the

*By illustrating this chart about various cumulative stories and songs, children learned to retell the stories in proper sequence.*
Highland Park Elementary School, South-Western City Schools, Grove City, Ohio. Kristen Kerstetter, teacher.

*Young children and parents can take delight in repeated visits to* Here Comes Mother Goose *in a superb collection by Iona Opie with vividly appealing illustrations by Rosemary Wells.*
*Here Comes Mother Goose* selection © 1999 Iona Opie. Illustrations © 1999 Rosemary Wells. Reproduced by permission of Walker Books Ltd., London. Published in the U.S. and Canada by Candlewick, Press, Inc., Cambridge, MA.

Mother Goose rhymes and jingles continue to be favorites of children 4 and 5 years old. What is the attraction of Mother Goose that makes her so appealing to these young children? What accounts for her survival through these many years? Much of the language in these rhymes is obscure; for example, modern-day children have no idea what curds and whey are, yet they delight in Little Miss Muffet. Nothing in current literature has replaced the venerable Mother Goose for the nursery school age.

## The Appeal of Mother Goose

Much of the appeal of Mother Goose lies in the musical quality of the varied language patterns, the rhythm and rhyme of the verses, the alliteration of such lines as "Wee Willie Winkie runs through the town" or "Deedle, deedle, dumpling, my son John."

Researchers have now linked children's experience with nursery rhymes and speech play to the development of sensitivity to the sounds within words, an ability they call "phonemic awareness." This ability to manipulate the sounds of words as they sing and chant nursery rhymes is a necessary foundation for understanding relationships between letters and sounds and contributes to children's emergent literacy development.[6]

More importantly, however, children love the sounds of the words, for they are experimenting with language in this period of their lives. The child learns new words every day; he likes to try them out, to chant them while playing. Mother Goose rhymes help the young child satisfy this preoccupation with language patterns and stimulate further language development.

Mother Goose rhymes also offer young children many opportunities for active participation and response. The young child loves to get bounced on Daddy's knee to the rhythm of "Ride a Cock Horse" or clap hands to the sound of "Pat-a-cake, pat-a-cake, baker's man." Some of the rhymes—such as "Pease Porridge Hot," "London Bridge," or "Ring a Ring o' Roses"—are games that involve direct action from the child. Other verses include counting rhymes—as in "1, 2, buckle my shoe, 3, 4, shut the door." Slightly older children enjoy answering the riddles in some of the Mother Goose verses or attempting to say their favorite tongue twisters. Every child likes to fool someone with the well-known riddle: "As I was going to St. Ives, I met a man with seven wives." And they never fail to delight in suc-

cessful recitation of the entire verse of "Peter Piper picked a peck of pickled peppers."

Another attraction of many of the Mother Goose rhymes is their narrative quality; they tell a good story with quick action. In just six lines "Little Miss Muffet" proves to be an exciting tale with action, a climax, and a satisfying conclusion. This is also true of "Simple Simon," "Sing a Song of Sixpence," "The Old Woman in the Shoe," and "Three Blind Mice." Preschool and kindergarten children enjoy pantomiming or dramatizing these well-known verse stories.

Many of the characters in Mother Goose have interesting, likable personalities: Old King Cole *is* a merry old soul; Old Mother Hubbard not only tries to find her poor dog a bone but she runs all over town at his special bidding; and although Tommy Lynn puts the pussy in the well, Johnny Stout pulls her out! Unpleasant but intriguing character traits are suggested by "Crosspatch," "Tom, the Piper's Son," and "Lazy Elsie Marley."

The content of the verses reflects the interests of young children. Many favorites are rhymes about animals—"The Three Little Kittens," "The Cat and the Fiddle," and the story of the mouse that ran up the clock in "Hickory Dickory Dock." Some of the verses are about simple everyday experiences and include such incidents as Lucy Locket losing her pocket, the Three Little Kittens losing their mittens, and Little Bo Peep losing her sheep. Children's pranks are enacted in "Ding, Dong, Bell!" and "Georgie Porgie." Peter, Peter, Pumpkin-Eater has a housing problem, as does the Old Woman in the Shoe. There are many verses about seasons and the weather, a concern of both young and old. The pleading request of one child in "Rain, Rain, Go Away" reflects the universal feelings of children.

A major appeal of Mother Goose is the varied humor. There is the jolly good fun of a ridiculous situation:

> One misty, moisty morning
> When cloudy was the weather,
> I chanced to meet an old man
> Clothed all in leather;
> He began to compliment
> And I began to grin—
> "How do you do" and "How do you do"
> And "How do you do" again!

Two 6-year-olds interpreted this verse in action by pretending to pass each other; as one moved to the left, the other moved in the same direction. Their movements were perfect for this amusing and familiar situation.

The young child's rather primitive sense of humor, which delights in other persons' misfortune, is satisfied by the verses in "Jack and Jill" and "Dr. Foster":

[6]Morag Maclean, Peter Bryant, and Lynette Bradley, "Rhymes, Nursery Rhymes, and Reading in Early Childhood," *Merrill-Palmer Quarterly, Journal of Developmental Psychology* 33 (July 1987): 255–281.

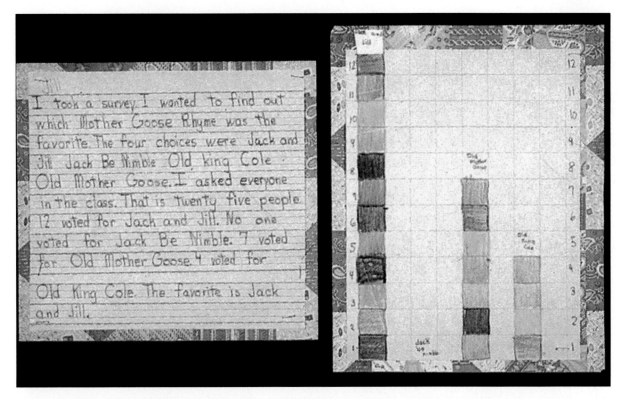

*Third graders conducted a survey of the children's favorite Mother Goose rhymes. They then wrote about how they had made the survey and graphed the results.*
Columbus Public Schools, Columbus, Ohio. Arleen Stuck, teacher.

Doctor Foster went to Gloucester
    In a shower of rain;
    He stepped in a puddle up to his middle
    And never went there again.

The pure nonsense in Mother Goose tickles children's funny bones. Chukovsky, a Russian poet, reminds us that there is sense in nonsense; a child has to know reality to appreciate the juxtaposition of the strawberries and the herrings in this verse:[7]

The man in the wilderness asked me
    How many strawberries grow in the sea.
    I answered him as I thought good,
    As many as red herrings grow in the wood.

## Different Editions of Mother Goose

Today's children are fortunate in being able to choose among many beautifully illustrated Mother Goose editions. There is no *one* best Mother Goose book, for this is a matter for individual preference. Some Mother Goose books seem to stay in print indefinitely. Each generation may have its favorite edition, yet older versions remain popular. The children in every

---

[7]Kornei Chukovsky, *From Two to Five*, trans. Miriam Morton (Berkeley: University of California Press, 1963), p. 95.

family deserve at least one of the better editions, however. Preschool and primary teachers will also want to have one that can be shared with small groups of children who might not have been fortunate enough ever to have seen a really beautiful Mother Goose.

### Collections
One of the most glorious nursery-rhyme collections is *Tomie de Paola's Mother Goose*. Each of the more than two hundred verses is illustrated with brilliant jewel tones against a clear white background. Characters of many races are included quite naturally. Pictures are large enough to be shared with a large group of children. Several include a full-page spread; many show a sequence of action. Careful placement of the rhymes provides interesting artistic contrasts, such as the jagged lines of the crooked man's house next to the rounded haystack of Little Boy Blue. The total format of this comprehensive Mother Goose is pleasing to the eye.

*The Random House Book of Mother Goose* should have been named for its editor/illustrator, Arnold Lobel, for it was one of the last books published before his death in 1987. Lobel illustrated over three hundred rhymes in this lively collection. Filled with fresh images and spontaneity, Lobel's Mother Goose book is a lasting contribution to children from this talented and well-loved illustrator. *Whiskers and Rhymes,* also by

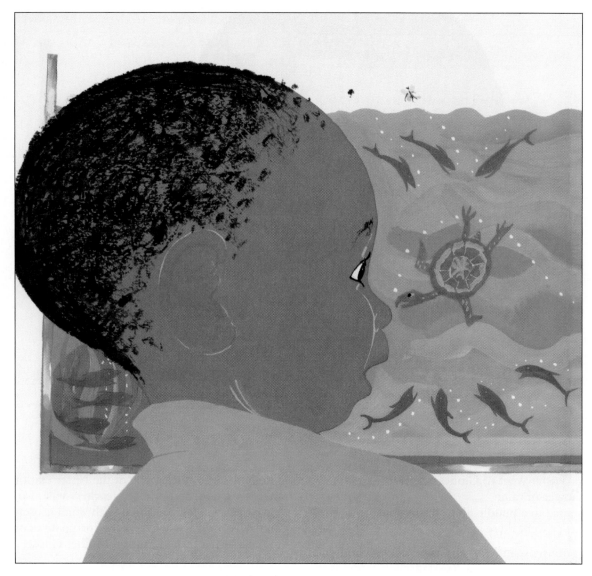

*Jan Ormerod has illustrated a short collection of Mother Goose rhymes for the very young in* To Baby with Love.

Illustration from *To Baby with Love* by Jan Ormerod. Used by permission of Lothrop, Lee & Shepard, an imprint of HarperCollins Publishers.

Lobel, is a lively collection of rhymes about cats. Although it features only several dozen rhymes, *James Marshall's Mother Goose* provides young children with a fresh and funny look at the venerable Old Goose. Most of the rhymes included in this collection are humorous, with hilarious illustrations to match. Children clever enough to spy the knife slipping through the pumpkin shell will realize that Peter is not going to be able to keep his wife forever, despite the last line of the rhyme. Sharing Marshall's funny parody on "Hey Diddle Diddle" might inspire older children to create their own original Mother Goose rhymes.

A recent collection by Zena Sutherland consists of some seventy-five verses under the title *The Orchard Book of Nursery Rhymes*. Brilliant detailed illustra-

tions by Faith Jaques depict an eighteenth-century setting of rural England, the source of many of these verses. A few, such as "How much wood would a woodchuck chuck," reveal their American origin. Adding to the authenticity of this edition are the carefully researched notes on the sources and variants of these verses by both author and illustrator.

Scholars of nursery rhymes are all indebted to Iona and Peter Opie for their definitive work *The Oxford Dictionary of Nursery Rhymes,* in which they assembled almost everything known about these verses. Maurice Sendak illustrated a new version of the Opies' first collection, *I Saw Esau,* which includes 170 rhymes, tongue twisters, jeers, and jump-rope rhymes. The many small pictures are just as sly and

# GUIDELINES

## *Evaluating Mother Goose Books*

With so many editions of Mother Goose, what factors should be considered when evaluating them? The following points might be useful in studying various editions:

### COVERAGE

How many verses are included? Are they well-known rhymes, or are there some fresh and unusual ones?

### ILLUSTRATIONS

What medium has been used? What colors? Are the illustrations realistic, stylized, or varied? Are the illustrations consistent with the text? Do they elaborate the text? What is the mood of the illustrations (humorous, sedate, high-spirited)? Has the illustrator created a fresh approach, avoiding cliché-ridden images?

### TEXT

Does the text read smoothly, or have verses been altered? Is the text all on the same page, or fragmented by turning the page?

### SETTING

What background is presented—rural or urban? Does the book take place in any particular country? Is the setting modern or in the past? What does the setting add to the collection?

### CHARACTERS

Do the characters come from a variety of ethnic backgrounds? Do the characters have distinct personalities? Are adults and children featured? Only children? How are animals presented—as humans or realistically?

### ARRANGEMENT

Is there a thematic arrangement of the verses? Is there a feeling of unity to the whole book, rather than just separate verses? Are pictures and verses well spaced or crowded? Is it clear which picture illustrates which verse?

### FORMAT

What is the quality of the paper and the binding? Is the title page well designed? Is there an index or table of contents? Is there harmony among endpapers, cover, and jacket?

No matter what edition is selected, children should be exposed to the rhythm and rhyme of Mother Goose. It is part of their literary heritage and might be their first introduction to the realm of literature.

---

naughty as the children's rhymes. Only 7 by 5 inches, this "Schoolchild's Pocket Book" is a superb example of fine bookmaking. Iona Opie and illustrator Rosemary Wells have collaborated on two beautiful collections, *My Very First Mother Goose* and *Here Comes Mother Goose*. The rhymes are attractively placed on each page and nicely paced throughout the book so as not to overwhelm parents and babies with too many images and too much black type. The layout gives young children time to make eye contact with the engaging illustrations and to wander around the page looking at all the little visual details, while Mother or Dad reads the rhyme. There are many full page illustrations facing a rhyme to attract baby's attention and keep her visually stimulated. In these cases the text is always accompanied by smaller pictures which elaborate on the visual narrative opposite.

With such a proliferation of nursery-rhyme books, parents, teachers, and librarians will want to examine a variety of collections before sharing them with their children. Even though you might have a favorite collection, try new ones with fresh images and unfamil-iar rhymes after you have read the more traditional ones. Mother Goose should never be enjoyed only once, but read over and over again. See Guidelines, "Evaluating Mother Goose Books," for some considerations to take into account when selecting Mother Goose editions.

### Single-Verse Editions

A recent publishing trend has been the production of picture books portraying only one Mother Goose rhyme or a limited number of rhymes around a single theme.

Maurice Sendak was one of the first to extend the text of two single verses with illustrations in his *Hector Protector and As I Went Over the Water*. The rhyme about Hector Protector is only five lines in length, but twenty-four action-filled pictures expand the story behind this five-line verse. Sendak has also combined two unrelated rhymes in *We Are All in the Dumps with Jack and Guy*. With its images of rats, box cities, and homeless people, this book is for older children, but Sendak's illustrations create strong visual links to the darker social and political origins of some of the earliest rhymes.

*Mary Had a Little Lamb* was first written by Sarah Josepha Hale in 1830 and then appeared in a McGuffey Reader. Since that time, however, it has been included in many Mother Goose collections. Bruce McMillan uses full-color photos of an African American child who poses for a rural Mary in his artfully crafted version of Hale's verse. Sally Mavor has used all kinds of fabrics and stitchery to construct the pictures for her version of Mary's tale. The old-fashioned costumes and setting and the subtle links to woolly fibers and American folk art add surprising depth to the familiar rhyme. Equally faithful, in very different ways, to the historical context of this verse, both these books would be good choices for sharing with children.

Two books make a kind of game based on children's knowledge of Mother Goose. The easiest one, Eric Hill's *Nursery Rhyme Peek-a-Book,* asks rhyming questions such as "Hickory, dickory, dock, what ran up the clock?" Lifting the flap covering the face of the clock, the child discovers not only a little mouse, but the text of the whole rhyme printed on the inside of the flap. Ten well-known rhymes, such as "Old Mother Hubbard," "Sing a Song of Sixpence," "Humpty Dumpty," and "Little Miss Muffet," are included. If children don't know these verses, they will after hearing this book. Sturdily made with lively, clear pictures, it provides for much participation and learning.

*Each Peach Pear Plum* by the Ahlbergs pulls together characters from Mother Goose and traditional folktales in a kind of "I Spy" game. Starting with Little Tom Thumb, each successive picture hides a new character somewhere in its design. Thus the picture of Baby Bunting carries the text "Baby Bunting fast asleep, I spy Bo-Peep," while the next picture of Bo-Peep challenges the viewer to find Jack and Jill. Children delight in playing this game, and they particularly love the ending, which pictures all of the characters together—eating plum pie, of course.

### Nursery Rhyme Collections from Other Lands

Although nursery rhymes are difficult to translate because they are based on sound and nonsense, several collections capture the elements of rhythm and sound that are so appealing to young children and several bilingual collections are available. Barbara Cooney creates authentic settings for her pictures of Latin American rhymes collected from Spanish-speaking communities in the Americas. Each rhyme in *Tortillitas Para Mama* by Margot Griego and others is written in both Spanish and English. The English verses do not rhyme, but the Spanish ones do. *Arroz Con Leche: Popular Songs*

*and Rhymes from Latin America,* collected by Lulu Delacre, is another source of rhymes of Spanish origin.

Sharing rhymes from other countries lets children of many cultures tap into their parents' memories to find rhymes in a variety of languages. The creation of nursery rhymes for the young child is a universal activity.

Young children enjoy all kinds of poetry besides nursery rhymes. See Chapter 8 for more about poetry. For a comparison of the unique features of various Mother Goose editions, see Resources for Teaching, "Mother Goose Books."

## Alphabet Books

In colonial days, children were first taught their ABCs from cautionary rhymes like "In Adam's Fall/we sinned all," which combined early literacy and religion. Later, pictures of animals beginning with certain letters were added to hornbooks and early primers for younger children. Alphabet books today can be equally deceptive. Many of them have moved beyond teaching children their alphabet to serving as a format to present detailed information about a particular subject for older boys and girls, to showcase an art book, or to create complicated puzzles. Most of the alphabet books and criteria for their evaluation discussed in this chapter are directed at ABC books for the young child, however. Ages are given when an older audience is implied.

Besides teaching the names and shapes of the letters, ABC books can also be used for identification or naming, as they provide the young child with large, bright pictures of animals or single objects to look at and talk about. One of the liveliest and jazziest alphabet books is Bill Martin, Jr., and John Archambault's *Chicka Chicka Boom Boom,* illustrated with vibrant colors by Lois Ehlert. An alphabet chant, this book helps children memorize the letters and identify them. It does not provide an object or animal that goes with a beginning sound as most alphabet books do, but it does provide for much fun and merriment as children chant these active letters.

Certain factors need to be considered in selecting alphabet books. Objects should be clearly presented on the page, and these should be easily identifiable and meaningful for the intended age level. Only one or two objects should be shown for the very young child, and it is best to avoid portraying anything that might have several correct names. For example, if a rabbit is presented for *R,* the very young child might refer to it as a "bunny." Since text is necessarily limited, the pictures usually "carry" the story. For this reason they should be both clear and consistent with the text, reflecting and creating the mood of the book.

# RESOURCES FOR TEACHING

## Mother Goose Books

### TRADITIONAL COLLECTIONS

| Author, Illustrator | Title | Unique Features |
|---|---|---|
| Leslie Brooke | *Ring o'Roses* | Published in 1923, this was the first collection to include humorous animals. |
| Kate Greenaway | *Mother Goose, or the Old Nursery Rhymes* | This has been a treasured classic since 1901. Tiny format and precise old-fashioned pictures of proper children. |
| Arthur Rackham | *Mother Goose, or the Old Nursery Rhymes* | Small, eerie pictures of pointed-eared elves and personified trees. |
| Feodor Rojankovsky | *The Tall Book of Mother Goose* | The illustrations depict natural-looking children showing real emotions. Humpty Dumpty is portrayed as Hitler, appropriate to the time of this book's publication in 1942. |
| Blanche Fisher Wright | *The Real Mother Goose* | With pale, flat, traditional pictures, this book has been divided into four narrow-sized board books with checkered covers. |

### CONTEMPORARY COLLECTIONS

| Author, Illustrator | Title | Unique Features |
|---|---|---|
| Marguerite de Angeli | *The Book of Nursery and Mother Goose Rhymes* | Some 250 soft watercolor illustrations portray the English countryside and show the author's love for and knowledge of children. |
| Tomie de Paola | *Tomie de Paola's Mother Goose* | See text. |
| Eric Hill | *The Nursery Rhyme Peek-a-Book* | See text. |
| Arnold Lobel | *The Random House Book of Mother Goose* | See text. |
| James Marshall | *James Marshall's Mother Goose* | See text. |
| Iona and Peter Opie, Maurice Sendak | *I Saw Esau* | See text. |
| Iona Opie and Rosemary Wells | *Here Comes Mother Goose* and *My Very First Mother Goose* | See text. |
| Jan Ormerod | *Jan Ormerod's To Baby With Love* | Four rhymes for baby. A short collection but perfect for bedtime reading. |
| Maud and Miska Petersham | *The Rooster Crows* | Includes many well-known American rhymes and jingles, such as "A bear went over the mountain" and "How much wood would a woodchuck chuck." |
| Robert Sabuda | *A Movable Mother Goose* | This glorious pop-up with modernized visuals of traditional rhymes will fascinate older readers. |
| Richard Scarry | *Richard Scarry's Best Mother Goose Ever* | Large brilliant-colored illustrations of animal characters make this a Mother Goose book that captures the attention of the youngest child. |
| Zena Sutherland, Faith Jaques | *The Orchard Book of Nursery Rhymes* | See text. |
| Tasha Tudor | *Mother Goose* | Small, soft pastel pictures are quaint and charmingly reminiscent of the work of Kate Greenaway. |

*continued*

# RESOURCES FOR TEACHING

## Mother Goose Books con't

### SINGLE-VERSE EDITIONS

| Author, Illustrator | Title | Unique Features |
|---|---|---|
| Lorinda Bryan Cauley | The Three Little Kittens | Appealing kittens that delight very young children. |
| Tomie de Paola | The Comic Adventures of Old Mother Hubbard and Her Dog | Comedy set behind a proscenium arch invites dramatic play. |
| Sarah Josepha Hale, Bruce McMillan | Mary Had a Little Lamb | See text. |
| Sarah Josepha Hale, Sally Mavor | Mary Had a Little Lamb | See text. |
| Susan Jeffers | Three Jovial Huntsmen | Three bumbling hunters search and search for their quarry and never see the many hidden animals watching them. |
| Tracey Campbell Pearson | Sing a Song of Sixpence | Children could compare this humorous version with Lubin's interpretation. |
| Janet Stevens | The House That Jack Built | Bright red yellow and black pictures portray the characters as country bumpkins. |
| Maurice Sendak | Hector Protector and As I Went Over the Water | See text. |
| Maurice Sendak | We Are All in the Dumps with Jack and Guy | See text. |

Alphabet books vary, in both their texts and their pictorial presentation, from very simple to intricate levels of abstraction. Authors and illustrators use a variety of organizing structures to create ABC texts. Four types of ABC books are discussed here (some books incorporate several types): (1) word-picture formats, (2) simple narratives, (3) riddles or puzzles, and (4) topical themes. Today there are so many alphabet books that only outstanding examples of each type are described here.

Striking pictures of realistic animals climb, poke through, or push large black block letters in *Animal Alphabet* by Bert Kitchen. A giraffe chins himself on the huge *G*, while a small snail climbs up the *S*. Each page contains only the letter and the picture of the animal. Names of animals are given on a page at the end of this handsome book.

Suse MacDonald creates an original and imaginative book in *Alphabatics*. Each letter grows or tilts to become part of a beautifully clear graphic picture on the next page. For example, a *C* moves sideways, stretches, and becomes the smile on the clown's face.

The *Y* moves off one page to become the head and horns of the yak on the other side. Children enjoy seeing the letters evolve and then finding them in the opposite picture.

Arnold and Anita Lobel combined their many talents to create a handsome and unique alphabet book. Starting with the picture of a small Victorian boy determinedly lacing up his high shoes, sailor hat ready to go and purse fat with change, we follow him on his journey to the page displaying the title, *On Market Street*. Then he proceeds on his way through the shops from A to Z. He returns home in the evening exhausted, with an empty purse but a gorgeous array of gifts, each purchased from a different shop. Rather than portray all the stores, Anita Lobel creates tradespeople and shopkeepers out of their own wares, making intriguing characters from books, clocks, eggs, quilts, toys, or zippers.

In brilliant watercolor collages, Lois Ehlert introduces children to a wide variety of fruits and vegetables in her book *Eating the Alphabet*. Sometimes as many as four vegetables appear on a single page, but they are clearly depicted. Children might not know all the items pictured, but it would extend their knowledge and be an excellent book to use prior to a trip to the grocery store.

In Anne Shelby's *Potluck,* Alpha and Betty decide to have a party, so they call all of their friends. Action-filled pictures by Irene Trivas show children of various racial and ethnic backgrounds bringing a variety of delectable foods. The foods are not stereotyped as to the child's background—for example, Ben, an African American child, brings bagels—but Hispanic triplets do turn up with tacos. Finally, they all sit down to a glorious feast, eating everything from A to Z. Children can also eat their way through the alphabet in Crescent Dragonwagon's *Alligator Arrived with Apples.* Dragonwagon's alliterative tale can serve as a model for children's own alphabet books.

Anita Lobel's *Alison's Zinnia* is a brilliant alphabet book glowing with flower paintings. Listen to the carefully planned sentences in this book:

Alison acquired an Amaryllis for Beryl
Beryl bought a Begonia for Crystal

and so it goes until

Yolanda yanked a Yucca for Zena
Zena zeroed in on a Zinnia for Alison.

Some alphabet books incorporate riddles or hidden puzzles in their formats. *Anno's Alphabet,* by one of Japan's leading illustrators and designers, Mitsumasa Anno, is filled with quirky illusions and puzzles. Each large letter looks three-dimensional, as if it has been carefully carved from wood. Suddenly, however, its perspective will appear to change and surprise you. The *M* is only half there as it disappears into its mirror image. Each letter is matched with a clear yet amusing picture, and hidden in all of the borders are even more surprises. A glossary at the end provides clues to the hidden pictures in this visually exciting ABC book.

*The Z Was Zapped* by Chris Van Allsburg is a highly sophisticated alphabet drama presented in twenty-six acts. The large black-and-white picture of a letter on a stage appears before the sentence describing how it meets its sinister demise. For example, a pair of gloved hands picks up the *K;* turn the page to find "The K was quietly Kidnapped." Older children delight in guessing what happened to each letter and may want to create their own alphabet drama. They will also enjoy comparing it to Richard Wilbur's *The Disappearing Alphabet.* In twenty-six poems, Wilbur speculates on the effects the lack of each letter might have on our language. If there were no letter *P,* banana peels would become slippery eels, and without

the *b* in *bat* or *ball* "there'd be no big or little leagues AT ALL." David Diaz's computer-created art is a lively accompaniment to the delightful word plays.

Topical themes are frequently used to tie the alphabet together. For example, *V for Vanishing: An Alphabet of Endangered Animals* by Patricia Mullins and Ann Jonas's *Aardvarks Disembark!* and *Gone Forever! An Alphabet of Extinct Animals* by Sandra and William Markle provide information on endangered or extinct animals. In *A Caribou Alphabet,* Mary Beth Owens portrays the world of the caribou, from "A for Antlers" to "Z for Below Zero Weather." A compendium at the end gives even more information about this endangered species.

Older students studying the Middle Ages will want to look at *Illuminations* by Peter Hunt. From *alchemist* to *zither,* Hunt depicts many aspects of the life, architecture, and legends of these times in a format that reflects the illuminated manuscripts. His *Bestiary: An Illuminated Alphabet of the Middle Ages* focuses on mythical creatures. Each book is an excellent example of theme alphabet books.

Children can explore the world around them or beyond their borders through alphabet books like Alma Flor Ada's *Gathering the Sun,* illustrated by Simon Silva, or Nikki Grimes's *C Is for City,* illustrated by Pat Cummings. Ada's bilingual poems introduce readers to the lives of field workers like Cesar Chavez. Silva's warm, richly textured paintings convey the quiet beauty of life on farms and the dignity of field workers. On the other hand, Grimes and Cummings show the lively multicultural world of a big city through rhyming text and detailed paintings. In this urban setting, for example, *H* is for handball, hopscotch, hot dogs, and Hasidim. Older children might enjoy creating their own alphabet book based on a chosen subject, using these two books as models. Such theme books suggest ways for older students to organize material they might be presenting for a particular study. Children could make their own ABC books of "Life at the Seashore," "Pioneer Life," or their favorite books. For a description of the unique features of many ABC books, see Resources for Teaching, "ABC Books."

## *Counting Books*

Ideally, girls and boys should learn to count by playing with real objects like blocks, boxes, bottle caps, or model cars. They can manipulate and group these as they wish, actually seeing what happens when you add one more block to nine or divide six blocks into two groups. Since time immemorial, however, we have been providing children with counting books, substituting pictures for real objects. Young children

D is for deli or doughnuts worth dunking
or doormen who jump double-Dutch while outside.
D is for drummers in dark-shaded glasses
who dazzle street-corner crowds from far and wide.

*The alliterative aspects of urban living are explored in* C Is for City *by Nikki Grimes.*

Illustration from *C Is for City* by Nikki Grimes, illustrated by Pat Cummings. Illustration copyright © 1995 by Pat Cummings. Used by permission of Lothrop, Lee & Shepard Books, an imprint of HarperCollins Publishers.

can make this transition from the concrete to its visual representation if they first experience the real objects and the visual illustrations are clearly presented.

In evaluating counting books, then, we look to see if the objects to be counted stand out clearly on the page. Groupings of objects should not look cluttered or confusing. Illustrations and page design are most important in evaluating counting books. Accuracy is essential.

Counting books, too, vary from the very simple to the more complex. For the purposes of this text they are discussed under three categories: (1) one-to-one correspondence, (2) other simple mathematical concepts, and (3) number stories and puzzles. Examples of each category are given; Resources for Teaching, "Counting Books," lists other titles by structure.

Tana Hoban's *1, 2, 3* is a sturdy, well-designed first counting book that presents simple one-to-one correspondence. Colored photographs picture well-known objects like two shoes, five small fingers, six

eggs, seven animal crackers, and ten toes. Numbers and names of the numerals are given in this first board book for very young children. Such a beginning counting book might serve more for identification of the object than for actual counting. Certainly it requires a lower level of associative thinking for the very young child.

Keith Baker's *Big Fat Hen* will attract children with its richly textured paintings and its familiar counting rhyme "1, 2, buckle my shoe." Bright white eggs are pictured on one double-page spread with numerals to match. On the next two pages the eggs have hatched into little chicks who act out buckling the shoe, shutting the door, and so on. The bright yellow chicks and white eggs stand out on the pages, making them easy to count. They also make a nice contrast to the beautifully patterned multicolored chickens.

Tana Hoban's *26 Letters and 99 Cents* is really two books in one. Clear magnetic letters are photographed with equally clear pictures of toys or objects beginning

# RESOURCES FOR TEACHING

## ABC Books

### WORD/PICTURE IDENTIFICATION

| Author, Illustrator | Illustrator | Age Level | Unique Features |
|---|---|---|---|
| John Burningham | *John Burningham's ABC* | 2–4 | One clear picture for each letter. Unusual choices: *T* is for tractor; *V* shows a volcano. |
| Tana Hoban | *A, B, See!* | 2–4 | Black-and-white photograms illustrate familiar objects. |
| C. B. Falls | *ABC Book* | 2–4 | A reissue of a classic originally published in 1923. |
| Bert Kitchen | *Animal Alphabet* | 2–5 | See text. |
| Flora MacDonald | *Flora MacDonald's ABC* | 2–5 | Large format and bright pictures give at least two words for each letter. |
| Suse MacDonald | *Alphabatics* | 3–8 | See text. |
| Helen Oxenbury | *Helen Oxenbury's ABC of Things* | 3–6 | Provides a small vignette for each letter. *H* is represented by a very funny picture of a hare and a hippopotamus lying in bed in a hospital. |

### SIMPLE NARRATIVE

| Author, Illustrator | Illustrator | Age Level | Unique Features |
|---|---|---|---|
| Deoborah Chandra, Keiko Narahashi | *A Is for Amos* | 4–7 | Poetic text and lovely watercolors show a little girl taking an imaginary ride on her rocking horse. |
| Crescent Dragonwagon, Jose Aruego, and Ariane Dewey | *Alligator Arrived with Apples* | 6–10 | See text. |
| Wanda Gág | *The ABC Bunny* | 2–4 | A little rabbit provides the story line for each letter. |
| Shirley Hughes | *Alfie's ABC* | 3–6 | Story shows favorite character Alfie and his family in their daily activities. |
| Anita Lobel, Arnold Lobel | *On Market Street* | 5–7 | See text. |
| Anne Shelby, Irene Trivas | *Potluck* | 6–10 | See text. |
| Clyde Watson, Wendy Watson | *Applebet* | 5–7 | A farmer and her daughter take a cart full of apples to the country fair. The accompanying verse asks the child to find the apple hidden in each picture. |

### RIDDLES OR PUZZLES

| Author, Illustrator | Illustrator | Age Level | Unique Features |
|---|---|---|---|
| Mitsumasa Anno | *Anno's Alphabet* | 5–10 | See text. |
| Jan Garten | *The Alphabet Tale* | 5–7 | Each letter is introduced on the preceding page by showing just the tail of an animal; turn the page and you see the whole animal. |
| Lucy Mickelwait | *I Spy: An Alphabet in Art* | 5–10 | Children are invited to play "I Spy" and find objects in famous paintings. |
| David Pellitier | *The Graphic Alphabet* | 7–14 | Letters turn into art in stunning visual designs. |
| Steve Schnur | *Fall: An Alphabet Acrostic* and *Spring: An Alphabet Acrostic* | 7–12 | The word representing each alphabet letter becomes an acrostic poem and invites children to try their own versions. |
| Chris Van Allsburg | *The Z Was Zapped* | 7–12 | See text. |

*continued*

# RESOURCES FOR TEACHING

## ABC Books con't

### TOPICAL THEMES

| Author, Illustrator | Illustrator | Age Level | Unique Features |
|---|---|---|---|
| Ada Alma Flor | *Gathering the Sun: An Alphabet in Spanish and English.* | 6–10 | See text. |
| Jim Aylesworth, Stephen Gammell | *Old Black Fly* | 6–10 | Marvelously funny illustrations portray this tiresome fly as he buzzes around the alphabet. |
| Mary Azarian | *A Farmer's Alphabet* | 5–12 | A handsome book that celebrates rural life in Vermont. Striking black-and-white woodcuts portray a barn, a quilt, and a wood stove, for example. |
| Betsy Bowen | *Antler, Bear, Canoe* | 6–10 | Hand-colored woodcuts show the four seasons in the North woods. Compare to Azarian's Vermont woodcuts. |
| Jo Bannatyne-Cugnet, Yvette Moore | *A Prairie Alphabet* | 6–14 | Highly detailed paintings provide a tour of the seasons and people of the northern prairie. |
| Lois Ehlert | *Eating the Alphabet* | 4–7 | See text. |
| Muriel Feelings, Tom Feelings | *Jambo Means Hello* | 6–14 | Muriel Feelings gives children a simple lesson in Swahili while introducing some important aspects of the geography and culture of East Africa. |
| Nikki Grimes, Pat Cummings | *C Is for City* | 6–10 | See text. |
| Lee Bennett Hopkins, Barry Root | *April, Bubbles, Chocolate* | 6–10 | Favorite poems to highlight the alphabet. Selections include "Foghorns" by Lilian Moore and Richard Brautigan's "Xerox Candy Bar." |
| Ted Harrison | *A Northern Alphabet* | 7–14 | This striking book about northern Canada and Alaska describes people, places, animals, and objects for each letter. |
| Peter Hunt | *Bestiary* | 8–14 | See text. |
| Peter Hunt | *Illuminations* | 8–14 | See text. |
| Rachel Isadora | *City Seen from A to Z* | 6–9 | This book captures the action of the city through body postures and storytelling vignettes. |
| Stephen Johnson | *Alphabet City* | 6–10 | Photo-realistic paintings capture the lines, shapes, and textures of the city. |
| Ann Jonas | *Aardvarks Disembark!* | 7–12 | See text. |
| Anita Lobel | *Alison's Zinnia* | 7–12 | See text. |
| Anita Lobel | *Away from Home* | 7–12 | Children travel to the far corners of the earth, beginning with Adam, who "arrived in Amsterdam," and ending with Zachary, who "zigzagged in Zaandam." |
| Michael McCurdy | *The Sailor's Alphabet* | 7–12 | This text is based on a sea chantey and introduces readers to the world of 18th-century sailing vessels. |
| Patricia Mullins | *V is for Vanishing* | 7–14 | See text. |
| Margaret Musgrove, Leo and Diane Dillon | *Ashanti to Zulu: African Traditions* | 7–14 | This is the only alphabet book to have won the Caldecott Medal. The illustrations picture the people, their homes, and an artifact and animal for each of 26 African tribes. |

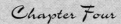

# RESOURCES FOR TEACHING

## ABC Books con't

### TOPICAL THEMES con't

| Author, Illustrator | Illustrator | Age Level | Unique Features |
|---|---|---|---|
| Ifeoma Onyefulu | A Is for Africa | 6–12 | Striking photographs and pleasing page design introduce African cultures and customs. |
| Mary Beth Owens | A Caribou Alphabet | 7–14 | See text. |
| Diana Pomeroy | Wildflower ABC | 6–12 | Pomeroy has created illustrations for each wildflower using potato prints and inviting similar efforts by children. |
| Alice Provensen, Martin Provensen | A Peaceable Kingdom: The Shaker ABCEDARIUS | 6–12 | The Provensens illustrated this old 1882 alphabet verse of the Shakers in a way that depicts the rhyme of the animals but also provides much information about the way the Shakers lived. |
| Marilyn Sanders, Eve Sanders | What's Your Name? From Ariel to Zoe | 6–10 | Twenty-six children from a variety of cultures talk about their names. Each class will want to create their own name alphabet book. |
| Luci Tapahonso, Eleanor Schick | Navajo ABC | 7–14 | Beginning with "A for Arroyo," lovely realistic illustrations give information about the Navajo, or Diné, culture. |
| Tobi Tobias | A World of Words | 7–14 | A beautifully illustrated collection of quotations accompany each letter. |
| Tasha Tudor | A Is for Annabelle | 5–7 | Delicate watercolors portray an old-fashioned doll with her different belongings representing different letters. |
| Richard Wilbur, David Diaz | The Disappearing Alphabet | 7–14 | See text. |
| Arthur Yorinks, Adrienne Yorinks, and Jeanyee Wong | The Alphabet Atlas | 7–12 | Beautiful calligraphy and stitchery pictures provide an introduction to countries and continents. |

with that letter. Turn the book around and you have number concepts with photos of magnetic numbers and all the possible sets of coins to make up that number. Although the number section is far more difficult than the alphabet section, primary children who are learning to count lunch money would find it very useful.

A watery theme can be found in Lois Ehlert's *Fish Eyes: A Book You Can Count On,* illustrated with brilliant colored graphics. A little black fish takes the reader on a journey through the ocean to discover "one green fish, two jumping fish, three smiling fish." Always the black fish adds himself to the group: "Three smiling fish plus me makes 4." Children delight in the spots and stripes of these gleaming fish with die-cut eyes.

Captivating language characterizes Charlotte Huck's *A Creepy Countdown,* illustrated by Jos. A. Smith. The tension mounts deliciously as Huck's fearsome creatures—scarecrows, toads, jack o'lanterns, owls, bats, witches, ghosts, cats, skeletons, and mice—gather together, say "boo to you!" and then disperse again until only "two lumpy toads hid beneath a stone, one tall scarecrow stood all alone." Smith's black-and-white scratchboard illustrations are wonderfully spooky, with touches of yellow and red that add to the supernatural atmosphere.

Many mathematical concepts are developed in one of the most inventive and perfect counting books of recent years, *Anno's Counting Book* by Mitsumasa Anno. Delicate watercolors portray a landscape changing with the various times of day, seasons, and

# RESOURCES FOR TEACHING

## Counting Books

### ONE-TO-ONE CORRESPONDENCE

| Author, Illustrator | Title | Age Level | Unique Features |
|---|---|---|---|
| Arlene Alda | Arlene Alda's 123: What Do You See? | 3–6 | Photos of everyday objects invite child's participation in finding hidden numerals. |
| Keith Baker | Big Fat Hen | 4–6 | See text. |
| Molly Bang | Ten, Nine, Eight | 4–6 | Starting with her ten toes, a father begins a countdown until his daughter is in bed. |
| Eric Carle | 1, 2, 3, to the Zoo | 4–6 | A circus train serves as the vehicle for this counting book as each passing car contains an increasing number of animals. |
| Cathryn Falwell | Feast for Ten | 4–7 | Beginning with one grocery cart, these bold, textured collages show an African American family shopping for, preparing, and eating a feast for ten. |
| Muriel Feelings, Tom Feelings | Moja Means One | 7–12 | This is as much an informational book on East Africa and the Swahili language as a counting book. |
| Tana Hoban | Let's Count | 1–6 | Clear bright pictures of everyday objects from 1 to 20, 50 and 100 are accompanied by large numerals and schematics. |
| S. T. Garne, Lisa Etre | One White Sail | 6–8 | Rhyming text and vivid watercolors reflect the climate and culture of the Caribbean. |
| Arthur Geisert | Pigs from 1 to 10 | 5–9 | Detailed etchings hide pigs to count and adventures to follow. |
| Tana Hoban | 1, 2, 3 | 1–3 | See text. |
| Bert Kitchen | Animal Numbers | 5–9 | A stunning counting book that begins with one baby kangaroo in its mother's pouch and ends with a hundred baby tadpoles and frog eggs. |
| Diana Pomeroy | One Potato: a Book of Potato Prints | 4–7 | Objects from the garden are created through lovely potato prints. Directions for making prints are included. |
| John J. Reiss | Numbers | 3–5 | Clear drawings of such common objects as shoes, kites, baseball players, etc., make this well within the young child's experience. |
| Ann Herbert Scott | One Good Horse: A Cowpuncher's Counting Book | 5–9 | From one good horse to a hundred cattle, this book provides a unique territory for a counting book. |
| Peter Sis | Waving: A Counting Book | 5–7 | Mary's mother waved to a taxi. Two bicyclists waved back to her while three boys waved to the bicyclists. A city background provides even more things to count. |

### OTHER MATHEMATICAL CONCEPTS

| Author, Illustrator | Title | Age Level | Unique Features |
|---|---|---|---|
| Mitsumasa Anno | Anno's Counting Book | 4–7 | See text. |
| Donald Crews | Ten Black Dots | 4–8 | A graphic counting book that shows what you can do with ten black dots. One can make a sun, two become fox's eyes, or eight the wheels of a train. |

# RESOURCES FOR TEACHING

## Counting Books

### OTHER MATHEMATICAL CONCEPTS con't

| Author, Illustrator | Title | Age Level | Unique Features |
| --- | --- | --- | --- |
| Lois Ehlert | Fish Eyes: A Book You Can Count On | 6–8 | See text. |
| Paul Giganti, Jr., Donald Crews | How Many Snails | 4–8 | A counting book that asks increasingly difficult questions: not only how many snails, but how many snails with stripes? how many striped snails with their head stuck out? |
| Tana Hoban | 26 Letters and 99 Cents | 6–8 | See text. |
| Ann Jonas | Splash! | 6–10 | See text. |
| Eve Merriam, Bernie Karlin | 12 Ways to Get to 11 | 5–7 | In an imaginative introduction to sets, eleven different combinations of things add up to twelve. |
| Bruce McMillan | Eating Fractions | 6–10 | Photographs show food divided into parts, and children are having a wonderful time eating up the parts. |
| Lloyd Moss, Marjorie Priceman | Zin! Zin! Zin! A Violin | 6–10 | Musical instruments come together to count to ten through musical groups, from solo to nonet to a chamber group that performs a stellar concert. |
| Pam Munoz Ryan, Benrei Huang | One Hundred Is a Family | 5–8 | The rhyming text first counts to ten, illustrated with pictures of families from many cultures. Then counting by tens shows families as larger communities working together for a better world. |

### NUMBER STORIES AND PUZZLES

| Author, Illustrator | Title | Age Level | Unique Features |
| --- | --- | --- | --- |
| Eric Carle | The Very Hungry Caterpillar | 5–7 | See text. |
| Sarah Hayes | Nine Ducks Nine | 5–7 | Nine ducks go for a walk, followed by a fox. One by one, the ducks take off for the rickety bridge where Mr. Fox receives his comeuppance. A wonderful story that helps children count down. |
| Charlotte Huck, Jos A. Smith | A Creepy Countdown | 5–7 | See text. |
| Pat Hutchins | 1 Hunter | 5–7 | See text. |
| Pat Hutchins | The Doorbell Rang | 5–7 | See text. |
| George Ella Lyon, Ann W. Olson | Counting on the Woods | 6–10 | Lovely poem illustrated with vivid photographs celebrates the woods. |
| Ifeoma Onyefulu | Emeka's Gift | 6–10 | Beautiful photographs celebrate family and community in a Nigerian village. |
| Charlotte Pomerantz, Jose Aruego and Ariane Dewey | One Duck, Another Duck | 5–7 | A grandmother owl teaches her grandson to count to ten. Easy and entertaining story. |

*In* Anno's Counting Book, *Mitsumasa Anno's delicate watercolors portray a landscape changing with the various times of day, seasons, and year. The clock in the church steeple tells the time of day while sets of adults, children, and animals go about their daily activities. How many sets of nine can you discover on this page?*

year. The clock in the church steeple tells the time of day while adults, children, and animals go about their daily activities. As the buildings in the village increase, so do the groups and sets of children, adults, trees, trains, boats, and so on. This is one of the few counting books to begin with zero—a cold winter landscape showing only the river and the sky, no village. It ends with a picture of the twelfth month, a snowy Christmas scene and twelve reindeer in the sky. *Anno's Counting Book* requires real exploration to find the sets of children, adults, buildings, and animals, generating a higher level of thought and discussion about numerical concepts than a simple one-to-one counting book.

Pat Hutchins provides both a number story and a puzzle in her creative book *1 Hunter*. This is an account of a hunter's humorous walk through a jungle filled with hidden animals. The hunter determinedly stalks past two trees; turn the page and "the trees" are the legs of two elephants. The hunter is oblivious to all he is missing, until the very last page when the animals come out of hiding and the one hunter runs away.

Hutchins's well-loved story *The Doorbell Rang* could also be used for its math concepts. Victoria and Sam's mother makes them a dozen cookies just like Grandmother's to share (six each). The doorbell rings and two friends are welcomed in to share the cookies (three each). The doorbell rings twice more until there are a dozen children and a dozen cookies. The doorbell rings again. Should they answer it? They do, and

it is their grandmother with an enormous tray of cookies!

Ann Jonas's *Splash!* will challenge primary children learning about adding and subtracting. The book begins on a lazy summer day at a backyard pond where two catfish and four goldfish swim lazily. On the bank three frogs, one turtle, and one dog are napping while one robin rests on a bird house. When one cat comes home, she startles the turtle, who jumps in the water. "How many are in my pond?" becomes the refrain that carries through the rest of the book as animals, amphibians, fish, birds, and insects get in and out of the pond.

Certainly there is no dearth of counting books and books that can be used for the development of math concepts. Because the criteria for evaluating counting books are similar to those for alphabet books, we have combined the criteria for both in Guidelines, "Evaluating ABC and Counting Books."

## Concept Books

A concept book describes various dimensions of an object, a class of objects, or an abstract idea. Concepts need to grow from firsthand experience as children gradually perceive common characteristics and relationships such as color, size, weight, or location. Some concepts, like shape or color, can be more easily presented in a book than abstract con-

## GUIDELINES

# *Evaluating ABC and Counting Books*

### ABC BOOKS

The objects or animals should be presented clearly.

For very young children, only one or two objects should be pictured on a page.

Common objects or animals that are easily identifiable are best for the young child.

ABC books should avoid the use of objects that might be known by several names.

The author/illustrator's purpose for the book should be clear.

The illustrations should be consistent with the text and reflect the mood of the book.

The organizing principle of the presentations should be clear.

The intended age level should be considered in both pictures and text.

### COUNTING BOOKS

Objects to be counted should stand out clearly.

Accuracy is essential.

Common objects that children know, such as fingers, toes, and eggs, are usually best for the young child.

Groupings or sets should be clearly differentiated.

Number concepts should not be lost in the story.

The level of thinking required should be challenging for appropriate ages.

---

cepts like growth, time, or distance. Certain concepts, like the concept of love or death, develop gradually over years and might be best understood in the themes of storybooks or informational books for older children.

The books discussed in this section are written for young children with the specific purpose of developing concepts. A concept book is really a young child's first informational book. It should stimulate much talk and help children develop their vocabularies while at the same time helping to sharpen their perceptions and enlarge their growing understanding of the world. Well-defined concepts are necessary for children's linguistic and cognitive development.

Notice how young children struggle to define their understanding of the concept "dog." At first "doggies" includes all dogs and maybe even a few cats and squirrels. Later, after they have abstracted the essential qualities of "dogginess," young children can tell the difference. Still later, they can make finer differentiations—among a St. Bernard, a cocker spaniel, and a German shepherd, for example. Concept books help children identify these essential elements of an object or a class of objects.

ABC books and counting books are really concept books. So, too, are the books that help children identify and discriminate colors. In *Colors Everywhere* Tana Hoban places photographs of a basket of buttons, a peacock in a field of daffodils, a carnival, and a pile of autumn leaves next to separate bands of color that a child could name and match in each picture. This task requires more-advanced perceptual skills, but even the very young child will be attracted to these brightly colored photographs.

*Color Dance* by Ann Jonas shows what happens when you mix colors, using four young dancers with colored scarves. The red dancer and yellow dancer unfurl their scarves to create orange. This is a joyous book of colors.

*Color Zoo* and *Color Farm,* both by Lois Ehlert, use sophisticated die-cut graphics to create the heads of stylized animals out of various shapes. A square, a triangle, and a circle produce a picture of a tiger's head. When you turn the page, each shape is then clearly shown and identified. Primary and even older children might use shapes to make their own animals after looking at these brilliant pictures.

In *Sea Shapes,* Suse MacDonald shows how abstract geometric shapes can be found in natural forms. In three small vignettes a circle becomes a whale's eye or a crescent turns into a leaping dolphin. A large picture facing each transformation shows the creature in its watery world. Tana Hoban has also written several books about shapes: *So Many Circles, So Many Squares, Shapes, Shapes, Shapes,* and *Spirals, Curves, Fanshapes, and Lines,* illustrated with full-color photographs.

In another fine photo concept book, *Is It Larger? Is It Smaller?* Hoban looks at relative size. Showing such familiar objects as three vases of flowers, or a large snowwoman and a baby snowman, she presents the concept of size in a way children can easily understand. In *Exactly the Opposite,* Hoban uses a variety of situations to show open and shut, front and back, empty and full, and far and near. Large colored photos capture children running up the stairs and the same children coming down the stairs. Children push a wagon, children pull a wagon. As always Hoban is

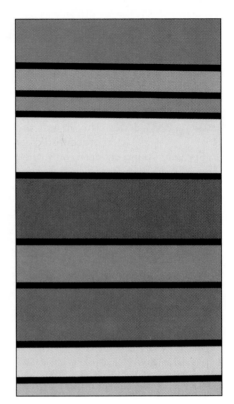

*Vividly colored photographs portray a full spectrum of color in Tana Hoban's* Colors Everywhere.

inclusive of various races and avoids any gender stereotyping.

Ann Morris has brought an international focus to the concepts of family, food, transportation, and the like in *Loving, Bread, Bread, Bread,* and *Houses and Homes. Work* and *Play* provide a multicultural survey of labor and leisure. In each of her books she provides photographs of children from a multitude of cultures. Simple text accompanies the pictures, and a simple glossary at the end matches photo to country with a brief fact.

Margaret Miller explores professions and trades in two well-conceived concept books, *Whose Hat?* and *Who Uses This?* A clear colored picture shows just a chef's hat. Turn the page and there is a picture of a chef in his kitchen. The opposite page pictures white and African American girls stirring a big pot, each wearing chef's hats. Nine professions are introduced by their hats. In *Who Uses This?* bakers, football players, and a conductor are identified by the tools of their trades. Miller has developed a similar question-and-answer format in *Can You Guess?* ("What do you comb in the morning?"), *Guess Who?* ("Who flies an airplane?"), and *Where Does It Go?* ("Where does a sock go?"). Photographs of four silly answers follow each question before the page is turned to reveal the correct response.

Many of Donald Crews's books, such as *Freight Train, Truck, School Bus,* and *Harbor,* could be classified as concept books or easy informational books. Certainly all of them explore the various dimensions of their subjects. In the first one, Crews pictures an empty track, then each of the different cars: the red caboose, orange tank car, yellow hopper car, green cattle car, blue gondola, purple box car, and finally the black steam engine. The train goes faster and faster through the tunnels and over bridges until it becomes a rainbow of speeding colors and then fades out of sight. Both colors and specific names for the cars provide real information for young children. In *Truck,* using bold graphics, Crews swings a big red truck across the country from east to west through cities, small towns, night and day, rain and shine. No text appears in this concept book except for all the environmental print one naturally encounters on a trip, such as names of other trucks, traffic signs, highway exit signs, tunnels, and truck stops. In *School Bus* children again have an opportunity to see common signs and symbols: the green "Walk" sign, the red "Don't walk" sign, the school bus stop, and others. The yellow buses are large and small, but all pick up students and bring them home when school is over.

*After exploring Lois Ehlert's style, children choose similar shapes and colors to respond to* Color Zoo.
Emerson and Central College Elementary Schools, Westerville, Ohio. Lisa Dapoz, Joan Fusco, and Jean Sperling, teachers. Photo by Connie Compton.

Other equally well-designed concept books by Crews include *Flying* and *Sail Away*. While these books seem geared for young children, some of them contain hidden messages that intrigue older children and adults.[8] For example, *Harbor* is dedicated "to the women in my life and Malcolm." Each boat is named after a woman: his wife, his daughter, his editor, and so on. Malcolm is his nephew.

Many of Lois Ehlert's books convey concepts for primary children as well as tell little stories. *Feathers for Lunch,* written with a rhyming text, tells about a little cat who would like to catch all the different birds that he sees, but luckily his bell fright-

ens them away. The birds are pictured with life-size brilliant collages, and plants and trees are labeled. In *Red Leaf, Yellow Leaf* Ehlert uses collage again to tell the story of her favorite maple tree. Using natural objects, fibers, and painted paper forms, she describes all the parts of the tree and the creatures it affects—at its beginning as a seed on the forest floor, then as a tree sprout in the nursery, and finally in her garden. In both books a brief appendix gives information about the concept dealt with in the story.

Aliki's two informational concept books, *My Feet* and *My Hands* from the Let's-Read-and-Find-Out Science Books series, seem just right for preschoolers. In simple words and with clear, attractive pictures, Aliki explores all of the things hands do and feet do. As always, Aliki pictures children of different races and cuts across gender stereotypes. For example, the title page of *My Hands* shows a young boy doing cross-stitching.

Dick King-Smith's *I Love Guinea Pigs* and *All Pigs Are Beautiful* are a particularly delightful pair from the Read and Wonder series, books that convey simple concepts about the natural world in the context of stories or poems. King-Smith's chatty format and his enthusiasm for his subjects provide just enough information for young children. For example, he explains immediately that guinea pigs aren't pigs but rodents. In smaller hand-printed captions he provides information about a major characteristic of rodents and mentions that guinea pigs and pigs have in common the fact that males and females are called "boars" and "sows." Anita Jeram's watercolor pictures add to the appeal of both books.

Concept books are really children's first nonfiction books. They help children see relationships between objects, develop awareness of similarities and differences, and grasp the various dimensions of an abstract idea. Often these books begin with the familiar and move to the unfamiliar or more complex. Many of them appear to be moving from totally obvious concepts for younger children to more abstract and less obvious concepts for older children. Concepts for the younger child should be presented in a clear, unconfusing manner, with one or more examples given. Where appropriate, the functions of objects should be made clear. Concepts should be within the developmental scope of the child. Concept books can be used to enrich or reinforce an experience, not substitute for it. Young children enjoy hearing these beginning nonfictional books along with fictional stories, for young children are curious and seek information. They want to know the *names* of things, *how* they work, and *why* this is so. Evaluative criteria for nonfiction books are presented in Chapter 11.

---

[8]See Susan Hepler, "Books in the Classroom," *Horn Book Magazine,* September/October 1988, pp. 667–669.

There's a silly old saying that

if you hold a guinea pig up

by its tail, its eyes

will drop out.

Well of course they wouldn't,

even if you could—which you couldn't,

because guinea pigs don't have tails.

*Anita Jeram's appealing illustrations will attract children to the information in Dick King-Smith's* I Love Guinea Pigs.

## Wordless Books

Wordless books are picture books in which the story line is told entirely through pictures. They are increasingly popular with today's TV-oriented child. Many of them are laid out in the same sequential manner as comic books and have wide appeal to different age levels.

Textless books are surprisingly helpful in developing some of the skills necessary for reading. Handling the book, turning the pages, beginning at the left-hand side and moving to the right are all skills that give the young child a sense of directionality and the experience of acting like a reader. These books are particularly useful in stimulating language development through encouraging children to take an active part in storytelling. As the child relates the story, she will become aware of beginnings, endings, the sequence of the story, the climax, the actions of the characters—all necessary for learning how a story works, and for developing a sense of story. "Reading" or telling what is happening in the pictures in a wordless book also requires specific comprehension skills. Teachers may want to record children's stories in language experience booklets. Older children might want to write their own creative stories to accompany the illustrations. To help the child tell the story, pictures must show action and sequence clearly so children will not be confused in their tellings. Also, children should be given an opportunity to examine the book and look through it completely before they try to tell the story orally. Otherwise, they will describe the action on each page but not understand the sequential relationship of the events.

In *Do You Want to Be My Friend?* Eric Carle gives the child latitude to create her own story about a little mouse who, in seeking a friend, follows the lead of one tail after another, only to be very surprised at what is at the other end! The brilliant collage pictures will delight children and provide the opportunity to tell their own versions of this story.

Nancy Tafuri provides an exciting wordless adventure story in *Junglewalk.* A boy puts down his book, "Jungles of the World," and turns off his light just as his cat slips out the window. The tail of the cat becomes a tiger, and the boy is off on his dream adventure seeing monkeys, elephants, zebras, and many other creatures in this brilliant jungle. The tiger brings him home, and the boy wakes from his dream just as his cat bounds in the window. In another wordless book, Tafuri uses exquisite large watercolors to show the explorations of a baby sea lion following a baby crab. Behind the baby sea lion is his mother carefully following him. When the crabs jump in the ocean, mother and child return to the herd. Tafuri's *Follow Me!* is a simple love story without words.

The concept in April Wilson's *Magpie Magic* is somewhat reminiscent of *Harold and the Purple Crayon*, but the execution is delightfully fresh. An artist's hands, drawn in black and white, pick up a pencil and draw a black magpie, who promptly flies off the paper. The hand reaches for a red pencil and draws cherries which the magpie gobbles down. A struggle of wits ensues as the artist draws other objects and the magpie gleefully interferes with each. When the artist draws a cage and entices the magpie inside, the story would seem to be over but several surprises are still in store in this imaginative story.

Alexandra Day tells a series of humorous stories about an almost human rottweiler dog named Carl. In each wordless story, when Carl is left to mind the baby, he gives the child a marvelous time and manages to keep the grown-ups ignorant of their escapades. This is the plot of *Good Dog, Carl.* In *Carl Goes Shopping,* Carl takes care of the baby in the lobby of an elegant department store. In *Follow Carl!* Carl and the toddler sneak out during nap time for a

*April Wilson's* Magpie Magic: A Tale of Colorful Mischief *invites children to create their own story for this wordless picture book.*

game of hide and seek. It is hard to tell who is the most lovable, dependable Carl or the delightful child.

A highly original wordless book is *Changes, Changes* by Pat Hutchins. Here, two wooden dolls arrange and rearrange wooden building blocks to tell a fast-paced circular story. When their block house catches fire, the resourceful couple dismantle it and build a fire engine, whose hose quickly douses the fire, thereby creating a flood! Undaunted, the wooden dolls then build a boat, which becomes a truck, which is changed to a train, until eventually they reconstruct their original block house. In *Rosie's Walk*, Hutchins has written and illustrated an even funnier story with the use of only one sentence. In this book Rosie—a very determined, flat-footed hen—goes for a walk, unmindful of the fact that she is being stalked by a hungry fox. At every turn of Rosie's walk, the hen unwittingly foils the fox in his plans to catch her. The brightly colored comic illustrations help youngsters tell Rosie's story. Primary children enjoy retelling this story from the point of view of the fox.

The first waking thought of a plump little lady is that this is the morning to have pancakes for breakfast. In *Pancakes for Breakfast,* Tomie de Paola pictures her persistent efforts to make the pancakes despite the fact that she has to gather the eggs from the hen house, milk the cow, and churn the butter. Finally thinking she has all the ingredients, she discovers she must go and buy some maple syrup. She returns with a self-satisfied expression on her face, only to discover that her dog and cat have tipped over the milk and flour and eaten the eggs. All is not lost, however, for from her neighbor's house comes the delicious aroma of pancakes. The recipe for the pancakes is given and asks to be tried out.

It is interesting to see when children recognize that *Deep in the Forest* by Brinton Turkle is really a variant of "Goldilocks and the Three Bears," with the unique twist that a baby bear wreaks havoc in a pioneer cabin. Usually when the children see baby bear eating porridge from three different-size bowls, they recall having "heard" something like this before.

Mercer Mayer was one of the first illustrators to create wordless books. His series that includes *A Boy, a Dog, and a Frog* is very popular with children aged 5 and up. Simple line drawings in green and black portray the friendship between a boy, his dog, his frog, and a turtle. The stories are amusing and full of slapstick fun, particularly *Frog Goes to Dinner,* in which frog hides in the boy's pocket and goes to the restaurant with the family. Jealousy is the theme of *One Frog Too Many* when the boy is given a new baby frog. These stories are humorous and easily told from their pictures.

Emily McCully tells delightful stories of a large mouse family and their seasonal fun in *Picnic,* and *School.* In *Picnic* a little mouse falls out of the truck when they go down a bumpy road. Her absence is not discovered until all eight of her brothers and sisters are ready to eat. Then the whole family piles into the truck to go find her. In *School,* the little mouse runs off to join her eight brothers and sisters. When the teacher discovers her, she calls her mother, only to have the little mouse cry. But after she holds the pointer, passes out milk and cookies, and listens to the teacher share *Picnic,* the little mouse is comforted and ready to go home with her mother. These books provide real narratives, with identifiable characters, exciting plots, and lush watercolors.

The story of Noah's ark has been translated from the Dutch by Peter Spier in *Noah's Ark* and appears in verse form on the first page. What follows, however, is the virtually wordless story of all that transpires both inside and outside the ark for forty days and forty nights. Various-size pictures portray Noah's many activities on the ark and capture his every mood, from deep concern to jubilant rejoicing over the dove's return with the olive branch. Mrs. Noah's washline of clothes contrasts sharply with the dirty, messy interior of the ark at the end of its long voyage. Humorous touches run throughout this book, including the number of rabbits that leave the ark and the slow final departure of the snails and tortoise. Each viewing of the book reveals more of Spier's wit and artistic talent. This book richly deserved the Caldecott Medal it received. Peter Spier's *Rain* is also a wordless book about rain but is set in the modern world.

Another beautiful wordless book is Raymond Briggs's *The Snowman.* Using soft colored pencils in a comic strip format, Briggs tells the story of a small boy and his snowman who comes to life one night. The boy invites the snowman inside to see the house but warns him away from the fireplace, the stove, and the hot water tap. The snowman has a childlike fascination for such simple things as an electric light switch, a skateboard, the father's false teeth in a glass, and the family car. The boy and the snowman share a meal and a fantastic predawn flight before returning to bed and the front lawn. In the morning the sun awakens the boy, and his first thought is for his snowman. He looks out the window—alas, his friend has melted. Children who have seen this lovely picture book want to look at it over and over again. It is the kind of story that invites revisiting and discussing all the details Briggs has included.

David Wiesner's fascinating book *Tuesday* is the second almost wordless book to receive the Caldecott Medal. On "Tuesday evening, around eight," all the frogs take off from their lily pads. Brilliant watercolors portray their joyous flight as they zoom through a house, chase birds and a dog, and return home at dawn. The next Tuesday evening, the pigs fly! Children could easily tell their own stories to accompany these action-filled pictures. Wiesner's other wordless books, such as *Free Fall,* and *Sector 7,* are of equally inventive artistic imagination. The age of the boy in each book would suggest that these wordless books are for older children.

Two other wordless picture books that also feature imaginary journeys play with unusual points of view. *Zoom* by Istvan Banyai begins in a barn with a close-up of a rooster's comb. The artist's eye pulls back like a movie camera to show the rooster and then moves back again to picture children looking through the barn window at the rooster. Banyai never lets viewers take the scenes for granted and includes many visual surprises as he takes the viewer farther and farther away from the barn until we are in outer space looking at Earth as a tiny dot of light. Steve Jenkins's *Looking Down* begins where *Zoom* ends, out in space looking at Earth. Now, however, we move in closer and closer through tissue paper clouds to the Maryland and South Carolina coasts, to cities and countrysides, to neighborhoods, to a small boy's house, and to the small boy who is looking at a ladybug through a magnifying glass. The last page pictures a close-up of that ladybug. These inventive books are lovely complements to one another and can help make the idea of point of view concrete for younger children while they will intrigue and instruct an older audience.

There appear to be fewer wordless books published today than five years ago. Increasingly, those being produced seem geared to an older audience than preschool or even kindergarten children.

## Books About the Common Experiences of Young Children

Increasingly, publishers are producing books that mirror the everyday common experiences and feelings of preschoolers across cultures. In these books for 2- through 5-year-olds the illustrations are simple and clear. The young child's activities and concerns are at the center of the action, but frequently the humor is directed at the parent reader.

David Shanon's *No David!* and Molly Bang's *When Sophie Gets Angry—Really, Really Angry* both do a superb job of capturing the terrible toddler in action. Shannon's lively illustrations show a preschooler doing his worst—stealing cookies from the cookie jar, playing with food, and running naked down the street. His antics are accompanied by a brief text, from an obviously harassed adult, which consists mostly of the words, "No David!" David is finally sent for a time out but in the end receives a hug and the words, "I love you!" Bang's Sophie is put upon by an older sister who grabs her favorite toy. Sophie gets so angry, "she kicks, she screams she wants to smash the world to smithereens." Bang's intensely colored illustrations represent Sophie's rage perfectly, following her outside as she runs away from her anger and then back home to the embrace of her now peaceful family. Both books acknowledge the mercurial emotions and sometimes difficult-to-control actions that characterize the preschooler yet provide a reassuring message of acceptance and love.

Amy Hest's Baby Duck is a difficult child of a different sort. When she's unhappy or fearful she pouts. Despite the reassurances of her parents, she has a difficult time adjusting to new experiences. In *Baby Duck Goes to School, In the Rain with Baby Duck,* and *Baby Duck and the Bad Eyeglasses,* it takes Grampa Duck coaxing the reluctant Baby to get past her fears and enjoy an adventure.

Jane Simmons's *Come Along Daisy* also offers reassurances to children suffering from separation anxiety. Despite Mama Duck's admonitions to "Come Along," Daisy is distracted while out for a swim and loses track of her mother. Simmons's thickly textured paintings portray Daisy's sudden panic, showing a very, very small duck in the middle of a suddenly frightening world. Daisy's face, peeking out from behind a bunch of water reeds as she hears a rustling along the riverbank, is priceless. Happily, the rustling is Mama Duck, who calls out "Daisy, Come Along!" Reunited, Daisy vows to stay close to Mama.

Eve Rice captures the feelings of a child whose birthday is almost a disaster. In *Benny Bakes a Cake,* Benny has a wonderful time helping his mother make his birthday cake. But when they go for a walk, Ralph, their dog, eats the cake. Benny is disconsolate until his father comes home with presents, birthday hats, *and* a beautiful birthday cake. A young child can easily follow the action of this story by looking at the large flat primary-color pictures against the clear white background.

Learning to get along in the family is another developmental task of the young child. In Ann Herbert Scott's *Sam,* an African American child, the youngest of his family, feels rejected by the other members of his family—all are so engrossed in their own activities that they tell him to go somewhere else to play. Finally, completely frustrated, Sam begins to cry. Then everyone in the family comes together and realizes the cumulative effect they have had on Sam. Consoled at last, Sam helps his mother make raspberry tarts.

The impulsiveness of the young child is typified by the character of Jamela in Niki Daly's *Jamela's Dress,* a warmhearted family story set in South Africa. Jamela's mother has bought some beautiful fabric to make herself a dress, and Jamela is so enamoured of it that she wraps herself up in the cloth and parades around town without considering the consequences. When she arrives home, Jamela is horrified to find that she has gotten the

In Molly Bang's When Sophie Gets Angry—Really, Really Angry *a young child finds space for a tantrum and room to calm down again.*

From *When Sophie Gets Angry—Really, Really Angry* . . . by Molly Bang. Published by The Blue Sky Press, an imprint of Scholastic, Inc. Copyright © 1999 by Molly Bang. Reprinted by permission.

So Jamela posed. The children pushed in. Taxi
pushed in. Mrs. Zibi and her chicken pushed in.
And the boy on the bicycle just s-q-u-e-e-z-e-d in.
They all smiled.

*click!*

*Young Jamela's impulsive behavior gets her into trouble in
Niki Daly's heart warming* Jamela's Dress.
From *Jamela's Dress* by Niki Daly. Copyright © 1999 Farrar, Straus &
Giroux by arrangement with The Inkman, Cape Town, S. A. Hand lettering
by Andrew van der Merwe, Francis Lincoln Limited, Great Britain.

fabric stained and torn. Luckily, a photographer who
has captured her picture wins a prize, and gives
Jamela some of the prize money. There is enough for
her mother to make her own dress and one for Jamela
as well. Any child who has ever acted without thinking will identify with Jamela's predicament and find
comfort in the happy outcome.

The youngest child frequently feels left out, the tag
end of the family. Pat Hutchins captures these feelings
in her well-loved books *Titch, You'll Soon Grow into
Them, Titch,* and *Tidy Titch.* In the first book Titch is
too small to ride a two-wheel bicycle or fly a kite or
use a hammer. But he is not too small to plant a seed,
and Titch's plant grows and grows. The ending of the
story is a classic example of poetic justice for the
youngest and smallest of a family. The classic story
*The Carrot Seed* by Ruth Krauss has a theme similar
to that in *Titch.* Here, the smallest in the family triumphs over all the doubts raised by his family. Little
children need to feel big, if only through their stories.

Young children also need much love and reassurance that they will always be needed and belong to
their family. This is the theme of the favorite story *The
Runaway Bunny* by Margaret Wise Brown. A little
bunny announces that he is going to run away, and his
mother tells him that she will run after him. The little
bunny thinks of all the things he will become—a fish
in a stream, a crocus, a sailboat. His mother in turn
says she will become a fisherman, a gardener, the
wind, and come after him. The little rabbit decides just
to stay and be her little bunny, after all. This story
might seem suffocating for older children, but it is just
what the preschool child wants to hear.

Bedtime stories provide the comfort
and reassurance that children need to
face the dark alone. There are several
recent bedtime books that have the
potential to become modern-day classics, although probably no book for
the very young child will ever replace
Margaret Wise Brown's *Goodnight
Moon.* First published in 1947, it was
reissued in 1975 in paperback and
made into a pop-up book, *The Goodnight Moon Room,* in 1984.

Kate Banks's lovely *And If the
Moon Could Talk,* with illustrations by
Georg Hallensleben, is reminiscent of
*Goodnight Moon* in its lyrical text and
vivid primary colors. A little girl is in
her room getting ready for bed, "and if
the moon could talk it would tell of evening stealing
through the woods and a lizard scurrying home to supper." As each part of the child's nighttime ritual is
completed, the refrain "and if the moon could talk" is
repeated and we see people and animals around the
world settling in for the night. Finally as the little girl
sleeps safely in her bed, the moon peeks in her window
and whispers "good night." Barbara Berger's *A Lot of
Otters* features Mother Moon, who has misplaced her
little baby. There is no reason to worry, however, for
the baby is safe with a loving family of otters who care
for him until Mother returns. The exquisitely beautiful
illustrations and gentle story will be enjoyed reading
after reading and generation after generation.

The musical text of Mem Fox's *Time for Bed* with
Jane Dyer's lovely watercolor illustrations will no
doubt have a similar soothing effect on toddlers. Beginning with a tiny mouse, animal and insect families
get ready for sleep. Finally, a human mother wishes
her baby sweet dreams against the background of a
starry pillow and a starry sky: "The stars on high are
shining bright—Sweet dreams, my darling, sleep
well . . . good night!" Molly Bang has written and
illustrated both a counting book and a loving bedtime
story in *Ten, Nine, Eight.* Starting with his daughter's
ten toes, a daddy counts backward until she is ready
for bed. This is a warm, reassuring story of an
African American father and his daughter.

Young children love the lilt and rhyme of *Jesse
Bear, What Will You Wear?* by Nancy Carlstrom.
Jesse Bear wears not only his red shirt but also such
unusual things as "the sun on his legs that run" or the
three kisses and bear hug that his dad gives him at
night. Exuberant paintings of Jesse Bear's day make
this a very special book to share with preschoolers
and kindergarten children.

*Goodnight, Gorilla* by Peggy Rathmann is an almost wordless book that is sure to delight toddlers. A

*A baby gorilla and a tiny mouse lead a parade of animals home with the zookeeper in* Goodnight, Gorilla.
From *Goodnight, Gorilla* by Peggy Rathmann, copyright © 1994 by Peggy Rathmann. Used by permission of G. P. Putnam's Sons, a division of Penguin Putnam Inc.

sleepy zookeeper is locking up for the night when a gorilla baby takes his keys. As the keeper says good night to the animals, one by one, the gorilla opens their cages and the animals all follow the keeper home and bed down in his room. His sleepy wife suddenly realizes what has happened and takes all the animals back to their cages—except for the little gorilla and a tiny mouse, who manage to follow her back to bed and slide in under the covers. Rathman's *10 Minutes to Bedtime* is a farcical look at bedtime, as a young child and his pet hamster entertain vacationing hamsters who want to experience the ten-minute countdown firsthand.

Martin Waddell's *Owl Babies* might be the perfect book to reassure a toddler who fears the nighttime separation from mother. In this charming predictable book, three little owl siblings find themselves alone on their leafy branch. "Where's Mommy?" asks Sarah, "Oh my goodness!" exclaims Percy, and "I want my mommy!" wails Bill, the smallest. Patrick Benson's expressive illustrations lend just the right amount of suspense to the story, in which the night seems to get darker and darker. Sarah and Percy try to reassure each other that Mom will be back, while Bill continues to cry for Mother until she swoops "soft and silent" through the trees and home to her children. Bill's plaintive wail will resonate with every child who is frightened of the dark, and the message that mother is never far away is a reassuring finale that will linger in sleepy memories.

Stories that have no relationship to bedtime make fine reading at this time, too, of course. So young children should see many of the appropriate picture storybooks described in Chapter 5 and hear the well-loved traditional tales of "The Three Bears," "The Three Billy Goats Gruff," and "The Gingerbread Man" discussed in Chapter 6. For although young children need books that mirror their own feelings and experiences, they also need books to take them beyond those experiences and to help their imaginations soar.

## Books for the Beginning Reader

Learning to read begins at home with children hearing stories on their parents' laps and seeing loved persons in their lives valuing books. The child lucky enough to have had such a wide exposure to books will usually learn to read easily and fluently. The importance of reading aloud to young children, if they are to be successful in learning to read, has been consistently proven by researchers in this country and abroad.[9]

The books for the very young child that have been discussed in this chapter can be read again when children of 5 or 6 start to become readers. Increasingly, theories of reading emphasize the importance of

---

[9]See Margaret Clark, *Young Fluent Readers* (London: Heinemann Educational Books, 1976); Dorothy Cohen, "The Effect of Literature on Vocabulary and Reading Achievement," *Elementary English* 45 (February 1968): 209–213; Dolores Durkin, *Children Who Read Early* (New York: Columbia Teachers College Press, 1966); Robert Ladd Thorndike, *Reading Comprehension, Education in 15 Countries: An Empirical Study,* vol. 3, International Studies in Education (New York: Holstead Wiley, 1973); Gordon Wells, *The Meaning Makers* (Portsmouth, N.H.: Heinemann, 1986).

*Kindergarten children enjoy reading their alternative version of* Goodnight Moon *by Margaret Wise Brown.*
Mission School, Redlands Public School, Redlands, California. Nancy Anderson, teacher and photographer.

reading for meaning and enjoyment from the very start of learning to read. Many preprimers and primers that are part of reading textbook series have stilted, unnatural language and pointless plots that thwart the child's spontaneous attempts to read; in contrast, stories that children love and have heard over and over again have natural language and satisfying plots that encourage reading. Many of these books utilize repetitious language and story patterns that help children learn to read naturally as they join in on the refrains or predict the action of the story.

Jerome Bruner was the first to use the term *scaffold* to characterize adult assistance to children's language development.[10] Some books can also be an instructional scaffold or a temporary help in the child's first attempts to read. Such books include familiar texts like Mother Goose rhymes or songs that children know by heart and can easily "read"; or they might be books with repetitive language or story patterns that help children remember or predict the story easily.

Margaret Meek points out that as children explore a variety of texts, they learn how books work.[11] She also emphasizes the importance of repeated readings, maintaining that each time a book is revisited, new understandings are gained.[12]

## Predictable Books

Books that can help an emergent reader can be identified by such characteristics as repetitive language patterns or story patterns or the use of familiar sequences like numbers, the days of the week, or hierarchical patterns. Frequently, texts combine several of these characteristics in a single story.

Many stories include repetitive words, phrases, or questions that invite children to share in the reading. Children quickly learn the language pattern of Eric Hill's *Where's Spot?* and chime in as the word *no* is revealed under each lifted flap. They will want to join in and repeat the word *suddenly!* in Colin McNaughton's

---

[10]Identified by C. B. Cazden, "Adult Assistance to Language Development: Scaffolds, Models, and Direct Instruction," in *Developing Literacy: Young Children's Use of Language*, ed. R. P. Parker and F. A. Davis (Newark, Del.: International Reading Association, 1983), pp. 3–18.

[11]Margaret Meek, *How Texts Teach What Readers Learn* (London: Thimble Press, 1988).

[12]See also Miriam Martinez and Nancy Roser, "Read It Again: The Value of Repeated Readings During Storytime," *Reading Teacher* 38 (1985): 782–786.

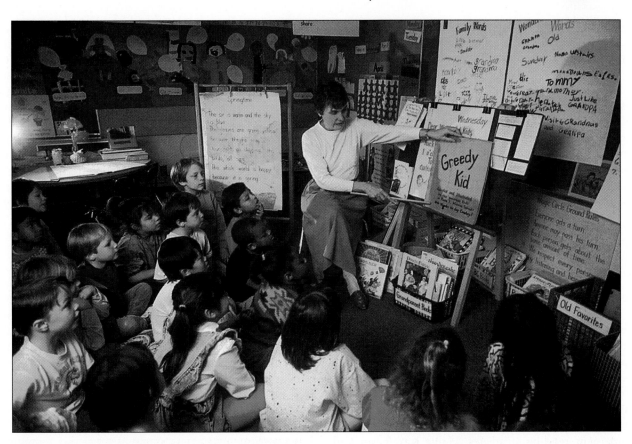

*Teacher and children share the reading of the alternative text they created, "Greedy Kid," following the pattern of* Greedy Cat *by Joy Cowley.*
Mission School, Redlands Public Schools, Redlands, California. Nancy Anderson, teacher. Photo by Larry Rose.

delightful book entitled *Suddenly!* They will also be tickled by the suspenseful plot as an ingenuous pig is set upon by a nasty wolf on his way home from school. Preston the pig escapes from each increasingly bizarre assault, seemingly unaware that the wolf is after him. Preston's further adventures can be followed in *Boo!, Yum!,* and *Preston's Goal!* The illustrations in these books, like those in Pat Hutchins's *Rosie's Walk,* give the real story away.

Denise Fleming's books, such as *In the Tall Tall Grass,* have predictable refrains that also convey simple concepts about animal behavior and habitats. In *In the Small Small Pond,* "wiggle, jiggle, tadpoles wriggle," and in *Barnyard Banter* "pigs in the wallow, muck muck muck." These visually appealing books also offer children interesting vocabulary within the context of the predictable text.

A well-liked patterned question-and-answer book is *Brown Bear, Brown Bear, What Do You See?* by Bill Martin, Jr. The question in the title is put to a large brown bear, who replies that he sees a redbird looking at him. The question is then directed at the redbird: "Redbird, redbird, what do you see?" He sees a yellow duck, who in turn sees a blue horse, and

so on. Identification of animal and color on the picture allows the child to chime in on the answer for each page. The large, bold collage pictures by Eric Carle are a perfect match for the text and support the child's reading of the story.

Other patterned language books might repeat certain words many times, as in *Snow on Snow on Snow* by Cheryl Chapman. In this simple narrative a little boy wakes up "under blankets under blankets under blankets" on a wintry day and goes sledding with his friends and his dog Clancy, who gets lost. The children look "behind trees behind trees behind trees" and "tears on tears on tears" result when they can't find him. Clancy finally appears from under a snowdrift to a triple happy-ever-after ending.

Rather than simply repeat words and phrases, some books play with the sounds of language in a more complex way. Many of Bill Martin, Jr.'s, books have refrains or patterns in which beginnings, endings, or internal parts of words are manipulated. In *The Happy Hippopotami,* "hippopotamuses climb aboard their picnic buses" for a trip to the beach. There are hippopotamamas wearing pajamas and hippopotapoppas who give their hippopotadaughters and their hippopotasons dimes and nickels to buy poppasicles, and they all give a "Hippo-ray! Hip-hippocheer!" for a jolly good time. Charlotte Pomerantz's *The Piggy in a Puddle* and *Here Comes Henny* also have irresistible refrains that will have children chanting along with enthusiasm. Piggy is in the middle of a "muddy little puddle" and dawdles and diddles there while daddy, mommy, and brother try to convince her to come out. In a rollicking ending they all dive in and join her in the "squishy-squashy, mooshy-squooshy, ooffy-poofy" mud. Henny is a mother chicken who plans a picnic for her chickies and packs it in her backpack,

which she carries
pickabacky
back and forth
and forth and backy.[13]

These are picky chickies, however, and they will only eat snacky snickies, not the snicky snackies that Henny has packed. In the end the chicks collect their own pack of snackies and have a happy picnic-nicky. In addition to being irresistible fun for children, this type of sound play helps make them more aware of the internal sounds of words and the fact that language is made up of individual sounds. This understanding—phonemic awareness—seems to be crucial to emergent reading strategies. Hallie Kay Yopp and other researchers suggest that a certain level of phonemic awareness is necessary for children to benefit from more-formal reading instruction.[14]

Building on children's knowledge of numbers and the days of the week provides a kind of scaffold for reading. Clear pictures by Tomie de Paola illustrate the predictable book *Cookie's Week* by Cindy Ward. If a child knows the days of the week, she can easily read the description of everything a mischievous little black-and-white cat does each day. Much to children's delight, it begins with "On Monday . . . Cookie fell in the toilet." The next page sets the pattern of the book: "And there was water everywhere." Knowledge of the days of the week and numbers help children read *The Very Hungry Caterpillar* by Eric Carle. They particularly enjoy reciting the part where the caterpillar eats through *one* apple on Monday, *two* pears on Tuesday, *three* plums on Wednesday, until he has a huge feast on Sunday. In *Today Is Monday* Carle illustrates the familiar nursery song with different animals. A snake eats spaghetti, a porcupine munches string beans, and so on.

The last picture shows children from many cultures, including a child in a wheelchair, sitting around a table for a feast. In Maurice Sendak's rhyming *Chicken Soup with Rice*, each verse begins with the month and ends with doing something to the soup, such as blowing on it or sipping it. Some groups have made up their own verses for the months, using Sendak's pattern and repeated phrases. Hierarchies based on such concepts as size can also help children to read stories. With one reading, children easily discern the pattern of being the littlest in Pat Hutchins's story *Titch*. They know that if his brother has a *great big bike* and his sister a *big bike*, then Titch will have a *tricycle*.

Repetitive story patterns also help the child predict the action in the story. The easy folktales with their patterns of three, such as *The Three Billy Goats Gruff* by Glen Rounds, *The Three Little Pigs* and *The Three Bears* by Paul Galdone, and *The Little Red Hen* by Byron Barton, support the child's reading. For once children recognize the story structure, they know that if the great big bear says, "Someone has been tasting my porridge," then the middle-size bear and the baby bear will both say the same thing.

*Synthia Saint James's bold collages reinforce the repetition of phrases in* Snow on Snow on Snow.

From *Snow on Snow on Snow* by Cheryl Chapman, illust. by Synthia Saint James, copyright © 1994 by Cheryl Chapman, text; copyright © 1994 by Synthia Saint James, illustrations. Used by permission of Dial Books for Young Readers, a division of Penguin Putnam Inc.

---

[13]Charlotte Pomerantz, *Here Comes Henny*, illus. Nancy Winslow Parker (New York: Greenwillow, 1994), p. 5.

[14]Hallie Kay Yopp, "Developing Phonemic Awareness in Young Children," *Reading Teacher* 45 (May 1992): 696–703; Steven A. Stahl, Ann M. Duffy-Hester, and Katherine Anne Doughty Stahl, "Everything You Wanted to Know About Phonics (But Were Afraid to Ask)," *Reading Research Quarterly* 33, no. 3 (1998): 338–355.

Cumulative tales have repeated patterns and phrases that become longer and longer with each incident. In Mem Fox's *Shoes from Grandpa* a simple gift for Jessie turns into a whole wardrobe as different members of her family decide to buy her an article of clothing "to go with the shoes from grandpa." There are lots of rhyming pairs here, such as "mittens soft as kittens" and a "skirt that won't show the dirt," that will invite children to make up their own special wardrobes. Patricia Mullins's lively collages include bits of fabric that reflect the theme and add to the humor of the story.

The familiar patterns of the cumulative nursery rhyme "This Is the House that Jack Built" can be found in many illustrated retellings and several modern-day variants. Children love Don and Audrey Wood's *The Napping House,* in which an old lady, a boy, a dog, a cat, and a mouse are sleeping until a flea "bites the mouse who scares the cat," and so on, until everyone wakes to a glorious day. Rose Robart creates a rollicking cumulative tale in *The Cake That Mack Ate.* Even though every verse ends in the title phrase, it is only in the last few pictures that children discover the identity of Mack, a huge dog.

Some modern stories contain predictable plots. *Rosie's Walk* by Hutchins is better for telling than reading, since the entire text is only one sentence long. However, children can learn how to predict what is going to happen to the fox by careful observation of where the unsuspecting hen takes her walk. Another tale of a narrow escape, *Across the Stream* by Mirra Ginsburg, is the story of a hen and chicks who cross a stream and foil the hungry fox. These and other stories like Colin McNaughton's *Suddenly!* help children begin to develop an understanding of how the character of a fox or a wolf will act in an animal tale. This developing sense of story also begins to help them predict action.

The popular song reprised in *Mary Wore Her Red Dress* by Merle Peek or familiar Mother Goose rhymes such as "Little Miss Muffet" or "Old Mother Hubbard" all enable the child to assume the role of reader. Children can hold the books or point to a large chart and "read the words" because they know the song or the verse. As they match sentences and phrase cards or point to individuals words in the text, they begin to read the story.

In the meantime, they are learning that those symbols stand for the words they already know. This enables them to behave like readers.

Some concept books, like *Truck* by Donald Crews give children an opportunity to read environmental print. Tana Hoban's books *I Read Signs* and *I Read Symbols* provide excellent photographs of the signs in their environmental context. Other books use print as an important part of the visual art and thus draw children's attention to letters and words. In Pat Hutchins's predictable *Little Pink Pig,* Mother Pig searches for her baby pig at bedtime. As she asks each animal for help, their animal responses are printed in a more decorative, larger, colored type. In Libba Moore Gray's *Small Green Snake,* Holly Meade uses torn-paper collage for some of the words

"I'm a grassy grassy garter snake a sassy sassy flashy flashy tail twisting tail turning tail snapping green snake hiss a hiss a hiss a hiss

*The printed words become part of the visual art in Holly Meade's lively illustrations for Libba Moore Gray's* Small Green Snake.

as well as the images and thus highlights important action and dialogue. With its wordplay and the large and colorful torn-paper words, the book will have children begging to join in the reading. In addition to being wonderful literature, books like these strengthen children's concepts about print and they can also help teachers see how aware of print children are becoming.

As more and more primary teachers begin to use real books for teaching children to read, textbook publishers are beginning to produce made-to-order predictable books written to a formula. These "little books" frequently lack the imaginative quality of true literature. They might use repetitive phrases or questions, but they have deadly dull plots and the unnatural language of primers. Look rather for imaginative trade books with natural language, a creative plot, and real child appeal. Look, too, for fine artwork such as that found in the books by Eric Carle, Denise Fleming, Pat Hutchins, Marisabina Russo, and many more outstanding author/illustrators.

The titles we have discussed here are all trade books that meet the criteria we have suggested. They help the emergent reader learn to read naturally and with real delight. For a list of predictable books by their characteristics, see Resources for Teaching, "Predictable Books."

## Big Books

As primary teachers begin to use real books to teach emergent readers, some of them put favorite stories and poems on large charts so that everyone in the class can see them. During shared reading time, the children read them together as one of them points to the words. Frequently, children illustrate these homemade charts with their own drawings and then the teacher puts them together as a big book. Teachers might chat about the words and ask a child to point to a particular word that they are certain the child knows, or to find all the words that begin with the same letter as their name. At other times, children might create their own original version of a favorite story. One group transposed the popular tale *Five Minutes' Peace* by Jill Murphy, which tells of a harassed mother elephant who could not get away from her family, to a schoolroom setting and a teacher's need for five minutes' peace.

Children love these alternative stories that they have a part in producing either by illustrating or by writing. They take ownership of them and read them to each other over and over again. In two trips we made to New Zealand to visit schools, these homemade big books were the only ones we saw.

Publishers have recognized a need for commercial big books and predictable books and created their own. Commercial big books are necessarily expensive

*First graders show much interest in reading the Big Book they have created.*
Idyllwild Elementary School, Idyllwild, California. Sharon Schmidt, teacher. Photo by Larry Rose.

*Using the structure of* Brown Bear, Brown Bear, What Do You See? *first graders created their own story about insects.*
Mission School, Redlands, California. Nancy Anderson, teacher. Photo by Larry Rose.

# RESOURCES FOR TEACHING

## Predictable Books

### LANGUAGE PATTERNS: REPETITIVE WORDS, PHRASES, QUESTIONS

Jill Bennett, *Teeny Tiny*

Ruth Brown, *A Dark Dark Tale*

Rod Campbell, *Dear Zoo*

Eric Carle, *Do You Want to Be My Friend?*

———, *Have You Seen My Cat?*

———, *The Very Busy Spider*

———, *The Very Quiet Cricket*

———, *The Very Lonely Firefly*

Denise Fleming, *Mama Cat Has Three Kittens*

———, *In the Tall Tall Grass*

———, *In the Small Small Pond*

———, *Barnyard Banter*

Phillis Gershator, *Greetings Sun*

Mirra Ginsburg, *The Chick and the Duckling*

———, *Good Morning, Chick*

Laura Godwin, *Little White Dog*

Eric Hill, *Where's Spot?*

Robert Kraus, *Where Are You Going, Little Mouse?*

———, *Whose Mouse Are You?*

Bill Martin, Jr., *Brown Bear, Brown Bear, What Do You See?*

Bernard Most, *Z-Z-Zoink!*

Charlotte Pomerantz, *Here Comes Henny*

———, *The Piggy in a Puddle*

Nancy Shaw, *Sheep in a Jeep*

Nancy Tafuri, *Have You Seen My Duckling?*

Martin Waddell, *Farmer Duck*

Sue Williams, *I Went Walking*

———, *Let's Go Visiting*

### FAMILIAR SEQUENCES: NUMBERS, DAYS OF WEEK, MONTHS, HIERARCHIES

Eric Carle, *The Very Hungry Caterpillar*

———, *Today Is Monday*

Eileen Christelow, *Five Little Monkeys Jumping on the Bed*

Paul Galdone, *The Three Bears*

———, *The Three Billy Goats Gruff*

Pat Hutchins, *Titch*

Eve Merriam, *Ten Rosy Roses*

Phyllis Root, *One Duck Stuck*

Maurice Sendak, *Chicken Soup with Rice*

Uri Shulevitz, *One Monday Morning*

Cindy Ward, *Cookie's Week*

### REPETITIVE STORY PATTERNS

Byron Barton, *Buzz Buzz Buzz*

Glen Rounds, *The Three Billy Goats Gruff*

Margaret Wise Brown, *Four Fur Feet*

Stephanie Calmenson. *The Teeny Tiny Teacher: A Teeny Tiny Ghost Story, Adapted a Teeny Tiny Bit*

Paul Galdone, *The Three Bears*

———, *The Little Red Hen*

———, *The Three Little Pigs*

Deborah Guarino, *Is Your Mama a Llama?*

Pat Hutchins, *Little Pink Pig*

Ruth Krauss, *The Carrot Seed*

Phyllis Root, *What Baby Wants*

Jeff Sheppard, *Splash Splash*

### PREDICTABLE PLOTS

Karen Beaumont Alarcón, *Louella Mae, She's Run Away!*

Margaret Wise Brown, *Goodnight Moon*

John Burningham, *Mr. Gumpy's Outing*

Pat Hutchins, *Good-Night, Owl!*

———, *Happy Birthday, Sam*

———, *Rosie's Walk*

———, *You'll Soon Grow Into Them, Titch*

Eve Rice, *Benny Bakes a Cake*

———, *Sam Who Never Forgets*

*continued*

# RESOURCES FOR TEACHING

## Predictable Books con't

### CUMULATIVE TALES

Alissa Capucilli, *Inside a House That Is Haunted*

Barbara Emberley, *Drummer Hoff*

Paul Galdone, *The Gingerbread Boy*

Sarah Hayes, *This Is the Bear*

Elizabeth MacDonald, *The Wolf Is Coming*

Shirley Neitzel, *The House I'll Build for the Wrens*

Rose Robart, *The Cake That Mack Ate*

Patricia Polacco, *In Enzo's Splendid Garden*

Cyndy Szerkeres, *The Mouse That Jack Built*

Linda Williams, *The Little Old Lady Who Was Not Afraid of Anything*

Audrey Wood, *The Napping House*

### FAMILIAR SONGS AND RHYMES

Alan Ahlberg, *Mockingbird*

Aliki, *Go Tell Aunt Rhody*

Marla Frazee, *Hush Little Baby*

Colin Hawkins and Jacqui Hawkins, *I Know an Old Lady Who Swallowed a Fly*

Eric Hill, *Nursery Rhyme Peek-a-Book*

Mary Ann Hoberman, *Miss Mary Mack*

Carol Jones, *Old MacDonald Had a Farm*

———, *This Old Man*

Merle Peek, *Mary Wore Her Red Dress and Henry Wore His Green Sneakers*

———, *Roll Over! A Counting Song*

Raffi, *Down By the Bay: Songs to Read*

———, *Five Little Ducks*

Simms Taback, *Joseph Had a Little Overcoat*

Alexandra Wallner, *The Farmer in the Dell*

Nadine Bernard Westcott, *Peanut Butter and Jelly: A Play Rhyme*

———, *Skip to My Lou*

### ARTISTIC USE OF PRINT

Katya Arnold, *Meow!*

Molly Bang, *When Sophie Gets Angry—Really, Really Angry*

Donald Crews, Night *At the Fair*

———, *School Bus*

———, *Truck*

Libba Moore Gray, *Small Green Snake*

Anna Grossnickle Hines, *Rumble Thumble Boom*

Tana Hoban, *I Read Symbols*

———, *I Read Signs*

Pat Hutchins, *Little Pink Pig*

Gail Jorgensen, *Crocodile Beat*

Karla Kuskin, *Roar and More*

Jonathon London, *Wiggle Waggle*

Phyllis Root, *One Windy Wednesday*

---

and do not provide the same sense of ownership that comes with the classmade books. This cost needs to be balanced against the number of trade books that can be purchased with the money. Some of the commercial big books use the same illustrations as the trade books; others have new illustrations. Almost all of the traditional tales, such as "The Three Bears," are available in big books. Teachers need to ask if this is the version they want to share with their class, or if they would prefer a different one.

Also, they must evaluate the text for ease of reading. Is this a version that helps students read the text? Does the placement of the text show the repetitious phrases, for example? Do the illustrations help the children read the story? Big books need to be evaluated before their purchase. The best of the commercial ones are those that replicate good, predictable trade books exactly; examples are *The Chick and the Duckling* by Mirra Ginsburg and *Rosie's Walk* by Pat Hutchins.

# Creating Big Books with Emergent Readers

**Teaching Feature**

At the end of the year, Nancy Anderson's group of kindergartners/first graders at Mission School in Redlands, California, did a unit on insects. They read informational books on insects and Eric Carle's stories about insects, including *The Very Hungry Caterpillar, The Very Busy Spider,* and *The Very Quiet Cricket.*

Using the structure of *Brown Bear, Brown Bear, What Do You See?* by Bill Martin, Jr., they wrote and illustrated their own big book with insects as their main characters. They read this together in shared reading time.

Later they decided to write their own story about a ladybug and illustrate it the way Eric Carle illustrated his stories. Using their fingerpaint

pictures, they cut out butterflies, ladybugs, and bumblebees to illustrate their story:

## LADY BUG SAVES THE DAY

Once there was a red shiny spotted ladybug. She lived in the forest. She kept busy eating aphids off the flowers and bushes.

Along came a black and orange butterfly who was being chased by a fierce mean bumblebee. The ladybug heard a terrible buzzing sound. The butterfly cried, "Help Help!" The ladybug waved and whispered, "Come over here, hide with me. Come in my house, it's safe."

The butterfly followed the ladybug to her house. She said, "Thank you for saving my life."

Both big books reflect what the children learned about insects. The first one shows how a book helped to provide structure to their story; the second one gives them an opportunity to illustrate like Eric Carle, their favorite illustrator.

*Nancy Anderson*
Mission School, Redlands, California

*The cover and one page from the story created by kindergarten and first graders about "Lady Bug Saves the Day." Notice their use of fingerpaint paper in their collage pictures, which they tried to do in the same way Eric Carle makes his.*
Mission School, Redlands Public Schools, Redlands, California. Nancy Anderson, teacher. Photo by Larry Rose.

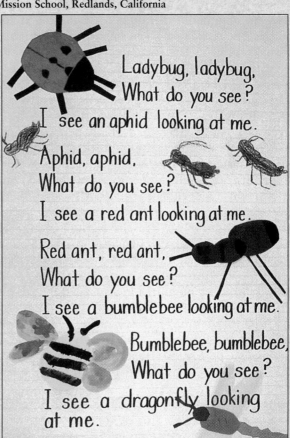

*Using the structure of* Brown Bear, Brown Bear, What Do You See? *first graders created their own story about insects.*
Mission School, Redlands, California. Nancy Anderson, teacher. Photo by Larry Rose.

## Controlled-Vocabulary Books

Most basal reading series control the number of words, the sounds of the words, and the length of the stories for beginning readers. Until the advent of books for babies and preschoolers, most picture storybooks were written to be read *to* children and thus were at a reading level of at least third grade. They were geared to the young child's interest and appreciation level, not reading ability level. That left very little for the beginning reader to read, except for preprimers and primers. This is no longer true, with the number of easy predictable books available today.

A new genre of book was created when Dr. Seuss wrote *The Cat in the Hat* in 1957. This book was written with a controlled vocabulary (derived from the Dolch vocabulary list of 220 words) for the young child to read independently. Since then many publishers have developed "easy-reading" books. In format, such books tend to look more like basal readers than picture storybooks, although they do have illustrations on every page. Some of these books, such as *Little Bear* by Else Minarik and illustrated by Sendak, and the superb *Frog and Toad* series by Arnold Lobel, are easy-reading books that do not use controlled vocabulary. They can take their rightful place in children's literature. In fact, *Frog and Toad Are Friends* was a Caldecott Honor Book and *Frog and Toad Together* was a Newbery Honor Book two years later, suggesting that quality writing can be achieved with a limited vocabulary.

Cynthia Rylant's *Henry and Mudge* series features Henry and his lovable 180-pound dog, Mudge. In *Henry and Mudge,* short episodes about these two inseparable friends are divided into chapters, just right for the newly independent readers who love them. The language is simple, but it has an almost poetic quality, particularly when the author contrasts Henry's life before and after acquiring Mudge. Before he had Mudge, he had to walk to school alone and he worried about "tornadoes, ghosts, biting dogs and bullies." But after he got Mudge, he'd think about "vanilla ice cream, rain, rocks and good dreams." Other well-loved Mudge stories include *Henry and Mudge and the Snowman Plan, Henry and Mudge and Annie's Good Move, Henry and Mudge and the Sneaky Crackers,* and *Henry and Mudge and the Starry Night.*

Today there are literally hundreds of these easy-reading books. Some are stories, some appeal to special interests such as sports, mysteries, science, or history. Not all achieve the literary excellence of the *Little Bear* series, *Frog and Toad* series, or *Henry and Mudge* series. Some appear contrived and restricted by the controlled vocabulary. Research has

*Beginning readers are supported by such "easy-reading" books as Cynthia Rylant's Henry and Mudge series. Reprinted with permission of Simon & Schuster Books for Young Readers from* Henry and Mudge: The First Book *by Cynthia Rylant, illustrated by Suçie Stevenson.*

From *Henry and Mudge: The First Book* by Cynthia Rylant, illustrated by Suçie Stevenson, illustrations copyright © 1987 Suçie Stevenson. Reprinted with permission of Simon & Schuster Books for Young Readers, an imprint of Simon & Schuster Children's Publishing Division.

shown that the meaning of the story is far more important for ease of reading than limiting vocabulary. We should not accept a book just because it has a beginning-to-read label. Each book must be evaluated for literary qualities, child appeal, and difficulty of reading.

Helping *children* choose the right book at the right time is an important aspect of literacy instruction.[15] We note with alarm the growing trend to sort trade books by levels of difficulty and then assign children to read through these levels. Sometimes children need to pick a book that is easy to read, just for the fun of it. At other times children have a fascination with a long book in which they search for familiar words and teach themselves to read. We need not limit the emergent reader's book exposure to just predictable books. One child, with whom one of the authors read in England, had taught himself to read with the *Frances* stories by Russell Hoban. He had learned to

---

[15]For insights on helping children choose their own books, see Marilyn Olhausen and Mary Jepson, "Lessons from Goldilocks: 'Somebody's Been Choosing My Books But I Can Make My Own Choices Now,' " *New Advocate* 5 (winter, 1992): 31–46.

read *Bread and Jam for Frances* and was working on *A Baby Sister for Frances*. These are difficult books, but Gerald wanted to read them, and that is the key to helping children learn to read.

Today, with the number of fine trade books available, it is quite possible to find books that children want to read and that they find pleasure in learning to read.

## INTO THE CLASSROOM

### Books to Begin On

**Room 201**

1. Select a wordless picture book to use with children of various ages. Record the retelling of the story by each child, noting differences in language development, sense of story, descriptive phrases, and complexity of plot. Be sure to let the child look through the book once before beginning to tell the story.
2. Select what you consider to be a predictable book. Share it with 5- and 6-year-olds, then reread it, waiting for them to join in at various places. What did you learn about your selection?
3. Read a story and an information book to a 5- or 6-year-old child. Ask that child to retell each book to you using only the pictures. What important ideas and vocabulary does the child remember? What additional details does the child give from the illustrations? What questions does the child ask about the book?
4. Make a big book with young children. Choose a favorite predictable book and ask 4-, 5-, or 6-year-olds to illustrate the pages on poster board after you have written in the words. How does this activity invite children to inspect written language? What aspects of the illustrator's work do the children incorporate into their book?
5. Learn several finger plays to try with young children. Can they do them? What is difficult for them?

## Personal Explorations

1. Share several stories with a child under 1 year of age. What appears to capture her or his attention? How many different ways can you provide for the child's active participation in the story?
2. Assume you are going to compile a small Mother Goose book of twenty to twenty-five rhymes. Which ones would you choose? How would you arrange them in your book?
3. Find a concept book about one particular subject. *Before* you read it, list all the possible dimensions of that concept. Then compare your list with what the author/artist chose to include.
4. Read three or four bedtime stories to one child or several children. Which ones do they ask to hear repeatedly? Can you find any patterns among their favorites?
5. Compare several preprimers and primers with the books for the beginning reader described in this text. What do you notice as being different or significant for an emerging reader?

## Related Readings

Barton, Bob, and David Booth. *Mother Goose Goes to School.* York, Maine: Stenhouse, 1995.

A collection of over a hundred nursery rhymes with ideas for teachers to extend the rhymes through creative drama, art activities, and examples of children's work.

Butler, Dorothy. *Babies Need Books.* New York: Atheneum, 1980.

A firm believer in the importance of books for the young child, this New Zealander writes from her experience as a mother, grandmother, and children's bookseller. She not only recommends books for ages 1 through 5, but she gives practical suggestions about when and how to read to wiggly children.

Cochran-Smith, Marilyn. *The Making of a Reader*. Norwood, N.J.: Ablex, 1984.

This book focuses on how adults and children observed over an eighteen-month period in a preschool collaborated on building meaning in books. It emphasizes what the children know about books and ways they seem to be coming to know it. The observational charts will prove useful to other researchers.

Fisher, Bobbi. *Joyful Learning*. Portsmouth, N.H.: Heinemann Educational Books, 1998.

———. *Thinking and Learning Together*. Portsmouth, N.H.: Heinemann Educational Books, 1995.

Written by an experienced primary-grade teacher, these two books describe a rich literature-based environment for children's literacy development. Practical suggestions are offered about organizing the day, developing emergent reading and writing activities, carrying out evaluation and portfolio assessment, and communicating with parents.

Hill, Mary W. *Home: Where Reading and Writing Begin*. Portsmouth, N.H.: Heinemann Educational Books, 1989.

Written for parents, this book is filled with children's literature titles and helpful suggestions of ways to create literate environments in the home.

Hart-Hewins, Linda, and Jan Wells. *Real Books for Reading: Learning to Read with Children's Literature*. Portsmouth, N.H.: Heinemann Educational Books, 1990.

The subtitle of this book evolved from the extensive experience of two former teachers in Canada using children's literature as the core of their classroom reading program. Practical suggestions for reading aloud, buddy reading,

conferencing with children, and writing opportunities are all given. An extensive bibliography of books for children is also included.

McConaghy, June. *Children Learning Through Literature*. Portsmouth, N.H.: Heinemann Educational Books, 1990.

A Canadian describes her experience of teaching first graders to read by using literature. She emphasizes discussing children's responses to books rather than quizzing them with questions. She describes literature's influence on children's writing and gives examples of children's stories. She also provides samples from her own journal entries to show her growth as a teacher.

Taylor, Denny, and Dorothy S. Strickland. *Family Storybook Reading*. Portsmouth, N.H.: Heinemann Educational Books, 1998 (1986).

These authors provide real-life experiences and photographs of the various ways parents share books in the home. Astute observers, the authors focus on the natural ways parents lead children to develop literacy.

Wells, Gordon. *The Meaning Makers: Children Learning Language and Using Language to Learn*. Portsmouth, N.H.: Heinemann Educational Books, 1986.

Wells reports on the importance of story and reading aloud to preschoolers for their later educational attainment. Based on fifteen years of longitudinal research, this is a significant book.

White, Dorothy. *Books Before Five*. Portsmouth, N.H.: Heinemann Educational Books, 1984 [1954].

A reissue of the first longitudinal study of a young child's response to books. Written by a young mother who was a former librarian, this book records how she and her daughter Carol explored books from the time Carol was 2 until she went to school. Long out of print, this new edition has a foreword by Marie Clay.

# Children's Literature

Ada, Alma Flor. *Gathering the Sun: An Alphabet in Spanish and English*. Translated by Rosa Zubizaretta. Illustrated by Simon Silva. Lothrop, Lee & Shepard, 1997.

Aesop. *Aesop's Fox*. Illustrated by Aki Sogabe. Browndeer, 1999.

Ahlberg, Alan. *Mockingbird*. Illustrated by Paul Howard. Candlewick, 1998.

Ahlberg, Janet, and Allan Ahlberg. *Each Peach Pear Plum*. Viking, 1979.

Alarcón, Karen Beaumont. *Louella Mae, She's Run Away!* Illustrated by Rosanne Litzinger. Holt, 1998.

Alda, Arlene. *Arlene Alda's 1 2 3 What Do You See?* Tricycle Press, 1998.

Alexander, Martha. *When The New Baby Comes I'm Moving Out*. Dial, 1992.

Aliki [Aliki Brandenberg]. *Go Tell Aunt Rhody*. Macmillan, 1986 [1974].

———. *My Feet*. Crowell, 1990.

———. *My Five Senses*. HarperCollins, 1990.

———. *My Hands*. Crowell, 1990.

Anno, Mitsumasa. *Anno's Alphabet*. Crowell, 1975.

———. *Anno's Counting Book*. Crowell, 1977.

Arnold, Katya. *Meow!* Holiday House, 1998.

Aruego, Jose. *We Hide. You Seek*. Illustrated by Ariane Dewey Greenwillow, 1979.

Aylesworth, Jim. *Old Black Fly*. Illustrated by Stephen Gammell. Holt, 1992.

Azarian, Mary. *A Farmer's Alphabet*. Godine, 1981.

Baker, Keith. *Big Fat Hen*. Harcourt Brace, 1994.

Bang, Molly. *Ten, Nine, Eight*. Greenwillow, 1983.

———. *When Sophie Gets Angry—Really, Really Angry.* Scholastic, 1999.

Banks, Kate. *And If the Moon Could Talk.* Illustrated by Georg Hallensleben. Foster Books, 1998.

Bannatyne-Cugnet, Jo. *A Prairie Alphabet.* Illustrated by Yevette Moore. Tundra Books, 1992.

Banyai, Istvan. *Zoom.* Viking, 1995.

Bennett, Jill. *Teeny Tiny.* Illustrated by Tomie de Paola. Putnam, 1986.

Berger, Barbara. *A Lot of Otters.* Philomel, 1997.

Bowen, Betsy. *Antler, Bear, Canoe: A Northwoods Alphabet Year.* Little, Brown, 1991.

Branley, Franklin. *Flash, Crash, Rumble, and Roll.* Illustrated by True Kelley, HarperCollins, 1999.

Brett, Jan. *The Gingerbread Baby.* Putnam, 1999.

———. *The Mitten: a Ukranian Folktale.* Putnam, 1999.

Briggs, Raymond. *The Snowman.* Random House, 1978.

Brown, Marcia. *Stone Soup.* Scribner's, 1947.

Brown, Margaret Wise. *Four Fur Feet.* Watermark, 1989. [William R. Scott. (Hopscotch Books), 1961].

———. *Goodnight Moon.* Illustrated by Clement Hurd. Harper & Row, 1947.

———. *The Goodnight Moon Room.* Illustrated by Clement Hurd. Harper & Row, 1984.

———. *The Runaway Bunny.* Illustrated by Clement Hurd. Harper & Row, 1972 [1942].

Brown, Ruth. *A Dark Dark Tale.* Dial, 1981.

Burningham, John. *John Burningham's ABC.* Crown, 1993 [1986].

———. *Mr. Gumpy's Outing.* Holt, 1971.

Byron, Barton. *Buzz Buzz Buzz.* Macmillan, 1973.

———. *The Little Red Hen.* HarperCollins, 1994.

———. *Machines at Work.* Crowell, 1987.

Calmenson, Stephanie. *The Teeny Tiny Teacher: A Teeny Tiny Ghost Story, Adapted a Teeny Tiny Bit.* Scholastic, 1998.

Campbell, Rod. *Dear Zoo.* Four Winds, 1983.

Capucilli, Alissa. *Inside a House That Is Haunted: A Rebus Read-Along Story.* Illustrated by Tedd Arnold. Scholastic, 1998.

Carle, Eric. *1, 2, 3, to the Zoo.* Philomel, 1968.

———. *Do You Want to Be My Friend?* Harper & Row, 1971.

———. *Have You Seen My Cat?* Picture Book Studio, 1987.

———. *Pancakes Pancakes!* Simon & Schuster, 1990.

———. *Today Is Monday.* Philomel, 1993.

———. *The Very Busy Spider.* Philomel, 1984.

———. *The Very Clumsy Click Beetle.* Philomel, 1999.

———. *The Very Hungry Caterpillar.* Philomel, 1969.

———. *The Very Lonely Firefly.* Philomel, 1995.

———. *The Very Quiet Cricket.* Philomel, 1990.

Carlstrom, Nancy White. *Jesse Bear, What Will You Wear?* Illustrated by Bruce Degen. Macmillan, 1986.

Cauley, Lorinda Bryan. *The Three Little Kittens.* Putnam, 1982.

Chandra, Deborah. *A is for Amos.* Illustrated by Keiko Narahashi. Farrar Straus Giroux, 1999.

Chapman, Cheryl. *Snow on Snow on Snow.* Illustrated by Synthia St. James. Dial, 1994.

Christelow, Eileen. *Five Little Monkeys Jumping on the Bed.* Clarion, 1989.

Cohen, Miriam. *Will I Have a Friend?* Illustrated by Lillian Hoban. Macmillan, 1967.

Cooke, Trish. *So Much.* Illustrated by Helen Oxenbury. Candlewick, 1994.

Cousins, Lucy. *Maisy Goes to Bed.* Little, Brown, 1990.

Cowley, Joy. *Greedy Cat.* Owens, 1988.

Crews, Donald. *Flying.* Greenwillow, 1986.

———. *Freight Train.* Greenwillow, 1978.

———. *Harbor.* Greenwillow, 1982.

———. *Sail Away.* Greenwillow, 1995.

———. *School Bus.* Greenwillow, 1984.

———. *Ten Black Dots.* Greenwillow, 1986 [1968].

———. *Truck.* Greenwillow, 1980.

Cummings, Pat. *Purrrrr.* HarperCollins, 1999.

Daly, Niki. *Jamela's Dress.* Farrar Straus Giroux, 1999.

Day, Alexandra. *Carl Goes Shopping.* Farrar Straus Giroux, 1989.

———. *Follow Carl!* Farrar Straus Giroux, 1998.

———. *Good Dog, Carl.* Green Tiger Press, 1985.

de Angeli, Marguerite. *The Book of Nursery and Mother Goose Rhymes.* Doubleday, 1954.

Delacre, Lulu, ed. *Arroz Con Leche: Popular Songs and Rhymes from Latin America.* Scholastic, 1989.

de Paola, Tomie. *The Comic Adventures of Old Mother Hubbard and Her Dog.* Harcourt Brace, 1981.

———. *Pancakes for Breakfast.* Harcourt Brace, 1978.

———. *Tomie de Paola's Mother Goose.* Putnam, 1985.

Dragonwagon, Crescent. *Alligator Arrived with Apples.* Illustrated by Jose Aruego and Ariane Dewey. Macmillan, 1987.

Earle, Ann. *Zipping Zapping Zooming Bats.* Illustrated by Henry Cole. HarperCollins, 1995.

Ehlert, Lois. *Color Farm.* Lippincott, 1990.

———. *Color Zoo.* Lippincott, 1990.

———. *Eating the Alphabet.* Harcourt Brace, 1989.

———. *Feathers for Lunch.* Harcourt Brace, 1990.

———. *Fish Eyes: A Book You Can Count On.* Harcourt Brace, 1990.

———. *Red Leaf, Yellow Leaf.* Harcourt Brace, 1991.

Emberley, Barbara. *Drummer Hoff.* Illustrated by Ed Emberley. Prentice Hall, 1967.

Falls, C. B. *ABC Book.* Morrow, 1998.

Falwell, Cathryn. *Feast for Ten.* Clarion, 1993.

Feelings, Muriel. *Jambo Means Hello: Swahili Alphabet Book.* Illustrated by Tom Feelings. Dial, 1974.

———. *Moja Means One: Swahili Counting Book.* Illustrated by Tom Feelings. Dial, 1971.

Fleming, Denise. *Barnyard Banter.* Holt, 1993.

———. *In the Small Small Pond.* Holt, 1993.

———. *In the Tall Tall Grass.* Holt, 1991.

———. *Mama Cat Has Three Kittens.* Holt, 1998.

Fox, Mem. *Shoes from Grandpa.* Illustrated by Patricia Mullins. Orchard, 1990.

———. *Time for Bed.* Illustrated by Jane Dyer. Harcourt Brace, 1993.

Frazee, Marla. *Hush, Little Baby: A Folk Song with Pictures.* Harcourt Brace, 1999.

Gág, Wanda. *The ABC Bunny.* Coward-McCann, 1933.

Galdone, Paul. *The Gingerbread Boy.* Clarion, 1975.

———. *The Little Red Hen.* Clarion, 1973.

———. *Over in the Meadow.* Prentice Hall, 1986.

———. *The Three Bears*. Clarion, 1972.

———. *The Three Billy Goats Gruff*. Clarion, 1981.

———. *The Three Little Pigs*. Clarion, 1970.

Garne, S. T. *One White Sail: A Caribbean Counting Book*. Illustrated by Lisa Etre. Simon & Schuster, 1994.

Garten, Jan. *The Alphabet Tale*. Illustrated by Muriel Batherman. Greenwillow, 1994 [1964].

Geisert, Arthur. *Pigs from 1 to 10*. Houghton Mifflin, 1992.

Gershator, Phillis. *Greetings Sun*. Illustrated by Synthia St. James. DK Ink, 1998.

Giganti, Paul, Jr. *How Many Snails?* Illustrated by Donald Crews. Greenwillow, 1988.

Ginsburg, Mirra. *Across the Stream*. Illustrated by Nancy Tafuri. Greenwillow, 1982.

———. *The Chick and the Duckling*. Illustrated by Jose Aruego and Ariane Dewey. Macmillan, 1972.

———. *Good Morning, Chick*. Illustrated by Byron Barton. Greenwillow, 1980.

Godwin, Laura. *Little White Dog*. Dan Yaccarino. Hyperion, 1998.

Gray, Libba Moore. *Small Green Snake*. Illustrated by Holly Meade. Orchard, 1994.

Greenaway, Kate. *Mother Goose, or the Old Nursery Rhymes*. Warne, n.d.

Greenfield, Eloise. *She Come Bringing Me That Little Baby Girl*. Illustrated by John Steptoe. Lippincott, 1974.

———. *Water, Water*. Illustrated by Jan Gilchrist Spivey. HarperCollins, 1999.

Griego, Margot C., et al. *Tortillitas Para Mama and Other Nursery Rhymes/Spanish and English*. Illustrated by Barbara Cooney. Holt, 1981.

Grimes, Nikki. *C Is for City*. Illustrated by Pat Cummings. Lothrop, Lee & Shepard, 1995.

Guarino, Deborah. *Is Your Mama a Llama?* Illustrated by Steven Kellogg. Scholastic, 1989.

Hale, Sarah Josepha. *Mary Had a Little Lamb*. Photo-illustrated by Bruce McMillan. Scholastic, 1990.

———. *Mary Had a Little Lamb*. Illustrated by Sally Mavor. Orchard, 1995.

Harrison, Ted. *A Northern Alphabet*. Tundra, 1982.

Hawkins, Colin, and Jacqui Hawkins. *I Know an Old Lady Who Swallowed a Fly*. Putnam, 1987.

Hayes, Sarah. *Nine Ducks Nine*. Lothrop, Lee & Shepard, 1990.

———. *This Is the Bear*. Illustrated by Helen Craig. Lippincott, 1986.

Henkes, Kevin. *The Biggest Boy*. Illustrated by Nancy Tafuri. Greenwillow, 1995.

Hest, Amy. *Baby Duck and the Bad Eyeglasses*. Illustrated by Jill Barton. Candlewick, 1996.

———. *In the Rain with Baby Duck*. Illustrated by Jill Barton. Candlewick, 1996.

———. *Off to School, Baby Duck!* Illustrated by Jill Barton. Candlewick, 1999.

Hill, Eric. *Good Night Spot*. Putnam, 1999

———. *Nursery Rhyme Peek-a-Book*. Price, Stern, 1982.

———. *Spot Bakes a Cake*. Putnam, 1994.

———. *Spot Goes to School*. Putnam, 1994.

———. *Where's Spot?* Putnam, 1980.

Hoban, Russell. *A Baby Sister for Frances*. Illustrated by Lillian Hoban. Harper & Row, 1964.

———. *Bread and Jam for Frances*. Illustrated by Lillian Hoban. Harper & Row, 1964.

Hoban, Tana. *1, 2, 3*. Greenwillow, 1985.

———. *26 Letters and 99 Cents*. Greenwillow, 1987.

———. *A, B, See!* Greenwillow, 1982.

———. *Black on White*. Greenwillow, 1993.

———. *Colors Everywhere*. Greenwillow, 1995.

———. *Exactly the Opposite*. Greenwillow, 1983.

———. *I Read Signs*. Greenwillow, 1983.

———. *I Read Symbols*. Greenwillow, 1983.

———. *Is It Larger? Is It Smaller?* Greenwillow, 1985.

———. *Let's Count*. Greenwillow, 1999.

———. *Red, Blue, Yellow Shoe*. Greenwillow, 1986.

———. *Shapes and Things*. Macmillan, 1970.

———. *So Many Circles, So Many Squares*. 1998.

———. *Spirals, Curves, Fanshapes, and Lines*. Greenwillow, 1992.

———. *What Is It?* Greenwillow, 1985.

———. *White on Black*. Greenwillow, 1993.

Hoberman, Mary Ann. *Miss Mary Mack*. Illustrated by Nadine Bernard Wescott. Little, Brown, 1998.

———. *The Seven Silly Eaters*. Illustrated by Marla Frazee. Browndeer, 1997.

Hogrogian, Nonny. *One Fine Day*. Macmillan, 1971.

Hopkins, Lee Bennett. *April, Bubbles, Chocolate: An ABC of Poetry*. Illustrated by Barry Root. Simon & Schuster, 1994.

Huck, Charlotte. *A Creepy Countdown*. Illustrated by Jos. A. Smith. Greenwillow, 1998.

Hughes, Shirley. *The Big Alfie and Annie Rose Storybook*. Lothrop, Lee & Shepard, 1989.

———. *Alfie's ABC*. Lothrop, Lee & Shepard, 1997.

———. *All About Alfie*. Lothrop, Lee & Shepard, 1997.

Hunt, Jonathon, *Bestiary: An Illuminated Alphabet of the Middle Ages*. Simon & Schuster, 1998.

Hunt, Peter. *Illuminations*. Bradbury, 1989.

Hutchins, Pat. *1 Hunter*. Greenwillow, 1982.

———. *Changes, Changes*. Macmillan, 1971.

———. *The Doorbell Rang*. Greenwillow, 1986.

———. *Good-Night, Owl!* Macmillan (Penguin), 1972.

———. *Happy Birthday, Sam*. Penguin, 1981.

———. *Little Pink Pig*. Greenwillow, 1994.

———. *Rosie's Walk*. Macmillan, 1968.

———. *Tidy Titch*. Greenwillow, 1991.

———. *Titch*. Macmillan, 1971.

———. *You'll Soon Grow into Them, Titch*. Greenwillow, 1983.

Isadora, Rachel. *City Seen from A to Z*. Greenwillow, 1983.

Jeffers, Susan. *Three Jovial Huntsmen*. Macmillan, 1989.

Jenkins, Steve. *Looking Down*. Houghton Mifflin, 1995.

Johnson, Angela. *Joshua by the Sea*. Illustrated by Rhonda Mitchell. Orchard, 1994.

———. *Joshua's Night Whisper*. Illustrated by Rhonda Mitchell. Orchard, 1994.

———. *Mama Bird, Baby Birds*. Illustrated by Rhonda Mitchell. Orchard, 1994.

———. *Rain Feet*. Illustrated by Rhonda Mitchell. Orchard, 1994.

Johnson, Stephen T. *Alphabet City*. Viking, 1995.

Jonas, Ann. *Aardvarks Disembark!* Greenwillow, 1989.

———. *Color Dance*. Greenwillow, 1989.

———. *Splash!* Greenwillow, 1995.

Jones, Carol. *Old MacDonald Had a Farm*. Houghton Mifflin, 1989.

———. *This Old Man*. Houghton Mifflin, 1990.

Jorgensen, Gail. *Crocodile Beat*. Illustrated by Patricia Mullins. Simon & Schuster, 1989.

Keats, Ezra Jack. *Over in the Meadow*. Four Winds, 1971.

Kellogg, Steven. *Chicken Little*. Morrow, 1987.

King-Smith, Dick. *All Pigs Are Beautiful*. Illustrated by Anita Jeram. Candlewick, 1993.

———. *I Love Guinea Pigs*. Illustrated by Anita Jeram. Candlewick, 1995.

Kitchen, Bert. *Animal Alphabet*. Dial, 1984.

———. *Animal Numbers*. Dial, 1987.

Kovalski, Maryann. *The Wheels on the Bus*. Little, Brown, 1987.

Kraus, Robert. *Where Are You Going, Little Mouse?* Illustrated by Jose Aruego and Ariane Dewey. Greenwillow, 1986.

———. *Whose Mouse Are You?* Illustrated by Jose Aruego and Ariane Dewey. Macmillan, 1970.

Krauss, Ruth. *The Carrot Seed*. Illustrated by Crockett Johnson. Harper & Row, 1945.

Kunhardt, Dorothy. *Pat the Bunny*. Golden, 1962 [1940].

Kunhardt, Edith. *Pat the Puppy*. Golden, 1993.

Kuskin, Karla. *Roar and More*. HarperCollins, 1990.

Lamont, Priscilla. *Playtime Rhymes*. Dorling Kindersley, 1998.

Langstaff, John. *Oh, A-Hunting We Will Go*. Illustrated by Nancy Winslow Parker. Atheneum, 1974.

———. *Over in the Meadow*. Illustrated by Feodor Rojankovsky. Harcourt Brace, 1967.

Lewis, Kevin. *Chugga-Chugga Choo-Choo*. Illustrated by Daniel Kirk. Hyperion, 1999.

Lobel, Anita. *Alison's Zinnia*. Greenwillow, 1990.

———. *Away from Home*. Greenwillow, 1994.

Lobel, Arnold. *Days with Frog and Toad*. Harper & Row, 1979.

———. *Frog and Toad All Year*. Harper & Row, 1976.

———. *Frog and Toad Are Friends*. Harper & Row, 1970.

———. *Frog and Toad Together*. Harper & Row, 1972.

———. *On Market Street*. Illustrated by Anita Lobel. Greenwillow, 1981.

———. *Whiskers and Rhymes*. Greenwillow, 1985.

———., ed. and illus. *The Random House Book of Mother Goose*. Random House, 1986.

London, Jonathon. *Wiggle Waggle*. Illustrated by Michael Rex. Harcourt Brace, 1999.

Lyon, George Ella. *Counting on the Woods*. Photographs by Ann W. Olson. DK Ink, 1998.

MacDonald, Elizabeth. *The Wolf Is Coming*. Illustrated by Ken Brown. Dutton, 1998.

MacDonald, Flora. *Flora MacDonald's ABC*. Candlewick, 1997.

MacDonald, Suse. *Alphabatics*. Bradbury, 1986.

———. *Sea Shapes*. Gulliver, 1994.

Manson, Christopher. *The Tree in the Wood: An Old Nursery Song*. North-South, 1993.

Markle, Sandra, and William Markle. *Gone Forever! An Alphabet of Extinct Animals*. Illustrated by Felipe Dávalos. Atheneum, 1998.

Marshall, James. *James Marshall's Mother Goose*. Farrar Straus Giroux, 1979.

Martin, Bill, Jr. *Brown Bear, Brown Bear, What Do You See?* Illustrated by Eric Carle. Holt, 1983.

———. *The Happy Hippopotami*. Illustrated by Betsy Everitt. Harcourt Brace, 1991.

———. *Polar Bear, Polar Bear, What Do You Hear?* Illustrated by Eric Carle. Holt, 1991.

Martin, Bill, Jr., and John Archambault. *Chicka Chicka Boom Boom*. Illustrated by Lois Ehlert. Simon & Schuster, 1989.

Mayer, Mercer. *A Boy, a Dog, and a Frog*. Dial, 1967.

———. *Frog Goes to Dinner*. Dial, 1974.

———. *One Frog Too Many*. Dial, 1975.

McCully, Emily Arnold. *Picnic*. Harper & Row, 1984.

———. *School*. Harper & Row, 1987.

McCurdy, Michael. *The Sailor's Alphabet*. Houghton Mifflin, 1998.

McMillan, Bruce. *Eating Fractions*. Scholastic, 1991.

McNaughton, Colin. *Boo!* Harcourt Brace, 1996.

———. *Preston's Goal*. Harcourt Brace, 1998.

———. *Suddenly!* Harcourt Brace, 1994.

———. *Yum!* Harcourt Brace, 1999.

Merriam, Eve. *12 Ways to Get to 11*. Illustrated by Bernie Karlin. Simon & Schuster, 1993.

———. *Ten Rosy Roses*. Illustrated by Julia Gorton. HarperCollins, 1999.

———. *What in the World?* Illustrated by Barbara J. Phillips-Duke. HarperCollins, 1998.

Mickelwait, Lucy. *I Spy: An Alphabet in Art*. Greenwillow, 1992.

Miller, Margaret. *Can You Guess?* Greenwillow, 1993.

———. *Guess Who?* Greenwillow, 1994.

———. *Where Does It Go?* Greenwillow, 1992.

———. *Who Uses This?* Greenwillow, 1990.

———. *Whose Hat?* Greenwillow, 1988.

Minarik, Else Holmelund. *Father Bear Comes Home*. Illustrated by Maurice Sendak. Harper & Row, 1959.

———. *A Kiss for Little Bear*. Illustrated by Maurice Sendak. Harper & Row, 1968.

———. *Little Bear*. Illustrated by Maurice Sendak. Harper & Row, 1957.

———. *Little Bear's Friend*. Illustrated by Maurice Sendak. Harper & Row, 1960.

———. *Little Bear's Visit*. Illustrated by Maurice Sendak. Harper & Row, 1961.

Mora, Pat. *Pablo's Tree*. Illustrated by Cecily Lang. Macmillan, 1994.

Morgan, Pierr. *The Turnip: An Old Russian Folktale*. Paper Star, 1996.

Morris, Ann. *Bread, Bread, Bread*. Photographs by Ken Heyman. Lothrop, Lee & Shepard, 1989.

———. *Houses and Homes*. Photographs by Ken Heyman. Lothrop, Lee & Shepard, 1992.

———. *Loving*. Photographs by Ken Heyman. Lothrop, Lee & Shepard, 1990.

———. *Play*. Lothrop, Lee & Shepard, 1998.

————. *Work.* Lothrop, Lee & Shepard, 1998.

Moss, Lloyd. *Zin! Zin! Zin! A Violin.* Illustrated by Marjorie Priceman. Simon & Schuster, 1995.

Most, Bernard. *The Cow That Went Oink.* Harcourt Brace, 1990.

————. *Z-Z-Zoink!* Harcourt Brace, 1999.

Mullins, Patricia. *V for Vanishing: An Alphabet of Endangered Animals.* HarperCollins, 1993.

Murphy, Jill. *Five Minutes' Peace.* Putnam, 1986.

Musgrove, Margaret. *Ashanti to Zulu: African Traditions.* Illustrated by Leo and Diane Dillon. Dial, 1976.

Neitzel, Shirley. *The House I'll Build for the Wrens.* Greenwillow, 1997.

Onyefulu, Ifeoma. *A Is for Africa.* Cobblehill, 1993.

————. *Chidi Only Likes Blue: An African Book of Colors.* Cobblehill, 1997.

————. *Emeka's Gift: An African Counting Story.* Cobblestone, 1995.

Opie, Iona. *Here Comes Mother Goose.* Illustrated by Rosemary Wells. Candlewick, 1999.

————. *My Very First Mother Goose.* Illustrated by Rosemary Wells. Candlewick, 1996.

Opie, Iona, and Peter Opie. *I Saw Esau.* Illustrated by Maurice Sendak. Candlewick Press, 1992.

————. *The Oxford Dictionary of Nursery Rhymes.* Oxford, 1951.

Ormerod, Jan. *Jan Ormerod's To Baby with Love.* Lothrop, Lee & Shepard, 1994.

Owens, Mary Beth. *A Caribou Alphabet.* Illustrated by Mark McCollough. Tilbury House, 1988.

Oxenbury, Helen. Baby Board Books. *Dressing. Family. Friends. Playing. Working.* All Simon & Schuster, 1995 [1981].

————. Baby Board Books. *I Can. I Hear. I See. I Touch.* All Candlewick, 1995 [Random House, 1986].

————. *Helen Oxenbury's ABC of Things.* Watts, 1972.

Peek, Merle. *Mary Wore Her Red Dress and Henry Wore His Green Sneakers.* Clarion, 1985.

————. *Roll Over! A Counting Song.* Clarion, 1981.

Pellitier, David. *The Graphic Alphabet.* Orchard, 1996.

Petersham, Maud, and Miska Petersham. *The Rooster Crows.* Macmillan, 1945.

Pinkney, Andrea. *I Smell Honey.* Illustrated by Brian Pinkney. Harcourt Brace, 1997.

————. *Pretty Brown Face.* Illustrated by Brian Pinkney. Harcourt Brace, 1997.

————. *Shake Shake Shake.* Illustrated by Brian Pinkney. Harcourt Brace, 1997.

————. *Watch Me Dance.* Illustrated by Brian Pinkney. Harcourt Brace, 1997.

Pomerantz, Charlotte. *Here Comes Henny.* Illustrated by Nancy Winslow Parker. Greenwillow, 1994.

————. *One Duck, Another Duck.* Illustrated by Jose Aruego and Ariane Dewey. Greenwillow, 1984.

————. *The Piggy in a Puddle.* Illustrated by James Marshall. Macmillan, 1974.

Pomeroy, Diana. *One Potato: A Counting Book of Potato Prints.* Harcourt Brace, 1996.

————. *Wildflower ABC.* Harcourt Brace, 1997.

Provensen, Alice, and Martin Provensen *A Peaceable Kingdom: The Shaker ABCEDARIUS.* Viking, 1978.

Rackham, Arthur. *Mother Goose, or the Old Nursery Rhymes.* Appleton, 1913.

Raffi. *Down By the Bay: Songs to Read.* Illustrated by Nadine Bernard Westcott. Crown, 1987.

————. *Five Little Ducks.* Illustrated by Jose Aruego and Ariane Dewey. Crown, 1989.

Rathman, Peggy. *10 Minutes Till Bedtime.* Putnam, 1999.

————. *Goodnight, Gorilla.* Putnam, 1994.

Rice, Eve. *Benny Bakes a Cake.* Greenwillow, 1981.

————. *Sam Who Never Forgets.* Greenwillow, 1977.

Robart, Rose. *The Cake That Mack Ate.* Illustrated by Maryann Kovalski. Joy Street/Little, Brown, 1986.

Rojankovsky, Feodor. *The Tall Book of Mother Goose.* Harper & Row, 1942.

Root, Phyllis. *One Duck Stuck.* Illustrated by Jane Chapman. Candlewick, 1998.

————. *What Baby Wants.* Illustrated by Jill Barton. Candlewick, 1998.

Rosen, Michael. *We're Going on a Bear Hunt.* Illustrated by Helen Oxenbury. Macmillan, 1989.

Root, Phyllis. *One Windy Wednesday.* Illustrated by Helen Craig. Candlewick, 1996.

Rounds, Glen. *Old MacDonald Had a Farm.* Holiday House, 1981.

————. *The Three Billy Goats Gruff.* Holiday House, 1993.

Ryan, Pam Munoz. *One Hundred Is a Family.* Illustrated by Benrei Huang. Hyperion, 1994.

Rylant, Cynthia. *Henry and Mudge.* Illustrated by Suçie Stevenson. Bradbury, 1987.

————. *Henry and Mudge and Annie's Good Move.* Illustrated by Suçie Stevenson. Simon & Schuster, 1998.

————. *Henry and Mudge and the Sneaky Crackers.* Illustrated by Suçie Stevenson. Simon & Schuster, 1998.

————. *Henry and Mudge and the Snowman Plan.* Illustrated by Suçie Stevenson. Simon & Schuster, 1999.

————. *Henry and Mudge and the Starry Night.* Illustrated by Suçie Stevenson. Simon & Schuster, 1998.

Sabuda, Robert. *The Movable Mother Goose.* Simon & Schuster, 1999.

Sanders, Marilyn. *What's Your Name? From Ariel to Zoe.* Photographs by Eve Sanders. Holiday House, 1995.

Scarry, Richard. *Richard Scarry's Best Mother Goose Ever.* Golden Press, 1970.

Schnur, Steve. *Autumn: An Alphabet Acrostic.* Illustrated by Leslie Evans. Clarion, 1997.

————. *Spring: An Alphabet Acrostic.* Illustrated by Leslie Evans. Clarion, 1999.

Schwartz, Amy. *Old MacDonald.* Scholastic, 1999.

Scott, Ann Herbert. *Sam.* Illustrated by Symeon Shimin. McGraw-Hill, 1992 [1967].

Sendak, Maurice. *Chicken Soup with Rice.* HarperCollins, 1962.

————. *Hector Protector and As I Went over the Water.* HarperCollins, 1990 [1965].

————. *We Are All in the Dumps with Jack and Guy: Two Nursery Rhymes with Pictures.* HarperCollins, 1993.

Seuss, Dr. [Theodor S. Geisel]. *The Cat in the Hat.* Beginner Books, 1957.

Shannon, David. *No David!* Scholastic, 1998.

Shaw, Nancy. *Sheep in a Jeep.* Illustrated by Margot Shaw. Houghton Mifflin, 1986.

Shelby, Anne. *Potluck*. Illustrated by Irene Trivas. Orchard, 1991.

Sheppard, Jeff. *Splash, Splash*. Illustrated by Dennis Panek. Macmillan, 1994.

Shulevitz, Uri. *One Monday Morning*. Scribner's, 1967.

Simmons, Jane. *Come Along Daisy!* Little, Brown, 1998.

Sis, Peter. *Waving: A Counting Book*. Greenwillow, 1988.

Slobodkina, Esphyr. *Caps for Sale*. Addison, 1947.

Spier, Peter. *The Fox Went Out on a Chilly Night*. Doubleday, 1961.

———. *Noah's Ark*. Doubleday, 1977.

———. *Peter Spier's Rain*. Doubleday, 1982.

Steptoe, John. *Baby Says*. Lothrop, Lee & Shepard, 1988.

Stevens, Janet. *The House That Jack Built*. Greenwillow, 1983.

Stevens, Janet, and Susan Crummel Stevens. *Cook-a-Doodle-Doo!* Harcourt Brace, 1999.

Sutherland, Zena. *The Orchard Book of Nursery Rhymes*. Illustrated by Faith Jaques. Orchard, 1990.

Sturges, Philemon. *The Little Red Hen (Makes a Pizza)*. Illustrated by Amy Walrod. Dutton, 1999.

Sweet, Melissa. *Fiddle-I-Fee*. Little, Brown, 1992.

Szerkeres, Cyndy. *The House That Jack Built*. Scholastic, 1997.

Taback, Simms. *Joseph Had a Little Overcoat*. Viking, 1999.

———. *There Was an Old Lady Who Swallowed a Fly*. Viking, 1997.

Tafuri, Nancy. *Early Morning in the Barn*. Greenwillow, 1983.

———. *Follow Me!* Greenwillow, 1990.

———. *Have You Seen My Duckling?* Greenwillow, 1984.

———. *Junglewalk*. Greenwillow, 1988.

Tapahonso, Luci, and Eleanor Schick. *Navajo ABC: A Diné Alphabet Book*. Illustrated by Eleanor Schick. Little, Brown, 1995.

Tobias, Tobi. *A World of Words: An ABC of Quotations*. Illustrated by Peter Malone. Lothrop, Lee & Shepard, 1998.

Tudor, Tasha. *A Is for Annabelle*. Walck, 1954.

———. *Mother Goose*. Walck, 1944.

Turkle, Brinton. *Deep in the Forest*. Dutton, 1976.

Van Allsburg, Chris. *The Z Was Zapped: A Play in Twenty-Six Acts*. Houghton Mifflin, 1987.

Waddell, Martin. *Farmer Duck*. Illustrated by Helen Oxenbury. Candlewick, 1993.

———. *Owl Babies*. Illustrated by Patrick Benson. Candlewick, 1992.

Wallner, Alexandra. *The Farmer in the Dell*. Holiday House, 1998.

Ward, Cindy. *Cookie's Week*. Illustrated by Tomie de Paola. Putnam, 1988.

Watson, Clyde. *Applebet*. Illustrated by Wendy Watson. Farrar Straus Giroux, 1982.

Weiss, Nicki. *Where Does the Brown Bear Go?* Greenwillow, 1989.

Wells, Rosemary. *Old Macdonald*. Scholastic, 1998.

———. Very First Books. *Max's Bath*, 1985. *Max's Bedtime*, 1985. *Max's Birthday*, 1985. *Max's Breakfast*, 1985. *Max's First Word*, 1979. *Max's Ride*, 1979. *Max's Toys*, 1979. All Dial.

Westcott, Nadine Bernard. I *Know an Old Lady Who Swallowed a Fly*. Little, Brown, 1980.

———. *Peanut Butter and Jelly: A Play Rhyme*. Dutton, 1987.

Wiesner, David. *Free Fall*. Lothrop, Lee & Shepard, 1988.

———. *Sector 7*. Clarion, 1999.

———. *Tuesday*. Clarion, 1991.

Wilbur, Richard. *The Disappearing Alphabet*. Illustrated by David Diaz. Harcourt Brace, 1999.

Wildsmith, Brian. *Brian Wildsmith's Mother Goose*. Watts, 1963.

Williams, Linda. *The Little Old Lady Who Was Not Afraid of Anything*. Illustrated by Megan Lloyd. Harper & Row, 1986.

Williams, Sue. *I Went Walking*. Illustrated by Julie Vivas. Harcourt Brace, 1990.

———. *Let's Go Visiting*. Illustrated by Julie Vivas. Harcourt Brace, 1998.

Williams, Vera B. *"More More More," Said the Baby*. Greenwillow, 1990.

Wilson, April. *Magpie Magic: A Tale of Colorful Mischief*. Dial, 1999.

Wood, Audrey. *Heckedy Peg*. Illustrated by Don Wood. Harcourt Brace, 1987.

———. *The Napping House*. Illustrated by Don Wood. Harcourt Brace, 1984.

Wood, Jakki. *Fiddle-I-Fee*. Bradbury, 1994.

Wright, Blanche Fisher. *The Real Mother Goose*. Running Press, 1992 [1916].

Yorinks, Arthur. *The Alphabet Atlas*. Illustrated by Adrienne Yorinks and Jeanyee Wong. Winslow Press, 1999.

Zelinsky, Paul O. *The Wheels on the Bus*. Dutton, 1990.

Zemach, Margot. *It Could Always Be Worse: A Yiddish Folktale*. Farrar Straus, 1990.

# Picture Books

Courtesy of Linda Rozenfeld/Images Marmor Rozenfeld

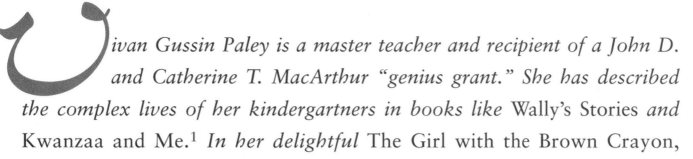

*ivan Gussin Paley is a master teacher and recipient of a John D. and Catherine T. MacArthur "genius grant." She has described the complex lives of her kindergartners in books like* Wally's Stories *and* Kwanzaa and Me.[1] *In her delightful* The Girl with the Brown Crayon,

Paley details a year-long odyssey that began when she read Leo Lionni's *Frederick* to her 5- and 6-year-olds. In *Frederick* Lionni creates his own version of the fable of the ant and the grasshopper, only this tale celebrates the contribution of Frederick, a mouse poet. The other mice bring in the harvest for the long winter, but Frederick does not work. He is gathering a harvest of sights and feelings. When the wind is cold and there is no food, Frederick shares his contribution of words and colors with his friends. He makes up poetry about the sun and the flowers and warms their souls. Paley describes the responses of a little 5-year-old girl following the first reading of the book.

> Reeny, a five-year-old, has fallen in love with Leo Lionni's Frederick, "because that brown mouse seem to be just like me! . . . Because I'm always thinking 'bout colors and words the same like him."

Paley reports that having identified with Frederick, Reeny is compelled to investigate further.

> She takes the book to a table and turns the pages, slowly tracing the mice with her finger. "They so . . . ," she sighs, unable to complete the sentence. But she puts her brown crayon to the task. The first picture Reeny copies is of Frederick sitting with his eyes closed under a warm yellow sun, while the other mice struggle to carry ears of corn to their hideout in the stones. "He is so quiet." In his stillness Reeny finds her word.
>
> "Frederick's not as nice as them," Cory argues, puzzled at her new friend's interest. "He's being mean."
>
> Reeny touches Cory's arm. "That's not the same as mean. He's thinking. Anyway, those others is nicer but I still like Frederick. Look how his tail is, Cory, don't you love his tail the way it goes?"
>
> "Can you do the eyes for me?" Cory asks, pushing her paper in front of Reeny.

When Paley looks again, five more children are drawing mice. "By some unspoken agreement they [the children] are following a new curriculum."[2]

This sensitively written book shows how an artist and one little girl transformed a whole classroom community. Lionni's books inspired the children's visual, mental, and verbal imaginations, and this wonderful teacher related his books to their life experiences, and life experiences back to the books! Repeated readings heightened the children's appreciation for the language and art of the story. Their experiences with art helped them see what they could do with media, and talking and writing about their own pictures enhanced their vocabularies.

---

[2]Vivian Gussin Paley, *The Girl with the Brown Crayon* (Cambridge, Mass.: Harvard University Press, 1997).

*Leo Lionni's* Frederick *provided the motivation for a study of Lionni's books by Vivian Gussin Paley's kindergarten class.*

From *Frederick* by Leo Lionni, copyright © 1997 by Leo Lionni. Copyright renewed 1995 by Leo Lionni. Reprinted by permission of Random House Children's Books, a division of Random House, Inc.

---

[1]Vivian Gussin Paley, *Wally's Stories: Conversations in Kindergarten* (Cambridge, Mass.: Harvard University Press, 1987) and *Kwanza and Me: A Teacher's Story* (Cambridge, Mass.: Harvard University Press, 1995).

In the process of looking at one illustrator in depth, children learned much about the way text and illustrations work together to create a story. Even more important, they learned so much about life. A picture book had provided for the development of these students' visual, mental, and verbal imaginations. Moreover, in following the curriculum that the children created, their teacher discovered critical life lessons about race, identity, gender, and human needs.

## The Picture Book Defined

Although we discuss picture books in Chapters 4, 6, and 11, this chapter is primarily concerned with picture books as art objects. These are books in which images and ideas join to form a unique whole. In the best picture books, the illustrations extend and enhance the written text, providing the reader with an aesthetic experience that is more than the sum of the book's parts.

Barbara Bader maintains:

> As an art form [the picture book] hinges on the interdependence of picture and words, on the simultaneous display of two facing pages, and on the drama of the turning of the page.[3]

In discussing the art of children's picture books, Perry Nodelman states:

> We perceive new experiences in terms of the experiences preceding them. . . . Each picture in a picture book establishes a context for the picture that follows—it becomes a schema that determines how we will perceive the next picture.[4]

Any book with a picture-book format can be included under the umbrella term *picture book*. A picture book might be an alphabet book, a counting book, a first book, or a concept book (the books discussed in Chapter 4). In these the pictures must be accurate and synchronized with the text; however, it is not essential that they provide the continuity required by a story line. The illustrations for a concept book or an alphabet book can depict a different object or an animal on each page, providing for much variety in the pictures. Examples would be Bert Kitchen's *Animal Alphabet,* which shows large individual pictures for each letter, or Tana Hoban's *Shadows and Reflections,* which explores various dimensions of a concept with stunning photographs. In a nonfiction book (discussed in Chapter 11) the illustrations can help support important concepts and clarify ideas.

In a picture book that tells a story, the message is conveyed equally through two media—picture and word. In a well-designed book in which the total format reflects the meaning of the story, both the illustrations and the text must bear the burden of narration. The pictures help tell the story, showing the action and expressions of the characters, the changing settings, and the development of the plot.

Paul O. Zelinsky's illustrations for *Swamp Angel* by Anne Isaacs are a fine example of the integral partnership between pictures and text. This original story is based on a particularly American folktale form, the tall tale. In a tall tale, heroes and heroines are larger than life and perform impossible feats, all in a spirit of comic

*Paul Zelinsky's richly layered paintings extend and enhance the written text of Anne Isaacs's* Swamp Angel.

From *Swamp Angel* by Anne Isaac, illustrated by Paul O. Zelinsky, copyright © 1994 by Paul O. Zelinsky, illustrations. Used by permission of Dutton, a division of Penguin Putnam Inc.

---

[3]Barbara Bader, *American Picturebooks from Noah's Ark to the Beast Within* (New York: Macmillan, 1976), introduction.

[4]Perry Nodelman, *Words About Pictures* (Athens: University of Georgia Press, 1988), p. 176.

horseplay that children love. For his illustrations, Zelinsky has looked to another American folk art that has been identified with America's past, the landscapes and portraits done during the colonial period by mostly untrained painters called limners. Inspired by their style, Zelinsky chose to work in oils on wood veneers that subtly recall the tall forests of the Appalachian mountains of Tennessee where the story takes place. On these warm and glowing woods, he paints the story of Angelica Longrider, who is "born scarcely taller than her mother" but grows up to save the people of Tennessee from Thundering Tarnation, a bear so big that his pelt covered the entire state of Montana and his bear soul became the big dipper. The portrait of Angelica opposite the title page introduces the wide-eyed heroine, and the look of unassuming innocence on her face sets the tone of the story: what is to come is good fun and not to be taken seriously. Throughout the book Zelinsky adds a wealth of visual detail to Isaacs's story. On the first double-page spread, for example, he shows Angelica stopping a flash flood with her apron, harnessing a rain cloud to put out a cabin fire, and knitting herself striped pantaloons with two tree trunks. His choice of color scheme creates a sense of lively action throughout the book. To heighten the excitement, aqua blue skies and soft grey-green mountains are set against the warm reds and oranges of his figures and the oak, ash, and cherry veneers of the background. In addition, the page design also has great energy. Zelinsky varies the frame for each picture from oval to semicircle to rectangle. On some double-page spreads he shows multiple scenes; on others he highlights the action in single frames. He also moves the story along by varying the point of view from a close-up to a distant shot and from looking straight at the scene to looking down from a bird's-eye view. Zelinsky's artistic choices add to the delight of the story, so that the reader closes the book with an experience that is more than the sum of its parts. This book represents the type of real marriage between pictures and text that we hope to find in good picture books.

An illustrated book is different from a picture book. In an illustrated book only particular incidents in the story might be illustrated to create interest. Chris Van Allsburg, noted for his fine picture books, provided full-color plates for the trilogy by Mark Helprin that began with *Swan Lake* and ended with *The Veil of Snows*. These books are beautiful examples of fine bookmaking, but they are not picture books.

## The Art & Artists of Picture Books

A picture book, then, must be a seamless whole conveying meaning in both the art and the text. Moreover, in a picture book that tells a story the illustration does not merely reflect the idea or action on a single page but shares in moving a story forward and in engaging the reader with the narrative on both an intellectual and an emotional level. Throughout the narration the pictures should convey and enhance the meaning behind the story. Artists create meaning in picture books in a variety of subtle and interesting ways. In Chapter 4 we described how the illustrations contributed to the meaning of various picture books formats for very young children. In this chapter we will extend understandings of artistic meaning-making in picture books.

### Creating Meaning in Picture Books

An outstanding example of illustrations that help move the plot can be found in the classic *Blueberries for Sal* by Robert McCloskey. This is a story that children can tell by themselves just by looking at the clear blue-and-white pictures. The illustrations help the reader anticipate both the action and the climax, as Sal and her mother are seen going berry picking up one side of Blueberry Hill, and Little Bear and his mother are seen coming up the other side. McCloskey uses a false climax, a good storytelling technique. Sal hears a noise and starts to peer behind an ominously dark rock; the reader expects her to meet the bears, but instead she sees a mother crow and her children. On the next page she calmly meets Mother Bear and tramps along behind her. A parallel plot gives Little Bear a similar experience, but Sal's mother is not so calm about meeting him! The human expressions of surprise, fear, and consternation on the faces of both mothers express emotion as well as action.

Artwork might show mounting tension by increasing the size of the pictures. One of the best-known examples of this is in Maurice Sendak's fine story *Where the Wild Things Are*. The pictures in this book become larger and larger as Max's dream becomes more and more fantastic. Following the climactic wild rumpus, which is portrayed on three full-sized spreads with no text whatsoever, Max returns home. The pictures decrease in size, although never down to their original size—just as, symbolically, Max will never be quite the same again after his dream experience.

Picture-book artists also provide clues to the future action of a story. A close look at the first and second pages of *Where the Wild Things Are* shows the mischievous Max dressed in his wild-thing suit and stringing up a homemade tent. A plush toy looking vaguely like a wild thing hangs nearby. Later the tent and wild things appear in Max's dream trip to the far-off land of the wild things. His drawing of a wild thing on page 2 shows his preoccupation with creating these creatures that later inhabit his dreams.

# *Learning About the Art of Picture Books*

During Book Week in the fall, teachers in the Highland Park School in Grove City, Ohio, presented several minicourses on the making of books. One minicourse gave an overview of all the kinds of books a child might want to write. The teacher showed the children various kinds of ABC books and counting books. They looked at concept books for the young child, collections of poetry, and many informational books, from Aliki's simple books *My Feet* and *My Hands* to more complicated books such as Patricia Lauber's *The News About Dinosaurs*. Special books that are takeoffs on fairy tales, such as *The Jolly Postman* by the Ahlbergs or *The Principal's New Clothes* by Stephanie Calmenson, were discussed. Children then started to write their own stories in their classrooms.

Another minicourse emphasized the use of art media, introducing children to the collages of Eric Carle, Ezra Jack Keats, and Jeannie Baker. The teachers had cloth and newspapers available as they discussed the material Keats used in *The Snowy Day* or *Whistle for Willie*. They had fingerpaint paper to make large animals like those in Eric Carle's stories,

and natural materials like the grasses, sponges, and mosses that Jeannie Baker uses.

Another teacher had collected books with interesting endpapers, like *The Great White Man-Eating Shark* by Margaret Mahy, *At Grammy's House* by Eve Rice, and *Henny Penny* by Stephen Butler. Then children made stamps from inner tubes, vegetables, or plastic foam meat trays to create their own endpapers. This same teacher had a collection of books with interesting title pages. In all instances, the teacher talked about the ways the artwork strengthened the theme of the book.

Another minicourse emphasized different ways to bind books with cloth or wallpaper covers.

At the end of the week, the children had all created their own books. More importantly, they had learned about the ways text and art work together to create a unified impression. They had developed a greater appreciation for picture storybooks and the amount of work involved in creating a fine books, and they looked at books differently after this experience.

*Faculty of Highland Park School*
*Kristen Kerstetter, project coordinator*
Grove City, Ohio

---

Some picture-book illustrations use visual metaphors in the same way that poets add to the image-making qualities of their poems. In *Once a Mouse*, Marcia Brown reinforces the drama of the little mouse who is about to be snatched up in the beak of a crow by making the shape of a hill in the background look like an open beak. Again, as she creates shadows of the animals, the reader can see that the shadow of the tiger is that of a dog, his former self before the hermit transformed him.

Pictures not only should reflect the action and climax of the plot, they should help create the basic mood of the story. Uri Shulevitz used increasing light and color in *Dawn* to portray his quietly beautiful story of a man and his grandson rowing out on a lake to see the dawn break. The book begins before dawn and the colors are monochromatic, shades and tints of deepest blue that convey the cool quiet beauty of the lake. As living creatures awake and enter the landscape, the color scheme begins to broaden until finally the sun rises to reveal a full color vista. Don Wood used a similar technique in illustrations for *The Napping House* by Audrey Wood. When everyone in the house is sleeping, the overall color is a restful blue-gray. As the house's inhabitants wake up, the illustra-

tions move to all the bright colors of the rainbow that appears on the final page.

Pictures not only should reflect the action and climax of the plot, they should help to create the basic mood of the story. In Janice Del Negro's *Lucy Dove*, Leonid Gore has used dark values to lend an air of mystery and menace to a tale set in a moonlit graveyard. Lucy Dove, a poor seamstress, takes on the challenge offered by the superstitious squire: she will sew him a pair of lucky trousers in the old abandoned graveyard in return for a bag of gold. Confronted by a fearsome monster, Lucy keeps her cool and finishes her task. The monster, taken by surprise by her cleverness and courage, hesitates a moment and Lucy escapes to claim her prize. Gore works back into his painted surface with scumbles and scratches that evoke the claws of the monstrous creature and add texture and tension to the setting. Yet his heroine is portrayed with touches of subtle color, highlighting her character and adding intensity to the story. Two wordless double-page spreads of Lucy confronting the monster are added at just the right moments to emphasize the shivery mood.

Besides creating the basic mood of a story, illustrations also help create convincing character delineation

*Janice Del Negro's use of dark values creates the spooky mood of the story* Lucy Dove.

From *Lucy Dove* by Janice Del Negro, illustration by Leonid Gore, copyright © 1998 Leonid Gore. Reprinted by permission of DK Publishing, Inc., New York, NY.

*Patricia Polacco captures the expression of amazement and concern on the faces of the two young Amish girls when they see their peacock spread his tail feathers for the first time.*

From *Just Plain Fancy* by Patricia Polacco, copyright © 1990 by Patricia Polacco. Reprinted by permission of Random House Children's Books, a division of Random House, Inc.

and development. Characters like Kevin Henkes's Lilly, Ezra Jack Keats's Peter, Rosemary Wells's Max, and Arnold Lobel's Frog and Toad become real and remain memorable to us because of the illustrations' power rather than the strength of the words.

The characterization in the pictures must correspond to that in the story. There is no doubt that David Shannon's antihero in *No David!* and *David Goes to School* is a holy terror. Yet David's vulnerable side is revealed in Shannon's spare line drawings that add just the right dimension of complexity to David's character. Mordecai Gerstein's *Wild Boy* tells of a child who never left the developmental stage of the preschooler. But this story of Victor, an adolescent boy found wandering in the forests near Saint-Sernin in southern France, is a tragic one. Victor, who had somehow survived apart from human contact for years, became the object of intense study by French experts who labeled him as hopelessly retarded when they failed to communicate with him. However, a young doctor named Jean-Marc-Gaspard Itard was intrigued by the boy and took him into his home, where he was cared for until his death in 1828. Itard's

careful observations and sensitive teaching allowed Victor to learn something of civilized life, although he never learned to talk. Gerstein has imagined Victor's life with great sympathy. His illustrations, executed in textured paint strokes and rough, crosshatched lines, evoke the untamed freedom of a child who lives purely for himself. The page design heightens the emotional tension and moves the story forward. Bright colors portray Victor's joyous connection to his natural world, while a darker palette shows him in captivity. Softer hues portray the warmth of the Itard household but the overall blue tones of the final pictures convey Victor's lost innocence and the human potential that was never realized.

Expression and gesture can also reveal character and move the action forward. In *Just Plain Fancy*, Patricia Polacco tells the story of Naomi, an Amish girl, and her little sister, who hatch a peacock from a fancy egg they find. Frightened that their bird is too fancy for Amish ways, they decide to hide it. The expression of awe and amazement on their faces when they first see Fancy raise his peacock feathers provides the emotional climax of this delightful story. Peggy Rathman's comical drawings carry the weight of the narrative in *Officer Buckle and Gloria*, the Newbery Medal–winning story of two friends who learn the value of partnership. The expressions on the faces of these characters convey a range of emotions and help the reader empathize with the predicament of Officer Buckle.

One of the few picture books to portray character development is the Japanese story *Crow Boy* by Taro Yashima. In the very first picture of this wonderfully sensitive story, Chibi is shown hidden away in the

That night, Officer Buckle watched himself on the 10 o'clock news.

*Peggy Rathmann portrays a wealth of emotions with a few tiny lines in* Officer Buckle and Gloria.

From *Officer Buckle and Gloria* by Peggy Rathmann, copyright © 1995 by Peggy Rathmann. Used by permission of G. P. Putnam's Sons, a division of Penguin Putnam Inc.

dark space underneath the schoolhouse, afraid of the schoolmaster, afraid of the other children. Once Chibi is inside the school, he and his desk are pictured as being far removed from all the other children. The artist's use of space helps emphasize Chibi's isolation and intensifies the representation of his feelings of loneliness. In subsequent pictures Chibi is always alone, while the other children come to school in twos and threes. With the arrival of the friendly schoolmaster and his discovery of Chibi's ability to imitate crows, we see Chibi grow in stature and courage.

In illustrating Paul Hein's version of the Grimm brothers' *Snow White,* Trina Schart Hyman shows the gradual deterioration of the stepmother until, in the last picture, she has the stare of a mad woman as she stands in front of a mirror framed with skulls and jeering faces. Nancy Burkert, on the other hand, in her interpretation of *Snow White* by the Grimm brothers, never shows the evil queen's face, only her back. But on the queen's workbench is every conceivable symbol of evil and death, including deadly nightshade, the thirteenth tarot card, a skull, spiders, bats, mushrooms, and an open book of formulas for poisonous concoctions. These symbols of evil are as eloquent as the mad queen's face. Each illustrator manages to bring a very personal interpretation to this old tale.

Another requirement of an excellent picture book is that the art be accurate and consistent with the text. If the story states, as in Ludwig Bemelmans's *Madeline,* "In an old house in Paris that was covered with vines

lived twelve little girls in two straight lines," children are going to look for the vines, they are going to count the little girls, and they are going to check to see that the lines are straight. Bemelmans was painstakingly careful to include just eleven little girls in his picture after Madeline goes to the hospital. Six-year-olds are quick to point out his one failure in a small picture that shows twelve girls breaking their bread, even though Madeline was still hospitalized. Accuracy is a requirement of all types of picture books.

## The Matter of Style

Style is an elusive quality of an artist's work based on the arrangement of line, color, and mass into a visual image. According to Barbara Kiefer,

style might be defined as a "manner of expressing." The meaning of the word *express*—to make known, reveal, show—is in keeping with the dual nature of style. The word *manner* can encompass all the conscious as well as unconscious choices the artist embraces to "make known." Aspects of style such as formal elements, techniques, and pictorial conventions, then, are among the choices the artist makes to accomplish the primary purpose of expressing meaning.[5]

---

[5]Barbara Z. Kiefer, *The Potential of Picturebooks: From Visual Literacy to Aesthetic Understanding* (Columbus, Ohio: Merrill/Prentice Hall, 1995), p. 120.

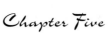
An illustrator's style will be influenced by her or his own skill as an artist and the vision of the story that is being interpreted. The primary decision for the artist to make is how to create visual images that will harmonize with and enhance the meaning of the text. The illustrator also needs to consider how the art might extend or add a new dimension to the message of the story.

## Elements of Design

Crucial to the visual meaning in a picture book are the choices artists make about certain elements of design, particularly the use of line, shape, color, and space, as they decide what to illustrate in the story and how best to do it.

### Line and Shape

Line is so inherently a part of every illustration that we forget that this element, too, can convey meaning. A horizontal line suggests repose and peace, a vertical line gives stability, and a diagonal line suggests action and movement. Uri Shulevitz has used diagonal rain lines superbly in the pictures and even endpapers of his book *Rain Rain Rivers*. Even the size of a line can convey meaning. In *Stevie*, John Steptoe uses a heavy black outline for his figures to emphasize Robert's resentment of Stevie, the little boy his mother takes care of during the day. The tiny, sketchy lines in Marcia Brown's version of Perrault's *Cinderella* suggest the somewhat fussy elegance of the story's setting at the sixteenth-century French court. Chris Raschka uses the element of line to great effect in books like *Yo! Yes?* and *Like Likes Like*. His lines predominate the otherwise empty space, defining the characters and moving the plot forward. The simplicity of line underscores Raschka's fundamental themes: our fears of our isolation and the unknown, and our overwhelming need for human companionship.

A line that encloses space creates shape, and this element is equally evocative of meaning. Richard McGuire chooses line and shape to create the flowing movement in two picture books, *Night Becomes Day* and *What Goes Around Comes Around*. Dan Yaccarino is another illustrator who uses the element of shape to great effect, in *Circle Dogs* by Kevin Henkes and *Little White Dog* by Laura Godwin. In all these books the reliance on shape rather than on realistic depiction of objects creates pleasing pictorial designs that subtly evoke themes for the intended audience of young children.

Shapes with sharp edges and corners can evoke tension and movement, as they do in Christopher Meyers's *Black Cat*. On the other hand, when shapes have nongeometric curving forms found in nature, they can breathe a sense of life into illustrations. Peter

Ocean becomes wave

And wave becomes beach

*The clean-edged shapes in Richard McGuire's* Night Becomes Day *echo the simple text and create a feeling of movement throughout the book.*

From *Night Becomes Day* by Richard McGuire, copyright © 1994 by Richard McGuire. Used by permission of Viking Penguin, a division of Penguin Putnam Inc.

Parnall's many horizontal lines convey movement and create rounded womblike shapes for Byrd Baylor's *Your Own Best Secret Place* and *The Way to Start a Day*. These reaffirm Baylor's reverence for the natural world and suggest peace and a tapping of inner strength.

### Use of Color

Many classic picture books did not use color in the illustrations—the sepia pictures of Robert McCloskey's *Make Way for Ducklings*, the black-and-white humorous illustrations by Robert Lawson for *The Story of Ferdinand* by Munro Leaf, and the well-loved black-and-white illustrations for *Millions of Cats* by Wanda Gág.

Modern publishing techniques make it much easier and less expensive to publish full-color books, but many illustrators are still using black-and-white graphics to create exciting picture books. The unique story *Round Trip* by Ann Jonas describes a trip to the city past farms, silos, and steel highway wires, to ride on the subway; turn the book around and the reader returns in the dark. The farm and silos become factories, the highway poles support the freeway, and the subway becomes a parking garage. Black and white are the appropriate colors for this triumph of design. David Weisner uses black and white to spooky effect for Eve Bunting's *Night of the*

*Gargoyles,* a story of stone sculptures that come alive to roam the city after the sun goes down. Chris Van Allsburg's black-and-white illustrations help create an eerie otherworldly cast in *The Widow's Broom, The Garden of Abdul Gasazi, Jumanji,* and *The Mysteries of Harris Burdick.*

The choice of colors depends on the theme of the book. Certainly, the choice of blue for both pictures and text in *Blueberries for Sal* by McCloskey was appropriate. Tawny yellow and black were the natural choices for Don Freeman's wonderfully funny *Dandelion,* the story of Dandelion the lion who suddenly decided to live up to the double meaning of his name. Uri Shulevitz's *Snow,* a quiet, nostalgic story, demands soft tones that suggest the breathless anticipation of the first snowfall of winter. By way of contrast, Joe Cepeda's intense colors are an appropriate choice for Julius Lester's *What a Truly Cool World,* a lively and energetic creation tale. Choice of color, then, can set the mood of the story.

Certain artists have made effective use of color to show a change in mood for the story. Allen Say uses color most effectively in his picture-book biography of the very first Chinese matador. Titled *El Chino,* it is the account of a Chinese American who longs to be a great athlete. He is an ace basketball player in high school but too short to compete in college. Following his graduation as an engineer, he goes on a vacation in Spain and falls in love with bullfighting. For the first half of the book, the pictures are in brownish-gray tones reminiscent of old photographs. However, after Billy Wong finds his true vocation, the pictures change to full color, symbolizing his joy at finding his life's work. To signify danger, Marcia Brown has added red to her pictures for *Once a Mouse.* Starting with cool forest green, mustard yellow, and a trace of red, the red builds up in increasing amounts until the climax is reached and the tiger is changed back to a mouse. Only cool green and yellow are seen in the last picture as the hermit is once again "thinking about big—and little."

It is this rich use of many layers of color to create meaning that helps distinguish the really fine picture books. The splashy use of color for color's sake, so frequently seen in the grocery store or mass-produced books, does little to develop children's artistic eye. It is the appropriate use of color that is significant.

*Uri Shulevitz's soft color palette evokes the visual hush of the year's first snowfall in* Snow.

Illustration from *Snow* by Uri Shulevitz. Copyright © 1998 by Uri Shulevitz. Reprinted by permission of Farrar, Straus and Giroux/Canada: Douglas & McIntyre.

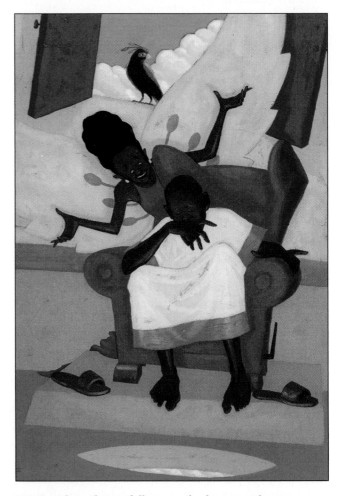

*Joe Cepeda's vibrant, full range of colors provides an ebullient mood for Julius Lester's* What A Truly Cool World.

Illustrations by Joe Cepeda from *What a Truly Cool World* by Julius Lester. Published by Scholastic Press, a division of Scholastic, Inc. Copyright © 1999 by Joe Cepeda. Reprinted by permission.

### Value

If we were to make a black and white photocopy of a page from a full-color book like Lester's *What a Truly Cool World,* we would see how illustrator Joe Cepeda considered the element of value, the amount of light-ness or darkness in a picture, just as carefully as he chose his colors. There is great contrast in the values on each page, and this lends extra energy and zing to the book. On the other hand, the values in Shulvitz's *Snow* are more uniform and give the book its gentle mood of innocence. Illustrator Chris Van Allsburg uses the element of value to create a dramatic three-dimensional effect for all his books. His masterful depiction of light and dark in books like *The Polar Express* and *Jumanji* suggest that the figures and objects might leap off the page at any moment.

### Space

The creative use of space can produce a feeling of isolation, as we have seen in Taro Yashima's *Crow Boy,* or the blurred line between reality and legend, as in the illustrations by Stephen Gammell for *Where the Buffaloes Begin* by Olaf Baker. Shirley Hughes uses the gutter between pages to represent the door into the house in *Alfie Gets in First* and to separate Alfie from his family and neighbors outside. In *Come Along Daisy!*—Jane Simmons's story about a wayward duck who becomes separated from her mother—we see a tiny Daisy almost invisible in the expanse of an huge blue-green world. Simmons's use of space effectively emphasizes Daisy's fright at being separated from her mother.

Molly Bang makes use of negative space in her surrealistic wordless book *The Grey Lady and the Strawberry Snatcher.* The gray lady appears to fade into the background of trees as she runs away from the strawberry snatcher. Part of the fun of David Macaulay's experimental book *Black and White* is his use of negative space to hide an escaping convict in a herd of Holstein cows. In *Little White Dog,* Dan Yaccarino provides preschoolers with a visual riddle by hiding the colored shapes of various animals against the same colored background. The white dog, for example, is hidden against a white snow bank and only his black eyes and nose can be seen.

The decision to use borders also involves the artist's use of space. The borders in Vera Williams's *A Chair for My Mother* or Trina Hyman's interpretation of *Little Red Riding Hood* provide a kind of coziness to these stories and help create a unified whole out of each double-page spread.

In inexpensive mass-marketed books, or in basal reading textbooks, which frequently must conform to one size for all, artists cannot afford the creative use of space. In a well-designed picture book, however, the illustrators can use space to enhance the meaning of the story.

### Point of View, or Perspective

Just as an author decides what would be the best point of view from which to tell a story, so too does an artist think about perspective. One way to obtain action in what might otherwise be a static series of pictures is to change the focus, just as a movie camera changes perspective or shows close-ups and then moves back to pan the whole scene. In *The Napping*

*John Schoenherr uses shifting perspectives to provide action in Jane Yolen's quiet story* Owl Moon.

From *Owl Moon* by Jane Yolen, illustrated by John Schoenherr, copyright © 1988 by John Schoenherr. Used by permission of Philomel Books, a division of Penguin Putnam Inc.

*House* by Audrey Wood, for example, the scene is almost always in the bedroom, where the granny, the dog, the cat, the mouse, and the flea are seen in various postures as they sleep during the quiet rain. Don Wood shows us a fish-eye view of the scene, with the bed growing increasingly concave until its final collapse. As the story progresses, Wood moves the point of view slowly upward until he is directly above the sleeping figures for the climax, when the flea bites the cat and wakes them and the bed falls down.

Part of the perfection of the poetic Caldecott Medal book *Owl Moon* by Jane Yolen is the way John Schoenherr uses shifting perspectives to provide the action. It is the quiet story of a father and child who go out late one snowy night to look for owls. Starting with an owl's view of the farm bathed in moonlight, the artist shifts his focus, showing the pair trudging through the snow from the side, from the front, and finally looking up in awe at the huge owl landing on the tree. This picture of the owl is the only close-up in the story, a fact that underlines the climax of the story and intensifies the excitement of finally seeing the owl.

The perspective in Chris Van Allsburg's surrealistic pictures for *Jumanji* changes from a worm's-eye point of view to a bird's-eye view, adding to the constant shifts between reality and fantasy in that story. Seen from the floor level of an ordinary living room, two charging rhinoceroses look much more frightening than in the zoo! Again in *The Polar Express,* Van Allsburg shows dramatic shifts in perspective from the aerial views from Santa's sleigh to the floor-level view of the children opening their presents.

*A double-page spread of David Macaulay's award-winning book* Black and White *shows four different stories done in four different media; or are there connections in this intriguing book?*

From *Black and White*. Copyright © 1990 by David Macaulay. Reprinted by permission of Houghton Mifflin Company. All rights reserved.

Not all artists work with changing perspectives, but when they do, it is interesting to ask why and look to see how this adds to the meaning of the story.

## The Artist's Choice of Media

Children accept and enjoy a variety of media in the illustrations of their picture books. The illustrator's choice of original media can be as important to the meaning of the book as the choice of the elements of art. Many artists today are using the picture book as a vehicle for experimentation with new and interesting media and formats. (See also "Exploring Artists' Media" in Chapter 13.) For example, David Macaulay's award-winning *Black and White* is really four stories, elements of which enter each story. Each story uses different media, including transparent watercolors, torn paper, opaque paint, and pen and sepia ink. This highly inventive book is like a game or puzzle. *Black and White* appeals to older children capable of interpreting four stories at the same time.

Illustrators are also experimenting with interesting materials that would have been difficult to reproduce prior to modern printing technology. Christopher

Meyers evocative *Black Cat* is created using a combination of photographs, ink, and opaque paint. This mixed media heightens the emotional depth of this poetic story of a lonely cat wandering the streets of a city. The layers created in Meyers's paintings also suggest underlying metaphors for human survival in urban environments. In this kind of creative experimentation that is taking place in picture books today, the medium the artist uses is not nearly as important as the appropriateness of the choice for a particular book and how effectively the artist uses it. Nevertheless, teachers and children are fascinated with the various aspects of illustrating and always ask what medium is used. This is becoming increasingly difficult to answer, as artists these days use a combination of media and printing techniques to achieve a particular effect. Some publishing houses provide information on the art techniques of some of their outstanding books. This might be found in a foreword, on the copyright page, or on a jacket flap. It is a service that teachers and librarians hope more companies will provide.

The following section gives a brief overview of some of the media choices open to the artist.

*Mary Azarian's Caldecott Medal-winning woodcuts for Jacqueline Briggs Martin's* Snowflake Bentley *evoke the time and place of nineteenth-century Vermont.*

Excerpt from *Snowflake Bentley* by Jacqueline Briggs Martin. Text copyright © Jacqueline Briggs Martin. Illustrations copyright © 1998 by Mary Azarian. Reprinted by permission of Houghton Mifflin Company. All rights reserved.

### Woodcuts and Similar Techniques

In the beginning of the history of printing, the woodcut or wood engraving was the only means of reproducing art. These methods are still used effectively today. In the making of a woodcut, the nonprinting areas are cut away, leaving a raised surface that, when inked and pressed on paper, duplicates the original design. If color is to be used, the artist must prepare as many woodcuts as colors, or the printed picture can be painted by hand. Woodcut illustrations produce a bold simplicity and have a power not found in any other medium.

Caldecott Award winner Mary Azarian uses this medium to illustrate Jacqueline Briggs Martin's *Snowflake Bentley,* the story of a Vermont farmer whose fascination with snowflakes led him to devise a way to photograph them and show their unique beauty to all the world. Azarian, an accomplished woodcut artist, creates lovely hand-colored prints that convey the rough edges of life on Vermont farms in the late 1800s. Her strong, black lines create pleasing patterns and echo the patterns of individual snowflakes. The woodcut technique thus effectively imparts the setting and themes of Bentley's story.

David Frampton uses this traditional medium in a fresh way to illustrate Jim Aylesworth's retelling of the traditional rhyme "Diddle Diddle Dumpling" in *My Son John.* The text for each of these fourteen new verses is cut into a wood block and is accompanied by pictures of fourteen lively children, each with a rhyming verse for her or his name. In *Once a Mouse,* a fable of India, Marcia Brown takes full advantage of her medium, allowing the texture or grain of the wood to show through. This adds depth and interesting patterns to these dramatic illustrations.

Wood engravings are cut on the end grain of very hard wood (usually boxwood) rather than with the grain on the plank side of a soft wood. This process gives a delicate, finer line to the illustrations than a woodcut has. Barry Moser has used this technique to illustrate Patricia MacLachlan's *What You Know First,* an evocative memoir that examines the importance of one's roots. Rooted in this centuries-old printing method, the book's text is quietly enhanced.

Etching is another type of engraving technique. A design is drawn with a tool on a waxed metal plate, then the plate is dipped in acid, which eats thin lines into the metal. The wax is removed, and prints are then made from the inked plate. Arthur Geisert makes use of this medium in his many books. His puzzle alphabet book *Pigs from A to Z* is illustrated with detailed etchings of seven little pigs constructing a tree house. Each picture shows five hidden forms of the letter and the seven pigs, and part of the fun of the book is to find them. The fine lines of these intricate etchings make superb hiding places for the letters. In *Haystack, Prairie Town,* and *River Town,* written with his wife Bonnie, Geisert hand-colors the etchings and gives a lovely timeless feeling to these stories about passing time in the heartlands of America.

Linoleum block prints also give a finer line than woodcuts. Mary Wormell uses this technique to add a lively charm to her stories of a sweet, rather egocentric hen in *Hilda Hen's Search* and *Hilda Hen's Happy Birthday.* Ashley Wolff uses linoleum block prints to illustrate many of her books such as *Goody O'Grumpity* by Carol Ryrie Brink. The crisp black lines of the linoleum cuts seem to make the animals, birds, and people stand out in relief against brilliant skies and seasonal landscapes.

Scratchboard illustrations can be confused with wood engravings, because their appearance is similar. However, the process of making them is very different. In the making of scratchboard illustrations, a very black ink is usually painted on the smooth white surface of a drawing board or scratchboard. When the ink is thoroughly dry, the picture is made by scratching through the black-inked surface with a sharp instrument. Color can be added with a transparent overlay, painted on the white scratchboard prior to applying the black ink, or applied after the drawing is complete. Scratchboard techniques produce crisply textured illustrations. Michael McCurdy, who has been a wood engraver for many years, uses a similar painstaking technique for the scratchboard drawings in two books by Donald Hall, *Lucy's Christmas* and *Lucy's Summer.* These stories have personal connections to Hall's mother's childhood in New Hampshire, and the fine linear work that McCurdy achieves on scratchboard resembles old wood engravings and evokes a lovely sense of the past as well as the hardy nature of family connections. Brian Pinkney creates stunning effects with scratchboard in books like *Max Found Two Sticks, Cosmo and the Robot* and Kim Siegelson's *In the Time of the Drums*. By adding color in inventive ways, he creates interesting textures that give his illustrations drama and excitement. Barbara Cooney has achieved an equally dramatic effect with this technique combined with brilliant color overlays for her award-winning book *Chanticleer and the Fox*.

### Collage and Construction

The use of collage for illustrating children's books has become very popular. The effect of this medium is simple and childlike, not unlike pictures children might make themselves. The word *collage,* derived from the French verb *collar,* meaning "to paste," refers to the kind of picture that is made by cutting out a variety of different kinds of materials—newspaper clippings, patterned wallpaper, fabric, and the like—and assembling them into a unified, harmonious

A strong breeze shook the tree in front of his house, and Max saw two heavy twigs fall to the ground.

*Scratchboard techniques allow illustrator Brian Pinkney to explore a range of textures and colors in books like* Max Found Two Sticks.

illustration. Ezra Jack Keats proved himself a master of this technique with his award-winning *The Snowy Day*. Using patterned and textured papers and pen and ink, Keats captured young Peter's delight in a snowy day.

Leo Lionni is known for his highly original use of collage in his many books. Circles of torn paper convey a satisfying story of families in *Little Blue and Little Yellow*. Lionni also uses his familiar collage techniques and brilliant colors to tell a fable of art, love, and the role of the imagination in seeing beauty in all things in *Matthew's Dream*. In *An Extraordinary Egg*, three frogs find what they believe to be a chicken egg. When the egg hatches into an alligator, they continue to believe it is a chicken, despite evidence to the contrary. In this book Lionni uses collage with oil pastels, a mixture that adds texture to the pictures but allows the white of the paper to show through, giving a much lighter tone to this funny story.

Eric Carle first paints many sheets of paper with various colors to achieve texture. Then he cuts them out and pastes them together to create interesting characters, as in *The Very Hungry Caterpillar*. Australian artist Patricia Mullins uses brilliant tissue-paper collages to create the animals in Gail Jorgensen's foot-stomping *Crocodile Beat* and Mem Fox's whimsical tale *Hattie and the Fox*.

Lois Ehlert combines handmade papers and natural materials in highly inventive ways in her picture books. Her illustrations for books such as *Cukoo=Cuco, Snowballs,* and *Hands* intrigue and delight children of all ages. Other artists who make skillful use of collage include Elizabeth Cleaver, Bettina Paterson, and Susan Roth.

Modern reproduction techniques have freed illustrators to go beyond collage, which is relatively flat, and work in three dimensions. Jeannie Baker makes what she calls "collage constructions" or "assemblage" to illustrate her fine books. Made from a multitude of materials, including modeling clay, papers, textured materials, preserved grass, leaves, feathers, hair, and paints, her pictures stand out in relief. In *Where the Forest Meets the Sea*, a story of a visit to a tropical rain forest in North Queensland, Australia, a young boy imagines who else might have played there before him, including the dinosaurs and later the aboriginal children. Baker also uses this technique effectively for her environmental statements in *The Hidden Forest, The Story of Rosy Dock* and *Window*, a wordless book.

Children will be intrigued by Barbara Reid's plasticine, or modeling clay, art for her books. Reid's *Two by Two* introduces animals who sailed with Noah on the Ark. The detail Reid can achieve with this modeling clay material is quite amazing.

Other artists are working in innovative ways with paper. Molly Bang, who used found-object constructions to illustrate her own original story *One Fall Day,* used folded-paper sculpture, cutout figures, and furniture for her modern folktale *The Paper Crane.* This medium seems the perfect choice to illustrate the story of the folded-paper bird who comes to life and restores the restaurant bypassed by a freeway.

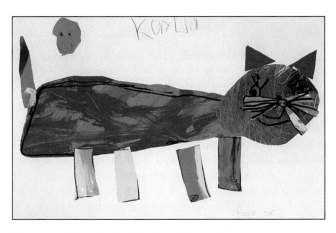

*Illustrator Eric Carle's bright collages inspire a kindergartener to experiment with forms.*

Your friends eat with you—juice from golden oranges, corn muffins and butter, eggs from clucking chickens, and milk from Jersey cows.

*Molly Bang experiments with constructions that recreate the intensely imaginative world of the child in* One Fall Day.

Another master of the art of cut-paper sculpture is David Wisniewski. *The Wave of the Sea-Wolf* is one of his many stories illustrated with intricately cut paper. Placed in layers that provide a feeling of depth to the pictures and add excitement and tension, the meticulously cut shapes tell an original story of a young Tlingit princess who saves her people from natural and human threats. Wisniewski won the Caldecott Award in 1997 for his hair-raising retelling of *The Golem.*

Other artists have used the traditional Asian technique of paper cutting to create their illustrations. Ed Young's illustrations for Jane Yolen's *The Emperor and the Kite* imply a subtle relationship to the paper kite that is at the center of the story. The lacy linear design that results also gives a feeling of airy lightness that suits the book's ending. Aki Sogabe illustrated *Aesop's Fox, Cinnamon, Mint, and Mothballs* by Ruth Tiller, and *The Loyal Cat* by Lensey Namioka using single sheets of black paper that she cut freehand and then placed over hand-painted rice papers. The result is a jewel-like quality well suited to these stories.

*David Wisniewski's intricate cut-paper illustrations add excitement to books like* The Wave of the Sea-Wolf.

Denise Fleming works with cotton rag fibers colored with pigments to create handmade papers for the illustrations in such books as *Mama Cat Has Three Kittens* and *Barnyard Banter*. Debra Frasier has experimented with paste paper cutouts in William Stafford's *The Animal That Drank Up Sound* and with collages made from tie-dyed papers for Kim Stafford's *We Got Here Together*. In all these books the abstracted shapes and the textures that result from these artistic processes match the poetic texts of the printed words.

*Jon Muth's transparent water colors mirror the watery puddles in Karen Hesse's* Come On Rain.

Illustrations by Jon J. Muth from *Come on Rain* by Karen Hesse. Published by Scholastic Press, a division of Scholastic, Inc. Copyright © 1999 by Jon J. Muth. Reprinted by permission.

### Computer Generated Art

As technology improves, we are likely to see more artwork that has been created on the computer. Currently many of these books, such as David Kirk's *Nova's Ark* and William Joyce's *Rolie Polie Olie*, recall computer-animated motion pictures and are likely to be popular with children familiar with this imagery. Mercer Mayer's *Shibumi and the Kitemaker* is more a promising indicator of the future of computer-created illustration. This fantasy, set in ancient Japan, concerns Shibumi, an overprotected royal daughter who flees her palace prison on a beautiful kite. In grief at the loss of his daughter, the emperor begins to make the social changes for which she had argued. After many years have passed, a young samurai finds Shibumi and returns her to her father and to a transformed kingdom. Mayer's style is recognizable in his illustrations, but the computer has allowed him to incorporate and enhance images from ancient Japanese art in a way that provides captivating compositions and richly textured patterns, transformations that echo those in the written text. These images, combined with his linear work, adds a satisfying dimension to the story. We will continue to hope for other such surprises in computer generated art in picture books.

### Paints and Pen and Ink

The vast majority of illustrations for children's books are done in paint, pen and ink, or combinations of these media. The creation of materials like plastic paints, or acrylics, and new techniques frequently make it very difficult to determine what medium has been used.

Generally, paint can be divided into two kinds: paint that is translucent and has a somewhat transparent quality, such as watercolor, and paint that is opaque and impenetrable to light, such as tempera, gouache, and oils.

The transparency of watercolor can be seen in books like Uri Shulevitz's *Rain Rain Rivers* and Karen Hess's *Come On Rain* illustrated by Jon Muth. For both books, watercolor is the perfect choice of medium, for

it allows the artists to convey the feeling of clouds bleeding into rainy skies and light reflected in watery puddles. Allen Say makes fine use of transparent watercolor in his many books. In *Grandfather's Journey* and *Tea With Milk*, the effect of the medium conveys a sense of quiet dignity to the stories of his grandfather and his mother. David Small's soft watercolor washes seem just right for the gently humorous stories, *The Library* and *The Gardiner*, both books by Sarah Stewart.

We might think of old-fashioned, delicate pictures when we think of watercolor, but watercolors do not have to look dated. Ted Lewin's rich watercolors flow with energy in books such as *The Storytellers* and *Peppe the Lamplighter*, written by Elisa Bartone. Edward Ardizzone, England's master of watercolor and pen-and-ink sketches, has produced full-color watercolor seascapes that have tremendous vitality and movement for his *Little Tim and the Brave Sea Captain*. The storm scenes in McCloskey's *Time of Wonder* have this same power, contrasted with the soft, diffused light of the fog scene.

Watercolors can be warm and cozy, too, as we see in Vera Williams's *A Chair for My Mother*. In this story of a family's struggle to recover from a household fire, we celebrate the day they have saved enough money to buy a big fat comfortable chair for the little girl's mother. Watercolors create the symbolic borders of these pictures and the velvet texture of the chairs in the furniture store.

Opaque paints can give an intense brilliant look, like Mollie Bang's *When Sophie Gets Angry—Really, Really Angry,* or they can produce the flatter colors of Amy Walrod's *Horace and Morris but Mostly Dolores* written by James Howe. Maurice Sendak contrasted dark green and blue tempera with shades of purple to create Max's weird fantasy world in *Where the Wild Things Are*. Texture and shading are achieved with pen-and-ink crosshatch strokes.

Gouache (pronounced "gwash") paint is water-color with the addition of chalk and has an effect similar to tempera. Marisabina Russo uses gouache to produce vivid paintings for books like *Hannah's Baby Sister* and *Mama Talks too Much*. Russo's subject matter is the everyday world of the younger child, and the choice of medium allows a style that is childlike and suits the subject matter perfectly. The use of gouache is also characteristic of the many books illustrated by Alice and Martin Provensen, including their well-known *A Visit to William Blake's Inn* by Nancy Willard and the Caldecott Medal winner *The Glorious Flight: Across the Channel with Louis Blériot.*

Acrylics (plastic paints) produce vibrant, almost glowing colors. When mixed with water, acrylics resemble transparent watercolors. More often acrylics are used straight from the tube. Like oils, they can be built up on the painting surface to give a dense texture; however, they dry faster than oils. Barbara Cooney used acrylic paints to create the pictures for her well-loved *Miss Rumphius*. After her many travels throughout the world, Miss Rumphius settles down in her little gray house in Maine beside a shimmering ocean. Crisp clear colors beautifully capture the Maine landscape, with its purple and blue blooming lupines.

We can also find picture books illustrated with oil paints. Because the medium is slower drying than acrylic, it allows the artist to build up layers and to work back into the colors as well as to create thick surface textures. Floyd Cooper uses oil paint on canvas board and works back into the paint with a soft malleable eraser before the paint dries. This technique gives his paintings layers of subtle color tones that seem to glow with a rich sheen and that add depth and drama to his scenes. This medium is particularly suited to the warm human stories Cooper illustrates, such as *Coming Home: From the Life of Langston Hughes* and Sandra Belton's *From Miss Ida's Front Porch.*

Thomas Locker, a well-known landscape artist, illustrates his picture books with majestic full-color oil paintings. Locker's rendering of light in such books as *Where the River Begins, The Mare on the Hill, Family Farm,* and *Sky Tree* reminds us of the early landscape painters of the Hudson River School. Locker's *The Young Artist* reflects the influence of the early Dutch masters. Oil paint is used to good effect by Mike Wimmer in Patricia MacLachlan's *All the Places to Love* and Robert Burleigh's *Home Run: The Story of Babe Ruth*. These are warm, richly textured stories, and the medium of oil paint enhances the emotional mood of the books.

### Crayon, Chalk, Charcoal, and Pencil

Crayon and soft-pencil illustrations are frequently employed for children's books. The subtle texture of crayon is easily discernible. In *Fish Is Fish*, Leo Lionni creates an underwater world with crayons, but he

*In books like* Coming Home: From the Life of Langston Hughes, *Floyd Cooper builds up many layers of transparent oil washes to give figures and landscapes a warm glow.*

From *Coming Home: From the Life of Langston Hughes*, by Floyd Cooper, copyright © 1994 by Floyd Cooper. Used by permission of Philomel Books, a division of Penguin Putnam Inc.

portrays the fish's conception of the frog's world with the brilliant colors of acrylics. The difference in color and media helps to separate the imagined world from the real one.

Pastels and charcoal are most appropriate media for Thomas Allen's rich illustrations for books that have strong connections to people and places. *Climbing Kansas Mountains* by George Shannon tells of a long-ago summer on a Kansas farm where the only mountains to climb were the grain elevators. Scott Russell Sander's *A Place Called Freedom* follows a family of former slaves as they establish an African American community in Indiana. In both books, the colored pastels are built up from the surface of the page, and the rich textures mingle with the tinted charcoal papers like the love that surrounds these families. Ed Young also uses pastel effectively in books like *Little Plum* and Rafe Martin's *Foolish Rabbit's Big Mistake*. Here he makes full use of brilliant color applied thickly to add intensity and life to the stories. In stories that convey a quieter mood, Young chooses softer tones and applies the colors more delicately. He often keeps his edges rough and lets the texture of the paper show through. This gives his illustrations something of a dreamlike quality and is very effective for stories like *The Dreamcatcher*, written by Audrey Osafsky.

Stephen Gammell's soft-pencil drawings create a mystical mood for the legend *Where the Buffaloes Begin* by Olaf Baker. The large full-page and double-page pictures capture the wide sweep of the prairie

*Wendy Anderson Halperin uses colored pencils to capture the soft light of a sleepy countryside in Tres Seymour's* Hunting the White Cow.

From *Hunting the White Cow* by Tres Seymour, illustrated by Wendy Anderson Halperin. Text copyright © 1993 by Tres Seymour. Illustrations copyright © 1993 by Wendy Anderson Halperin. Reprinted by permission of Orchard Books, New York. All rights reserved.

*Shelley Jackson's mixed media in* The Old Woman and the Wave *reflect the old woman's mixed-up priorities.*

From *The Old Woman and the Wave* by Shelley Jackson. Copyright © 1998 by Shelley Jackson. Reprinted by permission of DK Publishing, Inc. New York.

and the immensity of the buffalo. Yet the impressionistic, indefinite shapes suggest the legendary nature of a story in which the buffalo arise from a misty lake and stampede an enemy tribe, thereby saving Little Wolf's people. Wendy Anderson Halperin's pencil drawings overlaid with soft watercolor washes in Tres Seymour's *Hunting the White Cow* and Anne Shelby's *Homeplace* convey the lovely pastoral settings that frame these two folksy stories.

Using a conté pencil, a rather hard drawing pencil, Chris Van Allsburg creates a surrealistic world for the playing of the game in *Jumanji*. Sandpapering the conté pencil and applying the dust with cotton balls, he gives the pictures a spooky, dreamlike feeling. Van Allsburg is adept in the use of a variety of drawing materials; he used carbon pencil for his first book, *The Garden of Abdul Gasazi,* full-color pastels for *The Wreck of the Zephyr,* and oil pastels for *The Polar Express.*

Increasingly, artists are using combinations of many media. Erik Blegvad used drawing materials and watercolor paints to create the illustrations for N. M. Bodecker's *Hurry, Hurry, Mary Dear.* The rough

edges of the drawn lines and shadows are perfect to convey Mary's agitation as she rushes around getting the house ready for winter while her lazy husband gives directions. The watercolor washes provide the right balance of light humor to the funny tale that ends with Mary getting her revenge. In *The Old Woman and the Wave* Shelley Jackson combines paint, collage, drawing materials and an etching technique to convey the delightful story of a woman who lives with a giant wave hanging over her house. Her entire life is spent preparing for the worst, waiting for the water to fall, and she fails to appreciate the beautiful gifts the wave offers her. It takes a young wanderer and her own dog, Bones, to show her that the wave is there not to threaten her but to offer her the world to explore. The foreign words and maps that are worked into the paintings offer subtle clues to the wave's promise. Jackson's inventive combination of media lends just the right touch of whimsy to the story.

## Artistic Conventions

Style can also refer to the particular artistic properties associated with eras, like Renaissance art or Impressionism, or with cultures, such as the culture of the people of Tibet or of Northern Plains Indian tribes. Pictorial styles can be distinguished by certain constant elements or "umbrella conventions," which are widely accepted ways of depicting.[6] Illustrators often

---

[6]Ibid. pp. 118–120.

borrow these conventions to enhance or extend their visual message. Teachers might want to know these terms and conventions, just as they develop an understanding of literary terms for more careful evaluation of books for children. However, it is more important to teach children to look and really see how an illustrator creates meaning than it is to be glib with terms they might not understand. Also, these terms were developed to describe the art of single paintings hung on walls, not the cumulative effect of many images seen by turning the pages of a picture book.

### Realism, or Representational Art

No designation of an art style can be precise, because of the infinite variation within styles; however, realism is perhaps the easiest to recognize, because it presents a picture of the world as we see it in real life. Of course, the pictures still incorporate the artist's interpretation of the story, the choice of scenes to visualize, point of view, expressions, and so forth. Barry Moser's realistic watercolor illustrations for Cynthia Rylant's *Appalachia: The Voices of Sleeping Birds* have the feeling of arrested motion, almost like Depression-era photographs. The beauty of the countryside contrasts sharply with the harshness of the life, as seen in the face of the exhausted coal miner. Realism also emphasizes the message of family ties and warm affection in Mike Wimmer's glowing paintings for Patricia MacLachlan's *All the Places to Love*. In this story a young boy recalls the places his family introduced him to when he was born and plans to show these special spots to his new baby sister.

Canadian illustrator Ron Lightburn creates detailed drawings that have a wonderful three-dimensional quality. *Eagle Dreams*, written by Sheryl McFarlane, tells of a young farm boy who fights to save a wounded bald eagle and return it to the wild. Lightburn's rectangular pictures actually look like photographs and add believability to this story's important theme. Lightburn and McFarlane also collaborated on *Waiting for Whales*, a lovely story about a grandfather who teaches his young granddaughter the mysteries of the natural world.

### Impressionistic Art

The term *Impressionism* is associated with the French artists who worked in and around Paris in the latter part of the nineteenth century, including such well-known painters as Monet, Sisley, and Pissarro. They were concerned with observing nature as it really was and so attempted to capture their first visual impressions before intellect or emotion could define the image further.

A wonderful example of an homage to Impressionism can be found in the Monet-like paintings by Maurice Sendak for *Mr. Rabbit and the Lovely Pre-*

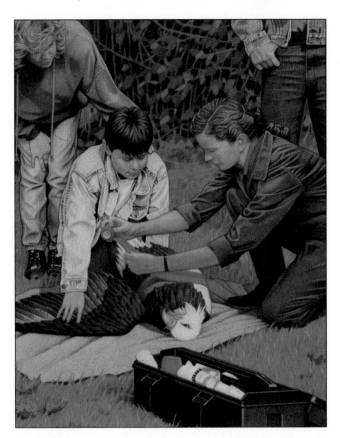

*Ron Lightburn's realistic drawings provide an intense immediacy to Sheryl McFarlane's* Eagle Dreams.
From *Eagle Dreams* by Sheryl McFarlane, illustrated by Ron Lightburn, copyright © 1995 by Ron Lightburn, illustrations. Used by permission of Philomel Books, a division of Penguin Putman Inc.

*sent*, written by Charlotte Zolotow. In luscious shades of blues and greens, Sendak has created a dreamlike world where a very sophisticated rabbit and a little girl wander about the countryside looking for presents of red, yellow, green, and blue (her mother's favorite colors) for the little girl's mother. The dappled endpapers for this book are examples of impressionistic techniques in themselves.

Raúl Colón's method of working paint into a textured surface provides an impressionistic atmosphere to books such as *My Mama Had A Dancing Heart* by Libba Moore Gray and *Celebration* by Jane Resch Thomas. The softened figures and glowing light in the paintings convey a warm emotional undertone to these family stories.

G. Brian Karas uses impressionistic rendering to create a very different mood for Megan MacDonald's *The Bone Keeper*. This spooky story tells of the old Bone Woman who lives in a deep cave by night and by day "sifts and searches the sand, searches and sifts for bones, bones bleached white in the desert sun." Karas's unfinished edges, hazy images, and textured surfaces perfectly visualize MacDonald's haunting story. Karas's work does not echo the subject matter of the Impressionists, but his technique certainly recalls their methods.

## Expressionistic Art

Aspects of expressionistic art include shocking colors, figures slightly out of proportion, and rough, rapid brushwork. The emphasis is on the artist's own inner emotions and on self-expression rather than the reproduction of what he or she sees.

In illustrations for children's books, expressionism might take the form of brilliant blue horses or blue cats, as seen in some of Eric Carle's pictures for very young children. In *Chato's Kitchen* Gary Soto tells the tale of a low-riding cat from East L.A. who has designs on a family of mice. The mice find an ally in Chorizo, the dog, and Chato and his friend Novio Boy decide to have a fiesta instead of fight. Susan Guevara's expressionistic paintings add heat to this lively tale and visually convey a wonderful rhythm of the barrio.

David Diaz's illustrations for *Smoky Night* are aptly suited to Eve Bunting's story of a community torn apart by riots. This is a difficult subject to present to children, and Bunting's text is quietly understated. She provides a glimpse of these upheavals through the eyes of a young narrator who is puzzled, then frightened, by events but also concerned about his missing cat. Diaz's paintings, framed in collages of papers, broken glass, shoe leather, and other found objects, provide emotional punch to the story without overwhelming children with concepts that might be beyond their understanding. The faces of the people are done in vivid greens, purples, and blues that heighten the tensions yet avoid racial stereotypes. The thick paint and black lines that frame the figures add movement and texture that also increase the emotional power of the illustrations.

Perhaps no book has captured musical expression as well as Chris Raschka's *Mysterious Thelonious*, Raschka's homage to jazz musician Thelonious. This prose poem in words and images can be viewed as a series of jazz riffs or read in chromatic scales. However one approaches the book, the experience of seeing music and hearing art is intense and exciting.

## Surrealistic Art

Surrealism is characterized more by subject matter than by technique, for the surrealist combines realistic yet incongruous images in unnatural juxtapositions. To make the viewer believe in this unreal scene, the artwork will be meticulously realistic in detail. Anthony Browne creates a surreal world in his picture books *Voices in the Park, Changes,* and *The Piggybook.* In *The Tunnel,* Jack and his sister Rose do not get along. She wants to read fairy tales, while he insists on exploring a tunnel. Finally, when he doesn't come back, Rose must go

*The intense colors and thick textures in Susan Guevara's paintings for Gary Soto's* Chato's Kitchen *convey the culture of East Los Angeles.*

From *Chato's Kitchen,* by Gary Soto, illustrations Susan Guevara, copyright © 1995 by Susan Guevara, illustrations. Used by permission of G. P. Putnam's Sons, a division of Penguin Putnam Inc.

through the frightening tunnel and find him. Once on the other side, she enters a dark forest of trees whose roots and branches form weird, threatening shapes. Finally, in a clearing, she spies the figure of her brother Jack, turned to stone. Fearing she is too late, she throws her arms around him and he is slowly transformed back to his original self. The transformation is also apparent in their friendship. This modern fairy tale becomes very real and frightening in this surrealistic setting.

In explaining his choice of surrealism, Browne is quoted as saying:

> It's a part of not losing that visual openness that kids have . . . surrealism corresponds to a childlike view of the world, in that everything can be made new by putting unrelated objects together.[7]

Chris Van Allsburg's surrealistic world in *Jumanji* is certainly well known, since this story won a Caldecott Medal. The fourteen pictures that make up *The Mysteries of Harris Burdick* are beautiful examples of surrealism. Houses lift off their foundations, schooners

---

[7]In Douglas Martin's *The Telling Line* (New York: Delacorte Press, 1990), p. 283.

*Kathy Jakobsen uses a folk art style to express her very personal view of New York City.*
From *My New York* by Kathy Jakobsen. Copyright © 1993 by Kathy Jakobsen. By permission of Little, Brown and Company (Inc.).

magically appear, and a nun sits in a chair suspended thirty feet above the cathedral floor! Even though the pictures have no connecting narrative, they stimulate children to tell their stories. Van Allsburg is a master of juxtaposition of the real with the unreal.

### Naive or Folk Art

One form of naive art is the style often found in self-taught artists like Grandma Moses, Henri Rousseau, and the itinerant painters, or limners, of colonial America. It can be characterized by a lack of such conventions as perspective and so-called real appearances. It also suggests the art of common people and thus implies art that is centered in community.

We have seen how Paul Zelinsky used these conventions in Anne Isaacs's *Swamp Angel*. Barbara Cooney also adapted her style to imitate that of the early American limners for *Ox-Cart Man* by Donald Hall. Tomie de Paola uses gouache paints reminiscent of the paintings on wood done by the early itinerant painters for *The Quilt Story* by Tony Johnston. His brightly colored illustrations for *Tomie de Paola's Mother Goose* echoes the early folk art style.

Kathy Jakobsen's folk art paintings for Woodie Guthrie's *This Land Is Your Land* and Reeve Lindbergh's narrative poem *Johnny Appleseed* seem most appropriate for celebrating America's history and heroes. Brightly colored pictures show journeys across the country and through the seasons. In *This Land Is Your Land,* originally written in the late 1940s, Jakobsen visually conveys a half century of social history in a style that seems to belong to all the people. Her *My New York* is a feast of visual details that represent a personal view of Jakobsen's years in New York City. Although set in modern times, the story is told in the form of a letter to a friend from a child who has moved from the Midwest to the city. Jakobsen's childlike paintings are appropriate to the theme and invite children everywhere to represent their own home places in art and writing.

Frané Lessac's brilliantly colored paintings represent naive art and capture her love for her native islands in the West Indies in such books as *My Little Island* and *Caribbean Canvas*. These books portray the people, places, sights, and sounds of the islands. Lessac also illustrated *The Chalk Doll* by Charlotte Pomerantz, in which a mother tells her daughter stories of her happy childhood growing up in Jamaica. These detailed paintings are childlike and beautiful in their simplicity of style.

### Cartoon Art

Many children's books are illustrated in a style that depends on a lively line to create movement and humor. The term *cartoon* was originally used to refer to the large, fully developed line drawings that artists prepared and then transferred to frescoes or easel paintings. This style has often been called comic art or comic book style. However, the best comic art in picture books has more in common with the works of eighteenth-century artists such as painter William Hogarth or political caricaturist Thomas Rowlandson than it does with superheroes comic books or the Sunday color comics of today.

Certainly the gross exaggerations of the zany animals of Dr. Seuss are representative of comic art. From the weird birds in *Scrambled Eggs Super!* to the mess created in *The Cat in the Hat*, Seuss utilized cartoon art to tell his far-fetched stories. Sendak used this style very effectively in some of his early art for *A Hole Is to Dig* and *A Very Special House*, both by Ruth Krauss. The little boy who swings on doors and jumps on beds in *A Very Special House* is the only one painted in color, so the reader knows that all the other goings-on in this very special house are "root in the noodle" of his "head head head."

Steven Kellogg's wonderful drawings are fine examples of the expression and humor that can be achieved with this style of art. *The Rattlebang Picnic* by Margaret Mahy is surely the silliest of summer getaways, and the McTavish family manages to escape from an erupting volcano none too soon. Kellogg's illustrations for Tom Paxton's *Engelbert the Elephant* are as hilarious as the story of this elephant who is invited to the queen's ball. Bursting with action and slapdash humor, Kellogg's illustrations always fill in many details that are never mentioned in the text.

William Steig creates his sophisticated dressed animals in line-and-wash drawings for *Pete's a Pizza*, *The Amazing Bone*, and *Doctor DeSoto*. Although

*William Steig's fine style lends a sense of lighthearted farce to* Zeke Pippin, *the story of a musician who puts his audiences to sleep with his music.*
Copyright © 1995 by William Steig. Used by permission of HarperCollins Publishers, New York, NY.

Steig uses background in many of his pictures, the flat-looking characters and clever lines carry the weight of visual storytelling.

James Stevenson, a fellow cartoonist at the *New Yorker*, has also created many books utilizing the cartoon style of art. His tall-tale stories about Grandpa use cartoon balloons for speech and watercolor illustrations. All children enjoy Grandpa's story in *That Terrible Halloween Night* when as a child he went into a haunted house and was so frightened he came out an old man. Comic art requires skilled drawing and vivid imagination. It creates and extends much of the humor in children's books.

Several artists have made use of the visual layout and linear qualities of the art found in comic books. The flat painted figures and speech balloons that are typical of this cultural icon can be seen in the pictures for *In the Night Kitchen* by Maurice Sendak and works by British artist Raymond Briggs. Briggs's *Father Christmas* and *Fungus the Bogeyman* are masterpieces of visual irony that have great appeal for older children. *The Bear* is a gentler story about a little girl who is convinced that a huge polar bear has come to live with her. As in his wordless book *The Snowman*, in *The Bear* Briggs gives a unique visual interpretation to a common childhood fantasy.

### Cultural Conventions

Many artists illustrating stories, folktales, or legends make use of the conventions found in art forms of their respective countries or cultures. David Diaz uses elements of Mexican folk art to tell contemporary stories set within the Mexican and Mexican/American cultures. In Eve Bunting's *Going Home*, the story of a farm family returning to Mexico for Christmas, Diaz creates endpapers that feature close-up photographs of brilliant "artesanias Mexicanas," decorative objects, figures, and other popular arts found in the market places of Mexico. This "arté popular" then forms the background on which the paintings and type are placed. Folk art silhouettes outline these panels; they are also found on the title page and the final page, set against brilliant presidential blue background.

Paul Goble's use of Plains Indian designs in his folktales, such as *Star Boy* and *Iktomi and the Buzzard*, recall the hide paintings of these Native Americans. Just as they made use of African motifs and art in Margaret Musgrove's *Ashanti to Zulu*, Leo and Diane Dillon have created vibrant, powerful illustrations for Leontyne Price's retelling of the opera *Aïda*, using borders and motifs from the one-dimensional Egyptian style of art. Deborah Nourse Lattimore always uses the style of art of the culture from which her tales come. For example, her Mayan tale *Why There Is No Arguing in Heaven* is illustrated with many bluish-gray figures that suggest the stone carvings of the ancient Mayas. In *The Sailor Who Captured the Sea,* she recreates the extraordinary art and design of the ancient Irish *Book of Kells* while telling its story. Chapter 6 details other works of traditional literature in which artists have used cultural conventions to enhance the meaning of the story.

### Personal Styles

Few picture-book artists use only one style of art; they adapt their work to meet the requirements of a particular story. At the same time, many of them do develop a recognizable personal style that can be identified by their preference for a particular pictorial style of art, use of medium, even choice of content. Thus we have come to associate the use of collage with Leo Lionni, Ezra Jack Keats, and Eric Carle, even though they differ in how they use it. The delicate, old-fashioned style of Tasha Tudor's watercolors is as easily recognizable as the flowing, massive look of Warwick Hutton's watercolors. Tomie de Paola's use of the symbols of folk art, such as hearts, doves, and rabbits, is another recognizable mark of his work. The amusing animals in the stories by Pat Hutchins are frequently stylized with patterned fur and feathers. Her birds and animals in *What Game Shall We Play?* and that self-assured hen in *Rosie's Walk* are obviously vintage Hutchins. Frequently, hers are the first illustrations children can identify by the artist's name. And yet Hutchins employs a very different style in *The Very Worst Monster* and *Its My*

*David Diaz's Mexican folkart motifs provide a culturally rich visual setting for Eve Bunting's* Going Home.

*Birthday*. Roy Gerrard always paints little chunky people, as in his riotous spoof on westerns in *Rosie and the Rustlers* and his journey to ancient Rome in *The Roman Twins* and to ancient Egypt in *Croco'nile*. Wordplay and visual fun are also characteristic of Gerrard's books.

Several artists are experimenting with both style and media and seem to gather strength with each new book. Paul O. Zelinsky is a talented artist who is able to choose styles that are beautifully suited to the mood and meaning of each of his books. His *The Maid, the Mouse and the Odd Shaped House* is a lighthearted tale, based on an old nursery rhyme, about an old woman and her pet mouse who make themselves at home in a very odd house. Zelinsky's softened tints and stylized figures evoke the decorative arts of the nineteenth century. He also relies primarily on the elements of line and shape to reveal clues to the real nature of the odd house as the story progresses. On the other hand, he uses oil paints and borrows conventions from Renaissance art to retell *Rapunzel, Hansel and Gretel,* and *Rumpelstiltskin*. This style beautifully evokes the setting and the origin of these old tales. His illustrations for *Swamp Angel* by Anne Isaacs are more playful, and here his style makes a direct connection to early American art and folklore.

Maurice Sendak's pictures for *Mr. Rabbit and the Lovely Present* by Charlotte Zolotow, *Where the Wild Things Are, In the Night Kitchen, Outside*

*Over There,* and *We Are All in the Dumps with Jack and Guy* vary, despite the fact that each has a moonlight setting. The impressionistic Monet-like pictures for Zolotow's *Mr. Rabbit and the Lovely Present* are easily identifiable. The trees and endpapers of *Where the Wild Things Are* have been compared to Henri Rousseau's French primitive paintings. However, Max with his roguish smile and the big ludicrous beasts with their "terrible eyes and terrible teeth" are very much Sendak. While the illustrations for *In the Night Kitchen* reflect the influence that Disney and the comics had on Sendak in his youth, they are very definitely Sendak's own creation. Max has now become Mickey, who sheds the last of his inhibitions in a dream in which he falls out of his clothes and into the night kitchen. Comic book characters have been refined into a work of art that captures the feelings and dream wishes of childhood. The lush watercolors in *Outside Over There* represent another direction in Sendak's work. Here he is reaching the child at a deeper psychological level through symbolic art. His artistic metaphors call forth the same inner feelings that Ida is struggling with as she imagines in a momentary daydream what it would be like to be rid of the responsibility of her baby sister. Even though the art is very different in *Where the Wild Things Are, In the Night Kitchen,* and *Outside Over There,* Sendak refers to these books as a trilogy, all united by the fact that they represent childhood dreams. Each new book of Sendak's seems to represent a deeper involvement with his "child within."

Style, then, is an elusive quality. It includes signature features like the big hands and feet that Sendak always draws and the small chunky figures in Roy Gerrard's amusing illustrations. Style can be the use of characteristic media, like Eric Carle's collages or Pat Hutchins's patterned animals and birds or Anthony Browne's surrealism. Style is an elusive quality of the artist, which changes and varies over the years and with the particular demands of the work. Today there is more freedom to experiment in illustrating children's picture books. Many of our artists are taking advantage of this new freedom and producing fresh and original art.

Exposure to a variety of art styles through fine picture books can help children develop visual maturity and appreciation. Certainly there is no *one* style that is appropriate for children or preferred by children. The major consideration in evaluating style is how well it conveys and enhances *meaning.* Exploring the work of an illustrator through an intense classroom study can give children time to articulate their responses to an artist's work and to identify some of the many components that can be part of an illustrator's style. The web "Brian Pinkney: A Web of Possibilities" shows how teachers might plan to study the work of Brian Pinkney.

## The Format of the Book

A picture book is not made up of single illustrated pictures but conveys its message through a *series* of images. The impact of the total format of the book is what creates the art object known as the picture book.

Book size and shape are often decisions made jointly by the illustrator and the art director of the publishing house. They might search for a size that will enhance the theme of the story. *The Bear* by Raymond Briggs is almost fifteen inches tall—big enough, it seems, to contain the huge bear within. *The Biggest Boy* by Kevin Henkes is also a large book, and Nancy Tafuri's close-up pictures make the little boy character seem even bigger, in keeping with his lively imagination. *Goose* by Molly Bang tells the story of an orphaned goose. Raised by a family of woodchucks, the little goose feels different and longs desperately for something else. She sets out to find it, but finds herself instead in an overwhelmingly frightening world. When by accident she discovers that she can fly, she flies home to her loving woodchuck family. The book's small size speaks to its small preschool audience and implies the character's feeling lost in a great big world.

The shape of some books suggests their content. The horizontal shape of Donald Hall's *Ox-Cart Man,* illustrated by Barbara Cooney, is very appropriate for portraying the long trek to the Portsmouth market to sell the family's produce in the early fall and the long walk home through leafless trees in late autumn after the father has sold everything, including the ox and his cart. The shape of *Fish Eyes* by Lois Ehlert is long and narrow like a fish or small aquarium. *Giants in the Land* by Diana Applebaum, illustrated by Michael McCurdy, and *A Tree Is Nice* by Janice Udry, illustrated by Marc Simont, are tall and vertical in shape, much like the trees described in the books.

Both the cover and dust jacket of a book should receive careful attention. The primary purpose of the jacket is to call attention to the book. The jacket for the award-winning *Puss in Boots* illustrated by Fred Marcellino certainly calls attention to itself, for it features the huge head of a hat-bedecked puss in a ruffled collar that could only be the famous *Puss in Boots* by Charles Perrault. But the cover carries no title. Turn the book over and there is the title on the back. A dark brown cloth cover and golden brown endpapers harmonize well with the picture on the jacket. Good cloth designs are usually small and symbolic of the content. For example, for *A Chair for My Mother,* Vera Williams uses an imprint of a chair,

## ART TECHNIQUES

Celebrate Brian Pinkney's work. How has his style changed over time? Set up an illustrator corner with books he has illustrated as well as work done by the children.

How does Pinkney's work convey the theme of each book? Affect its mood?

Display art media used in his illustrations.

Create your own scratchboard pictures. Use oil, pastel, paint, or other media to color the picture.

Compare Pinkney's scratchboard illustrations to other illustrators such as Barbara Cooney or Marcia Sewall.

*I Smell Honey, Pretty Brown Face* (A. Pinkney) Compare Pinkney's technique in his board books for young children to his books for older children.

Compare the techniques of scratchboard with block prints, wood engravings, and etchings. How are they similar/different? Can you tell the difference between these art techniques?

## THE STORY DRUM

*Cut from the Same Cloth* (San Souci) Make a graph of the most popular characters/tall tales among the boys and girls in the class. Label the locations of each legendary character on a map.
Read *Her Stories* (Hamilton). Try to find more female characters in other folklore, or create a heroine in your own tall tale.

*The Elephant's Wrestling Match* (Sierra) Write your own talking drum story with animal characters from Africa.
Make a story drum. Try using various containers with string or bands wrapped from end to end.

*Sukey and the Mermaid* (San Souci) Following Pinkney's scratchboard technique, create a picture of the mermaid's world. Explore and compare other tales of mermaids. Find their origins.

*A Wave in Her Pocket* (Joseph) *Cendrillon* (San Souci) Ask a family member or relative to come into class to tell stories passed down from generation to generation.

## DISCOVERING PEOPLE IN THE PAST

*Bill Pickett: Rodeo Riding Cowboy* (A. Pinkney)
*Alvin Ailey* (A. Pinkney) (see "Sing and Swing to the Beat")
*Dear Benjamin Banneker* (A. Pinkney)
*Happy Birthday, Martin Luther King* (Marzollo)
*Harriet Tubman and Black History Month* (Carter)
*The Dreamkeeper and Other Poems* (L. Hughes)
Make a timeline of African Americans who have contributed to American life and history.

## POETRY

*The Dream Keeper* (Hughes)
*I Never Told* (cover art) (Livingston)
*A Time to Talk* (Livingston)

Find favorite poems to read aloud.
Create scratchboard pictures for individual.
Research the lives of the poets Langston Hughes and Myra Cohn Livingston. What are the similarities and differences between the two? Their work?

## MAGIC, MYSTERY, & DISCOVERY

*In the Time of the Drums* (Siegelson)
*The Faithful Friend* (San Souci)
*The Ballad of Belle Dorcas* (Hooks)
*The Dark Thirty* (McKissack)
*The Boy and the Ghost* (San Souci)

Compare southern tales with tales from other regions or cultures.
Have a ghost-telling celebration at a pretend "dark-thirty" time, one-half hour of supernatural stories.
List the spells and the effects of each.
Find other folktales that contain three characters similar to the three witches, spells, or transformations.

*Where Does the Trail Lead?* (Burton)
Take a nature walk by the seashore.
Go on a scavenger hunt looking for specific objects along the trails.
Follow a guidebook of trails along seashores and sand dunes.

## CELEBRATE!

*Seven Candles for Kwanzaa* (Pinkney)

Discuss the seven principles of Kwanzaa, and discover the origins of Kwanzaa.
Weave your own straw "mkeka" placemat.
Make some Kwanzaa gifts: a fabric doll or a bead necklace.

*Day of Delight* (Schur)
Examine Jewish traditions. How are they alike and different from other religious traditions.
Discover kosher recipes.

*Happy Birthday, Martin Luther King* (Marzollo)
Plan a Birthday celebration in honor of Martin Luther King.

## ALL IN THE FAMILY

Explore the life of the illustrator through family members.

Father: Jerry Pinkney (illustrator)
Mother: Gloria Jean Pinkney (writer)
Wife: Andrea Davis Pinkney (writer and editor).

Make a comparison chart of various books created by each family member comparing story content, art techniques, and connection to authors.
Collect data in the library involving the work of the illustrator.
Write a letter to editors who publish the works of the Pinkney family to obtain background information.
Research how and why authors and illustrators work together on projects.

## CELEBRATE KID POWER

*Jojo's Flying Side Kick*
*Max Found Two Sticks*
*The Adventures of Sparrowboy*
*Cosmo and the Robot*

How did each of these characters do something extraordinary?
Choose something that you like to do and write a story about how you became a superpower at it.

## SING AND SWING TO THE BEAT

*Alvin Ailey* (A. Pinkney)
*Duke Ellington, The Piano Prince and His Orchestra* (A. Pinkney)
Visit a ballet class.
Listen to the music of jazz and blues bands. Create your own music and dance to celebrate these famous lives.

*Watch Me Dance* (A. Pinkney)
*Shake Shake Shake* (A. Pinkney)
*Max Found Two Sticks*
Make a list of the sounds that are similar to the sounds that Max's sticks made.
Collect different natural objects to represent different instruments.

## BRIAN PINKNEY
## A WEB OF POSSIBILITIES

Web prepared by Jean M. Norman

heart-shaped to show the family's intense desire for a beautiful, comfortable chair for their mother. Publishers are increasingly duplicating the image from the dust jacket on the book's cover rather than preparing a separate cloth cover that few people ever see. However, a peek beneath a dust jacket can still reveal pleasant surprises. In *Rushmore* by Lynn Currie, the front of the dust jacket shows a close-up of artisans working on the statue of Washington, while the back shows the mountain half finished and covered by scaffolds. The cover underneath the jacket is a different picture—the finished sculptures are shown spread out over the back and front covers. The cloth cover beneath the lovely full-color dust jacket of George Ella Lyon's *Book,* illustrated by Peter Catalanoto, has a wide green binding and a dark blue cover vertically embossed with the letters *B O O K.* This careful attention to detail evokes the lovingly crafted, handmade books of earlier centuries.

The endpapers of a picture book can also add to its attractiveness. These are the first and last pages of the book; one half of each is glued to the inside of the cover, while the other is not pasted down. Endpapers are usually of stronger paper than printed pages. In picture books, endpapers are often of a color that harmonizes with the cover or other pictures in the book, and frequently they are illustrated. Decorated endpapers can reflect the setting, the theme, or the content of the book and serve as a special invitation into the book. Jerry Pinkney's exquisitely painted endpapers for Hans Christian Andersen's *The Ugly Duckling* are as much a part of the storytelling as the other pages in the book. The opening endpapers show a parade of ducks swimming and diving in a pristine stream with an odd-looking bird struggling to bring up the rear. At the book's end a glorious, full-grown white swan is depicted in the same locale. In Kevin Hawkes's *Weslandia,* by Paul Fleischman, the main character is a social outcast who invents his own civilization for his summer project. Wesley's invented hieroglyphic alphabet appears on the endpapers and will have kids scrambling to figure out the code. Leo and Diane Dillon created stylized lotus blossoms and seedpods on marbelized paper for *Aïda,* retold by Leontyne Price. The endpapers of *Crow Boy* by Taro Yashima show a flower and a butterfly alone against a dark background. They seem to symbolize the metamorphosis of Crow Boy's life from dark despair to brilliant hope.

Even the title page of a picture book can be beautiful and symbolic. Marcia Brown has created a striking title page for Cendrars's *Shadow*. She por-

*Jerry Pinkney's exquisitely painted endpapers for Hans Christian Andersen's* The Ugly Duckling *reflect thoughtful care and book design.*

Illustration from *The Ugly Duckling* by Jerry Pickney. Copyright © 1999 by Jerry Pinkey. Used by permission of William Morrow Company, an imprint of HarperCollins Publishers.

trays a young boy in silhouette anxiously looking back at his long shadow, which falls across a double-page spread, while the spirits of his ancestors, shown as white masks, look on. This primitive fear of and respect for shadows permeates the book. William Steig emphasizes the friendship of a mouse and a whale at the same time as he contrasts their size with his title page for *Amos & Boris.* The title page of *Just Plain Fancy* by Patricia Polacco provides the clue to the origin of the fancy peacock egg that Naomi and Ruth found in the tall grass by the drive. All aspects of a book can reinforce or extend the meaning of the story.

The layout of pictures and text on each double-page spread and on succeeding pages can have an important impact on the meaning and movement of a story. Full-size pictures might be interspersed with smaller ones, or a page might show a sequence of pictures. Beatriz Vidal's placement of pictures and use of shapes complement the rhythm of Verna Aardema's *Bringing the Rain to Kapiti Plain.* This African tale from the Nandi tribe is cumulative, reminiscent of the nursery rhyme "The House That Jack Built." First, Vidal shows a verdant plain mostly on the right-hand page; then she switches to the left, while the third page rests the eye with a double-page spread showing a heavy cloud mass spreading over the entire plain. Then once again she places her masses on the right and then left page—readers anticipate this shift just as they anticipate the cumulative rhyme. This is not done throughout the book, however; it would be too monotonous. This is a beautiful example of how one image on a page blends into the next to create the total impact of the book.

The spacing of the text on the page, the choice of margins, and the white space within a book contribute to the making of a quality picture book. In Virginia Lee Burton's *The Little House,* the arrangement of the text on the page suggests the curve of the road in the opposite picture. In the very funny story of the dog poet in *Max Makes a Million* by Maira Kalman, Max dreams of going to Paris. These longings are printed on the paper in the shape of the Eiffel Tower.

Appropriate type design is also a matter for consideration. *Type* is the name given to all printed letters, and *typeface* refers to the thousands of letter styles available today. Before the advent of computer-created fonts, printers chose from some six thousand different styles then available. Nicolas Sidjakov describes the difficulty he and his editor had in finding a suitable typeface for Ruth Robbins's *Baboushka and the Three Kings.* When they did find one they liked, it was obsolete and not easily available. They finally located enough fonts to handset *Baboushka* a page at a time.[8]

Now the computer allows artists much more freedom. David Diaz designed the fonts for *Coming Home* to resemble the linear forms of the Mexican folk art that fills the book. Joe Cepeda created the display type for Julius Lester's *What a Truly Cool World,* and the remainder of the book was printed in a font called "smile and party."[9]

Whether they are traditional or computer created, typefaces or fonts vary in legibility and the feeling they create. Some seem bold, others delicate and graceful, some crisp and businesslike. The type should enhance or extend the overall design of the book. It is also important that the text can be read easily and is not printed on dark paper. In Paul Goble's *The Girl Who Loved Wild Horses,* the text was changed to white when it was placed on the dark pages that represented night. The result is far more pleasing aesthetically than had the type been printed in white rectangles and placed on the dark background.

Other factors in a picture book must be considered from a utilitarian standpoint. The paper should be dull enough so that it does not easily reflect light, opaque enough to prevent print from showing through, and strong enough to withstand heavy usage. Side sewing in the binding of many picture books makes them more durable, but it might distort double-page spreads unless the artwork is prepared

with the gutter separation in mind. Tall narrow books with side sewing will not lie flat when the book is open. Many librarians complain that today's bindings are of poor quality and will not last for the life of the book. These, then, are some of the practical considerations that can affect a book's beauty and durability.

In sum, no single element creates an outstanding picture book. What does create one is all elements working together to create a cohesive whole that pleases the eye and delights the imagination.

# The Language of Picture Books

The words of picture books are as important as the illustrations; they can help children develop an early sensitivity to the imaginative use of language and add to their overall experience with a picture book. Since most of these books are read to children rather than by them, there is no reason to oversimplify or write down to today's knowledgeable and sophisticated child. Beatrix Potter knew that, given the context of *The Tale of Peter Rabbit* and the picture of Peter caught in the gooseberry net, most children would comprehend the words "his sobs were overheard by some friendly sparrows, who flew to him in great excitement, and implored him to exert himself" (p. 45).

Steig's *Amos & Boris* is a comical story of the unlikely friendship between a mouse and a whale. Amos, the mouse, delighted by all things nautical, builds himself a jaunty little boat, which he names *Rodent.* Admiring the starry skies one night, he rolls overboard and is saved by a huge whale, who is amazed to find that the mouse is also a mammal. He gives him a ride to safety, and, true to the lion and rat fable on which the story is based, Amos is able to reciprocate at a later time. Steig's luxuriant use of language and superb pictures make this an unusual picture book. The description of their trip home details their growing friendship:

> Swimming along, sometimes at great speed, sometimes slowly and leisurely, sometimes resting and exchanging ideas, sometimes stopping to sleep, it took them a week to reach Amos's home shore. During that time, they developed a deep admiration for one another. Boris admired the delicacy, the quivering daintiness, the light touch, the small voice, the gemlike radiance of the mouse. Amos admired the bulk, the grandeur, the power, the purpose, the rich voice, and the abounding friendliness of the whale. (unpaged)

These words might seem difficult words to understand, but children do make sense of the story, using the context of both the pictures and the text. They

[8]Nicolas Sidjakov, "Caldecott Award Acceptance," in *Newbery and Caldecott Medal Books: 1956–1965,* ed. Lee Kingman (Boston: Horn Book, 1965), pp. 223–225.

[9]Kathryn Falwell's picture book *The Letter Jesters* (Boston: Ticknor and Fields, 1994) provides a sprightly overview of printing.

sweep back and forth from one to the other, obtaining the general feeling for this unusual friendship even if they do not know the exact meaning of every single word. This is the way children increase their vocabularies—by hearing or reading words they do not know but in a context that provides a general sense of the meaning.

In contrast to Steig's exuberant use of words in *Amos & Boris*, the well-known New England poet Donald Hall portrays the journey of *Ox-Cart Man* in cadenced language that is as slow and deliberate as the pace of the ox on the ten-day journey to Portsmouth. When the father packs the family's products, which had taken them a whole year to make, the author describes them in a kind of litany of words:

> He packed a bag of wool he sheared from the sheep in April.
>
> He packed a shawl his wife wove on a loom from yarn spun at the spinning wheel from sheep sheared in April.
>
> He packed five pairs of mittens his daughter knit from yarn spun at the spinning wheel from sheep sheared in April. (unpaged)

All children can appreciate figurative language, provided the comparisons are within the realm of their experience. The vivid word pictures in Alvin Tresselt's *White Snow, Bright Snow* are thoroughly enjoyed by 5- and 6-year-olds and reflect a child's point of view:

> In the morning a clear blue sky was overhead and blue shadows hid in all the corners. Automobiles looked like big fat raisins buried in snow drifts.
>
> Houses crouched together, their windows peeking out from under great white eyebrows. Even the church steeple wore a pointed cap on its top. (p. 20)

The dialogue of a story can be rich and believable or it can be stilted, as in a *Dick and Jane* basal reader. Arnold Lobel was a master at creating understated humorous dialogue in his *Frog and Toad* series. Similarly, part of the charm of the *Frances* stories by Russell Hoban is the natural-sounding dialogue of everybody's favorite badger, Frances. The expressive pictures are as humorous as the dialogue in both of these well-written series.

In evaluating picture books, it is important to remember that a story should be told quickly because the action must be contained within a 32- to 64-page book. Even with this limitation, the criteria developed in Chapter 1 for all fiction apply equally well to picture books that tells stories. Both text and illustrations should be evaluated. The artistry of the words should be equal to the beauty of the illustrations. See Guidelines, "Evaluating Picture Books," for some questions that can help you evaluate picture books.

## The Content of Picture Books

Several recent changes can be noted in the content of picture books. One is the increasing publication of books that are based on sharing memories of times past with children. Frequently these are told by grandparents, much as they might once have been told around the dinner table. Perhaps these books compensate for the lack of frequent contact with extended families in our fast-paced lives. These books seldom have a real plot but are based on what life was like when grandfather, or grandmother, or parents were children.

Another development in the content of picture books is a tremendous increase in books that are geared to children in the middle grades and older. This seems appropriate for today's visually minded child. As the age range for picture books increases, it becomes imperative to evaluate the appropriateness of the content for the age level of its intended audience. You do not want to share *Hiroshima No Pika* (The Flash of Hiroshima) by Toshi Maruki with young children any more than you would read *Goodnight Moon* by Margaret Wise Brown to older children.

Other considerations regarding the content of picture books need to be examined. For example, does the book avoid race, gender, and age stereotyping? Gender stereotyping begins early. Examples can be found in pictures as well as in text. In the imaginative story *Can I Keep Him?* by Steven Kellogg, Albert asks his mother if he can keep one pet after another, ranging from real to imaginary to human. His distraught mother is always pictured attending to such household chores as scrubbing, ironing, and cleaning the toilet bowl. She explains in very literal terms why Albert cannot keep his pets; for example, a snake's scales could clog the vacuum. While the contrast between Albert's highly original ideas and his mother's mundane preoccupation with household duties is funny, it is also a stereotyped image of the traditional housewife.

Books that counteract gender stereotyping are not as hard to find as they were when *William's Doll*, by Charlotte Zolotow, was published in 1972. William is a little boy who desperately wants a doll but is misunderstood by family and teased by friends. Only his grandmother understands how he feels, and so she brings him a baby doll "to hug . . . so that when he's a father . . . he'll know how to care for his baby."

More and more books portray characters who are willing to step outside of traditional roles to have fulfilling lives. In *Max* by Rachel Isadora, a young

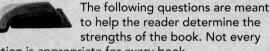

## Evaluating Picture Books

The following questions are meant to help the reader determine the strengths of the book. Not every question is appropriate for every book.

### CONTENT

How appropriate is the content of the book for its intended age level?

Is this a book that will appeal to children, or is it really written for adults?

When and where does it take place? How has the artist portrayed this?

Are the characters well delineated and developed?

Are race, gender, and other stereotypes avoided?

What is the quality of the language of the text?

How is the theme developed through text and illustrations?

### ILLUSTRATIONS

In what ways do the illustrations help create the meaning of the text?

How are pictures made an integral part of the text?

Do the illustrations extend the text in any way? Do they provide clues to the action of the story?

Are the pictures accurate and consistent with the text?

Where the setting calls for it, are the illustrations authentic in detail?

### MEDIUM AND STYLE OF ILLUSTRATIONS

What medium has the illustrator chosen to use? Is it appropriate for the mood of the story?

How has the illustrator used line, shape, and color to extend the meaning of the story?

How would you describe the style of the illustrations? Is the style appropriate for the story?

How has the illustrator varied the style and technique? What techniques seem to create rhythm and movement?

How has the illustrator created balance in composition?

### FORMAT

Does the size of the book seem appropriate to the content?

Does the jacket design express the theme of the book?

Do the cover design and endpapers convey the spirit of the book?

In what way does the title page anticipate the story to come?

Is the type design well chosen for the theme and purpose of the book?

What is the quality of the paper?

How durable is the binding?

### OVERALL EVALUATION

How is this work similar to or different from other works by this author and/or illustrator?

How is this story similar to or different from other books with the same subject or theme?

What comments have reviewers made about this book? Do you agree or disagree with them?

What has the artist said about her or his work?

Will this book make a contribution to the growing body of children's literature? How lasting do you think it will be?

---

baseball player decides to take ballet lessons. He finds that it is a super way to warm up for baseball.

We have picture books that portray the experiences of more diverse cultures than ever before, although the total number of multicultural books is still small compared to the proportion of ethnic and racial groups in the population.[10] Native Americans, who have been maligned in print, on television, and in commercial games as bloodthirsty warriors, are still underrepresented in books. *In My Mother's House* by Ann Nolan Clark, a poetic story of life among Pueblo Indians, has been reissued with handsome black-and-white and colored illustrations by Velino Herrera.

*This House Is Made of Mud*, by Ken Buchanan, celebrates the joy of living in a Navajo hogan. The desert is its yard, the mountains its fence, and all the animals and birds are welcome visitors. Lovely clear watercolors by Libba Tracy add to the beauty of this simple story. A few stories attempt to tell stories of family relationships in Native American communities, with mixed results.

*Annie and the Old One*, by Miska Miles, is a story of a Navajo girl and her grandmother. However, this book has been criticized by Native Americans for not being authentic in its representation of the Navajo way of life. Bill Martin, Jr., and John Archambault's *Knots on a Counting Rope* tells about a warm relationship between a blind child and his grandfather. Text and illustrations suggest that this is a story about a Native American family,

---

[10]See *New Advocate* 8 (winter 1995) and *Horn Book Magazine* (May/June 1995) for several articles on multicultural literature.

*In Arthur Dorros's* Isla, *vibrant paintings by Elisa Kleven sparkle like an island in the sea.*

From *Isla* by Arthur Dorros, illustrated by Elisa Kleven, copyright © 1995 by Elisa Kleven, illustrations. Used by permission of Dutton Children's Books, a division of Penguin Putnam Inc.

but Native Americans have objected to the portrayal of tribal life in this book.[11] The continuing popularity of books like these suggests the need for more Native American authors, or at least for teachers to have more resources on Native Americans to consult for authenticity.

The last few years have seen an increase in books about Latino cultures, in bilingual books and translated books. A picture book can often bridge linguistic barriers and introduce all children to cultures and languages other than their own. Brilliant collage paintings by Elisa Kleven illustrate the imaginary trips Rosalba and her grandmother take in *Abuela* and *Isla*. Rosalba narrates their marvelous journeys in English spiced with Spanish phrases that children who do not speak Spanish can easily understand in the context of these jewel-like settings. The author, Arthur Dorros, provides a glossary and pronunciation guide at the end. Edith Hope Fine's *Under the Lemon Moon*, illustrated by Rene King

Moreno, is a charming story of a little girl who carefully nurtures her lemon tree only to have the lemons stolen one night and the tree badly damaged. When Anciana, a mysterious old wise woman, helps restore the tree to abundant health, Rosalinda shares the harvest of lemons with the whole community, even the poor thief who took her lemons to help feed his family.

Many more cultures are now represented in stories about contemporary children as well as in folktales, but we need to continue to encourage authors, illustrators, and publishers to portray a variety of cultural experiences in books for children.

Though there are now more books about elderly people than ever before, we can find stereotypes among these, too. One young-appearing grandfather went to a bookstore recently and said he wanted "a book about a grandfather in which the main character doesn't die." Many grandparents today in their sixties and seventies are vigorous and healthy; we might well ask if they are being portrayed this way.

Picture books frequently give children their first impressions of various ethnic and racial groups. Only when our books portray characters of both sexes, all ages, and all ethnic and racial groups in a wide range of occupations, and from a great variety of socioeconomic backgrounds and settings, will we have moved away from stereotyping to a more honest portrayal of the world for children.

---

[11]Native Americans maintain that Native American children would not interrupt their grandfather as the boy does in this story, because elders are always respected. Clothing and hairstyles are not authentic to any one nation, and the naming ceremony is incorrect. See "Book Reviews" in *Books Without Bias: Through Indian Eyes*, eds. Beverly Slapin and Doris Seale (Berkeley, Calif.: Oyate, 1988), pp. 273–278. For a list of recommended books, see their website at http://www.oyate.org.

# Themes & Subjects in Picture Books

It is important that we, as teachers and librarians, know all the criteria by which to judge a quality picture book. Children are more interested in one criterion—does it tell a good story? They will respond most deeply to books that touch their interests and their imagination with words and pictures. In this section we briefly discuss picture books by theme for the benefit of those selecting particular books or preparing units of study.

## Family Stories

Contemporary realistic family stories include single-parent families, divorced and remarried (blended) families, adoptive and foster families, and the extended family. Children always beg to hear stories about when their parents were small. The little African American girl in *Tell Me a Story, Mama* by Angela Johnson knows exactly what family stories she wants to hear, and she knows them so well that she can tell them herself with her mother adding just the right comment. This is the story of a tender parent-child relationship.

Sibling conflict is portrayed more frequently in picture books than love and compassion. In Shirley Hughes's *Dogger,* a big sister, Bella, lovingly gives up the huge teddy bear she won at the fair in order to obtain her little brother's lost, much-loved plush-toy dog. Hughes always portrays real, believable characters in messy, confusing households in both her pictures and her text. In this story Bella shows her love for Dave in her actions, whereas many family mood stories only talk about love.

Relatives are an important part of a child's world, and many picture books explore the closeness between children and the members of their extended families. The warm, jubilant picture book by Cynthia Rylant, *The Relatives Came,* celebrates the joys of family reunions. Illustrated by Stephen Gammell, the book describes the summer when some six or seven relatives arrive, having driven up from Virginia in an old station wagon. The relatives stay for weeks and weeks, helping tend the garden and mend any broken things. Stephen Gammell used brightly colored pencil drawings for this award-winning book. The perfect companion to Rylant's book is Jacqueline Woodson's *We Had a Picnic This Sunday Past,* illustrated by Diane Greenseid. Although the time frame is only one day instead of weeks, this extended African American family is just as joyous and loving, and the culinary delights will have readers' mouths watering.

Several themes can be discerned in the many stories about grandparents. One theme is helping the child overcome a fear or learn something new, or just enjoyment of the relationship. A second type is learning to say good-bye and adjusting to the death of a grandparent. A third is the sharing of family stories, frequently including the cultural feeling for the country from which the grandparents emigrated.

In *Storm in the Night* by Mary Stolz, a storm has cut off the electricity, so a grandfather and grandson sit together in the dark and enjoy the sounds and smells of the rain. The grandfather recounts the story of a stormy night from his childhood and how he overcame his fear of the dark. Pat Cummings's pictures show a loving relationship in an African American family. Patricia Polacco tells a memorable story of how a little girl is terrified of thunder until her Russian "babushka" (grandmother) teaches her to make a special *Thunder Cake.* As child and grandmother scurry around to get the ingredients for the Thunder Cake, the little girl doesn't have time to be frightened of the storm.

Tomie de Paola has written several stories about grandparents. *Tom* describes his relationship with his irrepressible maternal grandfather, who must have given him his sense of humor as well as his name. *Nana Upstairs & Nana Downstairs* is more serious, describing a boy's visits with his bedridden great-grandmother. *Now One Foot, Now the Other* is de Paola's story of the little boy helping his grandfather recover from a stroke and learn to walk again.

Every family makes its own history, creates its own mythology by retelling family stories many times over. Three stories of African American families carry on this theme. In Valerie Flournoy's *The Patchwork Quilt,* Tanya loves to hear her grandmother tell the stories of the material she is using to make a quilt. She helps her cut the squares and listens to her story of the quilt of memories. Flournoy's story and the realistic pictures by Jerry Pinkney capture a young girl's love for her treasured grandmother. In Elizabeth Fitzgerald Howard's *Aunt Flossie's Hats (and Crab Cakes Later),* Sarah and Susan hear the history of their Great-Great-Aunt Flossie's many hats, including the time a dog retrieved her "favorite best Sunday hat" from the water. Sumptuous oil paintings by James Ransome convey the joy of the children's visit to their very special aunt. Howard's own 98-year-old aunt who never threw anything away was the inspiration for this delightful family story. In *Uncle Jed's Barbershop,* by Margaree King Mitchell, Sarah Jean remembers her uncle who sacrificed dreams of having his own barbershop to help his family and neighbors. Uncle Jed, a remarkable man, struggled through the Great Depression and the years of segregation in the South until finally, at the age of seventy-nine, he

*Seven-year-olds create a collage mural of the book* Hi, Cat! *by Ezra Jack Keats.*
Barrington Road School, Upper Arlington Public Schools, Ohio. Marlene Harbert, teacher.

opened his barbershop. James Ransome's richly textured paintings add to the warmth of this lovely story.

In *The Keeping Quilt* by Patricia Polacco, Great Gramma Anna, a Russian Jew who was an immigrant to this country, made a quilt to help the family always remember their homeland. Through four generations the quilt is a Sabbath tablecloth, a wedding canopy, and a blanket that welcomes babies warmly into the world. To this day, Patricia Polacco still treasures this family quilt. The warm sepias of the drawings set against the full color in the quilt itself visually recreate the textures of memory and the fabric of tradition.

## Familiar Everyday Experiences

Everything is new to the young child the first time it happens—going to school, making friends, losing teeth, taking a trip, moving away, the death of a pet. Children soon become accustomed to familiar experiences; nevertheless, books can help keep alive the wonder and anticipation of many such experiences. They can also alleviate some of children's concerns and worries about the new and unknown.

Ezra Jack Keats has used collage and bright acrylic paints for his well-loved stories of Peter and his friends. Beginning with *The Snowy Day, Peter's Chair, Whistle for Willie,* and *A Letter to Amy,* the stories deal with simple events that are central to a young child's life. As Peter grows up, he is joined by his friend Archie in *Goggles, Hi Cat!* and *Pet Show!* All these stories take place in the inner city and have exciting story lines and convincing characterization. In *Goggles,* Peter, Archie, and Willie, Peter's dachshund, fool some big boys who want to take away the motorcycle goggles that the two friends have found. In *Hi Cat!* Peter is adopted by a crazy cat. In *Pet Show!* the crazy cat disappears just when Archie

needs him for his entry. Being highly creative, Archie substitutes an empty bottle that contains his pet, a germ! He receives an award for the quietest pet.

Birthdays are extra-special events for children, and Vera Williams's brightly colored paintings add extra warmth to her stories about Rosa and her family. In *Something Special for Me,* Williams makes very real the decision that Rosa, the little girl in *A Chair for My Mother,* must make. Soon it will be her birthday, and this time she can have the money in the large money jar that contains her mother's waitressing tips to buy anything she wants. After much soul-searching, Rosa decides to spend the money on a used accordion. In *Music, Music for Everyone,* Rosa's grandmother becomes ill and the money jar is empty from paying her bills, so Rosa uses her birthday accordion to earn money.

## Appreciating Cultural Diversity

 American children of the twenty-first century will need to develop a worldview that appreciates the richness of other cultures at the same time as they preserve and celebrate their uniqueness. In this text we integrate multiracial and ethnic stories throughout chapters just as we would hope they will be used in schools. A global view requires books about other cultures and countries that children might not be able to visit. Fortunately, we have an increasing number of titles of both nonfiction and fiction that will introduce children to others who share this earth and who are like them in so many ways.

In *Elizabeti's Doll,* Elizabeti desperately wants a baby of her own to care for after her little sister is born. She doesn't have a doll, but she finds a special rock that she cares for just as lovingly. Stephanie

Stuve-Bodeen's delightful story is set in Tanzania and illustrated by Christy Hale. The story celebrates the power of a child's imagination and every child's longing for something to call her own. *Galimoto* is titled after a popular toy car that boys in Malawi, Africa, make out of scraps of wire. In this story by Karen Williams, Kondi, a resourceful 7-year-old boy, is determined to make one. He persists in finding enough wire and finally constructs what looks like a pickup truck from scraps and bits he has scavenged from various places. Vibrant watercolors by Catherine Stock portray this ingenious young boy and reflect her weeks spent sketching in Malawi. Williams and Stock have also collaborated on several other books, including *Painted Dreams,* the tender story of Marie, a young Haitian girl who dreams of being an artist. Like the character in Galimoto, this determined youngster uses materials at hand, including paints discarded by a local artist, to transform her neighborhood and achieve her dreams.

Stock has also told and illustrated the story of another African child in *Where Are You Going, Manyoni?* Manyoni wakes early. After breakfast, when the sun is just rising, she sets out on a journey. She travels past the baobab tree, across a ridge, under the wild fig trees, past the malala palms, through the fever-tree pan, over the place where impala feed beside the red sandstone, above the dam, and on and on until finally, when the sun is high over the Veld, she arrives at the end of her journey. She has come to school. The lovely watercolor illustrations give us an education while Manyoni travels to hers. We learn about the flora and fauna of Zimbabwe and come to appreciate the very real effort children like Manyoni must make to get an education. Another book that demonstrates children's determination to go to school is *Running the Road to ABC* by Dennis Lauture. Although the title makes the book sound like an alphabet book, these Haitian children are running to learn. "On the white turf and roads of red clay they run. On roads of rocks and roads of mud they run." For one more letter, and one more sound, and one more word, they run. Reynold Ruffins's vivid paintings capture lively Haitian culture and the intensity of the children's passions for learning

In Florence Parry Heide and Judith Heide Gilliland's *The Day of Ahmed's Secret,* Ahmed, a young *butagaz* boy in Cairo, Egypt, makes his daily rounds through sun-bleached streets and daily market stalls to deliver cooking oil. Ahmed hugs a special secret to his heart. Home, at last, he can finally show his newly acquired skill to his family: Ahmed has learned how to write his name. In *Sami and the Time of the Troubles,* Heide and Gilliland tell of a young boy who must struggle to maintain a normal life during the war in Lebanon. Ted Lewin's realistic water-

*In Dennis Lauture's* Running The Road To ABC *artist Reynold Ruffins's illustrations evoke Haitian children's passionate yearning for schooling.*

From *Running the Road to ABC* by Denize Lauture, illustrated by Reynold Ruffins, illustrations copyright © 1996 Reynold Ruffins. Reprinted with permission of Simon & Schuster Books for Young Readers, an imprint of Simon & Schuster Children's Publishing Division.

colors capture the sounds and sights of these two countries and visually convey the emotional power of the two stories.

Tololwa Mollel's *My Rows and Piles of Coins* is a story that will resonate with many young children. Saruni, a young Tanzanian boy, is trying to save enough money to buy a bicycle so that he can help his mother deliver her goods to market. He takes his hard-earned coins to the bicycle seller, who only laughs at him. However, his father is so proud of his son that he "sells" Saruni his own bike when he buys a motorcycle.

In Holly Keller's *Grandfather's Dream,* the war in Vietnam is over and Nam's family is rebuilding their lives. As the rice fields are replanted, Grandfather hopes that the beautiful Saurus cranes will return to nest in the wetlands. Some of the villagers think the land should be used for planting and not set aside for wildlife. Keller's lovely watercolors evoke the patterns of Vietnamese art and convey the beauty of the rural setting. Although the book has a happy ending, in reality the Vietnamese are still waiting for the cranes to return. Keller is honest about the dilemmas that face a community that has been torn apart by war.

*Holly Keller captures the essence of Vietnamese culture in her illustrations for* Grandfather's Dream.

Illustration from *Grandfather's Dream* by Holly Keller, copyright © 1994 by Holly Keller. Used by permission of Greenwillow Books, an imprint of HarperCollins Publishers.

Riki Levinson has told a more serious story of the families who lived on the boats in Hong Kong harbor in *Our Home Is the Sea.* The boy journeys from his school through the bustling city down to his family's houseboat. He can't wait for the day when he too will be a fisherman. Dennis Luzak's handsome oil paintings portray the huge gray city of Hong Kong and the boat the boy calls home. Eve Bunting has written a moving story of the flight of a Cuban family to America in their very small boat. These people are pilgrims in their search for freedom, so Bunting titled her story *How Many Days to America? A Thanksgiving Story.*

In the *Very Last First Time,* Jan Andrews gives us a picture of life in the Inuit village of Ungava Bay in northern Canada. This is a special day for Eva Padlyat, for she is going to go alone below the sea ice and gather mussels. Eva is so intrigued with all she sees that she nearly doesn't make it back up before the tide comes in again. When at last she is safe with her mother, she says, "That was my very last *first* time for walking alone on the bottom of the sea." Ian Wallace's full-color illustrations picture an Inuit family, with their modern-day kitchen but still gathering food in the traditional manner.

Naomi Shihab Nye makes connections between two countries half a world apart in *Sitti's Secret.* Back home in America, after a trip to Palestine, Mona recalls her experiences and thinks about Sitti, her grandmother who lives on the West Bank. Although the two speak different languages and have very different ways of life, they are joined by universal bonds of family feeling and the wish for peace. Like the secrets Sitti hears her lemon tree whisper each morning, Nancy Carpenter's illustrations have secrets, too. Maps, pieces of fabric, and photographs of cityscapes, desert mountains, and the planets form the background for the textured paintings of Mona and Sitti's world and reinforce the connections these two share.

Nigel Gray contrasts the story of two children, one black, one white, who wake, sleep, play, eat, and share in family life on opposite sides of the globe. The fascinating contrast between an African boy in his village and a Western child in his suburb is made clear by Philippe Dupasquier's detailed illustrations for *A Country Far Away.* This story could lead to much discussion of the contrast between wealthy Western countries and those of the third world. Children need to develop a world vision at an early age.

*Julie Vivas's illustrations show grandmothers with unique personalities and "can-do" attitudes in Mem Fox's* Our Granny.

Illustration by Julie Vivas from *Our Granny* by Margaret Wild. Illustration copyright © 1994 Julie Vivas. Reprinted by permission of Houghton Mifflin Company/Ticknor & Fields Books for Young Readers. All rights reserved. In Canada © Omnibus Books, reprinted by permission of Scholastic Australia.

## Picture Books About Older People

For many years we believed that children identified only with stories about children their own age. More recently we have given them literature that includes persons of all ages.

Mem Fox's *Wilfrid Gordon McDonald Partridge* is the story of a small redheaded boy who makes friends with the old folks who live next door in a home for people who are elderly. He likes them all, but his particular friend is 96-year-old Miss Nancy. When he hears his parents say she has lost her memory, he decides to help her find it. Julie Vivas's exuberant pictures provide unique characterizations that are painted almost larger than life and seen from unusual perspectives.

Vivas teams up with Margaret Wild for the loving and wonderfully funny *Our Granny*. The book is as much a positive look at older women as it is a celebration of one grandmother. Vivas's quirky illustrations and varied points of view show grannies who come in all shapes and sizes and do all manner of interesting things. They exercise, they drive trucks, they march in demonstrations, and they tuck their grandbabies in at night. Fox's descriptions of grannies who wear "jeans and sneakers, pantsuits, silky dresses, big bras, and baggy underwear" will delight children as much as Vivas's zany pictures.

Barbara Cooney illustrated two popular stories about older people, *Emma* and *Miss Rumphius*. *Emma*, written by Wendy Kesselman, is about a woman the author knew who didn't start painting until she was in her late eighties. In this story Barbara Cooney depicts her as a kind of Grandma Moses character who creates many primitive paintings based on her memories of her town. Cooney's *Miss Rumphius* is a fine model of an independent older person. As a youngster she told her grandfather that she, too, wished to travel to faraway places as he had and live by the sea. He told her there was a third thing she must do—make the world more beautiful. And so, years later she planted lupine all over her little seacoast village. Repetition of the story line is reflected as a very elderly Miss Rumphius passes along her grandfather's advice to her grandniece. The continuity of life is nicely portrayed by the many objects that we first saw in the grandfather's house, or on her travels, and that now comfortably reside in Miss Rumphius's home by the sea.

Another remarkable person who dreams of going to faraway places is Arizona in Gloria Houston's *My Great-Aunt Arizona*. Born in a log cabin in the Blue Ridge Mountains, Arizona never goes to those faraway places. Instead she stays at home and becomes one of those special teachers whom fortunate students hold in their hearts. Great-Aunt Arizona dies on her ninety-third birthday, but she goes to those faraway places with all of the students she taught. "She goes with us in our minds."

## The Child's World of Nature

Sometimes young children seem more attuned to the world about them than adults do. Watch children on the first day of snow, for example, and see the excitement in their eyes and their eagerness to go outside. Adults might complain about having to shovel the snow or getting the car stuck, but for children a snowstorm is pure joy. It is this very contrast between adults' and children's reactions to snow that formed the basis for Alvin Tresselt's well-loved book *White Snow, Bright Snow,* illustrated with Roger Duvoisin's sparkling pictures. Repeating the same pattern in *Hide and Seek Fog,* Tresselt describes the children's joyous response to a fog that came and stayed for three days in a little seaside village on Cape Cod, while their parents grumbled about spending their vacations in the middle of a cloud. Duvoisin's hazy pearl-gray illustrations effectively convey the mystery of a fog-shrouded day.

In *Come On Rain* by Karen Hesse, Tessie endures the summer heat in the city but longs for rain. When a storm finally arrives, she and her friends begin a joyous dance on the rain-drenched streets, and to their surprise their mothers come out to join in the fun. Jon Muth's transparent watercolors manage to capture the breathless shimmering heat and to convey the blissful feel of a soaking shower.

*Twister,* by Carleen Bailey Beard, is a reassuring look at a terrifying weather experience. Two children must sit out a tornado in a storm cellar while their mother has gone to help a neighbor. Nancy Carpenter's swirling pastel paintings add vivid reality to the storm and bring the final sunny pages to life.

Henry Cole invites young children to tune into the natural world in two delightful books. In *Jack's Garden,* Jack builds a garden in his back yard to the refrain from "This Is the House That Jack Built." The book shows a young child diligently caring for the seeds he has planted and gives details of the important ecosystem that supports his garden. In *I Took a Walk,* Jack moves out of the garden and investigates the ecology of the forest, meadow, stream and pond. Books like Cole's and those by Byrd Baylor such as *Your Own Best Secret Place* and *I'm In Charge of Celebrations* help children appreciate and value the thousands of natural treasures that make up their world.

Rachel Carson tells us in the sensitive essay that she wrote about her grandnephew Roger just a few years before her death: "If a child is to keep alive his inborn sense of wonder . . . he needs the companionship of at least one adult who can share it, rediscovering with him the joy, excitement and mystery of the world we live in."[12] Books are not a substitute for real experiences, but through the sharing of beautiful

The illustrations in Henry Cole's I Took a Walk *call attention to the simple beauty of the natural world.*
From *I Took a Walk* by Henry Cole. Copyright © 1998 by Henry Cole. Used by permission of Greenwillow Books, a division of William Morrow/HarperCollins Publishers.

picture books, teachers can enhance a real experience and keep the wonder of it alive with their own enthusiasm and appreciation for nature. See Resources for Teaching, "Picture Books About the Child's Everyday World," for a list of many picture books about children's everyday experiences.

## Animals as People

Ever since the day Peter Rabbit disobeyed his mother and squeezed through Mr. MacGregor's garden fence, children have enjoyed stories in which animals act like people, frequently like small children. In fact, many of these stories would be listed as family stories if you read just the text, since only in the pictures are the characters revealed as animals. Usually the animals are dressed and live in cozy furnished homes, hollow trees, or burrows and face the same problems as their child readers, whose lives are mirrored in these stories.

*Small Green Snake* by Libba Moore Gray is really Peter Rabbit in reptilian guise. Holly Meade's expressive collages add to the fun of this story of a little garter snake who is "grassy," "sassy," and "flashy" and likes to wander far from home. Despite his mother's warning, he is tempted over the garden wall and is captured in a glass jelly jar. A striped yellow cat provides the exciting climax and the means of escape for this wily snake, who is only slightly chastened by his adventures. Gray's vivid writing makes this a particularly wonderful book to read aloud.

[12]Rachel Carson, *The Sense of Wonder,* photographs by Charles Pratt and others (New York: Harper & Row, 1956, 1965), p. 45.

# RESOURCES FOR TEACHING

## Picture Books About the Child's Everyday World

### FAMILY STORIES

| Author, Illustrator | Title | Description |
| --- | --- | --- |
| Jeannine Atkins | *Get Set Swim* | The story of a young girl's first year on the swim team and the warm support she receives from her proud family. |
| Carrie Best, Dale Gottlieb | *Taxi Taxi* | A story of the loving relationship between a little girl, a child of divorced parents, and her Papi, who comes to pick her up every Sunday in his yellow taxi. |
| Judith Caseley | *Mama Coming and Going* | Mama is distracted by a new baby and doesn't know if she's coming or going. A warm and funny story about imperfections and affections. |
| Carmen Lomas Garza | *Family Pictures: Cuadros de Familia* | A family album of all the special events the author remembers from her childhood days of growing up in Kingsville, Texas. |
| Angela Johnson, David Soman | *Tell Me a Story, Mama* | See text. |
| Mavis Jukes, Lloyd Bloom | *Like Jake and Me* | Bloom's bold illustrations capture the strong personalities in a sensitive story about stepfather and son. |
| Patricia MacLachlan, Ruth Lercher Bornstein | *Mama One and Mama Two* | A foster child is reassured that she will be loved and cared for until her real mother recovers from her mental depression and the two of them can be together again. |
| Jan Ormerod | *Who's Whose?* | A delightful look at three families whose close friendship have intertwined them into one huge extended family. |
| Eileen Roe | *Con Mi Hermano: With My Brother* | Joyous times that a little boy spends with his older brother—playing ball, helping him deliver newspapers, and sharing picture books together. |
| Ann Turner, James-Graham Hale | *Through Moon and Stars and Night Skies* | Lovely, tender, but not sentimental watercolor pictures illustrate this story of a brave little boy coming to a strange land to his adoptive parents. |

### SIBLING RIVALRY

| Author, Illustrator | Title | Description |
| --- | --- | --- |
| Martha Alexander | *When the New Baby Comes, I'm Moving Out* | The anticipation of a new baby in the family is clearly expressed through words and humorous pictures. |
| Eloise Greenfield, John Steptoe | *She Come Bringing Me That Little Baby Girl* | Kevin dislikes all the attention given to his new sister until his uncle tells him how he used to take care of his baby sister, Kevin's mother. |
| Elizabeth Starr Hill, Sandra Speidel | *Evan's Corner* | Evan takes a corner of his family's two-room apartment for his special place and then decides to help his brother fix up his own place. |
| Shirley Hughes | *Dogger* | See text. |
| Ezra Jack Keats | *Peter's Chair* | Peter decides to run away before all of his possessions are painted pink for his new baby sister. However, when he discovers that he no longer fits in his chair, he decides that maybe it would be fun to paint it pink himself. |
| Jeanne Titherington | *A Place for Ben* | Ben invites his baby brother to come and play in his special place. |
| Mildred Pitts Walter, Pat Cummings | *My Mama Needs Me* | Bright illustrations show an African American older child's desire to be of help, as well as his resentment, when a baby sister arrives. |

*continued*

# RESOURCES FOR TEACHING

## Picture Books About the Child's Everyday World con't

### RELATIVES

| Author, Illustrator | Title | Description |
| --- | --- | --- |
| Eve Bunting, Donald Carrick | *The Wednesday Surprise* | For Dad's birthday surprise Anna teaches her grandmother to read by sharing books every Wednesday night when she comes to babysit. |
| Jeannette Caines, Pat Cummings | *Just Us Women* | Realistic illustrations detail the fun that African American women plan to have on their special trip to North Carolina in Aunt Martha's new car. |
| Judith Caseley | *Dear Annie* | Annie's grandfather celebrates his love for her through his many letters and postcards. |
| Tomie de Paola | *Watch Out for the Chicken Feet in Your Soup* | Joey and his friend Eugene visit Joey's Italian grandmother. |
| Tomie de Paola | *Nana Upstairs & Nana Downstairs* | See text. |
| Tomie de Paola | *Now One Foot, Now the Other* | See text. |
| Tomie de Paola | *Tom* | See text. |
| Helen Griffith, James Stevenson | *Grandaddy's Place* | Janetta meets her granddaddy for the first time. |
| Helen Griffith, James Stevenson | *Georgia Music* | Janetta's grandaddy's health is failing and he has been brought to live with her family in the city. |
| Mary Hoffman, Caroline Binch | *Amazing Grace* | Remarkably expressive watercolors help convey the story of an African American child whose mother and grandmother tell her she can be anything she wants to be, including Peter Pan in the school play. |
| Mary Hoffman, Caroline Binch | *Boundless Grace* | The sequel follows Grace to a visit with her father and his new family in Africa. |
| Patricia MacLachlan, Deborah Ray | *Through Grandpa's Eyes* | A tender story in which the grandson realizes that his blind grandfather has many ways of seeing. |
| Pat Mora, Cecily Lang | *Pablo's Tree* | Pablo's grandfather planted a tree when Pablo was born, and each year he decorates it as Pablo's special birthday surprise. |
| Susan Pearson, Ronald Himler | *Happy Birthday, Grampie* | Lovely realistic watercolors capture a moment of love when a little girl makes a very special birthday card that her blind grandfather can feel. |
| Patricia Polacco | *Thunder Cake* | See text. |
| Jama Kim Rattigan, Lillian Hsu-Flanders | *Dumpling Soup* | Marisa is finally old enough to contribute to her family's New Year festival in Hawaii. |
| Cynthia Rylant, Stephen Gammell | *The Relatives Came* | See text. |
| Mary Stolz, Pat Cummings | *Storm in the Night* | See text. |
| Jacqueline Woodson, Diane Greenseid | *We Had a Picnic this Sunday Past* | See text. |

## RESOURCES FOR TEACHING

## Picture Books About the Child's Everyday World con't

### FAMILY HISTORY

| Author, Illustrator | Title | Description |
|---|---|---|
| Barbara Cooney | *Island Boy* | Stunning pictures portray seascapes and the family members who make up four generations of a New England family who settled on Tibbett's Island. |
| Barbara Cooney | *Hattie and the Wild Waves* | Cooney describes the affluent life of her mother growing up in Brooklyn and then Long Island while searching for her life's work. |
| Valerie Flournoy, Jerry Pinkney | *The Patchwork Quilt* | See text. |
| Elizabeth Fitzgerald Howard, James Ransome | *Aunt Flossie's Hats (and Crab Cakes Later)* | See text. |
| Ina Friedman, Allen Say | *How My Parents Learned to Eat* | Delicate watercolors illustrate a young girl's story about her parents' meeting. Her father, an American sailor, learned to eat with chopsticks in order to invite his future wife, a Japanese girl, out to dinner. |
| Deborah Hopkinson, Raúl Colón | *A Band of Angels: A Story Inspired by the Jubilee Singers* | Little girl imagines herself as her great-great-grandmother, one of the Jubilee singers who became so popular they were able to raise money to establish Fisk University. |
| Riki Levinson, Diane Goode | *Watch the Stars Come Out* | Impressionistic watercolors detail the journey two young children made alone on a ship from Europe to their strange new home in America. |
| Margaree King Mitchell, James Ransome | *Uncle Jed's Barbershop* | See text. |
| Patricia Polacco | *The Keeping Quilt* | See text. |
| Alan Say | *Grandfather's Journey* | See text. |
| Alan Say | *Tea with Milk* | See text. |

### FAMILIAR EXPERIENCES

| Author, Illustrator | Title | Description |
|---|---|---|
| Carol Carrick, Donald Carrick | *The Accident* | This story describes Christopher's dismay when his dog, Bodger, is run over by a truck and killed. Children facing the death of a pet may find comfort in the book. |
| Miriam Cohen, Lillian Hoban | *Will I Have a Friend?, The New Teacher, When Will I Read?, Best Friends,* and others | Illustrations of a multicultural first-grade classroom are as warm and reassuring as Jim's teachers and friendly classmates as they face the everyday worries of young children. |
| Patricia Lee Gauch, Satomi Ichikawa | *Presenting Tanya, Ugly Duckling,* and others | One of a series of warm-hearted stories about Tanya, who loves to dance. |
| Juanita Havill, Anne Sibley O'Brien | *Jamaica and the Substitute Teacher,* and others | Jamaica is an irrepressible young African American girl whose experiences are warmly related. In this book a special teacher helps her to understand that copying someone else work isn't necessary and that she doesn't have to be perfect to be special. |
| Paul B. Johnson and Celeste Lewis | *Lost* | A child never gives up hope that her lost dog will be found. |

*continued*

# RESOURCES FOR TEACHING

## Picture Books About the Child's Everyday World con't

### FAMILIAR EXPERIENCES con't

| Author, Illustrator | Title | Description |
|---|---|---|
| Ezra Jack Keats | *The Snowy Day, Whistle for Willie*, and others | See text. |
| Robert McCloskey | *One Morning in Maine* | Sal announces her loose tooth to anyone who will listen. Story and illustrations show how important such changes are to young children. |
| Isaac Millman | *Moses Goes to a Concert* | Moses and his other deaf classmates go to a concert where they hold balloons on their laps to feel the vibrations and are introduced to the orchestra's deaf percussionist. |
| John Steptoe | *Stevie* | Robert resents Stevie, who stays at his house every day while his mother goes to work, but he realizes that he misses him after he goes back to his family. |
| Judith Viorst, Ray Cruz | *Alexander and the Terrible, Horrible, No Good, Very Bad Day*, and others | Cruz's illustrations add to the wonderfully funny stories about the frustrations of being a kid. |
| Judith Viorst, Erik Blegvad | *The Tenth Good Thing About Barney* | The little black-and-white ink sketches by Erik Blegvad underscore the sincerity of this story of a boy's first experience with death. |
| Bernard Waber | *Ira Sleeps Over* | Illustrations reflect Ira's dilemma as he tries to decide if he will take his teddy bear to his first sleep over. |
| Vera Williams | *Something Special for Me, A Chair for My Mother, Music, Music for Everyone* | See text. |

### APPRECIATING CULTURAL DIVERSITY

| Author, Illustrator | Title | Description |
|---|---|---|
| Jan Andrews, Ian Wallace | *Very Last First Time* | Andrews gives us a picture of life in the Inuit village of Ungava Bay in northern Canada. |
| Eve Bunting, Beth Peck | *How Many Days to America? A Thanksgiving Story* | See text. |
| Michelle Edwards | *Chicken Man* | A lighthearted story about the rotation of work at a kibbutzim in Israel. |
| Nigel Gray, Philippe Dupasquier | *A Country Far Away* | See text. |
| Ann Grifalconi | *Darkness and the Butterfly* | A wise woman helps Osa learn to overcome her fear of the dark. |
| Ann Grifalconi | *Osa's Pride* | Osa is too proud to make friends with the children in her Cameroon Village. |
| Florence Parry Heide, Judith Heide Gilliland, Ted Lewin | *The Day of Ahmed's Secret* | See text. |
| Florence Parry Heide, Judith Heide Gilliland, Ted Lewin | *Sami in the Time of the Troubles* | See text. |
| Rachel Isadora | *At the Crossroads* | After children wait all day and all night for their fathers to come home after ten months of working in the mines in South Africa, they share a joyful reunion. |

# RESOURCES FOR TEACHING

## Picture Books About the Child's Everyday World con't

### APPRECIATING CULTURAL DIVERSITY con't

| Author, Illustrator | Title | Description |
|---|---|---|
| Holly Keller | *Grandfather's Dream* | See text. |
| Dennis Lauture, Reynold Ruffins | *Running the Road to ABC* | See text. |
| Riki Levinson | *Our Home Is the Sea* | A serious story of the families who lived on the boats in Hong Kong harbor. |
| Naomi Shihab Nye | *Sitti's Secret* | See text. |
| Soyoung Pak and Susan Kathleen Hartung | *dear juno* | A young Korean American boy draws picture letters to stay in touch with his Korean grandmother. |
| Charlotte Pomerantz, Frané Lessac | *The Chalk Doll* | A mother shares stories of her growing up in Jamaica with her little daughter, Rose. |
| Catherine Stock | *Where Do You Think You're Going Manyoni?* | See text. |
| Stephanie Stuve-Bodeen, Christy Hale | *Elizabeti's Doll* | See text. |
| Karen Williams, Catherine Stock | *Galimoto* | See text. |
| Karen Williams, Catherine Stock | *Painted Dreams* | See text. |

### BOOKS ABOUT OLDER PEOPLE

| Author, Illustrator | Title | Description |
|---|---|---|
| Nancy White Carlstrom, Amy Schwartz | *Blow Me a Kiss, Miss Lilly* | Small, precise illustrations add to the appeal of this story of a friendship between a young child and a very old lady. After Lilly's death, young Sara remembers her in a special way. |
| Mem Fox, Terry Denton | *Night Noises* | Strange noises can't wake Lily Laceby, who has drifted off to sleep. Finally the commotion wakes her, and she discovers that her family has come to wish her a happy birthday. |
| Mem Fox, Julie Vivas | *Wilfrid Gordon McDonald Partridge* | See text. |
| Gloria Houston, Susan Condie Lamb | *My Great-Aunt Arizona* | See text. |
| Wendy Kesselman, Barbara Cooney | *Emma* | See text. |
| Barbara Cooney | *Miss Rumphius* | See text. |
| Margaret Wild, Julie Vivas | *Our Granny* | See text. |
| Margaret Wild, Julie Vivas | *The Very Best of Friends* | A poignant story of the loving friendship between James and Jessie, and James and his cat, William. |

### THE CHILD'S WORLD OF NATURE

| Author, Illustrator | Title | Description |
|---|---|---|
| Carleen Bailey Beard, Nancy Carpenter | *Twister* | See text. |

*continued*

## RESOURCES FOR TEACHING

## Picture Books About the Child's Everyday World con't

### THE CHILD'S WORLD OF NATURE con't

| Author, Illustrator | Title | Description |
| --- | --- | --- |
| Byrd Baylor, Peter Parnall | *Everybody Needs a Rock, Your Own Best Secret Place, The Other Way to Listen, The Way to Start a Day* | All of Baylor's books develop sensitivity to all aspects of the natural world. |
| Henry Cole | *I Took a Walk, Jack's Garden* | See text. |
| Sheila Cole, Virginia Wright-Frierson | *When the Tide Is Low* | The illustrations provide watery seascapes and accurate pictures of sea animals and shells for this quiet story of a mother and daughter's delightful day. |
| Karen Hesse, Jon Muth | *Come On Rain* | See text. |
| Katherine Lasky, Mike Bostock | *Pond Year* | This story details the changes that occur in the ecology of a backyard pond and describes the rich playground it provides for two friends. |
| Allen Say | *The Lost Lake* | Glowing watercolors portray the wilderness trip a Japanese American father and his son take to a lost lake. |
| Mary Serfozo, Keiko Narahashi | *Rain Talk* | The various sounds the rain makes are explored in the poetic picture book portray the child's delight in this summer rain. |
| Uri Shulevitz | *Rain Rain Rivers* | Watercolors in greens and blues are the appropriate medium and colors for a book that expresses the mood of a rainy day in the city and the country. |
| Peter Spier | *Peter Spier's Rain* | All the dimensions of a rainstorm are included here—children's and animals' reactions, indoor and outdoor fun in the rain. |
| Alvin Tresselt, Roger Duvoisin | *White Snow, Bright Snow, Hide and Seek Fog* | See text. |
| David Wiesner | *Hurricane* | Detailed watercolors capture all of the excitement of two boys waiting out a hurricane in their snug home. |
| Taro Yashima | *Umbrella* | A little Japanese American girl is impatient for rain because she wants to wear her new red rubber boots and carry her new umbrella to nursery school. |

Rosemary Wells creates many lovable animal characters that mirror the behavior of young children. *Shy Charles* is the interesting tale of a shy mouse who doesn't want to take ballet lessons or play football. He just wants to stay home and play by himself. However, in an emergency Charles comes through as a real hero, but still a shy one.

Kevin Henkes is the creator of a remarkable mouse child named Lilly, who was the very best until the arrival of her baby brother in *Julius, the Baby of the World*. Lilly thinks he is disgusting and hopes he will go away; she hates Julius and the way her parents fawn over him. When no one is looking, Lilly pinches his tail, teaches him his numbers backward, and tells him, "If he was a number, he would be zero. " Lilly spends a great deal of time in what her parents call "the uncooperative chair." But then Cousin Garland comes to visit and says Julius is disgusting. Suddenly

Lilly has a complete change of heart. Lilly is a real character wearing her queen's crown and red cowboy boots. She was first introduced in *Chester's Way*, a story of the friendship between Chester and Wilson and, finally, Lilly. In *Lilly's Purple Plastic Purse*, Lilly is an irrepressible second grader who finds it hard to keep her zippy new plastic purse in her desk until show and tell. When her beloved teacher takes it away from her, she lets her anger get the best of her. It takes a patient teacher and loving parents to restore Lilly's equilibrium. A new mouse character joins the crew in the hilarious *Wemberly Worried*.

First graders faced with the (for some of them) formidable task of learning to read can sympathize with *Leo the Late Bloomer* by Robert Kraus. Leo, a baby tiger, can't do anything right; he can't read, write, or draw; he is a sloppy eater and never talks. His mother assures his father that Leo is a late bloomer. And she is right. Eventually, and in his own good time, Leo blooms! Stunning pictures by José Aruego add much to the humor of this story.

Children might recognize a familiar situation in Erica Silverman's *Don't Fidget a Feather*. Gander and Duck are so full of self-adulation that they hold contests to see who is the best swimmer and who can fly the highest. When neither of these competitions has a clear winner, Duck suggests a freeze-in-place contest. Through many distractions they don't "fidget a feather," even when a fox takes the two back to his stew pot. When the fox prepares to cook Gander, however, Duck decides that winning the contest is not as important as saving Gander's life. S. D. Schindler's pastel drawings manage to maintain a state of high tension and add a note of realism to this story with its underlying note of conflict.

Children will also recognize the rift that occurs between three best mouse friends in James Howe's *Horace and Morris but Mostly Dolores*, illustrated by Amy Walrod. The three are inseparable until the boys decide that "a boy mouse must do what a boy mouse must do," and form a boys-only club. Dolores has her revenge however, and shows how silly the boys have been. In the end, intergender friendship triumphs over separation of the sexes.

## Modern Folktale Style

Perhaps Rudyard Kipling started the trend of writing modern folktales. The humor of his pourquoi tales, *Just So Stories*, is based on his wonderful use of words and his tongue-in-cheek asides to the reader. A favorite with children is *The Elephant Child,* the story of how a young elephant got his trunk. Originally his nose was no bigger than a bulgy boot. His "satiable curiosity" causes him all kinds of trouble and spankings. To find out what the crocodile has for dinner, he departs for

*Animal characters are involved with very human conflicts in James Howe's* Horace and Morris but Mostly Dolores.

the "banks of the great grey-green, greasy Limpopo River, all set about with fever-trees." Here he meets the crocodile, who whispers in his ear that today he will start his meal with the elephant's child! Then the crocodile grabs his nose and pulls and pulls. When the poor elephant is free, he has a trunk for a nose.

Some of these stories—such as *The Elephant's Child, How the Camel Got His Hump,* and *How the Leopard Got His Spots*—have been attractively illustrated in single picture-book editions by Jan Mogensen, Lorinda Cauley, Caroline Ebborn, and Quentin Blake. Children need to hear the language in these tales read aloud by an enthusiastic teacher or librarian.

Leo Lionni frequently writes modern folktales. In *Frederick* Lionni makes a statement about the role of the artist in society that is direct and to the point. His *Alexander and the Wind-Up Mouse* includes a purple pebble, a magic lizard, and a transformation. Alexander envies a wind-up mouse, Willie, and wants to become one himself. However, fortunes change, and in order to save his friend, Alexander asks the magic lizard to make Willie a real mouse, just like Alexander.

Certain contemporary stories provide modern twists on well-loved tales and require a previous knowledge of the folktales. Steven Kellogg's retelling and illustrations for *Chicken Little* are very funny

"No, no, no," said Rooster. "Don't cut the butter with scissors. Use these two table knives, like this." Rooster cut in the butter until the mixture was crumbly.

"Looks mighty dry in there," said Pig. "Perhaps I should taste it."

Butter and margarine are two types of solid shortening, or fat, used in cooking. The name "shortcake" doesn't mean the cake is short—it refers to the shortening in the recipe.

Cool butter is "cut in" to dry ingredients by using two table knives or a pastry blender. Cut the butter into tiny pieces.

"Not yet, Pig," said Turtle. "Now the recipe says to beat one egg."

"I can do that!" cried Iguana.

*Janet Stevens and Susan Crummel Stevens have provided a wonderfully wacky update of the Little Red Hen story in* Cook-a-Doodle-Do!

indeed. The story starts out with Chicken Little's famous warning that "The sky is falling" after she has been hit on the head by an acorn. Foxy Loxy hears the animals cry for the police and quickly changes his "poultry" truck sign to read "poulice." Thinking his Thanksgiving dinner is safely locked in the truck, he shows the foolish fowls the harmless acorn and tosses it up in the air. It gets caught in Sergeant Hippo Hefty's helicopter, which crashes to the earth, landing on the truck and freeing all the birds while Sergeant Hefty "flattens the fleeing fox." Foxy Loxy is sent to prison and Chicken Little plants the acorn. It grows into a fine tall tree by the side of her house, where her grandchildren come to hear her retell her famous story. Action-packed illustrations accompany this hilarious retelling of the Chicken Little story.

Other books take known characters or the bones of a traditional tale and flesh them out in new and intriguing ways. In Eugene Trivias's *The Three Little Wolves and the Big Bad Pig,* three wolf cubs go out into the world and build a house of bricks, only to have a mean pig attack it with a sledgehammer. Their next house, of concrete, is no match for the pig's pneumatic drill, and their metal bunker succumbs to his dynamite. Finally, they try a house of flowers. When the bad pig huffs to blow it down, he is transformed by the floral scents, and the four live happily ever after. This modern-day story about the power of aroma therapy is made all the more appealing through Helen Oxenbury's expressive characterizations.

Janet Stevens is well known for her interpretations of folktales, and in *Cook-a-Doodle-Do!* she and her sister have adapted the format of "The Little Red Hen" to tell a very funny farce. Big Brown rooster is so tired of eating chicken feed that he is determined to cook his own meals. He consults "The Joy of Cooking Alone," written by his great granny (The Little Red Hen) and decides that strawberry shortcake would be just the thing. History seems to repeat itself when, one after another, the dog, the cat, and the goose answer "Not I" to his requests for help. But then along come Turtle, Iguana, and Potbellied Pig, who are eager to join in. These very unexperienced cooks face some very funny kitchen disasters before they get the recipe right. Philemon Sturges has used the same familiar tale as the basis for *The Little Red Hen (Makes a Pizza),* illustrated by Amy Walrod.

Author Jon Scieszka and illustrator Lane Smith have great fun playing with traditional tales in *The True Story of the Three Little Pigs* and *The Stinky Cheese Man and Other Fairly Stupid Tales.* Their hilarious version of "The Three Pigs" is told from the wolf's point of view. His explanation is that he just wanted to borrow a cup of sugar to bake a cake for his old granny, when he accidentally sneezed and blew the pigs' houses down. It seemed like a shame to leave a perfectly good warm dinner lying there in the straw. So he eats one pig, and the second one too. He blames the whole bad rap on the reporters and the fact that when the third pig insulted his granny, he went berserk. Older students love this retelling, which easily invites them to write from a different point of view. In *The Stinky Cheese Man* the two turn ten familiar tales, such as "The Ugly Duckling," "Chicken Little," and "Jack and the Bean Stalk," inside out and upside down. They do the same thing and more with the format of the picture book, inserting the endpapers in the middle of the book, moving the table of contents to page 9, altering typeface, and changing size. Scieszka and Lane continue the silliness in *Squids Will Be Squids*.

As we have seen in Chapter 4, the nursery rhyme "The House That Jack Built" has provided many authors and illustrators with a model for inventive new versions. Will Hillenbrand's delightfully ghoulish illustrations for Judy Sierra's *The House That Drac Built* are scary enough to please the horror story crowd without sending them to bed with nightmares. As one might expect, the house that Drac built has a mummy, a manticore, and other monsters who precipitate a chain of events that is put to rights by a group of Halloween trick-or-treaters. In *The Book That Jack Wrote*, Jon Scieszka takes traditional nursery rhyme characters and creates a series of cause-and-effect events that will have readers wondering if they are coming or going. Daniel Adel manipulates the visual images in equally intriguing ways. Rather than looking like illustrations in a picture book, these framed paintings seem to hang on the page like pictures on a wall. But are these illusions or the real thing? Such questions will surely intrigue older readers.

One of children's favorite modern retellings involves a roundup of fairy tale characters on the postman's route in *The Jolly Postman* by Janet and Allan Ahlberg. In this rhymed tale, a postman delivers letters that readers can remove from real envelopes (which form the actual page), such as a letter of apology from Goldilocks to the Three Bears, a postcard from Jack to the Giant, and a business letter to the Wolf from the Three Pigs' lawyer representing the firm of Meany, Miny, Mo, and Company. This cleverly designed book synthesizes children's knowledge of folktales, besides providing them a model for writing all kinds of letters and making them laugh in the process.

## Humor

Young children's sense of fun is simple and obvious. Illustrations in picture books often provide the humor that they might miss through words alone. Steven Kellogg is a master at drawing utter confusion and slapstick. A bored young girl gives her mother a deadpan account of the class trip to the farm in the hilarious story of *The Day Jimmy's Boa Ate the Wash* by Trinka Noble. The contrast between the girl's reporting of the events and the exuberant illustrations is ex-

*After Martha the dog swallows alphabet soup, her ability to communicate takes an unusual turn in Susan Meddaugh's* Martha Calling.

treme. The same approach is used in *Jimmy's Boa Bounces Back,* written and illustrated by the same team. The low-key narration is nicely balanced by the action-packed pictures. Kellogg has also produced many books of his own, which are equally funny. The tales of his own Great Dane in *Pinkerton, Behave!, A Rose for Pinkerton,* and *Prehistoric Pinkerton* provide the frame for his madcap pictures.

Martha is another indomitable dog who takes matters into her own paws in Susan Meddaugh's *Martha Speaks.* When Martha swallows a bowl of alphabet soup, the letters go straight to her brain and convert Woof to English. At first her family is delighted, but soon Martha won't shut up and becomes an embarrassment. Her talents are finally appreciated when she saves the family treasures from a burglar. Martha in turn learns to appreciate the finer points of conversational etiquette. Martha's adventures are continued in *Martha Calling* and *Martha Walks the Dog.*

Children also enjoy books about funny weird characters who appear in a series of stories. Seven- and 8-year-olds find the deadpan humor of Harry Allard's *The Stupids Die* very funny. When the lights go out, the Stupids decide that they have died. When the lights come back on, they think they are in heaven, until Grandpa sets them right: "This isn't Heaven—This is

Cleveland." Children love to look for the visual jokes in the Stupids' house; for example, the framed picture of beach balls is labeled "The Pyramids" and one of a dog is titled "Fish." *The Stupids Have a Ball* and *The Stupids Step Out* are other titles in this series. James Marshall's lumpy figures seem just right for the Stupid family. Marshall has created his own funny friends in his many stories, such as *George and Martha,* about two large hippopotamuses. Each book contains about five episodes, which gives the feeling of a chapter book for 6- and 7-year-olds. The two hippo friends continue their antics in *George and Martha Tons of Fun, George and Martha Round and Round,* and *George and Martha Back in Town.*

Another favorite character of children this age is Harry Allard and James Marshall's Miss Nelson, the lovely sweet teacher who cannot make the class behave. In *Miss Nelson Is Missing,* she is replaced by Miss Viola Swamp, who wears a dark black dress and is a witch, the children decide. After one week with Miss Swamp's rules and homework, the children are delighted to welcome Miss Nelson back. At home Miss Nelson takes off her coat and hangs it right next to an ugly black dress. Viola Swamp returns to coach the worst team in the state in *Miss Nelson Has a Field Day.* Readers will be delighted with the coach's ugly black sweatshirt, which reads "Coach and Don't You Forget It." Children will have to solve the puzzle of how Miss Nelson and her alter ego can be in the same place at the same time.

Marc Brown's *Arthur* stories are equally popular and include a variety of animal characters. Arthur bears the brunt of a good deal of teasing in *Arthur's Nose* and *Arthur's Eyes* (when he must wear glasses). Never very brave, Arthur is seen as very courageous when he goes into a large spooky house on Halloween to find his baby sister in *Arthur's Halloween.* A surprise ending to *Arthur's Valentine* delights children, who have to guess the identity of his secret admirer. In *Arthur's Chicken Pox,* Arthur is afraid his spots will keep him from going on the annual family outing to the circus. All these *Arthur* books satisfy 6- and 7-year-olds' sense of humor and demand for poetic justice.

## Fantasy

The line is blurred between humorous picture stories for children and fanciful ones. Talking beasts and modern spin-offs on folktales are certainly fanciful stories, yet they can be very humorous. However, children appear to see a difference between the make-believe story and the funny one.

Imaginary trips are a common theme in picture books. In Arthur Dorros's *Abuela* and *Isla,* discussed previously, Rosalba and her grandmother visit favorite places in the city and Abuela's island home by flying over them. In Faith Ringgold's *Tar Beach,* Cassie Louise Lightfoot has a dream to be free, to go anywhere she wants. One night up on Tar Beach, the rooftop of her family's Harlem apartment building, her dream comes true. Cassie can fly over the city. This magical story was originally written by Ringgold for a story quilt of the same name.

In *How to Make Apple Pie and See the World* by Marjorie Priceman, an ordinary recipe for apple pie is made extraordinary when the grocery store is closed and the young heroine must seek the ingredients at their origin. She travels to Italy for semolina wheat, to Sri Lanka for cinnamon, to Jamaica for sugar, and so on. The childlike paintings echo the narrator's voice and make a nice model for researching and writing other imaginary cooking trips.

Paul Fleischman's *Weslandia* involves an entire imaginary civilization created by a boy who simply won't conform to childhood norms. When Wesley is told to work on a project over the summer, he decides to create his own civilization. He nurtures a group of seeds that have mysteriously appeared overnight in his garden patch (he has learned the fact "that seeds are carried great distances on the wind"). Because he has also learned that each civilization has its staple food crop, he cares for the unusual plants that appear. Once the plants mature, Wesley is on his way. He devises a full range of products from the plants, creates his own shelter and clothing, and establishes an economic system, a recreational system, and a language. His once-scornful classmates are intrigued and then won over by Wesley's incredible imagination. This entertaining fantasy will surely encourage readers to try to top Wesley in devising their own imaginary civilizations, although perhaps not to quite the same extent.

Another form of young children's fantasy involves anthropomorphism, or the personification of inanimate objects, such as toys and machines. Most children know and love Watty Piper's story *The Little Engine That Could* and Hardie Gramatky's story *Little Toot.* Most of the books written by Virginia Lee Burton contain personification: *Katie and the Big Snow, The Little House,* and *Mike Mulligan and His Steam Shovel.* The modern problem of obsolescence is solved easily in the story of Mike and his beloved steam shovel, Mary Ann. After proving that Mary Ann could dig a basement for the new town hall in a day, Mike is forced to convert her into a furnace, since he has neglected to plan a way for Mary Ann to get out of the excavation. Katie is a snowplow who saves the day by plowing out a whole village. The encroachment of the city on the country is portrayed in

*In Paul Fleischman's* Weslandia, *illustrated by Kevin Hawkes, a boy genius gets a little help from magic and turns his back yard into a unique and self-sustaining civilization.*

Weslandia text © 1999 Paul Fleischman. Illustrations © 1999 Kevin Hawkes. Reproduced by permission of Walker Books Ltd., London. Published in the U.S. and Canada by Candlewick Press, Inc., Cambridge, MA.

Burton's classic story *The Little House,* about a house that stands on the hill and watches day and night as the seasons pass. Gradually a road is built and cars come, and soon the city grows up around the little house. Elevated cars speed by her; subway trains speed under her; and people rush to and fro in front of her. One day the great-great-granddaughter of the original owner sees the little house, buys her, and has her moved back to the country where she can once again see the stars.

Several picture books personify toys and dolls. There are many editions of Margery Williams's sentimental classic *The Velveteen Rabbit: Or How Toys Become Real.* The most attractive ones are those illustrated by Michael Hague, Ilse Plume, and David Jorgensen. Any child who has loved a stuffed animal of her own will understand the conversation between the old skin horse and the velveteen rabbit on the subject of becoming real.

Today there might be more stories about monsters than there are about toys and dolls. Pat Hutchins's monster books present a family that is monstrously delightful. Sibling rivalry is the theme of Hutchins's *The Very Worst Monster* and *It's My Birthday Too.* In *Where's the Baby?* mother monster, grandmother monster, and Hazel (sister monster) all search for the baby. All they can find are clues to where he had been by the monstrous messes he left behind. At last they find him safe in bed—but not for long. Hutchins's green-colored monsters live in very cozy, well-furnished houses.

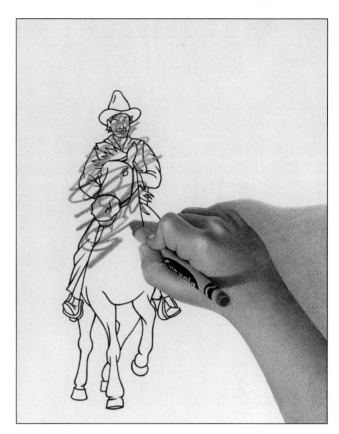

*Chris Van Allsburg combines visual styles to manipulate reality in* Bad Day at Riverbend.

Illustration from *Bad Day at Riverbend.* Copyright © 1995 by Chris Van Allsburg. Reprinted by permission of Houghton Mifflin Company. All rights reserved.

Chris Van Allsburg is certainly the best-known creator of fantasy in children's picture books. *Jumanji* has been discussed previously. *The Garden of Abdul Gasazi* was Van Allsburg's first book. Children are intrigued with the stark black-and-white pictures portraying the strange garden and huge house of the magician. The puzzling ending of the story gives them much to discuss. *Two Bad Ants* provides a useful perspective on another point of view. The ending for *The Wreck of the Zephyr* is another of Van Allsburg's puzzles. Superb full-color pictures illustrate this fantasy of the one time a boat could fly. The identity of the title character (who might be a relative of Jack Frost) is never fully revealed in the mysterious tale *The Stranger. The Polar Express* by Van Allsburg is a haunting Christmas story for all children and for those who remain children at heart. This picture book richly deserved the Caldecott Medal it received. See Resources for Teaching, "Picture Books About the Child's Imaginary World," for a list of many picture books exploring children's imaginary experiences.

# RESOURCES FOR TEACHING

## Picture Books About the Child's Imaginary World

### ANIMALS AS PEOPLE

| Author, Illustrator | Title | Description |
|---|---|---|
| Jean de Brunhoff | *The Story of Babar* | Well-loved stories about an elephant king and his friends and family. Continued in sequels by de Brunhoff's son, Laurent. |
| Roger Duvoisin | *Petunia* | A silly goose thinks she has acquired wisdom when she finds a book but does not know that it is important to learn to read what is in the book. |
| Mem Fox, Pamela Lofts | *Koala Lou* | A little koala bear feels neglected when new brothers and sisters arrive, and she tries to win her mother's attention. Her mother assures her that she always has, and always *will*, love her. |
| Don Freeman | *Dandelion* | The story of a lion who becomes such a "dandy" in order to go to a party that his hostess does not recognize him and shuts the door in his face. |
| Bob Graham | Benny | Graham's exuberant illustrations bring this tale of a hobo dog to life and to the story's final happy conclusion. |
| Libba Moore Gray, Holly Meade | *Small Green Snake* | See text. |
| Kevin Henkes | *Lilly's Purple Plastic Purse, Chester's Way, Julius, the Baby of the World* | See text. |
| Kevin Henkes | *Chrysanthemum* | A lively mouse thinks her name is "absolutely perfect" until she goes to school and is teased about her long flower name. |
| Kevin Henkes | *Owen* | Owen must deal with an interfering neighbor, Mrs. Tweezers, who convinces Owen's parents that he is too old for his security blanket. |
| James Howe, Amy Walrod | Horace and Morris but Mostly Dolores | See text. |
| Pat Hutchins | *Good-Night, Owl!* | A beautifully designed book about a poor owl who is kept awake by noisy animals during the day and then gets his revenge at night. |
| Russell Hoban, Garth Williams | *Bedtime for Frances* and other *Frances* stories | Frances is an engaging, uproariously funny badger who mirrors the behavior of young children. |
| Robert Kraus, José Aruego | *Leo the Late Bloomer* | See text. |
| Robert Kraus, José Aruego and Ariane Dewey | *Owliver* / *Milton the Early Riser* | More charming animal stories. |
| Petra Mathers | *Lottie's New Friend* | Herbie Duck and Lottie are best friends until Dodo arrives. Lottie is smitten with Dodo's exotic experiences and Herbie feels left out. |
| David McKee | *Elmer* | Lovely story about a patchwork-colored elephant who wanted to be gray like all the other elephants. |
| David McPhail | *Pig Pig Grows Up* | An overprotected pig refuses to grow up and act his age until disaster occurs. |

# RESOURCES FOR TEACHING

## Picture Books About the Child's Imaginary World con't

### ANIMALS AS PEOPLE con't

| Author, Illustrator | Title | Description |
|---|---|---|
| H. A. Rey | *Curious George* | A comical monkey has one escapade after another, but the man in the yellow hat always manages to save him from real danger. |
| Dr. Seuss | *Horton Hatches the Egg, Thidwick, the Big-Hearted Moose* | These two are among the many wonderfully original stories by a favorite author of young children. |
| Erica Silverman, S. D. Schindler | *Don't Fidget a Feather* | See text. |
| Bernard Waber | *The House on East 88th Street, Lyle, Lyle Crocodile* | Lyle, a performing crocodile, lives happily with the Pimm family in several comic stories. |
| Rosemary Well | *Noisy Nora* | See text. |
| Rosemary Wells | *Shy Charles* | See text. |

### MODERN FOLKTALE STYLE

| Author, Illustrator | Title | Description |
|---|---|---|
| Janet and Allan Ahlberg | *The Jolly Postman* | See text. |
| Raymond Briggs | *Jim and the Beanstalk* | A sequel to "Jack and the Beanstalk." |
| Stephanie Calmenson, Denise Brunkus | *The Principal's New Clothes* | Hysterically funny modern-day version of "The Emperor's New Clothes." |
| Pamela Edwards, Henry Cole | *Dinorella* | Prehistoric fairytale. A stone age version told in alliterative prose. |
| Mem Fox, Julie Vivas | *Possum Magic* | Grandma Poss and Hush set off on what becomes a culinary visit of the cities of Australia to find the proper magic food to turn Hush from invisible to visible. |
| Tony Johnston, James Warhola | *Bigfoot Cinderella* | Hilarious reversal has an oversize heroine and hero and a beary godmother. |
| Steven Kellogg | *Chicken Little* | See text. |
| Rudyard Kipling, various illustrators | *How the Camel Got His Hump, The Elephant's Child, How the Leopard Got His Spots* | See text. |
| Kathryn Lasky, David Catrow | *The Emperor's Old Clothes* | A comical sequel in which a farmer finds the emperor's old clothes. |
| Leo Lionni | *Alexander and the Wind-Up Mouse, Frederick* | See text. |
| Arnold Lobel | *Fables* | These modern fables include a pirouetting camel in a tutu and an elephant reading the *Daily Trumpet*. |
| David Martin, Susan Meddaugh | *Five Little Piggies* | The true story of what happened to the famous five including the one who ran home crying wee wee wee. |
| Mary Rayner | *Mr. and Mrs. Pig's Evening Out, Garth Pig and the Ice Cream Lady* | A family of pigs outsmarts the wicked wolf at every funny turn. |

*continued*

# RESOURCES FOR TEACHING

## Picture Books About the Child's Imaginary World con't

### MODERN FOLKTALE STYLE con't

| Author, Illustrator | Title | Description |
|---|---|---|
| Jon Scieszka, Lane Smith | *Squids Will Be Squids*<br>*The True Story of the Three Little Pigs*<br>*The Stinky Cheese Man* | See text. |
| Jon Scieszka, Steve Johnson | *The Frog Prince Continued* | Shows that every marriage has its rocky places after the "They lived happily ever after" ending. |
| Judy Sierra, Will Hillenbrand | *The House That Drac Built* | See text. |
| William Steig | *Sylvester and the Magic Pebble, The Amazing Bone, Doctor DeSoto, Brave Irene, Shrek!, Zeke Pippin* | Steig continues to enchant children with his superbly written stories and appealing illustrations. |
| Janet Stevens, Susan Stevens Crummel | *Cook-a-Doodle Do!* | See text. |
| Eugene Trivias, Helen Oxenbury | *The Three Little Wolves and the Big Bad Pig* | See text. |
| Jane Yolen, Victoria Chess | *King Langshanks* | The Frog Prince meets the Emperor's New Clothes in the amusing amphibian version of Andersen classic tale. |

### HUMOROUS PICTURE BOOKS

| Author, Illustrator | Title | Description |
|---|---|---|
| Harry Allard and James Marshall | *Miss Nelson Is Missing*<br>*Miss Nelson Has a Field Day* | See text. |
| Harry Allard, James Marshall | *The Stupids Die*<br>*The Stupids Have a Ball*<br>*The Stupids Step Out* | See text. |
| Judi Barrett, Ron Barrett | *Animals Should Definitely Not Wear Clothing*<br>*Animals Should Definitely Not Act Like People* | Children love the visual ridiculousness of animals garbed in highly inappropriate clothing. |
| Marc Brown | *Arthur's Chicken Pox* and other *Arthur* stories | See text. |
| Beatrice Schenk de Regniers, Beni Montresor | *May I Bring a Friend?* | Slapstick and nonsense are the order of the day. |
| Steven Kellogg | *Pinkerton, Behave!* and other stories | See text. |
| Margaret Mahy, Jonathan Allen | *The Great White Man-Eating Shark* | Norvin, a boy who looks rather like a shark, takes to swimming with a dorsal fin strapped to his back. He has the beach to himself until a female shark falls in love with him. |

# RESOURCES FOR TEACHING

## Picture Books About the Child's Imaginary World con't

### HUMOROUS PICTURE BOOKS con't

| Author, Illustrator | Title | Description |
|---|---|---|
| James Marshall | George and Martha stories | See text. |
| Susan Meddaugh | Martha Walks the Dog | Martha finds out that kind words are better than negative slurs in changing a neighborhood bully. |
| Susan Meddaugh | Martha Calling | Martha again takes charge, this time of the family vacation. |
| Susan Meddaugh | Martha Speaks<br>Martha Calling | See text. |
| Trinka Noble, Steven Kellogg | The Day Jimmy's Boa Ate the Wash<br>Jimmy's Boa Bounces Back | See text. |
| Tom Paxton, Steven Kellogg | Engelbert the Elephant | The illustrations are as uproarious as the antics of the guests when Engelbert crashes the queen's party. |
| Dav Pilkey | Dog Breath | Hally, the pet dog of the Tosis family, has breath problems, but she conquers a bunch of crooks—not with teeth but with odors. |
| James Stevenson | Could Be Worse! That Terrible Halloween Night<br>What's Under My Bed?<br>Worse Than Willy!<br>That Dreadful Day<br>Grandpa's Too-Good Garden | Children appreciate the humor of Grandpa's exaggerated tall tales. Stevenson's watercolor and cartoon-style illustrations are as funny as his stories. |
| Nancy Van Laan, George Booth | Possum Come A-Knockin' | Booth's wry cartoons illustrate this silly story about a little old possum just trying to have fun. |

### FANTASY IN PICTURE BOOKS

| Author, Illustrator | Title | Description |
|---|---|---|
| Eve Bunting, David Christiana | I Am the Mummy Heb-Nefert | In a wonderfully haunting book for older readers, a mummy recalls her days of glory and muses on the brevity of life. |
| Virginia Lee Burton | The Little House<br>Mike Mulligan and His Steam Shovel<br>Katie and the Big Snow | See text. |
| Pam Conrad, Richard Egielski | The Tub People and The Tub Grandfather | These stories of the adventures of seven wooden toys, including a father, mother, grandmother, boy, dog, doctor, and policeman, show the helplessness of dolls. |
| Robert Crowe | Clyde Monster | Clyde is afraid to go to bed because people might be hiding in his cave. |
| Don Freeman | Corduroy | Satisfying story of a plush-toy bear who waits patiently in the department store for someone to buy him. |
| Hardie Gramatky | Little Toot | See text. |

*continued*

# RESOURCES FOR TEACHING

## Picture Books About the Child's Imaginary World con't

<u>FANTASY IN PICTURE BOOKS con't</u>

| Author, Illustrator | Title | Description |
|---|---|---|
| Pat Hutchins | *It's My Birthday*<br>*The Very Worst Monster*<br>*Where's the Baby?* | See text. |
| William Joyce | *George Shrinks* | George dreams he is small and wakes to find it is true. |
| William Joyce | *Dinosaur Bob and His Adventures with the Family Lazardo* | Bob, discovered while the family is on a safari, scares off burglars, dances, and plays baseball. |
| William Joyce | *A Day with Wilbur Robinson* | Strange incongruities occur when Wilbur invites a friend to his house for the day. |
| Maira Kalman | *Max Makes a Million*<br>*Ooh La La, Max in Love*<br>*Max in Hollywood* | The wacky adventures of Max, a dog, a poet, and a dreamer. |
| Rafe Martin, Stephen Gammell | *Will's Mammoth* | Wonderful action-filled pictures capture this joyous imaginary adventure of Will and his very own mammoth. |
| Mercer Mayer | *There's a Nightmare in My Closet* | A small boy who is afraid of the dark ends up comforting a monster who has a nightmare. |
| Petra Mathers | *Victor and Christobel* | Two alligator characters meet through more magical circumstances. Victor is a guard in an art museum and falls in love with the beautiful alligator who has been trapped in the painting by her evil magician cousin. |
| Jerdine Nolan, Elise Primavera | *Raising Dragons* | Daughter of farmers puts her agricultural knowledge to use raising a dragon. |
| Watty Piper | *The Little Engine That Could* | See text. |
| Marjorie Priceman | *How to Make Apple Pie and See the World* | See text. |
| Faith Ringgold | *Tar Beach* | See text. |
| Toby Speed, Barry Root | *Two Cool Cows* | Millie and Maude, two Holsteins, break the contented-cow stereotype in their sunglasses and black boots as they travel to the other side of the moon. |
| Chris Van Allsburg | *Jumanji, The Garden of Abdul Gasazi, Two Bad Ants, The Wreck of the Zephyr, The Stranger, The Polar Express* | See text. |
| Chris Van Allsburg | *Bad Day at Riverbend* | A brave sheriff rides out to find the villain when a slimy substance begins to attack people, beasts, and countryside. |
| Chris Van Allsburg | *Just a Dream* | Predicts the kind of future we are going to have if we keep polluting the earth. |

# RESOURCES FOR TEACHING

## Picture Books About the Child's Imaginary World con't

### FANTASY IN PICTURE BOOKS con't

| Author, Illustrator | Title | Description |
|---|---|---|
| Chris Van Allsburg | *The Wretched Stone* | A message book that suggests the evils of watching television. |
| Chris Van Allsburg | *The Sweetest Fig* | A little dog receives poetic justice after years of mistreatment by a despicable dentist. |
| Chris Van Allsburg | *The Widow's Broom* | The title character needs a little help from the Widow Shaw to overcome its tormentors. |
| Margery Williams, Michael Hague, Ilse Plume, David Jorgensen | *The Velveteen Rabbit* | See text. |

## Social and Environmental Concerns

As more and more picture books are written for older children, more are dealing with major social and environmental concerns.

Eve Bunting's moving story *Fly Away Home* tells of a homeless boy and his father who live in a large airport, moving from terminal to terminal and trying never to be noticed. A trapped bird who finally manages to fly free becomes the boy's metaphor for hope. Ronald Himler's watercolors are as understated and honest as this story. In *Uncle Willie and the Soup Kitchen* by DyAnne DiSalvo-Ryan, a young boy goes with his uncle who volunteers at a soup kitchen. They stop and pick up chickens at the butcher shop. Then the boy meets the other volunteers and helps set tables for "the guests" as Uncle Willie calls them. Uncle Willie is a wonderful model as he stands at the door and greets the guests and shares his zest for living. The warm, sensitive story and pictures were inspired by the author's own experience as a soup kitchen volunteer.

Books sometimes portray the wrenching changes that often occur in the name of progress. In Jane Yolen's *Letting Swift River Go*, the change is bittersweet. Barbara Cooney's lovely transparent watercolors portray the landscapes that will remain in memory long after a little girl's community is drowned beneath the reservoir created by a new dam. She realizes in the end that although she has lost a physical place, she has not lost the stories of that place.

Jeannie Baker's collage pictures for *Where the Forest Meets the Sea* combine both the past and the future. As the young boy explores the forest, shadows of dinosaurs can be seen in the trees; and on the last page, shadows of a future Star Hotel, skyscrapers, homes, and swimming pools are superimposed on the picture of the beach and bay. *Window*, also by Jeannie Baker, is a wordless book that depicts the view from a boy's window changing from wilderness, to country, to small town, to city. The boy, now 25 and with a baby of his own, looks through a window in his new house in the country and sees an ominous sign advertising "House blocks for sale," suggesting that the whole destructive cycle will continue. Other books previously discussed, such as Van Allsburg's *Just a Dream* and Allen Say's *The Lost Lake*, also have an environmental theme.

Ann Turner's *Heron Street* provides a tale of so-called progress from wilderness to the arrival of settlers, the Revolutionary War, and the coming of houses, gaslights, cars, trolleys, and airplanes. One night a heron circles the house and flies higher and higher, "its legs like a long, thin good-bye." Lisa Desimini's jewel-like paintings perfectly complement this progression of change.

A story with a happier outcome is Lynne Cherry's *A River Ran Wild*. This stunning book details the history of the Nashua River in New Hampshire. Beginning long ago when the river ran so clear that its pebbled bottom was visible, Cherry shows how the ecology of the river gradually changed as the land was

*Lynne Cherry's detailed borders provide a visual history of life along the Nashua River in* A River Ran Wild.

Cover from *A River Ran Wild* copyright © 1992 by Lynne Cherry, reproduced with permission of Harcourt, Inc.

colonized and then industrialized. Eventually the river became so badly polluted that nothing lived in it. However, a community campaign led by one determined woman reversed this terrible decline and the river became a thriving ecosystem once again. The book is a model for action in other communities, and Cherry's illustrations, and her detailed borders showing wildlife and other artifacts from various eras, will invite children to create similar social and ecological histories.

## War and Its Aftermath

Art can portray the devastation of war in ways that mere words cannot. Picture books that tell of effects of war in times past and present may help a new generation bring about a peaceful future. Patricia Polacco's *Pink and Say* is a tremendously moving

book based on events that happened to her great-grandfather during the American Civil War. Sheldon Russell Curtis was a young white Union soldier badly wounded in Georgia and left to die when he was found by young Pinkus Aylee, an African American soldier. Pink risks his life to take Sheldon, or Say, to his mother, Moe Moe, who nurses him at great danger to herself. As he recuperates, the two share family stories and memories of the war. Say tells the two of shaking President Lincoln's hand before the Battle of Bull Run. Before they can get to safety, however, southern marauders kill Moe Moe, and on their way to rejoin their units, Pink and Say are captured by Confederate soldiers. In their last moments together, Pink reaches out to touch Say's hand, the hand that touched Mr. Lincoln. An afterword tells that Say survived (barely) the terrible Andersonville prison and that Pink was hanged.

Polacco meant the book to serve as a written memory because Pinkus had no descendants to preserve it for him.

*My Hiroshima* by Junko Morimoto describes Junko's life before the war and immediately after the atomic bomb was dropped. She was the youngest in a family of four children. Miraculously they all escaped being killed. Pictures and photographs of the events, in which 70,000 persons died instantly and another 70,000 died by the end of the first year, are devastating. This story is not as moving, however, as that told by Toshi Maruki in *Hiroshima No Pika* (The Flash of Hiroshima). Seven-year-old Mii and her family are calmly eating their breakfast of sweet potatoes on 6 August 1945, at 8:15 A.M., when the flash occurs. Mii's mother carries her wounded husband to the river. There they all sleep for four days. Mii's father recovers, only to die later from radiation sickness. Mii herself never grows in mind or body beyond her 7 years. The expressionistic pictures of the fires, the thunder and lightning, and the wounded and dying all recreate the horror of an atomic attack. Yet the book was written in the hope that such horrors would never happen again. This, of course, is the reason teachers should share this book. For somehow when pain is particularized for a specific family, it becomes more real and immediate than when it is depersonalized into mass numbers who were killed that day.

For many years children have been moved by Eleanor Coerr's chapter book *Sadako and the Thousand Paper Cranes*. In the picture book *Sadako*, Coerr rewrote the story of a young girl who died of leukemia as a result of the atomic bomb. Ed Young created the moving illustrations that are a fine example of how visual art can work with and empower fine writing. Young's soft pastels mediate this tragic story for children but do not lessen its emotional impact. Figures are hazily drawn, particularly when the most frightening scenes are rendered. Instead of using realistic depictions, Young lets color convey the feelings that underlie the story. As Sadako gets sicker and sicker, the colors darken, until the pages on which she dies are predominantly the blue-black color of night. On the following page, however, Young changes the colors to the soft blues and peaches of a sunrise. The paper cranes that Sadako tried so hard to make have become real cranes flying toward heaven. Young's moving artwork and Sadako's statue in Hiroshima suggest that Sadako left behind a powerful legacy of peace.

The kindness of one child who cared for and provided food for children in a concentration camp is told in the moving story *Rose Blanche* by Christophe Gallaz and Roberto Innocenti. Illustrated with paintings of almost photographic clarity, this picture

A *close-up of two hands is a particularly moving climax to* Patricia Polacco's Pink and Say.

book is certainly for older children. The courage of Rose Blanche and all persons who in their small ways try to maintain humanity in the midst of inhumanity is something that needs to be discussed with older children.

In *The Wall*, a little boy visits Washington, D.C., with his father and they find the name of his grandfather on the Vietnam Memorial. Eve Bunting tells this poignant story, and Ronald Himler creates stark watercolor pictures for it. The pain the boy's father feels is contrasted with the young child's comments. His father tells him he is proud that his grandfather's name is on this wall. The boy replies:

> "I am, too."
> I am.
> But I'd rather have my grandpa here, taking me to the river, telling me to button up my jacket because it's cold.
> I'd rather have him here. (p. 32)

Picture books are for all ages, and they can be about all subjects. They can enlarge children's lives, stretch their imaginations, increase their sensitivity, and enhance their living. The phenomenal growth of beautiful picture books for children of all ages is an outstanding accomplishment of the past fifty years of publishing. Children do not always recognize the beauty of these books, but early impressions do influence the development of children's permanent tastes as they grow up.

# INTO THE CLASSROOM

Room 201

## *Picture Books*

1. Form a mock Caldecott award committee and review the Honor Books and Medal-winning book for one specific year. What criteria do the children think are important? Would they have made the same decision as the ALA committee? Why or why not?

2. Find three or four books that are examples of the use of one medium, such as scratchboard or collage. Invite children to experiment with the materials used in this medium to make a picture of their own.

3. Help children plan a study of a favorite illustrator. What resources are available to find out more about that artist? How would they categorize the artist's books? Brainstorm ways to display the artist's work and to invite other children to learn more about that illustrator.

4. Enlist your art teacher to help children make connections between the historical and cultural conventions used by illustrators and works of art they might find in a museum. Find out more about these traditional works of art.

5. Study the history of bookmaking. Hold a bookmaking workshop and have children write and illustrate their own bound books.

# *Personal Explorations*

1. Look closely at three or more picture books to discover how the illustrations extend the story's meaning beyond the words. Note the effect of the artist's choice of medium, style, and color; look for content details present in the pictures but not in the text.

2. Study the work of one Caldecott Medal–winning illustrator. What medium does this artist use? What terms would you use to describe the style? How do earlier books compare to the artist's most recent ones? Read the artist's acceptance speech for the Caldecott. How has the illustrator's style been influenced by her or his concepts of childhood?

3. Find examples of picture books that you think might increase children's sensitivity to well-used language. Look for vivid descriptions, repetition of unusual words or phrases, and figures of speech within the child's experience.

4. Select a group of stories based on a single subject or theme, such as stories about grandparents, "Be yourself" themes, or environmental concerns. Discuss which ones you would use to introduce a unit, which ones you would read aloud as a teacher, and which ones would be appropriate for children's reading.

5. Collect stories written by one author, such as Mem Fox, Eve Bunting, or Cynthia Rylant, but illustrated by different artists. How do the artists' visions affect the moods of the stories?

# *Related Readings*

Brown, Marcia. *Lotus Seeds: Children's Pictures and Books.* New York: Scribner's, 1986.

A noted illustrator writes eloquently on picture books, the hero within, publishing, and her own work. Her three Caldecott acceptance speeches are included among these thought-provoking essays.

Cianciolo, Patricia. *Picture Books for Children.* 4th ed. Chicago: American Library Association, 1997.

A thorough discussion of the art of picture books, with an annotated listing of all kinds of picture books for children. Particular attention is given to the media and style of illustrating for each entry as well as the ethnic and racial backgrounds of the characters in the stories.

Cummins, Julie. *Children's Book Illustration and Design.* PBC International. 1997.

This beautiful volume includes biographical information and personal reflections of 56 picture-book illustrators and information about their techniques. The book is a follow-up to the first volume published in 1992 (currently out of print) and includes large full-color reproductions.

Kiefer, Barbara Z. *The Potential of Picturebooks: From Visual Literacy to Aesthetic Understanding.* Columbus, Ohio: Merrill/Prentice Hall, 1995.

This book discusses classroom research on children's responses to picture books, provides a history of picture books, looks at some of the modern-day artists who create them, and suggests a theory for evaluating the art of the picture book. The last section provides practical suggestions for classroom activities.

Kingman, Lee, ed. *Newbery and Caldecott Medal Books: 1956–1965.* Boston: Horn Book, 1965.

———. *Newbery and Caldecott Medal Books: 1966–1975.* Boston: Horn Book, 1975.

———. *Newbery and Caldecott Medal Books: 1976–1985.* Boston: Horn Book, 1985.

These volumes contain the acceptance speeches and biographies of the Newbery and Caldecott Medal winners, reprinted from August issues of *Horn Book Magazine.* In the most recent volume, Barbara Bader gives a very critical review of the committee's choices. She far prefers some of the Honor Books over the Medal winners and tells you why.

Marantz, Kenneth, and Sylvia Marantz. *Artists of the Page: Interviews with Children's Book Illustrators.* Jefferson, NC: McFarland, 1992.

Marantz, Kenneth, and Sylvia Marantz. *Creating Picturebooks: Interviews with Editors, Art Directors, Reviewers, Booksellers, Professors, Librarians and Showcasers.* Jefferson, NC: McFarland, 1997.

These two volumes offer a complete picture of the world of picture books and those who are involved in every professional way. The Marantzes' depth of experience with libraries, art education, and picture-book criticism allow them to provide penetrating insights.

Nodelman, Perry. *Words About Pictures: The Narrative Art of Children's Picture Books.* Athens: University of Georgia Press, 1988.

Nodelman explores the various means by which pictures tell stories. These elements include design, style, code, tension, action, irony, and rhythm. Nodelman draws on a number of aesthetic and literary theories in his discussions. Unfortunately this significant book contains few pictures.

Schwarcz, Joseph H., and Chava Schwarcz. *The Picture Book Comes of Age.* Chicago: American Library Association, 1991.

A remarkable book that reveals knowledge of the creative process, children, artistic and literary expertise, and books from several different countries. A professor at the University of Haifa, Joseph Schwarcz taught children's literature for many years before his death in 1988.

Shulevitz, Uri. *Writing with Pictures: How to Write and Illustrate Children's Books.* New York: Watson-Guptill, 1997 [1985].

This superb explanation of the illustrator's art is written by a master illustrator/author. The book includes information on writing and illustrating picture books, picture-book conventions, composition, design and layout of picture books, and technical information on reproduction and publishing.

# *Children's Literature*

Aardema, Verna. *Bringing the Rain to Kapiti Plain.* Illustrated by Beatriz Vidal. Dial, 1981.

Ahlberg, Janet, and Allan Ahlberg. *The Jolly Postman.* Little, Brown, 1986.

Albert, Burton. *Where Does the Trail Lead?* Illustrated by Brian Pinkney. Simon & Schuster, 1993.

Aliki [Aliki Brandenberg]. *Feelings.* Greenwillow, 1984.

Allard, Harry. *The Stupids Die.* Illustrated by James Marshall. Houghton Mifflin, 1981.

———. *The Stupids Have a Ball.* Illustrated by James Marshall. Houghton Mifflin, 1977.

———. *The Stupids Step Out.* Illustrated by James Marshall. Houghton Mifflin, 1978.

Allard, Harry, and James Marshall. *Miss Nelson Has a Field Day.* Illustrated by James Marshall. Houghton Mifflin, 1985.

———. *Miss Nelson Is Missing.* Illustrated by James Marshall. Houghton Mifflin, 1977.

Andersen, Hans Christian. *The Ugly Duckling.* Illustrated by Jerry Pinkney. Morrow, 1999.

Andrews, Jan. *Very Last First Time.* Illustrated by Ian Wallace. McElderry, 1985.

Applebaum, Diana. *Giants in the Land.* Illustrated by Michael McCurdy. Houghton Mifflin, 1993.

Ardizzone, Edward. *Little Tim and the Brave Sea Captain.* Penguin, 1983.

Atkins, Jeannine. *Get Set, Swim.* Lee & Low, 1998.

Aylesworth, Jim. *My Son John.* Illustrated by David Frampton. Henry Holt, 1994.

Baker, Jeannie. *The Hidden Forest.* Greenwillow, 2000.

———. *The Story of Rosy Dock.* Greenwillow, 1995.

———. *Where the Forest Meets the Sea.* Greenwillow, 1987.

———. *Window*. Greenwillow, 1991.

Baker, Olaf. *Where the Buffaloes Begin*. Illustrated by Stephen Gammell. Warne, 1981.

Bang, Molly. *Goose*. Scholastic, 1996.

———. *The Grey Lady and the Strawberry Snatcher*. Four Winds, 1980.

———. *One Fall Day*. Greenwillow, 1994.

———. *The Paper Crane*. Greenwillow, 1985.

———. *When Sophie Gets Angry—Really, Really Angry*. Scholastic, 1999.

Barrett, Judi. *Animals Should Definitely Not Act Like People*. Illustrated by Ron Barrett. Atheneum, 1980.

———. *Animals Should Definitely Not Wear Clothing*. Illustrated by Ron Barrett. Atheneum, 1970.

Bartone, Elisa. *Peppe the Lamplighter*. Illustrated by Ted Lewin. Lothrop, Lee & Shepard, 1993.

Baylor, Byrd. *Everybody Needs a Rock*. Illustrated by Peter Parnall. Scribner's, 1974.

———. *I'm in Charge of Celebrations*. Illustrated by Peter Parnall. Scribner's, 1986.

———. *The Other Way to Listen*. Illustrated by Peter Parnall. Scribner's, 1978.

———. *The Way to Start a Day*. Illustrated by Peter Parnall. Scribner's, 1978.

———. *Your Own Best Secret Place*. Illustrated by Peter Parnall. Scribner's, 1979.

Beard, Carleen Bailey. *Twister*. Illustrated by Nancy Carpenter. Farrar, Straus & Giroux, 1999.

Belton, Sandra. *From Miss Ida's Front Porch*. Illustrated by Floyd Cooper. Four Winds, 1993.

Bemelmans, Ludwig. *Madeline*. Viking, 1962 [1939].

Best, Carrie. *Taxi Taxi*. Illustrated by Dale Gottlieb. Little, Brown, 1994.

Bodecker, N. M. *Hurry, Hurry, Mary Dear*. Illustrated by Erik Blegvad. McElderry, 1998.

Briggs, Raymond. *The Bear*. Random House, 1994.

———. *Father Christmas*. Random House, 1973.

———. *Fungus the Bogeyman*. Random House, 1979.

———. *Jim and the Beanstalk*. Coward-McCann, 1970.

———. *The Snowman*. Random House, 1978.

Brink, Carol Ryrie. *Goody O'Grumpity*. Illustrated by Ashley Wolff. North South, 1996.

Brown, Marc. *Arthur's Chicken Pox*. Little, Brown, 1994.

———. *Arthur's Eyes*. Little, Brown, 1979.

———. *Arthur's Halloween*. Little, Brown, 1983.

———. *Arthur's Nose*. Little, Brown, 1976.

———. *Arthur's Valentine*. Little, Brown, 1980.

Brown, Marcia. *Once a Mouse*. Scribner's, 1961.

Brown, Margaret Wise. *Goodnight Moon*. Illustrated by Clement Hurd. Harper & Row, 1975 [1947].

Browne, Anthony. *Changes*. Knopf, 1986.

———. *The Piggybook*. Knopf, 1986.

———. *The Tunnel*. Knopf, 1990.

———. *Voices in the Park*. Knopf, 1998.

Buchanan, Ken. *This House Is Made of Mud*. Illustrated by Libba Tracy. Northland, 1991.

Bunting, Eve. *Fly Away Home*. Illustrated by Ronald Himler. Clarion, 1991.

———. *Going Home*. Illustrated by David Diaz. HarperCollins, 1996.

———. *How Many Days to America? A Thanksgiving Story*. Illustrated by Beth Peck. Houghton Mifflin, 1988.

———. *I Am the Mummy Heb-Nefert*. Illustrated by David Christiana. Harcourt Brace, 1997.

———. *Night of the Gargoyles*. Illustrated by David Weisner. Clarion, 1994.

———. *Smoky Night*. Illustrated by David Diaz. Harcourt Brace, 1994.

———. *The Wall*. Illustrated by Ronald Himler. Clarion, 1990.

———. *The Wednesday Surprise*. Illustrated by Donald Carrick. Clarion, 1989.

Burleigh, Robert. *Home Run: The Story of Babe Ruth*. Illustrated by Mike Wimmer. Silver Whistle, 1998.

Burton, Virginia Lee. *Katie and the Big Snow*. Houghton Mifflin, 1943.

———. *The Little House*. Houghton Mifflin, 1942.

———. *Mike Mulligan and His Steam Shovel*. Houghton Mifflin, 1939.

Caines, Jeanette. *Just Us Women*. Illustrated by Pat Cummings. Harper & Row, 1982.

Calmenson, Stephanie. *The Principal's New Clothes*. Illustrated by Denise Brunkus. Scholastic, 1989.

Carle, Eric. *The Very Hungry Caterpillar*. World, 1968.

Carlstrom, Nancy White. *Blow Me a Kiss, Miss Lilly*. Illustrated by Amy Schwartz. HarperCollins, 1990.

Carrick, Carol. *The Accident*. Illustrated by Donald Carrick. Clarion, 1976.

Carter, Polly. *Harriet Tubman*. Illustrated by Brian Pinkney. Silver Press, 1992.

Caseley, Judith. *Dear Annie*. Greenwillow, 1991.

———. *Mama Coming and Going*. Greenwillow, 1994.

———. *Mr. Green Peas*. Greenwillow, 1995.

Cendrars, Blaise. *Shadow*. Illustrated by Marcia Brown. Scribner's, 1982.

Cherry, Lynne. *A River Ran Wild*. Gulliver/Harcourt Brace, 1992.

Clark, Ann Nolan. *In My Mother's House*. Illustrated by Velino Herrera. Viking, 1991 [1941].

Coerr, Eleanor. *Sadako*. Illustrated by Ed Young. Putnam, 1993.

———. *Sadako and the Thousand Paper Cranes*. Illustrated by Ron Himler. Putnam, 1977.

Cohen, Miriam. *Best Friends*. Illustrated by Lillian Hoban. Macmillan, 1971.

———. *When Will I Read?* Illustrated by Lillian Hoban. Greenwillow, 1977.

———. *Will I Have a Friend?* Illustrated by Lillian Hoban. Macmillan, 1967.

Cole, Henry. *I Took a Walk*. Greenwillow, 1998.

———. *Jack's Garden*. Greenwillow, 1995.

Cole, Sheila. *When the Tide Is Low*. Illustrated by Virginia Wright-Frierson. Lothrop, Lee & Shepard, 1985.

Conrad, Pam. *The Tub Grandfather*. Illustrated by Richard Egielski. HarperCollins, 1993.

———. *The Tub People*. Illustrated by Richard Egielski. Harper & Row, 1989.

Cooney, Barbara. *Chanticleer and the Fox*. Crowell, 1958.

———. *Hattie and the Wild Waves*. Viking, 1990.

———. *Island Boy*. Viking, 1988.

———. *Miss Rumphius*. Viking, 1982.

Cooper, Floyd. *Coming Home: From the Life of Langston Hughes*. Philomel, 1994.

Crowe, Robert. *Clyde Monster*. Illustrated by Kay Chorao. Dutton, 1976.

Currie, Lynn. *Rushmore*. Scholastic, 1999.

Daly, Niki. *Jamela's Dress*. Farrar Straus Giroux, 1999.

de Brunhoff, Jean. *The Story of Babar*. Random House, 1960.

de Paola, Tomie. *Nana Upstairs & Nana Downstairs*. Penguin, 1978.

———. *Now One Foot, Now the Other*. Putnam, 1981.

———. *Strega Nona*. Prentice Hall, 1975.

———. *Tom*. Putnam, 1993.

———. *Tomie de Paola's Mother Goose*. Putnam, 1985.

———. *Watch Out for the Chicken Feet in Your Soup*. Prentice Hall, 1974.

de Regniers, Beatrice Schenk. *May I Bring a Friend?* Illustrated by Beni Montresor. Atheneum, 1964.

Del Negro, Janice. *Lucy Dove*. Illustrated by Leonid Gore. DK Ink, 1998.

DiSalvo-Ryan, DyAnne. *Uncle Willie and the Soup Kitchen*. Morrow, 1991.

Dorros, Arthur. *Abuela*. Illustrated by Elisa Kleven. Dutton, 1991.

———. *Isla*. Illustrated by Elisa Kleven. Dutton, 1995.

Duvoisin, Roger. *Petunia*. Knopf, 1950.

Edwards, Michelle. *Chicken Man*. Lothrop, Lee & Shepard, 1991.

Edwards, Pamela. *Dinorella: A Prehistoric Fairytale*. Illustrated by Henry Cole. Hyperion, 1997.

Egielski, Richard. *The Gingerbread Boy*. HarperCollins, 1997.

Ehlert, Lois. *Cukoo=Cuco: A Mexican Folktale=Un Cuento Folklorico Mexicano*. Harcourt Brace, 1997.

———. *Fish Eyes: A Book You Can Count On*. Harcourt Brace, 1990.

———. *Hands*. Harcourt Brace, 1997.

———. *Snowballs*. Harcourt Brace, 1995.

Fine, Edith Hope. *Under the Lemon Moon*. Illustrated by Rene King Moreno. Lee & Low, 1999.

Fleischman, Paul. *Weslandia*. Illustrated by Kevin Hawkes. Candlewick, 1999.

Fleming, Denise. *Barnyard Banter*. Holt, 1994.

———. *Mama Cat Has Three Kittens*. Holt, 1998.

Flournoy, Valerie. *The Patchwork Quilt*. Illustrated by Jerry Pinkney. Dial, 1985.

Fox, Mem. *Hattie and the Fox*. Illustrated by Patricia Mullins. Bradbury Press, 1988.

———. *Koala Lou*. Illustrated by Pamela Lofts. Harcourt Brace, 1989.

———. *Night Noises*. Illustrated by Terry Denton. Harcourt Brace, 1989.

———. *Possum Magic*. Illustrated by Julie Vivas. Harcourt Brace, 1990.

———. *Wilfrid Gordon McDonald Partridge*. Illustrated by Julie Vivas. Kane Miller, 1985.

Freeman, Don. *Corduroy*. Viking, 1968.

———. *Dandelion*. Viking, 1964.

Friedman, Ina. *How My Parents Learned to Eat*. Illustrated by Allen Say. Houghton Mifflin, 1984.

Gág, Wanda. *Millions of Cats*. Coward-McCann, 1928.

Gallaz, Christophe, and Roberto Innocenti. *Rose Blanche*. Illustrated by Roberto Innocenti. Harcourt Brace, 1996.

Garza, Carmen Lomas. *Family Pictures: Cuadros de Familia*. Children's Book Press, 1990.

Gauch, Patricia Lee. *Presenting Tanya, Ugly Duckling*. Illustrated by Satomi Ichikawa. Philomel, 1999.

Geisert, Arthur. *Pigs from A to Z*. Houghton Mifflin, 1986.

Geisert, Bonnie, and Arthur Geisert. *Haystack*. Houghton Mifflin, 1998.

———. *Prairie Town*. Houghton Mifflin, 1998.

———. *River Town*. Houghton Mifflin, 1998.

Gerrard, Roy. *Croco'nile*. Farrar, Straus & Giroux, 1994.

———. *The Roman Twins*. Farrar, Straus & Giroux, 1998.

———. *Rosie and the Rustlers*. Farrar, Straus & Giroux, 1989.

Gerstein, Mordecai. *Wild Boy*. Farrar, Straus & Giroux, 1998.

Goble, Paul. *The Girl Who Loved Wild Horses*. Bradbury Press, 1978.

———. *Iktomi and the Buzzard: A Plains Indian Story*. Orchard, 1994.

———. *Star Boy*. Bradbury Press, 1983.

Godwin, Laura. *Little White Dog*. Illustrated by Dan Yaccarino. Hyperion, 1998.

Graham, Bob. *Benny: An Adventure Story*. Candlewick, 1999.

Gramatky, Hardie. *Little Toot*. Putnam, 1939.

Gray, Libba Moore. *My Mama Had a Dancing Heart*. Illustrated by Raúl Colón. Orchard, 1995.

———. *Small Green Snake*. Illustrated by Holly Meade. Orchard, 1994.

Gray, Nigel. *A Country Far Away*. Illustrated by Philippe Dupasquier. Orchard, 1989.

Greenfield, Eloise. *She Come Bringing Me That Little Baby Girl*. Illustrated by John Steptoe. Lippincott, 1974.

Grifalconi, Ann. *Darkness and the Butterfly*. Little, Brown, 1987.

———. *Osa's Pride*. Little, Brown, 1990.

———. *The Village of Round and Square Houses*. Little, Brown, 1986.

Griffith, Helen. *Georgia Music*. Illustrated by James Stevenson. Greenwillow, 1986.

———. *Grandaddy's Place*. Illustrated by James Stevenson. Greenwillow, 1987.

Grimm brothers. *Hansel and Gretel*. Retold by Rika Lesser. Illustrated by Paul Zelinsky. Dodd Mead, 1984.

———. *Rumpelstiltskin*. Retold and illustrated by Paul O. Zelinsky. Dutton, 1986.

———. *Snow White*. Translated by Paul Heins. Illustrated by Trina Schart Hyman. Little, Brown, 1974.

———. *Snow White*. Translated by Randall Jarrell. Illustrated by Nancy Ekholm Burkert. Farrar, Straus & Giroux, 1972.

Guthrie, Woodie. *This Land Is Your Land*. Illustrated by Kathie Jakobsen. Little, Brown, 1998.

Hall, Donald. *Lucy's Christmas*. Illustrated by Michael McCurdy. Browndeer/Harcourt Brace, 1994.

———. *Lucy's Summer*. Illustrated by Michael McCurdy. Browndeer/Harcourt Brace, 1995.

———. *Ox-Cart Man.* Illustrated by Barbara Cooney. Viking, 1979.

Hamilton, Virginia. *Her Stories: African American Folktales, Fairy Tales and True Tales.* Illustrated by Leo and Diane Dillon. Scholastic, 1995.

Havill, Juanita. *Jamaica and the Substitute Teacher.* Illustrated by Anne Sibley O'Brien. Houghton Mifflin, 1999.

Heide, Florence Parry, and Judith Heide Gilliland. *The Day of Ahmed's Secret.* Illustrated by Ted Lewin. Lothrop Lee & Shepard, 1990.

———. *Sami and the Time of the Troubles.* Illustrated by Ted Lewin. Clarion, 1992.

Helprin, Mark. *Swan Lake.* Illustrated by Chris Van Allsburg. Houghton Mifflin, 1989.

———. *The Veil of Snows.* Illustrated by Chris Van Allsburg. Viking, 1997.

Henkes, Kevin. *The Biggest Boy.* Illustrated by Nancy Tafuri. Greenwillow, 1995.

———. *Circle Dogs.* Illustrated by Dan Yaccarino. Greenwillow, 1998.

———. *Chester's Way.* Greenwillow, 1988.

———. *Chrysanthemum.* Greenwillow, 1991.

———. *Julius, the Baby of the World.* Greenwillow, 1990.

———. *Lilly's Purple Plastic Purse.* Greenwillow, 1996.

———. *Owen.* Greenwillow, 1993.

———. *Wemberly Worried.* Greenwillow, 2000.

Hesse, Karen. *Come On Rain.* Illustrated by Jon Muth. Scholastic, 1999.

Hill, Elizabeth Starr. *Evan's Corner.* Illustrated by Sandra Speidel. Viking, 1991 [1967].

Hoban, Russell. *Bedtime for Frances.* Illustrated by Garth Williams. Harper & Row, 1960.

Hoban, Tana. *Shadows and Reflections.* Greenwillow, 1990.

Hodges, Margaret. *Saint George and the Dragon.* Illustrated by Trina Schart Hyman. Little, Brown, 1984.

Hoffman, Mary. *Amazing Grace.* Illustrated by Caroline Binch. Dial, 1991.

———. *Boundless Grace.* Illustrated by Caroline Binch. Dial, 1995.

Hooks, William H. *The Ballad of Belle Dorcas.* Illustrated by Brian Pinkney. Knopf, 1990.

Hopkinson, Deborah. *A Band of Angels: A Story Inspired by the Jubilee Singers.* Illustrated by Raúl Colón. Simon & Schuster, 1999.

Houston, Gloria. *My Great-Aunt Arizona.* Illustrated by Susan Condie Lamb. HarperCollins, 1992.

Howard, Elizabeth Fitzgerald. *Aunt Flossie's Hats (and Crab Cakes Later).* Illustrated by James Ransome. Houghton Mifflin, 1991.

Howe, James. *Horace and Morris but Mostly Dolores.* Illustrated by Amy Walrod. Atheneum, 1999.

Hughes, Langston. *The Dream Keeper.* Illustrated by Brian Pinkney. Knopf, 1994.

Hughes, Shirley. *Alfie Gets in First.* Lothrop, Lee & Shepard, 1982.

———. *Dogger.* Lothrop, Lee & Shepard, 1988.

Hutchins, Pat. *Good-Night, Owl!* Macmillan, 1972.

———. *Its My Birthday!* Greenwillow, 1999

———. *Rosie's Walk.* Macmillan, 1968.

———. *The Very Worst Monster.* Greenwillow, 1985.

———. *What Game Shall We Play?* Greenwillow, 1990.

———. *Where's the Baby?* Greenwillow, 1988.

Hyman, Trina Schart. *Little Red Riding Hood.* Holiday House, 1983.

Isaacs, Anne. *Swamp Angel.* Illustrated by Paul O. Zelinsky. Dutton, 1994.

Isadora, Rachel. *At the Crossroads.* Greenwillow, 1991.

———. *Max.* Macmillan, 1976.

Jackson, Shelley. *The Old Woman and the Wave.* DK Ink, 1998.

Jakobsen, Kathy. *My New York.* Little, Brown, 1993.

Johnson, Angela. *Tell Me Story, Mama.* Illustrated by David Soman. Orchard, 1989.

Johnson, Paul Brett, and Celeste Lewis. *Lost.* Illustrated by Paul Brett Johnson. Orchard, 1996.

Johnston, Tony. *Bigfoot Cinderella.* Illustrated by James Warhola. Putnam, 1998.

———. *The Quilt Story.* Illustrated by Tomie de Paola. Putnam, 1985.

Jonas, Ann. *Round Trip.* Greenwillow, 1983.

Jorgensen, Gail. *Crocodile Beat.* Illustrated by Patricia Mullins. Bradbury Press, 1989.

Joseph, Lynn. *A Wave in Her Pocket: Stories from Trinidad.* Illustrated by Brian Pinkney. Clarion, 1991.

Joyce, William. *A Day with Wilbur Robinson.* HarperCollins, 1990.

———. *Dinosaur Bob and His Adventures with the Family Lazardo.* Harper & Row, 1988.

———. *George Shrinks.* Harper & Row, 1985.

———. *Rolie Polie Olie.* HarperCollins, 1999.

Jukes, Mavis. *Like Jake and Me.* Illustrated by Lloyd Bloom. Knopf, 1984.

Kalman, Maira. *Max in Hollywood.* Viking. 1995.

———. *Max Makes a Million.* Viking, 1990.

———. *Ooh La La, Max in Love.* Viking, 1991.

Keats, Ezra Jack. *Goggles.* Macmillan, 1969.

———. *Hi Cat!* Macmillan, 1970.

———. *A Letter to Amy.* Harper & Row, 1968.

———. *Pet Show!* Macmillan, 1972.

———. *Peter's Chair.* Harper & Row, 1967.

———. *The Snowy Day.* Viking, 1962.

———. *Whistle for Willie.* Viking, 1964.

Keller, Holly. *Grandfather's Dream.* Greenwillow, 1994.

Kellogg, Steven. *Can I Keep Him?* Dial, 1971.

———. *Chicken Little.* Morrow, 1985.

———. *Pinkerton, Behave!* Dial, 1979.

———. *Prehistoric Pinkerton.* Dial, 1987.

———. *A Rose for Pinkerton.* Dial, 1981.

Kesselman, Wendy. *Emma.* Illustrated by Barbara Cooney. Doubleday, 1980.

Kipling, Rudyard. *The Elephant's Child.* Illustrated by Lorinda B. Cauley. Harcourt Brace, 1983.

———. *The Elephant's Child.* Illustrated by Jan Mogensen. Crocodile Books/Interlink, 1989.

———. *How the Camel Got His Hump.* Illustrated by Quentin Blake. Bedrick, 1985.

———. *How the Camel Got His Hump.* Illustrated by Krystyna Turska. Warne, 1988.

———. *How the Leopard Got His Spots.* Illustrated by Caroline Ebborn. Bedrick, 1986.

———. *Just So Stories.* Illustrated by David Frampton. HarperCollins, 1991 [1983].

Kirk, David. *Nova's Ark*. Scholastic, 1999.

Kitchen, Bert. *Animal Alphabet*. Dial, 1984.

Kraus, Robert. *Leo the Late Bloomer*. Illustrated by José Aruego. Crowell, 1971.

———. *Milton the Early Riser*. Illustrated by José Aruego and Ariane Dewey. Windmill, 1972.

———. *Owliver*. Illustrated by José Aruego and Ariane Dewey. Windmill, 1974.

Krauss, Ruth. *A Hole Is to Dig*. Illustrated by Maurice Sendak. Harper & Row, 1952.

———. *A Very Special House*. Illustrated by Maurice Sendak. Harper & Row, 1953.

Lasky, Kathryn. *The Emperor's Old Clothes*. Illustrated by David Catrow. Harcourt Brace, 1999.

———. *Pond Year*. Illustrated by Mike Bostock. Candlewick, 1995.

Lattimore, Deborah Nourse. *The Sailor Who Captured the Sea*. HarperCollins, 1991.

———. *Why There Is No Arguing in Heaven*. Harper & Row, 1989.

Lauber, Patricia. *The News About Dinosaurs*. Bradbury Press, 1989.

Lauture, Dennis. *Running the Road to ABC*. Illustrated by Reynold Ruffins. Simon & Schuster, 1996.

Leaf, Munro. *The Story of Ferdinand*. Illustrated by Robert Lawson. Viking, 1936.

Lessac, Frané. *Caribbean Canvas*. Lippincott, 1989.

———. *My Little Island*. Tambourine, 1985.

Lester, Julius. *What A Truly Cool World*. Illustrated by Joe Cepeda. Scholastic, 1999.

Levinson, Riki. *Our Home Is the Sea*. Illustrated by Dennis Luzak. Dutton, 1988.

———. *Watch the Stars Come Out*. Illustrated by Diane Goode. Dutton, 1985.

Lewin, Ted. *The Storytellers*. Lothrop, Lee & Shepard, 1998.

Lindbergh, Reeve. *Johnny Appleseed*. Illustrated by Kathy Jakobsen. Little, Brown, 1990.

Lionni, Leo. *Alexander and the Wind-up Mouse*. Pantheon, 1969.

———. *An Extraordinary Egg*. Knopf, 1994.

———. *Fish Is Fish*. Pantheon, 1970.

———. *Frederick*. Pantheon, 1967.

———. *Little Blue and Little Yellow*. Astor-Honor, 1959.

———. *Matthew's Dream*. Knopf, 1991.

Livingston, Myra Cohn. *I Never Told and Other Poems*. Cover art by Brian Pinkney. McElderry, 1992.

———. *A Time to Talk: Poems of Friendship*. Illustrated by Brian Pinkney. McElderry, 1992.

Lobel, Arnold. *Days with Frog and Toad*. Harper & Row, 1979.

———. *Fables*. Harper & Row, 1980.

———. *Frog and Toad All Year*. Harper & Row, 1976.

———. *Frog and Toad Are Friends*. Harper & Row, 1970.

———. *Frog and Toad Together*. Harper & Row, 1972.

Locker, Thomas. *Family Farm*. Dial, 1988.

———. *The Mare on the Hill*. Dial, 1985.

———. *Sky Tree*. With Candace Christiansen. HarperCollins, 1995.

———. *Where the River Begins*. Dial, 1984.

———. *The Young Artist*. Dial, 1989.

Lyon, George Ella. *Book*. Illustrated by Peter Catalanoto. DK Ink, 1999.

Macaulay, David. *Black and White*. Houghton Mifflin, 1990.

MacDonald, Golden [Margaret Wise Brown]. *The Little Island*. Illustrated by Leonard Weisgard. Doubleday, 1946.

MacDonald, Megan. *The Bone Keeper*. Illustrated by G. Brian Karas. DK Ink, 1999.

MacLachlan, Patricia. *All the Places to Love*. Illustrated by Mike Wimmer. HarperCollins, 1994.

———. *Mama One, Mama Two*. Illustrated by Ruth Lercher Bornstein. Harper & Row, 1982.

———. *Through Grandpa's Eyes*. Illustrated by Deborah Ray. Harper & Row, 1979.

———. *What You Know First*. Illustrated by Barry Moser. HarperCollins, 1995.

Mahy, Margaret. *The Great White Man-Eating Shark*. Illustrated by Jonathan Allen. Dial, 1990.

———. *The Rattlebang Picnic*. Illustrated by Steven Kellogg. Dial, 1994.

Marshall, James. *George and Martha*. Houghton Mifflin, 1972.

———. *George and Martha Back in Town*. Houghton Mifflin, 1984.

———. *George and Martha Round and Round*. Houghton Mifflin, 1984.

———. *George and Martha Tons of Fun*. Houghton Mifflin, 1972.

Martin, Bill, Jr., and John Archambault. *Knots on a Counting Rope*. Illustrated by Ted Rand. Henry Holt, 1987.

Martin, David. *Five Little Piggies*. Illustrated by Susan Meddaugh. Candlewick, 1998.

Martin, Jaqueline Briggs. *Snowflake Bentley*. Illustrated by Mary Azarian. Houghton Mifflin, 1998.

Martin, Rafe. *Foolish Rabbitt's Big Mistake*. Illustrated by Ed Young. Putnam, 1985.

———. *Will's Mammoth*. Illustrated by Stephen Gammell. Putnam, 1989.

Maruki, Toshi. *Hiroshima No Pika* (The Flash of Hiroshima). Lothrop, Lee & Shepard, 1980.

Marzollo, Jean. *Happy Birthday, Martin Luther King*. Illustrated by Brian Pinkney. Scholastic, 1993.

Mathers, Petra. *Lottie's New Friend*. Simon & Schuster, 1999.

———. *Victor and Christobel*. Knopf, 1993.

Mayer, Mercer. *Shibumi and the Kite Maker*. Marshall Cavendish, 1999.

———. *There's a Nightmare in My Closet*. Dial, 1968.

McCloskey, Robert. *Blueberries for Sal*. Viking, 1963.

———. *Make Way for Ducklings*. Viking, 1941.

———. *One Morning in Maine*. Viking, 1952.

———. *Time of Wonder*. Viking, 1957.

McFarlane, Sheryl. *Eagle Dreams*. Illustrated by Ron Lightburn. Philomel, 1995.

———. *Waiting for Whales*. Illustrated by Ron Lightburn. Philomel, 1993.

McGuire, Richard. *Night Becomes Day*. Viking, 1994.

———. *What Goes Around Comes Around*. Viking, 1995.

McKee, David. *Elmer*. Lothrop, Lee & Shepard, 1989 [1968].

McKissack, Patricia C. *The Dark Thirty: Southern Tales of the Supernatural.* Illustrated by Brian Pinkney. Knopf, 1992.

McPhail, David. *The Bear's Toothache.* Little, Brown, 1972.

———. *Pig Pig Grows Up.* Dutton, 1980.

Meddaugh, Susan. *Martha Calling.* Houghton Mifflin, 1994.

———. *Martha Speaks.* Houghton Mifflin, 1992.

———. *Martha Walks the Dog.* Houghton Mifflin, 1998.

Meyers, Christopher. *Black Cat.* Scholastic, 1999.

Miles, Miska. *Annie and the Old One.* Illustrated by Peter Parnall. Little, Brown, 1971.

Millman, Isaac. *Moses Goes to a Concert.* Farrar, Straus & Giroux, 1998.

Minarik, Else. *Father Bear Comes Home.* Illustrated by Maurice Sendak. Harper & Row, 1959.

———. *A Kiss for Little Bear.* Illustrated by Maurice Sendak. Harper & Row, 1968.

———. *Little Bear.* Illustrated by Maurice Sendak. Harper & Row, 1957.

———. *Little Bear's Friend.* Illustrated by Maurice Sendak. Harper & Row, 1960.

———. *Little Bear's Visit.* Illustrated by Maurice Sendak. Harper & Row, 1961.

Mitchell, Margaree King. *Uncle Jed's Barbershop.* Illustrated by James Ransome. Simon & Schuster, 1993.

Mollel, Tololwa. *My Rows and Piles of Coins.* Illustrated by E. B. Lewis. Clarion, 1999.

Mora, Pat. *Pablo's Tree.* Illustrated by Cecily Lang. Macmillan, 1994.

Musgrove, Margaret. *Ashanti to Zulu: African Traditions.* Illustrated by Leo and Diane Dillon. Dial, 1976.

Namioka, Lensey. *The Loyal Cat.* Illustrated by Aki Sogabe. Browndeer/Harcourt Brace, 1995.

Noble, Trinka H. *The Day Jimmy's Boa Ate the Wash.* Illustrated by Steven Kellogg. Dial, 1980.

———. *Jimmy's Boa Bounces Back.* Illustrated by Steven Kellogg. Dial, 1984.

Nolan, Jerdine. *Raising Dragons.* Illustrated by Elise Primavera. Harcourt Brace, 1998.

Nye, Naomi Shihab. *Sitti's Secret.* Illustrated by Nancy Carpenter. Four Winds, 1994.

Ormerod, Jan. *Who's Whose?* Lothrop, Lee & Shepard, 1998.

Osafsky, Audrey. *Dreamcatcher.* Illustrated by Ed Young. Orchard, 1992.

Pak, Soyung. *dear juno.* Illustrated by Susan Kathleen Hartung. Viking, 1999.

Paxton, Tom. *Engelbert the Elephant.* Illustrated by Steven Kellogg. Morrow, 1990.

Pearson, Susan. *Happy Birthday, Grampie.* Illustrated by Ronald Himler. Dial, 1987.

Perrault, Charles. *Cinderella.* Illustrated by Marcia Brown. Scribner's, 1954.

———. *Puss in Boots.* Illustrated by Fred Marcellino. Farrar, Straus & Giroux, 1990.

Pilkey, Dav. *Dog Breath: The Horrible Trouble with Hally Tosis.* Blue Sky, 1994.

Pinkney, Andrea Davis. *Alvin Ailey.* Illustrated by Brian Pinkney. Hyperion, 1993.

———. *Bill Pickett: Rodeo Riding Cowboy.* Illustrated by Brian Pinkney. Harcourt Brace, 1996.

———. *Dear Benjamin Banneker.* Illustrated by Brian Pinkney. Harcourt Brace, 1994.

———. *Duke Ellington, The Piano Prince and His Orchestra.* Illustrated by Brian Pinkney, Hyperion, 1998.

———. *I Smell Honey.* Illustrated by Brian Pinkney. Harcourt Brace, 1997.

———. *Pretty Brown Face.* Illustrated by Brian Pinkney. Harcourt Brace, 1997.

———. *Seven Candles for Kwanzaa.* Illustrated by Brian Pinkney. Dial, 1993.

———. *Shake Shake Shake.* Illustrated by Brian Pinkney. Harcourt Brace, 1997.

———. *Watch Me Dance.* Illustrated by Brian Pinkney. Harcourt Brace, 1997.

Pinkney, Brian. *The Adventures of Sparrowboy.* Simon & Schuster, 1997.

———. *Cosmo and the Robot.* Greenwillow, 2000.

———. *Jojo's Flying Side Kick.* Simon & Schuster, 1995.

———. *Max Found Two Sticks.* Simon & Schuster, 1994.

Piper, Watty. *The Little Engine That Could.* Illustrated by George Hauman and Doris Hauman. Platt & Munk, 1954 [1930].

Polacco, Patricia. *Just Plain Fancy.* Bantam/Doubleday, 1990.

———. *The Keeping Quilt.* Simon & Schuster, 1988.

———. *Pink and Say.* Philomel, 1994.

———. *Thunder Cake.* Philomel, 1990.

Politi, Leo. *Song of the Swallows.* Scribner's, 1949.

Pomerantz, Charlotte. *The Chalk Doll.* Illustrated by Frané Lessac. Lippincott, 1989.

Potter, Beatrix. *The Tale of Peter Rabbit.* Warne, 1902.

Price, Leontyne. *Aïda.* Illustrated by Leo and Diane Dillon. Harcourt Brace, 1990.

Priceman, Marjorie. *How to Make Apple Pie and See the World.* Knopf, 1994.

Provensen, Alice, and Martin Provensen. *The Glorious Flight: Across the Channel with Louis Blériot.* Viking, 1983.

Raschka, Chris. *Like Likes Like.* DK Ink, 1999.

———. *Mysterious Thelonious.* Orchard, 1997.

———. *Yo! Yes?* Orchard, 1993.

Rathman, Peggy. *Officer Buckle and Gloria.* Putnam, 1995.

Rattigan, Jama Kim. *Dumpling Soup.* Illustrated by Lillian Hsu-Flanders. Little, Brown, 1993.

Rayner, Mary. *Garth Pig and the Ice Cream Lady.* Atheneum, 1977.

———. *Mr. and Mrs. Pig's Evening Out.* Atheneum, 1976.

Reid, Barbara. *Two by Two.* Scholastic, 1992.

Rey, H. A. *Curious George.* Houghton Mifflin, 1941.

Ringgold, Faith. *Tar Beach.* Crown, 1991.

Robbins, Ruth. *Baboushka and the Three Kings.* Illustrated by Nicholas Sidjakov. Parnassus, 1960.

Roe, Eileen. *Con Mi Hermano: With My Brother.* Illustrated by Robert Casilla. Bradbury Press, 1991.

Russo, Marisabina. *Hannah's Baby Sister.* Greenwillow, 1998.

———. *I Don't Want to Go Back to School.* Greenwillow, 1994.

———. *Mama Talks Too Much.* Greenwillow, 1999.

Rylant, Cynthia. *Appalachia: The Voices of Sleeping Birds.* Illustrated by Barry Moser. Harcourt Brace, 1991.

———. *The Relatives Came.* Illustrated by Stephen Gammell. Bradbury Press, 1985.

———. *When I Was Young in the Mountains.* Illustrated by Diane Goode. Dutton, 1982.

San Souci, Robert D. *The Boy and the Ghost.* Illustrated by Brian Pinkney. Simon & Schuster, 1989.

———. *Cendrillon: A Caribbean Cinderella.* Illustrated by Brian Pinkney. Simon & Schuster, 1998.

———. *Cut from the Same Cloth: American Women of Myth, Legend, and Tall Tale.* Illustrated by Brian Pinkney. Putnam/Philomel, 1993.

———. *The Faithful Friend.* Illustrated by Brian Pinkney. Simon & Schuster, 1995.

———. *Sukey and the Mermaid.* Illustrated by Brian Pinkney. Four Winds, 1992.

Sanders, Scott Russell. *A Place Called Freedom.* Illustrated by Thomas B. Allen. Atheneum, 1997.

Say, Allen. *El Chino.* Houghton Mifflin, 1990.

———. *Grandfather's Journey.* Houghton Mifflin, 1993.

———. *The Lost Lake.* Houghton Mifflin, 1989.

———. *Tea with Milk.* Houghton Mifflin, 1999.

Schur, Maxine R. *Day of Delight.* Illustrated by Brian Pinkney. Dial, 1994.

———. *When I Left My Village.* Illustrated by Brian Pinkney. Dial, 1996.

Scieszka, Jon. *The Book That Jack Wrote.* Illustrated by Daniel Adel. Viking, 1994.

———. *The Frog Prince Continued.* Illustrated by Steve Johnson. Viking, 1991.

———. *Squids Will Be Squids.* Illustrated by Lane Smith. Viking, 1998.

———. *The Stinky Cheese Man and Other Fairly Stupid Tales.* Illustrated by Lane Smith. Viking, 1992.

———. *The True Story of the Three Little Pigs.* Illustrated by Lane Smith. Viking, 1989.

Sendak, Maurice. *In the Night Kitchen.* Harper & Row, 1970.

———. *Outside Over There.* Harper & Row, 1981.

———. *We Are All in the Dumps with Jack and Guy.* HarperCollins, 1993.

———. *Where the Wild Things Are.* Harper & Row, 1963.

Serfozo, Mary. *Rain Talk.* Illustrated by Keiko Narahashi. McElderry Books/Macmillan, 1990.

Seuss, Dr. [Theodor S. Geisel]. *And to Think That I Saw It on Mulberry Street.* Vanguard, 1937.

———. *The Cat in the Hat.* Random House, 1957.

———. *Horton Hatches the Egg.* Random House, 1993 [1940].

———. *Scrambled Eggs Super!* Random House, 1953.

———. *Thidwick, the Big-Hearted Moose.* Random House, 1948.

Seymour, Tres. *Hunting the White Cow.* Illustrated by Wendy Anderson Halperin. Orchard, 1993.

Shannon, David. *David Goes to School.* Scholastic, 1999.

———. *No David!* Scholastic, 1998.

Shannon, George. *Climbing Kansas Mountains.* Illustrated by Thomas B. Allen. Bradbury, 1993.

Shelby, Anne. *Homeplace.* Illustrated by Wendy Anderson Halperin. Orchard, 1995.

Shulevitz, Uri. *Dawn.* Farrar, Straus & Giroux, 1974.

———. *Rain Rain Rivers.* Farrar, Straus & Giroux, 1969.

———. *Snow.* Farrar, Straus & Giroux, 1998.

Siegelson, Kim L. *In the Time of the Drums.* Illustrated by Brian Pinkney. Hyperion, 1999.

Sierra, Judy. *The Elephant's Wrestling Match.* Illustrated by Brian Pinkney. Lodestar/Dutton, 1992.

———. *The House That Drac Built.* Illustrated by Will Hillenbrand. Gulliver, 1995.

Silverman, Erica. *Don't Fidget a Feather.* Illustrated by S. D. Schindler. Macmillan, 1994.

Simmons, Jane. *Come Along Daisy!* Little Brown, 1998.

Sogabe, Aki. *Aesop's Fox.* Browndeer, 1999.

Soto, Gary. *Chato's Kitchen.* Illustrated by Susan Guevara. Putnam, 1995.

Speed, Toby. *Two Cool Cows.* Illustrated by Barry Root. Putnam, 1995.

Spier, Peter. *Peter Spier's Rain.* Doubleday, 1982.

Stafford, Kim. *We Got Here Together.* Illustrated by Debra Frasier. Harcourt Brace, 1992.

Stafford, William. *The Animal That Drank Up Sound.* Illustrated by Debra Frasier. Harcourt Brace, 1992.

Steig, William. *The Amazing Bone.* Farrar, Straus & Giroux, 1976.

———. *Amos & Boris.* Farrar, Straus & Giroux, 1971.

———. *Brave Irene.* Farrar, Straus & Giroux, 1986.

———. *Doctor DeSoto.* Farrar, Straus & Giroux, 1982.

———. *Pete's a Pizza.* HarperCollins, 1998.

———. *Shrek!* Farrar, Straus & Giroux, 1990.

———. *Sylvester and the Magic Pebble.* Windmill, 1979.

———. *Zeke Pippin.* HarperCollins, 1994.

Steptoe, John. *Stevie.* Harper & Row, 1969.

Stevens, Janet, and Susan Crummel Stevens. *Cook-a-Doodle-Doo!* Harcourt Brace, 1999.

Stevenson, James. *Could Be Worse!* Greenwillow, 1977.

———. *The Dreadful Day.* Greenwillow, 1985.

———. *Grandpa's Too-Good Garden.* Greenwillow, 1988.

———. *That Terrible Halloween Night.* Greenwillow, 1983.

———. *What's Under My Bed?* Greenwillow, 1983.

———. *Worse Than Willy!* Greenwillow, 1984.

Stewart, Sarah. *The Gardener.* Illustrated by David Small. Farrar, Straus & Giroux, 1997.

———. *The Library.* Illustrated by David Small. Farrar, Straus & Giroux, 1995.

Stock, Catherine. *Where Are You Going, Manyoni?* Morrow, 1993.

Stolz, Mary. *Storm in the Night.* Illustrated by Pat Cummings. Harper & Row, 1988.

Sturges, Philemon. *The Little Red Hen (Makes a Pizza).* Illustrated by Amy Walrod. Dutton, 1999.

Stuve-Bodeen, Stephanie. *Elizabeti's Doll.* Illustrated by Christy Hale. Lee & Low, 1998.

Thomas, Jane Resch. *Celebration.* Illustrated by Raúl Colón. Hyperion, 1997.

Tiller, Ruth. *Cinnamon, Mint, and Mothballs: A Visit to Grandmother's House.* Illustrated by Aki Sogabe. Browndeer/Harcourt Brace, 1993.

Titherington, Jeanne. *A Place for Ben.* Greenwillow, 1987.

Tresselt, Alvin. *Hide and Seek Fog.* Illustrated by Roger Duvoisin. Lothrop, Lee & Shepard, 1988 [1965].

———. *White Snow, Bright Snow.* Illustrated by Roger Duvoisin. Lothrop, Lee & Shepard, 1988 [1947].

Trivias, Eugene. *The Three Little Wolves and the Big Bad Pig.* Illustrated by Helen Oxenbury. McElderry, 1993.

Turner, Ann. *Heron Street.* Illustrated by Lisa Desimini. Harper & Row, 1989.

———. *Through Moon and Stars and Night Skies.* Illustrated by James-Graham Hale. HarperCollins, 1990.

Udry, Janice May. *A Tree Is Nice.* Illustrated by Marc Simont. Harper & Row, 1956.

Van Allsburg, Chris. *Bad Day at Riverbend.* Houghton Mifflin, 1995.

———. *The Garden of Abdul Gasazi.* Houghton Mifflin, 1979.

———. *Jumanji.* Houghton Mifflin, 1981.

———. *Just a Dream.* Houghton Mifflin, 1990.

———. *The Mysteries of Harris Burdick.* Houghton Mifflin, 1984

———. *The Polar Express.* Houghton Mifflin, 1985.

———. *The Stranger.* Houghton Mifflin, 1986.

———. *The Sweetest Fig.* Houghton Mifflin, 1993.

———. *Two Bad Ants.* Houghton Mifflin, 1988.

———. *The Widow's Broom.* Houghton Mifflin, 1992.

———. *The Wreck of the Zephyr.* Houghton Mifflin, 1983.

———. *The Wretched Stone.* Houghton Mifflin, 1991.

Van Laan, Nancy. *Possum Come a-Knockin'.* Illustrated by George Booth. Knopf, 1990.

Viorst, Judith. *Alexander and the Terrible, Horrible, No Good, Very Bad Day.* Illustrated by Ray Cruz. Atheneum, 1972.

———. *The Tenth Good Thing About Barney.* Illustrated by Erik Blegvad. Atheneum, 1971.

Waber, Bernard. *The House on East 88th Street.* Houghton Mifflin, 1962.

———. *Ira Sleeps Over.* Houghton Mifflin, 1972.

———. *Lyle, Lyle Crocodile.* Houghton Mifflin, 1965.

Walter, Mildred Pitts. *My Mama Needs Me.* Illustrated by Pat Cummings. Lothrop, Lee & Shepard, 1983.

Wells, Rosemary. *Noisy Nora.* Dial, 1973.

———. *Shy Charles.* Dial, 1988.

Wiesner, David. *Hurricane.* Clarion, 1990.

Wild, Margaret. *Our Granny.* Illustrated by Julie Vivas. Ticknor & Fields, 1994.

———. *The Very Best of Friends.* Illustrated by Julie Vivas. Harcourt Brace, 1990.

Willard, Nancy. *A Visit to William Blake's Inn.* Illustrated by Alice and Martin Provensen. Harcourt Brace, 1981.

Williams, Karen Lynn. *Galimoto.* Illustrated by Catherine Stock. Lothrop, Lee & Shepard, 1990.

———. *Painted Dreams.* Illustrated by Catherine Stock. Lothrop, Lee & Shepard, 1998.

Williams, Margery. *The Velveteen Rabbit: Or How Toys Become Real.* Illustrated by Michael Hague. Henry Holt, 1983.

———. *The Velveteen Rabbit: Or How Toys Become Real.* Illustrated by David Jorgensen. Knopf, 1985.

———. *The Velveteen Rabbit: Or How Toys Become Real.* Illustrated by William Nicholson. Doubleday, 1958 [1922].

Williams, Vera B. *A Chair for My Mother.* Greenwillow, 1982.

———. *Music, Music for Everyone.* Greenwillow, 1984.

———. *Something Special for Me.* Greenwillow, 1983.

Wisniewski, David. *The Golem.* Clarion, 1996.

———. *The Wave of the Sea-Wolf.* Clarion, 1994.

Wood, Audrey. *The Napping House.* Illustrated by Don Wood. Harcourt Brace, 1984.

Woodson, Jacqueline. *We Had a Picnic This Sunday Past.* Illustrated by Diane Greenseid. Hyperion, 1998.

Wormell, Mary. *Hilda Hen's Happy Birthday.* Harcourt Brace, 1995.

———. *Hilda Hen's Scary Night.* Harcourt Brace, 1997.

Yashima, Taro [Jun Iwamatsu]. *Crow Boy.* Viking, 1955.

———. *Umbrella.* Viking Penguin, 1958.

Yolen, Jane. *The Emperor and the Kite.* Illustrated by Ed Young. Philomel, 1988 [1967].

———. *King Langshanks.* Illustrated by Victoria Chess. Harcourt Brace, 1998.

———. *Letting Swift River Go.* Illustrated by Barbara Cooney. Little, Brown, 1992.

———. *Owl Moon.* Illustrated by John Schoenherr. Philomel, 1987.

Young, Ed. *Little Plum.* Philomel, 1994.

Zelinsky, Paul O. *The Maid, the Mouse and the Odd Shaped House.* Dodd Mead, 1981.

———. *Rapunzel.* Dutton, 1997

Zolotow, Charlotte. *Mr. Rabbit and the Lovely Present.* Illustrated by Maurice Sendak. Harper & Row, 1962.

———. *William's Doll.* Illustrated by William Pène duBois. Harper & Row, 1972.

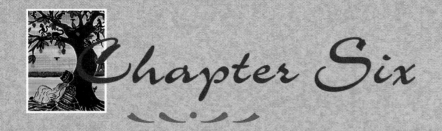

# Chapter Six

## Traditional Literature

*Ever since human beings realized they were unique among animals in that they could think and talk, they have tried to explain themselves and their world. Who were the first humans? How did they come to be? What made the sun and the moon and the stars? Why are the*

animals made the way they are? What caused night and day, the seasons, the cycle of life itself? Why are some people greedy and some unselfish, some ugly and some handsome, some dull and some clever? As people pondered these questions and many more, they created stories that helped explain the world to their primitive minds. The storytellers told these tales again and again around the fires of the early tribes, by the hearths of humble cottages, before the great fire in the king's hall; they told them as they sat in the grass huts of the jungle, the hogans of the southern plains, and the igloos of the northern tundra. Their children told them, and their children's children, until the stories were as smooth and polished as the roundest stones in a stream. And so people created their myths and their folktales, their legends and epics—the literature of the fireside, the poetry of the people, and the memory of humankind.

## A Perspective on Traditional Literature

Traditional literature can provide a window on cultural beliefs and on the spiritual and psychological qualities that are part of our human nature. These stories also form the basis for many works of more-modern literature, drama, and other art forms. It is important to help children become familiar with the rich heritage of stories that have come down to us from cultures around the world.

### The Origin of Folk Literature

We have no one word that encompasses all of the stories born of the oral tradition. The stories most often are labeled "folklore," "folk literature," or "mythology." Generally we say that myths are about gods and the creation of things; legends are about heroes and their mighty deeds before the time of recorded history; and folktales, fairytales, and fables are simple stories about talking beasts, woodcutters, and princesses who reveal human behavior and beliefs while playing out their roles in a world of wonder and magic.

Children sometimes identify these stories as "make-believe," as contrasted with "true" or "stories that could really happen." Unfortunately, the word *myth* has sometimes been defined as "imagined event" or "pagan falsehood" and contrasted with "historical fact" or "religious truth." In literary study, however, a myth is not "untrue"; rather, it is a story with a generalized meaning, or a universal idea, that expresses a significant truth about humans and their lives. A single myth is a narrative that tells of origins,[1] explains natural or social phenomena, or suggests the destiny of humans through the interaction of people and supernatural beings. A *mythology* is a group of myths of a particular culture. Myth making is continuous and still in process today.[2] Usually myth is a product of a society rather than of a single author.

The origin of the myths has fascinated and puzzled folklorists, anthropologists, and psychologists. How, they wonder, can we account for the similarities among these stories that grew out of ancient cultures widely separated from each other? The Greek myth Cupid and Psyche retold by M. Charlotte Craft is very much like the Norwegian tale told in George Dasent's *East o'the Sun and West o'the Moon*. The Chinese "Cinderella" story recounted in Ai-Ling Louie's *Yeh-Shen* is similar to Perrault's French *Cinderella* except that a fish acts on the poor girl's behalf. And the Cinderella story is found throughout the world, with nearly five hundred variants in Europe alone.

In trying to explain this phenomenon, one group of early mythologists proposed the notion of *monogenesis,* or inheritance from a single culture. The Grimm brothers, who were among the first nineteenth-century

---

[1]X. J. Kennedy, *Literature: An Introduction to Fiction, Poetry and Drama* (Boston: Little, Brown, 1983), p. 610.

[2]Joseph Campbell, with Bill Moyers, *The Power of Myth* (New York: Doubleday, 1988).

*Readers will recognize many aspects of the "Cinderella" story in the Ojibwa tale* Sootface *by Robert D. San Souci.*

From *Sootface* by Robert D. San Souci, copyright Text © 1994 by Robert San Souci, illustration by Daniel San Souci. Reprinted by permission of Random House Children's Books, a division of Random House, Inc.

scholars of folklore, theorized that all folktales originated from one prehistoric group called Aryans, later identified as Indo-Europeans by modern linguists. As this group migrated to other countries, the scholars reasoned, they took their folklore with them; such reasoning led scholars to the theory of *diffusion.*

Another approach to folklore involves the theory of *polygenesis,* or multiple origins. It is argued that each story could have been an independent invention growing out of universal human desires and needs. Early anthropologists viewed myth as the religion of the people derived from rituals that were recounted in drama and narratives. They identified recurrent themes in myths of different cultures. Clyde Kluckhohn's study of the myths of fifty cultures revealed recurring themes like the flood, the slaying of monsters, incest, sibling rivalry, and castration.[3] Kluckhohn also found several patterns repeated in the myth of the hero. Sir James Frazer's twelve-volume analysis of ritual, taboos, and myths, *The Golden Bough,*[4] was of major importance. This anthropological study ascribed sexual symbolic meaning to primitive myths and greatly influenced modern literature.

Sigmund Freud's analysis of myth as dream, or disguised wish fulfillment, was the beginning of psychological literary criticism.[5] Freud held the view that all myths expressed the Oedipus theme with its incest motive, guilt, and punishment. Another psychological viewpoint was that of Carl Jung, a contemporary of Freud, who thought that a "collective unconscious" is "inherited in the structure of the brain."[6] These unconscious, recurring images created the primitive mythic heroes and still exist as individual fantasies for the civilized person as a kind of "race memory," according to Jung. The folklorist, however, might disagree with such psychological interpretations. Richard Dorson argues that "folk literature cannot all be prettily channeled into the universal monomyth" and that "the folklorist looks with jaundiced eye at the excessive straining of mythologists to extort symbols from folk tales."[7]

Folktales are also of special interest to scholars of narrative theory. Because of the way the tales are honed by many generations of telling, only the most important elements of the story survive. Close study of the patterns of action and character relationships show how language shapes a form we recognize as a story. Vladimir Propp, for instance, analyzed Russian tales and identified a set sequence of thirty-one "functions" that might occur in a tale, such as these: The hero leaves home (departure); one member of a family lacks or desires something (lack); or a villain attempts to deceive his victim (trickery).[8] Other researchers have used simplified folktale structures to develop models of children's story comprehension. Although looking at tales in such a technical way is definitely an adult perspective, children who have heard and enjoyed many traditional stories begin to discover for themselves that folktales seem to follow certain structural rules. One 10-year-old girl who wrote instructions for "making a fairy story" summed up by saying, "Fairy tales have to have a sort of pattern or they would just be regular stories."

However scholars choose to look at them, folktales and myths are literature derived from human imagination to explain the human condition. Literature today continues to express our concern about human strengths and weaknesses and the individual's relationships to the world and to other people.

[3]Clyde Kluckhohn, "Recurrent Themes in Myth and Mythmaking," in *The Making of Myth,* ed. Richard M. Ohrmann (New York: Putnam, 1962), pp. 52–65.

[4]Sir James Frazer, *The Golden Bough,* 3rd ed. (London: Macmillan, 1911–1915).

[5]Stanley E. Hyman, *The Armed Vision,* rev. ed. (New York: Vintage, 1955).

[6]Carl C. Jung, "On the Relation of Analytic Psychology to Poetic Art," in *Modern Continental Literary Criticism,* ed. O. B. Hardison, Jr. (New York: Appleton, 1962), pp. 267–288.

[7]Richard Dorson, "Theories of Myth and the Folklorist," in *The Making of Myth,* p. 45.

[8]Vladimir Propp, *The Morphology of the Folktale* (Austin: University of Texas Press, 1968).

Traditional literature forms the foundation of understandings of life as expressed in modern literature.

## The Value of Folk Literature for Children

When Jacob and Wilhelm Grimm published the first volume of their *Household Stories* in 1812, they did not intend it for children. These early philologists were studying the language and grammar of such traditional tales. In recent years, as we have seen, anthropologists study folklore in order to understand the inherent values and beliefs of a culture. Psychologists look at folktales and myths and discover something of human motivation and feelings. Folklorists collect and categorize various stories, types, and motifs from around the world. These are all adult scholars of folk literature, which itself was first created by adults and usually told to an adult community. How, then, did folk literature become associated with children's literature, and what value does this kind of literature have for children?

Originally folklore was the literature of the people; stories were told to young and old alike. Families or tribes or the king's court would gather to hear a famous storyteller in much the same way that an entire family today will watch their favorite television program together. With the age of scientific enlightenment, these stories were relegated to the nursery, often kept alive by resourceful nursemaids or grandmothers, much to the delight of children.

Children today still enjoy these tales because they are good stories. Born of the oral tradition, these stories usually are short and have fast-moving plots. They frequently are humorous and almost always end happily. Poetic justice prevails; the good and the just are eventually rewarded; the evil are punished. This appeals to children's sense of justice and their moral judgment. Wishes come true, but usually not without the fulfillment of a task or trial. The littlest child, the youngest child, or the smallest animal succeeds; the oldest or the largest is frequently defeated. Youngsters, who are the little people of their world, thrive on such turns of events.

Beyond the function of pure entertainment, folktales can kindle the child's imagination. Behind every great author, poet, architect, mathematician, or diplomat are that person's dreams of what she or he hopes to achieve. These dreams or ideals have been created by the power of imagination. If we always give children stories of "what is," stories that only mirror the living of today, then we have not helped them to imagine what "might have been" or "what might be."

Bruno Bettelheim, in his remarkable book *The Uses of Enchantment,* maintains that fairy tales help children cope with their dreams and inner turmoil. "Each fairy tale," he says, "is a magic mirror which reflects some aspects of our inner world and of the steps required by our evolution from immaturity to maturity."[9]

Kornei Chukovsky, the Russian poet, tells of a time when it was proposed that all folktales and fairy tales be eliminated from the education of the Russian child in favor of simple realistic stories. Then one of the major Russian educators began keeping a diary of her child's development. She found that her child, as if to compensate for the loss of the fairy tales he had been denied, began to make up his own. He had never heard a folktale, but his world became peopled with talking tigers, birds, and bugs. Chukovsky concludes: "Fantasy is the most valuable attribute of the human mind and should be diligently nurtured from earliest childhood."[10]

Our speech and vocabulary reflect many contributions from traditional literature. Think of the figures of speech that come from Aesop's fables: "sour grapes," "dog in the manger," "boy who cried wolf." Our language is replete with words and phrases from the myths—*narcissistic, cereal, labyrinth, siren,* and many more.

Traditional literature is a rightful part of a child's literary heritage and lays the groundwork for understanding all literature. Poetry and modern stories allude to traditional literature, particularly the Greek myths, Aesop's fables, and Bible stories. Northrop Frye maintains that "all themes and characters and stories that you encounter in literature belong to one big interlocking family."[11] As you meet recurring patterns or symbols in mythlike floods, savior heroes, cruel stepmothers, the seasonal cycle of the year, the cycle of a human life, you begin to build a framework for literature. Poetry, prose, and drama become more emotionally significant as you respond to these recurring archetypes.

## Folktales

Folktales have been defined as "all forms of narrative, written or oral, which have come to be handed down through the years."[12] This definition would include epics, ballads, legends, and folk songs, as well as myths and fables. In using folk literature in the elementary school, we have tended to confine the rather

---

[9] Bruno Bettelheim, *The Uses of Enchantment* (New York: Knopf, 1976), p. 309.

[10] Kornei Chukovsky, *From Two to Five,* trans. and ed. Miriam Morton (Berkeley: University of California Press, 1963), p. 119.

[11] Northrop Frye, *The Educated Imagination* (Bloomington: Indiana University Press, 1964), p. 48.

[12] Ibid.

simple folktales—such as the popular "Three Billy Goats Gruff," "Little Red Riding Hood," and "Rumpelstiltskin"—to the primary grades; we recommend the so-called fairy tales or wonder tales—such as "Snow White" and "Cinderella"—for slightly older children, because these tales are longer and contain romantic elements. Such a division appears arbitrary; it is based more on use than on any real difference in the stories. To complicate matters even further, modern fanciful stories created by known authors are often also referred to as fairy tales. Hans Christian Andersen's stories are becoming part of the heritage that might be described as folktales, but *many originated in written rather than oral form.* Thus they are distinguished from the stories told by the common folk that were finally collected and recorded. Stories that are written in a folktale style but originated in an author's imagination are often referred to as "literary folktales" (see "Modern Folktale Style" in Chapter 5 and Modern Fairy Tales in Chapter 7).

Questions often arise about which of the available print versions of a tale is the "correct" or authentic text. From a folklorist's point of view, a tale is re-created every time it is told and therefore *every* telling is correct in its own way. A great deal of variation is also acceptable in print versions, where literary style carries the same uniqueness as the teller's voice. Authors and illustrators may also add original twists, customize their stories for a chosen audience, or adapt a familiar tale to an unfamiliar setting, as oral storytellers do. There might be a problem, however, when a print version suggests by its title, or lack of an author's note, that it represents a tale derived directly from a previously printed source. Readers of a story identified as recorded and published by the Grimm brothers, for instance, have a right to find that this tale has been subsequently published without major additions, omissions, or distortions.

This chapter discusses folktales in children's literature that come from the oral tradition. It also includes a description of epics, myths, and stories from the Bible, which are all a part of traditional literature. Modern fanciful stories written by known authors are discussed in Chapter 7.

## Types of Folktales

The many folktales that have found their way into the hands and hearts of children come from many cultures. There will be features of these stories that are unique to each culture, but children will also find particular aspects of plot or characterization that occur across cultures. Recognizable literary patterns can be found in cumulative tales, beast tales, pourquoi tales, wonder tales, and realistic tales.

### Cumulative Tales

Very young children are fascinated by such cumulative stories as "The Old Woman and Her Pig" with its "Rat! rat! gnaw rope; rope won't hang butcher; butcher won't kill ox; ox won't drink water; water won't quench fire; fire won't burn stick; stick won't beat dog; dog won't bite pig; piggy won't get over the stile; and I shan't get home tonight." (See versions by Eric Kimmel and Roseanne Litzinger.) The story itself is not as important as the increasing repetition of the details building up to a quick climax. The story of the gingerbread boy who ran away from the old woman, defiantly crying "Catch me if you can!" as in Paul Galdone's *The Gingerbread Boy*, has been told in many different versions, including Jim

*Children in a kindergarten/first-grade create their interpretations of "Little Red Riding Hood," a favorite folktale.*

Highland Park Elementary School, South-Western City Schools, Grove City, Ohio. Kristen Kerstetter, teacher.

## Creating Pourquoi Stories with Fifth Graders

A fifth-grade teacher assembled many African *pourquoi* stories and led her class in reading and discussing the patterns. Children noted that most explained animal characteristics or habits and natural phenomena. Children also discussed the illustrations and were particularly impressed with the clear colors and white-outlined shapes that Leo and Diane Dillon used for the Caldecott Medal–winning pictures in Verna Aardema's *Why Mosquitoes Buzz in People's Ears.* When the teacher asked children to produce their own "how" or "why" stories and illustrate them, here is what one child created:

### WHY FLIES EAT ROTTEN FOOD
A long time ago, in a jungle, Fly was very hot. So he flew to the river and rolled around in the mud. After that Fly was very hungry so he flew home. On the way he looked down and saw a big juicy steak lying on the ground.

Now fly was *very* hungry so he flew down and started eating it. But he was so dirty that when he landed he got mud on the steak and as he walked around eating it he got even more mud on it.

By the time Fly was done eating, the whole steak was covered with mud. Just then King Lion (the owner of the steak who had been taking a nap) walked into the clearing. "What have you done to my steak you stupid fly?" roared his majesty.

"Oh," said Fly, "I was just—." Then he looked at the steak. "Oh your majesty! I am very sorry. So very sorry," apologized Fly.

Then the King said, "As a punishment you can never eat fresh food again. You must always eat things like this steak."

Fly was so ashamed that he flew off with his head down but because he does not dare oppose King Lion he has eaten dirty and rotten food ever since.

*Allison Fraser, fifth grade*
*Susan Steinberg, teacher*
George Mason Elementary School, Alexandria, Virginia

---

Aylesworth's *The Gingerbread Man* and Ruth Sawyer's Appalachian version, *Journey Cake, Ho!* Richard Egielski has created an entirely modern setting for the traditional tale, *The Gingerbread Boy.* Construction workers, street musicians, and other urban mainstays chase the mischievous cookie through the streets of New York City instead of the countryside.

In another familiar cumulative tale, one day an acorn falls on Henny Penny (see the version in Helen Oxenbury's *Nursery Story Book).* Thinking the sky is falling down, she persuades Cocky-Locky, Ducky-Daddles, Goosey-Poosey, and Turkey-Lurkey to go along with her to tell the king. Children delight in the sound of the rhyming double names, which are repeated over and over. Young children, especially, enjoy extending and personalizing these cumulative tales through dramatic play. You will find repetitive stories in practically all folklore.

### Pourquoi Tales
Some folktales are "why," or *pourquoi,* stories that explain certain animal traits or characteristics or human customs. In "How the Animals Got Their Tails" in *Beat the Story-Drum, Pum-Pum,* Ashley Bryan tells an African tale of a time when all animals were vegetarians. Then Raluvhimba created a mistake, the flies who were flesh eaters and bloodsuckers. "I can't take back what I've done. After all, that's

life," the god said. But he did give the rest of the animals tails with which to swish away the flies.

Many Native American stories are "why" stories that explain animal features, the origin of certain natural features, or how humans and their customs came to be. Paul Goble's retelling of a Cheyenne myth in *Her Seven Brothers* explains the origins of the Big Dipper. The Cherokee *Story of the Milky Way* has been retold by Joseph Bruchac and Gayle Ross. Kristina Rodanas's *Follow the Stars* is an Ojibwa story that tells how the North Star was placed in the sky. [13]

### Beast Tales
Probably the favorite folktales of young children are beast tales in which animals act and talk like human beings. The best known of these frequently appear in newly illustrated versions. In his version of *The Three Little Pigs,* Paul Galdone portrays the wolf as a ferocious doggy creature. James Marshall's red-capped wolf looks like a thug in his red-striped polo shirt. In his *The Three Pigs,* Tony Ross shows a modern-day wolf in a gray flannel topcoat pursuing the pigs, who have moved to the country to escape an overcrowded city high-rise apartment! Other beast tales found in several versions include *The Three Billy Goats Gruff* (versions by Asbjørnsen and Moe, and Glen Rounds),

---

[13]For modern pourquoi tales, see the section on Rudyard Kipling's *Just-So Stories* in Chapter 7.

*The Little Red Hen* (Paul Galdone, Margot Zemach), and *Puss in Boots* (Galdone, Perrault).

Many African stories are "wise beast/foolish beast" tales of how one animal, such as a spider or rabbit, outwits a lion, hyena, leopard, or other foe. In Verna Aardema's *Rabbit Makes a Monkey of Lion,* Rabbit and Turtle steal Lion's honey and continually trick him into letting them go. So Lion hides in Rabbit's house in hopes of eating him for supper. But Rabbit notices the beast's footprints and calls out, "How-de-do, Little House." When the house doesn't reply, Rabbit pretends to be puzzled. "Little House, you always tell me *how-de-do.* Is something wrong today?" Of course, the confused Lion answers for the house, reveals his presence, and is tricked once again. Many beast tales that traveled to the United States with enslaved Africans were collected by Joel Chandler Harris in the late 1800s. These have been retold in two series, one by Julius Lester that begins with *The Tales of Uncle Remus: The Adventures of Brer Rabbit,* and the other by Van Dyke Parks, beginning with *Jump: The Adventures of Brer Rabbit.*

Talking animals appear in folktales of all cultures. Fish are often in English, Scandinavian, German, and South Seas stories. Tales of bears, wolves, and the firebird are found in Russian folklore. Spiders, rabbits, tortoises, crocodiles, monkeys, and lions are very much a part of African tales; rabbits, badgers, monkeys, and even bees are represented in Japanese stories. A study of just the animals in folklore would be fascinating.

## Wonder Tales

Children call wonder tales about magic and the supernatural "fairy tales." Very few tales have fairies or even a fairy godmother in them, but the name persists. These are the stories that include giants, such as Steven Kellogg's *Jack and the Beanstalk,* or fairies, as in Susan Cooper's *Tam Lin.* Wicked witches, Baba Yaga in Russian folklore, demons such as the *oni* of Japanese tales, or monsters and dragons abound in these stories. Traditionally we have thought of the fairy tale as involving romance and adventure. "Cinderella," "Snow White and the Seven Dwarfs," and "Beauty and the Beast" all have elements of both. The long quest tales—such as the Norwegian tale told in George Dasent's *East o'the Sun and West o'the Moon*—are complex wonder tales in which the hero, or heroine, triumphs against all odds to win the beautiful princess, or handsome prince, and makes a fortune. Children know that these tales will end with ". . . and they lived happily ever after." In fact, part of the appeal of the fairy tale is the secure knowledge that no matter what happens, love, kindness, and truth will prevail—and hate, wickedness, and evil will be punished. Wonder tales have always represented the glorious fulfillment of human desires.

*Rapunzel, retold and illustrated by Paul O. Zelinsky, is a wonder tale, a story that involves romance, magic, and difficult tasks.*

From *Rapunzel* by Paul O. Zelinsky, copyright © 1997 by Paul O. Zelinsky. Used by permission of Dutton Children's Books, a division of Penguin Putnam Inc.

## Realistic Tales

Surprisingly, there are a few realistic tales included in folklore. The story in Marcia Brown's *Dick Whittington and His Cat* could have happened; in fact, there is evidence that a Richard Whittington did indeed live and was mayor of London. Like the American story in Reeve Lindbergh's *Johnny Appleseed,* the tale began with a real person but has become so embroidered through various tellings that it takes its place in the folklore of its culture.

"Zlateh the Goat," the title story in a collection of Jewish tales by Isaac Bashevis Singer, is a survival story. The son of a poor peasant family is sent off to the butcher to sell Zlateh, the family goat. On the way, he and the goat are caught in a fierce snowstorm. They take refuge in a haystack, where they stay for three days. Zlateh eats the hay while the boy survives on Zlateh's milk and warmth. When the storm is over, they return home to a grateful family. No one ever again mentions selling Zlateh.

Resources for Teaching, "A Cross-Cultural Study of Folktale Types," is the first of three boxes in this chapter that *groups folktales from various countries*

# RESOURCES FOR TEACHING

## A Cross-Cultural Study of Folktale Types

### CUMULATIVE TALES

| Tale, Author | Culture |
| --- | --- |
| *The Gingerbread Man* (Aylesworth) | England |
| *Chicken Little* (Kellogg) | England |
| *One Fine Day* (Hogrogian) | Armenia |
| *Knock, Knock, Teremok!* (Arnold) | Russia |
| *Rooster Who Went to His Uncle's Wedding* (Ada) | Cuban |

### POURQUOI TALES

| Tale, Author | Culture |
| --- | --- |
| *The Great Ball Game* (Bruchac) | Native American |
| *Why Lapin's Ears Are So Long* (Doucet) | Cajun |
| "Jack and the Devil," in *The People Could Fly* (Hamilton) | African American |
| *The Cat's Purr* (Bryan) | West Indian |
| *Why the Sun and the Moon Live in the Sky* (Dayrell) | Africa |
| "How Animals Got Their Tails," in *Beat the Story-Drum* (Bryan) | Africa |
| "Tia Miseria's Pear Tree," in *The Magic Orange Tree* (Wolkstein) | Puerto Rico |

### BEAST TALES

| Tale, Author | Culture |
| --- | --- |
| *The Three Billy Goats Gruff* (Absjørnsen and Moe) | Norway |
| *The Bremen-Town Musicians* (Grimm brothers) | Germany |
| *Rabbit Makes a Monkey of Lion* (Aardema) | Africa (Tanzania) |
| *Three Little Pigs and the Big Bad Wolf* (Rounds) | England |
| *Foolish Rabbit's Big Mistake* (Martin) | India |
| "Brer Terrapin," in *Jump!* (Parks and Jones) | African American |
| *Beat the Story-Drum, Pum-Pum* (Bryan) | Africa |
| *Rockaby Crocodile* (Aruego and Dewey) | Philippines |
| *The Rabbit's Tail* (Han) | Korea |

### WONDER TALES

| Tale, Author | Culture |
| --- | --- |
| *Lily and the Wooden Bowl* (Schroeder) | Japan |
| *Ali Baba and the Forty Thieves* (McVitty) | Middle East |
| *Jack and the Beanstalk* (Kellogg) | England |
| *Beauty and the Beast* (de Beaumont) | France |
| *Snow White* (Grimm brothers) | Germany |
| *Tam Lin* (Cooper) | Scotland |
| *Vasilissa the Beautiful* (Winthrop) | Russia |
| *A Weave of Words* (San Souci) | Armenian |

### REALISTIC TALES

| Tale, Author | Culture |
| --- | --- |
| *Fire on the Mountain* (Kurtz) | Ethiopia |
| *Dick Whittington and His Cat* (Brown) | England |

# RESOURCES FOR TEACHING

## A Cross-Cultural Study of Folktale Types con't

### REALISTIC TALES con't

| Tale, Author | Culture |
| --- | --- |
| *Something from Nothing* (Gilman) | Jewish |
| *The Boy of the Three-Year Nap* (Snyder) | Japan |
| "The Case of the Uncooked Eggs," in *The Magic Orange Tree* (Wolkstein) | Haiti |
| *Two Brothers* (Waldman) | Jewish |
| *My Mother Is the Most Beautiful Woman in the World* (Reyher) | Russia |
| *The Empty Pot* (Demi) | China |
| *Zlateh the Goat* (Singer) | Jewish |

*in specific ways* to help teachers more easily plan curricula. This box groups together titles that tell similar tales. The other two boxes group tales by motif and by variants.

## Characteristics of Folktales

Because folktales have been told and retold from generation to generation within a particular culture, we may ask how they reflect the country of their origin and its oral tradition. An authentic tale from Africa will include references to the flora and fauna of Africa and to the tribespeople's food, huts, customs, foibles, and beliefs. It will sound like it is being *told*. Although folktales have many elements in common, it should not be possible to confuse a folktale from Japan with a folktale from the fjords of Norway. What then are the characteristics common to all folktales?

### Plot Structures

Of the folktales best known in children's literature, even the longer stories are usually simple and direct. A series of episodes maintains a quick flow of action. If it is a "wise beast/foolish beast" story, the characters are quickly delineated, the action shows the inevitable conflict and resolution, and the ending is usually brief. If the tale is a romance, the hero or heroine sets forth on a journey, often helps the poor on the way, frequently receives magical power, overcomes obstacles, and returns to safety. The plot that involves a weak or innocent child going forth to meet the monsters of the world is another form of the "journey-novel." In the Grimm brothers' *Hansel and Gretel* the children go out into a dark world and meet the witch, but goodness and purity triumph. Almost all folktale plots are success stories of one kind or another (unlike many myths where characters meet a sad end through their own human failings).

Repetition is a basic element in many folktale plots. Frequently three is the magic number. There are three little pigs whose three houses face the puffing of the wolf. The wolf gives three challenges to the pig in the brick house—to get turnips, to get apples, and to go to the fair. In the longer tales, each of the three tasks becomes increasingly more difficult, and the intensity of the wonders becomes progressively more marvelous. This repetition satisfies listeners or readers with its orderliness.

The repetition of responses, chants, or poems is frequently a part of the structure of a tale. "Mirror, mirror on the wall, who is fairest of them all?" And "Fee, fi, fo, fum" are repetitive verses familiar to all. Some versions of *Hansel and Gretel* end with a storyteller's coda, such as Elizabeth Crawford's: "My tale is done, and there a mouse does run. Whoever catches it can make a big fur cap of it." These serve both the storyteller and the listener as memory aids and familiar markers of the unfolding plot.

Time and place are established quickly in the folktale. Suzanne Crowder Han's *The Rabbit's Judgment*, a Korean tale, begins: "Long, long ago, when plants and animals talked, a tiger fell into a deep pit while roaming through the forest in search of food." Time is always past, and frequently described by such conventions as "Once upon a time" or "In olden times when wishing still helped." Time also passes quickly in the folktale. In Trina Schart Hyman's version of the Grimms' *Sleeping Beauty,* the woods and brambles encircled Sleeping Beauty's palace in a quarter of an hour, and "when a hundred years were gone and passed," the prince appeared at the moment the enchantment ended. The setting of the folktale is not specific, but in some faraway land, in a cottage in the woods, in a beautiful palace.

The introduction to the folktale usually presents the conflict, characters, and setting in a few sentences. In "Anansi and Nothing Go Hunting for Wives" (in Courlander and Herzog's *The Cow-Tail Switch*) the problem is established in the first two sentences:

> It came to Anansi one time, as he sat in his little hut, that he needed a wife. For most men this would have been a simple affair, but Anansi's bad name had spread throughout the country and he knew that he wouldn't be likely to have much luck finding a wife in near-by villages. (p. 95)

With little description, the storyteller goes to the heart of his story, capturing the interest of his audience.

The conclusion of the story follows the climax very quickly and includes few details. In the Grimm brothers' *The Seven Ravens,* after the small sister finds her brothers who have been bewitched as ravens, she leaves her tiny ring in the cup belonging to one of the ravens. He sees it and makes a wish:

> "Would God that our own little sister were here, for then we should be free . . . !"
>
> When the maiden, who was standing behind the door listening, heard the wish, she came out, and then all the ravens regained human forms again. And they embraced and kissed one another and went joyfully home. (unpaged)

Even this is a long ending compared with "And so they were married and lived happily ever after."

The structure of the folktale, with its quick introduction, economy of incident, and logical and brief conclusion, maintains interest through suspense and repetition. Because the storyteller has to keep the attention of the audience, each episode must contribute to the theme of the story. Written versions, then, should follow the oral tradition, adding little description and avoiding lengthy asides or admonitions.

### Characterization

Characters in folktales are shown in flat dimensions, symbolic of the completely good or entirely evil. Character development is seldom depicted. The beautiful girl is usually virtuous, humble, patient, and loving. Stepmothers are ugly, cross, and mean. The hero, usually fair-haired or curly-haired, is strong, virile, brave, kind, and sympathetic. The poor are often kind, generous, and long-suffering; the rich are imperious, hardhearted, and often conniving, if not actually dishonest. Physical characteristics may be described briefly, but readers form their own pictures as they read. In describing the

daughter of the Dragon King, the Chinese grandmother says: "Now this young woman was poorly dressed, but her face was as fair as a plum blossom in spring, and her body was as slender as a willow branch."[14]

Qualities of character or special strengths or weaknesses of the characters are revealed quickly, because this factor will be the cause of conflict or lead to resolution of the plot. The trickster character of Brer Rabbit in Van Dyke Parks's *Jump Again!* is established in a few swift phrases: "Brer Rabbit could cut more capers than a hive has bumbly-bees. Under his hat, Brer Rabbit had a mighty quick thinking apparatus" (p. 2).

Seeing folktale characters as symbols of good, evil, power, trickery, wisdom, and other traits, children begin to understand the basis of literature that distills the essences of human experience.

### Style

Folktales offer children many opportunities to hear rich qualitative language and a wide variety of language patterns. Story introductions may range from the familiar "Once upon a time" to the Persian "There was a time and there wasn't a time"; and then there is the African tale that starts: "We do not mean, we do not really mean that what we are going to say is true."

The introductions and language of the folktale should maintain the "flavor" of the country but still be understood by its present audience. Folktales should not be "written down" to children, but they might need to be simplified. Wanda Gág described her method of simplification in adapting folktales for children:

> By simplification I mean:
>   (a) freeing hybrid stories of confusing passages
>   (b) using repetition for clarity where a mature style does not include it
>   (c) employing actual dialogue to sustain or revive interest in places where the narrative is too condensed for children.
>   However, I do not mean writing in words of one or two syllables. True, the careless use of large words is confusing to children; but long, even unfamiliar words are relished and easily absorbed by them, provided they have enough color and sound value.[15]

Some folktales include proverbs of the country. For example, in Diane Wolkstein's *The Magic Orange Tree* a king says to his followers after hearing a story of a man whose second wife murdered his son: "Choose whom you want to marry, but if you choose a tree that has fruit, you must care for the fruit as much as for the tree" (p. 97). In Elizabeth Winthrop's Russian story *Vasilissa the Beautiful,* a small doll

---

[14]Frances Carpenter, *Tales of a Chinese Grandmother,* illustrated by Malthe Hasselriis (New York: Doubleday, 1949), p. 75.

[15]Wanda Gág, *Tales from Grimm* (New York: Coward-McCann, 1936), p. ix.

counsels the sorrowful Vasilissa to shut her eyes and sleep, for "The morning is wiser than the evening."

Although there is a minimum of description in the folktale, figurative language and imagery are employed by effective narrators. In *Mazel and Shlimazel,* Isaac Singer uses delightful prose to introduce the Jewish tale about the wager between the spirits of good luck and bad luck:

> In a faraway land, on a sunny spring day, the sky was as blue as the sea, and the sea was as blue as the sky, and the earth was green and in love with them both. (p. 1)

In Verna Aardema's East African story *Bimwili & the Zimwi,* a little girl, Bimwili, was playing by the ocean, and "something that looked like a daytime moon came rolling in with a wave, and it tumbled at Bimwili's feet." The daytime moon, a simile for a seashell, begins all of Bimwili's many nights of troubles.

Frequently storytellers imitate the sounds of the story. In Katherine Paterson's poetic translation from Sumiko Yagawa's traditional Japanese tale *The Crane Wife,* Yohei goes out into the winter snow on an errand. "Suddenly, *basabasa,* he heard a rustling sound. It was a crane dragging its wing, as it swooped down and landed on the path." In Verna Aardema's retelling of a West African tale in *Why Mosquitoes Buzz in People's Ears,* a python slithers into a rabbit's hole *wasawusu, wasawusu, wasawusu,* and the terrified rabbit scurries away *krik, krik, krik.* These onomatopoeic words help listeners hear the story and are wonderful additions for those who tell and read stories to children.

When the tales are written as though the storyteller is speaking directly to the reader, the oral tradition is more clearly communicated. Joyce Arkhurst uses this style effectively in *The Adventures of Spider:*

> I have already told you, and you have already seen for yourselves, that Spider was very full of mischief. He was often naughty and always greedy. But sometimes, in his little heart, he wanted very much to be good. . . . He tried hard, but his appetite almost always got in the way. In fact, that is why Spider has a bald head to this day. Would you like to hear how it got that way? (p. 21)

Surely children in the primary grades would be cheated linguistically if the only version they heard was Gerald McDermott's *Anansi the Spider:*

> One time Anansi went a long way from home. Far from home. He got lost. He fell into trouble. Back home was See Trouble. "Father is in danger!" he cried. He knew it quickly and he told those other sons. (unpaged)

This kind of simplification of text deprives children not only of the meaning but also of the language of the folktale, a key feature of literature based on an oral tradition. Without the pictures, it would be difficult to comprehend McDermott's story.

Dialect enhances a story, but it is difficult for children to read. The teacher will need to practice reading or telling a story with dialect, but it is worth the effort if it is done well. Julius Lester, in his retellings of the Uncle Remus stories collected by Joel Chandler Harris, tried to do what Harris had done: namely, to write tales "so that the reader (listener) would feel as if he or she were being called into a relationship of warmth and intimacy with another human body."[16] His contemporary storyteller communicates through asides, imagery, and allusions. For instance, in "Brer Rabbit Gets Even," in Julius Lester's *The Tales of Uncle Remus,* Brer Rabbit decides to visit with Miz Meadows and the girls:

> "Don't come asking me who Miz Meadows and her girls were. I don't know, but then again, ain't no reason I got to know. Miz Meadows and the girls were in the tale when it was handed to me, and they gon' be in it when I hand it to you. And that's the way the rain falls on that one. . . ." (p. 16)

The major criteria for style in the written folktale, then, are that it maintain the atmosphere of the country and culture from which it originated and that it sound like a tale *told* by a storyteller.

## Themes

The basic purpose of the folktale is to tell an entertaining story, yet these stories do present important themes. Some tales might be merely humorous accounts of foolish people who are so ridiculous that the listeners see their own foolish ways exaggerated in them. Many of the stories once provided an outlet for feelings against the kings and nobles who oppressed the poor. Values of the culture are expressed in folklore. Humility, kindness, patience, sympathy, hard work, and courage are invariably rewarded. These rewards reflect the goals of people—long life, a good spouse, beautiful homes and fine clothing, plenty of food, freedom from fear of the ogre or giant. In Verna Aardema's *Koi and the Kola Nuts: A Tale from Liberia,* a young man who has inherited a seemingly useless nut tree packs up some of the nuts and sets off on a journey. To his surprise, Koi encounters three people who desperately need the very nuts he carries. Koi shares them willingly and is, of course, justly rewarded. The power of love, mercy, and kindness is one of the major themes of folktales. The thematic wisdom of Mme. de Beaumont's *Beauty and the Beast* and Alan Schroeder's *Lily and the Wooden Bowl* is that we should not trust too much to appearances. The valuing of the inner qualities of kindness and a loving heart above outward appearance is dramatically presented.

[16]Julius Lester, "The Storyteller's Voice: Reflections on the Rewriting of Uncle Remus," *New Advocate* 1, no. 3 (summer 1988): 144.

*Inner beauty being valued over outward appearances is a common theme in such folktales as* Lily and the Wooden Bowl *by Alan Schroeder.*

From *Lily and the Wooden Bowl* by Alan Schroeder, illustrations by Yoriko Ito, copyright © 1994 by Alan Schroeder. Reprinted by permission of Random House Children's Books, a division of Random House, Inc.

Many folktales feature the small and powerless achieving good ends by perseverance and patience. In Gail Haley's African tale *A Story, a Story,* Anansi the spider man wins stories for his people by outsmarting a leopard, the hornets, and a fairy, and presenting them all to the Sky God. Both Marina, the good child in Eric Kimmel's *Baba Yaga,* and Sasha, the kind girl in Joanna Cole's *Bony-Legs,* have good luck when they are kind to objects and animals. Thus they are able to outwit the formidable old Russian witch, Baba Yaga.

Feminists have expressed concern that folktale themes most often favor courageous, independent boy adventurers and leave girl characters languishing at home. Though it is true that it is easier to find tales that feature plucky boys, there are folktales that portray resourceful, courageous, clever, and independent girls. In Jane Yolen's *Tam Lin,* an outspoken heroine perseveres in saving a young man bewitched by the fairies even though they change him into many fearsome animals. In the Grimm brothers' *Princess Furball,* the heroine doesn't need a fairy godmother; she wins a prince because of her own cleverness. In Harve Zemach's *Duffy and the Devil,* the heroine makes a

pact with the devil, but she finally outwits him—and manages to get out of spinning and knitting for the rest of her days. Anait in Robert D. San Souci's *A Weave of Words* is independent and goal directed. She rejects the pretty prince until he learns to read and write and learn a skill, then she is the one to save him from a three-headed ogre. In Anthony Manna's *Mr. Semolina-Semolinus: A Greek Folktale,* the heroine is so dissatisfied with her suitors that she creates the perfect mate out of almonds, sugar, and semolina. Tales that feature spirited and courageous heroines have been gathered in several collections. Robert D. San Souci's *Cut from the Same Cloth: American Women of Myth, Legend and Tall Tale,* Virginia Hamilton's *Her Stories: African American Folktales,* Ethel Johnston Phelps's *The Maid of the North,* and Rosemary Minard's *Womenfolk and Fairy Tales* are examples of collections from the world over that preserve and honor stories of strong, clever, and often brave women.

Parents, teachers, and some psychologists have expressed concern about themes of cruelty and horror in folktales. "Little Red Riding Hood," for example, has been rewritten so that the wolf eats neither the grandmother nor the heroine. Goals are not accomplished easily in folktales; they frequently require sacrifice. But usually harsh acts occur very quickly with no sense of pain and no details. In the Grimm brothers' *Seven Ravens,* no blood drips from the sister's hand when she cuts off a finger; not an "ouch" escapes her lips. Children accept these stories as they are—symbolic interpretations of life in an imaginary land of another time.

## Motifs

Folklorists analyze folktales according to motifs or patterns, numbering each tale and labeling its episodes.[17] *Motif* has been defined as the smallest part of a tale that can exist independently. Motifs can be seen in the recurring parade of characters in folktales—the younger brother, the wicked stepmother, the abused child, the clever trickster—or in supernatural beings like the fairy godmother, the evil witch, and the terrifying giant. The use of magical objects (a slipper, a doll, a ring, a tablecloth) is another pattern found in many folktales. Stories of enchantment, long sleeps, or marvelous transformations are typical motifs. Some motifs have been repeated so frequently that they have been identified as a type of folk story. Thus we have beast tales about talking animals and wonder tales about supernatural beings.

Even the story plots have recurring patterns—three tasks to be performed, three wishes that are granted, three trials to be endured. A simple tale will have several motifs; a complex one will have many. Recognizing some of the most common motifs in folklore will help a

---

[17]Stith Thompson, *Motif Index of Folk Literature* (Bloomington: Indiana University Press, 1955–1958), 6 vols.

teacher to suggest points of comparison and contrast in a cross-cultural approach to folk literature.

**Magical Powers** Magical powers are frequently given to persons or animals in folktales. A common motif in folklore is the presence of "helpful companions" who all have magical talents. In Arthur Ransome's *The Fool of the World and the Flying Ship*, the fool sails away with eight companions who can eat huge quantities, hear long distances, and drink whole lakes. Later these talents help them overcome trials the czar imposes on the fool. In the tale of *Marushka and the Month Brothers*, retold by Philemon Sturges, the brothers have magical powers to control the coming of the seasons, and each brother oversees his month. In William Hooks's *Moss Gown*, the gris-gris woman can make a girl fly as well as create a gown for her out of moss, in which she is able to attend the Carolina plantation owner's ball. Of course, the Grimms' Rumpelstiltskin can spin straw into gold. The possessors of magical powers always aid heroes and heroines in obtaining their goals.

**Transformations** The transformation of an animal into a person, or the reverse, is a part of many folktales. Mme. de Beaumont's *Beauty and the Beast* and the Grimm brothers' *The Frog Prince* are perhaps the best known of tales in which a bewitched animal is transformed by love. A crane turns into a woman and back into a crane when her spouse is disloyal in the Japanese tale recounted in Odds Bodkin's *The Crane Wife*. "Selkies" are seals that have shed their skins and assumed human form in Susan Cooper's *Selkie Girl* and Mordicai Gerstein's *The Seal Mother*. Children who feel caught between two cultures or between the world of childhood and the world of adolescence might see themselves reflected in such stories. In fact, in *The Star Fisher*, a work of historical fiction, Lawrence Yep uses a tale similar to *The Crane Wife* to represent the conflict felt by a young Chinese girl whose family moves to West Virginia from China.

**Magical Objects** Magical objects are essential aspects of many tales that also reflect other themes or motifs. Both a ring and a lamp play essential parts in the story recounted in Andrew Lang's *Aladdin and the Magical Lamp*. In Elizabeth Winthrop's *Vasilissa the Beautiful*, the heroine is able to outwit Baba Yaga's demands with the help of a magical little doll given to her by her mother. In Tomie de Paola's *Strega Nona*, the title character owns a magical cooking pot that can be started by saying "Bubble, bubble, pasta pot" to make all the pasta anyone needs. But Big Anthony, a true noodlehead, starts the pot without observing Strega Nona's method of getting it to stop: blowing three kisses. The title character of Arlene Mosel's *The*

Zomo is not big.
Zomo is not strong.
But now Zomo has wisdom.
And he is very, very fast.

*Tricksters like Zomo, in Gerald McDermott's* Zomo the Rabbit, *a West African story, are found in almost every culture.*

Text and illustration from *Zomo the Rabbit: A Trickster Tale from West Africa* copyright 1992 by Gerald McDermott, reprinted with permission of Harcourt, Inc.

*Funny Little Woman* has a magical rice paddle that she uses to good advantage both underground and above. Other magical objects that figure in folktales are purses, harps, hens that lay golden eggs, tables, sticks, and tinderboxes. A magical object often heightens a good character's courage and cleverness, while in other stories the misuse of a magical object can cause disaster for a bad character.

**Wishes** Many stories are told of wishes that are granted and then used foolishly or in anger or greed. In *The Three Wishes* Margot Zemach recounts the tale of the woodsman who was so hungry that he wished for a sausage; his wife was so angry at this wish that she wished the food would stick to his nose; then, of course, they have to use the third wish to get it off. In Gerald McDermott's *The Stonecutter*, a character wishes to have more power but ends up in a position of powerlessness. In the Grimm brothers' *The Fisherman and His Wife*, as in these other stories, greed destroys any gains a character might make.

In a Native American tale, *Gluskabe and the Four Wishes* retold by Joseph Bruchac, Gluskabe gives four men wishing pouches but warns them not to look inside until they get home. Three men cannot resist and are justly punished. The fourth man is rewarded for his patience in an unusual way.

**Trickery** Both animals and people trick their friends and neighbors in folk literature. The wolf tricks Little Red Riding Hood into believing he is her grandmother; Hansel and Gretel trick the mean old witch into crawling into the oven.

# RESOURCES FOR TEACHING

## A Cross-Cultural Study of Folktale Motifs

### MAGICAL POWERS

| Tale, Author | Culture |
| --- | --- |
| *The Fool of the World and the Flying Ship* (Ransome) | Russia |
| *Rumpelstiltskin* (Galdone) | Germany |
| *Marushka and the Month-Brothers* (Sturges) | Russia |
| *Uncegila's Seventh Spot* (Rubalcaba) | Native American |
| *The Seven Chinese Brothers* (Mahy) | China |
| *Moss Gown* (Hooks) | United States |
| *Yeh-Shen* (Louie) | China |

### TRANSFORMATIONS

| Tale, Author | Culture |
| --- | --- |
| *White Wave* (Wolkstein) | China |
| *The Girl, the Fish, and the Crown* (Heyer) | Spain |
| *Beauty and the Beast* (de Beaumont) | France |
| *The Crane Wife* (Bodkin) | Japan |
| *The Story of Jumping Mouse* (Steptoe) | Native American |
| *The Little Snowgirl* (Croll) | Russia |
| *Cinderella* (Perrault) | France |
| *Tam Lin* (Yolen) | Scotland |
| *Snow White and Rose Red* (Grimm brothers) | Germany |
| *The Princess and the Frog* (Grimm brothers) | Germany |
| *The Orphan Boy* (Mollel) | Africa (Kenya) |

### MAGICAL OBJECTS

| Tale, Author | Culture |
| --- | --- |
| *The Talking Eggs* (San Souci) | African American |
| *Vasilissa the Beautiful* (Winthrop) | Russia |
| *Aladdin* (Lang) | Middle East |
| *Two of Everything* (Hong) | China |

Almost every culture has an animal trickster in its folklore. In European folktales it is usually a wolf or a fox; in Japan it is a badger or a hare; Indonesia has Kantjil, a tiny mouse deer; Africa has three well-known tricksters—Anansi the spider, Zomo the rabbit, and Ijapa the tortoise. Coyote and Raven play this role in Native American tales.

Three realistic tales feature humans tricking others. In the familiar tale in Marcia Brown's *Stone Soup,* three poor soldiers dupe greedy peasants into contributing all of the ingredients for a pot of soup, save one—a stone, with which they generously start off the pot. In Diane Snyder's *The Boy of the Three-Year Nap,* the lazy boy tricks a rich merchant, but then is tricked into a lifetime occupation by his wise old mother. In Demi's *One Grain of Rice: A Mathematical Tale,* a village girl tricks a raja into giving up a billion grains of rice.

Magical powers, transformations, the use of magical objects, wishes, and trickery are just a few of the motifs that run through the folklore of all countries, as we have seen. Others might include the power of naming, as in Paul Galdone's *Rumpelstiltskin;* the ability to make yourself invisible, as the man did in Marianna

# RESOURCES FOR TEACHING

## A Cross-Cultural Study of Folktale Motifs con't

### MAGICAL OBJECTS con't

| Tale, Author | Culture |
| --- | --- |
| *The Rose's Smile* (Kerdian) | Middle East |
| *The Twelve Dancing Princesses* (Mayer) | France |
| *The Magic Purse* (Uchida) | Japan |
| *The Three Princes* (Kimmel) | Middle East |

### WISHES

| Tale, Author | Culture |
| --- | --- |
| *The Stonecutter* (McDermott) | Japan |
| *The Fisherman and His Wife* (Grimm brothers) | Germany |
| *The Seven Ravens* (Grimm brothers) | Germany |
| *The Three Wishes* (M. Zemach) | Germany |
| *The Fool and the Fish* (Afanasyev) | Russia |
| *Gluskabe and the Four Wishes* (Bruchac) | Native American |

### TRICKERY

| Tale, Author | Culture |
| --- | --- |
| *The Man Who Tricked a Ghost* (Yep) | China |
| *The Tale of Rabbit and Coyote* (Johnston) | Mexico |
| "Shrewd Todie and Lyzer, and Mizer," in *When Shlemiel Went to Warsaw* (Singer) | Jewish |
| *Rabbit Makes a Monkey of Lion* (Aardema) | Africa (Tanzania) |
| *Stone Soup* (Brown) | France |
| *The Boy of the Three-Year Nap* (Snyder) | Japan |
| "Firefly and the Apes," in *More Stories to Solve* (Shannon) | Philippines |
| *Clever Tom and the Leprechaun* (Shute) | Ireland |
| *Lon Po Po* (Young) | China |
| *Three Sacks of Truth* (Kimmel) | France |
| *Finn MacCoul and His Fearless Wife* (Byrd) | Ireland |

Mayer's *The Twelve Dancing Princesses;* becoming stuck to a person or object, as in the African American tale "The Wonderful Tar-Baby Story" in Van Dyke Parks's *Jump Again;* or an enchanted or lengthy sleep, as in "Urashimo Taro and the Princess of the Sea," in Yoshiko Uchida's *The Dancing Kettle;* or in the Grimms' *Snow White.* One way to understand the common elements of all folklore is to make your own lists of motifs or have the children in your classroom do so.

Resources for Teaching, "A Cross-Cultural Study of Folktale Motifs," mentions both well-known and lesser-known tales as a beginning for those wishing to pursue a study of motifs. There are many other titles that could be listed for these five motifs, and, of course, there are many more motifs around which to group folklore.

### Variants

The number of variants of a single folktale can fascinate beginning students of folklore. Each variant has basically the same story or plot as another, but it might have different characters and a different setting or it might use different motifs. For example, in Robert D. San Souci's retelling of an African American

# RESOURCES FOR TEACHING

## A Cross-Cultural Study of Folktale Variants

### CINDERELLA

| Theme | Culture |
|---|---|
| *Cinderella* (Perrault) | France |
| *Yeh Shen* (Louie) | China |
| *Sootface* (San Souci) | Native American |
| *The Egyptian Cinderella* (Climo) | Egypt |
| *The Korean Cinderella* (Climo) | Korea |
| *Moss Gown* (Hooks) | United States |
| *The Way Meat Loves Salt* (Jaffe) | Jewish |
| *Vasilissa the Beautiful* (Winthrop) | Russia |
| *Cendrillon* (San Souci) | Caribbean |
| *The Golden Sandal* (Hickox) | Middle East |
| *Princess Furball* (Grimm brothers) | Germany |

### MAGICAL GIFTS

| Theme | Culture |
|---|---|
| *The Table, the Donkey, and the Stick* (Grimm brothers) | Germany |
| "The Lad Who Went to the North Wind," in *East o'the Sun and West o'the Moon* (Asbjørnsen and Moe) | Norway |
| *The Magic Purse* (Uchida) | Japan |

### MAGICAL POTS

| Theme | Culture |
|---|---|
| *The Magic Porridge Pot* (Galdone) | Germany |
| *Strega Nona* (de Paola) | Italy |
| *The Funny Little Woman* (Mosel) | Japan |
| *Master Maid* (Shepard) | Norway |

story in *The Talking Eggs,* a poor girl is kind to an old woman and in return is given some plain eggs that become riches when tossed behind her. Later her greedy stepsister is critical and unhelpful to the old woman. She chooses to take fancy eggs instead of plain ones, but when these are tossed, out come stinging insects. In the Philippine tale retold by Jose Aruego and Ariane Dewey in *Rockaby Crocodile,* a kind boar and a greedy one end up in similar situations when one rocks a cranky baby crocodile while the other ignores it. In John Steptoe's *Mufaro's Beautiful Daughter,* the sister who takes time to stop and help people is the one who wins the prince's love. The theme of rewards for a generous and willing person and punishment for a greedy and disobedient one seems to be universal.

A comparison of the variants of the Cinderella story illustrates differences in theme and motif.

Scholars have found versions of this story in ancient Egypt, in ninth-century China, and in tenth-century Iceland. Cinderella receives her magical gifts in many different ways. In the French and most familiar version (see Charles Perrault's), a fairy godmother gives them to her; in the Grimms' version, a dove appears on the tree that grew from the tears she had shed on her mother's grave; in the Chinese version in Ai-Ling Louie's *Yeh-Shen,* magical fish bones bestow gifts on her. She attends three balls in some stories, and her treatment of the stepsisters varies from blinding them to inviting them to live at the palace. The Vietnamese version, "The Brocaded Slipper," recounted by Lynette Dyer Vuong, is made longer by the narrative of the stepsister's finally meeting her own death after "killing" her Cinderella sister, Tam, three times. In Rafe Martin's *The*

## RESOURCES FOR TEACHING

### A Cross-Cultural Study of Folktale Variants con't

#### GENEROUS PERSON/GREEDY PERSON

| Theme | Culture |
| --- | --- |
| *Mufaro's Beautiful Daughters* (Steptoe) | Africa (Zimbabwe) |
| *Baba Yaga* (Kimmel) | Russia |
| *The Talking Eggs* (San Souci) | African American |
| *Rockaby Crocodile* (Aruego and Dewey) | Philippines |
| *Toads and Diamonds* (Huck) | France |
| *Marushka and The Month-Brothers* (Sturges) | Russia |

#### HELPFUL COMPANIONS

| Theme | Culture |
| --- | --- |
| *The Loyal Cat* (Namioka) | Japan |
| *The Seven Chinese Brothers* (Mahy) | China |
| *The Fool of the World and the Flying Ship* (Ransome) | Russia |
| *The Little Humpbacked Horse* (Winthrop) | Russia |
| *Anansi the Spider* (McDermott) | West Africa |
| *Ouch!* (Babbitt) | Germany |
| *Iron John* (Kimmel) | Germany |

#### NAMING

| Theme | Culture |
| --- | --- |
| *Rumpelstiltskin* (Grimm brothers) | Germany |
| *Duffy and the Devil* (H. Zemach) | England |
| *Whuppity Stoorie* (White) | Scotland |
| *Tom Tit Tot* (Ness) | England |

*Rough-Face Girl,* an Algonquin story, the daughter of a poor man is made to sit by the fire by her cruel elder sisters. After a time her face and hands become horribly scarred and she is rejected by the villagers. For this reason she is often called "Little Burnt Face" in other versions of this tale.

Variants of the Rumpelstiltskin story (see the retelling by Paul Zelinsky) include the hero's need to know the antagonist's name in order to have his services or to be safe from his magical powers. A character in these stories is able to discover the name and trick an imp, dwarf, or fairy. Variations on this theme can be found in Harve Zemach's Cornish *Duffy and the Devil,* Evaline Ness's English *Tom Tit Tot,* and the Scottish *Whuppity Stoorie* by Carolyn White, all of which are discussed later in this chapter in the section entitled "British Folktales."

Knowledge of the variants of a tale, common motifs, and common types of folktales enable a teacher to help children see similar elements in folktales across cultures. Knowledge of the folklore of a particular country or cultural group aids in identifying the uniqueness and individuality of that group. Both approaches to a study of folklore seem essential. Resources for Teaching, "A Cross-Cultural Study of Folktale Variants" can help the teacher organize tales by variants for classroom presentation.

### Folktales of the World

 Every culture has produced folklore. A study of the folktales of West Africa, Russia, Japan, or North America can provide insights into the beliefs of these peoples, their values, their jokes, their lifestyles, their histories. At the same time, a cross-cultural study of folk literature can help children discover the universal qualities of humankind.

### British Folktales

The first folktales that most children in the United States hear are the English ones. This is because Joseph Jacobs, the folklorist who collected many of the English tales, deliberately adapted them for young children, writing them, he said, "as a good old nurse will speak when she tells Fairy Tales." His collection includes cumulative tales such as "The Old Woman and Her Pig" and "Henny Penny," and the much-loved talking-beast stories "The Little Red Hen," "The Three Bears," and "The Three Little Pigs." James Marshall's flippant tellings of several of these tales seldom stray in content from the "bones" of the originals yet are wonderfully humorous in their visual portrayals. His Goldilocks cries "Patooie" as she tastes the too-hot porridge, and his cartoonish illustrations show Baby Bear's room as a mess of football pennants, books, and toys. Marshall has also given *The Three Little Pigs* verbal and visual topspin.

In the original British tale "Henny Penny" the fox eats the accumulation of animals rushing to tell the king that the sky is falling. However, Steven Kellogg gives Foxy Loxy his comeuppance in *Chicken Little* by having a police helicopter pilot—a hippopotamus—fall onto the fox's poultry truck. The hapless fox is sentenced to jail and a diet of green bean gruel, and the foolish fowl are freed. While purists may object, these humorous treatments of well-known beast tales keep the stories alive for slightly older elementary school audiences who are familiar with the original story from having heard it in preschool, on television, or at library story hours.

An element of realism runs through some English folktales. The story of Dick Whittington and his cat has its basis in history. There was once a real Richard Whittington who was three times mayor of London, in 1396, 1406, and 1419. And what an exceptional mayor he must have been—enacting prison reforms, providing the first public lavatory and drinking fountain, and building a library and a wing on the hospital for unmarried mothers. It is no wonder that the common people made him the popular hero of one of their most cherished tales. The story "Dick and His Cat" was found in some of the very earliest chapbooks of the day. Marcia Brown's picture storybook *Dick Whittington and His Cat* portrays this realistic tale with handsome linoleum block prints appropriately printed in gold and black.

A Cornish variation on the German "Rumpelstiltskin" is presented in Harve Zemach's *Duffy and the Devil.* Illustrator Margot Zemach depicts the devil as a "squinny-eyed creature"; he dances and sings:

Tomorrow! Tomorrow! Tomorrow's the day!
I'll take her! I'll take her! I'll take her away!
Let her weep, let her cry, let her beg, let her pray—
She'll never guess my name is Tarraway! (unpaged)

However, Duffy's outwitting of the devil makes all of her husband's handspun clothes disappear! Both the language and the pen-and-wash illustrations retain the Cornish flavor of this folklore comedy. In the Scottish *Whuppity Stoorie* by Carolyn White, an evil fairy cures a poor woman's prize pig and demands her daughter Kate in return unless she can guess her name. The noble pig earns her keep by leading Kate deep into the forest where she overhears the fairy call herself "Whuppity Stoorie."

Two versions of the story told in the Scottish ballad "Tamlane" show how storytellers and illustrators give new meanings to a story. In Jane Yolen's *Tam Lin,* Jennet MacKenzie has a mind of her own: "No man would want her, even for all her beauty and her father's name. For she always spoke what she thought. And *what* she thought was never quite proper for a fine young lady." On her sixteenth birthday, she wishes to claim her inheritance, the ancient family home of Carterhaugh stolen by the fairies many years ago and left in ruins. In the garden she plucks a rose, the only thing of beauty left, and suddenly a young man appears. Claimed by the fairies over a hundred years ago, he is Tam Lin, and if she cannot save him by Hallow's Eve, he will die. The way she must save him is to pull him from his horse when the fairy procession passes, and hold him no matter what shape he assumes. Vivid and bold illustrations by Charles Mikolaycak depict Tam Lin's transformation from a serpent still partially clad in tartan to a lion. Jennet perseveres, outwits the fairies, and wins herself a husband and a home.

In Susan Cooper's retelling, Margaret meets Tam Lin in the forest in June and must save him by Midsummer's Eve. Warwick Hutton's ethereal watercolors give this version a more dreamlike appearance, and his depiction of Tam Lin's transformation is dramatically rendered over three pages.

In *The Selkie Girl,* Cooper and Hutton present another legend of Scottish or Irish origin, concerning a man who takes as his wife a selkie, who is a gray seal in the water but a woman on land. He hides her sealskin and for many years the woman lives as his wife and mother to their five children. But when the youngest child finds his mother's sealskin, she confesses that she also has a family of five children in the sea, bids farewell to her landbound family, and disappears into the sea. Mordicai Gerstein's *The Seal Mother* softens the ending by having the son accompany his mother under water. Each Midsummer's Eve thereafter, the

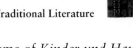

*Richard Egielski sets* The Gingerbread Boy *in modern day New York City, but its roots can be found in the German "Gingergread Man" or the British "Johnny-cake."*

From *The Gingerbread Boy* by Richard Egielski. Copyright © 1997 by Richard Egielski. A Laura Geringer book, an imprint of HarperCollins Publishers. Used by permission.

human and the selkie branches of the family meet to cavort on the rocks. Children familiar with Tam Lin or selkie stories can recognize the shape-changing or transformation motif, which is found in ancient mythology as well as modern fantasy (see Chapter 7). Cooper and Hutton have produced another tale of transformation in their Welsh story *The Silver Cow.* In this story the Scottish fairies, the Fey, turn cows into waterlilies when a farmer's greed gets the better of his judgment.

British folklore includes giants and wee folk but has developed relatively few of the complicated wonder tales that abound in French and Russian folklore. It is often more robust and humorous than some other European tale traditions. Its greatest contribution has been made to the youngest children in providing such nursery classics as "The Three Little Pigs," "Henny Penny," "The Little Red Hen," and "Johnny-cake."

### German Folktales

 Next in popularity to the English folktales are those of German origin. Jacob and Wilhelm Grimm spent more than twelve years collecting the tales they published in

1812 as the first volume of *Kinder und Hausmärchen* (Household Stories). They did not adapt their stories for children, as Joseph Jacobs did for British folktales, but were very careful to preserve (without benefit of a tape recorder) the form and content of the tales as they were told. In 1823 to 1826, these were then translated into English by Edgar Taylor.

Beautiful collections and single tales of the Grimms' stories continue to be published. Maurice Sendak visited Kassel, Germany, before illustrating his two volumes of *The Juniper Tree and Other Tales from Grimm.* In the museum there, he was fortunate to find a version illustrated by the Grimms' younger brother, Ludwig. The size of this little-known version with only six engravings served as the inspiration for Sendak's small volumes. Mindful of the fact that these tales were told to country folk, Sendak used adults as his subjects. His view of Rapunzel is from within her room looking out, rather than the cliché of Rapunzel hanging her hair out of the castle window. Sendak has pictured a pregnant Rapunzel, for the story states that she had her twin babies with her when she was at last united with her prince. This is an authentic and distinguished edition of Grimm that reflects the origin of the stories yet makes us look at them with new wonder and delight. In *The Fairy Tales of the Brothers Grimm* Neil Philip has collected twenty of the tales, some of which might not be as familiar as others. Isabelle Brent's brightly colored illustrations are lavishly edged in gold.

German folklore is enlivened by elves, dwarfs, and devils, rather than the fairies of other cultures. The Grimm brothers' *The Elves and the Shoemaker* tells of a kindly but poor shoemaker who is aided in his work by elves until he and his wife return the favor by making the elves clothes. Then, off the elves scamper, never to be seen again. Natalie Babbitt has written an amusing version of the Grimms' "The Devil with the Three Golden Hairs" in her story *Ouch!* Similar to the Russian story in Sally Scott's *The Three Wonderful Beggars,* it tells of a young man who wins the hand of the king's daughter by obtaining three hairs from the devil with the help of the devil's grandmother. Fred Marcellino creates an elaborate Renaissance setting in his sprightly illustrations.

Paul O. Zelinsky's elegant paintings for his edition of the Grimm brothers' *Rumpelstiltskin* set the tale in a medieval castle, and the gold of the spun straw shines richly from the pages. Paul Galdone's version presents a weepier daughter, a less elegant castle, and a more dwarflike little man. In comparing these versions, children would discover these subtle differences in aspects of the illustrations, as well as the demise of the little man, the verse in which he reveals his name, and the name guesses the miller's daughter offers.

Many children know a version of "Snow White" only from the cartoon story created by Walt Disney Studios. However, Nancy Ekholm Burkert's illustrations and Randall Jarrell's retelling in *Snow-White and the Seven Dwarfs* more faithfully recreate the original Grimm story. Burkert used her own 14-year-old daughter as the model for Snow White. Her drawings of dwarfs are based on weeks of medical library research studying characteristic proportions of dwarfs. And so Burkert's dwarfs are not grotesque elves, but real people who are loving and proud. The medieval cottage of the dwarfs is an authentic depiction; every architectural detail, the rich fabrics on floor and wall, the very plates and mugs on the table, were copied from museum pieces. In keeping with artistic styles of the late Middle Ages, Burkert used images symbolically: the white dog, the basket of cherries, and the lilies on the table signify virginity; the meadow rue embroidered on the girl's apron was supposed to protect the wearer against witches; a Tarot card, the red mushrooms, spiders, and other articles in the witch's workroom signify evil. In Disney's version, a "Sleeping Beauty" kiss awakes the sleeping girl. But Randall Jarrell was true to the Grimm story, in which the apple lodged in Snow White's throat is shaken free when the prince carries her off to Italy. Such a beautiful edition of this story restores its dignity, beauty, and symbolic meaning. Another edition of *Snow White* has been faithfully translated by Paul Heins and illustrated with robust, more romantic pictures by Trina Schart Hyman. In this version, the artist skillfully portrays the ravaging effects of the queen's jealous madness through the changing appearance of her face.

The villain in the few beast tales in German folklore is usually a wolf. Perhaps the best-known wolf appears in the Grimm story "Little Red Cap." In the familiar story, the heroine ignores her mother's warnings, and as a result she and her grandmother are eaten. Both escape through the intervention of a passing hunter who thinks that the wolf's loud snores couldn't be coming from a healthy grandmother. After her adventure, the little girl vows always to obey her mother's advice. Lisbeth Zwerger, in *Little Red Cap,* and Trina Schart Hyman, in *Little Red Riding Hood,* have portrayed this story with striking but differing illustrations. Hyman presents a younger, more innocent child distracted by the wolf. Small vignettes depicting household details, wildflowers, and insects are enclosed in changing border frames, giving the whole book a delightfully old-fashioned look. Beautiful, spare watercolors by Zwerger portray a contrasting older Red Cap, and only essential props are set against a soft and muted backdrop. James Marshall has illustrated his version of this tale in his characteristically humorous way.

Some of the Grimm tales can be grim, dark, and forbidding. Small children can be frightened by *Hansel and Gretel,* the somber tale of a brother and sister abandoned in the woods by their parents and nearly eaten by a horrible witch. However, justice does prevail in this wonder tale. The witch dies in the same way as she had intended to kill the children; the stepmother also dies; and the children, laden with wealth, are reunited with their joyful father. Several very different illustrated versions present this tale to children. Paul Zelinsky's oil paintings somberly recreate the forest settings and the interior of the poor woodcutter's house, and we can almost smell the witch's tasty house. Lisbeth Zwerger's illustrations portray characters against a brown wash that gives the action a dreamlike, long-ago appearance. Anthony Browne, in his startling contemporary illustrations, makes a visual connection between the stepmother and the witch by placing a mole on each woman's cheek. Browne's illustrations are full of reflected images, symbols of cages and flight, and the triangular shape that resembles a witch's hat. While adults might feel that Browne's interpretation brings the story too close to children today, this violation of the folktale convention of distancing in "a long time ago" might be treated by older children simply as one more interesting variation.

Other Grimm stories featuring witches have been illustrated and retold. In *Rapunzel,* a witch, though never unkind to Rapunzel, nevertheless keeps her locked in a tower until a prince climbs her braids. When the witch discovers the prince, she throws him from the tower and he is blinded by the sharp thorns below. A year later, he and Rapunzel are reunited and her tears restore his sight. Paul O. Zelinsky received the Caldecott Medal for his painstakingly rendered illustrations for *Rapunzel.* As he explains in a detailed afterword, he chose to set the story in Renaissance Italy in keeping with Italian elements of the story that he included. Trina Schart Hyman's dark and mysterious illustrations for this story have a Slavic appearance and owe a debt to Russian illustrator Ivan Biliban's use of small rectangular vignettes and borders. In Alix Berenzy's version, the illustrations and page design recall the miniatures and decorations in illuminated manuscripts.

Another Grimm tale with a moral is *The Frog Prince,* which stresses the importance of keeping a promise, even if it is made by a princess to a frog. So the king makes his daughter honor her promise to welcome a frog that has retrieved her golden ball from a deep, dark pond. After the princess lets the frog sit by her side, eat from her plate, and sleep in her bed for three nights, the frog becomes a prince and the two are married. Binette Schroeder has created an eerie surrealistic version that includes the prince's faithful servant, Henry, who has bound iron rings around his heart in grief at his master's bewitchment.

Wicked enchantments and magical transformations are typical of German folktales. In the Grimms' *The Seven Ravens,* seven boys are changed into ravens by their father's curse when they break a jug of water that was to be used to christen their new baby sister. When the sister is old enough to realize what has happened, she sets off for the glass mountain to find them. Coming at last to a locked door, she must cut off her finger in order to pass through. There she is able to release her brothers.

Charlotte Huck's "Cinderella" variation on the Grimm story of "Many Furs" is titled *Princess Furball.* A cruel king betroths his motherless daughter to an ogre in exchange for fifty wagonloads of silver. But the princess hopes to foil his plan by first demanding that her father give her three dresses, one as golden as the sun, another as silvery as the moon, and the last as glittering as the stars, as well as a coat made of a thousand pieces of fur, one from every animal in the kingdom. When the king actually fulfills these demands, the princess runs away with her dresses and three tiny treasures that had belonged to her mother. Disguised in her fur coat, she is discovered and taken to another king's castle, where she becomes a scullery maid known as Furball. When the king gives a ball, she appears in one of her dresses and the following day leaves a token in the king's soup. At the third ball, the king slips a ring on Furball's finger and is later able to identify the scullery maid as his own true love, saying, "You are as clever as you are lovely." Practical, independent, and resourceful, Furball has capably managed to create a happy future. Anita Lobel uses opening portraits to personify Furball's dead mother, while a portrait of the ogre looks like the father-king. A series of imprisoning enclosures such as long hallways, deep forests, and windowless kitchens symbolically give way to more open scenes in lighter and brighter colors, with more windows, and finally to the fresh air of an outdoor wedding. In contrast to many other Cinderella characters, Princess Furball is a strong, responsible female who actively brings about her own happy end.

Although there is little mercy for the wicked in these German tales, there is much joy for the righteous. The plots are exciting, fast-moving, and a little frightening. Evil stepmothers, wicked witches, and an occasional mean dwarf hold princes and princesses in magical enchantments that can be broken only by kindness and love. Such were the dreams and wishes of the common folk of Germany when the Grimm brothers recorded their tales.

## Scandinavian Folktales

 Most of the Scandinavian folktales are from the single Norwegian collection titled *East o'the Sun and West o'the Moon.* These stories were gathered in the early 1840s by Peter Christian Asbjørnsen and Jorgen Moe. The collection ranks in popularity with the Grimms' fairy tales for much the same reason; they capture the vigorous language of the storyteller. Ten years after their publication in Norway, they were ably translated by an Englishman, George Dasent, and made available to the English-speaking world.

Perhaps the best known of all of these stories is *The Three Billy Goats Gruff* (see the versions by Asbjørnsen and Moe and by Glen Rounds). These billy goats "trip-trapped" across the troll's bridge to eat the green grass on the other side in a tale that is a perfect example of folktale structure: the use of three billy goats, the increasing size of each one, and the anticipated downfall of the mean old troll. Fast action and an economy of words lead directly to the storyteller's conventional ending: "Snip, snap, snout/This tale's told out." Marcia Brown's matchless illustrations for the version by Asbjørnsen and Moe is faithful to the Norwegian origin of this tale in both the setting of her lively illustrations and in the text. Paul Galdone's picture-book version, showing large close-up illustrations of the goats and the troll, will appeal particularly to the younger child. Norse writer Lise Lunge-Larsen has included the story with nine other troll tales in *The Troll with No Heart in His Body,* a wonderful collection illustrated with woodcuts by Betsy Bowen.

Another story that delights young children is Nancy Polette's *The Little Old Woman and the Hungry Cat.* When his owner leaves him alone, the cat eats the sixteen cupcakes she left cooling and proceeds down the road eating everyone and everything in his path. When he meets his owner, he gobbles her up as well. But her sewing scissors save the day when she is able to cut her way out, and she and the rest of the cat's victims escape. Now free, all have a party—except for the hungry cat, who has to stitch himself up.

Eric Kimmel has placed one of Asbjørnsen tales in a pioneer setting in *Easy Work.* A husband thinks his wife has it pretty easy staying at home each day. When he chides her, she offers to exchange jobs with him. At first he thinks it is "easy work" and devises some Rube Goldberg inventions to help him mind the baby, churn the butter, bake the biscuits, and watch the cow. When his overconfident macho attitude ends in disaster, he finally admits how hard his wife has to work. Andrew Glass's illustrations bring glorious life to this funny story. In an end note, Kimmel explains that he retold the Asbjørnsen story in honor of Oregon women's rights crusader Abigail Scott Duniway.

George Dasent's *East o'the Sun and West o'the Moon* is a complex tale in which a poor man gives his youngest daughter to a white bear, who promises to make the family rich. The white bear comes to her every night and throws off his beast shape, but he leaves before dawn so she never sees him. When her mother tells her to light a candle and look into his face, she sees a handsome prince, but three drops of hot tallow awaken him. He then tells her of his wicked enchantment in which for one year he must be a bear by day. Now that she has seen him, he must return to the castle that lies east of the sun and west of the moon and marry the princess with a long nose. So the girl seeks the castle, finally arriving there on the back of the North Wind. Before the prince will marry, he sets one condition: he will only marry the one who can wash out the tallow spots on his shirt. Neither his long-nose troll bride-to-be nor an old troll hag can do it, but the girl who has posed as a beggar can wash it white as the snow. The wicked trolls burst, and the prince and princess marry and leave the castle that lies east of the sun and west of the moon. Gillian Barlow's framed paintings in the style of folk art glow with warm colors. Children who know the Greek myth of Cupid and Psyche (see the retelling by M. Charlotte Craft) will recognize similarities in the girl's nighttime curiosity and the trouble it begets. Kathleen and Michael Hague's retelling in their *East of the Sun and West of the Moon* follows the original structure of the story faithfully.

In many of the Norwegian tales, the hero is aided in the accomplishment of such seemingly impossible tasks by animals or people that he has been kind to. The hero of Eric Kimmel's *Boots and His Brothers* sets out with his two brothers, Peter and Paul, to seek his fortune. They meet an old woman along the way who tells them that their fortune can be gained from an old king who needs an oak tree chopped down and a well dug. The two older boys push the old woman out of the way and hurry off. But because Boots stops and takes time to talk to her, she gives him three magical objects and some good advice. These help him chop down the enchanted oak tree, dig a well in iron rocks, and fill it with cool clear water from a hundred leagues away. The king is so delighted with Boots, he gives him his weight in gold and half his kingdom. For the greedy brothers, the king has a job as dogkeepers.

Scandinavian tales often seem to reflect the harsh elements of the northern climate. Animal helpmates assist heroes in overcoming giants or wicked trolls. Frequently heroes are human beings who are held by an evil spell. The Scandinavian tales, characterized by many trolls, magical objects, and enchantments, often are also humorous, exciting, and fast-moving. The youngest son performs impossible tasks with ease and a kind of practical resourcefulness.

## French Folktales

French folktales were the earliest to be recorded, and they are also the most sophisticated and adult. This is probably because these tales were the rage among the court society of Louis XIV. In 1697, Charles Perrault, a distinguished member of the French Academy, published a little volume of fairy tales. The title page bore no name, and there has been some debate as to whether they were the product of Charles Perrault or his son, Pierre. While the stories were probably very close to the ones told to Pierre by his governess, they have the consciously elegant style of the "literary tale" rather than the "told tale" of the Grimms.

The fairy godmother in *Cinderella* is Perrault's invention, as are the pumpkin coach, the six horses of dappled mouse gray, and the glass slipper. In this French version, Cinderella is kind and forgiving of her two stepsisters, inviting them to live at the palace with her. Marcia Brown was faithful to both the French setting and the original text in her Caldecott Medal–winning illustrations for Perrault's *Cinderella*. Ethereal illustrations in delicate blues and pinks portray the splendid palace scenes. Cinderella's stepsisters are haughty and homely, but hardly cruel. Younger children will enjoy James Marshall's colorful and humorous illustrations in a version retold by Barbara Karlin.

The sister story to "Cinderella" is the well-known "Sleeping Beauty," and Perrault's version closely parallels the one collected by the Grimms. It is interesting to compare the wishes that the fairies gave to the newborn baby. In the German tale they endow Briar Rose with virtue, beauty, riches, and "everything in the world she could wish for"; in the French version they bestow on her beauty, an angelic disposition, and the abilities to dance, sing, and play music. In both versions the jealous uninvited fairy predicts that the child will prick her finger on a spindle and die. This wish is softened by the last fairy, who changes it to the long sleep of a hundred years to be broken by the kiss of a prince.

Margaret Early, an Australian, illustrated Perrault's *The Sleeping Beauty* with beautiful paintings filled with details of French costume design and architecture. The elaborate borders that frame the text and illustrations recall the interlacing of a French Book of Hours. Trina Schart Hyman has painted robust romantic scenes for her interpretation of the Grimms' *Sleeping Beauty*. Her many close-up pictures of the characters place the reader in the midst of the scenes rather than providing the distancing and mystical mood of the others.

On the cover of the version of Perrault's *Puss in Boots* illustrated by Fred Marcellino, a very French Puss looks out past the reader as if plotting his next moves. While he is the only inheritance of the youngest son of a poor miller, he proves his worth by fooling the king into believing the miller's son is the imaginary Marquis of Carabas. He then tricks an ogre out of his gold and proclaims the ogre's castle as his master's. The king is delighted to give his daughter in marriage to the "Marquis," and Puss retires to a life of luxury. Marcellino's illustrations and large type crowd the page as if the story would burst the confines of the book. Children familiar with this version and with Alain Vasës's elegant illustrations could compare it with Paul Galdone's swashbuckler cat.

The French telling of "The Twelve Dancing Princesses" is more ornate than the German version. In this story a poor soldier discovers an underground kingdom where twelve girls dance their shoes to pieces nightly. Marianna Mayer's cumbersome retelling of the story introduces new elements as well, but Kinuko Y. Craft's luminous paintings are well suited to the spirit of the original tale.

The best-known French wonder tale, other than those by Perrault, is "Beauty and the Beast," adapted from a long story written in 1757 by Madame de Beaumont. This story of love based on essence rather than appearance has been variously illustrated. Jan Brett's economical text and rich illustrations are framed in jeweled borders, and the elegant tapestries in the background reveal the boar-beast's true identity.

Marcia Brown's *Stone Soup* has long been staple primary-grade fare. As the French villagers clad in wooden shoes and smocks hurry their contributions to the huge soup kettle, the three soldiers maintain a subtly earnest but amused look. In John Stewig's version, Grethel is a solo hungry traveler. When villagers turn down their mouths "like unlucky horseshoes" at her request for food, the girl goes to work with her magic stone and soon has created an evening, and a soup, to remember. Margot Tomes's soft flat tones give the Stewig story a homespun look.

Eric Kimmel's *Three Sacks of Truth* also revolves around trickery and contains many other traditional folktale motifs as well. In Kimmel's retelling, a greedy king declares that he will marry his daughter to the suitor who brings him the perfect peach. When Petit Jean, the youngest of three brothers, does just that, the king finds additional tasks for him to perform. With the aid of a magical fife, given to him by an old woman he helped, Jean outwits the king and then performs one last difficult task. When the king asks him to show him three sacks of truth, Jean reveals that he knows a highly embarrassing truth—the king has kissed his donkey's muzzle. To save face, the king insists that Jean and the princess marry immediately. In *Three Perfect Peaches*, by Cynthia De Felice and Mary DeMarsh, the tale is retold from the

*Petit Jean's kindness to an old woman is rewarded in Eric Kimmel's* Three Sacks of Truth: A Story From France.
Illustration copyright © 1993 by Robert Rayevsky. Reprinted from *Three Sacks of Truth* by Eric A. Kimmel by permission of Holiday House.

same source, but in this version Jean receives a magical whistle instead of a fife and must fill a glass bucket to overflowing with truth. In addition, the king's secret is a bit more ribald—he has kissed the other end of his donkey. Both versions are sure to delight children.

The folktales of France are usually not the tales of the poor but those of the rich. Most have all the trappings of the traditional fairy tale, including fairy godmothers, stepsisters, and handsome princes. Tales of romance and sophisticated intrigue, they must surely have been the "soap operas" of their day.

### Russian Folktales

 Folktales from Russia feature universal patterns of tasks and trials, tricks, and transformations. Russian folktales are often longer and more complicated than those of other countries and frequently involve several sets of tasks. Elizabeth Winthrop's retelling of the story *The Little Humpbacked Horse* is quite complex and begins with a tale of how a modest hero, Ivan, tamed a mare with a golden mane. In return for her freedom, she gives him three horses—two fit as gifts for the tsar, and the other a little humpbacked horse. These gifts take Ivan to the tsar, where he becomes stablemaster, but it is the little humpbacked horse who becomes Ivan's helpful companion and helps him through many trials to his final triumph.

Russian folklore is replete with other stories of poor but lucky men. With the help of an irresistible magic sack, an old soldier outwits some devils in Michael McCurdy's *The Devils Who Learned to Be Good,* and another soldier saves a helpless tsar in Uri Shulevitz's *Soldier and Tsar in the Forest.* In Arthur Ransome's *The Fool of the World and the Flying Ship,* a youngest son goes forth, accompanied by eight companions, each of whom has a magical power that helps in outwitting the treacherous tsar; the fool wins the princess and riches for them both in this Caldecott Medal book. A poor archer in Diane Wolkstein's *Oom Razoom, or Go I Know Not Where, Bring Back I Know Not What* keeps his beautiful wife from the clutches of the king while gaining riches and a magical servant.

The witch Baba Yaga is a complex character who figures in many Russian tales, including Eric Kimmel's *I Know Not What, I Know Not Where* and Diane Wolkstein's *Oom Razoom.*[18] Elizabeth Winthrop's *Vasilissa the Beautiful* is often called "the Russian Cinderella." In this tale, Vasilissa is sent by her stepmother to Baba Yaga to get a light for the cottage with the hope that the witch will eat her up. But Vasilissa carries with her a doll that her mother gave her before she died. When Baba Yaga gives Vasilissa impossible tasks to perform, the unfortunate girl is saved by the doll's magic and its advice: to go to sleep, for "the morning is wiser than the evening." The renowned Russian illustrator Alexander Koshkin richly paints the story in a seventeenth-century setting. The arrival of Baga Yaga in her mortar and pestle is boldly lit by the glowing eyes of the picketed skulls surrounding her chicken-footed house. K. Y. Craft's paintings for Marianna Mayer's *Baba Yaga and Vasilisa the Brave* are reminiscent of the miniatures found on Russian lacquer boxes.

Other stories about Baba Yaga present the fearsome witch in less frightening terms. Joanna Cole's *Bony-Legs* tells how Sasha meets Baba Yaga under a different name but escapes being eaten by the witch because she is kind to a cat, a dog, and a squeaky gate. In *Baba Yaga,* Eric Kimmel adds a "generous person/greedy person" motif in this story of Marina, a child with a horn growing out of her forehead, who is sent by her stepmother to Baba Yaga to get a needle. Her kindness to a frog earns her good advice in

*Gennady Spirin's elegant paintings recreate the grandeur of old Russia in J. Patrick Lewis's* The Frog Princess.
From *The Frog Princess* by J. Patrick Lewis, illustrated by Gennady Spirin, copyright © 1994 by Gennady Spirin, illustrations. Used by permission of Dial Books for Young Readers, a division of Penguin Putnam Inc.

tricking the witch and good luck in having her horn removed. But when the stepsister Marusia rudely ignores the frog on her way to visit Baba Yaga so as to become "just like my stepsister," she is sent away with a horn on her forehead. Humorous illustrations in both stories remove some of the power of Baba Yaga's evil while providing an invitation to younger children to meet a well-known witch.

The same characters reappear in different guises in many Russian tales, and one story often braids into another. In J. Patrick Lewis's *The Frog Princess,* Prince Ivan marries a frog who sheds her skin and turns into the beautiful Princess Vasilisa at night. Ivan burns her frog skin, thinking this will keep her in the guise of a woman, only to find that he has interfered with the working out of a curse. Vasilisa is then imprisoned by Koschey the Invincible, another stock Russian character. It is only with the help of Baba Yaga that Ivan tricks the terrible demon and breaks the curse on Vasilisa. Gennady Spirin's stunningly beautiful illustrations lend a wonderful sense of the old Imperial Russia to this complex tale.

Not all Russian folktales are dark and complex. The theme of cooperation is addressed in Aleksei

---

[18]See the vivid description of one classroom's discovery of patterns when a teacher presented students with versions of "Baba Yaga" tales, in Joy F. Moss's *Focus on Literature: A Context for Literacy Learning* (Katonah, N.Y.: Richard C. Owen, 1990), pp. 49–62.

Tolstoy's *The Gigantic Turnip*. An old man plants a turnip seed, which grows so big that he needs to call his wife, to help by pulling him as he pulls. Eventually they are able to pull up the turnip with the help of their daughter, a dog, a cat, and finally a mouse. This humorous story would make a good primary drama.

The theme of beauty being in the eye of the beholder is presented in another story. A child lost in the wheatfields, separated from her mother, sobs and proclaims her mother's beauty in Becky Reyher's *My Mother Is the Most Beautiful Woman in the World*. After the townsfolk assemble all of the local beauties for Varya's inspection, a large toothless woman pushes through the crowd and mother and child are reunited.

Jan Brett's *The Mitten* is a Ukrainian tale in which animals small and large accumulate in Nicki's dropped mitten. Jan Brett divides the pages with a birchbark window through which the increasingly stuffed mitten can be seen. A mitten-shaped panel on the left depicts Nicki's busy day; on the right, the next animal who will try to squeeze into the mitten is shown. Alvin Tresselt's version features different animals and reads aloud as if it were a reminiscence. Both Yaroslava, the illustrator of this version, and Jan Brett have included traditional Ukrainian details, costumes, and patterns.

Carolyn Croll carefully researched Russian architecture, furnishings, toys, and clothing before illustrating a story set at Christmas, *The Little Snowgirl*. An old couple who wish for a child are delighted when the little girl the husband has made from snow comes to life. Caterina loves the snowgirl but cannot bear to let her stay outside on Christmas Eve. In the morning, all the two find is a small puddle by the fireplace, but a soft laugh reveals that the little snowgirl has been granted one wish by Baboushka, who gives good children what they want most on that special night. Reading aloud Charles Mikolaycak's *Baboushka*, about this woman who is destined to wander the world forever bestowing gifts on children, would forge a compelling link in the chain of Russian folklore.

In Philemon Sturges's *Marushka and the Month Brothers*, a girl is given an impossible task by her stepmother: to go out in the winter snow and not return until she has gathered violets. However, she luckily comes upon the twelve months of the year gathered about a fire in the forest. January and February agree to give the youngest month-brother, March, one hour to create a forest floor dappled with violets, and the girl is able to complete her task. When the greedy stepmother demands strawberries and then apples, brothers June and September oblige Marushka. However, the greedy stepmother next sends her own spoiled

daughter into the snow to demand more apples. The rude girl accosts the men and is frozen in snow by old January. The greedy mother also perishes while searching for her daughter. The "generous person/greedy person" motif accompanies this personification and explanation of the changing seasons.

In Mirra Ginsburg's *Clay Boy*, an old childless couple make themselves a boy out of clay. But in typical Russian style the clay boy comes alive and devours the population until he is stopped by a wily goat. Happily, his victims emerge unscathed when he is smashed to bits. This tale will remind children of Scandinavian versions such as Nancy Polette's *The Little Old Woman and the Hungry Cat*.

A tale with a musical theme has been retold by Aaron Shepard in *The Sea King's Daughter*. Sadko, a poor musician from Novgorod chances to play his gusli while sitting on the banks of the River Volkhov. The King of the Sea is so impressed by his music that he gives him a golden fish and invites Sadko to play in his undersea palace. When Sadko arrives, he finds an amazing kingdom and, as promised, he plays for the Sea King's banquet. Eventually the King offers him one of his daughters in marriage, but Sadko is homesick for Novgorod and wishes to return. When the Sea Queen warns him that he'll never go home if he kisses his bride, he restrains himself. The next morning he finds himself back home. Gennady Spirin's exquisite paintings bring the Russian settings to life and lend sumptuous mystery to the undersea kingdom. Celia Barker Lottridge has retold the same story with a different focus in *Music for the Tsar of the Sea*. In this version there is no river Volkov when the story begins. Sadko, the poor musician, charms the Sea King and journeys to his kingdom to play for the feast. When the king offers him his choice of wife, Sadko marries the King's daughter Volkova. Volkova realizes, however, that Sadko belongs in the bright world, not under the sea. Sadko falls asleep, and when he awakes, he is back at home with a beautiful river flowing beside him. Volkova has chosen this way to remain close to him, and thus the river Volkov was created. Harvey Chan's richly glowing pastel paintings add a warm intensity to this more emotionally satisfying version of the story.

## Jewish Folktales

 Jewish tales have a poignancy, wit, and ironic humor unmatched in any other folklore. Many of them have been preserved by the masterful writing of Isaac Bashevis Singer, who has retained the flavor of both the oral tradition and the Yiddish origin. Singer's warm, humorous stories in *Zlateh the Goat* and *When Shlemiel Went to Warsaw* are based on tradition and his own childhood memories. The amiable fools of Chelm (that fabled village where only fools live), lazy shlemiels, and shrewd poor peasants who outwit rich misers are familiar characters in Singer's tales. In Chelm the wise elders are the most foolish of all, and their "solutions" to people's problems make for some hilarious stories. One night they plan to gather the pearls and diamonds of the sparkling snow so the jewels can be sold for money. Worried about how they can prevent the villagers from trampling the snow, they decide to send a messenger to each house to tell the people to stay inside. But the "wise elders" realize the messenger's feet will spoil the snow, so they have him carried on a table supported by four men so that he will not make any footprints as he goes from house to house! David Adler has readers celebrate *Chanukah in Chelm* with silly Mendel, the caretaker of Chelm's synagogue. Francine Prose offers stories about the origins and endings of Chelm in *The Angel's Mistake.*

In *It Could Always Be Worse,* Margot Zemach tells the familiar tale of the poor farmer whose house is so crowded that he seeks the rabbi's advice. Following the rabbi's wise counsel, the farmer brings one animal after another into the house, until the noise and confusion become unbearable. The rabbi then advises their removal, and the house appears to be very large and peaceful. Zemach has created a humorous version of this tale with large robust pictures that seem to swarm with squalling children, rambunctious animals, and horrified adults.

Phoebe Gilman's *Something from Nothing* tells of a boy whose grandfather makes him a precious blanket. As Joseph grows older the blanket is made into smaller and smaller pieces of clothing, first a jacket, then a vest, a handkerchief, and finally a button. When he loses the button, the boy is told, "You can't make something from nothing." But Joseph does—he writes a story about his blanket. Gilman's illustrations set the story in the villages of the old country. Susan Gaber's pictures for Steve Sanfield's *Bit by Bit,* another version, have a more modern setting, but they still capture the flavor of Jewish culture and the lighthearted yet poignant tone of the Jewish folktale style. Simms Taback's Caldecott Medal-winning *Joseph Had a Little Overcoat* is based on a musical version of the story and aimed at an audience of younger children.

Francine Prose's *You Never Know* is also a quiet story with a subtle message. The townspeople make fun of Schmuel the shoemaker because he often gives away shoes for free. When his prayers for the town's safety are answered, however, they realize Schmuel is one of the Lamed-vavniks, a man so righteous that he has God's ear. Schmuel leaves town when he is discovered, but the townspeople are much kinder to the new shoemaker because "You never know."

Isaac Singer retells a Hebrew legend in *Elijah the Slave,* which is magnificently illustrated by Antonio Frasconi. In this story Elijah, a messenger from God, sells himself as a slave in order to help a poor, faithful scribe. The pictures appear to be woodcut prints cut out and pasted on radiant backgrounds. The effect is breathtaking and reminiscent of medieval art.

*The Diamond Tree,* by Howard Schwartz and Barbara Rush, is a collection of fifteen Jewish tales from around the world. Here readers meet the giant Og, the fools of Chusham, King Solomon, and even a Jewish Thumbelina, Katanya. Uri Shulevitz illustrated most of these tales with brilliant paintings. *A Coat for the Moon and Other Jewish Tales* illustrated by Micheal Iofin is another collection by the same pair.

### Folktales from the Middle East and India

Folktales from Middle Eastern countries and from India would take several books, for these areas are the birthplace of many of our Western stories. Unfortunately, these tales are not as well known in the United States as they deserve to be. Rather than describe many unfamiliar stories available only in out-of-print collections, this section discusses only available tales or books that might serve as an introduction. Nonny Hogrogian's *One Fine Day* is an Armenian cumulative story that begins when an old woman catches a fox licking up her pail of milk and cuts off his tail. She agrees to sew it back on only when he replaces the milk, which proves to be a difficult task. The simplicity of Hogrogian's drawings is perfect for the rustic humor and setting of this circular tale. In Robert San Souci's lovely Armenian tale *A Weave of Words,* a weaver's daughter refuses the hand of a young prince because he can neither read nor write nor earn a living with his hands. He learns for her sake and weaves her a beautiful carpet. They are married and live happily for many years as king and queen. When the king is captured by a three-headed monster, the queen's skills of reading, writing, and weaving enable her to rescue her husband. Raul Colon's glowing, finely textured paintings resemble the lovely patterns and colors of the very rugs that form the basis of the story. David Kherdian and Nonny Hogrogian have retold a version of this story in *The Golden Bracelet.* Both versions offer a strong heroine who knows her own mind and sets her own course.

Scheherazade's Arabian Nights tales have provided stories for generations since they were first published in 1712. Sir Richard Burton's translation made them available to English speakers and has been used as the basis for such collections such as Neil Philip's lavishly illustrated *The Arabian Nights.* In David Kherdian's *The Rose's Smile,* Farizad sets out to find three treasures and right a terrible wrong. Deborah Nourse Lattimore selected three of the stories to retell in *Arabian*

*Aladdin finds happiness with the royal princess in Deborah Nourse Lattimore's* Arabian Nights: Three Tales.
Illustration copyright © 1995 by Deborah Nourse Lattimore. Used by permission of HarperCollins Publishers, New York, NY.

*Nights:* the well-known "Aladdin," "The Queen of Serpents," and "The Lost City of Brass." In this last tale, Scheherazade describes how three men—a storyteller, a wise man, and a ruler—travel to find the lost city of Ubar in order to find the ancient brass bottles in which King Solomon imprisoned all the evil Jinn of the earth. Despite many terrible impediments along the way, the three are righteous men, praising Allah, doing good deeds, and thinking good thoughts. They reach the lost city and finally retrieve one of Solomon's bottles. In an author's note Lattimore tells that the remains of this ancient city, which was long thought to be mythical, have recently been unearthed. The city had disappeared into a sinkhole sometime between A.D. 200 and A.D. 400, and it now seems that Scheherazade's story was rooted in fact.

Andrew Lang retold Burton's version in *Aladdin*, and Errol Le Cain depicted it in pictures that resemble Persian miniature paintings. Details, ornate borders, and patterned surfaces lend an authenticity to the story. Eric Kimmel's *The Tale of Aladdin and the Wonderful Lamp* is a more inclusive story whose text captures some of the flavor of the told tale. Ju-Hong Chen's warmly colored, impressionistic paintings evoke the textured surfaces of desert landscapes and ancient cities of the story's origin.

John Yeoman has retold *The Seven Voyages of Sinbad* in a volume illustrated by Quentin Blake. Blake's sense of humor adds the right touch to these light-hearted adventures about a well-known hero. Sinbad is really a merchant, not a sailor, and Yeoman suggests that the tales arose out of yarns spun by real travelers. Sinbad's adventures recall the exaggerated antics of American tall-tale heroes.

Ehud Ben-Ezer has told a quieter tale in *Hosni The Dreamer*. Here a gentle shepherd, who loves to listen to the old stories of his elders, dreams one night of visiting a marvelous city. He soon travels to just such a city when he is among those chosen to take the sheikh's herd to market. When Hosni spends his earnings on a verse instead of on something substantial, he is chided by his fellow shepherds. However, the verse turns out to be a warning, and Hosni is the only one who heeds it and survives, winning a lovely princess in the process. The golden illustrations by Uri Shulevitz capture the desert setting and convey a subtle warmth to the story.

Readers will recognize recurring folktale motifs in several other tales from the Middle East. *Rimonah of the Flashing Sword*, a retelling by Eric Kimmel, has its origins in North Africa but contains many elements of "Snow White." When Rimonah's mother dies, her father is tricked into marriage by an evil sorceress. Instead of a magic mirror to answer her questions, however, Rimonah's wicked stepmother has a magic bowl. When her stepmother orders a huntsman to take her into the desert and kill her, Rimonah escapes and is taken in by a tribe of Bedouins. Later she lives with forty thieves. In this version Rimonah is not at all passive. When her prince awakens her from her enchanted sleep, she takes charge and leads her friends in battle against the wicked sorceress.

In Kimmel's *The Three Princes*, three cousins hope to win the hand of a wise and beautiful princess. Realizing that she loves Moshen, the youngest and poorest of the three, the princess sets the cousins the difficult task of finding the greatest wonder in the world. After a year's journey the three meet and compare their treasures. Prince Fahad has found a crystal ball, Prince Muhammed has obtained a magic carpet, and Prince Moshen has been given an orange. When the crystal ball tells them that the princess is dying, they climb aboard the magic carpet to return to the palace. Moshen feeds his orange to the princess and saves her life, but the princess's councilors cannot decide whose gift was the most wondrous. The princess declares that Fahad and Muhammed both still have their treasures but since Moshe gave up everything for her, he is the one she will marry. Leonard Everett Fisher's boldly colored and textured paintings add a sense of visual magic to this tender story.

Other rich sources of stories are the Hodja stories, known throughout the Mediterranean countries, Turkey, the Balkans, and Greece. Nasredden Hodja was thought to have lived several hundred years ago in Turkey, where he served as a religious teacher or judge when the occasion demanded. The wisdom of the Hodja is seen in the way he settles disputes. One day he watches a man cut wood while his companion rests nearby but groans helpfully each time the man swings his axe (see Barbara Walker's *Watermelons, Walnuts, and the Wisdom of Allah*). When the woodcutter finally sells his wood at the bazaar, the companion demands half the pay. The Hodja listens to both sides, takes the coins, and drops them one by one on a stone. He awards the sound to the companion and the coins to the woodcutter.

Indian folklore tradition has its share of wise men, too. "The Sticks of Truth" in George Shannon's collection *Stories to Solve* tells of an Indian judge asked to determine who stole a gold ring. He gives each suspect a stick and says that only the stick of the thief will grow in the night. In the morning, he is able to accuse the one with the shortest stick of the thievery. Why? In this collection of short pieces, the reader is invited to guess before turning the page to discover the answer. In this case, the girl trims her stick in an effort to hide its growth, thereby proving her guilt.

The Jataka (birth) stories found in India tell of the previous reincarnations of the Buddha and are known to have existed as early as the fifth century A.D. Many of these tales are moralistic or religious in nature. In Margaret Hodges's *Hidden in the Sand*, a caravan of traders becomes lost in the desert and is in danger of dying of thirst. A young boy finds a small plant growing in the sand and urges the men to dig for water. When they have dug a deep hole and found only hard rock, they ridicule the boy. But the youngster won't give up and climbs down into the hole. When he strikes the rock with a hammer, it bursts in two, and cool clean water gushes out. *The Brave Little Parrot* retold by Rafe Martin is a story of a small grey bird who desperately tries to put out a forest fire even though his fellows think the task is hopeless. His ef-

forts elicit tears from the eagle god and these quench the flames. In return for his bravery, the parrot is rewarded with feathers in flaming colors. These stories of faith and persistence are typical of many of the early Jataka tales but have few other elements of traditional folktales. Later, beast tales were drawn from this collection to form the *Panchatantra*, stories that were used to instruct young princes in morality. When these stories are translated into English, their morals and teaching verses are usually eliminated. The resulting Indian tales sound more like folktales.

Rafe Martin retells an ancient ancestor of "Henny Penny" or "Chicken Little" in the Jataka tale *Foolish Rabbit's Big Mistake*. Rabbit hears an apple fall from a tree and wonders if the earth is breaking up. He panics and arouses a chain of animals who thoughtlessly run with him until a wise lion stops the stampede. He carries the silly rabbit back to the scene, proves it was only an apple that fell from the tree, and finally defends the rabbit from the anger of his friends by pointing out that they, too, ran without trying to find out the true cause of the alarm. Ed Young's large-scale paintings depict the action in dramatic close-ups and vibrant explosions of color.

In vigorous woodcuts, Marcia Brown illustrates the fable *Once a Mouse*, which must have warned young princes about the folly of pride in one's origins. Seeing a mouse about to be eaten by a crow, a hermit rescues it. But a cat stalks the pet, so the hermit changes the mouse into a bigger cat. Each change results in new dangers, until finally the meek mouse is transformed into a huge tiger. But he "peacocked about the forest" until the hermit reminds him that he was once a mouse. When the tiger threatens the hermit, the hermit reduces it to its original shape of a mouse.

While these tales represent but a small portion of stories from the Middle Eastern countries and India, they are indicative of a rich source on which children's literature has yet to draw fully. Perhaps the next decades will provide a greater number of single-tale editions of stories such as these so that children might become more familiar with this important literary tradition.

### Folktales from Asia

Although fewer folktales are available from Asia, there are increasing numbers of outstanding, well-illustrated single-tale editions of the folktales from Japan, China, Korea, and Southeast Asia.

Ai-Ling Louie's *Yeh-Shen* is based on one of the oldest written variants of "Cinderella," predating European versions by a thousand years. Left in the care of a stepmother and stepsister, Yeh-Shen is made to do the heaviest chores. Her only friend is a fish, which she feeds and talks with each day until the stepmother kills and eats it. However, its magical power lives on in its bones. Through it, Yeh-Shen is able to go to a festival dressed in a gown, a cloak made of kingfisher feathers, and gold slippers. There, the suspicious stepsister causes the girl to run away and lose a slipper. Immediately Yeh-Shen's fine clothes turn to rags. But the king, struck by her beauty, places the slipper in a roadside pavilion and hides to wait for the girl who will reclaim it. When Yeh-Shen creeps, under cover of darkness, to retrieve the slipper, they are united, and later they marry. As in the German version of the Cinderella story, however, the stepsister and mother are punished, "crushed to death in a shower of flying stones." Ed Young's depictions of costumes and footwear reflect his research into textiles, costuming, and festivals of the ancient Hmong people. In addition, each shimmering pastel and watercolor illustration reminds us, in shape or shadow, of the contours of the magic fish. A much longer but similar version of the tale is the title story in Lynette Dyer Vuong's *The Brocaded Slipper and Other Vietnamese Tales.*

Young's Caldecott Medal book *Lon Po Po* tells a tale that comes from an ancient oral tradition and is thought to be more than a thousand years old. Child readers will recognize similarities between this story and "Red Riding Hood." However, this wolf perishes by falling from the gingko tree as a result of three children's trickery and resourceful teamwork. Combining Chinese panel format with contemporary pastel and watercolors, Young creates a mysterious nighttime setting illuminated by candles, moonlight, and the shining eyes of the wolf.

One of the most popular stories in the Chinese storytelling tradition is recounted in Margaret Mahy's *The Seven Chinese Brothers.* Each brother looks like the others but has one unique feature, such as unusual strength, amazing eyesight, acute hearing, bones that will not break, or unhappy tears that will flood an entire village. When Third Brother is imprisoned by the Emperor, the other brothers use their talents to bring about the Emperor's downfall. The carefully researched details of Jean and Mou-Sien Tseng's watercolors reflect our contemporary concerns with authenticity in illustration as well as text. This version contrasts with Claire Huchet Bishop's simpler retelling and Kurt Weise's black-line stereotyped illustrations from an earlier era for *The Five Chinese Brothers.*

Eric Kimmel's *Ten Suns* tells of the dilemma that arises on earth of long ago. At this time there were ten suns, and when they all decide to go walking together in the heavens at the same time they cause havoc. The earth's emperor begs the sun's father for help. When the ten suns ignore him, their father sends

*In* The Long-Haired Girl *by Doreen Rappaport, a girl is willing to sacrifice her life for her neighbors, a common theme in Asian folktales.*

From *The Long-Haired Girl* by Doreen Rappaport, pictures by Yang Ming-Yi, copyright © 1995 by Doreen Rappaport, pictures copyright © 1995 by Yang Ming-Yi. Used by permission of Dial Books for Young Readers, a division of Penguin Putnam Inc.

the heavenly archer Hu Yi to shoot them out of the sky. Nine of the suns are turned into black crows when they are pierced by the arrows. Just in time, however, the emperor realizes that if all the suns are gone the earth will die. He sends a messenger who steals Hu Yi's last arrow. The last sun is spared, and from that time crows greet their remaining brother sun each morning at dawn with loud cawing.

Caring for one's parents or others above oneself is also a theme of Chinese folktales. In Demi's *The Magic Tapestry,* as well as in Marilee Heyer's *The Weaving of a Dream,* a poor woman's weaving comes to life due to her youngest son's efforts and sacrifices. In Doreen Rappaport's *The Long-Haired Girl,* the heroine, Ah-mei, is willing to sacrifice her life for her fellow villagers. When a drought threatens the lives of her people, she climbs up into the mountains and discovers the secret stream of Lei-gong, the God of Thunder. He warns her not to tell of her discovery, on pain of death, and at first Ah-mei obeys. However, keeping her terrible secret causes her long, beautiful hair to turn white. Finally, moved by the awful suffering of an old man, she decides to sacrifice her life and leads the villagers to the hidden spring. In return for her goodness, the old man helps her to outwit Lei-gong, using her white hair as bait. The hair eventually becomes a beautiful waterfall, and Ah-mei returns safely to her people. Yang Ming-Yi's beautiful woodcuts, printed on rice paper and then painted with watercolor, capture the story's mood and reflect its theme.

Demi's *The Donkey and the Rock* is an amusing story that gently chides the human propensity to be sold a bill of goods. A merchant on the way to market rests his jar of oil on a large rock. When the donkey of another merchant accidentally smashes the jar of oil against the rock, no one can decide who is responsible. The king agrees to try the case in court, and curious people rush to witness the trial between a rock and a donkey. The king charges each of them a fee for being so silly as to believe anyone could judge a rock or a donkey. He uses the money to compensate the merchant.

Lily Toy Hong's *Two of Everything* is a lighthearted farce that contains elements of many magical pot stories. When poor old Mr. Haktak finds a brass pot in his field, he brings it home to his wife. They discover that this pot duplicates anything that they put into it, even Mrs. Haktak, who has fallen in by accident. In his consternation over his two identical wives, the farmer trips and falls in, too. Now there are two Mr. Haktaks and two Mrs. Haktaks. The clever solution will appeal to younger children, who might also discover the concept of multiplication.

Japanese folktales contain miniature people, monsters called *oni*, and, like Chinese tales, themes of gentleness toward animals and other people, the value of hard work, and respect for the elderly.

"Momotaro, or the Story of the Son of a Peach" is said to be the most popular folktale in Japan, where Momotaro is held up to children as an example of kindness, courage, and strength. In Virginia Haviland's retelling in *Favorite Folktales Told in Japan*, a tiny boy who has stepped out of a huge split peach must fight the *horned demons*, who are robbing and attacking the people. With the help of three companions, Momotaro storms the stronghold of the blue-bodied monsters. He returns victorious, bringing home all the gold and silver the *oni* had stolen from the people. Ed Young has used vivid pastel chalks to illustrate a Chinese version in his *Little Plum*. Little Plum, a boy no bigger than a plum seed, promises his parents to fight the evil lord who is terrorizing the people of his village and return their stolen goods. He outwits the lord through trickery, and when his parents realize that Little Plum "was as big as his promise," they are no longer troubled by his tiny size.

Another well-known Japanese story is retold in two beautiful editions. Sumiko Yagawa's *The Crane Wife* is a tale of the results of succumbing to poor advice and greed. Yohei, a poor peasant, removes an arrow from a wounded crane and dresses the injury. Later, a beautiful young woman appears at his door and asks to be his wife. To help pay for the extra mouth to feed, the woman offers to weave cloth but warns Yohei that he must never look at her as she works. One day, forgetting the warning, he looks in on her, only to see a crane plucking feathers from her own breast in order to weave the beautiful cloth. No longer wishing to remain in human form, she flies away. Sue-kichi Akaba applied water-thinned ink to textured paper to create haunting and beautiful illustrations. Odds Bodkin and Gennady Spirin have also created a sumptuous retelling of the story with some minor variations. The illustrations capture the gorgeous images of medieval Japanese screens and positively glow with visual energy. It would be interesting for children to compare Molly Bang's literary use of the tale in *Dawn,* which is set in nineteenth-century New England. The alert reader might spot clues to Dawn's true identity, such as pieces of eggshell under her bed when she gives birth to a daughter and the quilt pattern she is piecing, called "Wild Geese Flying."

Diane Snyder's *The Boy of the Three-Year Nap* is a humorous realistic folktale involving trickery. A poor widow, tired of supporting her son Taro, who is "lazy as a rich man's cat," pesters him to go to work for a rich rice merchant. Declining to work, the boy tricks the merchant into betrothing him to his daughter. Taro's mother works her own ruse, however, and in the end Taro is caught in his own tricks. Allen Say's precise watercolor illustrations reflect the Japanese love of order. The expressive faces of both the tricksters and the duped make readers laugh at the humorous situations.

Katherine Paterson's *The Tale of the Mandarin Ducks* presents a Japanese tale of a greedy lord who captures a magnificently plumed drake so as to have a beautiful caged bird. Shozo, a former mighty samurai who has lost an eye in battle, warns the lord that the wild bird will surely die in captivity, but the lord shuns his advice. When Yasuko, a kitchen maid, takes pity on the bird and frees him, the lord blames Shozo, strips him of his rank, and puts him to work in the kitchen, where he falls in love with Yasuko. The jealous and vindictive lord sentences them to death by drowning for releasing the duck. On their way to be executed, the condemned couple are rescued and taken to a hut in the forest. In the morning, they wish to thank their saviors but find instead the mandarin duck and his mate, who seem to bow before flying away. Shozo and Yasuko live on for many years in their forest hut in great happiness, for they had learned that "trouble can always be borne when it is shared." Leo and Diane Dillon studied *ukiyo-e,* a

Japanese art movement that depicted the everyday life of common people, before creating their lovely watercolor and pastel illustrations for the story that suggest the natural beauty of a simple life. Although the art superbly recalls this traditional form, the illustrations are less accurate. For example, women would not wear their zori or shoes on a tatami mat as pictured in the third double-page spread, nor would they wear their Zori without the little socks called tabi.

Some Korean folktales, such as Nami Rhee's *Magic Spring,* deal with themes of hard work, loyalty, and greed; others have a wonderful sense of playful humor. Rabbit is a familiar character in Asian folktales and often appears in the role of a clever trickster who also might be petty and vain. In *The Rabbit's Escape,* Suzanne Crowder Han's retelling of a Korean story, the Dragon King of the East Sea is told that he needs a rabbit's liver to cure his sickness. Unwilling to leave his watery kingdom, the king sends Turtle to bring him a rabbit from the land. Turtle lures a curious rabbit back to the sea kingdom, but when the rabbit discovers what his fate is to be, he tells the king that he has left his liver at home and must return to land to get it. Turtle takes the rabbit home, where he promptly runs away. Discovering that he has been tricked, Turtle weeps bitterly, and a god takes pity on him, giving him a piece of ginseng root. The king is cured, and from that day ginseng has been used to treat all sorts of illnesses. Han and illustrator Yumi Heo also collaborated on *The Rabbit's Judgment.* Both of these books are bilingual, printed in English and Han-gul, the Korean alphabet. Heo's abstracted paintings, with their strong linear designs, seem to mirror the Korean letter forms and recall the fantasy paintings of artist Paul Klee. They add a wonderfully light and humorous touch to these delightful tales. Crowder's *The Rabbit's Tale* has been illustrated in a very different style by Richard Wehman. In this story a proud tiger is tricked into believing that a persimmon is more frightening than he is. He runs through the jungle and sees images of the scary persimmon monster wherever he goes. This convoluted plot involves a poor farmer who gets into the middle of the tiger's terror and a curious rabbit whose curiosity loses him his tail.

The Korean tale *The Sun Girl and the Moon Boy* by Yangsook Choi is reminiscent of *Little Red Riding Hood* and *Lon Po Po.* In the time before there is a sun and a moon, a tiger gobbles up a woman who has gone out to get food for her children. Still hungry, the tiger tries to trick her children into believing he is their mother. When the children outwit him, they are reunited with their mother in the sky and they become the sun and the moon.

The many beautiful single-tale editions of folktales from Asia have made these old and magical tales

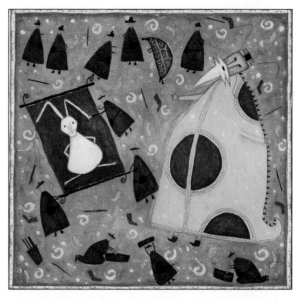

*Yumi Heo's stylistic illustrations help establish the magical setting and lighthearted mood in* The Rabbit's Escape *by Suzanne Crowder Han.*

From *The Rabbit's Escape* by Suzanne Crowder Han, illustrated by Yumi Heo. Illustrations copyright © 1995 by Yumi Heo. Reprinted by permission of Henry Holt and Company, LLC.

more widely available to an English-speaking audience. Often illustrated in the pictorial style of a particular period of Asian art, these stories can educate a child's artistic eye.

### Folktales from Africa

Children today are the fortunate recipients of a rich bounty of African folktales collected by folklorists such as Harold Courlander.[19] Many of these tales have been retold in single editions by authors like Verna Aardema and Ashley Bryan, and many of these stories have received Caldecott awards. The trickster tale of Anansi the spider told in *A Story, a Story* by Gail Haley won a Caldecott Medal, as did Aardema's pourquoi story *Why Mosquitoes Buzz in People's Ears* with illustrations by Leo and Diane Dillon. Caldecott Honor Books have included two other African pourquoi stories, Elfinstone Dayrell's *Why the Sun and the Moon Live in the Sky* with Blair Lent's distinguished illustrations, and *The Village of Round and Square Houses* by Ann Grifalconi; a second story of the trickster, *Anansi, the Spider* illustrated by Gerald McDermott; and John Steptoe's tale of a greedy and a generous sister, *Mufaro's Beautiful Daughters.*

Storytelling is a highly developed art in Africa, particularly in West Africa. These tales have an aural

---

[19]See Nina Jaffe's biography *A Voice for the People: The Life and Work of Harold Courlander* (Holt, 1997).

cadence found in no other stories of the world. They come from the oral tradition and are frequently written in the storyteller's voice. Short sentences, frequent use of parallel constructions, repetition, and dialogue characterize the style of many of the African tales. In Ashley Bryan's rhythmical tale from the Antilles, *The Dancing Granny*, Granny can't resist the song of Spider Ananse, who lures her to dance far out of sight while he raids her vegetable plot. The story sings with rhythmic prose and repeated refrains. Bryan's *The Story of Lightning and Thunder*, a story from Southern Nigeria, is filled with similar word music. It begins,

> A long time ago, I mean a long, long time ago, if you wanted to pat Lightning or chat with Thunder, you could do it. Uh huh, you could! (unpaged)

This tale of how thunder and lightning went to live in the sky is accompanied by Bryan's sparkling paintings, which, with their colorful abstracted patterns, seem to flash with a special lightning all their own.

Many similar African tales are about personified animals, including those tricksters Anansi the spider, a rabbit, and a tortoise. In Gerald McDermott's *Zomo the Rabbit*, Zomo asks the Sky God for wisdom. The Sky God agrees but sets the rabbit three difficult tasks. This speedy trickster accomplishes the tasks but wreaks havoc in the jungle, angering Big Fish, Wild Cow, and Leopard. Sky God gives him the wisdom he has asked for, but warns him that he might have a lot of courage, a little good sense, but no caution whatsoever. Therefore, warns the Sky God, he better learn to run very very fast. Gerald McDermott's illustrations recall the patterned designs of African textiles and bring Zomo's tricky character to life. In Tolowa Mollel's *Ananse's Feast,* Ananse the spider and the turtle Akye have a battle of wits over a meal. Ananse wins the first round but as often happens in trickster stories, the trickster spider is outtricked by the long-suffering turtle. Verna Aardema's *Anansi Does the Impossible* is a retelling of the three impossible tasks Anansi must accomplish in order to win the Sky God's stories. Readers will recognize a similar version in Gail Haley's *A Story, a Story.*

Trickster Rabbit appears in a more helpful mood in *The Hunterman and the Crocodile*, a charming retelling of a West African tale by Baba Wagué Diakité. Diakité has also told *The Hat Seller and the Monkeys*, an African tale that children will recognize as similar to the favorite *Caps for Sale* by Esphyr Slobodkina. In this version BaMusa, a hat seller on his way to market with a load of hats, falls asleep under a mango tree. When he awakens he finds that the monkeys in the tree have taken his hats. He tries everything he can think of to get his hats back, until he realizes that the monkeys are imitating his every move. When he takes off his hat and

*Some mischievous monkeys are tricked out of their stolen hats by the merchant BaMusa in Baba Wagué Diakité's delightful* The Hatseller and the Monkeys.

From *The Hatseller and the Monkeys* by Baba Wagué Diakité. Published by Scholastic Press, a division of Scholastic, Inc. Copyright © 1999 by Baba Wagué Diakité. Reprinted by permission.

throws it at the monkeys, they take off theirs and throw them at him. Diakité's paintings are executed on ceramic tile, and the bright patterns he creates in his pictures are a fresh addition to the folktale genre.

Verna Aardema has retold a West African tale in *Why Mosquitoes Buzz in People's Ears*. In this cumulative story the mosquito tells the iguana a tall tale, setting off a chain reaction that ends in disaster for a baby owl. Until the animals can find the culprit who is responsible for the owlet's death, Mother Owl refuses to hoot and wake the sun. King Lion holds a council and listens to everyone's excuse until the blame comes to rest on the mosquito. The white outline of the stylized watercolors gives a cool but brilliant atmosphere to this story. Leo and Diane Dillon won the Caldecott Medal for their beautiful illustrations of this story and also illustrated Aardema's humorous Masai tale *Who's in Rabbit's House?* as a play featuring masked actors.

Verna Aardema has retold many other folktales from Africa. *Misoso,* Aardema's collection of "once upon a time tales," is a delightful literary tour of the continent. In addition to a map showing each tale's place of origin, every story is introduced with a glossary and pronunciation guide and followed with notes about the tale and its place in African folklore. Accompanied by beautiful stylized illustrations by Reynold Ruffins, this book is a superb introduction to serious study of African folklore for older children.

Many other African stories may also be described as pourquoi stories. Ashley Bryan's wonderful retelling of "How the Animals Got Their Tails" in his *Beat the Story Drum, Pum-Pum* tells of the origins of characteristic features of African animals. Raouf Mama's *Why Goats Smell* is a collection of twenty traditional stories from Benin. Gail Haley's *A Story, a Story* explains the origins of a different type of tale—how humans got their stories. Ann Grifalconi's *The Village of Round and Square Houses* explains why, in a particular Cameroon village located at the base of a volcano, the women live in round huts while the men live in square ones, and the way in which people came to be farmers is explained in Mary-Joan Gerson's *Why the Sky Is Far Away.*

A play on words is a favored form of humor in some African tales. In *The Cow-Tail Switch,* Harold Courlander and George Herzog retell the story of the very wealthy man named Time. Change of fortune reduces him to a beggar, and persons remark, "Behold, Time isn't what it used to be!" (p. 77). The same collection has a story about the young hunters who try to capture "The One You Don't See Coming," which is their name for sleep. In another Anansi story in this collection, there is a character named Nothing. Anansi kills him, and all the villagers "cry for nothing!"

Tololwa Mollel's *The King and the Tortoise* is another humorous story in which a king who considers himself the cleverest one in the world challenges the creatures of his kingdom to make him a robe of smoke. A tortoise agrees to make the robe on the condition that the king give him seven days and provide any materials he needs. The tortoise returns on the day the robe is promised and explains that he must have a thread of fire to finish the robe of smoke. The king, realizing that he has been tricked and thinking fast, tells the tortoise that he doesn't really want the robe anymore. "You have proven to me that you are clever enough to make one, and that is all I really wanted to know. " He declares that two cleverest creatures in the world live in his kingdom, "You and I."

Frequently an African tale will present a dilemma and then the storyteller will invite the audience to participate in suggesting the conclusion. The problem of which son should be given the cow-tail switch as a reward for finding his lost father is asked in the title story *The Cow-Tail Switch* in the collection by Courlander and Herzog. The boys undertake the search only after the youngest child learns to speak and asks for his father. Each of the sons has a special talent he uses to help restore his father to life. It is then that the storyteller asks who should receive the father's cow-tail switch.

A more serious dilemma is presented in Nancy Day's *The Lion's Whiskers,* an Ethiopian tale about a stepmother whose stepson refuses to accept her as his new mother. After trying every kindness, she visits a medicine man, who tells her that she must bring back three whiskers of a lion. She is terrified but, loving her stepson, she sets out into the desert. Over the course of several months she patiently feeds a lion, getting closer and closer until she is able to pluck three hairs from his snout. When she returns to the wise man, he tells her she does not need the whiskers anymore, she has learned what she needs to know. "Approach your stepson as you did the lion and you will win his love." Indeed, when she returns home, it is her quiet and loving patience that finally draws her stepson into the circle of her arms. Ann Grifalconi's inventive photocollages embrace African symbols and objects and give this story an unusual but warm visual setting.

While searching for an African variant of "Cinderella," John Steptoe came upon the story he retells in *Mufaro's Beautiful Daughters,* turning it into a strikingly illustrated tale about conflict and contrast. Manyara, the bad-tempered, selfish sister, predicts that one day she will be queen and her sister will be a servant. Nyasha, the humble and hardworking sister, is happy to work in her garden and care for their father. When a message arrives from the king inviting all the worthy daughters in the land to appear before him so that he can choose a bride, Manyara hurries on ahead, thinking to beat her sister to the king's palace. Along the way she meets a hungry boy with whom she haughtily refuses to share her food, and she ignores the advice of an old woman. The next day, however, Nyasha shares her food with both people. When her sister arrives, Manyara comes running from the palace in hysterics because she has seen a five-headed serpent on the throne. But Nyasha bravely approaches and is relieved to find a little garden snake that transforms itself into the king. He reveals that he had also taken the shape of the little boy and the old woman and thus knows that she is the most beautiful daughter in the land, worthy to be his wife. Steptoe's careful research creates an accurate picture of the region. The intensely colored plants and animals living in the forest, architectural details from the actual ruined city of Zimbabwe, and a pair of crowned cranes that symbolize the royal couple all contribute authenticity to this Caldecott Honor winner.[20]

Obviously there is no dearth of folk literature from Africa, where oral tradition has been maintained. Children who hear these tales will become familiar with other cultures and the rhythmical chord

[20]Darcy Bradley, "John Steptoe: Retrospective of an Imagemaker," *New Advocate* 4, no. 1 (winter 1991): 21.

of ancient African storytellers. They will learn of a land where baobab trees grow and people fear lions, leopards, droughts, and famines. More importantly, they will learn something about the wishes, dreams, hopes, humor, and despair of other peoples. They may begin to see literature as the universal story of humankind.

### Folktales of North America

When the early settlers, immigrants, and slaves came to North America, they brought their folktales with them from Europe, China, and West Africa. As they repeated their folktales, some of the tales took on an unmistakable North American flavor. Indigenous to the continent are folktales told by Native Americans and tall tales that developed from the pioneer spirit of the young American country.

In a discussion of folktales of North America, it is impossible to describe any one body of folklore such as the Grimms discovered in Germany. However, the folklore of North America may be sorted into four large categories:

1. Native American, Eskimo, and Inuit tales that were originally here
2. Tales that came from other countries, primarily from West Africa, and were changed in the process to form the basis of African American and African Caribbean folktales
3. Tales that came primarily from Europe and were modified into new variants
4. Tall tales, legends, and other Americana that developed here

Virginia Haviland's collection *North American Legends*[21] presents tales from each of these categories and gives a broad overview of folklore in the United States. *From Sea to Shining Sea,* Amy Cohn's extensively researched collection of American folklore and folk songs, offers children a stirring journey into an America that consists of many cultures, many stories, and many songs. Fourteen Caldecott Medal–winning artists provide the visual map for this marvelous exploration. A glossary, extensive footnotes, and suggested readings add to the book's value as a classroom resource.

Other notable collections include Laurence Yep's *The Rainbow People* and *Tongues of Jade,* tales Chinese immigrants told not only to remind themselves of home but to show how a wise person could survive in a strange new land. Paul Yee's *Tales from Gold Mountain* draws on the wellspring of stories told by the Chinese who settled in Vancouver's Chi-

natown. Eighteen stories from Americans of European descent are collected in Neil Philip's *Stockings of Buttermilk* illustrated by Jacqueline Mair. Nancy Van Laan's *With a Whoop and a Holler* includes stories from the Deep South, and readers will find familiar characters such as Jack and Brer Rabbit as well as superstitions and riddles. African Americans are represented in such fine collections as Virginia Hamilton's *The People Could Fly* and *Her Stories.* Both collections have been illustrated by Leo and Diane Dillon in their distinctive style. Native American tales have been assembled in thematic collections, such as Maria Brusca and Tona Wilson's *When Jaguars Ate the Moon and Other Stories About Animals and Plants of the Americas,* and in tribal collections such as Joseph Bruchac's *The Boy Who Lived with the Bears and Other Iroquois Stories.* Increasingly, readers will find that many other well-written collections and beautifully illustrated tales represent the many colorful threads that make up America's rich tapestry of story.

### Native American Folktales

To try to characterize all the folklore of the various Native American tribes as one cohesive whole is as unreasonable as it would be to lump all of the folklore of Europe together. Variations in Native American dwellings, such as pueblos, longhouses, and teepees, or in the symbolic artwork of totem poles, beading, story skins, and carvings are mirrored in the variations of Native American folktales. Resources for Teaching, "Some Native American Folktales by Region" is a useful grouping of tales for those wishing to study Native American folktales, specifically of a particular geographical area. However, there are some common characteristics among the various tribes and between the folklore of Native Americans and that of northern Europeans.

Many Native American tales might be categorized as mythology, for they include creation myths and sacred legends. Jean Monroe and Ray Williamson's *They Dance in the Sky* is a collection of Native American star myths that includes stories of the origin of the Pleiades, the Big Dipper, and other constellations. Manitonquat's *The Children of the Morning Light* brings together creation myths and other legends from the Wampanoag people of southeastern Massachusetts. Some myths attempt to explain religious beliefs while telling people about tribal customs and how to act. Some of these tales were told as separate stories, but as with Greek or Roman mythology, they were heard by insiders who understood these tales within the context of a large interlocking set of stories.

Native American tales, when originally told, were loosely plotted rather than highly structured like European fairy tales. Thomas Leekley, who retold some

---

[21]Virginia Haviland, *North American Legends,* illustrated by Ann Strugnell (New York: Collins, 1979).

# RESOURCES FOR TEACHING

## Some Native American Folktales by Region

### PLAINS

Caron Lee Cohen, *The Mud Pony* (Pawnee)

Joe Medicine Crow, *Brave Wolf and the Thunderbird* (Crow)

Paul Goble, *Iktomi and the Berries: A Plains Indians Story* (Lakota Sioux)

John Steptoe, *The Story of Jumping Mouse: A Native American Legend*

Nancy Van Laan, *Buffalo Dance: A Blackfoot Legend*

Nancy Van Laan, *Shingebiss, an Ojibwe Legend*

Douglas Wood, *Rabbit and the Moon* (Cree)

### WOODLAND

John Bierhorst, ed., *The White Deer and Other Stories Told by the Lenape*

Barbara Juster Esbensen, *Ladder to the Sky* (Ojibwa)

————, *The Star Maiden* (Ojibwa)

Virginia Hamilton, "Divine Woman the Creator" (Huron), in *The Beginning: Creation Stories from Around the World*

Rafe Martin, *The Rough-Face Girl* (Algonquin)

Robert D. San Souci, *Sootface: An Ojibwa Cinderella*

William Toye, *How Summer Came to Canada* (Micmac)

### SOUTHWEST

Byrd Baylor, ed., *And It Is Still That Way*

John Bierhorst, *Doctor Coyote: A Native American Aesop's Fables*

Tomie de Paola, *The Legend of the Bluebonnet: An Old Tale of Texas* (Comanche)

Gerald Hausman, *Coyote Walks on Two Legs: A Book of Navajo Myths and Legends*

Gerald McDermott, *Arrow to the Sun* (Pueblo)

————, *Coyote* (Zuni)

Kristina Rodanas, *Dragonfly's Tale* (Zuni)

Michael Rosen, *Crow and Hawk: A Traditional Pueblo Indian Story*

Nancy Wood, *The Girl Who Loved Coyote: Stories of the Southwest*

### NORTHWEST

Fionna French, *Lord of the Animals* (Mikwok)

Gerald McDermott, *Raven: A Trickster Tale from the Pacific Northwest*

Jean Guard Monroe and Ray A. Williamson, "How Coyote Arranged the Night Stars" (Wasco), in *They Dance in the Sky: Native American Star Myths*

Laura Simms, *The Bone Man* (Modoc)

William Toye, *The Loon's Necklace* (Tsimshian)

### SOUTHEAST

Joseph Bruchac, *The First Strawberries: A Cherokee Story*

————, *The Great Ball Game: A Muskogee Story* (Creek)

Beatice Orcutt Harrell, *How Thunder and Lightning Came to Be* (Choctaw)

Gretchen Will Mayo, "Ice Man Puts Out the Big Fire" (Cherokee), in *Earthmaker's Tales: North American Indian Stories from Earth Happenings*

Jean Guard Monroe and Ray A. Williamson, "What the Stars Are Like" (Cherokee), in *They Dance in the Sky*

*continued*

## RESOURCES FOR TEACHING

## Some Native American Folktales by Region con't

### FAR NORTH

Emery Bernhard, *How Snowshoe Hare Rescued the Sun: A Tale Told from the Arctic* (Yuit)

John Bierhorst, *The Dancing Fox* (Arctic region)

Dale De Armond, *The Seal Oil Lamp* (Eskimo)

Virginia Hamilton, "Raven the Creator," in *In the Beginning: Creation Stories from Around the World* (Eskimo)

James Houston, *The White Archer: An Eskimo Legend*

Rafe Martin, *The Eagle's Gift* (Inuit)

Howard Norman, *The Girl Who Dreamed Only Geese* (Inuit)

---

of the stories of the Chippewa and Ottawa tribes in his *The World of Manobozho,* says:

> Indian folklore is a great collection of anecdotes, jokes, and fables, and storytellers constantly combined and recombined these elements in different ways. We seldom find a plotted story of the kind we know. Instead, the interest is usually in a single episode; if this is linked to another, the relationship is that of two beads on one string, seldom that of two bricks in one building. (pp. 7–8)

The very act of storytelling was considered to be of ceremonial importance in various tribal groups. Storytelling took place at night and, in certain tribes such as the Iroquois, it was permitted only in the winter. Men, women, and children listened reverently to stories, some of which were "owned" by a teller and could not be told by any other person. The sacred number four is found in all Indian tales, rather than the pattern of three common to other folktales. Four hairs might be pulled and offered to the four winds; or four quests must be made before a mission will be accomplished.

Many Native American tales are nature myths, pourquoi stories that explain how animals came to earth or why they have certain characteristics. Paul Goble tells of the origin of the first horses in *The Gift of the Sacred Dog,* in which the gift is the Great Spirit's attempt to help the Plains tribes hunt the buffalo more efficiently.

In William Toye's *The Loon's Necklace,* the loon receives his markings as a reward for his kindness in restoring the sight of a blind old man. Elizabeth Cleaver created stunning collage illustrations for this picture-book story of the origin of the "necklace." In

*How Turtle's Back Was Cracked,* Gayle Ross recounts how Turtle, who used to have a smooth shell, became so full of himself that he annoyed a group of wolves who heard his bragging. They determine to kill him, but Turtle tricks them into throwing him in the river, where they think he'll drown. Instead of landing in the water, however, he falls on a large boulder and his shell cracks in a dozen places. Being a good healer, Turtle fixes his shell, but today if you look closely you can still see where his back was cracked. Marvin Jacob's paintings, executed in natural earth tones with patterned borders, nicely capture the story's Cherokee origin. Ashley Wolff's appealing linoleum block prints illustrate Gerald Hausman's *How Chipmunk Got Tiny Feet,* a collection of seven Native American animal origin stories.

Perhaps one of the best known stories of explanation, which combines religious beliefs, how-and-why explanations, and references to Indian custom, is "Star Boy," which has many versions. Paul Goble retells this tale in *Star Boy* with beautiful illustrations drawn from careful references to Blackfoot artistic traditions. In this story, Star Boy, expelled from the sky world with his mother and marked with a mysterious scar because of her disobedience, becomes known as Scarface. In order to marry, he must make a journey to the Sun, who removes the scar. To commemorate and honor the Sun's gesture, the Blackfeet have a sacred Sun Dance each summer. In Goble's version, Star Boy becomes another star and joins his father, Morning Star, and his mother, Evening Star.

The heavens hold special significance for native peoples, as can be seen in such tales as Joseph Bruchac's *The Story of the Milky Way,* a Cherokee tale; Paul Goble's *Her Seven Brothers,* a Cheyenne

*Murv Jacob's color scheme and his use of Cherokee designs add authenticity to* How Turtle's Back Was Cracked *by Gayle Ross.*

From *How Turtle's Back Was Cracked* by Gayle Ross, illustrated by Murv Jacob, copyright © 1995 by Murv Jacob, illustrations. Used by permission of Dial Books for Young Readers, a division of Penguin Putnam Inc.

myth about the origin of the Big Dipper; and Goble's *The Lost Children,* a Blackfoot story about the origin of the Pleiades. Beatrice Harrell's *How Thunder and Lightning Came to Be* is set closer to earth and is a humorous story from the Choctaw about two birds who agree to help the Great Sun Father warn the people when a bad storm is coming. Their silly attempts only amuse the people, however, until one day when Helotha's eggs roll off the clouds, creating a great thumping and bumping. When her husband, Melatha, races to catch them, sparks fly from his heels. The Sun Father was pleased with the effect this made. Now every time Helotha lays her eggs and Melatha chases them, Sun Father sends wind and rain to the earth. Susan Roth's textured collages capture the essence of the story's motifs and reflect the rich and varied patterns of Native American stories.

Almost all Native American folklore traditions contain a trickster figure who mediates between the sky world and earth. The woodland tribes tell tales of Manabozho, a kind of half god, half superpower among the eastern tribes. The Great Plains trickster Coyote snatches fire from the burning mountain and to this day, says the legend, Coyote's fur is singed and

yellow along his sides where the flames blew backward as he ran down the mountain carrying the burning brand. A version of this story can be found in Gerald Hausman's *Coyote Walks on Two Legs,* a collection of Navajo myths and legends about this well-known trickster that includes a version of the Great Flood. Paintings by Floyd Cooper lend the poetic text a sense of the glowing warmth of the deserts of the Southwest.

Paul Goble has illustrated many tales from the Plains tribes, including several about the Plains trickster, Iktomi. Amusing stories that often have moral lessons within, they were to be told only after the sun had set. These stories were meant to elicit audience participation, and Goble has incorporated this in an inviting way. Asides like "It looks like the end of Iktomi, doesn't it?" and Iktomi's often self-serving remarks would make this very funny as a shared reading. *Iktomi and the Coyote* and *Iktomi Loses His Eyes* are two of many stories about this Plains Indian trickster. Goble's illustrations for other titles, such as his *The Great Race of the Birds and the Animals* and *Buffalo Woman,* are filled with patterns of flowers, trees, birds, and other animals indigenous to the prairie. Goble received the Caldecott Medal for his stunning illustrations for *The Girl Who Loved Wild Horses.* All of Goble's work draws on Native American artistic traditions as well.

The trickster of the Pacific Northwest is Raven. While he is a wily, crafty being who loves to get the better of others, he is also a friend to humankind. Gerald McDermott's version of this story, *Raven: A Trickster Tale from the Pacific Northwest,* is illustrated in watercolors, but Raven in his many guises wears the more abstract and solidly colored patterns of Northwest tribal art. In an Eskimo version, another Raven story tells how he created the first human from a peavine (Virginia Hamilton, *In the Beginning*).

The stories of many tribes often revolved around a cultural hero like the woodland character Gluskap, Glooscap, or Gluskabe. This hero accomplished great deeds and often served as helper to the Great Spirit. In Joseph Bruchac's *Gluskabe and the Four Wishes,* Gluskabe has retired across the big water to take a rest after making the world a better place for his children. Four Abenaki men decide to undertake a difficult journey to ask Gluskabe for their hearts' desires. Impressed by the difficulties they have faced to get to him, Gluskabe gives them each a pouch but warns them not to look inside until they get home. The first three men cannot resist a peek and are justly punished. The fourth man, who only asked to be a good hunter to provide food for his people, resists temptation, but when he returns home he finds the pouch is empty. As he is about to despair, however, he hears the voices of the animals, who speak to him of the proper ways to prepare for the hunt and how to show respect for the animals. "From that day on he was the best hunter among the people. He never took more game than was needed, yet he always provided enough to feed his people." Perhaps this is one of the "Glooskabe" stories Attean told to Matt as the two boys survived the long winter in Speare's *Sign of the Beaver* (see Chapter 10).

Other, more human, heroes can be found in many Native American stories. Rafe Martin's *The Rough-Face Girl* is a retelling of an Algonquin story and has many elements of the Cinderella tales. In this version, Rough Face is the youngest of three sisters and has become scarred from sitting too close to the fire in order to feed the flames. Although her sisters both hope to be the ones to marry the Invisible Being, Rough Face is the only one who can see his face in the beauty of the world around her. When she has passed the tests set her, the Invisible Being appears and sees her true beauty. Then she is sent to bathe in the lake and her physical scars disappear, revealing her true form to all. David Shannon's carefully modeled paintings bring the characters in the story to life.

San Souci's *Sootface* is an Ojibwa story that is very similar to many other Native American versions of this tale. In this variant, Sootface, the youngest sister, is only dirty with the soot from the fire rather than physically scarred. When she goes to meet the invisible warrior, she dresses in a gown of birch bark and wears a crown of wildflowers on her head. Daniel San Souci's realistic illustrations are based on thoroughly researched details of mid-1700s Ojibwa life.

Rafe Martin's poignant *The Boy Who Lived with the Seals* is based on a Chinook legend and tells of a boy who is torn between the world of The People and the undersea world of the seals. Although he does not transform physically into a seal as do the Selkies of North Atlantic legend, he eventually chooses to live in their kingdom, returning only once a year to leave a beautiful carved canoe for the humans he has left behind.

Barbara Diamond Goldin has retold *The Girl Who Lived with the Bears,* the story of a young girl of the Raven clan in the Pacific Northwest. When she insults the bears who interfere with her berry picking, she is kidnapped by the Bear People to be a servant. With the help of Mouse Woman, she makes the Bear Chief believe she has great power, and he marries her to his nephew. Eventually she grows to love the handsome man and gives him twin sons. Her life with the Bear People is happy until her husband dreams that her brother is searching for her and will kill him. He tells her the way in which her people must honor the Bear People when they kill them for food. Grief stricken when her husband's dream proves true, she and her two sons return home with her brother. She passes on the songs and ceremonies of the Bear People, and she teaches her own people to honor and respect all living creatures.

The character of Mouse Woman figures prominently in Dale De Armond's *The Seal Oil Lamp,* another story about a child caught between two worlds. Because Allegua was blind and Eskimo tribal law stated that no child may live if it cannot grow up to support itself, his family sadly left him behind when they moved to the summer fish camp. But the 7-year-old had fed a starving mouse that winter, so the Mouse Woman and her family take care of Allegua and he comes to know and love their world.

> They told him wonderful stories about the mouse world and about the owls and foxes and eagles who try to catch them, and how the mouse people outwit their enemies. They told him about Raven and the magic that lives under the earth and in the sky country. And the mouse people sang their songs for him and did their dances on the back of his hand so he could feel how beautiful their dances were. (p. 20)

De Armond's stylized wood engravings suggest dramatically the powerful beauty of Eskimo artwork.

Although survival themes are constant in Indian tales, they are particularly strong in Eskimo stories. James Houston, who spent many years among the Inuit, is especially sensitive to authentic depictions of Eskimo art and culture. His illustrations often look like renderings of Eskimo carvings. In his *Tikta Liktak,* a legendary hunter is isolated when an ice pan breaks away. In a dream, he gains courage, kills a seal, and is able to find his way home. *The White Archer* is a tale of a revengeful hunter who finally succumbs to the kindness and wisdom of an Eskimo couple.

Resources for Teaching, "A Study of Folktales by Culture" provides a start for comparing characteristics, characters, collectors, and typical tales representative of specific areas around the world.

### European Variants in the United States

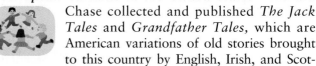 Richard Chase collected and published *The Jack Tales* and *Grandfather Tales*, which are American variations of old stories brought to this country by English, Irish, and Scottish settlers in the seventeenth and eighteenth centuries. They are as much a part of Americana as the Brer Rabbit stories. In some respects Jack is an equivalent to Brer Rabbit. He is a trickster hero who overcomes his opponent through quick wit and cunning, rather than through the strength that triumphs in the tall tales that originated in the United States. All of these variants come from the mountain folk of the southern Appalachians. Cut off from the mainstream of immigration and changing customs, these people preserved their stories and songs in the same way that they continue to weave the Tudor rose into their fabrics.

# RESOURCES FOR TEACHING

## A Study of Folktales by Culture

| CULTURES AND COLLECTORS | TYPICAL TALES, AUTHOR | CHARACTERS | CHARACTERISTICS |
|---|---|---|---|
| **BRITISH FOLKTALES** | | | |
| Joseph Jacobs (1854–1916) | *The Three Little Pigs* (Rounds) <br> *The Little Red Hen* (Galdone, M. Zemach) <br> *Tam Lin* (Yolen) <br> *Jack and the Beanstalk* (Kellogg, Benaduce) <br> *Finn MacCoul and His Fearless Wife* (Byrd) | Lazy Jack <br> Giants <br> "Wee folk" <br> Dick Whittington | Cumulative tales for youngest children <br> Beast tales <br> Droll humor <br> Transformations <br> Giant Killers |
| **GERMAN FOLKTALES** | | | |
| The Grimm brothers <br> Jacob (1785–1863) <br> Wilhelm (1786–1859) | *Little Red Cap* (Grimm brothers) <br> *Rumpelstiltskin* (Grimm brothers) <br> *Hansel and Gretel* (Grimm brothers) <br> *The Frog Prince* (Grimm brothers) <br> *Snow White and the Seven Dwarfs* (Grimm brothers) <br> *The Elves and the Shoemaker* (Grimm brothers) | Tom Thumb <br> Rumpelstiltskin <br> Hansel and Gretel <br> Red Riding Hood <br> Witches, elves, dwarfs <br> Bears, wolves <br> Snow White <br> King Thrushbeard | Somber stories <br> Children as characters <br> Harsh punishments <br> Romances <br> Transformations |
| **SCANDINAVIAN FOLKTALES** | | | |
| Peter Christian Asbjørnsen (1812–1885) <br> Jorgen E. Moe (1813–1882) <br> Translated into English by George Webbe Dasent (1817–1896) | *The Three Billy Goats Gruff* (Galdone, Rounds) <br> "The Lad Who Went to the North Wind," in *East o'the Sun and West o'the Moon* (Asbjørnsen and Moe) <br> *East o'the Sun and West o'the Moon* (Dasent) <br> *The Little Old Woman and the Hungry Cat* (Polette) <br> *Boots and His Brothers* (Kimmel) | Trolls, Tomte <br> Many-headed giants <br> Youngest sons or "Boots" <br> North Wind <br> White bears <br> Salmon <br> Cats <br> Reindeer, elk | Tongue-in-cheek humor <br> Helpful animals <br> Magical objects <br> Magical enchantments <br> Many trials and tasks <br> Poor boy succeeds |

*continued*

# RESOURCES FOR TEACHING

## A Study of Folktales by Culture con't

| CULTURES AND COLLECTORS | TYPICAL TALES, AUTHOR | CHARACTERS | CHARACTERISTICS |
|---|---|---|---|
| **FRENCH FOLKTALES** | | | |
| Charles Perrault (1628–1703) | *Puss in Boots* (Perrault) | Fairy godmothers | Traditional fairy tale |
| | *Cinderella* (Perrault) | Jealous stepsisters | Romance |
| | *The White Cat* (San Souci) | Royalty | Wicked enchantments |
| | *Beauty and the Beast* (de Beaumont) | Talking cats | Long sleep |
| | *The Sleeping Beauty* (Perrault) | Unselfish youngest daughter | |
| | *Stone Soup* (Brown) | | |
| **RUSSIAN FOLKTALES** | | | |
| Alexander Afanasyev (1855–1864) | *Baba Yaga* (Kimmel) | Vasilissa, beautiful and wise | Peasants outwit tsars |
| | *Baba Yaga and Vasilisa* (Mayer) | Ivan, youngest brother | Many tasks |
| | *The Frog Princess* (Lewis) | Baba Yaga, the witch | Quest for firebird |
| | *The Fool of the World and His Flying Ship* (Ransome) | Wolves, bears | Dire punishments |
| | *The Little Humpbacked Horse* (Winthrop) | Firebird | Helpful animals |
| | | Koschey the Deathless | Fool or youngest triumphs |
| **JAPANESE FOLKTALES** | | | |
| | *The Boy of the Three-Year Nap* (Snyder) | Momotaro | Transformation to birds |
| | *The Crane Wife* (Bodkin) | Wicked *oni*, ogres | Childless couples have "different" children |
| | *Momotaro, the Peach Boy* (Haviland) | Trickster badger | Respect for elderly |
| | *The Inch Boy* (Morimoto) | Urashima Taro | Self-sacrifice |
| | *The Wise Old Woman* (Uchida) | Poor farmers, fisherman | |
| | *The Farmer and the Poor God* (Wells) | | |
| **AFRICAN FOLKTALES** | | | |
| Harold Courlander and other present-day collectors | *Mufaro's Beautiful Daughters* (Steptoe) | Anansi, trickster spider | Pourquoi stories |
| | *Rabbit Makes a Monkey of Lion* (Aardema) | Zomo, trickster rabbit | Talking-beast tales |
| | *A Story, a Story* (Haley) | Various animals | Animal tricksters |
| | *The Cow-Tail Switch* (Courlander and Herzog) | | "Why" humor |
| | | | Onomatopoeia |
| | | | Wordplay |

# RESOURCES FOR TEACHING

## A Study of Folktales by Culture con't

| CULTURES AND COLLECTORS | TYPICAL TALES, AUTHOR | CHARACTERS | CHARACTERISTICS |
|---|---|---|---|
| **AFRICAN FOLKTALES con't** | | | |
| | *How Many Spots Does a Leopard Have?* (Lester) | | |
| | *A Promise to the Sun* (Mollel) | | |
| | *Zomo the Rabbit* (McDermott) | | |
| **NATIVE AMERICAN FOLKTALES** | | | |
| Henry Rowe Schoolcraft (1820s–1850s) | *Gluskabe and the Four Wishes* (Bruhac) | Gluskap, Gluskabe | Nature myths |
| | *Star Boy* (Goble) | Manabozho | Tricksters |
| | *The Gift of the Sacred Dog* (Goble) | Hare | Transformation tales |
| | *Ladder to the Sky* (Esbensen) | Coyote | Pattern of four |
| | *The Deekatoo* (Bierhorst) | Raven | Pourquoi stories |
| | *Iktomi and the Buzzard* (Goble) | Iktomi | Interaction with spirit world |
| | *The Dark Way* (Hamilton) | Sky People | |
| | | Little People | |
| | | Mouse Woman | |

*The Jack Tales* is a cycle of stories in which Jack is always the central figure. You'd expect to find him playing this role in "Jack in the Giant's Newground" and "Jack and the Bean Tree." However, he shows up again in "Jack and the Robbers," which is a variant of "The Bremen Town Musicians." The delightful aspect of these tales is Jack's nonchalance about his exploits and the incongruous mixing of the mountaineer dialect with unicorns, kings, and swords.

In *Moss Gown*, William H. Hooks retells an old story from North Carolina that melds elements of "Cinderella" with motifs from *King Lear*. Rejected by her father and banished from home by her two sisters, Candace meets a gris-gris woman who gives her a shimmering gown that will change back into Spanish moss when the morning star sets. Candace finds work in the kitchen of a plantation where the Young Master is about to give a series of balls. Calling on the gris-gris woman for help, Candace goes to each of the three balls and falls in love with the Young Master. When Candace finally reveals herself, the Young Master has come to know her through conversation and, it is implied, to love her for more than her beauty. Although the moss gown has magic to help her, Candace is more similar in spirit to Princess Furball and The Rough-Face Girl than to the Disney and Perrault Cinderellas, for it is her own intelligence and spirit that wins her a husband, a home, and her father's love once again.

Authors continue to Americanize European folktales. Hooks has also written an Appalachian *The Three Little Pigs and the Fox* that depends on local detail, colloquial language, and mountain customs for flavor. In it, Hamlet rescues her two pig brothers from a "drooly-mouth fox" and comes home in time for Sunday dinner. Alan Schroeder's *Smoky Mountain Rose* is a version of Cinderella with a hog as fairy godmother and a man who has made his fortune in sowbellies and grits as her "prince."

*African American Folktales*  Africans who were brought to North America as slaves continued to tell the tales they remembered, particularly the talking-beast tales. Some of these stories took on new layers of meaning about the relationship between the slaves and their masters. In the late 1800s, Joel Chandler Harris, a Georgia newspaperman, recorded these tales in a written approximation of the Gullah dialect in which the tales were told to him. In his *Uncle Remus: His Songs and His Sayings*, Harris invented Uncle Remus, an elderly plantation slave who told these talking-beast tales to a little white boy (see Harris's *The Complete Tales of Uncle Remus*). Harris was later criticized for his portrayal of the Old South, but the "Brer Rabbit" stories live on in retellings by other people.

Two excellent series have adapted these stories for today's children. In *Jump Again!* Van Dyke Parks and Malcolm Jones present "The Wonderful Tar-Baby Story," in which Brer Fox sets up a sticky contraption and then, "Brer Fox, he lay low." When Brer Rabbit is finally stuck, Brer Fox saunters forth and laughs threateningly, showing "his teeth all white and shiny, like they were brand-new." Of course, Brer Rabbit pleads with the fox to do anything but throw him into a briar patch, and the gullible fox is tricked once again into sparing the rabbit's life, for Brer Rabbit was "bred and born in a briar patch" (p. 9). In contrast, Julius Lester's "Brer Rabbit and the Tar Baby" from his *Tales of Uncle Remus* is a more rambunctious version that sounds as if it is being told directly to the reader. Asides, contemporary allusions, creative figurative language, and interjections are characteristic of this storyteller. Lester describes Brer Rabbit as strutting "like he owned the world and was collecting rent from everybody in it" (p. 11). But by the time the poor rabbit is stuck, Brer Fox saunters out "as cool as the sweat on the side of a glass of ice tea" (p. 14). Full-colored watercolors by Jerry Pinkney depict incidents in the story. Julius Lester's foreword for his three collections dispel many of the myths surrounding the "Brer Rabbit" stories, discuss the nature of storytelling, and reflect on the role of the trickster figure in valuing a little disorder in today's society. Lester has also included several talking-beast tales in *The Knee-High Man and Other Tales*.

Folktales from the African Caribbean tradition have been collected in several books for children, and the islands have certainly contributed many stories to the mainland African American tradition. *Dr. Bird* by Gerald Hausman presents three tales about a humming bird whose advice is not always well received by the animals he tries to help. Lynn Joseph's *A Wave in Her Pocket: Stories from Trinidad*, illustrated by Brian Pinkney, and *The Mermaid's Twin Sister: More Stories from Trinidad*, illustrated by Donna Perronne, present traditional stories within modern-day narratives. Amber loves hearing her Tantie's tales about Trinidad, and both of these books place those traditional tales within stories about Amber and her island family. Robert D. San Souci has relied on several Creole tales from the French West Indies to tell *Cendrillon: A Caribbean Cinderella*. The story is narrated by Cendrillon's godmother, a washerwoman whose only treasure is a mahogany wand that changes one thing into another. When Cendrillon wishes to go to the ball given by Monsieur Thibault for his son Paul, the godmother turns a breadfruit into a carriage, rodents into horses, and lizards into footmen. The story has its traditional happy ending.

*The Talking Eggs* by San Souci is also a Creole folktale that seems to have its roots in European tales like those in Charlotte Huck's *Toads and Diamonds*. A poor widow and her two daughters live on a farm that looks like "the tail end of bad luck." Blanche, who has to do all the work, runs into the forest one day and meets a strange old woman who gives her the gift of special eggs, which will turn into riches when she throws them over her shoulder. But she is warned to take only the ones that say "Take me." Blanche follows this advice even though the ones she leaves are jewel-encrusted. When she arrives home with fancy clothes and a carriage, her mother plots to steal Blanche's things and send Rose for more. But Rose steals the jeweled eggs and is paid for her greediness by the release of whip snakes, wasps, and a cloud of bad things that chase her home. Jerry Pinkney's rich and colorful illustrations magically evoke the forest and swamp settings of this Louisiana "generous person/greedy person" tale.

San Souci and Jerry Pinkney have also collaborated on *The Hired Hand*, a somewhat macabre version of "The Sorcerer's Apprentice." Young Sam, the lazy son of a hardworking sawmill owner, sees the hired hand work magic on an old man by making him young again. When the greedy boy tries to perform the same trick on the man's wife, his victim ends up dead. It is only when he is on trial for his life and expresses repentance that the hired hand appears and saves him.

San Souci has retold a longer version of a short tale from the Sea Islands of South Carolina in *Sukey and the Mermaid*. In this story, Sukey has a mean stepfather who works her from dawn to dusk. Mama Jo, a mermaid, befriends her and gives her a gold coin whenever she calls her to the shore. Sukey's stepfather eventually discovers the mermaid's existence and tries to capture her for her gold. Sukey is led on several journeys between the world of the sea and that of her home on land, but eventually she decides to give up the mermaid's treasure for the love of a simple man.

Her greedy stepfather, who has caused her so much trouble and pain, drowns as he tries to escape with Mama Jo's gold. Brian Pinkney's scratchboard illustrations help shape this wonderfully textured and complex story.

Virginia Hamilton is responsible for several superior collections of stories representing African American folktales. In *The People Could Fly,* she has collected twenty-four stories, including animal tales, stories with motifs of transformation and trickery, Jack tales and a tale of John de Conquer, and slave tales of freedom, including one handed down in the author's own family. In *Her Stories,* Hamilton follows a similar organizational format, but these tales have their roots in the history and folklore of African American women. They include animal stories, fairy tales, stories of the supernatural, and stories about real-life heroines. Hamilton has preserved the individual voices of the storytellers from whom the stories were collected. Some of the stories are in Gullah or plantation dialect, and others include African words whose meanings are lost to us today. Excellent classroom resources, these collections contain author notes and extensive bibliographies. Bold black-and-white illustrations by Leo and Diane Dillon evoke the humor, beauty, and liveliness of these traditional stories.

According to Steve Sanfield's introduction to his *Adventures of High John the Conqueror,* the High John stories were popular among slaves but for obvious reasons were never shared with white people. Although John was a slave, he spent his time doing as little slaving as possible, tricking the Old Master out of a roasting pig or a few hours of rest. Sanfield prefaces eight of the sixteen tales with notes explaining historical context or giving background. In "Tops and Bottoms," titled after a motif found in many tales, John asks Boss which half of the planting he wants. Thinking that High John will plant cotton, Boss chooses the top. But John has planted sweet potatoes. Each of the next three years, Boss is tricked by John. Finally, he chooses *both* tops and bottoms, which leaves High John the middle. But John, no fool, plants corn, and Boss is left with a heap of tassels and stalks while High John takes the corn. Virginia Hamilton extended the adventures of this sometimes mythical hero into a folktale-like novel, *The Magical Adventures of Pretty Pearl.*

**Tall Tales**  Ask any visitors to the United States what they have seen, and they are apt to laugh and reply that, whatever it was, it was the "biggest in the world"—the longest hot dog, the highest building, the largest store, the hottest spot. This is the land of superlatives, of "the best." Many countries have tall tales in their folklore, but only the United States has developed so many huge legendary heroes. Perhaps the vast frontier made settlers seem so puny that they felt compelled to invent stories about superheroes. Whatever the reasons, North American tall tales contain a glorious mixture of the humor, bravado, and pioneer spirit that was needed to tame a wilderness.

Paul Bunyan was a huge lumberjack who bossed a big gang of lumbermen in the North Woods of Michigan, Minnesota, and Wisconsin. Paul's light lunch one day was "three sides of barbecued beef, half a wagon load of potatoes, carrots and a few other odds and ends," Glenn Rounds reports in *Ol' Paul, the Mighty Logger* (p. 28). Rounds asserts, as do most chroniclers of Paul's doings, that he worked for Paul and was the biggest liar ever in camp. By switching from past to present tense, Rounds gives these eleven tales special immediacy. Steven Kellogg synopsizes Paul Bunyan's life in his humorously illustrated picture-book version, *Paul Bunyan.* Tidy endpapers depict Paul's New England seacoast beginnings, and a map of the States highlights Paul's feats. This action-packed version serves as an introduction to Bunyan's exploits, but the extended text of the other versions fleshes out individual tall tales and makes them better choices for reading aloud.

Kellogg's *Pecos Bill* tells the tale of a Texan who, as a child, fell out of his parents' wagon as they moved west and was raised by coyotes. Bill's exploits include squeezing the poison from a rattler to create the first lasso, and inventing cattle roping. He also bred cattle with shorter legs on the uphill side so that they could graze steep pinnacles without falling off. His taming of a wild horse eventually won him a bride, Slue-Foot Sue. Kellogg's depiction of this exuberant tall-tale hero is full of humor, exaggeration, and boundless energy.

Of all the heroes, only Johnny Appleseed was a gentle, tame person who lived to serve others. His real name was John Chapman, and he grew up in the Connecticut Valley before setting out for Pennsylvania, Ohio, and Indiana. Kathy Jakobsen's full-page folk-art paintings for Reeve Lindbergh's *Johnny Appleseed* capture the changing face of the land as settlers moved west in this poetic retelling. Steven Kellogg's *Johnny Appleseed,* in contrast, focuses on the more rollicking incidents that grew around the tales Chapman told to settlers and their own embellishments of these stories. Both authors include notes that help readers see how storytellers select events to shape into tales.

Industry has its heroes, too. "Joe Magarac," in Adrien Stoutenberg's *American Tall Tales,* tells of a man of steel who came to Hunkietown. The word *magarac* means "jackass" (which to steelworkers was a term of admiration), and Joe Magarac worked and ate like one. He finally melted himself down to become part of a new steel mill. John Henry was a powerful African American who swung his mighty hammer in a contest with a steam drill to build the

*Jerry Pinkney portrays a magnificent American tall-tale hero in Julius Lester's retelling of* John Henry.

From *John Henry* by Julius Lester, illustrated by Jerry Pinkney, copyright © 1994 by Jerry Pinkney, illustrations. Used by permission of Dial Books for Young Readers, a division of Penguin Putnam Inc.

transcontinental railroad. Jerry Pinkney won a Caldecott Honor Medal for his sparkling watercolor illustrations for Julius Lester's robust retelling in *John Henry*. Steve Sanfield's illustrated short story *A Natural Man* also chronicles John Henry's life from childhood to his death after defeating the steam drill. Ezra Jack Keats created bold figures to depict this legendary hero in his picture book *John Henry*. "The Working of John Henry," in William J. Brooke's *A Telling of the Tales*, is a variation in which the steel-driving man triumphs by changing with the times and learning to use the newfangled machine.

Mary Pope Osborne tells the stories of nine heroes in *American Tall Tales*. In the tradition of nineteenth-century storytellers, she uses figurative language easily and has combined, edited, and added her own touches to these stories. Michael McCurdy's watercolor-washed bold wood engravings of Pecos Bill, John Henry, and Stormalong perfectly suit the exaggerated language of the tall tale.

In *Cut from the Same Cloth,* Robert San Souci has assembled a marvelous multicultural collection of tall tales with women heroines. Illustrated by Brian Pinkney, the stories are arranged by region and include such characters as Sal Fink, wife of the famous

Mike; Annie Christmas, an African American heroine; and Otoonah, a member of the Sugpiaq people of the Aleutian Islands. Although not all of these stories can be strictly defined as tall tales, they do feature women who are tall in courage and strong in will. Anne Isaacs has surely based *Swamp Angel,* her original tall tale, on these wonderful heroines. (See Chapter 5.)

Resources for Teaching, "Some American Tall-Tale Heroes" outlines some of the characteristics of eight of these legendary heroes. Others whom children might research and add to the list include Casey Jones, Old Stormalong, Slue-Foot Sue, Febold Feboldson, Tony Beaver, and Mike Fink.

### Folktales from Central and South America

Each year a little more of the rich story heritage of Central and South America becomes available. Many stories from this area appear in excellent collections of folktales, myths, or fables edited by John Bierhorst. *The Monkey's Haircut and Other Stories Told by the Maya* includes stories collected in Guatemala and southeastern Mexico from Mayan Indians since 1900. Some are obvious variations of European tales, and other are *ejemplos* (explanatory myths). Robert Andrew Parker's gray-washed drawings and Bierhorst's informative introduction both contribute appeal for middle-grade readers. (See the sections "Fables" and "Myths" in this chapter for other Bierhorst titles.) Lucia M. Gonzalez's carefully researched *Senor Cat's Romance* contains six stories from Latin America and is illustrated by Latina artist Lulu Delacre. Nicholasa Mohr's *The Song of el Coqui and Other Tales of Puerto Rico* includes stories with Taino, African, and Spanish origins and is indicative of the rich interweaving of cultures that contributed to the folklore of this vast region.

In Verna Aardema's Mexican tale *Borreguita and the Coyote,* a crafty "little lamb" outwits a coyote. Petra Mathers's stylish watercolor paintings feature bright saturated colors and primitive figures reminiscent of Henri Rousseau. Harriet Rohmer's *The Invisible Hunters* is a Nicaraguan Miskito Indian folktale about an isolated tribe's first contact with the outside world when a magic vine bestows the gift of invisibility on three brother hunters

Emery and Durga Bernhard's *The Tree That Rains* is a complex story from the Huichol Indians of Mexico that has a great flood as one of its episodes. In this version Great-Grandmother Earth warns the hardworking Nakawe that the great flood is coming, and he escapes with his faithful dog in a canoe he has made out of his fig tree. He sails the floodwaters for five years, and when the flood recedes he plants the seeds he has brought and prays for rain to grow them. He awakes the next morning to find a full-grown fig tree that gushes water to nourish his crops.

# RESOURCES FOR TEACHING

## Some American Tall-Tale Heroes

### JOHNNY APPLESEED (JOHN CHAPMAN) (1774–1845)

| Hero and Tales | Occupation/Locale | Characteristics |
| --- | --- | --- |
| *Johnny Appleseed* (Kellogg, Lindbergh)<br><br>"Johnny Appleseed," in *American Tall Tales* (Osborne)<br><br>"Rainbow Walker," in *American Tall Tales* (Stoutenberg) | Born in Massachusetts, wanderer in Pennsylvania, Indiana, and Ohio; planter of apple trees | Selfless; friend to animals; dressed in rags with cook pot for hat |

### PAUL BUNYAN

| Hero and Tales | Occupation/Locale | Characteristics |
| --- | --- | --- |
| *Ol' Paul, the Mighty Logger* (Rounds)<br><br>*Paul Bunyan* (Shephard, Kellogg)<br><br>"Sky Bright Axe," in *American Tall Tales* (Stoutenberg)<br><br>"Paul Bunyan," in *American Tall Tales* (Osborne) | Lumberjack; North American woods; created the Great Lakes, St. Lawrence Seaway, and Grand Canyon | Huge; strong even as a baby; Babe the Blue Ox was the pet; inventive problem solver |

### JOE MAGARAC

| Hero and Tales | Occupation/Locale | Characteristics |
| --- | --- | --- |
| "Steelmaker," in *American Tall Tales* (Stoutenberg) | Steelworker; Pittsburgh, or "Hunkietown" | Made of steel; works and eats like a mule; born from an ore pit; stirs steel with bare hands |

### PECOS BILL

| Hero and Tales | Occupation/Locale | Characteristics |
| --- | --- | --- |
| *Pecos Bill* (Kellogg, Dewey)<br><br>"Coyote Cowboy," in *American Tall Tales* (Stoutenberg)<br><br>"Pecos Bill," in *American Tall Tales* (Osborne)<br><br>"Slue-Foot Sue and Pecos Bill" (San Souci) | Cowboy; first rancher; Texas panhandle and the Southwest | Raised by coyotes; Widowmaker was his horse; Slue-Foot Sue was his wife; invented lasso, six-shooter, cattle roping |

### SALLY ANN THUNDER ANN WHIRLWIND CROCKETT

| Hero and Tales | Occupation/Locale | Characteristics |
| --- | --- | --- |
| *Sally Ann Thunder Ann Whirlwind Crockett* (Kellogg) | Kentucky, Mississippi River | Could outwrestle, outrun, and outfish her brothers even as a child. Rescued Davy Crockett then married him |

*continued*

# RESOURCES FOR TEACHING

## Some American Tall-Tale Heroes con't

### JOHN HENRY

| Hero and Tales | Occupation/Locale | Characteristics |
|---|---|---|
| *John Henry* (Keats, Lester)<br>*A Natural Man* (Sanfield)<br>"Hammerman," in *American Tall Tales* (Stoutenberg)<br>"John Henry," in *American Tall Tales* (Osborne)<br>"The Working of John Henry," in *A Telling of the Tales* (Brooke)<br>"John Henry the Steel Driving Man," in *Larger Than Life* (San Souci) | Railroad man; West Virginia west to the Mississippi | African American wanderer, exceedingly strong even as a baby; Polly Ann was his wife; companion was Little Willie |

### DAVY CROCKETT (1786–1836)

| Hero and Tales | Occupation/Locale | Characteristics |
|---|---|---|
| "Davy Crockett," in *American Tall Tales* (Osborne)<br>"Frontier Fighter," in *American Tall Tales* (Stoutenberg) | Frontiersman; Tennessee | Tall; good hunter and fighter; Betsy was his rifle; tamed a bear; wore coonskin cap |

### ALFRED BULLTOP STORMALONG

| Hero and Tales | Occupation/Locale | Characteristics |
|---|---|---|
| "Five Fathoms Tall," in *American Tall Tales* (Stoutenberg)<br>"Stormalong," in *American Tall Tales* (Osborne)<br>"Old Stormalong: The Deep Water Sailor," in *Larger Than Life* (San Souci) | Sailor whaler, ship's captain; Massachusetts and northern coasts | Giant man, huge appetite; ship called the Tuscarora; made the White Cliffs of Dover with soap |

Now every year the Huichol people remember this story at the Festival of the New Corn. An Argentinean tale by Nancy Van Laan also focuses on water. In *The Magic Bean Tree*, the Great Bird of the Underworld has caused a drought that is threatening all the wild life on the Argentinean Pampas. Little Topec figures out how to scare away the miserable bird with the help of the beans from a Carob Tree.

The folk art pictures by Beatriz Vidal lend a range of emotional moods to this story.

Pourquoi stories are as common in Central and South America as they are in other cultures. Lois Ehlert's *Moon Rope* is a bilingual retelling of a Peruvian tale in which Mole and Fox try to climb to the moon on a grass rope. Mole falls off the rope and is so embarrassed by the other animals' teasing that he

*Emery and Durga Bernhard use traditional Indian motifs to illustrate their version of a Mexican flood myth in* The Tree That Rains.

Illustration copyright © 1994 by Durga Bernhard. Reprinted from *The Tree That Rains* by Emery Bernhard by permission of Holiday House.

goes to live underground. As for Fox, Lois Ehlert's illustrations, adapted from Peruvian folk arts, show his face, just visible in the silvery moon. A pourquoi story tells how birds became brightly colored. "Humming-Bird and the Flower" appears in Charles Finger's *Tales from Silver Lands,* a collection of South American stories, illustrated with woodcuts, that won a Newbery Medal in 1925. The story attributes the hummingbird's colors to clay, jewels, the color of the sunset, and the greens of the forests, which Panther helped the bird to gather after it helped restore Panther's eyesight. Nancy Van Laan has retold another pourquoi tale for younger readers. *So Say the Little Monkeys* tells why black-mouth monkeys live in the trees; they mean to be industrious but end up playing all the time instead. Gerald McDermott explains how music came into the world in his *Musicians of the Sun,* a retelling of an Aztec myth.

With the changing population of North America, we need more editions of traditional folktales, myths, and legends that reflect South and Central American cultural heritage. Small publishers have begun to feature folktales of the region, and teachers will need to be persistent in finding these sources.

The "Exploring Folktales" web on page 276 suggests the rich possibilities inherent in a study of this genre of literature. It provides for a serious look at the types of folktales and certain motifs found in the tales that would appeal to younger children. A study of more-complex tales or myths or a cross-cultural study could be planned for older children.

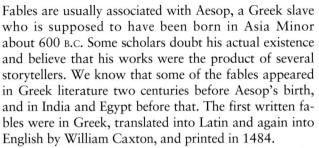

# Fables

Fables are usually associated with Aesop, a Greek slave who is supposed to have been born in Asia Minor about 600 B.C. Some scholars doubt his actual existence and believe that his works were the product of several storytellers. We know that some of the fables appeared in Greek literature two centuries before Aesop's birth, and in India and Egypt before that. The first written fables were in Greek, translated into Latin and again into English by William Caxton, and printed in 1484.

Other sources for fables, as we have seen, were the Jataka tales—animal stories that told of the previous births of the Buddha—and the *Panchatantra,* which was written for the purpose of instructing the young princes of India. These stories, longer than Aesop's fables, have moralistic verses interspersed throughout. When these are removed, the tales are closer to folktales. (See the earlier section "Folktales.")

A third common source for fables is the work of Jean De La Fontaine, a French poet, who wrote his fables in verse form. However, he drew largely on the collections of Aesop's fables that were available in the seventeenth century.

## Characteristics of Fables

Fables are brief, didactic tales in which animals, or occasionally the elements, speak as human beings. Examples of these might be the well-known race between the hare and the tortoise or the contest between the sun and the north wind. Humans do appear in a few fables, such as "The Country Maid and the Milk Pail" or "The Boy Who Cried Wolf." The characters are impersonal, with no name other than "fox," rabbit," or "cow." They do not have the lively personalities of Anansi the spider or Raven the trickster of folktale fame. The animals merely represent aspects of human nature—the lion stands for kingliness, the fox for cunning, the sheep for innocence and simplicity, and so on. Fables seldom have more than three characters, and the plots are usually based on a single incident. Fables were primarily meant to instruct. Therefore, all of them contain either an implicit or an explicit moral.

Because of their brevity, fables appear to be simple. However, they convey an abstract idea in relatively few words, and for that very reason they are highly complex. In selecting fables, then, it is wise to look at the quality of both language and illustrations. Compare the following two beginnings for "The Town Mouse and the Country Mouse." The first is Lisbeth Zwerger's, in her *Aesop's Fables:*

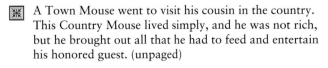

A Town Mouse went to visit his cousin in the country. This Country Mouse lived simply, and he was not rich, but he brought out all that he had to feed and entertain his honored guest. (unpaged)

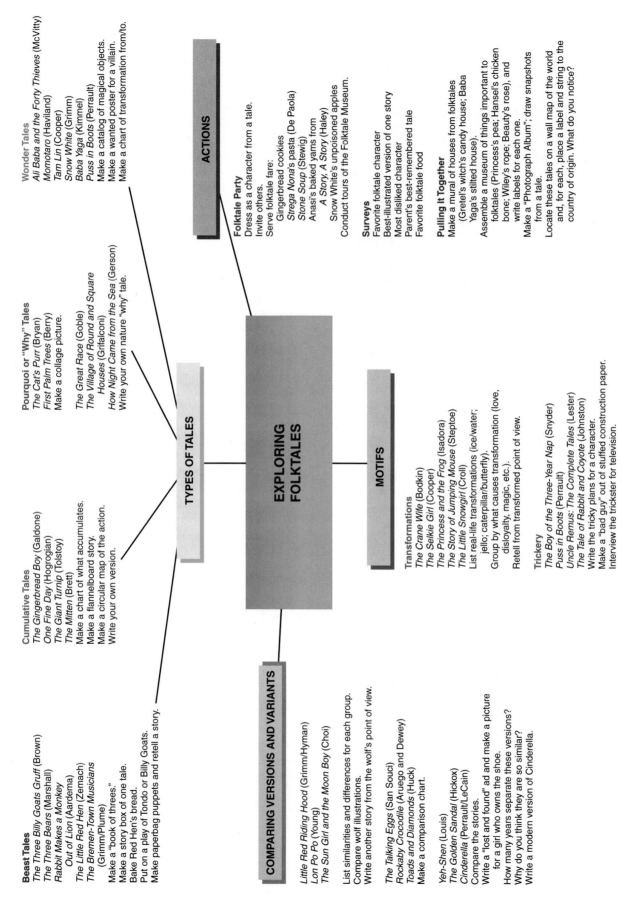

**EXPLORING FOLKTALES**

## TYPES OF TALES

**Beast Tales**
*The Three Billy Goats Gruff* (Brown)
*The Three Bears* (Marshall)
*Rabbit Makes a Monkey Out of Lion* (Aardema)
*The Little Red Hen* (Zemach)
*The Bremen-Town Musicians* (Grimm/Plume)
Make a "book of threes."
Make a story box of one tale.
Bake Red Hen's bread.
Put on a play of Tondo or Billy Goats.
Make paperbag puppets and retell a story.

**Cumulative Tales**
*The Gingerbread Boy* (Galdone)
*One Fine Day* (Hogrogian)
*The Giant Turnip* (Tolstoy)
*The Mitten* (Brett)
Make a chart of what accumulates.
Make a flannelboard story.
Make a circular map of the action.
Write your own version.

**Pourquoi or "Why" Tales**
*The Cat's Purr* (Bryan)
*First Palm Trees* (Berry)
Make a collage picture.
*The Great Race* (Goble)
*The Village of Round and Square Houses* (Grifalconi)
*How Night Came from the Sea* (Gerson)
Write your own nature "why" tale.

**Wonder Tales**
*Ali Baba and the Forty Thieves* (McVitty)
*Momotaro* (Haviland)
*Tam Lin* (Cooper)
*Snow White* (Grimm)
*Baba Yaga* (Kimmel)
*Puss in Boots* (Perrault)
Make a catalog of magical objects.
Make a wanted poster for a villain.
Make a chart of transformation from/to.

## ACTIONS

**Folktale Party**
Dress as a character from a tale.
Invite others.
Serve folktale fare:
　Gingerbread cookies
　*Strega Nona*'s pasta (De Paola)
　*Stone Soup* (Stewig)
　Anasi's baked yams from
　　*A Story, A Story* (Haley)
　Snow White's unpoisoned apples
Conduct tours of the Folktale Museum.

**Surveys**
Favorite folktale character
Best-illustrated version of one story
Most disliked character
Parent's best-remembered tale
Favorite folktale food

**Pulling It Together**
Make a mural of houses from folktales (Gretel's witch's candy house; Baba Yaga's stilted house).
Assemble a museum of things important to folktales (Princess's pea; Hansel's chicken bone; Wiley's rope; Beauty's rose), and write labels for each one.
Make a "Photograph Album"; draw snapshots from a tale.
Locate these tales on a wall map of the world and, for each, place a label and string to the country of origin. What do you notice?

## MOTIFS

**Transformations**
*The Crane Wife* (Bodkin)
*The Selkie Girl* (Cooper)
*The Princess and the Frog* (Isadora)
*The Story of Jumping Mouse* (Steptoe)
*The Little Snowgirl* (Croll)
List real-life transformations (ice/water; jello; caterpillar/butterfly).
Group by what causes transformation (love, disloyalty, magic, etc.).
Retell from transformed point of view.

**Trickery**
*The Boy of the Three-Year Nap* (Snyder)
*Puss in Boots* (Perrault)
*Uncle Remus: The Complete Tales* (Lester)
*The Tale of Rabbit and Coyote* (Johnston)
Write the tricky plans for a character.
Make a "bad guy" out of stuffed construction paper.
Interview the trickster for television.

## COMPARING VERSIONS AND VARIANTS

*Little Red Riding Hood* (Grimm/Hyman)
*Lon Po Po* (Young)
*The Sun Girl and the Moon Boy* (Choi)

List similarities and differences for each group.
Compare wolf illustrations.
Write another story from the wolf's point of view.

*The Talking Eggs* (San Souci)
*Rockaby Crocodile* (Aruego and Dewey)
*Toads and Diamonds* (Huck)
Make a comparison chart.

*Yeh-Shen* (Louis)
*The Golden Sandal* (Hickox)
*Cinderella* (Perrault/LeCain)
Compare the stories.
Write a "lost and found" ad and make a picture for a girl who owns the shoe.
How many years separate these versions?
Why do you think they are so similar?
Write a modern version of Cinderella.

Jan Brett's version, *Town Mouse, Country Mouse* begins,

> One morning the town mouse woke up shivering from a dream about the kitchen cat who prowled the house. "I need a vacation," he said to his wife. "Let me take you to the countryside where I was born. Life is quiet and peaceful there. The sun shines brightly every day and the air is so clear that you can see the stars every night. And nothing will prepare you for the taste of wild blackberries." (unpaged)

Zwerger's illustrations feature a simple picture of two mice conversing on a hillside. Brett's highly detailed drawings have woodland borders that contain visual subplots. In addition she introduces two new characters to the traditional fable, an owl and a cat. These reflect some of the unique and various treatments given to Aesop's stories for today's readers.

## Editions

Younger children might appreciate some fables, but they are not usually able to extract a moral spontaneously until about second or third grade. Fulvio Testa's *Aesop's Fables* recounts its fables concisely, with morals concealed in the conversation rather than appended. Testa's use of crisp line and bright borders makes this version especially useful in reading aloud to larger groups.

In *A Sip of Aesop,* Jane Yolen has also used rhymes to retell thirteen of the fables, including "The Dog in the Manger" and "Counting Your Chickens." Her amusing introduction sets the tone for these decidedly modern retellings. Brightly colored paintings by Karen Barbour recall the work of Henri Matisse and are vivid reminders of the timeliness of the stories. Eric Carle, in *Twelve Tales from Aesop,* took some liberties in retelling, so that in "The Grasshopper and the Ant," instead of being left out in the cold as a result of his lack of foresight, the grasshopper is invited into a second house as an honored musician.

A reissue of *The Caldecott Aesop* shows how Randolph Caldecott applied the moral of a fable to a contemporary (for Caldecott) setting. Each fable has two pictures—one, a literal animal scene, and the second, a human one. The title character of "The Ass in the Lion's Skin" impresses the other animals until the disguise blows off. In Caldecott's satiric second interpretation, a pompous art critic is discovered to know nothing. In *Aesop & Company,* Barbara Bader has sandwiched nineteen of Aesop's fables between an introduction to the origins of the stories and an afterword that retells the legends that surround Aesop's life. Detailed etchings by Arthur Geisert add visual complexity to the brief fables and provide a nice feel of timelessness.

John Bierhorst, a distinguished collector and editor of Native American literature, discovered that

MORAL:
You may not have time
For a final correction.
Don't open your mouth
Without proper reflection.

*Karen Barbour's lively illustrations add to the appeal of Jane Yolen's retellings in* A Sip of Aesop.

Illustration by Karen Barbour from *A Sip of Aesop* by Jane Yolen. Published by Blue Sky Press, an imprint of Scholastic Inc. Illustration copyright © 1995 by Karen Barbour. Reprinted by permission.

Aesop's fables had been recorded by the Aztecs in the sixteenth century. His *Doctor Coyote* is a collection of these stories, translated from the Aztec manuscript, in which the main character of each fable became Coyote, a Native American trickster. Bierhorst's cohesive collection of twenty fables weaves one story into the next and shows Coyote getting a little wiser with each "lesson." With ample use of blues and roses, Wendy Watson's full-color illustrations warmly depict the desert and mountain settings of New Mexico.

Other illustrators have chosen fewer tales for interpretation. Illustrator Aki Sogabe has woven several of Aesop's fox fables into a single tale in *Aesop's Fox.* Paul Galdone's *Three Aesop Fox Fables* includes two stories in which the same fox is outsmarted and one in which he triumphs. Galdone has also illustrated a Jataka tale, *The Monkey and the Crocodile,* as did Marcia Brown in *Once a Mouse.* Startling close-ups heighten the drama of "little and big" in Ed Young's black-and-white illustrations for *The Lion and the Mouse.* By contrast, Young's vividly colored collages for the Indian fable *Seven Blind Mice* highlight the patchwork nature of understanding that these mice bring to their definition of an elephant.

Older children might enjoy comparing treatments of several of these fables. In this way they would become familiar with the spare language, the conventional characters, and the explicit or implied morals of fables. They might appreciate modern writers of fables, such as Leo Lionni, whose *Frederick* is similar to Carle's version of "The Grasshopper and the Ant," or William Steig, whose *Amos & Boris* mirrors "The Lion and the Mouse." After such comparisons, discussions, and readings, they would then be well prepared to write their own fables and variations.

# *Myths*

Mythology evolved as primitive peoples searched their imaginations and related events to forces, as they sought explanations of the earth, sky, and human behavior. These explanations moved slowly through the stages of a concept of one power or force in human form, who controlled the phenomena of nature; to a complex system in which the god or goddess represented such virtues as wisdom, purity, or love; to a worshiping of the gods in organized fashion. Gods took the forms of men and women, but they were immortal and possessed supernatural powers.

Myths deal with human relationships with the gods, with the relationships of the gods among themselves, with the way people accept or fulfill their destiny, and with people's struggles with good and evil forces both within themselves and outside themselves. The myths are good stories, too, for they contain action, suspense, and basic conflicts. Usually each story is short and can be enjoyed by itself, without deep knowledge of the general mythology. Geraldine McCaughrean has written several fine collections of myths and legends from around the world in *The Golden Hoard, The Silver Treasure,* and *The Bronze Cauldron.* The fine illustrations by Bee Wiley and the source notes in each volume mark these volumes as essential to any study of mythology.

## Types of Myths

Many myths can be characterized by the type of explanation they offer about the beginnings of the world or about some natural phenomenon. Other myths might focus on difficult tasks or obstacles to be overcome by the hero or heroine.

### *Creation Myths*

Every culture has a story about how the world began, how people were made, how the sun and the moon got into the sky. These are called creation myths, or origin myths; they give an explanation for the beginnings of things. John Bierhorst's *The Woman Who Fell from the Sky* is an Iroquois creation story in which First Woman falls from her home in the sky and lands on Turtle's back, creating the world. She soon gives birth to two boys, Sapling and Flint. Sapling busies himself creating gifts for the people who are soon to come. Flint, whose heart is hard, injects difficulties into every gift. Then Flint invents terrible troubles for people, but Sapling mediates and makes these easier to bear. Finally Sapling takes some earth and makes human beings, teaching them to make houses and light fires. Then he and Flint return to the sky, each taking a separate path that becomes the Milky Way. Their mother leaps into a campfire and rises with the smoke into the air. To this day the people give her their thanks as smoke rises from their fires. Robert Andrew Parker's flowing watercolor illustrations bring a sense of magic and mystery to this lovely story.

Virginia Hamilton chose creation stories from around the world for her collection *In the Beginning.*

> These myths from around the world were created by people who sensed the wonder and glory of the universe. Lonely as they were, by themselves, early people looked inside themselves and expressed a longing to discover, to explain who they were, why they were, and from what and where they came. (p. xi)

Barry Moser's watercolor portraits and representations are mysterious and dramatic accompaniments to these tales. An Eskimo story tells how Raven the Creator made a pea pod from which humans sprang. A Chinese story explains how Phan Ku burst from a cosmic egg to create the world. A California Indian legend, "Turtle Dives to the Bottom of the Sea," begins with a sea turtle that dives underwater to bring up enough earth to make dry land.

John Bierhorst's expertise in Aztec literature is the basis for his *Mythology of Mexico and Central America.* This book traces twenty basic myths and explains how they functioned among the ancient Aztec and Maya people and how they survive today. This volume, as well as its two companions, *The Mythology of South America* and *The Mythology of North America,* would give teachers and older students the background needed to understand these creation stories. Bierhorst's *The Hungry Woman: Myths and Legends of the Aztecs* is for a younger audience and includes reproductions of early Aztec paintings that functioned as a way of preserving stories.

Children who compare myths may marvel at the human imagination and see the world in a different way. Comparing myths also often raises interesting questions for children about the similarities, connections, and migrations of early peoples.

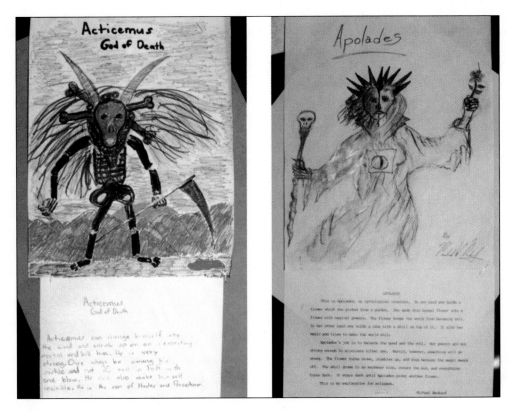

*As part of a study of myths, sixth graders created stories and illustrations describing their own mythological creatures.*
George Mason Elementary School, Alexandria City Public Schools, Alexandria, Virginia. Susan Steinberg, teacher.

## Nature Myths

The nature myths include stories that explain seasonal changes, animal characteristics, earth formations, constellations, and the movements of the sun and earth. Many Native American nature myths are easier for young children to comprehend than are the creation myths. Some of these myths have been previously discussed in the section "Native American Folktales."

The Greek story of Demeter and Persephone explains the change of seasons. Hades, god of the underworld, carried Persephone off to the underworld to be his bride, and Demeter, her mother, who made plants grow, mourned so for her daughter that she asked Zeus to intercede. It was granted that the girl might return if she had eaten nothing in Hades. Because she had eaten four seeds of a pomegranate, she was compelled to return to Hades for four months each year, during which time the earth suffered and winter came. In *Daughter of Earth,* Gerald McDermott tells the Roman version of the myth, visually contrasting the cool greens of earth above with the smoke reds of the underworld.

## Hero Myths

The hero myths, found in many cultures, do not attempt to explain anything at all. These myths have some of the same qualities as wonder stories—the hero is given certain tasks or, in the case of Heracles, labors, to accomplish. Frequently the gods help (or hinder) a particular favorite (or disliked) mortal. Monsters, such as gorgons, hydras, and chimeras, are plentiful in the Greek stories, but these provide the hero with a challenge. Characteristic of the hero or heroine is that he or she accepts all dangerous assignments and accomplishes the quest or dies in one last glorious adventure.

## Greek Mythology

The myths with which we are most familiar are those of the ancient Greeks collected by the poet Hesiod sometime during the eighth century B.C. The Roman versions of these myths were adapted by the poet Ovid during the first century B.C. in his well-known *Metamorphoses.* This has caused some confusion, in that the Roman names for the gods are better known than the Greek, even though the stories originated with the Greeks. However, the more recent versions of these myths are using Greek names. In working with children, it is best to be consistent in your choice of names, or they will become confused. You might wish to reproduce Resources for Teaching, "Some Gods and Goddesses of Greek and Roman Mythology" for

# RESOURCES FOR TEACHING

## Some Gods and Goddesses of Greek and Roman Mythology

| Greek | Roman | Title | Relationship |
|---|---|---|---|
| Zeus | Jupiter or Jove | Supreme Ruler, Lord of the Sky | |
| Poseidon | Neptune | God of the Sea | Brother of Zeus |
| Hades or Pluto | Pluto | God of the Underworld | Brother of Zeus |
| Hestia | Vesta | Goddess of the Home and Hearth | Sister of Zeus |
| Hera | Juno | Goddess of Women and Marriage | Wife and sister of Zeus |
| Ares | Mars | God of War | Son of Zeus and Hera |
| Athena | Minerva | Goddess of Wisdom | Daughter of Zeus |
| Apollo | Apollo | God of Light and Truth, the Sun God | Son of Zeus and Leto |
| Aphrodite | Venus | Goddess of Love and Beauty | Daughter of Zeus, wife of Hephaestus |
| Hermes | Mercury | Messenger of the Gods | Son of Zeus and Maia |
| Artemis | Diana | Goddess of the Moon and Hunt | Twin sister of Apollo |
| Hephaestus | Vulcan | God of Fire | Son of Hera |
| Eros | Cupid | God of Love | Son of Aphrodite (in some accounts) |
| Demeter | Ceres | Goddess of Grain | Daughter of Cronus and Rhea |
| Dionysus or Bacchus | Bacchus | God of Wine | Son of Zeus and Semele |
| Persephone | Proserpine | Maiden of Spring | Daughter of Demeter |

their reference. Leonard Everett Fisher's *The Olympians* provides an introduction to the pantheon. Each double-page spread features a painting as well as a paragraph about a particular god or goddess, and lists both Greek and Roman names, parentage, and the symbols representing that deity.

Greek mythology is composed of many stories of gods and goddesses, heroes, and monsters. The Greeks were the first to see their gods in their own image. As their culture became more sophisticated and complex, so too did their stories of the gods. These personified gods could do anything that humans could do, but on a much mightier scale. The gods, although immortal, freely entered into the lives of mortals, helping or hindering them, depending on their particular moods. Their strength was mighty and so was their wrath. Many of the myths are concerned with the gods' conflicts and loves. Their jealousy and their struggles for power often caused trouble for humans. (Some of the stories concerning the loves and quarrels of the immortals are inappropriate for children.)

Greek mythology includes the creation story that Earth and Sky were the first gods. Their children were the giant Cyclopes and the Titans, one of whom was Cronus, who drove his father away with a scythe (the source of the traditional picture of Father Time). Cronus swallowed his children so they would not usurp his place, but his wife gave him a stone in place of her last child, Zeus. Of course, Zeus overthrew his father and made him disgorge his brothers and sisters, who were still alive. Zeus married the jealous Hera, who caused all kinds of trouble. Prometheus was a Titan who defied the other gods in order to give fire to humankind. Zeus punished his disobedience by chaining him to Mount Caucasus, where each day his liver was devoured by an eagle but each night it was renewed. Zeus also sent Pandora and a box of trouble to punish Prometheus and humankind (see "Pandora" in Virginia Hamilton's *In the Beginning*). Warned not to open the box, Pandora was so curious that she could not help herself. All the evils of the world were released, but hope remained in the box and gave humans the ability to endure.

Another story concerned Zeus's punishment of the greedy King Midas (see the versions by Alice Low, Neil Philip, and John Stewig). Midas's curse was that everything he touched, including his little daughter, turned to gold. Children who have a good background in folktales will find that many of the same elements are present in the Greek myths. In the *D'Aulaires' Book of Greek Myths* the story of King Midas is economically told in two pages with a bold stone lithograph illustration. The D'Aulaires's collection presents a well-woven selection of tales ranging from the birth of Cronus's children to the stories of the mortal descendants of Zeus.

The gods could not tolerate human pride, which the Greeks called *hubris*. Arachne was transformed into a spider because of her pride when she foolishly challenged the goddess Athena to a weaving contest. Bellerophon slew the monster Chimaera, defeated the Amazons, and rode Pegasus. But when he boasted that he would fly to Olympus, the offended Zeus caused a gadfly to sting Pegasus, who bucked and tossed Bellerophon to his death.

Other stories of the disastrous results of *hubris* include the myths of Daedalus and Phaethon. In Jane Yolen's *Wings,* Daedalus is presented as a proud Athenian inventor who is banished for inadvertently killing a nephew. Exiled to Crete, he designs and builds a labyrinth for King Minos but years later gives the Athenian Theseus the key to its maze. In punishment for this, Daedalus and his young son, Icarus, are imprisoned in a high tower. Using candle wax, Daedalus makes a framework of wings from bird feathers. As they are about to escape, he warns his son not to fly too high or the sun will melt the wax, but Icarus does not heed his father's warning and falls to his death in the ocean. In italics, Yolen's text provides a Greek chorus, or commentary by the gods, who give approval, observe, laugh, or listen gravely. Dennis Nolan's illustrations show the faces of the gods hidden in the clouds, looking on, mourning, but doing nothing to prevent Icarus's death. The story of the winged horse Pegasus also involves a mortal whose pride gets the best of him. This myth has been retold by Marianna Mayer in *Pegasus* and by Jane Yolen in *Pegasus the Flying Horse.*

Descended from the sun god, Helios, Phaethon desires to drive the sun chariot to prove his parentage to his friends. When his father is finally tricked into agreeing, Phaethon cannot control the sun chariot and nearly burns up the earth. Zeus saves humankind by killing Phaethon with a thunderbolt. Alice Low retells both of these stories and many others in *The Macmillan Book of Greek Gods and Heroes.* An excellent, insightfully illustrated collection of stories that feature more dialogue than the d'Aulaire versions, Low's book also includes hero tales of Perseus, Heracles, Jason, Theseus, and Odysseus.

Pride is also the downfall of Atalanta, a young woman who is a skillful hunter and the swiftest of runners in Shirley Climo's *Atalanta's Race.* Reluctant to marry and give up her life of freedom, Atalanta finally agrees to wed the man who can beat her in a foot race. Melanion, a suitor whom she has admired, is given three golden apples by Aphrodite, who is angered by Atalanta's lack of reverence for the gods. As the two race side by side, Melanion throws an apple in Atalanta's path, distracting her so that he can win the race. The two marry and live relatively happily for many years, but because they have ignored the gods, Aphrodite punishes the two by changing them into lions. Alexander Kohskin's painted illustrations are set in Corinthian columns and resemble the murals found in Greek and Roman dwellings.

In *Cupid and Psyche* Charlotte M. Craft retells the story of Cupid, who has been sent by the jealous Aphrodite to find a horrible mate for the beautiful Psyche. Instead he falls in love with her. Invisible, cupid woos Psyche, and she falls in love with him sight unseen. When Psyche's sisters talk her into lighting a lamp in order to see her husband, Cupid flees. To win him back, Psyche must perform difficult tasks, and the last one kills her. Cupid carries her to Olympus, where the gods honor her for her steadfastness by making her immortal. Children will be struck by the similarity of patterns in this tale with the folktales in *East o'the Sun and West o'the Moon* (see the version by Asbjørnsen and Moe).

Older children who have been introduced to Greek mythology through the simpler stories will be ready for the longer hero tales of Perseus, the gorgon-slayer; Theseus, killer of the minotaur; Heracles and his many labors; Jason and his search of the golden fleece; and the wanderings of Odysseus. Fortunately, several of these stories are now published in single-tale editions. Leonard Everett Fisher's *Jason and the Golden Fleece* is told in spare prose with dramatic paintings to underscore Jason's trials in overcoming the Harpies, avoiding the crashing rocks of the Symplegades, and numerous other tasks. Jason wins the fleece with the help of Medea, sails home victoriously, but then betrays his wife, finally coming to a lonely end. Fisher has also illustrated and retold *Theseus and the Minotaur.*

Warwick Hutton has also undertaken a series of Greek myths, including *Perseus* and *Theseus and the Minotaur.* His Theseus is more poetic and evocative of an Aegean setting than Fisher's version. Theseus promises his father that he will go with the fourteen youths sacrificed each year to King Minos's monster, the Minotaur. There, with the help of Ariadne, who has fallen in love with him and gives him a cord to follow to find his way out again, he is able to find his way into the labyrinth and kill the evil creature. Theseus's tragedy is that he must abandon Ariadne to the god Dionysus and in his misery he forgets to

*Barry Moser's paintings provide a romantic realism for Doris Orgel's retelling of Theseus's betrayal of Ariadne in* Ariadne, Awake!

From *Ariadne, Awake!* by Doris Orgel, illustrated by Barry Moser, copyright © 1994 by Bear Run Publishing, Inc., illustrations. Used by permission of Viking Penguin, a division of Penguin Putnam Inc.

change the sail of his boat from black to white to indicate to his father that he is alive. Seeing the black sail, the grief-stricken King Aegeus hurls himself into the sea, from whence comes its name—the Aegean Sea. Theseus later becomes king of Athens, but he is never truly happy and finally steps down. Hutton's artwork reflects designs and motifs of Minoan architecture, clothing, and artifacts.

Doris Orgel has told this myth from Ariadne's point of view in the short chapter book *Ariadne, Awake!* illustrated by Barry Moser. The first-person narrative has an exciting immediacy as Ariadne, a sheltered teenager, tells of falling in love with the beautiful but callow Theseus. After he has used her to gain his own ends, his abandonment of her is especially heart-rending. Left alone on the island of Naxos, Ariadne is visited by the god Dionysus. He comforts her with the thought that even love that ends in pain is merely a stop along the way to greater love. His advice seems to be true, for eventually these two are married and live a long and happy life. This powerfully romantic version will have special appeal for early adolescents.

Bernard Evslin's *Hercules,* part of a series that includes *Jason and the Argonauts,* is told in modern

language and allusion, which makes for an exciting and fast-paced narrative. By heightening the action and emphasizing characterization of the villainous Hera or the faithful and brave Iole, Evslin makes Hercules into a hero very much in keeping with the heroes children already know from television and fantasy movies. Evslin also employs modern vernacular in *Heroes and Monsters of Greek Myth.*

Like Evslin, Robert Graves in *Greek Gods and Heroes* utilizes the same rather flippant approach in his telling. This style makes the stories seem more contemporary, but they lose part of their mystery and grandeur. *Tales of the Greek Heroes* by Roger Lancelyn Green is a somewhat more difficult but well-written collection.

## Norse Mythology

 A mythology derives its characteristics from the land and peoples of its origin. The land of the Norse was a cold, cruel land of frost, snow, and ice. Life was a continual struggle for survival against these elements. It seems only natural that Norse mythology was filled with gods who had to battle against huge frost giants, also. These were heroic gods who, unlike the immortal Greek gods safe in their home on sunny Mount Olympus, knew that they and their home on Asgard would eventually be destroyed. And in a way their prophecy was fulfilled, for Christianity all but extinguished talk of the old gods, except in Iceland. There, in the thirteenth century, Snorri Sturluson—a poet, scholar, and historian—collected many of the Norse myths and legends into a book called the *Prose Edda*. Much of his writing was based on an earlier verse collection called the *Poetic Edda*. These two books are the primary sources for our knowledge of Norse mythology.

It is too bad that children do not know these myths as well as they know those of the Greeks. In some ways the Norse tales seem more suited to children than the highly sophisticated Greek tales. These stories appeal to the child's imagination, with their tales of giants and dwarfs, eight-legged horses and vicious wolves, magic hammers and rings. Primarily they are bold, powerful stories of the relationships among the gods and their battles against the evil frost giants. Odin is the serious protector of the humans he created, willingly sacrificing one of his eyes to obtain wisdom that would allow him to see deep into their hearts. The largest and the strongest of the gods is Thor, owner of a magic hammer that will hit its mark and then return to his hands. And Balder, the tragic god of light, is the most loved by all the other gods.

Some of the stories are amusing. Seven- and 8-year-olds would enjoy the picture-book versions of the story of Thor's stolen hammer by Shirley Climo. In

*Stolen Thunder* the enormous Thor, the god of Thunder, is dressed as a bride and goes with Loki, who is his "bridesmaid," to trick the giant Thrym into returning Thor's magic hammer. Loki is a mischievous sidekick in Climo's version, although in the original myths he became increasingly evil. One of the best collections of these myths is the classic *The Children of Odin* by Padraic Colum.

If children have time to become acquainted with only one mythology, they should know the Greek stories (or their Roman adaptations). No other tales have so influenced the literature and art of the Western world. Norse mythology, too, has left its marks on Western culture, as in the names *Thursday* ("Thor's day") and *Friday* ("Freya's day"). Also, these tales have a special appeal for children. However, there are many other important mythologies that might be sampled as a part of the study of a culture or simply be enjoyed as literature.

## Epic & Legendary Heroes

An epic is a long narrative or a cycle of stories clustering around the actions of a single hero. Epics grew out of myths or along with them, since the gods still intervene in earlier epics like the *Iliad* and the *Odyssey*. Gradually, the center of action shifted from the gods to human heroes, so that in tales like "Robin Hood" the focus is completely on the daring adventures of the man himself.

The epic hero is a cultural or national hero embodying all the ideal characteristics of greatness in his time. Thus Odysseus and Penelope, his wife, represented the Greek ideals of intelligence, persistence, and resourcefulness. Odysseus survived by his wit rather than his great strength. Both King Arthur and Robin Hood appealed to the English love of justice and freedom: King Arthur and his knights represented the code of chivalry; Robin Hood was the champion of the commoner—the prototype of the "good outlaw." The epics, then, express the highest moral values of a society. A knowledge of the epics gives children an understanding of a particular culture; but more importantly, it provides them with models of greatness through the ages.

### The Epic of Gilgamesh

The Epic of Gilgamesh, recorded more than four thousand years ago in Mesopotamia, is one of the oldest hero stories. The epic poem, first discovered written on clay tablets in the library of Assur-Bani-Pal, an Assyrian king who ruled from 668 to 626 B.C.,

*Mila Zeman's* The Revenge of Ishtar *is one of a trilogy of picture books that provide a retelling of the Gilgamesh epic for children.*
From *The Revenge of Ishtar* © 1993 by Ludmila Zeman, published by Tundra Books of Northern New York/McClelland & Stewart Children's Books.

is probably the compilation of many earlier myths. The original stories actually concerned three figures: Gilgamesh, a Sumerian King; Endiku, a primitive wild man; and Utnapishtim, the man we would call Noah. Canadian author Ludmila Zeman has retold and illustrated these three episodes in a highly readable trio of picture books. In *Gilgamesh the King* we are introduced to the god-king who plays the central role in the three books. He is a bitter and cruel king because he has not experienced the power of human companionship. When his desire to build a great wall threatens his people's survival, the sun god sends Endiku, another man as strong as Gilgamesh, to earth, where he lives in the forest and cares for the animals. When he threatens one of Gilgamesh's hunters, Gilgamesh sends the lovely singer Shamat to tempt Endiku out of the forest. In spite of his beastly appearance, she teaches him about human love and they leave the forest to confront Gilgamesh. The two men engage in a terrible struggle on Gilgamesh's famous wall, but because their powers are equal they seem to be at an impasse. Then Gilgamesh stumbles on a stone and would fall to his death except that Enkidu reaches out a hand to help him. Gilgamesh's experience with human kindness is transforming, and the two become like brothers. In the second book, *The Revenge of Ishtar*, the two meet the goddess *Ishtar*, who offers to marry Gilgamesh and give him a chariot of gold.

When he spurns her, he makes a great enemy who will plague him all his life and cause the deaths of Shamat and Enkidu. In *The Last Quest of Gilgamesh,* the great king is so heartbroken by the death of his friends that he sets out to find the secret of immortality. When he learns that Utnapishtim is the only human who knows that secret, Gilgamesh endures a terrible journey across the waters of death to Utnapishtim's island. Utnapishtim explains that he arrived on the island on a great ark after he had been warned of a terrible flood that would destroy the earth. Gilgamesh cannot accomplish the task that Utnapishtim sets him to become immortal, and after one more battle with Ishtar he returns home heartbroken at his failure. Enkidu is sent by the gods to show him that the immortality he craves is there in the great civilization he has created. Zeman's majestic illustrations, done in mixed media and incorporating motifs from Mesopotamian art, have a wonderful sense of timelessness.

## The *Iliad* and the *Odyssey*

According to tradition, a blind minstrel named Homer composed the epic poems the *Iliad* and the *Odyssey* about 850 B.C.; but scholars generally believe that parts of the stories were sung by many persons and that they were woven into one long narrative before they were written. The *Iliad* is an account of the Trojan War fought over Helen, the most beautiful woman in the world. When Helen is kidnapped by Paris, a Trojan, her Greek husband, King Menelaus, enlists the Greeks in a ten-year siege of Troy that is led by the Greek warriors Agamemnon and Achilles. The complex story is long and difficult to understand, although specific incidents, such as the final defeat of the Trojans by the cunning device of the Trojan Horse, do intrigue some children.

The *Odyssey* is the story of the hazardous ten-year journey of Odysseus (called Ulysses by the Romans) from Troy to his home in Ithaca, following the end of the war. Odysseus has one terrifying experience after another, which he manages to survive by his cunning. For example, he defeats the horrible one-eyed Cyclops by blinding him and then strapping his men to the undersides of sheep, which were allowed to leave the cave. His ship safely passes between the whirlpool of Charybdis and the monster Scylla, but later is shipwrecked and delayed for seven years. A loyal servant and his son aid the returned hero in assuming his rightful throne and saving his wife; Penelope has had a difficult time discouraging the many suitors who wished to become king. While children or teachers might be acquainted with episodes from the story, it is the total force of all his trials that presents the full dimensions of this hero. Geraldine McGaughrean has

written a version for middle-grade readers that has been illustrated by Victor Ambrus. Padraic Colum's *The Children's Homer* keeps the essence of the traditional poem, and Pogany's illustrations distinguish this book from others. An edition suitable for older readers is Colum's *The Trojan War and the Adventures of Odysseus,* illustrated by Barry Moser. Leonard Everett Fisher and Warwick Hutton both created a picture-book retelling of Odysseus's battle with the Cyclops.

## The *Ramayana*

The *Ramayana* is the great epic tale of India that tells how the noble Rama, his devoted brother, and his beautiful, virtuous wife, Sita, manage to defeat the evil demon Ravana. Heir to the throne, Rama is banished from his home through the trickery of his stepmother. Prince Rama, his brother, and the devoted Sita spend fourteen years in wandering and adventure. One day Sita vanishes, kidnapped by Ravana. Rama searches for her unsuccessfully and then turns to a tribe of monkeys for help. Finally Sita is found, and with the help of an entire army of monkeys, Rama rescues her. To be cleansed from her association with the demon, Sita must withstand a trial by fire. Her faithfulness proved, she is united with her beloved Rama. Peace and plenty prevail during Rama's reign.

Composed in India by the sage Vlamiki during the fourth century B.C., the *Ramayana* represented some 24,000 couplets that were memorized and repeated. It constitutes part of the gospel of Hindu scripture, for Rama and his wife are held as the ideal man and woman. Rama is believed to be an incarnation of the god Vishnu come to earth in human form.

Surely Western children should know something of this epic hero who is so important to a large part of the world. Jamake Highwater has written *Rama,* a novel based on the Ramayana, for older readers. Joseph Gaer relates the story for children in *The Adventures of Rama.* Jessica Souhami's *Rama and the Demon King* is a picture-book version that focuses on Rama's exile and his battle with Ravana. Souhami's cut-paper illustrations recall Indian folk art forms and provide the story with a dramatic touch. It's easy to visualize these pictures in an Indian puppet theater.

## Heroes of the Middle Ages

Some historians believe there was a King Arthur who became famous around the sixth century. Defeated by the invading Saxons, his people fled to Wales and Brittany and told stories of his bravery and goodness. Other stories became attached to these, and the exploits of Tristram, Gawaine, and Lancelot were added to the Arthurian cycle. The religious element of the quest for the Holy Grail, the cup used by Christ at the Last Supper, was also added. Whether or not the chalice actually existed, it remains as a symbol of purity and love. In the fifteenth century, Sir Thomas Malory's *Morte d'Arthur* was one of the first books printed in England and became a major source of later versions.

In the short novel *The Dragon's Boy,* Jane Yolen tells of the boyhood of Arthur, here called Artos. Artos has been raised by Sir Ector in a small castle. One day while searching for a prized dog he discovers a cave in which a dragon dwells. Both fascinated and terrified, Artos agrees to seek wisdom from the dragon when he is not doing his work at the castle. Children will find this a compelling introduction to the Arthur legends as they sympathize with the lonely boy who confronts his fears to discover the truth about the supposed dragon, his own parentage, and his future as the great King Arthur.

Other illustrated books about Arthur and Merlin will also introduce children to these stories. In Robert D. San Souci's *Young Merlin,* Merlin, whose parentage was thought to be half human and half fairy, is dragged before Vortigern, King of Britain, to be sacrificed to save Vortigern's defense tower. Merlin instead is able to see that underneath the tower's foundation, a red dragon fights a white one. When the dragons are freed, the tower will stand. Merlin foretells the victory of Uther Pendragon over Vortigern as well, and is taken into the new king's household. Daniel Horne depicts the magician's childhood in paintings fittingly lit by eerie yellows and diffused by mists and smoke. In *Young Guinevere,* San Souci presents a courageous and resourceful heroine who explores the magical kingdoms around her father's palace and faces a terrible monster to bring Arthur to her castle to relieve a siege. When Arthur falls in love with her, she overhears Merlin warn him that she will prove to be his downfall. However, she finally agrees to the marriage when Merlin tells her that without her love Arthur will die all the sooner. Hudson Talbott's *King Arthur and the Round Table* and *Excalibur* recount single episodes in Arthur's life, and his vivid watercolors reflect the romance of the tale. T. H. White's *The Sword in the Stone* is an imaginative retelling of Arthur's boyhood and growth under Merlin's tutelage. Middle-school readers enjoy this novel for its humor.

Arthur himself is the narrator of nine episodes of his life in Michael Morpugo's *Arthur, High King of Britain.* The book begins in modern times when a small boy is trapped on an offshore island and is rescued by an old man who claims to be Arthur Pendragon. In telling the boy his story, Arthur provides a poignant and honest portrayal of a youth grown to manhood, a man with faults as well as strengths. When Arthur finishes his tale, he gives the boy an acorn from Merlin's tree in the courtyard at Camelot. Arthur urges him to plant it and remember him. This beautifully complex retelling will ensure that older readers do, indeed, remember these ancient tales.

Rosemary Sutcliff brings thirteen stories from the Arthurian cycle to life in *The Sword and the Circle.* Beginning with the events surrounding Arthur's accession to the throne, she weaves other stories into the text in separate chapters. "Tristan and Iseult," "Beaumains, the Kitchen Knight," "Sir Gawain and the Green Knight," and "Gawain and the Loathly Lady" are but a few of the tales included. Two other volumes, though concerning important parts of Arthurian legend, deal with less adventurous or romantic aspects of the story and might be of less interest to middle-grade readers. *The Light Beyond the Forest: The Quest for the Holy Grail* details the wanderings of Lancelot, Galahad, Percival, and others in search of the Grail but also in search of their own salvation. *The Road to Camlann* tells of the sad end of Arthur and the Round Table fellowship. Sutcliff has also retold the romantic *Tristan and Iseult* in a full-length novel by that title. The language has a lyrical quality reminiscent of the old storytellers:

> It was young summer when they came to the hidden valley; and three times the hawthorn trees were rusted with berries and the hazelnuts fell into the stream. And three times winter came and they huddled about the fire in the smoky bothie and threw on logs from the woodstore outside. (p. 90)

Sidney Lanier's *The Boy's King Arthur,* which first appeared in 1880, and Howard Pyle's *The Story of King Arthur and His Knights,* which was published as a four-volume work between 1902 and 1910, are classic works told in a stately mode.

Children who wish to learn more about the legendary King Arthur would appreciate Kevin Crossley-Holland's *The World of King Arthur and His Court.* Crossley-Holland presents the many King Arthur legends and carefully explores the historical facts behind them. In addition he provides wonderful anecdotes about daily life in the Middle Ages.

Several stories set in King Arthur's time and retold with pictorial conventions of the Middle Ages are available in picture storybook format. Margaret Hodges retells the first part of "The Tale of Sir Gareth of Orkney," taken from Malory's *Le Morte D'Arthur,* in *The Kitchen Knight.* In this story, Gareth, who is a nephew of King Arthur, wishes to earn his knighthood by deeds, not by birthright. So he becomes a kitchen lad in Arthur's castle and accepts a quest that no other knight will undertake, that of saving the beautiful Linette's sister, Linesse,

*The Lady of the Lake appears in her various guises in Kevin Crossley-Holland's* The World of King Arthur and His Court: People, Places, Legends, and Lore.

from imprisonment in the castle of the Knight of the Red Plain. He vanquishes the Red Knight, but it takes extra effort to win the gratitude of Linette and the acceptance of the highly selective Lady Linesse, whom he has rescued. Trina Schart Hyman researched weaponry, enabling her to accurately depict a leather rather than metal shield and an early horned helmet that was discovered recently in the Thames River.

Hyman also conducted painstaking research to produce accurate illustrations for Hodges's *Saint George and the Dragon,* set in fourth-century England. She studied ancient lore of wildflowers and herbs in order to use them symbolically in the borders of each picture. For example, when Saint

George engages the dragon in battle, agrimony, which was a charm against serpents, appears in the borders. The fourth century was a time in which Christianity and ancient beliefs competed, so red-winged angels and pale fairies are both part of the borders. A pre-Norman sailing vessel appears in small pictures as a symbol of the hero's progress. Children are appropriately awed and thrilled by the truly terrible dragon, which Hyman drew after a long siege she had with a snapping turtle in her New Hampshire pond. While the story of St. George has little to do with King Arthur, it shares similar time, theme, and conventions with other tales told in the Middle Ages.

All of these books contribute to a child's knowledge of the mystique that surrounds the story of King Arthur. Students seldom discover these tales on their own, but once introduced to them, they delight in taking their place at that round table of adventure.

Another legendary hero who captures children's imagination is Robin Hood. Scholars have been unable to agree on whether there was indeed a medieval outlaw by the name of Robin Hood or whether he was really a mythical character derived from festival plays that took place in France at Whitsuntide. But by the fifteenth century, May Day celebrations in England were called "Robin Hood's Festivals," and the story of Robin Hood had become a legend for all time.

Children love this brave hero who lived in Sherwood Forest, outwitted the Sheriff of Nottingham, and shared his stolen goods with the poor. Others in the band included the huge Little John, Friar Tuck, the minstrel Alan-a-Dale, and Robin's sweetheart, Maid Marian. These characters can be found in Howard Pyle's classic, *The Merry Adventures of Robin Hood.* Ann McGovern retells this familiar legend in clear, direct language; a few words, such as *perchance* and *thou,* retain the spirit of the medieval language without making her *Robin Hood of Sherwood Forest* too difficult to read.

Robin McKinley's *The Outlaws of Sherwood* presents a Robin Hood for modern times. Robin is not much of a shot, but others in his band do the hunting while Robin broods over how to manage, shelter, and feed his ever-growing group. McKinley fleshes out the emotions of Little John, Robin Hood, Maid Marian, and others while exploring various dimensions of heroism. Theresa Tomlinson tells Marion's story in *The Forestwife.* In this version Marian runs away to the forest with her nurse Agnes in order to escape an unwanted marriage. As she and Agnes provide aid to other poor refugees, Marion meets Agnes's son Robert, who, falsely accused of murder, has also made the forest his home. The story continues in

*Child of May.* Older readers who understand loyalty and appreciate the romance of a good tale will find these stories rewarding and compelling.

# The Bible as Literature

The Bible has an important and rightful place in any comprehensive discussion of traditional literature because it is a written record of people's continuing search to understand themselves and their relationships with others and their creator. It makes little sense to tell children the story of Jack the Giant Killer but to deny them the stories about David and Goliath or Samson. They read of the wanderings of Odysseus, but not those of Moses. They learn in Gilgamesh that Utnapishtim built an ark and survived a flood, but do not know the story of Noah. Our fear should not be that children will know the Bible; rather it should be that they will *not* know it. Whatever our religious persuasion or nonpersuasion, children should not be denied their right to knowledge of the traditional literature of the Bible. Children cannot fully understand other literature unless they are familiar with the outstanding characters, incidents, poems, proverbs, and parables of this literature of the Western world of thought.

We must clarify the difference between the practice of religious customs and indoctrination in one viewpoint and the study of the Bible as a great work of literature. In 1963 the Supreme Court asserted that "religious exercises" violated the First Amendment, but the Court also encouraged study of the Bible as literature:

> In addition, it might well be said that one's education is not complete without a study of comparative religion or the history of religion and its relationship to the advancement of Civilization. It certainly may be said that the Bible is worthy of study for its literary and historic qualities.[22]

The literary scholar Northrop Frye believes it is essential to teach the Bible, for it presents humans in all their history. "It's the *myth* of the Bible that should be the basis of literary training, its imaginative survey of the human situation which is so broad and comprehensive that everything else finds its place inside it."[23] Some critics will be disturbed by the use of the term *myth* unless they understand its larger literary context as the human search for and expression of truth and meaning.

## Collections of Bible Stories

When a school staff agrees that children should have an opportunity to hear or read some of the great stories from the Bible, it faces the task of selecting material. Walter de la Mare provides an excellent background for understanding the problems of translation. He compares versions of the story of Ruth in the Geneva Bible (1560), the Douai Bible (1609), and the Authorized Version (1611). The old form of spelling is used in his quotations from Wycliffe of 1382, John Purvey of 1386, and Miles Coverdale of 1536. He clearly explains the differences between the literal, allegorical, oral, and analogical meanings of given words and phrases. This book presents the Creation, the Flood, and the stories of Moses, Joseph, Samson, Samuel, Saul, and David. The text combines modern descriptive imagery with a biblical style of narration. For example: "As Joseph grew older, and in all that he was and did showed himself more and more unlike themselves, jealousy gnawed in their hearts like the fretting of a cankerworm."[24]

In *Moses' Ark,* a collection ranging from Genesis through Kings, Alice Bach and J. Cheryl Exum retain the spirit of the original stories as they expand the narration with subtle details. Conversation, based on archaeological and anthropological research, and borrowings from other parts of the Bible enrich our understanding. In *Miriam's Well* these authors focus on the role of women in the Old Testament. In both books, stunning illustrations by Leo and Diane Dillon depict the stories of familiar Biblical figures.

In *Does God Have a Big Toe?* Marc Gellman, a rabbi, follows a long-held Jewish tradition of telling *midrashim,* stories about stories in the Bible. These involve readers with their often humorous, contemporary tellings. For instance, Noah doesn't have the heart to tell his friends what God has told him, so he hints: "You know, Jabal, this might be a very good time for you to take those swimming lessons you have been talking about for so long" (p. 31). Miriam Chaikin's *Clouds of Glory* and Jan Mark's *God's Story* are two other beautifully designed and written collections informed by the Midrash. In *When the Beginning Began: Stories About God the Creatures, and Us,* Julius Lester retells tales from Genesis and includes other creation stories from Jewish and other traditions. Lester's unique wit and special storytelling voice bring these stories to marvelous life.

---

[22]Quoted by Betty D. Mayo, "The Bible in the Classroom," *Christian Science Monitor,* 30 September 1966, p. 9.

[23]Northrop Frye, *The Educated Imagination* (Bloomington: Indiana University Press, 1964), p. 111.

---

[24]Walter de la Mare, *Stories from the Bible,* illustrated by Edward Ardizzone (New York: Knopf, 1961), p. 62.

A more complete undertaking is *The Bible Story,* written by Philip Turner and illustrated by Brian Wildsmith. Presented in chronological order, stories from both the Old Testament and the New Testament are told with dignity and illustrated with colorful flair.

## Single Bible Stories

Many individual picture books based on individual stories from the Bible are especially useful to introduce children to this literature. The story of the creation in Genesis has inspired several wonderful editions for children. *Light* by Sarah Waldman is a simple retelling of the story of creation brought vividly to life through Neil Waldman's glowing impressionistic paintings. Ed Young's *Genesis* is more primeval and mysteriously haunting. Leonard Everett Fisher also told this story in his adaptation, *The Seven Days of Creation,* and used bold colorful paintings to excite readers' imagination. Fisher followed this book with retellings of two other Old Testament stories in *David and Goliath* and *Moses.* Several illustrators, including Mordecai Gerstein, Warwick Hutton, Charles Mikolaycak, and Tomie de Paola, have also contributed beautiful editions of single Bible stories. Hutton's *Adam and Eve* is illustrated with quietly powerful watercolors depicting the Garden of Eden in all its splendor. A snake encircles the final illustration of two people walking away.

Hutton's *Moses in the Bulrushes* is more intimate in scale. Hutton uses close-up views of Moses being cared for by his mother and the Pharaoh's daughter discovering him as she bathes in a gossamer bathing dress. This version ends with a short paragraph and an illustration of the resolute Moses followed by his people as they leave Egypt. Miriam Chaikin's *Exodus* reveals what happened from the time Moses arrived in the Pharaoh's palace until his final march across the desert; among the scenes portrayed in Charles Mikolaycak's dramatic illustrations bordered in weathered browns are Moses confronting the Pharaoh as he conveys God's words "Let my people go," the plagues that were visited on the Egyptians, Moses receiving the Ten Commandments, and the Israelites' march toward the Promised Land. A contrast in artistic styles, these two books show how two different illustrators can depict the same story in unique but equally compelling ways.

Leo and Diane Dillon have illustrated a full-length picture book around the well-known Bible verses from Ecclesiastes in *To Everything There is a Season.* Each double-page spread presents the viewpoint of a different cultural and historical period to emphasize the meaning of the verses, and the Dillon's pictorial style changes to further enhance the passage. An afterword gives information about the pictorial style chosen to represent each culture.

Charles Mikolaycak has illustrated two New Testament stories adapted by Elizabeth Winthrop. His illustrations for Winthrop's *A Child Is Born* give a more active and protective role to Joseph. In Winthrop's *He Is Risen,* he portrays the central events of the Easter story in strong diagonals and a muted palette of rusts, browns, and reds. As in all of his illustrations of stories from the Bible, Mikolaycak's authentic depiction of textile patterns, everyday details, armor, and headgear are based on research he conducted in places like the Metropolitan Museum of Art in New York.

The Christmas story has been retold in words and pictures many times. Among the traditional tellings, Maud and Miska Petersham's *The Christ Child* has long been a favorite. Isabelle Brent's *The Christmas Story* resembles medieval manuscripts with its burnished gold, illuminated capitals, patterned backgrounds, and embellishments. Jan Pienkowski also uses gilt for the borders in his exquisite *Christmas: The King James Version.* Detailed black silhouettes against softly colored backgrounds give this telling the look of a pageant. Jacqueline Rogers's *The Christmas Pageant,* on the other hand, is a real modern-day version. While the text is from the traditional King James version, the pictures humorously and lovingly depict contemporary families gathering in a country meeting house to see the children's annual play. Julie Vivas also used the King James text for her exuberantly childlike vision of the Christmas story, *The Nativity.* Mary is shown in a cosy tête-à-tête with the angel Gabriel, and her look of surprise and delight as she tells Joseph his news is priceless. After she gives birth, Mary leans exhaustedly against Joseph, who lovingly cradles the baby Jesus. These glowing pictures must surely present the story as seen through the innocent eyes of a child. John Bierhorst recounts an Aztec version in *Spirit Child;* Barbara Cooney's beautiful paintings portray the story against a background of Central American mountains abloom with yucca and poinsettia.

Told from Mary's point of view, Cecil Bødker's *Mary of Nazareth* is an insightful narrative of Mary's life from the time she receives the bewildering news from an angel until her son begins to learn the carpenter's trade. This psychological portrait of a young woman is illustrated in richly detailed watercolors depicting everything from quiet evenings in outdoor courtyards to the busy work of a shipyard. The

*Neil Waldman's lovely paintings convey a sense of dignity and wonder in Sarah Waldman's* Light, *a retelling of the Genesis creation story.*

Illustration from *Light: The First Seven Days* retold by Sarah Waldman, illustrations copyright © 1993 by Neil Waldman, reprinted with permission of Harcourt, Inc.

everyday life of people two thousand years ago is richly realized. Tomie de Paola's *Mary, the Mother of Jesus* reflects the stately power of Early Renaissance frescoes yet has the warm and earthy reality of de Paola's other books.

Many legends are associated with the Christmas story as well. *The Cobweb Curtain* by Jenny Koralek tells how a friendly spider wove a web across a cave where Mary and Joseph hid from soldiers. Mikolaycak's *Babushka* presents the Russian story of the old woman who was too busy sweeping to follow the three wise men and so is destined to wander the world forever. Tomie de Paola's Italian version is *The Legend of Old Befana.* His *The Story of the Three Wise Kings* begins with a historical note about how this story has developed over the centuries. It would make a good companion to either of the previous stories, as would Ruth Robbins's *Baboushka and the Three Kings.* The stories concerning Befana would be ripe for reading on 6 January, or Twelfth Night, the traditional Feast of the Three Kings.

The Bible, myths and legends, fables, and folktales represent literature of people through the ages. Folk literature has deep roots in basic human feelings. Through this literature, children can form a link with the common bonds of humanity from the beginnings of recorded time, as well as form a foundation for much of their future reading.

## INTO THE CLASSROOM

Room 201

# Traditional Literature

1. The variants on a folktale make excellent comparison material, and elementary children enjoy discovering the similarities and differences. Classroom-made charts, with the tale titles going down the left margin and topics listed across the top, allow children to compare aspects like these:

   - Opening and ending conventions
   - Origin of the tale
   - Clues to the country or region of origin
   - Talents of the characters
   - Tasks to be done
   - Verses, refrains, chants, and their outcomes
   - Illustrations
   - Special or unique vocabulary

   Each group of variants will have other categories to compare as well. For example, categories might be "Instructions for Stopping a Pot from Cooking," "How Rumpelstiltskin's Name Is Discovered," or "Greedy Person's Reward." Children should be encouraged to develop their own category titles whenever possible.

2. Read folktales and myths from one country or one geographical or cultural region. Assume that these stories provide your only basis for understanding the country. Chart what you might derive from these tales, using categories like climate, food, animals, typical occupations, customs, geography, values, expressions, and story conventions.

3. Find as many different editions as you can of well-known stories like "Cinderella," "Hansel and Gretel," "Sleeping Beauty," "Noah's Ark," or "Puss in Boots." Chart or compare both the language of the retellings and the illustrations.

4. Study fables or myths and then write your own versions.

# Personal Explorations

1. Choose one motif, such as transformations, wishes, or magical objects, and see how many different tales you can find with this motif, and how many different cultures or countries your collection represents.

2. Select one folktale that you think you would like to learn to tell. Prepare it and tell it to four or five members of your class or to a group of children. What suggestions do they or you have for improving your presentation?

3. Beginning with a moral chosen from one of the fable collections, write a modern fable. Use present-day animals, people, or objects.

4. Collect advertisements and references that show our use of words from the myths: for example, *Ajax* cleanser, *Mercury* as a floral delivery symbol, or *Atlas* tires. Using a collection of myths, determine the story behind the reference and decide why the advertiser might wish consumers to connect this reference with their product.

5. On the basis of your knowledge of the characteristics of an epic, what do you think the hero of a North American epic might be like? Consider personal qualities, obstacles, achievements, and so forth.

6. Develop a simple inventory of names from folktales, myths, legends, and the Bible. Give it to your class or ask to give it to a group of children. How well known is traditional literature today?

# Related Readings

Bettelheim, Bruno. *The Uses of Enchantment.* New York: Knopf, 1976.

This noted child psychologist maintains that fairy tales have a unique place in children's development, satisfying many of their deepest emotional needs. He offers detailed analysis of several individual tales to show how they enable children to cope with their emotions and their world.

Bosma, Betty. *Fairy Tales, Fables, Legends, and Myths: Using Folk Literature in Your Classroom.* 2nd ed. New York: Teachers College Press, 1992.

This practical handbook provides a brief overview and rationale for using folktales, then lists classroom activities for exploring this genre with children. The emphasis is on reading, writing, and oral language activities, but suggestions also include responding to these stories with puppetry, art, drama, and music. An annotated bibliography is included.

Caduto, Michael J., and Joseph Bruchac. *Keepers of the Earth: Native American Stories and Environmental Activities for Children.* Foreword by N. Scott Momaday. Illustrated by John Kahionhes and Carl Wood. Golden, Col.: Fulcrum, 1989.

This is a collection of Native American folktales grouped under such headings as Creation, Fire, Earth, and Life/Death/Spirit, retold and illustrated with black-line drawings. Stories are followed by discussion and many far-ranging activities for the elementary-age child. The map of Native American tribes and cultural boundaries is a helpful organizer for teachers. See also, by the same authors, *Keepers of the Animals,* illustrated by John K. Fadden (Fulcrum, 1991); *Keepers of Life,* illustrated by John K. Fadden (Fulcrum, 1994); and *Keepers of the Night,* illustrated by John K. Fadden (Fulcrum, 1994).

Campbell, Joseph, and Bill Moyers. *The Power of Myth.* New York: Doubleday, 1988.

Campbell, a preeminent teacher and scholar of mythology, converses with Moyers about myth in the modern world, the first storytellers, the power of myth in our lives, and mythical themes across cultures.

Dundes, Alan, ed. *Cinderella: A Casebook.* New York: Wildman Press, 1989.

This is a collection of scholarly essays spanning the history of folklore research on the Cinderella theme. Of special interest to teachers and librarians are the essay "Cinderella in Africa," the Jungian approach in the essay "The Beautiful Wassilissa," and Jane Yolen's look at Cinderella in the mass market in "America's Cinderella."

Frye, Northrop. *The Great Code: The Bible in Literature.* San Diego: Harcourt Brace Jovanovich, 1982.

The eminent literary critic develops a theory of literature based on patterns found in the Bible.

Hamilton, Edith. *Mythology.* New York: New American Library, 1953.

The introduction to this literary standard summarizes the emergence of Greek ideas, followed by a readable presentation of Creation, Stories of Love and Adventure, and Heroes of the Trojan War. Genealogical tables are helpful inclusions.

Moss, Joy F. *Focus on Literature: A Context for Literacy Learning.* Katonah, N.Y.: Richard C. Owen, 1990.

With classroom examples, Moss presents ten "focus units" developed around such themes as "Baba Yaga Tales," "Cat Tales," "Magic Object Tales," and "Bird Tales." Units involve traditional and other genres of literature, thoughtful discussions of children's learning and curriculum development, and excellent bibliographies. This is a valuable teacher resource and a companion volume to Moss's *Focus Units in Literature* (Urbana, Ill.: National Council of Teachers of English, 1984).

Opie, Iona, and Peter Opie. *The Classic Fairy Tales.* New York: Oxford University Press, 1974.

This volume presents twenty-four of the best-known fairy tales as they first appeared in print in English. Pictures are gleaned from two centuries of illustrators. Invaluable sources of information on primary sources are the Opies' introductory essays for the tales.

Schmidt, Gary D., and Donald R. Hettinga, eds. *Sitting at the Feet of the Past: Retelling the North American Folktale for Children.* Westport, Conn.: Greenwood Press, 1992.

This collection of essays focuses on tales told in the context of a North American setting and raises issues of concern to authors, illustrators, critics, and teachers. Authors of selections include Paul Goble, Patricia McKissack, William H. Hooks, and Steven Kellogg.

Thompson, Stith. *The Folktale.* Berkeley: University of California Press, 1978.

Various theories of the origins of folktales and folktale themes are presented in a thorough manner in this book.

# Children's Literature

Except where obvious from the title, the country or culture of origin follows each entry in parentheses. Modern stories with strong folktale roots are referred to as "Modern Literary." The notation (S) stands for single-tale edition. Dates in square brackets are original publication dates.

## Folktales

Aardema, Verna. *Anansi Does the Impossible: An Ashanti Tale.* Illustrated by Lisa Desimini. Atheneum, 1997. (S)
————. *Bimwili & the Zimwi.* Illustrated by Susan Meddaugh. Dial, 1985. (S)(Africa, Zanzibar)
————. *Borreguita and the Coyote.* Illustrated by Petra Mathers. Knopf, 1991. (S)(Mexico)
————. *Koi and the Kola Nuts: A Tale from Liberia.* Illustrated by Joe Cepeda. Atheneum, 1999. (S)
————. *Misoso: Once Upon a Time Tales from Africa.* Illustrated by Reynold Ruffins. Applesoup/Knopf, 1994.

———. *Rabbit Makes a Monkey of Lion.* Illustrated by Jerry Pinkney. Dial, 1989. (S)(Africa, Tanzania)

———. *Who's in Rabbit's House?* Illustrated by Leo and Diane Dillon. Dial, 1977. (S)(West Africa)

Ada, Alma Flor. *The Rooster Who Went to His Uncle's Wedding.* Illustrated by Kathleen Kuchera. Putnam, 1993. (S)(Cuba)

Adler, David. *Chanukah in Chelm.* Illustrated by Kevin O'Malley. Lothrop, Lee & Shepard, 1997. (S)(Jewish)

Afanasyev, Alexander Nikolayevich. *The Fool and the Fish.* Retold by Lenny Hort. Illustrated by Gennady Spirin. Dial, 1990. (S)(Russia)

Arkhurst, Joyce Cooper. *The Adventures of Spider: West African Folk Tales.* Illustrated by Jerry Pinkney. Little, Brown, 1964.

Arnold, Katya. *Knock, Knock, Teremok!* North-South, 1994. (S)(Russia)

Aruego, Jose, and Ariane Dewey. *Rockaby Crocodile.* Greenwillow, 1988. (S)(Philippines)

Asbjørnsen, Peter Christian. *The Three Billy Goats Gruff.* Illustrated by Marcia Brown. Harcourt Brace, 1957. (S)(Norway)

Asbjørnsen, Peter Christian, and Jorgen E. Moe. *East o'the Sun and West o'the Moon.* Translated by George Webbe Dasent. Dover, 1970 [1842–1843]. (Norway)

Aylesworth, Jim. *The Gingerbread Man.* Illustrated by Barbara McClintock. Scholastic, 1998. (S)(English)

Babbitt, Natalie. *Ouch!* Illustrated by Fred Marcellino. HarperCollins, 1998. (S)(Germany)

Bang, Molly. *Dawn.* Morrow, 1983. (S)(United States)

Baylor, Byrd. *And It Is Still That Way: Legends Told by Arizona Indian Children.* Scribner's, 1976. (Native American)

Benaduce, Ann Keay. *Jack and the Beanstalk.* Illustrated by Gennady Spirin. Philomel, 1999. (S)(English)

Ben-Ezer, Ehud. *Hosni the Dreamer: An Arabian Tale.* Illustrated by Uri Shulevitz. Farrar, Straus & Giroux, 1997. (S)

Berenzy, Aliz. *Rapunzel.* Holt, 1995. (S)(Germany)

Bernhard, Emery. *How Snowshoe Hare Rescued the Sun: A Tale Told from the Arctic.* Illustrated by Durga Bernhard. Holiday House, 1993. (S)(Yuit)

———. *The Tree That Rains: The Flood Myth of the Huichol Indians of Mexico.* Illustrated by Durga Bernhard. Holiday House, 1994. (S)

Berry, James. *First Palm Trees: An Anacy Spiderman Story.* Illustrated by Greg Shed. 1997. (S)(West Indies)

Bierhorst, John. *The Dancing Fox: Arctic Folktales.* Illustrated by Mary K. Okheena. Morrow, 1997.

———. *The Deetkatoo: Native American Stories About Little People.* Illustrated by Ron Hilbert Coy. Morrow, 1998.

———, ed. *The Monkey's Haircut and Other Stories Told by the Maya.* Illustrated by Robert Andrew Parker. Morrow, 1986. (Central American)

———, ed. *The White Deer and Other Stories Told by the Lenape.* Morrow, 1995.

Bishop, Claire Huchet. *The Five Chinese Brothers.* Illustrated by Kurt Wiese. Coward-McCann, 1938. (S)

Bodkin, Odds. *The Crane Wife.* Illustrated by Gennady Spirin. Harcourt Brace, 1998. (S)(Japan)

Brett, Jan. *The Mitten.* Putnam, 1989. (S)(Ukrainian)

Brooke, William J. *A Telling of the Tales: Five Stories.* Illustrated by Richard Egielski. HarperCollins, 1990. (Modern Literary)

Brown, Marcia. *Dick Whittington and His Cat.* Scribner's, 1950. (S)(England)

———. *Once a Mouse.* Scribner's, 1961. (S)(India)

———. *Stone Soup.* Scribner's, 1947. (S)(France)

Bruchac, Joseph. *The Boy Who Lived with the Bears and Other Iroquois Stories.* Illustrated by Murv Jacob. HarperCollins, 1995.

———. *The First Strawberries: A Cherokee Story.* Illustrated by Anna Vojtech. Dial, 1993. (S)

———. *Gluskabe and the Four Wishes.* Illustrated by Christine Nyburg Shrader. Cobblehill, 1995. (S)(Native American)

———. *The Great Ball Game: A Muskogee Story.* Illustrated by Susan L. Roth. Dial, 1994. (S)(Native American)

Bruchac, Joseph, and Gayle Ross. *The Story of the Milky Way.* Illustrated by Virginia Stroud. Dial, 1995. (S)(Cherokee)

Brusca, Maria Christina, and Tona Wilson. *When Jaguars Ate the Moon and Other Stories About Animals and Plants of the Americas.* Illustrated by Maria Christina Brusca. Holt, 1995.

Bryan, Ashley. *Beat the Story-Drum, Pum-Pum.* Atheneum, 1980. (Africa)

———. *The Dancing Granny.* Atheneum, 1977. (S) (Antilles)

———. *The Story of Lightning and Thunder.* Atheneum, 1993. (S)(West Africa)

Byrd, Robert. *Finn MacCoul and His Fearless Wife: A Giant of a Tale from Ireland.* Dutton, 1999.

Chase, Richard. *Grandfather Tales.* Houghton Mifflin, 1973 [1948]. (United States)

———. *The Jack Tales.* Illustrated by Berkeley Williams, Jr. Houghton Mifflin, 1993 [1943]. (United States)

Choi, Ynagsok. *The Sun Girl and the Moon Boy.* Knopf, 1997. (S)(Korea)

Climo, Shirley. *The Egyptian Cinderella.* Illustrated by Ruth Heller. Crowell/Harper & Row, 1989. (S)

———. *The Korean Cinderella.* Illustrated by Ruth Heller. HarperCollins, 1993. (S)

Cohen, Caron Lee. *The Mud Pony.* Illustrated by Shonto Begay. Scholastic, 1988. (S)(Native American)

Cohn, Amy. *From Sea to Shining Sea.* Illustrated by various artists. Scholastic, 1993.

Cole, Joanna. *Bony-Legs.* Illustrated by Dirk Zimmer. Four Winds, 1983. (S)(Russia)

Cooper, Susan. *The Selkie Girl.* Illustrated by Warwick Hutton. McElderry, 1986. (S)(Scotland)

———. *The Silver Cow: A Welsh Tale.* Illustrated by Warwick Hutton. McElderry, 1983. (S)

———. *Tam Lin.* Illustrated by Warwick Hutton. McElderry, 1991. (S)(Scotland)

Courlander, Harold, and George Herzog. *The Cow-Tail Switch and Other West African Stories.* Illustrated by Madye Lee Chastian. Holt, 1947.

Croll, Carolyn. *The Little Snowgirl.* Putnam, 1989. (S) (Russia)

Dabovich, Lydia. *The Polar Bear Son: An Innuit Tale.* Clarion, 1997. (S)

Dasent, George. *East o'the Sun and West o'the Moon.* Illustrated by Gillian Barlow. Philomel, 1988. (S)(Norway)

Day, Nancy Raines. *The Lion's Whiskers: An Ethiopian Folktale.* Illustrated by Ann Grifalconi. Scholastic, 1995. (S)

Dayrell, Elphinstone. *Why the Sun and the Moon Live in the Sky.* Illustrated by Blair Lent. Houghton Mifflin, 1968. (S)(Africa)

De Armond, Dale. *The Seal Oil Lamp.* Sierra Club/Little, Brown, 1988. (S)(Eskimo)

de Beaumont, Mme. *Beauty and the Beast.* Illustrated by Jan Brett. Houghton Mifflin, 1989. (S)(France)

De Felice, Cynthia, and Mary DeMarsh. *Three Perfect Peaches.* Illustrated by Irene Trias. Orchard, 1995. (S)(France)

de Paola, Tomie. *The Legend of the Bluebonnet: An Old Tale of Texas.* Putnam, 1983. (S)(Comanche)

———. *Strega Nona.* Prentice Hall, 1975. (S)(Italy)

Demi. *The Donkey and the Rock.* Holt, 1999. (S)(China)

———. *The Empty Pot.* Holt, 1990. (S)(China)

———. *The Magic Tapestry.* Holt, 1994. (S)(China)

———. *One Grain of Rice: A Mathematical Tale.* Scholastic, 1997. (S)(India)

Diakité, Baba Wagué. *The Hatseller and the Monkeys: A West African Folktale.* Scholastic, 1999. (S)

———. *Hunterman and the Crocodile: A West African Folktale.* Scholastic, 1997. (S)

Doucet, Sharon Arms. *Why Lapins Ears Are So Long: And Other Tales from the Louisiana Bayou.* Orchard, 1997. (S)

Egielski, Richard. *The Gingerbread Boy.* HarperCollins, 1997. (S)(English)

Ehlert, Lois. *Moon Rope/Un Lazo de la Luna.* Harcourt Brace, 1992. (S)(South America)

Esbensen, Barbara Juster. *Ladder to the Sky.* Illustrated by Helen K. Davie. Little, Brown, 1989. (S)(Native American)

———. *The Star Maiden.* Illustrated by Helen K. Davie. Little, Brown, 1988. (S)(Native American)

Finger, Charles. *Tales from Silver Lands.* Illustrated by Paul Honore. Doubleday, 1924. (Central and South America)

French, Fionna. *Lord of the Animals: A Miwok Indian Creation Myth.* Millbrook, 1997. (S)

Galdone, Paul. *The Gingerbread Boy.* Clarion, 1984 [1968]. (S)(England)

———. *The Little Red Hen.* Clarion, 1979 [1974]. (S)(England)

———. *The Magic Porridge Pot.* Clarion, 1979 [1976]. (S)(France)

———. *Puss in Boots.* Clarion, 1979 [1976]. (S)(France)

———. *Rumpelstiltskin.* Houghton Mifflin, 1985. (S)(Germany)

———. *The Three Billy Goats Gruff.* Clarion, 1979 [1970]. (S)(Norway)

———. *The Three Little Pigs.* Clarion, 1981 [1973]. (S)(Norway)

Gerson, Mary-Joan. *Why the Sky Is Far Away.* Illustrated by Carla Golembe. Joy Street, 1992. (S)(Nigeria)

Gerstein, Mordicai. *The Seal Mother.* Dial, 1986. (S)(Scotland)

Gilman, Phoebe. *Something from Nothing.* Scholastic, 1992. (S)(Jewish)

Ginsburg, Mirra. *Clay Boy.* Illustrated by Jos. A. Smith. Greenwillow, 1997. (S)(Russia)

Goble, Paul. *Buffalo Woman.* Bradbury Press, 1984. (S)(Plains Indian)

———. *The Gift of the Sacred Dog.* Bradbury Press, 1980. (S)(Plains Indian)

———. *The Girl Who Loved Wild Horses.* Bradbury Press, 1978. (S)(Plains Indian)

———. *The Great Race of the Birds and the Animals.* Bradbury Press, 1985. (Plains Indian)

———. *Her Seven Brothers.* Bradbury Press, 1988. (S)(Native American)

———. *Iktomi and the Berries: A Plains Indian Story.* Orchard, 1989. (S)

———. *Iktomi and the Coyote.* Orchard, 1998. (S)(Plains Indian)

———. *Iktomi Loses His Eyes.* Orchard, 1999. (S)(Plains Indian)

———. *The Lost Children.* Bradbury Press, 1993. (S)(Blackfoot)

———. *Star Boy.* Bradbury Press, 1983. (S)(Plains Indian)

Gonzalez, Lucia M. *Senor Cat's Romance: And Other Favorite Stories from Latin America.* Illustrated by Lulu Delacre. Scholastic, 1997.

Grifalconi, Ann. *The Village of Round and Square Houses.* Little, Brown, 1986. (S)(West Africa, Cameroon)

Grimm brothers. *The Bremen-Town Musicians.* Retold and illustrated by Ilse Plume. Doubleday, 1980. (S)(Germany)

———. *The Elves and the Shoemaker.* Illustrated by Bernadette Watts. North-South, 1986. (S)(Germany)

———. *The Fisherman and His Wife.* Retold by John Warren Stewig. Illustrated by Margot Tomes. Holiday House, 1988. (S)(Germany)

———. *The Frog Prince or Iron Henry.* Translated by Naomi Lewis. Illustrated by Binette Schroeder. North-South, 1998. (S)(Germany)

———. *Hansel and Gretel.* Illustrated by Anthony Browne. Knopf, 1988 [1981]. (S)(Germany)

———. *Hansel and Gretel.* Illustrated by Paul Galdone. McGraw-Hill, 1982. (S)(Germany)

———. *Hansel and Gretel.* Retold by Rika Lesser. Illustrated by Paul O. Zelinsky. Dodd Mead, 1984. (S)(Germany)

———. *Hansel and Gretel.* Translated by Elizabeth D. Crawford. Illustrated by Lisbeth Zwerger. Morrow, 1979. (S)(Germany)

———. *Household Stories of the Brothers Grimm.* Translated by Lucy Crane. Illustrated by Walter Crane. Dover, n.d. [1886].

———. *The Juniper Tree and Other Tales from Grimm.* Translated by Lore Segal and Maurice Sendak. Illustrated by Maurice Sendak. Farrar, Straus & Giroux, 1973. (Germany)

———. *Little Red Cap.* Translated by Elizabeth D. Crawford. Illustrated by Lisbeth Zwerger. Morrow, 1983. (S)(Germany)

———. *Little Red Riding Hood.* Illustrated by Trina Schart Hyman. Holiday House, 1983. (S)(Germany)

———. *Princess Furball.* Retold by Charlotte Huck. Illustrated by Anita Lobel. Greenwillow, 1989. (S)(Germany)

———. *Rapunzel.* Retold by Barbara Rogasky. Illustrated by Trina Schart Hyman. Holiday House, 1982. (S) (Germany)

———. *Rumpelstiltskin.* Illustrated by Paul Galdone. Clarion, 1985. (S)(Germany)

———. *Rumpelstiltskin.* Retold and illustrated by Paul O. Zelinksy. Dutton, 1986. (S)(Germany)

———. *The Seven Ravens.* Translated by Elizabeth D. Crawford. Illustrated by Lisbeth Zwerger. Morrow, 1981. (S)(Germany)

———. *The Sleeping Beauty.* Retold and illustrated by Trina Schart Hyman. Little, Brown, 1974. (S) (Germany)

———. *Snow White and the Seven Dwarfs.* Translated by Randall Jarrell. Illustrated by Nancy Ekholm Burkert. Farrar, Straus & Giroux, 1972. (S) (Germany)

———. *Snow White.* Translated by Paul Heins. Illustrated by Trina Schart Hyman. Little, Brown, 1974. (S) (Germany)

———. *The Table, the Donkey, and the Stick.* Illustrated by Paul Galdone. McGraw-Hill, 1976. (S) (Germany)

Hague, Kathleen, and Michael Hague. *East of the Sun and West of the Moon.* Illustrated by Michael Hague. Harcourt Brace, 1980. (S)(Norway)

Haley, Gail E. *A Story, a Story.* Atheneum, 1970. (S)(Africa)

Hamilton, Virginia. *The Dark Way: Stories from the Spirit World.* Illustrated by Lambert Davis. Harcourt Brace, 1990. (Native American)

———. *Her Stories: African American Folktales.* Illustrated by Leo and Diane Dillon. Blue Sky, 1995. (S)(African American)

———. *In the Beginning: Creation Stories from Around the World.* Illustrated by Barry Moser. Harcourt Brace, 1988.

———. *The Magical Adventures of Pretty Pearl.* Harper & Row, 1983. (African American)

———. *The People Could Fly.* Illustrated by Leo and Diane Dillon. Knopf, 1985. (African American)

Han, Suzanne Crowder. *The Rabbit's Escape.* Illustrated by Yumi Heo. Holt, 1995. (S)(Korea)

———. *The Rabbit's Judgment.* Illustrated by Yumi Heo. Holt, 1994. (S)(Korea)

———. *The Rabbit's Tail: A Tale from Korea.* Illustrated by Richard Wehrman. Holt, 1999. (S)

Harrell, Beatrice Orcutt. *How Thunder and Lightning Came to Be.* Illustrated by Susan L. Roth. Dial, 1995. (S)(Native American)

Harris, Joel Chandler. *The Complete Tales of Uncle Remus.* Compiled by Richard Chase. Illustrated by Arthur Frost and others. Houghton Mifflin, 1955. (African American)

Haviland, Virginia. *Favorite Folktales Told in Japan.* Morrow, 1996.

Hausman, Gerald. *Coyote Walks on Two Legs: A Book of Navajo Myths and Legends.* Illustrated by Floyd Cooper. Putnam, 1994.

———. *Doctor Bird: Three Lookin' Up Tales from Jamaica.* Illustrated by Ashley Wolff. Philomel, 1998.

———. *How Chipmunk Got Tiny Feet: Native American Animal Origin Stories.* Illustrated by Ashley Wolff. HarperCollins, 1995.

Heyer, Marilee *The Girl, the Fish and the Crown: A Spanish Folktale.* Viking, 1995.

———. *The Weaving of a Dream: A Chinese Folktale.* Penguin, 1986. (S)

Hickox, Rebecca. *The Golden Sandle: A Middle Eastern Cinderella.* Illustrated by Will Hillenbrand. Holiday House, 1998.

Highwater, Jamake. *Anpao.* Illustrated by Fritz Scholder. HarperCollins, 1992 [1977].

Ho, Minfong. *Brother Rabbit: A Cambodian Tale.* Illustrated by Jennifer Hewiston and Jou-Sien Tseng. Lothrop, Lee & Shepard, 1997. (S)

Hodges, Margaret. *Hidden in the Sand.* Illustrated by Paul Birling. Scribner's, 1994. (S)(Middle East)

Hogrogian, Nonny. *One Fine Day.* Macmillan, 1971. (S)(Armenia)

Hong, Lily Toy. *Two of Everything.* Whitman, 1993. (S)(China)

Hooks, William. *Moss Gown.* Illustrated by Donald Carrick. Clarion, 1987. (United States)

———. *The Three Little Pigs and the Fox.* Illustrated by S. D. Schindler. Macmillan, 1989. (S)(United States)

Houston, James. *Tikta Liktak: An Eskimo Legend.* Harcourt Brace, 1965. (S)

———. *The White Archer: An Eskimo Legend.* Harcourt Brace, 1967. (S)

Huck, Charlotte. *Toads and Diamonds.* Illustrated by Anita Lobel. Greenwillow, 1996. (S)(French)

Isaacs, Anne. *Swamp Angel.* Illustrated by Paul O. Zindel. Dutton, 1994. (Modern Literary)

Jaffe, Nina. *A Voice for the People: The Life and Work of Howard Courlander.* Holt, 1997.

———. *The Way Meat Loves Salt: A Cinderella Tale from the Jewish Tradition.* Illustrated by Louise August. Holt, 1998. (S)

Johnston, Tony. *The Tale of Rabbit and Coyote.* Illustrated by Tomie de Paola. Putnam, 1994. (S)(Mexico)

Joseph, Lynn. *The Mermaid's Twin Sister: More Stories from Trinidad.* Illustrated by Donna Perrone. Clarion, 1994.

———. *A Wave in Her Pocket: Stories from Trinidad.* Illustrated by Brian Pinkney. Clarion, 1991.

Karlin, Barbara. *Cinderella.* Illustrated by James Marshall. Little, Brown, 1989. (S)(France)

Keats, Ezra Jack. *John Henry: An American Legend.* Pantheon, 1965. (S)(African American)

Kellogg, Steven. *Chicken Little.* Morrow, 1988. (S)(United States)

———. *Jack and the Beanstalk.* Morrow, 1991. (S)(England)

———. *Johnny Appleseed.* Morrow, 1988. (S)(United States)

———. *Paul Bunyan.* Morrow, 1986. (S)(United States)

———. *Pecos Bill.* Morrow, 1986. (S)(United States)

———. *Sally Ann Thunder Ann Whirlwind Crockett.* Morrow, 1995. (S)(United States)

Kherdian, David *The Golden Bracelet.* Illustrated by Nonny Hogrogian. Holiday House, 1998. (S)(Armenian)

———. *The Rose's Smile: Farizad of the Arabian Nights.* Stephano Vitale. Holt: 1997. (S)

Kimmel, Eric A. *Baba Yaga: A Russian Folktale.* Illustrated by Megan Lloyd. Holiday House, 1991. (S)

———. *Boots and His Brothers.* Illustrated by Kimberly Bulken Root. Holiday House, 1992. (S)(Norway)

———. *Easy Work: An Old Tale.* Illustrated by Andrew Glass. Holiday House, 1998. (S)(Norway)

———. *I Know Not What, I Know Not Where.* Illustrated by Robert Sauber. Holiday House, 1994. (S)(Russia)

———. *Iron John.* Illustrated by Trina Schart Hyman. Holiday House, 1994. (S)(German)

———. *The Old Woman and Her Pig.* Illustrated by Giora Carmi. Holiday House, 1993. (S)(English)

———. *Rimonah of the Flashing Sword.* Illustrated by Omar Rayyan. Holiday House, 1995. (S)(Middle East)

———. *The Tale of Aladdin and the Wonderful Lamp.* Illustrated by Ju-Hong Chen. Holiday House, 1992. (S)(Middle East)

———. *Ten Suns: A Chinese Legend.* Illustrated by Yong-sheng Xuan. Holiday House, 1998. (S)

———. *The Three Princes.* Illustrated by Leonard Everett Fisher. Holiday House, 1995. (S)(Middle East)

———. *Three Sacks of Truth: A Story from France.* Illustrated by Robert Rayevsky. Holiday House, 1993. (S)(France)

Kurtz, Jane. *Fire on the Mountain.* Illustrated by E. B. Lewis. Simon & Schuster, 1994. (S)(Ethiopia)

Lang, Andrew. *Aladdin and the Wonderful Lamp.* Illustrated by Erroll LeCain. Viking, 1993. (S)(Middle East)

Lattimore, Deborah Nourse. *Arabian Nights: Three Tales.* HarperCollins, 1995. (S)(Middle East)

Lester, Julius. *How Many Spots Does a Leopard Have? and Other Tales.* Illustrated by David Shannon. Scholastic, 1989. (Africa)

———. *John Henry.* Illustrated by Jerry Pinkney. Dial, 1994. (S)(African American)

———. *The Knee-High Man and Other Tales.* Illustrated by Ralph Pinto. Dial, 1972. (African American)

———. *The Last Tales of Uncle Remus.* Illustrated by Jerry Pinkney. Dial, 1994. (African American)

———. *More Tales of Uncle Remus: Further Adventures of Brer Rabbit, His Friends, Enemies, and Others.* Illustrated by Jerry Pinkney. Dial, 1988. (African American)

———. *The Tales of Uncle Remus: The Adventures of Brer Rabbit.* Illustrated by Jerry Pinkney. Dial, 1987. (African American)

———. *Uncle Remus: The Complete Tales.* Illustrated by Jerry Pinkney. Dial, 1999.

Lewis, J. Patrick. *The Frog Princess.* Illustrated by Gennady Spirin. Dial, 1994. (S)(Russia)

Lindbergh, Reeve. *Johnny Appleseed.* Illustrated by Kathy Jakobsen. Little, Brown, 1990. (S)(United States)

Litzinger, Roseanne. *The Old Woman and Her Pig: An Old English Tale.* Harcourt Brace, 1992. (S)

Lottridge, Celia Baker. *Music for the Tsar of the Sea.* Illustrated by Harvey Chan. Groundwood, 1998. (S)(Russia)

Louie, Ai-Ling. *Yeh-Shen: A Cinderella Story from China.* Illustrated by Ed Young. Philomel, 1982. (S)

Mahy, Margaret. *The Seven Chinese Brothers.* Illustrated by Jean and Mou-Sien Tseng. Scholastic, 1990. (S)

Mama, Raouf. *Why Goats Smell Bad and Other Stories from Benin.* Illustrated by Imna Arroyo. Linnet Books, 1998.

Manitonquat. *The Children of the Morning Light: Wampanoag Tales.* Illustrated by Mary F. Arguette. Macmillan, 1994. (Native American)

Manna, Athony. *Mr. Semolina-Semolinus: A Greek Folktale.* Illustrated by Giselle Potter. Atheneum, 1997. (S)

Marshall, James. *Goldilocks and the Three Bears.* Dial, 1988. (S)(England)

———. *Red Riding Hood.* Dial, 1987. (S)(Germany)

———. *The Three Little Pigs.* Dial, 1989. (S)(England)

Martin, Rafe. *The Boy Who Lived with the Seals.* Illustrated by David Shannon. Putnam, 1993. (S)(Native American)

———. *The Brave Little Parrot.* Illustrated by Susan Gaber. Putnam, 1998. (S)(India)

———. *The Eagle's Gift.* Illustrated by Tatsuro Kiuchi. Putnam, 1997. (S)(Inuit)

———. *Foolish Rabbit's Big Mistake.* Illustrated by Ed Young. Putnam, 1985. (S)(India)

———. *The Rough-Face Girl.* Illustrated by David Shannon. Putnam, 1992. (S)(Native American)

Mayer, Marianna. *Baba Yaga and Vasilisa the Brave.* Illustrated by Kinuko Y. Craft. Morrow, 1994. (S)(Russia)

———. *The Twelve Dancing Princesses.* Illustrated by Kinuko Y. Craft. Morrow, 1989. (S)(France)

Mayo, Gretchen Will. *Earthmaker's Tales: North American Indian Stories from Earth Happenings.* Walker, 1989.

McCurdy, Michael. *The Devils Who Learned to Be Good.* Little, Brown, 1987. (S)(Russia)

McDermott, Gerald. *Anansi the Spider.* Holt, 1972. (S)(Africa)

———. *Arrow to the Sun.* Viking, 1974. (S)(Native American)

———. *Coyote: A Trickster Tale from the American Southwest.* Harcourt Brace, 1994. (S)(Native American)

———. *Musicians of the Sun.* Simon & Schuster, 1997. (S)(Mexico)

———. *Raven: A Trickster Tale from the Pacific Northwest.* Harcourt Brace, 1993. (S)(Native American)

———. *The Stonecutter: A Japanese Folk Tale.* Penguin, 1975. (S)

———. *Zomo the Rabbit: A Trickster Tale from West Africa.* Harcourt Brace, 1992. (S)

McVitty, Walter. *Ali Baba and the Forty Thieves.* Illustrated by Margaret Early. Abrams, 1989. (S)(Middle East)

Medicine Crow, Joe. *Brave Wolf and the Thunderbird.* Illustrated by Linda R. Martin. Abbeville, 1998. (S)(Native American, Crow).

Mikolaycak, Charles. *Babushka: An Old Russian Folktale.* Holiday House, 1984. (S)

Minard, Rosemary, ed. *Womenfolk and Fairy Tales.* Illustrated by Suzanne Klelin. Houghton Mifflin, 1975.

Mohr, Nicholasa. *The Song of el Coqui and Other Tales of Puerto Rico.* Illustrated by Antonio Martorell. Viking, 1995.

Mollel, Tolowel M. *Ananse's Feast: An Ashanti Tale.* Illustrated by Andrew Glass. Clarion, 1997. (S)

———. *The King and the Tortoise.* Illustrated by Kathy Blankley. Clarion, 1993. (S)(Africa, Cameroon)

———. *The Orphan Boy.* Illustrated by Paul Morin. Clarion, 1991. (S)(Africa, Maasai)

———. *A Promise to the Sun.* Illustrated by Beatriz Vidal. Little, Brown, 1992. (S)(Native American)

Monroe, Jean Guard, and Ray A. Williamson. *They Dance in the Sky: Native American Star Myths.* Illustrated by Edgar Stewart. Houghton Mifflin, 1987. (Native American)

Mosel, Arlene. *The Funny Little Woman.* Illustrated by Blair Lent. Dutton, 1972. (S)(Japan)

Namioka, Lensey. *The Loyal Cat.* Illustrated by Aki Sogabe. Browndeer, 1995. (S)(Japan)

Ness, Evaline. *Tom Tit Tot.* Scribner's, 1965. (S)(England)

Norman, Howard. *The Girl Who Dreamed Only Geese: And Other Tales of the Far North.* Illustrated by Leo and Diane Dillon. Harcourt Brace, 1997.

Osborne, Mary Pope. *American Tall Tales.* Illustrated by Michael McCurdy. Knopf, 1991.

Oxenbury, Helen. *The Helen Oxenbury Nursery Story Book.* Knopf, 1985.

Parks, Van Dyke. *Jump Again! More Adventures of Brer Rabbit.* Illustrated by Barry Moser. Harcourt Brace, 1987. (African American)

———. *Jump on Over! The Adventures of Brer Rabbit and His Family.* Illustrated by Barry Moser. Harcourt Brace, 1989. (African American)

Parks, Van Dyke, and Malcolm Jones. *Jump! The Adventures of Brer Rabbit.* Illustrated by Barry Moser. Harcourt Brace, 1986. (African American)

Paterson, Katherine. *The Tale of the Mandarin Ducks.* Illustrated by Leo and Diane Dillon. Lodestar, 1990. (S)(Japan)

Perrault, Charles. *Cinderella.* Illustrated by Marcia Brown. Scribner's, 1954. (S)(France)

———. *Cinderella, or the Little Glass Slipper.* Illustrated by Errol Le Cain. Bradbury Press, 1973. (S)(France)

———. *Puss in Boots.* Retold by Lincoln Kirstein. Illustrated by Alain Vaës. Little, Brown, 1992. (S)(France)

———. *Puss in Boots.* Translated by Malcolm Arthur. Illustrated by Fred Marcellino. Farrar, Straus & Giroux, 1990. (S)(France)1993. (S)(France)

———. *The Sleeping Beauty.* Illustrated by Margaret Early. Abrams, 1993. (S)(France)

Phelps, Ethel Johnston. *The Maid of the North: Feminist Folk Tales from Around the World.* Illustrated by Lloyd Bloom. Holt, 1981.

Philip, Neil. *The Arabian Nights.* Illustrated by Sheila Moxley. Orchard, 1994. (S)(Middle East)

———. *The Fairy Tales of the Brothers Grimm.* Illustrated by Isabelle Brent. Viking, 1997.

———. *Stockings of Buttermilk: American Folktales.* Illustrated by Jacqueline Mair. Clarion, 1999.

Polette, Nancy. *The Little Old Woman and the Hungry Cat.* Illustrated by Frank Modell. Greenwillow, 1989. (S)(Norway)

Prose, Francine. *The Angel's Mistake: Stories of Chelm.* Illustrated by Mark Podwall. Greenwillow, 1997. (S)(Jewish)

———. *You Never Know: A Legend of the Lamed-Vavniks.* Illustrated by Mark Podwall. Greenwillow, 1998. (S)(Jewish)

Ransome, Arthur. *The Fool of the World and the Flying Ship.* Illustrated by Uri Shulevitz. Farrar, Straus & Giroux, 1968. (S)(Russia)

Rappaport, Doreen. *The Long-Haired Girl.* Illustrated by Yang Ming-Yi. Dial, 1995. (S)(China)

Reyher, Becky. *My Mother Is the Most Beautiful Woman in the World.* Illustrated by Ruth Gannett. Lothrop, Lee & Shepard, 1945. (S)(Russia)

Rhee, Nami. *Magic Spring: A Korean Folktale.* Putnam, 1993. (S)

Rodanas, Kristina. *Dragonfly's Tale.* Clarion, 1991. (Zuni/Native American)

Rohmer, Harriet. *The Invisible Hunters.* Illustrations by Joe Sam. Children's Book Press, 1987. (S)(Nicaragua)

Rosen, Michael. *Crow and Hawk: A Traditional Pueblo Indian Story.* Illustrated by John Clementson. Harcourt Brace, 1995. (S)

Ross, Gayle. *How Turtle's Back Was Cracked.* Illustrated by Marvin Jacob. Dial, 1995. (S)(Native American)

Rounds, Glen. *Ol' Paul, the Mighty Logger.* Holiday House, 1949. (S)(United States)

———. *The Three Billy Goats Gruff.* Holiday House, 1993. (S)(Norway)

———. *Three Little Pigs and the Big Bad Wolf.* Holiday House, 1992. (S)(England)

Rubalcaba, Jill. *Uncegila's Seventh Spot: A Lakota Legend.* Illustrated by Irving Toddy. Clarion, 1995. (S)

San Souci, Robert D. *Cendrillon, a Caribbean Cinderella.* Illustrated by Brian Pinkney. Simon & Schuster, 1998. (S)

———. *Cut from the Same Cloth: American Women of Myth, Legend and Tall Tale.* Illustrated by Brian Pinkney. Philomel, 1993. (United States)

———. *The Hired Hand.* Illustrated by Jerry Pinkney. Dial, 1997. (S)(African American)

———. *Larger Than Life: The Adventures of American Legendary Heroes.* Illustrated by Andrew Glass. Doubleday, 1991. (United States)

———. *Sootface: An Ojibwa Cinderella.* Illustrated by Daniel San Souci. Doubleday, 1994. (S)

———. *Sukey and the Mermaid.* Illustrated by Brian Pinkney. Four Winds, 1992. (S)(African American)

———. *The Talking Eggs.* Illustrated by Jerry Pinkney. Dial, 1989. (S)(African American)

———. *A Weave of Words: An Armenian Tale.* Raul Colon. Orchard, 1998.

———. *The White Cat.* Illustrated by Gennady Spirin. Orchard, 1990. (S)(France)

Sanfield, Steve. *The Adventures of High John the Conqueror.* Illustrated by John Ward. Orchard, 1989. (African American)

———. *A Natural Man.* Illustrated by Peter J. Thornton. Godine, 1986. (S)(African American)

———. *Bit by Bit.* Illustrated by Susan Gaber. Philomel, 1995. (S)(Jewish)

Sawyer, Ruth. *Journey Cake, Ho!* Illustrated by Robert McCloskey. Viking, 1953. (S)(United States)

Schroeder, Alan. *Lily and the Wooden Bowl.* Illustrated by Yoriko Ito. Doubleday, 1994. (S)(Japan)

———. *Smoky Mountain Rose: An Appalachian Cinderella.* Illustrated by Brad Sneed. Dial, 1997. (S)(American)

Schwartz, Howard, and Barbara Rush. *A Coat for the Moon and Other Jewish Tales.* Illustrated by Michael Iofin. Jewish Publication Society, 1999.

————. *The Diamond Tree: Jewish Tales from Around the World*. Illustrated by Uri Shulevitz. HarperCollins, 1991.

Scott, Sally. *The Three Wonderful Beggars*. Greenwillow, 1987. (S)(Russia)

Shannon, George. *More Stories to Solve: Fifteen Folktales from Around the World*. Illustrated by Peter Sis. Greenwillow, 1990.

————. *Stories to Solve: Folktales from Around the World*. Illustrated by Peter Sis. Greenwillow, 1985.

Shepard, Aaron. *Master Maid: A Tale from Norway*. Illustrated by Pauline Ellison. Dial, 1997.

————. *The Sea King's Daughter*. Illustrated by Gennady Spirin. Atheneum, 1997. (S)(Russia)

Sherlock, Philip M. *West Indian Folktales*. Illustrated by Joan Kindell-Monroe. Oxford University Press, 1988.

Shulevitz, Uri. *Hosni the Dreamer: An Arabian Tale*. Farrar, Straus & Giroux, 1997. (S)

————. *Soldier and Tsar in the Forest: A Russian Tale*. Translated by Richard Lourie. Farrar, Straus & Giroux, 1972. (S)

Shute, Linda. *Clever Tom and the Leprechaun*. Lothrop, Lee & Shepard, 1988. (S)(Ireland)

————. *Momotaro, the Peach Boy*. Lothrop, Lee & Shepard 1986. (S)(Japan)

Simms, Kaura. *The Bone Man: A Native American Modoc Tale*. Illustrated by Michael McCurdy. Hyperion, 1997. (S)

Singer, Isaac Bashevis. *Elijah the Slave*. Translated by the author and Elizabeth Shub. Illustrated by Antonio Frasconi. Farrar, Straus & Giroux, 1970. (S)(Jewish)

————. *Mazel and Shlimazel, or the Milk of a Lioness*. Illustrated by Margot Zemach. Farrar, Straus & Giroux, 1967. (S)(Jewish)

————. *When Shlemiel Went to Warsaw and Other Stories*. Translated by the author and Elizabeth Shub. Illustrated by Margot Zemach. Farrar, Straus & Giroux, 1968. (Jewish)

————. *Zlateh the Goat, and Other Stories*. Translated by the author and Elizabeth Shub. Illustrated by Maurice Sendak. Harper & Row, 1966. (Jewish)

Slobodkina, Esphyr. *Caps for Sale*. HarperCollins, 1987.

Snyder, Diane. *The Boy of the Three-Year Nap*. Illustrated by Allan Say. Houghton Mifflin, 1988. (S)(Japan)

Speare, Elizabeth George. *The Sign of the Beaver*. Houghton Mifflin, 1983.

Steptoe, John. *Mufaro's Beautiful Daughters: An African Tale*. Lothrop, Lee & Shepard, 1987. (S)(Zimbabwe)

————. *The Story of Jumping Mouse: A Native American Legend*. Morrow, 1984. (S)

Stewig, John Warren. *Stone Soup*. Illustrated by Margot Tomes. Holiday House, 1991. (S)(France)

Stoutenberg, Adrien. *American Tall Tales*. Illustrated by Richard M. Powers. Penguin, 1976.

Sturges, Philemon. *Marushka and the Month Brothers*. Illustrated by Anna Vojtech. Chronicle, 1996. (S)(Russia)

Taback, Simms. *Joseph Had a Little Overcoat*. Viking, 1999.

Tolstoy, Aleksei. *The Gigantic Turnip*. Illustrated by Niamh Sharkey. Barefoot Books, 1999. (S)(Russia)

Toye, William. *The Loon's Necklace*. Illustrated by Elizabeth Cleaver. Oxford University Press, 1977. (S)(Native American)

Tresselt, Alvin. *The Mitten*. Illustrated by Yaroslava. Lothrop, Lee & Shepard, 1964. (S)(Ukrainian)

Uchida, Yoshiko. *The Dancing Kettle and Other Japanese Folk Tales*. Illustrated by Richard C. Jones. Harcourt Brace, 1949.

————. *The Magic Purse*. Illustrated by Keiko Narahasi. McElderry, 1993. (S)(Japan)

————. *The Wise Old Woman*. Illustrated by Martin Springetti. McElderry, 1994. (S)(Japan)

Van Laan, Nancy. *Buffalo Dance: A Blackfoot Legend*. Illustrated by Beatriz Vidal. Little, Brown, 1993. (S)

————. *The Magic Bean Tree: A Legend from Argentina*. Illustrated by Beatriz Vidal. Houghton Mifflin, 1998. (S)

————. *Shingebiss: An Ojibwe Legend*. Illustrated by Betsy Bowen. Houghton Mifflin, 1997. (S)

————. *So Say the Little Monkeys*. Illustrated by Umi Heo. Atheneum, 1998. (S)(Brazil)

————. *With a Whoop and a Holler: A Bushel of Lore from Way Down South*. Illustrated by Scott Cook. Atheneum, 1998.

Vuong, Lynette Dyer. *The Brocaded Slipper and Other Vietnamese Tales*. Illustrated by Vo-Dinh Mai. HarperCollins, 1991.

Waldman, Neil. *Two Brothers; A Legend of Jerusalem*. Athenum, 1997. (S)

Walker, Barbara. *Watermelons, Walnuts, and the Wisdom of Allah and Other Tales of the Hoca*. Illustrated by Harold Berson. Texas Tech University Press, 1991 [1967]. (Middle East)

Wattenberg, Jane. *Henny Penny*. Scholastic, 2000.

Wells, Ruth. *The Farmer and the Poor God*. Illustrated by Yoshi. Simon & Schuster, 1996. (S)(Japan)

White, Carolyn. *Whuppity Stoorie*. Illustrated by S. D. Schindler. Putnam, 1997. (S) (Scotland)

Winthrop, Elizabeth. *The Little Humpbacked Horse*. Illustrated by Alexander Koshkin. Clarion, 1997. (S)(Russia)

————. *Vasilissa the Beautiful*. Illustrated by Alexander Koshkin. HarperCollins, 1991. (S)(Russia)

Wolkstein, Diane. *The Magic Orange Tree and Other Haitian Folktales*. Illustrated by Elsa Henriquez. Knopf, 1978.

————. *Oom Razoom, or Go I Know Not Where, Bring Back I Know Not What*. Illustrated by Dennis McDermott. Morrow, 1991. (S)(Russia)

————. *The White Wave*. Illustrated by Ed Young. Harcourt Brace, 1996 [1979]. (S)(China)

Wood, Nancy. *The Girl Who Loved Coyote: Stories of the Southwest*. Illustrated by Diana Bryer. Morrow, 1995.

Yagawa, Sumiko. *The Crane Wife*. Translated by Katherine Paterson. Illustrated by Suekichi Akaba. Morrow, 1981. (S)(Japan)

Yee, Paul. *Tales from Gold Mountain*. Illustrated by Simon Ng. Macmillan, 1990. (Chinese American)

Yeoman, John. *The Seven Voyages of Sinbad*. Illustrated by Quentin Blake. McElderry, 1997. (Middle East)

Yep, Laurence. *The Man Who Tricked a Ghost*. Illustrated by Isadore Seltzer. Bridgewater, 1993. (S)(China)

————. *The Rainbow People*. Illustrated by David Wiesner. Harper & Row, 1989. (Chinese American)

————. *The Star Fisher*. Morrow, 1991.

————. *Tongues of Jade*. Illustrated by David Wiesner. HarperCollins, 1991. (Chinese American)

Yolen, Jane. *Tam Lin.* Illustrated by Charles Mikolaycak. Harcourt Brace, 1990. (S)(Scotland)

Young, Ed. *Little Plum.* Philomel, 1994. (S)(China)

———. *Lon Po Po: A Red Riding Hood Story from China.* Philomel, 1989. (S)

Zelinsky, Paul O. *Rapunzel.* Dutton, 1997. (S)(Italian)

Zemach, Harve. *Duffy and the Devil.* Illustrated by Margot Zemach. Farrar, Straus & Giroux, 1973. (S)(England)

Zemach, Margot. *It Could Always Be Worse.* Farrar, Straus & Giroux, 1977. (S)(Jewish)

———. *The Little Red Hen.* Farrar, Straus & Giroux, 1983. (S)(England)

———. *The Three Wishes: An Old Story.* Farrar, Straus & Giroux, 1986. (S)(England)

## Fables

Aesop. *Aesop's Fox.* Illustrated by Aki Sogabe. Browndeer, 1999.

Bader, Barbara. *Aesop & Company.* Illustrated by Arthur Geisert. Houghton Mifflin, 1991.

Bierhorst, John. *Doctor Coyote: A Native American Aesop's Fables.* Illustrated by Wendy Watson. Macmillan, 1987.

Brett, Jan. *Town Mouse Country Mouse.* Putnam, 1994. (S)

Brown, Marcia. *Once a Mouse.* Scribner's, 1961. (S)

Caldecott, Randolph. *The Caldecott Aesop.* Doubleday, 1978 [1883].

Galdone, Paul. *The Monkey and the Crocodile.* Seabury, 1969. (S)

———. *Three Aesop Fox Fables.* Seabury, 1971.

Lionni, Leo. *Frederick.* Pantheon, 1967. (S)(Modern Literary)

Steig, William. *Amos & Boris.* Farrar, Straus & Giroux, 1971. (S)(Modern Literary)

Testa, Fulvio. *Aesop's Fables.* Barron's, 1989.

Yolen, Jane. *A Sip of Aesop.* Illustrated by Karen Barbour. Blue Sky, 1995.

Young, Ed. *The Lion and the Mouse.* Doubleday, 1980. (S)

———. *Seven Blind Mice.* Philomel, 1992. (S)

Zwerger, Lisbeth. *Aesop's Fables.* Picture Book Studios, 1989.

## Myths and Legends

Bierhorst, John. *The Hungry Woman: Myths and Legends of the Aztecs.* Morrow, 1984.

———. *The Mythology of Mexico and Central America.* Morrow, 1990.

———. *The Mythology of North America.* Morrow, 1985.

———. *The Mythology of South America.* Morrow, 1988.

———. *The Woman Who Fell from the Sky.* Illustrated by Robert Andrew Parker. Morrow, 1993. (S)

Climo, Shirley. *Atalanta's Race.* Illustrated by Alexander Koshkin. Clarion, 1995. (S)

———. *Stolen Thunder.* Illustrated by Alexander Koshkin. Clarion, 1994. (S)

Colum, Padraic. *The Children's Homer: The Adventures of Odysseus and the Tale of Troy.* Illustrated by Willy Pogany. Macmillan, 1962.

———. *The Trojan War and the Adventures of Odysseus.* Illustrated by Barry Moser. Morrow, 1997.

Craft, M. Charlotte. *Cupid and Psyche.* Illustrated by Kinuko Craft. Morrow, 1996. (S)

Crossley-Holland, Kevin. *The World of King Arthur and His Court: People, Places, Legends, and Lore.* Illustrated by Peter Malone. Dutton, 1999.

D'Aulaire, Ingri, and Edgar Parin d'Aulaire. *D'Aulaires' Book of Greek Myths.* Doubleday, 1962.

Evslin, Bernard. *Hercules.* Illustrated by Joseph A. Smith. Morrow, 1984. (S)

———. *Jason and the Argonauts.* Illustrated by Bert Dodson. Morrow, 1986.

Evslin, Bernard, Dorothy Evslin, and Ned Hoopes. *Heroes and Monsters of Greek Myth.* Illustrated by William Hunter. Scholastic, 1970.

Fisher, Leonard Everett. *Jason and the Golden Fleece.* Holiday House, 1990. (S)

———. *The Olympians.* Holiday House, 1984.

———. *Theseus and Minotaur.* Holiday House, 1988. (S)

Gaer, Joseph. *The Adventures of Rama.* Illustrated by Randy Monk. Little, Brown, 1954.

Graves, Robert. *Greek Gods and Heroes.* Laurel Leaf, 1995 [1960].

Green, Roger Lancelyn. *Tales of the Greek Heroes.* Penguin, 1958.

Hamilton, Virginia. *In the Beginning: Creation Stories from Around the World.* Illustrated by Barry Moser. Harcourt Brace, 1988.

Highwater, Jamake. *Rama.* Illustrated by Kelli Glancey. Replica, 1997.

Hodges, Margaret. *The Kitchen Knight: A Tale of King Arthur.* Illustrated by Trina Schart Hyman. Holiday House, 1990. (S)

———. *Saint George and the Dragon.* Illustrated by Trina Schart Hyman. Little, Brown, 1984. (S)

Hutton, Warwick. *Odysseus and Cyclops.* McElderry, 1994. (S)

———. *Perseus.* McElderry, 1994. (S)

———. *Theseus and the Minotaur.* McElderry, 1989. (S)

Lanier, Sidney. *The Boy's King Arthur.* Illustrated by N. C. Wyeth. Scribner's, 1989 [1917].

Low, Alice. *The Macmillan Book of Greek Gods and Heroes.* Illustrated by Arvis Stewart. Macmillan, 1985.

Lunge-Larsen, Lise. *The Troll with No Heart in His Body: And Other Tales of Trolls from Norway.* Illustrated by Betsy Bowen. Houghton Mifflin, 1999.

McDermott, Gerald. *Daughter of Earth: A Roman Myth.* Delacorte, 1984. (S)

McGovern, Ann. *Robin Hood of Sherwood Forest.* Illustrated by Tracy Sugarman. Scholastic, 1970.

McCaughrean, Geraldine. *The Bronze Cauldron: Myths and Legends of the World.* Illustrated by Bee Willey. McElderry, 1998.

———. *The Golden Hoard: Myths and Legends of the World.* Illustrated by Bee Willey. McElderry, 1995.

———. *Greek Gods and Goddesses.* Illustrated by Emma Chichester Clark. McElderry, 1998.

———. *The Oddyssey.* Illustrated by Victor Ambrus. Oxford University Press, 1997.

———. *The Silver Treasure: Myths and Legends of the World.* Illustrated by Bee Willey. McElderry, 1996.

McKinley, Robin. *The Outlaws of Sherwood Forest.* Greenwillow, 1988.

Morpugo, Michael. *Arthur, High King of Britain.* Illustrated by Michael Foreman. Harcourt Brace, 1995.

Orgel, Doris. *Ariadne, Awake!* Illustrated by Barry Moser. Viking, 1994. (S)

Philip, Neil. *King Midas.* Illustrated by Isabelle Brent. Little, Brown, 1994. (S)

Pyle, Howard. *The Merry Adventures of Robin Hood.* Scribner's, 1946 [1888].

———. *The Story of King Arthur and His Knights.* Scribner's, 1954.

San Souci, Robert D. *Young Guinevere.* Illustrated by Jamichael Henterly. Doubleday, 1993. (S)

———. *Young Merlin.* Illustrated by Daniel Horne. Doubleday, 1990. (S)

Souhami, Jessica. *Rama and the Demon King: An Ancient Tale from India.* DK Publishing, 1997. (S)

Stewig, John. *King Midas.* Illustrated by Omar Rayyan. Holiday House, 1999. (S)

Sutcliff, Rosemary. *The Light Beyond the Forest: The Quest for the Holy Grail.* Dutton, 1980.

———. *The Road to Camlann.* Dutton, 1982.

———. *The Sword and the Circle.* Dutton, 1981.

———. *Tristan and Iseult.* Dutton, 1981.

Talbott, Hudson. *Excalibur.* Illustrated by Peter Glassman. Morrow, 1996.

———. *King Arthur and the Round Table.* Illustrated by Peter Glassman. Morrow, 1995.

Tomlinson, Theresa. *Child of May.* Orchard, 1998.

———. *The Forestwife.* Orchard, 1995.

White, T. H. *The Sword in the Stone.* Putnam, 1939.

Yolen, Jane. *The Dragon's Boy.* HarperCollins, 1990. (S)

———. *Pegasus the Flying Horse* Illustrated by Li Ming. Dutton, 1998. (S)

———. *Wings.* Illustrated by Dennis Nolan. Harcourt Brace, 1991. (S)

Zeman, Ludmila. *Gilgamesh the King.* Tundra, 1995. (S)

———. *The Last Quest of Gilgamesh.* Tundra, 1995. (S)

———. *The Revenge of Ishtar* Tundra, 1995. (S)

## Bible

Bach, Alice, and J. Cheryl Exum. *Miriam's Well: Stories About Women in the Bible.* Illustrated by Leo and Diane Dillon. Delacorte, 1991.

———. *Moses' Ark: Stories from the Bible.* Illustrated by Leo and Diane Dillon. Delacorte, 1989.

Bierhorst, John, trans. *Spirit Child: A Story of the Nativity.* Illustrated by Barbara Cooney. Morrow, 1984. (S)(Mexico)

Brent, Isabelle. *The Christmas Story.* Dial, 1989. (S)

Chaikin, Miriam. *Clouds of Glory: Jewish Stories and Legends About Bible Times.* Illustrated by David Frampton. Clarion, 1998.

———. *Exodus.* Illustrated by Charles Mikolaycak. Holiday House, 1987. (S)

de Paola, Tomie. *The Legend of Old Befana.* Harcourt Brace, 1980. (S)

———. *Mary, Mother of Jesus.* Holiday House, 1995. (S)

———. *The Story of the Three Wise Kings.* Putnam, 1983. (S)

Dillon, Leo, and Diane Dillon. *To Everything There Is a Season.* Scholastic, 1998.

Fisher, Leonard Everett. *David and Goliath.* Holiday House, 1993. (S)

———. *Moses.* Holiday House, 1995. (S)

———. *The Seven Days of Creation.* Holiday House, 1981.

Gellman, Marc. *Does God Have a Big Toe? Stories About Stories in the Bible.* Illustrated by Oscar de Mejo. Harper & Row, 1989.

Hutton, Warwick. *Adam and Eve: The Bible Story.* McElderry, 1987. (S)

———. *Moses in the Bulrushes.* McElderry, 1986. (S)

Lester, Julius. *When the Beginning Began: Stories About God, The Creatures and Us.* Harcourt Brace, 1999.

Mark, Jan. *God's Story.* Illustrated by David Parkins. Candlewick, 1998.

Mayer, Marianna. *Pegasus.* Illustrated by Kinuko Y. Craft. Morrow, 1998.

McCaughrean, Geraldine. *God's People: Stories from the Old Testament.* McElderry, 1998.

Mikolaycak, Charles. *Babushka: An Old Russian Folktale.* Holiday House, 1984. (S)

Petersham, Maud, and Miska Petersham. *The Christ Child.* Doubleday, 1931. (S)

Pienkowski, Jan. *Christmas: The King James Version.* Knopf, 1984. (S)

Robbins, Ruth. *Baboushka and the Three Kings.* Illustrated by Nicolas Sidjakov. Parnassus, 1960. (S)

Turner, Philip. *The Bible Story.* Illustrated by Brian Wildsmith. Oxford University Press, 1987.

Vivas, Julie. *The Nativity.* Harcourt Brace, 1986. (S)

Waldman Sarah. *Light.* Illustrated by Neil Waldman. Harcourt Brace, 1993. (S)

Winthrop, Elizabeth. *A Child Is Born.* Illustrated by Charles Mikolaycak. Holiday House, 1983. (S)

———. *He Is Risen.* Illustrated by Charles Mikolaycak. Holiday House, 1985. (S)

Young, Ed. *Genesis.* HarperCollins, 1997.

# Chapter Seven

# Modern Fantasy

Barbara Z. Kiefer

A wonderfully perceptive teacher maintained a diary in which she recorded significant events in her teaching day. These excerpts reveal her students' responses to a reading aloud of the well-known fantasy Charlotte's Web *by E. B. White:*

*January 18*

A wisp of a girl with dark dreaming eyes, Judy F. sits transfixed, listening to *Charlotte's Web.* When I read aloud, I'm aware of an irreplaceable group feeling. But beyond that, if children aren't read to, how will they see the purpose of such a difficult skill?

*February 6*

Judy came in glowing.

"We've bought a baby pig. Mother took me to a nearby farm."

"How marvelous. What's his name?"

"Wilbur," she said, in a matter-of-fact voice—as if the name of the pig in *Charlotte's Web* was the only one possible. "He's quite cuddly for a pig. We bathe him every day."

*February 20*

When I'm alone with Judy, I ask about Wilbur.

"Oh, he's getting along just fine. We bought him a large pink ribbon and only take it off when he goes to bed."

"Where does he sleep?"

"In my bed," said Judy, as if I ought to know.

*March 2*

Everyone was silent at the end of *Charlotte's Web.* David wept when Charlotte died. Later he asked to borrow the book. It'll be interesting to see how he maneuvers such difficult reading. But there's the motivation they talk about.

*April 3*

Judy's mother hurried over to me at the P.T.A. meeting.

"What's all this about your pig?" she queried.

"My pig?" I answered incredulously. "You mean your pig; the one you and Judy bought at the farm."

"Come now," said Mrs. F. "This is ridiculous. Judy's been telling me for weeks about the class pig. The one you named for Wilbur in *Charlotte's Web.*"

We looked at each other, puzzled, and suddenly the truth dawned upon us.

Wilbur, that immaculately clean pig in his dazzling pink ribbon, belonged to neither Mrs. F. nor me. He was born in dreams—a creature of Judy's wonderful imagination.[1]

A book of fantasy had seemed so real to these children that 7-year-old David had cried at its end, and Judy had continued the story in her imagination, convincing both her teacher and her mother that Wilbur did indeed exist.

---

## *Fantasy for Today's Child*

Some educators and parents question the value of fantasy for today's child. They argue that children want contemporary stories that are relevant and speak to the problems of daily living—"now" books about the real world, not fantasies about unreal worlds. Others object to any fantasy at all for children, afraid that reading about goblins, trolls, and witches will lead children to practices of satanism or belief in the occult.[2]

But good fantasy might be critical to children's understanding of themselves and of the struggles they will face as human beings. Lloyd Alexander argues that fantasy is of the utmost value for children.

> We call our individual fantasies dreams, but when we dream as a society, or as a human race, it becomes the sum total of all our hopes. Fantasy touches our deepest feelings and in so doing, it speaks to the best and most hopeful parts of ourselves. It can help us learn the most fundamental skill of all—how to be human.[3]

The great fantasies frequently reveal new insights into the world of reality. Both *Charlotte's Web* and *The Wind in the Willows* detail the responsibilities and loyalties required of true friendship. The fundamental truth underlying Ursula Le Guin's story *A Wizard of Earthsea* is that each of us is responsible

[1] Jean Katzenberg, "More Leaves from a Teacher's Diary: On Reading," *Outlook* issue 2 (spring 1974): 28–29. Published by the Mountain View Center for Environmental Education, University of Colorado.

[2] According to the *Newsletter on Intellectual Freedom* (March 1994, p. 54), for example, a group who objected to Lloyd Alexander's classic *Prydain Chronicles* said that the series "contained religious themes that are pagan in nature and young minds would be drawn to the allure of witchcraft and black magic that runs through the books."

[3] Lloyd Alexander, "Fantasy and the Human Condition," *New Advocate* 1, no. 2 (spring 1983): 83.

for the wrong that we do and are free of it only when we face it directly. In a book of realism, such a theme might appear to be a thinly disguised Sunday school lesson; in fantasy it becomes an exciting quest for identity and self-knowledge. Fantasy consistently asks the universal questions concerning the struggle of good versus evil, the humanity of humankind, and the meaning of life and death.

A modern realistic fiction novel can be out of date in five years, but well-written fantasy endures. Hans Christian Andersen's *The Nightingale* speaks directly to this century's adoration of mechanical gadgetry to the neglect of what is simple and real. Lois Lowry's *The Giver* asks how the freedom of an individual can be weighed against the needs of the group. Natalie Babbitt's *Tuck Everlasting* questions whether anything or anyone would wish to live forever.

More importantly, however, fantasy helps the child develop imagination. To be able to imagine, to conceive of alternative ways of life, to entertain new ideas, to create strange new worlds, to dream dreams—these are all skills vital to human survival. Maxine Greene argues that "of all our cognitive capacities, imagination is the one that permits us to give credence to alternative realities."[4]

> It is imagination—with its capacity to both make order out of chaos and open experience to the mysterious and the strange—that moves us to go in quest, to journey where we have never been.[5]

Susan Cooper suggests that because of the heterogeneous mix of cultures in the United States, children here have no shared myths to inherit as children in more homogeneous cultures do. She believes that the role of fantasy, with its heroes, struggles, and allegories, becomes even more important because it satisfies our modern-day hunger for myth.[6]

These arguments aside, children themselves have shown that they continue to want books that satisfy this hunger. D. K. Rowlings's *Harry Potter* books are undoubtedly the most popular children's books to be published in the past fifty years. E. B. White's *Charlotte's Web,* Brian Jacques's *Redwall* series, C. S. Lewis's *Narnia* series, and Madeleine L'Engle's *A Wrinkle in Time* are all fantasies that rank among children's favorite books. And many of the classics, books that have endured through several generations—such as *Winnie-the-Pooh, The Wind in the Willows,* and *Alice's Adventures in Wonderland*—are

*Natalie Babbitt's* Tuck Everlasting *asks children to consider what it means to be mortal.*
Jacket design from *Tuck Everlasting* by Natalie Babbitt. Copyright © 1975 by Natalie Babbitt. Reprinted by permission of Farrar, Straus and Giroux, LLC.

also fantasies. As Molly Hunter suggests, children (and writers of fantasy) are the ones who "never pass a secret place in the woods without a stare of curiosity for the mystery implied . . . who still turn corners with a lift of expectation at the heart."[7] And who still open a book of fantasy with that same sense of anticipation.

The modern literature of fantasy is diverse. We have contemporary fairy tales; stories of magic, talking toys, and other wonders; quests for truth in lands that never were; and narratives that speculate on the future. Though these types of stories might seem very different, they do have something in common: they have roots in earlier sources—in folktales, legends, myths, and the oldest dreams of humankind.

All literature borrows from itself, but the fantastic genre is particularly dependent. The motifs, plots,

---

[4]Maxine Greene, *Releasing the Imagination: Essays on Education, the Arts, and Social Change* (San Francisco: Jossey-Bass, 1995), p. 3.
[5]Ibid., p. 23.
[6]Susan Cooper, "Fantasy in the Real World," *Dreams and Wishes: Essays on Writing for Children* (New York: Simon & Schuster, 1996), pp. 57–71.

[7]Molly Hunter, "One World," in *Talent Is Not Enough* (New York: Harper & Row, 1976), p. 77.

characters, settings, and themes of new fantasy books often seem familiar. And well they should, for we have met them before, in other, older stories.

Jane Yolen, in an essay on the importance of traditional literature, says:

> Stories lean on stories, art on art. This familiarity with the treasure-house of ancient story is necessary for any true appreciation of today's literature. A child who has never met Merlin—how can he or she really recognize the wizards in Earthsea? The child who has never heard of Arthur—how can he or she totally appreciate Susan Cooper's *The Grey King?*[8]

Many authors borrow directly from the characters and motifs of folklore. The African American folk heroes John de Conquer and John Henry Roustabout enliven the unusual fantasy *The Magical Adventures of Pretty Pearl* by Virginia Hamilton. Mollie Hunter's fantasy books are filled with the magic folk of her native Scotland. There are, among others, worrisome trows; water sprites called kelpies, often seen as horses; and the Selkies, who are seals capable of taking human form on land.[9]

Such shape shifting often occurs in folk and fairy tales, and similar transformations are frequently arranged by authors of modern fantasy. In *The Cat Who Wished to Be a Man*, Lloyd Alexander's wizard transforms his cat Lionel into a young man whose catlike ways wear off only gradually. The wizard himself, of course, is a character drawn from the magician figures of old tales. In the same book, a good-hearted rogue named Tudbelly invites inhospitable townspeople to a feast, promising them a special stew, and then tricks them into furnishing the ingredients themselves. Readers who have had prior experience with folktales may recognize that Alexander's "delicious Pro Bono Publico" stew is made from the same basic recipe as *Stone Soup* in the retelling by Marcia Brown.

In the case of Robin McKinley's *Beauty*, the debt to Mme. de Beaumont's *Beauty and the Beast* is immediately clear. McKinley recasts the tale in the form of a novel by exploring character, motive, and the everyday details that do not fit within the frame of a conventional fairy tale. The result is a rich and satisfying book that manages to sustain a sense of anticipation even in readers who know the outcome. In *The Magic Circle*, a powerful tale for older readers,

Donna Jo Napoli's healer gives a gripping yet sensitive account of how she came to be bewitched and fled deep into a magic forest so that she might do no harm to humans. Here she lives for years until one day two children named Hansel and Gretel stumble upon her cottage. Although they will prove to be her undoing, they will also be her salvation from the evil powers that have held her in their grip for so many years. In this book, and in others such as *Zel* and *Spinners,* Napoli explores the complex nuances of human relationships within the framework of traditional tales.

Some bodies of traditional lore have proven to be more popular than others as sources of new stories. Echoes of King Arthur—both the Arthur of the medieval romances (as in Malory's *Le Morte d'Arthur*) and his historic precursor, Arthur the tribal chieftain of early Britain—are found in a great many modern fantasies. William Mayne's *Earthfasts,* Nancy Springer's *I Am Mordred,* and Gerald Morris's *The Squire's Tale* and its sequel, *The Squire, His Knight, and His Lady,* are books much in Arthur's debt. Susan Cooper's five books that make up the *Dark Is Rising* sequence weave together elements of the Arthurian legends and broader themes from Celtic mythology, with its emphasis on ancient powers. Lloyd Alexander's *Prydain Chronicles* and T. A. Barron's *The Lost Years of Merlin* series borrow extensively from the Welsh stories known as the "Mabinogion."

Many fantasies incorporate motifs and elements from multiple sources. Perhaps it is this striking of several familiar notes at once that brings them such enduring popularity. *The Hobbit,* by J. R. R. Tolkien, places the archetypal hero of mythology against a smaller-scale setting more common in folk tales. C. S. Lewis's *Narnia* series puts centaurs and fauns from classical myths in company with modern children fighting medieval battles parallel to those recounted in Christian theology. Madeleine L'Engle draws on a similar array of referents. The volumes of her Time Trilogy (*A Wrinkle in Time, A Wind in the Door, A Swiftly Tilting Planet*) explore intriguing possibilities of astrophysics and cellular biology, as befits science fiction, but the books also reflect her knowledge of theology, classical literature, myths, legends, and history.

The ultimate taproot of all fantasy is the human psyche. Like the ancient tale-tellers and the medieval bards, modern fantasy writers speak to our deepest needs, our darkest fears, and our highest hopes. Maurice Sendak, for instance, relies on such themes in his picture storybooks and in the singular small volume entitled *Higglety, Pigglety, Pop!* In this book a dog named Jennie sets out on an unspecified quest because "There must be more to life than having

[8]Jane Yolen, "How Basic Is Shazam?" in *Touch Magic: Fantasy, Faerie and Folklore in the Literature of Childhood* (New York: Philomel Books, 1981), p. 15.

[9]See Barbara Z. Kiefer, "Exploring the Roots of Fantasy with Mollie Hunter's *Stranger Came Ashore.*" In *Children's Literature in the Classroom: Extending Charlotte's Web*, eds. Janet Hickman, Bernice E. Cullinan, and Susan Hepler (Norwood, MA: Christopher Gordon, 1994), pp. 103–122.

everything."[10] Her experiences are childlike and highly symbolic: the comforts of eating, and the fear of being eaten in turn by a lion; the importance of one's own real name; the significance of dreams. Jennie's quest, as it turns out, may be read as the search for maturity and personal identity.

Ursula K. Le Guin conducts a similar psychic adventure for an older audience in *A Wizard of Earthsea,* where a young magician must learn the power of naming and recognize the Shadow that pursues him as part of himself. Adults might find, in these and similar stories, many of the collective images or shared symbols called archetypes by the great psychologist Carl Jung. Children will simply recognize that such a fantasy is "true." All our best fantasies, from the briefest modern fairy tale to the most complex novel of high adventure, share this quality of truth.

# Modern Fairy Tales

The traditional folklore or fairy tale had no identifiable author but was passed on by retellings by one generation to the next. Even though the names Grimm and Jacobs have become associated with some of these tales, they did not *write* the stories; they compiled and edited the folktales of Germany and England. The modern literary fairy tale utilizes the form of the old but has an identifiable author.

## The Beginnings of the Modern Fairy Tale

Hans Christian Andersen is generally credited with being the first *author* of modern fairy tales, although even some of his stories, such as *The Wild Swans,* are definite adaptations of the old folktales. (Compare Andersen's *The Wild Swans* with the Grimm brothers' "The Six Swans," for example.) Many of Andersen's stories bear his unmistakable stamp of gentleness, melancholy, and faith in God. Often even his retellings of old tales are embellished with deeper meanings, making them very much his creations.

Some of Andersen's tales are really commentaries on what he saw as the false standards of society. In *The Emperor's New Clothes,* farce is disclosed by a child who tells the truth—that the Emperor indeed has no clothes. Others of Andersen's tales are thought to be autobiographical commentaries. In *The Ugly Duckling* the jest of the poultry yard became a beautiful swan, just as the gawky Andersen suffered in his youth but was later honored by the Danish king and

the world. *The Steadfast Tin Soldier* was rejected by his ballerina love just as Andersen was rejected by the woman he loved.

Andersen was not afraid to show children cruelty, morbidity, sorrow, and even death in his stories. *The Little Match Girl* freezes to death on Christmas Eve while seeing a vision of her grandmother, the only person who truly loved her, in the flames of her unsold matches. The grandmother carries the girl to heaven. In the long tale of *The Snow Queen,* a glass splinter enters Kai's (or Kay's) eye and stabs his heart. He becomes spiteful and angry with his friend Gerda, who is hurt by the change in his behavior. When he disappears with the Snow Queen, Gerda searches for and finds him, and her tears melt the splinter and dissolve his icy demeanor.

Other early authors of the modern literary fairy tale are Oscar Wilde and George MacDonald. Wilde's *The Happy Prince* is the sentimental story of a bejeweled statue who little by little gives his valuable decorations to the poor. His emissary and friend is a swallow who faithfully postpones his winter migration to Egypt to do the prince's bidding, only to succumb to the cold at the statue's feet. When the town councilors melt down the now shabby statue for its lead, all burns except the heart, which is cast on the same ash heap as the body of the dead bird. Together, the two are received in Heaven as the most precious things in the city. Wilde's *The Selfish Giant* has even more religious symbolism.

Many of MacDonald's fairy tales are also religious in nature, including *The Golden Key,* which has been sensitively illustrated by Maurice Sendak. Sendak also illustrated MacDonald's *The Light Princess,* the story of a princess deprived of gravity by an aunt who was angry at not being invited to her christening. MacDonald is also remembered for *At the Back of the North Wind,* published in 1871 and one of the foundation stories of modern fantasy.

Other well-known authors have been captivated by the possibilities of the literary fairy tale. Kenneth Grahame's *The Reluctant Dragon* is the droll tale of a peace-loving dragon who is forced to fight Saint George. The dragon's friend, called simply "Boy," arranges a meeting between Saint George and the dragon, and a mock fight is planned. Saint George is the hero of the day, the dragon is highly entertained at a banquet, and Boy is pleased to have saved both the dragon and Saint George. Black-line drawings by Ernest Shepard add to the subtle humor of this book. James Thurber's *Many Moons* is the story of a petulant princess who desires the moon. The characterizations of the frustrated king, the perplexed wise men, and the understanding jester are well realized. Princess Lenore solves the problem of obtaining the moon in a completely satisfying and childlike manner.

---

[10]Maurice Sendak, *Higglety, Pigglety, Pop!* (New York: Harper & Row, 1967), p. 5.

*As Christmas revelers dance in the background, the Tin Soldier gazes longingly at the beautiful ballerina in Fred Marcellino's illustrations for Hans Christian Andersen's poignant story* The Steadfast Tin Soldier.
Pictures copyright © 1992 by Fred Marcellino. Used by permission of HarperColllins Publishers, New York, NY.

A popular fairy tale of our time for adults and children is the haunting story *The Little Prince* by Antoine de Saint-Exupéry. Written in the first person, the story tells of the author's encounter with the Little Prince in the Sahara Desert, where he has made a forced landing with his disabled plane. Bit by bit, the author learns the strange history of the Little Prince, who lives all alone on a tiny planet no larger than a house. He possesses three volcanoes, two active and one extinct, and one flower unlike any other flower in all the galaxy. However, when he sees a garden of roses, he doubts the uniqueness of his flower until a fox shows him that what we love is always unique to us. This gentle story means many things to different people, but its wisdom and beauty are for all.

## Fairy Tales Today

In many instances modern authors have written farcical versions of the old fairy tales that play with characters and twist familiar situations with hilarious results (see the section on Modern Folktale Style in Chapter 5). Other authors set their stories in the days of kings and queens and beautiful princesses with language that reflects the manners of the period. The usual "Once upon a time" beginning and "They lived happily ever after" ending will be present. True to most fairy tales, virtue will be rewarded and evil overcome.

*The sad-faced hero of Laurence Yep's* The City of Dragons *causes the dragon maidens to weep tears of pearls.*
Illustration by Jean and Mou-Sien Tseng from *The City of Dragons* by Laurence Yep. Illustrations copyright © 1995 by Jean and Mou-Sien Tseng. Reprinted by permission of Scholastic, Inc.

## RESOURCES FOR TEACHING

### Books That Introduce Aspects of Fantasy Novels

| Book, Author | Motif, Theme, or Topic | Fantasy Novel |
|---|---|---|
| *Tam Lin* (Yolen) | Shape changing | *Owl in Love* (Kindl) |
| *Tam Lin* (Cooper) | | *The Moorchild* (McGraw) |
| *The Frog Prince* (Grimm) | | *I Was a Rat* (Pullman) |
| *The Tunnel* (Browne) | Transformation by love | *The Lion, the Witch, and the Wardrobe* (Lewis) |
| *The Snow Queen* (Andersen) | | *A Wrinkle in Time* (L'Engle) |
| *Beauty and the Beast* (de Beaumont) | | *Skellig* (Almond) |
| | | *Kit's Wilderness* (Almond) |
| | | *The Golden Compass* (Pullman) |
| *The Seal Mother* (Gerstein) | Selkie legend | *The Folk Keeper* (Billingsley) |
| *The Selkie Girl* (Cooper) | | *Daughter of the Sea* (Doherty) |
| | | *A Stranger Came Ashore* (Hunter) |
| | | *Seal Child* (Peck) |
| *Rumpelstiltskin* (Grimm brothers) | Power of naming | *A Wizard of Earthsea* (Le Guin) |
| *Duffy and the Devil* (Zemach) | | *A Stranger Came Ashore* (Hunter) |
| | | *The Wings of Merlin* (Barron) |
| *Dove Isabeau* (Yolen) | Nature of dragons | *The Hobbit* (Tolkien) |
| *St. George and the Dragon* (Hodges) | | *Dragon's Blood* (Yolen) |
| *The City of Dragons* (Yep) | | *Dealing with Dragons* (Wrede) |
| | | *The Dragon of the Lost Sea* (Yep) |
| | | *The Fires of Merlin* (Barron) |

Jane Yolen writes lyrical tales that make use of modern psychological insights while following the traditional patterns in folk literature. Ed Young's illustrations in the style of Chinese cut-paper artwork grace Yolen's *The Emperor and the Kite,* in which the youngest daughter rescues her emperor father from imprisonment by means of a kite. In *Dove Isabeau* the heroine, Dove, is pure of heart, but when her mother dies and her father remarries a witch, Dove is transformed into a terrible dragon. Her destiny is to kill young men beneath her claws and to be cursed by all. While kisses may save Isabeau, the one who bestows them will himself turn to stone. This story of a spirited heroine and faithful love is a fine introduction to many longer fantasy novels.

Several other modern folktales present contrasting characterizations of dragons. Jay Williams suggests in *Everyone Knows What a Dragon Looks Like* that appearances can be deceiving, for no one except a small boy will believe that a small fat man with a long white beard is really a dragon come to defend the city. Laurence Yep also tells a tale about appearances in *The City of Dragons.* In this story a small boy has such a sad face that he is banished from his village. He is employed by a band of merchant Giants who take him to the undersea Dragon Kingdom to trade for silk and pearls. Having heard all the sad stories in the world, however, the dragons, who normally weep tears of pearls, have not been able to cry. When they see the boy's face they imagine such sad tales that their tears produce baskets of pearls. The boy returns home to find that his neighbors have decided to judge him by his deeds rather than his appearance.

A study of traditional tales and modern fairy tales can provide children with the framework for reading longer and more complex works of fantasy. Resources for Teaching, "Books That Introduce Aspects of Fantasy Novels" lists some of the stories and motifs and themes that connect to some of the novels discussed in the next section.

# Modern Fantasy

Fantasy, like poetry, means more than it says. Underlying most of the great books of fantasy is metaphorical commentary on society today. Some children will find deeper meanings in a tale like *The Little Prince,* others will simply read it as a good story, and still others will be put off from reading it altogether because it isn't "real." Children vary in their capacity for imaginative thinking. The literal-minded child finds the suspension of reality a barrier to the enjoyment of fantasy; other children relish the opportunity to enter the world of enchantment. Children's reactions to books of modern fantasy are seldom predictable or mild; they appear to be vehemently either for or against them. Frequently teachers can help children develop a taste for fantasy by reading aloud books such as Beverly Cleary's *Ralph S. Mouse,* Avi's *Poppy,* or Sid Fleischman's *The Whipping Boy.*

## Evaluating Modern Fantasy

Well-written fantasy, like other fiction, has a well-constructed plot, convincing characterization, a worthwhile theme, and an appropriate style. However, additional considerations must guide the evaluation of fantasy. The primary concern is the way the author makes the fantasy believable. A variety of techniques can be used to create belief in the unbelievable. Many authors firmly ground a story in reality before gradually moving into fantasy. Not until Chapter 3 in *Charlotte's Web* does author E. B. White suggest that Fern can understand the farm animals as they talk. And even then, Fern never talks to the animals; she only listens to them. By the end of the story Fern is growing up and really is more interested in listening to Henry Fussy than to the animals. White's description of the sounds and smells of the barnyard allows readers to experience the setting as well.

Creating belief by careful attention to the detail of the setting is a technique also used by Mary Norton in *The Borrowers.* Her graphic description of the Borrowers' home beneath the clock enables the reader to visualize this domestic background and to feel what it would be like to be as small as the Borrowers. J. K. Rowling has created such wonderfully detailed settings for *Harry Potter and the Sorcerer's Stone, Harry Potter and the Chamber of Secrets, Harry Potter and the Prisoner of Azkaban,* and *Harry Potter and the Doomspell Tournament* that children have no trouble accepting the magical creatures and the fantastic events that occur at Hogwarts School of Witchcraft and Wizardry.

Having one of the characters mirror the disbelief of the reader is another device for creating convincing fantasy. In *Jeremy Visick,* David Wiseman has portrayed his protagonist, Matthew, as a boy who thinks history is rubbish. Therefore, when even he is persuaded that the past lives again, the reader shares Matthew's terror as he descends to sure disaster within the depths of the Wheal Maid mine.

The use of appropriate language adds a kind of authenticity to fantasy. Underground for nearly two hundred years, the drummer uses such obsolete words as *arfish* for "afraid" in *Earthfasts,* by William Mayne, and his lack of understanding of modern words like *breakfast* seems very authentic indeed. In *The Fox Busters,* a clever story full of wordplay and puns, Dick King-Smith creates languages for a farm community in which chickens speak Hennish while the foxes speak Volpine. When one of the hens curses, using "fowl language," she tells a fox, "Go fricassee yourself," and calls a human a "stupid scrambled boy." The hens are named after famous farm-implement companies like Massey-Harris or Allis-Chalmers, which adds further authenticity to this delightful fantasy.

The proof of real objects gives an added dimension of truth in books. How can we explain the origin of Greta's kitten or her father's penknife if not from Blue Cove in Julia Sauer's story *Fog Magic?* In *Tom's Midnight Garden* by Philippa Pearce, it is the discovery of a pair of ice skates that confirms the reader's belief in Tom's adventures.

Another point to be considered when evaluating fantasy is the consistency of the story. Each fantasy should have a logical framework and an internal consistency in the world set forth by the author. For instance, characters should not become invisible whenever they face difficulty unless invisibility is a well-established part of their natures. The laws of fantasy may be strange indeed, but they must be obeyed.

Lloyd Alexander, master of the craft of writing fantasy, explains the importance of internal consistency within the well-written fantasy:

 Once committed to his imaginary kingdom, the writer is not a monarch but a subject. Characters must appear plausible in their own setting, and the writer must go along with the inner logic. Happenings should have logical implications. Details should be tested for consistency. Shall animals speak? If so, do *all* animals speak? If not, then which—and how? Above all, why? Is it essential to the story, or lamely cute? Are there enchantments? How powerful? If an enchanter can perform such-and-such, can he not also do so-and-so?[11]

---

[11]Lloyd Alexander, "The Flat-Heeled Muse," in *Children and Literature,* ed. Virginia Haviland (Glenview, Ill.: Scott, Foresman, 1973), p. 243.

---

## GUIDELINES

### *Evaluating Modern Fantasy*

The following specific questions might guide an evaluation of modern fantasy.

What are the fantasy elements of the story?
How has the author made the story believable?
Is the story logical and consistent within the framework established by the author?

Is the plot original and ingenious?
Is there a universal truth underlying the metaphor of the fantasy?
How does the story compare to other books of the same kind or by the same author?

---

Finally, while all plots should be original, the plots of fantasy must be ingenious and creative. A contrived or trite plot seems more obvious in a fanciful tale than in a realistic story.

Modern fantasy makes special demands on authors. The Guidelines box "Evaluating Modern Fantasy" summarizes the criteria that need to be considered when evaluating this genre for children.

### Animal Fantasy

Children might first be introduced to fantasy through tales of talking animals, toys, and dolls. The young child frequently ascribes powers of thought and speech to pets or toys and might already be acquainted with some of the Beatrix Potter stories or the more sophisticated tales of William Steig.

A humorous introduction to animal fantasy is *Bunnicula* by Deborah and James Howe. When the Monroe family return from seeing the movie *Dracula* with a small rabbit they found on a theater seat, the family cat, Chester, is immediately suspicious. Evidence mounts up: A note written in an obscure Transylvanian dialect is tied around the rabbit's neck; in the kitchen a white tomato and other vegetables appear drained of their juices; and the rabbit can go in and out of his locked cage. Is Bunnicula a vampire? Chester is convinced of it, and his efforts to protect the Monroes are laconically observed and recounted by Harold, the family dog. Older children can appreciate Harold's clever observations and his very doglike concern for food. There are several pun-filled sequels in this series, including *The Celery Stalks at Midnight, Howliday Inn,* and *Bunnicula Strikes Again!*

Other introductions to animal fantasy are Beverly Cleary's *The Mouse and the Motorcycle, Runaway Ralph,* and *Ralph S. Mouse.* In the first story, Ralph makes friends with a boy who gives him a small toy motorcycle. *Runaway Ralph* continues Ralph's ad-

ventures with the motorcycle. In the third story, to escape his jealous mouse relatives, Ralph goes to school in the pocket of his friend Ryan, becomes a class project, and loses his precious motorcycle but gains a sports car. Cleary's excursions into the world of fantasy are as well accepted by children, as are her realistic humorous stories of Henry Huggins and Ramona Quimby.

Michael Bond's *Paddington* series continues to please children who are just discovering the pleasures of being able to read longer books. Bond's first book, *A Bear Called Paddington,* introduces readers to the bear found in a London railway station and taken home by the Brown family. Paddington earnestly tries to help the Browns, but invariably ends up in difficulty. There are many other books in the series, and the numerous commercial spin-offs from this popular series have made Paddington a household word.

British writer Dick King-Smith introduces Thomas, Richard, and Henry Gray, three intrepid mouse brothers, in *The Terrible Trins.* Their mother is determined that the boys will not meet the same unhappy fate as their father, who was killed at the paws of Bertha the cat. She undertakes a rigorous training schedule, the outcome of which is to produce three guerrilla fighters in the cause of mousedom. In a hilarious sequence of events the trins not only rid the house of cats but also convince Farmer and Mrs. Budge, the human owners, that mice are pretty good companions to have around. The title character of Avi's *Poppy* is an equally fearless mouse heroine who is willing to brave the terrible Mr. Oxcax, an owl bully who has run a protection racket in Dimwood Forest for years. Poppy defeats the owl bully with the help of a grumpy porcupine and finds a desperately needed new home for her large mouse family.

In another mouse story, poet Lilian Moore gives younger readers a chance to think about the art of poetry. In *I'll Meet You at the Cucumbers,* Adam, a country mouse, shares his love for his natural surroundings with his mouse pen-pal friend, Amanda, who lives in the city. When he finally visits Amanda, Adam is nearly overwhelmed by all that the city has to offer. But his best discovery is the library, where Amanda tells him about human story hour and all the wonderful stories humans have written about mice. Amanda finally shows Adam that the thoughts he has written to her are really poems when she reads aloud poetry by Judith Thurman and Valerie Worth. In this gentle and humorous book, Moore skirts the "city mouse/country mouse" issue of which place is best in order to deal with larger themes. She helps readers think about the value of new experiences and new friendships, and the way poetry helps us see the world from a fresh perspective.

Adam and Amanda might have enjoyed the gentle and poignant tale of *The Mousewife* by Rumer Godden, a story of the friendship between an industrious mouse and a caged turtledove. Reminiscent of Hans Christian Andersen tales, this story has been realistically illustrated by Heidi Holder with soft-pencil drawings emphasizing the limited sphere of the mousewife's world.

The same qualities of wonder and tenderness are found in the story of a small brown bat who becomes a poet in Randall Jarrell's *The Bat-Poet*. A perfect story and a commentary on the writing of poetry itself, it features a bat who cannot sleep during the day and makes up poems. The other bats aren't interested, and the mockingbird comments only on the form of his poem. The chipmunk, however, is delighted with his poems and believes them. The fine pen-and-ink drawings by Maurice Sendak are as faithful to the world of nature as are the animals and the poetry in this story.

Unquestionably the most beloved animal fantasy of our time is E. B. White's delightful tale *Charlotte's Web*. While much of our fantasy is of English origin, *Charlotte's Web* is as American as the Fourth of July and just as much a part of our children's heritage. Eight-year-old Fern can understand all of the animals in the barnyard—the geese who always speak in triplicate ("certainly-ertainly-ertainly"), the wise old sheep, and Templeton, the crafty rat—yet she cannot communicate with them. The true heroine of the story is Charlotte A. Cavatica—a beautiful large gray spider who befriends Wilbur, a humble little pig. When the kindly old sheep inadvertently drops the news that as soon as Wilbur is nice and fat he will be butchered, Charlotte promises to save the hysterical pig. By miraculously spinning words into her web that describe the pig as "radiant," "terrific," and "humble," she makes Wilbur famous. The pig is saved, but Charlotte dies alone at the fairgrounds. Wilbur manages to bring Charlotte's egg sac back to the farm so that the

*A loyal Charlotte spins out her opinion of her friend Wilbur in Garth Williams's illustration for E. B. White's* Charlotte's Web.

continuity of life in the barnyard is maintained. Wilbur never forgets his friend Charlotte, though he loves her children and grandchildren dearly. Because of her, Wilbur may look forward to a secure and pleasant old age:

> Life in the barn was very good—night and day, winter and summer, spring and fall, dull days and bright days. It was the best place to be, thought Wilbur, this warm delicious cellar, with the garrulous geese, the changing seasons, the heat of the sun, the passage of swallows, the nearness of rats, the sameness of sheep, the love of spiders, the smell of manure, and the glory of everything.[12]

This story has humor, pathos, wisdom, and beauty. Its major themes speak of the web of true friendship and the cycle of life and death. All ages find meaning in this most popular fantasy.

Children also enjoy two other animal fantasies by White, *Stuart Little* and *The Trumpet of the Swan*. Neither book has all the strengths of *Charlotte's Web*, but both appeal to children for their curious blend of fantasy and reality.

The English counterpart of Wilbur the pig is Daggie Dogfoot, the runt hero of Dick King-Smith's *Pigs*

---

[12]E. B. White, *Charlotte's Web*, illustrated by Garth Williams (New York: Harper & Row, 1952,) p. 183.

*Might Fly.* Saved from the Pigman's club by luck and his own determination, Daggie watches birds and aspires to fly. He discovers instead a talent for swimming that allows him to help rescue all the pigs from a flood. Like E. B. White's barn, the pigyard and pastures here are described in sharp, sensory detail, and the animals' conversation reflects the author's shrewd perceptions about human as well as animal nature. Another pig hero is King-Smith's *Babe: The Gallant Pig,* whose remarkable ability to speak politely to sheep gains him a stunning victory in a sheepdog trial meet. In *Ace: The Very Important Pig,* Babe's great-grandson even manages to communicate with his owner in this joyful and absurd continuation of a barnyard saga.

In *Rabbit Hill,* Robert Lawson has written a satisfying and tender story about all the little animals who live on Rabbit Hill. When they discover that new folks are moving into the big house on the hill, they are worried: Will they be planting folks who like small animals, or shiftless, mean people? Although on probation for several days after their arrival, the new folks win approval by putting up a large sign that says: "Please Drive Carefully on Account of Small Animals."

The urban counterpart of *Charlotte's Web* and *Rabbit Hill* is *The Cricket in Times Square* by George Selden. A fast-talking Broadway mouse named Tucker and his pal, Harry the Cat, initiate a small country cricket called Chester into the vagaries of city living. Chester spends the summer in New York City, having been transported there in someone's picnic basket. The climax of Chester's summer adventures comes when the cricket begins giving nightly concerts from the Bellinis' newsstand, saving his benefactors from bankruptcy. In several sequels the animal friends reunite for further adventures. In all these warm and witty books, illustrator Garth Williams creates human expressions for the animals to complement their very real personalities.

In chronicling the year-long survival of a mouse on an island, William Steig firmly establishes himself as a superb author as well as illustrator. *Abel's Island* details the survival of Abel, a very Victorian mouse, who is trapped on an island after being caught in a torrential rainstorm. Left on his own, this rodent Crusoe finds a hollow log and learns to feed off the land. In addition to battling physical elements, he overcomes the psychological fears of loneliness and overwhelming despair. Finally, after almost a year of foraging for himself, Abel is able, and easily swims the distance to shore. Creating more than a mouse melodrama, Steig shows us what qualities help a mouse or person survive. Abel relies on his resourcefulness, but he is kept alive by his love for his wife, Amanda, his art, his friendship with a forgetful frog, and his joy of life.

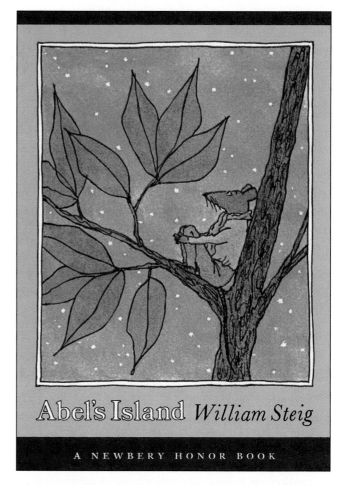

*Abel contemplates his fate from the sheltered branch of his home away from home in William Steig's* Abel's Island.
Jacket design from *Abel's Island* by William Steig. Copyright © 1976 by William Steig. Reprinted by permission of Farrar, Straus and Giroux, LLC.

Tor Seidler has created a memorable cast of animal and human characters in *Mean Margaret.* The story begins when Fred, a fastidious bachelor woodchuck, finally gives in to matrimonial urges and marries the lovely Phoebe. Soon a little one arrives in the burrow. Unfortunately for Fred, the newcomer is not a baby woodchuck but an utterly terrible 2-year-old human child who has been abandoned in a ditch by her older siblings. Kindhearted Phoebe can not bear to leave the helpless child out in the cold, and Margaret (whom they name for Phoebe's mother) is brought home to the burrow, where she wreaks havoc and turns Fred's cozy life upside down. When Margaret is finally returned to her rightful human family, she has been oddly humanized by her stay with the animals. In addition, the lives of her animal guardians, particularly Fred's, have been changed, one might even say humanized, by the sacrifices they had to make for her.

What E. B. White did to popularize and humanize spiders, Robert C. O'Brien has accomplished for rats in *Mrs. Frisby and the Rats of NIMH.* Part of the

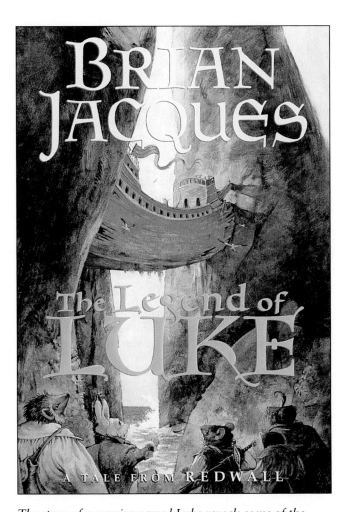

*The story of a warrior named Luke reveals some of the mysteries of the early years of Redwall Abbey.*

From *The Legend of Luke: A Tale from Redwall* by Brian Jacques, jacket art copyright © 2000 by Troy Howell. Used by permission of Philomel books, a division of Penguin Putman Inc.

story, which could be categorized either as animal fantasy or as science fiction, concerns the widowed mouse Mrs. Frisby and her efforts to save her family and their cement-block house in the garden from the spring plowing. The other part gradually reveals the history of a remarkable band of rats who—along with Mrs. Frisby's late husband—were trained to read and write in a laboratory at NIMH (National Institute for Mental Health—although it is never so identified in the story). When Mrs. Frisby meets the rats of NIMH, they are just completing a plan to move to a wilderness preserve where they can establish a self-sufficient community. The rats agree to help move the cement block, thus saving Mrs. Frisby's family, and she returns the favor by warning them about government exterminators who are coming with cyanide gas. Jane Conly, O'Brien's daughter, has written two sequels. In *Racso and the Rats of NIMH*, Mrs. Frisby's son Timothy meets Racso, a cocky and streetwise rat from the city, locates the rat preserve, and cooperates with the rats to thwart the building of a dam that

would flood their home. Short chapters, fast-moving plots advanced frequently by conversation, and memorable characters help make this longer book accessible and exciting to readers. The Teaching Feature on keeping journals shows how journals helped sixth graders respond to *Mrs. Frisby and the Rats of NIMH.*

The well-loved *The Wind in the Willows* by Kenneth Grahame endures even though it is slow-paced, idyllic, and more sentimental than more-modern animal fantasy. It is the story of four friends: kindly and gruff old Badger, practical and good-natured Ratty, gullible Mole, and boisterous, expansive, and easily misled Toad. Toad gets into one scrape after another, and the other three loyally rescue their errant friend and finally save his elegant mansion from a band of wicked weasels and stoats. The themes of friendship, the importance of a home place, and the love of nature pervade this pastoral fantasy. Not all children have the experience or patience with words to appreciate this book, but generations of parents have read it aloud a chapter at a time, which is perhaps the best way to introduce the book.

The villainous animals threatening Toad Hall in *The Wind in the Willows* are the same sorts who threaten Redwall Abbey in Brian Jacques's *Redwall* books. But this series is swiftly told, complexly plotted, and action-packed by comparison. *Redwall* tells of Matthias, a clumsy, young, and peace-loving mouse who galvanizes himself to defeat the evil rat, Cluny the Scourge. Aided by Cornflower the Fieldmouse, Constance the Badger, and Brother Methuselah, Matthias's efforts to fortify the Abbey alternate with chapters of the terrible Cluny subduing woodland creatures to his will. The sinister names of Cluny's band (Fangborn, Cheesethief, Ragear, Mangefur) alert young readers to the evil characters. In fact, one of the major appeals of the story is that one never doubts that good will triumph. *Mossflower* and *Martin the Warrior* are prequels to *Redwall* and detail the escapades of the founder of Redwall. Other titles like *Mattimeo, Mariel of Redwall, and The Legend of Luke* continue the *Redwall* saga. The series resembles high fantasy (discussed later in this chapter), in that good and evil battle for possession of the Redwall Abbey world; quests are undertaken; the heroes are small, unprepared, and sometimes unwilling; and courage, truth, wisdom, and goodness are finally rewarded. Even though these books are long, they provide satisfaction to readers who enjoy adventurous quests, humor, and intrigue but are not yet ready for the deeper themes, ambiguous characters, or created worlds of high fantasy.

When *Watership Down* by Richard Adams was first published in England, one reviewer maintained that the "story is what one might expect had *The Wind in the*

## Journals Help Children Understand Fantasy

**Teaching Feature**

In September, a sixth-grade language arts teacher asked her students to keep a journal and react to Robert C. O'Brien's *Mrs. Frisby and the Rats of NIMH*. She divided the book into about ten parts, and children responded in their journals after reading each assignment. The diversity of the children's responses showed how differently individual readers engage with a story.

One girl challenged the believability of this fantasy: "I wonder where Mr. Ages gets the paper for the bags for medicine? . . . I wonder how Mrs. Frisby can hold on to Jeremy's back. She's too small to wrap her 'arms' around it. I also wonder how mice can understand people talk." The teacher acknowledged her concerns and invited her to try to find some answers. She also reminded her that this was an animal fantasy that had its own rules.

Another girl sympathized with Mrs. Frisby's very modern predicament and mused about the humor of the story: "Mrs. Frisby has a lot on her mind being a single parent with four children and one sick in bed with pneumonia. I would feel really pressured like that and Moving Day coming. . . . I like the crow Jeremy. He's funny and stupid. He picked up the string because it was *sparkly*. (That's cute.)" The teacher called attention to the way an author creates believability when she wrote back, "O'Brien has given the crow some human characteristics but has kept the animal habits faithful to the species."

Children asked questions: "I don't understand what the Boniface Estate is," said one. "I still have a question. What does *NIMH* stand for?" asked another. A third lamented, "All my questions aren't answered yet. I may seem like a bottomless pit of questions." The teacher reassured them that it is fine to have questions, clarified meanings, or referred a child to a classmate or back to a page in the book.

Some children worried about the morality of experimenting on animals: "I am very very very very very mad that they give those poor rats shocks plus giving the rats injections. I think it is very mean." "It made me wonder if given injections, animals are in as much pain as they look." The teacher asked children to talk about the animal experimentation in this story and scientific experimentation in general.

In their final journal entries, some children were dissatisfied with the ending. "I think he should have put more pictures in and made the story a couple of chapters longer. He should have said something about like how Jeremy had a family." "Who died in the rat hole?" Others found the sequels and filled themselves in on what happened next.

Writing journals allowed the children to work out the meaning of the story for themselves. They also revealed themselves to the teacher in ways that would help her plan discussions, choose books, select writing topics, and diversify instruction for the rest of the school year.

*Based on journals selected from the sixth-grade language arts class taught by Susan Steinberg*
George Mason Elementary School, Alexandria, Virginia

---

*Willows* been written after two world wars, various marks of nuclear bomb, the Korean and Vietnam obscenities and half a dozen other hells created by the inexhaustibly evil powers of man."[13] Published as adult fiction in the United States, this is the remarkable story of a rabbit band who cherish their freedom enough to fight for it. The book is lengthy and complex, but many older children have found it compelling. Adams has created a complete rabbit civilization, including a history, a religion, a mythology, and even a lapine language with a partial set of accompanying linguistic rules. The central character is Hazel, a young buck who leads a little band of bucks away from their old warren, which is doomed by a new housing tract. He does so reluctantly but at the urging of his younger and weaker brother, Fiver, who has a form of extrasensory perception. The slow, steady growth of Hazel as a leader is told in this surprisingly unsentimental, even tough, story. It is more realistic than most "realism," because the story is firmly rooted in a world we know: Rabbits mate, make droppings, and talk and joke about both, very much as humans do. They get hurt, bleed, and suffer; they grow ugly with age, and they die. During their storytelling sessions, readers learn of El-ahrairah, the great chief rabbit and trickster. In a remarkable creation legend and a deeply moving story, a rabbit redeemer braves the palace of death to offer his own life for his people. And at the end of the book, when one of the does tells her little one a new story of El-ahrairah, we know that she is telling a garbled version of the story of the establishment of Watership Down and adding Hazel's accomplishments to those of the legendary rabbit—a comment on the entire process of mythmaking.

---

[13]Aidan Chambers, "Letter from England: Great Leaping Lapins!" *Horn Book Magazine*, June 1973, p. 255.

*A Hive for a Honeybee* by Soinbhe Lally is an unusual animal fantasy that begins as an aged Queen bee and many of her attendants leave their hive to find another home. The bees left behind await the arrival of a new Queen and carry on with the life of the hive. We meet Thora, a young worker bee who dares to imagine a life of contemplation; Mo, a drone who is a political radical; and Alfred, another drone who composes poems and ponders the meaning of life. Each of them reacts in different ways to the demands of their position within the hive, but like the rabbits in *Watership Down* these bees cannot escape the limitations of their nature. At the close of the book with winter approaching, Mo, Alfred, and the other drones are refused entrance to the hive and fly off to their predetermined end. Thora too, now old and tired, makes her last flight in the dying rays of the autumn sun. This allegory demands sophisticated readers, but it is richly imagined and raises intriguing questions about human behavior that could evoke thoughtful discussion among such children.

## The World of Toys and Dolls

As authors have endowed animals with human characteristics, so, too, have they personified toys and dolls. Young children enjoy stories that bring inanimate objects such as a tugboat or a steam shovel to life. Seven-, 8-, and 9-year-olds still like to imagine that their favorite playthings have a life of their own. Hans Christian Andersen appealed to this in "The Steadfast Tin Soldier," "The Fir Tree," and many other stories.

Probably no one has made toys seem quite so much like people as has A. A. Milne in his well-loved Pooh stories. Each chapter contains a separate adventure about the favorite stuffed toys of Milne's son, Christopher Robin. The good companions introduced in *Winnie-the-Pooh* include Winnie-the-Pooh, "a bear of little brain"; Eeyore, the doleful donkey; Piglet, the happy follower and devoted friend of Pooh; and Rabbit, Owl, Kanga, and little Roo. A bouncy new friend, Tigger, joins the group in Milne's second book, *The House at Pooh Corner*. They all live in the "100 Aker Wood" and spend most of their time getting into—and out of—exciting and amusing situations. Eight- and 9-year-olds thoroughly enjoy the humor of the Heffalump story, the self-pity of gloomy Eeyore on his birthday, and kindly but forgetful Pooh, who knocks at his own door and then wonders why no one answers. The humor in these stories is not hilarious but quiet, whimsical, and subtle. Such humor is usually lost on young children but greatly appreciated by third graders. However, younger children might enjoy the Pooh stories when they are read within a family circle. Parents' chuckles are contagious, and soon everyone in the family becomes a Pooh admirer.

*Miss Hickory* by Carolyn Bailey is the story of a unique country doll whose body is an applewood twig and whose head is a hickory nut. Miss Hickory has all the common sense and forthright qualities that her name implies. She survives a severe New Hampshire winter in the company of her friends—Crow, Bull Frog, Ground Hog, and Squirrel.

In her books about the Mennyms, Sylvia Waugh has created a family of three generations of dolls who have survived after the death of the old woman who made them.

> They were not human you see—at least not in the normal sense of the word. They were not made of flesh and blood. They were just a whole lovely family of life-size ragdolls. They were living and walking and talking and breathing, but they were made of cloth and kapok. They each had a little voicebox, like the sort they put in teddy bears to make them growl realistically. Their frameworks were strong but pliable. Their respiration kept their bodies supplied with oxygen that was life to the kapok and sound to the voices. (p. 17)

These are fully realized characters, doll-like only in that they are made of cloth and stuffing. Otherwise they have the same idiosyncrasies, quarrels, and desires as any other family, and these conflicts are played out in all five tautly paced stories. In *The Mennyms* they are faced with the threat of discovery after successfully hiding their secret for forty years. In trying to avoid this disaster, they discover a new sister hidden in an old trunk in the attic. In *The Mennyms in the Wilderness*, Brocklehurst Grove, the only home they have ever known, is threatened by a superhighway. In *The Mennyms Under Siege,* the family secret is in danger of being revealed by an impetuous Mennym and a nosy neighbor. *The Mennyms Alone* and *The Mennyms Alive* complete this unusual series. The Mennym family members are so beautifully realized that children will be reluctant to close the covers of these imaginative books.

In *The Indian in the Cupboard* by Lynne Reid Banks, a toy plastic Indian comes to life when Omri puts it inside a cupboard, locks it, and then unlocks it with a special key. Nine-year-old Omri feels pride and responsibility in caring for "his" Indian, Little Bear, and is quickly involved in providing for his needs. But trouble begins when Omri's friend Patrick places a cowboy in the cupboard. The British author uses stereotypical language in this and the other books in the series ("Little Bear fight like mountain lion. Take many scalps!"), but the characters transcend this in their growing concern for each other's welfare. Banks suggests once again to readers that we are responsible for what we have tamed or brought to life.

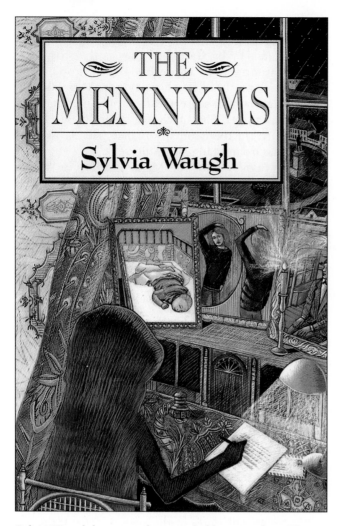

*Sylvia Waugh has created a remarkable series about* The Mennyms, *a family of life-size rag dolls.*

Jacket illustration from *The Mennyms* by Sylvia Waugh. Jacket illustration by Richard Ross, jacket illustration copyright © 1994 by James McMullan. Used by permission of Greenwillow Books, an imprint of HarperCollins Publishers.

Elizabeth Winthrop's *The Castle in the Attic* also examines responsibility for one's own actions. Although an accomplished gymnast, 10-year-old William lacks confidence in himself. When he hears that Mrs. Phillips, his lifelong friend and live-in baby-sitter, is returning to her native England, he is crushed but determined to find a way to make her stay. Inside her parting gift, a huge model of a castle that has been in her family for generations, William discovers a tiny lead knight that comes to life at his touch. The knight shows William a charm that can be used to miniaturize objects or people, and William uses it to reduce his baby-sitter to toy size and keep her in the castle. Regretting this hasty act, he submits himself to the charm, travels back in time with the knight, and recovers the amulet that will reverse the spell. On this quest William discovers unexpected strengths in himself. He returns victorious, prepared to wish Mrs. Phillips

farewell. In *The Battle for the Castle* Mrs. Phillips sends William a magic token for his twelfth birthday; twelve was the age at which a young man could be trained as a squire in the Middle Ages. The token allows William to return to the land of the castle, where further adventures teach him about love, courage, and loyalty. The strong grounding in reality and the elaborately described castle give these fantasies special appeal for upper elementary students.

Another strangely cruel yet tender tale by Russell Hoban, *The Mouse and His Child*, tells of two windup toys and their efforts to become "self-winding." New and shiny in the toy shop the day before Christmas, the naive little toys end up on the rubbish heap in the cruel clutches of Manny Rat. In their long and tedious journey, they search for a home, a family, and "their territory." The story is not a gentle one. It is filled with images of death and decay, violence and vengeance, tears and laughter. Like *Alice's Adventures in Wonderland*, the complex ideas, satire, and symbolism might appeal more to mature readers than to young children. Yet it is a fantasy that is not easily forgotten.

## Eccentric Characters and Preposterous Situations

Many fantasies for children are based on eccentric characters or preposterous situations. Cars or people might fly, eggs might hatch into dinosaurs or dragons, ancient magical beings might come up against modern technology. Often these characters and situations occur in otherwise very normal settings—which allows readers to believe more readily.

Pippi Longstocking, a notoriously funny character created by Astrid Lindgren, has delighted children for more than forty years. Pippi is an orphan who lives alone with her monkey and her horse in a child's utopian world where she tells herself when to go to bed and when to get up! Although she is only 9 years old, Pippi can hold her own with anyone, for she is so strong that she can pick up a horse or a man and throw him into the air. Children love this amazing character who always has the integrity to say what she thinks, even if she shocks adults. Seven-, 8-, and 9-year-olds enjoy her madcap adventures in *Pippi Longstocking* and in the sequels, *Pippi Goes on Board, Pippi in the South Seas,* and *Pippi on the Run.*

When the east wind blew the title character of P. L. Travers's *Mary Poppins* into the Bankses' house in London to care for Michael and Jane, it blew her into the hearts of many thousands of readers. Wearing her shapeless hat and white gloves, carrying her parrot-handled umbrella and a large carpetbag, Mary Poppins is as British as tea, yet many children in the United States also love this nursemaid with strange magical powers. Nothing seems impossible for this prim autocrat of the nursery, and she goes serenely on her way through other funny adventures in *Mary Poppins Comes Back, Mary Poppins Opens the Door,* and *Mary Poppins in the Park.*

*Mr. Popper's Penguins* by Richard and Florence Atwater has long been the favorite funny story of many primary-grade children. Mr. Popper is a mild little house painter whose major interest in life is the study of the Antarctic. When an explorer presents Mr. Popper with a penguin, he promptly names him Captain Cook, and he obtains Greta from the zoo to keep Captain Cook company. After the arrival of ten baby penguins, Mr. Popper puts a freezing plant in the basement of his house and moves his furnace upstairs to the living room. The Atwaters' serious account of a highly implausible situation adds to the humor of this truly funny story.

In *James and the Giant Peach* by Roald Dahl, James, one of the saddest and loneliest boys in the world, lives with his wicked aunts in an old, ramshackle house on a high hill in the south of England. Given a bag of green crystals by an old man, James hurries home with them, but he trips and falls, and all of the magic crystals disappear into the ground under an old peach tree. In the enormous peach that grows on the tree, James discovers six amazing creatures who have been waiting for him—a grasshopper the size of a large dog, a giant ladybug, an enormous spider, a centipede, an earthworm, and a silkworm. Early the next morning the centipede gnaws off the stem, the huge peach rolls down the hill, incidentally crushing the aunts, and the marvelous adventure begins. This wonderful spoof on Victorian morality tales features well-drawn characters whose grumbling conversations are very believable. This book is popular with children of all ages. Its short chapters make it a good read-aloud selection for first and second graders, as well as for older children.

Allan Ahlberg's *The Giant Baby* is another book that will delight 7- to 9-year-olds. Alice Hicks desperately wants a baby brother, but her parents insist there's no room in their little house. When late one night thunderous footsteps approach the Hicks house and then fade off into silence, Alice is delighted to discover a big bundle left on the doorstep. Inside is an amazingly large baby. The Hickses are flabbergasted. Feeding the baby is a bit of a problem, and changing nappies is an even bigger difficulty. Pretty soon the giant baby is no secret in the neighborhood. The press gets wind of the story, and this brings onto the scene the Grubbling Brothers, circus people who are down on their luck, and other villains. The giant baby keeps falling into the wrong hands, but Alice and her friends keep rescuing him. Finally the biggest rescue of all occurs when the giant baby's giant mother returns for

her "little baby." Alice, who "had wanted a baby brother, got one and lost him," is inconsolable. But happily after all, Mr. and Mrs. Hicks had gotten quite attached to the big baby, so at the very end Alice is invited to the hospital to meet her new and "proper size" baby brother. This is a delightful story told with wit and warm good humor that is given added zest by Fritz Wegner's pen-and-ink illustrations.

Older readers will find similar enjoyment in Patricia Kindl's *Owl in Love.* Owl Tycho is an unusual 14-year-old who belongs to a family of shape shifters, and she has the ability to change into an owl. This causes great distress for her as she tries to fit into the teenage world. She can't eat in the cafeteria because her diet consists of grasshoppers and mice. She can't participate in the science class experiment on blood types because her blood is black. And worst of all she is madly in love with her science teacher and state law says they cannot marry for several more years. This hilarious story finds Owl as troubled and torn as any other youngster trying to deal with the changing body and shifting emotions of adolescence, and her journey to self-understanding is no less poignant because it takes place in a tree in the cool night air as often as at a desk in a brightly lit classroom. Kindl's characterization is flawless and her sense of humor right on target for middle-school readers.

Younger children will fall in love with Hob, a brownie-like creature whose job is to be helpful to humans in William Mayne's *Hob and the Goblins.* "He tidies away abandoned things, like scraps of quarrel, or pieces of spite. He banishes small troubles, makes ghosts happy, soothes tired curtains, charms kettles into singing, and stops milk sulking" (p. 6). He has been out of practice for some time when he adopts a new family. They don't realize that their new house sits atop a crock of gold that is coveted by all manner of dwarfs, witches, gremlins, and a goblin king, but Hob does—and his humble talents are put to the test in a charming tale with a rollicking finale. This endearing character's adventures, continued in *Hob and the Peddler,* will be familiar to children who have read "The Elves and the Shoemaker" and other stories about mythical creatures, and who may be delighted to find his relatives in Tolkien's *The Hobbitt.*

The title character of Susan Cooper's *The Boggart* is another ancient sort who must wrestle with the modern world. When a Canadian family inherits an old Scottish castle, they do not realize that the property includes the Boggart, an ancient and mischievous spirit. Trapped in a desk that the family ships back to Canada, the Boggart discovers a new world of technological wonders. His pranks, however, wreak havoc on the Volnik family, who blame each other for the Boggart's tricks. A solution is found only when the Volnick children and the Boggart enter the world of computer "magic" and the Boggart is returned to his familiar world. There he continues to play his tricks on the new owner of his castle home in *The Boggart and the Monster*. The beauty of Cooper's stories lies as much in the Boggart's thoroughly developed character as in the stories' well-paced plots. The Boggart is not simply a naughty spirit but one who has feelings and needs friends and companionship as much as any human child does.

Technology of a different sort is encountered in *The Twenty-One Balloons* by William Pène DuBois. Professor Sherman leaves San Francisco on 15 August 1883 in a hot air balloon, telling reporters that he hopes to be the first person to fly across the Pacific Ocean. He is picked up three weeks later in the Atlantic Ocean clinging to the wreckage of a platform that has been flown through the air by twenty-one balloons. The story, told as the professor's speech to the Explorers' Club, recounts his forced landing on the volcanic island of Krakatoa, where he discovers twenty families who live over the most fabulous diamond mine in the world. The professor describes in graphic detail the inventions and customs of Krakatoans and their escape when the volcano erupts. As usual, DuBois's minute descriptions are matched only by the meticulous perfection of his pen-and-ink drawings.

It seems preposterous to try to raise a dinosaur in a small New Hampshire town. However, that is precisely what Nate Twitchell does in Oliver Butterworth's *The Enormous Egg* when the egg he is taking care of hatches into a baby triceratops. Consulted about the problem, members of Congress attempt to have "Uncle Beazley" (the dinosaur) destroyed, since he is extinct and probably un-American! This satire on U.S. politics is a delightful mixture of humor and truth.

A preposterous situation is presented in one of the few satires really enjoyed by children, Jean Merrill's *The Pushcart War*. The story is presented as a "documented report" of the famous Pushcart War of 1996 (more than thirty years in the future when the book was first published). Believing that we cannot have peace in the world unless people understand how wars start, the "author-historian" proceeds to describe the beginning of the war, between the giant trucks of New York City and the pushcarts, that began when Mack, driver of the Mighty Mammoth, rode down the cart of Morris the Florist. The straight-faced account of the progress of the war and the eventual triumph of the pushcart peddlers provides a funny and pathetic commentary on life today. Children thoroughly enjoy this satire; in fact, when one fifth-grade class returned for report cards on the last day of school, they stayed an extra hour to hear their teacher finish reading the book. Few books can claim such devotion!

## Extraordinary Worlds

When Alice followed the White Rabbit down his rabbit hole and entered a world that grew "curiouser and curiouser," she established a pattern for many modern books of fantasy. Often starting in the world of reality, they move quickly into a world where the everyday becomes extraordinary, yet still believable. The plausible impossibilities of Lewis Carroll's *Alice's Adventures in Wonderland* include potions and edibles that make poor Alice grow up and down like an elevator. At the famous "Mad Hatter's tea party" no one has the time to drink tea. The Mad Hatter, the Dormouse, and the Rabbit are just a few of the individuals Alice meets in her wanderings. Other characters include the Red Queen, who has to keep running in order to stay "in the same place"; the hurrying White Rabbit, who keeps murmuring that he'll be late yet no one knows where he is going; Humpty Dumpty, whose words mean exactly what he chooses them to mean; and the terrifying Queen of Hearts, who indiscriminately shouts, "Off with her head!" Always the proper Victorian young lady, Alice maintains her own personality despite her bizarre surroundings, and her acceptance of this nonsense makes it all seem believable. She is the one link with reality in this amazingly fantastic world.

The cyclone that blew Dorothy into the Land of Oz continues to blow swirling controversies around this series of books by L. Frank Baum and others. Some maintain that *The Wizard of Oz* is a skillfully written fantasy, a classic in its own right. Others condemn the first book because some of the forty-plus volumes that followed are poorly written. Dorothy and her companions eventually achieve their particular wishes, but the wizardry is what they do for themselves, rather than anything that the Wizard does for them. For the most part this fantasy depends on the strange situations and creatures that Dorothy and her companions meet. Readers never doubt that the four will overcome all odds and achieve their wishes. Even the Wizard holds no terror for practical, matter-of-fact Dorothy. This lack of wonder and awe—the basic ingredients of most fantasy—makes *The Wizard of Oz* seem somewhat pedestrian when compared with other stories of its kind.

This sense of wonder is very much present in the character of Harry Potter, a young orphan who is amazed to discover his magical talents and remains awestruck and apprehensive in the face of each of the difficult tasks he must undertake. *Harry Potter and the Sorcerer's Stone*, the first book in J. K. Rowling's phenomenally popular series, begins in what seems to be a run-of-the-mill middle-class neighborhood as a Mr. Dursley picks up his briefcase, bids his wife and son goodbye, and heads off to work. As he drives off, however, he fails to notice a cat sitting on the street reading a map. Mr. Dursley might be clueless, but readers know immediately that this is no ordinary work of realism. They are soon immersed in the magical world of Harry Potter, his awful Dursley relatives, and a host of magical and muggical characters (*muggle* being the term for people who have no magical powers). Rowling has adapted the familiar characters of school stories—a well-meaning and earnest hero and his likable friends, a school bully, an acerbic teacher and a kindhearted one, and finally a wise if uneducated janitor to whom the kids go for advice and comfort. Her plots are fast moving and straightforward. The hero is confronted with a serious problem that, in spite of many obstacles, is eventually solved. What make these books so enjoyable are the good humor and obvious zest with which Rowling writes and the wonderful details of Harry's extraordinary world. Harry's required school equipment includes such textbooks as "A Beginner's Guide to Transfiguration" by Emeric Switch, "a cauldron (pewter, standard size 2)" and "one pointed hat (black) for day wear." He arrives at school, not in a yellow bus, but on a train that departs King's Cross Station from platform nine and three quarters or a flying car. His homework assignments include a three-foot-long composition on "The Medieval Assembly of European Wizards" for a History of Magic course. His mail is delivered by owls, his dorm is haunted by a ghost fondly known as Headless Nick, and he plays the intricate sport of Quidditch, on a Nimbus Two Thousand broomstick (later replaced by an awesome Firebolt). In addition to all these elements, the very real dangers that confront Harry and his own sense of vulnerability are likely reasons for the sustained popularity of the series.

Eva Ibbotson's *The Secret of Platform 13,* published in the same year as *Harry Potter and the Sorcerer's Stone,* is equal to the *Harry Potter* books in its richly imagined world. The book's fantastic yet humorous characters and situations will be familiar to Harry Potter fans. Platform 13 is located in an abandoned railway station under the River Thames. It is a "gump," a magical place where every nine years for nine days a door opens into another world inhabited by ogres, wizards, fairies, and other creatures. The story takes place nine years after a baby prince was taken through the door to London by his nurse, who certainly planned to return him before the door closed. Unfortunately the prince was kidnapped by the wicked Larina Trottle, who just happened to decide she wanted a baby. The delightful tale centers on a unique band of monsters, led by the young hag

*A secret entry way from the city of London to a magical world is found in Eva Ibbotson's* The Secret of Platform 13.

Odge Gribble, who decide to return to London and rescue the prince. Ibbotson's *Which Witch?* has an equally weird group of characters who are all witches pitted against one another in a contest to win the hand of Arriman the Awful, Loather of Light and Wizard of the North. The wonderfully unearthly personalities, the ghoulish magic, and the mistaken identities in both books will be hard for children to resist.

Mary Norton tells a fascinating story about tiny people and their miniature world under the grandfather clock in *The Borrowers.* The Borrowers derive their names from their occupation, which is "borrowing" from human "beans," those "great slaves put there for them to use." "Borrowing" is a dangerous trade, for if one is seen by human beings, disastrous things may happen. Therefore, Pod and Homily Clock are understandably alarmed when they learn of their daughter Arrietty's desire to explore the world upstairs. Finally Pod allows Arrietty to go on an expedition with him. While Pod is borrowing fibers from the hall doormat to make a new brush for Homily,

*Mary Norton creates a memorable miniature world in* The Borrowers.

Illustration from *The Borrowers* copyright © 1952, 1953 by Mary Norton and renewed 1981, 1980 by Mary Norton, Beth Krush and Joe Krush, reproduced by permission of Harcourt, Inc.

Arrietty wanders outside, where she meets the boy. Arrietty's disbelief about the number of people in the world who are the boy's size, compared to those of her size, is most convincing:

> "Honestly—" began Arrietty helplessly and laughed again. "Do you really think—I mean, whatever sort of world would it be? Those great chairs . . . I've seen them. Fancy if you had to make chairs that size for everyone? And the stuff for their clothes . . . miles and miles of it . . . tents of it . . . and the sewing! And their great houses, reaching up so you can hardly see the ceilings . . . their great beds . . . the food they eat . . . great smoking mountains of it, huge bags of stew and soup and stuff." (p. 78)

In the end, the Borrowers are "discovered" and flee for their lives. This surprise ending leads directly to the sequel, *The Borrowers Afield*. Strong characterizations, apt descriptions of setting, and detailed illustrations by Beth and Joe Krush make the small-scale world of the Borrowers come alive. Other titles continue the series.

The story of the Minnipins, mostly sober, sedate, and tradition-bound little folk in the Land Between the Mountains, is told in *The Gammage Cup* by Carol Kendall. When a "best village" contest is announced, the people of Slipper-on-the-Water decide that in order to win the coveted Gammage Cup, all homes must be painted green and all Minnipins must wear green. Muggles is the spokesperson for the nonconforming few who insist on bright doors and orange sashes. The rebellious ones are exiled to the mountains, where by chance they discover a threat to the village from the Minnipins' ancient enemies, the Mushrooms. Muggles and her companions sound the alarm, save the village, and are welcomed back as heroes. This well-written fantasy offers tart commentary on false values in society and the theme of the individual versus the group. Ironically, the gentle Minnipins prove to be surprisingly fierce in their encounter with the Mushrooms.

In *The Minpins*, Roald Dahl relates an illustrated story about tiny people with a similar name who live in the Forest of Sin behind Little Billy's house. One day Little Billy, who has been warned never to go beyond his garden wall, gets fed up with being coddled and heads for adventure in the forest. When he encounters the terrible Gruncher, he climbs a tree and discovers the Minpins, who live in rooms and staircases of the hollow trees. Riding on the back of a swan, Little Billy lures the Gruncher into the lake, where it dissolves into steam and smoke. He returns home safely, but his sheltered life is changed forever. Patrick Benson's charming illustrations make this a perfect read-aloud for younger children and a fine introduction to extraordinary and magical worlds.

One of the most popular fantasies for children is Dahl's tongue-in-cheek morality tale *Charlie and the Chocolate Factory*. Mr. Willie Wonka suddenly announces that the five children who find the gold seal on their chocolate bars will be allowed to visit his fabulous factory. And what an assortment of children win—Augustus Gloop, a greedy fat pig of a boy; Veruca Salt, a spoiled little rich girl; Violet Beauregarde, the world's champion gum chewer; Mike Teevee, a fresh child who spends every waking moment in front of the television set; and Charlie Bucket, a hero who is honest, brave, trustworthy, obedient, poor, and starving. One by one the children disobey and meet with horrible accidents in the chocolate factory. Nothing, of course, happens to the virtuous Charlie, who by the story's conclusion has brought his poor family to live in the chocolate factory and is learning the business from his benefactor. The 1964 edition of this book was criticized for its stereotypical depiction of the Oompa-Loompas, black pygmies supposedly imported from Africa by Mr. Wonka and exploited as factory workers.[14] In the 1973 edition, Dahl revised the text so that the Oompa-Loompas

---

[14] Lois Kalb Bouchard, "A New Look at Old Favorites: 'Charlie and the Chocolate Factory,'" *Interracial Books for Children* 3 (winter/spring 1971): 3, 8.

were long-haired little people imported from Loompaland. The sequel to this book, *Charlie and the Great Glass Elevator,* lacks the humor and the imaginative sparkle of the first book.

In Norton Juster's *The Phantom Tollbooth,* when Milo goes through a peculiar tollbooth he discovers a strange and curious world indeed—"The Lands Beyond," which include the Foothills of Confusion, the Mountains of Ignorance, and the Sea of Knowledge. Here Milo meets King Azaz the Unabridged, the unhappy ruler of Dictionopolis, the Mathemagician who serves them subtraction stew and increases their hunger, and the watchdog Tock, who keeps on ticking throughout their adventures. The substance of this fantasy is in its play on words rather than its characters or situations. Its appreciation is dependent on the reader's knowledge of the definitions of various words, phrases, and allusions. For this reason children with mature vocabularies particularly enjoy its humor.

## Magical Powers

The children in books of fantasy often possess a magical object, know a magical saying, or have magical powers themselves. In *Half Magic* by Edward Eager, the nickel that Jane finds turns out to be a magical charm, or at least half of a magical charm, for it provides half of all the children's wishes, so that half of them will come true. Eager's *Seven-Day Magic* tells of a magical book that the children borrow from the library. When they open the book, they find it is about themselves. Everything they did that morning is in the book, and the rest of the book is shut tight waiting for them to create it. Logic and humor are characteristic of the many books of fantasy that were Eager's legacy of modern magic to today's children.

Frequently, less demanding fantasy relies on magical powers, slight characterization, and fast-moving plots to interest less able readers. Scott Corbett's "trick" books, such as *The Lemonade Trick,* rely on Kirby Maxwell's use of a magic chemistry set belonging to Mrs. Greymalkin, a neighborhood witch. Greedy John Midas suffers the consequences of his newly acquired magical power, *The Chocolate Touch,* in Patrick Skene Catling's new twist on an old story. Many children come to discover the pleasures of wide reading and build skills for more complex stories through books such as these.

The magical object in Jon Scieszka's eight *Time Warp Trio* stories is "The Book." In *Knights of the Kitchen Table,* the Book, a birthday present from his magician uncle, whisks Joe and his friends Fred and Sam back into King Arthur's time. The boys' quick thinking saves them from the Black Knight, a foul-smelling giant, and a fire-breathing dragon before they find their way back to modern time. In *The Not-So-*

*A magic book enables three boys to travel through time in Jon Scieszka's* Tut Tut.

From *Tut, Tut* by Jon Scieszka, illustrated by Lane Smith, copyright © 1996 by Lane Smith, illustrations. Used by permission of Viking Penguin, a division of Penguin Putman Inc.

*Jolly Roger* the boys materialize on the island where Blackbeard is about to bury his treasure. In *It's All Greek to Me, Summer Reading Is Killing Me, Tut, Tut, The Good, the Bad, and the Goofy, Your Mother Was a Neanderthal,* and *2095* the boys travel back to the past and into the future for more wacky adventures. Short chapters, broad humor and gross characters, Lane Smith's quirky line illustrations, a fast-moving plot, and contemporary-sounding dialogue appeal especially to boys in second to fifth grade.

Jane Langton has created several stories of mystery and magical powers surrounding the Halls, who live in a strange old turreted house in Concord, Massachusetts. In *The Diamond in the Window,* Uncle Freddy had been a world-renowned authority on Emerson and Thoreau until the mysterious disappearance of his younger brother and sister left him slightly deranged. In the tower room two beds are made up in a vain hope for the return of the two children. Edward and Eleanor move to the tower room and search in their dreams for the two missing members of the family.

Another story of the Hall family, *The Fledgling,* centers upon 8-year-old Georgie's desire, and eventual ability, to fly. She is befriended by the Goose Prince, who takes her on his back and teaches her to glide in the air by herself. Although Georgie outgrows her gift and the goose falls prey to a gun, he leaves her with a magical present—a ball that projects an image of the whole world, and the admonition "Take good care of it." Langton's descriptions give the story a warm and comfortable tone; her evocation of flying might make earthbound readers' spirits soar.

In a much lighter vein, Sid Fleischman sets his fantasy *The Midnight Horse* near the New England town of Cricklewood, New Hampshire: "Population 217. 216 Fine Folks & 1 Infernal Grouch." An orphan comes to claim his inheritance from the infernal grouch, a shady judge who is his great-uncle. Fleischman, in setting the scene, minces no words:

> It was raining bullfrogs. The coach lurched and swayed along the river road like a ship in rough seas. Inside clung three passengers like unlashed cargo.
>
> One was a blacksmith, another was a thief, and the third was an orphan boy named Touch. (p. 1)

When Touch arrives in Cricklewood, Judge Wigglesforth tries to force him to sign for his inheritance, thirty-seven cents. No fool, Touch refuses to sign and escapes to a ramshackle inn. In fast-paced, humorous, short chapters, Touch discovers his real inheritance, saves the inn, and unmasks both the thief and the judge. Fleischman's ear for comic dialogue, his inspired similes, and his ability to strip a tale to its essentials make this a lively story in the same vein as his *The Whipping Boy.*

Like the characters in "The Fisherman and His Wife" and other traditional tales, the characters in Franny Billingsley's *Well Wished* don't always use their wishes wisely. Due to one of these misguided wishes, made on a magic wishing well, the townspeople of Bishop Mayne have lost all their children, except for Catty, a young girl in a wheelchair. When Nuria arrives to live with her grandfather, she and Catty soon become friends. Catty, who wants desperately to walk again, convinces Nuria that she can outsmart the wishing well, and despite her grandfather's repeated warnings, Nuria makes a wish. However, she is soon trapped by the terrible consequences that are the result of that wish, and Nuria must put a devilishly complex scheme into play in order to make things right. The magic in *Well Wished* is dark magic and the story has overtones of the supernatural, but the important themes such as the power of love and the sacrifices made for friendship will also appeal to children.

Older readers with a tolerance for invented worlds and the ability to follow a large cast of characters will enjoy the many books by Diana Wynne Jones. Stories featuring the magician Chrestomanci are a good place to begin. In *Charmed Life,* young Eric Chant (called "Cat" for short) and his conniving sister Gwendolyn are invited to live at Chrestomanci's castle. Cat is unaware of his own magical talents, but his sister has been using minor witchcraft to borrow power from him. Chrestomanci must help Cat realize his own powers while he preserves his household against the evil that assails them from outside the castle walls. *The Lives of Christopher Chant,* a prequel, is about the boyhood of Chrestomanci, who is able to dream himself into strange worlds and bring back from these places what others cannot. Like Eric he is naive about adult motives, an unwitting accomplice to his uncle's wicked plans, and an unwilling heir to the previous Chrestomanci's power. These imaginatively plotted stories reveal the author's wry humor, her love of language, and her ability to balance aspects of time and space in impossible but believable ways.

## Suspense and the Supernatural

Interest in the occult and the supernatural, always an adult preoccupation, also captures the imagination of children. They enjoy spooky, scary stories, just as they like being frightened by TV or theater horror stories.[15] This may in part explain the popularity of authors like John Bellairs, whose mysteries, such as *The House with a Clock in Its Walls,* are full of spooky old houses, scary characters, fast-moving plots, and plenty of dialogue. Increasingly, publishers issue finely crafted suspense fantasies that are often superior to the usual ghost story or mystery tale. These well-written tales of suspense and the supernatural deserve attention.

Paul Fleischman's *The Half-a-Moon Inn* has the tone of a folktale and a setting to match. Born mute, 12-year-old Aaron sets off to find his mother when she becomes lost in a great snowstorm. He accidentally stumbles into the Half-a-Moon Inn, where he is imprisoned by the evil Miss Grackle, who needs a boy to tend the bewitched fires that none but honest folk can kindle. Aaron's escape, his reunion with his mother, and the folktale-like demise of the witch (she freezes to death beside her unlit fireplace) provide a satisfying conclusion. The narration is lighter than the content, and the well-wrought dialogue makes this a challenging and entertaining choice for reading aloud to 9- and 10-year-olds.

---

[15]See Carl M. Tomlinson and Michael O. Tunnell, "Children's Supernatural Stories: Popular but Persecuted," in *Censorship: A Threat to Reading, Thinking and Learning,* ed. John S. Simmons (Newark, Del.: International Reading Association, 1994), pp. 107–113; and Jodi Wilgoren, " 'Don't Give Us Little Wizards,' The Anti-Potter Parents Cry," *New York Times,* 1 November 1999.

Eloise McGraw's *The Moorchild* is a haunting story that relies on elements from traditional folktales such as "Tam Lin" and other Celtic lore. Saaski is half fairy and half human, born to a fairy mother and fathered by a young man lured into their caverns by fairy magic. Because Saaski does not have the right fairy skills, she is banished from their kingdom and exchanged for a human baby. Here she grows up as an outsider, little understood by her perplexed parents and miserable at her failure to fit in. As the townspeople become more and more hostile and fearful of her strangeness, Saaski pieces together her origins and makes a courageous attempt to return her changling counterpart to her real home, knowing that she herself belongs in neither world.

In *The Mermaid Summer*, Molly Hunter explores the ancient legend of a mermaid who was thought to live near the "Drongs" and could lure poor fishermen to their deaths on these rocks. Eric Anderson refuses to believe in the legend until he nearly loses his entire fishing crew to her singing. No one will sail with Eric after that, and he is forced to leave his wife, son, and two grandchildren, named Jon and Anna, and find a place on a large ship leaving for faraway ports. When Anna and Jon trick the vain and deadly mermaid into removing the curse from their grandfather, he is able to return home. Filled with the cadenced language of the storyteller, this tale evokes the rich heritage of Scottish folklore.

Mollie Hunter has based another eerie tale, *A Stranger Came Ashore*, on the old legends of the Shetland Islands that tell of the Selkie Folk, seals who can take on human form. Only young Robbie Henderson and his grandfather are suspicious of the handsome stranger who appears in their midst on the stormy night of a shipwreck. After Old Da dies, Robbie must put together the clues that reveal the real identity of Finn Learson and the sinister nature of his interest in the golden-haired Elspeth, Robbie's sister. Events build to a fearsome climax on a night of ancient magic, when the dark powers of the sea are pitted against the common folk dressed as earth spirits and celebrating the last of the yule festival. Teachers who read aloud *A Stranger Came Ashore* find Jane Yolen's picture book *Greyling* or Susan Cooper's *The Selkie Girl* a good prior introduction to Selkie lore. Children familiar with these stories are much more sensitive to Hunter's use of foreshadowing, folk beliefs, mood, and setting in this finely crafted novel.

Selkies appear in two other fine works of fantasy for older readers, but in these books the selkies are not villains but victims. In *Daughter of the Sea* author Berlie Doherty uses a vivid storyteller's voice to reveal her story. Munroe, a young fisherman, finds a baby floating near his boat one night in a storm and he brings the child home to his wife Jannet. They name the baby Giogga, and they love her as their own. Although they try to ignore the fact that this child is different, eventually there is a price that must be paid for their happiness and for their refusal to accept the fact that Giogga is a child of the sea. In a moving climax, the sacrifices made by both human and selkie allow Giogga to follow her true nature and return to her real home.

In Franny Billingsley's *The Folk Keeper* the main character is Corinna, a sullen orphan with strange abilities to tame the Folk, malevolent creatures who haunt the caves and tunnels beneath the surface. Summoned from her orphanage to be the folk keeper at a great estate near the sea, Corinna finds a friend in the young stepson of the mansion's master. Plunged into dangerous intrigues and a battle of wits with both human and nonhuman opponents, Corinna comes to accept the qualities that have set her apart from other children. When she realizes her true heritage, she understands her strange and terrible longing for the sea. Told through the pages of Corinna's diary, *The Folk Keeper* is a complex and eerie interweaving of folklore and selkie legend that will demand the careful attention of older readers but reward them with an exciting and imaginative tale.

Stories about ghosts and spirits who haunt the real world are more likely to attract readers who don't have the attention span or the background knowledge for complex stories like *The Folk Keeper*. In Mary Downing Hahn's *Wait Till Helen Comes*, a ghost child named Helen has perished in a fire and now waits by a pond to drag children to their deaths as play companions. When Molly and Michael's mother remarries, their new father's child joins the family, but Heather is a brat who forever whines about imagined injustices. Nobody believes Heather's stories of the ghostly Helen until Molly begins to develop some sympathy for her stepsister's point of view. In a chilling ending, Molly pieces together the mystery, saves Heather from a sure death, and forges a hopeful beginning of a loving family. Hahn's fast-paced stories consistently win young-readers awards presented by various states, showing how much children appreciate a good and scary ghost story.

Betty Ren Wright is another writer who can spin a good ghost story. In *The Ghost Comes Calling*, a ghost comes to call on 9-year-old Chad Weldon, who is a reluctant camper at an old cottage his father is trying to restore. The ghost is old Tim Tapper, who years earlier was wrongly accused of misconduct by the townspeople and went to live in the old cabin as a recluse. When Chad proposes a solution that restores the old man's good name, the ghost can finally rest in peace. In Wright's *Out of the Dark*, a ghost appears to 12-year-old Jessica in a nightmare just after she and her family move in to house-sit for her grandmother. Jessie is even more terrified to find that the setting of her nightmare, an old one-room schoolhouse, exists in the middle of a nearby nature preserve and that her grandmother had attended the school as a young girl. The ghost of her dreams begins to appear in various places in and around Gran's house and is obviously trying to harm her. This apparition in white almost succeeds in locking her and a neighbor girl in a metal storage room in the floor of the old school. The mystery of the ghost's identity and Gran's role in a long-ago incident is finally resolved in a riveting conclusion.

Friendship binds a child from the present with a child from the past in Pam Conrad's *Stonewords*. Zoe, who lives with her grandparents in an old farmhouse while her flighty mother "shows up when she shows up," makes friends with a strange, transparent girl from the past named Zoe Louise, whom only she can see. The ghost girl appears, plays with Zoe, and enigmatically states that she is looking in Zoe's eyes for "the truth." On a rare visit, Zoe's mother points out the memory roses planted for a child who died on the property. When Zoe realizes that her ghost friend is that child, she must find out how her death occurs in order to prevent it from happening. A stack of old newspapers moldering away in the basement provides a clue, and the real Zoe is able to go up the back stairs into the past and change history and the present as well.

Margaret Mahy's *The Haunting* blends a ghost story with careful observations of family interactions. Shy Barney Palmer is receiving unwanted messages from a ghostly relative but is afraid to tell anyone, especially his beloved new stepmother, who is about to have a baby. At a family gathering, writing appears on a page of a book Barney is looking at. Barney soon discovers that on his real mother's side of the family, there is in each generation a magician or psychic. His black-sheep Uncle Cole, holder of the magical power for his generation, is lonesome for other psychics and is trying to possess Barney's mind. In an effort to remain normal, Barney struggles against his uncle's mounting frustration and anger. When the malevolent Uncle Cole finally arrives in Barney's house, different family members come to Barney's aid, revealing individual strengths with surprising results. Mahy's trenchant observations of family communications, her deft and often humorous turns of phrase, and a riveting plot make this an excellent choice for reading aloud to older elementary school children.

Another restless spirit is found in *The Ghost of Thomas Kempe* by Penelope Lively. Released from a bottle dislodged by workmen refinishing James Harrison's room, the ghost is determined to harass James into being his apprentice. This seventeenth-century poltergeist blows through rooms, causes some small accidents and a near tragedy, and leaves accusing notes in an effort to control James and make his own presence felt in this century. When at last the ghost is returned to his final resting place, James experiences a sense of the layers of time coexisting in his English village. Penelope Lively tells a good story with humor, and readers are left with the feeling of being, like James, in the middle of time that reaches away behind and before us.

The opening paragraph of *Sweet Whispers, Brother Rush* by Virginia Hamilton quickly draws the reader into a remarkable story:

> The first time Teresa saw Brother was the way she would think of him ever after. Tree fell head over heels for him. It was love at first sight in a wild beating of her heart that took her breath. But it was a dark Friday three weeks later when it rained, hard and wicked, before she knew Brother Rush was a ghost. (p. 9)

Fourteen-year-old Tree takes care of her older brother Dab while her mother, Viola, works in another city as a practical nurse. Tree painfully accepts her mother's absences and devotes her time to schoolwork and caring for her brother. As Dab's occasional bouts of sickness suddenly become more frequent, Brother Rush appears to Tree and shows her her family's recent past, which until now she has not questioned. Through Brother Rush, Tree begins to understand why her mother has always avoided Dab, the hereditary nature of Dab's sickness, and something about her father. When Dab succumbs to the disease, Tree's experiences with Brother Rush enable her to understand what has happened. But it is her mother's love and the gentle strength of her companion Silversmith that pull Tree through her anger and despair toward an acceptance of her brother's death and the promise of new extended family relationships. Making use of African American cadences and inflections, Hamilton moves surely from narration to dialogue and into Tree's thoughts. She has created complex characters whose steady or fumbling reachings for each other may linger with middle-school readers long past the end of this story.

David Almond's *Skellig* is a quietly beautiful story of faith, hope, and friendship. Michael, the protagonist and storyteller, has just moved into a new home with his mother and father and his prematurely born baby sister. The book begins as Michael finds an odd creature in the garage of his new home, a bag of bones, "sitting with his legs stretched out and his head tipped back against the wall. He was covered with dust and webs like everything else and his face was thin and pale. Dead bluebottles were scattered on his hair and shoulders" (p. 8). Michael's encounters with this mysterious creature, named Skellig, are interwoven with his interactions with his mother and father, who are

*Teresa reaches for images in the mirror held by her uncle's ghost to try to grasp what she has seen but has yet to understand in Leo and Diane Dillon's painting for the jacket of Virginia Hamilton's story* Sweet Whispers, Brother Rush.

Jacket art from *Sweet Whispers, Brother Rush* byVirginia Hamilton. Copyright © 1982 by Leo & Diane Dillon.

The book has four major plot threads woven around the character of 13-year-old Kit Watson. He and his family have returned to their roots, an old mining town in England where generations of Kit's family have lived. They are there to care for Kit's grandfather, who has deteriorated mentally and physically since the death of his wife. Although close to his grandfather, Kit finds the move difficult, and he finds himself both repelled by and drawn to an angry outsider, John Askew. John invites Kit to join a group of adolescents who play a game called Death in one of the abandoned cave mines nearby. There they take turns lying in the mine, waiting for the ghosts of children who died in the mine to appear. When the game eventually leads Kit and John into real peril, they find that their childish rituals and secret hideaways have not prepared them for the infinitely more complicated problems of life. They are saved by their own unique talents, and their connections to their families and to their past. The book's complicated plot structure and its interweaving of reality and fantasy demand careful reading. Even more important, older children may need guidance in discussing the game of Death, and the reasons why these and other children are drawn to such rituals. Despite the sensitive issues that are found here, *Kit's Wilderness* is a powerfully imaginative work and well worth sharing with mature readers.

## Time-Shift Fantasy

Probably everyone at one time or another has wondered what it would be like to visit the past. We have looked at old houses and wished they could tell us of their previous occupants; we have held antique jewelry in our hands and wondered about its former owners. Our curiosity has usually been more than just historical interest; we have wished to communicate, to enter into the lives of the past without somehow losing our own particular place in time.

Recognizing this, authors of books for children have written many fantasies that are based on characters who appear to shift easily from their particular moment in the present to a long-lost point in someone else's past. Usually these time leaps are linked to a tangible object or place that is common to both periods. In *Tom's Midnight Garden* by Philippa Pearce, the old grandfather clock that strikes thirteen hours serves as the fixed point of entry for the fantasy. And in *Playing Beatie Bow* by Ruth Park, Abby slips into the 1870s by virtue of the antique crochetwork she wears on her dress; she cannot return to her own time without it.

Julia Sauer's *Fog Magic* is the tender, moving story of Greta Addington, a young girl of Nova Scotia. One day while walking in the fog, Greta discovers a secret world, Blue Cove, a fishing village that is present only

distracted by their concern for the baby. His growing friendship with Mina, an oddly eccentric neighbor girl who is fond of quoting William Blake, provides relief from the tensions at home. As his baby sister, still unnamed, fights for her life amidst the tubes and machines of modern medicine, Michael and Mina care for Skellig, slowly bringing him health. The questions of Skellig's identity and the role he is meant to play in healing Michael's sister must ultimately be decided by reader. Quoting William Blake ("love is the child that breathes our breath/Love is the child that scatters death"), Almond makes the profound suggestion that love can heal when it is aided by the power of the imagination. This strangely moving story is a testament to the power of that belief.

Almond's *Kit's Wilderness* is a frightening and complex story of the supernatural for older readers.

in the fog. Here Greta forms a friendship with a girl her own age, whose mother senses that Greta is from "over the mountain" and quietly reminds her each time the fog is lifting that it is time to go home. On the foggy evening of her twelfth birthday, Greta enters Blue Cove, where her friend's mother gives her a soft gray kitten and quietly wishes her "Safe passage for all the years ahead." Greta senses that this will be the last time that she will be able to visit Blue Cove. She walks slowly down the hill to find her father waiting. As she shows him her kitten, he reaches into his pocket and pulls out an odd little knife that he had received on his twelfth birthday at Blue Cove. This is a hauntingly beautiful story, memorable for its mood and setting. Part of its appeal may come from the underlying view, common in mystical fantasy, that childhood confers special sensibilities that adults can no longer share.

No one is more skillful in fusing the past with the present than L. M. Boston in her stories of Green Knowe, that mysterious old English house in which the author lived. In *The Children of Green Knowe,* the first in this series, Boston tells the story of Tolly, who is sent to live with his great-grandmother. Over the large fireplace in the drawing room hangs a picture of three children who grew up at Green Knowe in the seventeenth century. When Tolly's great-grandmother tells him stories about the children, they seem so real that Tolly is convinced they often play hide-and-seek with him. His great-grandmother believes him, and soon the reader does too. Each story of Green Knowe blends a child of the present with characters and situations from previous centuries while creating for the reader a marvelous sense of place.

One of the finest time fantasies ever written is the mysterious and exciting *Tom's Midnight Garden* by Philippa Pearce. Forced to spend part of a summer with a rather boring aunt and uncle, Tom finds his visit quite dull until he hears the grandfather clock in the hall strike thirteen. Then he is able to slip into the garden and play with Hatty, a child of the past. Tom becomes so absorbed in his midnight visits, when "there is time no longer," that he does not wish to return home. One fateful night Tom opens the back door and sees only the paving and the fences that stand there in daylight—Hatty and her garden have vanished. When Tom meets the real Hatty Bartholomew, a little old lady, he understands why the weather in the garden has always been perfect, why some nights it has been one season and the next night a different one, why Hatty was sometimes young and sometimes older; it all depended on what old Mrs. Bartholomew had been dreaming. Lonely and bored, Tom joined her in her dreams. This is a fascinating story that should please both boys and girls in the middle grades.

While the characters in most time fantasies slip in and out of the past, the problem in *Tuck Everlasting* is that the Tuck family is trapped forever in the present. Natalie Babbitt's elegant prose leads the reader to expect a quiet Victorian fantasy, but the book holds many surprises—including a kidnapping, a murder, and a jailbreak. The story opens with Winnie Foster, an overprotected 10-year-old, sitting in front of her family's prim touch-me-not cottage on a hot August day talking to a large plump toad. She informs the toad that she wants to do something interesting, something that will make a difference to the world. The very next morning Winnie "runs away" to the nearby woods owned by her parents and sees a young man of 17 (although he first says he is 104 years old) drinking from a spring. When Winnie asks for a drink, Jesse Tuck warns her not to take one. Just at that moment his mother, Mae Tuck, and brother Miles arrive. With all due apologies to Winnie, they bundle her onto their horse to go back to their home to have a talk with Mae's husband, Angus Tuck. On the way, Mae tells Winnie that drinking the spring water has given them everlasting life. Back at the shabby three-room cottage of the Tucks, they gently try to persuade Winnie to guard their secret. In the morning Angus Tuck takes Winnie rowing on the lake and explains to her what it is like to live forever. He longs for a natural conclusion to his life. "I want to grow again, . . . and change. And if that means I got to move on at the end of it, then I want that, too" (p. 63). Although the Tucks intend to let Winnie make her own decision, they do not know that a man in a yellow suit, who has been searching for them for years, has overheard Mae Tuck reveal their secret to Winnie. Caught in the melodrama of the Tucks' lives, Winnie decides to protect and help them, a decision that does indeed change her life. The simplicity of the Tucks and their story belies the depth of the theme of *Tuck Everlasting*. With its prologue and epilogue, the story is reminiscent of a play, a kind of *Our Town* for children.

Mystery is also an important part of the complex fantasy by Eleanor Cameron titled *The Court of the Stone Children*. The story of modern-day Nina, who has a "Museum Feeling" and thinks she would like to be a curator, is intertwined with the story of Dominique, a young noblewoman of nineteenth-century France whose father was executed by Napoleon's regime and whose family possessions are now housed in a French museum in San Francisco. Domi enlists Nina's help in the task of clearing her father's name of the charge of murder. A suspenseful mystery, with telling clues foreshadowed in one of Nina's "real-life" dreams, leads to a painting that serves as evidence of the count's innocence. A Chagall painting, *Time Is a River Without Banks,* which also hangs in the museum, is used throughout the story as a symbol of Nina's unusual interest in the abstract nature of time. This is a profound theme explored by a truly accomplished writer. However, young readers will more likely value the book for its exciting events and for the haunting presence of Domi in her museum domain than for its eloquent abstractions.

Like the "Green Knowe" stories, *A String in the Harp* gains strength from its setting and also from its connection to legend. Nancy Bond tells of an American family's adjustment to living in Wales when their newly widowed father accepts a university post. It is a particularly difficult time for 12-year-old Peter, who is stubborn, lonely, and hateful until he finds a strange object later identified as the harp key of Taliesin, the great sixth-century bard who lived in this part of Wales. When the key draws Peter back in time, his present-day life is adversely affected. Eventually he is able to return the key to its proper place and assume a responsible place in his family. This strongly characterized but lengthy story mingles past and present time in a believable and involving way.

In *Earthfasts* William Mayne also draws on legendary characters to tell his story of three interwoven times. When two boys meet at a swelling in the earth, the ground begins to vibrate with the sound of drumming. Out of the earth emerges a stranger who is beating a drum and clutching a steady, cold white flame. It is Nellie Jack John, who according to local legend went underground two hundred years ago to seek the treasure of King Arthur. Nellie Jack John's disturbance of time causes many bizarre events: ancient stones called "earthfasts" work up in a farmer's field; a family's poltergeist returns after a long absence; and one boy vanishes in what looks like a flash of lightning. Only by restoring the candle to its proper place because "King Arthur's time has not yet come" can the boys right the imbalance of time. This unforgettable book owes much of its impact to Mayne's use of language and his finely realized setting.

Often, time travelers learn to deal with a troubled present through experiences in an equally troubled past. In the Australian prize winner *Playing Beatie Bow*, Ruth Park presents Abigail, a contemporary 14-year-old who has been deeply hurt—first by her father's defection from the family and then by her mother's quick agreement when he wants to come back. In this resentful mood, Abigail follows a strangely dressed child who has been watching a neighborhood street game called "Beatie Bow." The little girl, the original Beatie Bow, leads Abigail through increasingly unfamiliar streets to her home in the Rocks area of Sydney—in the year 1873. Injured in a fall and divested of the dress with antique crochetwork that has made her time passage possible,

Abigail is trapped with Beatie's family. She comes to care for them all, especially charming cousin Judah, who is engaged to Beatie's older sister but attracted to Abby as well. Through her courage during a fire in the Bow family candy shop, Abigail earns her return to the twentieth century, where she finds that she is now more tolerant of her father's lapse of affection.

Mary Downing Hahn's *Time for Andrew* is a gripping time-shift mystery. Staying at his great-grandfather's old house for the summer while his parents travel abroad, Drew is a nervous 12-year-old, afraid of bullies, bad storms, and bogeymen. Exploring the attic one day, he finds a bag of marbles that had belonged to Andrew, a distant relative who died of diphtheria at the age of 12. Disturbing the marbles has also disrupted time, however, and as the hour of his death approaches, Andrew is transported to Drew's bedroom. Andrew begs Drew to change places with him and give him a chance to live. Reluctantly Drew does so, going back to the early 1900s to live as Andrew. Here he must face bullies and frightening situations similar to those he feared in his own time. Most frightening of all, however, is Andrew's growing reluctance to trade places and allow Drew back into his own time. The longer Drew stays in Andrew's time, the more he begins to forget his own. Yet he also finds some of the courage he lacked in the modern world and grows to appreciate the close family life he has never had. Hahn is a master at building tension as the story approaches its resolution, and the question of Drew's and Andrew's futures is brought to a satisfying and wholly believable conclusion.

Self-understanding and better family relationships are also the outcomes for characters in two time-shift fantasies by Canadian authors. In *A Handful of Time* by Kit Pearson, a 12-year-old girl is sent to her cousins' camp on a lake near Edmonton while her parents' divorce becomes final. Patricia is definitely the "city cousin" who knows little about boating or horseback riding and is the constant butt of her cousins' jokes. When she discovers an old watch hidden under the floor of a guest house, she finds herself taken back in time to the same summer cabin when her mother was 12 and equally miserable. In her frequent trips to view the past, Patricia learns much about her short-tempered grandmother and her beautiful but reserved mother. By coming to understand her mother, Patricia moves toward understanding herself.

In some books where characters are shifted from modern times into specific periods of history, the concern with social and political issues of the past is very strong. Several notable examples serve the purposes of historical fiction as well as fantasy. In *A Chance Child* by Jill Paton Walsh, Creep, a present-day English boy who has been abused and kept locked in a closet, gets out by chance and follows a canal that takes him back to the Industrial Revolution. As a child laborer, he travels from one exhausting and dangerous job to another, eventually losing his grip on the present altogether. His half-brother, the only person with any clue to his disappearance, searches historical documents from the early 1800s and is at last satisfied that Creep has escaped into the past and lived out his life there. The amount of technological information about work in the coal mines, the nailer's forge, the pottery, and the textile mill attests to the research necessary for recreating these settings. Walsh's juxtaposition of the abusive treatment of children in the nineteenth century and Creep's contemporary plight makes a strong statement about children and society.

David Wiseman's *Jeremy Visick* explores the conditions of child laborers in England's nineteenth-century copper mines when Matthew's school assignment leads him into a mine disaster of a previous century. In *A Girl Called Boy* by Belinda Hurmence, an African American girl, Blanche Overtha Yancy ("Boy"), is bored by her father's obvious pride in their African American heritage. But a tiny African soapstone "freedom bird" sends her into the past when her father's ancestors were slaves, and she is taken for a runaway. The author's use of actual slave narratives and plantation records provides the same authenticity of background that would be expected in historical fiction. Using the device of time travel strengthens this story, however, for it allows the interjection of a contemporary perspective to balance the impact of that era's distorted values.

Welwyn Wilton Katz, a Canadian author, imagines a disastrous future for Earth in *Time Ghost*. In the year 2044, the natural world is far removed from most people, who live in large block buildings in crowded cities and rarely venture outdoors for fear of air pollution and ultraviolet radiation. Sara's grandmother is an environmental lawyer determined to protect the last remaining wild areas of the Arctic from oil industry tycoons, and Sarah joins her on a trip to the North Pole. Through a botched experiment, Sara is sent back in time to central Canada of 1993. Struggling to figure out a way to return to her own time, Sara comes to new understandings about the beautiful natural world she has lost. The story ends with real growth for Sara and other characters and real hope for the little natural wilderness they have left.

Janet Lunn, American born but now living in Canada, weaves together a haunting tale of a contemporary child, an old Canadian farmhouse, and the American Civil War in her book *The Root Cellar*. When her grandmother dies, Rose is sent to live with her Aunt Nan's family in their country home on the

northern shore of Lake Ontario. A shy child who has lived only with adults in New York City, 12-year-old Rose feels desperately lonely in the midst of Aunt Nan's and Uncle Bob's lively family. When she discovers an old root cellar door covered with vines and grass, she opens it and finds herself in a world more than a hundred years past. She is more comfortable in this world and easily makes friends with Susan and Will. When Will runs off to fight in the Civil War and does not return, Rose and Susan set out on a hazardous journey that eventually takes them to an army hospital in Washington, D.C. On the journey Rose discovers a strength and determination she did not know she had that helps her when she returns to her own time.

Susan Cooper has created a richly detailed time travel story in *King of Shadows*. Nat Field is a passionate actor and a member of a group of boys who have been chosen to perform William Shakespeare's *A Midsummer Night's Dream* at the recently opened replica of the Globe Theatre in London. Nat keeps himself busy with rehearsals and throws himself into his part of Puck, partly out of love for acting and partly to block out thoughts about his father's suicide. Soon after his arrival in London, Nat becomes ill and wakes from his fever to find himself in sixteenth-century London. There he is still called Nat Field and he is still an actor. But now he finds he is to play the part of Puck alongside Will Shakespeare on the boards of the original Globe. Cooper manages to fill the story with information about Shakespeare, his time, and the craft of acting, but the story is not driven by these details. Instead Nat's personal pain and his developing insight into himself as well as the elements of suspense and mystery in the plot remain central. Children should enjoy the well-told story and come to share Nat's affectionate attachment to Shakespeare and his passion for the man's beautiful plays.

## Imaginary Realms

Many authors of fantasy create believability by setting their stories in an imaginary society where kings and queens rule feudal societies that resemble the Middle Ages. Often lighter in tone than high fantasy, these stories might nonetheless feature some of its attributes—such as a human character's search for identity, a quest, or the struggle against evil—and are good introductions to the more complex and more serious works of high fantasy. Children are often drawn to this kind of fantasy, as it seems so closely related in many ways to folktales and traditional literature.

Two of Natalie Babbitt's stories, *The Search for Delicious* and *Kneeknock Rise*, are set in an imaginary medieval kingdom. In the first story, young Gaylen is sent out as the king's messenger to poll the

*In Susan Cooper's* King of Shadows *Nat Field, an aspiring young actor, is transported to Elizabethan London and finds work with Will Shakespeare's troop.*

Cover of *King of Shadows* by Susan Cooper. Copyright © 1999 by John Clapp, Illustrator.

has given her the gift of obedience, but the gift turns into a curse when her stepfamily starts ordering her around. This wily heroine eventually breaks the wish through willing self-sacrifice and wins the Prince through her own devices. Patricia Wrede's *Enchanted Forest Chronicles* feature the unconventional Princess Cimorene. In *Dealing with Dragons*, Cimorene runs off to be librarian and cook for the dragon Kazul rather than stay in the palace, sew, and wait for a suitor. Cimorene organizes the dragon's hoard, reads ancient books, and makes friends with neighboring princesses captured by dragons and awaiting rescue. Cimorene's gradual mastery of rudimentary magic and her friendship with the witch Morwen allow her to defeat an evil band of wizards who are trying to influence the choice of the new dragon ruler. Cimorene's further adventures are told in *Searching for Dragons* and *Calling on Dragons*. *Talking to Dragons* finds Cimorene's son Daystar and a feisty fire-witch named Shiara ready for their own adventure with Kazul. All the books make many sly references to folktale and fantasy conventions. While Cimorene and Menolly in Anne McCaffrey's high-fantasy *Dragonsinger* series (discussed in the next section) are sisters under the skin, the two series differ in tone. Children who enjoy Wrede's unconventional feminine adventurer would appreciate being guided to the works of McCaffrey, as well as those of Robin McKinley and Lloyd Alexander, whose heroines appeal to slightly older readers.

This same audience will appreciate the books of Tamora Pierce and Sherwood Smith, two other writers who have spun series that feature characters who will not stay put in the roles their societies have dictated for them. Tamora Pierce's Lioness Quartet is especially popular with early adolescents and follows the career of Alanna, a young girl whose dearest wish is to train as a warrior maiden. In the books *Alanna, In the Hand of the Goddess, The Woman Who Rides Like a Man,* and *Lioness Rampant* she faces many trials and tribulations as she attempts to restore the Dominion Jewel to the King of Tortall and a just peace to the kingdom. *Wild Magic, Wolf Speaker, The Realms of the Gods,* and *Emperor Mage* are set in the same imaginary land of Tortall and feature Daine, a heroine whose magical talent is the ability to communicate with animals. *First Test* features Keladry, a 10-year-old heroine who meets many obstacles in her quest to become a knight. These books feature fast-paced adventures with strong females. Pierce's *Circle of Magic* series, which begins with *Sandry's Book,* is told with the same attention to storytelling but with different characters, four male and female outcasts, who discover their special talents and inner strengths during their training at the Winding Circle Temple, a school of magic. *Magic Steps* is the first book in *The*

kingdom as to which food should stand for the word *delicious* in the dictionary the prime minister is compiling. Before he finishes, Gaylen uncovers Hemlock's plot to overthrow the king. With the help of supposedly fictitious creatures such as woldwellers, dwarfs, and Ardis the mermaid, Gaylen is able to foil Hemlock and save his king. In *Kneeknock Rise*, Egan climbs the mountain and finds a perfectly rational explanation for the groaning noises of the mythical Megrimum. When he eagerly relates his findings to the villagers, they refuse to listen to him, and Egan discovers that people do not relinquish their myths easily; harmless monsters may be preferable to facts.

Authors have long enjoyed playing with the characters and elements of traditional tales. Gail Carson Levine and Patricia Wrede are two writers who have relied on familiar fairy tales to create humorous, highly readable fantasies. In *Ella Enchanted* Levine has taken the Cinderella story and provided a reasonable interpretation for Cinderella's subservience to her stepmother and stepsisters. A well-meaning fairy

*Circle Opens,* a series that follows Sandry and her three friends beyond the school years into their teens, when they must assume their full-fledged responsibilities as magicians.

Although the orphan Wren is the central character in Sherwood Smith's *Wren to the Rescue, Wren's Quest,* and *Wren's War,* her friends Tess, Connor, and Tyron are strong supporting characters. As the four companions battle the evil wizard-king Andreus, they also struggle with the roles they are expected to play and seek to understand the gifts that are uniquely theirs. In this fully realized imaginary kingdom, Smith's appealing characters have the type of wonderful adventures that are the perfect introduction to the more-complex fantasy worlds of Ursula Le Guin and J. R. R. Tolkien.

In Zilpha Keatley Snyder's fast-paced adventure *Song of the Gargoyle,* 13-year-old Tymmon eludes capture when his court-jester father is mysteriously kidnapped. The boy is befriended by a huge and ugly dog, Troff, which he believes is a stone gargoyle come to life. Troff displays a talent for singing along with Tymmon's flute music, and the two are able to make a living as itinerant musicians. As Tymmon searches for his father, he sees the poverty and suffering that peasants endure because of the greed of the nobility, and he takes on responsibility for two homeless children. When the tale of a mysterious old man sends Tymmon to rescue or avenge his father, the boy and dog are thrown into a dungeon. Music again saves boy, dog, and father, who reunite with the two children in an exciting conclusion.

Sid Fleischman sets *The Whipping Boy,* his humorous variation on the prince-and-the-pauper theme, in a time of velvet britches, princely tutors, and robber brigands. Jemmy, the whipping boy for Prince Brat, has taken all the abuse for the prince that he can stand. Each time the bored prince makes mischief and is caught, Jemmy must receive the twenty whacks. But before Jemmy can leave, the prince commands the former street urchin to sneak away from the dull palace with him to see what the world holds. When the boys are kidnapped by two notorious outlaws, Hold-Your-Nose-Billy and Cutwater, one of the boys' identities is given away: Prince Brat had thoughtfully stowed his crown in his picnic basket. But which one is the prince? Because Jemmy had learned to read and write as a tutor futilely labored to teach the prince, the cutthroats consider the whipping boy the one to be ransomed. The exaggerated characters in humorous situations are balanced by the prince's gradual transition into a decent person when he finds that none of his future subjects think much of him. Fleischman's appealing use of colorful figurative language, witty repartee, broadly drawn characters, and clever chapter titles make this a good shared-reading choice for fourth or fifth graders. Peter Sis's quirky drawings and small chapter openings are perfectly suited to this spoof.

If Snyder and Fleischman have woven their stories around a nebulous medieval setting, Gerald Morris and Nancy Springer have placed their fantasies squarely within the tradition of Arthurian legend. Morris's *The Squire's Tale* and *The Squire, His Knight and His Lady* are the somewhat lighthearted stories of 14-year-old Terence Springer's apprenticeship to Sir Gawain and his adventures at King Arthur's court. Nancy Springer's *I Am Mordred* is a more tragic but ultimately uplifting story of Mordred, bastard son of Arthur who is destined to be the cause of his demise. The story takes place as Mordred arrives at Arthur's court and tells of his desperate attempts to avoid the fate foretold for him. *I Am Mordred* is a complex story of a love/hate relationship between father and son and an adolescent's need for self-understanding.

Readers will find a different mythical kingdom realistically realized in Susan Fletcher's *Shadow Spinner.* The setting here is ancient Persia, where Marjan, a young girl with a talent for storytelling, finds herself dragged from her home to the sultan's palace. Her storytelling talents are badly needed by a young princess named Sharazad who must entertain the sultan with a new tale every night in order to prolong her life. Marjan's role in bringing about the famous Arabian Nights tales is richly imagined and deftly woven into a suspenseful story that will engage middle-grade readers and send them off in search of all thousand and one tales.

Joan Aiken sets her stories within imaginary kingdoms with a nod to history as well. *The Wolves of Willoughby Chase* has all of the ingredients of a nineteenth-century chiller, including wicked wolves without and an outrageously wicked governess within. It takes place in a period of history that never existed—the Stuarts, in the person of good King James III, are on the throne in the nineteenth century. Readers will applaud Aiken's resourceful heroines and hiss the evil villains in all the *Wolf Chronicles.* Eleven-year-old Dido is the resourceful heroine of *The Wolves of Willoughby Chase, Black Hearts in Battersea, Nightbirds on Nantucket,* and *Dangerous Games.* Dido's distant relative, "Is" Twite, has her own hair-raising adventures in *Is Underground* and *Cold Shoulder Road.* In the latter book, Is and her cousin Arun come up against such sinister characters as Dominic de la Twite, Admiral Fishkin, a band of smugglers called the Merry Gentry, and the members of a religious group called the Silent Sect. Strange inventions, hidden treasure, and kidnapped children are other features of this thrilling story. As with all these titles, children will find the books hard to put down.

Philip Pullman has written two lighthearted fantasies for younger readers that take place in imaginary realms. *The Firework-Maker's Daughter,* set in an unnamed country with Asian aspects, revolves around Lila, a girl whose temperament somewhat resembles the fireworks her father manufactures. Raised in her father's workshop, Lila learns the pyrotechnic arts and contributes many of her own ideas to the dazzling displays. When she is told that her role in life is to become a wife and not a craftsperson, she rebels and sets off to face Razvani the Firefiend and obtain the magic sulphur that will set her up in her own business. Lila's quest includes help from her friend Chulak and his talking white elephant and encounters with bumbling bandits and other eccentric characters. All these elements form the basis for engaging episodes and a satisfying climax that takes place at a royal fireworks competition.

*I Was a Rat* is Pullman's hilarious spoof of old-fashioned fairy tales and modern tabloid publishing. Old Bob, a cobbler, and his wife Joan are a loving couple who have always missed having a child of their own. When they answer a knock at their door one evening, they find a little boy dressed in a tattered page's uniform. The child is confused about his origins and can only tell them, "I was a rat." The kindhearted couple take in the child, whom they name Roger, and they try to do their best by him. But rat nature and human nature soon complicate the plot. Roger can't seem to stop chewing things up, eating curtain tassels, pencils, and other strange fare. His strange behavior is spotted by a carnival shyster who kidnaps him and exhibits him as a half-human/half-rat monster. Bob and Joan are hot on his trail, however, and after a few more mishaps and some help from a newly married princess, Roger finds a happy home. The book makes the most of Cinderella and other traditional tales, and pokes fun at the media feeding frenzies that seem to accompany almost every aspect of modern life. Older children will enjoy the newspaper pages that are placed throughout the text, but the book would make a good read-aloud for younger children who don't need to understand the tabloid connection to sympathize with Roger's plight.

Lloyd Alexander has a gift for portraying comic adventures in which serious themes lie under a surface of fast action and polished wit. *Gypsy Rizka, The Cat Who Wished to Be a Man, The Marvelous Misadventures of Sebastian,* and *The Wizard in the Tree* are books of this sort. *The Arkadians* is equally lighthearted, with all the trappings of madcap adventure, but it also includes some serious ideas about the craft of storytelling. Lucian is a young accountant in the court of King Bomios who finds his life threatened when he discovers that Calchas, the king's royal soothsayer, is fiddling with the royal books. He must

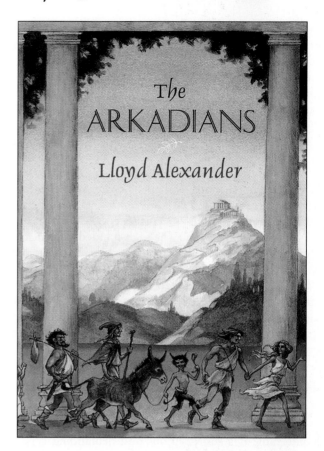

*Lloyd Alexander's* The Arkadians *includes a storyteller named Lucian who encounters a cast of characters who might have lived in mythical Greece.*

From *The Arkadians* by Lloyd Alexander, jacket art by Trina Schart-Hyman, copyright © 1995 by Trina Schart-Hyman. Used by permission of Dutton Children's Books, a division of Penguin Putnam Inc.

flee for his life, and his journey to restore his good name takes him throughout the hills and dales of Arkadia. In the company of Fronto, a poet who has been turned into a donkey, he encounters all manner of refugees from Greek myths as well as a charming but spirited young woman named Joy-in-the-Dance. The three sometimes-reluctant companions have wonderful adventures before all wrongs are righted and all characters are restored to their original forms. Alexander's *The Iron Ring* and *The Remarkable Journey of Prince Jen* are adventures interwoven with the mythologies of India and China. Alexander's books share certain common elements: rich use of language, comic tone, usually a strong-willed female foil to the likable, all-too-human hero, and a setting in an imaginary kingdom. Filled with humor, excitement, and wisdom, any of these books would make superb stories to read aloud to middle-grade students.

Older readers find satisfaction in the two series by Lloyd Alexander, both of which take place in unmagical but imagined settings. *Westmark* is the story of Theo, a printer's apprentice, who pursues questions of honor, justice, and freedom of the press as he tries to avoid the villainous chief minister of the realm. Theo helps restore his street-urchin friend Mickle to her rightful place as princess, but he also questions the concept of a monarchy: Does anyone have a rightful place on a throne? *The Kestrel* and *The Beggar Queen* are sequels in which Theo and Mickle, now the "Beggar Queen," prove their worth in battle but learn the cost of personal victory. In a lighter vein, Vesper Holly is the intrepid young woman who, with her guardian Brinnie, embarks on adventures in *The Illyrian Adventure, The El Dorado Adventure, The Drackenburg Adventure, The Jedera Adventure,* and *The Philadelphia Story.* The high-minded heroine and her guardian journey to imaginary places in Europe, Africa, and Central America where they discover treasure, recover important antiquities, foil villains, and narrowly escape all dangers. Told with Alexander's usual wit, these five stories invite middle-grade readers to create their own adventure "movies of the mind."

## High Fantasy

Many readers who learn to enjoy popular stories of magic, ghosts, time travel, and the like go on to become fans of a more serious and demanding type of story called high fantasy. These complex narratives, which often extend into sequels, are characterized by certain recurring themes and motifs. For instance, the stories frequently take place in created worlds or imaginary realms. Characters might call on ancient and fundamental powers, for good or ill. The conflict between these opposing forces becomes the focus of many stories. Frequently the protagonists of high fantasy have a quest to fulfill. Finally, although there may be touches of humor, the overall tone of high fantasy is serious, because its purpose is serious. High fantasy concerns itself with cosmic questions and ultimate values: goodness, truth, courage, wisdom.

In accepting the National Book Award for *The Farthest Shore,* Ursula K. Le Guin spoke about the intent of fantasy at this level:

> The fantasist, whether he uses the ancient archetypes of myth and legend or the younger ones of science and technology, may be talking as seriously as any sociologist—and a good deal more directly—about human life as it is lived, and as it might be lived, and as it ought to be lived. For after all, as great scientists have said and as all children know, it is above all by the imagination that we achieve perception, and compassion, and hope.[16]

High fantasy's best audience stretches over a wide age range, from preadolescents to adults. Some of its most enthusiastic readers are the same young people who are devoted to video games of imagined adventures. Many older readers simply call themselves science fiction fans and make little distinction between the two types of books. In fact, much science fiction is also high fantasy; Madeleine L'Engle's *A Wrinkle in Time* is one familiar example. Some stories, like Anne McCaffrey's *Dragonsong,* appear to be science fiction with their extraterrestrial settings and the use of precepts of science (in this case, the bonding of a newborn animal and a mother figure). But *Dragonsong* seems more fantasy than science, since the newborns are traditional dragons and "fire lizards."

Not all critics will agree about the proper categorization of books like these. But it is the book itself, not its label, that matters to the reader. However it might be identified, well-written high fantasy rewards its audience with new understandings as well as a good read.

### The Struggle between Good and Evil

The age-old conflicts between good and evil, light and darkness, life and death, are recurring themes in modern fantasy as well as in traditional literature. The setting for the struggle might be the world as we know it, or an invented land like Narnia, which some children know as well as their own backyards or city blocks. C. S. Lewis, a well-known English scholar and theologian, created seven fantasies about the country of Narnia. The best of the series is the first one published, *The Lion, the Witch, and the Wardrobe,* although it was the second in the sequence according to the history of Narnia. Beginning quite realistically in our time and world, four children find their way into the land of Narnia through the back of a huge wardrobe (or closet) in one of the large rooms of an old English house. The land, blanketed in snow and ice, is under the wicked Snow Queen's spell, which controls the weather so that it is "always winter and never Christmas." The children and the Narnians pit themselves against the evil witch and her motley assortment of ghouls, boggles, minotaurs, and hags. With the coming, sacrifice, and resurrection of the great Aslan the Lion, signs of spring are seen in the land. The children successfully aid the lion king in destroying the evil forces, and he crowns them Kings and Queens of Narnia. Narnia has its own history and time, and in *The Magician's Nephew* the reader is told of the beginnings of Narnia.[17] In the last of the

[16]Ursula K. Le Guin, "National Book Award Acceptance Speech," in *The Language of the Night: Essays on Fantasy and Science Fiction,* ed. Susan Wood (New York: Putnam, 1979), p. 58.

[17]See Brian Sibley's *The Land of Narnia,* with illustrations by Pauline Baynes (New York: HarperCollins, 1990) for help in sorting out the chronology of Narnia, notes on the creation of the series, and a simplified biography of C. S. Lewis.

books of Narnia, *The Last Battle,* King Tirian calls on the Earth Children to come to his aid. Narnia is destroyed; yet the real Narnia, the inner Narnia, is not. The children learn that no good thing is ever lost, and the real identity of Aslan is finally revealed to them. These stories are mysterious, intriguing, and beautifully written. Even if children do not always understand their religious allegory, they can appreciate them as wondrous adventures that somehow reveal more than they say.

Susan Cooper has written a series of five books about the cosmic struggle between good and evil. *Over Sea, Under Stone* introduces the three Drew children, who, on holiday in Cornwall, find an ancient treasure map linked to King Arthur. The third book in the series, *Greenwitch,* continues this quest story. Both stories are less complex than the remarkable second book, *The Dark Is Rising.* On Midwinter Day, his eleventh birthday, Will Stanton discovers that he is the last of the Old Ones, immortals dedicated throughout the ages to keeping the world from the forces of evil, the Dark. Will must find the six Signs of Life in order to complete his power and defeat, even temporarily, the rising of the Dark. Strange powers enable him to move in and out of time, where he meets Merriman Lyon, the first of the Old Ones, who becomes his teacher and mentor. While rich in symbolism and allegory, the story is grounded in reality so that both Will's "real" life and his quest in suspended time are distinct, yet interwoven. In the fourth book of the series, *The Grey King,* Will once again must prepare for the coming battle between the Dark and the Light. Special help comes from Bran, a strange albino boy, and his dog, Cafall. Set in Wales, the story works on many levels—with the feud over a sheep-killing dog taking on more significance when Bran's mysterious background is revealed. *Silver on the Tree* draws together characters from the previous four novels for a final assault on the Dark. Much that was hidden in the other tales is made explicit here, and knowledge of the major threads of the first four books is necessary to understand this exciting and fulfilling climax to the saga.

T. A. Barron has also drawn on myths surrounding King Arthur in *The Lost Years of Merlin.* This saga begins with a young boy who finds himself lying on a rocky shore robbed of his memory and his identity. Over the course of the five-book series this child will uncover his past and his magical gifts. More important, however, as he faces increasingly difficult trials, he will learn to control his marvelous talents and to accept the responsibilities that come with power. Barron has developed a multifaceted character in this young wizard, who grows from an impulsive and irresponsible child to a young person who accepts his

In T. A. Barron's The Wings of Merlin, *young Merlin finds his true identity and comes into his full power by working through age-old conflicts of good and evil.*

From *Wings of Merlin* by Thomas A. Barron, jacket art copyright © 2000 by Ian Schoenherr and Mike Wimmer. Used by permission of Philomel Books, a division of Penguin Putnam Inc.

dark side along with his great gifts. Only through such understandings can this young boy become Merlin, the mage who will guide King Arthur. Barron sees the story of Merlin's coming of age as a metaphor for the human spiritual journey. "Like the boy who washed ashore with no clue whatsoever about his wondrous future, each of us harbors hidden capacities, hidden possibilities. Though they may be undiscovered they are nonetheless there."[18] The revelation of these fundamental human needs interwoven with tests of courage and set in a mythical land peopled with marvelous characters typify the genre of high fantasy.

Philip Pullman, whose skillful writing has given us such fine books as the suspenseful *The Ruby in the Smoke,* the supernatural *Clockwork,* and the farcical

---

[18]T. A. Barron, "The Remarkable Metaphor of Merlin," *Book Links* 7, no. 3 (January 1998): 40–44.

# The Lure of The Golden Compass

Bree and Madeline are best friends and best book buddies. When Philip Pullman's *The Golden Compass* was first published, they were in fifth grade and their reaction to the book was passionate and heartfelt. They both felt it was "stupendous." Now ninth graders, the two reflected on their experiences with the book.

Our first encounters with *The Golden Compass* began a continuing dialogue about daemons, pronunciations, and auroras. One year, in September, we both had the same idea—to dress up as *Golden Compass* characters for Halloween. Bree ended up being Lyra, and Madeline went as a girl we imagined Lyra would meet on the other side of the Aurora. (The sequels, *The Subtle Knife* and *The Amber Spyglass*, weren't out yet.) Of course, the people giving away candy didn't guess what we were, but we didn't really expect them too. Since reading the book, we have both been "lured" by hopes of seeing the Aurora Borealis. Bree looked for it at camp in Quebec, and Madeline on her trip to Norway. We are both members of a mother-daughter book group, which read this book over one summer. During our meeting, we assigned daemons to each other, then created our adopted daemon out of socks and fabric markers. Madeline was a type of monkey, and Bree a griffin. During sleep-overs, while we were about to drift off to sleep, we would begin assigning each person we knew their *true* type of daemon. Factors to be considered: outer and inner personalities, interests, level of personal hypocrisy, animal stereotypes, and whether it *just seemed right*. We have yet to figure out what our own daemons really are, but it is a relief to realize that we are not quite grown up yet anyhow, and our daemons have not yet chosen their permanent form.

*The Golden Compass* is our measuring stick when comparing the caliber of other books. We ask each other, "But is it as good as *The Golden Compass*"? Are the characters as realistic? Is the setting as vivid? Is the plot as compelling? The currently popular *Harry Potter* books while very good, don't meet our *Golden Compass* standards, and the main problem is that nothing ever does.

*Bree Bang-Jensen, age 14, ninth grade*
Dobbs Ferry High School, Dobbs Ferry, New York
*Madeline Kerner, age 14, ninth grade*
Dobbs Ferry High School, Dobbs Ferry, New York

*The Firework-Maker's Daughter* and *I Was a Rat*, has created high fantasy of matchless proportion in his "His Dark Materials" series. The trilogy, which includes *The Golden Compass, The Subtle Knife,* and *The Amber Spyglass*, is a richly complex work of the imagination. Inspired by a phrase from Milton's *Paradise Lost*, Pullman wrestles with profound issues of innocence, individuality, and spirituality. Lyra, the central character in *The Golden Compass,* is a young waif who has been raised amid the corridors of intellectual power in a university that seems to be Oxford in a country that closely resembles England. We quickly surmise that there is something off kilter here. For one thing, Lyra is accompanied everywhere by a daemon, a shape-shifting creature that is her soul's companion. For another thing, Lyra's world has strange devices such as anbaric lamps and alethiometers. There are only five planets revolving around this world's sun. Most importantly, there is something mysterious and powerful called Dust. In *The Golden Compass* Lyra's burning desire to discover the importance of Dust propels her on a journey into the far North where she meets a complement of astounding characters. The most important of these is Iorek Brynison, outcast member of the panserbjørne, a race of armored bears. Iorek becomes an important companion for Lyra and a father figure who counters the evil actions of her parents. In *The Subtle Knife* Lyra is introduced to Will Parry, son of an adventurer who, like Lyra's father, has learned to travel between universes. Will's search for his father is intertwined with Lyra's quest for Dust as both seek understanding of the evil mysteries that bind their worlds. In *The Amber Spyglass* these characters' unequaled adventures see them travel between parallel worlds for a confrontation between the forces of good and evil. These compelling books, with their connections to Judeo-Christian traditions, their underpinnings in literary classics, and their references to theories of quantum physics, demand much of readers, but those willing to accept the challenging puzzles will be rewarded with an exceptionally satisfying experience. The Teaching Feature "The Lure of *The Golden Compass*" exemplifies the rich responses that arise from Pullman's wonderful works of high fantasy.

### Quests and Adventures

High fantasy is almost always the story of a search—for treasure, justice, identity, understanding—and of a hero figure who learns important lessons in the adventuring. One of the most famous seekers in all fantasy is J. R. R. Tolkien's Bilbo Baggins in *The Hobbit*. Generally hobbits are very respectable creatures who never have any adventures or do anything unexpected. Bilbo Baggins, however, has an adventure and finds himself doing and saying altogether unexpected things. He is tricked by the dwarfs and the elves into going on a quest for treasure when he would much rather stay at home where he could be sure of six solid meals a day rather than be off fighting dragons. On the way, he becomes lost in a tunnel and is nearly consumed by a ghoulish creature called Gollum, who is "dark as darkness except for his two big round pale eyes." Gradually the hobbit's inner courage emerges, as he struggles on through terrifying woods, encounters with huge hairy spiders, and battles with goblins to a somewhat enigmatic victory over the dragon (a more heroic figure is allowed to slay it). *The Hobbit* gives children an introduction to Middle Earth and its creatures. Later they may pursue this interest in Tolkien's vastly expanded view of Middle Earth in *The Lord of the Rings,* a 1,300-page trilogy that again draws on the author's scholarly knowledge of the myth and folklore of northwestern Europe.

Welsh legends and mythology are the inspiration for the intriguing chronicles of the imaginary land of Prydain as told by Lloyd Alexander. In *The Book of Three* the reader is introduced to Taran, an assistant pigkeeper who dreams of becoming a hero. With a strange assortment of companions he pursues Hen Wen, the oracular pig, and struggles to save Prydain from the forces of evil. The chronicles are continued in the most exciting of all of the books, *The Black Cauldron.* Once again the faithful companions fight evil as they seek to find and destroy the great cauldron in which the dread Cauldron-Born are created, "mute and deathless warriors" made from the stolen bodies of those slain in battle. Taran is proud to be chosen to fight for Lord Gwydion, for he believes he will have more opportunity to win honor than when washing pigs or weeding a garden. His wise and sensitive companion Adaon tells him:

> I have marched in many a battle host . . . but I have also planted seeds and reaped the harvest with my own hands. And I have learned there is greater honor in a field well plowed than in a field steeped in blood. (p. 43)

Gradually Taran learns what it means to become a man among men—the sacrifice of his gentle Adaon, the final courage of the proud Ellidyr, and the faithfulness of his companions. He experiences treachery, tragedy, and triumph; yet a thread of humor runs throughout to lighten the tension. Good does prevail, and Taran has matured and is ready for his next adventure. *The High King,* the masterful conclusion to this cycle of stories about the kingdom of Prydain, received the Newbery Medal. However, the recognition carried praise for all five of these chronicles. Each can be read independently, but together they present an exciting adventure in some of the best-written fantasy of our time.

In Robin McKinley's *The Blue Sword,* a book with closer ties to the world as we know it, a young woman called Harry discovers that her heritage has destined her to be a "Lady Hero." A ward of her brother, Harry feels vaguely out of place in the military outpost where he has brought her to live and is strangely drawn by the mountains where Free Hillfolk live. When Corlath the Hill-King comes to ask the Homelanders' cooperation in turning back the Northerners, who have demonic powers in battle, he is rebuffed. But his visionary gift of *kelar* drives him to kidnap Harry. She is treated as an honored captive and is destined to play a part in the Hillfolk's efforts against the hordes of the North. More and more at ease with her abductors, Harry trains for battle and earns the right to be a King's Rider and to bear the treasured Blue Sword, whose special power in her hand must finally stand between the Hillfolk and their enemies. The girl's poignant relationship with Corlath and his people is put in new perspective by her defiant courage and by her discovery of an ancestral link that proves she is in truth one of them. The story is rich with details of horsemanship, combat, and the romance of a nomadic life. It also speaks directly about women's roles and responsibilities, a message all the more intriguing for being set in a frame of military and desert life, where traditional roles for women are often rigid. *The Hero and the Crown* happens in time before *The Blue Sword* and features many of the same themes. It chronicles the coming of the king's only child, Aerin, into her powers, while leaving the reader with the desire to know more of what Aerin's future will bring.

In *Dragonsong,* Anne McCaffrey writes of another young woman, Menolly, whose special power is tied to her remarkable talent for music. Her family denies her dream of becoming a Harper because tradition dictates that the making of music is a man's task. Menolly runs away, taking shelter from her planet's fiery scourge of "Threadfall" in a hollow cliff by the sea. Here she stumbles on a hatching clutch of coveted fire lizards, kin to the great dragons that patrol the skies. Being the first to feed and touch the new creatures, she "bonds" with nine of them, commanding their loyalty for life. Menolly's beautiful lizards help give her the confidence she needs to take up a new life when she is rescued by a dragonrider and brought to the attention of the Master Harper. *Dragonsinger* tells of Menolly's trials and successes as an apprentice at Harper Hall, and *Dragondrums* takes up the story of her fellow student Piemur, who has his own role to play in protecting the kingdom of

Pern. Except for the unusual proper names, these books are less complex and easier to read than many of the high fantasies previously discussed. *Dragonsong* in particular has great reader appeal; but it may be worth noting that in comparison to other fantasy protagonists, Menolly pays a small price for getting her heart's desire.

*Dragon's Blood* by Jane Yolen has some similarity to the McCaffrey books although it embodies a sterner view of the world. On a mythical planet, dragons who fight for sport must be trained from hatchlings by one who has the gift for mind-bonding with them. Yolen tells the story of Jakkin, a bond servant who steals a newly hatched dragon and trains it in the hope of earning his bond price and his freedom. His surprising success is due in part to the help of a girl named Akki, who has distinct ideas about running her own life. In *Heart's Blood,* Jakkin's plans to enter his own dragon in the gaming pits are disrupted when he agrees to infiltrate a treacherous rebel group. *A Sending of Dragons* brings Jakkin and Akki together for the exciting conclusion to the series.

A superior tale against which other novels of high fantasy may be judged is *A Wizard of Earthsea* by Ursula K. Le Guin. Studying at the School for Wizards, Sparrowhawk is taunted by a jealous classmate to use his powers before he is ready. Pride and arrogance drive him to call up a dreadful malignant shadow that threatens his life and all of Earthsea. Thus begins a chase and the hunt between the young wizard and the shadowbeast across the mountains and the waters of this world. Sparrowhawk, or Ged, his true name known only by his most trusted friends, is a well-developed character who transforms from an intelligent, impatient adolescent into a wise and grateful mage, or wizard. A major theme of the story is the responsibility that each choice carries with it. When Ged asks one of his teachers at the school how transformation of objects can be made permanent, he is answered:

> . . . you will learn it, when you are ready to learn it. But you must not change one thing, one pebble, one grain of sand, until you know what good and evil will follow the act. The world is in Equilibrium. A wizard's power of Changing and of Summoning can change the balance of the world. It is dangerous, that power. It is most perilous. It must follow knowledge, and serve need. To light a candle is to cast a shadow. (p. 57)

The word *shadow* is one of the recurring motifs of the story: Ged's boat bears this name; the evil he releases into the world is called a shadow; and in the end, Ged recognizes this evil as a shadow of himself and his hasty deed. The power of knowing the true name of someone or something, a common motif in traditional literature, is of central importance to this story. So, too, is the value of self-knowledge:

> Ged's ultimate quest . . . had made him whole: a man who knowing his whole true self, cannot be used or possessed by another power other than by himself, and whose life therefore is lived for life's sake and never in the service of ruin, or pain, or hatred, or the dark. (p. 203)

The next story in this quartet of Earthsea is *The Tombs of Atuan,* the sinister tale of Tenar, a child priestess given at the age of 5 to a cult of darkness and evil. This more somber story provides important insights into trust and the price of freedom. *The Farthest Shore* in a sense completes the mighty deeds of Ged, as the wizard must use all of his wisdom to defeat evil forces threatening to overcome Earthsea. *Tehanu* returns to Tenar and her attempts to save a child who has been abused both physically and sexually. Ged returns to these hills entirely spent of his powers and humiliated, but it is his human act, rather than his powers of wizardry, that saves Tenar and the child. This final volume explores the many sources of a woman's strength—hearth, heart, and humanity— that she draws upon to arrive at mature and vital love. The metaphors in all four stories speak clearly and profoundly to today's world.

# *Science Fiction*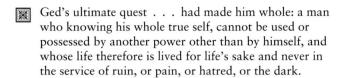

The line between fantasy and science fiction has always been difficult to draw, particularly in children's literature. Children are likely to use the label *science fiction* for any book that includes the paraphernalia of science, although critics make finer distinctions. It has been suggested that fantasy (even "science fantasy") presents a world that never was and never could be, whereas science fiction speculates on a world that, given what we now know of science, might just one day be possible. Sylvia Engdahl suggests that "science fiction differs from fantasy not in subject matter but in aim, and its unique aim is to suggest real hypotheses about mankind's future or about the nature of the universe."[19] Of course, the difficulty comes in deciding what constitutes a "real hypothesis." Are talking cats possible? Plants with a crystalline structure? Spaceships that think and are self-repairing? All these ideas have been put forth by science fiction writers asking themselves "What if . . . ?"

Science fiction is relevant for today's rapidly changing world. Writers must speculate about future technology and how new discoveries will affect our daily lives and thoughts. To do this, they must

---

[19]Sylvia Louise Engdahl, "The Changing Role of Science Fiction in Children's Literature," *Horn Book Magazine* (October 1971): p. 450.

construct a world in which scientific frontiers of genetic engineering, artificial intelligence, space exploration, or robotics have advanced beyond our present knowledge. As in modern fantasy, detailed descriptions of these "scientific principles" and the characters' acceptance of them make the story believable. H. M. Hoover speaks about the author's responsibility to be consistent with "facts":

> If the story takes place on an alien world, the reader must be able to believe humans can walk there. Everything, from gravity and atmosphere, geology and life forms, must fit and be a part of that world if it is to ring true. . . . If not, somewhere a bright child will say "baloney" or a less polite equivalent, and toss the book aside. Children may be gullible from lack of time to learn, but they're not stupid, and they remember details.[20]

In addition, authors who speak to today's reader about the future must consider the ethical or social implications inherent in the scientific issues they raise.

One of the values of science fiction is its ability to develop children's imagination and intuition as well as exercise their speculative and improvisational abilities. Most literature offers a view of society as it is; science fiction assumes a vastly different society. Madeleine L'Engle suggests that children enter this world of speculation more easily than adults do: "Children have always been interested in these cosmic questions and riddles that adults often attempt to tame by placing into categories fit only for scientists or adults or theologians."[21]

Much science fiction that considers cosmic questions falls within the realm of young adult novels. For instance, Peter Dickinson in *Eva* considers the consequences when the mind of a human girl is transferred from her ruined body to that of a healthy chimpanzee. *The Duplicate* by William Sleator gives a teenage boy the power to be in two places at once, with chilling results. Occasionally, however, older elementary and middle school readers, drawn by a love of science, might read well above what adults consider their usual reading levels. Because newer science fiction tends to emphasize a concern with the complex emotional and physical consequences of technological breakthroughs to the future of humankind rather than the dangers posed by aliens or intergalactic warfare, perhaps science fiction readers will be more compassionate and informed in choosing the future. The web *The Giver* on page 340 shows how such concerns might be explored.

---

[20]H. M. Hoover, "Where Do You Get Your Ideas?" *Top of the News* 39 (fall 1982): 61.

[21]Madeleine L'Engle, "Childlike Wonder and the Truths of Science Fiction," *Children's Literature* 10 (1982): 102.

*From the porthole of their departing spaceship, two sisters watch as the world diminishes and finally disappears in Lloyd Bloom's illustration from* The Green Book *by Jill Paton Walsh.*

Illustration by Lloyd Bloom from *The Green Book* by Jill Paton Walsh. Copyright © 1982 by Lloyd Bloom. Reprinted by permission of Farrar, Straus and Giroux, LLC.

## Through the Door

Many children come easily to science fiction by way of books that might not fit a purist's definition of the genre but that incorporate some of its trappings, such as robots, spaceships, futuristic settings, or scientific terminology. Eleanor Cameron's *The Wonderful Flight to the Mushroom Planet* begins a series of stories about Mr. Bass, who lives on the planet Basidium. Alfred Slote has written a popular series that begins with *My Robot Buddy,* in which Jack Jameson and his robot Danny One switch places to foil robotnappers. Older readers are often entertained by Isaac Asimov's *Norby* series about an adolescent boy and his robot. Few of these books tackle weighty themes, but they provide satisfaction to readers who can follow the characters through a series of adventures or who relish the ultimately happy conclusions in a science fiction setting.

An exceptional book that presents a hopeful view of the future is Jill Paton Walsh's *The Green Book.* A family escapes Earth with others in a preprogrammed spacecraft before the "Disaster." Father tells Joe, Sarah, and Pattie that they can take very little with them but that this includes "one book per voyager." Pattie is ridiculed for wasting her choice on a blank green-covered book. When they arrive at their destination planet, Pattie, as the youngest, has the privilege of naming their new home, a place of red foliage and shimmering silver plains. "We are at Shine, on the first day," says Pattie. Ironically, this shine is produced by the crystalline structure of the plant life on the planet. When the wheat seeds brought from Earth produce a crop of grains like "hexagonal yellow beads, shining like golden glass," it appears that the colony will face starvation. The children secretly grind the glasslike beads, mix and bake the dough, and eat the bread without harm. It is then that Pattie's blank book is needed to keep records, and the story-starved people discover that the green book is now full of the most satisfying story of all—their own. An excellent choice for reading aloud and discussing with third and fourth graders, this brief, high-quality book raises thought-provoking speculations about life and survival on another planet. The writing is vivid and tight, evocative without being obscure, and an interesting twist in the narrative voice neatly brings together the opening and closing sentences. Illustrations by Lloyd Bloom match the solemn tone of the text and are memorable for their rounded shapes softened by the light on Shine.

## Visitors to Earth

Television and motion pictures have eased our acceptance of the possibility of visitors from other parts of the universe. Whether the visitor arrives purposefully or inadvertently, young readers today are willing to suspend disbelief and are usually prepared to consider the dilemmas that interactions between visitors and humans present.

Alexander Key presents a visitor to Earth in *The Forgotten Door*, which explores the rights of individuals and challenges readers' assumptions about the nature of human society. Little Jon awakens cold and bruised in a mossy cave and cannot remember who he is or where he came from. He is found by the kindly Bean family, who gradually discover that he is not from this world. Rumors about his strange powers spread, however, and soon the federal government demands custody of Little Jon. Other political groups would like to use Jon's powers, and the Beans are desperate for help. Finally, Jon is able to hear his parents calling him, and he communicates his concern for his friends, the Beans. As various forces close in on their tiny cabin, Jon and the Beans disappear through the Forgotten Door to the world Jon has described to them—a world so simple as to need no laws, leaders, or money, and where intelligent people work together. The fast pace of the story and its substantial characters and challenging themes have made this a good discussion choice for small groups of fourth and fifth graders.

The title character in Dick King-Smith's *Harriet's Hare* is really a visitor from the planet Pars who has been dropped off on Earth for a brief vacation. He assumes the shape of a hare and is discovered by Harriet in the middle of a flattened circle in her father's wheat field. Harriet, a lonely child since her mother's death, is thrilled to have a new friend, whom she names Wiz. The two have a wonderful time exploring the countryside together. Wiz is certainly an extraordinary friend, and because he can communicate with animals he shows Harriet the natural world in a new and magical way. Dreading the end of his vacation, Harriet implores him to stay longer, but he reminds her that he misses his home and must return. He leaves behind several wonderful gifts, however—three little hare offspring and a new mother for Harriet. Although this is a lovely surprise to Harriet, it is no wonder at all to readers who have watched the romance grow between Harriet's father and a children's book author who has moved in nearby. King-Smith spins a warm and gentle tale for younger readers, filled with the wonders of the English countryside and brimming with likable and amusing characters.

The visitor to this planet in Daniel Pinkwater's *Borgel* moves into Melvin Spellbound's family's guest room as a sort of long-lost uncle. The special occasions when Melvin is invited into Uncle Borgel's room to drink Norwegian vole-moss tea lead to an invitation to travel in time, space, and "the other," a place Borgel compares to a tossed salad. Borgel, Melvin, and the unlovable family dog, Fafnir, who can suddenly speak, are off to outer space to visit a time traveler's root beer stand managed by a Bloboform. There they begin their search for the Great Popsicle, which is a coveted sort of energy bundle. Pinkwater's puns, jokes, and asides and the flip "science" he invents are bound to be traded back and forth by older readers who relish the social aspects of reading a truly funny book.

In Kate Gilmore's *The Exchange Student*, Fen, a seven-foot alien from the planet Chela, comes to Earth as an exchange student. When he arrives at his host family's abode, he is delighted to discover that 16-year-old Daria Wells, the Wells's youngest daughter, is in charge of a breeding zoo for endangered Earth animals. Fen's unusual interest in her animals does not surprise Daria, who feels such passion herself. But readers will soon suspect something more sinister. As Fen secretly communicates with his fellow exchange students, a plot to steal animal DNA from Earth's breeding center is revealed. The Chelan people, it turns out, have destroyed their own animals in an ecological disaster, and the planet is overrun with insect pests who are uncontrolled by natural predators. Fen's attempted theft and his strong love for Earth animals is a response to that disaster. There is a strong environmental message in *The Exchange Student*, but it does not overwhelm a good story or overshadow the likable characters, both human and alien.

In Lesley Howarth's *Maphead*, older readers will appreciate the adventures of a half-human, half-

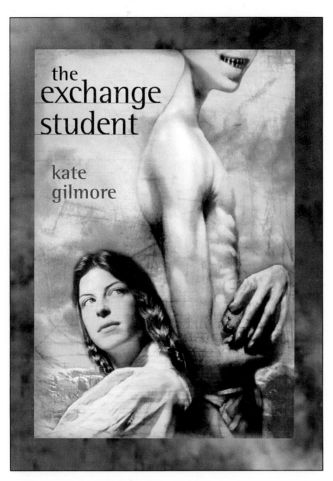

*Fen, Kate Gilmore's* The Exchange Student, *is from a world whose sentient inhabitants have so upset the ecological balance that lower forms of animal life no longer exist.*

From *The Exchange Student* by Kate Gilmore, © 1999. Reprinted by permission of Houghton Mifflin Company.

alien 12-year-old who has returned to Earth with his father. Their purpose is to meet his mother and to understand his roots so that he can come into his full power. This is as much a coming-of-age story as it is a power trip for Maphead. Like any young adolescent, he longs to know who he really is, aches for friends, and wishes for the love of a mother he has never known. He is also inept and clumsy, able to flash a map of any location on his head but unable to map the vagaries of the human heart. Howarth's wickedly funny descriptions of alien habits, particularly their diet, will appeal to the adolescent's sense of the gross, but good writing and strong characterization make this book and its sequel, *The Return,* more than a run-of-the-mill visit from aliens.

## Outer Space and Cyberspace

The technology of the early twenty-first century makes visits beyond Earth's surface much more plausible to

today's child, and many writers have tapped into the premise that interstellar travel is just around the corner. In Annette Klause's *Alien Secrets,* Robin Goodfellow, nicknamed "Puck," is a troubled 12-year-old expelled from her boarding school and traveling to join her parents on the distant planet of Shoon when she witnesses a murder. On board her spaceship she encounters an alien boy named Hush who has lost the Soo, a treasure of his people that he was entrusted with returning to them. It becomes apparent that, along with a few ghosts, the murderer is on board their spaceship, and that the Soo is at the center of a devious plot. Puck risks her life to help Hush find the treasure, but the two make a great team. The mystery is solved, the villains unmasked, and the Soo restored to its rightful place. Both Puck and Hush find their strengths in adversity and also come to accept their faults. This is a thrilling story, interwoven with subtle political themes of oppression and colonization that raise the book far above the level of most outerspace adventures.

Although outerspace adventures have been popular since Jules Verne wrote *From the Earth to the Moon,* there is now a growing subgenre of science fiction set in cyberspace. In the hilarious *Lost in Cyberspace* by Richard Peck, Josh Lewis's friend Aaron figures out a way to use his laptop computer to travel through time. The two sixth graders then carry out the ultimate research paper and plan to present their findings at their school's Parents' Night. They continue their tinkering with cyberspace in *The Great Interactive Dream Machine.* In *Cyberstorm,* Gloria Skurzynski's 11-year-old heroine, Darcy, escapes into a virtual reality machine in the year 2015. Trying to save her dog, Chip, from the Animal Control Division, Darcy is sent back in time with Mrs. Galloway, an elderly woman who rented the machine to revisit her youth. When the machine malfunctions, the two are caught in a terrifying world that might be real or surreal. Both books have the type of fast-moving plots that appeal to middle-grade readers, but they also deal with more serious problems that confront families and cut across generations.

Works like Orson Scott Card's *Ender's Game* and Joan Vinge's *Psion,* although published for adult readers, have been discovered by adolescents who are devotees of computer games and steeped in the language of the computer. These readers might have the background to enjoy such young-adult titles as Vivian Vande Velde's *User Unfriendly* and Monica Hughes's *Invitation to the Game,* and they will certainly find Gillian Cross's *New World* accessible. Cross tells a gripping tale in which Miriam, Will, and Stuart, three 14-year-olds unknown to each other, are recruited by a computer company to test a prototype of a new virtual reality game. As each becomes more and more hooked on the game, one of them begins to suspect that there is something sinister behind the fun. In circumstances that become increasingly threatening, the youngsters are forced to face questions about their own identities and the nature of reality itself. In a thought-provoking and chilling scenario, Cross manages to address issues such as manipulation, greed, and the lengths young people will go to for excitement.

## Views of the Future

Science fiction of the highest level presents the reader with complex hypotheses about the future of humankind. Many novels raise questions about the organization of society or the nature of the world following a massive ecological disaster. Writers such as John Christopher and Madeleine L'Engle imagine other life-forms and their interactions with our world. William Sleator in *The Green Futures of Tycho* asks how present time can be altered to affect the future; in L'Engle's *A Swiftly Tilting Planet*, the past is altered to change the present and future. Throughout these novels of speculation runs the question of which human qualities and responsibilities will become—or remain—essential in time to come. The web "*The Giver*" shows how these issues might be explored in Lois Lowry's Newbery Medal–winning novel.

*A Wrinkle in Time* suggests that love and individuality will continue to be important for the future. If there is a classic in the field of science fiction for children, it might be this Newbery Medal winner by Madeleine L'Engle. The exciting story concerns Charles Wallace, a 5-year-old brilliant beyond his age and time, and Meg, his 12-year-old sister, whose stubbornness later becomes an asset. With the help of Calvin O'Keefe, a 14-year-old on whose stability the two often rely, the children begin a frenzied search for their missing father, a scientist working for the government. They are aided in their search by three women who have supernatural powers—Mrs. Whatsit, Mrs. Who, and Mrs. Which. The children travel by means of a wrinkle in time, or a tesseract, to the evil planet Camazotz. The people of Camazotz, having given up their identities to "It," do everything in synchronization. When Charles Wallace attempts to resist It by reason, he, too, is captured. Though Meg is able to save her father, they must leave Charles Wallace behind. Exhausted and still under the evil influence of It, Meg is slowly nursed back to love and peace by another strange but loving creature, Aunt Beast. When Meg realizes that only she can save Charles Wallace, she returns to confront It with what she knows It does not have or understand—the power of love. This many-layered story can be read for the exciting plot alone or for the themes and the values it espouses.

*In her Newbery Medal–winning book* The Giver, *Lois Lowry raises fundamental questions about human nature and human society.*

From *The Giver* by Lois Lowry, © 1993. Reprinted by permission of Houghton Mifflin Company.

*A Wind in the Door,* also by L'Engle, is a companion story involving many of the previous characters with new situations and other creatures. The story concerns the fight to save Charles Wallace from a baffling illness. Meg, Calvin, and Mr. Jenkins, the cold, remote principal of the school, are led to a planet in galactic space where size does not exist. Here they are made small enough to enter Charles Wallace's body and help fight the attacking forces of evil, the Echthroi. Only when Meg names them with her own name does she overcome the Echthroi and save Charles. The story emphasizes the importance of every minuscule part of the universe in carrying out its purpose in living. *A Wind in the Door* is more complex than *A Wrinkle in Time,* but L'Engle is capable of conveying her message to perceptive children of 9 or 10 and up.

*A Swiftly Tilting Planet* completes L'Engle's Time Trilogy. Charles Wallace has been saved, first from the dehumanization of It, and second from a rare blood disease. Now, in this story, the reader discovers why Charles Wallace has been twice rescued, for his ultimate mission involves saving the world from total destruction. He must journey back in historical time to change some seemingly small part of past relationships so that a potential world war in the present can be averted. This is by far the most demanding of the three volumes, as there are many characters in several time frames to attend to. The Time Trilogy is a unique and wonderful combination of science fiction, modern fantasy, traditional lore, and religious symbolism by which L'Engle stretches the minds and the spirits of her readers.

Susan Butler's *The Hermit Thrush Sings* is set in a future where the earth's environment and political structure have been devastated by a meteor crash. The survivors have been isolated in walled towns controlled by a fearsome military government. Leora is an outsider, reviled because of her webbed hand, the result of genetic mutations. She is also a dreamer who longs to explore the woods outside her city prison. When she discovers a special bond with the feared apelike creatures called birmbas, she begins to question other information fed to her people by their cruel rulers. Leora flees to a town rumored to be full of rebels and finds an army of women led by a sister she had believed was dead. Leora's role in the rebels' subsequent battle for freedom is central to this suspenseful story.

*The Ear, the Eye, and the Arm* by Penelope Farmer is a complex, gripping, and funny story set in Zimbabwe in the year 2194. Thirteen-year-old Tendai and his younger brother and sister live in a protected enclave in a society that separates out the haves from the have-nots. Like children in other tales, however, they long for adventure, and when they venture out from behind the electrified fences one day, they get more than they bargained for. Kidnapped by the She Elephant's hooligans, they are taken to a toxic waste dump where this evil old woman holds court. They escape to an idyllic village where technology is banned and the people live in pastoral splendor. But they find that the price for this peace is often death for those who are weak or won't conform. Close behind the three children in their escapades is an unusual trio of detectives—Ear, Eye, and Arm, who have unusual powers because of genetic mutation and have been hired by the children's parents to bring them home. As in all good cliffhangers, however, they discover the children's whereabouts just a fraction too late to rescue them, and the children, particularly Tendai, must take responsibility for themselves. Farmer weaves Shona mythology, science fiction, and a little Hollywood action thriller into a book that has many layers. She raises searching questions about social and political issues without neglecting issues that are closer to the heart of a young boy's coming of age, all in the context of a strapping good yarn.

The White Mountains quartet by John Christopher describes a future world that has been reduced to a primitive society. However, people in this twenty-first-century world are controlled by machine creatures called Tripods. At age 14, each human being must be "capped," a ceremony in which a steel plate is inserted into the skull to make the wearer a servant of the state. Over the course of the four books, young Will leads the revolt that defeats the Tripods and leaves humans free to set up their own government. Christopher's second science-fiction series—*The Prince in Waiting, Beyond the Burning Lands,* and *The Sword of the Spirits*—deals with England in the twenty-first century following the "Disaster," a period of volcanic activity, earthquakes, and strong radiation from the sun that destroyed all of humanity's technical accomplishments. These books are much more violent than the White Mountain quartet, which is in keeping with their imagined setting. However, the violence may be justified because it raises the ethical questions of whether violence impersonalized by distance and machine is any different from hand-to-hand violence and whether it is possible to keep "rules" in war. Mature readers who enjoy the Christopher books will want to read Garth Nix's *Shade's Children* about refugees from an equally brutal future world where an alien race harvests the brains of children when they reach the age of 14.

Teenager Ann Burden in *Z for Zachariah* by Robert C. O'Brien thinks she is the last living person on Earth, following a nuclear war. She begins to carve out a solitary life, accompanied only by the family dog, when she sees what appears to be smoke from a campfire on the horizon. She finds another survivor, John Loomis. But instead of providing Ann with hoped-for companionship, he becomes more and more possessive. At last she decides on a plan of escape and leaves the valley in hopes that she will find other survivors she has dreamed about. Written in the form of a diary kept by Ann, this story is rich in the details of her survival and growing resolve. Ann relates her doubt and anger about the many choices she must make, but the reader does not doubt that Ann will find the others for whom she searches.

The authors of the previously discussed books have drawn clear distinctions between the world of reality and the world of fantasy. There are several books, however, that could be considered as works of contemporary realism yet seem best discussed in this section because their authors, rather than focus just on family relationships or on the difficulties of growing up in today's world, also speculate about human actions and interactions that might lead to dramatic alterations in humanity's future.

## Division of Labor

In Jonas's community everyone who was able worked. There was no unemployment. How did they determine who would do which job? Were all the jobs equally desirable or equally respected in the community? Do you think this is a good system?

Ask adults in your family if they would like to be guaranteed a job for life. Would they like someone else to choose it for them?

How does Pattie's community handle these problems in *The Green Book* (Walsh)?

## Family

Read *Families: A Celebration of Diversity, Commitment, and Love* (Jenness).

How do the contemporary families profiled in this book compare with Jonas's family? with your own family?

Compare how elderly people are treated in Jonas's community to the way they are treated in American society and in other countries.

Compare family structures in *Beginnings: How Families Came to Be* (Schuett).

Read *Families: Poems Celebrating the African American Experience* (Strickland), *Fathers, Mothers, Sisters, Brothers* (Hoberman).

What type of poetry might Jonas write about his family?

## Conformity

When Jonas asks, "What if we could hold up things that were bright red or bright yellow, and [Gabriel] could choose?" The Giver responds, "He might make wrong choices." What are the advantages and disadvantages of having choices? Have you ever made a wrong one? Have you ever regretted having to choose?

Jonas lives in a community that has turned to "Sameness." Are there times in your life when you choose sameness or conformity? What are they? When do you act independently?

Compare to issues of conformity in *A Wrinkle in Time* (L'Engle)

## Without Differences?

In Jonas's community there were no racial or ethnic differences. Is that desirable? What are the pros and cons? What about economic class differences?

## Without Conflict?

Jonas's community seemed to be so isolated that it almost seemed to be surrounded by an unknown wall.

Read *Talking Walls* and *Talking Walls: The Story Continues* (Knight)

What have been the functions of walls throughout history and in the present? To separate, unite, protect, etc.? Are there walls in your vision of a perfect future world? If so, describe them.

Is it right to impose order by taking away choice?

## LIVING IN A COMMUNITY

## Government and Rules

Describe the government and the rules in *The Giver*.

How do they compare with those in our democratic system? with communism or totalitarianism? With other governments past or present that you've studied? Create a comparison chart.

If you could make the rules for a group of people, where would you start?

## Censorship

It is easy to understand that the Giver, as the sole repository of memory, is the only one in the community permitted to have history books, but why can't the rest of the community have access to other types of books? What about films, visual arts, theater, music, and other art forms?

Read *The Day They Came to Arrest the Book* (Hentoff). Does your community have to deal with issues of censorship?

Has *The Giver* been the object of censorship? Consult the American Library Association website at http://www.ala.org/bbooksat and related websites.

Write a rationale for why *The Giver* should not be banned.

## COMMUNICATION

## Names

How are names used in the Community? How does that compare with the way we use names in our society today? Why do you think that all the "new children" are assigned numbers at birth, but not given names until the Ceremony of One? Why does Jonas's father think that calling Gabriel by his name might help him?

Research the meanings of characters' names. Read the biblical stories of the archangel Gabriel and Jonah. How do these stories change or add to your understanding of the novel?

Is there any significance to the fact that the Giver's daughter's name, Rosemary, has been associated with "remembrance"?

## Language

What are the effects of how language is used and controlled in the community?

How is lying or deception related to word choice?

Contrast Jonas's and Asher's use of language.

At the Ceremony of Twelve, the Chief Elder says: "Jonas has not been assigned. Jonas has been *selected.*" Is this distinction important? How?

What important words do we have in our language that are missing from theirs?

Trace the etymology of words such as *community*, *future*, and *utopia*.

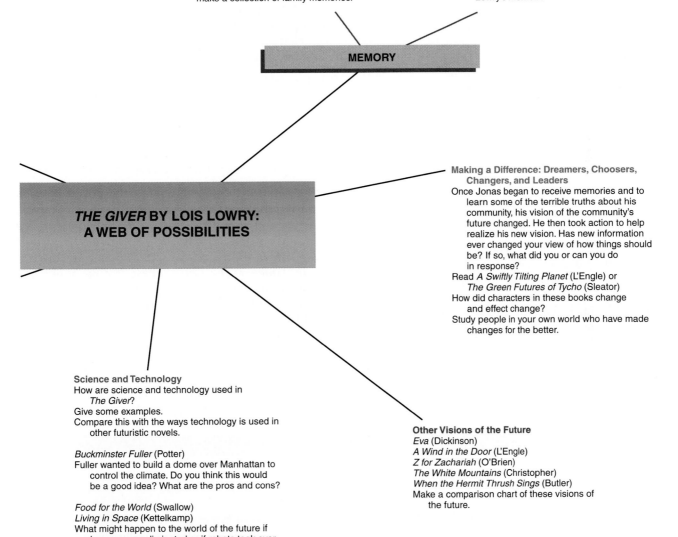

Recall the memories that Jonas receives.
How do they change him?

**Community Memory**
Record and preserve the memories of some of the
   older people in your community. Create a book of
   these memories and find an appropriate place for
   it in the community, such as the public library or
   the historical society.

**Personal and Familial Memory**
The Giver's favorite memory is of "families, and
   holidays, and happiness." If you could give Jonas
   your favorite memory, what would it be? How is
   yours similar to and different from the Giver's?
Read such memoirs as *Family Pictures* (Garza) and
   *Homesick* (Fritz). Interview your grandparents and
   make a collection of family memories.

**Lois Lowry's Memories**
Read "On Writing the Giver" (Lowry) and "Newbery
   Award Acceptance Speech" (Lowry) for
   background information. How have her memories
   affected her writing of *The Giver*?
Discuss Lowry's reason for writing the novel's
   dedication. What are its implications?

**Memory in Other Books by Lois Lowry**
Memory is an important topic in Lowry's
   *Anastasia Krupnik* and *Autumn Street*.
Compare and contrast what these books suggest
   about the value of and the pain associated
   with memory.

*Looking Back: A Book of Memories* (Lowry)
   How did memory influence the style of
   Lowry's memoir?

**MEMORY**

**THE GIVER BY LOIS LOWRY:
A WEB OF POSSIBILITIES**

**Making a Difference: Dreamers, Choosers,
   Changers, and Leaders**
Once Jonas began to receive memories and to
   learn some of the terrible truths about his
   community, his vision of the community's
   future changed. He then took action to help
   realize his new vision. Has new information
   ever changed your view of how things should
   be? If so, what did you or can you do
   in response?
Read *A Swiftly Tilting Planet* (L'Engle) or
   *The Green Futures of Tycho* (Sleator)
How did characters in these books change
   and effect change?
Study people in your own world who have made
   changes for the better.

**Science and Technology**
How are science and technology used in
   *The Giver*?
Give some examples.
Compare this with the ways technology is used in
   other futuristic novels.

*Buckminster Fuller* (Potter)
Fuller wanted to build a dome over Manhattan to
   control the climate. Do you think this would
   be a good idea? What are the pros and cons?

*Food for the World* (Swallow)
*Living in Space* (Kettelkamp)
What might happen to the world of the future if
   hunger were eliminated or if robots took over
   your school or if a nonpolluting, renewable
   fuel were discovered? Think through the
   impact of one such scientific advancement.

**Other Visions of the Future**
*Eva* (Dickinson)
*A Wind in the Door* (L'Engle)
*Z for Zachariah* (O'Brien)
*The White Mountains* (Christopher)
*When the Hermit Thrush Sings* (Butler)
Make a comparison chart of these visions of
   the future.

*Web prepared by Jennifer Madden O'Hear*

In *Phoenix Rising* by Karen Hesse, Nyle and her grandmother must deal with nuclear threat that is all the more chilling for being so possible. The setting for the story is rural Vermont, where the countryside has been contaminated by a terrible accident at the Cookshire nuclear power plant. Nyle is horrified when her grandmother takes in two survivors from the disaster, 15-year-old Ezra and his mother. Ezra is dying, and Nyle, deeply wounded by the deaths of her mother and grandfather, wants nothing to do with these refugees. She finds she is drawn to the boy, however, and gradually she grows to care deeply for him. In the end, accepting his death means that she accepts life. This lovely coming-of-age story is full of hope, for Nyle is no longer the angry child shut off from those around her, but a mature young woman who clearly sees her responsibility to others and to their future world.

In John Marsden's *Tomorrow When the War Began,* a group of teenagers returns from a camping trip in a remote Australian canyon to find their town invaded by an unknown army. In this book and the following volumes, *The Dead of Night* and *A Killing Frost,* the teens face critical issues of right and wrong as they attempt to fight a guerilla war against the totalitarian enemy. The books work beautifully as survival stories but they also raise important moral and political questions that link them to contemporary conflicts in the wider world, present, past, and future.

Lois Lowry's *The Giver* imagines a future that at first seems benign and idyllic. Pollution is gone, family life is tranquil, and communities are orderly and peaceful. In this world young Jonas approaches the Ceremony of Twelve with anticipation, for this is when he will be assigned to his life's work. He is stunned when his name is passed over during the ceremony, but then the Chief Elder announces that Jonas has been selected to be the next Receiver of Memory. This is the one person in the community who holds memories not just of events, but of feelings. As he is instructed by the old Receiver, now

the Giver, he comes to understand the fullness of human experience in all its color, joy, and pain. He also begins to see beneath the orderly surface of his existence and to understand the terrible price his people have paid for their serenity. Determined to change the course of the future, Jonas and the Giver plan for his escape. But at the last moment a terrible threat to Gabriel, a foster child about whom Jonas cares deeply, forces a change of plan, and Jonas sets out on a journey that might lead to his end or might bring him full circle to his humanity. *The Giver* is a richly rewarding fantasy, full of subtle clues, connections, and ideas. Lowry has given each reader the wonderful gift that Jonas's community lacked, the gift of choice. This is a book to be read, enjoyed, and understood on an intensely personal level. In her Newbery acceptance speech, Lowry remarked on the interpretation a young reader brought to the book.

> The child—as we all do—has brought her own life to a book. She has found a place, a place in the pages of a book, that shares her own frustrations and feelings. . . . Most of the young readers who have written to me have perceived the magic of the circular journey—the truth that we go out and come back, and that what we come back to is changed, and so are we.[22]

The ability to change lives is the power of such good writing. Fantasy for children needs no defense. Whether a modern fairy tale like *Many Moons* or *The Little Prince,* modern fantasy like *Charlotte's Web* or *The Dark Is Rising,* or the science fiction of *A Wrinkle in Time* or *The Giver,* these lasting books can speak for our time and the times to come. They stretch children's imaginations, present our own world in a new perspective, and ask readers to consider how present actions might affect Earth's ecological, political, and social future.

---

[22]Lois Lowry, "Newbery Medal Acceptance," *Horn Book Magazine* (July/August 1994): pp. 420–421.

## INTO THE CLASSROOM

### *Modern Fantasy*

**Room 201**

1. Make an illustrated map to show an extraordinary world or imaginary realm that you have discovered in a book. Make a key to locate events of the story.
2. Make a display or a chart of the many symbols and their meaning found in *The Dark Is Rising* by Susan Cooper or *A Stranger Came Ashore* by Mollie Hunter.
3. Think of some family heirloom that might act as a magical amulet that would take you back to the time when

your mother or father was 12 years old. How does the heirloom "work"? Where would you be? What might you witness?

4. Ask yourself what might happen to the world of tomorrow if hunger were eliminated, or if robots took over your school, or if hydrogen fusion were made a workable source of energy. Think through the impact of one such scientific advancement.

# Personal Explorations

1. Write a modern fairy tale, fable, or tall tale using the old forms, but with twenty-first-century content reflecting today's changing values. For example, you might want to consider reversing the stereotyped sex roles of the prince and princess.
2. Ask a group of your friends to list their ten favorite children's books. How many of these could be categorized as modern fantasy?
3. Compare the Chronicles of Narnia by C. S. Lewis with Lloyd Alexander's Prydain Chronicles; or compare two animal fantasies, such as *Charlotte's Web* and *Pigs Might Fly*. In what ways are they alike? How are they different?
4. Choose a book of high fantasy or time fantasy and identify motifs that seem derived from folklore, myth, or legend. Which of these motifs are common in other modern fantasies?

# Related Readings

Anderson, Douglas A. *The Annotated Hobbit*. Illustrated by J. R. R. Tolkien. New York: Houghton Mifflin, 1988.

Fascinating background information on Tolkien's sources for story, choices of names, scholarship, revisions, and illustrations, including many examples from foreign editions.

Campbell, Joseph. *The Hero with a Thousand Faces*. 2nd ed. Princeton, N.J.: Princeton University Press, 1968.

This standard scholarly work on the "monomyth," or the archetypal story of the hero, helps the serious student of high fantasy to see the protagonist of the quest in a universal perspective.

Cooper, Susan. *Wishes and Dreams: Essays on Writing for Children*. New York: McElderry, 1996.

This collection of speeches made by Cooper over the years shows her growth as a writer for children and the inspirations, ideas, and events that have fed her fantasy writing.

Egoff, Sheila. *Worlds Within: Children's Fantasy from the Middle Ages to Today*. Chicago: American Library Association, 1988.

A study of the development of children's fantasy from its roots in ancient myth and legend to the intense and sometimes violent novels being written today.

Gose, Elliott. *Mere Creatures: A Study of Modern Fantasy Tales for Children*. Toronto: University of Toronto Press, 1988.

In twelve thoughtful essays Gose focuses on creatures in fantasy, from the "real" rabbits of *Watership Down* to the toy animals in *Winnie-the-Pooh* to mythical creatures in *The Hobbitt*, and finds psychological as well as literary underpinnings.

Mahy, Margaret. "A Dissolving Ghost: Possible Operations of Truth in Children's Books and the Lives of Children." In the ALA *Arbuthnot Lectures 1980–1989*. Chicago: American Library Association, 1990.

Mahy's intriguing essay reveals the transformation of a real-life experience into a fantastic tale. See also Patricia Wrightson's essay "Stones in Pools," in the same volume, in which she discusses the continuity of story from ancient times and the wonder found in fantasy.

May, Jill P. *Lloyd Alexander*. New York: Twayne, 1991.

A twelve-page biographical essay is followed by a critical examination of each of Alexander's books. Among other things, May discusses Alexander's innovative abilities and the diverse sources his books draw on.

Tunnell, Michael O. *The Prydain Companion: A Reference Guide to Lloyd Alexander's Prydain Chronicles*. Westport, Conn.: Greenwood, 1989.

Major characters, places, objects, and themes from Alexander's ten Prydain books are examined in encyclopedic fashion. Entries include a pronunciation guide (helpful for Welsh names), a full discussion of the entry as it is found across the books, and information about the topic's roots in Welsh and Celtic folklore.

# Children's Literature

The books listed here are recommended, subject to the qualifications noted in the text. Original publication dates appear in square brackets. See Appendix C for publishers' complete addresses.

Adams, Richard. *Watership Down*. Macmillan, 1974.

Ahlberg, Allan. *The Giant Baby*. Illustrated by Fritz Wegner. Viking, 1994.

Aiken, Joan. *Black Hearts in Battersea*. Illustrated by Robin Jacques. Doubleday, 1964.

————. *Cold Shoulder Road*. Delacorte, 1996.

————. *Dangerous Games*. Delacorte, 1999.

————. *Is Underground*. Delacorte, 1995.

————. *Nightbirds on Nantucket*. Illustrated by Robin Jacques. Doubleday, 1966.

————. *The Wolves of Willoughby Chase*. Illustrated by Pat Marriott. Doubleday, 1963.

Alexander, Lloyd. *The Arkadians*. Dutton, 1995.

————. *The Beggar Queen*. Dutton, 1984.

————. *The Black Cauldron*. Holt, 1965.

————. *The Book of Three*. Holt, 1964.

————. *The Castle of Llyr*. Holt, 1966.

————. *The Cat Who Wished to Be a Man*. Dutton, 1973.

————. *The Drackenburg Adventure*. Dutton, 1988.

————. *The El Dorado Adventure*. Dutton, 1987.

————. *Gypsy Rizka*. Dutton, 1999.

————. *The High King*. Holt, 1968.

————. *The Illyrian Adventure*. Dutton, 1986.

————. *The Iron Ring*. Dutton, 1997.

————. *The Jedera Adventure*. Dutton, 1989.

————. *The Kestrel*. Dutton, 1982.

————. *The Marvelous Misadventures of Sebastian*. Dutton, 1970.

————. *The Philadelphia Adventure*. Dutton, 1990.

————. *The Remarkable Journey of Prince Jen*. Dutton, 1991.

————. *Taran Wanderer*. Holt, 1967.

————. *Westmark*. Dutton, 1981.

————. *The Wizard in the Tree*. Illustrated by Laszlo Kubinyi. Dutton, 1975.

Almond, David. *Kit's Wilderness*. Delacorte, 2000.

————. *Skellig*. Delacorte, 1999.

Andersen, Hans Christian. *The Emperor's New Clothes*. Illustrated by Virginia Lee Burton. Houghton Mifflin, 1949.

————. *Hans Christian Andersen: The Complete Fairy Tales and Stories*. Translated by Erik Haugaard. Doubleday, 1974.

————. *The Little Match Girl*. Illustrated by Jerry Pinkney. Phyllis Fogleman, 1999.

————. *The Nightingale*. Illustrated by Lisbeth Zwerger. North-South, 1999.

————. *The Snow Queen*. Translated by Anthea Bell. Illustrated by Bernadette Watts. Picture Book Studio, 1985.

————. *The Steadfast Tin Soldier*. Retold by Tor Seidler. Illustrated by Fred Marcellino. HarperCollins, 1992.

————. *The Ugly Duckling*. Illustrated by Jerry Pinkney. Morrow, 1999.

————. *The Wild Swans*. Retold by Amy Ehrlich. Illustrated by Susan Jeffers. Dial, 1981.

Atwater, Richard, and Florence Atwater. *Mr. Popper's Penguins*. Illustrated by Robert Lawson. Little, Brown, 1938.

Avi. *Poppy*. Illustrated by Brian Floca. Orchard, 1995.

Babbitt, Natalie. *Kneeknock Rise*. Farrar, Straus & Giroux, 1970.

————. *The Search for Delicious*. Farrar, Straus & Giroux, 1969.

————. *Tuck Everlasting*. Farrar, Straus & Giroux, 1975.

Bailey, Carolyn Sherwin. *Miss Hickory*. Illustrated by Ruth Gannett. Viking, 1962 [1946].

Banks, Lynne Reid. *The Indian in the Cupboard*. Illustrated by Brock Cole. Doubleday, 1981.

Barron, T. A. *The Fires of Merlin*. Philomel, 1998.

————. *The Lost Years of Merlin*. Philomel, 1996.

————. *The Mirror of Merlin*. Philomel, 1999.

————. *The Seven Songs of Merlin*. Philomel, 1997.

————. *The Wings of Merlin*. Philomel, 2000.

Baum, L. Frank. *The Wizard of Oz*. World, 1972 [1900].

Bellairs, John. *The House with a Clock in Its Walls*. Dial, 1973.

Billingsley, Franny. *The Folk Keeper*. Atheneum, 1999.

————. *Well Wished*. Atheneum, 1997.

Bond, Michael. *A Bear Called Paddington*. Illustrated by Peggy Fortnum. Houghton Mifflin, 1960.

Bond, Nancy. *A String in the Harp*. Atheneum, 1976.

Boston, L. M. *The Children of Green Knowe*. Illustrated by Peter Boston. Harcourt Brace, 1955.

————. *An Enemy at Green Knowe*. Illustrated by Peter Boston. Harcourt Brace, 1964.

————. *The River at Green Knowe*. Illustrated by Peter Boston. Harcourt Brace, 1959.

————. *The Treasure of Green Knowe*. Illustrated by Peter Boston. Harcourt Brace, 1958.

Brown, Marcia. *Stone Soup*. Scribner's, 1947.

Browne, Anthony. *The Tunnel*. Knopf, 1990.

Butler, Susan. *The Hermit Thrush Sings*. DK Ink, 1999.

Butterworth, Oliver. *The Enormous Egg*. Illustrated by Louis Darling. Little, Brown, 1956.

Cameron, Eleanor. *The Court of the Stone Children*. Dutton, 1973.

————. *The Wonderful Flight to the Mushroom Planet*. Illustrated by Robert Henneberger. Little, Brown, 1954.

Card, Orson Scott. *Ender's Game*. Tor, 1985.

Carroll, Lewis [Charles L. Dodgson]. *Alice's Adventures in Wonderland and Through the Looking Glass*. Illustrated by John Tenniel. Macmillan, 1963 [1865, 1872].

Catling, Patrick Skene. *The Chocolate Touch*. Illustrated by Margot Apple. Morrow, 1979 [1952].

Christopher, John. *Beyond the Burning Lands*. Macmillan, 1971.

————. *The City of Gold and Lead*. Macmillan, 1967.

————. *The Guardians*. Macmillan, 1968.

————. *The Pool of Fire*. Macmillan, 1968.

————. *The Prince in Waiting*. Macmillan, 1970.

————. *The Sword of the Spirits*. Macmillan, 1972.

————. *When the Tripods Came*. Dutton, 1988.

————. *The White Mountains*. Macmillan, 1967.

Cleary, Beverly. *The Mouse and the Motorcycle*. Illustrated by Louis Darling. Morrow, 1965.

————. *Ralph S. Mouse*. Illustrated by Paul O. Zelinsky. Morrow, 1982.

————. *Runaway Ralph*. Illustrated by Louis Darling. Morrow, 1970.

Conly, Jane. *Racso and the Rats of NIMH*. Illustrated by Leonard Lubin. Harper & Row, 1986.

————. *R-T, Margaret, and the Rats of NIMH*. Illustrated by Leonard Lubin. HarperCollins, 1990.

Conrad, Pam. *Stonewords*. HarperCollins, 1990.

Cooper, Susan. *The Boggart*. McElderry, 1993.

————. *The Boggart and the Monster*. Margaret McElderry, 1997.

————. *The Dark Is Rising*. Illustrated by Alan E. Cober. Atheneum, 1973.

————. *Greenwitch*. Atheneum, 1974.

————. *The Grey King*. Atheneum, 1975.

————. *King of Shadows*. McElderry, 1999.

————. *Over Sea, Under Stone*. Illustrated by Marjorie Gill. Harcourt Brace, 1966.

————. *The Selkie Girl*. Illustrated by Warwick Hutton. Macmillan, 1986.

————. *Silver on the Tree*. Atheneum, 1977.

————. *Tam Lin*. Illustrated by Warwick Hutton. Macmillan, 1990.

Corbett, Scott. *The Lemonade Trick*. Illustrated by Paul Galdone. Little, Brown, 1972 [1960].

Cross, Gillian. *New World*. Holiday House. 1995.

Dahl, Roald. *Charlie and the Chocolate Factory*. Illustrated by Joseph Schindelman. Knopf, 1972.

————. *Charlie and the Great Glass Elevator*. Illustrated by Joseph Schindelman. Knopf, 1972.

————. *James and the Giant Peach*. Illustrated by Nancy Ekholm Burkert. Knopf, 1961.

————. *The Minpins*. Illustrated by Patrick Benson. Viking, 1991.

de Beaumont, Mme. *Beauty and the Beast*. Illustrated by Jan Brett. Houghton Mifflin, 1989.

Dickinson, Peter. *Eva*. Delacorte, 1989.

Doherty, Berlie. *Daughter of the Sea*. DK Publishing, 1997.

DuBois, William Pène. *The Twenty-One Balloons*. Viking, 1947.

Eager, Edward. *Half Magic*. Illustrated by N. M. Bodecker. Harcourt Brace, 1954.

————. *Seven-Day Magic*. Illustrated by N. M. Bodecker. Harcourt Brace, 1962.

Farmer, Nancy. *The Ear, the Eye, and the Arm*. Orchard, 1994.

————. *The Warm Place*. Orchard, 1995.

Fleischman, Paul. *The Half-a-Moon Inn*. Illustrated by Kathy Jacobi. Harper & Row, 1980.

Fleischman, Sid. *The Midnight Horse*. Illustrated by Peter Sis. Greenwillow, 1990.

————. *The Whipping Boy*. Illustrated by Peter Sis. Greenwillow, 1986.

Fletcher, Susan. *Shadow Spinner*. Atheneum, 1998.

Fritz, Jean. *Homesick*: My Story. Putnam, 1982. (Biography)

Garza, Karen Lomas. *Family Pictures*. Children's Book Press, 1990. (Picture book)

Gerstein, Mordicai. *The Seal Mother*. Dial, 1986.

Gilmore, Kate. *The Exchange Student*. Houghton Mifflin, 1999.

Godden, Rumer. *The Dolls' House*. Illustrated by Tasha Tudor. Viking, 1962 [1947].

Grahame, Kenneth. *The Reluctant Dragon*. Illustrated by Ernest H. Shepard. Holiday House, 1938.

————. *The Wind in the Willows*. Illustrated by E. H. Shepard. Scribner's, 1940 [1908].

Grimm brothers. *The Frog Prince or Iron Henry*. Translated by Naomi Lewis. Illustrated by Binette Schroeder. North-South, 1998.

Grimm brothers. *Rumpelstiltskin*. Illustrated by Paul O. Zelinsky. Dutton, 1986.

Hahn, Mary Downing. *Time for Andrew: A Ghost Story*. Clarion, 1994.

————. *Wait Till Helen Comes: A Ghost Story*. Houghton Mifflin, 1986.

Hamilton, Virginia. *The Magical Adventures of Pretty Pearl*. Harper & Row, 1983.

————. *Sweet Whispers, Brother Rush*. Philomel, 1982.

Hentoff, Nat. *The Day They Came to Arrest the Book*. Dell, 1983. (Fiction)

Hesse, Karen. *Phoenix Rising*. Holt, 1994.

Hoban, Russell. *The Mouse and His Child*. Illustrated by Lillian Hoban. Harper & Row, 1967.

Hoberman, Mary Ann. *Fathers, Mothers, Sisters, Brothers*. Viking, 1993. (Poetry)

Hodges, Margaret. *St. George and the Dragon*. Illustrated by Trina Schart Hyman. Little, Brown, 1984.

Howarth, Lesley. *Maphead*. Candlewick, 1994.

————. *The Return*. Candlewick, 1997.

Howe, Deborah, and James Howe. *Bunnicula*. Illustrated by Leslie Morrill. Atheneum, 1983.

Howe, James. *Bunnicula Strikes Again!* Atheneum, 1999.

————. *The Celery Stalks at Midnight*. Illustrated by Leslie Morrill. Atheneum, 1983.

————. *Howliday Inn*. Illustrated by Lynn Munsinger. Atheneum, 1982.

Hughes, Monica. *Invitation to the Game*. Simon & Schuster, 1990.

Hunter, Mollie *The Mermaid Summer*. Harper & Row, 1988.

————. *A Stranger Came Ashore*. Harper & Row, 1975.

Hurmence, Belinda. *A Girl Called Boy*. Clarion, 1982.

Ibbotson, Eva. *The Secret of Platform 13*. Dutton, 1998.

————. *Which Witch?* Dutton, 1999.

Jacques, Brian. *The Legend of Luke*. Philomel, 2000.

————. *Mariel of Redwall*. Illustrated by Gary Chalk. Philomel, 1992.

————. *Martin the Warrior*. Philomel, 1994.

————. *Mattimeo*. Illustrated by Gary Chalk. Philomel, 1990.

————. *Mossflower*. Illustrated by Gary Chalk. Philomel, 1988.

————. *Redwall*. Illustrated by Gary Chalk. Philomel, 1987.

Jarrell, Randall. *The Bat-Poet*. Illustrated by Maurice Sendak. Macmillan, 1964.

Jenness, Lynette. *Families: A Celebration Of Diversity, Commitment, and Love*. Houghton Mifflin, 1990. (Nonfiction)

Jones, Diana Wynne. *Charmed Life*. Greenwillow, 1989.

———. *The Lives of Christopher Chant*. Greenwillow, 1988.

Juster, Norton. *The Phantom Tollbooth*. Illustrated by Jules Feiffer. Random House, 1961.

Katz, Welwyn Wilton. *Time Ghost*. McElderry, 1995.

Kendall, Carol. *The Gammage Cup*. Illustrated by Erik Blegvad. Harcourt Brace, 1959.

Kettelkamp, Larry. *Living in Space*. Morrow, 1993. (Nonfiction)

Key, Alexander. *The Forgotten Door*. Westminster, 1965.

Kindl, Patricia. *Owl in Love*. Houghton Mifflin, 1993.

King-Smith, Dick. *Ace: The Very Important Pig*. Illustrated by Lynette Hemmant. Crown, 1990.

———. *Babe the Gallant Pig*. Illustrated by Mary Rayner. Crown, 1985.

———. *The Fox Busters*. Illustrated by Jon Miller. Delacorte, 1988.

———. *Harriet's Hare*. Illustrated by Roger Roth. Crown, 1994.

———. *Pigs Might Fly*. Illustrated by Mary Rayner. Viking, 1982.

———. *Three Terrible Trins*. Illustrated by Mark Teague. Crown, 1994.

Klause, Annette Curtis. *Alien Secrets*. Delacorte, 1993.

Knight, Margery Burns. *Talking Walls*. Illustrated by Ann Sibley O'Brien. Tilbury House, 1995. (Fiction)

———. *Talking Walls: The Story Continues*. Illustrated by Ann Sibley O'Brien. Tilbury House, 1997. (Fiction)

Lally, Soinbhe. *A Hive for a Honeybee*. Illustrated by Patience Brewster. Scholastic, 1999.

Langton, Jane. *The Diamond in the Window*. Illustrated by Erik Blegvad. Harper & Row, 1962.

———. *The Fledgling*. Harper & Row, 1980.

Lawson, Robert. *Rabbit Hill*. Viking, 1944.

———. *The Tough Winter*. Viking, 1954.

Le Guin, Ursula K. *The Farthest Shore*. Illustrated by Gail Garraty. Atheneum, 1972.

———. *Tehanu: The Last Book of Earthsea*. Atheneum, 1990.

———. *The Tombs of Atuan*. Illustrated by Gail Garraty. Atheneum, 1971.

———. *A Wizard of Earthsea*. Illustrated by Ruth Robbins. Parnassus, 1968.

L'Engle, Madeleine. *A Swiftly Tilting Planet*. Farrar, Straus & Giroux, 1978.

———. *A Wind in the Door*. Farrar, Straus & Giroux, 1973.

———. *A Wrinkle in Time*. Farrar, Straus & Giroux, 1962.

Levine, Gail Carson. *Ella Enchanted*. HarperCollins, 1997.

Lewis, C. S. *The Horse and His Boy*. Illustrated by Pauline Baynes. Macmillan, 1962.

———. *The Last Battle*. Illustrated by Pauline Baynes. Macmillan, 1964.

———. *The Lion, the Witch, and the Wardrobe*. Illustrated by Pauline Baynes. Macmillan, 1961.

———. *The Magician's Nephew*. Illustrated by Pauline Baynes. Macmillan, 1964.

———. *Prince Caspian: The Return to Narnia*. Illustrated by Pauline Baynes. Macmillan, 1964.

———. *The Silver Chair*. Illustrated by Pauline Baynes. Macmillan, 1962.

———. *The Voyage of the "Dawn Treader."* Illustrated by Pauline Baynes. Macmillan, 1962.

Lindgren, Astrid. *Pippi Goes on Board*. Translated by Florence Lamborn. Illustrated by Louis S. Glanzman. Viking, 1957.

———. *Pippi in the South Seas*. Translated by Florence Lamborn. Illustrated by Louis S. Glanzman. Viking, 1959.

———. *Pippi Longstocking*. Illustrated by Louis S. Glanzman. Viking, 1950.

———. *Pippi on the Run*. Viking, 1976.

Lively, Penelope. *The Ghost of Thomas Kempe*. Illustrated by Anthony Maitland. Dutton, 1973.

Lowry, Lois. *Anastasia Krupnik*. Houghton Mifflin, 1979. (Fiction)

———. *Autumn Street*. Houghton Mifflin, 1980. (Fiction)

———. *The Giver*. Houghton Mifflin, 1993.

———. *Looking Back: A Book of Memories*. Houghton Mifflin, 1980. (Biography)

———. "Newbery Award Acceptance Speech." *Horn Book Magazine* 70, no. 4 (1994): 423–426.

———. "On Writing the Giver." *Book Links* (May 1994).

Lunn, Janet. *The Root Cellar*. Scribner's, 1983.

MacDonald, George. *At the Back of the North Wind*. Garland, 1976 [1871].

———. *The Golden Key*. Illustrated by Maurice Sendak. Farrar, Straus & Giroux, 1967 [1867].

———. *The Light Princess*. Illustrated by Maurice Sendak. Farrar, Straus & Giroux, 1969.

Mahy, Margaret. *The Haunting*. Macmillan, 1982.

Marsden, John. *The Dead of Night*. Houghton Mifflin, 1997.

———. *A Killing Frost*. Houghton Mifflin, 1998.

———. *Tomorrow When the War Began*. Houghton Mifflin, 1995.

Mayne, William. *Earthfasts*. Dutton, 1967.

———. *Hob and the Goblins*. Illustrated by Norman Messenger. Dorling Kindersley, 1994.

———. *Hob and the Peddler*. DK Publishing, 1997.

McCaffrey, Anne. *Dragondrums*. Illustrated by Fred Marcellino. Atheneum, 1979.

———. *Dragonsinger*. Atheneum, 1977.

———. *Dragonsong*. Illustrated by Laura Lydecker. Atheneum, 1976.

McGraw, Eloise. *The Moorchild*. McElderry, 1996.

McKillip, Patricia. *The Forgotten Beast of Eld*. Harcourt Brace, 1996.

McKinley, Robin. *Beauty: A Retelling of the Story of Beauty and the Beast*. Harper & Row, 1978.

———. *The Blue Sword*. Greenwillow, 1982.

———. *The Hero and the Crown*. Greenwillow, 1985.

Merrill, Jean. *The Pushcart War*. Illustrated by Ronni Solbert. W. R. Scott, 1964.

Milne, A. A. *The House at Pooh Corner*. Illustrated by Ernest H. Shepard. Dutton, 1928.

———. *Winnie-the-Pooh*. Illustrated by Ernest H. Shepard. Dutton, 1926.

Moore, Lilian. *I'll Meet You at the Cucumbers.* Illustrated by Sharon Wooding. Atheneum, 1988.

Morris, Gerald. *The Squire, His Knight and His Lady.* Houghton Mifflin, 1999.

———. *The Squire's Tale.* Houghton Mifflin, 1998.

Napoli, Donna. *The Magic Circle.* Dutton, 1993.

———. *Spinners.* Dutton, 1999.

———. *Zel.* Dutton, 1996.

Nix, Garth. *Shade's Children.* HarperCollins, 1997.

Norton, Mary. *The Borrowers.* Illustrated by Beth and Joe Krush. Harcourt Brace, 1953.

———. *The Borrowers Afield.* Illustrated by Beth and Joe Krush. Harcourt Brace, 1955.

———. *The Borrowers Afloat.* Illustrated by Beth and Joe Krush. Harcourt Brace, 1959.

———. *The Borrowers Aloft.* Illustrated by Beth and Joe Krush. Harcourt Brace, 1961.

———. *The Borrowers Avenged.* Illustrated by Beth and Joe Krush. Harcourt Brace, 1982.

O'Brien, Robert C. *Mrs. Frisby and the Rats of NIMH.* Illustrated by Zena Bernstein. Atheneum, 1971.

———. *Z for Zachariah.* Atheneum, 1975.

Park, Ruth. *Playing Beatie Bow.* Atheneum, 1982.

Pearce, Phillipa. *Tom's Midnight Garden.* Illustrated by Susan Einzig. Lippincott, 1959.

Pearson, Kit. *A Handful of Time.* Viking Penguin, 1988.

Peck, Richard. *The Great Interactive Dream Machine.* Dial, 1996.

———. *Lost in Cyberspace.* Dial, 1995.

Peck, Sylvia. *Seal Child.* Illustrated by Robert Andrew Parker. Morrow, 1989.

Pierce, Tamora. *Alanna, the First Adventure.* Atheneum, 1982.

———. *Emperor Mage.* Simon & Schuster, 1995.

———. *First Test.* Random House, 2000.

———. *In the Hand of the Goddess.* Atheneum, 1984.

———. *Lioness Rampant.* Atheneum, 1988.

———. *Magic Steps (The Circle Opens).* Scholastic, 2000.

———. *Realm of the Gods.* Random House, 1997.

———. *Sandry's Book (Circle of Magic Book 1).* Scholastic, 1997.

———. *Wild Magic.* Atheneum, 1992.

———. *Wolf-Speaker.* Atheneum, 1994.

———. *The Woman Who Rides Like a Man.* Atheneum, 1986.

Pinkwater, Daniel. *Borgel.* Macmillan, 1990.

Potter, Robert R. *Buckminster Fuller.* Silver Burdett, 1990. (Biography)

Pullman, Philip. *The Amber Spyglass.* Knopf, 2000.

———. *Clockwork: Or All Wound Up.* Scholastic, 1998.

———. *The Firework-Maker's Daughter.* Illustrated by S. Saelig Gallagher. Arthur A. Levine Books, 1999.

———. *The Golden Compass.* Knopf, 1996.

———. *I Was a Rat.* Knopf, 2000.

———. *The Ruby in the Smoke.* Knopf, 1994.

———. *The Subtle Knife.* Knopf, 1997.

Rowling, J. K. *Harry Potter and the Chamber of Secrets.* Scholastic, 1999.

———. *Harry Potter and the Prisoner of Azkaban.* Scholastic, 1999.

———. *Harry Potter and the Sorcerer's Stone.* Scholastic, 1998.

Saint-Exupéry, Antoine de. *The Little Prince.* Translated by Katherine Woods. Harcourt, 1943.

Sauer, Julia. *Fog Magic.* Illustrated by Lynd Ward. Viking, 1943.

Scieszka, Jon. *2095.* Illustrated by Lane Smith. Viking, 1995.

———. *The Good, the Bad, and the Goofy.* Illustrated by Lane Smith. Viking, 1992.

———. *It's All Greek to Me.* Illustrated by Lane Smith. Viking, 1999.

———. *Knights of the Kitchen Table.* Illustrated by Lane Smith. Viking, 1991.

———. *The Not-So-Jolly Roger.* Illustrated by Lane Smith. Viking, 1991.

———. *Summer Reading Is Killing Me.* Illustrated by Lane Smith. Viking, 1998.

———. *Tut, Tut.* Illustrated by Lane Smith. Viking, 1996.

———. *Your Mother Was a Neanderthal.* Illustrated by Lane Smith. Viking, 1993.

Selden, George. *Chester Cricket's Pigeon Ride.* Illustrated by Garth Williams. Farrar, Straus & Giroux, 1981.

———. *The Cricket in Times Square.* Illustrated by Garth Williams. Farrar, Straus & Giroux, 1960.

———. *Harry Cat's Pet Puppy.* Illustrated by Garth Williams. Farrar, Straus & Giroux, 1974.

———. *Tucker's Countryside.* Illustrated by Garth Williams. Farrar, Straus & Giroux, 1969.

Sendak, Maurice. *Higglety, Pigglety, Pop!* Harper & Row, 1967.

Skurzynski, Gloria. *Cyberstorm.* Macmillan, 1995.

Sleator, William. *The Duplicate.* Dutton, 1988.

———. *The Green Futures of Tycho.* Dutton, 1981.

Slote, Alfred. *My Robot Buddy.* Lippincott, 1975.

Smith, Sherwood. *Wren's Quest.* Harcourt Brace, 1993.

———. *Wren to the Rescue.* Harcourt Brace, 1990.

———. *Wren's War.* Harcourt Brace, 1995.

Snyder, Zilpha Keatley. *Song of the Gargoyle.* Delacorte, 1991.

Springer, Nancy. *I Am Mordred: A Tale from Camelot.* Philomel, 1998.

Steig, William. *Abel's Island.* Farrar, Straus & Giroux, 1976.

Stewig, John. *Stone Soup.* Illustrated by Margot Tomes. Holiday House, 1991.

Strickland, Dorothy, and Michael Strickland. *Families: Poems Celebrating the Africa American Experience.* Illustrated by John Ward. Boyds-Mills, 1994. (Poetry)

Thurber, James. *Many Moons.* Illustrated by Marc Simont. Harcourt Brace, 1990.

Tolkien, J. R. R. *The Fellowship of the Ring. The Two Towers. The Return of the King* (the Lord of the Rings trilogy). Houghton Mifflin, 1965.

———. *The Hobbit.* Houghton Mifflin, 1938.

Travers, P. L. *Mary Poppins.* Illustrated by Mary Shepard. Harcourt Brace, 1934.

———. *Mary Poppins Comes Back.* Illustrated by Mary Shepard. Harcourt Brace, 1935.

————. *Mary Poppins in the Park*. Illustrated by Mary Shepard. Harcourt Brace, 1952.

————. *Mary Poppins Opens the Door*. Illustrated by Mary Shepard and Agnes Sims. Harcourt Brace, 1943.

Vande Velde, Vivian. *User Unfriendly*. Harcourt Brace, 1991.

Vinge, Joan D. *Psion*. Delacorte, 1982.

Walsh, Jill Paton. *A Chance Child*. Farrar, Straus & Giroux, 1978.

————. *The Green Book*. Illustrated by Lloyd Bloom. Farrar, Straus & Giroux, 1982.

Waugh, Sylvia. *The Mennyms*. Greenwillow, 1994.

————. *The Mennyms Alive*. Greenwillow, 1997.

————. *The Mennyms Alone*. Greenwillow, 1996.

————. *The Mennyms in the Wilderness*. Greenwillow, 1995.

————. *The Mennyms Under Siege*. Greenwillow, 1996.

White, E. B. *Charlotte's Web*. Illustrated by Garth Williams. Harper & Row, 1952.

————. *Stuart Little*. Illustrated by Garth Williams. Harper & Row, 1945.

————. *The Trumpet of the Swan*. Illustrated by Edward Frascino. Harper & Row, 1970.

Wilde, Oscar. *The Happy Prince*. Illustrated by Ed Young. Simon & Schuster, 1989.

————. *The Selfish Giant*. Illustrated by Lisbeth Zwerger. Picture Book Studios, 1984.

Williams, Jay. *Everyone Knows What a Dragon Looks Like*. Illustrated by Mercer Mayer. Four Winds, 1976.

Winthrop, Elizabeth. *The Battle for the Castle*. Holiday House, 1993.

————. *The Castle in the Attic*. Holiday House, 1985.

Wiseman, David. *Jeremy Visick*. Houghton Mifflin, 1981.

Wrede, Patricia C. *Calling on Dragons*. Harcourt Brace, 1993.

————. *Dealing with Dragons*. Harcourt Brace, 1990.

————. *Searching for Dragons*. Harcourt Brace, 1991.

————. *Talking to Dragons*. Harcourt Brace, 1993.

Wright, Betty Ren. *The Ghost Comes Calling*. Scholastic, 1994.

————. *Out of the Dark*. Scholastic, 1995.

Yep, Laurence. *The City of Dragons*. Illustrated by Jean and Mou-Sien Tseng. Scholastic, 1995.

————. *The Dragon of the Lost Sea*. Harper & Row, 1982.

Yolen, Jane. *Dove Isabeau*. Illustrated by Dennis Nolan. Harcourt Brace Jovanovich, 1989.

————. *Dragon's Blood*. Delacorte, 1982.

————. *The Emperor and the Kite*. Illustrated by Ed Young. World, 1967.

————. *Heart's Blood*. Delacorte, 1984.

————. *A Sending of Dragons*. Delacorte, 1987.

————. *Tam Lin*. Illustrated by Charles Mikolaycak. Harcourt Brace Jovanovich, 1990.

Zemach, Harve. *Duffy and the Devil*. Illustrated by Margot Zemach. Farrar, Straus & Giroux, 1986.

# Chapter Eight

# Poetry

*A fifth-grade teacher finished reading aloud Katherine Paterson's* Bridge to Terabithia *to her class. This is the well-loved story of friendship between a highly imaginative girl, Leslie, and Jess—middle child in a rural family of five. It was Leslie's idea to create*

Terabithia, their secret kingdom in the woods that could be approached only by swinging across a stream on a rope. And it was this frayed rope that brought about the tragedy in the story. Following the completion of the story, the group was silent for a moment thinking about Leslie's death and the legacy she had left Jess. Wisely, the teacher respected their silence, recognizing that this book had moved them deeply. They did not discuss it immediately but quietly began to do other work. That evening one of the girls in the class wrote this poem:

As the stubborn stream swirls and pulls out a song,
The hillside stands in the cold dark sky.
Over the hillside stands a lonely palace.
Before it shook with joy
But now its queen is dead
So the sour sweet wind blows the tassels of the
   weak rope,

And the tree mourns and scolds the rope,
Saying "Couldn't you have held on a little
   longer?"

–Cheri Taylor, Highland Park School, Grove City, Ohio; Linda Charles, teacher

Poetry was as much a part of this classroom as prose was. The teacher shared some poetry every day, in addition to reading stories. Frequently she read a poem that reflected the same content or feeling as the novel she was reading. So it was natural for Cheri to write a poem in response to her feelings about *Bridge to Terabithia*.

Poetry is the language of emotions. It can encapsulate a deep response in a few words. For Cheri, poetry was the only way to capture her feelings about a book that had moved her as no other had ever done.

## The Meaning of Poetry

There is an elusiveness about poetry that makes it defy precise definition. It is not so much what it is that is important, as how it makes us feel. In her *Poems for Children*, Eleanor Farjeon tells us that poetry is "not a rose, but the scent of the rose. . . . Not the sea, but the sound of the sea."[1] Fine poetry is this distillation of experience that captures the essence of an object, a feeling, or a thought. Such intensification requires a more highly structured patterning of words than prose does. Each word must be chosen with care for both sound and meaning, because poetry is language in its most connotative and concentrated form. Laurence Perrine defines poetry as "a kind of language that says

more and says it more intensely than ordinary language."[2]

Poetry can both broaden and intensify experience, or it might present a range of experiences beyond the realm of personal possibility for the individual listener. It can also illuminate, clarify, and deepen an everyday occurrence in a way the reader never considered, making the reader see more and feel more than ever before. For poetry does more than mirror life; it reveals life in new dimensions. Robert Frost said that a poem goes from delight to wisdom. Poetry does delight children, but it also helps them develop new insights, new ways of sensing their world.

Poetry communicates experience by appealing to both the thoughts and the feelings of its reader. It has

---

[1] *Poetry* originally appeared in *Sing For Your Supper*. Copyright © 1938 by Eleanor Farjeon; renewed 1966 by Gervase Farjeon. Used by permission of HarperCollins Publishers, New York, NY.

[2] Laurence Perrine, *Sound and Sense: An Introduction to Poetry*, 5th ed. (New York: Harcourt Brace Jovanovich, 1981), p. 3.

the power to evoke in its hearers rich sensory images and deep emotional responses. Poetry demands total response from the individual—all the intellect, senses, emotion, and imagination. It does not tell *about* an experience as much as it invites its hearers to *participate in* the experience. Poetry can happen only when the poem and the reader connect. Eleanor Farjeon says this about poetry:

Poetry

What is Poetry? Who Knows?
Not a rose but the scent of the rose;
Not the sky but the light in the sky;
Not the fly but the gleam of the fly;
Not the sea but the sound of the sea;
Not myself but what makes me
See, hear, and feel something that prose
Cannot, and what it is, who knows?

–Farjeon, Eleanor. "Poetry" (in Bobbye Goldstein, ed., *Inner Chimes*)
Eleanor Farjeon. "Poetry" from *Poems for Children* by Eleanor Farjeon. Reprinted by permission of Harold Ober Associates Incorporated. Copyright 1938 by Eleanor Farjeon. Copyright renewed 1966 by Gervase Farjeon.

Much of what poetry says is conveyed by suggestion, by indirection, by what is not said. As Carl Sandburg put it, "What can be explained is not poetry. . . . The poems that are obvious are like the puzzles that are already solved. They deny us the joy of seeking and creating."[3] A certain amount of ambiguity is characteristic of poetry, for more is hidden in it than in prose. The poet does not tell readers "all," but invites them to go beyond the literal level of the poem and discover its deeper meanings for themselves.

Robert Frost playfully suggested that poetry is what gets lost in translation—and translation of poetry into prose is as difficult as translation of poetry into another language. To paraphrase a poem is to destroy it. Would it be possible to reduce Frost's "Mending Wall" to prose? The scene, the situation, the contrast of the two men's thoughts about the wall they are repairing can be described, but the experience of the poem cannot be conveyed except by its own words.

## Poetry for Children

Poetry for children differs little from poetry for adults, except that it comments on life in dimensions that are meaningful for children. Its language should be poetic and its content should appeal directly to children. Bobbi Katz describes the feel of cat kisses in a way that appeals to children's sensory experiences and helps them think about a cat in a new imaginative way.

Sandpaper kisses
on a cheek or a chin—
that is the way
for a day to begin!

Sandpaper kisses—
a cuddle, a purr
I have an alarm clock
that's covered with fur.

–Bobbi Katz, "Cat Kisses," from *Tomie de Paola's Book of Poems*, by Bobbi Katz. Copyright © 1974 by Bobbi Katz. Reprinted with permission of the author.

The comparison of the rough feel of a cat's tongue to sandpaper kisses and a cat's function as an alarm clock are both metaphors that will delight a child. These metaphors are childlike, but not "childish."

The emotional appeal of children's poetry should reflect the real emotions of childhood. Poetry that is cute, coy, nostalgic, or sarcastic might be *about* children, but it is not *for* them. Whittier's "The Barefoot Boy" looks back on childhood in a nostalgic fashion characteristic of adults, not children; "The Children's Hour" by Longfellow is an old man's reminiscences of his delight in his children (both poems can be found in Helen Ferris's *Favorite Poems Old and New*). Some poems patronize childhood as a period in life when children are "cute" or "naughty." Joan W. Anglund's poetry is as cute and sentimental as her pictures of "sweet little boys and girls."

Many poems are didactic and preachy. Unfortunately, some teachers will accept moralizing in poetry that they would never accept in prose. Sentimentality is another adult emotion that is seldom felt by children. The poem "Which Loved Best," frequently quoted before Mother's Day, drips with sentiment and morality. Poems that are *about* childhood or aim to instruct are usually disliked by children.

Yet children do feel deep emotions; they can be hurt, fearful, bewildered, sad, happy, expectant, satisfied. Almost all surveys show that adults believe children have a harder time growing up today than their parents did.[4] More and more modern poetry for children reflects the despair of struggling to grow up in America today. Some poets have been successful in capturing the real feelings of troubled children. For example, Elizabeth Smith, an African American poet, describes the mixed feelings of pride and loneliness felt by a latchkey child:

[3]Carl Sandburg, "Short Talk on Poetry," in *Early Moon* (New York: Harcourt Brace, 1930), p. 27.

[4]Kati Haycock, "Producing a Nation of Achievers," *Journal of Youth Services in Libraries* 4 (spring 1991): 237.

I don't go to daycare
Or a sitter any more.
Now that I am grown-up
I've a key to my front door.

I check my pocket through the day,
Making sure I have my key.
I call my mom when I get home
To tell her all is right with me.

I get a little scared sometimes
When there's no one else at home.
The TV keeps me company—
I'm not all that alone.

I like the grown-up feeling
Of having my own key.
But every now and then I wish
My mom was home with me.

> –Elizabeth A. Smith. "My Key," by Elizabeth A. Smith as appeared in *Through Our Eyes* edited by Lee Bennett Hopkins. Boston: Little, Brown. 1992.

Poets have many ways of speaking to the needs and interests of children.

## The Elements of Poetry

A child responds to the total impact of a poem and should not be required to analyze it. However, teachers need to understand the language of poetry if they are to select the best to share with children. How, for example, can you differentiate between real poetry and mere verse? Mother Goose, jump-rope rhymes, tongue twisters, and the lyrics of some songs are not poetry; but they *can* serve as a springboard for diving into real poetry. Elizabeth Coatsworth, who has written much fine poetry and verse for children, refers to rhyme as "poetry in petticoats."[5] Such rhymes might have the sound of poetry, but they do not contain the quality of imagination or the depth of emotion that characterizes real poetry.

It is a difficult task to identify elements of poetry for today's children, for modern poets are breaking traditional molds in both content and form. These poems speak directly to the reader about all subjects. Frequently the words are spattered across pages in a random fashion or they become poem-pictures, as in concrete poetry. As children become more sophisticated through their exposure to films and television, the dividing line between what is poetry for adults and what is poetry for children becomes fainter. It is, however, possible to identify those poems that contain the elements of fine poetry yet still speak to children.

[5]Elizabeth Coatsworth, *The Sparrow Bush*, illustrated by Stefan Martin (New York: Norton, 1966), p. 8.

### Rhythm

The young child is naturally rhythmical. She beats on the tray of her high chair, kicks her foot against the table, and chants her vocabulary of one or two words in a singsong fashion. She delights in the sound of "Pat-a-cake, pat-a-cake, baker's man," or "Ride a cock-horse to Banbury Cross" before she understands the meaning of the words. She is responding to the monotonous rocking-horse rhythm of Mother Goose. This response to a measured beat is as old as humans themselves. Primitive people had chants, hunting and working songs, dances, and crude musical instruments. Rhythm is a part of the daily beat of our lives—the steady pulse rate, regular breathing, and pattern of growth. The inevitability of night and day, the revolving seasons, birth and death provide a pattern for everyone's life. The very ebb and flow of the ocean, the sound of the rain on the window, and the pattern of rows of corn in a field reflect the rhythm of the world around us.

Poetry satisfies the child's natural response to rhythm. A poem has a kind of music of its own, and the child responds to it. The very young child enjoys the rocking rhythm of Mother Goose and expects it in all other poems. In the following poem from *The Llama Who Had No Pajamas*, Mary Ann Hoberman explores other rhythms in the child's life as she links weather and seasonal patterns to the rhythm of a child's swinging:

*Hello and good-by*
*Hello and good-by*
When I'm in a swing
Swinging low and then high,
Good-by to the ground
Hello to the sky.

Hello to the rain
Good-by to the sun,
Then hello again sun
When the rain is all done.

In blows the winter,
Away the birds fly.
*Good-by and hello*
*Hello and good-by.*

> –Mary Ann Hoberman. "Hello and Good-by" from *The Llama Who Had No Pajama: 100 Favorite Poems*, copyright © 1959 and renewed 1987 by mary Ann Hoberman, reprinted with permission of Harcourt, Inc.

This poem could be compared to Robert Louis Stevenson's well-known poem "The Swing" (in *Tomie de Paola's Book of Poems*), which suggests a different meter for the physical sensation of swinging.

In some poems, both the rhythm and the pattern of the lines are suggestive of the movement or mood of the poem. The arrangement of these poems forces the reader to emphasize a particular rhythm. For exam-

*Collections such as Mary Ann Hoberman's* The Llama Who Had No Pajamas *introduce children to the delights of poetry.*

Jacket from *The Llama Who Had No Pajama: 100 Favorite Poems* by Mary Ann Hoberman, jacket illustrations copyright © 1998 by Betty Fraser, reproduced by permission of Browndeer Press, a division of Harcourt, Inc.

ple, in Eleanor Farjeon's "Mrs. Peck-Pigeon" (in de Regnier et al., *Sing a Song of Popcorn*), "Mrs. Peck Pigeon is picking for bread, Bob-bob-bob goes her little round head"—the repetition of the hard sounds of *b* and *p* help create the bobbing rhythm of the pigeon herself.

A change of rhythm is indicative of a new element in the poem: a contrast in mood, a warning, or a different speaker, for example. The following poem by Lilian Moore gathers momentum with the sound of all the things the wind blows, and then becomes suddenly quiet when the wind dies down.

> When the wind blows
> the quiet things speak.
> Some whisper, some clang,
> Some creak.
>
> Grasses swish.
> Treetops sigh.
> Flags slap
> and snap at the sky.
> Wires on poles
> whistle and hum.
> Ashcans roll.
> Windows drum.

When the wind goes—
suddenly
then,
the quiet things
are quiet again.

–Lilian Moore. "Wind Song" from *I Feel the Same Way* by Lilian Moore. Copyright © 1967 by Lilian Moore. Copyright renewed 1995 Lilian Moore Reavin. Used by permission of Marian Reiner for the author.

### Rhyme and Sound

In addition to the rhythm of a poem, children respond to its rhyme—for rhyme helps to create the musical qualities of a poem, and children enjoy the "singingness of words." The Russian poet Kornei Chukovsky maintains that in the beginning of childhood we are all "versifiers," and that it is only later in life that we begin to speak in prose.[6] He is referring to the young child's tendency to double all syllables, so that *mother* is first "mama" and *water* "wa-wa." This, plus the regular patterning of such words as *daddy, mommy, granny,* and so on, makes for a natural production of rhyme. The young child's enjoyment of Mother Goose is due almost entirely to the rhyme and rhythm of these verses. This poem by Eloise Greenfield captures the rhythm of the turning rope and the slapping sound of the rope itself:

> Get set, ready now, jump right in
> Bounce and kick and giggle and spin
> Listen to the rope when it hits the ground
> Listen to that clappedy-slappedy sound
> Jump right up when it tells you to
> Come back down, whatever you do
> Count to a hundred, count by ten
> Start to count all over again
> That's what jumping is all about
> Get set, ready now,
> jump
>    right
>      out!

–Eloise Greenfield. "Rope Rhyme," from *Honey, I Love and Other Poems* by Eloise Greenfield. Text copyright © 1978 by Eloise Greenfield. Used by permission of HarperCollins Publishers.

If children have not heard any poetry or do not know any Mother Goose rhymes, teachers may want to introduce poetry with street rhymes, jump-rope rhymes, or raps through such books as Stephanie Calmenson and Joanna Cole's *Miss Mary Mack and Other Children's Street Rhymes.* But children need to be freed from the notion that all poetry must rhyme. They should be introduced to some poetry that doesn't rhyme, such as free verse or haiku, so that they begin to listen to the meaning of a poem as well as the sound of it.

---

[6]Kornei Chukovsky, *From Two to Five*, translated and edited by Miriam Morton (Berkeley: University of California Press, 1963), p. 64.

Rhyme is only one aspect of sound; alliteration, or the repetition of initial consonant sounds, is another; assonance, or the repetition of particular vowel sounds, is still another. Jack Prelutsky frequently uses alliteration to create the humor in his verse. For example, read "The Grobbles are Gruesome" in his *Snopp on the Sidewalk* (see p. 391) and listen to the repetition of the *gr* sounds. Younger children delight in the sounds of the mud that "splishes and sploshes" in Rhoda Bacmeister's well-known poem "Galoshes" (in *Tomie de Paola's Book of Poems*).

The quiet *s* sound and the repetition of the double *o* in *moon* and *shoon* suggest the mysterious beauty of the moon in Walter de la Mare's poem "Silver" (in Helen Ferris's *Favorite Poems Old and New*). The term *onomatopoeia* refers to the use of words that make a sound like the action represented by the word, such as *crack, hiss,* and *sputter.* Occasionally a poet will create an entire poem that resembles a particular sound. David McCord has successfully imitated the sound of hitting a picket fence with a stick in his popular chant:

The pickety fence
The pickety fence
Give it a lick it's
The pickety fence
Give it a lick it's
A clickety fence
Give it a lick it's
A lickety fence
Give it a lick
Give it a lick
Give it a lick
With a rickety stick
Pickety
Pickety
Pickety
Pick

    –David McCord, "The Pickety Fence," from *One at a Time* by
    David McCord. Copyright © 1961, 1962 by David McCord.
    Reprinted by permission of Little, Brown and Company.

Repetition is another way the poet creates particular sound effects in a poem. Certainly, David McCord employed repetition along with onomatopoeia to create "The Pickety Fence." Robert Frost frequently used repetition of particular lines or phrases to emphasize meaning in his poems. The repetition of the last line "miles to go before I sleep" in his famous "Stopping by Woods on a Snowy Evening" (in de Regniers et al., *Sing a Song of Popcorn*) adds to the mysterious element in that poem.

Children are intrigued with the sound of language and enjoy unusual and ridiculous combinations of words. The gay nonsense of Laura Richards's "Eletelephony" (also in the de Regniers et al. anthology) is as much in the sound of the ridiculous words as in the

*Sally Mavor's choice of poems and her delightful illustrations reflect the emotions and experiences of real children in* You and Me.

plight of the poor elephant who tried to use the "telephant." Children love to trip off the name "James James Morrison Morrison Weatherby George Dupree" in A. A. Milne's "Disobedience" (*The World of Christopher Robin*). Poets use rhyme, rhythm, and the various devices of alliteration, assonance, repetition, and coined words to create the melody and sound of poetry loved by children.

### Imagery

Poetry draws on many kinds of language magic. The imagery of a poem involves direct sensory images of sight, sound, touch, smell, or taste. This aspect of poetry has particular appeal for children, as it reflects one of the major ways they explore their world. The very young child grasps an object and immediately puts it in her mouth. Children love to squeeze warm, soft puppies, and they squeal with delight as a pet mouse scampers up their arms. Taste and smell are also highly developed in the young child.

In our modern society, children are increasingly deprived of natural sensory experiences. One of the first admonitions they hear is "Don't touch." On the end-

*Eric Beddows's illustration helps children understand Barbara Esbensen's delightful imagery in "Tell Me" found in* Who Shrank My Grandmother's House?

Copyright © 1992 by Eric Beddows. Used by permission of HarperCollins Publishers, New York, NY.

less pavements of our cities, how many children have an opportunity to roll in crunchy piles of leaves? Air pollution laws assure that they will never enjoy the acrid autumn smell of burning bonfires (rightly so, but still a loss). Many also miss the warm yeasty odor of homemade bread or the sweet joy of licking the bowl of brownie batter. Some of our newest schools are windowless, so children are even deprived of seeing the brilliant blue sky on a crisp cold day or the growing darkness of a storm or the changing silhouette of an oak tree on the horizon.

Poetry can never be a substitute for actual sensory experience. A child can't develop a concept of texture by hearing a poem or seeing pictures of the rough bark of a tree; he must first touch the bark and compare the feel of a deeply furrowed oak with the smooth-surfaced trunk of a beech tree. Then the poet can call up these experiences and extend them or make the child see them in a new way.

Because most children are visual-minded, they respond readily to the picture-making quality of poetry. Barbara Esbensen's images of autumn birch trees is perfectly childlike and sure to surprise and delight children:

Why do you think
the birches
tore off their yellow
sweaters

on the windiest coldest day
of all   waved good-bye
and watched them scatter
down the street?

Why do you think
the birches
are standing in our yard
in their underwear?

–Barbara Juster Esbensen. "Tell Me," from *Who Shrank My Grandmother's House?* by Barbara Juster Esbensen. Copyright © 1992 by Barbara Juster Esbensen. Used by permission of HarperCollins Publishers.

In Tennyson's "The Eagle" (in Nancy Larrick's *Piping Down the Valleys Wide*), the description of the eagle is rich in the use of visual imagery. In the first verse the reader can see the eagle perched on the crest of a steep mountain, posed ready for his swift descent whenever he sights his quarry. But in the second verse the poet "enters into" the eagle's world and describes it from the bird's point of view. Looking down from his lofty height, the might of the waves is reduced to wrinkles and the sea seems to crawl:

He clasps the crag with crooked hands;
Close to the sun in lonely lands,
Ringed with the azure world, he stands.

The wrinkled sea beneath him crawls;
He watches from his mountain wall,
And like a thunderbolt he falls.

–Alfred, Lord Tennyson, "The Eagle," in *Piping Down the Valleys Wide*, ed. Nancy Larrick.

The lonely, peaceful scene is shattered by the natural metaphor of the final line: "And like a thunderbolt he falls." In your mind's eye you can see, almost feel, the wind on your wings as you plunge down the face of the cliff.

Most poetry depends on visual and auditory imagery to evoke a mood or response, but imagery of touch, taste, and smell is also used. Valerie Worth's poem "Mud" makes fingers tingle with the feel of squishy earth:

Mud mixed
With a stick
To the right
Thickness,
Not too stiff
Nor too full
of rain,

Can then
Be picked up
In the hand,
Soft, still cold
As a stone,
And squeezed
Until it strains

Out between the fingers—
Warmed a bit,
But still heavy
With earth's
Rich grit and grain.

–Valerie Worth. "Mud" from *All the Small Poems and Fourteen More* by Valerie Worth. Copyright © 1987, 1994 by Valerie Worth. Reprinted by permission of Farrar Straus and Giroux, LLC.

Psychologists tell us that some of children's earliest memories are sensory, recalling particularly the way things smell and taste. Most children have a delicate sense of taste that responds to the texture and smell of a particular food. In "Hard and Soft," in his *Eats: Poems,* Arnold Adoff contrasts the crunch of eating a carrot with the quiet sound of swallowing raisins. Rose Rauter captures both the feel of a fresh-picked peach and its delicious taste in this poem:

Touch it to your cheek and it's soft
as a velvet newborn mouse
who has to strive
to be alive.
Bite in. Runny
honey
blooms on your tongue—
as if you've bitten open
a whole hive.

–Rose Rauter, "Peach," from X. J. Kennedy and Dorothy M. Kennedy, *Knock At a Star: A Child's Introduction to Poetry,* Little, Brown & Company, 1982.

Certain smells can recapture a whole experience that may have happened years earlier. We recall the sweet scent of lilacs that might have drifted by one wet spring day on reading James Stevenson's "May Morning" in his *Popcorn.* Constance Levy's "Greensweet," in her *A Tree Place,* evokes the summer smells of newly mown grass.

### Figurative Language: Comparison and Contrast

Because the language of poetry is so compressed, every word must be made to convey the meaning of the poem. Poets do this by comparing two objects or ideas with each other in such a way that the connotation of one word gives added meaning to another.

In "Peach," Rose Rauter compared the soft fuzzy feel of a peach to a velvety newborn mouse; its sweet taste made her think of a whole hive of honey. Kristine O'Connell George makes this observation about the surprise waiting on the branch of a winter tree.

Bud
A tiny velveteen satchel,
the color of pale cream,
Is perched on the tip
of this bare branch.

Snap open the clasp—
And you will find,
Inside this tiny valise,
One rolled and folded
neatly packed

leaf.

–Kristine O'Connell George. "Bud" from *Old Elm Speaks* by Kristine O'Connell George. Text copyright © 1998 by Kristine O'Connell George. Reprinted by permission of Clarion Books/Houghton Mifflin Company. All rights reserved.

When writers compare one thing with another, using such connecting words as *like* or *as,* they are using a *simile.* In a *metaphor* the poet speaks of an object or idea as if it *were* another object. In recent years we have paid little attention to the difference between these two techniques, referring to both as examples of metaphorical or figurative language.

It is not important that children know the difference between a simile and a metaphor. It is important that they know what is being compared and that the comparison is fresh and new and helps them view the idea or object in a different and unusual way. Two well-known poems containing metaphors that help children see their world afresh are Carl Sandburg's "Fog" and Vachel Lindsay's "The Moon's the North Wind's Cooky" (both in Jack Prelutsky's *Random House Book of Poetry for*

The watercolor sketch that accompanies "May Morning" in James Stevenson's Popcorn *brightens the eye as the poem lightens the heart.*

From *Popcorn* Poems by James Stevenson. Illustrations copyright © 1998 by James Stevenson. Used by permission of Greenwillow Books, a division of William Morrow Company/HarperCollins Publishers.

*Children*). Perhaps the reason these poems have endured is that they also reveal a true understanding of a child's point of view.

Some figurative language is so commonplace that it has lost its ability to evoke new images. Language and verse are filled with clichés like "it rained cats and dogs," "a blanket of snow," "quiet as a mouse," or "thin as a rail." Poet Eve Merriam described a cliché as what lazy people use in their writing. Good poetry helps look at the usual in un-usual ways.

Valerie Worth received the NCTE Award for Excellence in Poetry for Children for her *Small Poems* books. These have been combined and added to in her *All the Small Poems and Fourteen More*. Her simple free verse contains vivid metaphors that describe ordinary objects like chairs, earthworms, or a safety pin:

Closed, it sleeps
On its side
Quietly,
The silver image
Of some
Small fish

Opened it snaps
Its tail out
Like a thin shrimp
And looks
At the sharp
Point with a
Surprised eye

> –Valerie Worth. "Safety Pin" from *All the Small Poems and Fourteen More* by Valerie Worth. Copyright © 1987, 1994 by Valerie Worth. Reprinted by permission of Farrar, Straus and Giroux, LLC.

Some poets sustain a metaphor throughout the poem. Most children are intrigued with the subject of dinosaurs and readily respond to Charles Malam's poem that compares a steam shovel with those enormous beasts.

The dinosaurs are not all dead.
I saw one raise its iron head
To watch me walking down the road
Beyond our house today.
Its jaws were dripping with a load
Of earth and grass that it had cropped.
It must have heard me where I stopped,
Snorted white steam my way,
And stretched its long neck out to see,
And chewed, and grinned quite amiably.

> –Charles Malam. "Steam Shovel" from *Upper Pastures: Poems* by Charles Malam. Copyright © 1930, 1958 by Charles Malam. Reprinted by permission of Henry Holt and Company, LLC.

Personification is a way of speaking about inanimate objects and animals as though they were persons. Human beings have always personified inanimate objects. Young children personify their toys; adolescents and adults name their computers, their cars and boats. Poetry simply extends this process to a wider range of objects. James Stephens's well-known poem "The Wind" (in *Wider than the Sky*, ed. Scott Elledge) personifies the wind as a person who will "kill, kill." Diane Siebert personifies the desert in her book *Mojave* and the Sierra Nevada Mountains in *Sierra*. Debra Chandra sings winter's song with a mother's voice in this poem:

The leaves are gone,
The world is old,
I hear a whisper from the sky—
The dark is long,
The ground's grown cold,
I hear the snow's white lullaby.
She breathes it softly
Through the air,
While with her gown of flakes she sweeps
The sky, the trees, the ground grown cold,
Singing hush
Now hush.
   Now hush,
     Hush
       Sleep.

> –Deborah Chandra. "Snowfall" from *Balloons and Other Poems* by Deborah Chandra. Copyright © 1990 by Deborah Chandra. Reprinted by permission of Farrar, Straus and Giroux, LLC.

Another way of strengthening an image is through contrast. Elizabeth Coatsworth employs this device in much of her poetry. Her well-known "Poem of Praise" (in *Reflections on a Gift of Watermelon Pickle*, ed. Stephen Dunning et al.) contrasts the beauty of swift things with those that are slow and steady. Marci Ridlon presents two points of view concerning life in the city in her poem "City City" (in *The Random House Book of Poetry for Children*, ed. Jack Prelutsky). In the following poem Marcie Hans compares the launching of a man-made rocket with the miraculous growth of a seedling pushing its way through the earth. The first feat receives much acclaim; the second goes virtually unnoticed. There seems to be no doubt in the poet's mind which is the greater event, for she has even shaped her poem to resemble half of a tree:

Fueled
  by a million
  man-made
  wings of fire—
  the rocket tore a tunnel
  through the sky—
  and everybody cheered.
Fueled
  only by a thought from God—
  the seedling
  urged its way

through the thickness of black—
and as it pierced
the heavy ceiling of the soil—
and launched itself
up into outer space—
no
one
even clapped.

–Marcie Hans. "Fueled" from *Serve Me a Slice of Moon,*
copyright © 1965 by Marcie Hans and renewed 1993 by
Ernestine Hans, reprinted by permission of Harcourt, Inc.

Even though all children know about rockets and seeds, they might not be able to see the connection between the two images the poet has created. Among one group of educationally and economically advantaged 8-year-olds, not one child saw both of these ideas; yet 11-year-olds in the same school easily recognized them. This suggests the importance of knowing the developmental level of a group before selecting poetry for them.

## Shape

The first thing children notice about reading a poem is that it looks different from prose. And usually it does. Most poems begin with capital letters for each line and have one or more stanzas.

Increasingly, however, poets are using the shape of their poems to reinforce the image of the idea. In "The Grasshopper" (in his *One at a Time*) David McCord describes the plight of a grasshopper that fell down a deep well. As luck would have it, he discovers a rope and up he climbs one word at a time! The reader must read up the page to follow the grasshopper's ascent. Eve Merriam's "Windshield Wiper" (in *Knock at a Star,* ed. X. and D. Kennedy) not only sounds like the even rhythm of a car's wiper but has the look of two wipers (see p. 362). Lillian Morrison's poem about a sidewalk racer describes the thrill experienced by the rider at the same time as it takes the shape of a skateboard and strengthens her image.

Skimming
an asphalt sea
I swerve, I curve, I
sway; I speed to whirring
sound an inch above the
ground; I'm the sailor
and the sail, I'm the
driver and the wheel
I'm the one and only
single engine
human auto
mobile

–Lillian Morrison. "The Sidewalk Racer" from *The Sidewalk
Racer and Other Poems of Sports and Motion* by Lillian
Morrison. Copyright © 1965, 1967, 1968, 1977 by Lillian
Morrison. Used by permission of Marian Reiner for the
author.

Children enjoy mounting their own poems on a piece of paper shaped in the image of their poem, such as a verse about a jack-o'-lantern on a pumpkin shape or a poem about a plane mounted on the silhouette of a plane. Later the words themselves may form the shape of the content, as in concrete poetry.

## Emotional Force

We have seen how sound, language, and the shape of a poem can all work together to create the total impact of the poem. Considered individually, the rhyme scheme, imagery, figurative language, and appearance of the poem are of little importance unless all of these interrelate to create an emotional response in the reader. The craft of the poem is not the poem.

In the following poem, a modern poet writes of the way two children feel when caught in the vortex of their parents' quarrel:

Listening to grownups quarreling,

standing in the hall against the
wall with my little brother, blown
like leaves against the wall by their
voices, my head like a pingpong ball
between the paddles of their anger:
I knew what it meant
to tremble like a leaf.

Cold with their wrath, I heard
the claws of the rain
pounce. Floods
poured through the city,
skies clapped over me,
and I was shaken, shaken
like a mouse
between their jaws.

–Ruth Whitman. "Listening to Grownups Quarreling" from
*The Marriage Wig and Other Poems,* copyright © 1968 and
renewed 1996 by Ruth Whitman, reprinted by permission of
Harcourt, Inc.

A teacher could destroy the total impact of this poem for children by having them count the number of metaphors in it, looking at their increasing force and power. Children should have a chance to hear it, comment on it if they wish, or compare it with Debra Chandra's "The Argument" (see p. 371). All elements of these poems work together to create the feeling of being overpowered by a quarrel between those you love most.

Good poetry has the power to make the reader moan in despair, catch his breath in fear, gasp in awe, smile with delight, or sit back in wonder. For poetry heightens emotions and increases one's sensitivity to an idea or mood.

Teachers need to be able to identify the characteristics of good poetry in order to make wise selections to share with children. They need to know the various

# GUIDELINES

## Evaluating Poetry for Children

How does the rhythm of the poem reinforce and create the meaning of the poem?

If the poem rhymes, does it sound natural or contrived?

How does the sound of the poem add to the meaning? Does the poem use alliteration? onomatopoeia? repetition?

Does the poem create sensory images of sight, touch, smell, or taste?

Are these related to children's delight in their particular senses?

What is the quality of imagination in the poem? Does the poem make the child see something in a fresh, new way, or does it rely on tired clichés?

Is the figurative language appropriate to children's lives? Are the similes and metaphors ones that a child would appreciate and understand?

What is the tone of the poem? Does it patronize childhood by looking down on it? Is it didactic and preachy? Does it see childhood in a sentimental or nostalgic way?

Is the poem appropriate for children? Will it appeal to them, and will they like it?

How has the poet created the emotional intensity of the poem? Does every word work to heighten the feelings conveyed?

Does the shape of the poem—the placement of the words—contribute to the poem's meaning?

What is the purpose of the poem? To amuse? To describe in a fresh way? To comment on humanity? To draw parallels in our lives? How well has the poet achieved this purpose?

---

kinds of poetry and the range of content of poetry for children. Then they can select poetry that will gradually develop children's appreciation and sense of form. The questions listed in Guidelines, "Evaluating Poetry for Children" would not be appropriate to use for every poem. However, they can serve as a beginning way to look at poetry for children.

## Forms of Poetry for Children

Children are more interested in the "idea" of a poem than in knowing about the various forms of poetry. However, teachers will want to expose children to various forms of poetry and note their reactions. Do these children like only narrative poems? Do they think all poetry must rhyme, or will they listen to some free verse? Are they ready for the seemingly simple, yet highly complex, form of haiku? Understanding of and appreciation for a wide variety of poetry grow gradually as children are exposed to different forms and types of poems.

### Ballads

Ballads are narrative poems that have been adapted for singing or that give the effect of a song. Originally, they were not made or sung for children but were the literature of all the people. Characteristics of the ballad form are the frequent use of dialogue in telling the story, repetition, marked rhythm and rhyme, and refrains that go back to the days when ballads were sung. Popular ballads have no known authors, as they were handed down from one generation to the next; the literary ballad, however, does have a known author. Ballads usually deal with heroic deeds and include stories of murder, unrequited love, feuds, and tragedies.

Children in the middle grades enjoy the amusing story of the stubborn man and his equally stubborn wife in "Get Up and Bar the Door" (in *The Oxford Book of Poetry for Children,* ed. Edward Blishen) or the story of the "Wraggle Taggle Gypsies" (in *Wider than the Sky,* ed. Scott Elledge), in which the newlywed wealthy lady leaves her lord to run off with gypsies. (For discussions of the Scottish ballad "Tam Lin," see Chapters 6 and 7.)

American ballads frequently were popular songs, such as "On Top of Old Smoky" (in the Kennedys' *Knock at a Star*) and "The Foggy Foggy Dew" (in *Wider than the Sky,* ed. Scott Elledge). Few literary ballads are being written today. One, "Ballad of Birmingham" (in *Wider than the Sky*) by Dudley Randall, is a civil rights ballad about the tragic death of a child in the bombing of a church in Birmingham, Alabama, in 1963. When a young girl begs to go to the freedom march in the streets of Birmingham, her mother tells her it is too dangerous. Instead the mother sends the girl off to the children's choir, where she thinks she will be safe. That day the church is bombed and the daughter is killed. Ballads frequently have this ironic twist to their stories.

## Narrative Poems

The narrative poem relates a particular event or episode or tells a long tale. It may be a lyric, a sonnet, or free verse; its one requirement is that it must tell a story. Many of children's favorite poems are these so-called story poems. One of the best-known narrative poems is Robert Browning's *The Pied Piper of Hamelin*. First illustrated by Kate Greenaway in 1888, it continues to be published with new illustrators.

The most popular narrative poem in this country is Clement Moore's *The Night Before Christmas* (or *A Visit from St. Nicholas*). Every artist from Grandma Moses to Tasha Tudor to Ted Rand and Jan Brett has illustrated this Christmas story. Presently there are over fifty editions of *The Night Before Christmas*.

A. A. Milne's narrative poems are favorites of many young children. They love his story of a lost mouse in "Missing" and the disappearing beetle in "Forgiven." Six-, 7-, and 8-year-olds delight in Milne's "The King's Breakfast" and "King John's Christmas," poems about petulant kings, one of whom wants a "bit of butter" for his bread and the other of whom wants a big red India-rubber ball (all of these poems are in *The World of Christopher Robin*). Other favorite story poems for this age group are Karla Kuskin's ridiculous tale "Hughbert and the Glue" and her loving story about a plush toy, "Bear with Golden Hair" (both in *Dogs & Dragons, Trees & Dreams*). The long narrative tale "Custard the Dragon" by Ogden Nash, in *The Tale of Custard the Dragon*, has been illustrated by Lynn Munsinger.

Without a doubt the all-time favorite narrative poems of children today are the outrageously funny ones in Shel Silverstein's *Where the Sidewalk Ends*, *The Light in the Attic*, and *Falling Up*. Some of their favorite story verses include Shel Silverstein's "Sick," in which Peggy Ann McKay claims to have every known symptom of dreadful diseases until she realizes it is Saturday; the sad tale "Sarah Cynthia Sylvia Stout Who Would Not Take the Garbage Out"; and "Boa Constrictor," in which a man is slowly being swallowed alive (all are in Silverstein's *Where the Sidewalk Ends*).

Children also enjoy Jack Prelutsky's story verse, particularly his collection of poems about the bully Harvey and the children's ultimate revenge on him, *Rolling Harvey Down the Hill*. Middle graders delight in Prelutsky's macabre tales in *Nightmares* and *The Headless Horseman*, enriched by Arnold Lobel's grisly black-and-white illustrations.

Not all narrative poems for children are humorous. Older children, for example, respond to the pathos of Eve Merriam's poem "To Meet Mr. Lincoln" (in *Sing a Song of Popcorn*, ed. de Regniers et al.). They are stirred by the galloping hoofbeats in Longfellow's *Paul Revere's Ride*, illustrated with vibrant moonlit

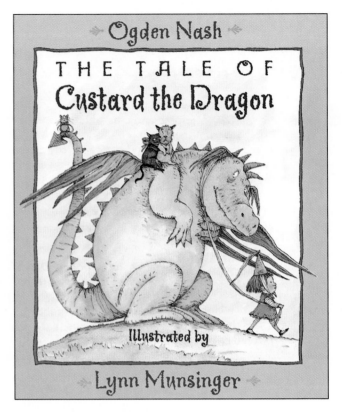

*Ogden Nash's well-loved* The Tale of Custard the Dragon *is made even more appealing by Lynn Munsinger's droll illustrations.*

From *The Tale of Custard the Dragon* by Ogden Nash, illustrated by Lynn Munsinger. © 1995 Little, Brown and Company.

pictures by Ted Rand. A favorite romantic tale is the dramatic *Highwayman* by Alfred Noyes, which has been portrayed in two stunning picture-book editions, illustrated by Charles Keeping and Neil Waldman.

One of the best ways to capture children's interest in poetry is to present a variety of narrative poems. Teachers will want to build a file of story poems appropriate to the interests of the children in their classes to use to introduce poetry to the children.

## Lyrical Poetry

Most of the poetry written for children is lyrical. The term *lyrical* derives from the word *lyric* and means poetry that sings its way into the minds and memories of its listeners. It is usually personal or descriptive poetry, with no prescribed length or structure other than its melody.

Much of William Blake's poetry is lyrical, beginning with the opening lines of his introductory poem to *Songs of Innocence*: "Piping down the valleys wild/Piping songs of pleasant glee" (in *Piping Down the Valleys Wide*, ed. Nancy Larrick). Robert Louis Stevenson's poems have a singing quality that makes them unforgettable. Everyone knows his poems "The Swing" and "The Wind" (both in *A Child's Garden of Verses*). Equally popular is his mysterious "Windy Nights," which compares the sound of the wind to a galloping horseman:

Whenever the moon and stars are set,
  Whenever the wind is high,
All night long in the dark and wet,
  A man goes riding by.
Late in the night when the fires are out,
Why does he gallop and gallop about?

Whenever the trees are crying aloud,
  And ships are tossed at sea,
By, on the highway, low and loud,
  By at the gallop goes he.
By at the gallop he goes, and then
By he comes back at the gallop again.

—Robert Louis Stevenson, "Windy Nights," in *Sing a Song of Popcorn*, ed. Beatrice de Regniers et al.

Eleanor Farjeon's lovely "The Night Will Never Stay" (in *Wider than the Sky*, ed. Scott Elledge) is another thoughtful lyrical poem. Masefield's well-known poem "Sea Fever" (in *Favorite Poems Old and New*, ed. Helen Ferris) would be a good one to read after sharing *The True Confessions of Charlotte Doyle* by Avi. Children always respond to the sound of the internal rhyme in Irene Rutherford McLeod's "The Lone Dog" (in Ferris's *Favorite Poems Old and New*), which begins with "I'm a lean dog, a keen dog, a wild dog and lone." Lyrical poetry is characterized by this lilting use of words that gives children an exhilarating sense of melody.

### Limericks

A nonsense form of verse that is particularly enjoyed by children is the limerick. This is a five-line verse in which the first and second lines rhyme, the third and fourth rhyme, and the fifth line rhymes with lines 1 and 2 and usually is a surprise or humorous statement. Freak spellings, oddities, and humorous twists characterize this form of poetry. David McCord, in his book *One at a Time*, suggests that "a limerick, to be lively and successful, *must* have *perfect* riming and *flawless* rhythm."

Other modern poets who continue to produce limericks include William Jay Smith and John Ciardi. Ciardi's collection *The Hopeful Trout and Other Limericks* offers limericks on a variety of themes from families to outer space. Arnold Lobel's *The Book of Pigericks* is a most humorous book of limericks, with verses about different pigs from various cities in the United States. His illustrations of humanized pigs are as funny as the limericks.

Children in the middle grades enjoy writing limericks, whether based on nursery rhymes, pigs, or their own names. It is certainly a far easier form for them to write than the highly abstract haiku.

### Free Verse

Free verse does not have to rhyme but depends on rhythm or cadence for its poetic form. It may use some rhyme, alliteration, and pattern. Though it frequently looks different on a printed page, it sounds very much like other poetry when read aloud. Children who have the opportunity to hear this form of poetry will be freed from thinking that all poetry must rhyme. Many of Valerie Worth's deceptively simple poems in *Small Poems* are written in free verse.

While much of Eve Merriam's poetry rhymes, she has also written free verse. Her well-known poem "How to Eat a Poem" (in *A Jar of Tiny Stars*, ed. Cullinan) is written in free verse. Langston Hughes's melodic "April Rain Song" (in *The Dream Keeper*) and Carl Sandburg's "Fog" (in *Rainbows Are Made*, ed. Lee Bennett Hopkins) are other examples of the effective use of free verse. Kristen O'Connell George's collections of poems, *Old Elm Speaks: Tree Poems*, *Little Dog Poems*, and *The Great Frog Race and Other Poems* contain many examples of free verse that will appeal to children.

### Haiku

Haiku is an ancient Japanese verse form that can be traced back to the thirteenth century. There are only seventeen syllables in the haiku; the first and third lines contain five syllables, the second line seven. Almost every haiku can be divided into two parts: first, a simple picture-making description that usually includes some reference, direct or indirect, to the season; and second, a statement of mood or feeling. A relationship between these two parts is implied, either a similarity or a telling difference.

The greatest of haiku writers, and the one who crystallized the form, was Basho. In his lifetime Basho produced more than eight hundred haiku. In the following poem the negative emotion expressed in the first line is reversed in the surprisingly pleasing image left by the last line. This image of black on white maintains the contrast of the two emotions that sustain the poem.

Detestable crow!
Today alone you please me—
black against the snow.

Matthew Gollub includes some of the poems of Issa, another famous Haiku poet, in his biography *Cool Melons Turn to Frogs*. The poet's life story and Gollub's note at the book's end should help demystify this ancient form. J. Patrick Lewis has written his own collection of haiku in *Black Swan/White Crow*. His thirteen poems are given visual expression by Chris Manson's lovely woodcuts, which subtly enhance images in the poems and recall the classic prints of Japanese artist Hokusai. Myra Cohn Livingston uses the form to celebrate the changing natural world over the course of the four seasons in *Cricket Never Does.*

The meaning of haiku is not expected to be immediately apparent. The reader is invited to add his or her own associations and meanings to the words, thus completing the poem in the mind. Each time the poem is read, new understandings will develop. Haiku is deceiving in that the form appears simple yet it requires much from its reader. Unless children have reached the Piagetian level of formal operations in their thinking, haiku might be too abstract a form of poetry for them to fully understand it. The common practice of asking young children to write haiku suggests that teachers do not understand its complexity. In this case, short is not simple!

### Concrete Poetry

Many poets today are writing picture poems that make the reader see what they are saying. The message of the poem is presented not only in the words (sometimes just letters or punctuation marks) but in the arrangement of the words. Meaning is reinforced, or even carried, by the shape of the poem. We have seen how Lillian Morrison formed her poem "The Sidewalk Racer" into the shape of a skateboard (p. 358) and how "Fueled" by Marcie Hans was shaped to resemble half a tree (p. 357).

Eve Merriam uses concrete poetry to create the image of a windshield wiper while her words imitate its sound:

| | |
|---|---|
| fog smog | fog smog |
| tissue paper | tissue paper |
| clear the blear | clear the smear |
| | |
| fog more | fog more |
| splat splat | downpour |
| rubber scraper | rubber scraper |
| overshoes | macintosh |
| bumbershoot | muddle on |
| slosh through | slosh through |
| | |
| drying up | drying up |
| sky lighter | sky lighter |
| nearly clear | nearly clear |
| clearing clearing veer | |
| clear here clear | |

–Eve Merriam. "Windshield Wiper" from *Out Loud* by Eve Merriam. Copyright © 1973 by Eve Merriam. Used by permission of Marian Reiner.

Joan Bransfield Graham has created attractive graphic forms for poems about water in *Splish, Splash,* illustrated by Steve Scott, and poems about light in *Flicker Flash,* illustrated by Nancy Davis. In *Doodle Dandies,* Lisa Desimini contributes mixed-

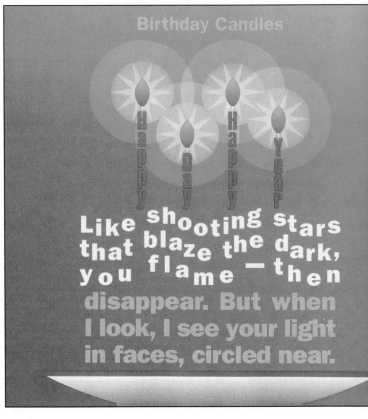

Art and words combine to create poems about light in Joan Graham's book of concrete poetry, Flicker Flash, *with illustrations by Nancy Davis.*

media collages that build upon J. Patrick Lewis's words so that these poems have a wonderful three-dimensional feel. They truly are *concrete.*

Once children have been exposed to concrete poetry, they invariably want to try creating some of their own. However, some children become so involved in the picture-making process, they forget that the meaning of the poem is carried by both words and arrangement. If emphasis is placed on the meaning first, then the shaping of the words will grow naturally from the idea of the poem.

## Selecting Poetry for Children

Before they enter school, children seem to have a natural enthusiasm for the sounds and rhythms of language. Schoolteachers and librarians will want to select poems and poets that will build upon these inclinations and that appeal to children's interests. They will also want to find ways to extend and deepen children's initial preferences into a lifelong love of poetry.

## Children's Poetry Preferences

Starting in the early 1920s, children's interest in poetry has been the subject of many research studies. The interesting fact about all these studies is the similarity of the findings and the stability of children's poetry preferences over the years. According to Ann Terry, these studies suggest the following:

1. Children are the best judges of their preferences.
2. Reading texts and courses of study often do not include the children's favorite poems.
3. Children's poetry choices are influenced by (1) the poetry form, (2) certain poetic elements, and (3) the content, with humor and familiar experience being particularly popular.
4. A poem enjoyed at one grade level may be enjoyed across several grade levels.
5. Children do not enjoy poems they do not understand.
6. Thoughtful, meditative poems are disliked by children.
7. Some poems appeal to one sex more than the other; girls enjoy poetry more than boys do.
8. New poems are preferred over older, more traditional ones.
9. Literary merit is not necessarily an indication that a poem will be liked.[7]

Terry also reports that in her study of children in grades 4 through 6, narrative poems, such as John Ciardi's "Mummy Slept Late and Daddy Fixed Breakfast" (in *A Jar of Tiny Stars*, ed. Cullinan), and limericks, including both modern and traditional, were the children's favorite forms of poetry. Haiku was consistently disliked by all grade levels. Elements of rhyme, rhythm, and sound increased children's enjoyment of the poems, as evidenced by their preference for David McCord's "The Pickety Fence" (in *Every Time I Climb a Tree*) and "Lone Dog" (in *Favorite Poems Old and New*, ed. Ferris). Poems that contained much figurative language or imagery were disliked. Children's favorite poems at all three grade levels contained humor or were about familiar experiences or animals. All children preferred contemporary poems containing modern content and today's language more than the older, more traditional poems.

Carol Fisher and Margaret Natarella[8] found similar preferences among first, second, and third graders,

as did Karen Kutiper[9] among seventh, eighth, and ninth graders. However, the younger children enjoyed poems about strange and fantastic events, such as Prelutsky's "The Lurpp Is on the Loose" (in *The Snopp on the Sidewalk*) and Nash's "Adventures of Isabel" (in *The Adventures of Isabel*), while the older children opted for more realistic content. Younger children also appeared to like traditional poems more than the older children did. They insisted that poetry must rhyme, and all of the traditional poems did, so they could have been selecting on the basis of rhyme rather than content. However, one consistent finding of these studies was that adults cannot accurately predict which poems children will like.

How then can we most effectively select poetry for children? Certainly a teacher will want to consider children's needs and interests, their previous experience with poetry, and the types of poetry that appeal to them. A sound principle to follow is to begin where the children are. Teachers can share poems that have elements of rhyme, rhythm, and sound, such as Rhonda Bacmeister's "Galoshes" (in *Sing a Song of Popcorn*, ed. Beatrice de Regniers et al.) or David McCord's "The Song of the Train" (in *One at a Time*). They can read many narrative verses and limericks and look for humorous poems and poems about familiar experiences and animals. They should share only those poems that they really like themselves; enthusiasm for poetry is contagious. However, teachers will not want to limit their sharing only to poems that they know children will like. For taste needs to be developed, too; children should go beyond their delight in humorous and narrative poetry to develop an appreciation for variety in both form and content. We want children to respond to more poetry and to find more to respond to in poetry.

It may well be that the consistency in children's poetry preferences over the years simply reflects the poverty of their experience with poetry. We tend to like the familiar. If teachers read only traditional narrative poems to children, then these children will like narrative poems. Or having had little or no exposure to fine imaginative poetry, children might not have gone beyond their natural intuitive liking for jump-rope rhymes or humorous limericks. In brief, the results of the studies of children's interests in poetry might be an indictment more of the quality of their literature program than of the quality of their preferences. We need to ascertain children's poetry preferences *after* they have experienced a rich, continuous exposure to poetry throughout the elementary school years. It is hoped that as children have increased experience with a wide range of quality poetry by various poets, they will grow in appreciation and understanding of the finer poems.

[7]Ann Terry, *Children's Poetry Preferences: A National Survey of the Upper Elementary Grades* (Urbana, Ill.: National Council of Teachers of English, 1974), p. 10.

[8]Carol J. Fisher and Margaret A. Natarella, "Young Children's Preferences in Poetry: A National Survey of First, Second and Third Graders," *Research in the Teaching of English* 16 (December 1982): 339–353.

[9]Karen Sue Kutiper, "A Survey of the Adolescent Poetry Preferences of Seventh, Eighth and Ninth Graders" (Ed.D. dissertation, University of Houston, 1985).

## Poets and Their Books

Recent years have seen an increase in the number of writers of verse for children and the number of poetry books published for the juvenile market. Poetry itself has changed, becoming less formal, more spontaneous, and imitative of the child's own language patterns. The range of subject matter has expanded with the tremendous variation in children's interests. It is difficult to categorize the work of a poet on the basis of the poems' content, for many poets interpret various areas of children's experience. However, an understanding of the general subject matter of the works of each poet will help the teacher select poems and make recommendations to children.

### Humorous Verse

In every preference study that has been done, children prefer narrative rhyme and humorous verse. Today the popularity of the verse of Shel Silverstein and Jack Prelutsky attests to this. The use of imaginative symbols and vivid imagery and metaphor mark the difference between real poetry and verse. The versifiers provide instant gratification but leave the reader with little to ponder. However, because children begin here in their enjoyment of poetry, it seems appropriate to start this section with writers of humorous verse.

Almost all poets have written some humorous verse, but only a few have become noted primarily for this form. In the nineteenth century the names of Edward Lear and Lewis Carroll became almost synonymous with humorous nonsense poems. Lear's limericks, alphabet rhymes, and narrative poems have been compiled into one book, *The Complete Nonsense Book*. Each absurd verse is illustrated by the poet's grotesque drawings, which add greatly to Lear's humor. Artist Fred Marcellino has collected three of Lear's narrative poems in *The Pelican Chorus and Other Nonsense*. In addition to the title poem, Marcellino's watercolor paintings add zest and humor to "The Owl and the Pussycat" and "The New Vestments."

Following in the tradition of Lear, J. Patrick Lewis has created a wonderful homage to Lear in his collection of original poems, *Bosh Blobber Bosh; Runcible Poems for Edward Lear*. Lewis also writes wonderfully funny verse in his books *Little Buggers, A Hippopotamusn't*, and *Ridicholas Nicholas*. Victoria Chess illustrates all these poems with most amusing pictures of silly and dumpy-looking creatures. The puns in the poem "Tom Tigercat" in *A Hippopotamusn't* are reminiscent of the work of Ogden Nash and John Ciardi. Lewis's *Riddle-Icious* and *Riddle-lightful* offer children riddles in the form of amusing verses.

Many of Douglas Florian's rhymes in *Beast Feast* are reminiscent of Ogden Nash's animal sketches in their brevity and their sense of playfulness:

Just when you think you know the boa
There's moa and moa and moa and moa.

> –Douglas Florian. "The Boa" from *Beast Feast*, copyright © 1994 by Douglas Florian, reprinted by permission of Harcourt, Inc.

Florian's witty artwork adds to the delight in his other collections about the animal world, *In the Swim, Insectlopedia, Mammalabilia*, and *On the Wing*. *Bing Bang Bong* and *Laugh-eteria* are longer collections of rhymes that place Florian in the company of Shel Silverstein and Jack Prelutsky as a writer of nonsense poems that delight children.

John Ciardi's light verse for children is enjoyed by girls and boys with enough sophistication to appreciate his tongue-in-cheek humor. His "Mummy Slept Late and Daddy Fixed Breakfast" (in *A Jar of Tiny Stars*, ed. Cullinan), was the most popular poem of the children in the fourth, fifth, and sixth grades in the Terry study (see p. 363). A former poetry editor for the *Saturday Review*, Ciardi could write serious verse as well as light verse. His "How to Tell the Top of the Hill" (in *The Reason for the Pelican*) and "The River Is a Piece of the Sky" (in Larrick's *Piping Down the Valleys Wild*) are both proof of this. Ciardi was an early winner of the NCTE Poetry Award.

Much of what children consider funny is frequently sadistic and ghoulish. Colin McNaughton's *Who's Been Sleeping in My Porridge?* and *Making Friends with Frankenstein* are collections that range from the stomach-turning "Cockroach Sandwich" to the mournful satire of "The Doom Merchant," with much pure silliness in between. McNaughton's bizarre illustrations add humor and clarify his wordplay, as in "Frankenstein's Monster Is Finally Dead." We see Frankenstein's feet, head, and other body parts sprouting angel wings ("may he rest in pieces"). Jack Prelutsky's macabre poems in *Nightmares* and *The Headless Horseman* and Arnold Lobel's black-and-white illustrations are splendidly terrifying. One seventh-grade teacher of children in the inner city maintained that this book got her through her first year of teaching! Prelutsky is also a master at creating such zany imaginary creatures as the "Wozzit," who is hiding in the closet, and the "Grobbles," who quietly wait to gobble someone up. Both of these poems are in *The Snopp on the Sidewalk*. He creates more appealing creatures in *The Baby Uggs Are Hatching*, including the "Sneezy-Snoozer," the "Dreary Dreeze," and the "Sneepies." *The Dragons Are Singing Tonight*, one of several collaborations with illustrator Peter Sis, includes a dragon whose cold is cured with a dose of turpentine and one whose fire is doused in a bout with a thunderstorm.

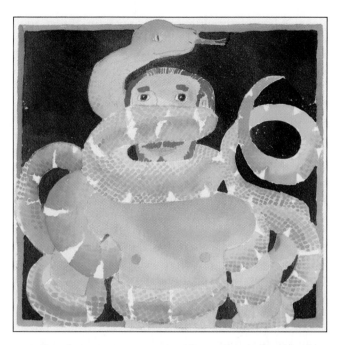

*Douglas Florian's "Boa" is one of many brightly colored paintings and poems that will delight young readers in* Beast Feast.

Illustration from *Beast Feast,* copyright © 1994 by Douglas Florian, reproduced by permission of Harcourt, Inc.

*Peter Sis creates the imaginative pictures for Jack Prelutsky's humorous collections* The Dragons Are Singing Tonight *and* Monday's Troll.

Illustration from *The Dragons Are Singing Tonight* by Jack Prelutsky, illustrated by Peter Sis. Illustration copyright © 1993 by Peter Sis. Used by permission of Greenwillow Books, an imprint of HarperCollins Publishers.

All ages enjoy Prelutsky's large collections (more than a hundred poems) titled *The New Kid on the Block, Something Big Has Been Here,* and *A Pizza The Size of the Sun,* which include humorous realistic poems such as "I'm Disgusted with My Brother," "The Wumpaloons, Which Never Were" and "My Sister Is a Sissy," plus many funny characters and more zany creatures.

Prelutsky has written some lighthearted realistic verse for younger children about special holidays and seasons. These include some useful poems in *It's Halloween* and *It's Thanksgiving.* His books *Ride a Purple Pelican* and *Beneath a Blue Umbrella* are filled with Mother Goose–type verses that appeal to preschoolers. Garth Williams has made large, handsome, colored illustrations for each of these joyous poems that play with place names—such as "Grandma Bear from Delaware" and "Cincinnati Patty" (both in *Ride a Purple Pelican*).

Shel Silverstein's *Where the Sidewalk Ends* was on the *New York Times* best-sellers list for three years. It is the one poetry book that all teachers, children, and parents seem to know. Librarians complain that they can't keep the book on the shelf, no matter how many copies they have. Here you meet a boy who turns into a TV set, a king who eats only a "Peanut-Butter Sandwich," and those three characters "Ickle Me, Pickle Me, Tickle Me Too." Much of the humor of these poems is based on the sounds of words, the preposterous characters, and amusing situations.

While some verses are slightly unsavory, others surprise you with their sensitivity, such as "Invitation," "Listen to the Mustn'ts," and the title poem, "Where the Sidewalk Ends." *The Light in the Attic* and *Falling Up* provide more of the same fun.

Poetry is neglected in our schools today, but there is no dearth of humorous verse. Children take to it as they do to a hamburger, fries, and a shake. And like a fast-food meal, it is enjoyable but not the only food to include in a balanced diet.

### Interpreters of the World of Childhood

Robert Louis Stevenson was the first poet to write of childhood from the child's point of view. *A Child's Garden of Verses,* published in 1885, continues to be popular today. Stevenson was himself a frail child and spent much of his early life in bed or confined indoors. His poetry reflects a solitary childhood, but a happy one. In "Land of Counterpane" and "Block City," he portrays a resourceful, inventive child who can create his own amusement. He found playmates in his shadow, in his dreams, and in his storybooks. The rhythm of Stevenson's "The Swing," "Where Go the Boats," and "Windy Nights" appeals to children today

*In* Where Go the Boats *Max Grover's illustrations for four of Robert Louis Stevenson's poems for children show how some classics never go out of date.*

Cover from *Where Go the Boats? Play-Poems of Robert Louis Stevenson* by Max Grover, cover art copyright © 1998 by Max Grover, reproduced by permission of Browndeer Press, a division of Harcourt, Inc.

as much as it did to the children of a century ago. In *Where Go the Boats?* Max Grover has illustrated four of Stevenson's poems with bright pictures that appeal to children. Ted Rand has created a stunning picture-book edition of Stevenson's *My Shadow,* expanding the meaning of this poem to incorporate children from all over the world. Stevenson's *Block City* has been illustrated by Ashley Wolff. All these editions make a fine introduction to Stevenson's poems.

Perhaps the best loved of British children's poets is A. A. Milne. Some of his poems, such as "Halfway Down" and "Solitude," show perceptive insight into the child's mind. "Happiness" captures a child's joy in such delights as new waterproof boots, a raincoat, and a hat. Most of Milne's poems are delightfully funny. The poetry from both of Milne's poetry books has now been collected into one volume, titled *The World of Christopher Robin.* Illustrations by Ernest Shepard seem to belong with Milne's poetry as much as Pooh belongs with Christopher Robin; it is hard to imagine one without the other.

Another well-loved British poet for children is Eleanor Farjeon. Her knowledge and understanding of children's thoughts and behavior are reflected in her many poems. Farjeon wrote the lovely nature poem "The Night Will Never Stay" (in *Wider than the Sky,* ed. Scott Elledge) and the graphically descriptive "Mrs. Peck-Pigeon" (in *Sing a Song of Popcorn,* ed. Beatrice de Regniers et al.). Before her death in 1965, Eleanor Farjeon had received notable recognition for her poetry and prose. She was the first recipient of the international Hans Christian Andersen Medal and she received the Regina Medal for her life's work. A prestigious British award "for distinguished services to children's books" that bears the name of this well-known poet and writer is given annually. No other poet who has written exclusively for children has received such recognition.

Dorothy Aldis was one of the first American poets to celebrate children's feelings and everyday experiences with simple childlike verses. With rhyme and singsong meter, she captures the child's delight in the ordinary routines of home life. Family relationships are lovingly portrayed in "Little" and "My Brother" (both in *Tomie de Paola's Book of Poems*). Poems from the first four books by Dorothy Aldis were collected in a single volume entitled *All Together,* which can still be found in most library collections.

Mary Ann Hoberman writes lively rhythmical verse for young children. The poems in her collection *The Llama Who Had No Pajamas* range from the delightful nonsense of the title poem to the swinging rhythm of "Hello and Goodbye" (see page 352). Hoberman's poem "Brother" (in *Sing a Song of Popcorn,* ed. Beatrice de Regniers et al.), about a boy who is a bit of a bother to everyone, is a favorite with children and could well be shared as an introduction to books on sibling rivalry. Primary children also enjoy the long, sustained poem in Hoberman's picture book *A House Is a House for Me.* In this book she plays with the concept of houses, including regular houses and animals' houses, and then looks at other possibilities, such as a glove becoming a house for a hand and a pocket as a house for pennies. All of Hoberman's poetry is distinguished by its fast-paced rhymes and marked rhythms.

Karla Kuskin also sees with the eyes of a child as she creates her well-known poems. Her book *Dogs & Dragons, Trees & Dreams* includes many of her best-known narrative poems, such as "I Woke Up This Morning," which tells of a child who feels she/he hasn't done anything right since "quarter past seven," or "Lewis Has a Trumpet," or "The Bear with the Golden Hair." She can write mysterious poems, such as the haunting "Where Would You Be?" or play with the sounds of words, as in "The Full of the Moon." Many of her poems contain both humor and wisdom, as in this quizzical one:

People always say to me
"What do you think you'd like to be
When you grow up?"

And I say "Why,
I think I'd like to be the sky
Or be a plane or train or mouse
Or maybe a haunted house
Or something furry, rough and wild . . .
Or maybe I will stay a child."

> –Karla Kuskin. "The Question," from *The Middle of the Trees*,
> by Karla Kuskin. Copyright © 1959, renewed 1986 by Karla
> Kuskin. Reprinted by permission of Scott Treimel New York.

Kuskin's *Soap Soup and Other Verses* is a collection of easy-to-read poems. Karla Kuskin often illustrates all her own poetry books with tiny, precise pen-and-ink drawings. She designed the artwork for the NCTE Poetry Award and then was the third recipient of that coveted prize. A recent collection of her poems has been gathered together in *The Sky Is Always in the Sky*.

### Multicultural Poetry

 Long before the experiences of African Americans became recognized in literature, Pulitzer Prize winner Gwendolyn Brooks wrote poignant poetry about African American children living in the inner city. *Bronzeville Boys and Girls* contains thirty-four poems, each bearing the name, thoughts, and feelings of an individual child. There is "John, Who Is Poor"; "Michael," who is afraid of the storm; "Beulah," who has quiet thoughts at church; and "Luther and Breck," who have a make-believe dragon fight. Unfortunately, this poet has written only one volume of poetry for children.

Langston Hughes was the first African American to write poems of black protest and pride, such as "What Happens to a Dream Deferred?" *The Dream Keeper and Other Poems* is a handsome collection of his poems illustrated by Brian Pinkney. "Dreams" and "April Rain Song" and "Mother to Son" are among the sixty-six poems that show the full range of this poet's powerful voice. The title poem reflects the lyrical beauty of Hughes's imagination.

Bring me all of your dreams,
You dreamers
Bring me all of your
Heart melodies
That I may wrap them
In a blue cloud cloth
Away from the too rough fingers
Of the world.

> –Langston Hughes. "The Dream Keeper" from *Collected Poems* by Langston Hughes. Copyright © 1994 by the Estate of Langston Hughes. Reprinted by permission of Alfred A. Knopf, a Division of Random House Inc.

The poetry of two other important but long neglected African American poets can be found in two recent collections for young people. Effie Lee New-

some was one of the first African American poets to write for an audience of children. Rudine Sims Bishop has selected many of her poems for the book *Wonders*. In *Jump Back, Honey* well-known African American illustrators have interpreted poems of the noted turn-of-the-century writer Paul Laurence Dunbar. The paintings of Ashley Bryan, Carol Byard, Jerry and Brian Pinkney, Faith Ringgold, and Jan Spivey Gilchrist provide backdrops for the varied moods, topics and language styles found in such poems as "Dawn," "Little Brown Baby" and "Rain-Songs." Both Newsome and Dunbar are important voices whose words still speak to children.

Today, we can find many wonderful African American poets represented in books for children. *Honey, I Love* is by Eloise Greenfield, who has a great capacity for speaking in the voice of a young African American child. This joyous little book of sixteen poems includes a chant, the jump-rope rhyme (see p. 353), and thoughtful observations on experiences like dressing up ("I look Pretty") or thinking about a neighbor who left her a nickel ("Keepsake") before she died. The Dillons' illustrations are as sensitive as these poems that celebrate the rich content of a child's world.

Greenfield portrays a slightly older child in the eighteen first-person poems in *Nathaniel Talking*. Nathaniel gives us his "philosophy" of life in these poems. Some are bittersweet memories; others look to the future. Sharp, clear pencil drawings by Jan Spivey Gilchrist help to make this a distinguished book of poetry. Gilchrist also illustrated the eighteen poems in Greenfield's *Night on Neighborhood Street*, poems about family, friends, and neighbors, and *Angels*, a collection of poems about the angels who watch over children at different moments in their lives. Greenfield, who has also written poems to go with Amos Ferguson's Bahamian folk-art paintings in *Under the Sunday Tree*, is a recipient of NCTE Poetry Award for Excellence in Children's Literature.

Nikki Giovanni is well known for her adult poetry, but she has also written for children. *Spin a Soft Black Song* has been reissued with new illustrations. "Poem for Rodney" expresses both a child's point of view and an adult's. Rodney is tired of everyone asking him what he is going to do when he grows up; his reply is simply that he'd like to grow up. Noted artist and storyteller Ashley Bryan has illustrated a collection of thirteen of Giovanni's poems in *The Sun Is So Quiet*.

*Sing to the Sun*, by Ashley Bryan, is a collection of his own poems that are as vibrant as the paintings that decorate the book's pages. While there is poignancy in poems such as "Leaving," there are also strong rhythms and bright images that fulfill the promise of the sunny title and evoke the warmth of

Caribbean culture. Bryan's special magic is present in the "Storyteller," about a storyteller whose stories were pieced together with bird song, and in "Artist," about an artist who can transform sorrow. James Berry, a noted Jamaican poet, has several collections of poetry that celebrate the life of the Caribbean islands with a unique voice. *Everywhere Faces Everywhere* includes a variety of topics and poetic forms, and Berry weaves a sense of magic with both formal English and Caribbean patois.

Arnold Adoff writes strong poems about the inner thoughts and feelings of a girl born of a mixed-race marriage. In *All the Colors of the Race*, as in his other work, he shapes each poem to balance the semantic and rhythmic lines of force. He wants his words to sing as well as say. His poem "The way I see any hope for later" is one that everyone should read and heed. His story-poem *Black Is Brown Is Tan* describes a biracial family growing up happy in a house full of love:

Black is brown is tan
  is girl     is boy
  is nose    is face
  is all the colors
  of the race
  is dark    is light
  singing songs
  in singing night
  kiss big woman     hug big man
  black   is brown  is tan

–Arnold Adoff. *Black Is Brown Is Tan* by Arnold Adoff. Copyright © 1973 by Arnold Adoff. Used by permission of HarperCollins Publishers.

These poems not only reflect Arnold Adoff's love for his own family but celebrate diversity and individuality. Adoff's *Love Letters* are loving poems that could be sent to family and friends at any time of year. While many of his poems are about caring and friendship between races, others are about seasons and eating. *In for Winter, Out for Spring* is a journal of poems of the changing seasons, capturing the joy of everything from the first snowflake in winter to pumpkins in late October. Adoff creates vivid images in these poems of people and seasons. His *Street Music: City Poems* presents the vigor of city life, its clangor and its vibrancy. *Eats* celebrates the poet's passion for tasty treats, particularly sweets. Adoff is also a 1988 recipient of the prestigious NCTE Poetry Award for Excellence in Children's Literature.

Gary Soto's poetry collections for older students, *Cantos Familiar* and *Neighborhood Odes*, capture the Latino experience. *Neighborhood Odes* sings the praises of everything from tortillas to tennis shoes. In "Ode to Senor Leal's Goat" a goat amuses the chickens and shocks Senor Leal when he runs away with

*"The Storyteller," in Ashley Bryan's* Sing to the Sun, *captures the warmth of the Caribbean culture portrayed in Bryan's poems and paintings.*

Copyright © 1992 by Ashley Bryan. Used by permission of HarperCollins Publishers, New York, NY.

his smoking pipe. "Ode to My Library" touches upon the rich life in, and out of, books that the library provides a young dreamer. Other notable books about the Latino experience can be found in Jane Medina's *My Name Is Jorge* and Pat Mora's *Confetti.*

Janet Wong, of Korean and Chinese descent, has several poetry collections that will appeal to adolescents, *A Suitcase of Seaweed and Other Poems, Good Luck and Other Poems,* and *The Rainbow Hand: Poems About Mothers and Daughters.* Her lovely *Night Garden* evokes the surrealistic world of dreams and will be appreciated by middle-grade children as well as those in middle school.

*In My Mother's House* by Ann Nolan Clark was a breakthrough book when it was first published in 1941. Now reissued, it contains poems describing a close-knit farming community of Pueblo Indians. Based on stories told by Pueblo children, it was the first book to represent a Native American point of view. Velino Herrera did the beautifully clear pictures for this fine book of poems.

Noted Navajo poet Luci Tapahonso has published several collections for children. *Songs of Shiprock Fair,* illustrated by Anthony Chee Emerson, relates the experiences of Nezbah and her family at the parade and carnival held during the Shiprock Fair. *A Breeze Swept Through* is a collection of Tapahonso's poems that includes "Note to a Younger Brother," and "For Misty Starting School."

There are many multicultural voices that are beginning to be heard through some of the fine collections of poetry that are now being published. Many of these anthologies are discussed in the section "Specialized Collections" later in this chapter.

## Poets of Nature

Like poets, children are very attuned to the world around them. They are fascinated by the constant changes in nature and enjoy poems that communicate their delight in the first snow, their sense of wonder when they touch a pussy willow or hear a foghorn or see a deer.

Aileen Fisher is adept at observing both nature and children. She views the natural world through the eyes of the child, preserving a remarkable sense of wonder, as in this poem:

Out in the Dark and Daylight—Title

Out in the dark and daylight
under a cloud or tree,

Out in the park or play light
out where the wind blows free,

Out in the March or May light
with shadows and stars to see,

Out in the dark and daylight . . .
that's where I like to be.

–Aileen Fisher. "Out in the Dark and Daylight" from *Out in the Dark and Daylight* by Aileen Fisher. Copyright © 1980 Aileen Fisher. Used by permission of Marian Reiner for the author.

Fisher's poems are simple and fresh, very much within the experience of a child. Aileen Fisher was the second recipient of the Award for Excellence in Poetry for Children given by the National Council of Teachers of English.

Lilian Moore describes the changing moods and seasons of both the city and the country in her short-line free verse. Her poems frequently appeal to the senses, as she talks about the moaning of foghorns or the "tree-talk" or "wind-swish" of the night. "Wind Song" (in *Sing a Song of Popcorn*, ed. Beatrice de Regniers et al.) describes the flapping and snapping noise the wind makes as it blows flags and ashcans, and "Until I Saw the Sea" (in de Regniers et al., *Sing a Song of Popcorn*) provides a fresh new image of the "wrinkled sea." A former teacher, reading specialist, and editor who lived in the city, Moore's most recent collection, *Poems Have Roots*, reflects her deep concern for the environment, her close observations of her surroundings, and a knowledge of what children enjoy. Moore is also a recipient of the NCTE Poetry Award.

Byrd Baylor writes story-length prose poems that reflect her appreciation for nature and the beauty of the landscape of the Southwest. In *The Other Way to Listen*, an older man tells a young girl how you can hear wildflower seeds burst open or a rock murmuring or hills singing—of course, it takes practice! *Your Own Best Secret Place, Everybody Needs a Rock,* and *I'm in Charge of Celebrations* are fine poetry workshop starters, as they inspire children to describe their secret places or plan special celebrations. Peter Parnall incorporates the text as part of his bold illustrations.

Constance Levy has written several volumes of poetry that make strong connections to children's experiences with nature. *When Whales Exhale* brings together poems about traveling, and *A Crack in the Clouds* focuses on the wonders of the world in the backyard. In *I'm Going to Pet a Worm Today*, Levy muses in "The Color Eater" about how night laps up the sunset. She wonders about bees in "The Business of Bees" and about butterflies in "Questions to Ask a Butterfly." The poems in *A Tree Place* introduce creatures like the black snake who can write his name, in "S Is for Snake," or the inchworm:

A little green inchworm
dropped from a tree,
and rode in my hair
unknown to me,
till I looked in the mirror.
"Aha!" I said,
"What is this green thing on my head?"
And the worm must have wondered
seeing me,
"What is this funny looking tree?"

–Constance Levy. "Inchworm" reprinted with the permission of Margaret K. McElderry Books, an imprint of Simon & Schuster Children's Publishing Division from *A Tree Place and Other Poems* by Constance Levy. Text copyright © 1994 Constance Kling Levy.

While Carl Sandburg is noted for his sage commentary on people, he did make two collections of poetry with young people in mind, *Early Moon* and *Wind Song*, both now out of print. Lee Bennett Hopkins has made a handsome new edition of selected poems of Carl Sandburg titled *Rainbows Are Made*, illustrated with six of Fritz Eichenberg's wood engravings—themselves as powerful as some of Sandburg's poetry. This collection includes selections from *The People, Yes* and poems about nature, people, the seasons, the sea, and the stars. In *Grassroots* Wendell Minor has illustrated a lovely picture-book collection that celebrates Sandburg's affinity for midwestern rural life. Ted Rand has illustrated a picture-book version of the old favorite by Sandburg, *Arithmetic*, using anamorphic, or distorted, pictures that must be viewed with a special mylar cylinder or by holding the book at a special angle. These handsome books will introduce children to the thoughtful, quizzical nature of Carl Sandburg's poetry.

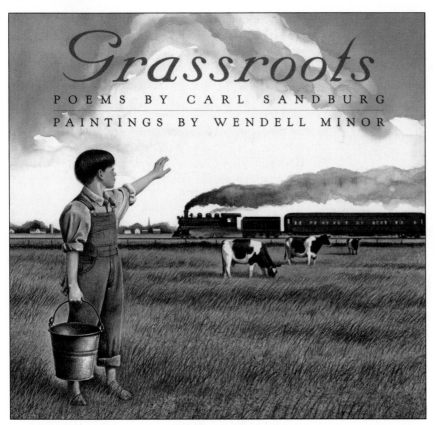

*In Carl Sandburg's* Grassroots *Wendell Minor's beautiful landscape paintings capture Sandburg's midwestern roots.*

Cover from *Grassroots: Poems* by Carl Sandburg, illustrated by Wendell Minor, cover art copyright © 1998 by Wendell Minor. Reproduced by permission of Browndeer Press, a division of Harcourt, Inc.

Many poems by Robert Frost are both simple enough for a child to understand and complex enough for graduate study. Before his death, Frost selected some of his poems to be read to, or by, young people. Interestingly, the title of this collection, *You Come Too,* was taken from a line of "The Pasture," the first poem in this book and the introductory poem of the very first book Frost ever published. Upon initial reading, this poem seems no more than a literal invitation to join someone as he cleans the pasture spring. However, the poem takes on more meaning when viewed in the context of its placement; the trip to the pasture to clean the spring might well be an invitation to the enjoyment of poetry itself—"you come too!" By reading *You Come Too,* children can enjoy "The Runaway," "Dust of Snow," "The Last Word of a Bluebird," and "The Pasture," poems on their level of understanding. Older children will begin to comprehend the deeper meanings in "Mending Wall," "The Road Not Taken," and "The Death of the Hired Man."

## Versatile Poets

It is almost impossible to characterize the wide variety of poems produced by certain poets. David McCord's poetry, for example, ranges in subject matter from poems about everyday experiences to nature poems to verses about verse. He plays with sound in "The Pickety Fence" and "Song of the Train"; with form, including couplets, quatrains, limericks, and triolets, in "Write Me a Verse"; and with words and their meanings in many of his poems, including "Glowworm," "Ptarmigan," and "Goose, Moose and Spruce." He can write with a lively wit or quietly enter the serious inner world of the child.

McCord's *Every Time I Climb a Tree* was one of the first poetry books to be illustrated by the well-known picture-book illustrator Caldecott Medal–winning Marc Simont. All of David McCord's poetry was collected in a single volume titled *One at a Time.* It is appropriate that this book was published in the same year that McCord received the first NCTE Award for Excellence in Poetry for Children.

Much of Eve Merriam's poetry has a lilt and bounce that will capture the most disinterested child's attention. *You Be Good & I'll Be Night, Blackberry Ink,* and *Higgle Wiggle* contain bouncy jump-rope rhymes such as "Jump, Jump," the rhythmical "Swing Me Swing Me," and the loving "You're My Turtle." Merriam has an extensive range as a poet and has written such biting commentary as *The Inner City Mother Goose,* a collection of parodies of the traditional rhymes. *The Singing Green* contains poems about indoors and outdoors, and one called "The Poem as a Door." The fresh images in *Fresh Paint,* a collection that is still available in libraries, shows how many of her poems are invitations for readers to write their own poems.

Fresh Paint
It glistens on this wall
that turns
whatever color I conjure
when I close my eyes:

green for the moss of
memories on a stone

blue for ice caves in August

scarlet for the banners of maple leaves
triumphant in the fall

yellow for the lights
of a homebound car in the fog

white for the drift of
cherry blossoms

orange for tiger flames
leaping in the bonfire

violet for daybreak
and violet for dusk

black for the warmth of darkness

and look
how the word *don't* is painted out
and the side reads

   *touch.*

–Eve Merriam. "Fresh Paint" from *Fresh Paint* by Eve Merriam. Copyright © 1986 Eve Merriam. Used by permission of Marian Reiner.

It seems obvious that such a versatile poet received the NCTE Poetry Award.

Another NCTE Poetry Award winner is Myra Cohn Livingston, a prolific and versatile writer of poetry for children of all ages. She handles a variety of styles and forms masterfully, including rhymes, free verse, limerick, triolet, haiku, concrete poems, and others. Her first books of poetry appealed more to the younger child and included such well-known poems as "Whispers," "The Night," and "Bump on My Knee." Many of these poems for younger children have been gathered together in a small-size book, *A Song I Sang to You*, illustrated with Margot Tomes's appropriately naïve ablack-and-white illustrations. In *Flights of Fancy* the poems range from a flight of imagination to images seen on a real airplane flight.

Livingston has also combined her poetry with the artwork of Leonard Everett Fisher to produce such striking books as *A Circle of Seasons*, *Sky Songs*, *Space Songs*, and *Up in the Air*. In *Celebrations*, both the art and the poems present a moving panorama of sixteen holidays, including Martin Luther King Day, Columbus Day, Presidents' Day, and all birthdays. *Festivals* includes poems and pictures to celebrate Chinese New Year, Kwanza, and Ramadan. Not only was Myra Cohn Livingston a versatile poet, but she was also a well-known anthologist and teacher of creative writing to children. A wonderful collection of poems written by many of her students at UCLA was published after her death. Titled *I Am Writing a Poem About . . . A Game of Poetry*, the collection came about when Livingston challenged the students to write a poem in which one word, *rabbit*, appeared. She then went on to give them three words, *blanket, ring,* and *drum* to incorporate in their poems. The group then agreed on a choice of six words, *hole, friend, candle, ocean, snake,* and either *bucket* or *scarecrow*. The results are truly delightful and illuminate the wonderful range of possibility that words offer the imagination. Included in the collection are poems by Deborah Chandra, Kristine O'Connell George, Tony Johnston, Alice Schertle, Janet Wong, Joan Bransfield Graham, and other well-known poets whose work honors the influence of Livingston as poet and teacher.

Deborah Chandra, one of those students, has been awarded the International Reading Association/Lee Bennett Hopkins Promising Poet Award for two volumes of poetry, *Balloons* and *Rich Lizard*. Many of her poems, such as "Snowfall" (in *Balloons and Other Poems*) and "The Wild Wood" (in *Rich Lizard*) focus on the natural world. Other poems show her ability to uncover fresh images in the everyday concerns of children. In "Bubble" (in *Balloons*) a child discovers "*my breath*—wrapped in a quivering skin, . . . so marble round and glistening." The following poem leaves a memorable image of angry words hanging in an empty room:

Her words rose, swarming round,
Ugly, stinging shapes of sound,
Circling the foe.

His words bristled, black with warning,
Arched and stiff, they met the swarming,
Hissing low

They sprang and clawed and stung in space,
But shaped as words, they left no trace
Of fur or fang around the place

–Deborah Chandra. "The Argument" from *Rich Lizard and Other Poems* by Deborah Chandra. Copyright © 1993 by Deborah Chandra. Reprinted by permission of Farrar, Straus and Giroux, LLC.

Barbara Esbensen, a well-known writer of fiction and nonfiction, is a winner of the NCTE Poetry Award for poems about such varied topics as dance, discoveries, and animals. In *Who Shrank My Grandmother's House?* she discovers something new in "Doors" and "Pencils" and invites children to make science connections through such poems as "Sand Dollar," "Geode," and "Prism in the Window." *Dance with Me* includes poems about movement and invites children to imagine dances with their bodies as well as in their heads. *Words with Wrinkled Knees* is a collection of poems in which she examines the images in the letters of animal names. The title poem shows the imaginative scope of her poet's ear and eye.

The word is too heavy
   to lift    too cumbersome to
   lead through a room filled with
   relatives or small
   glass trinkets

E L E P H A N T

He must have invented it
himself. This is a lumbering
gray word    the ears of it
are huge and flap like loose
wings    a word with
wrinkled knees and toes
like boxing gloves

This word E L E P H A N T
sways toward us      bulk
and skull-bones filling up
the space      trumpeting
its own wide name
through its nose!

–Barbara Juster Esbensen. "Elephant," from *Words with
Wrinkled Knees* by Barbara Juster Esbensen. Copyright ©
1986 by Barbara Juster Esbensen. Reprinted by permission of
Tory Esbensen.

Four collections of poetry by James Stevenson demonstrate the versatility of this longtime-favorite picture-book author and illustrator. In *Popcorn, Candy Corn, Sweet Corn* and *Cornflakes,* Stevenson examines the world around him with a careful eye. In *Popcorn* he muses about a beloved dog, morning mist, and a harbor dredge. In "Along the Rusty Railroad Track" he wonders about an old derelict building and the ghostly inhabitant who might come to visit. "Coming or Going," in *Candy Corn,* considers the meaningful sound of a slamming, screeching screen door. "The Morning After Halloween" imagines that pieces of candy corn scattered across the street are a dragon's lost teeth. All these poems are enriched by Stevenson's careful page design, his choice of typeface, and his lovely watercolors.

## Anthologies of Poems for Children

Today poetry anthologies do not stay in print as long as they used to, because time limits are usually placed on permissions to use certain poems. This has meant the publication of fewer large anthologies and the proliferation of many specialized collections containing fewer than twenty poems.

### Comprehensive Poetry Collections

Every family with children will want to own at least one excellent anthology of poetry for children. Teachers will want to have several, including some for their personal use and some for the children's use.

*Sing a Song of Popcorn,* edited by Beatrice Schenk de Regniers and others, is a stunning collection of poetry for all children. The poems were first selected for a popular paperback called *Poems Children Will Sit Still For* (now out of print, this Scholastic title sold more than a quarter of a million copies). The selection of poetry for *Sing a Song of Popcorn* has been updated and is now illustrated in full color by nine Caldecott Medal–winning artists. The volume contains 128 poems that had to meet the criterion of captivating children. The represented poets range from Mary Ann Hoberman to Emily Dickinson. Included are such well-known poems as "Galoshes," "Eletelephony," "Brother," and "Stopping by Woods on a Snowy Evening." If a teacher or parent

could only have one collection, this would be the one to buy.

*Tomie de Paola's Book of Poems* is also a handsome anthology. Emily Dickinson's poem "There is no frigate like a book" is used to symbolically unite the cover, title page, introduction, and final page. These eighty-six well-chosen poems include classics like Stevenson's "Land of Counterpane" and contemporary poems like Myra Cohn Livingston's "Secret Door" and Eve Merriam's funny "Alligator on the Escalator." A unique addition is some poems in Spanish.

Lee Bennett Hopkins has compiled two special collections for younger children. *Side by Side: Poems to Read Together* contains fifty-seven poems, ranging from traditional to poems by such modern poets as David McCord, Karla Kuskin, Lilian Moore, Robert Frost, and Lewis Carroll. Hopkins's *Climb Into My Lap* contains fifty-three well-chosen poems including the traditional "Eensy Weensy Spider" and poems by well-loved authors Dorothy Aldis and Mary Ann Hoberman. Both collections invite the shared intimacy that comes from many hours of family poetry sharing.

Many parents and teachers will be attracted to the large *Random House Book of Poetry,* with its 572 poems selected by Jack Prelutsky and profusely illustrated with Arnold Lobel's lively pictures. For children who have known only Shel Silverstein's and Prelutsky's humorous verse, this is a good place to begin. Though much of the book is dominated by humorous verse (including some 38 poems by Prelutsky himself), fine poems by Robert Frost, Eve Merriam, Eleanor Farjeon, Emily Dickinson, Myra Cohn Livingston, Dylan Thomas, and others are interspersed with them. Arnold Lobel's humorous full-color illustrations also draw children to this anthology.

David Booth's *Til All the Stars Have Fallen* is an exciting collection of over seventy poems for children ages 8 and up. These include poems by such well-known Canadian poets as Dennis Lee and Jean Little and some wonderful new voices such as Duke Redbird, A. M. Klein, Lois Simmie, and George Swede. Kady Denton has echoed the poetic imagery of many of these poems in her expressive watercolors and collage illustrations.

*Knock at a Star: A Child's Introduction to Poetry,* compiled by the well-known adult poet and anthologist X. J. Kennedy and his wife, Dorothy, is a memorable collection of poetry for children 8 years old and up. The poets represented range widely, from adult poets like James Stephens, Emily Dickinson, Robert Frost, and William Stafford to children's poets Aileen Fisher, David McCord, and Lillian Morrison. Many familiar poems are here, but most of them are new and fresh to children's collections. The three section headings in this book also are addressed to children and provide an understanding of how poetry does

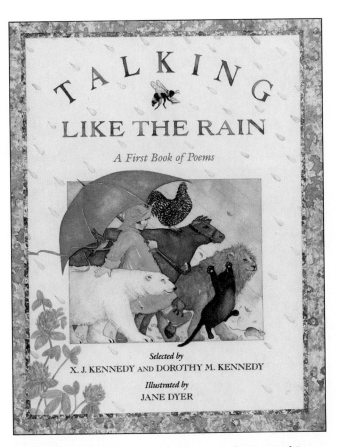

*X. J. and Dorothy M. Kennedy's poetry selection and Jane Dyer's lovely illustrations provide an inviting introduction of poetry for young children in* Talking Like the Rain.

From *Talking Like the Rain* by X. J. Kennedy and Dorothy Kennedy, illustrated by Jane Dyer. © 1992 Little, Brown and Company.

what it does: (1) "What Do Poems Do?" (make you laugh, tell stories, send messages, share feelings, start you wondering); (2) "What's Inside a Poem?" (images, word music, beats that repeat, likenesses); and (3) "Special Kinds of Poems." Teachers, librarians, and parents as well as children can learn from this wise book, which teaches at the same time as it develops enthusiasm for poetry.

X. J. and Dorothy Kennedy's *Talking Like the Rain,* illustrated by Jane Dyer, contains a mixture of old and new poems that have the kind of sound and word play that is particularly appealing to younger children. *Talking Like the Rain* contains 123 poems, ranging from Robert Louis Stevenson's "The Swing" to Myra Cohn Livingston's "Working with Mother."

Another anthology, which provides insight into how some thirty-nine poets work and feel about their poems, is Paul Janeczko's *The Place My Words Are Looking For.* Here Jack Prelutsky, X. J. Kennedy, Myra Cohn Livingston, and others talk about how they create their poetry, by providing personal comments and examples of their poems. Pictures of the poets accompany each section so children can see what their favorite poet looks like. For example, Lil-

lian Morrison comments on how she wrote "The Sidewalk Racer" (see p. 358):

Writing poems can be a way of pinning down a dream (almost); capturing a moment, a memory, a happening; and, at the same time, it's a way of sorting out your thoughts and feelings. Sometimes words tell you what you didn't know you knew.[10]

One of the most enduring current anthologies is *Reflections on a Gift of Watermelon Pickle and Other Modern Verses,* edited by Stephen Dunning and others. Illustrated with superb black-and-white photographs surrounded by much space, this anthology appeals to the eye as well as the ear of older students in middle school. They will take delight in "Sonic Boom" by John Updike, "Ancient History" by Arthur Guiterman, "Dreams" by Langston Hughes, and "How to Eat a Poem" by Eve Merriam. They will appreciate the honesty and realistic viewpoint of "Husbands and Wives," in which Miriam Hershenson tells of couples who ride the train from station to station without ever speaking to each other.

Several volumes of multicultural poetry for older children deserve to be considered among the "must-haves" in any home or classroom. Catherine Clinton has edited a fine anthology of poetry called *I, Too, Sing America: Three Centuries of African American Poetry.* Illustrated in muted tones by Stephen Alcorn, the book provides a chronological history of African American poetry by including poets from the 1700s to today. Naomi Shihab Nye has edited beautiful books that celebrate the arts of Mexico and the Middle East: *The Space Between Our Footsteps: Poems and Paintings from the Middle East* and *This Tree Is Older Than You Are: A Bilingual Gathering of Poems and Stories from Mexico with Paintings by Mexican Artists.* Nye has gathered poems, stories, and paintings from two widely separated and underrepresented peoples and provided important insights into their cultural, political, and social lives. In Nye's *This Same Sky: A Collection of Poems from Around the World,* 129 poets from 68 countries look at the world in poems rich with images and feeling. This is an international collection with universal connections.

### Specialized Collections

As mentioned above, as poetry permissions have become more expensive and more difficult to obtain for long lengths of time, anthologists have turned to making small, specialized collections. Most of these are organized for a particular age level or around certain subjects, such as dogs or seasons. Some are related to the ethnic origin of the poems, such as

---

[10]Lillian Morrison in Paul Janeczko, ed., *The Place My Words Are Looking For* (New York: Bradbury Press, 1990), p. 11.

poetry of Native Americans or poems that celebrate the experiences of African Americans. An increasing number of specialized collections contain stunning illustrations. Some of the best of these are noted in the text; others are listed in Resources for Teaching, "Specialized Collections of Poetry."

Children will find imaginative connections to themes such as "Time" or "Animals" and to subjects as varied as American history, music, and science through many of these anthologies. Barbara Rogasky's collection *Winter Poems*, beautifully illustrated by Trina Schart Hyman, recreates a cycle of time from late autumn to the first buds of spring with poems like Elizabeth Coatsworth's "Cat on a Night of Snow" and Robert Frost's "A Patch of Old Snow." Hyman has also illustrated John Updike's *A Child's Calendar*, a lovely collection of year-round poems that won a Caldecott Honor Medal in 2000. Ralph Fletcher takes older readers from winter into spring in *Ordinary Things: Poems from a Walk in Early Spring*, and Rebecca Dotlich extends the journey into summer with *Lemonade Sun and Other Summer Poems*.

Alice Schertle continues to delight children with her many special collections of poetry. Cows have never been more appealing than in the fifteen poems in her *How Now, Brown Cow?* Schertle ruminates on various topics in "The Cow's Complaint" (the grass is always greener) and "The Bull" (the title character wonders if the cows can see him bellowing, blowing, and striking a pose). Schertle's imaginative *Advice for a Frog* is a collection of poems about animals found in the wild, including "Black Rhino," "Iguana," and "Secretary Bird." Schertle explores the life of a cat in *I am the Cat* and life in a barn in *A Lucky Thing*.

Several books invite children to move to the beat and sing with the music of poetry. Michael R. Strickland has poems and songs about music and music makers, dancers and dance, in *My Own Song and Other Poems to Groove To* and *Poems That Sing to You*. Lee Bennett Hopkins's collection *Song and Dance* and Barbara Esbensen's *When I Dance* will have children dancing in the aisles. In *Singing America*, Neil Philip has collaborated with artist Michael McCurdy to tell America's history through the voices of Walt Whitman, Emily Dickinson, Gwendolyn Brooks, Woodie Guthrie, and seventy other poets. This handsome volume includes poems from many Native American tribes, traditional ballads, and Shaker anthems.

*Trina Schart Hyman has provided the details of a year's worth of family moments to accompany John Updike's* A Child's Calendar.

Illustration © 1999 by Trina Schart Hyman. Reprinted from *A Child's Calendar* by John Updike. Copyright © 1965, 1999 by John Updike. Used by permission of Holiday House.

*Artist Amanda Schaffer creates unique personalities for the bovines in Alice Schertle's collection of poetry,* How Now, Brown Cow?

Illustration from *How Now, Brown Cow?* by Alice Schertle, illustrations copyright © 1994 by Amanda Schaffer, reproduced by permission of Harcourt, Inc.

# RESOURCES FOR TEACHING

## Specialized Collections of Poetry

### CHILDREN'S EVERYDAY EXPERIENCES

| Compiler, Poet | Title | Age Level | Description |
|---|---|---|---|
| Arnold Adoff | *The Basket Counts* | 8 and up | Adoff celebrates the game of basketball. |
| Lee Bennett Hopkins | *Surprises* and *More Surprises* | 6–8 | With unerring taste for good poetry and what children enjoy, Hopkins has selected poems that children can read independently. |
| Lee Bennett Hopkins | *Extra Innings* | 10–12 | These poems about baseball will invite fans of the sport as well as non fans to enjoy the runs and the rhythms of the game. |
| Nikki Grimes | *A Dime a Dozen* | 12 and up | Twenty-eight poems explore the pleasure and pain of growing up. |
| Nikki Grimes | *It's Raining Laughter* | 6–8 | Bright photographs illustrate this sunny collection of poetry about everyday experiences. |
| Paul Janeczko | *Very Best (Almost) Friends* | 7–10 | A short but lively collection about the ups and downs of friendships. |
| Myra Cohn Livingston | *I Like You, If You Like Me* | 10 and up | Nearly a hundred poems that celebrate friends and comradeship. Some are funny, others are sad or lonesome. |
| Sally Mavor | *You and Me: Poems of Friendship* | 6–8 | Mavor's wonderful stitchery pictures illustrate these cheerful poems about friends. |
| Susan Marie Swanson | *Getting Used To the Dark* | 10–12 | Peter Catalanoto's pencil drawings enhance the mood of these poems about night. |
| Joyce Carol Thomas | *Gingerbread Days* | 7–12 | Floyd Cooper's warm paintings add to the glow of this collection about a child's world. |

### FAMILIES

| Compiler, Poet | Title | Age Level | Description |
|---|---|---|---|
| Ralph Fletcher | *Relatively Speaking* | 10–12 | Fletcher's poems about family reflect his upbringing in a large family. |
| Nikki Grimes | *Hopscotch Love* | 9–12 | Different characters experience love in different ways. |
| Myra Cohn Livingston | *Poems for Fathers* | 5–8 | Well-chosen poems that avoid typical stereotypes of father roles. |
| Marilyn Singer | *Family Reunion* | 5–10 | This collection about a summer reunion includes lyrical and amusing poems. |
| Dorthy and Michael R. Strickland | *Families: Poems Celebrating the African American Experience* | 5–8 | Poems celebrating African American family life. |
| Joyce Carol Thomas | *Gingerbread Days* | 7–12 | These poems follow an African American family throughout the year. |
| Janet Wong | *The Rainbow Hand: Poems About Mothers and Daughters* | 12 and up | This sensitive collection reveals the complex relations that exist between mothers and daughters. |

*continued*

# RESOURCES FOR TEACHING

## Specialized Collections of Poetry con't

### POETRY OF NATURE AND SEASONS

| Compiler, Poet | Title | Age Level | Description |
|---|---|---|---|
| Rebecca Kai Dotlich | *LemonadeSun* | 6–8 | Sunny poems about the pleasures of summertime. |
| Ralph Fletcher | *Ordinary Things* | 10 and up | These poems about a walk in the woods uncover the hidden treasures in ordinary things. |
| Josette Frank | *Snow Toward Evening* | 7–10 | Thirteen poems, one for each month plus an introductory poem. Thomas Locker has painted a full-page oil landscape for each poem. |
| Ed Young | *Birches* (Robert Frost) | 10 and up | Young never pictures the swinger of birches but leaves that to the reader's imagination. He does portray lovely birches seen from various perspectives. The complete poem is given at the end. |
| Tony Johnston | *An Old Shell* | 9 and up | Lovely poems written during a trip to the Galápagos Islands demonstrate the poet's versatility and sensitivity to nature. |
| Dorothy M. Kennedy | *Make Things Fly: Poems About the Wind* | 9–12 | A collection of poems about the wind includes old favorites by A. A. Milne and Robert Louis Stevenson. |
| J. Patrick Lewis | *Earth Verses and Water Rhymes* | 9–12 | Lewis begins with poems about the fall and progresses through the seasons. Among these poems' fresh images is his description of trees as "Earth umbrellas." |
| Myra Cohn Livingston | *If the Owl Calls Again* | 9 and up | Over 70 owl poems by poets ranging from Shakespeare to Eve Merriam and David McCord. Nursery rhymes and poems from the Navajo and Chippewa are included. |
| Charlotte F. Otten | *January Rides the Wind* | 6–8 | Otten uses poetic elements that young children will understand and enjoy in these short poems about each month of the year. |
| Barbara Rogasky | *Winter Poems* | 9 and up | See text. |
| Alice Schertle | *Advice for a Frog* | 9 and up | See text. |
| Alice Schertle | *A Lucky Thing* | 9 and up | A young writer sits at the window of an old barn and composes poems to the world she sees. |
| Marilyn Singer | *Sky Words* | 4–8 | Fifteen poems about the sky include reflections on the moon and the stars and fireworks and fog. |
| Marilyn Singer | *Turtle in July* | 4–8 | Singer focuses on a different animal for each month of the year, describing, for example, a deer who runs over the hard-packed January snow. |
| Jane Yolen | *One Upon the Ice* | 8–12 | Seventeen poets composed poems inspired by Jason Stemple's exquisite photographs of icy settings. |

### ANIMAL POEMS

| Compiler, Poet | Title | Age Level | Description |
|---|---|---|---|
| Kristine O'Connell George | *Little Dog Poems* | 5–8 | A little girl tells about a day in the life of her dog. |
| Bobbye S. Goldstein | *Bear in Mind* | 5–8 | Thirty poems about bears—live ones and teddy bears. Wonderful full-color pictures by William Pène DuBois. |
| David Greenburg | *Bugs!* | 5–8 | Delicious menu of funny poems about insects from the subversive author of *Slugs*. |
| Lee Bennett Hopkins | *Dinosaurs* | 8 and up | Eighteen poems, including "The Last Dinosaur" and "How the End Might Have Been." Good for discussion and dinosaur units. |

# RESOURCES FOR TEACHING

## Specialized Collections of Poetry con't

### ANIMAL POEMS con't

| Compiler, Poet | Title | Age Level | Description |
|---|---|---|---|
| Anne Isaacs | Cat up a Tree | 6–8 | Each separate poem provides the point of view of everyone concerned about a cat up in a tree. |
| Nancy Larrick | Cats Are Cats | 5–9 | Ed Young provides superb charcoal and pastel illustrations for these 25 well-chosen poems about cats. |
| Myra Cohn Livingston | Cat Poems | 5–9 | Over 20 poems about cats. Stylish black-and-white illustrations by Trina Schart Hyman. |
| Myra Cohn Livingston | Dog Poems | 5–9 | Some 20 poems, contemporary and traditional, illustrated by Leslie Morrow. |
| Jeff Moss | Bone Poems | 7–12 | Dinosaur lovers will devour these 40 poems inspired by a visit to the American Museum of Natural History. |
| Jack Prelutsky, ed. | The Beauty of the Beast | 7–12 | Meilo So's exquisite watercolor paintings make these beasts truly beautiful. Over 200 poems celebrate the animal world. |
| Alice Schertle | I Am the Cat | 7–12 | Schertle muses on the nine lives of a cat in these marvelous poems. |
| Judy Sierra | Antarctic Antics | 4–8 | Lively verses celebrate the emperor penguin (from the penguin's point of view). |
| Laura Whipple | Eric Carle's Animals Animals | 5–9 | See text. |
| Laura Whipple | Eric Carle's Dragons Dragons & Other Creatures That Never Were | 8 and up | See text. |

### HUMOROUS POETRY

| Compiler, Poet | Title | Age Level | Description |
|---|---|---|---|
| William Cole | Poem Stew | 6–12 | A hilarious feast of poems about food. Children love this collection. |
| William Cole | Oh, What Nonsense! | 7–12 | These collections contain some of Shel Silverstein's verses and other favorites of children. |
| Colin McNaughton | Who's Been Sleeping in my Porridge? Making Friends with Frankenstein | 7–12 | Two collections of wacky poems and pictures. |
| Dennis Lee | Dinosaur Dinner (with a Slice of Alligator Pie) | 5–10 | A wonderful collection of silly poems from a master at delighting children. |
| Jack Prelutsky | For Laughing Out Loud: Poems to Tickle Your Funnybone | 5–10 | Over 130 of the funniest poems. Lively colored illustrations by Marjorie Priceman add to the humor. |
| Jack Prelutsky | Poems by A. Nonny Mouse and A. Nonny Mouse Writes Again | 5–10 | The first volume contains over 70 of the silliest poems attributed by publishers to "anonymous." The sequel contains some 50 more poems that are short, silly, and fun to recite. |

*continued*

# RESOURCES FOR TEACHING

## Specialized Collections of Poetry con't

### HUMOROUS POETRY con't

| Compiler, Poet | Title | Age Level | Description |
| --- | --- | --- | --- |
| William Jay Smith | *Laughing Time* | 4–8 | Smith included limericks, rhyming ABCs, and imaginary dialogue in much of his nonsense verse. |
| Wallace Tripp | *Rose's Are Red and Violet's Are Blue* | 10 and up | Tripp's wonderful wacky illustrations bring a whole new interpretation to familiar verses and poems by poets such as Gertrude Stein, Edward Lear, and Henry Wadsworth Longfellow. |

### MULTIETHNIC POETRY COLLECTIONS

| Compiler, Poet | Title | Age Level | Description |
| --- | --- | --- | --- |
| Arnold Adoff | *My Black Me* | 8 and up | A collection of contemporary poems that mixes black pride with power and protest. Brief biographical notes on each of the poets add interest. |
| Arnold Adoff | *I Am the Darker Brother: An Anthology of Modern Poems by Black Americans* | 10 and up | Contains some of the best-known poetry of Langston Hughes, Gwendolyn Brooks, and Countee Cullen, as well as some modern poets. |
| Francisco X. Alarcon | *From the Belly Button of the Moon and Other Summer Poems* | 5–8 | Alarcon's joyous bilingual poems about summer in Mexico will delight young children. |
| James Berry | *When I Dance Everywhere Faces Everywhere* | 10 and up | See text. |
| John Bierhorst | *On the Road of Stars* | 5–8 | Native American night poems and sleep charms. |
| John Bierhorst | *In the Trail of the Wind* | 12 and up | See text. |
| Ashley Bryan | *Ashley Bryan's ABC of African American Poetry* | 5–8 | African American poets and their poems from A to Z, illustrated with Bryan's usual sunny style. |
| Lori M. Carlson | *Cool Salsa* | 12 and up | Bilingual poems about growing up Latino in the United States. |
| Lori M. Carlson | *Sol a Sol* | 5–8 | These vibrant poems follow a family from morning to sundown with poems in both English and Spanish. |
| Ann Nolan Clark | *In My Mother's House* | 6–10 | See text. |
| Paul Laurence Dunbar | *Jump Back, Honey* | 8 and up | See text. |
| Tom Feelings | *Soul Looks Back in Wonder* | 5–9 | See text. |
| Nikki Giovanni | *Genie in a Jar* | 4–8 | See text. |
| Nikki Giovanni | *The Sun Is So Quiet* | 4–8 | Thirteen of Giovanni's sensitive poems, illustrated by Ashley Bryan. |
| Eloise Greenfield | *Honey I Love* | 4–8 | See text. |
| Eloise Greenfield | *Angels* | 4–8 | See text. |

# RESOURCES FOR TEACHING

## Specialized Collections of Poetry con't

### MULTIETHNIC POETRY COLLECTIONS con't

| Compiler, Poet | Title | Age Level | Description |
|---|---|---|---|
| Nikki Grimes | *Is It Far to Zanzibar? Poems About Tanzania* | 8 and up | Thirteen evocative poems about life in Zanzibar. |
| bel hooks | *Happy to be Nappy* | 4–8 | See text. |
| Hettie Jones | *The Trees Stand Shining* | 5–9 | See text. |
| Monica Gunning | *Not a Copper Penny in Me House* | 4–8 | Every day life and special celebrations of the author's Jamaican childhood. |
| Minfong Ho | *Maples in the Mist* | 7 and up | Lovely watercolor illustrations accompany these fine translations of Tang Dynasty poems. |
| Wade Hudson | *Pass It On* | 5–9 | See text. |
| Michio Mado | *The Magic Pocket* | 4–8 | A lovely collection of verses for young children by a Japanese author. Mitsumasa Anno's illustrations add charm. |
| Pat Mora | *Confetti* | 4–8 | Bright pictures by Enrique O. Sanchez enliven this warm collection of poems about a young girl's life in the Southwest. |
| Effie Lee Newsome | *Wonders: The Best Children's Poems of Effie Lee Newsome* | 4–8 | See text. |
| Charlotte Pomerantz | *If I Had a Paka: Poems in Eleven Languages* | 4–8 | Poems build a child's cross-cultural vocabulary by repeating a key word in a different language, such as Swahili. English-language clues and the clear pictures by Nancy Tafuri help define meanings. |
| Cynthia Rylant | *Waiting to Waltz* | 9–12 | The poems in Rylant's book capture the essence of growing up in a small town in Appalachia. |
| Virginia Driving Hawk Sneve | *Dancing Teepees* | 8–12 | See text. |
| Jamake Steptoe | *In Daddy's Arms I Am Tall* | 6–9 | Steptoe's stunning collages bring energy and warmth to this collection of poems about African American fathers. |
| Brian Swann | *The House with No Door* | 6–9 | On each page a poem poses a riddle and Ashley Bryan's lively illustrations provide the possible answers. |
| Brian Swann | *Touching the Distance* | 6–9 | More riddle poems from Native American traditions. |
| Luci Tapahonso | *A Breeze Swept Through* | 10 and up | See text. |
| Luci Tapahonso | *Songs of Shiprock Fair* | 4–8 | See text. |
| Janet Wong | *Good Luck and Other Poems, A Suitcase of Seaweed and Other Poems* | 12 and up | Wong's versatility as a poet is evident in these two collections. |
| Janet Wong | *Night Garden: Poems From the World of Dreams* | 9 and up | See text. |

*Tom Feelings's striking artwork accompanies his selections of poetry by African Americans in* Soul Looks Back in Wonder.

From *Soul Looks Back in Wonder* by Tom Feelings, copyright © 1993 by Tom Feelings, illustrations. Used by permission of Dial Books for Young Readers, a division of Penguin Putnam Inc.

Collected African American poetry can be found in such attractive illustrated editions as Tom Feelings's *Soul Looks Back in Wonder,* a winner of the Coretta Scott King Award for illustration. Feelings has chosen selections from thirteen poets that celebrate African American heritage and sing of African pride. Wade Hudson's collection *Pass It On,* illustrated by Floyd Cooper, is broader in scope. It includes poems like Nikki Giovanni's "Prickled Pickles Don't Smile" and Henry Dumas's "Peas," which are light in tone, as well as more serious reflections such as Lucille Clifton's "Listen Children." All volumes include well-known poets and introduce newer voices.

Hettie Jones's *The Trees Stand Shining* represents Native American poets of the past century. These short song-poems are accompanied by Robert Andrew Parker's impressionistic watercolor paintings that evoke the Native American reverence for the sun and moon, the eagle and owl. Stephen Gammell illustrates *Dancing Teepees,* edited by Virginia Driving Hawk Sneve, with sensitive full-color watercolors. This is a handsome book of some twenty poems chosen from various tribes. John Bierhorst also emphasizes humanity's close relationship to nature in his anthologies, *In the Trail of the Wind: American Indian Poems and Ritual Orations* and *On the Road of Stars: Native American Night Poems and Sleep Chants.* These authentic collections include poems of the Aztec, Maya, and Eskimo as well as North American Indians. It is more appropriate for older students.

We can be grateful for the reissue of . . . *I Never Saw Another Butterfly,* edited by Hana Volavkova.

This book contains poems and pictures created by children in the Terezin concentration camp from 1942 to 1944. These drawings and poems are all that are left of the fifteen thousand children who passed through this camp on their way to Auschwitz. They are an eloquent statement of their courage and optimism in the midst of despair.

### Picture-Book Editions of Single Poems

It was inevitable that poetry should also follow the trend to single-poem editions already established by the many beautifully illustrated editions of single fairy tales and folk songs.

The first book of poetry to be presented with the Newbery Medal was *A Visit to William Blake's Inn* by Nancy Willard. In the same year, the illustrators for this book, Alice and Martin Provensen, received a Caldecott Honor Award. Inspired by Blake's work, Nancy Willard created a book of connected poems about life at an imaginary inn run by William Blake himself. Children ages 8 and up will be intrigued by the detailed pictures of the inn and its guests.

Susan Jeffers has illustrated two well-known poems in picture-book format. Her pictures for Frost's *Stopping by Woods on a Snowy Evening* evoke the quiet stillness of the forest in contrast to the staid New England village. In *Hiawatha,* she pictures the romantic Indian in keeping with Longfellow's poem and time. Lovely pictures of Nokomis and a growing Hiawatha hold children's interest. The artist is not always consistent in portraying the age of the Iroquois lad, however; he seems older, then younger, before he reaches manhood and leaves the tribe.

In some instances these stunning picture books may create new interest in a poem like *Hiawatha* or *Paul Revere's Ride.* It is generally a good idea to read the poem through once before sharing the pictures, because turning the pages to look at the illustrations interrupts the flow of the poem. Many of these picture/poetry books provide the text of the complete poem at the end of the book. Because poetry is the most concentrated and connotative use of language, it needs to be shared several times anyway.

Contemporary poets are also represented in single-poem editions. Eve Merriam's *Bam Bam Bam* and *Ten Tiny Roses* are vividly illustrated by Dan Yaccarino and Julia Gorton, respectively. These bouncing rhymes are invitations for younger readers to chant and move to. Chris Raschka's lively linear artistic style seems perfect for Nikki Giovanni's wonderfully hopeful poem *The Genie in the Jar* and bel hooks's *Happy to be Nappy.* Both of these books celebrate the uniqueness of African American culture yet speak joyfully to all children.

## Sharing Poetry with Children

There can be no question that very young children respond spontaneously to the sensory-motor action of "Ride a Cock Horse" or "Peas porridge hot/Peas porridge cold." Children in the primary grades love to join in with the wacky words and rhythm of Jack Prelutsky's "Bleezer's Ice Cream Store" in *The New Kid on the Block*. Younger children naturally delight in the sound, rhythm, and language of poetry.

We have seen that sometime toward the end of the primary grades, children begin to lose interest in poetry. The poet William Jay Smith comments: "How natural and harmonious it all is at the beginning; and yet what happens along the way later to make poetry to many children the dullest and least enjoyable of literary expressions?"[11] There may be many reasons for this lessening of enthusiasm. Some studies suggest that teachers tend to read traditional poems or sentimental poems that are *about* childhood rather than contemporary poems that would be more suited to the modern child's maturity, experiences, and interests.[12] Poems that are too difficult, too abstract for children to understand, will also be rejected.

Other studies have indicated that teachers neglect poetry. Ann Terry found, for example, that more than 75 percent of the teachers in the middle grades read poetry to their children only once a month or less.[13] Children can hardly be expected to develop a love of poetry when they hear it less than nine times a year! It is also possible to hear too much poetry, particularly at one time. Teachers who read poetry for an hour or have every child read a poem on a Friday afternoon are contributing to children's dislike of poetry as much as those who simply neglect it. This also happens when we relegate poetry to a "Poetry Week" in the spring. Poetry needs to be shared naturally every day by a teacher who loves it.

Another way to create distaste for poetry is by requiring children to memorize certain poems, usually selected by the teacher. It is especially dull when everyone has to learn the same poem. Many children do enjoy memorizing favorite poems, provided they can do it voluntarily and can select the poem. But

choosing to commit a certain poem to memory is quite different from being required to do so.

Too-detailed analysis of every poem is also detrimental to children's enjoyment of poetry. An appropriate question or comment to increase meaning is fine; but critical analysis of every word in a poem, every figure of speech, and every iambic verse, is lethal to appreciation. Jean Little captures one student's reaction to too much analysis in this poem:

I used to like "Stopping by Woods on a Snowy
    Evening,"
I liked the coming darkness,
The jingle of harness bells, breaking—and adding
    to—the stillness,
The gentle drift of snow . . .

But today, the teacher told us what everything
    stood for.
The woods, the horse, the miles to go, the sleep—
They all have "hidden meanings."
It's grown so complicated now that,
Next time I drive by,
I don't think I'll bother to stop.

> –Jean Little. "After English Class" from *Hey World, Here I Am!* by Jean Little. New York: Harper & Row, 1989.

### Creating a Climate for Enjoyment

There have always been teachers who love poetry and who share their enthusiasm for poetry with students. There are teachers who make poetry a natural part of the daily program of living and learning. They realize that poetry should not be presented under the pressure of a tight time schedule, but should be enjoyed every day. Children should be able to relax and relish the humor and beauty that the sharing of poetry affords. The web "In Praise of Poetry" describes some of the classroom experiences with poetry these teachers provide for their children.

### Finding Time for Poetry

Teachers who would develop children's delight in poetry will find time to share poetry with them sometime each day and find ways to connect poetry to the experiences in children's lives. They know that anytime is a good time to read a poem to children, but they will especially want to capitalize on exciting experiences like the first snow, a birthday party, or the arrival of a classmate's new baby brother. Perhaps there has been a fight on the playground and someone is still grumbling and complaining—that might be a good time to share poetry about feelings. The teacher could read Karla Kuskin's "I Woke Up This Morning" (in *Dogs & Dragons*), and then everyone could

---

[11]Virginia Haviland, and William Jay Smith, *Children and Poetry* (Washington, D.C.: Library of Congress, 1969), p. iv.

[12]Chow Loy Tom, "Paul Revere Rides Ahead: Poems Teachers Read to Pupils in the Middle Grades," *Library Quarterly* 43 (January 1973): 27–38.

[13]Ann Terry, *Children's Poetry Preferences*, p. 29.

# IN PRAISE OF POETRY

## POETRY CELEBRATIONS

*I'm in Charge of Celebrations* (Baylor)
Find something simple and special to celebrate every day. Compile a class list of special celebrations. Hold a Poetry Celebration Day. Invite parents and other special people to read or recite favorite poems. Display class poetry collections.

*Eats* (Adoff)
*Poem Stew* (Cole)
*Sweets and Treats* (Goldstein)
*Peas* (Levy)
*Spaghetti* (Silverstein)
Have a class feast, inspired by poems about food.

## SENSORY EXPLORATIONS

*Mud* (Worth)
*Peach* (Rauter)
*Greensweet* (Levy)
Blindfold group members. Have them touch, taste, or smell objects. List words or phrases they use to describe their sensory impressions. Compare these to ways that poets have compared similar experiences.

## POETRY CORNER

*Hailstones and Halibut Bones* (O Neill)
*Everybody Needs a Rock* (Baylor)
*These Small Stones* (Faber)
Establish a rotating display around special topics such as Small Things or Color. Display poems, artwork, and artifacts that fit the theme.

## READING ALOUD

*Harriet Tubman* (Greenfield)
Read poems together in one voice.

*Bam Bam 3am* (Merriam)
Read poems and create hand or body movements to accompany yourselves.

*The Grobbles* (Prelutsky)
*The Song of the Train* (McCord)
Plan choral reading with single and many voices, loud and soft sounds, high and low pitch.

*I Am Phoenix* (Fleischman)
*Joyful Noise* (Fleischman)
*Big Talk* (Fleischman)
Read poems in two, three, or four, voices. Write your own poems for several voices.

## POETRY MODELS

*Poetry from A to Z* (Janeczko)
*Prayers from the Ark* (Bernos de Gaztold)
*A House Is a House for Me* (Hoberman)
*Words with Wrinkled Knees* (Esbensen)
*I am Writing a Poem About A Game of Poetry* (Myra Cohn Livingston)
Use poems as springboards to try your own forms.

## POETRY CYCLES

Find and read poems about similar themes.
*Feelings Wrong Start* (Chute),
*When I Woke Up This Morning* (Kuskin)
*Weather Fog* (Sandburg),
*Fog* (Chandra)

## POETRY/PROSE CONNECTIONS

*Quiet Please* (Merriam)
Make a collection of quiet phrases.

*Hailstones and Halibut Bones* (O Neill)
*A Song of Colors* (Hindley)
Think of a favorite color. Write color poems or color phrases.

Find poems to match the mood, theme, etc. of favorite books.

*Until I Saw the Sea* (Moore)/
*Time of Wonder* (McCloskey)
*Mother to Son* (Hughes)/
*Scorpions* (Myers)

## HAIKU

*Black Swan/White Crow* (Lewis)
*Cricket Never Does* (Livingston)
Write haiku or tanka poems.
Illustrate them with collage or prints.

## LIMERICKS

*The Hopeful Trout and Other Limericks* (Ciardi)
*The Book of Pigericks* (Lobel)
Make a class book of limericks on a theme or topic.

## POETRY AND THE ARTS

*Imaginary Gardens* (Sullivan)
*Families, Children, Seascapes* (Roalf)
Collect reproductions of paintings based on a theme and choose poems that match each painting.

*Poems That Sing to You* (Strickland)
Select poems about a topic. Choose music that matches the mood, rhythm, or theme of the poems. Put together a poetry reading to music.

## PATTERNED POEMS

*Splish Splash* (Graham)
*Doodle Dandies* (Lewis)
Write a poem about a concrete object like trees, waterfalls, or popsicles. Change it into a visual art form.

laugh the bad feelings away. Poetry can also be thought of as a delicious snack to nibble on during transition times between going out to recess or the last few minutes of the day. Anytime is a good time for a poetry snack!

Inspiring teachers frequently read poetry cycles, three or four poems with the same theme. One teacher capitalized on children's interest in "special places." She shared Byrd Baylor's poetic story *Your Own Best Secret Place* and Charlotte Huck's specialized collection of poems *Secret Places* with a group of third graders. Later the children wrote about their own secret places in both prose and poetry. Children also enjoy selecting a particular subject and creating their own poetry cycles from anthologies in the library or classroom.

One way to be sure to share poetry every day is to relate children's favorite prose stories to poetry. One teacher who keeps a card file of poems always slips one or two cards into the book that is to be read aloud that day. For example, after sharing *Whistle for Willie* by Ezra Jack Keats, Jack Prelutsky's "Whistling" (in *Read-Aloud Rhymes for the Very Young*) could be read. Librarians and teachers will want to make their own poetry/prose connections. We hope that Resources for Teaching, "Connections between Poetry and Prose" will get you started.

Other subjects and activities in the curriculum can be enriched with poetry. A "science discovery walk" could be preceded by reading Florence McNeil's "Squirrels in My Notebook" (in *Til All the Stars Have Fallen*, ed. David Booth), in which a child records his observations of a squirrel, including the fact that he couldn't repeat what the squirrel said to him! Older children would enjoy Moffitt's well-known poem "To Look at Anything" (in *Reflections on a Gift of Watermelon Pickle*, ed. Stephen Dunning et al.). A math lesson might be introduced with Carl Sandburg's "Arithmetic" (in his *Arithmetic*) or poems from Lee Bennett Hopkins's collection, *Marvelous Math*. Many poems can enhance social studies, including Neil Philip's *Singing America* and Rosemary and Stephen Vincent Benét's *A Book of Americans*, which includes the well-known poems "Nancy Hanks," "Abraham Lincoln," and "Western Wagons." The first poem in their collection is "Christopher Columbus," but the second one is "The Indians," about the people who were here first.

Several volumes pair poetry and art in unique ways. Charles Sullivan's *Imaginary Gardens* makes such matches as a Grandma Moses painting with Lydia Child's "Over the River and Through the Woods," and "Afternoon on a Hill" by Edna St. Vincent Millay or "Spring" by Marjorie Frost Fraser with Andrew Wyeth's painting of "Christina's World." This last pairing is pure genius. The repeated phrase *to tangled grass I cling* is so right for Christina, who must pull her body back to that bleak house on the hill. Norma Panzer has created similar matches with American art and poetry in *Celebrate America*. This attractive volume includes works and images that represent the many cultures in American life both past and present. These are books that middle graders would enjoy looking at and reading over and over again. In addition, books like these might inspire children to make their own connections between art and poetry.

Children will also be delighted with excellent poetry books on sports, such as Robert Burleigh's *Hoops*, Lee Bennett Hopkins's *Extra Innings*, and *American Sports Poems* selected by R. R. Knudson and May Swenson. All areas of the curriculum can be enhanced with poetry; teachers should realize that there are poems on *every* subject, from dinosaurs to quasars and black holes. The Teaching Feature "Studying Poetry and Nature" shows how one teacher found connections between poetry and the natural world.

## Reading Poetry to Children

Poetry should be read in a natural voice with a tone that fits the meaning of the poem. Generally, the appropriate pace for reading poetry is slower than for reading prose. It is usually recommended that a poem be read aloud a second time, perhaps to refresh children's memories, to clarify a point, or to savor a particular image. Most poetry, especially good poetry, is so concentrated and compact that few people can grasp its meaning in one exposure. Following the reading of a poem, discussion should be allowed to flow. In certain instances discussion is unnecessary or superfluous. Spontaneous chuckles might follow the reading of Kaye Starbird's "Eat-It-All Elaine" (in *The Random House Book of Poetry for Children*, ed. Prelutsky), while a thoughtful silence might be the response to Robert P. Tristram Coffin's "Forgive My Guilt" (in *Reflections on a Gift of Watermelon Pickle*, ed. S. Dunning et al.). It is not necessary to discuss or do something with each poem read, other than enjoy it. The most important thing you as a teacher or librarian can do when you are reading poetry is share your enthusiasm for the poem.

## Discussing Poetry with Children

After teachers or librarians have shared a poem with children, they may want to link it to other poems children have read, comparing and contrasting how the poet dealt with the concept. This could open up natural avenues for thoughtful discussion. Suppose a second-grade teacher reads the picture book *The Accident* by the Carricks to children. She or he may want to follow

# RESOURCES FOR TEACHING

## Connections between Poetry and Prose

| Subject/Theme | Age Level | Poems | Prose |
|---|---|---|---|
| Bears | 5–7 | "Algy Met a Bear," Anon., in *I Never Saw a Purple Cow*, ed. E. Clark | *The Bear's Toothache* (David McPhail) |
| | | "The Bear with Golden Hair" by Karla Kuskin, in *Dogs & Dragons, Trees & Dreams* | *Corduroy* (Don Freeman) |
| | | "Oh, Teddy Bear" by Jack Prelutsky, in *New Kid on the Block* | *Ira Sleeps Over* (Bernard Waber) |
| | | "Grandpa Bear's Lullaby" by Jane Yolen, in *Sing a Song of Popcorn*, ed. de Regniers et al. | *Where's My Teddy?* (Jez Alborough) |
| | | "Koala" by Karla Kuskin, in *Dogs & Dragons, Trees & Dreams* | *Koala Lou* (Mem Fox) |
| | | *Bear in Mind* by Bobbye Goldstein | *Goldilocks and the Three Bears* (Jan Brett) |
| | | *The Three Bears Rhyme Book* by Jane Yolen | *Jamberry* (Bruce Degen) |

| Subject/Theme | Age Level | Poems | Prose |
|---|---|---|---|
| Family | 5–7 | "Little" by Dorothy Aldis, in *Tomie de Paola's Book of Poems* | *A Chair for My Mother* (Vera Williams) |
| | | "My Brother" by Marci Ridlon, in *The Random House Book of Poetry for Children*, ed. Jack Prelutsky | *Dogger* (Shirley Hughes) |
| | | "My Father's Words" by Claudia Lewis, in *Poems for Fathers*, ed. Myra Cohn Livingston | *Mr. Rabbit and the Lovely Present* (Charlotte Zolotow) |
| | | "All Kinds of Grands" by Lucille Clifton, in *Sing a Song of Popcorn*, ed. Beatrice Shenk de Regniers et al. | *The Whales' Song* (Dyan Sheldon) |
| | | | *The Stories Julian Tells* (Ann Cameron) |

| Subject/Theme | Age Level | Poems | Prose |
|---|---|---|---|
| Feelings | 6–8 | "When I Woke Up This Morning" by Karla Kuskin, in *Dogs & Dragons, Trees & Dreams* | *Alexander and the Terrible, Horrible, No Good, Very Bad Day* (Judith Viorst) |
| | | "When I Was Lost" by Dorothy Aldis, in *The Random House Book of Poetry for Children*, ed. Jack Prelutsky | *The Hating Book* (Charlotte Zolotow) |
| | | "Wrong Start" by Marchette Chute, in *The Random House Book of Poetry for Children*, ed. Jack Prelutsky | *Lost in the Museum* (Miriam Cohen) |
| | | "Sometimes I Feel this Way" by John Ciardi, in *A Jar of Tiny Stars*, ed. Bernice Cullinan | *Will I Have a Friend?* (Miriam Cohen) |
| | | "A Small Discovery" by James Emannuel, in *Tomie de Paola's Book of Poetry* | *Osa's Pride* (Ann Grifalconi) |
| | | "I'm in a Rotten Mood" by Jack Prelutsky, in *The New Kid on the Block* | *When Sophie Gets Angry—Really, Really Angry* (Bang) |
| | | | *Lilly's Purple Plastic Purse* (Kevin Henkes) |

# RESOURCES FOR TEACHING

## Connections between Poetry and Prose con't

| Subject/Theme | Age Level | Poems | Prose |
|---|---|---|---|
| Sibling rivalry | 5–7 | "Brother" by Mary Ann Hoberman, in *Tomie de Paola's Book of Poems* | *A Baby Sister for Frances* (Russell Hoban) |
| | | "I'm Disgusted with My Brother" by Jack Prelutsky, in *New Kid on the Block* | *Julius the Baby of the World* (Kevin Henkes) |
| | | "For Sale" by Shel Silverstein, in *A Light in the Attic* | *She Come Bringing Me That Little Baby Girl* (Eloise Greenfield) |
| | | "Moochie" by Eloise Greenfield, in *Honey, I Love* | *Peter's Chair* (Ezra Jack Keats) |
| | | | *Titch* (Pat Hutchins) |
| | | | *Noisy Nora* (Rosemary Wells) |

| Subject/Theme | Age Level | Poems | Prose |
|---|---|---|---|
| Death/loss | 7–8 | "Chelsea" by James Stevenson, in *Popcorn* | *The Accident* (Carol and Donald Carrick) |
| | | "For a Bird" by Myra Cohn Livingston, in *A Song I Sang to You* | *Mustard* (Charlotte Graeber) |
| | | "Skipper" by Gwendolyn Brooks, in *Bronzeville Boys and Girls* | *The Tenth Good Thing About Barney* (Judith Viorst) |
| | | "For a Dead Kitten" by Sara Henderson Hay, in *Reflections on a Gift of Watermelon Pickle*, ed. Stephen Dunning et al. | *Blow Me a Kiss, Miss Lily* (Nancy W. Carlstrom) |
| | | "Poem" by Langston Hughes, in *The Dream Keeper* | *The Very Best of Friends* (Margaret Wild) |

| Subject/Theme | Age Level | Poems | Prose |
|---|---|---|---|
| Folktales | 7–8 | "Look Cinderella" by Myra Cohn Livingston, in *A Song I Sang to You* | *Cinderella* (Charles Perrault) |
| | | "The Gingerbread Man" by Rowena Bennett, in *Sing A Song of Popcorn*, ed. Beatrice Shenk de Regniers et al. | *The Gingerbread Boy* (Paul Galdone) |
| | | | *The Frog Prince* (Edith Tarcov) |
| | | "In Search of Cinderella" by Shel Siverstein, in *Where the Sidewalk Ends* | *The Frog Prince Continued* (Jon Scieszka) |
| | | "Spaghetti" by Shel Silverstein, in *A Light in the Attic* | *The Three Little Pigs* (James Marshall) |
| | | "The Builders" by Sara Henderson Hay, in *Reflections on a Gift of Watermelon Pickle*, ed. Stephen Dunning et al. | *The True Story of the 3 Little Pigs!* (Jon Scieszka) |
| | | | *Strega Nona* (Tomie de Paola) |

| Subject/Theme | Age Level | Poems | Prose |
|---|---|---|---|
| Secret places | 7–8 | "Hideout" by Aileen Fisher, in *Tomie de Paola's Book of Poems* | *The Little Island* (Golden MacDonald) |
| | | "Secret Place" by Dorothy Aldis, in *Climb Onto My Lap*, ed. Lee Bennett Hopkins | *Dawn* (Uri Shulevitz) |
| | | "Tree House" by Shel Silverstein, in *A Light in the Attic* | *When I Was Young in the Mountains* (Cynthia Rylant) |
| | | *Secret Places*, ed. by Charlotte Huck | *Wild Boy* (Mordecai Gerstein) |
| | | *Your Own Best Secret Place*, ed. Byrd Baylor | |

*continued*

## Connections between Poetry and Prose con't

| Subject/Theme | Age Level | Poems | Prose |
|---|---|---|---|
| Courage and pride | 10–12 | "Mother to Son" by Langston Hughes, in *The Dream Keeper*<br>"I Too Sing America" by Langston Hughes, in *The Dream Keeper*<br>"Otto" by Gwendolyn Brooks, in *Bronzeville Boys and Girls*<br>. . . *I Never Saw Another Butterfly*, ed. by Hana Volavkova<br>*It's a Woman's World*, ed. by Neil Philip | *Roll of Thunder, Hear My Cry* (Mildred Taylor)<br>*Sounder* (William Armstrong)<br>*The Most Beautiful Place in the World* (Ann Cameron)<br>*Running the Road to ABC* (Dennis Lauture)<br>*Number the Stars* (Lois Lowry)<br>*Lyddie* (Katherine Paterson)<br>*The Land I Lost: Adventures of a Boy in Vietnam* (Quang Nhuong Huynh) |

| Subject/Theme | Age Level | Poems | Prose |
|---|---|---|---|
| The environment | 12–13 | "To Look at Anything" by John Moffit, in *Reflections on a Gift of Watermelon Pickle*, ed. Stephen Dunning et al.<br>"Hurt No Living Thing" by Christina Rossetti, in *The Random House Book of Poetry for Children*, ed. Jack Prelutsky<br>*Sierra*, by Diane Siebert<br>"Tree Coming Up" by Constance Levy, in *I'm Going to Pet a Worm Today* | *Window* (Jeannie Baker)<br>*On the Far Side of the Mountain* (Jean George)<br>*Who Really Killed Cock Robin?* (Jean George)<br>*One Day in the Tropical Rain Forest* (Jean George)<br>*Hawk, I'm Your Brother* (Byrd Baylor)<br>*The Way to Start a Day* (Byrd Baylor)<br>*The Year of the Panda* (Miriam Schlein)<br>*The Great Kapok Tree* (Lynne Cherry)<br>*Ancient Ones* (Barbara Bash) |

| Subject/Theme | Age Level | Poems | Prose |
|---|---|---|---|
| Relationships | 10–14 | "Some People" by Charlotte Zolotow, in *Very Best (Almost) of Friends*, ed. Paul Janeczko<br>"Poem" by Langston Hughes, in *The Dream Keeper*<br>*Hey World. Here I Am!* by Jean Little<br>"Friendship" by Shel Silverstein, in *A Light in the Attic*<br>*I Like You, If You Like Me* by Myra Cohn Livingston | *Bridge to Terabithia* (Katherine Paterson)<br>*The Sign of the Beaver* (Elizabeth Speare)<br>*Other Bells for Us to Ring* (Robert Cormier)<br>*The Starplace* (Vicki Grove) |

| Subject/Theme | Age Level | Poems | Prose |
|---|---|---|---|
| Holocaust/war | 11–14 | . . . *I Never Saw Another Butterfly*, ed. Hana Volavkova<br>"Earth" by John Hall Wheelock, in *Relections on a Gift of Watermelon Pickle*, ed. Stephen Dunning et al.<br>*Music and Drum: Voices of War and Peace, Hope and Drums*, ed. Laura Robb<br>"The House That Fear Built: Warsaw, 1943" by Jane Flanders, in *War and the Pity of War*, ed. Neil Philip<br>"War" by Dan Roth, in *Sing a Song of Popcorn*, ed. Beatrice Shenk de Regniers et al.<br>"Inside" by Kim China, in *This Same Sky*, ed. Naomi Nye | *Anne Frank: Diary of a Young Girl* (Anne Frank)<br>*Hiroshima No Pika* (Toshi Maruki)<br>*Rose Blanche* (Christophe Gallaz and Roberto Innocenti)<br>*Number the Stars* (Lois Lowry)<br>*The Wall* (Eve Bunting)<br>*Year of Impossible Goodbyes* (Sook Choi)<br>*The Man from the Other Side* (Uri Orlev) |

## *Studying Poetry and Nature*

**Teaching Feature**

Linda Woolard combines poetry and nature study with her fifth-grade class on their visits to the school's William E. Miller Land Lab in Newark, Ohio. The students explore the land lab's trails on a wooded hillside by the school. Each student has selected a favorite spot and returns there each season. They usually spend the first ten minutes in silence to better use all their senses. They observe the woods carefully, sketching and recording their observations. They may list their sightings using books to identify wildflowers, rocks, animals, or other special finds. Linda encourages them to record their thoughts and feelings also.

Before they visit the wooded area, Linda reads to them from books and poems, such as Jean George's *My Side of the Mountain*, Jim Arnosky's books on sketching nature in different seasons, John Moffitt's poem "To Look at Anything" (in *Reflections on a Gift of Watermelon Pickle*, ed. S. Dunning et al.), Marcie Han's "Fueled" (in the same anthology), Lew Sarrett's "Four Little Foxes" (in *Piping Down the Valleys Wild*, ed. Nancy Larrick), and many more.

The children bring back their notebooks, nature specimens, such as interesting fossils, leaf rubbings, and sketches, lists of bird sightings and wildflowers, and so on. These are placed on a special bulletin board. Poems are reread, reference books consulted, and pictures mounted. Many of the careful observations now become part of poems. Two that came from these trips follow:

The Woods Are So Still
Still
Still
The woods are very
Still;
Water dripping, dripping
Off the trees.
Nothing moves
It all stays very
Still.
–*Katie Hopkins*

Eagle
Soaring high
   Soaring low
From mountain to hill
   And back
Wind whispering under his
magnificent wings
   gently falling
climbing
   falling
      climbing
      then he lands.
–*Brian Dove*

Linda writes poetry at the same time as her students do, and she is brave enough to ask them to make suggestions on how she can improve! Obviously, this is another classroom where a love of poetry is nurtured by much sharing of poetry, relating it to children's experiences, and modeling the joy of writing it by the teacher herself.

*Linda Woolard, teacher*
Miller Elementary School, Newark, Ohio

---

that book with Sarah Henderson Hay's "For a Dead Kitten" (in *Reflections on a Gift of Watermelon Pickle*, ed. S. Dunning et al.) or Myra Cohn Livingston's "For a Bird" (in *Poem Stew*, ed. William Cole). Children could then compare how the person in the poems felt about the cat and the little bird. Were they as hurt by their loss as Christopher was when Bodger was struck by a truck? How much detail can an author and artist give? How much can a poet give? With many such discussions, children will eventually see how poetry has to capture the essence of a feeling in very few words and how important each of the words must be. Starting then with the content (children will want to tell of their experiences of losing pets—and they should have a chance to link these real-life experiences with literature), the teacher can gradually move into a discussion of the difference between prose and poetry.

Discussion should center on meaning and feelings first. Only after much exposure to poetry does a teacher move into the various ways a poet can create meaning.

Children might help each other find meaning in a poem by meeting in small discussion groups, or the teacher might lead a whole-class discussion. In the following class discussion, the teacher had read aloud this short poem by Nikki Giovanni:

Daddy says the world
Is a drum
Tight and hard
And I told him
I'm gonna beat out my own rhythm.

–Nikki Giovanni. "The Drum" from *Spin a Soft Black Song Revised Edition* by Nikki Giovanni. Copyright © 1971, 1985 by Nikki Giovanni. Reprinted by permission of Farrar, Straus and Giroux, LLC.

This fifth- and sixth-grade group of children had heard and discussed many poems, so they were eager to talk about the meaning of this one with their teacher, Sheryl, and offered the following opinions in answer to her question "What do you think about this poem?"

"Well, when Mike said about when the father was telling what the world was going to be like—he said the world is a tight drum. He said it *is*, not it *will be*," Aaron answered, seemingly intent on examining each word carefully so he understood the poet's message.

"Yes," agreed Sheryl. "Why did the father say the world is a drum, tight and hard? Why did he say it *is* instead of it *will be*?"

"Because it is right now," answered many voices.

"Because he is the one that has to pay all the taxes and make a living," said Stacie.

"Why does the father know that and the girl doesn't," Sheryl asked again, intent on helping them delve as far into the poem as they could.

Many voices again responded: "Because he's out in the world." "He knows about life." "He's lived longer." And similar comments were offered. . . .

Carrie had an interesting observation. "This reminds me of that poem by . . . I forget . . . the one you read yesterday to us about the crystal stairs." She was referring to Langston Hughes's moving poem "Mother to Son," in which a black mother gives advice to her child about not giving up in the face of adversity. "The part . . . when he said the part about the drum, is tight," she continued, "that's the part that reminded me of the [Hughes] poem because it talks about nails and spots without any boards and no carpet. That sounded the same."

"That is an interesting connection because Langston Hughes and Nikki Giovanni could well have had similar experiences growing up," answered Sheryl. "Do people who heard 'Mother to Son' see any relationship between these poems?"

Jennifer had an idea. "They're both talking about how life is or was. Like the mother was talking about how hard hers was and the dad—he is talking about how hard his life was."

"It also seems like they're alive and it could happen," added Aaron.

"Like my dad," said Deon. "My mom and dad . . . he always says things like you can't get your own way—just like that poem."

"All right," responded Sheryl.

"I think that in both poems—that this one and the one we're comparing it to—that they're warning their children of what life will be and they should be ready for it," said Jennifer.

"And in 'The Drum,' how is the child responding to that?" Sheryl asked the group.

"She's gonna beat her own rhythm," answered Stacie and Deon together.

"Is it okay to do that?" Sheryl wanted to know. Many children shook their heads no. "If you didn't, what would you be like?"

"Boring," said Stacie, wrinkling up her nose in distaste.

"You would be the same as everybody else," added Mike.

"Or at least the same as what?" asked Sheryl. "Do you think the father was telling her she *had* to live her life in a certain way?"

Her question was greeted by a strong chorus of "No."

"She chose to live that way," added Angela.

"But he is trying to warn her what life is going to be like. Nevertheless she is going to try—just like the mother in Langston Hughes's poem, she is going to climb her stairs," said Sheryl.[14]

Not only did the children understand the meaning of this poem, they connected it with their own lives and with another poem. Notice that the teacher did not tell them the meaning of the poem but let them discover the meaning for themselves. In the total discussion, she reread the poem twice. By comparing this poem with the Langston Hughes poem "Mother to Son" (in his *The Dream Keeper*), the children extended their understanding of both poems. They also considered the idea of creating their own individual lives—beating their own rhythms.

## Children Writing Poetry

Children need to hear much poetry and discuss it before attempting to write it themselves. Teachers can invite children to write poetry by providing them with poetry models and by developing a workshop approach to writing that helps children to understand that writing poetry takes time and effort.

### Using Models from Literature

Children's early efforts at writing poetry are usually based on the false notion that all poetry must rhyme. Acting on this assumption, beginning efforts might be rhyme-driven and devoid of meaning. One third-grade teacher, in an effort to avoid this rhyming trap, read her children Aileen Fisher's poem "All in a Word" (in her *Always Wondering*), which is a Thanksgiving acrostic based on the word *thanks*. She also shared William Smith's poem "Elephant" (in his *Laughing Time*), which is laid out in the shape of that animal. One child created an acrostic "Winter Is" and another one did a shaped poem about a mouse. These were then included in a bound book of class poems for all to read. The mouse poem shows the influence of hearing Mary O'Neill's well-loved poems about color in *Hailstones and Halibut Bones*. The first time children try to write their own takeoffs on these poems, they are apt to make a kind of grocery list of all the objects that are a particular color. By returning to the book they can begin to appreciate the craft of the poems, realizing that all lines do not begin in the

---

[14]Amy A. McClure, Peggy Harrison, and Sheryl Reed, *Sunrises and Songs: Reading and Writing Poetry in an Elementary Classroom* (Portsmouth, N.H.: Heinemann Educational Books, 1990), pp. 61–62.

*A class poetry book includes third graders' poems that are expressed in both visual and verbal form.*
Greensview School, Upper Arlington Public Schools, Upper Arlington, Ohio. Susan Lee, teacher.

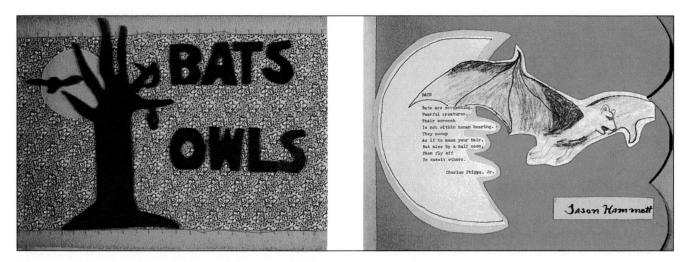

*Two sixth graders worked together to create this book of poems titled* Bats and Owls. *Charles Phipps, Jr., created the poetry while his friend Jason Hammet drew the illustrations. Notice how the pages are scalloped like the wings of owls.*

same way. They see that the poems contain objects that are that color but also describe the way the color made the poet feel, smell, and taste. One sixth grader made several revisions of her poem before she was satisfied with it:

MY RED MOOD
Red is the heat from a hot blazing fire,
A soft furry sweater awaiting a buyer.
Red is the sweet smell of roses in the spring,
Red are my cheeks that the winter winds sting.
Red is a feeling that rings deep inside
When I get angry and want to hide.
Red is a sunset waving good-bye.
Red is the sunrise shouting "Surprise!"

–Treeva. Ridgemont Elementary School, Mt. Victory, Ohio.
Sheryl Reed, Peggy Harrison, teachers.

Looking at the way other poets have described color can extend children's thinking. Examples are Rossetti's well-known poem "What Is Pink?" (in *The Random House Book of Poetry for Children*, ed. J. Prelutsky), David McCord's "Yellow" (in his *One at a Time*), or Eve Merriam's "Fresh Paint" (see p. 370).

Different forms of poetry can offer poetic structures to children and serve as models for creative poetry writing. We have seen how shaped poetry can get children started. Concrete poetry is another gateway. Using J. Patrick Lewis's *Doodle Dandies* or Joan Graham's *Splish, Splash,* children could try creating their own concrete poems. Again the emphasis should be on the meaning of the poem first, then its shape.

*Poetry Workshop*

Using models can be a way to get children started in writing poetry. It provides the opportunity to "write like a poet," and the given structures usually help the child produce an acceptable poem. This approach does not help a child *think* like a poet. That will happen only after much sustained writing and many revisions.

In a small rural school in Ohio, two teachers, Sheryl Reed and Peggy Harrison, began a year-long poetry program with their combined group of fifth and sixth graders. Amy McClure spent a year studying this poetry program and then writing an ethnographic research report on it.[15] Still later this study was rewritten into a fine book for teachers on how to include poetry in the classroom.[16]

These teachers begin their poetry workshop with reading poetry aloud several times a day. The classroom collection of over two hundred poetry books is extensive. Children read poetry for ten or fifteen minutes a day and keep poetry journals in which they write every day. They do not have to produce a poem a day—they can list possibilities, revise a poem they have been working on, or invite one of their friends to critique a poem. Frequently, they illustrate one of their best poems, or they make anthologies of their own poetry or create personal anthologies of their favorite poems from various books. This requires that the child read a wide variety of poetry and then decide on the organizing feature. Is it to be a book of animal poems or, as one child titled his, "deep feeling poems"?

One student wrote over four hundred poems in the two years he was in this class. He created an anthology with all the poems he had written about bats and owls, an interest that developed from his teacher's reading of Randall Jarrell's story of *The Bat-Poet.* He then asked one of his friends in the class who was known for his artistic ability to illustrate it with detailed black-and-white pencil drawings. These pictures were mounted on black, tan, and gray pages cut with scalloped edges to imitate the shape of an owl's wing. Their finished book reflected the subject as well as the carefully crafted poems. Here is one of the poems from their book:

A Bat

A bat
Feeds lavishly
On moths
And beetles
Flies loops
And twirls
Catches bugs
From behind
When the sun
Rises faintly
The bat
Retires to rest

–Charles Phipps, Jr., Ridgemont Elementary School,
Mt. Victory, Ohio. Sheryl Reed, Peggy Harrison, teachers.

In New York City, Georgia Heard, a published poet herself, also encourages children to write what they know and what they feel when she conducts poetry workshops with all age groups. In conferring with children, she frequently asks them to close their eyes and visualize their topic. Jason had written a first draft of a poem about cats:

Cats are cats
Cats are great
Cats can't be beat

After reading his poem, Georgia Heard writes:

The old me wants to evaluate Jason's poem. The researcher, the curious me, notices what Jason knows about poetry. There's some rhythm in his poem, repetition, and a little rhyme; it sounds like a chant or a cheer. He definitely knows the difference between a poem and a story. I tell him what I notice about his poem, but I also want to know why he chose cats as his subject.[17]

When she discovered that Jason owned a cat, she asked him to close his eyes again and visualize his cat. Slowly, he told her what he saw. She repeated his words back to him, and Jason wrote his poem again:

My Cat

My cat is black and white
I pretend he is my son
I love him.
His feet smell like popcorn.[18]

At another time, this child might want to play with the order of his lines. However, because he is just

---

[15]Amy A. McClure, "Children's Responses to Poetry in a Supportive Literary Context" (Ph.D. dissertation, Ohio State University, Columbus, 1984).

[16]McClure, Harrison, and Reed, *Sunrises and Songs.*

[17]Georgia Heard, *For the Good of the Earth and Sun: Teaching Poetry* (Portsmouth, N.H.: Heinemann Educational Books, 1989), pp. 40–41.

[18]Ibid., p. 41.

beginning to write poems, Georgia Heard wisely let his second draft stand. He has specifically described *his* cat and how he feels about him in this poem, a far cry from his first generic poem about all cats.

Children's poems do not have to be perfect. One of the reasons for having them write poetry is to increase their enjoyment of poetry; it is not necessary to produce poets. In critiquing children's poems, it is important to evaluate improvement. In Georgia Heard's evaluation conferences, she asks students to bring all of their poems to her, and then they spread them out on the floor. Here are some of the questions she offers as guidelines:

What things do you usually write about?

What kind of poems do you tend to write? Rhyming poems, long, short, narrative, lyric?

What kind of lines do you usually work with? Long or short?

What are you really good at? Titles, images, interesting words, repetition, rhyme?

What are you not so good at? How would you like to improve?

Do you revise? How do you do it? Do you change or add a word or overhaul the whole poem?

What is the hardest part of writing a poem for you? Where do you get stuck?

Are there any new things you'd like to learn?[19]

This process enables the child, rather than the teacher, to be the evaluator. It is a learning process for both of them, however. Children who hear poetry every day, who read poetry every day, and who write it every day develop a deep love for poetry. Writing honest poems that reflect their own thoughts and feelings helps children develop a real appreciation for poetry.

## Choral Reading

The reading and sharing of poetry through choral speaking is another way to foster interest in poetry. Choral speaking or reading is the interpretation of poetry by several voices speaking as one. At first, young children *speak* it as they join in the refrains. Middle-grade children might prefer to *read* their poems. They are not always read in unison; in fact, this is one of the most difficult ways to present a poem.

Several types of choral speaking are particularly suited for use in the elementary school. In the "refrain" type, one person (teacher or child) reads the narrative and the rest of the class joins in the refrain. The teacher might use the well-known folk poem that begins "In a dark, dark wood there was a dark dark house" and let children join in on the "dark darks." Eve Merriam's "Windshield Wipers" (in *Knock at a*

*Star,* ed. X. and D. Kennedy) and Vachel Lindsay's poem "The Mysterious Cat" (in *Cats Are Cats,* ed. N. Larrick) are good echo poems to try.

Another way to do a group reading, called antiphonal, is to divide the class into two groups and let the groups take turns reading each verse. An effective approach with young children is the "line-a-child" arrangement, where different children say, or read, individual lines, with the class joining in unison at the beginning or end of the poem. "One, Two, Buckle My Shoe" is a good rhyme to introduce this type of choral reading. The dialogue of David McCord's "At the Garden Gate" (in his *One at a Time*) lends itself to this approach for children in the middle grades. A more difficult and formal version of this method is part speaking. Groups are divided according to the sound of their voices into high, middle, and low parts. The poem is then interpreted much as a song might be sung in parts. This is usually done with mature groups, and is the method utilized by verse-speaking choirs. Another difficult method is to have children say the whole poem in unison, giving just one interpretation.

Many variations to these approaches will be used by creative teachers and children. A certain sound that complements both the rhythm and the meaning of the poem may be an accompaniment, such as "clickety clack" for David McCord's "The Song of the Train" (in his *One at a Time*). One group might repeat this phrase as another group says the words of the poem.

Children could also plan how to read Jack Prelutsky's "The Grobbles" (in his *The Snopp on the Sidewalk*). One child can be the innocent soul walking through the woods, while others can each give a line describing the grobbles. Then the poem can grow with scary intensity as the person walks closer to the grobbles:

| | |
|---|---|
| The grobbles are gruesome | (Child 1) |
| The grobbles are green | (Child 2) |
| The grobbles are nasty | (Child 3) |
| The grobbles are mean | (All) |
| The grobbles hide deep | (Child 4) |
| in a hollow tree | |
| just waiting to gobble | (All) |
| whomever they see | |
| | |
| I walk through the woods | (Solo) |
| for I'm quite unaware | |
| that the grobbles are waiting | |
| to gobble me there | |
| they suddenly spring | (Children 1–4) |
| from their hollowy tree | |
| Oh goodness! the grobbles | (Solo) |
| are gobbling m . . . | |

–Jack Prelutsky. "The Grobbles" from *The Snopp on the Sidewalk* by Jack Prelutsky. Text copyright © 1977 by Jack Prelutsky. Used by permission of HarperCollins Publishers.

---

[19]Ibid., p. 53.

This interpretation of how to read "The Grobbles" is only one of many that could be developed. After you have worked with children in choral reading, they will suggest variations of different ways to interpret poems. Try these out and see which ones are the most pleasing to the ear and the most appropriate for the meaning of the poem. More serious poetry can also be read effectively by a group.

Older children particularly enjoy practicing reading Paul Fleischman's poems for two voices found in his Newbery Medal book *Joyful Noise* and in his *I Am Phoenix*. All of the poems in *Joyful Noise* are about insects. In *I Am Phoenix*, all of the poems are about birds. With two columns of words placed side by side, sometimes each reader reads alone and at other times the readers are reading in unison or sometimes in opposition. The result is a wonderful image of each bird or insect that results as much from the sound of the reading as from the meaning of the words.

The values of children reading poetry together are many. They derive enjoyment from learning to respond as a group to the rhythm and melody of the poem. They learn much about the interpretation of poetry as they help plan various ways to read the poem. Shy children forget their fears when participating with the group, and all children learn to develop cooperation as they work together with a leader to present a poem. It is necessary to remember that the process of choral reading is much more important than the final product. Teachers must work for the enjoyment of poetry, not perfection of performance. Too frequently choral reading becomes a "stunt" or a quick way to entertain a PTA group. If teachers and children are pressured into a "production," interpretation of poetry will be exploited for unnatural ends.

Boys and girls should have many opportunities to share poetry in interesting and meaningful situations, if they are to develop appreciation for the deep satisfactions that poetry brings. Appreciation for poetry develops slowly. It is the result of long and loving experience with poetry over a period of years. Children who are fortunate enough to have developed a love of poetry will always be the richer for it.

## INTO THE CLASSROOM

### Poetry

**Room 201**

1. Select three different kinds of poems and read them to a group of children. Record their responses. What poems had the greatest appeal? Why?
2. Select one or two poems that contain figurative language. Share them with children at different developmental stages. When do children appear to understand the metaphors being used? One way to link into their understanding is to ask them to draw a picture of the images they see.
3. Work with a group of children or classmates in planning ways to present one of several poems chorally. If possible, tape-record these interpretations.

4. Create poetry self-portraits. Draw an outline of each child on a large piece of chart paper. Have the children find poems that they respond to in a personal way. Each child can then write or paste the poems inside their outline. A poem about food might be placed on the stomach, a sad or happy poem on the heart.
5. Create poetry spirals. Have one child choose a favorite poem and share it with a classmate. That child can choose a word or image from the poem and find another poem on that topic. Other children continue the connection. Rose Rauter's "Peach" might connect to Constance Levy's "Moon Peach" or Eve Merriam's "Sunset." These might be connected to Constance Levy's "Orange Lined Whelk" or "The Color Eater."

# Personal Explorations

1. Begin a poetry collection for future use with children. Make your own filing system. What categories will you include? Indicate possible uses for some poems, possible connections with prose, ways to interpret poems.

2. Make a study of one poet. How would you characterize her or his work in style and usual content? What can you find out about her or his background? How are these experiences reflected in the poetry?

3. Make a cycle of poems about one particular subject—for example, friends, secret places, the city, loneliness. Share these with the class.

4. Bring your favorite children's poem to present to the class or to tape-record. Invite class members to comment on both your selection and your presentation.

5. Find a poem to go with a passage in a book or with your favorite picture book.

6. Make a survey of the teachers in an elementary school to see how often they read poetry to their students, what their favorite poems are, what their favorite sources for poetry are. Make a visual presentation of your results.

7. Listen to some recordings of poetry read by authors and by interpreters. Contrast the presentations and appropriateness of the records for classroom use. Share these with children. Which ones do they prefer?

8. Try writing some poetry yourself. You may want to use some experimental verse forms, such as concrete poetry or found poetry.

# Related Readings

Chatton, Barbara. *Using Poetry Across the Curriculum: A Whole Language Approach.* Phoenix: Oryx Press, 1993.

An indispensable classroom resource for any classroom teacher, this book will enable teachers to immerse children in poetry throughout the school day. Chapters include suggestions for making connections to all the content areas, including science, mathematics, and social studies. Also included are thematic units that are filled with poems, multicultural resources, and ideas for sharing poetry with children.

Chukovsky, Kornei. *From Two to Five.* Translated and edited by Miriam Morton. Berkeley: University of California Press, 1963.

This is a classic review of the young child's delight in poetry. Written by a well-known Russian poet, it emphasizes that poetry is the natural language of little children.

Cullinan, Beatrice, Marilyn C. Scala, and Virginia C. Schroeder. *Three Voices: An Invitation to Poetry Across the Curriculum.* York, Maine: Stenhouse, 1995.

This practical book includes thirty-three detailed strategies for using poetry with children and provides three hundred additional brief suggestions. Teachers describe the classroom poetry activities in which their children were involved and include examples of student work.

Heard, Georgia. *Awakening the Heart: Exploring Poetry in the Elementary and Middle School.* Portsmouth, N.H.: Heinemann Educational Books, 1999.

A published poet provides marvelous ideas for engaging children with poetry. She shares ideas for introducing poetry to children and setting up poetry centers. Chapters also offer help for reading, writing and discussing poetry.

Heard, Georgia. *For the Good of the Earth and Sun: Teaching Poetry.* Portsmouth, N.H.: Heinemann Educational Books, 1989.

Heard describes her methods of teaching elementary children in New York City schools to enjoy poetry, to read poetry, and to write poetry. She describes the many poetry workshops she does with children from kindergarten through sixth grade. Filled with practical suggestions, this book offers the reader help and inspiration for ways to teach poetry to children.

Hopkins, Lee Bennett. *Pass the Poetry, Please.* Rev. ed. New York: Harper & Row, 1998.

This revised edition of a well-known book presents a wealth of ideas for making poetry come alive in the classroom. It contains suggestions for sparking children's interest in writing poetry. It also includes interviews with more than twenty contemporary poets.

Janeczko, Paul. *How to Write Poetry.* Scholastic, 1999.

———. *Poetry from A to Z: A Guide for Young Writers.* Bradbury, 1994.

Both books are aimed at an audience of children and young adults but teachers will enjoy them as resources. The first book addresses the finding of ideas, starting to write, and writing both rhyming poetry and free verse. In the second book Janeczko includes seventy-two poems that can serve as models and fourteen poetry-writing exercises that invite children to poetry in engaging, nonthreatening ways. The A-to-Z format is meant to show children that they can write poetry about anything. The excercises include patterns such as acrostics and haiku and themes such as prayer poems, memory poems, and opposites.

Livingston, Myra Cohn. *The Child as Poet: Myth or Reality?* Boston: Horn Book, 1984.

———. *Poem-Making: Ways to Begin Writing Poetry.* New York: HarperCollins, 1991.

In the first text, Livingston disputes the widely believed statement that the child is a natural poet. She reacts strongly to some techniques used in teaching children to write poetry. In the second book, she provides positive help for middle-grade students or teachers who want to learn more about the form and elements of poem making. She clearly presents the process of writing poetry and gives many poems as examples. Teachers will find this a very useful book.

McClure, Amy A., Peggy Harrison, and Sheryl Reed. *Sunrises and Songs: Reading and Writing Poetry in an Elementary Classroom.* Portsmouth, N.H.: Heinemann Educational Books, 1990.

This book has been rewritten for teachers from McClure's dissertation. The research voice is exchanged for an almost poetic description of one year in a classroom where poetry was the heart of the curriculum. This is a text middle-grade teachers should not miss.

# *Children's Literature*

## Poetry

Adoff, Arnold. *All the Colors of the Race.* Illustrated by John Steptoe. Lothrop, Lee & Shepard, 1982.

———. *The Basket Counts.* Illustrated by Michael Weaver. Simon, 2000.

———. *Black Is Brown Is Tan.* Illustrated by Emily McCully. Harper & Row, 1973.

———. *Eats: Poems.* Illustrated by Susan Russo. Lothrop, Lee & Shepard, 1979.

———, ed. *I Am the Darker Brother: An Anthology of Modern Poems by Black Americans.* Macmillan, 1970.

———. *In for Winter, Out for Spring.* Illustrated by Jerry Pinkney. Harcourt Brace, 1991.

———. *Love Letters.* Illustrated by Lisa Desimini. Blue Sky, 1997.

———, ed. *My Black Me: A Beginning Book of Black Poetry.* Dutton, 1994 [1974].

———. *Street Music: City Poems.* Illustrated by Karen Barbour. HarperCollins, 1995.

Alarcón, Francisco X. *From the Belly Button of the Moon and Other Summer Poems.* Illustrated by Maya Christina Gonzalez. Children's Book Press, 1998.

Aldis, Dorothy. *All Together.* Illustrated by Marjorie Flack, Margaret Frieman, and Helen D. Jameson. Putnam [1925, 1952; out of print].

Baylor, Byrd. *Everybody Needs a Rock.* Illustrated by Peter Parnall. Scribner's, 1974.

———. *I'm in Charge of Celebrations.* Illustrated by Peter Parnall. Scribner's, 1986.

———. *The Other Way to Listen.* Illustrated by Peter Parnall. Scribner's, 1978.

———. *Your Own Best Secret Place.* Illustrated by Peter Parnall. Scribner's, 1979.

Benét, Stephen Vincent, and Rosemary Benét. *A Book of Americans.* Illustrated by Charles Child. Henry Holt, 1984.

Bernos de Gasztold, Carmen. *Prayers from the Ark.* Translated by Rumer Godden. Illustrated by Barry Moser. Viking, 1992.

Berry, James. *Everywhere Faces Everywhere.* Illustrated by Reynold Ruffins. Simon & Schuster, 1997.

Bierhorst, John, ed. *In the Trail of the Wind: American Indian Poems and Ritual Orations.* Farrar, Straus & Giroux, 1971.

———, ed. *On the Road of Stars: Native American Night Poems and Sleep Charms.* Illustrated by Judy Pedersen. Macmillan, 1994.

Blishen, Edward, ed. *The Oxford Book of Poetry for Children.* Illustrated by Brian Wildsmith. Bedrick Books, 1984 [1963].

Booth, David, ed. *Til All the Stars Have Fallen: Canadian Poems for Children.* Illustrated by Kady MacDonald Denton. Kids Can Press, 1989.

Brooks, Gwendolyn. *Bronzeville Boys and Girls.* Illustrated by Ronni Solbert. Harper & Row, 1965.

Browning, Robert. *The Pied Piper of Hamelin.* Illustrated by Kate Greenaway. Random House, 1993 [1889].

Bryan, Ashley, ed. *Ashley Bryan's ABC of African American Poetry.* Atheneum, 1997.

———. *Sing to the Sun.* HarperCollins, 1992.

Burleigh, Robert. *Hoops.* Illustrated by Stephen T. Johnson. Silver Whistle, 1997.

Calmenson, Stephanie, and Joanna Cole. *Miss Mary Mack and Other Children's Street Rhymes.* Illustrated by Alan Tiegreen. Morrow, 1990.

Carlson, Lori M., ed. *Cool Salsa: Bilingual Poems on Growing Up Latino in the United States.* Holt, 1994.

————, ed. *Sol a Sol.* Illustrated by Emily Lisker. Holt, 1998.

Chandra, Deborah. *Balloons and Other Poems.* Illustrated by Leslie Bowman. Farrar, Straus & Giroux, 1990.

————. "Fog." In *Balloons and Other Poems.* Illustrated by Leslie Bowman. Farrar, Straus & Giroux, 1990.

————. *Rich Lizard and Other Poems.* Illustrated by Leslie Bowman. Farrar, Straus & Giroux, 1993.

Chute, Marchette. "Wrong Start." In *The Random House Book of Poetry for Children.* Edited by Jack Prelutsky. Illustrated by Arnold Lobel. Random House, 1983.

Ciardi, John. *The Hopeful Trout and Other Limericks.* Illustrated by Susan Meddaugh. Houghton Mifflin, 1992.

————. *The Reason for the Pelican.* Illustrated by Dominic Catalano. Boyds Mills, 1994.

Clark, Ann Nolan. *In My Mother's House.* Illustrated by Velno Herrera. Viking, 1991 [1941].

Clinton, Catherine. *I, Too, Sing America: Three Centuries of African American Poetry.* Illustrated by Stephen Alcorn. Houghton Mifflin, 1998.

Cole, Joanna, and Stephanie Calmenson. *Miss Mary Mack and Other Children's Street Rhymes.* Illustrated by Alan Tiegreen. Morrow, 1990.

Cole, William, ed. *Oh, What Nonsense.* Illustrated by Tomi Ungerer. Viking, 1966.

————, ed. *Poem Stew.* Illustrated by Karen Ann Weinhaus. Lippincott, 1981.

Cullinan, Bernice E., ed. *A Jar of Tiny Stars: Poems by NCTE Award-Winning Poets.* Wordsong, Boyds Mills, 1996.

de Paola, Tomie, ed. *Tomie de Paola's Book of Poems.* Putnam, 1988.

de Regniers, Beatrice Schenk, et al., eds. *Sing a Song of Popcorn.* Illustrated by nine Caldecott Medal artists. Scholastic, 1988.

Dotlich, Rebecca Kai. *Lemonade Sun: And Other Summer Poems.* Illustrated by Jan Spivey Gilchrist. Wordsong, 1998.

Dunbar, Paul Laurence. *Jump Back Honey: The Poems of Paul Laurence Dunbar.* Hyperion, 1999.

Dunning, Stephen, Edward Lueders, and Hugh Smith. *Reflections on a Gift of Watermelon Pickle and Other Modern Verses.* Lothrop, Lee & Shepard, 1966.

Elledge, Scott, ed. *Wider than the Sky: Poems to Grow Up With.* HarperCollins, 1990.

Esbensen, Barbara. *Dance with Me.* Illustrated by Megan Lloyd. HarperCollins, 1995.

————. *Who Shrank My Grandmother's House?* Illustrated by Eric Beddows. HarperCollins, 1992.

————. *Words with Wrinkled Knees.* Illustrated by John Stadler. Harper & Row, 1986.

Faber, Norma, and Myra Cohn Livingston, sel. *These Small Stones.* HarperCollins, 1987.

Farjeon, Eleanor. *Eleanor Farjeon's Poems for Children.* Lippincott, 1985 [1951].

Feelings, Tom. *Soul Looks Back in Wonder.* Dial, 1993.

Ferris, Helen, ed. *Favorite Poems Old and New.* Illustrated by Leonard Weisgard. Doubleday, 1957.

Fisher, Aileen. *Always Wondering.* Illustrated by Joan Sandin. HarperCollins, 1992.

Fleischman, Paul. *Big Talk.* Illustrated by Beppe Giacobbe. Candlewick, 2000.

————. *I Am Phoenix: Poems for Two Voices.* Illustrated by Ken Nutt. Harper & Row, 1985.

————. *Joyful Noise: Poems for Two Voices.* Illustrated by Eric Beddows. Harper & Row, 1988.

Fletcher, Ralph. *Ordinary Things: Poems from a Walk in Early Spring.* Illustrated by Walter Lyon Krudop. Atheneum, 1997.

————. *Relatively Speaking: Poems About Family.* Illustrated by Walter Lyon Krudop. Orchard, 1999.

Florian, Douglas. *Beast Feast.* Harcourt Brace, 1994.

————. *Bing Bang Bong.* Harcourt Brace, 1994.

————. *Insectlopedia: Insect Poems and Paintings.* Harcourt Brace, 1998.

————. *In the Swim: Poems and Paintings.* Harcourt Brace, 1997.

————. *Laugh-eteria.* Harcourt Brace, 1999.

————. *Mammalabilia.* Harcourt Brace, 2000.

————. *On the Wing: Bird Poems and Paintings.* Harcourt Brace, 1996.

Frank, Josette, ed. *Snow Toward Evening.* Illustrated by Thomas Locker. Dial, 1990.

Frost, Robert. *Birches.* Illustrated by Ed Young. Henry Holt, 1988.

————. *Stopping by Woods on a Snowy Evening.* Illustrated by Susan Jeffers. Dutton, 1978.

————. *You Come Too.* Illustrated by Thomas W. Nason. Henry Holt, 1995 [1959].

George, Kristine O'Connell. *The Great Frog Race and Other Poems.* Illustrated by Kate Kiesler. Clarion, 1997.

————. *Little Dog Poems.* Illustrated by June Otani. Clarion, 1999.

————. *Old Elm Speaks: Tree Poems.* Illustrated by Kate Kiesler. Clarion, 1998.

Giovanni, Nikki. *The Genie in the Jar.* Illustrated by Chris Raschka. Holt, 1996.

————. *Spin a Soft Black Song: Poems for Children.* Illustrated by George Martins. Hill & Wang, 1985 [1971].

————. *The Sun Is So Quiet.* Illustrated by Ashley Bryan. Holt, 1996.

Goldstein, Bobbye S., ed. *Bear in Mind.* Illustrated by William Pène DuBois. Viking, 1989.

————, ed. *Inner Chimes: Poems on Poetry.* Illustrated by Jane Breskin Zalben. Birdsong/Boyds Mills. 1992.

————. *Sweets and Treats: Dessert Poems.* Illustrated by Katherine A. Couri. Hyperion, 1998.

Gollub, Matthew. *Cool Melons Turn to Frogs: The Life and Poems of Issa.* Illustrated by Kazuko G. Stone. Lee & Low, 1998.

Graham, Joan Bransfield. *Flicker Flash.* Illustrated by Nancy Davis. Houghton Mifflin, 1999.

————. *Splish, Splash.* Illustrated by Steve Scott. Ticknor & Fields, 1994.

Greenberg, David. T. *Bugs!.* Illustrated by Lynn Munsinger. Little, Brown, 1997.

Greenfield, Eloise. *Angels.* Illustrated by Jan Spivey Gilchrist. Hyperion, 1998.

————. "Harriet Tubman." In *Honey I Love: And Other Poems.* Illustrated by Leo and Diane Dillon. Harper & Row, 1978.

————. *Honey, I Love: And Other Poems.* Illustrated by Leo and Diane Dillon. Harper & Row, 1978.

———. *Nathaniel Talking*. Illustrated by Jan Spivey Gilchrist. Black Butterfly Children's Books, 1988.

———. *Night on Neighborhood Street*. Illustrated by Jan Spivey Gilchrist. Dial, 1991.

———. *Under the Sunday Tree*. Illustrated by Amos Ferguson. Harper & Row, 1988.

Grimes, Nikki. *A Dime a Dozen*. Illustrated by Angelo. Dial, 1998.

———. *Hopscotch Love: A Family Treasury of Love Poems*. Illustrated by Melodye Rosales. Lothrop, Lee & Shepard, 1999.

———. *Is It Far to Zanzibar, Poems About Tanzania*. Illustrated by Betsy Lewin. HarperCollins, 2000.

———. *It's Raining Laughter*. Photographs by Myles C. Pinkney. Dial, 1997.

Gunning, Monica. *Not a Copper Penny in Me House: Poems from the Caribbean*. Illustrated by Frané Lessac. Wordsong, 1993.

Hindley, Judy. *A Song of Colors*. Illustrated by Mike Bostock. Candlewick, 1998.

Ho, Minfong. *Maples in the Mist: Children's Poems from the Tang Dynasty*. Illustrated by Jean Tseng and Mou-Sien Tseng. Lothrop, Lee & Shepard, 1996.

Hoberman, Mary Ann. *A House Is a House for Me*. Illustrated by Betty Fraser. Penguin, 1982.

———. *The Llama Who Had No Pajamas*. Illustrated by Betty Fraser. Harcourt Brace, 1998.

hooks, bel. *Happy to be Nappy*. Illustrated by Chris Raschka. Hyperion, 1999.

Hopkins, Lee Bennett. *Climb Into My Lap: First Poems to Read Together*. Illustrated by Kathryn Brown. Simon & Schuster, 1998.

———, ed. *Dinosaurs*. Illustrated by Murray Tinkelman. Harcourt Brace, 1987.

———, ed. *Extra Innings: Baseball Poems*. Illustrated by Scott Medlock. Harcourt Brace, 1993.

———, ed. *Marvelous Math*. Illustrated by Karen Barbour. Simon & Schuster, 1997.

———, ed. *More Surprises*. Illustrated by Megan Lloyd. Harper & Row, 1987.

———, ed. *Rainbows Are Made: Poems by Carl Sandburg*. Illustrated by Fritz Eichenberg. Harcourt Brace, 1984.

———, ed. *Side by Side: Poems to Read Together*. Illustrated by Hilary Knight. Simon & Schuster, 1991.

———. *Song and Dance*. Illustrated by Cheryl Munro Taylor. Simon & Schuster, 1997.

———, ed. *Surprises*. Illustrated by Megan Lloyd. Harper & Row, 1984.

———, ed. *Through Our Eyes: Poems and Pictures About Growing Up*. Photography by Jeffrey Dunn. Little, Brown, 1992.

———, ed. *Weather*. Photographs by Melanie Hale. HarperCollins, 1994.

Huck, Charlotte, ed. *Secret Places*. Illustrated by Lindsay Barrett George. Greenwillow, 1993.

Hudson, Wade, ed. *Pass It On: African American Poetry for Children*. Illustrated by Floyd Cooper. Scholastic, 1993.

Hughes, Langston "Mother to Son" in *The Dream Keeper and Other Poems*. Illustrated by Brian Pinkney. Knopf, 1994 (1932).

———. *The Dream Keeper and Other Poems*. Illustrated by Brian Pinkney. Knopf, 1992 [1932].

Isaacs, Anne. *Cat Up a Tree*. Illustrated by Stephen Mackey. Dutton, 1998.

Janeczko, Paul B., ed. *The Place My Words Are Looking For*. Bradbury Press, 1990.

———, ed. *Poetry from A to Z*. Bradbury Press, 1994.

———. *Very Best (Almost) Friends*. Illustrated by Christine Davenier. Candlewick, 1999.

Johnston, Tony. *An Old Shell: Poems of the Galapagos*. Illustrated by Tom Pohrt. Farrar, Straus & Giroux, 1999.

Jones, Hettie, ed. *The Trees Stand Shining: Poetry of the North American Indians*. Dial, 1993.

Kennedy, Dorothy M. *Make Things Fly: Poems About the Wind*. Illustrated by Sarah Meret. McElderry, 1998.

Kennedy, X. J., and Dorothy M. Kennedy, compilers. *Knock at a Star: A Child's Introduction to Poetry*. Illustrated by Karen Ann Weinhaus. Little, Brown, 1999 [1982].

———, compilers. *Talking Like the Rain*. Illustrated by Jane Dyer. Little, Brown, 1992.

Knudson, R. R., and May Swenson. *American Sports Poems*. Orchard, 1988.

Kuskin, Karla. *Dogs & Dragons, Trees & Dreams: A Collection of Poems*. Harper & Row, 1980.

———. *The Sky Is Always in the Sky*. Illustrated by Isabelle Dervaux. HarperCollins, 1997.

———. *Soap Soup and Other Verses*. HarperCollins, 1992.

———. "When I Woke Up This Morning" in *Dogs & Dragons, Trees & Dreams: A Collection of Poems*. Harper, 1980.

Larrick, Nancy, ed. *Cats Are Cats*. Illustrated by Ed Young. Philomel, 1988.

———, ed. *Piping Down the Valleys Wild*. Illustrated by Ellen Raskin. Delacorte, 1985 [1968].

Lear, Edward. *The Complete Nonsense Book*. Dodd, Mead, 1946.

———. *The Owl and the Pussycat*. Illustrated by James Marshall. HarperCollins, 1998.

———. *The Owl and the Pussycat*. Illustrated by Jan Brett. Putnam, 1991.

———. *The Pelican Chorus and Other Nonsense*. Illustrated by Fred Marcellino. HarperCollins, 1995.

Lee, Dennis. *Dinosaur Dinner (with a Slice of Alligator Pie): Favorite Poems*. Selected by Jack Prelutsky. Illustrated by Debbie Tilley. Knopf, 1997.

Levin, Jonathon, ed. *Walt Whitman: Poetry for Young People*. Illustrated by Jim Burke. Sterling, 1997.

Levy, Constance. *A Crack in the Clouds and Other Poems*. Illustrated by Robin Bell Corfield. McElderry, 1998.

———. "The Color Eater," in *I'm Going to Pet a Worm Today and Other Poems*. Illustrated by Ron Himler. Macmillan, 1991.

———. "Greensweet," in *A Tree Place and Other Poems*. Illustrated by Robert Sabuda. Macmillan 1994.

———. *I'm Going to Pet a Worm Today and Other Poems*. Illustrated by Ron Himler. Macmillan, 1991.

———. "Moon Peach," in *A Tree Place and Other Poems*. Illustrated by Robert Sabuda. Macmillan, 1994.

————. "An Orange-lined Whelk," in *A Tree Place and Other Poems*. Illustrated by Robert Sabuda. Macmillan, 1994.

————. "Rah, Rah Peas!" in *I'm Going to Pet a Worm Today and Other Poems*. Illustrated by Ron Himler. Macmillan, 1991.

————. *A Tree Place and Other Poems*. Illustrated by Robert Sabuda. Macmillan, 1994.

————. *When Whales Exhale and Other Poems*. Illustrated by Robin Bell Corfield. McElderry, 1997.

Lewis, J. Patrick. *Black Swan/White Crow*. Illustrated by Chris Manson. Atheneum, 1995.

————. *Bosh Blobber Bosh: Runcible Poems for Edward Lear*. Illustrated by Gary Kelley. Harcourt/Creative Editions, 1998.

————. *Doodle Dandies*. Illustrated by Lisa Desimini. Atheneum, 1998.

————. *Earth Verses and Water Rhymes*. Illustrated by Robert Sabuda. Atheneum, 1991.

————. *A Hippopotamusn't*. Illustrated by Victoria Chess. Dial, 1990.

————. *Little Buggers: Insect and Spider Poems*. Illustrated by Victoria Chess. Dial, 1998.

————. *Riddle-Icious*. Illustrated by Debbie Tilley. Knopf, 1996.

————. *Riddle-Lightful: Oodles of Little Riddle Poems*. Illustrated by Debbie Tilley. Knopf, 1998.

————. *Ridicholas Nicholas: More Animal Poems*. Illustrated by Victoria Chess. Dial, 1995.

Lindbergh, Reeve. *Johnny Appleseed*. Illustrated by Kathy Jakobsen. Little, Brown, 1990.

Little, Jean. *Hey World, Here I Am!* Illustrated by Sue Truesdell. Harper & Row, 1986.

Livingston, Myra Cohn. *Cat Poems*. Illustrated by Trina Schart Hyman. Holiday House, 1987.

————. *Celebrations*. Illustrated by Leonard Everett Fisher. Holiday House, 1985.

————, ed. *Christmas Poems*. Illustrated by Trina Schart Hyman. Holiday House, 1985.

————. *A Circle of Seasons*. Illustrated by Leonard Everett Fisher. Holiday House, 1982.

————. *Cricket Never Does: A Collection of Haiku and Tanka*. Illustrated by Kees de Kiefte. McElderry, 1997.

————, ed. *Dog Poems*. Illustrated by Leslie Morrill. Holiday House, 1990.

————. *Festivals*. Illustrated by Leonard Everett Fisher. Holiday House, 1996.

————. *Flights of Fancy and Other Poems*. McElderry, 1994.

————, ed. *I Am Writing a Poem About—A Game of Poetry*. McElderry, 1997.

————, ed. *I Like You, If You Like Me: Poems of Friendship*. McElderry, 1987.

————, ed. *If the Owl Calls Again: A Collection of Owl Poems*. Illustrated by Antonio Frasconi. McElderry, 1990.

————, ed. *Poems for Fathers*. Illustrated by Robert Assila. Holiday House, 1989.

————. *Sea Songs*. Illustrated by Leonard E. Fisher. McElderry, 1986.

————. *Sky Songs*. Illustrated by Leonard E. Fisher. McElderry, 1984.

————. *A Song I Sang to You: A Selection of Poems*. Illustrated by Margot Tomes. Harcourt Brace, 1984.

————. *Space Songs*. Illustrated by Leonard E. Fisher. McElderry, 1988.

————, ed. *Thanksgiving Poems*. Illustrated by Stephen Gammell. Holiday House, 1985.

————. *Up in the Air*. Illustrated by Leonard E. Fisher. McElderry, 1989.

————, ed. *Valentine Poems*. Holiday House, 1987.

Lobel, Arnold. *The Book of Pigericks*. Harper & Row, 1983.

Longfellow, Henry Wadsworth. *Hiawatha*. Illustrated by Susan Jeffers. Dial, 1983.

————. *Paul Revere's Ride*. Illustrated by Nancy Winslow Parker. Greenwillow, 1985.

————. *Paul Revere's Ride*. Illustrated by Ted Rand. Dutton, 1990.

Mado, Michio. *The Magic Pocket: Selected Poems*. Translated by Empress Michiko of Japan. Illustrated by Mitsumaso Anno. McElderry, 1998.

Mavor, Sally. *You and Me: Poems of Friendship*. Orchard, 1997.

McCord, David. *Every Time I Climb a Tree*. Illustrated by Marc Simont. Little, Brown, 1967.

————. *One at a Time*. Illustrated by Henry B. Kane. Little, Brown, 1977.

————. "The Song of the Train." In *One at a Time*. Illustrated by Henry B. Kane. Little, Brown, 1977.

McNaughton, Colin. *Making Friends with Frankenstein: A Book of Monstrous Poems and Pictures*. Candlewick, 1994.

————. *Who's Been Sleeping in My Porridge? A Book of Wacky Poems and Pictures*. Candlewick, 1998.

Medina, Jane. *My Name is Jorge: On Both Sides of the River*. Illustrated by Fabricio Vanden Broeck. Boyds Mills, 1999.

Merriam, Eve. *Bam Bam Bam*. Illustrated by Dan Yaccarino. Holt, 1995.

————. *Blackberry Ink*. Illustrated by Hans Wilhelm. Morrow, 1985.

————. *Fresh Paint*. Illustrated by David Frampton. Macmillan, 1986.

————. *Higgle Wiggle: Happy Rhymes*. Illustrated by Hans Wilhelm. Morrow, 1994.

————. *The Inner City Mother Goose*. Illustrated by David Diaz. Simon & Schuster, 1996.

————. *Quiet Please*. Illustrated by Sheila Hamanaka. Simon & Schuster, 1993.

————. *The Singing Green: New and Selected Poems for All Seasons*. Illustrated by Kathleen Collins Howell. Morrow, 1992.

————. *Ten Tiny Roses*. Illustrated by Julia Gorton. HarperCollins, 1999.

————. *You Be Good & I'll Be Night*. Illustrated by Karen Lee Schmidt. Morrow, 1988.

Milne, A. A. *The World of Christopher Robin*. Illustrated by E. H. Shepard. Dutton, 1958.

Moore, Clement. *The Night Before Christmas*. Illustrated by Jan Brett. Putnam, 1998.

————. *The Night Before Christmas.* Illustrated by Grandma Moses. Random House, 1962.

————. *The Night Before Christmas.* Illustrated by Ted Rand. North-South, 1995.

————. *The Night Before Christmas.* Illustrated by Tasha Tudor. Macmillan, 1975.

Moore, Lilian. *Poems Have Roots: New Poems.* Illustrated by Tad Hills. Atheneum, 1997.

————. "Until I Saw the Sea" in Beatrice Schenk de Regniers, et al., eds. *Sing a Song of Popcorn.* Illustrated by nine Caldecott medal artists. Scholastic, 1988.

Mora, Pat. *Confetti.* Illustrated by Enrique O. Sanchez. Lee & Low, 1996.

Moss, Jeff. *Bone Poems.* Illustrated by Tom Leigh. Workman, 1997.

Myers, Walter Dean. *Harlem.* Illustrated by Christopher Myers. Scholastic, 1997.

Nash, Ogden. *The Adventures of Isabel.* Illustrated by James Marshall. Little, Brown, 1991.

————. *The Tale of Custard the Dragon.* Illustrated by Lyn Munsinger. Little, Brown, 1995.

Newsome, Effie Lee. *Wonders: The Best Children's Poems of Effie Lee Newsome.* Boyds Mills, 1999.

Noyes, Alfred. *The Highwayman.* Illustrated by Charles Keeping. Oxford University Press, 1981.

————. *The Highwayman.* Illustrated by Neil Waldman. Harcourt Brace, 1990.

Nye, Naomi Shihab. *The Space Between Our Footsteps: Poems and Paintings from the Middle East.* Simon & Schuster, 1998.

————. *This Same Sky: A Collection of Poems from Around the World.* Four Winds, 1992.

————. *This Tree Is Older Than You Are: A Bilingual Gathering of Poems and Stories from Mexico with Paintings by Mexican Artists.* Simon & Schuster, 1995.

O'Neill, Mary. *Hailstones and Halibut Bones: Adventures in Color.* Illustrated by John Wallner. Philomel, 1989 [1961].

Otten, Charlotte F. *January Rides the Wind: A Book of Months.* Illustrated by Todd L. W. Doney. Lothrop, Lee & Shepard, 1997.

Panzer, Nora, ed. *Celebrate America: In Poetry and Art.* Hyperion, 1994.

Philip, Neil. *It's A Woman's World: A Century of Women's Voices in Poetry.* Dutton, 2000.

————. *Singing America: Poems That Define a Nation.* Illustrated by Michael McCurdy. Viking, 1995.

————. *War and the Pity of War.* Illustrated by Micheal McCurdy. Clarion, 1998.

Pomerantz, Charlotte. *If I Had a Paka: Poems in Eleven Languages.* Illustrated by Nancy Tafuri. Greenwillow, 1993 [1982].

Prelutsky, Jack, ed. *A. Nonny Mouse Writes Again.* Illustrated by Marjorie Priceman. Knopf, 1993.

————. *The Baby Uggs Are Hatching.* Illustrated by James Stevenson. Greenwillow, 1982.

————. *The Beauty of the Beast: Poems from the Animal Kingdom.* Illustrated by Meilo So. Knopf, 1997.

————. *Beneath a Blue Umbrella.* Illustrated by Garth Williams. Greenwillow, 1990.

————. *The Dragons Are Singing Tonight.* Illustrated by Peter Sis. Greenwillow, 1993.

————. *For Laughing Out Loud: Poems to Tickle Your Funnybone.* Illustrated by Marjorie Priceman. Knopf, 1991.

————. "The Grobbles" in *The Snopp on the Sidewalk and Other Poems.* Illustrated by Byron Barton. Greenwillow, 1977.

————. *The Headless Horseman: More Poems to Trouble Your Sleep.* Illustrated by Arnold Lobel. Greenwillow, 1977.

————. *It's Halloween.* Illustrated by Marylin Hafner. Greenwillow, 1977.

————. *It's Thanksgiving.* Illustrated by Marylin Hafner. Greenwillow, 1982.

————. *Monday's Troll.* Illustrated by Peter Sis. Greenwillow, 1996.

————. *The New Kid on the Block.* Illustrated by James Stevenson. Greenwillow, 1984.

————. *Nightmares: Poems to Trouble Your Sleep.* Illustrated by Arnold Lobel. Greenwillow, 1976.

————. *A Pizza the Size of the Sun.* Illustrated by James Stevenson. Greenwillow, 1996.

————, ed. *Poems by A. Nonny Mouse.* Illustrated by Henrik Drescher. Knopf, 1989.

————, ed. *The Random House Book of Poetry for Children.* Illustrated by Arnold Lobel. Random House, 1983.

————. *Ride a Purple Pelican.* Illustrated by Garth Williams. Greenwillow, 1986.

————. *Rolling Harvey Down the Hill.* Illustrated by Victoria Chess. Greenwillow, 1980.

————. *The Snopp on the Sidewalk and Other Poems.* Illustrated by Byron Barton. Greenwillow, 1977.

————. *Something Big Has Been Here.* Illustrated by James Stevenson. Greenwillow, 1990.

Rauter, Rose. "Peach." In *Knock at a Star: A Child's Introduction to Poetry,* compiled by X. J. Kennedy and Dorothy M. Kennedy, illustrated by Karen Ann Weinhaus. Little, Brown, 1982.

Robb, Laura. *Music and Drum: Voices of War and Peace Hope and Drums.* Illustrated by Debra Lill. Philomel, 1997.

Rogasky, Barbara. *Winter Poems.* Illustrated by Trina Schart Hyman. Scholastic, 1994.

Sandburg, Carl. *Arithmetic.* Illustrated by Ted Rand. Harcourt Brace, 1993.

————. *Early Moon.* Illustrated by James Daugherty. Harcourt Brace, 1930.

————. "Fog." In *The Random House Book of Poetry for Children,* edited by Jack Prelutsky, illustrated by Arnold Lobel. Random House, 1983.

————. *Grassroots,* Illustrated by Wendell Minor. Harcourt Brace, 1998.

————. *The People, Yes.* Harcourt Brace, 1936.

Schertle, Alice. *Advice for a Frog.* Illustrated by Norman Green. Lothrop, Lee & Shepard, 1995.

————. *How Now, Brown Cow?* Illustrated by Amanda Schaffer. Browndeer/Harcourt Brace, 1994.

————. *I Am the Cat.* Illustrated by Mark Buehner. Lothrop, Lee & Shepard, 1999.

————. *A Lucky Thing.* Illustrated by Wendell Minor. Browndeer, 1999.

Siebert, Diane. *Mojave.* Illustrated by Wendell Minor. Crowell, 1988.

———. *Sierra.* Illustrated by Wendell Minor. Crowell, 1991.

Sierra, Judy. *Antarctic Antics: A Book of Penguin Poems.* Illustrated by Jose Aruego and Ariane Dewey. Gulliver, 1998.

Silverstein, Shel. *Falling Up.* HarperCollins, 1996.

———. *A Light in the Attic.* Harper & Row, 1981.

———. "Spaghetti" in *Where the Sidewalk Ends: Poems and Drawings.* Harper, 1974.

———. *Where the Sidewalk Ends: Poems and Drawings.* Harper & Row, 1974.

Singer, Marilyn. *Family Reunion.* Illustrated by R. W. Alley. Macmillan, 1994.

———. *Sky Poems,* Illustrated by Deborah Ray. Atheneum, 1994.

———. *Turtle in July.* Illustrated by Jerry Pinkney. Macmillan, 1989.

Smith, William Jay. *Laughing Time.* Illustrated by Fernando Krahn. Delacorte, 1990 [1980].

Sneve, Virginia Driving Hawk. *Dancing Teepees.* Illustrated by Stephen Gammell. Holiday House, 1989.

Soto, Gary. *Canto Familiar.* Illustrated by Anneke Nelson. Harcourt, Brace, 1995.

———. *Neighborhood Odes.* Illustrated by David Diaz. Harcourt Brace, 1992.

Steptoe, Jamake. *In Daddy's Arms I Am Tall: African Americans Celebrating Fathers.* Lee & Low, 1997.

Stevenson, James. *Candy Corn.* Greenwillow, 1999.

———. *Cornflakes.* Greenwillow, 2000.

———. *Popcorn.* Greenwillow, 1998.

———. "May Morning" in *Popcorn.* Greenwillow, 1998.

———. *Sweet Corn.* Greenwillow, 1997.

Stevenson, Robert Louis. *Block City.* Illustrated by Ashley Wolff. Dutton, 1988.

———. *A Child's Garden of Verses.* Illustrated by Diane Goode. Morrow, 1998.

———. *A Child's Garden of Verses.* Illustrated by Tasha Tudor. Oxford University Press, 1947 [1885].

———. *A Child's Garden of Verses.* Illustrated by Brian Wildsmith. Oxford University Press, 1966 [1885].

———. *My Shadow.* Illustrated by Ted Rand. Putnam, 1990.

———. *Where Go the Boats?* Illustrated by Max Grover. Browndeer Press, 1998.

Strickland, Dorothy S., and Michael R. Strickland. *Families: Poems Celebrating the African American Experience.* Illustrated by John Ward. Boyds Mills/Wordsong, 1994.

Strickland, Michael. R. *My Own Song: And Other Poems to Groove To.* Illustrated by Eric Sabee. Wordsong, 1997.

———. *Poems That Sing to You.* Illustrated by Alan Leiner. Boyds Mills/Wordsong, 1993.

Sullivan, Charles, ed. *Imaginary Gardens: American Poetry and Art for Young People.* Abrams, 1989.

Swann, Brian. *The House with No Door: African Riddle Poems.* Illustrated by Ashley Brian. Browndeer/Harcourt Brace, 1998.

———. *Touching the Distance: Native American Riddle Poems.* Illustrated by Maria Rendon. Harcourt Brace, 1998.

Swanson, Susan Marie. *Getting Used to the Dark: 26 Night Poems.* Illustrated by Peter Catalanoto. DK Ink, 1997.

Tapahonso, Luci. *A Breeze Swept Through.* University of New Mexico Press, 1987.

———. *Songs of Shiprock Fair.* Illustrated by Anthony Chee Emerson. Kiva, 1999.

Thomas, Joyce Carol. *Brown Honey in Broomwheat Tea.* Illustrated by Floyd Cooper. HarperCollins, 1993.

———. *Gingerbread Days.* Illustrated by Floyd Cooper. HarperCollins, 1995.

Tripp, Wallace. *Rose's Are Red, Violet's Are Blue: And Other Silly Poems.* Little, Brown, 1999.

Updike, John. *A Child's Calendar.* Illustrated by Trina Schart Hyman. Holiday, 1999.

Viorst, Judith. *If I Were in Charge of the World and Other Worries.* Illustrated by Lynne Cherry. Atheneum, 1982.

Volavkova, Hana, ed. *. . . I Never Saw Another Butterfly: Children's Drawings and Poems from Terezin Concentration Camp, 1942–1944.* Schocken, 1992.

Whipple, Laura, ed. *Eric Carle's Animals Animals.* Philomel, 1989.

———, ed. *Eric Carle's Dragons Dragons & Other Creatures That Never Were.* Philomel, 1991.

Willard, Nancy A. *A Visit to William Blake's Inn.* Illustrated by Alice and Martin Provensen. Harcourt Brace, 1981.

Wong, Janet. *Good Luck and Other Poems.* McElderry, 1994.

———. *Night Garden: Poems From the World of Dreams.* Illustrated by Julie Paschkis. McElderry, 2000.

———. *The Rainbow Hand: Poems About Mothers and Daughters.* McElderry, 1999.

———. *A Suitcase of Seaweed and Other Poems.* McElderry, 1996.

Worth, Valerie. *All the Small Poems and Fourteen More.* Illustrated by Natalie Babbitt. Farrar, Straus & Giroux, 1994.

———. "Mud." In *All the Small Poems and Fourteen More,* illustrated by Natalie Babbitt. Farrar, Straus & Giroux, 1994.

———. *Small Poems.* Illustrated by Natalie Babbitt. Farrar, Straus & Giroux, 1972.

Yolen, Jane. *Once Upon the Ice, and Other Frozen Poems.* Illustrated by Jason Stemple. Wordsong, 1997.

## Prose

Alborough, Jez. *Where's My Teddy?* Candlewick, 1992.

Armstrong, William H. *Sounder.* Illustrated by James Barkley. Harper & Row, 1969.

Arnosky, Jim. *Sketching Outdoors in the Spring.* Morrow, 1997.

Avi. *The True Confessions of Charlotte Doyle.* Orchard, 1990.

Baker, Jennie. *Window.* Greenwillow, 1991.

Bang, Molly. *When Sophie Gets Angry—Really, Really Angry.* Scholastic, 1999.

Bash, Barbara. *Ancient Ones: The World of the Old Growth Firs.* Sierra Club, 1994.

Baylor, Byrd. *Hawk, I'm Your Brother.* Illustrated by Peter Parnall. Scribner's, 1976.

———. *The Way to Start a Day.* Illustrated by Peter Parnall. Scribner's, 1978.

Brett, Jan. *Goldilocks and the Three Bears.* Dodd, Mead, 1987.

Bunting, Eve. *The Wall.* Illustrated by Ronald Himler. Clarion, 1990.

Cameron, Ann. *The Most Beautiful Place in the World.* Illustrated by Thomas B. Allen. Knopf, 1988.

———. *The Stories Julian Tells.* Illustrated by Ann Strugnell. Knopf, 1981.

Carlstrom, Nancy W. *Blow Me a Kiss, Miss Lilly.* Illustrated by Amy Schwartz. HarperCollins, 1990.

Carrick, Carol, and Donald Carrick. *The Accident.* Seabury, 1976.

Cherry, Lynne. *The Great Kapok Tree.* Harcourt Brace, 1990.

Choi, Sook Nyul. *Year of Impossible Goodbyes.* Houghton Mifflin, 1991.

Christopher, John. *When the Tripods Came.* Dutton, 1988.

Cormier, Robert. *Other Bells for Us to Ring.* Illustrated by Deborah Kogan Ray. Delacorte, 1990.

Degen, Bruce. *Jamberry.* Harper & Row, 1983.

de Paola, Tomie. *Strega Nona.* Prentice Hall, 1975.

Fox, Mem. *Koala Lou.* Illustrated by Donald A. Mackay. Bradbury Press, 1968.

Frank, Anne. *Anne Frank: Diary of a Young Girl.* Doubleday, 1952.

Freeman, Don. *Corduroy.* Viking, 1968.

Galdone, Paul. *The Gingerbread Boy.* Clarion, 1979.

Gallaz, Christophe, and Roberto Innocenti. *Rose Blanche.* Illustrated by Roberto Innocenti. Creative Education, 1985.

George, Jean Craighead. *The Cry of the Crow.* Harper & Row, 1980.

———. *On the Far Side of the Mountain.* Dutton, 1990.

———. *One Day in the Tropical Rain Forest.* Illustrated by Gary Allen. Crowell, 1990.

———. *Who Really Killed Cock Robin?* HarperCollins, 1991 [1971].

Gerstein, Mordecai. *Wild Boy.* Farrar, Straus & Giroux Straus, 1998.

Greenfield, Eloise. *She Come Bringing Me That Little Baby Girl.* Illustrated by John Steptoe. Lippincott, 1974.

Grifalconi, Ann. *Osa's Pride.* Little, Brown, 1990.

Henkes, Kevin. *Julius, the Baby of the World.* Greenwillow, 1990.

———. *Lilly's Purple Plastic Purse.* Greenwillow, 1996.

Hoban, Russell. *A Baby Sister for Frances.* Illustrated by Lillian Hoban. Harper & Row, 1970.

Hughes, Shirley. *Dogger.* Lothrop, Lee & Shepard, 1988.

Hutchins, Pat. *Titch.* Macmillan, 1971.

Huynh, Quang Nhuong. *The Land I Lost: Adventures of a Boy in Vietnam.* Illustrated by Vo-Dinh Mai. Harper & Row, 1982.

Jarrell, Randall. *The Bat-Poet.* Illustrated by Maurice Sendak. Macmillan, 1964.

Keats, Ezra Jack. *Peter's Chair.* Harper & Row, 1967.

———. *Whistle for Willie.* Viking, 1964.

Lauture, Dennis. *Running the Road to ABC.* Illustrated by Reynold Ruffins. Simon & Schuster, 1996.

Lowry, Lois. *Number the Stars.* Houghton Mifflin, 1989.

MacDonald, Golden [Margaret Wise Brown]. *The Little Island.* Illustrated by Leonard Weisgard. Doubleday, 1946.

Marshall, James. *The Three Little Pigs.* Dial, 1989.

Martin, Bill, Jr. *Brown Bear, Brown Bear, What Do You See?* Illustrated by Eric Carle. Henry Holt, 1983.

Maruki, Toshi. *Hiroshima No Pika* (The Flash of Hiroshima). Lothrop, Lee & Shepard, 1980.

McCloskey, Robert. *Time of Wonder.* Viking, 1957.

McPhail, David. *The Bear's Toothache.* Little, Brown, 1972.

Mtesger, Lori. *Missing Girls.* Viking, 1999.

Myers, Walter Dean. *Scorpions.* Harper & Row, 1988.

Orlev, Uri. *The Man from the Other Side.* Translated by Hillel Ahlkin. Houghton Mifflin, 1984.

Paterson, Katherine. *Bridge to Terabithia.* Illustrated by Donna Diamond. Crowell, HarperCollins, 1977.

———. *Lyddie.* Dutton, 1991.

Perrault, Charles. *Cinderella.* Retold by May Ehrlich. Illustrated by Susan Jeffers. Dial, 1985.

Roalf, Peggy. *Children.* Hyperion, 1993.

———. *Families.* Hyperion, 1992.

———. *Seascapes.* Hyperion, 1992.

Rylant, Cynthia. *When I Was Young in the Mountains.* Illustrated by Diane Goode. Dutton, 1982.

Schlein, Miriam. *The Year of the Panda.* Illustrated by Kam Mak. Crowell, 1990.

Scieszka, Jon. *The Frog Prince Continued.* Illustrated by Steve Johnson. Viking, 1991.

———. *The True Story of the 3 Little Pigs!* Illustrated by Lane Smith. Viking, 1989.

Sheldon, Dyan. *The Whales' Song.* Illustrated by Gary Blythe. Dial, 1991.

Shulevitz, Uri. *Dawn.* Farrar, Straus & Giroux, 1974.

Speare, Elizabeth. *The Sign of the Beaver.* Houghton Mifflin, 1983.

Tarcov, Edith H. *The Frog Prince.* Illustrated by James Marshall. Scholastic, 1987.

Taylor, Mildred. *Roll of Thunder, Hear My Cry.* Dial, 1976.

Viorst, Judith. *Alexander and the Terrible, Horrible, No Good, Very Bad Day.* Illustrated by Ray Cruz. Atheneum, 1972.

———. *The Tenth Good Thing About Barney.* Illustrated by Erik Blegvad. Atheneum, 1971.

Waber, Bernard. *Ira Sleeps Over.* Houghton Mifflin, 1972.

Wells, Rosemary. *Noisy Nora.* Dial, 1973.

Wild, Margaret. *The Very Best of Friends.* Illustrated by Julie Vivas. Harcourt Brace, 1990.

Williams, Vera B. *A Chair for My Mother.* Greenwillow, 1982.

Zolotow, Charlotte. *The Hating Book.* Illustrated by Ben Shecter. Harper & Row, 1969.

———. *Mr. Rabbit and the Lovely Present.* Illustrated by Maurice Sendak. Harper & Row, 1962.

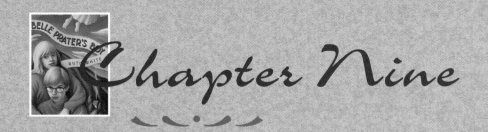

# Chapter Nine

# Contemporary Realistic Fiction

## *G*illy in Me

*I think I am a lot like Gilly in some ways. One way is everything somebody says I can't do, I have to show them that I can do it or something like it. I think Gilly and I feel the same way about foster parents.*

If I had foster parents, I probably would feel that my mother would come and get me; but I wouldn't run away or steal money.

In school I don't act like she does, going to the principal or slipping notes in teacher's books. It seems she doesn't like to be with her friends. I like to be around with my friends. I don't like to be by myself. I think Gilly gets mad easy. I get mad easy like getting called names. I always have to call them a name back.

–Amy Kauffman, seventh grade
Delaware Public Schools, Ohio
Christy Slavik, teacher

A small group of seventh graders read Katherine Paterson's *The Great Gilly Hopkins* in their in-depth reading group. One of their options when they finished the book was to write about ways they were like Gilly and different from Gilly. Obviously, Amy had identified with the character Gilly Hopkins. By contrasting her perception of herself with Gilly, she learned more about Gilly and developed insight into her own personality.

A well-written contemporary story should do more than just mirror modern life. It should take children inside a character and help them understand the causes of behavior; at the same time it should take them outside themselves to reflect on their own behavior. *The Great Gilly Hopkins* had opened a window of understanding for Amy and let her view herself and the world with slightly changed perception.

## *Realism in Contemporary Children's Literature*

Realistic fiction may be defined as imaginative writing that accurately reflects life as it was lived in the past or could be lived today. Everything in such a story can conceivably happen to real people living in our natural physical world, in contrast to fantasy, where impossible happenings are made to appear quite plausible even though they are not possible. Historical fiction (see Chapter 10) portrays life as it may have been lived in the past; contemporary realism focuses on the problems and issues of living today. Though other genres in children's literature, such as fantasy, are popular, children consistently are found to prefer realistic fiction. The books discussed in this chapter can be categorized as contemporary realistic fiction for children. Many of these are stories about growing up today and finding a place in the family, among peers, and in modern society. In addition, aspects of coping with the problems of the human condition may be found in contemporary literature for children. Books that are humorous or reflect special interests—such as animal or sports stories and mysteries—are also classified as realistic literature and so are included in this chapter.

The content of contemporary realism for children has changed dramatically in the past thirty years. These changes have provoked controversy among writers, critics, librarians, teachers, and parents. For this reason we give attention to some of the values of contemporary realism for children and some of these issues.

### The Value of Contemporary Fiction

Realistic fiction serves children in the process of understanding and coming to terms with themselves as they acquire "human-ness." Books that honestly portray the realities of life help children gain a fuller understanding of human problems and human relationships and, thus, a fuller understanding of themselves and their own potential. In describing her purpose in writing for children, Nina Bawden states:

> If a children's writer presents his characters honestly and is truthful about their thoughts and their feelings, he is giving his readers "a means to gain a hold on fate" by showing them that they can trust their thoughts and their feelings, that they can have faith in themselves. He can also show them a bit of the world, the beginning of the path they have to tread; but the most important thing he has to offer is a little hope and courage for the journey.[1]

This is not a function unique to contemporary realism. Other types of books can show children a slice of the world. Some fantasy is nearer to truth than realism; biography and autobiography frequently provide readers with models of human beings who offer "hope and courage for the journey." The ability to maintain one's

---

[1]Nina Bawden, "Emotional Realism in Books for Young People," *Horn Book Magazine*, February 1980, p. 33.

humanity and courage in the midst of deprivation is highlighted in *Number the Stars,* Lois Lowry's historical fiction about Danish efforts to save Jewish citizens in World War II. Personal bravery and responsible behavior under dire circumstances is also one of the themes of the high fantasy *A Wizard of Earthsea* by Ursula Le Guin. However, most children appear to identify more readily with characters in books of contemporary realism than with those of historical fiction or fantasy.

Realistic fiction helps children enlarge their frames of reference while seeing the world from another perspective. For example, human rights abuses in Haiti are memorably portrayed in Frances Temple's *Taste of Salt.* No one reading about the plight of these characters could think of them as "other." Instead Temple places the reader directly in her characters' shoes. Children who are repelled or frightened by the problems of the elderly might come to understand the elderly as real people through Janet Hickman's *Jericho* or Kazumi Yumoto's *The Friends.* Stories like these help young people develop compassion for and an understanding of human experiences.

Realistic fiction also reassures young people that they are not the first in the world to have faced problems. In Kimberly Willis Holt's *When Zachary Beaver Came to Town* and Marion Dane Bauer's *A Question of Trust,* they read of other children whose parents have separated or divorced. In Kevin Henke's *The Birthday Room* and Betsy Byars's *The Burning Questions of Bingo Brown,* they read about characters who are beginning to be concerned about relationships with the opposite sex. They gain some solace from recognizing the problems a ghetto environment poses for Jamal in Walter Dean Myers's *Scorpions* or Jazmin in Nikki Grimes's *Jazmin's Notebook.* This knowledge that they are not alone brings a kind of comfort to child readers. James Baldwin recognized the power of books to alleviate pain:

> You think your pain and your heartbreak are unprecedented in the history of the world, but then you read. It was books that taught me that the things that tormented me the most were the very things that connected me with all the people who were alive, or who had ever been alive.[2]

Realistic fiction can also illuminate experiences that children have not had. A child with loving parents whose only chore consists of making a bed may have a deeper need to read Marilyn Sachs's *The Bears' House* than a child of poverty whose life is more nearly reflected in the story. A child who takes school for granted might gain much from Ann Cameron's poignant *The Most Beautiful Place in the World,* about a Guatemalan who desperately wants

*Books such as Janet Hickman's* Jericho *help children view contemporary problems from many perspectives.*

Cover of *Jericho* by Janet Hickman, jacket illustration by James McMullan. Jacket illustration copyright © 1994 by James McMullan. Used by permission of Greenwillow Books, an imprint of HarperCollins Publishers.

an education. Realistic fiction can be a way of experiencing a world we do not know.

Some books also serve as a kind of preparation for living. Far better to have read Katherine Paterson's *Bridge to Terabithia* or Cynthia Voigt's *Dicey's Song* than to experience firsthand at age 10 or 12 the death of your best friend or your mother. For many years, death was a taboo subject in children's literature. Yet, as children face the honest realities of life in books, they are developing a kind of courage for facing problems in their own lives. Madeleine L'Engle, whose *Meet the Austins* was among the first works of modern children's literature to treat the subject of death, maintained that "to pretend there is no darkness is another way of extinguishing light."[3]

Realistic fiction for children does provide many possible models, both good and bad, for coping with problems of the human condition. As children experience these stories, they may begin to filter out some meaning for their own lives. This allows children to organize and shape their own thinking about life as they follow, through stories, the lives of others. The Web *"Growing Up is Hard to Do—A Web of Possibilities"* suggests how contemporary realistic fiction

[2]James Baldwin, "Talk to Teachers," *Saturday Review,* 21 December 1963, pp. 42–44, 60.

[3]Madeleine L'Engle, in a speech before the Florida Library Association, May 1965, Miami.

# GROWING UP IS HARD TO DO: A WEB OF POSSIBILITIES

## PARTINGS

*The Leaving Morning* (Johnson)
*Alexander, Who's Not (Do You Hear Me? I Mean It!) Going to Move* (Viorst)
*Amber Brown Is Not a Crayon* (Danzinger)
*The Ashwater Experiment* (Koss)
*Eagle Song* (Bruchac)
*Hey New Kid!* (Duffy)
*Aldo Applesauce* (Hurwitz)
*Morgy Makes His Move* (Lewis)
*My Name Is Marie Isobel* (Ada)
*Ola Shakes It Up* (Hippolite)

Post a map of the United States and the world; have students mark where they have lived.
Survey the school to find out: How many people have moved? How many times?

*Baby* (MacLachlan)
*Missing May* (Rylant)
*Jericho* (Hickman)
*Chasing Redbird* (Creech)
*Mick Harte Was Here* (Park)
*Getting Near to Baby* (Couloumbis)

How has each of the characters in these books been affected by death?
How does each of them learn to say goodbye?
Learn more about the stages of grief.

## FAMILY ADDITIONS, SUBTRACTIONS, SEPARATIONS

*Homecoming* (Voigt)
*Words of Stone* (Henkes)
*The Birthday Room* (Henkes)
*Vinegar Pancakes and Vanishing Cream* (Pryor)
*Afternoon of the Elves* (Lisle)
*Fig Pudding* (Fletcher)

Create Venn diagrams of families: girls and boys, hair color, eye color.
Invent variations of the family tree chart to show blended families.

## MEMORIES

*All the Places to Love* (MacLachlan)
*26 Fairmount Ave.* (de Paola)

Write about your first or your most vivid memory.
Make a timeline or a pictorial map of highlights in your life; include future as well as past events.
Write your own memoir.

*Trolls* (Horvath)
Interview a relative about their memorable moments.

## FRIENDSHIPS

*Arthur for the Very First Time* (MacLachlan)
*Flip-Flop Girl* (Paterson)
*All Alone in the Universe* (Perkins)
*Bluish* (Hamilton)
*Bridge to Terebithia* (Paterson)
*Bell Prater's Boy* (White)
*Crash* (Spinelli)
*The Cybil War* (Byars)
*The View from Saturday* (Konigsburg)

Share ideas about how a book's author makes a friendship seem real.
Learn to make friendship bracelets.
Write to pen pals.

## FEARS

*Dog Friday* (McKay)
*I Want Answers and a Parachute* (Peterson)
*What Are We Going to Do About David?* (Roberts)
*Alice the Brave* (Naylor)
*Chuck and Danielle* (Dickinson)
*The Fear Place* (Naylor)

What were some of the fears you used to have?
What helped you overcome them?
Create monster symbols for your fears; make them huge!

## COPING WITH SCHOOL

*Hey, World, Here I Am!* (Little)
*If You're Not Here, Please Raise Your Hand* (Dakos)
*Dear Mr. Henshaw* (Cleary)
*The Burning Questions of Bingo Brown* (Byars)
*The Landry News* (Clements)
*Flying Solo* (Fletcher)
*Flour Babies* (Fine)

Write letters of advice to younger students.
Write (anonymously) what you expect from the next school year or of a specific year yet to come; read and discuss each other's ideas.
Identify common school problems and explore solutions through creative drama.

## LIVING WITH DISABILITIES

*Joey Pigza Swallowed the Key* (Gantos)
*My Buddy* (Osofsky)
*Chesire Moon* (Butts)
*My Name is Brain Brian* (Betancourt)
*True Friends* (Wallace)
*Blabber Mouth* (Gleitzman)

Spend some time blindfolded or with your writing hand in your pocket; have a partner observe and take notes as you go about ordinary tasks.
Ask the school district special education specialist to visit your classroom and talk about helping children with special needs.

## GROWING UP AT RISK

*Fly Away Home* (Bunting)
*Home* (Rosen)
*Monkey Island* (Fox)
*Maniac Mcgee* (Spinelli)
*Against the Storm* (Hicyilmaz)
*Journey to Jo'burg* (Naidoo)
*Scorpions* (Myers)
*Zlata's Diary* (Filipovic)
*Smiling for Strangers* (Hicyilmaz)

Create a service project to help the homeless.
Establish a school-to-school partnership to allow children contacts with those of different ethnic or social backgrounds.
Make a file of new stories detailing problems children face.
Compare characters in two or more books; write letters from one character to another.

## RITES OF PASSAGE

*Kinaalda: A Navajo Girl Grows Up* (Roessel)
*Rites of Passage: Stories About Growing Up by Black Writers from Around the World* (Bolden)

Research rites of passage in other cultures.
Create a chart showing ages, ceremonies, etc. Find out what is expected of people of different ages in another culture.
Create your own rite of passage:
What ceremony would you invent?
Who would be invited?
What would be the initiation?

## PHYSICAL CHANGES

*Fit for Life* (Parsons)
*365 Foods Kids Love to Eat* (Ellison)

How does food contribute to your body's changes? Plan and cook meals that promote healthy growth.

*Isn't It Amazing* (Harris)
*Are You There God? It's Me, Margaret* (Blume)
*Then Again Maybe I Won't* (Blume)

Learn more about your body's physical changes.

## ENTERING THE WORLD OF WORK

*A Day's Work* (Bunting)
*Love as Strong as Ginger* (Look)
Interview an adult about their job.

*Help Wanted: Stores About Young People Working* (Silvey)
Ask a working teenager to come in and talk about work experiences.
Compare working wages of today with wages of 50 or 100 years ago.

*The Day of Ahmed's Secret* (Heide)
*Free the Children* (Kielburger)
*Iqbal Masih and the Crusaders Against Child Slavery* (Kuklin)
Study working conditions for children around the world. What can you do to help?

Based on *The Web: Wonderfully Exciting Books.*
Janet Hickman and Rudine Sims Bishop eds.
The Ohio State University, Vol. XVIII, 3 (Winter 1995)

Based on *The Web: Wonderfully Exciting Books.* Janet Hickman and Rudine Sims Bishop eds. The Ohio State Univesity—Vol XVII, 3 (Winter, 1995) could provide the foundation for a classroom exploration of problems and prospects facing the modern child.

## Issues Relating to Realistic Fiction

More controversy surrounds the writing of contemporary realistic fiction for children than perhaps any other kind of literature. Everyone is a critic of realism, for everyone feels he or she is an expert on what is real in today's world. But realities clash, and the fact that "what is real for one might not be real for another" is a true and lively issue. Some of the questions that seem uniquely related to contemporary realism in writing for children need to be examined.

### What is Real?

The question of what is "real" or "true to life" is a significant one. C. S. Lewis, the British author of the well-known Narnia stories (see Chapter 7) described three types of realistic content:

> But when we say, "The sort of thing that happens," do we mean the sort of thing that usually or often happens, the sort of thing that is typical of the human lot? Or do we mean "The sort of thing that might conceivably happen or that, by a thousandth chance, may have happened once?"[4]

Middle graders reading the Narnia series know that these stories are fantasy and couldn't happen in reality. However, middle graders might read stories like Vera and Bill Cleaver's *Where the Lilies Bloom* or Gary Paulsen's *Hatchet* and believe that children can survive any hardship or crisis if only they possess determination. These well-written books cast believable characters in realistic settings facing real problems. But an adult reader might question whether this is the sort of thing that "by a thousandth chance, may have happened once."

### How Real May a Children's Book Be?

Controversy also centers on how much graphic detail may be included in a book for children. How much violence is too much? How explicit may an author be in describing bodily functions or sexual relations? These are questions that no one would have asked thirty-five years ago. But there are new freedoms today. Childhood is not the innocent time we like to think it is (and it probably never was). Although youth might not need protection, they do still need the perspective that literature can give. A well-written book makes the reader aware of the human suffering resulting from inhumane acts by others, whereas television and films are more apt to concentrate on the acts themselves.

The TV newscasts of the local Saturday-night killings or the body count in the latest "peacekeeping" effort seldom show the pain and anguish that each death causes. The rebuilding of human lives is too slow and tedious to portray in a half-hour newscast. Even video games are based on violence. The winner of the game is the one who can eliminate or destroy the "enemy." Reasons or motivations are never given, and the aftereffects of violence are not a part of the game.

By way of contrast to the media world, a well-written story provides perspective on the pain and suffering of humankind. In a literary story the author has time to develop the characters into fully rounded human beings. The reader knows the motives and pressures of each individual and can understand and empathize with the characters. If the author's tone is one of compassion for the characters, if others in the story show concern or horror for a brutal act, the reader gains perspective.

A story that makes violence understandable without condoning it is Suzanne Fisher Staples's *Shabanu, Daughter of the Wind*. In the Pakistani desert culture in which 12-year-old Shabanu lives, obedience to rules has enabled many tribes to live in peace in an environment that offers little material comfort. When Shabanu runs away to avoid an arranged marriage to a middle-aged man, she discovers her favorite camel has broken its leg. In choosing to remain with the camel, Shabanu tacitly agrees to the rules of her clan. Her father catches up with her and beats her severely. But she is soaked with his tears as he does what he must, and the reader realizes both are trapped in roles their society has defined for them.

James Giblin, a former children's book editor, suggests that a book can be realistic without being overly graphic.

> For instance, if the young detective in a mystery story was attacked by a gang of bullies, I wouldn't encourage an author to have them burn his arms with a cigarette to get him to talk (although that might conceivably happen in an adult mystery). However, I would accept a scene in which the gang *threatened* to do so: that would convey the reality and danger of the situation without indulging in all the gory details.[5]

Giblin maintains that very few subjects are inappropriate in themselves; it is all in how the author treats them. The facts of a situation, ugly as they might be, can be presented with feeling and depth of emotion, which carry the reader beyond the particular subject.

[4]C. S. Lewis, *An Experiment in Criticism* (Cambridge: Cambridge University Press, 1961), p. 57.

[5]James Cross Giblin, *Writing Books for Young People* (Boston: The Writer, 1990), p. 73.

The same criteria are appropriate for evaluating explicitness about sex and bodily functions in books for children. Betty Miles raises this issue in *Maudie and Me and the Dirty Book*. When seventh grader Kate Harris teams up with a classmate to read aloud to first graders, one of her choices—a story about a puppy being born—triggers a discussion among the 6-year-olds about human birth and conception. Although Kate handles the discussion with poise, a parent complaint eventually brings about a town meeting concerning what is appropriate in the elementary classroom curriculum. Miles treats the topics of conception, birth, and censorship in an open and forthright way.

### Bias and Stereotyping

Children's books have always reflected the general social and human values of a society, so it is not surprising they are also scrutinized for implied attitudes or biases of that society. Contemporary realistic fiction is examined for racism, cultural inaccuracies, sexism, ageism, and treatment of people with physical or mental impairments. Because consciousness generally has been raised in the world of children's book publishing, there are now more books that present diverse populations positively and fairly.

The political and social activism of the 1960s contributed to an awareness of racism in children's books. In the 1980s and 1990s, children have been able to find fully realized African American characters in books such as Virginia Hamilton's *Cousins*, Jacqueline Woodson's *I Hadn't Meant to Tell You This*, Walter Dean Myers's *Darnell Rock Reporting*, and Angela Johnson's *Heaven*. These characters exist in their own right and not so that a white main character can "find" herself or himself. Still, adults need to be alert to reissues of books from an earlier era—such as the 1945 Newbery Honor Book *The Silver Pencil*,[6] which contains many racist descriptions of people in Trinidad. Books like this help us recognize the gains of recent decades.

Because feminists in the 1970s made us more aware of the subtle ways in which literature has perpetuated stereotypes, contemporary realistic fiction now does a much better job of portraying women in a variety of roles. Capable working mothers; caring female role models outside of a child's family; characters who fight sexism; intelligent, independent, and strong girls and women; and romance as a consequence of strong friendship are all found in realistic fiction of the present decade.

Decrying a work of historical realistic fiction as sexist has its own problems. Elizabeth George

---

[6]Alice Dalgliesh, *The Silver Pencil* (New York: Puffin, 1991 [1944]).

*Marley, the main character in Angela Johnson's* Heaven *struggles with questions of identity that are common to all children.*

Cover of *Heaven* by Angela Johnson. Copyright 1998 by John Jude Palencar, Illustrator.

Speare's *The Witch of Blackbird Pond* has been criticized for depicting the heroine as someone whose greatest problem is deciding who to marry. But in 1688, Kit had little other choice. Again, there is no point in denouncing fairy tales for their sexist portrayal of evil stepmothers, nagging wives, or beautiful young girls waiting for the arrival of princes. Such stories reflect the longings and beliefs of a society long past. To change the folktales would be to destroy our traditional heritage. A book should not, then, be criticized for being historically authentic or true to its traditional genre. However, we have every right to be critical when such stereotyped thinking is perpetuated in contemporary literature.

Boys have also been subtly victimized by the stereotypes of the past. They have been consistently reminded that men and boys don't cry, for example. But more-modern realistic fiction shows that everyone may cry as they grieve, as do a boy and his father following the drowning of a friend in *On My Honor* by

*Illustrator Ann Strugnell portrays a likable African American family in* More Stories Julian Tells *by Ann Cameron.*

From *More Stories Julian Tells* by Ann Cameron, illustrations coyright © 1986 by Ann Strugnell. Reprinted by permission of Alfred A. Knopf Children's Books, a division of Random House, Inc.

Marion Dane Bauer. Boys have also been frequently stereotyped in animal stories as having to kill an animal they have loved as an initiation rite. In Marjorie Kinnan Rawlings's *The Yearling,* for instance, Jody is ordered to shoot his pet deer because it is destroying the family crops: "He did not believe he should ever again love anything, man or woman or his own child, as he loved the Yearling. He would be lonely all his life. But a man took it for his share and went on" (p. 400). In Fred Gipson's *Old Yeller,* after the boy shoots his possibly rabid dog, his father tells him to try to forget and go on being a man. Stories such as these cause us to question the way some of our best literature conditions boys to be hard and unfeeling.

People with mental or physical impairments have in the past been depicted as "handicapped" or "disabled." A more enlightened view suggests that the person is more important than the impairment; one can be differently abled without necessarily being disabled. Older people (and other adults) in children's literature have often been dismissed to an irrelevant position in a young person's life, as ineffectual in contrast to the vibrancy of young spirits, or as unable to do certain things because of their age. (See the section "Coping with Problems of the Human Condition" later in this chapter.) High-quality contemporary realistic fiction stories depict adults and the elderly in many ways—as mentors to young people, for instance, and as having their own romances, problems, and triumphs.

Children's books have made great gains in the depiction of our changing society. However, today's books need to continue to reflect the wide ranges of occupations, education, speech patterns, lifestyles, and futures that are possible for all, regardless of race, gender, age, or belief.

### The Author's Background

 Another controversy swirls around authors' racial backgrounds. Must an author be black to write about African Americans, or Native American to write about Native Americans? As Virginia Hamilton states:

> It happens that I know Black people better than any other people because I am one of them and I grew up knowing what it is we are about. . . . The writer uses the most comfortable milieu in which to tell a story, which is why my characters are Black. Often being Black is significant to the story; other times, it is not. The writer will always attempt to tell stories no one else can tell.[7]

It has been generally accepted that an author should write about what she or he knows. But Ann Cameron, the white author of *The Stories Julian*

[7]Virginia Hamilton, "Writing the Source: In Other Words," *Horn Book Magazine,* December 1978, p. 618.

## GUIDELINES

## *Evaluating Contemporary Realistic Fiction*

Does the book honestly portray the realities of life for today's children?

Does the book illuminate problems and issues of growing up in today's world?

Does the story transcend the contemporary setting and have universal implications?

Are the characters convincing and credible to today's child?

Are controversial topics such as sexuality dealt with in an open and forthright way?

If violence or other negative behavior is part of the story, does the author provide motivations and show aftereffects?

Does the author avoid stereotyping?

Does the book truly represent the experience of the culture depicted?

Does the book help children enlarge their personal points of view and develop appreciation for our ever-changing pluralistic society?

---

*Tells, More Stories Julian Tells,* and other books about an African American family, maintains a different point of view:

 It seems to me that the people who advise "write about what you know" drastically underestimate the human capacity for imagining what lies beyond our immediate knowledge and for understanding what is new to us. Equally, they overestimate the extent to which we know ourselves. A culture, like a person, has blind spots. . . . Often the writer who is an outsider—an African writing about the United States, an American writing about China—sees in a way that enriches him as an observer, the culture he observes, and the culture he comes from.[8]

The hallmark of fine writing is the quality of imagining it calls forth from us. Imagination is not the exclusive trait of any race or gender but is a universal quality of all fine writers. No authors or artists want to be limited to writing about or portraying only the experiences of persons of a single race or cultural background, nor should they be. We need to focus on two aspects of every book: (1) What is its literary merit? and (2) Will children enjoy it? For some additional criteria to keep in mind, see Guidelines: "Evaluating Contemporary Realistic Fiction."

### Categorizing Literature

Reviewers, educators, and curriculum makers often categorize books according to their content. Categorizing serves textbook authors by allowing them to talk about several books as a group. It serves educators who hope to group books around a particular theme for classroom study. While one person might place Paterson's *Bridge to Terabithia* in a group of

books about "making friends," it could just as easily be placed in other groups, such as books about "growing up" or "learning to accept death," or "well-written books." It is a disservice to both book and reader if, in labeling a book, we imply that this is all the book is about. Readers with their own purposes and backgrounds will see many different aspects and strengths in a piece of literature. It is helpful to remember that our experiences with art occur at many different, unique, and personal levels. Even though teachers might wish to lead children to talk about a particular aspect of a book, they will not want to suggest that this is the only aspect worth pursuing. Author Jean Little argues that teachers need to trust children to find their own messages in books.

 Individual readers come to each story at a slightly different point in their life's journey. If nobody comes between them and the book, they may discover within it some insight they require, a rest they long for, a point of view that challenges their own, a friend they may cherish for life. If we, in the guise of mentor, have all the good messages listed or discussed in small groups . . . the individual and vitally important meeting of child and story may never happen.[9]

A second issue in the categorizing of literature is age-appropriateness. Realistic fiction is often categorized as being for upper elementary or middle-grade and junior high or young-adult (YA) readers. Yet anyone who has spent time with 9- to 14-year-old readers has surely noticed the wide ranges of reading interests, abilities, and perceptions present. Betsy Byars's *The Pinballs* and Judy Blume's *Are You There, God? It's Me, Margaret* have challenged and entertained readers from fourth grade through high school. To

---

[8]Ann Cameron, "Write What You Care About," *School Library Journal* 35, no. 10 (June 1989): 50.

[9]Jean Little, "A Writer's Social Responsibility," *New Advocate* 3 (spring 1990): 83.

suggest that these titles are only "for 10- to 12-year-old readers" would ignore the ages of half of the readership of these popular authors.

In this chapter, books are arranged according to categories based on theme and content merely for the convenience of discussion. They could have been arranged in many other ways. The ages of main characters are noted, where appropriate, as a clue to potential readership. In some instances we have also noted, with references to actual classroom teachers' experiences, at which grade levels certain titles seem to have the greatest impact.

# Becoming One's Own Person

The story of every man and every woman is the story of growing up, of becoming a person, of struggling to become one's own person. The kind of person you become has its roots in your childhood experiences—how much you were loved, how little you were loved; the people who were significant to you, the ones who were not; the places you've been, and those you did not go to; the things you had, and the things you did not get. Yet a person is always more than the totality of these experiences; the way a person organizes, understands, and relates to those experiences makes for individuality.

Childhood is not a waiting room for adulthood but the place where adulthood is shaped by one's family, peers, society, and, most importantly, the person one is becoming. The passage from childhood to adulthood is a significant journey for each person. It is no wonder that children's literature is filled with stories about growing up in our society today.

## Living in a Family

The human personality is nurtured within the family; here the growing child learns of love and hate, fear and courage, joy and sorrow. The first "family life" stories tended to portray families without moments of anger and hurt, emphasizing only the happy or adventurous moments. Today the balance scale has tilted in the other direction, and it is often more difficult to find a family story with well-adjusted children and happily married parents than it is to find a story about family problems.

Children still enjoy series such as Eleanor Estes's pre-television-era books *The Moffats, The Middle Moffat,* and *Rufus M,* or Sidney Taylor's All-of-a-Kind Family series, which recreates family life in a Lower East Side Jewish home in the 1930s, and adults often point to them as evidence of the pleasures of a less fast-paced life. However, many young readers prefer stories about today's children, those they might meet in the neighborhood, the shopping center, a playground, or the classroom. More recent books include adults with both strengths and weaknesses and show children interacting with them, although formula stories might depict parents and adults as completely inept and unable to cope with or understand their children. If children are to see life wholly and gain some perspective from their reading, educators must help children balance their reading choices.

### Family Relationships

Episodic stories centered comfortably in a warm family setting are often the first chapter-book stories younger children read independently. Young readers who more readily follow episodic rather than complicated plots find Johanna Hurwitz's Russell and Elisa stories satisfying reading. Chapters alternate between 4-year-old Elisa and her older brother, Russell, who is 7. Hurwitz portrays character through authentic dialogue and description of the small tensions that make up many children's lives. Sibling rivalry, an older child's scorn for the younger one and the younger one's revenge, and exasperated but patient parents who set limits and warn of consequences are familiar to most readers.

Beverly Cleary's perennially popular and humorous stories about Ramona are enjoyed both by 7- to 9-year-olds who identify with Ramona's problems, and by 10- and 11-year-olds who remember "how I used to be." Cleary's stories concern "the problems which are small to adults but which loom so large in the lives of children, the sort of problems children can solve themselves."[10] In *Ramona and Her Mother,* Ramona worries that her mother doesn't love her as much as she loves Beezus, her older sister. In *Ramona and Her Father,* Ramona is able to be with her father more often now that she returns from school to find him waiting for telephone calls about jobs he has applied for. In *Ramona's World,* Ramona is involved with her new baby sister and beginning to feel the first romantic stirrings for her old friend "Yard Ape." Now a fourth grader and a more mature, *older* sister, Ramona continues to be her irrepressible dramatic self. Ramona and her family are people worth knowing.

In Lois Lowry's *Anastasia Krupnik,* Anastasia is the only girl in fourth grade whose name will not fit on the front of a sweatshirt. To top off the list of "Things I Love/Things I Hate" that Anastasia keeps, one of the things she is sure she is going to hate is the arrival of a new baby brother. In an effort to appease

---

[10]Beverly Cleary, "The Laughter of Children," *Horn Book Magazine,* October 1982, p. 557.

her, Anastasia's parents let her choose the baby's name, and she considers the worst ones possible. But the death of her grandmother gives Anastasia some thoughts about the importance of family and of memories—and the new baby is named Sam after her grandfather, whom Anastasia knows only through the reminiscences of her grandmother. Sam's story is told in the hilarious *All About Sam.* Anastasia and Sam have both been featured in a succession of wonderful books. In each, the Krupnik parents treat Anastasia and Sam with openness, humor, and respect; they are both literate and concerned parents whose careers as artist and English teacher do not interfere with their interactions with Anastasia and Sam. Lowry has a gift for natural-sounding dialogue and situational humor, anchored by keen observations of human nature and family relationships.

No book has revealed the complexities of sibling rivalry with as much depth as Katherine Paterson's challenging Newbery Medal–winning story *Jacob Have I Loved.* Louise is convinced that she lives in her twin sister's shadow. Caroline, her beautiful, blond, delicate sister, is the talented one, who leaves their island home of Rass each week to take piano lessons. Louise, or "Wheeze," the hated name Caroline has given her, believes her sister has stolen everything from her: her parents' affection, her friends Call and the Captain, and her chance for an education. Her half-crazed Bible-quoting grandmother recognizes her burning resentment of Caroline and taunts her with the quote "Jacob have I loved but Esau have I hated."

Paterson has skillfully woven the Bible story of Esau, firstborn, who was tricked into giving up his birthright to Jacob, the younger of the twin brothers, into this modern novel of sibling rivalry. Only maturity and a family of her own can help Louise to put her hatred and resentment of her sister to rest. The novel ends on a theme of reconciliation as Louise, now a midwife in a mountain community, fights to save the life of the weaker second-born baby of a pair of twins. In her Newbery acceptance speech for *Jacob Have I Loved,* the author, herself the middle child of five, said: "Among children who grow up together in a family there run depths of feeling that will permeate their souls for good and ill as long as they live."[11]

Adolescence also seems to be a time for sometimes-bitter conflicts between parents and children. In Keven Henkes's *Protecting Marie,* 12-year-old Fanny finds it difficult to deal with her temperamental father's inconsistencies at the same time as she is thrust into the inconsistencies of early adolescence. When her artist father, Henry, presents her with the puppy

she has longed for all her life and then gives it away because it interferes with his painting, Fanny is devastated. Although her father repents and brings home Dinner, an older, better-trained dog, Fanny finds that she cannot trust her father, and their alienation increases. When the dog disappears one afternoon, Fanny is sure Henry has given this one away, too. When Henry returns home with Dinner, Fanny reveals her fear of him. "You don't understand me sometimes," she whispered, her voice changing sharply as her emotions rose. "I'm always worrying that you're going to take something away from me" (p. 177). In response Henry reveals something of his own vulnerability. There are strong enough bonds of love in this family that, with the stabilizing element of Fanny's mother, there is a final promise of an improved relationship for Fanny and Henry and a permanent home for Dinner.

In *The Birthday Room,* Henkes deals with long-held grudges between grown siblings. Twelve-year-old Ben's mother has never forgiven her brother Ian for an accident that maimed Ben's hand. When Ian asks Ben to come for a visit to Oregon, Ben's mother reluctantly agrees to accompany him. There they find that Ian's new wife, Nina, is soon to give birth. Even though sister and sister-in-law form an immediate bond, the tension continues between sister and brother. Ben, caught in the middle, is distracted by his feelings for Lynnie, a neighbor girl. However, Ben's efforts to help Lynnie's younger twin siblings, Kale and Elke, with a special project result in a near tragedy when Kale falls out of a tree and breaks his arm and leg. Ben's feelings of guilt and remorse are mirrored by those of his Uncle Ian and his mother for their own culpability in Ben's accident years before. Unlike these two, however, Ben accepts responsibility for his role in the accident and sets about to make amends to Kale. At the book's end, perhaps influenced by Ben's example, his mother and Uncle Ian are reconciled. In a lovely reference to the book's title, Ben, pleased to have reestablished these family connections, makes room in his life for his new baby cousin.

Several books for older readers examine complex mother-daughter relationships and the conflicts between two generations that seem to intensify during adolescence. In Maude Casey's *Over the Water,* Mary, a 14-year-old Irish Catholic girl living with her family in London, is isolated from friends by her own anger and her mother's fear and bitterness at having had to leave her beloved Irish farm. When the family returns to the farm for the summer. Mammy's strictness gets even worse and Mary's resentment deepens. But over the course of the visit, as her grandmother and Aunt Nuala act as buffers between the two, Mary comes to appreciate the strong community that exists

[11]Katherine Paterson, "Newbery Medal Acceptance," in *Gates of Excellence* (New York: Elsevier/Nelson Books, 1981), p. 118.

*Twelve-year-old Ben learns that the long-standing relationship between his mother and his uncle has an important effect on his own self-awareness.*

Jacket from *The Birthday Room* by Kevin Henkes. Jacket illustrations copyright © 1999 by Laura Dronzek. Used by permission of Greenwillow Books, a division of William Morrow Company/HarperCollins Publishers.

in the Irish countryside and to revel in its quiet beauty after the grimy, gray city landscape of London. She also begins to see how the loss of this place must affect her mother. There is no easy resolution to the conflict between Mary and her mother, but at the end Mary begins to understand something of her mother's sacrifices.

Canadian writer Budge Wilson's collection of exquisitely written short stories explores mother-daughter relationships and other conflicts of adolescence. *The Leaving,* which won the Canadian Library Association Young Adult Book Award, explores the painful, sometimes funny journeys of nine girls moving into the adult world. "The Pen Pal" holds a wonderfully funny surprise ending, but the other eight stories are more poignant, told by adult women looking back on their youth yet never losing the adolescent's point of view.

### Extended Families

The extended family of grandparents, uncles, aunts, cousins, and so on, often plays a significant role in a

child's developing perception of the world. Children's literature presents other adults, and sometimes even children, acting in the place of absent or incapacitated parents.

Patricia MacLachlan's *Arthur for the Very First Time* chronicles the summer of a 10-year-old boy. From the moment his parents drop him off at the farm of idiosyncratic Uncle Wrisby and Aunt Elda, Arthur begins to change. His aunt and uncle speak French to a pet chicken, sing to a pig, and allow Arthur to check off the foods he doesn't like to eat. His new friend Moira is bothered by Arthur's introspective nature. Refusing to call Arthur anything but "Mouse," she accuses him of spending so much time writing in his journal that he doesn't really see what is going on around him. When Arthur saves a piglet from dying and protects its mother from the rain with Moira's help, however, she excitedly tells everyone "Arthur did it . . . Arthur really *did* it." She has called him "Arthur" for the very first time. MacLachlan's story is full of warmth, humor, and quirky characters, both human and animal.

MacLachlan's *Journey* is the story of an 11-year-old boy named Journey who is devastated and angered when his mother leaves him with his grandparents. He cannot accept the fact that his mother is gone—not for the summer, but for good. His loving grandparents, a cat named Bloom, and his grandfather's photographs finally help him to accept the loss of his mother. His grandfather has told him that "sometimes pictures show us what is really there," and later his sister explains that the collection of photographs his grandfather has taken represent his grandfather's efforts to give him back everything that his mother took away. Journey understands then that his grandparents, unlike his mother, have given him the family he has longed for. MacLachlan's writing respects readers' intelligence, and these two books suggest that what is important or real is often at first difficult to see.

*I See the Moon* by C. B. Christiansen is written in the form of a letter to a young niece by her Aunt Bitte. At 12, Bitte is thrilled at the news that she is to become an aunt and imagines all of the things she will do with and for the baby when it arrives. She is shocked to find out that her unmarried 15-year-old sister is planning to give the baby up. Bitte goes on a campaign to change Kari's mind and is finally sent to stay with her favorite uncle and aunt until after the baby is born. Changes have also come to these two, for Bitte finds that Aunt Minna is in a nursing home, ill with Alzheimer's disease. When Bitte begins to menstruate, Uncle Axel helps her to accept these changes, and to leave behind her unrealistic childish daydreams. She meets Jacob and Hope, her niece's adoptive parents, and when they come to the hospital to take the baby home, she is able to let go. She understands finally that "love is a circle, full as the moon," and that, separate but linked together, she, her family, Jacob, Hope, and the baby are part of the same constellation.

In Betsy Byars's *The House of Wings,* Sammy's parents leave him behind with his aged grandfather, a recluse in an old run-down house, while they go ahead to find a place to stay in Detroit. When Sammy refuses to believe his parents have left and tries to follow them, the old man runs after the furious boy. But in the midst of the chase he calls him to come and look at a wounded crane. Together the two of them catch the crane and care for it. Suddenly the boy desperately wants his grandfather to know him the way he knows birds:

> He wanted his grandfather to be able to pick him out of a thousand birds the way he could pick out the blackbird, the owls, the wild ducks. . . . He said, "My name's Sammy." (p. 141)

His grandfather looks at Sammy and then, instead of calling him "Boy," calls him "Sammy," and the relationship is sealed. This is still one of Betsy Byars's best books. Her two characters are well drawn: the eccentric old man, more interested in birds than in his grandson; the boy Sammy, furious at being left, uncertain of himself, and desperately wanting to love and be loved.

Thirteen-year-old Jan Tucker, the title character of *The Outside Child* by Nina Bawden, has lived with her two loving but eccentric aunts for as long as she can remember. But when she discovers a photograph of two other children while visiting her father's ship, she learns of Annabel and George, the children of her father's second marriage. With her best friend, an asthmatic outsider named Plato Jones, Jane locates the family on the other side of London and spies on them, with near-tragic results. Even though Jane repairs her relationship with her aunts and her newfound family, at the end of the novel Jane sees the adult world and her own family a little less idealistically. Like Katherine Paterson, Nina Bawden suggests that what people most often wish for is not necessarily what is best for them.

Fourteen-year-old Marley must also come to terms with family secrets in Angela Johnson's *Heaven.* Raised in a loving family in an idyllic small town called Heaven, Marley is shocked to learn that her "parents" are really her aunt and uncle and that her real father is her itinerant uncle. She eventually comes to terms with her anger and feelings of betrayal, in large part because the members of the small community teach her that no family is perfect and that families are created by loving support rather than by genetics.

Among Virginia Hamilton's many books are those that draw on her family experiences as part of the fifth generation of free African Americans to have lived in southern Ohio. On one level, *Cousins* is the story of 10-year-old Cammy, who is consumed with jealousy for her beautiful and probably bulimic cousin, Patty Ann. During a summer camp outing, Patty Ann disappears in a sinkhole of a fast-moving river after saving another cousin from drowning, and Cammy is convinced the death is her fault for having hated this perfect cousin so much. In *Second Cousins,* set a year later, Cammy is still trying to deal with the effects of the drowning. A family reunion brings new relatives and new family secrets out into the open, yet these events threaten Cammy's recovery. Both stories, told with Hamilton's unsurpassed style, reveal how interconnected tensions, complex relationships, and surprising discoveries can nurture and sustain each member of an extended family. Hamilton's *Zeely,* another story set in Ohio, concerns 11-year-old Geeder Perry's need to make a Watusi queen out of Zeely Taber, a herder of pigs. It is Zeely who convinces Geeder that real beauty comes from accepting yourself and others for what they are.

Cynthia Voigt's saga about the Tillerman family spans at least six novels as it fills in the events of several families' lives in a small Chesapeake Bay town. *Homecoming* introduces 13-year-old Dicey Tillerman, who, along with her two younger brothers and a younger sister, was abandoned in the parking lot of a Connecticut shopping mall by her mentally ill mother. Dicey decides the children must walk south along the Connecticut shoreline to Bridgeport to live with an aunt. But the aunt has died and her daughter, Cousin Eunice, wants to divide the family into foster homes. From Eunice, Dicey discovers that they have a grandmother living in Maryland. Determined to keep her family together, Dicey manages against all odds to reach her grandmother's home on the Chesapeake Bay, only to find an eccentric, independent, and angry old lady. The children try to keep up the huge rundown house and garden and quickly grow to love the place. But they are less sure about their prickly grandmother. This believable survival story ends with a tentative understanding formed between Gram and the children. In the sequel, *Dicey's Song,* Dicey must learn to let her family change, accept her own move toward maturity, and acknowledge her feelings for others. It is the growing warmth the Tillermans take on as they learn to be a family that lets the children, and the reader, accept their mother's death at the story's end. Other stories carry on the Tillerman saga, and two young-adult novels, *The Runner* and *Seventeen Against the Dealer,* conclude the story. In all of her novels about the Tillerman family, Voigt explores love in its many forms—love that can't be expressed, love achieved through learning, manipulative love, and family love.

## Families in Transition

The 1990 U.S. census report found that one-fourth of American children live in single-parent families; although a majority of suburban children live with married parents, as many as two-thirds of city children do not. Nearly one out of every two marriages now ends in divorce. It is only natural, then, that books acknowledge children's attempts to deal with the disruption and confusion or pain and anger that often result from divorce, death, and other family upsets.

Beverly Cleary won the Newbery Medal for *Dear Mr. Henshaw,* the story of Leigh Botts, a child of divorce. The plot is skillfully revealed through a series of letters to an author, Mr. Henshaw. Sixth grader Leigh writes Mr. Henshaw and asks for an immediate answer to ten questions. Mr. Henshaw responds with ten questions of his own. In the process of answering these questions (his mother says he has to), Leigh reveals how much he misses his truck-driver father and Bandit, his dog, and his many other concerns. Though not as humorous as some of Beverly Cleary's other books, this one is more thoughtful and certainly presents an honest picture of a child living in a single-parent home. Cleary's ear for the way children think and speak is remarkably true. Cleary's *Strider,* a buoyant sequel, begins four years later when Leigh is in high school and his hurt over his father's abandonment has been lessened by new friends and his success in school.

Ruth White's *Belle Prater's Boy* tells of Woodrow Prater, cousin to Gypsy Leemaster of Coal City West Virginia. Although on the surface life seems "fresh and bright, pink and white" as Gypsy describes it, both cousins have secret pain that they hide and mysteries that they each need to solve. Woodrow's problems are out front for the world to see. Not only has his mother disappeared, leaving him with an alcoholic father who is unable to care for him, but his cross-eyed visage and hand-me-down clothes leave him open to pity as well as ridicule. Gypsy, who seems to have everything Woodrow lacks, suffers too—from strange nightmares and nameless fears. Her own family secret has been buried almost too deeply for her to acknowledge. As the story progresses, each cousin draws strength from the other, supported in their quest for truth about their family by a wonderfully quirky yet loving cast of characters. White's story is enriched by her intimate knowledge of small-town Appalachian life. She portrays this very human story with a sense of humor and warmth that seems to grow uniquely out of this setting.

Vinnie Matthews is the title character in Katherine Paterson's *Flip-Flop Girl,* about a family devastated

*Each of the main characters in Ruth White's warmly affecting* Belle Prater's Boy *must deal with the loss of a parent.*

Jacket design by Elizabeth Sayles from *Bell Prater's Boy* by Ruth White. Jacket art copyright © 1996 by Elizabeth Sayles. Reprinted by permission of Farrar, Straus and Giroux, LLC.

by a father's death and their forced move from the Washington suburbs to their grandmother's crowded house in rural Virginia. Nine-year-old Vinnie is miserable in her new home and isolated in her new school except for one very strange little girl named Lupe, who wears orange flip-flops to school and lives in a shack in the middle of a pumpkin patch. Vinnie's mother is distracted by her own grief and her younger brother Mason's refusal to talk. Vinnie displaces all the longing she feels for her absent father onto her fourth-grade teacher, who takes extra time with her. When she learns that Mr. Clayton is going to be married, she feels betrayed and lashes out at him by vandalizing his car and then blaming Lupe. Eventually an incident involving Lupe and Mason gives Vinnie the words to express her pain to her mother and to tell the truth to Mr. Clayton. The family begins to heal as Vinnie takes responsibility for her actions and accepts the new role she must play in her altered family.

In Cynthia Rylant's Newbery Medal book *Missing May,* Summer has finally found a family only to lose its heart. Following her mother's death, Summer had been bounced around from one relative to another until her Aunt May and Uncle Ob had shown up and taken her home with them. Home was only a trailer in the West Virginia hills, but it was heaven to the little 6-year-old, and May was its center.

> May was the best person I ever knew. Even better than Ob. She was a big barrel of nothing but love and while Ob and me were off in our dreamy heads, May was there in this trailer seeing to it there was a good home for us when we were ready to land. She understood people and she let them be whatever way they needed to be. She had faith in every single person she ever met, and this never failed her, for nobody ever disappointed May. Seems people knew she saw the very best of them and they'd turn that side to her to give her a better look. (pp. 15–16)

Summer is 12 when May dies, and she and Ob cannot seem to find their way without her. *Missing May* is about the grieving that people need to do and the healing that comes with time, with love, and—in this case—with a little help from Summer's strange friend Cletus, a dead medium named Miriam Young, and perhaps a guardian angel named May. And while Summer, Ob, and Cletus set out on a real journey to cure their pain, it is the journey of the spirit that finally brings them home, ready to be a family to each other with May's memory at the center.

In *Baby* Patricia MacLachlan tells of a family that is in transition following the death of an infant son. When baby Sophie is left in their driveway, she becomes a foil for their grief and deflects their unspoken inner pain in their efforts to care for her. But eventually Sophie's real mother returns to claim her and the family cannot hide from their sorrow any longer. Byrd, a 70-year-old friend, insists that they need to find the words for their grief. "If we talk about Sophie, we can talk about Larkin's brother who died. The Baby she never saw. The Baby with no name" (p. 122). Slowly her mother and father begin to describe the baby's blue eyes and his "long serious thoughtful look," and the infant, now finally named Michael, is given a proper funeral service. MacLachlan's beautiful story of healing is filled with wonderful characters and interwoven with a subtle message about the healing power of poetry and music.

The words of a storyteller also prove healing in Sharon Creech's *Walk Two Moons*. Salamanca Tree Huddle has found it difficult to reconcile herself to the changes in her family's situation. Living in suburban Cleveland, she longs for the family's beautiful Kentucky farm, but most of all she desperately misses her mother, who went West to find herself following the death of her newborn baby. Sal is convinced that if she can only get to her mother in Idaho in time for her birthday, she can bring her home. Her grandparents

agree to undertake the long journey, and in the car Salamanca regales them with stories of her friend Phoebe Winterbottom, Phoebe's mother's disappearance, a kidnapping, and an ax murder that the two girls set out to solve. Interwoven with this story and the ongoing story of their trip are Salamanca's memories of her mother and their life in Kentucky. Her grandparents, wonderfully warm and funny characters, give her the help she needs to accept the truth about her family. Sal comes to understand the purpose that these stories have served for her.

> It seems to me that we can't explain all the truly awful things in the world like war and murder and brain tumors, and we can't fix these things so we look at the frightening things that are closer to us and we magnify them until they burst open. Inside is something that we can manage, something that isn't as awful as it had at first seemed. (p. 277)

*Walk Two Moons* is a complex narrative peopled by quirky yet fully realized characters. As the plot evolves, Salamanca's stories to herself burst open to involve and surprise the reader in a story that has all the action of a great read yet all the depth of great literature.

Betsy Byars frequently writes about children who live in single-parent families and are often left on their own. Even though adult intervention eventually helps allay a crisis, Byars's main characters generally work things out for themselves while realizing a "little moment of growth." In *Cracker Jackson*, 11-year-old Cracker suspects that his much-loved former baby-sitter Alma is being abused by her husband. *The Night Swimmers* is about three children who are raising themselves while their father tries to pursue a career as a country western singer. *The Pinballs* deals with three children who have been placed in a foster home. Carlie is a tough, likable 12-year-old girl who has repeatedly been beaten up by her third stepfather. She endures her world by watching television and making caustic comments. Harvey comes to the Masons in a wheelchair because his alcoholic father accidentally ran him over and broke both his legs. The third child in this mismatched group is Thomas J., a boy who is 8 going on 80. Elderly twin spinsters had tried to raise him without notifying the authorities, so Thomas J. had never gone to school. Carlie maintains that they are all "just like pinballs. Somebody put in a dime and punched a button and out we come, ready or not, and settled in the same groove" (p. 29). By the end of the story, Carlie has learned that life is determined not only by blind chance but also by initiative, for it is her creative planning that finally breaks through Harvey's depression and gives him some reason to live. Carlie's change, from being a defensive, self-centered person into becoming a compassionate

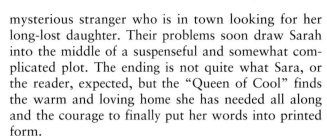

human being, is gradual and believable, and she never loses her comical perspective on life. Middle-grade students enjoy hearing this story read aloud and meeting this fine cast of characters. A keen ear for dialogue and humor and an accurate eye for the memorable incidents of childhood typify the novels by Betsy Byars.

In Katherine Paterson's *The Great Gilly Hopkins,* Gilly is not nearly the likable character that Carlie is. When Gilly arrives at her next foster home, she can't bear the huge, semiliterate Maime Trotter and her "retard" 7-year-old ward. So she sends a letter to her beautiful mother in California greatly exaggerating her situation. When she steals over a hundred dollars of Trotter's foster-care money and tries to buy a ticket to California, she is stopped by the police. Finally she understands the real love and trust that Trotter has for her as she refuses to let the social worker move Gilly to yet another home. It is too late, however, as Gilly receives an answer to her letter in the form of a visit from her grandmother, who she never knew existed. Desperately sad about leaving Trotter, Gilly learns then that one has to accept responsibility for one's own actions. One of the consistent themes in Paterson's writings is that main characters always get their wishes—but not in the way they expected.[12] At the end of the story Gilly's wish for a real home comes true, but it is a home with her grandmother, not with Courtney, the beautiful idealized mother she has created in her dreams. However, life with Maime Trotter, in which she had learned to accept and give love for the first time, made her ready for her real family. The reader knows that Gilly is capable of healing the hurt in Nonnie's life and that her own will be healed in the process. These larger-than-life characters are superbly drawn and most believable. Children delight in the swearing, self-sufficient young Gilly, but they admire the more mature Gilly who has to learn her lessons the hard way.

Sara Moon, in Julie Johnston's *Adam and Eve and Pinch-Me,* could be an older Gilly, an adolescent who has been passed around from one foster home to another. At 15, however, she'll soon be able to be on her own, and there is nothing this isolated teen wants more than to be left alone. Like the computer that she types her thoughts into, Sara is a cold machine, unable to show emotions to the outside world. And just as her computer is without a printer, she is without the ability to reveal her thoughts to anyone. Impinging on this isolation are the Huddlestons, her new foster parents, their two other foster children, and a

mysterious stranger who is in town looking for her long-lost daughter. Their problems soon draw Sarah into the middle of a suspenseful and somewhat complicated plot. The ending is not quite what Sara, or the reader, expected, but the "Queen of Cool" finds the warm and loving home she has needed all along and the courage to finally put her words into printed form.

The themes surrounding the need for a family unit and the love and acceptance that can be found within that unit has intrigued writers of literature for children for more than a century. In books such as *Heidi* by Johanna Spyri (1884) and *Anne of Green Gables* by Lucy Montgomery (1908), the circumstances of the orphaned child seemed mainly to thrust the plot forward to a happy ending. At the end of the twentieth century, orphans in books such as Richard Peck's *Strays like Us* or Heather Quarles's *A Door Near Here* are presented with such realities as addictions, AIDS, and an overburdened welfare system. These characters don't always achieve success, happiness, and the perfect nuclear family. However, they do find a measure of self-understanding and self-respect over the course of the book, and their need to be part of a supportive and loving unit is as strong as it was in books written a century ago.

## Living with Others

Three- and 4-year-olds show momentary concern for their sandbox companions, but it is usually only when children go to school that the peer group becomes important. By the time children approach the middle of elementary school, what other children think is often more significant than what parents, teachers, or other adults think. By the time children reach middle school or junior high school, the peer group and making friends are all-important.

### Finding Peer Acceptance

A classic example of children's cruelty to others who are "different" is the well-known, somewhat didactic story *The Hundred Dresses* by Eleanor Estes. Wanda, a poor Polish girl, attempts unsuccessfully to win a place in the group by telling of the hundred dresses she owns. It is only after she moves away, and the hundred dresses—all drawings—are displayed, that her peers understand that their cowardice in not befriending Wanda and their meanness have deprived them of both a friend and their own self-respect.

Louise Fitzhugh's *Harriet the Spy* has also achieved the status of a modern classic. It is the story of a precocious child who finds it difficult to relate to either her parents or her peers. Harriet tells her own story, interspersed with her notes about people she observes

[12]Christy Richards Slavik, "The Novels of Katherine Paterson: Implications for the Middle School" (Ph.D. dissertation, Ohio State University, 1983).

at school and after school. Her baby-sitter, Ole Golly, has been Harriet's consistent source of security, and when she leaves, Harriet's loneliness is compounded when her classmates find her journal. The underlying theme of this 30-year-old story is still relevant today. It contains serious statements about how children respond to teachers, to cliques, and to each other.

Amy Goldman Koss examines peer relationships from the point of view of the outsider in *The Ashwater Experiment*. Hillary has spent her life traveling from craft fair to craft fair with her hippie parents. She has never had a chance to form friendships and has learned to shut herself off from relationships. When her parents take on a long-term house-sitting job in Ashwater, California, Hilary decides to be more open to her classmates as an experiment, and this "exercise" allows her to be more vulnerable. She finds, to her surprise, that she is welcomed into the clique surrounding Serena, one of the most popular girls in the school, but she is also drawn to Cass, another loner. Hillary is able to maintain both friendships without being drawn in by the lure of the in-crowd. Although she must move away, in the end she has learned that friendships are not a matter of place but of feelings. She is now confident that she will remain connected to the friends in Ashwater at the same time as she makes new friends in her new home.

Several books, such as Walter Dean Myers's *Scorpions* and Dennis Haseley's *Getting Him,* examine the serious consequences of peer pressure. In Jerry Spinelli's *Wringer,* 9-year-old Palmer is pushed to be "one of the boys" by enduring physically painful rituals. In addition, he is pressured into taunting his one-time friend Dorothy. Worst of all he is expected to be part of a right of passage that requires 10-year-old boys to attend the community pigeon shoot to act as "wringers." These boys seek out the pigeons that have been wounded in the shoot and wring their necks, with a prize given to the boy who collects the most pigeons. Palmer is uncomfortable with the new role he is forced to play, but he is downright sickened by the thought of being a "wringer," especially after he makes a pet of a pigeon that has landed on his windowsill. Spinelli, with his usual wry sense of humor still in evidence, examines important issues of peer pressure and gender roles in a serious way. This is a fine book to invite classroom discussion on topics critically important to today's middle graders.

In two books by Mary Stolz, the same characters and events are examined from different points of view. In the first story, *A Dog on Barkham Street,* Edward is frightened of Martin, the bully next door, who threatens him each day. When his uncle comes with his collie dog to visit the family, he helps Edward learn how to handle a bully. When he leaves, he gives Edward what he has always wanted, his own dog. In the other book, *The Bully of Barkham Street,* the reader learns that Martin Hastings had once had a dog but that his parents had given it away when Martin had failed to care for it. Then the reader knows why Martin is so resentful of Edward and his collie dog.

### Making Friends

The theme of building friendships is often a part of realistic fiction. Stories about life in families often include one child's relationship with someone outside the home. Popular fiction traces the ups and downs of friendships in the classroom. Other stories, such as Nina Bawden's *The Outside Child,* Kazumi Yumoto's *The Friends,* Ann Cameron's *Julian's Glorious Summer,* or Beverly Cleary's depiction of Ramona and her friends, have multiple themes besides the tentative ways boys and girls form important friendships. In Kimberly Willis Holt's *When Zachary Beaver Came to Town,* 13-year-old Toby must deal with his mother's absence from their small Texas town, his crush on a neighbor girl, and his longing for a brother like his best friend Cal's. The arrival in his small Texas town of Zachary Beaver, an immensely overweight boy who has been abandoned by his side-show manager, is the catalyst for the book's adventures and its many subthemes. But all these events center around friendships—the ups and downs of longtime friends and the forging of a new friendships.

Two fifth-grade friendships are presented in Betsy Byars's *The Cybil War;* the first is a long-standing one between Simon Newton and Cybil Ackerman, and the other is a rocky one between Simon and his boastful, lying friend Tony Angott. While both boys vie for Cybil's attention, Tony tricks her into going out on a first date with him. However, his scheme backfires, for Cybil recognizes Tony's true nature. Simon's triumphant bicycle ride with Cybil provides a satisfying conclusion to this lighthearted tale of friendship.

Characters in Zilpha Keatley Snyder's books are often intelligent children from differing backgrounds who develop strong friendships. In *The Egypt Game,* six young children in a Berkeley, California, neighborhood set up in an abandoned storage yard an imaginary game based on their research into the ceremonies and culture of ancient Egypt. When one of the game players is attacked and another neighborhood child is murdered, the children's outdoor play is curtailed. In this mystery, Snyder leads readers to believe that a junk dealer/professor who owns the storage yard is the murderer. But he is instrumental in apprehending the criminal, which forces the children to reconsider their appraisal of him. The children continue their friendship, this time with a game based on gypsies.

Snyder's *Libby on Wednesday* is about an 11-year-old who, because of her home schooling by well-educated adults, is placed in the eighth grade. Her actress mother, away in New York, thinks Libby needs to be "socialized." But Libby hates school because she is ridiculed for her height and intelligence. When she wins a writing competition and is placed in a five-person writers group, she retreats to her Victorian treehouse where she writes in her journal about the others in her group: Alex, a brilliant parodist with cerebral palsy; Wendy, whose clichéd writing reflects her concern for clothes and boyfriends; Tierney, angry because she did not inherit her family's good looks; and G. G., whose searing sarcasm and angry comments cover his fear of an alcoholic father. As Libby finds the courage to share herself, beginning with a tour of the run-down family mansion and the treehouse her eccentric-author grandfather built, her views of those in her writing group begin to change.

Four highly unusual characters find friends in each other in E. L. Konigsburg's Newbery Medal–winning *The View from Saturday*. This richly layered story is woven around a middle school academic bowl and is put in motion by Mrs. Olinsky, the teacher who has chosen Noah, Ethan, Julian, and Nadia to represent the sixth grade. As the story unfolds at the state finals, flashbacks reveal the personalities and vulnerabilities as well as the special talents that will make each character so important to winning the match. Better than a trophy, however, is what the four gain from each other's friendship. Gathered together for one of their Saturday teas at Sillington House, Julian's father's inn, Ethan reflects on the way his friendship with the other three has changed him.

> Something in Sillington House gave me permission to do things I had never done before. Never even thought of doing. Something there triggered the unfolding of those parts that had been incubating. Things that had lain inside me, curled up like the turtle hatchlings newly emerged from their eggs, taking time in the dark of their nest to unfurl themselves. (p. 93)

Indeed, all four are changed profoundly by the sense of acceptance and affection they glean from one another. Konigsburg's wonderful sense of humor is firmly in place here, but she also manages to create highly believable characters who are linked together by surprising connections. Like Madeleine L'Engle and Zilpha Keatley Snyder, Konigsburg creates exceptional and gifted child characters whose intelligent thoughts and actions often lead older readers to reflect more widely on their own lives.

In Katherine Paterson's Newbery Medal book *Bridge to Terabithia*, imaginary play is the basis for a friendship that develops between 10-year-old Jess Aarons, an artistic boy who is a misfit in his family, and Leslie Burke, a newcomer who is a misfit at school. Her parents, both writers, have moved to rural Virginia in pursuit of a simpler lifestyle. These two lonely children invent an imaginary realm based on Leslie's image of Narnia and other fantasy worlds in literature. Their "Terabithia" is a real place, however, a private hideout in the woods reached by swinging on a rope across a dry creek bed. On a day when spring rains turn the creek into a torrent, Leslie goes alone to their meeting place, falls off the rope swing, and drowns. As Jess works through his complex feelings of grief, he comes to see a more supportive side of his usually unsympathetic family and realizes that Leslie's gifts to him—a wider perspective and confidence in his own imaginative powers—are gifts that last and can be shared.

> Now it occurred to him that perhaps Terabithia was like a castle where you came to be knighted. After you stayed for a while and grew strong you had to move on. . . . Now it was time for him to move out. She wasn't there, so he must go for both of them. It was up to him to pay back to the world in beauty and caring what Leslie loaned him in vision and strength. (p. 126)

With lumber given him by Leslie's father, Jess builds a bridge to Terabithia, a safe entry for his younger sister, May Belle, as he leads her into the shining realm with the unspoken hope that her world, like his own, will grow. By asking fourth and fifth graders if there are any other "bridges" in this story, teachers have allowed children to discuss the many emotional or metaphorical bridges portrayed in Paterson's beautifully written book.

Virginia Hamilton presents an achingly tender story of friendship that revolves around questions of illness and death in *Bluish*. Dreenie, new to her Manhattan school, has been slow in making new friends. Her little sister and a wacky classmate, Tuli, occupy her time but both are needy in different ways. They seem to demand more of Dreenie than they give back in the way of friendship. When Natalie Winburn arrives in their fifth-grade class in a wheelchair, her head covered by a knitted cap, Dreenie writes in her journal, "This girl is like moonlight. So pale you see the blue veins all over. You can tell though once she had some color." Dreenie and her classmates are fascinated and yet repelled by her strangeness. They "call her Bluish and grin and look at her hard." Eventually we find out that Natalie has leukemia and has endured the terrible pain of a bone marrow transplant. Her physical suffering and her desire to not seem different have made her angry and hard to know. But Dreenie reaches out to Bluish in small ways at first and then gets past her own fear of Bluish's illness to form a firm friendship. This lovely story unfolds in alternating chapters through the pages of Dreenie's journal and through a third-person voice. In this way we come to see the loving connections that are slowly built within the classroom community by Dreenie, two concerned teachers, and the other children. Eventually those bonds extend beyond the classroom to the families of Dreenie, Bluish, and Tuli. Bluish is not the passive recipient of friendship and compassion but has real contributions of her own to make to their lives. Although we do not know if Bluish will be one of the 85 to 90 percent who survive treatment, the story ends with a warmly hopeful scene in which Bluish reveals her profound trust in the girls by removing her knitted cap and revealing her newly growing hair.

> They jumped up and down. "You have hair!" Dreenie shouted. It had to be the shortest copper-red hair anybody'd ever seen.
>
> "Looks just like peach fuzz," Willie said.
>
> "No, it's shiny and curlier than fuzz. It's gonna be ringlets. It's cute!" Dreenie said. "Bluish!"
>
> "No Reddish!" They all yelled it at once. And the color of a new penny. Hollering and laughing until Dreenie's Mom knocked and opened the door, to see what in the world was going on. (p. 124)

The topic of making friends seldom focuses on broken friendships, but in reality two children who have shared years of closeness might suddenly grow apart. This process can be particularly painful to the friend who feels left behind or left out when a new person enters the relationship. Such is the case in Lynne Rae Perkins's poignant and funny *All Alone in the Universe*. Thirteen-year-olds, Debbie and Maureen have been friends since third grade when Glenna enters the picture. Suddenly the other two girls have little secrets and rituals that leave Debbie out in the cold. "I'm just left by myself, like we were never friends, like I don't even exist," Debbie cries. She wants to blame Glenna for the rift, but eventually she comes to understand that it is Maureen who has left her all by herself with no urging from Glenna. Debbie's heartbreak is very real, but she has the warm support of family, neighbors, teachers, and other adults who help her to see that she is a a good person capable of having friends. Her thirteenth year is painful, but she emerges with new understandings about her self and others—and with a new best friend.

## Growing Toward Maturity

In building a concept of self, each person begins to answer questions like "What kind of person am I?" "How am I changing?" "What do others think of me?" "What are my roles in society?" Based on their experiences, children begin to see themselves as worthy and successful people who can give and receive love and respect.

As children move toward adulthood, they may experience brief moments of awareness of this growth

*In Lynne Rae Perkins's* All Alone in the Universe *13-year-old Debbie is devastated when Maureen, her long time friend, finds a new best friend.*

From *All Alone in the Universe* by Lynne Rae Perkins. Jacket illustration copyright © 1999 by Lynne Rae Perkins. Used by permission of Greenwillow Books, a division of William Morrow Company/HarperCollins Publishers.

process. A conversation, an event, or a literary experience might give a child the sudden realization that he or she has taken a step toward maturity. The step might be toward understanding complex human emotions, acknowledgment of sexuality, or acceptance of responsibility for one's actions. This process of becoming is never easy or painless. In modern realistic fiction, there are models of ordinary girls and boys who find the courage to grow and change, or to stand up for their beliefs.

### Developing Sexuality

The first children's story to discuss menstruation, *The Long Secret* by Louise Fitzhugh, was published in 1965. In it, a girl explains menstruation to her friend in a matter-of-fact manner to correct misinformation the friend's grandmother had given her. Neither of the girls is pleased with the prospect, but they take some satisfaction in the fact that when they have their periods, they'll be able to skip gym. In contrast, Margaret, in the story *Are You There, God? It's Me, Margaret* by Judy Blume, prays for her period because she doesn't want to be the last of her secret club to start menstruating. She regularly does exercises that she hopes will increase her 28-inch bust, and she practices wearing a sanitary napkin. Mixed with her desire for physical maturation is a search for a meaningful relationship with God. Adults find this book very funny and reminiscent of their own preadolescence, but it is extremely serious for 10- and 11-year-old girls who share Margaret's concern for their own physical maturation. Mavis Jukes's *Expecting the Unexpected: Sex Ed with Mrs. Gladys B. Furley R.N.* is aimed at middle school students and is even franker about matters of maturation, in keeping with its 1990s view of the world. At the book's outset, 12-year-old River hasn't gotten her period yet, but she has gotten just enough information from her sex education class. This information causes her to make some hilariously erroneous conclusions about her older sister, whom she suspects is pregnant, at the same time as she misses all the signs of her mother's middle-age pregnancy. The adventures of River and her classmates continue to center on their "human interaction" class in a sequel, *Planning the Impossible.*

Judy Blume has also written a book about the physical and emotional maturing of a boy, *Then Again, Maybe I Won't.* One strand of the story concerns the sexual awakening of Tony, a 13-year-old boy who is embarrassed and concerned about erections and nocturnal emissions. The other concerns the conflicts that Tony feels about his family's sudden adoption of a new lifestyle when they move from a cramped two-family house in Jersey City to an acre of land on Long Island. The title conveys the same ambiguity as the direction of Tony's life. There is no doubt that Tony has achieved physical maturation, but will he be able to sustain his personal values in the difficult task of growing toward psychological and emotional maturity?

In Brock Cole's remarkable novel *The Goats,* a boy and girl are stripped of their clothes and left on an island in the night as a summer camp prank. Angry and humiliated, the two outcasts, or "goats," decide not to return to camp and instead to escape from the island. They float ashore holding on to a floating log, and break into a cabin and find some clothes, crackers, and ginger ale. Then, penniless, they begin an aimless journey, finding food, coping with various new problems (including the arrival of the girl's period), and making do until the Saturday when the girl's mother plans to visit camp. As a friendship gradually develops between them, the two become awkwardly aware of each other and more self-aware. When they cleverly figure out a way to stay in a motel at someone else's expense, a suspicious cleaning woman accuses them of "spending the afternoon in the same bed." Ironically, it is the adult suspicion of

*Author Jacqueline Woodson deals with sensitive issues of abuse in the moving* I Hadn't Meant to Tell You This.

From *I Hadn't Meant to Tell You This* (Jacket Cover) by Jacqueline Woodson, coyright © 1994 by Jacqueline Woodsen. Designed by Joseph Run. Reprinted by permission of Random House Children's Books, a division of Random House, Inc.

sexual activity, rather than the thievery of clothes, food, or a motel room, that leads to the two fugitives' being caught. The girl and boy, nameless to each other until the final chapter, are reunited with the girl's mother and other adults who will straighten things out. But Laura and Howie are different now: more self-reliant, able to form real friendships based on their own inner sense of themselves, and unlikely ever again to be gullible victims of peer cruelty or thoughtlessness. Emotionally gripping and thought provoking, this story leads individual young-adult readers to consider what it means to be alienated from one's peers and what it means to have a trusted friend. Cole has written another book, *The Facts Speak for Themselves,* that provides a grim look at a young teenager. Thirteen-year-old Linda has been abused both emotionally and sexually by so many people in her short life that she refuses to look below the surface to accept the psychological trauma that she has suffered. This book is notable for its literary style and its level of honesty, but the callous treatment of sex requires a very mature reader.

Jacqueline Woodson's *I Hadn't Meant to Tell You This* is a powerfully moving story that deals with sexual abuse in the context of larger social issues. The town of Chauncey, Ohio, is divided along racial lines but in an unexpected way. Poor white families live on one side of town and prosperous middle-class African Americans on the other. Twelve-year-old Marie is from the latter group, a confident, popular black girl who is somehow drawn to the new white girl, Lena Bright, perhaps because they have both lost their mothers. Marie is isolated from her unemotional professor father, who seems even more distant since her mother left him. Marie wonders why he never touches her. Lena has the opposite problem—her father touches her in the wrong ways. She confides in Marie but exacts a promise that she will tell no one; caught in a social service system that has not served her well, Lena is afraid that if she reports the abuse she will be taken away from her younger sister again, the only loving connection she has had since her mother died. Marie must struggle with her own hurt at the same time as she desperately tries to protect Lena without violating her confidence. This is not a typical problem novel, nor is it a book that provides easy answers. Rather, Woodson raises critical questions about class, race, prejudice, and loyalty in the context of this beautifully realized friendship.

Published in 1969 and now out of print, John Donovan's sensitively told story *I'll Get There, It Better Be Worth the Trip* was the first book for young readers to confront questions of homosexuality. Young-adult authors have dealt frankly with issues of homosexuality in books such as such as Francesca Lia Block's *Weetzie Bat,* M. E. Kerr's *Hello I Lied,* and Nancy Garden's *Annie on My Mind.* Perhaps because of groundbreaking books such as these, authors will now able to incorporate sexuality and sexual preference issues into stories suitable for the younger readers.

### Finding Oneself

Most of the stories about physical maturing also suggest a kind of emotional growth or coming to terms with oneself. The process of becoming a mature person is a lifelong task that begins in the later stages of childhood and continues for as long as a person lives. Many stories in children's literature chronicle the steps along the way to maturity.

Told in blank verse, Robert Cormier's *Frenchtown Summer* takes place "in the days in which I knew my name but did not know who I was," as young Eugene tells us. During a brief summer, small everyday occurrences and larger tragedies shape Eugene's reflections about himself. His relationship with his father, whom he finds remote and unapproachable, is especially troubling to him. Yet as the summer progresses Eugene gleans unexpected insights from the members of his family and his larger community. These, in turn, help him shape a clearer understanding of his identity and the role his father has played in shaping that identity. Cormier's distilled writing is lyrical and subdued,

but it evokes a powerful emotional response that lingers long after the book is closed.

In Pam Conrad's short novel *Staying Nine,* Heather wishes in the week before her tenth birthday that she "could stay just the same for millions of years." She doesn't like change, and she especially doesn't want to lose the ability to edge up to the ceiling by way of the kitchen doorway. So Heather decides not to have a birthday party, to wear the same clothes for her school picture that she wore last year, and to stay the passing of time by ignoring it. Her mother wisely agrees to an unbirthday party, but it is Rose Rita, her uncle's young girlfriend, who sympathetically and humorously conveys to Heather that growing up just might be fun and that her wall-climbing skills won't atrophy with age. Conrad's depiction of a week in the life of a child who has trouble accepting changes is both humorous and poignant.

In Lois Lowry's memorable *Rabble Starkey,* the title character, a 12-year-old, tells her own story of accepting growth and change, "about all kinds of loving, and about saying good-bye. And about moving on to where more things are in store" (p. 191). Rabble (short for Parable Ann) lives with her mother Sweet Hosanna above the Bigelow family's garage, where they take care of two children whose mother is hospitalized for depression. Veronica Bigelow and Rabble are like sisters; Mr. Bigelow even buys both girls new dresses, treating Rabble as if he were the father she has never known. She feels she finally has a family. Her mother, Sweet-Ho, an abandoned wife at 14, is also trying to grow as she acknowledges she doesn't want to be a housekeeper or a waitress forever. Rabble is a sympathetic character, a clear-eyed and unsentimental observer, a lover of words, and a person who initially has trouble accepting her mother's decision to start college when Mrs. Bigelow returns to the family. But the strength of the story is its quiet assurance that while it is all right to be wary of change, love and a plan make growth not only bearable but rewarding.

Another aspect of growing up is accepting people as they are, including their small pretenses and idiosyncrasies. This is one of the themes of E. L. Konigsburg's *Journey to an 800 Number,* in which highly proper prep-school student Maximilian Stubbs must come to terms with his father, Woody, a camel keeper who moves through the Southwest giving rides at shopping centers, state fairs, and conventions. Konigsburg's first-person narrative is sharp, humorous, and insightful. The gradual revelation to Max of the strange and wonderful possibilities in a world outside prep school suggests to him new definitions of "normal" and "first class."

Joan Bauer has dealt with similar issues of identity with great insight and good humor in such titles as

*Squashed, Rules of the Road,* and *Backwater.* Although she depicts older teenage protagonists, Bauer speaks to middle school students who remain outside the pale, those nonconformists who for one reason or another don't fit in with the in-crowd. In *Squashed,* Ellie is a slightly overweight teen determined to grow the biggest pumpkin in Rock River, Iowa. Jenna, in *Rules of the Road,* is quite tall, somewhat plain, and an unexceptional student, but she is a master shoe salesperson. Ivy of *Backwater* is the only child in her family uninterested in following in her ancestor's footsteps and becoming a lawyer. Over the course of the books, each of these likable heroines take a personal journey that crystallizes her self-understanding and reaffirms her worth.

In Virginia Euwer Wolff's *Make Lemonade,* when 14-year-old LaVaugn takes a job baby-sitting for a teenage mother, she's interested only in the extra money to put into her college account. But 17-year-old Jolly is as much a child as her two children Jilly and Jeremy, and LaVaugn is soon so involved with this family that she begins to neglect her studies. As she tries desperately to give Jolly the kind of moral support that her own mother has given her, LaVaugn must also struggle with being a mother to the two children. With LaVaugn's help, Jolly begins to pull her life together. Each of these young women has learned to "make lemonade" from whatever lemons life hands her. Virginia Euwer Wolff tells the story in LaVaugn's voice, placing the words like poetry on the page in phrasing that rings of the rhythms of speech patterns. This lends a sense of immediacy to the telling and underscores the important truths in this coming-of-age story.

Another psychologically complex novel, *One-Eyed Cat* by Paula Fox, begins when 11-year-old Ned Willis receives from his favorite uncle an unexpected birthday present—an air rifle. But Ned's minister father banishes the gun to the attic until Ned is older. Longing to shoot just once, Ned steals into the attic at night, points the gun out the window, and fires toward something moving near a shed. He is immediately guilt-stricken. Was it an animal? As he broods on his disobedience, he begins to lie, and each lie "makes the secret bigger." He can't confide in his mother, who is wheelchair-bound by arthritis, or in his preoccupied father. Carrying his uncomfortable secret, Ned does odd jobs after school for an elderly neighbor, Mr. Scully. There he and the old man see a sickly one-eyed cat that they feed and observe during the winter. When Mr. Scully suffers a stroke, Ned is afraid he has lost both his friend and the cat. Finally, on a visit to the home where Mr. Scully, unable to speak, resides, Ned gathers enough courage to tell his guilty secret to his friend. This release brings a change in Ned and enables him to repair the pains of separation and assuage his guilt. Ned's rich interior monologues contrast with his own inability to talk to anyone; this motif of being unable to speak about some of life's most important moments recurs throughout the story. Paula Fox's carefully chosen images, such as "people aging the way trees do, getting gnarled and dried out" or "the gun was a splinter in his mind," lend real depth to this perceptive and well-written story. Although it is set in 1935, children are likely to see the book not as historical fiction but rather as a story of the moral dilemmas that result from Ned's disobedience and lying.

Readers know that Ned has made it through a difficult time; they are not so sure that 12-year-old Joel will be able to do the same in the powerful story *On My Honor* by Marion Dane Bauer. Goaded by his friend Tony, Joel asks his father if the two boys can ride their bicycles to the bluffs outside of town and is surprised when his father gives permission. Joel promises on his honor to be careful, but when the two boys come to a bridge across a swiftly moving river, they agree to stop for a swim. When they reach the fast current, Tony, who can't swim, is swept away and drowned. Joel, horrified, doesn't know what to do. When he reaches his home, he can't tell anyone what has happened and withdraws to his bed. Finally, the arrival of the police at Tony's house and the anguish of the adults forces Joel to tell his story. He angrily blames his father and himself. In a moving scene by Joel's bedside, his father says: "We all made choices today, Joel. You, me, Tony. Tony's the only one who doesn't have to live with his choice" (p. 88). His father's admission of partial responsibility frees Joel to cry and begin to grieve. While for some children the book ends abruptly, it is not a story of dealing with the death of a friend. Instead, it is a story about facing the tragic consequences of your own actions with the help of a loving family. After reading this story, fifth graders are anxious to discuss honor, conscience, and parental obligations versus self-responsibility. They are also eager to predict a hopeful future for Joel.

Several of Katherine Paterson's novels are concerned with similar themes of growing up. *Preacher's Boy* is a lighthearted story of the son of a minister who has a hard time living up to his personal view of what his father's religion demands of him. Yet amid the Mark Twain–inspired adventures that Robbie encounters, Paterson raises very real questions of self-understanding and spirituality that are very real to the modern reader although the story takes place at the end of the 19th century. In *Come Sing, Jimmy Jo,* James struggles to reconcile his singing talent and his growing love of performance in his Appalachian family's country western band with his need for the quiet security of his grandmother and her country life. His friendship with an African American classmate, Eleazer Jones, who is uncowed by adults, helps him acknowledge his real father as he confronts his feelings about his stepfather. James finds support for his growth from both inside and outside his family. The boy in Paterson's *Park's Quest* journeys from his home near Washington, D. C., to the home where his dead father once lived in rural Virginia. Like James, Park is trying to discover who he is, and his family both supports and interferes with his desire to know more. Park's father died in Vietnam, and his mother wants nothing to do with Park's grandfather, who has suffered a stroke and cannot speak. When he visits his ancestral home, Park finally has a glowing moment of understanding and communication with the old man. He also forms a prickly friendship with a girl on the farm called Thanh, her Vietnamese mother, and the mother's husband, but the reader realizes who this girl is long before Park does. Like the characters in *Bridge to Terabithia*, Park loves books, especially the story of King Arthur. Paterson's many allusions reinforce points in the story where Park demonstrates heroism as he seeks to know about his parents and their past, himself, and his future.

His real name is Jeffrey Lionel Magee but the kids of Two Mills call the homeless boy who became a legend "Maniac Magee." Jerry Spinelli's Newbery Medal book *Maniac Magee* is more a tale of a modern-day superman than it is realistic fiction. There is nothing Maniac can't do. He beats a kid called Mars Bar in a race running backward; he hits home runs, scores touchdowns; he teaches old Mr. Grayson to read and gets the famous McNab twins to go to school. Most importantly, he brings together the town, which is racially divided. Yet Maniac continues running. He finds many shelters for himself, but no home. He lives for a while with the Beals, a kind African American family, and later with the McNabs, who are racist whites. He is happiest with Mr. Grayson, a locker room attendant at the YMCA who lives with him under a band shell. But when Grayson dies, Maniac is running again. Only when Amanda Beal goes to the zoo where Maniac is now spending his nights and forces Maniac to listen does he finally know that someone is calling him home. Maniac is bigger than life, a legend in his own world. Short chapters, punchy dialogue, and nonstop action make this a book that readers will not want to put down.

In *Scorpions* by Walter Dean Myers, 12-year-old Jamal reluctantly takes his brother's place as leader of a Harlem gang, the Scorpions, after his brother is sent to prison. His best friend, Tito, constantly counsels him not to get involved with the gang, while his long-suffering mother and his sister, Sassy, fear that he might follow in his brother's footsteps. When Jamal is given the gang's gun, he briefly displays it to get away from a school bully. On his way to a meeting with dissatisfied older boys in the gang, Tito and Jamal reflect on their lives:

> "I don't like this park, man," Tito spoke under his breath to Jamal.
>
> "How come?"
>
> "You got guys laying on the ground, you got guys laying on the grass, you even got some women laying around in here."
>
> "They either winos or crackheads," Jamal said.
>
> "They look like they thrown-away people," Tito said. "That makes me scared, because I don't want to be no thrown-away guy."
>
> "That's why we got to be like this"—Jamal held up two fingers close together—"So we don't let nobody throw us away." (p. 161)

But in a nighttime encounter with two older boys in the gang, Jamal is beaten and Tito, who is holding the gun, shoots the assailants. Both boys are stunned by the incident, but Tito worries and finally goes to the police. Because he is a minor, he may return to Puerto Rico to avoid prosecution. The novel leaves readers to wonder if Jamal, who has lost his best friend and his innocence, is strong enough to follow his own conscience and resist becoming a "thrown-away guy" himself.

## Survival Stories

Survival stories have powerful appeal to children in middle grades. Numerous stories in all genres portray an individual child or a small group of children, without adults, in situations that call for ingenuity, quick thinking, mastery of tools and skills, and strength of character. Survivors return to civilization or their former lives knowing that they have changed as a result of their experiences. In primitive societies, surviving a hazardous experience often marked the transition from childhood to adulthood. Today, we have forms of this in "survival training" conducted in schools, camps, or juvenile homes. Children in middle grades avidly read survival stories and wonder, "Could I do it? How? What would I do in this same situation?"

Armstrong Sperry's quintessential survival story *Call It Courage* begins and ends in the manner of a story told in the oral tradition:

> It happened many years ago, before the traders and the missionaries first came into the South Seas, while the Polynesians were still great in numbers and fierce of heart. But even today the people of Hikueru sing this story in their chants and tell it over the evening fires. It is the story of Mafatu, the Boy Who Was Afraid. (p. 7)

Taunted for his fears, Mafatu sets out to conquer his dread of the water by sailing to some other island, accompanied only by his pet albatross and his dog. On a distant island his character gradually develops as he proves his courage to himself: He defies a taboo, steals a much-needed spear from an idol, fights dangerous animals, and escapes from cannibals. These heroic deeds, which represent the many faces of courage, build his self-esteem. As in so many survival stories, having proven to himself that he can carve out an existence, Mafatu is ready to return to his former life as a changed person who knows his own worth. The first paragraph of the book is repeated at the end—only the last sentence is left off.

Nancy Farmer's *A Girl Named Disaster* is an 11-year-old Shona girl whose real name is Nhamo. Living as a poor relation with her dead mother's family, Nhamo's only source of support is her beloved grandmother. Because of her father's earlier misdeeds, she is blamed for an outbreak of cholera in her village, and a shaman insists that she marry a despicable man to appease the angry spirits. Her grandmother urges her to run away from their village and travel by river from Mozambique to Zimbabwe to find her father. Lost on the river, Nhamo faces terrible obstacles, including hunger, dangerous leopards, and marauding baboons. In mystical dream states she calls on companions from tribal lore to give her the strength to survive. Nhamo is eventually rescued and taken in by researchers in a tsetse fly station before she sets off to find her father. The book is long and complex, but Nhamo is a compelling heroine and the book stands alongside such other survival stories as Jean George's *Julie of the Wolves* and Scott O'Dell's *Island of the Blue Dolphins*.

In George's Newbery Medal novel *Julie of the Wolves*, Miyax, the Eskimo heroine of this beautiful story, finds herself alone on the Alaskan tundra. She realizes that her salvation or her destruction depends on a nearby pack of wolves. Julie (Miyax is her Eskimo name) watches the wolves carefully and gradually learns to communicate with them by glance, movement, and caress until Amaroq, their leader, acknowledges her as a friend. Because of the wolves, Julie survives and finds her way back to civilization. But civilization kills Amaroq, as white hunters wantonly shoot him down from a plane for the "sport" of killing. Much of the story is based on research on wolves conducted at the Arctic Research Laboratory.[13] In the sequel *Julie,* Julie has returned to her father's home near Point Barrow and finds she must deal with the changes in the community as well as a new stepmother. Her father, concerned about the fledgling herd of musk oxen that is to become part of a new native industry, insists he will kill any wolf that attacks the herd. Julie is frantic to protect her beloved pack, and in an exciting climax she leads them away from the village and out on the tundra in search of a

*Wendell Minor creates a beautiful portrait of Julie for the cover of* Julie, *Jean Craighead George's sequel to* Julie of the Wolves.
Illustration copyright © 1994 by Wendell Minor.

herd of caribou. George weaves a complex story of cultures in the middle of change, a young girl in the midst of becoming a woman, and a natural world in danger of disappearing forever.

George's well loved *My Side of the Mountain* is about a city boy who chooses to spend a solitary winter in the Catskills on family land. Armed with knowledge from reading, he makes a home in a hollow tree, tames a falcon, sews buckskin clothing, and lays up stores for the winter. In his journal, he records his observations as he goes about the business of living. When a reporter discovers him in the spring, Sam realizes he is ready to be found. Thirty years after the publication of this story, George wrote a bittersweet but worthy sequel, *On the Far Side of the Mountain,* which picks up the plot immediately following the first story. Sam allows his younger sister Alice to become his neighbor while he continues to enrich his environment and his life in the wild. But a criminal posing as a conservation officer steals Sam's falcon and his sister vanishes. In both books George expresses concern about our relationship to the natural world and our responsibility to preserve it.

Canadian author James Houston has based his survival story *Frozen Fire* on the actual survival experiences of a boy in the Canadian Arctic. Two boys,

---

[13]See Jean Craighead George's Newbery Medal acceptance speech in *Horn Book Magazine,* August 1973, pp. 337–347.

Matthew Morgan and his Inuit friend Kayak, set forth on a snowmobile to search for Matthew's prospector father, whose plane has been downed by a snowstorm. Carelessness in securing the cap of the gas can leaves them stranded seventy miles from Frobisher Bay. Kayak is able to use the skills taught him by his grandfather and helps both boys eventually walk out on the ice, where they are seen and rescued. They discover that Matthew's father has also been saved. Houston's crisp telling and cliffhanger chapter endings make this a fast-paced story. Where the strengths of George's book lies in her naturalist's knowledge of wolf behavior, Houston spent twelve years among the Inuit people and he is able to weave aspects of a changing Eskimo culture and folk wisdom into the text.

Gary Paulsen's survival story *Hatchet* also begins with a crash of a bush plane. On his way to meet his father when the pilot suffers a heart attack, Brian Robeson manages to land the plane in a lake in the Canadian wilderness and swim to shore. Alone, 13-year-old Brian lets self-pity and anxiety over his parents' impending divorce distract him from the immediate needs of survival, and he is soon sick and frightened. But gradually he begins to act intelligently—building a shelter, finding ripe berries, fending off a bear, and discovering respect for a cow moose that nearly kills him. A hatchet his mother had given him as a parting gift becomes essential to his survival. When a huge storm disturbs the plane enough to raise its tail in the water, Brian ventures out to seek the survival kit all pilots carry with them. But his carelessness when he loses his hatchet in the water and his horror of what he might find when he dives to the cockpit nearly prevents him from retrieving the kit. Ironically, Brian is cooking a delicious meal of trail food in a real pot and has survived for over two months when he is finally spotted from the air by a mapping plane. In *Brian's Winter*, Paulsen speculates on what it might have been like had Brian been forced to spend the winter in the wilderness. In *The River*, Brian is once again pitted against the elements when he agrees to make a film to teach survival techniques to the military. But the man recording Brian's experiences is struck by lightning and will die unless Brian can build a raft and navigate himself and Derek downriver to a trading post. Brian's experiences finally lead to the realization that he belongs in the wilderness rather than the city, and he leaves his old life behind for a permanent home in *Brian's Return*. Other survival stories by Paulsen include *Dogsong*, which is partially based on the author's own experiences of training sled dogs for the Iditarod trail race, and *The Voyage of the Frog*, which reveals the courage of a boy who ventures out on the ocean to scatter his dead uncle's ashes and is caught unprepared in a sudden storm.

Vera and Bill Cleaver's *Where the Lilies Bloom* is a well-known survival story set in Appalachia. The torturous death of Roy Luther from "worms in the chest" puts the full responsibility for the survival of the family on Mary Call, his 14-year-old daughter. She and Romey, her younger brother, bury him secretly so the "county people" will not find out that they are orphaned and separate them. Then Mary Call strives to keep her "cloudy-headed" older sister, Devola, and her two younger siblings alive through the winter. Mary Call's fierce pride gives her fortitude to overcome a severe winter, a caved-in roof, and the constant pretense that Roy Luther still lives. At 14, Mary Call's strength and responsibility have made her mature beyond her years, but she pulls the family through the crisis:

> My name is Mary Call Luther, I thought, and someday I'm going to be a big shot. I've got the guts to be one. I'm not going to let this beat me. If it does, everything else will for the rest of my life. (p. 144)

Mary Call and her family do survive, through wildcrafting on the mountains, scheming, and pure grit. The authors have captured the beauty of the Smokies and of this memorable family who live in what an old hymn calls the land "Where the Lilies Bloom So Fair."

This story's tone stands in sharp contrast to that in E. L. Konigsburg's *From the Mixed-Up Files of Mrs. Basil E. Frankweiler*, in which two children decide to run away from home and live in comfort in the Metropolitan Museum of Art. Claudia, feeling unappreciated at home and bored with the sameness of her straight-A life, wants to do something that is different and exciting. She chooses her brother Jamie to go along with her because he has the money they need. Claudia is a good organizer, and the two of them take up residence in the museum. They take baths in the museum's fountain, eat meals at the automat and the museum's cafeteria, and join tour groups for their education. Their adventure grows more exciting when Claudia becomes involved in the mystery surrounding the statue of a little angel. The children's research finally takes them to the home of Mrs. Basil E. Frankweiler, who arranges for Claudia to return home the way she had hoped she would—different in some aspect. Now she is different because she knows the secret of the angel. In return for this knowledge the two children tell Mrs. Frankweiler the details of their survival; she carefully records it and then writes their story. This story-within-a-story is a sophisticated and funny account of two very resourceful survivors.

Three other survival stories set in New York City take place in much grimmer circumstances. In Felice Holman's *Slake's Limbo*, Slake is a 13-year-old nearsighted orphan who lives with his aunt and thinks of himself as a worthless lump. Slake has no friends; his vision makes him a poor risk for any gang, and a severe reaction to smoke and drugs makes him useless in other ways. Hunted and hounded for sport, Slake takes refuge in the subway, staying for 121 days. He earns a little money reselling papers he picks up on the trains and makes his home in a hidden cave in the subway wall. One day when the subway repair crew comes through, Slake realizes that his "home" will be destroyed. He becomes ill and is taken to the hospital, where he is given nourishment and proper eyeglasses. Later he slips out of the hospital. His first reaction is to return to the subway, but when he hears a bird sing he looks up and decides he could perhaps exist on the roofs of some of the buildings: "He turned and started up the stairs and out of the subway. Slake did not know exactly where he was going but the general direction was up" (p. 117). Neil Shusterman's *Downsiders,* also set beneath the New York subway tunnels, is a survival tale that reads more like science fiction than realism, but Shusterman raises interesting questions about the fate of outsiders in today's world. The book makes compelling reading and serves as a good companion to Holman's story.

A more hopeful story is told in Paula Fox's *Monkey Island.* Eleven-year-old Clay Garrity is abandoned by his despondent and pregnant mother, and not wishing to let his neighbor in the New York welfare hotel report him to the social worker, Clay runs away. On the street, he manages to survive because two homeless men share with him their place in a park, a box where they sleep. Calvin and Buddy become his family, sharing their food and their life stories. Clay learns to wear all his clothes at once, where to find food, and how not to attract attention during the day. One terrifying November night, a street gang destroys the makeshift shelters of the homeless people living in the park, Calvin disappears, and Clay catches pneumonia. Realizing his friend needs help, Buddy makes the choice of taking him to a hospital even though it means Clay will lose his freedom. But in a hopeful conclusion, Clay, his mother, and his new baby sister are reunited. Paula Fox's story prompts readers to consider the causes of homelessness and to consider what may happen. Clay's dangerous journey is made at least partially bearable by the dog-eared copy of *Robinson Crusoe* he carries from the welfare hotel. Later, a copy of *David Copperfield,* the story of a life outside a lost family, lends Clay some courage. Paula Fox creates memorable characters in an unsentimental but hopeful survival story in which the social services of a large city, as well as caring individuals who take action, are able to do well for at least one boy and one family.

There are intriguing patterns in stories of survival. Many deal with questions and themes basic to humankind. Some survival stories suggest that surviving with another person provides comforting benefits as well as difficulties. Questions readers might ask while comparing survival stories of all genres include these: What qualities make one able to survive? How does surviving an ordeal change a person's outlook? After basic wants are satisfied, what other needs do survivors seem to have? Which is more difficult, physical survival or emotional survival? What role does art or beauty play in the survivor's ability to endure?

## Coping with Problems of the Human Condition

People in all times and places must cope with problems of the human condition—birth, pain, and loneliness; poverty, illness, and death. Children do not escape these problems, but literature can give them windows for looking at different aspects of life, show them how some characters have faced personal crises, and help them ask and answer questions about the meaning of life.

In discussing the portrayal of emotionally significant themes in children's literature, Mollie Hunter points out:

> A broken home, the death of a loved person, a divorce between parents—all these are highly charged emotional situations once considered unsuitable for children's reading, but which are nevertheless still part of some children's experience; and the writer's success in casting them in literary terms rests on the ability to create an emotional frame of reference to which children in general can relate.[14]

David Elkind, a psychologist, warns that we might nonetheless be overburdening our children with the ills of society before they have an opportunity to find themselves. He says:

> This is the major stress of the literature of young children aimed at making them aware of the problems in the world about them before they have a chance to master the problems of childhood.[15]

Certainly teachers and librarians should balance the reading of "problem books" with those that emphasize joy in living.

### Physical Disabilities

Good stories about people with physical disabilities serve two purposes. They provide positive images

---

[14]Mollie Hunter, *Talent Is Not Enough* (New York: HarperCollins, 1990), p. 20.
[15]David Elkind, *The Hurried Child: Growing Up Too Fast Too Soon* (Reading, Mass.: Addison-Wesley, 1981), p. 84.

with which youngsters with disabilities can identify, and they can help children who do not have disabilities develop a more intelligent understanding of some of the problems that persons with disabilities face. In stories, disabilities should be neither exaggerated nor ignored, neither dramatized nor minimized, neither romanticized nor belittled.[16] It is particularly important that stories of people with disabilities be well written, not sentimental or maudlin. They should not evoke pity for what children with disabilities cannot do, but respect for what they *can* do. As in all well-written stories, characters should be multidimensional persons with real feelings and frustrations rather than serve as a foil for another character's good deeds. The author should be honest in portraying the condition and future possibilities for the character. Illustrations should also portray disabilities in an honest and straightforward manner.

Literary treatment of disabilities might rely on time-honored themes: a person with disabilities has special powers, grace, or a predetermined destiny; a person with a disability serves as a catalyst in the maturation of others; a disability is a metaphor for society's ills, such as a blind person who can "see" what others do not choose to acknowledge or are too insensitive to see. Occasionally, disabilities are somewhat misleadingly portrayed as something that can be overcome with determination, faith, and grit,[17] but in the hands of a fine writer, themes like these avoid becoming clichés and can present the reader with fresh insight into coping with the human condition.

Older stories have depicted children with cerebral palsy and families who deal courageously with this illness. The theme "what kind of help and how much" is evident in Jean Little's *Mine for Keeps.* When Sally, who has cerebral palsy, returns from a special school to live at home, she attends regular school and faces several problems. But a dog that may be hers "for keeps" helps her gain physical skill and the emotional courage to help another child who has been ill. In *The Alfred Summer,* Jan Slepian presents a 14-year-old boy with cerebral palsy who also chafes resentfully at the strings that he feels bind him to his overprotective mother and ignoring father. Lester describes himself self-mockingly as a walking "perpetual motion machine." One day he makes a friend of Alfred, a retarded boy he sees collecting tinfoil from the gutters. Alfred's total acceptance of him frees Lester, and the two discover a third friend in Myron. As the three friends make a boat, each accomplishes something he thought he could not do and gains some self-respect. When the boat is finally launched, it sinks, but Myron and Lester realize that what they have built over the summer is much more important than a leaky old boat. By using Lester as a narrator in several chapters, Slepian injects humor and insight into this well-characterized, compassionate story.

Ben Mikaelsen's moving *Petey* is based on a true story of a boy born with cerebral palsy but diagnosed as mentally retarded. Hospitalized in a state home for years, Petey is finally rediagnosed and released to a nursing home. Here he meets a young eighth grader whose own life is changed dramatically by his friendship with Petey. Although the book is long and somewhat sentimentalized, Petey's character is portrayed with great dignity. The message is clear that each of us deserves respect and the chance to realize our potential.

Rowena Batts, the heroine of Australian writer Morris Gleitzman's *Blabber Mouth,* has been born, as she puts it, with "some bits missing from my throat." She is mainstreamed into a regular classroom after her special school is shut down, and like any middle-grade child, she wants to fit in and find friends. She stumbles a bit at first, but her ability as a runner brings her a new friend named Amanda who had learned rudimentary sign language for a community service project. Her real problem, as she sees it, is her quirky father, who dresses in wild cowboy clothes and sings country western at the top of his lungs. He is constantly embarrassing her in front of her new classmates. This upbeat story of how Ro and her father make peace and how Ro makes it in her new environment is moving and funny and incidentally provides a positive picture of a child who is differently abled but not disabled.

## Developmental and Learning Disabilities

Betsy Byars won a Newbery Medal for her story about an adolescent girl and her retarded brother in *The Summer of the Swans.* Sara feels very much like the ugly duckling in her difficult fourteenth summer. She weeps over her big feet, her skinny legs, and her nose, even over her gross orange sneakers. But when her brother is lost in the woods, her tears vanish in the terror she feels for Charlie. In her anguish Sara turns to Joe Melby—whom she had despised the day before—and together they find Charlie. It is the longest day of the summer and Sara knows that she will never be the same again. Like the awkward flight of the swans with their "great beating of wings and ruffling of feathers," Sara is going to land with a long, perfect glide. Sara's love for her brother and concern for his safety help her break through her shell of adolescent moodiness.

---

[16]Barbara H. Baskin and Karen H. Harris, *More Notes from a Different Drummer: A Guide to Juvenile Fiction Portraying the Disabled* (New York: Bowker, 1984).

[17]Baskin and Harris, *More Notes from a Different Drummer,* chap. 2.

The ambivalent feelings of siblings are examined with compassion in Colby Rodowsky's *What About Me?* and Paula Fox's *Radiance Descending.* Rodowsky's Dorrie, a rebellious 15-year-old, feels that her own life is swallowed up in the family's constant concern for Fred, her retarded 11-year-old brother. Her frustration and anger boil to the surface as expressions of hatred for her brother; yet when she is left alone with him and his heart condition becomes critical, she finds herself caring for him, loving him, just as her parents have always done. In the story's poignant resolution Fred dies and, like Dorrie, the reader is left to consider what it means to grow up in a family that includes a retarded child. Paula Fox's Paul is also tired of the attention focused on his younger brother, Jacob, who was born with Down syndrome, and embarrassed by Jacob's actions. Only his grandfather seems to understand Paul's feelings, and his patient willingness to listen finally helps Paul begin to reach out to Jacob.

In *My Louisiana Sky* Kimberly Willis Holt's Tiger Ann Parker must cope with adults with developmental disabilities, her own parents. Raised by her grandmother, who also looks after her childlike mother and learning-disabled father, Tiger Ann is ashamed of her parents, especially when her classmates make fun of her family situation. She longs for the type of life her sophisticated Aunt Doreen can give her. However, when her beloved grandmother dies and her aunt takes her to Baton Rouge to live, Tiger Ann understands that there is a trade-off between big city sophistication and her small but close-knit rural community. She begins to recognize that her parents have unusual talents and she reaches out to grasp the role that she can play in this loving if eccentric family.

Sue Ellen Bridgers portrays an important summer in 12-year-old Casey Flanagan's life in *All Together Now.* Casey has come to spend the summer with her grandparents in a small southern town. There she meets Dwayne Pickens, a retarded man who is her father's age. Dwayne has the mind of a 12-year-old and a passion for baseball. Their friendship grows when Dwayne, who dislikes girls but mistakes Casey for a boy, includes her in his endless baseball sessions. Casey contracts what might be polio, and her anxious family sits with her through several terrible August days. Dwayne faithfully visits during the long convalescence that follows and keeps her spirits up. By summer's end, Casey has grown in awareness of herself and the nature of friendship.

Joey Pigza has problems of a different sort in Jack Gantos's *Joey Pigza Swallowed the Key.* As if an abusive grandmother and an absent father aren't enough to deal with, Joey's attention deficit hyperactivity disorder (ADHD) is out of control. Despite medication, Joey cannot seem to stop his impulsive behavior. He sticks his finger in a pencil sharpener, swallows his house key, and drives his classmates to distraction. When his impetuous actions injure another student, he is sent to a special education program in another school. Here Joey finds a knowledgeable teacher who has the time to help him learn how to deal with his behavior. A physical evaluation identifies a medication that is more suitable for him and eventually he is able to return to his original school. Gantos does a fine job of letting us inside Joey's head to experience his behavior, his feelings, and his frustrations at his loss of control. This understanding and sympathetic portrait of the different child will resonate with all children.

## Mental Illness

Few stories in which the protagonist suffers from mental illness have been written for the elementary school child, but several well-written books for adolescents and young adults feature characters that are struggling with mental illness. In a demanding and serious book, *3 NBs of Julian Drew* by James Deem, 15-year-old Julian has been traumatized and abused both physically and mentally. Writing in a code he has invented as a way of escaping his pain, he keeps a series of notebooks, which this book is named after. Deem has told the story through this cryptic code, mirroring Julian's mental state in a way conventional spelling could not. Thus the book is for mature and accomplished readers who will be intrigued by the device and moved by Julian's struggle to escape the tyranny of his home and the prison of his disturbed mind.

Thirteen-year-old Carrie Stokes, in Zibby Oneal's *The Language of Goldfish*, does not like what is happening to her. She wishes her family could return to the days when they lived in a cramped Chicago apartment rather than in an affluent suburb. If only things hadn't changed, she would still be close to her sister, Moira, and they would share all that they had as children. Instead, Carrie is under pressure from her mother and sister to wear more appropriate and stylish clothes, to go to school dances, and, somehow, be someone Carrie feels she is not. When she attempts suicide by overdosing on pills, her mother still avoids dealing with the real Carrie. Gradually, as Carrie mends, she is better able to understand her mother's denial. She is helped in this by a therapist, a trusted art teacher, and a new friend, a neighbor boy. Finally she learns to accept changes in others and herself while those closest to her display various ways in which they, too, cope with mental illness.

While there are few books about mentally ill children, there are several that present a child or children dealing with a mentally ill adult. Cynthia Voigt's

*Homecoming* and *Dicey's Song,* for instance, portray the aftereffects of a depressed mother's abandonment of her children. Paula Fox's *The Village by the Sea* concerns a girl's two-week stay with a mentally ill aunt. Bruce Brooks, in *The Moves Make the Man,* shows through the eyes of a compassionate and articulate boy narrator how the mental breakdown of his friend's mother nearly brings about the breakdown of the friend as well.

In Kristine L. Franklin's *Eclipse,* sixth grader Trina must deal with the changes in her father's mental state following an accident that disabled him. As she looks forward to the birth of a sibling the family has wanted for years, her normally outgoing father either sleeps all the time or lashes out irrationally at Trina. Trina is troubled by his behavior and the fear that the new baby could be born retarded because of her mother's age. Her mother tries to protect her from the truth but finally admits to Trina that her father has attempted suicide. When the baby is born prematurely, her father cannot seem to cope and, refusing to take his medication, falls further into depression. On the night of a lunar eclipse, in a tremendously tense and painful conclusion, he takes a rifle into their barn and a shot rings out just as Trina and her mother realize what his calm goodnight must have meant. The consequences to families of mental illness are painfully clear in this moving yet ultimately hopeful story.

## Aging and Death

In the early part of this century the aging and death of loved ones were accepted as a natural part of a child's firsthand knowledge. However, most modern children are removed from any such knowledge of senility and death. Few grandparents live with their families anymore, and many relocate to apartments or retirement communities. When older relatives become ill, they are shunted off to hospitals and nursing homes. Few people die at home today, and many children have never attended a funeral. Seldom is death discussed with children. Contemporary authors realize that there is enough genuine mystery about death, without hiding it under this false cloak of secrecy.

Today, realistic fiction for children reflects society's concern for honesty about aging and dying. We have moved from a time when the subject of death was one of the taboos of children's literature to a time when it is being discussed openly and frankly.

### Aging

Many recent picture books have portrayed young people learning to accept older people as they are or to recall them fondly as they were (see Chapter 5). Realistic fiction portrays older people in all their rich variety, as treasured grandparents, as activists or as passive observers, as senile or vitally involved in events around them, and as still-valuable contributors to a society they have helped to build.

*The Hundred Penny Box,* written by Sharon Bell Mathis and illustrated by Leo and Diane Dillon, tells of the love between Great-Great-Aunt Dew, an aged African American woman, and Michael, a young boy. Aunt Dew is 100 years old and she keeps a box full of pennies, one for each year of her life. Michael loves to count them out while Aunt Dew tells him the story behind each one, relating it to life and historical events. Michael's mother wants to give the old box away, but Michael plans a special hiding place for it. This story is remarkable for presenting perspectives on aging from the viewpoints of three different persons: Aunt Dew, who is content to sing her long song and recall the past with her pennies; Michael's mother, who has to take care of her; and Michael, who loves her but in his childlike way also wants to be entertained by her storytelling.

The title character of Peter Härtling's *Old John* is an independent, cantankerous, lovable, and opinionated 75-year-old when he comes to live with Laura and Jacob's family. One of his prized possessions is a poster of Albert Einstein sticking out his tongue, a comment on Old John's belief that people should give themselves the freedom to put people on a little bit. While each person in the family must cope with exasperation over the old man's habits, each loves him and learns from him. Old John finds raucous companions in the small German village where he now lives, paints and decorates his bedroom to his own tastes, picks up his former profession as a dyer, and even falls in love. However, he suffers a stroke, and as the next year passes he becomes progressively more disoriented and crotchety. But the family rallies to care for him and he dies peacefully at home. Härtling lets incidents speak for themselves, leaving the reader to observe what life with an older person can be like for one family. Though Old John will "never be there again" on his favorite corner of the couch, the reader knows that he will be there in the minds of Jacob and Laura, who are richer people for having known their grandfather so well.

In Janet Hickman's *Jericho,* Angela's great-grandmother, Grandmin, is also old and disoriented. When her family decides to spend the summer helping fix up the old woman's house, Angela resents having to leave home and her friend Tessa. She is repulsed by the old woman's physical needs and angry that Grandmin cannot remember who she is. But in her mind, Grandmin *is* remembering; she has gone back to the time when she was a young girl like Angela. As Angela's summer progresses, Min's story runs parallel to hers, and as we experience Angela's frustration and adolescent longing, we see Min's even more clearly. This is a lovely story about the gulf that often separates generations. Although she never learns Min's story, after Min's death Angela is looking at some old photographs and comes across one of her great-grandmother as a young woman. "For that first speechless moment she feels a sense of connection so strong and so unsettling that she thinks she cannot bear it" (p. 135). Looking at the picture is like looking in a mirror. Grandmin is Angela in ways that go deeper than the flat surface of an old photograph.

There are also books that portray older people as active, lively, and engaging. British author Nina Bawden portrays vital and energetic older people in many of her books. In the humorous *Granny the Pag*, Catriona Brooke's beloved Granny is a psychiatrist who tools around town on her Harley-Davidson motorcycle. In *The Friends* by Kazumi Yumoto, three boys have a horrified fascination with death and begin to spy on a reclusive old neighbor, hoping to observe the process firsthand. But the old man turns out to be a vital if somewhat curmudgeonly character, and the boys find themselves taken in by his personality and his needs. In the witty and often poignant *Tiger, Tiger, Burning Bright* by Ron Koertge, Pappy, Jesse's grandfather, is also an independent spirit. When Pappy reports that he has seen a tiger in the hills surrounding their desert home, Jesse is afraid that this vital, funny man is becoming senile as his mother believes. Jesse gradually comes to accept the normal processes of aging and to understand that he cannot pretend that his grandfather is not changing. But Pappy also proves to be more alert than anyone had realized, and although he may need some extra help, he still isn't ready for a nursing home. Jesse's mother acknowledges, "Neither one of us ever had it right about Pappy. So now I think we just take it one day at a time" (p. 174).

In Lois Lowry's *Anastasia Again*, Anastasia devises a scheme for involving her grouchy neighbor with a group of lively older people at a local senior citizen center. In Eth Clifford's *The Rocking Chair Rebellion*, 14-year-old "Opie" (short for Penelope) is volunteering at the Maple Ridge Home for the Aged when a former neighbor takes up residence there. Opie eventually is instrumental in helping several of the residents leave and set up their own group home in her neighborhood. Although events are somewhat improbable, both Lowry and Clifford present older people as diverse, intelligent, active, and interesting as potential friends.

Another book that suggests that different generations have much to offer each other is Angela Johnson's *Toning the Sweep*. Fourteen-year old Emily and her mother have traveled to the desert Southwest to bring her sick grandmother back to Cleveland.

Grandma Ola has built a rich life for herself in this desert land she loves so much, and the summer visit is the opportunity for Emily to discover her grandmother's present and her own past. She undertakes a video project and interviews Ola, her mother, and the people who make up her grandmother's community. The story that emerges includes the awful facts about her grandfather's death in Alabama and the painful truth that her grandmother is coming home to die. But this story is not about dying. Rather, it is a celebration of a remarkable woman who has lived a full, if unconventional, life. Emily's project becomes a fitting way to "tone the sweep" for her, the opportunity to ring her soul to heaven as her ancestors in South Carolina might have done in previous generations.

### Death and Dying

A child's first experience with death is frequently the loss of a pet. While picture books for younger children portray this experience with younger protagonists, several longer books have depicted slightly older children dealing with the death of a pet. In *Growing Time* by Sandol Stoddard Warburg, Jamie's old collie dog King dies and Jamie is desolate. Eventually the family buys Jamie a puppy, but he doesn't even want to look at it. In the middle of the night, however, the new pup cries and needs someone to love it. Jamie comes downstairs to comfort and claim him.

Other children's first experience with death is the loss of a grandparent. Two warmly illustrated short stories show a child coping with the death of one grandparent while continuing a rewarding relationship with the remaining one. In Mavis Jukes's *Blackberries in the Dark*, Austin spends the summer on the farm with Grandma and everywhere around him are reminders of his grandfather: the tire swing he built, his fishing reel hanging in the barn, and his treasured old fishing knife now strangely out of place in the dining room cupboard. Grandpa had promised to teach him how to fish this summer, and with him gone, there's no one to teach him or to help him pick blackberries at night. After Grandma and Austin recall the past summer, however, Austin starts out to pick blackberries on his own, only to have his grandmother follow, complete with her husband's fishing gear, so the two of them can teach each other to fish. Readers can almost feel the two resolve to move on from grief to new challenges, and the decision is neatly punctuated by Grandma's gift of Grandpa's fishing knife to Austin. Thomas B. Allen's black-and-white soft-pencil illustrations capture poignancy, accept the pleasant loneliness of the farm, and depict the humor of Austin's story.

*A Taste of Blackberries* by Doris Smith is a believable story of the sudden death of a young boy. Jamie and his friends are catching Japanese beetles for Mrs. House when Jamie shoves a slim willow limb down a bee hole. The bees swarm out and Jamie is stung. Allergic to bee stings, Jamie screams and gasps and falls to the ground. His best friend thinks Jamie is just showing off, until the ambulance arrives. Jamie is dead by the time he arrives at the hospital. His friend goes to the funeral, and the author graphically describes his reaction to seeing Jamie:

> There was Jamie. He was out straight with one hand crossed over his chest. He didn't look like he was asleep to me. Jamie slept all bunched up. Jamie looked dead. (p. 34)

After the funeral Jamie's friend picks blackberries because the two of them had planned to do so together. He shares the berries with Jamie's mother, who is very loving toward him. Because the story is told in the first person, the reader views death through a child's eyes. Simple, yet direct, this story seems very real. Paterson's *Bridge to Terabithia* and Bauer's *On My Honor*, which were discussed earlier in this chapter, are each about a child who suffers after the death of a friend.

In *A Family Project* by Sarah Ellis, 11-year-old Jessica is delighted when her parents announce that Mum is pregnant. She embarks on a class project of researching babies with her best friend, Margaret. Baby Lucie's arrival creates the expected chaos but also provides Jessica with special moments of love and appreciation. One night when Jessica is at a friend's slumber party, Lucie dies suddenly of sudden infant death syndrome. Following the funeral and a large gathering of friends and relatives, each member of the family grieves. Mum withdraws, Dad is frenetically busy, her brother Simon is curt, and Jessica feels as if her life will never be joyous or whole again. Margaret acknowledges her friend's grief, saying that while time will help her feel less sad, she will always have a small sad spot in her memory for this baby sister. Weeks pass, and it is finally Simon and Jessica who help each other accept their sister's death. Ellis creates a totally believable contemporary family whose grief over the sudden death of a baby will be healed by their love for each other.

Several other stories deal with the process of grieving the death of a brother or sister. Barbara Park's *Mick Harte Was Here* begins after the bike accident that killed 13-year-old Phoebe's younger brother, Mick. As she remembers this lively boy and deals with her guilt at the petty quarrels they had, Phoebe learns that her mother and father are struggling under the burden of their own guilt. The family members finally acknowledge the "if onlys" each of them has carried silently. When Phoebe cries, "If only I had ridden his bike home Mick would still be here" (p. 84),

her father sits her down and makes a list of all the other "if onlys" the family has used to blame themselves. Bringing these out into the open signals a new and healthier stage in their grieving. *Beat the Turtle Drum* by Constance Greene is narrated by 13-year-old Kate and tells of the summer when Joss saved her money, rented a horse, and finally, in an accidental fall from a tree, was killed. Readers who have come to know the two sisters feel, along with Kate and her parents, the tragedy of Joss's death. *A Summer to Die* by Lois Lowry presents two sisters who quarrel constantly until the older one contracts leukemia. Lowry juxtaposes the celebration of birth with the sadness of a death, and Meg moves through the stages of dealing with her sister's death, but the other two stories seem more compelling.

*Getting Near to Baby* by Audrey Couloumbis reveals the heartbreaking aftereffects of the death of a baby sister on her family. Younger Sister has stopped talking and mother has fallen apart in her effort to overcome her guilt and grief. Willa Jo, the 13-year-old eldest sister, tries to carry the burden of care for her family. The story concerns the conflict between Willa Jo and Aunt Patty, Willa Jo's mother's oldest sister. When Aunt Patty and Uncle Hob insist that the two girls come to stay with them, Willa Jo resents her Aunt's interference and her fussy, class-conscious ways. The book begins as Willa Jo crawls out on the roof of the house one morning to watch the sun rise. Joined by Little Sister, she decides to just stay on the roof, to the consternation of Aunt Patty and the bemusement of Uncle Hob and the neighbors. Gradually, in between episodes on the roof, the story of Baby's death and the resulting events is revealed in flashbacks. Through these finely interwoven strands of story the terrible burden of sadness that each of the characters carries is revealed. We also come to see the complex personalities of Willa Jo and Aunt Patty, both of them more alike than they want to admit. In the end they find that all of them have had something important to contribute to the healing process that has occurred.

In Janet Taylor Lisle's *The Lost Flower Children* we also find two sisters who have been traumatized by a death. After their mother dies, Olivia and her younger sister Nellie are sent to live with their Great Aunt Minty. This circumstance appalls 9-year-old Olivia, who takes the move as a betrayal by her father. Olivia, who is fiercely protective of her demanding and explosive younger sister, focuses all her energy on caring for Nellie, perhaps as a way of vanquishing her own pain. Olivia views Aunt Minty's spinsterish, old-lady habits with disdain, and Aunt Minty seems to be at a loss to know how to care for the two girls. Her efforts at entertaining them and finding friends for them seem to end in disaster. But

*In Janet Taylor Lisle's beautifully written* The Lost Flower Children *two young sisters find a way to accept their mother's death with the help of their Great Aunt Minty.*

From *Lost Flower Children* by Janet Taylor Lisle, jacket illustration by Satomi Ichikawa, copyright © 1999 by Satomi Ichikawa. Used by permission of Philomel Books, a division of Penguin Putman Inc.

when she unearths a little china cup in her overgrown garden, the two girls are curious despite themselves. When Olivia finds an old storybook hidden in Aunt Minty's vast library, the meaning of the tiny tea cup is revealed. The children are soon captivated by the task of finding the other pieces of the tea set, which they believe will release a party of children transformed into flowers by a spell of enchantment. The search for the lost tea set becomes the focal point of their lives and the unconscious channel into which they pour their grief. Gradually the girls bloom just as Aunt Minty's garden is revived. One of Janet Taylor Lisle's great strengths as a writer is her ability to create magic and enchantments that seem absolutely real. Whether this is a work of fantasy or realism will be up to individual children to decide. Whether the characters have been enriched and healed by giving free reign to their imagination is not in dispute.

Crescent Dragonwagon's *Winter Holding Spring* is a simple poetic story with complex ideas about death, time, hope, and love. It begins as 11-year-old Sarah

and her father can tomatoes just as her mother used to before she died. Both adult and child find it difficult to talk about their feelings, but they observe, as a yellow leaf falls, that the season of summer holds fall. As the seasons progress, the two go about the daily chores of living, and Sarah uses the idea of a future embedded in the present to give herself hope and courage. In Kevin Henkes's *Sun and Spoon,* young Spoon attempts to hold on to something concrete from his grandmother following her death. He takes a deck of her solitaire cards, not realizing how disturbing this will prove to his grandfather. Eventually he gives the cards back and his Grandfather and his loving parents help him understand how to hold on to memories. In both books the philosophical discussion of death in the midst of life is grounded realistically for child readers in the ordinary events of everyday lives.

Two books face the issue of AIDS and the death of a parent from this disease. In Teresa Nelson's *Earthshine,* Slim McGranahan's father is an out-of-work actor who is being cared for by his friend Larry when Slim leaves her mother and stepfather and moves in with the two. As Mack McGranahan deals with his sickness in his own indomitable way, Slim attends a support group for children and meets Isaiah, whose mother has the AIDS virus. Isaiah convinces Slim to take a pilgrimage to a healer as her father moves closer to death. Their strange journey does not bring a cure to her father, but it lifts the burden of anger and guilt from her own spirit. Gillian is the feisty, somewhat eccentric central character in Barbara Ann Porte's *Something Terrible Happened.* When her mother dies of AIDS, Gillian is sent to her deceased father's family in Tennessee. Gillian is angry that she could not stay with her grandmother and still grieving at losing her mother. But being with her father's family gives her a part of herself that this biracial child had not known, and brings her a stable family structure that is just what she needs to work through her grief. Porte tells the story through an unusual point of view: The unknown narrator recounts events as they were pieced together from multiple sources—eyewitness accounts, Gilly's letters, and the wonderful folktales that feature in Gilly's heritage.

Previously discussed books deal with a child who recovers from the death of a friend, sibling, parent, or grandparent. *Hang Tough, Paul Mather* tells a memorable story of a boy who is anticipating his own death. Alfred Slote writes of Paul, a Little Leaguer who develops leukemia. The family moves from California to Michigan to be close to the university hospital where Paul will have special treatments. He is not supposed to play baseball, but the neighborhood team needs a pitcher for their big game. Paul slips out without his parents' knowledge, forges the permission slip, and pitches a great game. However, he injures himself and endures a long stay in the hospital. There, a young doctor becomes his friend. Their discussion of death is one of the most honest in children's literature. Paul leaves the hospital in his wheelchair, at least long enough to watch and help win another game. While Paul sounds hopeful at the end of the story, he is back in the hospital and his condition has worsened.

A powerful story that asserts that coming to terms with death can be an affirmation of life and hope is Madeleine L'Engle's *A Ring of Endless Light.* Vicky Austin, whom readers met in *Meet the Austins,* begins her sixteenth summer at graveside services for a family friend who has suffered a heart attack after rescuing a spoiled teenager from an attempted suicide. While Vicky is already grieving for the impending death of her beloved grandfather, she tries to understand what mortality and immortality mean. She also deals with the attentions of three different young men. Zachary, the boy who attempted suicide, is rich, impulsive, and exciting; Leo, whose father had tried to save Zachary, is plain and awkward but reliable and candid; and Adam, a marine biologist studying dolphin communication, is warm, kind, and intensely eager to involve Vicky in his research after he sees her natural ability to communicate with dolphins. When the death of a child numbs Vicky, it is her experience with the dolphins that brings her back to an emotional present. Throughout the story shines the "ring of endless light" that her grandfather has been leading her to see. He tells Vicky, in the depths of her grief and denial:

> You have to give the darkness permission. It cannot take over otherwise. . . . Vicky, do not add to the darkness. . . . This is my charge to you. You are to be a light-bearer. You are to choose the light. (p. 318)

## *Living in a Diverse World*

 In a true pluralistic society it is essential that we learn to respect and appreciate cultural diversity. Books can never substitute for firsthand contact with other people, but they can deepen our understanding of different cultures. Rather than falsely pretend that differences do not exist, children need to discover what is unique to each group of persons and universal to the experience of being human.

### African American Experiences in Books for Children

 In the last decades many fine books have been published that reflect the social and cultural traditions associated with growing up as an African American child in Amer-

ica. This "culturally conscious fiction," says Rudine Sims Bishop, has certain recurring features that offer all children, but especially African American children, a unique perspective in fiction. In culturally conscious fiction there often appear references to distinctive language patterns and vocabulary; relationships between a young person and a much older one; extended or three-generational families; descriptions of skin shades, including positive comparisons, such as "dark as a pole of Ceylon ebony"; and acknowledgment of African American historical, religious, and cultural traditions.[18]

Today, the number of chapter books for younger readers is still small but increasing. For instance, Ann Cameron's Julian and Huey series portrays a small-town family consisting of a soft-spoken mother, a stern but fun-loving father, and two brothers. Another chapter book that children aged 7 or 8 can read easily is Lucille Clifton's *The Lucky Stone.* In four short chapters, Clifton traces the path of a black stone with a letter scratched on it as it is passed from generation to generation of African Americans, from slave times to now.

Mildred Pitts Walter's *Justin and the Best Biscuits in the World* draws on information about African American cowboys on the American frontier in the late 1800s while telling a contemporary story. Tired of his family of sisters and his mother, 10-year-old Justin is relieved when his grandfather invites him to stay at his Missouri ranch. From Grandpa, Justin learns family history and how to clean fish, keep his room in order, and cook. When he goes home, Justin has developed self-confidence and his family is more appreciative of his talents. Walter's digressions about African Americans in the old West, under the guise of books read by Justin, might send some children to the library for further research. Walter's *Suitcase* is about a sixth grader whose height seems ideal for a basketball player. His physical ability is more suited to drawing than to dribbling, however, and this artistic talent both puzzles and disappoints his father. *Have a Happy . . . ,* by Walter, traces an 11-year-old boy's feelings as he tries to earn money to help out his family during the Christmas season. His participation in the events of Kwanza is presented so that even readers unfamiliar with this modern African American holiday can visualize the celebration and understand its significance.

In *Sister,* using the device of a secret diary about her "special days," Eloise Greenfield has presented an intimate picture of Doretha, called "Sister" by her family. The diary begins when Doretha is 10, and de-

---

[18]Rudine Sims Bishop, *Shadow and Substance: Afro-American Experience in Contemporary Children's Fiction* (Urbana, Ill.: National Council of Teachers of English, 1982), pp. 49–77.

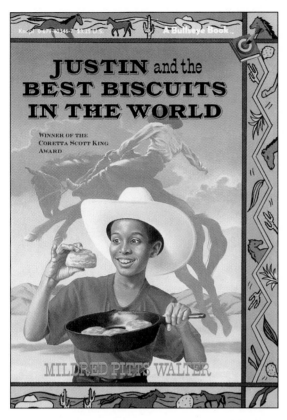

In *Justin and the Best Biscuits in the World* *Mildred Pitts Walter interweaves the story of a contemporary African American boy with information about African American cowboys in the old West.*

From *Justin and the Best Biscuits in the World* by Mildred Pitts Walter. Cover illustration copyright © 1991 by Paul Tankersley 1991. Reprinted by permission of Alfred A. Knopf Children's Books, a division of Random House, Inc.

tails the sudden death of her father while they are all attending a picnic. At 11 Doretha learns the family's story of her freedom-fighting ex-slave ancestor. When she is 12 she records her tears and her mother's disappointment when her mother's friend jilts her. Throughout the book Doretha worries about her alienated sister, but gradually Doretha emerges from the pages of her book and from her role as sister to become a very real person in her own right.

A four-time winner of the Coretta Scott King Award, Walter Dean Myers sets many of his stories in Harlem, but he portrays a less grim, and even humorous, city existence in some of his stories. *The Mouse Rap,* which alternates between poetry and prose, is written in the vernacular of jive-talking, rapping, 14-year-old Mouse Douglas, boy "hoop" player. Mouse's parents are separated but his father wants to rejoin the family, and Mouse and his best friend Styx like the same girl. In addition, Mouse and his friends know an old man who used to be part of Tiger Moran's gang. The old fellow says there is money from a 1930s bank robbery hidden in an abandoned

Harlem building. In an exciting and humorous conclusion, Mouse cleverly uses a television news reporter who is in the neighborhood covering a dance contest he and his friends have entered to gain a chance to explore the abandoned building. Myers also relies on the keen observations of an intelligent boy narrator in his *Fast Sam, Cool Clyde, and Stuff,* a story of the interdependence of a group of basketball-playing boys who inadvertently become involved with drugs while trying to help a former addict. The author's lighter books also show boys coping successfully with urban life.

Nikki Grimes also chooses an urban setting to provide a glimpse of pressures and problems faced by an adolescent girl living in Harlem in the 1960s in *Jazmin's Notebook.* Jazmin's problems, not the least of which are a dead father and an alcoholic mother, would seem almost stereotypical but her response to them is not. Jazmin keeps a notebook to record her observations of life and to write her poetry. Her strong character, her dreams of college, and her determination to succeed are revealed within its pages. Eventually, the stable home she finds with an older sister and the support of the other caring adults she meets promise a positive future for Jazmin.

In 1975, Virginia Hamilton became the first African American to win the Newbery Medal, with *M. C. Higgins, the Great.* Like *Cousins,* it is set in southern Ohio where 13-year-old Cornelius Higgins and his family live on old family property just beneath a slagheap created by strip miners. M. C. dreams of moving his family away from the slow-moving heap that threatens to engulf their home. His place of refuge from which he surveys the world is a 40-foot steel pole. From there M. C. sees a "dude" who he imagines will make his mother a singing star and enable them to move. Another outsider, Lurhetta, who is hiking through this section of Appalachia, awakens M. C.'s initiative and makes him see that he is never going to solve his problems by daydreaming about them. M. C. is finally moved to a small but symbolic action. (Mildred Taylor in 1977 was the second African American author to win the Newbery Medal. Her books are discussed in Chapter 10.)

Hamilton has also written *The Planet of Junior Brown,* which is really a story about three complementary "planets." The first planet is a huge mass added to a model solar system that Mr. Poole, the custodian, and Buddy have set up in the school basement. Like the 300-pound Buddy, the planet is larger than anything else in its area. The second is a set of sanctuaries for homeless boys throughout the forgotten places of New York City, held together by boys like Junior Brown who act as leaders of children who do not have homes or families. The final planet is the one that readers see as possible if people like Junior

Brown could lead us there. This planet could be a place where everyone belongs, where people respect each other, and where all value themselves as well. Hamilton's books celebrate the uniqueness of an African American experience in elegant and approachable prose. Her books speak to all readers, encouraging young people to take risks on behalf of others, to love all members of their immediate or extended or adopted families, and to do their best to act responsibly and honorably, for all of these actions will improve a small part of humankind.

Several books look at middle-class African Americans and the special pressures they face as they try to succeed in an often-hostile white world. Jacqueline Woodson's Margaret and Maizon are best friends growing up in Brooklyn when Maizon wins a scholarship to a mostly white private school. Her struggles to fit into a world that is alien and alienating are detailed in *Maizon at Blue Hill.* Margaret's own year apart from Maizon is related in *Last Summer with Maizon.* The two are reunited in *Between Madison and Palmetto* when Maizon drops out of Blue Hill and returns home to Madison Street. In all these books the girls confront difficult issues of race and class, but first and foremost these are stories about real young people whose friendship is strengthened through a variety of trials.

The Willis family in Andrea Davis Pinkney's *Hold Fast to Dreams* must confront similar issues when they move to suburban Connecticut from urban Baltimore. Dee's father has been promoted to vice president of sales at the Kentwood Corporation. Dee has a hard time fitting into the all-white environment of Wexford Middle School and misses her close friends in Baltimore. Eventually she finds that everyone in the family has had to confront some form of racism. She has had to deal with muffled whispers and "beady eyed" stares of classmates who know nothing of her world. Her sister has responded to her private-school classmates by "trying to act white" but is humiliated by her lacrosse teammates. Her father is harassed by a security guard at work, and her mother is trying desperately to pretend everything is fine. Mr. Willis admits his own problems and tells the girls that he finally had to stand up to the guard,

> When white folks stare and wonder and show disrespect, it's best to kindly—but firmly—let them know that you won't stand for it. Then you've just got to go on about your business. I figure if they don't have anything better to do than watch every blink I make, then boo-*hoo* for *them.* (p. 82)

His actions serve as a model for each of the girls to find a way to deal honorably with her own situation. Dee wins acceptance at an important all-school talent assembly when she presents her photographs and a

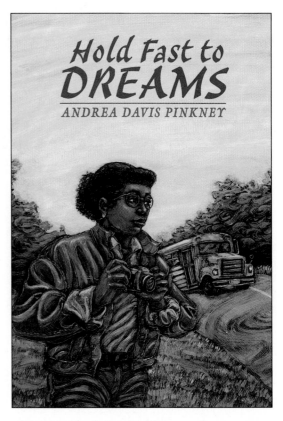

In Andrea Davis Pinkney's Hold Fast to Dreams, *Dee Willis is a middle-class African American girl who must face an all-white environment when her family moves to the suburbs.*

Illustration from the cover of *Hold Fast to Dreams* by Andrea Davis Pinkney. Illustration copyright © 1995 by Brian Pinkney. Used by permission of William Morrow & Company, an imprint of HarperCollins Publishers.

reading of Langston Hughes's poems. She also accepts something of the realities of the new world her family must live in and comes to value the loyalty and good humor of a new white friend.

## Books About Other Cultures

 For some years the quality and range in novels about African Americans have been far better than for other ethnic or racial groups. Informational books, folktales, biographies, and picture books have done a much better job of reflecting the multicultural society in which we now live. In older books about Hispanic Americans, for instance, forced stories and thin characterizations tended to perpetuate stereotypes rather than dispel them. Other titles, such as *Felita* by Nicholasa Mohr, suggested that "stick to your own kind" is the only way 9-year-old Felita and her family can cope with prejudice from their new neighbors. They return to the ghetto rather than stay in an apartment building where they have no friends. In *Going Home,* Felita, now a sixth grader, spends a summer in Puerto Rico and recognizes the universality of prejudice when her friendliness and artistic talents cause jealousy from her Puerto Rican peers.

In striking contrast, more-recent publications provide honest and memorable portrayals of many aspects of Latino and Hispanic culture. Nicholasa Mohr's *El Bronx Remembered* and Judith Ortiz Coffer's *An Island Like You* are excellent collections of short stories for older adolescents. Gary Soto's *Baseball in April and Other Stories, Local News,* and *Petty Crimes* are inspired collections of short stories that depict a variety of Hispanic children and adolescents in daily life. In *Baseball in April* Fausto longs for a guitar but his scheme to raise the money to buy one makes him feel so guilty that he finally gives the money to a church. His honorable behavior is amply rewarded when he becomes the owner of his grandfather's *guitarron.* In other stories one girl becomes marbles champ while another learns that it can be more painful to stay home when your family goes on vacation than it is to endure their company. *Local News* includes the wonderfully funny "School Play" and the sweetly gentle "New Year's Eve." In *Petty Crimes* Soto takes a more serious tone in several of the stories, depicting adolescents who struggle with poverty and gang violence. Soto's portrayal of these central-Californian youngsters, through description and dialogue, reflects sympathy for the universal experiences of growing up.

Soto's fine novels explore these experiences further. In *Taking Sides,* Lincoln Mendoza finds that he has divided loyalties when he moves from a barrio school to a suburban junior high school and competes in basketball against his former teammates. In *Pacific Crossing,* Lincoln and his friend Tony travel to Japan for a summer exchange program and find a further mixture of culture. *Crazy Weekend* and *Summer on Wheels* follow the adventures of Hector and Mando, two teenage friends, and in *Boys at Work* and *The Pool Party* 10-year-old Rudy Herrera is the main character. Soto adds a female protagonist, Miata Ramirez, to his extended family of books in *The Skirt* and *Off and Running.* In the latter, Miata runs against Rudy Herrera for school president. In all his books Soto writes gentle stories of family and friends that are infused with the rhythms and images of Mexican American culture. Glossaries in the books help those readers who cannot use context to translate the Spanish words and phrases that flow naturally through the story.

An older story of a boy of Spanish descent is Joseph Krumgold's *. . . And Now Miguel.* Miguel is the middle brother of a Hispanic family living on a New Mexico sheep ranch. Pedro, the younger brother, seems satisfied with what he has, but Miguel thinks his 19-year-old brother Gabriel not only can

*When a fancy invitation arrives from beautiful Tiffany, 10-year-old Rudy Herrera gets all decked out for a party in* The Pool Party *by Gary Soto.*

From *The Pool Party* by Gary Soto, Illustrated by Robert Casilla, copyright © 1993 illustrated by Robert Casilla. Reprinted by permission of Random House Children's Books, a division of Random House, Inc.

do everything but also has everything. Miguel has one all-consuming desire, and that is to be able to go with the men when they take the sheep to the Sangre de Cristo Mountains. His prayers are answered, but not as Miguel wished. Because Hispanics are one of the fastest-growing groups of immigrants to the United States, we still urgently need more contemporary realistic fiction that reflects Hispanic culture.

Asian Americans are among the most rapidly growing groups in North America. Many of the excellent stories set in this country that include children from countries in Asia are historical fiction titles such as Yoshiko Uchida's books that build on her experiences in the 1930s and in relocation camps for Japanese Americans in World War II. Jean Fritz's *Homesick: My Own Story* and Bette Bao Lord's *In the Year of the Boar and Jackie Robinson* are also set in the past.

Notable exceptions are Laurence Yep's fine contemporary novels. *Child of the Owl* is the story of a Chinese American girl who finds herself and her roots when she goes to live with Paw Paw, her grandmother, in San Francisco's Chinatown. At first Casey doesn't like the narrow streets and alleys or the Chinese schools. But Paw Paw tells her about Jeanie, the mother Casey never knew, about her true Chinese name, and the story of the family's owl charm. Gradually she comes to appreciate it all and to realize that this place that has been home to Paw Paw, Jeanie, and Barney is her home, too. *Child of the Owl* is as contemporary as the rock music that Paw Paw enjoys and as traditional as the owl charm, but Casey and Paw Paw are true originals. *Thief of Hearts* follows Casey's daughter Stacy on her own journey to understanding. Set in contemporary suburbia south of San Francisco, the book explores more subtle issues of prejudice and belonging. A mixed-race child, Stacy has her father's blond hair and her mother's Chinese eyes. She is a confident adolescent, at home in her multiethnic middle school, until her mother urges a new friend upon her. Hong Ch'un and her family are newly arrived from China and the girl is aloof and critical of American society. She and Stacy do not hit it off at all. When Hong Ch'un is accused of theft, however, Stacy stands up for her and finds that friends whom she has trusted hold her mixed-race status against her. Suddenly she sees her world in a different light.

> All my life I thought I had lived in a safe warm secure world where I was just like everyone else, but it had only been my little fantasy. I looked too Chinese. And yet, even if I learned Chinese and the culture, I looked too American. (p. 45)

Fortunately Paw Paw is there to set things right. Now called Tai-Paw, Stacy's great-grandmother, the wonderful old woman, has moved in with the family. She, too, has lost her familiar world, and this becomes even clearer when she and Stacy return to Chinatown to solve the mystery regarding Hong Ch'un. The Chinatown that existed when she raised Stacy's mother is almost unrecognizable and many of her old friends are dead. But the old woman is as wise as ever and she helps heal some of Stacy's hurt at the same time as she smooths a growing rift between Stacy and her mom. Well written, with fully developed, likable characters and a wonderful story, *Thief of Hearts* is a worthy sequel to *Child of the Owl*.

Yep has written many other titles for the middle-grade child. Although they are not as richly textured as *Child of the Owl*, they still provide satisfying stories and offer insights into Chinese American culture. Among these books are the warmly funny *Later, Gator,* and mysteries such as *The Case of the Firecrackers* that feature a young protagonist and her Great Aunt as a crime-solving duo in San Francisco's Chinatown. In *The Amah, The Cook's Family* and *Ribbons,* Yep presents Stephanie Chin, a young girl determined to be a ballet dancer despite the many setbacks that beset her family.

Lensey Namioka addresses a younger audience in *Yang the Youngest and His Terrible Ear.* Nine-year-old Yingtao Yang would rather play baseball than practice the violin with his musical siblings. His American friend Matthew has the opposite problem. Unlike Yingtao, he has quite an ear for music and would love to have violin lessons. With the help of Third Sister everyone gets to play the instrument of his or her choice. The stories of other irrepressible family members are continued in *Yang the Third and Her Impossible Family, Yang the Second and Her Secret Admirers,* and *Yang the Eldest and His Odd Jobs.* All of these warm, amusing books tell of a Chinese immigrant family and their attempts to fit in with the people and customs of their new country.

Jamie Gilson's novel *Hello, My Name Is Scrambled Eggs* takes its name from the stick-on labels Harvey Trumble uses to teach Vietnamese refugee Tuan Nguyen to speak English while Tuan, his father, and his grandmother are staying with Harvey until their own home is ready. But 12-year-old Tuan, eager to please, is nonetheless his own person, too, and he decides that although he will be American, he will also keep his Vietnamese name. Gilson allows Tuan to reveal parts of his

*In Lensey Namioka's* Yang the Second and Her Secret Admirers *Yinglan Nang, the oldest sister in a Chinese family who has immigrated to America, has more trouble fitting in than her siblings.*

From *Yang the Second and Her Secret Admirer* by Lensey Namioka. Illustrated by Kees de Kiefte. © 1998 Little, Brown & Company.

harrowing boat escape from Vietnam, and a classmate's current-events report fills in other details. Like Barbara Cohen's historical story *Molly's Pilgrim,* this novel culminates symbolically in a Thanksgiving celebration. Both would be excellent catalysts for discussing the many reasons, including political repression, that have caused people to emigrate to the United States.

Novels about Native Americans told with an authentic view of culture are hard to find. Joseph Bruchac, best known perhaps for his retellings of Native American folktales, has written two works of contemporary fiction that feature Native American characters. In *Eagle Song,* Danny Bigtree is a young Mohawk whose family moves to Brooklyn where his ironworker father can find work. In *Heart of a Chief* Chris Nicola, a Penacook Indian, lives on a reservation where his people face multiple issues including the opening of a gambling casino. Both books provide details of the warm family relationships that sustain each protagonist as he deals with problems that, though they might be particular to his culture, speak to universal issues facing children growing up in today's world.

Other books about Native Americans have geographically diverse settings but depict adolescents in-

*Joseph Bruchac's warm and realistic* Eagle Song *is one of the few books for children that feature a Native American character in a contemporary setting.*

From *Eagle Song* by Joseph Bruchac, illustrated by Dan Andreasen, copyright © 1997 by Dan Andreason. Used by permission of Dial Books for Young Readers, a division of Penguin Putman Inc.

volved in survival who must draw on their Native American heritage in various ways. In Kirkpatrick Hill's well-crafted survival story *Toughboy and Sister,* the title characters are suddenly on their own at the family summer fish camp in Canada's Yukon Territory after their widowed father, an alcoholic, literally drinks himself to death. Eleven-year-old Toughboy, an Athabascan Indian, and his sister expect to be rescued in a few days because their father's boat with his corpse in it will float downriver by their village. But when no one comes, the two must work together to cook, fish, make bread, deal with a pesky bear, and keep their clothes and cabin clean. The trials of these two resourceful children don't compare to those in many other stories in the survival genre, which usually feature greater dangers and deprivations. However, this story does provide fourth- and fifth-grade readers with a sympathetic glimpse into the life of two self-reliant and strong Native American children.

In Jean Craighead George's *The Talking Earth,* Billy Wind, a Seminole Indian girl who has been to school at the Kennedy Space Center, scoffs at the legends of her ancestors. As punishment, she is sent to stay in the Everglades for one night and two days to see if she then will believe in talking animals and little people who live under the ground. In the company of a baby panther, a pet otter, and a turtle, she survives a swamp fire, a hurricane, and a tidal wave; after twelve weeks in the wilderness, she arrives home convinced that the animals do indeed know the earth as she and others do not. As in *Julie of the Wolves* (discussed previously in this chapter), George states a powerful ecological message.

*Bearstone* by Will Hobbs tells the story of 14-year-old Cloyd Atcitty, a Ute Indian who has lived resentfully in a group home in Durango, Colorado, for much of his life. Cloyd is placed for the summer on a ranch where he will work for an old widower named Walter. Angry, Cloyd runs off after he is driven to the remote ranch in the Colorado/Utah mountain country. Taking refuge in a small cave, he discovers a small carved stone bear, an animal important to Ute tribal beliefs. Adopting this bear as his totem, Cloyd decides to give Walter and ranch life a try. While Cloyd and Walter develop respect for each other, Cloyd finds respect for himself. More important, in this excellent coming-of-age story, Cloyd's knowledge of his people's ways finally gives him the power to control his own life. *Beardance* continues Cloyd's story.

## Understanding Various World Cultures

Despite the increasing number of fine books of nonfiction and folklore and picture books from and about other countries, there are fewer novels that attempt to portray the lives of modern children and their families living in other places. Yet, as children study Australia or the countries of South America, Europe, or Africa, it is critical that they also be made aware of the stories that reveal the feelings of people in those countries. Children will find descriptions of Australian culture in books by such fine writers as Ivan Southall, Colin Thiele, Patricia Wrightson, Ruth Park, and Robin Klein. In addition, the American Library Association annually gives the Batchelder Award to the publisher of the most outstanding book of that year originally published in a foreign language in a foreign country. These books are excellent firsthand accounts of life in other countries (see Appendix A). However, children might need to be reminded that no single book can convey a complete picture of a country and its people. To make this point clear, one might ask students to consider what book, if any, they would like to have sent to other countries as representative of life in the United States.

One of the few books for younger children that reflect urban life in a Central American country is Ann Cameron's *The Most Beautiful Place in the World,* which tells of 7-year-old Juan, who lives in Guatemala. His young mother has remarried, but her new husband can't support Juan, so Juan moves in with his grandmother. His grandmother makes her living by selling *arroz con leche* in the market every day, and she puts Juan to work helping her in the marketplace. As he waits for customers, he practices reading on scraps of newspaper, produce signs, and other print that comes his way. When Juan asks to go to school, his grandmother tries to enroll him, but they are nearly turned away until Juan shows that he has learned to read. When his grandmother explains why she never went to school, Juan realizes how important an education could have been to her. He might live in the most beautiful place in the world, as the travel poster says, but he knows that truly the best place is where there is someone like his grandmother who loves him. Thomas B. Allen's black-line drawings capture the warmth of Juan's life, yet the artist also reveals the cold realities of the boy's poverty and abandonment. Third- or fourth-grade children who read this story learn something of the geography of Guatemala, the distant volcanoes and the cornfields, the customary stroll through the streets in the evening, and what a marketplace is like. However, they learn nothing about the political realities or the pervasive military influence in this country.

In contrast, one child's discovery of political realities is the focus of several books about South Africa. In Beverley Naidoo's *Journey to Jo'burg,* 13-year-old Naledi is forced to face the terrible realities of apartheid when she must journey from her sheltered village to Johannesburg. On the way, Naledi contrasts her own family's values and lifestyle with those of the white families and begins to question the political system that divided South Africa. In a sequel for older readers, *Chain of Fire,* Naledi learns that the people of her village are to be relocated to a "homeland." A peaceful student demonstration is violently terminated by police, some of Naledi's neighbors betray their own people, and homes are bulldozed. The move will eventually transpire, but not before Naledi and others unify to fight injustice.

Sheila Gordon's *The Middle of Somewhere* depicts the effects on two families of relocating their village. Nine-year-old Rebecca's family refuses to leave, and when Rebecca's father is arrested in a demonstration, the family must struggle to survive without him. Outside observers at his trial help gain his release at the time when Nelson Mandela is also released. This story of a family helping itself through difficult times is written for a younger reader than Gordon's earlier *Waiting for the Rain,* which also captures a feel for the geography, the people, and the language of South Africa. Happily, these books can now be read as historical fiction, but they give young readers a powerful glimpse of human rights abuses that continue in other parts of the world.

Such issues are still very much at the center of many countries in the Western Hemisphere, and several excellent novels for middle school readers provide a powerful glimpse of what it is like to live in poverty and fear. In Frances Temple's *Taste of Salt,* two voices retell events in recent Haitian history as Djo, one of Father Jean-Bertrand Aristide's street boys, lies near death from a fire bombing by Aristide's enemies. Jeremie, a Haitian girl, has been sent to record Djo's story and perhaps to give him reason to live. At first Djo's voice, full of the rhythms of the native Creole, remembers his childhood in the streets and alleys of Port-au-Prince, the harshness of his life, and the political realities of Haiti. When Djo slips into a coma, Jeremie's distinctive voice takes up the narrative. Born into poverty like Djo, she has been fortunate to fall under the protection of Catholic nuns and to be educated at the same time as she has been sheltered from important truths. As she reflects on her own and Djo's stories, she is faced with difficult choices about the future. The title *Taste of Salt* comes from the books that one of the priests is using to teach Djo and others to read. The term is taken from the belief that giving a zombie a taste of salt will open his true eyes and he will become free of his master. It is a powerful hope to give an oppressed people.

The story of a young Haitian girl, Paulie, and a small group of refugees desperately trying to escape to the United States is told in Temple's *Tonight, by Sea,* while Temple's *Grab Hands and Run* follows the journey of a family from El Salvador who must flee

*Francis Temple tells a moving story of Haitians trying to escape from their country's brutality in* Tonight, by Sea.

government soldiers after the father disappears. Their journey on a modern-day underground railroad to freedom in Canada is full of danger, despair, and betrayal. Temple's books give vivid and compelling accounts of the human yearning for freedom and security, and the terrible price that some must pay to obtain the rights too many of us take for granted.

While these books give young people a glimpse of political and economic realities that children face in other countries, Joan Abelove's *Go and Come Back* provides insights into cultural realities and points of view. Mature readers will be fascinated by this view of another culture, although in this case it is their own. Told by Alicia, a Peruvian teenager, the story centers on her experiences with two American anthropologists who come to "study" her people. Alicia is a critical and astute observer of the habits and attitudes of the American women whom she finds amusing, stingy, and ignorant. Alicia's descriptions of her people's customs and concerns are set against the women's attempts at fitting in with the life in this Amazon region and their struggles to remain objective observers. In this thought-provoking story, Abelove, an anthropologist herself, reveals that the worldview that one person holds can, in effect, be very different from the reality experienced by someone else.

Several excellent books about countries in the Middle East provide young people with insights into social and political issues at the same time as they involve readers with compelling characters in exciting stories. Elizabeth Laird's *Kiss the Dust* follows the journey of 13-year-old Tara and her family of middle-class Kurds. They have a comfortable home in Iraq, but because the father has been involved with the Kurdish resistance movement, the family is forced to flee. They journey first to the mountains of northern Iraq, where they experience rural Kurdish culture, and then they are forced into a refugee camp in Iran. Finally they are able to emigrate to England, but their lives are drastically altered by the events that have taken place. In Gaye Hiçyilmaz's *Against the Storm*, 12-year-old Mehmet and his family try to escape the circumstances of poverty. When they leave their beautiful country village to move to Ankara, their previously close family is torn apart by the crowded and dehumanizing conditions of the city. Only Mehmet seems to have the energy to fight against this storm and seek a better life. Vedat Dalokay's view of Turkey is more benign in *Sister Shako and Kolo the Goat*. Suitable for a younger audience, this evocative memoir centers on an old woman whose family has been killed in a vendetta and who moves into a deserted stable on the narrator's father's land. Kolo is the unusual and somewhat miraculous goat who appears at Sister Shako's door one day. This "Guest of God," as Sister calls her, becomes the leader of the village flock and the perpetrator of some funny and strangely supernatural incidents. The book is memorable not so much for its facts about Turkish life but for its sense of a Turkish culture, which is conveyed through the cadences of the prose and the images in the writing.

One of the few books to provide a Palestinian point of view of recent events in Israel is Naomi Shihab Nye's *Habibi*. Liyana Abboud is a 14-year-old who has grown up in St Louis. Her father, a doctor, decides to move his family back to his native Jerusalem, and the main focus of the story is on Liyana's attempts to fit into her new home and to find her true identity. But these events are set within Arab-Israeli conflict, the effects of the conflict on Liyana's family, and her growing friendship with a Jewish boy. The purpose here is not to champion any one point of view but to raise questions about the roots of conflict. Nye's beautifully written story also raises hopes for a lasting peace.

Other books give readers a glimpse of the environments and cultures of Asian and South Asian countries. In *The Year of the Panda* by Miriam Schlein, Lu Yi rescues a starving baby panda against his father's wishes and names it Su Lin. The pandas are moving down from the high ground, where their food source, bamboo, has died out as it does every seventy years. Their needs conflict with those of the people in Su

Lin's village, and the government urges the villagers to relocate so that their land can be made into a refuge for wild pandas. His family refuses to move, and Lu Yi agrees to accompany his pet by helicopter to a panda rescue center. There he witnesses what American and Chinese scientists are doing to save the giant pandas. His sadness at leaving Su Lin behind is tempered by the center's invitation for him to be a student aide the following year. Schlein's notes at the end of the story satisfy third and fourth graders' need to know "what happened next" while her research suggests the ways countries work together to save endangered species.

*The Land I Lost: Adventures of a Boy in Vietnam* by Quang Nhuong Huynh is a series of portraits remembered from the author's home village in the central highlands of Vietnam. Although it is "endless years of fighting" that make his homeland lost, his reminiscences barely mention war. Instead, his stories focus on people: farmers, hunters, bandits, his karate-expert grandmother, and his older cousin who could capture pythons and train birds to sing popular tunes. Each episode is sparely told, often humorous, and infused with the elusive meanings of folklore. *The Land I Lost* personalizes the Vietnamese people and can help children become acquainted with what has so often been represented as an alien land.

A Vietnamese girl comes to terms with the trauma of escaping from her country without knowing what has happened to the rest of her family in Diana Kidd's brief *Onion Tears*. In first-person narrative, Nam reveals her life with Auntie and another refugee, Chu Minh, who cooks in Auntie's restaurant. As time passes, Nam is able to shed real tears over the sickness of her teacher instead of the onion tears she sheds as she helps in Auntie's kitchen. Instead of being a lonely survivor, she is now a part of a school and a neighborhood community. Based on interview accounts of girls who journeyed from Southeast Asia to Australia, this story has many gaps that readers must fill in by inference. Children might be misled by Lucy Montgomery's line drawings, which misrepresent the characters' ages. This book would be a good small-group choice for its excellent discussion possibilities about Nam and the qualities she possesses that make her, too, a survivor.

Two moving books for children are rich in details of many aspects of Indian culture. In Gloria Whelan's *Homeless Bird* Koli, daughter of an impoverished village family, is married early and just as soon widowed when her young husband dies before the marriage is ever consummated. Unable by custom to return to her own family, she is abused and mistreated by her mother-in-law. When her father-in-law dies her mother-in-law abandons Koli in Vrindavan, "the city of widows." At first she joins the hundreds of homeless widows who struggle for survival while living on the streets, but with the help of Raji, a young rickshaw driver, Koli eventually finds shelter at a refuge for widows. Here Koli's talent for embroidery and her growing love for Raji open up a future of promise. Koli's strong character, her need for friends and family, and her perseverance in the face of so many obstacles will resonate with children of any culture.

Suzanne Fisher Staples' *Shiva's Fire* is a magical work of fiction that is also set in India. The book's main character, Parvati, is born in the middle of a devastating cyclone that kills her father and almost wipes out her village in Southern India. From the moment of her birth she seems to burn with a need to dance just as the Hindu God Shiva dances in flames on the little wooden statue carved by her late father. Parvati's unearthly talents and uncanny vision isolate her from the other villagers and she grows up a reserved, introverted child fiercely protected by her loving mother. When a famous Indian guru and dance teacher offers her a place at his school she is torn at the thought that she will be separated from her mother but thrilled at the chance to become a devadasi, a dancer whose life and art are devoted to the gods. *Shiva's Fire* is a fascinating look at a world that will be unfamiliar to most Western children. Although Parvati may be unusual in her single-minded determination to dance and in her willingness to sacrifice so much for her art, she is also achingly familiar in her need for human connections.

The Cholistan desert area of modern Pakistan is the setting for the coming-of-age story *Shabanu: Daughter of the Wind,* also by Suzanne Fisher Staples. Staples, a former UPI correspondent, was based in India and Pakistan and spent three years participating in a study of women in the deserts of Pakistan. *Shabanu,* based on some of her experiences living among these women, is a riveting portrait of a young girl in a family of nomadic camel herders. Shabanu, nearly 12, knows that she must accept an arranged marriage in the next year following the wedding of her older sister, Phulan. However, as the time of Phulan's marriage draws near, the two girls are accosted by a rich landowner's hunting guests, who threaten to abduct and rape the pair. In seeking revenge, Phulan's intended husband is killed. Phulan is quickly married to her sister's betrothed, and Shabanu is promised against her will to an older man as his fourth wife. Shabanu struggles to reconcile her own independent spirit with her loyalty to her family. An aunt offers support, saying, "Keep your wits about you. Trust yourself. Keep your inner reserves hidden." Shabanu chooses to run away, but when a much loved camel she has raised breaks his leg in the desert, she decides to stay with him and accept the beating she knows will follow when her father finds her. She will accept her marriage, too, but she vows to herself that no one can

## *Teachers Discuss Literature by and About Parallel Cultures*

**Teaching Feature**

Three curriculum specialists in the Fairfax County Public Schools in northern Virginia were concerned that teachers were not incorporating books by and about parallel cultures into their classroom reading programs. With a significant and growing multicultural population, the school system needed to modify its choices of assigned reading. The specialists noted that although they provided annually updated book lists and library media specialists added multicultural titles to school collections, these titles did not then become a part of classroom study. They concluded that teachers would not work recent books into their curriculum unless they had read and discussed the books. Providing book lists was not enough to change teacher behaviors.

A modest sum of grant money was available for programs that would "improve minority achievement." So they invited teachers in grades 4 through 12 to hold book discussion groups. Groups of at least three teachers agreed to discuss one book per month for a three-, four-, or five-month period. In-service credits could be earned for time spent in discussion. They supplied a list of paperback books (purchased with grant and other money) that could be checked out from a central office location and were available in multiple copies. Titles included Gary Soto's *Baseball in April, El Chino* by Allen Say, *The Talking Earth* by Jean Craighead George, Virginia Hamilton's *Cousins,* Diana Kidd's *Onion Tears,* and Mildred Taylor's *The Friendship.*

They were overwhelmed by the response. More than three hundred administrators and teachers in all

subject areas formed groups in 35 of the 37 schools in their area. The three facilitators drew up charts of which schools needed which books and shipped them via interoffice mail. The facilitators' advice to discussion leaders was to talk about the book. "Talk about whatever you want. Did you like it? Was it good? And save the inevitable question of how you would use it in the classroom for the very last." The groups began to meet.

As a result of these discussions, teachers discovered many books that were new to them and also read beyond the book list to find additional titles to add to it. Their book evaluation skills increased. They became risk takers as they ventured opinions and discovered how others' responses meshed with, illuminated, or conflicted with their own. In fact, in evaluating the program, teachers indicated that what was most important to them was the experience of discussing books with their peers. Many of the books are now in children's hands. A grant provided some extra funding so that participating schools could purchase multicultural literature. The discussion groups are still meeting and continuing to add new books to their classroom reading plans.

This could happen anywhere, couldn't it? What it takes is some planning, some seed money to purchase multiple paperbacks of selected titles, and the belief that teachers are willing to change if given support.

*This program was designed and carried out by Joan Lewis, Shirley Bealor, and Patricia M. Williams, Curriculum Specialists in Area II*
Fairfax County Public Schools, Virginia

---

ever unlock the secrets of her heart. Telling her compelling story in present tense, Shabanu faces giving up her life as a camel herder, discovers and accepts her sexuality, and finds a place in the adult world. Vivid details of camel behavior, camel-trading fairs, feasts and celebrations, the differing roles of men and women, and the ever-changing desert are brilliantly evoked for older readers. It is difficult for Western readers to imagine that this story takes place in the modern world. Reading *Shabanu* and its sequel *Haveli* would certainly lead readers to discuss women's roles in other countries as well as in their own.

Many young-adult novels also deal with contemporary life in other lands. *The Honorable Prison* by Lyll Becerra de Jenkins depicts the internment of Marta's family in an Andean Mountain village when her father's political opinions fall out of favor. In *The Forty-Third War* by Louise Moeri, 12-year-old Uno is

conscripted into the army and forced, like the reader, to learn of the harsh realities of a Central American military state. *The Return* by Sonia Levitin is a survival story of Ethiopian Jews trying to escape to Jerusalem. Minfong Ho's *Rice Without Rain* presents the class struggles for land reform in Thailand in the 1970s as seen by 17-year-old Jinda. Some middle schoolers might be ready for the complex political and emotional scopes of young-adult novels such as these, but teachers should first read any of these titles before introducing them into the classroom.

All children deserve a chance to read about the lives of children in other lands. As modern technology reduces the distances between cultures, books such as these contribute to a deeper, richer, more sympathetic and enduring communication between people.

The Teaching Feature "Teachers Discuss Literature by and About Parallel Cultures" shows how three teachers began an effort to introduce their district to some of the many books that represent the cultures of their community and the children of the world.

# Popular Types of Realistic Fiction

Certain categories of realistic fiction are so popular that children ask for them by name. They want a good animal story, usually about a dog or horse; a sports book; a "funny" book; or a good mystery. Each decade seems to have a popular series, as well, that lingers on the bookshelves. From Gertrude Chandler Warner's Boxcar Children to Ann Martin's Baby-Sitters Club series, from Nancy Drew and the Hardy Boys to Patricia Reilly Giff's Kids of Polk Street School series, children read one volume of a series and demand the next. Many of these books are not high-quality literature, and we would hope that children would not read these titles to the exclusion of other books. Yet many of these stories do serve the useful function of getting children hooked on books so that they will move on to better literature.[19] Children also develop fluency and reading speed as they quickly read through popular books or a series. Teachers and librarians need to identify and evaluate these popular books. Knowing and honoring the books children like increases an adult adviser's credibility, while also allowing him or her to recommend other titles that can broaden children's reading choices. Resources for Teaching, " 'To Be Continued': Popular Series Books for Children" lists some of the popular series books for children.

## Humorous Stories

Children like to laugh. The humorous verses of contemporary poets like Shel Silverstein and Jack Prelutsky are some of children's favorite poetry (see Chapter 8). Collections of jokes and riddles circulate at all levels of the elementary school. Humorous realistic fiction often presents characters involved in amusing or exaggerated predicaments that are solved in clever or unique ways. Sometimes these stories are episodic in plot structure—each chapter might stand alone as a complete story.

Beverly Cleary's stories about Ramona have probably made more real readers than any basal reading series has. Cleary has written another genuinely funny

---

series of books about a very normal boy, starting with *Henry Huggins.* In this first book, Henry's problems center on a stray dog named Ribsy and Henry's efforts to keep him. In *Henry and Beezus,* Henry's major interest is in obtaining a new bicycle. At the opening of the Colossal Market he is delighted when he wins one of the door prizes but then horrified to find out it is fifty dollars' worth of Beauty Shoppe services. Cleary's intimate knowledge of boys and girls is evident as she describes their problems, adventures, and hilarious activities.

The opening chapter of Barbara Park's *Skinnybones* is also hilarious. The self-acclaimed funniest person in the sixth grade is telling his story about trying to enter a cat food commercial contest. In addition, Alex (also known as "Skinnybones") has been a size "small" in Little League for six years, never is able to catch the ball or make a hit, and is the butt of the class bully's jokes. The bully wins the baseball trophy, but Alex wins, too, in this story of a wisecracker with a knack for getting into trouble.

*My Life as a Fifth Grade Comedian* by Elizabeth Levy also has its wildly funny moments but also makes a serious attempt to portray the personal pain that is sometimes masked by a class clown. Bobby Garrick has always been a champion jokester, but life doesn't seem so funny as his once-close relationships with his father and brother fall apart when his father kicks his brother out of the house. Bobby's clowning in school masks his unhappiness but also leads to poor grades and constant visits to the principal's office. When a sympathetic teacher helps him channel his energies into a school comedy contest, he finds an outlet for his energies and the self-esteem he needs to change his behavior.

Peter Hatcher's endless problems with his brother begin in Judy Blume's *Tales of a Fourth Grade Nothing.* In this story, 2-year-old Fudge, whose real name is Farley Drexel Hatcher, eats Peter's pet turtle but the long-suffering Peter earns a pet dog. In *Superfudge,* Peter narrates further complications in his life—his new baby sister Tootsie, new school, and new friends—when his family moves to New Jersey. Fudge begins kindergarten much to Peter's embarrassment and dismay. Dialogue and plot unfold like television situation comedies in these entertaining stories appealing to children in second through fifth grades.

*How to Eat Fried Worms* by Thomas Rockwell begins with a dare and a fifty-dollar bet. To win it, Billy plans to eat fifteen worms in fifteen days. They are fried, boiled, and smothered with catsup, horseradish, and other toppings. Each ingestion becomes more bizarre the closer Billy comes to winning his bet. The brief chapters, extensive and amusing dialogue, and plot make this a favorite story of less-able middle-grade readers.

---

[19]See Margaret Mackey's "Filling the Gaps: *The Baby-Sitters Club,* the Series Book, and the Learning Reader," *Language Arts* 67, no. 5 (September 1990): 484–489; and *Bookbird* 33, no. 3/4, special issue "Bad Books, Good Reading" (fall/winter 1995–1996).

## RESOURCES FOR TEACHING

### "To Be Continued": Popular Series Books for Children

| Author | Titles | Description | Grade level |
| --- | --- | --- | --- |
| Betsy Byars | *Death's Door* and others | Mysteries starring Herculeah Jones and her friend Meat | 4–6 |
| Betsy Byars | *Bingo Brown, Gypsy Lover* and others | A funny look at a young adolescent boy's problems as he grows up | 4–8 |
| Betsy Byars | *Wanted . . . Mud Blossom* and others | The continuing adventures of the wacky Blossom family | 3–6 |
| Ann Cameron | *The Stories Julian Tells, The Stories Huey Tells,* and others | Easy-reading adventures of two young African American boys | 1–4 |
| Judith Caseley | *Harry and Arney* and others | A funny series that centers on Harry and the everyday occurrences in his Jewish family | 1–3 |
| Matt Christopher | *The Captain Contest* and others | Sports stories for younger readers | 2–4 |
| Matt Christopher | *Spike It!* and others | A long list of titles by Christopher that center on the thrill of the play and action of a sport | 3–7 |
| Ilene Cooper | *Choosing Sides* and others | The Kids from Kennedy Middle School series, which treats middle school themes both humorously and seriously | 5–8 |
| Paula Danzinger | *Amber Brown Goes Fourth* and others | A feisty heroine gives an appealing first-person account of her trials and tribulations | 2–4 |
| Judy Delton | *Angel Spreads Her Wings* and others | A series of warmly funny stories that center on Angel and her extended family | 2–4 |
| Walter Farley | *The Black Stallion* and others | Popular horse and dog adventures | 4–7 |
| Jack Gantos | *Jack on the Tracks* and others | Hilarious misadventures of an adolescent boy, told in episodic hard-to-put-down chapters | 3–6 |
| Patricia Reilly Giff | *The Beast in Ms. Rooney's Room* and others | Adventures of the Kids of Polk Street School through second grade | 1–3 |
| Jamie Gilson | *Hobie Hanson, Greatest Hero of the Mall* and others | A fourth grader's antics in and out of school | 2–4 |
| Sheila Greenwald | *Rosy Cole, She Walks in Beauty* and others | The ups and downs of an indomitable grade school girl | 2–5 |
| Carolyn Haywood | *"B" is for Betsy* and others | A classic series about Betsy and Eddie that provides a safe, predictable experience for fledgling readers | 1–3 |
| Marguerite Henry | *Misty of Chincoteague* and others | Well-researched, well-written, and well-loved horse stories | 3–6 |
| James Howe | *Dew Drop Dead* and others | Sebastian Barth mysteries, which develop situations and characters to a depth seldom found in a mystery series | 4–6 |
| Johanna Hurwitz | *Busybody Nora* and others | Episodic family stories featuring Elisa, Russell, Nora, and her brother Teddy, who all live in the same apartment building | 1–3 |
| Johanna Hurwitz | *Aldo Applesauce* and others | Humorous stories featuring fifth grader Aldo and his friend DeDe | 2–5 |
| Rebecca Jones | *Germy Blew It* and others | A hilarious series centering on Jeremy Bluett and life in the sixth grade | 3–6 |

*continued*

# RESOURCES FOR TEACHING

## "To Be Continued": Popular Series Books for Children con't

| Author | Titles | Description | Grade level |
|--------|--------|-------------|-------------|
| Suzy Kline | *Orp Goes to the Hoop* and others | Sports stories with a middle school hero | 5–8 |
| Ellen Leverich | *Best Enemies Forever* and others | Two girls, one so nice and one so nasty, face off in an ongoing series of funny confrontations | 2–4 |
| Janet Taylor Lisle | *The Gold Dust Letters* and others | Well-written books featuring "Investigators of the Unknown," friends who solve mysteries that might or might not involve the supernatural | 2–4 |
| Maude Hart Lovelace | *Betsy-Tacy* and others | A popular series, originally published in the 1940s, that details the adventures of two best friends | 2–5 |
| Lois Lowry | *Anastasia Krupnik* and others | Sensitive, funny, and well-written books with a strong-minded heroine | 4–7 |
| Lois Lowry | *All About Sam* and others | Anastasia's younger genius brother has a unique viewpoint on growing up | 2–5 |
| Christine McDonnell | *Don't Be Mad, Ivy* and others | Books that follow the friendships of a group of first graders | 1–2 |
| Claudia Mills | *Dynamite Dinah* and others | A well-written series that follows an intrepid middle grader through the trials and tribulations of childhood | 4–8 |
| Phyllis Reynolds Naylor | *Alice In-Between* and others | Growing up female in an all-male household | 4–8 |
| Barbara Park | *Junie B. Jones Is Almost a Flower Girl* and others | An irrepressible kindergartner stars in a series of hilarious adventures | 1–3 |
| Peggy Parrish | *Amelia Bedelia* and others | A longtime favorite easy-to-read series that features the literal-minded maid of the Rogers family | 1–3 |
| Robert Newton Peck | *Soup* and others | Boys especially enjoy following the antics of Soup and friends | 4–8 |
| Cynthia Rylant | *Henry and Mudge* and others | An easy-to-read series about likable Henry and his lovable dog | 1–3 |
| Louis Sachar | *Marvin Redpost: Why Pick on Me?* and others | Hilarious misadventures of Marvin and his classmates in an easy-to-read format | 1–4 |
| Louis Sachar | *Wayside School Gets a Little Stranger* and others | Crazy misadventures at the thirty-story Wayside School | 2–5 |
| Marjorie Wiseman Sharmat | *Nate the Great* | Entertaining detective stories for beginning readers | 1–4 |
| Janice Lee Smith | *Serious Science* and other Adam Joshua stories | A funny series that follows Adam Joshua and his friends through the trials and tribulations of elementary school | 1–4 |
| Zilpha Keatly Snyder | *Libby on Wednesday* and others | A gifted child and her adventures in middle school | 4–8 |
| Eileen Spinelli | *Lizzie Logan, Second Banana* and others | Lizzie and her best friend Heather deal with friends and family | 2–4 |

One of the funniest books to be published for children is Barbara Robinson's *The Best Christmas Pageant Ever.* The six Herdman children are the terror of the public school, so it is not surprising that they extend their reign of terror to Sunday school and take over the Christmas pageant. The poor unsuspecting substitute teacher cannot understand why only the Herdmans volunteer for parts in the pageant, unaware that they have threatened to stuff pussy willows down the ears of any other children who raise their hands to volunteer. The Herdmans have never heard the Christmas story before, and their interpretation is contemporary, humorous, and surprisingly close to the true meaning of Christmas.

Several books have a more sophisticated brand of humor that will appeal particularly to middle school audiences. Gary Paulsen takes a break from his more serious and intense stories in *Harris and Me.* In a memorable and riotously funny voice, Paulsen's narrator recalls a summer spent with relatives on a farm in the Midwest in the 1950s and the many hilarious adventures that revolved around his cousin Harris, who at age 9 was a wicked combination of Huck Finn and Holden Caulfield. This city-boy narrator, who had been shuffled from relative to relative because of alcoholic parents, knew nothing of farm life or of loving family relationships. By the end of the summer he became an expert in agricultural science, but, even more important, he discovered what it means to belong to a loving, if slightly wacky, family. Australian novelist Tim Winton has an immensely funny hero in Lockie Leonard, a surfer dude with a wonderfully wacky attitude toward life. In *Lockie Leonard Scum Buster,* Lockie deals with problems of love and life in addition to trying to save the world. Lockie's hip Australian slang might challenge some young adolescent readers but, as with Paulsen's protagonist in *Harris and Me,* Lockie is an adolescent antihero who is sure to attract an audience of teenage boys.

In *The Exiles,* a funny novel by British writer Hilary McKay, the four Conroy sisters, Ruth, Naomi, Rachel, and Phoebe, ranging in age from 6 to 13, don't mean to be difficult, they just gravitate to trouble the way rain ends up in puddles. They hold races with their father's fishing maggots. They collect cast-off school projects and attract disorder and disaster. Their parents are driven by frustration and the happy circumstance of a house-remodeling job to send the girls to imposing Big Grandma's house in the country for the summer, and they become "the exiles." Big Grandma looks on their visit as an opportunity to instill discipline, fresh air and exercise, and a little hard work. Moreover, Big Grandma thinks they read too much, so she hides all her books away in a locked room. The girls, starved for reading materials, discover adventures outside the covers of books (some that Big Grandma wishes they hadn't). The outcome of this family conflict is poetic *and* hilarious. There are lessons to be learned by everyone and more than one surprise in store for all concerned, including the reader. Their adventures continue in *The Exiles at Home* and the *Exiles in Love.* McKay has also written several warmly humorous stories featuring ten-year-old Robie Brogan and his uninhibited next-door neighbors, the Robinson family. *Dog Friday, The Amber Cat,* and *Dolphin Luck* are more poignant stories than are *The Exiles* books, but in all three books McKay writes with warm good humor and a keen eye to events and people that capture the imagination of middle-grade readers.

Louis Sachar, well loved for his humorous Wayside School and Marvin Redpost series has written a highly original comedy in the Newbery Award–winning *Holes.* Because of an implausible circumstance with a sneaker, the totally unassuming, somewhat overweight Stanley Yelnats is introduced to Camp Green Lake, a Texas camp that is really a reform school, on a lake that is really as dry and brown as yesterday's leftover toast. The setting is as wild as the host of ludicrous

*Understated humor, unique characters, and a finely constructed plot provide the winning elements for Louis Sachar's Newbery Award–winning* Holes.

characters, both past and present, who populate the story. At first, each wacky character seems unconnected to the events that unfold, yet they all are interrelated in surprising and satisfying ways. In the end, Stanley Yelnats, Victim, becomes Stanley Yelnats, Hero; and the curse that shaped the destiny of Stanley and his family is finally put to rest. This highly entertaining comedy might stretch the definition of realistic contemporary fiction, but part of the fun of the book is believing that all these coincidences might really have happened.

There are certainly many other books in which humor plays a part. The fantasies of Roald Dahl, and Daniel Pinkwater, for instance, often portray absurd situations that children find funny. The animal antics in stories by Farley Mowat or Nina Bawden cause readers to laugh out loud. The snappy retorts of Carlie in Betsy Byars's *The Pinballs* or the accurate and humorous observations about everyday school situations in *The Burning Questions of Bingo Brown* give readers a smile of recognition. The Magic School Bus series by Joanna Cole and Bruce Degen is an example of nonfiction packaged in child-appealing humorous asides and funny conversation balloons. Humorous books need no justification other than that they provide pure enjoyment. They are a healthy contrast to a reading diet that might be overburdened with contemporary social problems. Funny stories also beg to be shared with other readers in the classroom and are powerful reading catalysts. Children who laugh with books are building a love of reading in which enjoyment is the foundation.

## Animal Stories

Stories about animals provide children with the vicarious experience of giving love to and receiving devotion and loyalty from an animal. Frequently these animal tales are really stories of the maturing of their major characters. For example, the well-loved story *The Yearling* by Marjorie Kinnan Rawlings is as much the story of Jody's growth and realization of the consequences of giving love as it is the story of a boy's discovery and raising of a pet deer. Sterling North's *Rascal: A Memoir of a Better Era* presents a boy who shares happy outings with his father, worries about his older brother serving in World War I, builds a canoe in the living room, and raises a crow and a raccoon as pets. But Sterling gradually and painfully realizes that his beloved companion raccoon, Rascal, will survive only in the wild.

Jean Craighead George draws on her own experiences with animals to imbue her many stories with fascinating insights into animal behavior to provide fascinating information. In *Frightful's Mountain* and *Julie's Wolfpack,* George returns to the setting of previous books to tell the stories of Frightful, Sam Gribley's Peregrine falcon in *My Side of the Mountain* and the wolf pack that Julie has guarded and cared for in *Julie of the Wolves* and *Julie.* In *The Cry of the Crow* George provides many humorous anecdotes about crows as part of the story. Mandy is accustomed to roaming the piney woods surrounding her family's Florida strawberry farm and rescues a fledgling crow shot from its nest. Naming it Nina Terrance, she secretly raises it over the summer, learns to recognize crow calls, and teaches it to make some human speech sounds. Torn between letting the maturing crow go with the flock and keeping it as a pet, she opts to keep the crow. But crows have been known to seek revenge, and when Mandy, and finally Nina Terrance, discover that it was Mandy's brother who shot at the crow's nest, she must face the consequences of having kept a wild animal as a pet when the crow attacks her brother. Jean George's careful research is skillfully woven into this story of the difficult choices people must make as they grow to maturity.

Dogs respond to human affection and return it warmly. This bond of love is one of the themes in Sidney's Taylor's *The Trouble with Tuck,* based on a true story. Helen lacked self-confidence until she became involved in raising Tuck, a beautiful golden Labrador retriever given to her by her parents. Tuck once saved Helen from drowning and is devoted to her. By the time Helen reaches 13, Tuck has grown totally blind. Rejecting the advice of the veterinarian to give Tuck to the university for research or have him put to sleep, Helen finds an alternative—she obtains a seeing-eye dog for Tuck. Jealous and confused, Tuck refuses to accept this stranger until Helen's patient and innovative training methods teach Tuck to follow the guide dog. As the two dogs parade before Helen and her proud family, the reader rejoices in both canine and human triumphs. In a sequel, *Tuck Triumphant,* the focus shifts from Tuck to a Korean boy the family adopts.

In Jane Resh Thomas's *The Comeback Dog,* Daniel must decide if he is once again going to risk his love on a dog that has already rejected him. While 9-year-old Daniel is still grieving for the loss of his old dog, Captain, he discovers a starved and nearly drowned English setter in the culvert near his family's Michigan farm. He brings the dog home, names her Lady, and nurses her back to health, assuming that she will return his love in the same way Captain did. But Lady, who has been mistreated, cringes at Daniel's touch and refuses to wag her tail for him. One day, in anger at her lack of affection, Daniel releases Lady from her chain, and she bounds away over the fields. She is gone, only to return a week later bristling with porcupine quills. Sympathetic parents who show their love finally help Daniel show his.

Troy Howell's frequent illustrations, the believable dialogue, and short chapters make this book easily approachable by independent 8- and 9-year-old readers.

The same age group will enjoy Karen Hesse's *Sable,* which is also about a stray dog. Tate is determined to keep Sable when she turns up one day in the family's yard, even though her mother is afraid of dogs. An uneasy compromise is arrived at, and Sable is allowed to stay on the property. But the dog keeps roaming and causing trouble with the neighbors. When Sable is given to a family friend, Tate is heartbroken but determined to prove she is responsible enough to take care of a dog. After much reading and planning, she builds a fence to keep Sable out of trouble, but when she goes to bring Sable home she finds that the dog has run away. Her parents are impressed with her hard work and softened by her devotion to the dog, so that when Sable finally turns up weeks later, skinny and torn, they accept the fact that they have a dog in the family.

Colby Rodowsky's short chapter book *Not My Dog* presents a different sort of dilemma. Eight-year-old Ellie has been dreaming of having a puppy of her own for years, but her parents insist that she wait until she is 9 and old enough to take care of it. Then her great-aunt Margaret must move into an apartment that doesn't allow dogs and she asks Ellie's family to take her dog, Preston. Ellie is horrified. This "square brown dog with sort of sticking up ears and a skinny tail" is not at all what she imagined her puppy would be like, and Ellie exclaims to her family that Preston is "not *my* dog." Not hers, that is, until Preston begins to work his wiles on her. She is gradually won over by Preston's intelligence, his obvious preference for her company, and his ability to get her home when she gets lost. When her teacher asks Ellie to write about someone important in her life, she writes about Preston, and realizes that he has indeed become *her* dog.

Meindert DeJong's moving story *Hurry Home, Candy* tells of another dog's search for love and security. Candy had first been owned by two children and punished with a broom by their impatient mother. In a storm Candy is separated from the family, and fear of a broom across the ditch prevents him from crossing to them. Alone, hungry, lost, and sorrowful, he at last finds shelter with a lonely old man, a retired captain turned artist. One night, the artist interrupts some thieves, and the news story brings Candy's original owners. But the children want only the reward, not the small dog. Candy hides again, but is drawn to the house by hunger. Once more, a broom stands between the dog and love and security. The captain discovers the source of the dog's fear; at the same time he gains understanding of his own. The big man tosses the broom aside, and the dog edges his way to food, to love, and home.

Colby Rodowsky's *Not My Dog* *is a heart-warming animal story for younger readers.*

Jacket design by Thomas F. Yezerski from *Not My Dog* by Colby Rodowsky. Jacket art coyright © 1999 by Thomas F. Yezerski. Reprinted by permission of Farrar, Straus and Giroux, LLC.

In Phyllis Reynolds Naylor's Newbery Medal–winning *Shiloh,* Marty Preston befriends a cringing stray beagle that surrounds the boy with joy. The dog, however, belongs to a neighbor known for abusing his animals; Marty, reluctantly but obedient to his father, returns the puppy. When the half-starved dog later slinks back to the field by the Preston home, Marty decides to hide the dog in the woods of his West Virginia mountain hollow. He deceives his family until a crisis forces him to fight for his principles and confront the owner of the dog, whom he has named Shiloh. Well-drawn characters, a strongly realized setting, and a quick-paced plot are woven into the first-person narrative that continues in *The Shiloh Season* and *Saving Shiloh.*

Marion Dane Bauer's *A Question of Trust* raises similar problems for Brad and his brother, who are hurt and angered by their parents' divorce. Although their father, with whom they are living, forbids them to have any pets, Brad comes across a stray mother cat and her two newborn kittens. He is determined to care for them even though he risks losing his father's trust. However, he finds that he is in over his head when things go dreadfully wrong with one of the kittens. Like Bauer's *On My Honor,* these two stories ask upper elementary students to think about what constitutes honorable and responsible behavior when rebelling against parents and their beliefs.

Heroic dogs who overcome obstacles are the subject of popular animal stories for children. Sheila Burnford's *The Incredible Journey* recounts the odyssey of courage and endurance of three runaway pets, a young Labrador retriever, an old bull terrier, and a Siamese cat. Left with a friend of their owner, the animals try to reach their home more than 250 miles away. Hunger, storms, dangerous river crossings, and fights are the nearly insurmountable problems of these three animals. Their survival and care for each other make a remarkable story.

A sled dog named Searchlight and his owner, little Willy, are the heroes of John Reynolds Gardiner's well-loved *Stone Fox.* Little Willy needs five hundred dollars to pay off the back taxes on his grandfather's farm or it will be taken from them. So the two enter a dogsled race. But among the contestants is the legendary Indian Stone Fox with his five Samoyed sled dogs. Willy nearly wins the race, but Searchlight's heart gives out in a final burst of speed just before the finish line. In the moving conclusion, Stone Fox and his team halt just short of the finish while Willy carries his dog across the line to win the race and save his farm. This short story, an excellent read-aloud choice, causes fourth- and fifth-grade readers to ask for tissues and more animal stories.

*Where the Red Fern Grows* by Wilson Rawls is a heartwarming sentimental tale of the love between two hound dogs and their master. Young Billy trains his two dogs, Old Dan and Little Ann, to be the finest hunting team in the Cherokee country of the Ozarks in northeastern Oklahoma. Twenty-five sets of hounds are entered in the big coon hunt. After five nights of hunting, catching raccoons, skinning them, and turning in the hides, Billy's hounds win three hundred dollars and the first-place cup. During the hunt, Old Dan and Little Ann nearly freeze to death after getting lost during an unexpected blizzard. When the family decides to move, Billy plans to remain behind with his beloved grandfather and the two dogs. But when the dogs die, one defending Billy against a mountain lion attack and one pining away, he regretfully departs with his family. Billy's decision is reaffirmed when a legendary red fern springs up at the dogs' gravesite. This story is memorable to 10-, 11-, and 12-year-olds because of its warmth and its strong portrayal of devotion between humans and animals.

Occasionally books intended for an adult audience become part of the reading of older children. Jack London's *The Call of the Wild* was written for adults but is read by some gifted middle-grade students. The men in the story are ruthless, and the dog Buck re-turns to the wildness of nature just as the men revert to force and cruelty to survive. Jim Kjelgaard communicates a love of wilderness through exciting dog stories like *Big Red,* a tale of an Irish setter groomed for championship showing who, along with his 17-year-old trainer, faces the bear Old Majesty. Farley Mowat's *The Dog Who Wouldn't Be* tells of his boyhood on the Saskatchewan prairie in the company of his Prince Albert retriever, Mutt, and a score of other animal pets. In his shorter novel *Owls in the Family,* Mowat recounts in hilarious detail his adventures in acquiring and training two pet great horned owls, the intrepid Wol and his timid companion, Weeps.

## Sports Stories

Sports fiction for children reflects their energetic participation and interest in a variety of individual and team sports. Recent fiction includes books about team sports, like baseball, football, soccer, and basketball, and popular individual sports like tennis, running, gymnastics, dirt-bike racing, skateboarding, and swimming. Fiction, biography, and informational books about sports extend and enrich the personal experiences of the child who participates in or observes sports.

It is sometimes difficult to find well-written sports stories. In many books the characters are flat and one-dimensional. The dialogue tends to be stilted, and the plots predictable. Nevertheless, children continue to select these stories because they are so personally involved and interested in the activities. Series like Dean Hughes's Angel Park All-Stars series and the Rookies series, by various authors, cater to sports fans.

Even though there are now many more stories that feature girls in sports, there are still few female athletes in formula sports fiction. The same clichés—making the team through hard work or overcoming fear and triumphing over pain—are prevalent in both stories for boys and stories for girls. One important change, however, is that girls on boys' sports teams are no longer greeted with disbelief and protest.

A serious story that portrays characters of real depth and understanding is *Thank You, Jackie Robinson* by Barbara Cohen. Though the story takes place in 1947–1948, it is written in the first person and told as a reminiscence to a contemporary child. Sam Green is the only son of a Jewish widow who runs an inn in New Jersey. He doesn't care much about sandlot ball, but he can recite the batting order and play-by-play for every Dodgers game since the time he became a fan. Sam's best friend is the inn's African American cook, Davy, who takes Sam to his first Dodgers game. The two see other games together, and the hero of all the games for both of them is Jackie Robinson. In midseason Davy has a heart attack. Sam gathers his courage, buys a baseball, and goes alone to a Dodgers game, where he asks Jackie Robinson to autograph the ball for Davy. Then Davy's son-in-law, Elliott, helps Sam sneak into the hospital in a laundry cart so he can personally present the ball to Davy. This book succeeds at many levels: as a warm and understanding consideration of friendship across ages and races, as a realistic presentation of death, and as a retrospective look at Jackie Robinson and the Brooklyn Dodgers during the height of their baseball fame.

Another book that succeeds on many levels is Alfred Slote's *The Trading Game.* Andy Harris, who loves to play baseball and collect baseball cards, receives the cards his deceased father had bequeathed to him. Among them is a precious 1953 Mickey Mantle card worth over two thousand dollars. But the card Andy truly wants is Ace 459, the card of his grandfather, a former major league player, whom he idolizes. Greedy Tubby Watson owns the card and won't part with it unless Andy will trade the Mickey Mantle card. When Grampa comes to visit, it is clear to Andy that the cards his father collected are of no importance to the old man and that Grampa has not reconciled himself to his son's death. Andy eventually realizes that friendships and the memories the cards represent are more important than winning and the money the cards are worth. Slote's books, many of which are told in first person, capture the emotions, actions, and conversation of typical fifth- and sixth-grade boys.

Upper elementary school students have laughed at the antics of Orp, or Orville Rudemeyer Pygenski, Jr. In one story in the series by Suzy Kline, *Orp Goes to the Hoop,* the seventh grader is trying to make the basketball team of his Connecticut middle school. With a mother who was a free-throw champion and a father with a terrific lay-up, Orp receives great advice. Even though Orp's story is one of near-continuous successes both on the court and in the social arena, readers will appreciate Orp's long pass to a teammate for the winning basket.

Middle schoolers ready to move into more-complex novels that use sports to explore other subjects might be guided to Scott Johnson's *Safe at Second,* Ilene Cooper's *Choosing Sides,* Bruce Brooks's *The Moves Make the Man,* Robert Lipsyte's *The Contender,* Virginia Euwer Wolff's *The Mozart Season,* or Chris Crutcher's *Stotan!* Sports fiction at its best provides readers with the vicarious satisfactions of playing the sport as well as struggling with the problems and issues that arise in practice, in play, and at home.

## School Stories

Stories that take place in school offer children the solace of the familiar. All schoolchildren recognize settings furnished with desks and lockers; characters like the friendly custodian or principal, the class bully, the understanding teacher, the hatchet-faced teacher, the cheating student; and situations such as the looming deadline for a project or paper, misunderstandings between friends, and seasonal celebrations. Books like these do not always encourage readers to stretch their abilities, but they do provide a kind of support for horizontal growth as children learn to read faster with more satisfaction. Unfortunately (or fortunately for the readers), many of these stories are part of a numbered series and children want to read them in order. This challenges teachers and parents to help children find other books while they are "waiting for number 7 of the series."

Susan Shreve's school story *The Flunking of Joshua T. Bates* is about being held back. Joshua hasn't mastered reading, but through the thoughtful tutoring and friendship of his new teacher he is able to pass a test at Thanksgiving and join his old class. Adults will wince as Joshua vents his frustration by threatening to move to East Africa or become a custodian in Japan, and they might find unrealistic the implication that children can be promoted after two months of tutoring. But children applaud the subduing of the bully in Joshua's former class and the satisfying happy ending.

Beverly Cleary, Jamie Gilson, and Johanna Hurwitz make use of the humor of school situations for

*Ramona, Beverly Cleary's irrepressible character, has been promoted to the fourth grade in* Ramona's World.

From *Ramona's World* by Beverly Cleary, illustrated by Alan Tiegreen. Jacket illustration copyright © 1999 by Alan Tiegreen. Used by permission of Morrow Junior Books, a division of William Morrow Company/ HarperCollins Publishers.

third and fourth graders. In Cleary's *Ramona Quimby, Age 8*, Ramona arrives in third grade, where she enjoys her teacher's "Dear" (Drop Everything and Read) time. She also stages a hilarious parody of a cat food commercial for her book report, makes a friend of "Yard Ape," and realizes that her teacher likes her. In *Class Clown*, Hurwitz introduces Lucas Cott, the most obstreperous boy his third-grade teacher has ever seen. Lucas finally settles down when he stands in for a sick classmate to become the ringmaster of the class circus. Gilson's *4-B Goes Wild* and *Thirteen Ways to Sink a Sub* and her Hobie Hansen books are also popular school tales. Gilson's stories are fast moving and full of pranks and funny dialogue, with reasonable adults who remain very much in the background.

Andrew Clements explores the often complex power of language and the relationships between students and teachers in several books. In *Frindle*, Nick Allen is a clever smart aleck who loves to outwit his teachers. When Mrs. Granger, the veteran fifth-grade teacher who loves vocabulary lessons, asks him to do a report on the origin of words, Nick's somewhat devious mind goes to work. Steeped in etymological knowledge as a result of a study of word origins, Nick decides to coin a new word for "pen," *frindle*. Neither Nick nor Mrs. Granger has any idea of how this incident will build into a war of wits and words that will have unexpected results for Nick, Mrs. Granger, and the children of the Westfield school district. Cara Landry is another bright fifth grader whose editorial for *The Landry News* has unexpected consequences for herself and her teacher. Cara finds herself in the middle of a controversy about freedom of speech and responsible reporting.

Avi also develops a student-teacher conflict in *Nothing but the Truth,* but this book takes a much more serious tone than *The Landry News*. Ninth-grader Philip Malloy has dreams about being a track star, but a D in English has kept him off the school track team. When Philip challenges a school rule for silence during the singing of the national anthem, Mrs. Narwin, the English teacher who has given him the poor grade, sends him to the office. This begins a chain of events that spirals out of control for both student and teacher. Philip is eventually suspended, and his story attracts media attention. A variety of administrators, community leaders, and media mavens enter the fray, and Philip and Mrs. Narwin become the pawns of people with their own personal and political agendas. Eventually Mrs. Narwin, a dedicated and caring teacher, resigns. Philip is forced to change schools and to give up his dreams of being a running legend. His new school can't afford to support a track team. Avi composes this powerful story through dialogue, journal entries, letters, memos, and other primary source materials and in-

vites readers to a deeper understanding about the meaning of truth. The manipulation of truth by those in positions of power has critical importance in today's world.

In Walter Dean Myers's *Darnell Rock Reporting*, Darnell is a normal underachieving middle school student who spends as much time in the principal's office as he does in a classroom. To get the principal off his back, he mentions that he is thinking of joining the school newspaper, and this is the delaying tactic he needs to keep his parents ignorant of his little problems. As he attends staff meetings, Darnell's interest is piqued and he begins to get involved. When he sets out to interview Seebie, a homeless man, he begins to see the man as a human being and takes on his cause. At the same time, his success at writing begins to have an effect on the way he sees himself. Trying to establish a community garden for the homeless, Darnell makes a speech to the town council and draws this analogy:

> If you're a kid who isn't doing so good, people start off telling you what you should be doing, and you know it, but sometimes you still don't get it done and mess up some more. Then people start expecting you to mess up, and then *you* start expecting you to mess up. (p. 156)

Darnell realizes that being on the newspaper has changed how he sees himself and also made people look at him differently. Believing that the garden is a way of helping them become self-sufficient, he is asking the same chance for Seebie and the other homeless people in the area. Myers writes with a keen understanding of adolescent concerns and creates funny, likable characters. In this case he shapes to perfection a picture of an underachieving middle-class boy, and mirrors a segment of the population who don't often see themselves reflected in books.

Anne Fine zeroes in on a similar group of young teens in her very funny, but ultimately very poignant, *Flour Babies*. Room 8 at St. Boniface's School is a teacher's nightmare, the classroom where the "Sads and the Bads" end up. It is time for the school science fair, and in an effort to avoid repeating previous disasters, Mr. Cassidy presents the boys with some pretty tame choices. In a glorious misunderstanding, Simon Martin, a "clumsy young giant," convinces his classmates to choose the child development experiment, eighteen days of caring for flour sacks as if they were babies. Simon believes that the boys will be allowed to explode the sacks at the end of the experiment. But before this end occurs, Simon finds he has grown quite attached to his sack. He paints eyes on it and confides his innermost thoughts to it. Not only does the experiment teach the boys the weighty responsibilities of parenting, but it also gives Simon, whose own father skipped out when he was 6 weeks

## Ralph Fletcher

*A group of sixth graders take over their classroom for the day in Ralph Fletcher's* Flying Solo.

From *Flying Solo* by Ralph Fletcher, © 1998. Jacket design © 1998 by Ben Caldwell. Reprinted by permission of Clarion Books/Houghton Mifflin Company.

old, some important insights about fathering. Simon gets his explosive ending, but he also ends up knowing that "if keeping what you care for close and safe counts for any thing" (p. 127), he'll make a better father than most.

Ralph Fletcher, whose *Fig Pudding* provided a warm and insightful story of family life, has written a thought-provoking school story in *Flying Solo*. When Mr. Fabiano calls in sick and the substitute fails to show up, the kids take over the class. The tension builds as readers try to anticipate the outcome—Will they be discovered? Will anarchy reign? Surprisingly, these sixth graders are, for the most part, mature, thoughtful adolescents. As the day proceeds, they manage to hide their lack of adult supervision, conduct and complete class business, discuss a host of ethical questions that their experiment raises, and come to grips with some of their individual problems and heartaches. There are consequences for their actions in the end, but *Flying Solo* is a well-written, realistic story that will raise smiles of recognition as well as important questions of responsibility in the middle-grade audience.

Other authors also set their stories for older readers within the cozy confines of a school. Gordon Korman's private school Macdonald Hall has been the setting for many of his slapstick stories. The characters of the popular Sweet Valley High and Sweet Valley Twins paperback series (created by Francine Pascal but written by a stable of authors) use school as a backdrop for their interactions. A giant step up from these series is Ilene Cooper's Kids from Kennedy Middle School series, in which deeper themes and situations are treated both humorously and seriously. In *Choosing Sides*, for instance, sixth grader Jonathan Rossi is trying to be the basketball player his father wants him to be and his older brother already is. But Jonathan's heart isn't in it. His friend Ham Berger purposely gets cut from the team, but Jon continues to put up with pressure and lessons from his father. When his teacher Mrs. Volini asks the class to write about "moral dilemmas," Jon suddenly sees that his is not how to skip basketball practice but how to reconcile his own feelings with his father's unreasonable demands. *Queen of the Sixth Grade* introduces readers to Jon's friend Robin, who suddenly becomes a class outcast when she rebels against the cruel Veronica's jokes. Each of Cooper's stories deals with a major theme against the backdrop of everyday school concerns, such as what to do at a first sixth-grade coed dance, peer groups and making friends of both sexes, dealing with bad and good teachers, or handling difficult school assignments.

## Mysteries

Most children enjoy mystery stories during some period in their lives. James Howe, author of the popular Sebastian Barth mysteries, has said that in adult mysteries "Who done it?" is the question to be answered but in children's mysteries the question is more likely to be "What's going on here?"[20] Children enjoy figuring out the "rules of the game" in a mystery, and they are proud to be masterful solvers of the problem. They enjoy the order of a mystery's universe, where loose ends are tied up, everything is explained, and evil is punished. They like escapist reading just as much as adult mystery fans do.

Even first- and second-grade readers demand mysteries. Whole series, such as the Something Queer books by Elizabeth Levy, the Miss Mallard and Sherlock Chick animal detective stories by Robert Quackenbush, Crosby Bonsall's mystery stories, or Patricia Reilly Giff's Polka Dot Private Eye books, satisfy a child's need to keep reading.

[20]James Howe, "Writing Mysteries for Children," *Horn Book Magazine*, March/April 1990, pp. 178–183.

Slightly older children usually become enmeshed in the Nancy Drew or Hardy Boys series. These formula books have predictable plots, one-dimensional characters, stilted dialogue, and cliché-ridden prose. Although most librarians and teachers do not order these books, they continue to sell well. Rather than discount mystery stories in general because of popular series, teachers and librarians should look for better-written mysteries and other books that contain the elements of mystery, such as "suspense and supernatural fantasy" (see Chapter 7), to expand children's interests.

Two popular mystery series give the reader a chance to match wits with clever boys. Both boys and girls enjoy the Encyclopedia Brown stories by Donald Sobol. In *Encyclopedia Brown Takes a Case,* Mr. Brown, chief of police of Idaville, brings home all the cases his detectives cannot solve. At dinner he describes them to his son, Encyclopedia Brown, who usually solves them before it is time for dessert. Each Encyclopedia Brown book presents ten cases whose solutions are included in the back of the book. Seymour Simon, author of many nonfiction titles, also features short mysteries in his Einstein Anderson series. In *Einstein Anderson Lights Up the Sky,* the brainy Einstein applies his knowledge of science to show that mysterious UFOs are really spotlights reflected off low nighttime clouds, and he "solves" another nine problems. While each series features both consistent format and a continuing case of characters, Einstein's incidental jokes, puns, and riddles and the scientific observations give this series extra appeal and depth.

An attic holds clues to the past and keys to the future for a horse-loving girl in Rumer Godden's *The Rocking Horse Secret.* Eight-year-old Tibby discovers a rocking horse in the attic playroom of the old Pomeroy mansion. When the horse's tail falls off and a piece of paper falls out, she repairs the damage and hopes no one will notice. But the paper proves to be a will that holds the secret of the old house, and Tibby is the one who solves the mystery and saves the house. Godden creates memorable characters and provides a satisfying ending sure to delight middle elementary mystery and horse lovers.

Alison Lester combines a mystery with a horse story, survival tale, and family saga in *The Quicksand Pony.* Biddy, a 10-year-old girl, is finally allowed to go on the family muster that rounds up the cattle that have been grazing wild in the Australian back country. Just after the trip begins, Biddy's dearly loved pony, Bella, is caught in quicksand that dots the shoreline. Biddy is inconsolable when she is forced to leave the horse to its fate. When she returns to the spot the next day, however, she finds that Bella has escaped, and she notices small human footprints in the sand. As she sets off to find Bella, Biddy begins to uncover the mystery of a disappearance that had affected her family years before. This gentle, warmly satisfying story unfolds through Biddy's experiences in the present as well as through past events that lead up to her discovery of her long-lost cousin.

A mystery of a different sort confronts two sisters in Adele Griffins's *The Other Shepards.* In this case the mystery centers on dead siblings killed in a car accident years before Holland and Geneva were born. The girls' mother and father have been traumatized, and the girls feel that their lives are controlled and overshadowed by these absent children. Geneva suffers from a severe panic disorder, and Holland suffers from the energy expended in trying to mother her. When Annie, a young artist, arrives to paint a mural in their kitchen she sets into motion the events that will finally help the family heal. The mystery here lies in questions of Annie's origins. Is she a real person or a figment of the girls' needy imaginations? Or perhaps she represents some unearthly power that is present to help the girls sort out their problems. Wisely, Griffin does not provide easy answers that would diminish the emotional power of the story or take away from Holland and Geneva's ultimate accomplishments. Readers are asked to be the detectives here and determine the solution according to their own understanding of the novel's characters and events.

*The House of Dies Drear* by Virginia Hamilton is a compelling story of the weird and terrifying happenings that threaten and mystify an African American professor and his family when they rent a house that was formerly an underground railway station. The brooding old house holds many secrets for Thomas Small and his family, who are threatened by dangers from outside as well as inside the house. The treasure of fleeing slaves that is discovered by Thomas in this title becomes one of the problems in a sequel, *The Mystery of Drear House.* Now the Small family must help determine the fate of the abolitionist's house and the disposal of the goods. Hamilton's finely crafted plot, elegant prose, and well-developed characters provide gripping reading.

In Ellen Raskin's *The Westing Game,* millionaire Sam Westing cut out the words to the song "America the Beautiful" and distributed them among his heirs as clues to his murderer.[21] At the reading of his will, the sixteen characters are presented with a directive to discover the identity of his murderer and other clues cleverly hidden within the will. The characters, all with their own physical, moral, or emotional imperfections, play in pairs. They include a judge, a Chi-

---

[21]See Ellen Raskin, "Newbery Medal Acceptance," *Horn Book Magazine,* August 1979, pp. 385–391.

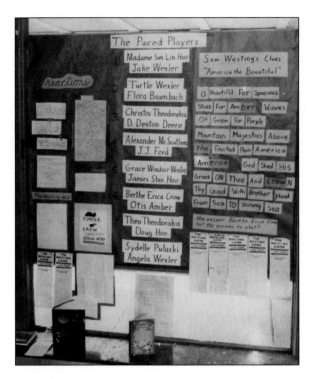

*Fourth graders keep track of Ellen Raskin's intricate mystery* The Westing Game *by listing character pairs, assembling cut-up clues, and making predictions.*

Barrington Road Elementary School, Upper Arlington Public Schools, Ohio. Pat Enciso, teacher.

nese restaurateur, a dressmaker, a track star, a 15-year-old palsied boy, a reluctant bride-to-be, and a 13-year-old terror, Turtle Wexler. It is Turtle who begins to link clues and discover patterns as she and readers piece together Westing's amazing game. In a tightly constructed story divided into many short sections, Raskin piles detail upon detail; rereading shows that what appears to be insignificant always proves otherwise. Warmly realized characters interrelate and grow in this Newbery Medal winner, but it is Turtle who, unbeknownst to any of the other players, quietly solves the puzzle and bikes up to the Westing house to receive her prize in the satisfying ending.

Popular mystery writer Vivien Alcock skirts the fantastic in novels such as *The Mysterious Mr. Ross,* in which 12-year-old Felicity suspects that the man she has saved from drowning, Albert Ross, may well be the human incarnation of an injured albatross. Readers are kept in suspense, however, as this young, gullible girl on the edge of adolescence moves through sympathy, doubt, anger, and remorse before defending Mr. Ross from nosy seacoast villagers. Alcock's numerous other titles, such as *The Monster Garden* and *The Stonewalkers,* venture into supernatural and science fiction territory and appeal to middle schoolers for their mixture of mystery, fantasy, and adolescent awareness of the adult world.

Joan Lowery Nixon's riveting story *The Other Side of Dark* won the Edgar Allan Poe Mystery Writer's Award for its distinctive portrayal of a girl who, after witnessing the murder of her mother and being shot herself, loses her memory for four years. At 17, Stacy McAdams regains some of her memory and is adjusting to being an adolescent. When publicity suggests that she might remember the face of the killer, Stacy is again in danger and she attempts to identify the killer before he kills her. The plot is complicated when it appears that new friends might not be what they seem. Stacy's first-person narrative reveals her desire for revenge, her confusion over who she is, and her growth toward adulthood in this thriller. Another of Nixon's thrillers, *A Candidate for Murder,* concerns Cary and the crank calls she begins to receive when her father runs for governor of Texas. Cary has unknowingly witnessed something that places her in the midst of political intrigue and danger. Older readers enjoy Nixon's compelling mysteries for their skilled combination of human emotions, suspense, romance, and terror with a fast-moving plot and cliffhanger chapters.

Like Nixon, Lois Duncan writes about high school students who inadvertently stumble into mysteries. *The Twisted Window,* for instance, is the story of high school junior Tracy Lloyd, who believes Brad Johnson when he says his stepfather has stolen his little sister from his mother's house. Three days later she is involved in a kidnapping, a case of mistaken identity, and a dangerous game with a disturbed boy. Middle school girl readers pass Duncan's young-adult mysteries from hand to hand.

Popular fiction should be evaluated with the same criteria used to consider all fiction, with the recognition that its major appeals are fast action, contemporary characters in familiar settings, straightforward plot development, humor, and suspense. Children develop the skills of rapid reading, vocabulary building, prediction, and the ability to notice relevant details when they read popular fiction. They develop a love of reading with popular novels, and skillful teachers can extend and diversify readers' choices with all that realistic fiction has to offer.

Contemporary realistic fiction is diverse. It has moved away from the problem novels of the 1960s and 1970s to serious fiction balanced with characters less prone to despair. Contemporary novels encompass diverse themes and writing styles. While paperback series and popular novels continue to attract readers, these selections are now counterbalanced by many well-written and compelling stories. The diverse cultures of the United States and many other world cultures are represented in literature for children, and the number of titles available continues to grow. Contemporary realistic fiction, the most popular genre among child readers, continues to thrive in this new century.

# INTO THE CLASSROOM

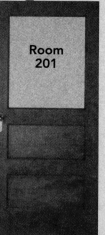

Room 201

## Contemporary Realistic Fiction

1. Discuss with a small group of children a novel such as Lowry's *Rabble Starkey*, MacLachlan's *Arthur for the Very First Time*, Creech's *Walk Two Moons*, Paterson's *Flip-Flop Girl*, or Bawden's *The Outside Child*. How is the main character influenced by other characters in the book? When the child character becomes an adult, which of these other characters might he or she want to thank? Why?

2. Compare the relationships of parents and children in several titles discussed in the section of this chapter entitled "Living in a Family."

3. Compare several survival stories discussed in this chapter. After basic wants are satisfied, what else does the surviving person seem to need? What qualities does each person possess or develop in order to survive? How does (or might) surviving change a person?

4. Compare several humorous stories. Where does the humor lie? (slapstick? exaggeration? puns or wordplay? situations? satire?) How would you rank these titles from lesser to greater sophistication?

# Personal Explorations

1. Find books about a specific culture. Look for poetry, biography, fiction, picture storybooks, nonfiction, and websites that would deepen understanding of these books in a classroom. What kinds of books were the easiest to find, and which were the most difficult to find?

2. Select a current subject in realistic fiction, such as single-parent families, foster children, immigration, or disability, and create an annotated bibliography. Find some nonfiction that can be grouped with the fiction.

3. Compare the treatment of a topic, such as the death of a pet, a child, or a grandparent, in a picture book, a novel, poetry, and informational books. Select several books from various decades that portray a particular culture. Do you find stereotypes? What themes prevail?

# Related Readings

Barrera, Rosalinda Benevides, and Verlinda D. Thompson, eds. *Kaleidoscope: A Multicultural Booklist for Grades K–8*. Urbana, Ill.: National Council of Teachers of English, 1974.

This annotated bibliography includes a discussion of criteria and a list of resources pertaining to multicultural literature. Titles are grouped by genre or theme.

Bernstein, Joanne E., and Marsha K. Rudman. *Books to Help Children Cope with Separation and Loss*. 4th ed. New York: Bowker, 1994.

This book-selection guide summarizes 600 recent fiction and nonfiction titles grouped by topics such as divorce, mental illness, moving, tragic loss, and disabilities.

Bishop, Rudine Sims. *Presenting Walter Dean Myers*. New York: Twayne, 1990.

A discussion and criticism of Myers's books about young urban African Americans, including an analysis of humor, theme, characterization, and other patterns found in Myers's work. Other titles in this critical series discuss works by authors such as Sue Ellen Bridgers, Robert Cormier, Richard Peck, and Judy Blume.

Day, Frances. *Multicultural Voices in Contemporary Literature*. Portsmouth, N.H.: Heinemann, 1999.

This updated and revised edition of an earlier work provides a highly useful classroom resource. Day provides a wealth of information on more than forty multicultural authors and includes classroom activities and reviews of more than 120 of their books to help teachers thoroughly explore the books and authors. Appendixes include lesson plans, additional activities, and lists of resources.

Dreyer, Sharon Spredeman. *The Bookfinder: A Guide to Children's Literature About the Needs and Problems of Youth Aged 2–15*. Vols. 1–5. Circle Pines, Minn.: American Guidance Service, 1981, 1985, 1989, 1994.

Titles are indexed and annotated under headings that suggest a range of problems in growing up: responsibility, parental absence, disabilities, friendship, and so on. The introductory essay discusses ways parents and teachers might plan thematic studies to develop children's understandings.

Hunter, Mollie. *The Pied Piper Syndrome*. New York: HarperCollins, 1992.

A collection of speeches and essays that shows how Scotland's best-known children's author sees her craft. Because Hunter's first language is not English, her essay "Writing from a Minority Literature" rings true. In an earlier collection, *Talent Is Not Enough* (New York: Harper & Row, 1976, 1990), Hunter reflects on the challenges and demands of writing for children.

Lehr, Susan, ed. *Battling Dragons: Issues and Controversy in Children's Literature*. Portsmouth, N.H.: Heinemann, 1995).

Teachers, librarians, parents, and authors offer essays on difficult and controversial issues in children's books. Authors include Beverly Naidoo, Alan Baillie, and Brian Jacques. This volume provides unique and important perspectives on topics of concern to adults who work with children's literature.

Paterson, Katherine. *A Sense of Wonder: Thoughts on Reading and Writing Books for Children*. New York: Plume Books, 1995.

A collection of essays, speeches, and book reviews that develop the author's views on three themes: story, imagina-

tion, and hope. The essays were previously published in two volumes, *The Spying Heart* and *Gates of Excellence*.

Rees, David. *Painted Desert, Green Shade: Essays on Contemporary Writers of Fiction for Children and Young Adults*. Boston: Horn Book, 1984.

Rees critiques the work of thirteen American and British writers, focusing on such authors as Betsy Byars, Katherine Paterson, Jan Mark, Robert Westall, Virginia Hamilton, and John Rowe Townsend. See also the companion volume, *Marble in the Water: Essays on Contemporary Writers of Fiction for Children and Young Adults* (Boston: Horn Book, 1980).

Rudman, Masha. *Children's Literature: An Issues Centered Approach*. Reading, Mass.: Addison-Wesley, 1994.

Rudman organizes a discussion of children's books according to contemporary issues such as divorce, death, gender roles, aging, death, and war. She provides an overview of the topic, special criteria and activities for exploring each issue, then follows with an annotated book list for each topic.

http://www.ala.org/parentspage/greatsites/amazing.html
This site is organized by the Children and Technology Committee of the Association of Library Services to Children, a division of the American Library Association. It lists over 700 approved websites for children up to the age of 14. Sites are organized under such topics as Literature and Language and People Past and Present.

http://www.wolfsden.org/nactr/ The Wolf's Den is a Native American Resource Center website that provides a clearinghouse for information on Native peoples.

http://www.library.uiuc.edu/edx/s-guides.htm This site, developed by the University of Illinois Education and Science Library, provides links to a range of multicultural resources and book lists.

# *Children's Literature*

The books listed here are recommended, subject to the qualifications noted in this chapter. See Appendix C for publishers' complete addresses. References to books of genres other than realism are noted in parentheses. Original publication dates are in square brackets.

Abelove, Joan. *Go and Come Back*. DK Ink, 1998.

Ada, Alma Flor. *My Name Is Marie Isobel*. Atheneum, 1993.

Alcock, Vivien. *The Monster Garden*. Delacorte, 1988. (Fantasy)

———. *The Mysterious Mr. Ross*. Delacorte, 1987.

———. *The Stonewalkers*. Delacorte, 1983. (Fantasy)

Avi. *Nothing but the Truth*. Orchard, 1991.

Bauer, Joan. *Backwater*. Putnam, 1999.

———. *Rules of the Road*. Putnam, 1998.

———. *Squashed*. Delacorte, 1992.

Bauer, Marion Dane. *On My Honor*. Houghton Mifflin, 1986.

———. *A Question of Trust*. Houghton Mifflin, 1994.

Bawden, Nina. *Granny the Pag*. Clarion, 1996.

———. *The Outside Child*. Lothrop, Lee & Shepard, 1989.

Betancourt, Jean. *My Name is Brain Brian*. Scholastic, 1993.

Block, Francesca Lia. *Weetzie Bat*. Harper, 1999.

Blume, Judy. *Are You There, God? It's Me, Margaret*. Bradbury, 1970.

———. *Superfudge*. Dutton, 1980.

———. *Tales of a Fourth Grade Nothing*. Illustrated by Roy Doty. Dutton, 1972.

———. *Then Again, Maybe I Won't*. Bradbury, 1971.

Bolden, Tonya. ed. *Rites of Passage: Stories About Growing Up by Black Writers from Around the World*. Hyperion, 1994.

Bridgers, Sue Ellen. *All Together Now*. Knopf, 1979.

Brooks, Bruce. *The Moves Make the Man*. Harper & Row, 1984.

Bruchac, Joseph. *Eagle Song*. Dial, 1997.

———. *The Heart of a Chief*. Dial, 1998.

Bunting, Eve. *A Day's Work*. Illustrated by Ron Himler. Clarion, 1991.

———. *Fly Away Home*. Illustrated by Ron Himler. Clarion, 1991.

Burnford, Sheila. *The Incredible Journey*. Illustrated by Carl Burger. Little, Brown, 1961.

Butts, Nancy. *Chesire Moon*. Front Street, 1996

Byars, Betsy. *Bingo Brown, Gypsy Lover*. Viking, 1990.

———. *The Burning Questions of Bingo Brown*. Viking, 1988.

———. *Cracker Jackson*. Viking, 1985.

———. *The Cybil War*. Illustrated by Gail Owens. Viking, 1981.

———. *Death's Door: A Herculeah Jones Mystery*. Viking, 1998.

———. *The House of Wings*. Illustrated by Daniel Schwartz. Viking, 1972.

———. *The Night Swimmers*. Delacorte, 1980.

———. *The Pinballs*. Harper & Row, 1977.

———. *The Summer of the Swans*. Illustrated by Ted CoConis. Viking, 1970.

———. *Wanted . . . Mud Blossom*. Delacorte, 1991.

Cameron, Ann. *Julian, Dream Doctor*. Illustrated by Ann Strugnell. Random House, 1990.

———. *Julian's Glorious Summer*. Illustrated by Dora Leder. Random House, 1987.

———. *More Stories Julian Tells*. Illustrated by Ann Strugnell. Knopf, 1986.

———. *The Most Beautiful Place in the World*. Illustrated by Thomas B. Allen. Knopf, 1988.

———. *The Stories Huey Tells*. Illustrated by Roberta Smith. Knopf, 1995.

———. *The Stories Julian Tells*. Illustrated by Ann Strugnell. Knopf, 1981.

Caseley, Judith. *Harry and Arney*. Greenwillow, 1994.

Casey, Maude. *Over the Water*. Holt, 1994.

Christiansen, C. B. *I See the Moon*. Atheneum, 1994.

Christopher, Matt. *The Captain Contest*. Illustrated by Daniel Vasconcellos. Little, Brown, 1999.

———. *Spike It!* Little, Brown, 1999.

Cleary, Beverly. *Dear Mr. Henshaw*. Illustrated by Paul O. Zelinsky. Morrow, 1983.

———. *Henry and Beezus*. Illustrated by Louis Darling. Morrow, 1952.

——— *Henry Huggins*. Illustrated by Louis Darling. Morrow, 1950.

———. *Ramona and Her Father*. Illustrated by Alan Tiegreen. Morrow, 1977.

———. *Ramona and Her Mother*. Illustrated by Alan Tiegreen. Morrow, 1979.

———. *Ramona Quimby, Age 8*. Illustrated by Alan Tiegreen. Morrow, 1981.

———. *Ramona's World*. Illustrated by Alan Tiegreen. Morrow, 1999.

———. *Strider*. Illustrated by Paul O. Zelinsky. Morrow, 1991.

Cleaver, Vera, and Bill Cleaver. *Where the Lilies Bloom*. Illustrated by James Spanfeller. Lippincott, 1969.

Clements, Andrew. *Frindle*. Simon & Schuster, 1996.

———. *The Landry News*. Simon & Schuster, 1996.

Clifford, Eth. *The Rocking Chair Rebellion*. Houghton Mifflin, 1978.

Clifton, Lucille. *The Lucky Stone*. Illustrated by Dale Payson. Delacorte, 1979.

Coffer, Judith Ortiz. *An Island Like You: Stories of the Barrio*. Orchard, 1995.

Cohen, Barbara. *Molly's Pilgrim*. Illustrated by Michael J. Deraney. Lothrop, Lee & Shepard, 1983. (Historical fiction)

———. *Thank You, Jackie Robinson*. Illustrated by Richard Cuffari. Lothrop, Lee & Shepard, 1974.

Cole, Brock. *The Facts Speak for Themselves*. Front Street, 1997.

———. *The Goats*. Farrar, Straus & Giroux, 1987.

Conrad, Pam. *Staying Nine*. Illustrated by Mike Wimmer. Harper & Row, 1988.

Cooper, Ilene. *Choosing Sides*. Morrow, 1990.

Cormier, Robert. *Frenchtown Summer*. Delacorte, 1999.

Couloumbis, Audrey. *Getting Near to Baby*. Putnam, 1999.

Creech, Sharon. *Walk Two Moons*. HarperCollins, 1994.

Crutcher, Chris. *Stotan!* Greenwillow, 1986.

Dakos, Kalli. *If You're Not Here, Please Raise Your Hand: Poems About School*. Illustrated by G. Brian Karas. Four Winds, 1990.

Dalokay, Vedat. *Sister Shako and Kolo the Goat*. Translated by Güner Ener. Lothrop, Lee & Shepard, 1994.

Danziger, Paula. *Amber Brown Goes Fourth*. Illustrated by Tony Ross. Putnam, 1995.

———. *Amber Brown is Not a Crayon*. Putnam, 1994.

Davis, Gabriel. *The Moving Book. A Kids' Survival Guide*. Illustrated by Suse Dennen. Little, Brown, 1997.

Deem, James. *3 NBs of Julian Drew*. Houghton Mifflin, 1994.

de Jenkins, Lyll Becerra. *The Honorable Prison*. Dutton, 1988.

DeJong, Meindert. *Hurry Home, Candy*. Illustrated by Maurice Sendak. Harper & Row, 1953.

Delton, Judy. *Angel Spreads Her Wings*. Houghton Mifflin, 1999.

de Paola, Tomie. *26 Fairmount Ave*. Putnam, 1999.

Dickinson, Peter. *Chuck and Danielle*. Dell, 1997.

Dragonwagon, Crescent. *Winter Holding Spring*. Illustrated by Ronald Himler. Macmillan, 1990.

Duffy, Betsy. *Hey New Kid!* Viking, 1996.

Duncan, Lois. *The Twisted Window*. Delacorte, 1987.

Ellis, Sarah. *A Family Project*. Macmillan, 1988.

Ellison, Sarah. *365 Foods Kids Love to Eat*. Sourcebooks, 1995.

Estes, Eleanor. *The Hundred Dresses.* Illustrated by Louis Slobodkin. Harcourt, 1944.

———. *The Middle Moffat.* Illustrated by Louis Slobodkin. Harcourt, 1942.

———. *The Moffats.* Illustrated by Louis Slobodkin. Harcourt, 1941.

———. *Rufus M.* Illustrated by Louis Slobodkin. Harcourt, 1943.

Farley, Walter. *The Black Stallion.* Illustrated by Keith Ward. Random House, 1944.

Farmer, Nancy. *A Girl Named Disaster.* Orchard, 1996.

Filipovic, Zlata. *Zlata's Diary.* Viking, 1994.

Fine, Anne. *Flour Babies.* Little, Brown, 1994.

Fitzhugh, Louise. *Harriet the Spy.* Harper & Row, 1964.

———. *The Long Secret.* Harper & Row, 1965.

Fletcher, Ralph. *Fig Pudding.* Clarion, 1995.

———. *Flying Solo.* Clarion, 1999.

Fox, Paula. *Monkey Island.* Orchard, 1991.

———. *One-Eyed Cat.* Bradbury Press, 1984.

———. *Radiance Descending.* DK Ink, 1998.

———. *The Village by the Sea.* Orchard, 1988.

Franklin, Kristine L. *Eclipse.* Candlewick, 1995.

Fritz, Jean. *Homesick: My Own Story.* Illustrated by Margot Tomes. Putnam, 1982. (Historical fiction)

Gantos, Jack. *Jack on the Tracks: Four Seasons of Fifth Grade.* Farrar, Straus & Giroux, 1999.

Garden, Nancy. *Annie On My Mind.* Farrar, Straus & Giroux, 1992.

Gardiner, John Reynolds. *Stone Fox.* Illustrated by Marcia Sewall. Crowell, 1980.

George, Jean Craighead. *The Cry of the Crow.* Harper & Row, 1980.

———. *Frightful's Mountain.* HarperCollins, 1999.

———. *Julie.* Illustrated by Wendell Minor. HarperCollins, 1994.

———. *Julie of the Wolves.* Illustrated by John Schoenherr. Harper & Row, 1972.

———. *Julie's Wolfpack.* HarperCollins, 1997.

———. *My Side of the Mountain.* Dutton, 1959.

———. *On the Far Side of the Mountain.* Dutton, 1990.

———. *The Talking Earth.* Harper & Row, 1983.

Giff, Patricia Reilly. *The Beast in Mrs. Rooney's Room.* Dell, 1985.

Gilson, Jamie. *4-B Goes Wild.* Illustrated by Linda S. Edwards. Lothrop, Lee & Shepard, 1983.

———. *Hello, My Name Is Scrambled Eggs.* Illustrated by John Wallner. Lothrop, Lee & Shepard, 1985.

———. *Hobie Hanson, Greatest Hero of the Mall.* Illustrated by Anita Riggio. Lothrop, Lee & Shepard, 1989.

———. *Hobie Hanson, You're Weird.* Illustrated by Elise Primavera. Lothrop, Lee & Shepard, 1987.

———. *Thirteen Ways to Sink a Sub.* Illustrated by Linda S. Edwards. Lothrop, Lee & Shepard, 1982.

Gipson, Fred. *Old Yeller.* Illustrated by Carl Burger. Harper & Row, 1956.

Gleitzman, Morris. *Blabber Mouth.* Harcourt Brace, 1995.

Godden, Rumer. *The Rocking Horse Secret.* Illustrated by Juliet S. Smith. Viking, 1978.

Gordon, Sheila. *The Middle of Somewhere: A Story of South Africa.* Orchard, 1990.

———. *Waiting for the Rain.* Orchard, 1987.

Greene, Constance C. *Beat the Turtle Drum.* Illustrated by Donna Diamond. Viking, 1976.

Greenfield, Eloise. *Sister.* Crowell, 1974.

Griffin, Adele. *The Other Shepards.* Hyperion, 1998.

Grimes, Nikki. *Jazmin's Notebook.* Dial, 1998.

Hamilton, Virginia. *Bluish.* Scholastic, 1999.

———. *Cousins.* Philomel, 1990.

———. *The House of Dies Drear.* Illustrated by Eros Keith. Macmillan, 1968.

———. *M.C. Higgins, the Great.* Macmillan, 1974.

———. *The Mystery of Drear House.* Greenwillow, 1987.

———. *The Planet of Junior Brown.* Macmillan, 1971.

———. *Second Cousins.* Scholastic, 1998.

———. *Zeely.* Illustrated by Symeon Shimin. Macmillan, 1967.

Harris, Robie, H. *It's So Amazing: A Book About Eggs, Sperm, Birth, Babies and Families.* Illustrated by Michael Emberley. Candlewick, 1999.

Härtling, Peter. *Old John.* Translated by Elizabeth D. Crawford. Lothrop, Lee & Shepard, 1990.

Haseley, Dennis. *Getting Him.* Farrar, Straus & Giroux, 1994.

Haywood, Carolyn. *"B" Is for Betsy.* Harcourt Brace, 1956.

Heide, Florence Parry, and Judith Heide Gilliland. *The Day of Ahmed's Secret.* Illustrated by Ted Lewin. Lothrop, 1990.

Henkes, Kevin. *The Birthday Room.* Greenwillow, 1999.

———. *Owen.* Greenwillow, 1993.

———. *Protecting Marie.* Greenwillow, 1995.

———. *Sun and Spoon.* Greenwillow, 1997.

Henry, Marguerite. *Misty of Chincoteague.* Illustrated by Wesley Dennis. Macmillan, 1947.

Hesse, Karen. *Sable.* Illustrated by Marcia Sewall. Holt, 1994.

Hickman, Janet. *Jericho.* Greenwillow, 1994.

Hiçyilmaz, Gaye. *Against the Storm.* Joy Street, 1990.

———. *Smiling for Strangers.* Farrar, Straus & Giroux, 2000.

Hill, Kirkpatrick. *Toughboy and Sister.* McElderry, 1990.

Hippolite, Joanne. *Ola Shakes It Up.* Bantam, 1998.

Ho, Minfong. *Rice Without Rain.* Lothrop, Lee & Shepard, 1988.

Hobbs, Will. *Beardance.* Atheneum, 1993.

———. *Bearstone.* Atheneum, 1989.

Holman, Felice. *Slake's Limbo.* Scribner's, 1974.

Holt, Kimberly Willis. *My Louisiana Sky.* Holt, 1998.

———. *When Zachary Beaver Came to Town.* Holt, 1999.

Horvath, Polly. *Trolls.* Farrar Straus, 1999.

Houston, James. *Frozen Fire.* Atheneum, 1977.

Howe, James. *Dew Drop Dead: A Sebastian Barth Mystery.* Atheneum, 1990.

Hurwitz, Johanna. *Aldo Applesauce.* Illustrated by John Wallner. Morrow, 1979.

———. *Busybody Nora.* Illustrated by Susan Jeschke. Morrow, 1976.

———. *Class Clown.* Illustrated by Sheila Hamanaka. Morrow, 1987.

———. *Russell and Elisa.* Illustrated by Lillian Hoban. Morrow, 1989.

Huynh, Quang Nhuong. *The Land I Lost: Adventures of a Boy in Vietnam*. Illustrated by Vo-Dinh Mai. Harper & Row, 1982.

Johnson, Angela. *Heaven*. Simon & Schuster, 1998.

———. *The Leaving Morning*. Illustrated by David Soman. Orchard, 1992.

———. *Toning the Sweep*. Orchard, 1993.

Johnson, Scott. *Safe at Second*. Philomel, 1999.

Johnston, Julie. *Adam and Eve and Pinch-Me*. Little, Brown, 1994.

Jukes, Mavis. *Blackberries in the Dark*. Illustrated by Thomas B. Allen. Knopf, 1985.

———. *Expecting the Unexpected: Sex Ed with Mrs. Gladys B. Furley R.N.* Delacorte, 1996.

———. *Planning the Impossible*. Delacorte, 1999.

Kerr, M. E. *Hello I Lied*. Harper, 1997.

Kielburger, Craig. *Free the Children: A Young Man's Personal Crusade Against Child Labor*. HarperCollins, 1999.

Kidd, Diana. *Onion Tears*. Illustrated by Lucy Montgomery. Orchard, 1991.

Kjelgaard, Jim. *Big Red*. Illustrated by Bob Kuhn. Holiday House, 1956.

Kline, Suzy. *Herbie Jones*. Illustrated by Richard Williams. Putnam, 1985.

———. *Orp*. Putnam, 1989.

———. *Orp Goes to the Hoop*. Putnam, 1991.

Koertge, Ron. *Tiger, Tiger, Burning Bright*. Orchard, 1994.

Konigsburg, E. L. *From the Mixed-Up Files of Mrs. Basil E. Frankweiler*. Atheneum, 1967.

———. *Journey to an 800 Number*. Atheneum, 1982.

———. *The View from Saturday*. Atheneum, 1996.

Korman, Gordon. *This Can't Be Happening at Macdonald Hall*. Scholastic, 1978.

Koss, Amy Goldman. *The Ashwater Experiment*. Dial, 1999.

Krumgold, Joseph. *. . . And Now Miguel*. Illustrated by Jean Charlot. Crowell, 1953.

Kuklin, Susan. *Iqbal Masih and the Crusaders Against Child Slavery*. Holt, 1998.

Laird, Elizabeth. *Kiss the Dust*. Dutton, 1992.

Lasky, Kathryn. *The Night Journey*. Illustrated by Trina Schart Hyman. Warne, 1981.

Le Guin, Ursula K. *A Wizard of Earthsea*. Illustrated by Ruth Robbins. Houghton Mifflin, 1968. (Fantasy)

L'Engle, Madeleine. *Meet the Austins*. Dell, 1981 [1960].

———. *A Ring of Endless Light*. Farrar, Straus & Giroux, 1980.

Lester, Allison. *The Quicksand Pony*. Houghton Mifflin, 1998.

Leverich, Ellen. *Best Enemies Forever*. Greenwillow, 1995.

Levitin, Sonia. *The Return*. Atheneum, 1987.

Levy, Elizabeth. *My Life as a Fifth Grade Comedian*. HarperCollins, 1997.

Lewis, Maggie. *Morgy Makes His Move*. Houghton Mifflin, 1999.

Lipsyte, Robert. *The Contender*. Harper & Row, 1967.

Lisle, Janet Taylor. *Afternoon of the Elves*. Orchard, 1989.

———. *The Gold Dust Letters*. Orchard, 1994.

———. *Looking for Juliette*. Orchard, 1994.

———. *The Lost Flower Children*. Philomel, 1999.

———. *A Message from the Match Girl*. Orchard, 1995.

Little, Jean. *Hey World, Here I Am!* Illustrated by Sue Truesdell. Harper & Row, 1989.

———. *Mine for Keeps*. Viking, 1995.

London, Jack. *The Call of the Wild*. Illustrated by Charles Pickard. Dutton, 1968 [1903].

Look, Lenore. *Love as Strong as Ginger*. Illustrated by Stephen T. Johnson. Atheneum, 1999.

Lord, Bette Bao. *In the Year of the Boar and Jackie Robinson*. Illustrated by Marc Simont. Harper & Row, 1984. (Historical fiction)

Lovelace, Maude Hart. *Betsy-Tacy*. Illustrated by Lois Lensky. Harper & Row, 1940.

Lowry, Lois. *All About Sam*. Houghton Mifflin, 1988.

———. *Anastasia Again!* Illustrated by Diane de Groat. Houghton Mifflin, 1981.

———. *Anastasia Krupnik*. Houghton Mifflin, 1979.

———. *Attaboy, Sam*. Illustrated by Diane de Groat. Houghton Mifflin, 1992.

———. *Number the Stars*. Houghton Mifflin, 1989. (Historical fiction)

———. *Rabble Starkey*. Houghton Mifflin, 1987.

———. *A Summer to Die*. Illustrated by Jenni Oliver. Houghton Mifflin, 1977.

MacLachlan, Patricia. *All the Places to Love*. Illustrated by Mike Wimmer. HarperCollins, 1994.

———. *Arthur for the Very First Time*. Illustrated by Lloyd Bloom. Harper & Row, 1980.

———. *Baby*. Delacorte, 1993.

———. *Journey*. Delacorte, 1991.

Martin, Ann. *Kristy's Great Idea: The Baby-Sitters Club, #1*. Scholastic, 1986.

Mathis, Sharon Bell. *The Hundred Penny Box*. Illustrated by Leo and Diane Dillon. Viking, 1975.

McKay, Hillary. *The Amber Cat*. Simon & Schuster, 1998.

———. *Dog Friday*. Simon & Schuster, 1995.

———. *Dolphin Luck*. Simon & Schuster, 1999.

———. *The Exiles*. McElderry, 1992.

———. *The Exiles at Home*. McElderry, 1994.

———. *Exiles in Love*. McElderry, 1998.

Mikaelsen, Ben. *Petey*. Hyperion, 1998.

Miles, Betty. *Maudie and Me and the Dirty Book*. Knopf, 1980.

Moeri, Louise. *The Forty-Third War*. Houghton Mifflin, 1989.

Mohr, Nicholasa. *El Bronx Remembered: A Novella and Stories*. HarperCollins, 1988.

———. *Felita*. Illustrated by Ray Cruz. Dial, 1979.

———. *Going Home*. Dial, 1986.

Montgomery, L. M. *Anne of Green Gables*. Bantam, 1976 [1908].

Mowat, Farley. *The Dog Who Wouldn't Be*. Little, Brown, 1957.

———. *Owls in the Family*. Little, Brown, 1961.

Myers, Walter Dean. *Darnell Rock Reporting*. Delacorte, 1994.

———. *Fast Sam, Cool Clyde, and Stuff*. Viking, 1975.

———. *The Mouse Rap*. HarperCollins, 1990.

———. *Scorpions*. Harper & Row, 1988.

Naidoo, Beverley. *Chain of Fire*. Illustrated by Eric Velasquez. Lippincott, 1990.

———. *Journey to Jo'burg*. Illustrated by Eric Velasquez. Lippincott, 1986.

Namioka, Lensey. *Yang the Eldest and His Odd Jobs*. Little, Brown, 2000.

———. *Yang the Second and Her Secret Admirers*. Little, Brown, 1998.

———. *Yang the Third and Her Impossible Family*. Illustrated by Kees de Kiefte. Little, Brown, 1995.

———. *Yang the Youngest and His Terrible Ear*. Illustrated by Kees de Kiefte. Little, Brown, 1992.

Naylor, Phyllis Reynolds. *The Agony of Alice*. Atheneum, 1985.

———. *Alice the Brave*. Atheneum, 1995.

———. *Alice In-Between*. Atheneum, 1994.

———. *The Fear Place*. Atheneum, 1994.

———. *Saving Shiloh*. Atheneum, 1997.

———. *Shiloh*. Atheneum, 1991.

———. *The Shiloh Season*. Atheneum 1996.

Nelson, Theresa. *Earthshine*. Orchard, 1994.

Nixon, Joan Lowery. *A Candidate for Murder*. Delacorte, 1991.

———. *The Other Side of Dark*. Delacorte, 1986.

North, Sterling. *Rascal: A Memoir of a Better Era*. Illustrated by John Schoenherr. Dutton, 1963.

Nye, Naomi Shihab. *Habibi*. Simon & Schuster, 1997.

Oneal, Zibby. *The Language of Goldfish*. Viking, 1980.

Osofsky, Audrey. *My Buddy*. Illustrated by Ted Rand. Holt, 1992.

Parish, Peggy. *Amelia Bedelia*. Illustrated by Fritz Siebel. Harper & Row, 1963.

Park, Barbara. *Junie B. Jones Is Almost a Flower Girl*. Random House, 1999.

———. *Mick Harte Was Here*. Apple Soup, 1995.

———. *Skinnybones*. Knopf, 1982.

Parsons, Alexandra. *Fit for Life*. Watts, 1996.

Paterson, Katherine. *Bridge to Terabithia*. Illustrated by Donna Diamond. Crowell, 1977.

———. *Come Sing, Jimmy Jo*. Dutton, 1985.

———. *Flip-Flop Girl*. Lodestar, 1994.

———. *The Great Gilly Hopkins*. Crowell, 1978.

———. *Jacob Have I Loved*. Harper & Row, 1980.

———. *Park's Quest*. Dutton, 1988.

———. *Preacher's Boy*. Clarion, 1999.

Paulsen, Gary. *Brian's Return*. Delacorte, 1999.

———. *Brian's Winter*. Delacorte, 1996.

———. *Dogsong*. Bradbury Press, 1985.

———. *Harris and Me*. Harcourt Brace, 1993.

———. *Hatchet*. Bradbury Press, 1987.

———. *The River*. Delacorte, 1991.

———. *The Voyage of the Frog*. Bradbury Press, 1989.

Peck, Richard. *Strays Like Us*. Dial, 1998.

Peck, Robert Newton. *Soup*. Illustrated by Charles Gehm. Knopf, 1974.

Perkins, Lynne Rae. *All Alone in the Universe*. Greenwillow, 1999.

Peterson, P. J. *I Want Answers and a Parachute*. Simon & Schuster, 1993.

Pinkney, Andrea Davis. *Hold Fast to Dreams*. Morrow, 1995.

Porte, Barbara Ann. *Something Terrible Happened*. Orchard, 1994.

Pryor, Bonnie. *Vinegar Pancakes and Vanishing Cream*. Morrow, 1987.

Quarles, Heather. *A Door Near Here*. Delacorte, 1998.

Raskin, Ellen. *The Westing Game*. Dutton, 1978.

Rawlings, Marjorie Kinnan. *The Yearling*. Illustrated by Edward Shenton. Scribner's, 1938.

Rawls, Wilson. *Where the Red Fern Grows*. Doubleday, 1961.

Roberts, Willo David. *What Are We Going to Do About David?* Atheneum, 1993.

Robinson, Barbara. *The Best Christmas Pageant Ever*. Illustrated by Judith Gwyn Brown. Harper & Row, 1972.

Rockwell, Thomas. *How to Eat Fried Worms*. Watts, 1973.

Rodowsky, Colby. *Not My Dog*. Farrar, Straus & Giroux, 1999.

———. *What About Me?* Watts, 1976.

Roessel, Monty. *Kinaalda: A Navajo Girl Grows Up*. Lerner, 1993.

Rosen, Michael. *Home: A Collaboration of Thirty Distinguished Authors and Illustrators of Children's Books to Aid the Homeless*. HarperCollins, 1992.

Rylant, Cynthia. *Henry and Mudge: The First Book of Their Adventures*. Illustrated by Suçie Stevenson. Bradbury Press, 1987.

———. *Missing May*. Orchard, 1992.

Sachar, Louis. *Holes*. Farrar, Straus & Giroux, 1998.

———. *Marvin Redpost: Why Pick on Me?* Illustrated by Neal Hughes. Random House, 1993.

———. *Wayside School Gets a Little Stranger*. Illustrated by Joel Schick. Morrow, 1995.

Sachs, Marilyn. *The Bears' House*. Illustrated by Louis Glanzman. Doubleday, 1971.

Schlein, Miriam. *The Year of the Panda*. Illustrated by Kam Mak. Crowell, 1990.

Sharmat, Marjorie Wiseman. *Nate the Great*. Illustrated by Marc Simont. Putnam, 1986.

Shreve, Susan. *The Flunking of Joshua T. Bates*. Illustrated by Diane de Groat. Knopf, 1984.

Shusterman, Neil. *Downsiders*. Simon & Schuster, 1999.

Silvey, Anita. *Help Wanted: Stories About Young People Working*. Little, Brown, 1997.

Simon, Seymour. *Einstein Anderson Lights Up the Sky*. Illustrated by Fred Winkowski. Viking, 1982.

Slepian, Jan. *The Alfred Summer*. Macmillan, 1980.

Slote, Alfred. *Hang Tough, Paul Mather*. Lippincott, 1973.

———. *The Trading Game*. Lippincott, 1990.

Smith, Doris Buchanan. *A Taste of Blackberries*. Illustrated by Charles Robinson. Crowell, 1973.

Smith, Janice Lee. *Serious Science: An Adam Joshua Story*. Illustrated by Dick Gackenbach. HarperCollins, 1993.

Snyder, Zilpha K. *The Egypt Game*. Illustrated by Alton Raible. Atheneum, 1967.

———. *Libby on Wednesday*. Delacorte, 1990.

Sobol, Donald. *Encyclopedia Brown Takes a Case.* Illustrated by Leonard Shortall. Nelson, 1973.

Soto, Gary. *Baseball in April and Other Stories.* Harcourt Brace, 1990.

———. *Boys at Work.* Delacorte, 1995.

———. *Crazy Weekend.* Scholastic, 1995.

———. *Local News.* Harcourt Brace, 1993.

———. *Off and Running.* Delacorte, 1996.

———. *Pacific Crossing.* Harcourt Brace, 1992.

———. *Petty Crimes.* Harcourt Brace, 1998.

———. *The Pool Party.* Delacorte, 1993.

———. *The Skirt.* Delacorte, 1992.

———. *Summer on Wheels.* Scholastic, 1995.

———. *Taking Sides.* Harcourt Brace, 1991.

Speare, Elizabeth George. *The Witch of Blackbird Pond.* Houghton Mifflin, 1958. (Historical fiction)

Sperry, Armstrong. *Call It Courage.* Macmillan, 1968.

Spinelli, Eileen. *Lizzy Logan, Second Banana.* Simon & Schuster, 1998.

Spinelli, Jerry. *Crash.* Knopf, 1996.

———. *Maniac Magee.* Little, Brown, 1990.

———. *Wringer.* HarperCollins, 1997.

Spyri, Johanna. *Heidi.* Illustrated by Troy Howell. Messner, 1982 [1884].

Staples, Suzanne Fisher. *Haveli.* Knopf, 1993.

———. *Shabanu: Daughter of the Wind.* Knopf, 1989.

———. *Shiva's Fire.* Farrar, Straus & Giroux, 2000.

Stolz, Mary. *The Bully of Barkham Street.* Illustrated by Leonard Shortall. Harper & Row, 1963.

———. *A Dog on Barkham Street.* Illustrated by Leonard Shortall. Harper & Row, 1960.

Taylor, Mildred. *The Friendship.* Illustrated by Max Ginsburg. Dial, 1987. (Historical fiction)

Taylor, Sidney. *More All-of-a-Kind Family.* Illustrated by Mary Stevens. Follett, 1954.

———. *The Trouble with Tuck.* Doubleday, 1981.

———. *Tuck Triumphant.* Doubleday, 1991.

Temple, Frances. *Grab Hands and Run.* Orchard, 1993.

———. *Taste of Salt.* Orchard, 1992.

———. *Tonight, by Sea.* Orchard, 1995.

Thomas, Jane Resh. *The Comeback Dog.* Illustrated by Troy Howell. Houghton Mifflin, 1981.

Viorst, Judith. *Alexander, Who's Not (Do Your Hear Me? I Mean It!) Going to Move.* Illustrated by Robin Price Glasser. Atheneum, 1995.

Voigt, Cynthia. *Dicey's Song.* Atheneum, 1983.

———. *Homecoming.* Atheneum, 1981.

———. *The Runner.* Atheneum, 1985.

———. *Seventeen Against the Dealer.* Atheneum, 1985.

Wallace, Bill. *True Friends.* Holiday House, 1994.

Walter, Mildred Pitts. *Have a Happy. . . .* Lothrop, Lee & Shepard, 1989.

———. *Justin and the Best Biscuits in the World.* Illustrated by Catherine Stock. Knopf, 1986.

———. *Suitcase.* Lothrop, Lee & Shepard, 1999.

Warburg, Sandol Stoddard. *The Growing Time.* Illustrated by Leonard Weisgard. Harper & Row, 1969.

Whelan, Gloria. *Homeless Bird.* HarperCollins, 2000.

White, Ruth. *Belle Prater's Boy.* Farrar, Straus & Giroux, 1996.

Wilson, Budge. *The Leaving.* Philomel, 1992.

Winton, Tim. *Lockie Leonard Scum Buster.* Simon & Schuster, 1999.

Wolff, Virginia Euwer. *Make Lemonade.* Holt, 1993.

———. *The Mozart Season.* Holt, 1991.

Woodson, Jacqueline. *Between Madison and Palmetto.* Delacorte, 1993.

———. *I Hadn't Meant to Tell You This.* Delacorte, 1994.

———. *Last Summer with Maizon.* Delacorte, 1990.

———. *Maizon at Blue Hill.* Delacorte, 1992.

Yep, Laurence. *The Amah.* Putnam, 1999.

———. *The Case of the Firecrackers.* HarperCollins, 1999.

———. *The Case of the Goblin Pearls.* HarperCollins, 1997.

———. *The Case of the Lion Dance.* HarperCollins, 1998.

———. *Child of the Owl.* Harper & Row, 1977.

———. *The Cook's Family.* Putnam, 1998.

———. *Later, Gator.* Hyperion, 1995.

———. *Ribbons.* Putnam, 1998.

———. *Thief of Hearts.* HarperCollins, 1995.

Yumoto, Kazumi. *The Friends.* Farrar, Straus & Giroux, 1996.

# Chapter Ten

## Historical Fiction

Barbara Z. Kiefer

*t*he author of a historical novel visited a public library's after-school program to meet with a group of children. In her talk she described the research she had done to establish an authentic Civil War background for her book. To make these efforts more concrete for the children,

she had brought along many examples of source material: maps, reproductions of nineteenth-century photographs, books and pamphlets, and a three-ring binder bulging with notes. One 10-year-old girl regarded this display with a troubled expression; when time came for questions, she quickly raised her hand.

"You found out a lot of things that you didn't put in the book, didn't you?" she asked. The author agreed, and the girl smiled. "Good!" she said. "If you had put all *that* stuff in, there wouldn't have been any room for the imagining!"

This child intuitively knew that historical fiction must draw on two sources, fact and imagination—the

author's information about the past and her or his power to speculate about how it was to live in that time.

Biography for children also draws on both sources (see Chapter 12). Although biography is by definition a nonfiction genre, its success depends as much on its imaginative presentation of facts as on accuracy. Both historical fiction and biography have narrative appeal. By personalizing the past and making it live in the mind of the reader, such books can help children understand both the public events that we usually label "history" and the private struggles that have characterized the human condition across the centuries.

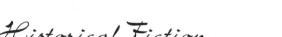

## Historical Fiction for Today's Child

Historical fiction is not as popular with readers today as it was a generation or two ago. Today's children generally select realistic fiction, the so-called "I" stories with modern-day characters and settings. Even so, children have more historical fiction available now than in the 1980s.

Publishers have capitalized on children's interest in series books by developing collectible sets of historical fiction titles. The American Girl books offer six different series, each chronicling the adventures of a girl in a particular time. These books, along with the expensive dolls and period costumes that go with them, have been phenomenally successful. Other publishers have also targeted the 7-to-11 age range. Viking's Once Upon America books, written by many different authors, vary widely in quality. However, they offer an unusually wide range of settings, such as the Oklahoma land rush (*Beautiful Land* by Nancy Antle) and the polio epidemic of 1952 (*Close to Home* by Lydia Weaver). In 1996, Scholastic introduced the Dear America series of fictional journals by young girls, which provide "eyewitness" accounts of events in American history. All the books are written by well-known authors, though with mixed results. Joyce

Hansen's *I Thought My Soul Would Rise and Fly* received a Coretta Scott King Honor medal in 1998; other titles have been severely criticized.[1] Perhaps most disturbing is the series' attempt to look like authentic diaries rather than like fiction. No author's name is given on the cover or spine. Following the diary entries is an epilogue, describing what happened to the character following the accounts in the diary. A historical note and archival photographs follow. Buried at the back of the book is a brief "About the Author" section, and the dedication, acknowledgments, and CIP information is given on the final page. It is no wonder that many children and teachers believe these stories are real accounts. The popularity of the series has spawned two others that use a similar format. The My Name Is America series features fictional boys' reports of significant happenings in American history, and the Royal Diaries series provides fictional chronicles of famous young women such as Elizabeth I and Cleopatra. Teachers who want to share these books with children will want to select titles carefully and ensure that children read them with a critical eye.

---

[1]See Marlene Atleo et al., "A Critical Review of Ann Rinaldi's *My Heart Is on the Ground*," and Beverly Slapin's "A Critical Review of Ann Turner's *The Girl Who Chased Away Sorrow*," available on the World Wide Web: http://www.oyate.org.

*Greg Shed's illustration represents the isolation of life on the prairie in Eve Bunting's* Dandelions.

Illustration from *Dandelions* by Eve Bunting, illustrations copyright © 1995 by Greg Shed, reproduced by permission of Harcourt, Inc.

*Ted Lewin received a Caldecott Honor Medal for his dramatic illustrations of immigrant life in Elisa Bartone's* Peppe the Lamplighter.

Illustration from *Peppe the Lamplighter* by Elisa Bartone, illustrated by Ted Lewin. Illustration copyright © 1993 by Ted Lewin. Used by permission of Lothrop, Lee, and Shepard, an imprint of HarperCollins Publishers.

Another noticeable trend in historical fiction is the number of picture storybooks that portray the life of a particular period. For example, children can sail on the Mayflower through picture books like Jean Van Leeuwen's *Across the Wide Dark Sea;* Thomas B. Allen's impressionistic pastel drawings help them visualize details of seventeenth-century life. In Eve Bunting's *Dandelions* they can travel across the prairie, helped by Greg Shed's textured paintings to experience the vast distances and huge skies of a land in which the closest neighbors were three hours away. They can walk among the tenements of an immigrant community in New York City in Elisa Bartone's *Peppe the Lamplighter.* Here Ted Lewin's flowing watercolors will light their way through the frightening darkness of city streets and overwhelming demands of a new land and a new culture.

The increased use of books across the curriculum has created a demand for more historical fiction and biography in the social studies curriculum. Many books that were written in the 1950s—such as Eloise McGraw's *Moccasin Trail* and William Steele's *Winter Danger, The Buffalo Knife,* and *Flaming Arrows*—have been reissued in paperback. These are still exciting, well-written stories of frontier living and will capture children's interest. Based on a true story, *On to Oregon!* by Honoré Morrow is an almost unbelievable tale of the courage of the six Sager children, who, after their parents' deaths, walked more than a thousand miles by themselves through the wilderness until they reached the Whitman missionary station. First published in 1926, then again in 1946 and 1954, and then in paperback in the 1990s, this novel proves the lasting quality of a true survival story.

While many books of American historical fiction are being reissued, many fine books, such as Rosemary Sutcliff's books about early Britain, have been allowed to go out of print in the United States. Except for an increase in the number of titles about the Holocaust, we have fewer books of historical fiction about other lands. This is a loss, indeed, in a world in which we are all becoming increasingly interdependent. We need to know our history *and* the history of other countries. One way for teachers to overcome this problem is to seek out some of these important titles through Internet book stores. These give teachers access to titles in the United Kingdom that were heretofore almost impossible to find in the United States. Those we discuss here are well worth the time it takes to locate them.

## The Value of Historical Fiction

Historical novels for children help a child to experience the past—to enter into the conflicts, the suffering, the joys, and the despair of those who lived before us. There is no way children can feel the jolt of a covered wagon, the tediousness of the daily trek in the broiling sun, or the constant threat of danger unless they take an imaginative journey in books like

Jean Van Leeuwen's *Bound for Oregon* or *Beyond the Divide* by Kathryn Lasky. Well-written historical fiction offers young people the vicarious experience of participating in the life of the past.

Historical fiction encourages children to think as well as feel. Every book set in the past invites a comparison with the present. In addition, opportunities for critical thinking and judgment are built into the many novels that provide conflicting views on an issue and force characters to make hard choices. Readers of *My Brother Sam Is Dead* by the Colliers can weigh Sam's patriot fervor against his father's Tory practicality as young Tim tries to decide which one is right. Readers will question Will Page's dislike of his uncle because he refused to fight the Yankees in Carolyn Reeder's *Shades of Gray*. And yet there have been conscientious objectors to every war this nation has participated in. Mary Downing Hahn deals with the same issue in *Stepping on the Cracks*, a story set during World War II.

A historical perspective also helps children see and judge the mistakes of the past more clearly. They can read such books as *Ajeemah and His Son* by James Berry, *Hide and Seek* by Ida Vos, or *Under the Blood-Red Sun* by Graham Salisbury and realize the cruelty people are capable of inflicting on each other, whether by slavery, persecution, or the internment of Japanese Americans in "relocation centers." Such books will quicken children's sensibilities and bring them to a fuller understanding of human problems and human relationships. We hope that our children will learn not to repeat the injustices of the past. Many years ago George Santayana cautioned: "Those who cannot remember the past are condemned to repeat it."

Stories of the past help children see that times change, nations do rise and fall, but universal human needs have remained relatively unchanged. All people need and want respect, belonging, love, freedom, and security, regardless of whether they lived during the period of the Vikings or the pioneers or are alive today. It matters not how many different "Little Houses" the Ingalls family lived in as long as Pa's fiddle sang a song of love and security in each one. Children today living in tenements, trailers, or suburban homes seek the same feeling of warmth and family solidarity that Laura Ingalls Wilder portrayed so effectively in her Little House series.

Historical fiction also enables children to see human interdependence. We are all interconnected and interrelated. We need others as much as Matt needed Attean and Saknis in Elizabeth George Speare's *The Sign of the Beaver* or Ellen Rosen needed Annemarie Johansen's family in order to escape the Nazis in Lois Lowry's award-winning book *Number the Stars*. Such books also dramatize the

*Illustrator Beth Peck shows a Native American father burying an arrowhead that will be found years later in* The House on Maple Street *by Bonnie Pryor.*

Illustration from *The House on Maple Street* by Bonnie Pryor, illustrated by Beth Peck. Illustration copyright © 1987 by Beth Peck. By permission of Morrow Junior Books, an imprint of HarperCollins Publishers.

courage and integrity of the thousands of "common folk" who willingly take a stand for what they believe. History does not record their names, but their stories are frequently the source of inspiration for books of historical fiction.

Children's perceptions of chronology are inexact and develop slowly. Even so, stories about the past can develop a feeling for the continuity of life and help children to see themselves and their present place in time as part of a larger picture. Books such as Bonnie Pryor's *The House on Maple Street* provide this sense for younger elementary students. In Pryor's book, lost objects from early times are unearthed in a contemporary child's yard. Paintings by Beth Peck link past and present, showing changes that came to that specific setting over the intervening centuries. Reading historical fiction is one way children can develop this sense of history and begin to understand their place in the sweep of human destiny.

## Types of Historical Fiction

The term *historical fiction* can be used to designate all realistic stories that are set in the past. Even though children tend to see these in one undifferentiated category (because all the action happened "in the olden days" before they were born), students of literature will want to keep in mind that various distinctions can be made on the basis of the author's purpose and the nature of the research and writing tasks required. Teachers and librarians should help children differentiate between the fictionalized aspects and the factual aspects in all types of historical fiction.

In the most obvious type of historical fiction, an author weaves a fictional story around actual events and people of the past. *Johnny Tremain* by Esther Forbes, the story of a fictional apprentice to Paul Revere, is a novel of this sort. The author had previously written a definitive adult biography of Revere and had collected painstakingly accurate details about life in Boston just before the Revolutionary War: the duties of apprentices, the activities of the Committee for Public Safety, and much, much more. Johnny Tremain's personal story, his development from an embittered boy into a courageous and idealistic young man, is inextricably connected with the political history and way of life of his place and time.

In other stories of the past, fictional lives are lived with little or no reference to recorded historical events or real persons. However, the facts of social history dictate the background for how the characters live and make their living; what they wear, eat, study, or play; and what conflicts they must resolve. Rachel Anderson's *Black Water* is of this type. Set in Victorian England, the book focuses on the problems of Edward, a child with epilepsy in a time when such conditions were little understood. As he grows toward adulthood, the boy learns to accept his limitations but also to understand that his talents hold hope for a rich and fulfilling life. Though the details of nineteenth-century life enrich the story and shape the action, the book's theme and the character's development could be placed in any time period. Authors who write within this generalized frame of social history have more freedom to imagine their story, because they are not bound to the chronology of specific historical events.

If we look at the author's task in another way, we can see that some authors deliberately reconstruct, through research, the life and times of a period long past. Others recreate, largely from memory, their own personal experiences of a time that is "history" to their child audience. The Little House books, for example, are all based on actual childhood experiences in the life of their author, Laura Ingalls Wilder, or those of her husband. Such books require searching one's memory for details and then the sorting and imaginative retelling of significant events, but extensive research is seldom done.

In other instances, a purely contemporary story about a significant event might endure until it acquires historical significance. *Snow Treasure* by Marie McSwigan is the exciting story of Norwegian children who heroically strapped gold bullion under their sleds and slid downhill to the port past the watchful Nazi commandant. Written as realism in 1942, this book is read by children today as historical fiction. We must also realize that Katherine Paterson's *Park's Quest* and other books about the Vietnam War might be read as historical fiction by today's child.

Some essentially historical stories defy commonly accepted classifications. Pam Conrad's *My Daniel* looks back on the past from the present. It concerns the pilgrimage of 80-year-old Julia Creath Summerwaite to a natural history museum where lie the bones of a dinosaur her brother once discovered. In the course of a day, Julia takes her grandchildren, Ellie and Stevie, to the museum and tells them bits about her brother Daniel, silently recalls other moments, and gradually reveals to the children how he died. This powerful story about Julia's life on the prairie and her love for her brother also captures the time when the discovery of dinosaur bones was beginning to suggest to humankind the evolution of life on this planet.

Other stories that appear to be historical fiction might better be classified as fantasy. Diane Matchek's *The Sacrifice* is a powerful survival story with vividly drawn characters and a richly complex plot. The fiercely independent heroine is prevented from taking any leadership role in her tribe because her dead twin brother was believed destined to become a "Great One." When her father is killed, the young woman sets out into the Yellowstone region to avenge his death and prove her courage. Over the course of this many-layered story we find that she has grown from a reckless and arrogant girl into a young woman who understands that the title *Great One* entails not glory but duty to others. Matcheck sets the book in the 1700s among the Apsaalooka Indian people who lived in Wyoming and Montana during that time. This particularity of setting suggests that we read the book as historical fiction, and in that case it does not stand up to close examination when held to the criteria for authenticity in its depiction of culture. The heart and soul of the book lies in the author's exploration of the traditional quest pattern, what Northrup Frye referred to as the quest of the human imagination for identity.* As such it works beautifully as fantasy but not as historical fiction.

A few authors tell stories of the past in the guise of another genre to draw the hesitant reader in more quickly. Jane Yolen's devastating story of the Holocaust, *The Devil's Arithmetic*, begins in the present when Hannah, bored with all the remembering of the Passover Seder, opens the door to welcome symbolically the prophet Elijah and finds herself in the

---

*See Glenna Sloan. *The Child as Critic: Teaching Literature in the Elementary and Middle School* (New York Teachers College Press, 1984), p. 27.

unfamiliar world of a Polish village in the 1940s. In Lois Ruby's *Steal Away Home,* 12-year-old Dana Shannon finds a skeleton in a closet after her family moves into an old house in Kansas. A small black diary found with the skeleton helps Dana discover that the skeleton is that of Lizbeth Charles, who had died 130 years earlier. In addition, alternate chapters take the reader back to the 1850s, when the house was owned by a Quaker family and was part of the underground railroad. Other devices are used to transport the main character (and the reader) from the present day to a carefully researched past in books like Janet Lunn's *The Root Cellar* (see Chapter 7).

Cynthia De Felice's *Lostman's River* is an exciting adventure set in the Florida Everglades in the early 1900s. Children will learn more about the fragile ecology of the Everglades than they will about historical details, but the story is based on real events—particularly the murder of an Audubon Society game warden hired to protect the rookeries of birds who were being wiped out for their feathers. E. L. Konigsburg's unique story of Eleanor of Aquitaine, *A Proud Taste for Scarlet and Miniver,* combines fantasy, historical fiction, and biography. Geraldine McCaughrean's *The Pirate's Son,* set in eighteenth-century England and Madagascar, is as much a classic adventure story as it is historical fiction. Categorizing books like these is far less important than bringing them to the attention of children, for they all tell good stories and make their subjects memorable.

No type of historical story is intrinsically better than another. However, the type of story might influence a teacher's selection process when choosing books for specific classroom purposes. And in applying the criteria for evaluating historical fiction, which are described in the following section, standards of authenticity must be applied most rigorously to stories that give a prominent place to real people and real events.

## Criteria for Historical Fiction

Books of historical fiction must first of all tell a story that is interesting in its own right. The second, and unique, requirement is balancing fact with fiction. Margery Fisher maintains that a good story should not be overwhelmed by facts:

 For the more fact he [the author] has to deal with, the more imagination he will need to carry it off. It is not enough to be a scholar, essential though this is. Without imagination and enthusiasm, the most learned and well-documented story will leave the young reader cold, where it should set him on fire.[2]

---

[2]Margery Fisher, *Intent upon Reading: A Critical Appraisal of Modern Fiction for Children* (New York: Watts, 1962), p. 225.

Historical fiction *does* have to be accurate and authentic. However, the research should be thoroughly digested, making details appear as an essential part of the story, not tacked on for effect. Mollie Hunter, a well-known Scottish writer of fine historical fiction for children, maintains that an author should be so steeped in the historical period of the book that "you could walk undetected in the past. You'd wake up in the morning and know the kind of bed you'd be sleeping in, . . . even to the change you'd have in your pocket!"[3] The purpose of research, she said, is

 to be able to think and feel in terms of a period so that the people within it are real and three-dimensional, close enough to hear the sound of their voices, to feel their body-warmth, to see the expression in their eyes.[4]

This obligation applies not only to details of person, place, and time but also to the values and norms of the culture or cultures depicted. To provide a faithful representation of a culture, an author needs to grasp the language, emotions, thoughts, concerns, and experiences of her character rather than shape that character to fit a mainstream point of view. In Ann Rinaldi's *My Heart Is on the Ground: The Diary of Nannie Little Rose, a Sioux Girl,* in addition to many factually inaccurate details, there are cultural miscues as well. For example, Lakota (Sioux) children are taught to be deferential and respectful to their elders and would be unlikely to criticize their mothers. Yet Nannie's disdain for her mother is a thread that runs throughout the book. Her continuing disapproval of her brother's actions also conflicts with the special bond that existed between Lakota brother and sister, one that even exceeded the bond between husband and wife.[5] Comparing these relationships with those of the Ojibway family in Louise Erdrich's *The Birchbark House* can reveal the importance of accurate depiction of culture in historical fiction for children. To fail in this regard is, at the very least, insensitive to children who are members of that culture. Such a failure also does a disservice to children from outside that culture whose worldview and understanding could be enriched by exposure to the attitudes, values, and goals of another group.

Although fictional characters and invented turns of plot are accepted in historical novels, nothing should be included that contradicts the actual record of history. If President Lincoln was busy reviewing Union

---

[3]Mollie Hunter, lecture, the Ohio State University, Columbus, Ohio, November 1968.

[4]Mollie Hunter, "Shoulder the Sky," in *Talent Is Not Enough* (New York: Harper & Row, 1976), pp. 43–44.

[5]Atleo et al., "A Critical Review of Ann Rinaldi's *My Heart Is On The Ground.*"

troops in Virginia on a given day in 1863, an author must not "borrow" him for a scene played in New York City, no matter how great the potential dramatic impact. It breaks the unwritten contract between author and child reader to offer misinformation in any form.

Stories must accurately reflect the spirit and values of the times, as well as the events. Historical fiction can't be made to conform to today's more enlightened point of view concerning women or minorities or medical knowledge. You can't save George Washington with a shot of penicillin any more than you can have the African American mother in William Armstrong's *Sounder* become a militant in the 1890s. Characters must act in accordance with the values and beliefs of the time. In Carol Ryrie Brink's *Caddie Woodlawn,* Caddie's father allowed her to be a tomboy while she was growing up in the Wisconsin backwoods, but she had to become a "proper lady" during the Victorian era; there was no other choice. Avi's *The True Confessions of Charlotte Doyle* is a dramatic sea adventure story in the manner of Robert Louis Stevenson's *Kidnapped.* In 1832, 13-year-old Charlotte Doyle boards the *Seahawk* to sail from Liverpool, England, to Providence, Rhode Island. Fresh from her proper boarding school experience in England, Charlotte is dismayed to find that she is the only passenger and the only female on the ship. Within hours of her arrival onboard, the ship's cook gives her a dagger for her protection. And that is just the beginning of this exciting sea yarn. Charlotte is a strong female character, yet some of her adventures stretch credibility as tightly as the full-blown sails that she climbs. Despite the many awards this book has received, we cannot help wondering if it wasn't written with today's values in mind rather than the New England of the early 1830s.

The historian Christopher Collier, who has collaborated with his brother James Lincoln Collier on several novels set during the era of the American Revolution, maintains that authors should pay careful attention to historiography, "that is, the way that professional historians have approached and interpreted the central episode of the story."[6] Collier believes that authors should weigh opposing views on the causes or meaning of a conflict and decide which should be predominant in the story, but also find a way to include the other significant interpretations. One way is to have different characters espouse different points of view. In *Bull Run,* Paul Fleischman deals with this reality by telling the story of this early

battle of the Civil War through the voices of sixteen different characters—northerners and southerners, male and female, civilian and military, slave and free. However, fiction that draws the reader into the thoughts and feelings of a central character cannot be truly impartial. In the middle of a massacre scene, a bleeding settler who cries "But the Indians are only fighting for what is theirs!" will sacrifice the story's credibility. Many other fine books, like Carolyn Reeder's *Shades of Gray* and Avi's *The Fighting Ground,* do let the reader feel more than one side of an issue. But for a more inclusive viewpoint, teachers and librarians will want to provide a variety of books, each with its own point of view and approach to the topic.

The authenticity of language in historical fiction should be given careful attention. We have no recordings of the speech of people from much earlier times, but the spoken word in a book with a historical background should give the flavor of the period. However, too many *prithees* and *thous* will seem artificial and might discourage children's further reading. Some archaic words can be used if they are explained in the content. For example, the book *The Cabin Faced West* notes that George Washington "bated" at the Hamiltons. The author, Jean Fritz, makes it very clear by the action in the story that "bated" meant "stopped by for dinner."

Some words commonly used in earlier times are offensive by today's standards. Authors must consider whether or not it would be misleading to omit such terms entirely and how necessary such language is for establishing a character. In Graham Salisbury's *Under the Blood-Red Sun,* "haoles," or white Hawaiians, refer to the Japanese as "Japs." It would have defeated the purpose and ruined the tensions of the story to have these people use more acceptable language. The same is true for James and Christopher Collier's use of language in their Revolutionary War trilogy that includes *War Comes to Willy Freeman.* In all their books, the Colliers provide detailed authors' notes to explain their background sources. For this series the notes also explain their choice of language, including the use of the term *nigger* in dialogue:

> The language used in this book is a case in point. It is almost certainly not how people spoke at the time for the reason that nobody knows how they spoke. We know how they wrote, because we have their diaries and letters, but of course the spoken language perishes with the time. We have therefore tried to give something of the flavor of how an uneducated black person might have spoken then. In truth, Willy's way of expressing herself is much too modern for the times, but once again we cannot be sure. We are more sure about the attitudes that Willy and others around her had—the idea that women were inferior to men, blacks to whites, children to adults.

---

[6]Christopher Collier, "Criteria for Historical Fiction," *School Library Journal* 28 (August 1982): 32.

## RESOURCES FOR TEACHING

### Recurring Themes in Historical Fiction

| Theme | Title, Author | Setting |
|---|---|---|
| The clash of cultures | *The Lantern Bearers* (Sutcliff) | Fifth-century England |
| | *The Sign of the Beaver* (Speare) | Maine Territory, 1760s |
| | *The Arrow over the Door* (Bruchac) | American Revolution, 1777 |
| | *The Man from the Other Side* (Orlev) | Poland, World War II |
| | *Year of Impossible Goodbyes* (Choi) | North Korea, 1940s |
| The human cost of war | *My Brother Sam Is Dead* (Collier and Collier) | American Revolution |
| | *The Slopes of War* (Perez) | U.S. Civil War |
| | *After the Dancing Days* (Rostkowski) | World War I |
| | *The Eternal Spring of Mr. Ito* (Garrigue) | Canada, World War I |
| In quest of freedom | *Jump Ship to Freedom* (Collier and Collier) | United States, 1780s |
| | *The Captive* (Joyce Hansen) | United States, 1840s |
| | *North to Freedom* (Holm) | Europe, 1940s |
| | *The Clay Marble* (Ho) | Cambodia, 1980s |
| Overcoming handicaps | *A Way of His Own* (Dyer) | Prehistoric America |
| | *The King's Shadow* (Alder) | Medieval England |
| | *Door in the Wall* (de Angeli) | Medieval England |
| | *Black Water* (Anderson) | Victorian England |
| | *Apple Is My Sign* (Riskind) | United States, early 1900s |

Almost all historians agree that such ideas were held by nearly all Americans of the Revolutionary era.

In particular, we had to consider very carefully our use of the word *nigger*. This term is offensive to modern readers and we certainly do not intend to be insulting. But it was commonly used in America right into the twentieth century and it would have been a distortion of history to avoid it entirely. (pp. 177–178)

Teachers should try to be aware of the reasoning behind authors' decisions and should be ready to discuss controversial issues that arise in books like these with their students.

Well-written historical fiction also makes use of figurative language that is appropriate for the times and characters in the story. For example, in Katherine Paterson's powerful story *Lyddie,* about a farm girl who goes to work in the fabric mills of Lowell, Massachusetts, in the 1840s, all allusions and metaphors are those of an uneducated rural girl. In the very beginning of the story a bear gets into their farm cabin and Lyddie stares him down while the other children climb the ladder to the loft. Finally she herself backs up to the ladder, climbs it, and pulls it up behind her. Throughout the book Lyddie alludes to "staring down the bears." She thinks of the huge machines as "roaring clattering beasts . . . great clumsy bears" (p. 97). And when she throws a water bucket at the overseer to get him to let go of a young girl, she laughs as she imagines she hears the sound of an angry bear crashing the oatmeal bucket in the cabin. Everything about this book works together to capture Lyddie's view of the world. At the same time, the long thirteen hours a day of factory work, life in the dormitories, the frequency of TB, and the treatment of women all reflect the spirit and the values of the times. More important than the authenticity of the writing is the fast-paced story and Lyddie's grit, determination, and personal growth.

A book of historical fiction should do even more than relate a good story of the past authentically and imaginatively. It should illuminate today's problems by examining those of other times. The themes of many historical books are basic ones about the meaning of freedom, loyalty and treachery, love and hate, acceptance of new ways, closed minds versus questing ones, and, always, the age-old struggle between good and evil. Many tales of the past echo recent experience. Books like *Catherine, Called Birdy* by Karen Cushman, *Lyddie* by Katherine Paterson, *Prairie Songs* by Pam Conrad, and *The Pirate's Son* by Geraldine McCaughrean could well be used in a discussion of the history of women's roles. All these books can shed light and understanding on today's problems.

To summarize, historical fiction must first meet the requirements of good writing, but it demands special criteria beyond that. In evaluating historical fiction the reader will want to consider whether the story meets these specialized needs.

Historical fiction can dramatize and humanize the facts of history that can seem sterile in so many textbooks. It can give children a sense of participation in the past and an appreciation for their historical heritage. It should enable the child to see that today's way of life is a result of what people did in the past and that the present will influence the way people live in the future. For some of the most important criteria to keep in mind, see Guidelines, "Evaluating Historical Fiction."

One way to approach historical fiction is to look at common topics or themes as they are presented in different settings across the centuries; the Resources for Teaching box (p. 468) groups titles by such themes. Another approach is to discuss books chronologically, according to the periods and settings they represent; the following sections are organized in this fashion.

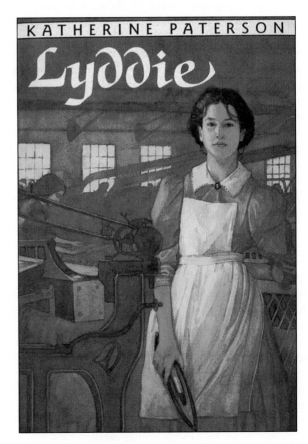

*The cover of Katherine Paterson's* Lyddie *introduces a main character whose fortitude is written on her face.*

# Stories of Prehistoric Times

Anthropologists and geologists are slowly uncovering scientific data that make it possible to imagine what life in prehistoric times might have been like. Authors and their readers have been fascinated with trying to reconstruct the minds and feelings of primitive people. How did they discover that there were others living in the world? Were all the tribes at the same level of development, or did different groups mature ahead of others? What happened when two groups met? These and other questions have provided the stimulus for some remarkably fine stories, many of which center on a character who is an outsider and independent thinker.

T. A. Dyer's *A Way of His Own* deals with early people of North America, a small band of hunters and gatherers on an inland prairie. According to their way, they abandon young Shutok because he cannot keep up and because they believe his "crippled" back houses an evil spirit responsible for all their misfortunes. But Shutok, a well-developed character with great determination, does not die as expected. He is joined by the escaped slave girl Uita, and together the two outcasts kill the fearsome jaguar that invades their cave, struggle against bitter cold and hunger, and live to reclaim a position of worth with Shutok's people. The story is fast-paced, with lively dialogue. Justin Denzel's *Boy of the Painted Cave* and its sequel *Return to the Painted Cave* also center on a hero with disabilities. Tao, a young adolescent, is rejected by his tribe because of a "lame" foot until his wall paintings are believed to bring luck to his tribe. Both stories are strongly plotted, with believable details of Stone Age life.

Strong female characters can be found in Marjorie Cowley's *Anooka's Answer* and Ruth Craig's *Malu's Wolf*. In Cowley's book, Anooka questions the tribal traditions that forbid her to create sculptures from riverbank clay. Cowley, a teacher of prehistoric archaeology, establishes a credible dilemma for Anooka as she must decide whether to accept the strictures of her clan or to set off to find a place that will accept her individual talents. Craig's Malu is an equally independent character who, in spite of a clan taboo, adopts a wolf pup and establishes a strong bond with the pup, whom she names Kono. When Kono attacks a clan member to protect her, Malu must flee her home and learn to survive on her own.

# Stories of the Old World

Children in the United States are often more interested in stories of the American frontier, the Civil War, or World War II than they are in fiction about ancient or medieval days. However, there is some fine historical fiction that portrays the old world in vivid and exciting terms.

## Ancient Times

The ancient world of Egypt with all of its political intrigue provides a rich background for Eloise McGraw's *Mara, Daughter of the Nile*. Mara, the mistreated slave of a wealthy jewel trader, is bought by a mysterious man who offers her luxury in return for her services as a spy for the queen. On a Nile riverboat Mara meets Lord Sheftu, who employs her as a spy for the king. In this exciting and sinister story of espionage and counterespionage, the transformation of Mara from a selfish, deceitful slave into a loyal and courageous young woman is made slowly and believably. Eloise McGraw has written another exciting, complex story of this period of ancient history titled *The Golden Goblet*, which has recently been reissued in paperback. Jill Rubalcaba's *A Place in the Sun* is a shorter but highly readable adventure set in thirteenth-century Egypt. Senmut, the young hero, is exiled to work in the gold mines in Nubia after he accidentally kills a sacred dove. This is a fate worse than death except that his talent for stone carving comes to the attention of Ramses II and he is eventually freed.

In Elizabeth George Speare's *The Bronze Bow*, Daniel Bar Jamin has one all-consuming purpose in life, to avenge the cruel death of his father and mother by driving the Romans out of his land, Israel. First with an outlaw band, and then with a group of boy guerrillas, Daniel nurses his hatred and waits for the hour to strike. He takes comfort in the verse 2 Samuel 22:35: "He trains my hands for war, so that my arms can bend a bow of bronze." A bronze bow is a symbol for what no one can do. *The Bronze Bow* is the story of Daniel's tormented journey from blind hatred to his acceptance and understanding of love. Only after he has nearly sacrificed his friends and driven his sister, Leah, deeper into mental darkness, does he seek the help of Simon's friend, Jesus. The healing strength of Jesus cures Leah, and at that moment Daniel can forgive the Romans. He understands at last that only love can bend the bow of bronze. Each character stands out in this startling story of conflict between good and evil.

## Tales of Early Britain

No one has surpassed Rosemary Sutcliff in her ability to recreate the life and times of early Britain. In books such as *Sun Horse, Moon Horse* and *Warrior Scarlet*, she vividly portrays the Iron and Bronze Age peoples of Britain, of whom there is no written record. Equally remarkable, she writes of the native peoples of Britain and of the Roman occupation forces with equal skill and sympathy. Sutcliff's *The Eagle of the Ninth, The Silver Branch,* and *The Lantern Bearers* form a trilogy that describes the period when Britain was ruled by Romans. In the third book, the last of the Roman auxiliaries set sail in their galleys and abandon Britain to internal strife and the menace of invasion by Saxons. At the final moment, one Roman officer decides that his loyalties lie with Britain rather than with the legions. Aquila returns to his family villa, only to see all that he loves destroyed by the Saxons. His father is killed, his sister is captured, and he is enslaved by a band of invaders. Three years later he escapes his thralldom, but it is many years before he can rid himself of the black bitterness of his sister's marriage to a Saxon.

In *The Shining Company,* Sutcliff tells of the king's betrayal of his war host of three hundred young men sent to fight the invading Saxons. Among them is his own son, Gorthyn, and his shieldbearer, Prosper. Set in A.D. 600, the story is based on *The Gododdin,* the earliest surviving North British poem. It is a story of adventure and heroism, loyalty and betrayal. Sutcliff's *Sword Song* is a fine coming-of-age story that focuses on the Viking occupation of Britain and on Bjarni Sigurdson, a young Viking warrior who is banished from his village in Northern Scotland for accidentally killing a man.

## Medieval Times and Tales

In the Dark Ages, the chivalrous deeds of the knights were a window to the light. Young children of 7 and 8 are intrigued with stories of the days of knighthood. Some of them will be able to read Clyde Bulla's *The Sword in the Tree,* the story of a boy who saved his father and Weldon Castle by bravely going to King Arthur. Through treachery, Shan's uncle makes his own brother a captive and takes control of the castle. Remembering where he hid his father's sword in a tree, Shan establishes his identity as the rightful owner of Weldon Castle. This is an easy-reading book with excitement on every page. It has more than just a lively plot, however, for it presents an interesting picture of the justice of the time.

Medieval entertainers were minstrels, whose special way of life provides a natural frame for journey or chase stories. Thirteenth-century England is the setting for the Newbery Medal winner *Adam of the Road* by Elizabeth Janet Gray. It is the story of Adam, his minstrel father, Roger, and Adam's devoted dog, Nick. Nick is stolen on their way to the great Fair of St. Giles, and in the frantic chase that follows, Adam is separated from his father. It takes him a whole long winter to find both Nick and Roger again. Adam has many adventures and some disas-

ters, but he learns that the road is home to the minstrel and that people generally are kind.

Marguerite de Angeli has written many books, but her finest is *The Door in the Wall,* a Newbery Medal winner. Setting the book in fourteenth-century England, de Angeli painted in words and pictures the dramatic story of Robin, son of Sir John de Bureford. Robin is to become a page to Sir Peter de Lindsay. He becomes ill with a strange malady, however, and is taken to the monastery by Brother Luke. There, Robin learns many things: to whittle, to swim, to read, to write, and above all to have patience—all "doors in the wall," according to Brother Luke:

> Whether thou'lt walk soon I know not. This I know. We must teach thy hands to be skilled in many ways, and we must teach thy mind to go about whether thy legs will carry thee or no. For reading is another door in the wall, dost understand, my son? (p. 28)

Eventually Robin is reunited with his father and mother. Robin's rebellion, final acceptance, and then challenge to live a rich life *with* his disability should provide inspiration for children today.

Frances Temple's *The Ramsey Scallop* centers upon Eleanor and Thomas, two youngsters who have been betrothed by their families but have grown up with little knowledge of one another. Fourteen-year-old Eleanor is frightened of marriage and the burdens that will be placed upon her as an adult woman. Thomas, just returned from the Crusades, is sick at heart and in spirit, and he doesn't think much of marriage either. Father Gregory, their village priest, proposes a pilgrimage of penance to the shrine of Saint James in Spain. The journey of these two young people (who promise chastity as part of their penance) takes them from England to France and Spain, and gives Temple the opportunity for rich descriptions of life in the Middle Ages. At the same time, however, she never loses sight of Eleanor and Thomas, and she skillfully tells the story of their coming of age and their gaining of faith. Their pilgrimage successfully accomplished, they return home committed to each other and to the future of their community. A companion book, *The Beduin's Gazelle,* follows Etienne, one of the characters Eleanor and Thomas met on their pilgrimage, to the Middle East. Here the young scholar becomes involved with a young Beduin couple and aids in a daring rescue.

Author Karen Cushman has given us two memorable heroines whose experiences provide insights into women's roles in the Middle Ages. The title character of *Catherine, Called Birdy* is the daughter of a minor baron whose schemes to marry her off to one appalling husband after another form the center of the plot. Catherine, called "Birdy" because of the birds she keeps as pets, wishes desperately for the freedom to move about the countryside and beyond the limitations placed upon her. The birds' cages represent her own constraints, and although she escapes from confinement long enough to have an adventure with a dancing bear, she must return to her cage like this performing animal and step into the role she has been given. The outcome is not tragic, however, for Catherine escapes marriage with the worst of her ancient suitors and ends up with a husband who can match her wit and independent spirit. Told in the form of Catherine's journal, the book is earthy and funny. The wonderfully descriptive and often obscure Saints Days that mark each diary entry, as well as her descriptions of the more vulgar aspects of medieval life, lend Catherine's voice an unusual ring of truth that will appeal especially to middle school readers.

Cushman's *The Midwife's Apprentice* strikingly contrasts the lot of a midwife's apprentice with Catherine's more privileged life. In fact, this young girl cannot get much farther from a castle keep than the midden heap into which she crawls for warmth at the book's beginning. She has little memory of her origins, and none of her name, and so she is called "Brat" by the urchins who tease and torment her, "Dung Beetle" by the sharp-tongued midwife who takes her in, and "Midwife's Apprentice" by the people in the community to which she has come. As she finds companionship with a stray cat and kindness from some of the people she meets, she also begins to discover her identity. At St. Swithin's Day Fair, she is given a comb, a wink, and a compliment and then is mistaken for a woman named Alyce who knows how to read. These experiences lead her to stop and examine her reflection in a horse trough as she heads for home.

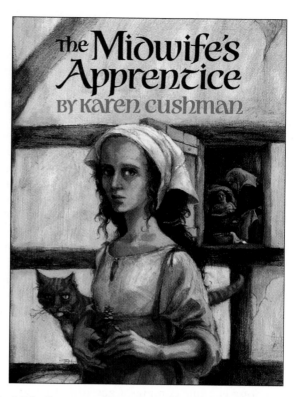

The Midwife's Apprentice, *Karen Cushman's vivid portrayal of life in the Middle Ages, reflects the dreams and difficulties of modern-day adolescents.*

From *The Midwife's Apprentice* by Karen Cushman, Trina Schart Hyman, illustrator, © 1995. Reprinted by permission of Clarion Books/Houghton Mifflin Company.

"And this is me Beetle." She stopped. Beetle was no name for a person, no name for someone who looked like she could read.

Frowning she thought a minute, and then her face shone as though a torch were fired inside her. "Alyce," she breathed. Alyce sounded clean and friendly and smart. You could love someone named Alyce. She looked back at the face in the water. "This then is me Alyce." It was right. (pp. 31–32)

This incident does not end Alyce's story but begins the real tempering-through-adversity that is at the heart of a good book. This Newbery Medal–winning story is almost heartbreakingly beautiful in its portrait of a child who comes to a full understanding of her true self. Cushman's writing captures the speech patterns of a medieval village and the rhythms of life in a different age, but her character and theme speak to all that is universal in human longing for identity.

In *The King's Shadow* by Elizabeth Alder, it is the year 1053 and Evyn, a young Welsh boy, loses rather than finds his name. He must also give up his dreams

of being a "storiawr" (storyteller) when, in revenge for his uncle's misdeed, his tongue is cut out and he is sold into slavery to Lady Ealdgyth, the consort of the Saxon leader, Harold Godwinson. Evyn is called "Shadow" because of his black hair, and his bitterness at his fate is just as dark. Yet Lady Ealdgyth is kind to him, and when he breaks his arm she sends him to Lewys, a Welsh monk, who teaches him how to read and write. This ability opens up new doors for him. When he finally accepts the identity fate has handed him, he finds a greater destiny than he had ever imagined. Shadow eventually becomes the squire and then the foster son of Harold Godwinson and witnesses events leading up to the Battle of Hastings. When Harold is defeated and killed by William the Conqueror, Shadow is rescued at the point of death. Nursed back to health by Lewys, he spends his remaining days writing his eyewitness account of these momentous events, an account that will become part of the Anglo-Saxon Chronicle.

Joan Elizabeth Goodman's *The Winter Hare* is set just over a hundred years later during the struggle for power between Empress Matilda and King Stephen. Following his recovery from a long illness, 12-year-old Will Belet is sent to his Uncle's manor as a page. He dreams of bringing honor to England but never imagines the important role he will play in thwarting a plot by an evil villain to betray his queen. Will is an immensely likable character, typical of adolescents across the ages, full of spirit, emotionally fragile, but never lacking integrity or a sense of honor.

Henrietta Branford provides an unusual perspective on the Middle Ages in *Fire, Bed and Bone.* Branford unfolds the events leading up to the Peasant's Revolt in the England of 1381 through the eyes of an old farm dog. The author remains faithful to her character's canine characteristics and perceptions, focusing on sights and smells of the time and revealing the human suffering that abounded. The book is highly believable, a moving account of a period of history that is on the cusp of consequential social change.

## The Emergence of the Modern World

In *The King's Swift Rider* Mollie Hunter has woven an exciting story around the fourteenth-century Scottish hero, Robert the Bruce. Young Martin Crawford, the story's narrator, wants to be a scholar rather than a soldier but when he encounters the fugitive Bruce their lives are entwined. Martin becomes the king's swift rider, a spy who passes information about the English army. Over the course of seven years Martin is witness to the brilliant tactics of a man whose forces are outnumbered by the merciless English yet who finally wins Scottish freedom at the battle of Bannockburn. Hunter writes with passion and insight about a crowning moment in Scottish history but never neglects the human relationships and desires that bring good historical fiction to life.

Fifteenth-century Eastern Europe is vividly portrayed as the background of Eric Kelly's Newbery Medal winner *The Trumpeter of Krakow.* This is a complex tale of the quest for the shimmering Great Tarnov Crystal, coveted by a Tartar chieftain for its supposed magical powers and zealously guarded by the ancestral oath of a Ukrainian family.

The Renaissance and the centuries that followed were particularly remarkable for the flowering of art and architecture that occurred in Europe. Several books have given us glimpses of what life might have been like for the young people who inhabited the world of the great masters. In *The Second Mrs. Giaconda,* E. L. Konigsburg hypothesizes the true identity of the Mona Lisa through the point of view of a young apprentice to Leonardo da Vinci. Set in a later time period, Elizabeth Borton de Trevino's *I, Juan de Pareja* is the fictionalized account of the real apprentice of Spanish master Diego Velázquez. Pilar Molina Llorente's *The Apprentice,* winner of the Batchelder Award, is the story of a Florentine boy whose greatest wish is to be-

come a painter. His father, who is one of the finest tailors in the city, is against this, but he agrees to give Arduino one chance at success in the workshop of Cosimo di Forli. Arduino discovers that the life of an apprentice is tedious at best, and that his new master is mean-spirited and worse. Jealous of the talents of Donato, his head assistant, Cosimo has imprisoned him in an attic room. Arduino discovers this secret and befriends Donato, sneaking to his prison late at night, where Donato gives him drawing lessons and talks about painting. When di Forli falls ill and cannot complete a commission, Arduino convinces him to give Donato the chance. Although somewhat melodramatic, the story provides a vivid picture of a time in history that is not often addressed in children's books.

The flourishing world of Renaissance theater is portrayed in Gary Blackwood's exciting *The Shakespeare Stealer.* Fourteen-year-old Widge is a young orphan who has been taught a system of shorthand by an unscrupulous clergyman. Apprenticed to the mysterious Simon Bass, Widge is ordered to attend performances of Will Shakespeare's "Hamlet" in order to copy down the script, a common custom in a time before copyright laws. Instead, he ends up employed at the Globe theatre and befriended by many members of the acting company. Widge soon learns for the first time what it means to belong to a "family," and he is torn between his loyalty to the company and his fear of reprisal at the hands of his master. Blackwood does a fine job of portraying Shakespeare's world, yet the fascinating details never overwhelm the exciting story or detract from the engaging characters.

Stories in English about life in China and Japan during this period are less numerous than those depicting life in Europe, but those that are available give older children a fascinating glimpse of life in Asia as well as a satisfying tale. These include Katherine Paterson's masterful stories of feudal Japan, *The Sign of the Chrysanthemum, Of Nightingales That Weep,* and *The Master Puppeteer.* Lensey Namioka has set three exciting stories, *The Den of the White Fox, The Coming of the Bear,* and *Island of Ogres,* in the same time period with young samurai warriors as heroes. Dorothy and Thomas Hoobler's *The Ghost in the Tokaido Inn* is a fast-paced mystery story set in eighteenth-century Japan. Malcolm Bosse's *The Examination* is a fascinating look at life in China during the late sixteenth century. The examination is one that Chen, a brilliant scholar, decides to undertake. If he passes, his future will be assured. But as the poor and unworldly son of a disgraced father, he faces many obstacles on the road to Beijing, where the exam will be given. His younger brother Hong, who makes up in quick wit for what he lacks in intellectual abilities, decides to travel with his brother to keep him safe. This long and complexly plotted novel is demanding yet has enough excitement to maintain interest. The picture Bosse presents of this period in Chinese history will have mature readers hungry for more details.

# Stories of the Americas

 Although recorded history in the Americas is relatively brief in comparison to European and Asian chronicles, the years from the fifteenth century to the present have been of interest to many writers of historical fiction. Many of these books show how the past has shaped present events in the United States and in the world.

## Colonial America

The varied settings and conflicts of colonial America have inspired an unusually large number of books about this period. *A Lion to Guard Us* by Clyde Bulla tells of three motherless London children who sail to Jamestown in hopes of finding their father, who has gone ahead to the new colony. The carefully limited historical detail and simple writing style make this book accessible to readers as young as 8 or 9. Several fine picturebooks also bring this time period alive for younger readers. Jean Van Leeuwen's *Across The Wide Dark Sea*, based on entries in William Bradford's diary, tells the story in the imagined voice of 9-year-old Love Brewster, who was aboard the ship. *The Thanksgiving Story* by Alice Dalgliesh details the life of one family on the Mayflower, including their hardships on the voyage and during their first winter. It tells, too, of joy in the arrival of their new baby, of spring in their new home, of planting, harvest, and giving thanks. *The Pilgrims of Plimoth*, written and illustrated with full-color illustrations by Marcia Sewall, provides a descriptive text that discusses the travels of the Pilgrims and their way of life at the settlement. Using George Ancona's black-and-white photographs of the reconstructed settlement at Plymouth Plantation, Joan Anderson presents her concept of the first Thanksgiving in *The First Thanksgiving Feast*. The text includes dialogue based on historical accounts from the era. All these picture books are appropriate for children in grades 2 and up. They can serve to celebrate Thanksgiving or as an introduction to a serious study of the Pilgrims.

Such a study might begin with Patricia Clapp's *Constance: A Story of Early Plymouth,* which is written in the form of a diary and details the story of Constance Hopkins, a young girl who sailed on the *Mayflower*. Constance describes the grim first winter at Plymouth—the fear of Indians, the deaths of many of the colonists, and difficulties with the English backers of the settlement. The device of a diary allows the author to use first-person narrative, which pro-

*Thomas B. Allen's pastel drawings provide a lovely accompaniment to Jean Van Leeuwen's* Across The Wide Dark Sea, *a story based on William Bradford's diary.*

motes the reader's immediate identification with Constance. An excellent romance, it is all the more fascinating for being the story of real people.

The Puritans soon forgot their struggle for religious freedom as they persecuted others who did not follow their beliefs or ways. Older students will thoroughly enjoy the superb story *The Witch of Blackbird Pond* by Elizabeth Speare. Flamboyant, high-spirited Kit Tyler is a misfit in the Puritan household of her aunt and stern-faced uncle. Her colorless cousins are as different from Kit as the bleak barren shoreline of Wethersfield, Connecticut, is from the shimmering turquoise bay of Barbados that had been Kit's home for sixteen years. The only place where Kit feels any peace or freedom is in the meadows near Blackbird Pond. Here she meets the lonely, bent figure of Quaker Hannah, regarded as a witch by the colonists. Here, too, Kit meets Nathaniel Eaton, the sea captain's son, with his mocking smile and clear blue eyes. Little Prudence, a village child, also comes to the sanctuary in the meadows. One by one, outraged townspeople draw the wrong conclusions, and the result is a terrifying witch hunt and trial. The story is fast-paced and the characters are drawn in sharp relief against a bleak New England background.

*Tituba of Salem Village* by Ann Petry and *Witches' Children* by Patricia Clapp both focus on

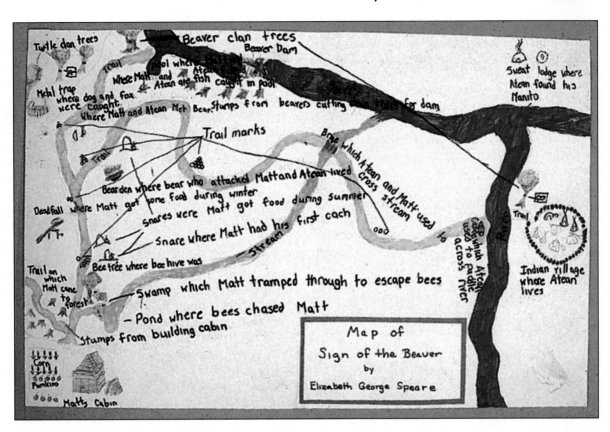

*One of the projects that grew out of an in-depth study of Elizabeth George Speare's* The Sign of the Beaver *was this imaginary map of the places in the story.*
Barrington Road School, Upper Arlington, Ohio. Marlene Harbert, teacher.

the witch-hunting frenzy that occurred in Salem Massachusetts in 1692. Tituba is from sunny Barbados but has been sold as a slave to the self-seeking, pious minister Samuel Parris. The fact that Tituba is both a slave and a black makes her particularly vulnerable to suspicion and attack from the obsessed witch hunters in Salem. A sense of foreboding, mounting terror, and hysteria fills the story of great evil done in the name of God. In Clapp's *Witches' Children* the first-person narrator is Mary Warren, a bond servant and one of ten girls who are "possessed." Mary admits to herself that the ravings began as "sport," a way to vent boredom and high spirits, and grew into group hysteria. When she tries to explain, she is not believed and is herself accused. In spite of the grim subject, the story moves at a fast and readable pace. A comparison of *Tituba of Salem Village* with *Witches' Children* would provoke much critical thinking by mature readers, especially in considering the two characterizations of Tituba.

During the eighteenth century, colonists pushed farther and farther into the wilderness. Many favorite stories have been set against this background. *In The Cabin Faced West* Jean Fritz has written the poignant story of lonely 10-year-old Ann Hamilton, who was the only girl in the wilderness of early eastern Pennsylvania. Ann longs for the books and other niceties she formerly owned, but her father urges the family to

look forward, or westward, toward their new life. At last, a special occasion arises when George Washington stops at the Hamilton cabin for dinner. Ann wears ribbons in her hair and sets the table in the way she has longed to do. This final episode is based on fact and really happened to Ann Hamilton, who was the author's great-great-grandmother.

Another lonely girl has been immortalized for children of 7 and 8 by Alice Dalgliesh in her popular book *The Courage of Sarah Noble*. This is the true and inspiring story of 8-year-old Sarah, who accompanies her father into the wilderness to cook for him while he builds a cabin for their family. Many times Sarah has to remind herself of her mother's final words to her when she left home: "Keep up your courage, Sarah Noble!" Sarah faces the real test of her courage when her father tells her that he must leave her with Tall John, a friendly Indian, while he returns to Massachusetts for the rest of the family. Symbolic of Sarah's courage is the cloak that Sarah's mother had fastened around her just before she left home. When her family are finally reunited in their new home in the wilderness, Sarah is secure in the knowledge that she has "kept up her courage."

The situation in *The Sign of the Beaver* by Elizabeth George Speare is much like that in Sarah Noble's story, as young Matt is left to tend the new cabin in

Maine territory while his father goes back to Massachusetts for the rest of the family. Matt eventually learns essential survival skills from Attean, grandson of the chief of the Beaver clan. The story explores their growing friendship, their changing attitudes, and the shifting balance between their two cultures. Speare has included carefully researched details of colonial life, and she has also considered some of the ethical questions that may have faced the early settlers. Joseph Bruchac's *The Arrow Over the Door*, establishes a similar relationship between Stands Straight, an Abenaki boy, fighting for the British during the revolutionary War, and Samuel Russell, a Quaker lad whose family adheres to their pacifist principles. Although Bruchac's book is set in a later time period than Speare's, it presents a Native American point of view and would allow opportunity for discussion and comparison. The Web "*The Sign of the Beaver*" suggests opportunities for study of this book and the connections teachers might make to other books and other events in colonial history.

Other books, like *The Matchlock Gun* by Walter D. Edmonds, show that the differences between white and Native American people could not always be bridged. This book, based on the experiences of a Dutch family living in the Hudson Valley in 1756, focuses on the terror as well as the courage of settlers who were victims of fierce Indian raids. This story, which won the Newbery Medal in 1942, has since been criticized for presenting Native Americans as bloodthirsty savages and for having a child shoot them. Obviously, this account of events is told from the colonists' point of view.

Two books centering on events surrounding King Phillip's War, a Native American uprising that took place in Massachusetts in 1675, try to imagine a Native American point of view. Paul Samuel Jacobs's *James Printer: A Novel of Rebellion* is based on the true account of a Nipmuck Indian who was raised by a white family and apprenticed in the printing shop of Samuel Green. Green's son Bartholomew narrates the story, describing the brutality of the war and the tragic choices Printer must make between his love for his craft and his loyalty to his people. Paul Fleischman's *Saturnalia* takes place six years later and follows the experiences of 14-year-old William, a survivor of a vicious attack during the war by the Massachusetts Militia. William is also apprenticed to a printer, who has the boy taught Greek and Latin and the Bible and treats him as a member of his family. Fleischman weaves the complex stories of good and evil characters back and forth like a musical fugue. Only William is a part of all worlds depicted here: night and day, servant and family, Indian and Colonial, educated and nonliterate. His is the melody that holds this many-layered novel together.

## The Revolutionary Era

One of the best-known stories of the American Revolution for children is *Johnny Tremain* by Esther Forbes. Johnny Tremain is a silversmith's apprentice, a conceited, cocky young lad who is good at his trade and knows it. The other apprentices are resentful of his overbearing manner and are determined to get even with him. Their practical joke has disastrous results, and Johnny's hand is maimed for life. Out of a job and embittered, Johnny joins his new friend Rab and becomes involved in pre-Revolutionary activities. As a dispatch rider for the Committee of Public Safety he meets such men as Paul Revere, John Hancock, and Samuel Adams. Slowly, Johnny regains his self-confidence and overcomes his bitterness. Rab is killed in the first skirmish of the Revolution, and Johnny is crushed but not defeated. Somehow, this greatest of blows makes him a man of fortitude and courage, a new man of a new nation.

For Johnny Tremain, the decision to join the Patriot cause was clear. In many other books, because the Loyalist tradition and point of view are presented in a more compelling way, the characters are perceived to have a more difficult choice. In *John Treegate's Musket* by Leonard Wibberly, the title character is a solid citizen of Boston who has fought for his king at the Battle of Quebec. Not until he sees hundreds of troops marching through a peaceful countryside to seize two men does he arm himself and join his son Peter to fight the British at the Battle of Bunker Hill. In *Early Thunder* by Jean Fritz, 14-year-old Daniel adopts his father's loyalty to the king. Daniel hates the rowdy Liberty Boys who creep up on Tory porches and distribute their "Liberty Gifts" of manure, but he becomes equally disillusioned by the British attitudes. Daniel's struggle to sort out his loyalties will help children see that issues in war are seldom clear-cut.

*My Brother Sam Is Dead* by the Colliers tells of conflicting loyalties within a family and the injustices that are always inflicted on the innocent in time of war. Sam is the only member of his Connecticut family who is fighting for the rebel cause. Ironically, Sam is falsely accused of stealing his own cattle and is executed as an example of General Putnam's discipline. No one will believe the real facts of the case, for despite Sam's excellent war record, his family are Tories. This story takes on special poignancy because it is told by the younger brother, Tim, who loves and admires Sam.

Some of the same dreams of glory that drew Sam into the Patriot army plague 13-year-old Jonathan in *The Fighting Ground* by Avi. In 1778, near Trenton, Jonathan desperately wants to be in on the "cannons and flags and drums and dress parades." When he is

# THE SIGN OF THE BEAVER
## BY ELIZABETH GEORGE SPEARE: A WEB OF POSSIBILITIES

## SETTING

Map the trip that Matt's father made from Maine to Massachusetts and back.

Make a time line showing events during Matt's long wait. How many ways could you represent time passing?

Make an illustrated catalog of items that would have been familiar to Matt but are not common today. Consider tools, household items, clothing; see *Colonial Living* (Tunis), *Book of the New American Nation* (Smith-Barazini). Arrange a display of artifacts (or make your own reproduction) of colonial life or the Northeast Native Americans.

Build a model of Matt's cabin, or Attean's village. Compare and discuss—what differences in lifestyles are dictated by shelter and its surroundings?

## STYLE AND TECHNIQUE

### Pace of Plot
How long are the chapters? What kinds of things happen as the chapters end? How do "cliff-hangers" help keep the reader interested?

### Predictions
What does the cover make you think the book will be about? Read and predict from chapter endings what might happen in the following chapter. Make up your own chapter titles.

### Foreshadowing
What bits of warning does the author give that there might be trouble from a bear? that something might happen to Matt's father's gun? Can you find early clues for other events?

### Use of Language
Notice descriptions that are comparisons (simile and metaphor). Compile a list, and suggest others of your own. Why would the author say that the gun was "smooth as a silk dress" rather than "shiny as a no-wax floor"? How does the author make Attean's speech different from Matt's? What problems do you think an author has in deciding how people might have talked more than 200 years ago? Write a story about Matt's family. How might they have felt about being separated from Matt?

## MOTIFS

### Signs and Symbols
What makes *The Sign of the Beaver* a good title? How many examples of signs and symbols can you find in the book? Which are Abenaki signs? signs of the white man? animal signs?

### Animals
How are animals important to this story? Make a chart picturing the animals. Describe their role in the story's events; explain what that shows about setting, character, or theme.

### Gifts and Exchanges
What gifts are given in this story by Matt? by the Abenaki Indians? Think of some that are not material things. What gifts would you have to share with a friend like Matt or Attean? What gifts did Matt make for his family? What does that show you about how he felt?

## BOOK CONNECTIONS

### Clash of White and Native American Cultures in Colonial Times
*The Double Life of Pocahontas* (Fritz)
*Saturnalia* (P. Fleischman)
*The Arrow over the Door* (Bruchac)
*King Philip, the Indian Chief* (Averill)
*Thunder from the Clear Sky* (Sewall)
*Guests* (Dorris)
*James Printer: A Novel of Rebellion* (Jacobs)

### Other Books by Speare
*Calico Captive*
Compare portrayal of Native American characters with Attean and family.

*The Witch of Blackbird Pond*
*The Bronze Bow*

## THEMES

### The Value of Stories
What does this book have to say about the importance of stories and storytelling? How might Matt tell his story when he is a grandfather? What books does Matt's family own? Can you find any parallels between *The Sign of the Beaver* and *Robinson Crusoe* (Defoe)? What stories did Attean's family tell? What traditional tales might they have known? Read folktales of the Northeastern Indians; *The Winter Wife* (Crompton); *Gluskabe and the Four Wishes* (Bruchac).

### Survival
What survival skills did Matt develop? Which did he learn by observation? Without the Indians, what might have happened to Matt? Read other stories of survival: *My Side of the Mountain* (George); *The Talking Earth* (George); *Toughboy and Sister* (Hill); *Hatchet* (Paulsen). How does the predicament of the main character in any of these books compare to Matt's?

*The Heritage Sampler* (Hopple)
*Slumps, Grunts and Snickerdoodles* (Perl)
Try out some of Matt's survival skills. What did he cook? What were common foods in colonial times?

Make johnnycake.

### Changing Relationships
Trace the development of friendship between Matt and Attean. What events or passages from the story show a change in ideas about each other's culture? Think about Matt and Attean as teacher and student. How did Matt become a better teacher? How would you teach someone to read? What did Attean teach Matt? How did he conduct the lessons? Discuss the changes in the balance between the Beaver clan's existence and the coming of white settlers. Find out what really happened to Attean's people in the years that followed. What other changes do you see in characters' attitudes toward one another?

### Growing Up
How does Attean mark his preparation for manhood? What tests must he pass? What does Matt do that shows he is a man? Which of his actions earns the respect of Attean's people? Keep a journal for Matt that shows his feelings about passing events.

### Freedom
Who is more free, Matt or Attean? As winter sets in, Matt's snowshoes "set him free." What other things gave him more freedom?

477

caught up in a real battle and captured by Hessians who seem no worse than the Patriots, Jonathan does not know which way to turn. The action takes place in little more than one day, with the text divided into many short segments labeled by the hour and minute. This makes the book look simpler than it is, for although the print is not dense on the page, the story makes strong emotional demands on the reader.

The title character in Scott O'Dell's *Sarah Bishop* hates war, and with good reason. Her father, a British Loyalist, dies after being tarred and feathered by Patriot sympathizers. Her brother dies on a British prison ship, and Sarah herself is arrested on a false pretense. She escapes and flees to the Connecticut wilderness, where she struggles against the elements instead of soldiers. Her biggest battle is with herself, however, as she brings herself to face the world of towns and people once again. This story is based on the experiences of a real Sarah Bishop during the Revolutionary period.

Another little-known story of the American Revolution is that of a spunky young girl named Tempe Wick, who hid her horse in her bedroom for three days to save it from Revolutionary soldiers looting the countryside around their New Jersey camp. Finally, when a soldier demanded to search the house, the feisty Tempe threw him out in the snow. This humorous legend of the Revolutionary War is told by Patricia Lee Gauch in a brief book, *This Time, Tempe Wick?* A fuller characterization of this heroine is given in Ann Rinaldi's novel for older readers, *A Ride into Morning*.

Few stories are available about the role of African Americans prior to and during the Revolutionary era. Older readers will enjoy the extensive period details in Ann Rinaldi's *Hang a Thousand Trees with Ribbons*, the tragic story of Phillis Wheatley, an African American poet whose talents were largely unrecognized during her short lifetime. The Collier brothers have featured black characters in several books, however, including a trilogy that deals with the wartime problems of blacks in the northern colonies and their futile hope for a guarantee of liberty under the new government. In *Jump Ship to Freedom*, the memory of the late Jack Arabus, who had won his freedom in the courts as a result of his service in the Continental army, serves as inspiration for his son Dan. The boy's first problem is keeping the soldiers' notes earned by Jack to buy his family's freedom. Even if the notes can be saved, they might be worth nothing under the terms of the new Constitution just being written. Exciting action brings Dan as a messenger to the site of the Constitutional Convention. Because he is bringing important word about the slavery compromise (which will, ironically, set up a fugitive slave law), he gets to meet George Washington, Alexander Hamilton, and

other statesmen. A strong theme of this book is Dan's growing belief in himself and his abilities. The other titles in this trilogy are *War Comes to Willy Freeman* and *Who Is Carrie?* Each features a young African American woman as the central character.

Novels about Revolutionary America offer an intriguing variety of viewpoints. Individual books will help children feel the intense emotions of the time, but the impact of several read for comparison and contrast will be much greater. Children can also increase their knowledge of details about a time period in this way. Knowing more background each time, they will read each succeeding book with greater ease.

## Native Americans

Too often in historical fiction, Native Americans have been portrayed as cruel, bloodthirsty savages attacking small groups of helpless settlers. The provocations for the attacks are seldom explained. Thus, in Walter Edmonds's story *The Matchlock Gun*, the reader can only guess the Indians' reasons for wounding Edward's mother and burning their cabin. In Rachel Field's *Calico Bush*, the Indians seem equally cruel as they burn the settler's house.

More recently, several Native American authors have written fine works of historical fiction that begin to balance the picture of Native American cultures that children have seen in books. In *The Birchbark House*, the first in a planned series, Louise Erdrich has created a moving and significant counterpart to Laura Ingalls Wilder's Little House books. Little Frog, an Ojibwa girl living on an island in Lake Superior, relates her experiences over the course of a single year, detailing the small details of family and tribal life and customs and the tragedies that almost overcome her people. Erdrich's exquisite writing lends great power to the story. Although Little Frog's voice is more sophisticated than we would expect from a child of 7, her emotions and reactions to the events seem authentic, and young readers will have no trouble identifying with Little Frog just as they do with Laura Ingalls. The book would make a fine read-aloud for children in the middle grades and, shared with Wilder's *Little House in the Big Woods*, would provide many opportunities for comparison and discussion.[7]

Joseph Bruchac, well known for his many picture books and collections of legends and Native lore, has written several works of historical fiction that focus on the peoples of the northeastern woodlands. *The*

---

[7]See Michael Dorris, "Trusting the Words," *Booklist* 89, nos. 1 & 15 (June 1993): pp. 1820–1822, for the perspective of a Native American parent on the Little House books.

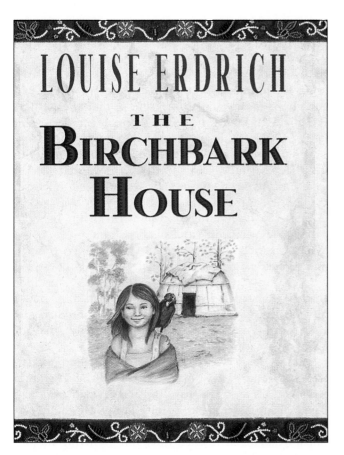

*In* The Birchbark House *Louise Erdrich provides a moving account of Native American life in the mid-nineteenth century through the eyes of a seven-year-old Ojibwa girl.*

From *The Birchbark House* by Louise Erdrich. Copyright © 1999 by Louise Erdrich. Reprinted by permission of Hyperion Books for Children, an imprint of Disney Children's Book Group, LLC.

*Arrow Over the Door,* mentioned earlier, is a readable and engaging story of the clash between Abenaki and European cultures. *Children of the Longhouse* is set in the late 1400s before European contact and tells an exciting story of Ohkwa'ri', a young Mohawk boy who overhears plans by young warriors in his village to raid a neighboring village. Such an act would violate the terms of the Great League of Peace, which bound the Iroquois nations. Ohkwa'ri' prevents the raid but earns the enmity of the older boys. Their conflict is played out in a game of Tekwaarathon (which later became lacrosse). Bruchac's *Dawn Land,* set during the Ice Age, is a richly detailed novel for older readers that weaves together Native American folklore and spiritual values with an exciting coming-of-age story.

Author Michael Dorris wrote three books that evoke generalities of a Native American way of life, drawing his reader emotionally close to his characters rather than providing specific details of time and place. In *Morning Girl* Dorris gives us an almost ethereal portrait of an island culture and two children who are the central members of a loving family unit. Morning Girl and Star Boy tell their stories in alter-

nate chapters, providing insights into their own personalities as well as details of their day-to-day life on the island. A terrible storm, their mother's miscarriage, and Star Boy's running away are events that emerge in a circular pattern characteristic of Native American storytelling. One day, curious to know what people see when they look at her, Morning Girl asks her mother and her brother, but their answers do not satisfy her. Finally her father motions her to stand beside him. He kneels down beside Morning Girl and tells her to look into his eyes. She explains,

> I leaned forward, stared into the dark brown circles, and it was like diving into the deepest pools. Suddenly I saw two tiny girls looking back. Their faces were clear, their brows straight as canoes, and their chins as narrow and clean as lemons. As I watched their mouths grew wide. They were pretty.
>
> "Who are they?" I couldn't take my eyes off those strange new faces. "Who are these pretty girls who live inside your head?"
>
> "They are the answer to your question," Father said. "And they are always here when you need to find them." (p. 36)

It is through such evocative reflecting, rather than through the relating of particular facts, that we learn most about these people. The ending, an excerpt from Christopher Columbus's journal describing Morning Girl's people, is all the more powerful because we have come to know them with such intimacy.

Dorris's *Guests* and *Sees Behind Trees* offer additional perspectives on Native American cultures. In *Guests* Dorris enlarges our understanding of the American Thanksgiving holiday, an event that has long been portrayed from a European point of view. *Guests* begins as an unnamed people are preparing to share their yearly harvest meal with some strange outsiders. These people are never named, nor is Moss's tribe identified, but children are likely to make the connection to Pilgrim and Pawtuxet. Young Moss is angered that this special time will be ruined by ignorant people who don't know how to behave properly. He runs off into the forest, hoping to learn his true identity during a special coming-of-age event, but he really discovers that the world is much more complicated than he had first considered. "Sees Behind Trees" is the name eventually earned by young Walnut, a boy who cannot live up to tribal expectations for males because of his poor eyesight. Walnut learns to compensate for his near-sightedness by increasing his sensitivity to his surroundings through other senses. Then through a series of events he truly discovers his identity and earns his new name. In all his books Dorris's skill with characterization lends emotional power to our reading.

Another fine book that relates historical events about Native Americans, although it might lack nuances of cultural details, is Scott O'Dell's *Sing Down the Moon.* O'Dell's title takes on tragic significance when compared to the southwestern Indians' creation myths that tell of "singing up the mountains." His book describes the "Long Walk," the disastrous three-hundred-mile march the Navajo were forced to make from their canyon homes to Fort Sumner. One of the most popular stories about Native Americans is O'Dell's Newbery Medal book *Island of the Blue Dolphins.* Based on fact, the story concerns Karana, an Indian girl who lived alone on an island off the coast of California for some eighteen years. Following an attack by Aleuts who had come to kill otters, all of Karana's people leave their island home by boat. When Karana realizes that her younger brother has been left on the island, she jumps overboard and returns to him. Within a few hours the boy is killed by wild dogs, and memories of the tribe are all Karana has left. Despite her despair when she realizes the boat will not return, Karana creates a life for herself. She makes a house and utensils, and fashions weapons, although in so doing she violates a tribal taboo against women making weapons. Eventually she makes friends with the leader of the dog pack, and thereafter enjoys his protection and companionship. When Spanish priests "rescue" Karana, she leaves in sadness. The reader may question whether she will find as much happiness at the mission with human companionship as she had known alone on the island. The question is answered in a sequel, *Zia,* in which Karana's last days are witnessed through the eyes of her niece.

Several books are based on accounts of Indians' capture of white settlers. *Calico Captive* by Elizabeth Speare is for more mature readers. Based on real people and events, this is a fictionalized account of the experiences of young Miriam Willard, who had just been to her first dance when she was captured by Indians. Her sister, brother-in-law, three children, and a neighbor are captured with her, taken to Montreal, and sold as slaves. Their hardships and ordeals are taken from a diary kept by a real captive in 1754. Speare tells this story with her usual fine characterizations and attention to authentic detail. Katherine Kirkpatrick's *Trouble's Daughter,* also for older readers, is the story of Susanna Hutchinson, the daughter of religious radical Anne Hutchinson, who in 1663 moved with her family to Long Island to avoid persecution. When Lenape Indians massacre the family, they take Susannah prisoner. At first terrified, Susannah grows to love and respect her captors by the time she returns to white society. In both these books the author's careful research never overwhelms the emotionally charged and moving story.

In *Moccasin Trail* by Eloise McGraw, Jim Heath is rescued from a grizzly bear by Crow Indians and brought up to think and feel like an Indian. Eventually reunited with his younger sister and brothers, Jim begins to long for the sensible Indian ways. Everything he does seems to be wrong. He steals a horse as a gift for Jonnie—the grandest present a Crow Indian can give—and is rebuffed in front of the other settlers and made to return the horse. A loner, Jim decides to leave. Little Daniel is heartbroken and runs away, only to be captured by the Umpqua Indians, who keep slaves. Jim rescues him but knows that for his sake and his brother's he must forsake the moccasin trail forever. *Jenny of the Tetons* by Kristiana Gregory is the fictionalized account of an Englishman called "Beaver Dick" and his Shoshone wife, Jenny. When an Indian attack leaves Carrie Hill wounded and alone, she decides to join Beaver Dick and help care for his family. She is horrified when she finds that he is married to a Native American. But gradually she learns to respect this gentle person who carefully tends her wound. This is a moving story of changing relationships.

Mature readers will also enjoy the highly fictionalized biography *Ishi, Last of His Tribe* by Theodora Kroeber. Most of the Yahi Indians of California had been killed or driven from their homes by the invading gold seekers and settlers during the early 1900s, but a small band resisted their fate by living in concealment. Ishi is the last survivor of this tribe, and hungry and ill, he allows himself to be found. Haltingly, he tells his story to an anthropologist who takes him to live at the University of California's museum. Here he dwells happily for five years, helping to record the language and ways of the Yahi world.

## The American Frontier

No other period in U.S. history has been more dramatized in films and television than that of the westward movement of the American pioneers. Because civilization grows with a ragged edge, nineteenth-century frontier stories are set in widely scattered locations. Some settlers moved with the wilderness, like Pa Ingalls in what might be the best loved of all American historical fiction, the nine Little House books by Laura Ingalls Wilder. These stories describe the growing up of the Ingalls girls and the Wilder boys. In the first book of the series, *Little House in the Big Woods,* Laura is only 6 years old; the last three books—*Little Town on the Prairie, These Happy Golden Years,* and *The First Four Years*—tell of Laura's teaching career and her marriage. Based on the author's own life, these books portray the hardships and difficulties of pioneer life in the 1870s and 1880s and describe the fun and excitement that were also a part of daily living in those days. Throughout the stories the warmth and security of family love run like a golden thread that binds the books to the hearts of their readers. The family faces many hardships but there are wonderful moments as well. Best of all are the long winter evenings of firelight and the clear singing of Pa's fiddle. These mean love and security, whether the home is in Wisconsin, in the wild Kansas country as described in *Little House on the Prairie*, in the Minnesota of *On the Banks of Plum Creek*, or in Dakota Territory as in *By the Shores of Silver Lake*. The last book of the series, *The First Four Years*, describes the years immediately following Laura and Manley's marriage in 1885. The manuscript for this story was found among Laura's papers after her death in 1957. Garth Williams illustrated a uniform edition of all the books in the series. His black-and-white pictures capture the excitement and terror of many of the episodes in the books, but they also convey the tenderness, love, amusement, and courage that were necessary in the life of the early settlers.

Another favorite book of pioneer days is *Caddie Woodlawn* by Carol Ryrie Brink. This story takes place in the Wisconsin wilderness of the 1860s, but it is primarily the story of the growing up of tomboy Caddie. Caddie had been a frail baby, and so her father persuaded her mother to allow her to be reared more freely than her older sister, Clara, who was restricted by the rules of decorum for young ladies. Caddie was free to run about the half-wild Wisconsin frontier with her two brothers. Their escapades and adventures read like a feminine *Tom Sawyer*. Caddie is a self-willed, independent spirit who is assured a memorable place in children's literature.

Like Caddie, May Amelia Jennifer L. Holm's *Our Only May Ameila* is an independent female somewhat limited by the strictures of her day. She is the only girl in a family of seven brothers, and even worse, the only girl born into her rural Finnish American community. Expected to work on her family's farm as well as take on more traditional female jobs, May Amelia has a hard time conforming to the role of "Proper Young Lady." She dreams of growing up to sail the world like her sea captain uncle but in the meantime has some marvelously funny adventures chasing sheep, fishing for salmon, running from bears, and encountering ghosts. This warm and lighthearted account of growing up in early-twentieth-century Washington state is told in May Amelia's appealingly fresh voice. This Newbery Honor story was inspired by the author's grandaunt's diary.

The Texas frontier has provided a distinctive setting for many exciting stories. One of the best known is Fred Gipson's *Old Yeller*, the story of a boy's integrity and love for his dog on an early Texas homestead. Patricia Beatty's *Wait for Me, Watch for Me, Eula Bee* takes place at the time of the Civil War, when the absence of men who had joined the Confederate army made West Texas homesteads especially vulnerable to Indian attack. Lewallen's mother, brother, and uncle are killed by Comanches, but he and his 3-year-old sister, Eula Bee, with her bouncy red curls that fascinate the warriors, are taken captive. When Lewallen manages at last to escape, he vows to return for his sister. Many months later he makes good his promise, but Eula Bee has forgotten him and has to be carried away, kicking and struggling. Long after they have reached safety, she is won to remembrance by the chance hearing of a song, the popular tune "Lorena," which Lewallen had whistled over and over during their captivity to assure her he was near.

Following the Civil War, Sam White and his family leave the safety and security of their grandparents' white house in Kentucky and head for Dakota Territory. In *The Grasshopper Summer*, Ann Turner details the hardships faced by this determined southern family. After staking their claim, they built a sod house facing south and planted their first crops; then the grasshoppers came, eating everything green in sight. Sam's younger brother, Bill, said, "They ate up all the pretty things and left all the ugly things" (p. 134). Their neighbors, the Grants, give up and go back home, but the Whites meet the challenge of the harsh land and decide to stay on in their sod house. *Dakota Dugout*, also by Ann Turner, is the perfect picture storybook to read either before or after *Grasshopper Summer*. The black-and-white illustrations by Ronald Himler show both the beauty and the ruggedness of living in a sod house sandwiched between the wide prairie and the endless sky.

By the mid nineteenth century, the far western frontier was in California and Oregon. Karen Cushman's *The Ballad of Lucy Whipple* is for the most part a lighthearted account of the California gold rush seen through the eyes of an 11-year-old girl. Lucy feels highly put out when her widowed mother decides to run a boarding house for miners and drags her and her two siblings from their comfortable home in Massachusetts to the rough-hewn and roughhouse life of a mining camp. Lucy does everything in her power to get back home, yet when she is finally given the chance she turns it down to remain as the town librarian. *On to Oregon!* by Honoré Morrow and Jean Van Leeuwen's *Bound for Oregon* are based on the accounts of real people who braved the Oregon Trail and make fascinating reading for middle graders. *Trouble for Lucy* by Carla Stevens uses information from first-person accounts of a journey in 1843 to set the scene for each of its brief chapters. Appropriate for 8- and 9-year-old readers, the story focuses on Lucy's efforts to keep her fox terrier puppy from being a nuisance to the oxen and drivers and the adventures that ensue. There is no pretending here that the pioneers' way was easy, yet the story is more concerned with the universal feelings of childhood than it is with hardship.

Kathryn Lasky's *Beyond the Divide* is a dramatic story for mature readers about an Amish father and daughter bound for the California gold rush. The plain ways of Meribah Simon, 14, are thought peculiar by some of her fellow travelers, but she makes many friends among them. The author creates a community of characters who bring very different pasts and problems to the challenging journey they share. Because they do seem like a community, it is all the more shocking that they should decide to abandon Will Simon along the trail when his wagon is disabled and he seems too weak to continue. Angry and disillusioned, Meribah elects to stay with her father. From that point the story hinges on her efforts to save him and then herself.

Another vivid story for older readers is *Prairie Songs* by Pam Conrad. It contrasts two points of view of homesteading in the new lands, that of the Downing family, who had settled in a "soddy," and that of the beautiful, cultured wife of the new doctor in Howard County, Nebraska, who has come to live in the next soddy. The story is told by young Louisa Downing and reflects her wonder at the back-East world of wealth and learning that Mrs. Emmeline Berryman represents. Never able to adjust to her life on the prairie, Mrs. Berryman is terrified out of all reason one winter day by the visit of two Indians and she flees. She is finally found, sitting in the snow, frozen to death. Louisa's narration is vivid, and her casual acceptance of life in a soddy points up the irony of Mrs. Berryman's inability to cope. The woman Louisa had admired could not match her own mother in strength of spirit or the special kind of beauty that made Louisa feel good inside.

Moving westward and settling the frontier was a major force in the life of many Americans throughout the nineteenth century. Farming the vast mid-American prairies put special demands on families. In *Sarah, Plain and Tall*, a beautifully written short novel by Patricia MacLachlan, motherless Anna and Caleb are delighted when Papa's advertisement for a mail-order bride brings Sarah to their prairie home. Sarah comes from the coast of Maine, with mementos of the sea she loves, her gray cat Seal, a moon shell for Caleb, and a round sea stone for Anna. She has agreed only to a month's visit, and the children, who quickly learn to love her lively, independent ways, are afraid that they will lose her. On the day Sarah goes to town for colored pencils to add the blue, gray, and green of the ocean to the picture she has drawn of the prairie, they realize that she will stay. She misses the sea, she tells them, but she would miss them more. The rhythm and lyrical simplicity of the writing are especially effective

when read aloud. MacLachlan continues the story in *Skylark,* an equally well written sequel. In *Three Names,* a slice-of-life picture book that would make a good companion piece for the two books, MacLachlan tells of her great-grandfather when he went to a one-room schoolhouse on the prairie with his dog, Three Names. Alexander Pertzoff's lovely watercolors show the beauty and spaciousness of the wide-open prairie.

Not all stories of this period take place in the West, however. Although set in the early 1900s, Mary Riskind's *Apple Is My Sign* is less a historical novel than a story of a 10-year-old deaf child learning to live among the hearing with his disability. Harry Berger, called "Apple" because of his family's orchards, is sent to a school for the deaf in Philadelphia. His whole family is deaf, but Harry is the first one to go away, and his early days at the school are difficult and lonely at first. Harry tells his family that he thinks he'd like to be a teacher, but a family friend signs "Hearing best teacher." His mother, however, reassures Harry: "I-f you want teach deaf, must try. That's-all. Never know, i-f never try. In head must think can. Brave" (p. 119). Riskind conveys the rapidity of signed talk by approximating its actual meanings, eliminating the little words or word endings, as signers do, and spelling out meanings for which there are no signs. Through Harry's story, readers may come to realize that opportunities for people with disabilities have changed over the years.

Two fine books explore largely unexamined episodes in the history of this period through themes of family ties and conflicted loyalties. Cynthia DeFelice has focused on the topic of medicine and healing in the early 1800s in *The Apprenticeship of Lucas Whitaker.* Lucas's family has been decimated by tuberculosis, and after a period of homeless wandering he is taken in as an apprentice to the local doctor. The local townspeople want to exhume the bodies of tuberculosis victims in order to burn their hearts and breath the smoke, believing that this can cure the illness. Lucas is torn between science and superstition as he struggles with his loyalty to Dr. Beecher and his desire to find a cure for the awful disease.

In the beautifully written *Susannah,* Janet Hickman explores the topic of families broken apart by tenets of religion rather than by the finality of death. In 1810, following the death of her mother, Susannah's father brings her into a Shaker community in Southern Ohio. In keeping with Shaker beliefs, 14-year-old Susannah is separated from her father and must live with the other children in the community. She longs for the remembered warmth of her mother's love and wants desperately to leave the community. However, she finds it difficult to leave a little 6-year-old girl she has come to care for. Like

Lucas Whitaker, Susannah must deal with the loss of her family and the difficult choices that ensue between self-satisfaction and self-sacrifice. Hickman provides fascinating details of Shaker life, but her greatest strength is the ability to deal with universal human problems.

## The Civil War Era

Attention to American history in the nineteenth century often seems to be centered on the Civil War. The events leading up to the war and those that followed also need to be considered if children are to have an accurate picture of this volatile period.

### Resistance and Freedom

 The country was involved and concerned with the issue of slavery long before the Civil War. *Nettie's Trip South* by Ann Turner is a picture book based on the real diary of the author's great-grandmother. When Nettie is 10 years old, she goes with her older brother, a reporter, and her 14-year-old sister on a trip from Albany, New York, to Richmond, Virginia. As Nettie writes to her friend Addie, she remembers all of the things she saw in that prewar city, including Tabitha, a black slave, in the hotel, who had no last name, and the slave auction where two children clasping hands were bought by different masters. Ronald Himler illustrated this moving account of a young girl's horror at her first exposure to slavery.

That cruelty is viewed from a variety of perspectives in several fine books for older children. In smoky tones of gray and black Tom Feelings's powerful *The Middle Passage* presents vivid images of the slaves' journey across the Atlantic. The pictures are preceded by a lengthy introduction that provides background about Feelings's work and provides details about the slave trade. The artwork is presented without words, however, because no written text could express the horror that these pictures convey.

Two fine novels, Joyce Hansen's *The Captive* and James Berry's *Ajeemah and His Son,* give readers an understanding of the lives their characters lived in Africa prior to their enslavement. At the beginning of Hansen's *The Captive,* Kofi, the 12-year-old son of an Ashanti chief, is attending a ceremony honoring Ashanti kings. When Kofi's father is murdered in a plot to weaken the Ashanti tribes, Kofi is captured and eventually placed aboard a "water house" bound for Boston. Kofi is sold to a white merchant and must adjust to his master's cruelties and the terrible bleakness of New England winters, but he never gives up his dreams of returning home. When he runs away, he is helped by Paul Cuffe, a free black merchant sea captain. Because the importing of slaves is illegal in

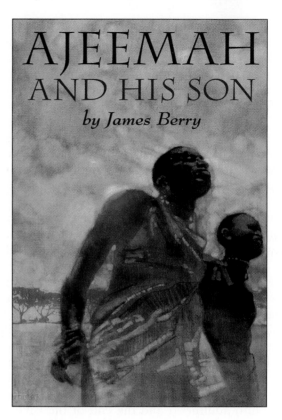

Ajeemah And His Son, *by James Berry, shows how one family was affected by the brutality of the slave trade.*
Jacket copyright © 1991 by Bernie Fuchs. Jacket copyright © 1991 by HarperCollins Publisher. Used by permission of HarperCollins Publishers, New York, NY.

Massachusetts, a judge declares that Kofi cannot be held as a slave and he is given into Paul Cuffe's custody. In Cuffe's caring home Kofi comes of age and eventually joins Cuffe in fighting slavery. In Berry's *Ajeemah And His Son,* Ajeemah and his son, Atu, are on their way to present the dowry for Atu's bride when they are captured and sent aboard a slaver to Jamaica. There the two are separated, and parallel chapters portray their experiences of slavery in moving detail. Atu is killed in an escape attempt, but Ajeemah is freed in 1838 when the British outlawed slavery. Although he creates a new family for himself, Ajeemah forever misses Atu and the loved ones he left behind in Africa.

Andrea Davis Pinkney also provides two points of view of life as a slave in the highly readable *Silent Thunder.* Eleven-year-old Summer and her older brother Roscoe have grown up on the Parnell plantation in Virginia. In 1862, as events of the Civil War envelop them, they are old enough to rebel against their circumstances and long to choose their own futures. Summer's heart's desire is to learn to read; Roscoe longs to run away and join the Union army. As the story evolves we see how both of them manage to achieve their goals. Pinkney, although mistakenly placing the Battle of Vicksburg in 1862 instead of 1863, does a fine job of depicting the terrible injustice of slavery. Her real strength lies in her portrayal of complex personalities and relationships and in her ability to show the courage and determination of people filled with silent thunder.

Gary Paulsen's *Nightjohn* is a graphic and emotionally wrenching account of the terrible cruelties of slavery. Sarny, a young slave on the Waller plantation, narrates the story of Nightjohn, who is brought to the plantation in a most inhumane way by owner Clel Waller. Although he has been brutally used, that night in the slave quarters Nightjohn offers Sarny a wonderful gift in exchange for a bit of tobacco. He gives her the first three letters of the alphabet and begins to teach her to read and write. When Waller discovers Sarny writing a letter in the dirt, Nightjohn pays a terrible price. Waller informs Nightjohn that it is against the law for slaves to learn to read and that punishment "according to the law, is removal of an extremity." Even the loss of two toes does not defeat this heroic figure, however, and Nightjohn runs away only to return later to teach Sarny and other slaves to read and write. In *Sarny* Paulsen continues the girl's story into adulthood and the end of the Civil War when Sarny sets off for New Orleans to find her two young children.

Mary Lyons's *Letters from a Slave Girl* is a fictionalized account of Harriet Jacob's early life as a slave in North Carolina. The letters, addressed to her dead or absent relatives, provide a moving account of her growing-up years, her longing for freedom, and her love for her family. Although not as horrifying as in those in Paulsen's book, Harriet's experiences still portray the dehumanizing effects of slavery, particularly for women. After hiding for seven years in an attic storeroom, Harriet escapes, and later her memoir becomes important to the abolitionist movement.

Elisa Lynn Carbonne's *Stealing Freedom* is also based on a real person, Ann Maria Weems. Ann Maria is the daughter of a free father and slave mother in Maryland of the 1850s. When her brothers are sold South, her father seeks help from abolitionists, who raise funds to buy Ann Marie, her mother, and her sister. Her master refuses to sell Ann, and she determines to run away. Traveling on the Underground Railroad, she hides in Baltimore for some months and finally reaches relatives in Canada. Carbonne does not stint on details of slave life, but this is really a book about the importance of family ties and the terrible pain of families torn apart by this cruel institution.

In Sandra Forrester's *Sound the Jubilee,* Maddie bears witness to the cruelties of human bondage on her North Carolina plantation. When the war breaks out, she and her family manage to escape to Roanoke Island, where the Union army provides sanctuary for runaway slaves. Forrester shows that mistreatment of African Americans was not limited to southerners, however, as Union promises of land and education are withdrawn with the end of the war.

Another eyewitness account of slavery is provided in *The Slave Dancer* by Paula Fox. Jessie Bollier is a 13-year-old white boy who is shanghaied in New Orleans and made to join the crew of a slave ship. In this grim story, Jessie is forced to play his fife and "dance the slaves" so their muscles will remain strong and they will bring a higher price on the slave market. Jessie is young, innocent, and still capable of feeling shock. Everyone else on board the ship is so hardened that they have become indifferent to human suffering. And this is the real message of the story—the utter degradation that eventually engulfs everyone connected with slavery, including the captain, the black Portuguese broker, the depraved Ben Stout, and even Jessie himself. In one of the most compelling and symbolic scenes in the book, Jessie is forced into the hold of the ship to look for his fife. Here he must touch, literally step on, the bodies of the captives, who were so crowded together that there was no room to walk. Jessie's descent into that hold somehow represents the descent of the whole of humankind.

Many stories of the pre–Civil War period relate to slavery and the activities of the underground railroad, when people faced the moral issue of breaking laws out of compassion for other human beings. F. N. Monjo titled his easy-reading book *The Drinking Gourd* after the "code song" that the slaves sang. The song was used to point the direction for escape by following the North Star, using the Big Dipper as a guide. The words to the song are included in this short story of how a young mischievous boy helps a family on their way to freedom.

In *Brady,* Jean Fritz tells the story of a very believable boy who discovers that his father is an agent for the Underground Railroad. His parents had not told him of their forbidden activities, for Brady just cannot keep a secret. However, Brady discovers the secret for himself when his father suffers a broken leg during a fire in the barn and Brady must carry out the plan for moving a fugitive slave.

A fugitive slave whom Catherine never meets brings changes to her life in *A Gathering of Days: A New England Girl's Journal, 1830–32* by Joan Blos. Catherine and her friend Cassie agonize over a plea for help slipped into her writing book when she leaves it in the woods. They have heard about slavery and the abolitionist movement from their teacher, yet their activities are circumscribed by strict but loving families. Finally compassion and a sense of justice outweigh their respect for authority, and they leave food and a quilt where the fugitive will be sure to find them. Much later a packet arrives from Canada with a cryptic message and two bits of lace as a thank-you; the runaway is safe and free.

Paul Fleischman tells the moving story of Georgina Lott's life in *The Borning Room*. In one of the episodes, Georgina recalls hiding a runaway slave in the barn loft. Later, when her mother is giving birth and they cannot get the midwife, Georgina goes out to the barn and brings in Cora to help her mother. When her father comes home that night, he drives Cora by moonlight to the home of Mr. Reedy, a Quaker. Georgina's mother says:

> It's been a day of deliverance, . . . Cora brought Zeb here out of the womb. And we helped deliver her from slavery. . . . We must continue with that work, Georgina. (p. 33)

In *Jip: His Story* Katherine Paterson relates the story of a young boy who is affected by the long arm of slavery in rural Vermont in 1855. Jip is a foundling who has been raised in a charity orphanage. This American Oliver Twist is just as independent as Dickens's hero and involved with some equally memorable characters. Jip's dream of a real home turns into a nightmare when a mysterious stranger claims him as his son. Caught in a tug of war between abolitionists and slave hunters, Jip finally breaks free and finds a place where he belongs.

Patricia Beatty's *Jayhawker* is the story of Lije Tulley, a Kansas 12-year-old who joins in his family's abolitionist activities. Lije rides in his dead father's place in raids to free slaves across the border in Missouri. As war begins, he becomes a spy to serve the cause, posing as a supporter of the South while working on a Missouri farm. Courage, loneliness, and conflicting loyalties are highlighted in this well-crafted story with a dramatic conclusion.

### The Civil War

There are many fine stories for children about the Civil War itself. Most of these describe the war in terms of human issues and suffering, rather than political issues. Two books focus on very different adventures of young drummer boys in the Civil War. *Charley Skedaddle*, written by Patricia Beatty, tells the story of 13-year-old Charley Quinn, a tough kid from the New York Bowery who, after his older brother is killed at Gettysburg, enlists in the Union army as a drummer boy. When the horrors of war become a reality to him, he runs away to the Blue Ridge Mountains. Here he must prove his courage in a different way. Charley's gradual change from a boy filled with bravado into one who shows real bravery is made very believable in this fast-paced story.

Ransom Powell is not as lucky as Charley Skedaddle, for two years after joining the Tenth West Virginia Regiment as a drummer boy for the Union army, he is captured with eighteen others and sent to Andersonville Prison. Well loved by his company for his humor, helpfulness, and red cap, Powell beat taps on his drum for every member of his group. G. Clifton Wisler has told Ransom Powell's story in *Red Cap*, based on authentic records and other men's reminiscences. This is the only Civil War story for children that details the horrors of Andersonville Prison.

In *Thunder at Gettysburg*, Patricia Lee Gauch tells the story of Tillie Pierce, a little girl caught in the midst of battle. She had gone out to a farm for safety and to help a neighbor with her children. The farm was right by Little Round Top, and for three days battle roared around them. Tillie carried water and helped with the wounded. The high drama of this three-day battle is also the focus of a story for older readers, *The Slopes of War* by N. A. Perez. Buck Summerhill returns to Gettysburg, his home town, as a soldier in the Army of the Potomac and loses his leg in the fight for Little Round Top. His sister Bekah cares for a wounded Union officer, Captain Waite, upstairs in the family's home while injured rebels are taken into the parlor. *The Slopes of War* is packed with authentic information about real officers and battle strategies, as well as several threads of fictional story line. The effect of the war on a frontier family in Illinois has been told by Irene Hunt in the fine historical novel *Across Five Aprils*. Jethro Creighton is only 9 years old at the outbreak of the war that at first seemed so exciting and wonderful. As the war continues, Jethro learns that it is not glorious and exciting, but heartbreaking and disruptive to all kinds of relationships. This book makes difficult reading because the device of letter writing is used to carry the action of the story to different places and provide historical detail; but it is beautifully written and thought provoking.

*Rifles for Watie* by Harold Keith tells of the life of a Union soldier and spy engaged in fighting the western campaign of the Civil War. Jefferson Davis Bussey, a young farm boy from Kansas, joins the Union forces and becomes a scout and, quite accidentally, a member of Stand Watie's Cherokee Rebels. Jeff is probably one of the few soldiers in the West to see the Civil War from both sides. This vibrant novel is rich in detail, with fine characterizations.

*With Every Drop of Blood* by James and Christopher Collier is the first-person narrative of 14-year-old Johnny. After his father is killed fighting for the Confederate army, Johnny is desperately worried that he will not be able to keep his family alive. He is lured into transporting food for Confederate troops despite his promise to his family to stay out of the fighting. He is captured by Cush, an African American Union soldier, but as the war disintegrates into chaos, the two find that their dependence on each other overrides their enmity. Their bond of friendship grows as their questions about the war and its savagery deepen. At the war's end, the two have survived, but they wonder about the future in a world that is so full of meanness and hate. Patricia Polacco's *Pink and Say* is a moving picture book that deals with a similar friendship, this one between two Union soldiers (see Chapter 5).

In Patricia Beatty's *Turn Homeward, Hannalee,* the story of 12-year-old Hannalee Reed from Roswell, Georgia, Hannalee, her little brother Jem, and hundreds of other young millworkers in Yankee-occupied Georgia are branded as traitors for making cloth and rope for the Confederacy. They are sent north by Sherman's soldiers to work in mills in Kentucky and Indiana or hired out as servants to northern families. This book emphasizes the point that few southerners were slaveholders, and it forces readers to consider the war's effects on the common people of the South—a good balance to the many books that present northerners' views. The sequel to this story is *Be Ever Hopeful, Hannalee,* which tells of the family's struggle to survive the aftermath of the war.

*Shades of Gray* by Carolyn Reeder is also a story about the aftermath of the Civil War. Twelve-year-old Will Page blames the Yankees for the loss of his entire family. He is sent to live with his aunt and uncle out in the Virginia Piedmont. He can endure living in the country, but he finds it hard to accept the hospitality of his uncle, who had refused to fight the Yankees because he did not believe in war. It is even more difficult for Will to hang on to his resentment because his uncle is so fair and kind and can do everything well. Gradually Will begins to understand the courage it took for his uncle to stand up for his beliefs. When his uncle shelters a wounded Yankee on his way home to Pennsylvania, Will learns that there were good men fighting on both sides of the war. Well plotted, this is an exciting story that will make readers think of the many "shades of gray" that surround all prejudices.

### The Rise of Industry

Although a runaway slave is part of the many-layered *Lyddie* by Katherine Paterson, the main focus of the story is on the rights of child laborers in the eighteenth and early nineteenth century. When Lyddie's mother abandoned their farm, she hired out 13-year-old Lyddie to a hotel for fifty cents a week. Determined to find a better job in order to buy back her beloved farm, Lyddie travels to Lowell, Massachusetts, to work in the textile mills. Lyddie must adjust to the long hours and miserable conditions of nineteenth-century mills, but her indomitable spirit as well as the friendships she forms allow her to survive. On a visit

*Ellen Howard's warmly engaging* The Gate in the Wall *provides a view of the effects of industrialization on the children of mid-nineteenth century England.*

home, Lyddie finds a runaway slave hidden next door and is tempted to turn him in for the reward. But the more she talks with Ezekiel, the more she sees a parallel with her own life. In the end she gives him all the money she has and wishes him a safe journey. He in turn hopes she will find her freedom. This is something Lyddie thinks about frequently, as she realizes she is no more than a slave at the textile mills that enslave young women to provide cheap labor for cruel industrialists.

Younger readers will enjoy Ellen Howard's lovely story *The Gate in the Wall*, set in late-nineteenth-century England. Ten-year-old Emma is an orphan who works ten hours a day in the spinning mills to help support her older sister, her brutal brother-in-law, and their sickly baby. Shut out of the mill for being late one day, Emma is afraid to go home. She discovers an old gate that leads her to a nearby canal and a beautiful boat filled with a cargo of potatoes. Seeing no one around, she hungrily takes some of the potatoes but is discovered by the boat's owner, Mrs. Minshull, who offers her work instead of turning her in to the law for stealing. As she and Mrs. Minshull travel the canals with their various cargoes, Emma finds that she has a job that makes the most of her talents rather than victimizes her. However, her loyalty and anxiety for her sister hang over her head, and she temporarily deserts Mrs. Minshull to return home. Her sister recognizes that Emma's future lies with Mrs. Minshull and a home that nourishes both her body and her spirit, and she sends Emma back to the canal boat. Other viewpoints on the effects of an industrialized society, particularly on children, can be found in fine books such as Jill Paton Walsh's *A Chance Child* and David Wiseman's *Jeremy Visick*, time fantasies discussed in Chapter 7.

# Into the Twentieth Century

The twentieth century has been a period of new hopes for many people and of broken dreams for others. As we look back on this century from the new millennium, we can see how many different stories have shaped our world.

## Immigrants

Immigrants who came to North America in the nineteenth and early twentieth centuries had many different origins and destinations. Still, like the immigrants who came before them in previous centuries, they shared common dreams of a better life and faced similar difficulties in making a place for themselves in a new country.

These themes are universal and seem to resonate with children of all ages. For that reason the stories of immigrants seem an appropriate place to introduce young children to their own family roots through many fine picture books such as *Immigrant Girl* by Brett Harvey, *When Jesse Came Across the Sea* by Amy Hest, *The Memory Coat* by Elvira Woodruff, and *The Dream Jar* by Bonnie Pryor.

Older readers will be captivated by Laurence Yep's *Dragon's Gate.* The story begins in China, where Otter and his community have welcomed Otter's father and Uncle Foxfire home from "Gold Mountain," the United States, where they earned money they sent back to support the family and help the people of the Middle Kingdom drive out the hated Manchus. The two men return to America to work on the railroad and eventually Otter, held responsible for the death of a Manchu soldier, must be sent to join them. Otter arrives in the Sierra Nevada Mountains in February of one of the worst winters on record, and he finds the

*Otter, a young Chinese boy, travels to the Sierra Nevada Mountains to join the Chinese laborers building the transcontinental railroad in Laurence Yep's* Dragon's Gate.
Illustration copyright © 1993 by Charles Lilly. Used by permission of HarperCollins Publishers, New York, NY.

Chinese engaged in a brutal battle to tunnel through mountains that seem made of iron. The story of how they accomplished this, their tremendous contributions to the building of the transcontinental railroad, and the unfairness of their treatment by the white bosses is told in the remainder of the book, with Otter, his father, and his uncle as the central characters. As in his earlier books—*Dragonwings, The Serpent's Children,* and *Mountain Light*—Yep weaves fascinating cultural and historical details into a story that is both gripping and emotionally satisfying.

Set some sixty years later, Yep's *The Star Fisher* is lighter in tone and describes the trials of a Chinese American family who move from Ohio to Clarksburg, West Virginia, in 1927. With a mixture of humor and real emotion, the family realizes that their laundry has no customers in this narrow-minded town that cannot accept outsiders. Only when they conquer their pride and allow Miss Lucy to help them, by teaching Mama how to make apple pie, do they finally become a part of the community. The Chinese folktale "The Star Fisher," which the oldest daughter tells to the youngest, becomes an extended metaphor throughout this fine story of adjustment to a new life.

## Civil Rights

The history of civil rights has centered on the struggles of African Americans from the late 1800s through the twentieth century. This is a bitter record of high hopes brought low by others' prejudice, hatred, and greed. Because novels that explore these situations examine issues that are still sensitive today, critics with a sociological point of view sometimes disagree about the merits of these books just as they do about portrayals of Native Americans. Some question the authenticity or appropriateness of portraying racist attitudes for today's children. Others argue that only members of the culture are capable of portraying these experiences in an authentic manner. Still others point to the inherent drama of the stories and their intended themes of tolerance and understanding. The books we will discuss in this section, whether written by African Americans or authors outside that culture, present memorable characters facing the uncertain future common to African Americans in the South during the first half of the twentieth century. These stories are worth sharing with children in a classroom context where careful reflection and discussion about these issues and events are encouraged.

Mildred Taylor, one of the first African American authors to win a Newbery Medal, has written with understanding about the experiences of African Americans in rural Mississippi during the 1930s. *Roll of Thunder, Hear My Cry* is the story of the Logan family, their pride in the land they have owned since Reconstruction, and their determination not to let injustice go unchallenged. The crucial action in the narrative is the conflict that 9-year-old Cassie observes in the adult world around her: night riders who terrorize the black community; her mother's teaching job gone as a result of her efforts to organize a boycott of the store whose white owners are among those night riders; and her father's dramatic part in rescuing a black teenager, T. J., from a lynch mob. The grim nature of the events is offset by the portrayal of the family caught up in them, the warmth of their concern for one another, the strength of their pride, and their courage. A direct sequel, *Let the Circle Be Unbroken*, follows the tragic trial of T. J. and carries Cassie's family saga into 1935.

Taylor has written several shorter stories of the Logan family. In *Mississippi Bridge*, blacks and whites meet briefly at the Wallace store while they wait for the weekly bus. Jeremy Simms, a 10-year-old white boy and would-be friend of the Logan children, watches as the bus splashes through a heavy rainstorm to stop at the store. When it is fully loaded, Jeremy is dismayed to see the bus driver order the black passengers off to make room for late-arriving white passengers. In the next few minutes the bus skids off the bridge and all are drowned. In *The Well*, a drought has dried up the water sources for all of the Logans' neighbors, and they freely share their own well water with both black and white families. The Simmses, white sharecroppers, cannot accept this gift gracefully, however, and animosity builds between David's older brother Hammer and the Simms boy Charlie, with near-tragic results. Both books portray the terrible effects of prejudice and the fear that was a daily part of life in rural Mississippi in the 1930s.

For the title character of Karen English's *Francie*, the everyday humiliations and injustices she and her family experience in the Jim Crow South are just as debilitating as the experiences that confront Taylor's characters. Like Cassie, Francie has a strong sense of self and a strong role model in her mother. Her father, a Pullman porter, has moved to Chicago and has promised to send for the family as soon as he is able. Looking forward to the move, Francie finishes up eighth grade and takes on the task of teaching 16-year-old Jesse to read. She must also cope with a school bully and an insufferable white girl whose mother employs Francie's mother as cleaner and cook. When Jesse is accused of attacking a white employer, Francie takes some awful risks to help him hide out and then hop a train to California. Eventually Francie and her family will also board a train to what promises to be a better life. Throughout this warmly told story Francie remains a strong and likable character, a young adolescent whose intelligence and courage serve her well in any setting she finds herself in.

*Sounder* by William Armstrong is another story about this time period. This Newbery Medal book tells the stark tale of a black sharecropper and his family who endure cruel injustice within a setting so inhumane that they seem to be nameless, in contrast to their dog. That very namelessness and the family's helplessness, however, have been debated among critics who see the protagonist in Sounder as a stereotype of the "good Negro, humble and honest, hard working, God-fearing, and content to keep his place" (p. 130).[8] One can find examples of African Americans who, throughout our history, offered resistance of one kind and another to their terrible circumstances just as there were those who were defeated by oppression. Today, the increase in books about African American experiences makes it likely that children will have better access to portrayals of the full range of human suffering and ascendancy that occurred as a result of slavery.

---

[8]Trousdale, Ann M., "A Submission Theory for Black Americans: Religion and Social Action in Prize-Winning Children's Books About the Black Experience in America," *Research in the Teaching of English* 24 (1990): 177–140.

## The Great Depression

In the past few years the Great Depression has served as a rich source for writers to explore important human themes. Karen Hesse's Newbery Medal winner *Out of the Dust* is the emotionally wrenching story of a young girl's grim existence in the dust bowl of the Oklahoma panhandle. In the midst of the terrible external presence of dust, wind, and dying crops, Billie Jo must cope with her inner pain—her complicity in her mother's terrible death by fire and her anger at her father's helpless surrender to grief. Her one solace, playing the piano, is no longer available because of the burns she sustained in trying to help her mother. Hesse's narrative, written in free verse, magnifies Billie Jo's anguish and brings the red Oklahoma dust off the printed page and into the reader's heart.

Other titles such as Cynthia DeFelice's *Nowhere to Call Home* and Tracey Porter's *Treasures in the Dust* also feature strong girl characters. DeFelice's heroine, 12-year-old Frances, finds herself riding the rails with other victims of the Great Depression after her father commits suicide. Porter's book is told in alternating chapters by two friends separated by events of the 1930s. Annie stays in Oklahoma as her family struggles to hold onto their farm. Violet travels to California with her family and tells of her own experiences with prejudice and mistreatment. *Treasure in the Dust* would make a good companion book to Zilpha Keatley Snyder's *Cat Running*. Cat's family lives comfortably in California, and Cat's challenges have more to do with conflicts with her father and her own struggle to break away from gender sterotypes than with economic realities. However, her encounters with a family of "Okies" changes her attitude about her own family and gives her courage to find her own way.

Christopher Paul Curtis's Newbery Medal book *Bud, Not Buddy* is set in the mid 1930s in Michigan. Although the main character lives in a world where African Americans must face the results of strong prejudice in addition to the effects of the Great Depression, his main struggle lies in finding his own identity and a place to call home. Raised in orphanages and foster homes following the death of his mother, 10-year-old Bud is a feisty, street-smart kid. His decision to head to Grand Rapids from Flint, to find his father, leads him on a journey to self-discovery that has an unexpected but satisfying outcome. The setting is rich with detail about African American life in the North during this time, especially the world of jazz. Bud is a highly engaging character, and Curtis, as he did in *The Watson's Go to Birmingham*, draws us into the story with wonderfully humourous episodes only to unexpectedly seize our hearts with an emotionally wrenching climax.

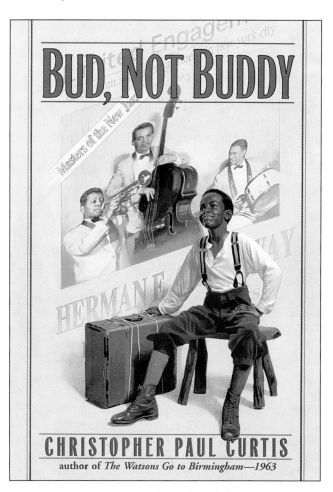

*In Depression era Michigan, 10-year-old Bud undertakes a journey to find his father in Christopher Paul Curtis's Newbery Award–winning* Bud, Not Buddy.

From *Bud Not Buddy* (Jacket Cover) by Christopher Paul Curtis, copyright © 1999. Reprinted by permission of Random House Children's Books, a division of Random House, Inc.

## The World at War

 Unfortunately, much of the history of the twentieth century is the story of a world at war. Many books for young people chronicle its horrors. In these stories the common enemy is war itself. Though most of them depict people's inhumanity to each other, they also show many individual acts of humanity and extreme courage.

Oddly enough, very few books for children about World War I have been published. *Goodbye Billy Radish* by Gloria Skurzynski tells the story of Hank, aged 11 when America enters the war. He sees the war from the distant but no less painful perspective of a child working in the factories that feed the war machine. In an unusual touch, black-and-white photographs introduce each chapter, lending a sense of reality to this story of a time many modern children know little about. *After the Dancing Days* by Margaret I.

Rostkowski is a moving story of the aftermath of that war for those who were wounded. Annie's father is a doctor in one of the veterans hospitals, and despite her mother's disapproval, Annie goes to visit the soldiers with her father. There she meets Andrew, a bitter, withdrawn young veteran with a disfigured face. In time, Annie no longer sees his face as horrible and begins to draw him out of his shell. At the end of the summer Andrew is beginning to heal both physically and psychologically, and Annie has matured while confronting the ironies of war.

The majority of the war stories are about World War II and the Holocaust. Several picture storybooks might be used to introduce the topic or as companion books to longer stories. *Rose Blanche* by Christophe Gallaz and Roberto Innocenti is the story of a girl of about 10 who observes the actions of the Nazis and one day follows a van out to a concentration camp. Later she visits the camp and slips food to the inmates. Her actions would not actually have been possible, but they symbolize all of the little efforts made by people who resisted the war in small ways. The very name *Rose Blanche* was derived from a group of young German citizens who protested the war. They were all killed, as is the Rose Blanche in this story. *Let the Celebrations Begin!* by Margaret Wild is the poignant story of a group of Polish women in the Belsen concentration camp who are determined to make toys for the children in the camp to have on the day of their liberation. So out of scraps of materials, rags, buttons, and pockets, they secretly make stuffed elephants, owls, and other toys. Based on a reference to a small collection of toys found at the Belsen concentration camp, this is a moving testament to all that is good in humankind.

World War II in Asia is touched upon in *Hiroshima No Pika* (The Flash of Hiroshima) by Toshi Maruki, *Shin's Tricycle* by Tatsuharu Kodama, and *Sadako* by Eleanor Coerr. These books record in pictures and stories the horror of the atomic bomb and the tragic aftermath. These picture books (see Chapter 5) are for older children and could well serve as an introduction to units on World War II or units on peace.

### Escape and Resistance

Some of the most popular war stories are about families who escaped to freedom or endured long years of hiding from the Nazis. *Journey to America* by Sonia Levitin tells of a German Jewish family who become refugees when Hitler comes to power. Pap goes ahead to the United States, but Mama and the girls must wait in Switzerland. There Mama is an alien and cannot work, and other living arrangements are made for the children. After a difficult separation, the family are all reunited in America. Simple language and the

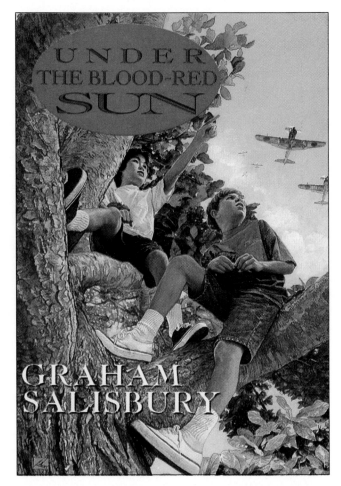

The lives of two friends are unalterably affected by the bombing of Pearl Harbor in Graham Salisbury's Under the Blood-Red Sun.

From *Under the Blood-Red Sun* (Jacket Cover) by Graham Salisbury, copyright © 1994 by Graham Salisbury. Reprinted by permission of Random House Children's Books, a division of Random House, Inc.

emphasis on family solidarity and mutual love make this story appealing for 8- to 10-year-olds.

Along with its intriguing title, *When Hitler Stole Pink Rabbit* by Judith Kerr also has the validity of solid detail that comes from personal experience. This is the story of another family's escape to Switzerland and their trials in trying to earn a living there, then in France, and finally in England. Again, this is a prewar story taking place in the 1930s. It is a happier account than Levitin's *Journey to America;* yet as they leave France for England, Anna wonders if they will ever really belong anywhere.

Others made their escape by hiding for the duration of the war. *The Upstairs Room* by Johanna Reiss is a moving account based on the author's own experiences when she and her sister were hidden by a farm family, the Oostervelds. The girls spent most of the time in an upstairs room so that they wouldn't be seen. The greatest excitement occurs when German soldiers make the Oosterveld house their temporary headquarters. Mostly, however, this is a story of the reactions of all the characters in close confinement and secrecy—the irritability, tension, and fear. The real delight of the book is the Oosterveld family with their plain-folks values, salty language, and generosity. Annie's story is continued in *The Journey Back,* which shows the aftereffects of war on her family and her difficulties with a perfectionistic stepmother.

In *Hide and Seek* Ida Vos tells the story of one Jewish family in the Netherlands after the arrival of the German army. Rachel is bewildered by the constant change of laws, the confiscation of the family's bicycles, the yellow stars that must be sewn on coats, the disappearances of friends and relatives. Rachel and her sister eventually go into hiding, sheltered by various "uncles" and "aunts" who are willing to risk their lives to hide the girls. At the end of the story the children are reunited with their parents, but 105 of her parents' family members have been killed. More than a hundred thousand Dutch Jews were killed in German concentration camps.

Uri Orlev's *The Island on Bird Street* takes the reader into an almost deserted Polish ghetto where Alex, not yet 12, has an ingenious hiding place high in the ruins of building No. 78. His mother, a Zionist, has disappeared, and his father is taken away by the Germans along with the last workers cleared from the ghetto. But Alex's instructions are to wait for his return at No. 78—for a day, a week, or even a year, if necessary. As the months pass, Alex proves to be a clever and courageous survivor, avoiding detection even when German soldiers come to blast open a secret bunker under the cellar. The story ends as Alex and his father, now a part of the Underground, are miraculously reunited. The author's confident tone comes from experience; he spent two years in hiding in the Warsaw ghetto as a child. Orlev's *The Man from the Other Side* is also set in Warsaw. In this Batchelder Award–winning book, Marek is a young Polish boy who must help his stepfather smuggle food into the ghetto for monetary rather than altruistic reasons. These activities give him access to the ghetto through the sewers and bring him into the middle of the ghetto uprising. When he finds out that his real father was Jewish, he reflects on his own attitude toward the Jews, and he begins to examine the anti-Semitism that is so prevalent in Polish society. Based on the experiences of a Polish journalist, this is an exciting story that raises important questions about community attitudes and the terrible consequences of prejudice.

One of the best survival stories is *The Endless Steppe* by Esther Hautzig. This is the author's own account of growing up in a slave labor camp in Siberia. The Rudomins, a wealthy Jewish family, live in Vilna, a city in Poland. The Russians occupy Vilna and confiscate the family business; then one day they arrest the whole family as "capitalists and therefore enemies of the people." They are shipped in filthy, stiflingly hot cattle cars across Siberia—the barren flat land that is to be their home for five endless years. Despite the poverty and privation, Esther manages to satisfy her adolescent needs and find hope in a hopeless situation. During the time the Rudomins are in Siberia, the Nazis enter Poland and kill all their Jewish relatives and friends; in retrospect they consider themselves supremely lucky to have been deported to "The Endless Steppe." The ending of this story is less grim than that of *Anne Frank,* but both stories are a tribute to the courage of the human spirit.

Many refugees were helped to flee or hide from authorities by common folk who did what they could to resist the Nazis. Many stories relate the roles that children played in helping these resisters. Two stories of enduring popularity with young readers are Claire Bishop's *Twenty and Ten,* in which French orphans manage to hide ten Jewish children during a Nazi investigation, and Marie McSwigan's *Snow Treasure,* which tells how a brave group of Norwegian children helped smuggle gold out of the country to keep it from the Nazis.

Lois Lowry tells the dramatic story of the Danish Resistance as they successfully smuggled nearly seven thousand Jews across the sea to Sweden. In *Number the Stars,* she details the story of how one family saved the lives of the Rosens, their friends. Perhaps the most exciting scene is when the German soldiers come to the house where Ellen Rosen is staying and pretending to be a member of the family. She still wears her Star of David necklace and Annemarie hisses to her to take it off. She is unable to get it unclasped, so Annemarie yanks it off just before the Nazis enter the room. When they leave,

> Annemarie relaxed the clenched fingers of her right hand, which still clutched Ellen's necklace. She looked down, and saw that she had imprinted the Star of David into her palm. (p. 49)

Only through the cooperation and extraordinary bravery of the common people were the Danes able to save most of their Jewish population. This theme of community responsibility is explored in Carol Matas's moving *Greater than Angels.* Older readers will enjoy this story of the French citizens of Le Chambon-Sur-Lignon who risked their lives to shelter Jews who had taken refuge in the town.

Another story of a dramatic rescue of Jewish children by a whole French town is told in *Waiting for Anya* by Michael Morpurgo. A reclusive widow's farm set high in the hills close to Spain is the perfect escape point for Jewish children. Benjamin, the widow's son-in-law, is waiting for the arrival of his own daughter, Anya, but when German soldiers start patrolling the borders, he and Jo, a young boy in the village, form a plan to help a group of children escape. The plan works, but Benjamin is captured with Leah, a young child who refused to leave him at the border, and they are sent to Auschwitz. Ironically, the war is over in a few weeks and Anya comes home at last. This is a moving story of uncommon bravery by the small village of Vichy, France.

Some of the most dramatic stories about young people who lived through the conflict in Europe are autobiographical. However, they employ many of the techniques of fiction, including the creation of dialogue. Ilse Koehn's *Mischling, Second Degree* describes her childhood of active participation in the Hitler Youth movement, made ironic by the secret kept even from her at the time: Her father's mother was Jewish, and Ilse would have been classified as an enemy of the Third Reich had that fact been known. Aranka Siegal's own story of her Hungarian childhood, *Upon the Head of the Goat,* is filled with dread, for the Davidowitz family is Jewish. The final scene is emotionally shattering, as Piri and her mother, brother, and two sisters are forced to board a train for a destination with a name that is unfamiliar to them—Auschwitz. Books like these are really for adolescents, but they require maturity of their readers, whatever their age level.

Children in Asia also suffered during the war years. *The House of Sixty Fathers* by Meindert DeJong is an example of a book that does not glorify war. It clearly and vividly tells of the horror of being in a rain of bullets and the pains of hunger. DeJong's descriptions of Tien Pao's fear, loneliness, and hunger are starkly realistic but couched in terms that even 9- or 10-year-olds can well understand. The Chinese boy and his family flee before the Japanese invasion, but they are separated. Clutching his pet pig, Tien Pao struggles on, not knowing where to go. He finds a U.S. flier who helps him survive. The boy is taken to the barracks and becomes a mascot of the soldiers, his sixty fathers. Although it seems impossible, he continues to believe his parents will be found. In a rather contrived but satisfying ending he does identify his mother from a plane as she is working on the construction of an airfield.

Many authors from England have written about children's experiences there at the time of the bombing raids. Susan Cooper's *Dawn of Fear* and Robert Westall's *The Machine Gunners* are frequently read by young adolescents. One of the best selections for elementary readers is Nina Bawden's *Carrie's War,* about three children who are evacuees living in a Welsh mining town. Nick and Carrie, brother and sister, are sent to live with stern Mr. Evans and his sister, Auntie Lou. The story moves ahead on two

levels—the family's feud with Mr. Evans's older sister, Dilys, and the children's involvement in it. The characters are seen from a child's-eye view, with a child's perception of adults. This is a remarkable story that tells much more of the personal wars of living, both for children and for adults, than of the war of bombs and blitzes.

An unusual story that concerns itself with the aftermath of a war is *North to Freedom* by Anne Holm. A boy named David is given a chance to escape from the prison camp in Eastern Europe where he has been imprisoned for most of his 12 years. He has no knowledge of his own background or of the world at large, and no feeling about people except that no one can be trusted. Although David is able to read and has learned seven languages from the other prisoners, much of his learning has been without the essential experience that brings meaning. He finds it difficult to relate to the world, avoids people, and makes only tentative gestures toward others. Slowly his trust in human beings grows, and with it the desire to live and be part of the world of sunshine, beauty, and color that is in such contrast to the drabness of the prison camp. David's change from an imprisoned creature completely shut off from normal human feelings into a responsive and responsible boy makes for a remarkable story.

### The Impact of World War II in North America

 Thousands of American families lost parents, husbands, wives, children, brothers sisters, friends, and relatives in World War II, but we never endured the physical horror of war in North America. For this reason, perhaps, we have fewer stories about the impact of the war in the West.

Two popular stories tell of the English children who were sent to Canada for the duration of the war. *Searching for Shona* by Margaret Anderson is more about trading identities than it is about the war, but it could not have happened except for the children's evacuation. In *The Sky Is Falling* by Kit Pearson, Norah and her younger brother, Gavin, are sent to live with a rich woman and her sister in Toronto. This story details the difficult adjustment of the children, particularly since "Aunt Florence" obviously prefers Gavin to Norah. This well-written story tells a believable tale of the gradual change in relationships between 10-year-old Norah and her sponsor.

*The Summer of My German Soldier* by Bette Greene is the story of 12-year-old Patty Bergen, who is Jewish and the awkward elder daughter of a small-town Arkansas department store owner. Except for the real love of Ruth, the Bergens' African American cook, Patty lives in a loveless situation. Perhaps this explains her compassion for a handsome, well-educated German prisoner of war named Anton who lives in a prison camp near town and comes to her father's store. Patty begins to think of him as her friend, and later, when she sees him running down the railroad tracks, she offers him the safety of her special hideout room over the garage. Only after Anton has gotten away and is captured elsewhere is Patty's role in his escape uncovered. She is arrested and sent to a reform school, clinging to the knowledge that one day she will be free to leave her family and become a "person of value," a term Anton had used.

The painful family separations that were the effect of the war can be seen in several books that are as pertinent to today's child as they are true to the time period. Patricia Reilly Giff's *Lily's Crossing* concerns a lonely 10-year-old girl who is frustrated and angry at the way the war has changed her life, separating her from her father and her best friend. She spends much of her time making up fantasies that turn more and more destructive. Only when she befriends a Hungarian refugee boy does she come to realize the real consequences of the war and those of her own behavior. The main character in Carolyn Reeder's *Foster's War* is an 11-year-old boy who has lost his older brother to the army and his best friend to the Japanese internment camps. When the family learns that the brother, Mel, who enlisted to get away from their abusive father, has been killed in action they come close to falling apart. *Foster's War* is a moving portrayal of the everyday sacrifices and the devastating losses the war inflicted on families.

Two authors have written children's books about the aftermath of the Holocaust. In Myron Levoy's *Alan and Naomi*, Alan Silverman does not want to have to make friends with crazy-acting Naomi Kirshenbaum, but at the insistence of his parents he visits her. Her haunted face and her horrifying experiences during the war in France challenge him, and by acting silly with his puppet, he gets her to laugh and speak. When Alan gets into a bloody fight with the school bully, however, Naomi is traumatized and retreats again into her shell. Alan and his father go to visit her at a nursing home, but it is of no use. Alan cannot reach her. The outcome of Ida Vos's *Anna Is Still Here* is more hopeful though no less painfully achieved. Anna was a hidden child in Holland during the war, and at the war's end she is struggling to overcome her fears and come to terms with the guilt of being a survivor. Reunited with her parents and helped by Mrs. Neuman, another adult survivor who is looking for her daughter, Anna's rage and grief eventually are tempered by the rebuilding of community.

Citizens of the United States can take no pride in the treatment of Japanese Americans at the beginning of the war against Japan. Graham Salisbury's *Under the Blood-Red Sun* vividly recreates the paranoia that occurred in Hawaii following the attack on Pearl

Harbor. Until that time Tomi was a typical eighth grader, more interested in baseball than in his studies, and eager to help out on his father's fishing boat. But the attack turns his world upside down. His father's boat is scuttled and his father imprisoned. Tomi is further torn between his need to fit in with his "haoli" (white) friends and his loyalty to his grandfather, who cannot give up his Japanese identity. In *Journey to Topaz*, Yoshiko Uchida has given a fictionalized account of her family's evacuation and internment in a relocation camp. Yuki's father, a businessman, is taken away from his family on the very day of Pearl Harbor. Taken first to a temporary center at an old race track, Yuki and her mother and older brother eventually end up in the "permanent" camp in Topaz, Utah. The author writes the story with restraint and no bitterness. The quiet courage, dignity, and loyalty with which this Japanese family endures their unjust internment makes its own statement to the reader. Citizens of Japanese descent in Canada were subjected to similar treatment. Sheila Garrigue's *The Eternal Spring of Mr. Ito* helps the reader experience the passionate anti-Japanese feeling along the Pacific Coast even as it demonstrates the blamelessness of those who were shunned, jeered, vandalized, and interned. On the surface Virginia Euwer Wolff's *Bat 6* is a book about a girl's baseball league set in a small Oregon community in 1949. However, Wolff uses the framework of the game as the setting for the playing out of rivalries and hatreds not unlike those that led to World War II in the first place. The people in this rural community have all been affected by Japanese internment as well as other tragedies of war. In multiple points of view the twenty-one girls who make up two opposing baseball teams reveal the events of the war on the home front and its effects on the community. Moreover, they find that when left unexamined, the aftereffects linger on, with results just as tragic as those in the battlefield.

*War Continues*

Unfortunately war did not end with World War II but continued in other conflicts, such as those in Korea, Vietnam, Iraq, and the Balkans. Sook Nyul Choi writes a poignant story of her childhood in northern Korea in the 1940s in *Year of Impossible Goodbyes*. As the war rages, 10-year-old Sookan, her mother, her brother, and Aunt Tiger endure the cruelties of the Japanese occupation. Her father is a resistance fighter in Manchuria and her brothers have been taken to Japanese labor camps. When the war is over in 1945, the Koreans hope for a permanent peace, but then communist Russian troops come. By now Sook Choi and her family have lost everything dear to them. They decide to escape to the Americans at the

38th parallel, but their guide double-crosses them and their mother is taken into custody. Left alone, Sook Choi and her little brother escape after a terrifying dash through barbed wire. The two children finally make it to the Red Cross center and are later reunited with their parents. This is a story that emphasizes that all the so-called victors of a war always make the people of a country their victims. Again it relates the uncommon courage of the common people.

Set in a similar time period, *So Far from the Bamboo Grove* by Yoko Kawashima Watkins is also a true story that tells of a Japanese family living in northern Korea at the close of the war. Fleeing from the Korean communists, 11-year-old Yoko, her older sister Ko, and their mother head south, hoping their brother, Hideyo, and their father will catch up with them on their journey. Their nightmarish trip is described in harrowing detail, and when they reach Japan they find a country devastated by the war and all their relatives killed. Their mother places the two girls in school, but when she dies suddenly they must struggle to survive, selling cloth toys, shining shoes, and picking food from garbage cans. Eventually Hideyo finds them in Kyoto and this unforgettable story ends on a note of hope. Watkins continues their story of survival in the equally moving *My Brother, My Sister, and I*.

*The Clay Marble* by Minfong Ho tells of 12-year-old Dara and her family, who are among the thousands forced to flee from their villages in war-torn Cambodia during the early 1980s. In the refugee camp, there is peace and plenty of food, and Dara makes a new friend, Jantu. Then the shells and bombs start falling again, this time in the middle of camp. In the chaos, Dara is separated from her family and from Jantu. Alone, she must find the strength to reunite her family. When she finally finds them, her brother wants to enlist in the army rather than go home to help them plant their rice crop. Listening to the propaganda over the loudspeaker, Jantu says:

> They all say the same thing. They seem to think it's a game. . . . They take sides, they switch sides, they play against each other. Who wins, who loses, whose turn it is to kick next—it's like an elaborate soccer game. Except they don't use soccer balls. They use us. (p. 141)

The author grew up in Thailand and worked as a nutritionist with an international relief organization on the Thai-Cambodian border in 1980. Dara and Jantu's story is the story of every child in that refugee camp.

Well-written historical fiction like that reviewed in this chapter can enable children to see the continuity of life and their own places in this vast sweep of history. The power of good historical fiction can give children a feeling for a living past. History can become an extension of their own personal experiences, rather than a sterile subject assigned to be studied in school. Such books can offer children new perspectives by which they come to realize that people make and shape their destinies through their own decisions and actions. The events that are happening today do become the history of tomorrow.

# INTO THE CLASSROOM

## *Historical Fiction*

**Room 201**

1. Prepare a decorated portfolio or box of materials of a particular event or period of time to help children build a background for selected books of historical fiction. You might want to include copies of newspaper clippings, artifacts, an annotated bibliography, copies of appropriate paperback books, and examples of art, music, and handicrafts. Plan activity cards for children's use and extension of these materials. (See the description of jackdaws in Chapter 13.)

2. Work with classmates or middle-grade students in role-playing dramatic confrontations in historical fiction. Some possible choices would be the witch trial of Kit Tyler in *The Witch of Blackbird Pond* by Speare or Sam Meeker's argument with his father about going to war in *My Brother Sam Is Dead* by the Colliers.

3. Compare the values and attitudes of the heroine of *Lyddie* by Katherine Paterson with those of a young heroine in a contemporary novel, such as Dicey in *Dicey's Song* by Cynthia Voigt. What are their hopes and expectations? How do they express themselves? How are their priorities different or alike?

4. Compare a picture storybook such as *Rose Blanche* by Christophe Gallaz and Roberto Innocenti, a fantasy such as *The Devil's Arithmetic* by Jane Yolen, and a realistic adventure like *Hide and Seek* by Ida Vos. What does each genre do that is unique? How much information do you receive from each? Chart the differences and similarities.

# Personal Explorations

1. Read four or five books about one particular period or place and chart the references to kinds of food, clothing, houses, transportation, language, and so on. Which books give the most authentic picture?
2. Collect examples of dialogue and descriptive language from several books of historical fiction. You might want to include something by Patricia Beatty, Paul Fleischman, or Rosemary Sutcliff in this sample. What techniques do the authors use to indicate the setting?
3. Analyze a work of historical fiction, for accuracy of facts as well as literary qualities.
4. Make a list of text sets on a historical theme or time period. Include works of fiction, nonfiction, poetry, and picturebooks. Find additional primary source materials that support exploration of your theme.

# Related Readings

Collier, Christopher. "Johnny and Sam: Old and New Approaches to the American Revolution." *Horn Book Magazine,* April 1976, pp. 132–138.

One of the co-authors of popular novels about the American Revolution discusses three historiographic interpretations of that conflict and contends that modern historical fiction should not present historical events in simple or one-sided terms.

Collier, Christopher, ed. *Brother Sam and All That: Historical Context and Literary Analysis of the Novels of James and Christopher Collier.* Clearwater, Fl.: Clearwater Press, 1999.

This highly useful resource offers essays about many of the Colliers' books, background information and photographs of many of their settings, and classroom activities including dramatizations of *The Clock* and *My Brother Sam Is Dead.*

Haugaard, Erik Christian. " 'Before I Was Born': History and the Child." *Horn Book Magazine,* October 1979, pp. 514–521.

The author writes of the relationship between history and truth and makes an eloquent case for the value of history in showing that people always have choices.

Hunter, Mollie. "Shoulder the Sky." In *Talent Is Not Enough* (pp. 31–56). New York: Harper & Row, 1976.

A fine writer reveals her sense of history as human drama while discussing several issues critical to historical fiction, including the portrayal of violence and the relationship of contemporary attitudes to those of the past.

Levstik, Linda S., and Keith C. Barton. *Doing History: Investigating with Children in the Elementary and Middle Schools.* Mahwah, N.J.: Erlbaum, 1997.

This superb book's content builds strong connections from historical study to the broader fields of social studies, reading, science, mathematics, and the arts with children's literature at the center of the curriculum. The book, grounded in sound learning theory filtered through the voices of teachers and children engaged in critical inquiries, provides a framework for extending such studies into all classrooms.

Segel, Elizabeth. "Laura Ingalls Wilder's America: An Unflinching Assessment." *Children's Literature in Education* 25 (summer 1977): 63–70.

Segel examines the values portrayed in the Little House series, particularly *Little House on the Prairie,* and points out that Wilder, through the character of Laura, not only presented the attitudes and beliefs of nineteenth-century America but also questioned them.

Stanley, Diane. "Picture Book History." *New Advocate* 1 (fall 1988): 209–220.

The author and illustrator of several picture-book biographies of historical figures describes the difficulties of providing accurate pictures. The background details about *Shaka, King of the Zulus* are interesting to children as well as adults.

# Children's Literature

Alder, Elizabeth. *The King's Shadow.* Farrar, Straus & Giroux, 1995.

Anderson, Joan. *The First Thanksgiving Feast.* Photographs by George Ancona. Clarion, 1983.

Anderson, Margaret. *Searching for Shona.* Knopf, 1978.

Anderson, Rachel. *Black Water.* Holt, 1995.

Antle, Nancy. *Beautiful Land: A Story of the Oklahoma Land Rush.* Illustrated by John Gampert. Viking, 1994.

Armstrong, William H. *Sounder*. Illustrated by James Barkley. Harper & Row, 1969.

Averill, Esther. *King Philip: The Indian Chief*. Illustrated by Vera Belsky. Linnet, 1993 [1950].

Avi [Avi Wortis]. *Beyond the Western Sea. Book One: The Escape from Home*. Orchard, 1996.

———. *Beyond the Western Sea. Book Two: Lord Kirkle's Money*. Orchard, 1996.

———. *The Fighting Ground*. Lippincott, 1984.

———. *The True Confessions of Charlotte Doyle*. Orchard, 1990.

Bartone, Elisa. *Peppe the Lamplighter*. Illustrated by Ted Lewin. Lothrop, Lee & Shepard, 1993.

Bawden, Nina. *Carrie's War*. Illustrated by Colleen Browning. Lippincott, 1973. (In print in UK)

Beatty, Patricia. *Be Ever Hopeful, Hannalee*. Morrow, 1988.

———. *Charley Skedaddle*. Morrow, 1987.

———. *Jayhawker*. Morrow, 1991.

———. *Turn Homeward, Hannalee*. Morrow, 1984.

———. *Wait for Me, Watch for Me, Eula Bee*. Troll, 1986.

Berry, James. *Ajeemah and His Son*. HarperCollins, 1992.

Bishop, Claire Huchet. *Twenty and Ten*. As told by Janet Jolly. Illustrated by William Pène DuBois. Viking, 1964.

Blackwood, Gary. *The Shakespeare Stealer*. Dutton, 1998.

Blos, Joan W. *A Gathering of Days: A New England Girl's Journal, 1830–32*. Scribner's, 1979.

Bosse, Malcolm. *The Examination*. Farrar, Straus & Giroux, 1994.

Branford, Henrietta. *Fire, Bed and Bone*. Candlewick, 1998.

Brink, Carol Ryrie. *Caddie Woodlawn*. Illustrated by Trina Schart Hyman. Macmillan, 1973.

———. *Caddie Woodlawn*. Illustrated by Kate Seredy. Macmillan, 1936.

Bruchac, Joseph. *The Arrow over the Door*. Dial, 1998.

———. *Children of the Longhouse*. Dial, 1996.

———. *Dawn Land*. Fulcrum, 1993.

Bulla, Clyde Robert. *A Lion to Guard Us*. Illustrated by Michelle Chessare. Harper Trophy, 1990 [1981].

———. *The Sword in the Tree*. Illustrated by Paul Galdone. Crowell, 1956.

Bunting, Eve. *Dandelions*. Illustrated by Greg Shed. Harcourt Brace, 1995.

Carbonne, Elisa Lynn. *Stealing Freedom*. Knopf, 1999.

Chana Byers Abells. *The Children We Remember*. Greenwillow, 1986.

Choi, Sook Nyul. *Year of Impossible Goodbyes*. Houghton Mifflin, 1991.

Clapp, Patricia. *Constance: A Story of Early Plymouth*. Lothrop, Lee & Shepard, 1968.

———. *Witches' Children*. Lothrop, Lee & Shepard, 1982.

Coerr, Eleanor. *Sadako*. Illustrated by Allen Say. Philomel, 1993.

Collier, James Lincoln, and Christopher Collier. *Jump Ship to Freedom*. Delacorte, 1981.

———. *My Brother Sam Is Dead*. Four Winds, 1974.

———. *War Comes to Willy Freeman*. Delacorte, 1983.

———. *Who Is Carrie?* Delacorte, 1984.

———. *With Every Drop of Blood*. Delacorte, 1994.

Conrad, Pam. *Prairie Songs*. Illustrated by Darryl Zudeck. Harper & Row, 1985.

Cooper, Susan. *Dawn of Fear*. Illustrated by Margery Gill. Harcourt Brace, 1970.

Cowley, Marjorie. *Anooka's Answer*. Clarion, 1999.

Craig, Ruth. *Malu's Wolf*. Orchard, 1995.

Crompton, Anne Eliot. *The Winter Wife*. Illustrated by Robert Andrew Parker. Little, Brown, 1975.

Curtis, Christopher Paul. *Bud, Not Buddy*. Delacorte, 1999.

———. *The Watson's Go to Birmingham—1963*. Delacorte, 1995.

Cushman, Karen. *The Ballad of Lucy Whipple*. Clarion, 1996.

———. *Catherine, Called Birdy*. Clarion, 1994.

———. *The Midwife's Apprentice*. Clarion, 1995.

Dalgliesh, Alice. *The Courage of Sarah Noble*. Illustrated by Leonard Weisgard. Scribner's, 1954.

———. *The Thanksgiving Story*. Illustrated by Helen Sewell. Scribner's, 1954.

de Angeli, Marguerite. *The Door in the Wall*. Doubleday, 1949.

DeFelice, Cynthia C. *The Apprenticeship of Lucas Whitaker*. Farrar, Straus & Giroux, 1996.

———. *Lostman's River*. Macmillan, 1994.

———. *Nowhere to Call Home*. Farrar, Straus & Giroux, 1999.

DeJong, Meindert. *The House of Sixty Fathers*. Illustrated by Maurice Sendak. Harper & Row, 1956.

Denzel, Justin. *Boy of the Painted Cave*. Philomel, 1988.

———. *Return to the Painted Cave*. Philomel, 1997.

de Trevino, Elizabeth Borton. *I, Juan de Pareja*. Farrar, Straus & Giroux, 1965.

Dorris, Michael. *Guests*. Hyperion, 1994.

———. *Morning Girl*. Hyperion, 1992.

———. *Sees Behind Trees*. Hyperion, 1996.

Dyer, T. A. *A Way of His Own*. Houghton Mifflin, 1981.

Edmonds, Walter D. *The Matchlock Gun*. Illustrated by Paul Lantz. Dodd, Mead, 1941.

English, Karen. *Francie*. Farrar, Straus & Giroux, 1999.

Erdrich, Louise. *The Birchbark House*. Hyperion, 1999.

Feelings, Tom. *The Middle Passage: White Ships/Black Cargo*. Introduction by Dr. John Henrik Clarke. Dial, 1995.

Field, Rachel. *Calico Bush*. Illustrated by Allen Lewis. Macmillan, 1931.

Fleischman, Paul. *The Borning Room*. HarperCollins, 1991.

———. *Bull Run*. HarperCollins, 1993.

———. *Saturnalia*. HarperCollins, 1990.

Forbes, Esther. *Johnny Tremain*. Illustrated by Lynd Ward. Houghton Mifflin, 1946.

Forrester, Sandra. *Sound the Jubilee*. Lodestar, 1995.

Fox, Paula. *The Slave Dancer*. Illustrated by Eros Keith. Bradbury Press, 1973.

Fritz, Jean. *Brady*. Illustrated by Lynd Ward. Coward-McCann/Penguin, 1987 [1960].

———. *The Cabin Faced West*. Illustrated by Feodor Rojankovsky. Coward-McCann, 1958.

———. *The Double Life of Pocahontas*. Illustrated by Ed Young. Putnam, 1983.

———. *Early Thunder*. Illustrated by Lynd Ward. Coward-McCann, 1967.

Gallaz, Christophe, and Roberto Innocenti. *Rose Blanche*. Illustrated by Roberto Innocenti. Creative Education, 1985.

Garrigue, Sheila. *The Eternal Spring of Mr. Ito*. Bradbury Press, 1985.

Gauch, Patricia L. *This Time, Tempe Wick?* Illustrated by Margot Tomes. Putnam, 1974.

———. *Thunder at Gettysburg*. Illustrated by Stephen Gammell. Putnam, 1990 [1975].

Giff, Patricia Reilly. *Lily's Crossing*. Delacorte, 1997.

Gipson, Fred. *Old Yeller*. Illustrated by Carl Burger. Harper & Row, 1956.

Goodman, Joan Elizabeth. *The Winter Hare*. Houghton Mifflin, 1996.

Gray, Elizabeth Janet. *Adam of the Road*. Illustrated by Robert Lawson. Viking, 1942.

Greene, Bette. *The Summer of My German Soldier*. Bantam, 1984 [1973].

Gregory, Kristiana. *Jenny of the Tetons*. Harcourt Brace, 1989.

Hahn, Mary Downing. *Stepping on the Cracks*. Clarion, 1991.

Hansen, Joyce. *The Captive*. Scholastic, 1994.

———. *I Thought My Soul Would Rise and Fly: The Diary of Patsy a Freed Girl*. Scholastic, 1997.

Harvey, Brett. *Immigrant Girl: Becky of Eldridge Street*. Illustrated by Deborah K. Ray. Holiday House, 1987.

Hautzig, Esther. *The Endless Steppe: Growing Up in Siberia*. Crowell, 1968.

Hesse, Karen. *Out of the Dust*. Scholastic, 1997.

Hest, Amy. *When Jessie Came Across the Sea*. Illustrated by P. J. Lynch. Candlewick, 1997.

Hickman, Janet. *Susannah*. Greenwillow, 1998.

Ho, Minfong. *The Clay Marble*. Farrar, Straus & Giroux, 1991.

Holm, Anne. *North to Freedom*. Translated by L. W. Kingsland. Harcourt Brace, 1965.

Holm, Jennifer L. *Our Only May Amelia*. HarperCollins, 1999.

Hoobler, Dorothy, and Thomas Hoobler. *The Ghost in the Tokaido Inn*. Philomel, 1999.

Hoople, Cheryl. *The Heritage Sampler: A Book of Colonial Arts and Crafts*. Dial, 1975.

Howard, Ellen. *The Gate in the Wall*. Atheneum, 1999.

Hunt, Irene. *Across Five Aprils*. Follett, 1964.

Hunter, Mollie. *The King's Swift Rider: A Novel on Robert the Bruce*. HarperCollins, 1998.

Jacobs, Paul Samuel. *James Printer: A Novel of Rebellion*. Scholastic, 1997.

Keith, Harold. *Rifles for Watie*. Crowell, 1957.

Kelly, Eric P. *The Trumpeter of Krakow*. Rev. ed. Illustrated by Janina Domanska. Macmillan, 1966 [1928].

Kerr, Judith. *When Hitler Stole Pink Rabbit*. Coward-McCann, 1972.

Kirkpatrick, Katherine. *Trouble's Daughter*. Delacorte, 1999.

Kodama, Tatsuharu. *Shin's Tricycle*. Translated by Kazuko Hokuman-Jones. Illustrated by Noriyuki Ando. Walker, 1995.

Koehn, Ilse. *Mischling, Second Degree: My Childhood in Nazi Germany*. Greenwillow, 1977.

Konigsburg, E. L. *A Proud Taste for Scarlet and Miniver*. Atheneum, 1973.

———. *The Second Mrs. Giaconda*. Macmillan, 1978.

Kroeber, Theodora. *Ishi, Last of His Tribe*. Illustrated by Ruth Robbins. Parnassus, 1964.

Lasky, Kathryn. *Beyond the Divide*. Macmillan, 1983.

Levitin, Sonia. *Journey to America*. Illustrated by Charles Robinson. Atheneum, 1970.

Levoy, Myron. *Alan and Naomi*. Harper Trophy, 1987 [1977].

Llorente, Pilar Molina. *The Apprentice*. Translated by Robin Longshaw. Illustrated by Juan Ramón Alonso. Farrar, Straus & Giroux, 1993.

Lowry, Lois. *Looking Back: A Book of Memories*. Houghton Mifflin, 1998

———. *Number the Stars*. Houghton Mifflin, 1989.

Lunn, Janet. *The Root Cellar*. Macmillan, 1983.

Lyons, Mary E. *Letters from a Slave Girl: The Story of Harriet Jacobs*. Scribner's, 1992.

MacLachlan, Patricia. *Sarah, Plain and Tall*. Harper & Row, 1985.

———. *Skylark*. HarperCollins, 1994.

———. *Three Names*. Illustrated by Alexander Pertzoff. HarperCollins, 1991.

Maruki, Toshi. *Hiroshima No Pika* (The Flash of Hiroshima). Lothrop, Lee & Shepard, 1980.

Matas, Carol. *Greater than Angels*. Simon & Schuster, 1998.

Matchek, Diane. *The Sacrifice*. Farrar, Straus & Giroux, 1998.

McCaughrean, Geraldine. *The Pirate's Son*. Scholastic, 1998.

McGraw, Eloise Jarvis. *The Golden Goblet*. Viking Penguin, 1986 [1961].

———. *Mara, Daughter of the Nile*. Viking Penguin, 1985 [1953].

———. *Moccasin Trail*. Viking Penguin, 1986 [1952].

McSwigan, Marie. *Snow Treasure*. Illustrated by Alexander Pertzoff. HarperCollins, 1991.

Monjo, F. N. *The Drinking Gourd*. Illustrated by Fred Brenner. Harper & Row, 1970.

Morpurgo, Michael. *Waiting for Anya*. Viking, 1990.

Morrow, Honoré. *On to Oregon!* Beech Tree, 1991 [1946].

Namioka, Lensey. *The Coming of the Bear*. HarperCollins, 1992.

———. *Den of the White Fox*, Browndeer, Harcourt, 1997.

———. *Island of Ogres*. Harper & Row, 1989.

O'Dell, Scott. *Island of the Blue Dolphins*. Houghton Mifflin, 1960.

———. *Sarah Bishop*. Houghton Mifflin, 1980.

———. *Sing Down the Moon*. Houghton Mifflin, 1970.

———. *Zia*. Illustrated by Ted Lewin. Houghton Mifflin, 1976.

Orlev, Uri. *The Island on Bird Street*. Translated from the Hebrew by Hillel Halkin. Houghton Mifflin, 1984.

———. *The Man from the Other Side*. Translated by Hillel Halkin. Houghton Mifflin, 1991.

Park, Ruth. *Playing Beatie Bow*. Atheneum, 1982.

Paterson, Katherine. *Jip: His Story*. Lodestar, 1996.

———. *Lyddie*. Lodestar, 1988.

———. *Of Nightingales That Weep*. Harper & Row, 1974.

————. *The Master Puppeteer.* Harper & Row, 1975.

————. *Park's quest.* Dutton, 1991.

————. *The Sign of the Chrysanthemum.* Harper & Row, 1973.

Paulsen, Gary. *Hatchet.* Bradbury, 1987.

————. *Nightjohn.* Delacorte, 1993.

————. *Sarny.* Delacorte, 1997.

Pearson, Kit. *The Sky Is Falling.* Viking, 1989.

Perez, N. A. *The Slopes of War.* Houghton Mifflin, 1984.

Petry, Ann. *Tituba of Salem Village.* Crowell, 1964.

Pinkney, Andrea Davis. *Silent Thunder.* Hyperion, 1999.

Polacco, Patricia. *Pink and Say.* Philomel, 1994.

Porter, Tracey. *Treasures in the Dust.* HarperCollins, 1997.

Pryor, Bonnie. *The Dream Jar.* Illustrated by Mark Graham. Morrow, 1996.

————. *The House on Maple Street.* Illustrated by Beth Peck. Morrow, 1987.

Reeder, Carolyn. *Foster's War.* Scholastic, 1998.

————. *Shades of Gray.* Macmillan, 1989.

Reiss, Johanna. *The Journey Back.* Crowell, 1976.

————. *The Upstairs Room.* Crowell, 1972.

Richter, Hans Peter *Friedrich.* Holt, Rinehart and Winston, 1956.

Rinaldi, Ann. *Hang a Thousand Trees with Ribbons.* Harcourt, 1996.

————. *My Heart is on the Ground: The Diary of Nannie Little Rose a Sioux Girl (Dear America).* Scholastic, 1999.

————. *A Ride into Morning: The Story of Tempe Wick.* Gulliver, 1991.

Riskind, Mary. *Apple Is My Sign.* Houghton Mifflin, 1981.

Rostkowski, Margaret I. *After the Dancing Days.* Harper & Row, 1986.

Rubalcaba, Jill. *A Place in the Sun.* Clarion, 1997.

Ruby, Lois. *Steal Away Home.* Macmillan, 1994.

Salisbury, Graham. *Under the Blood-Red Sun.* Delacorte, 1994.

Sewall, Marcia. *The Pilgrims of Plimoth.* Atheneum, 1986.

————. *Thunder from the Clear Sky.* Atheneum, 1995.

Siegal, Aranka. *Upon the Head of the Goat: A Childhood in Hungary, 1939–1944.* Farrar, Straus & Giroux, 1981.

Skurzynski, Gloria. *Goodbye Billy Radish.* Bradbury, 1992.

Snyder, Zilpha Keatley. *Cat Running.* Delacorte, 1994.

Speare, Elizabeth George. *The Bronze Bow.* Houghton Mifflin, 1961.

————. *Calico Captive.* Illustrated by W. T. Mars. Houghton Mifflin, 1957.

————. *The Sign of the Beaver.* Houghton Mifflin, 1983.

————. *The Witch of Blackbird Pond.* Houghton Mifflin, 1958.

Steele, William O. *The Buffalo Knife.* Illustrated by Paul Galdone. Harcourt Brace, 1952.

————. *Flaming Arrows.* Illustrated by Paul Galdone. Harcourt Brace, 1957.

————. *Winter Danger.* Illustrated by Paul Galdone. Harcourt Brace, 1954.

Stevens, Carla. *Trouble for Lucy.* Illustrated by Ronald Himler. Clarion, 1979.

Stolz, Mary. *Bartholomew Fair.* Greenwillow, 1990.

Sutcliff, Rosemary. *The Eagle of the Ninth.* Illustrated by C. W. Hodges. Walck, 1954.

————. *Flame-Colored Taffeta.* Farrar, Straus & Giroux, 1986.

————. *The Lantern Bearers.* Illustrated by Charles Keeping. Walck, 1959.

————. *The Shining Company.* Farrar, Straus & Giroux, 1990.

————. *The Silver Branch.* Illustrated by Charles Keeping. Walck, 1959.

————. *Sun Horse, Moon Horse.* Dutton, 1978.

————. *Sword Song.* Farrar, Straus & Giroux, 1998.

————. *Warrior Scarlet.* Walck, 1958.

Taylor, Mildred. *Let the Circle Be Unbroken.* Dial, 1981.

————. *Mississippi Bridge.* Illustrated by Max Ginsburg. Dial, 1990.

————. *Roll of Thunder, Hear My Cry.* Illustrated by Jerry Pinkney. Dial, 1976.

————. *The Well.* Dial, 1995.

Taylor, Theodore. *The Cay.* Doubleday, 1989 [1969].

Temple, Frances. *The Bedouin's Gazelle.* Orchard, 1996.

————. *The Ramsey Scallop.* Orchard, 1994.

Tunis, Edwin. *Colonial Living.* HarperCollins, 1999 [1976].

Turner, Ann. *Dakota Dugout.* Illustrated by Ronald Himler. Macmillan, 1985.

————. *Grasshopper Summer.* Macmillan, 1989.

————. *Nettie's Trip South.* Illustrated by Ronald Himler. Macmillan, 1987.

Uchida, Yoshiko. *Journey to Topaz.* Illustrated by Donald Carrick. Scribner's, 1971.

Van Leeuwen, Jean. *Across the Wide Dark Sea.* Illustrated by Thomas B. Allen. Dial, 1995.

————. *Bound for Oregon.* Illustrated by James Watling. Dial, 1994.

Vos, Ida. *Anna Is Still Here.* Translated by Terese Edelstein and Inez Smidt. Houghton Mifflin, 1994.

————. *Hide and Seek.* Translated by Terese Edelstein and Inez Smidt. Houghton Mifflin, 1991.

Walsh, Jill Paton. *A Chance Child.* Farrar, Straus & Giroux, 1978.

Watkins, Yoko Kawashima. *My Brother, My Sister, and I.* Bradbury Press, 1994.

————. *So Far from the Bamboo Grove.* Lothrop, Lee & Shepard, 1986.

Weaver, Lydia. *Close to Home: A Story of the Polio Epidemic.* Illustrated by Aileen Arrington. Viking, 1993.

Westall, Robert. *The Machine Gunners.* Greenwillow, 1976.

Wibberley, Leonard. *John Treegate's Musket.* Farrar, Straus & Giroux, 1959.

Wild, Margaret. *Let the Celebrations Begin!* Illustrated by Julie Vivas. Orchard, 1991.

Wilder, Laura Ingalls. *By the Shores of Silver Lake.* Illustrated by Garth Williams. Harper & Row, 1953 [1939].

————. *The First Four Years.* Illustrated by Garth Williams. Harper & Row, 1971.

————. *Little House in the Big Woods.* Illustrated by Garth Williams. Harper & Row, 1953 [1932].

————. *Little House on the Prairie.* Illustrated by Garth Williams. Harper & Row, 1953 [1935].

————. *Little Town on the Prairie.* Illustrated by Garth Williams. Harper & Row, 1953 [1932].

————. *On the Banks of Plum Creek.* Illustrated by Garth Williams. Harper & Row, 1953 [1937].

————. *These Happy Golden Years.* Illustrated by Garth Williams. Harper & Row, 1953 [1943].

Wisler, G. Clifton. *Red Cap.* Dutton, 1991.

Wiseman, David. *Jeremy Visick.* Houghton Mifflin, 1981.

Wolff, Virginia Euwer. *Bat 6.* Scholastic, 1998.

Woodruff, Elvira. *The Memory Coat.* Illustrated by Michael Dooling. Scholastic, 1999.

Yep, Laurence. *Dragon's Gate.* HarperCollins, 1993.

————. *Dragonwings.* Harper & Row, 1977.

————. *Mountain Light.* Harper & Row, 1985.

————. *The Serpent's Children.* Harper & Row, 1984.

————. *The Star Fisher.* Morrow, 1991.

Yolen, Jane. *The Devil's Arithmetic.* Viking Penguin, 1990.

# Chapter Eleven

# Nonfiction Books

Barbara Z. Kiefer

*W*e know a 6-year-old who loves to go to the school library because there he can choose any book he wants. At story time he listens eagerly to picture storybooks and other fiction, but the books he chooses to check out, to keep for a time and to pore over at home, are nonfiction. His favorites are about airplanes, rockets, space travel, and complex machinery. He often chooses books far above his level of understanding (once it was an encyclopedia of space facts so big that he could barely carry it by himself). Part of his fun is looking at the illustrations over and over again, but he also wants an adult to "read" these difficult books to him. In this case he means reading the picture captions and talking through main ideas or intriguing details in response to his many questions. He joins in the reading by looking for words he knows or can figure out in the boldface headings or diagram labels.

We call attention to this common scenario because it demonstrates so much about the special role of nonfiction literature in children's lives. The audience for nonfiction books is broad, including young children as well as older students. Adult ideas about what is appropriate for a given age level are often less important than a child's desire to know about a particular topic. A reader's approach to a nonfiction book might not always be to read pages in order from first to last, as fiction demands. In this type of reading, illustration plays a vital part by focusing interest and clarifying or extending information. Most of all, our example shows how nonfiction literature can provide powerful motivation to read and to enjoy experiences with books. Children are curious about the world and how it works, and they develop passionate attachments to the right books at the right time. They deserve teachers and librarians who can help them discover this particular kind of satisfaction in reading.

## Trends in Nonfiction Books

For many years children's literature scholars have used the term *informational books* rather than *nonfiction books* to designate literature for children that is based in the actual rather than the imagined. One recent trend in children's literature is the movement to the term *nonfiction* rather than *informational*. Author Penny Colman argues that the term *informational* tends to make people think of encyclopedias and textbooks.

> The term does not readily trigger associations with the variety of nonfiction books—biographies, history, true adventures, science, sports, photographic essays, memoirs, etc.—that are available and accessible for children and young adults and that can be just as compelling, engaging and beautifully written as good fiction.[1]

In this chapter and in Chapter 12, "Biography," we will most often use the term *nonfiction* rather than *informational* to refer to this body of literature, as is common with adult literature.

New worlds and new interests lie waiting for children between the covers of nonfiction books. The secrets of a water droplet, mummies, and doll making have all been revealed in attractive and inviting formats. For proof, have a look at Walter Wick's *A Drop of Water*, Patricia Lauber's *Tales Mummies Tell*, and Susan Kuklin's *From Head to Toe: How a Doll Is Made*. Nonfiction books also offer children new perspectives on familiar topics, as can be found in Jennifer Owings Dewey's *Mud Matters* or in Cathryn Falwell's *The Letter Jesters*. Some nonfiction books, like *Inside and Outside Spiders* by Sandra Markle, have tremendous eye appeal and invite browsing. Others are designed to reward sustained attention, like James Cross Giblin's explanation of the unraveling of an ancient mystery in *The Riddle of the Rosetta Stone*. Nonfiction books for children are more numerous, more various, and more appealing than ever. Only recently have they begun to receive the critical recognition and classroom attention that

[1]Penny Colman, "Nonfiction Is Literature Too," *New Advocate* 12, no. 3 (summer 1999): 217.

they have long deserved. We begin here by looking briefly at some of these changes and the current trends in nonfiction books for today's child.

In many ways the current trends mirror recent changes in the larger world of children's books. The following overview covers the more obvious developments of recent years.

*Nonfiction books such as Susan Kuklin's* From Head to Toe: How a Doll Is Made *offer children fascinating details about familiar objects.*

From *From Head To Toe: How A Doll Is Made* by Susan Kuklin. Text and photographs copyright © 1994 Susan Kuklin. Reprinted by permission of Hyperion Books for Children.

## Increased Quantity and Quality

More trade book publishers are producing nonfiction books—and more attractive ones—than ever before. New companies and new imprints have been created to keep up with the demand generated by more teachers using literature in the classroom and more people buying books in retail stores. Some publishers' catalogs that in the past only rarely offered nonfiction now show many new titles on a regular basis. Frequently these titles are edited, designed, and produced with the same care that was once reserved for picture books. Jean George's *Everglades*, with illustrations by Wendell Minor, is one example. The result is a stunning array of nonfiction books from which teachers, librarians, and children of all ages can choose.

## A New Focus on the Very Young

Part of the increased production of nonfiction books can be attributed to a growing awareness of a new market. In keeping with the recent emphasis on the importance of early childhood education, there is a new focus on the preschool and early primary audience for nonfiction books. Concept books and identification books that provide the names of objects have long been a popular type of nonfiction picture book for young children (see Chapter 4). Recently, however, many types of nonfiction formats have been offered for the very young. Books in the See How They Grow series (published by Dorling Kindersley) use clear photos and minimal text to show how baby animals change in the first few weeks of life. Angela Royston's *Insects*

*Wendell Minor's lovely illustrations for* Everglades *by Jean Craighead George help create a nonfiction book that is also aesthetically pleasing.*

Illustration copyright © 1995 by Wendell Minor. Used by permission of HarperCollins Publishers, New York, NY.

*and Crawly Creatures,* a book in the Eye-Openers series, focuses on naming and identification but adds information about each insect and close-up drawings of significant details. Both series are printed on extra-heavy stock to allow for hard wear by preschoolers. Both also originate in England and share some of the visual characteristics of the popular Eyewitness Books series for older readers and their simpler counterparts in the Eyewitness Juniors series (published by Knopf).

The photo essay is another format sometimes directed now to a very young audience, as in Ron Hirschi's gentle commentaries on the seasons in *Spring, Summer, Fall,* and *Winter.* Even experiment books, usually the province of older students, can be appropriate for younger classes if they are as simple and inviting as Neil Ardley's *The Science Book of Weather.* Although nonfiction series for young children account for many of the new titles, some authors and illustrators do produce fine nonfiction picture books that are one of a kind. Byron Barton's *I Want to Be an Astronaut* and *Bones, Bones, Dinosaur Bones* fit this category.

## The Growing Importance of Illustration

Another feature of nonfiction books that has changed in recent years is the increased reliance on visuals, especially photography. In our media-conscious society, both children and adults have become more visually oriented, more likely to expect pictures in magazines, newspapers, and other print materials. At the same time, technological improvements in making and reproducing pictures have made it possible to satisfy the demand for color, close-ups, and novel perspectives.

Nonfiction books for all ages often sell themselves, and their topic, on the basis of sophisticated photography or ingenious illustration. In *A Drop of Water,* Walter Wick's exquisite photographs of different states of water brings a sense of wonder to something that we take for granted most of the time. Richard Platt's "Incredible Cross Sections" books are full of facts, but the real fascination of these books lies in Stephen Beisty's intricate illustrations.

## Unconventional Formats and Approaches

A related trend in nonfiction books today is enthusiasm for unconventional approaches, including experimental formats and combinations of fact and fiction. Pop-ups and lift-the-flap books are part of this trend. Nancy Willard's pop-up book *Gutenberg's Gift* allows children to get an idea of how the first printing press worked. Scholastic's First Discovery books, such as Pascale de Bourgoing's *Under the Ground,* have clear plastic overlays that help children visualize important concepts. Dorling Kindersley's Eyewitness 3D series includes a mirror device that provides a three-dimensional look at books like *Insect* by Teresa Greenaway. This is the next best thing to holding the

*Many nonfiction books for the very young child feature attractive photographs, like these in Angela Royston's* Insects and Crawly Creatures.

little bugs in your hand. The text of Sheila Hamanaka's distinguished book *The Journey: Japanese Americans, Racism, and Renewal* is organized around a mural painted by the author; each segment of text accompanies and describes one or two details of the larger painting.

Other books that look like conventional picture books might be innovative in the ways they deliver information, often using a fictitious story as the vehicle or at least borrowing from the techniques of fiction. *The Magic School Bus Explores the Senses* and other books in this series by Joanna Cole and Bruce Degen could be classified as fantasy picture books, with their miniaturized school bus and impossible field trips led by the intrepid teacher, Ms. Frizzle. Student dialogue is presented in speech balloons borrowed from the comics and a wisecracking tone reminiscent of television situation comedy. Yet the books are clearly designed to present information, both in the details of the bus's journey and in the student "reports" displayed as insets in almost every illustration.

## Specialized Topics

During the last decade, more nonfiction books have been published about highly specialized topics. There have always been specialized books, but today there are more and more books that reflect very specific interests. They might report personalized perspectives, give detailed information about a narrowly defined topic, or cut across subject matter in a new way. For instance, Hana Machotka focuses on single features of animal anatomy in *Breathtaking Noses*. There are books about special topics like lacrosse (Diane Hoyt-Goldsmith's *Lacrosse: The National Game of the Iroquois*), adjectives (Ruth Heller's *Many Luscious Lollipops*), and feuding bone hunters (Thom Holmes's *Fossil Feud: The Rivalry of the First American Dinosaur Hunters*). Although students might not identify these topics as something they want or need to read about, the books frequently create interest in the topics.

## Recognition and Awards

Many of the trends we have looked at here indicate that nonfiction books are innovative and creative. They carry the unique perspective of individual authors and of artists free to experiment with formats and media. It is not surprising, then, that nonfiction books for children are finally being recognized for their aesthetic qualities as literature. In the past, nonfiction books have not earned their fair share of critical attention and recognition. In 1981, author Betty Bacon pointed out that nonfiction books had won the Newbery Medal only six times in fifty-eight years, and those winners were from history or biography, in which the chronological narrative form is very much like fiction.[2] This is quite a contrast to literature for adults, where authors like John McPhee and Tracy Kidder regularly win critical acclaim for their work and nonfiction frequently dominates the best-sellers lists. As a result of this imbalance, the Association of Library Services to Children has established the Robert F. Sibert Informational Book Award. This new award is meant to honor an author whose work of nonfiction has made a significant contribution to the field of children's literature in a given year.

Recent works of nonfiction that have appeared on the Newbery list include Russell Freedman's *Lincoln: A Photobiography*, which received the Newbery Medal. Freedman's *The Wright Brothers*, and *Eleanor Roosevelt: A Life of Discovery*, Katherine Lasky's *Sugaring Time*, Rhoda Blumberg's *Commodore Perry in the Land of the Shogun*, Patricia Lauber's *Volcano: The Eruption and Healing of Mt. St. Helens*, and Jim Murphy's *The Great Fire* have received Newbery Honor medals.

The Boston Globe-Horn Book Awards have included a nonfiction category for many years. Some of the books recognized in this category have been Natalie S. Bober's *Abigail Adams: Witness to a Revolution*, Robie H. Harris's *It's Perfectly Normal: A Book About Changing Bodies, Growing Up, Sex, and Sexual Health*, and Steve Jenkins's *The Top of the World: Climbing Mount Everest*.

In 1990 the National Council of Teachers of English established the Orbis Pictus Award for Outstanding Nonfiction for Children. Its name commemorates what is thought to be the first book of facts produced for children, dating back to the seventeenth century. Recent winners include Jennifer Armstrong's *Shipwreck at the Bottom of the Worlds: the Extraordinary True Story of Shakleton and the Endurance* and *An Extraordinary Life: The Story of the Monarch Butterfly* by Laurence Pringle. In general, biography continues to win more awards than other types of nonfiction, but now at least there are opportunities for all kinds of nonfiction books to receive the acclaim they deserve.

## Criteria for Evaluating Nonfiction Books

One critic who has given close attention to nonfiction books for children is Jo Carr.[3] Teachers and librarians who want to choose the very best books available

---

[2]Betty Bacon, "The Art of Nonfiction," *Children's Literature in Education* 12 (spring 1981): 3.

[3]Jo Carr, "Writing the Literature of Fact," in *Beyond Fact: Nonfiction for Children and Young People* (Chicago: American Library Association, 1982), pp. 3–12.

# GUIDELINES

## Evaluating Nonfiction Books

### ACCURACY AND AUTHENTICITY

Is the author qualified to write about this topic? Has the manuscript been checked by authorities in the field?

Are the facts accurate according to other sources?

Is the information up-to-date?

Are all the significant facts included?

Do text and illustrations reveal diversity and avoid stereotypes?

Are generalizations supported by facts?

Is there a clear distinction between fact and theory?

Do text and illustrations omit anthropomorphism and teleological explanations?

### CONTENT AND PERSPECTIVE

For what purpose was the book designed?

Is the book within the comprehension and interest range of its intended audience?

Is the subject adequately covered? Are different viewpoints presented?

Does the book lead to an understanding of the scientific method? Does it foster the spirit of inquiry?

Does the book show interrelationships? If it is a science book, does it indicate related social issues?

### STYLE

Is information presented clearly and directly?

Is the text appropriate for the intended audience?

Does the style create the feeling of reader involvement?

Is the language vivid and interesting?

### ORGANIZATION

Is the information structured clearly, with appropriate subheadings?

Does the book have reference aids that are clear and easy to use, such as table of contents, index, bibliography, glossary, appendix?

### ILLUSTRATIONS AND FORMAT

Do illustrations clarify and extend the text or speak plainly for themselves?

Are size relationships made clear?

Are media suitable to the purposes for which they are used?

Are illustrations explained by captions or labels where needed?

Does the total format contribute to the clarity and attractiveness of the book?

---

can be guided by her view that a nonfiction writer is first a teacher, then an artist, and should be concerned with feeling as well as thinking, passion as well as clarity. Specific criteria can be used to help identify this level of achievement. Being familiar with these criteria and with the types of books in which information is presented will make it easier to choose the best books at the right time. The individual reviewer must judge the relative value of the various criteria in terms of particular books. Sometimes a book's strengths in one or two categories may far outweigh its weakness in others. See Guidelines, "Evaluating Nonfiction Books" for an overview of these criteria.

## Accuracy and Authenticity

Accuracy is of primary importance in nonfiction books for children. No one wants inaccurate information, no matter how well it is presented, especially because many children believe that anything printed in a book is true. The author's qualifications, the way in which the author presents facts and generalizations, the correctness of the illustrations, and many other factors need to be considered in evaluating a book's accuracy and authenticity.

### The Author's Qualifications

Nonfiction books are written by people who are authorities in their fields, or they are written by writers who study a subject, interview specialists, and compile the data. A few, like naturalist Jean Craighead George, are both specialists and writers. It is always a good idea to check the book's jacket copy, title page, introduction, or "About the Author" page at the back for information about the author's special qualifications, often expressed in terms of professional title or affiliation. Expertise in one field does not necessarily indicate competency in another, however, so we expect a high degree of authenticity only if the author has limited the book to what appears to be his or her specialty.

If a book is written by a "writer," not by an expert in the field, facts can be checked by authorities and the authority cited. For example, the book *Get the Message: Telecommunications in Your High-Tech World* was written by Gloria Skurzynski, a writer better known for fiction than for information. However, the acknowledgments name a long list of experts she interviewed and consulted, corporations that provided materials and information, and experts who reviewed her manuscript. Photo credits show that the illustrations were furnished by companies and universities on the cutting edge of this technology. The record of sources and research provided here gives assurance that the book is accurate.

A number of authors have earned the reputation of writing dependably good nonfiction books. When in doubt, teachers and librarians are likely to turn first to writers who have proved their integrity with facts—Penny Colman, Patricia Lauber, James Cross Giblin, Russell Freedman, Milton Meltzer, Laurence Pringle, Seymour Simon, and Helen Roney Sattler, among others. But authorship, while it may be a valuable rule of thumb, is a dangerous final criterion. Each book must be evaluated on its own merits.

### Factual Accuracy

Fortunately, many of the errors of fact in children's nonfiction books are minor. Children who have access to a variety of books on one topic should be encouraged to notice discrepancies and pursue the correct answer, a valuable exercise in critical reading.

Errors that teachers and children recognize are less distressing than those that pass for fact because the topic is unfamiliar or highly specialized; then the reader must depend on a competent reviewer to identify inaccuracies. Ideally, a book with technical information should be reviewed by someone with expertise in that field. *Appraisal: Science Books for Young Readers* is a periodical that offers paired reviews, one by a science professional and one by a teacher or librarian. *Science Books and Films* includes reviews by specialists in the field. *Horn Book Magazine* singles out science books for special reviewing efforts, although other nonfiction is included. The *School Library Journal* often provides helpful criticism. *Social Education* and *Science and Children* magazines also give some attention to appropriate books, and both publish a list of outstanding books in their respective fields each year. Both of these lists can be accessed through the Children's Book Council website at *http://www.cbcbooks.org*. Generally speaking, science books are more likely to be challenged by experts than are those about history or other topics in the humanities.

### Being Up-to-Date

Some books that are free of error at the time of writing become inaccurate with the passage of time, as new discoveries are made in the sciences or as changes occur in world politics. Books that focus on the past are less likely to be rapidly outdated, although new discoveries in archaeology or new theories in history and anthropology call for a reevaluation of these materials also. Shelley Tanaka's *Graveyards of the Dinosaurs* discusses scientists Michael Novacek and Mark Norell's discoveries

about the oviraptor. Scientists had once believed that these beasts were solitary animals who would eat their eggs if given the chance. Novacek and Norell showed that the oviraptor actually sat on its nest and incubated its eggs. This type of information helps children to understand how what we know about an extinct species changes as scientists continue to ask questions. Books that focus on subjects on which vigorous research and experimentation are being done, such as viruses and disease or space technology, are even more quickly outdated. It is worth noting, however, that the latest trade books are almost always more up-to-date than the latest textbooks or encyclopedias.

It is also difficult, but important, to provide children with current information about other countries where national governments are emerging or where future political developments are uncertain. Current events that generate an interest in books about a particular country also call attention to the fact that those books might be out-of-date. Internet sites would be an excellent way to keep track of current events, although these too require critical evaluation. The American Library Association lists more than 700 Great Sites for Children at *www.ala.org/ parentspage/greatsites/amazing.html*. Teachers will want to make note of other sites vetted by professional organizations, such as the website for the National Council for the Social Studies (*www.ncss.org*) and the Website for the National Science Teachers Association (*www.nsta.org*).

Books about minority cultures also need to include material on contemporary experience, as well as heritage. Books like *Apache Rodeo* and *Potlatch: A Tsimshian Celebration,* both by Diane Hoyt-Goldsmith, show families who take pride in continuing their traditions but also are clearly people of today's world. Being up-to-date is one of the ways that books of this kind can combat stereotypes.

### Inclusion of All the Significant Facts

Though the material presented in a book might be current and technically correct, the book cannot be totally accurate if it omits significant facts. Thirty years ago science books that dealt with animal reproduction frequently glossed over the specifics of birth or mating. In Robert McClung's *Possum*, the process was explained like this: "All night long the two of them wandered through the woods together. But at dawn each went his own way again. Possum's babies were born just twelve days later."[4] Fortunately, changing social mores that struck down taboos in children's fiction also encouraged a new frankness in nonfiction books. For instance, close-up photographs

---

[4]Robert McClung, *Possum* (New York: Morrow, 1963), p. 41.

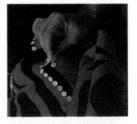

Hundreds of white mother-of-pearl buttons are sewn on the back of this button blanket to make a design.

David's father works hard for many months to make the gifts and the new regalia necessary for a large potlatch. He paints a drum as his friend Evelyn finishes sewing a button blanket.

Friends from all over the Northwest come to help David's father finish the potlatch gifts.

—*In her many books such as* Potlatch: A Tsimshian Celebration *Diane Hoyt-Goldsmith portrays the lives of modern day Native Americans.*

Photographs copyright © 1995 by Lawrence Migdale. Reprinted from *Potlatch* by Diane Hoyt-Goldsmith by permission of Holiday House.

and a forthright text in *My Puppy Is Born* by Joanna Cole show the birth and early development of a terrier's litter. *Egg to Chick* by Millicent Selsam pictures the mating of a rooster and a hen.

Human reproduction and sexuality have so often been distorted by omissions that books with accurate terminology and explicit information are particularly welcome. Older children will find that Robie H. Harris's *It's So Amazing: A Book About Eggs, Sperm, Birth, Babies, and Families* and *It's Perfectly Normal: A Book About Changing Bodies, Growing Up, Sex, and Sexual Health* are thorough and frank guides to adolescent and adult sexuality. Michael Emberley's detailed illustrations add a wonderful touch of humor to what is often a touchy subject for this age group.

The honest presentation of all information necessary for understanding a topic is just as important in historical or cultural accounts as in the sciences. This can be difficult to achieve because social issues are complex and writing for a young audience requires that the author be brief. Judging whether a book does include all the significant facts can also be difficult, for deciding what really counts is a matter of interpretation, often dependent on the book's intended audience. A. P. Porter's *Kwanzaa,* a book de-

signed for early elementary readers, does an admirable job of explaining in simple terms the purpose and symbolism of this seven-day African American holiday. The presentation of historical context, however, might be more helpful if it were more complete. How does Kwanza reflect a heritage that predates slavery? Was the origin of Kwanza related to changes brought about by the civil rights movement? Is Kwanza recognized and celebrated by a large percentage of African Americans? If a book leaves important questions unanswered, it has not included all the significant facts.

### Avoiding Stereotypes

A book that omits significant facts tells only part of the truth; a book that presents stereotypes pretends, wrongly, to have told the truth. One very common sort of stereotyping is by omission. If we never see women or minorities in science books, for instance, we are left with the incorrect impression that all scientists must be white males. In recent years, fortunately, more authors, illustrators, and publishers have made conscious efforts to represent the great variety of roles that women and minorities play in science and the world of work. Harlow Rockwell's *My Doctor* was a leader in portraying a woman physician in a book for the very young, and Gail Gibbons has made many similar contributions, including a woman surveyor on the work crew of *New Road!* George Ancona's lively photographs in *Let's Dance!* include boys and men and a woman dancing in a wheelchair. This no-fanfare approach helps combat stereotypes because it encourages children to accept the contributions of all people as a matter of course.

Books about countries around the world and those that describe life in a minority culture are the most likely to include stereotypes. Children can be taught to watch for sweeping general statements and for unwarranted claims about what "everybody" thinks or does. However, all readers need to realize that it is almost impossible to portray a country or region completely in *all* its diversity of people, terrain, industry, lifestyles, and the like. When the region is large and the book is limited in length, it is good if the author deliberately highlights differences rather than generalizing too freely. In *Chidi Only Likes Blue: An African Book of Colors,* Ifeoma Onyefulu provides lovely pictures of the colors found in a child's village in Nigeria. From the title, however, one might generalize these images to all of Africa. Only a map on the end pages indicates that this is a small country on a large continent. Onyefulu's *Ogbo: Sharing Life in an African Village* is much more successful. The title itself focuses our attention on the village and then a large map and author's note opposite the first page provide the background we need for understanding the pictures and the information that follow.

Another way authors try to avoid stereotyping is by relating the story of one individual within a community. Diane Hoyt-Goldsmith's books about Native Americans focus on one tribe and then on a particular child's family, school, and community experiences. Readers associate the facts in these books with specific persons and places. Consequently, they will be less likely to assume that this description of Native American life represents the way *all* people of Native American heritage live.

### Using Facts to Support Generalizations

To be distinguishable from stereotype or simple opinion, a proper generalization needs facts for support. In *What's the Deal? Jefferson, Napoleon and the Louisiana Purchase*, Rhoda Blumberg explains that there were many conspiracies by Americans, living in what was then the West, to separate from the Union.

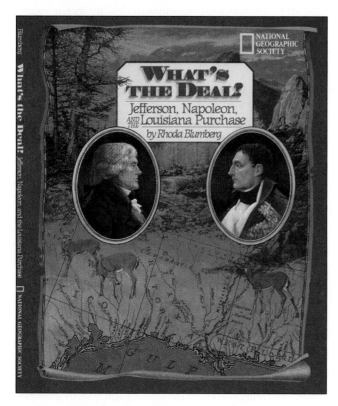

*Author Rhoda Blumberg provides supporting evidence for generalizations throughout her fine* What's the Deal? Jefferson, Napoleon and the Louisiana Purchase.

Jacket art from *What's the Deal? Jefferson, Napoleon, and the Louisiana Purchase* by Rhoda Blumberg. Front cover artwork by John Buxton, © 1998 National Geographic Society.

She states, "The most malevolent plotter was James Wilkinson, one of Thomas Jefferson's friends." She supports this broad statement in the next three paragraphs with examples of Wilkinson's perfidy.

Laurence Pringle says in *Vanishing Ozone: Protecting Earth from Ultra Violet Radiation* that the ozone layer in the atmosphere is shrinking as a result of chemicals released into the atmosphere. He explains how scientists proved that the ozone layer was being depleted and then offers evidence to support the role of chemicals such as CFCs in this phenomenon. Critical readers need to be aware of generalizations and judge for themselves whether adequate facts are offered for support.

### Making the Distinction Between Fact and Theory

Careful writers make careful distinctions between fact and theory; but even so, children need guidance in learning to recognize the difference. Often the distinction depends on key words or phrases—such as *scientists believe, so far as we know,* or *perhaps.* Consider the importance of the simple phrase *may have* in this description of a prehistoric reptile: "Pterodactyls lived near the shores of prehistoric seas and may have slept hanging from tree branches by their feet, like bats."[5] Some discussion of different kinds of possible evidence might be in order as children are led to see that one-half of this statement is presented as fact, the other as theory.

Books about the disappearance of the dinosaurs make good material for helping children sort out the difference between fact and theory, because the problem is dramatic and the evidence provides for legitimate disagreement among scientists. Franklin Branley's *What Happened to the Dinosaurs?* does a particularly good job of helping primary-age children understand what a theory is.

Although it is important to distinguish between fact and theory in all of the sciences, including the social sciences, the matter receives most attention in books dealing with evolution and human origins. In some communities this is a very sensitive topic, but it would seem that children everywhere have a right to information about scientists' discoveries and theories regarding our origins. *Traces of Life* by Kathryn Lasky, now out of print, presented "the origins of humankind" in terms of particular fossil discoveries and scientists' sometimes differing interpretations of these. In contrast, David Peters's *From the Beginning: The Story of Human Evolution* fails to acknowledge the process by which ideas about evolution have become accepted in the scientific community. It is disturbing to note that balanced coverage of this important topic is becoming more difficult to find in nonfiction books

[5]David C. Knight, *Dinosaurs That Swam and Flew,* illus. Lee J. Ames (Englewood Cliffs, N.J.: Prentice Hall, 1985), p. 39.

at a time when many school districts are also reluctant to include the topic in their curricula.

## Avoiding Anthropomorphism

In poetry and fiction, the assignment of human feelings and behavior to animals, plants, or inanimate objects is called *personification*—an accepted literary device that can be used with great effect. In science, however, this device is unacceptable and is known as *anthropomorphism*. Science writer Millicent Selsam addressed the problem of interpreting what animals do in one of her early books on animal behavior:

It is hard to keep remembering that animals live in a different kind of world from our own. They see, hear, smell, and taste things differently. And they do not have human intelligence or emotions, so we must avoid interpreting their behavior in terms of our own feelings and thoughts. For example, it looks to us as though parent birds are devoted to their young in the same way that human parents are devoted to theirs. But only experimental work can show whether this interpretation is true.[6]

Many books with these anthropomorphic touches are still in print. In *Antarctica,* an otherwise lovely book about the animal life on this great continent, Helen Cowcher tries to convey the negative impact of human intrusion on the animal life. She states, "Out at sea anxious songs ring out from the depths. Weddell seals call to their friends under the ice."[7] The words *anxious* and *friends* attribute human emotions and human relationships to the seals and may lead children to the types of interpretation that Selsam cautions against.

On the other hand, knowing that young children perceive new things in terms of their experiences and feelings, writers have often given names to their animal subjects or expressed animal behavior in childlike terms. In *To the Top of the World: Adventures with Arctic Wolves,* Jim Brandenburg names the wolves he observes after one of his relatives (Buster), their role in the pack (Mom), or their physical characteristics (Scruffy, Midback). Describing Midback's behavior, Brandenburg writes, "There is no way to know why this alpha female did not give birth, but she was the most fiercely protective 'parent' the pups had. She behaved like a dominant aunt who was often jealous of the pups' mother" (p. 12). This is *not* anthropomorphism, just good reporting and clear writing.

Closely related to anthropomorphism is another error called *teleological* explanation of phenomena.

Briefly, teleology attempts to account for natural phenomena by assigning a purpose to the plants, animals, or forces involved. Science books should not suggest that leaves turn toward the light in order to bask in the sun or that "Mother Nature," capitalized and personified, is at work carving the walls of canyons. Such a description has a certain poetic effect, but it also conveys a basically unscientific attitude.

## Content and Perspective

Consideration of the purpose of a book, its intended audience, and the objectivity of its author can help readers evaluate a nonfiction book's content and perspective. A good nonfiction book should also foster reflective inquiry in children and enable them to see relationships across disciplines.

## Purpose

It is futile to try to pass judgment on the content of a nonfiction book without first determining the purpose for which the book was designed. Identifying the scope of the book lets us know what we can reasonably expect. A quick look at Vicki Cobb's *Why Can't I Live Forever? And Other Not So Dumb Questions About Life* reveals a fascinating collection of questions and explanations for browsing, whereas both the title and the appearance of Martin Redfern's *The Kingfisher Young People's Book of Space* indicate a comprehensive treatment of the topic. Titles can be misleading, particularly those that promise to tell "all about" a subject but offer limited coverage instead. At best, titles indicate the scope of the book's content and pique the reader's curiosity, as do the titles of two of James Cross Giblin's books, *The Truth About Unicorns* and *The Mystery of the Mammoth Bones.* More about the scope and purpose of nonfiction books can be found in the section "Types of Nonfiction Books" later in this chapter.

## Intended Audience

Before evaluating content, we have to know not just for what the book was intended, but for whom. Book jackets and book reviews often indicate an age range according to reading level or interest. It is difficult to know whether one or both of these factors are reflected in the age recommendation. Generally, a book's reading level is not as important as its content in relation to the reader's actual interest in a subject. Older students and adults might turn to children's nonfiction books for introductory material on an unfamiliar topic. In using nonfiction books, children will read "beyond their abilities" when reading for particular facts. Children will frequently turn to difficult books if they contain many pictures or useful diagrams. At the same time,

---

[6]Millicent Selsam, *Animals as Parents,* illus. John Kaufmann (New York: 1965), p. 16.

[7]Helen Cowcher, *Antarctica* (New York: Farrar, Straus & Giroux, 1990), unpaged.

vocabulary, sentence length, size of type, and the book's organization are factors to be considered. Children might reject a book that contains useful information if they see crowded pages, relatively small type, and few pictures.

The choice of topic, then, is an important factor in determining whether a book will be suitable for its intended audience. Books for young children most often reflect their basic egocentric concerns and their curiosity about themselves and other living things; it is a mistake to assume that they will not be interested in other subjects, however. Many early primary children enjoy browsing through the widely diverse titles of the Eyewitness series, such as Andrée Grau's *Dance*, Theresa Greenaway's *Jungle,* or *Pyramid* by Jane McIntosh, even though these books are designed for an older audience. On the other hand, books that look like picture books are frequently aimed at upper-grade children. Some of these may require readers to keep track of some complex concepts while they follow the ins and outs of the visual and verbal narrative.

Examples chosen by an author to clarify concepts are related to the level of cognitive ability needed to get the most out of a book. In *Samuel Eatons' Day* and *Sarah Morton's Day,* Kate Waters caters to a young child's need to approach historical understanding through concrete details. Double-page spreads of sequenced color photos show Sarah and Samuel, the pilgrim children, getting dressed in their overgarments. For Sarah, first comes the petticoat, then stockings, garters, two more petticoats, a waistcoat, coif, apron, "pocket," and shoes. For Samuel, stockings, garters, breeches, doublet, shoes, "points," and hat—a clear contrast to sweatsuits and sneakers!

## Adequate Coverage

Recognizing the purpose of a book and its intended level, the reader has a basis for deciding if the author has said too much about the topic or too little. Jim Murphy's many fine books, such as *The Great Fire* and *Gone A-Whaling: The Lure of the Sea and The Hunt for the Great Whale,* are close to 200 pages. The focus of the topic is limited but the treatment is detailed.

Broader topics, like the history or culture of a nation, might require many pages in order to give even brief attention to all the significant material. History textbooks have earned particularly harsh criticism for faulty coverage,[8] and good trade books help fill in perspectives that the textbooks omit. A generation ago, Gerald Johnson expressed the need for careful writing in the introduction to his book *America Is Born:*

 Part of the story is very fine, and other parts are very bad, but they all belong to it, and if you leave out the bad parts you never understand it all. (pp. viii–ix)*

Authors who fail to acknowledge more than one viewpoint or theory fail to help children learn to examine issues. Even young children should know that authorities do not always agree, though the context might be simple. It is far more common, though, and certainly more necessary, for books about complex issues to deal with varying points of view. Laurence Pringle's *Nuclear Energy: Troubled Past, Uncertain Future* outlines efforts for and against a "second nuclear era" and identifies proponents of both sides. Anything less would have been inadequate coverage of the topic.

### Demonstration of the Scientific Method

Because we are concerned about *how* as well as *what* children learn, it is important to note what kind of thinking a book encourages, as well as the body of facts it presents. Nonfiction books should illustrate the process of inquiry, the excitement of discovery. James Cross Giblin's *The Mystery of the Mammoth Bones and How It Was Solved* and Johann Reinhard's *Discovering the Inca Ice Maiden* give readers a good idea of the problems scientists try to solve and the kind of day-to-day work that is involved.

While these are fine accounts of the scientific method at work, the reader's involvement is still vicarious. Some books are designed to give children more-direct experience with the skills of inquiry. Millicent Selsam's *How to Be a Nature Detective* encourages children to ask "What happened, who was here, and where did he go?" in order to learn how to read animal tracks. At each step of the process, Marlene Donnelly's illustrations help children follow this sequence as if they were actually outdoors tracking various animals. Sandra Markle's guides for observing ants in *Exploring Autumn* provide simple directions (no pictures needed), ask questions that direct attention to important features like the relation between the size of an ant's burden to its body, and give background information that helps children interpret what they see.

The photographs in Patricia Lauber's *Dinosaurs Walked Here and Other Stories Fossils Tell* are chosen and placed to help children make their own observations about the fossil record. A photo of a present-day horseshoe crab beside the fossil print of its

---

[8]See Frances FitzGerald, *America Revised* (Boston: Atlantic/Little, Brown, 1979).

*Johnson, Gerald White. *America is Born.* Illustrated by Leonard Everett Fisher. New York: William Morrow, 1959.

140-million-year-old ancestor allows readers to conclude that these creatures have scarcely changed over time; a companion picture lets us discover how beavers have shrunk in the past fifteen thousand years. All of Lauber's books demonstrate this commitment to presenting scientific evidence in such a way that children can confirm some conclusions for themselves.

The scientific method applies to the social sciences, too. Jean Fritz has illustrated techniques of historical research in a fictionalized account that children like very much—*George Washington's Breakfast.* The story illustrates the role of perseverance and good luck in problem solving. After young George, who is trying to find out what George Washington customarily ate for breakfast, has asked questions, exhausted library resources, and gone on a futile fact-finding trip to Mt. Vernon, he happens to find the answer in an old book written during Washington's lifetime, about to be discarded from his own attic. When he finds the answer to his question, he has discovered the usefulness of primary source materials. Intermediate children can also find out about using primary sources for studying personal history in *The Great Ancestor Hunt* by Lila Perl. *The Riddle of the Rosetta Stone: Key to Ancient Egypt* by James Cross Giblin and Kathy Pelta's *Discovering Christopher Columbus: How History Is Invented* demonstrate how historians study evidence and develop hypotheses.

### Interrelationships and Implications

A list of facts is fine for an almanac, but nonfiction books should be expected to put facts into some sort of perspective. After all, linking facts in one way or another transforms information into knowledge. Thomas Locker's *Sky Tree* shows how the same tree changes through the seasons and how it interacts with the animals, the earth, and the sky around it throughout the year. *Come Back Salmon* by Molly Cone intersperses information about Coho salmon, the watershed, and water pollution in a story about a class of fifth graders who cleaned up a dead stream near their school and saw the salmon return to spawn there.

Interrelationships of a different sort are pointed out in Barbara Brenner's *If You Were There in 1492.* This book helps readers see the cultural context in which a major event, Columbus's first voyage, took place. The author describes the world as it would have been known to ordinary people in Spain in terms of food, clothing, education, books, the arts, crime, ships, and many other aspects. The vivid presentations of the 1492 expulsion of Jews from Spain and the everyday life of the Lucayan people on the island where Columbus would land are especially good for prompting discussion about the relationship of one culture to another.

It is the remembered smell of its home stream that tells a salmon when its journey is over. Its nostrils quiver as it recognizes the smell. Its body quickens. At last it is home again. Where it finally comes to a stop may be only yards from its birthplace, or, in the case of the Jackson School salmon, from the spot where it was released into the creek.

But not all salmon migrating from stream to ocean will return.

Many smolt-size salmon are gobbled up almost as soon as they enter the sea. Water birds such as mergansers, kingfishers, sea gulls, and great blue herons feed on the tiny fish. Whales, seals, and sea lions eat larger salmon, as do eagles and

**GROWING UP IN THE OCEAN**

All species of Pacific salmon leave their home streams to feed and to grow to maturity in the salty waters of the Pacific Ocean. But different species of Pacific salmon stay in the ocean for different lengths of time. A Coho, or "Silver," usually lives in the ocean for about one and a half to two years before returning to its home stream to spawn. However, some early-maturing Cohos, known as "Jacks," return from the ocean after less than a year.

The Pacific salmon that stays in the ocean the longest is the Chinook. This "king of salmons" sometimes grows to more than a hundred pounds (while a fully grown Coho usually weighs no more than twelve pounds). No other species grows as big. The Chinook may take four years or more of feeding in the ocean to reach its immense size.

During their life in the ocean, Chinook and Coho salmon may journey as far north as Baranof Island, Alaska, and as far south as the coast of northern California. Pacific salmon generally travel in a counterclockwise direction until the time comes for them to begin their race toward their home streams.

ALASKAN BROWN BEARS ARE EXPERTS AT FISHING. ►

*Molly Cone's* Come Back Salmon *provides facts about Pacific salmon alongside the story of fifth graders who restored salmon spawning grounds.*

Text copyright © 1992 by Molly Cone from *Come Back Salmon.* Used by permission of Sierra Club Books for Children. Photo copyright © Jim Nilsen.

Intertwining science and technology with modern culture has become crucial, and many recent nonfiction books have taken this issue as a focus. *A Home by the Sea: Protecting Coastal Wildlife* by Kenneth Mallory discusses effects of commercial and residential development on coastal wildlife in New Zealand and the efforts being made to protect wildlife species. Even books not specifically designed to call attention to the related social problems of science and technology ought to acknowledge that such problems exist. Where the uses of science have serious implications for society, the relationships should be made clear. (See the discussion of the study theme "Stewards of the Earth" in Chapter 13 for more about this issue.)

### Style

The style of a nonfiction book can be crucial in attracting children to the book and in helping them understand the concepts presented there. The clarity of presentation and the appropriateness of the language for its intended audience are important matters to consider in evaluating a book's style. In addition, the writing should involve readers in the topic and provide them with an absorbing and vivid learning experience. Author Penny Colman suggests that in evaluating nonfiction writing we should ask how authors effect transitions, craft the ending, "establish a point of view, create a sense of time, use adjectives, adverbs, metaphors, or varied sentence lengths."[9] These qualities of style are just as important in nonfiction as they are in fiction.

### Clarity and Directness

It is difficult to list all of the criteria that influence clarity. The use of precise language and specific detail is one important factor. Nothing is vague in Miriam Schlein's description of a vampire bat's dinner in *Billions of Bats*. She names the animals that are likely prey ("a horse, a cow, a donkey, or even chicken"), describes the approach and the bite ("only about a tenth of an inch long"), and goes on to explain how the bat curves its tongue into a funnel shape and sucks in blood ("for about a half hour"). The language is simple and direct, giving the reader a clear picture of the process.

In earlier decades we could say with some certainty that information presented in the guise of fiction was confusing and ought to be avoided. A few recent books, however, have offered skillful combinations of fact and fiction in which information is clearly presented. One of these, *Merrily Ever After* by Joe Lasker, contrasts two stories of ruling class and peasant weddings during the Middle Ages. Still, the center of interest is the book's information about medieval life and customs. Patricia and Frederick McKissack use a similar technique to contrast the lives of white and African American families prior to the Civil War in *Christmas in the Big House, Christmas in the Quarters*. By placing the facts about life on a plantation in the context of two imaginary families, the contrast between the two cultures and between free whites and enslaved blacks is given greater impact. The story element in books like this can help children understand facts that might otherwise seem too distant. On the other hand, not every author is this successful in making the combination; some fail to do a very good job of entertaining or of informing. When a picture book is only loosely based in fact, as in Emily Arnold McCully's *The Bobbin Girl* or Pam Conrad's *Call Me Ahnighito*, we cannot call it nonfiction (perhaps *informational fiction* or *faction*[10] would be good terms)—and we need to make sure children understand the difference. Each book must be judged on its own merits.

### Level of Difficulty

Although the vocabulary does have to be within the child's range, books for primary-grade children need not be restricted to a narrow list of words. New terms can be explained in context. In *Follow the Water from Brook to Ocean*, Arthur Dorros provides a two-paragraph description of the effects of moving water before introducing the word *erosion*. He also gives helpful context through examples and illustrations for the words *meanders* and *reservoir*. Context does not serve to explain everything, however; a writer aware of the background of the intended audience takes pains to make new words clear.

Words that look unpronounceable are another stumbling block for most children. A glossary is helpful, but youngsters who are intent on a book's content might not take time to look in the back. In some cases authors provide pronunciation guides in parentheses for daunting words. Such is the case in Caroline Arnold's *Dinosaurs Down Under: And Other Fossils from Australia* and Miriam Schlein's *Discovering Dinosaur Babies*.

### Reader Involvement

Authors use many different techniques to engage readers' attention and help them stay involved with a book's subject matter. David Getz's *Frozen Man*, about a five-thousand-year-old man found frozen in the ice in the Alps, begins with this enticing statement: "Nobody knew what stories the body could tell." Jim Arnosky's *All About Turtles* and *All About Owls* asks questions that alert readers to important information in the text.

Nonfiction authors also use direct address—sentences that speak to the reader as "you." Sometimes an author asks direct questions to claim a bond of communication with the reader. Paul Showers hooks the primary audience for *How Many Teeth?* with a variety of rhymes interspersed throughout the text to ask "How many teeth have you?"

One technique that lends itself to nonfiction for children is called "creative nonfiction." Such writers of adult nonfiction as Annie Dillard and Frank Conroy have long used this approach to invigorate their topics.[11] Author Penny Colman Colman explains that in writing creative nonfiction, "I adhere to the basic tenets of nonfiction writing as well as use stylistic and narrative strategies traditionally found in fiction."[12] Colman begins *Corpses, Coffins and*

[9]Colman, "Nonfiction Is Literature Too," p. 220.

[10]See Carol Avery, "Nonfiction Books: Naturals for the Primary Level," in *Making Facts Come Alive: Choosing Quality Nonfiction for Children*, ed. Rosemary Banford and Janice Kristo (Norwood, Mass.: Christopher Gordon, 1998).

[11]Lee Gutkind, "From the Editor: The 5R's of Creative Nonfiction," *Creative Nonfiction* 6 (1996): 1–16.

[12]Colman, "Nonfiction Is Literature Too," p. 219.

*Crypts: A History of Burial* with her own reflection about spending the day with her uncle's dead body, and in subsequent chapters she relays the real-life experiences of many others to cover subjects such as autopsies, embalming and cremation, and burial customs. These real-life experiences and personal reflections add zest to her explanations, yet her meticulous research and attention to detail are evident not only in her writing but also in her extensive use of archival material and site visits. The results are highly engaging books like *Corpses, Coffins and Crypts, Rosie the Riveter: Woman Working on the Home Front in World War II,* and *Girls: A History of Growing Up Female in America.*

### Vivid Language

The writer of nonfiction books uses the same techniques as the writer of fiction to bring a book to life, although the words must be accurate as well as attractive. Imagery is used to appeal to the senses, as in Barbara Bash's *Ancient Ones: The World of the Old-Growth Douglas Fir:*

> Walking into an old-growth forest, you enter a strangely silent world. The Earth feels moist and springy underfoot, and the air is thick with the fragrance of decomposing needles. (p. 7)

This quiet beginning in Jim Murphy's *Gone A-Whaling* provides a sense of anticipation:

> The water in the bay was calm. Mewing gulls soared and dipped feverishly, searching for fish, before gliding off toward the rocky shore. For a few seconds, all was quiet. (p. 9)

When a forty-ton whale erupts out of the sea, the reader's emotional leap is all the more exciting.

Metaphorical language, because it is based on comparison, can be used to contribute to clarity in nonfiction. Older readers appreciate the vivid comparisons in *Predator!* by Bruce Brooks. In describing killer whales in pursuit of a large prey, Brooks says:

> two of them will taunt a large baleen whale by cruising alongside one to a side, nipping and nudging and poking, like two hoods in stock cars hassling a stern old gent riding in a Cadillac between them. (p. 23)

This book's frequent references to sport and to the contemporary scene present the world of nature in an unusually appealing way, especially for young adolescents.

Children probably will not be able to describe an author's style, but they certainly will respond to it. They know that a well-written nonfiction book somehow does not sound the same as an encyclopedia essay, and they enjoy the difference.

## Organization

Even if a book is vividly written, accurate, and in command of its topic, children will not find it very useful unless it also furnishes a clear arrangement of information. The way a book's content is structured and the reference aids it includes should help readers find and then understand key concepts and facts.

### Structure

Every author must choose a structure, or organizing principle, as a basis for presenting facts. Sometimes an author uses a very obvious principle, such as organizing a collection of facts alphabetically. This format allows Seymour Simon to introduce older readers to important understandings about the global ecosystem in *Earth Words: A Dictionary of the Environment.* In this book, as in others, the alphabet device makes a good format for browsing and is easily understood by children, although it pays less attention to the relationship among facts.

The question-and-answer approach has become more widely used in recent years. For very young children, questions and pictured answers can change a concept book into an engaging guessing game. Several of Margaret Miller's books such as *Guess Who?* repeat a question and suggest four silly answers; turn the page and discover a word or phrase and the photographs of the correct answer. One of the many question books for older readers is Vicki Cobb's *Why Can't I Live Forever? And Other Not So Dumb Questions About Life.* This book presents interesting details about biology, reproduction and death.

Another structure closely related to questions and answers is the true/false approach that states common myths or misconceptions and then offers corrected or updated information. One of the best of these books is Seymour Simon's *Animal Fact/Animal Fable.* On each right-hand page Diane de Groat has a lively illustration to highlight statements such as "bats are blind," "[an] owl is a wise bird," and "some fish can climb trees." When the page is turned, Simon provides the information that explains whether the statement is fact or fable. Another fine example of this approach is Patricia Lauber's *The News About Dinosaurs,* with its meticulous but not too technical updates on the scientific interpretations of information about the dinosaurs.

A common and sensible arrangement for many books, especially about history or biological processes, is based on chronology. Sarah Waters's *Samuel Eaton's Day* and *Kate Morton's Day* allow modern-day children to compare their own morning-to-nighttime activities to those of children who lived almost four hundred years ago. *Cactus Hotel* by

Brenda Guiberson reveals both history and science in its account of the two-hundred-year growth of a giant saguaro cactus.

Regardless of its topic, a general-survey type of book should have a system of headings that help the reader get an overview of the content, unless the book is very brief and has pictures that serve as graphic guides for skimming. The longer the book and the more complex its topic, the greater the need for manageable division. Subheadings are more helpful as indicators of structure, especially for less-practiced readers.

### Reference Aids

With the exception of certain simple and special types, factual books should offer help at both front and back for the reader who needs to locate information quickly. It is important for children to develop reference skills early, so a table of contents and an index should be included in any book whose structure warrants it. Two of Ann Morris's concept books for younger children, *Weddings* and *Shoes, Shoes, Shoes,* provide visual indexes with additional information about each of the countries that she has visited in photographs in the books. A map identifies each of the countries shown in the pictures. This is a good way to introduce younger readers to indexes and other reference aids. For older children an index will be truly useful only if it is complete and has necessary cross-references. It is difficult to think of all the possible words children might use to look up a topic or to answer a question, yet writers should consider as many possibilities as seem reasonable.

Other helpful additions to a book are glossaries, bibliographies, suggestions for further reading, and nonfiction appendixes. Picture glossaries are on the increase with the growing number of nonfiction picture books. Nancy Winslow Parker and Joan Richards Wright include illustrated glossaries that summarize growth patterns and add detail about anatomy in their joint productions *Bugs* and *Frogs, Toads, Lizards, and Salamanders.* Either book would be good for demonstrating to children the use of reference aids, because both have touches of humor that add appeal as well as a full range of devices for locating and extending information.

If children are to understand methods of inquiry, they need to learn that a writer uses many sources of information. Penny Colman's *Corpses, Coffins and Crypts* has five pages of references. In an author's note Colman provides information about the people whose experiences she related, and she lists the sources that were particularly helpful to her. Photo credits that include many of her own photographs show how thorough and wide ranging her research was.

Appendixes are used to extend information in lists, charts, or tabulations of data that would seem cumbersome in the text itself. *Commodore Perry in the Land of the Shogun,* Rhoda Blumberg's award-winning account of the opening of Japanese harbors to American ships, seems all the more credible because of the documents and lists presented in the appendixes. Having read that lavish gifts were exchanged during the negotiations, children can discover in an appendix that the emperor was offered more than thirty items, including two telegraph sets, a copper lifeboat, champagne, tea, muskets, swords, and two mailbags with padlocks.

## Illustrations and Format

In our visually oriented culture, readers of all ages demand that a book's illustrations make it more interesting and attractive. In a nonfiction book, the illustrations and design must do that, and much more.

### Clarification and Extension of Text

One of the basic functions of illustrations is to clarify and extend the text. *Our Patchwork Planet* by Helen Roney Sattler has photographs of Earth taken from space, photos of nature features on Earth, and computer-generated images that show Earth's shifting surface. It also has drawings and diagrams by Guilio Maestro that help make complicated ideas about plate tectonics more understandable. Cutaway views and clear labeling are other good features of the pictures in this book.

The more abstract the topic, the more important it is that pictures help children "see" explanations. Latitude, longitude, and other mapping concepts, for instance, are often hard for children to grasp, so it is especially important that they be illustrated clearly, as Harriet Barton has done for Jack Knowlton's introductory book *Maps and Globes.* These big, bright pictures use color to focus attention on the equator, contour lines, and other specific aspects of simplified maps.

Illustrations are especially important in clarifying size relationships. Paul Facklam's illustrations for Margery Facklam's *The Big Bug Book* show the actual size of really big bugs and then place them with familiar objects to help children visualize just how large they really are. Not many topics lend themselves to life-size portrayals, of course, and that makes it important for artists to find other ways to be clear. Photographs and drawings often show magnified parts or wholes, and often some information about actual size is needed. When the reader has no frame of reference for the size of an object, comparison with something familiar is effective. If it weren't for the human hands holding the "Brazilian princess" topaz pictured in

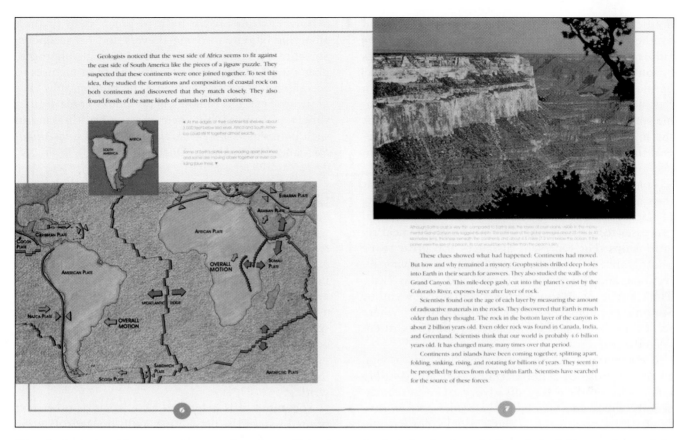

*The photographs and computer-generated images in Helen Roney Sattler's* Our Patchwork Planet *help children understand the concept of plate tectonics.*

From *Our Patchwork Planet* by Helen Roney Sattler, illustrated by Guilio Maestro. Illustration copyright © 1995 by Guilio Maestro. Used by permission of Lothrop, Lee & Shepard Books, an imprint of HarperCollins Publishers. Photo © American Museum of Natural History, Dept. of Library Services.

*Paul Facklam's drawing of a Goliath beetle shows its size in relation to familiar objects in Margery Facklam's* The Big Bug Book.

From *Big Bug Book* by Margery Facklam. Copyright © 1994 by Margery Facklam (text); copyright © 1994 by Paul Facklam (illustrations). By permission of Little, Brown and Company (Inc.).

*Earth Alive!* by Sandra Markle, most readers would fail to appreciate its tremendous size.

In many books the illustrations add detail and extend the information of the text; in others the illustrations themselves provide the bulk of the information, or become the subject of the text. In Walter Wick's *A Drop of Water*, the amazing photographs invite the reader to ask questions about such things as how a straight pin can indent the surface of water in a glass or how a huge bubble can rest on a metal frame. The text functions here to clarify and extend the pictures rather than the other way around. When illustrations are this important to a book, they need to have substantive content, high-quality reproduction, and a logical presentation or layout. For other good examples of effective presentation, look at Seymour Simon's books about the planets or Patricia Lauber's *Volcano: The Eruption and Healing of Mt. St. Helen's.*

### Suitability of Media

Illustrations in any medium can be clear and accurate, but one medium might be more suitable than another for a given purpose. Three-dimensional illustrations are used for clarity and interest in some nonfiction books. People of all ages are fascinated by the paper engineering in Jonathan Miller's *The Human Body,* designed by David Pelham. This goes beyond the entertainment value of a pop-up book; its movable parts reveal more about anatomy than flat pictures can possibly do. For instance, one double spread of the torso allows the reader to flip back the muscular diaphragm, spread the rib cage to reveal the lungs, and open the lungs to study their connection to the heart.

Diagrams and drawings have an impact of their own and also have many uses especially appropriate to science books. Diagrams can reduce technological processes to their essentials or show astronomical relationships that represent distances too great to be photographed. Diagrams are also fine for giving directions, and they can be charming as well as clear. This is true of Byron Barton's work for Seymour Simon's popular *The Paper Airplane Book,* where scenes are interspersed with how-to drawings to enliven the text.

Sometimes the perception of a graphic artist is vital to the purpose of a book. David Macaulay's *Ship* traces the modern-day discovery of a sixteenth-century wreck and then takes the reader back in time to watch its construction. Using various color schemes to indicate changes in time and place, Macaulay intersperses realistic drawings with sketches, diagrams, letters, and other documents to show how archaeologists painstakingly research and reconstruct the Spanish caravel *Magdelena.* Then through a "newly" discovered diary from archives in Seville he reveals how the ship was built and launched. The same standard of excellence, attention to detail, and touches of humor can be found in Macaulay's *The Way Things Work, Cathedral, City, Castle, Pyramid, Underground,* and *Mill.*

In spite of the range of media available for nonfiction books, the medium of choice is now photography. Photographs help establish credibility for real-life stories like Diane Hoyt-Goldsmith's *Las Posadas: An Hispanic Christmas Celebration* and add to the fascination of such topics as bog people in James M. Deem's *Bodies from the Bog.* Photographs reveal the natural world in its astonishing variety, recording minute detail in an instant. The photos by Nic Bishop for Joy Cowley's *Red-Eyed Tree Frog* (see p. 519) reveal marvels of skin textures, colors, and patterns that would be difficult to reproduce with complete accuracy in a painting.

Photographs in nonfiction books furnish more than technical accuracy, however. Photographers can be artists as well as recorders of information. Ken Robbins uses hand-tinted photographs in *Air* and other books in his Elements series. In *A Flower Grows,* he shows the sequence of stages in the life of a flower, from brown bulb to green stem to pink amaryllis blooms to dying flowers and fat seedpods. Sometimes artistry results not from a single photographer's work but from the careful choice of pictures to accompany a nonfiction text. The photographs that illustrate Seymour Simon's many books come from a variety of sources, but their effect is breathtaking in such books as *Bones, Galaxies Crocodiles and Alligators,* and *Spring Across America.*

## Captions

Children need to be able to look at an illustration and know what they are seeing, and that requires a wise use of captions and labels. Many writers use the text itself, if it is brief, to explain the pictures, eliminating the need for additional captions. Patricia Lauber's words and Jerome Wexler's photographs are combined in this way for *Seeds: Pop Stick Glide,* a handsome book that explains how plant life spreads. The arrangement of the text on the page and occasional references like "As you can see . . ." or "In this photo, . . ." help readers get maximum information from the illustrations as well as from the writing.

Sometimes it is helpful to have labels or other text printed within the illustration itself. In *Maps: Getting from Here to There* by Harvey Weiss, many drawings and diagrams include labels and arrows to show specifically where items like "a south latitude" or "an east longitude" are represented on the globe. Explanation within the pictures also helps identify contour lines and the features of a marine chart. Only occasionally does Weiss use a conventional caption to refer to an entire illustration. However an author chooses to use captions, they should be clear.

## Format

The total look of a book is its *format,* involving type size, leading, margins, placement of text and pictures, and arrangement of front and back matter—these include title and copyright pages in the front and indexes, bibliographies, and other aids at the back. *Mummies Made in Egypt* by Aliki incorporates hieroglyphic writing on the dedication and half-title pages, and many of the illustrations are arranged like the friezes that decorated the tombs of antiquity. This author frequently arranges sequences of pictures on the page in a comic strip or storyboard variation.

There are no absolute rules for format; the look of a book should be responsive to its purpose and its content. The broad coverage of topic intended in the Eyewitness series published by Knopf makes the busy layout of its pages seem rich rather than crowded. *Think of an Eel* by Karen Wallace is aimed at younger audiences and has wide margins, uncluttered

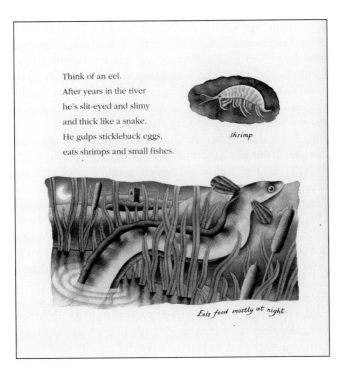

Think of an eel.
After years in the river
he's slit-eyed and slimy
and thick like a snake.
He gulps stickleback eggs,
eats shrimps and small fishes.

*shrimp*

*Eels feed mostly at night.*

*Mike Bostock's illustrations and page designs for Karen
Wallace's* Think of an Eel *are particularly inviting to young
readers.*

Think of an Eel *text copyright © 1993 Karen Wallace. Illustrations
© 1993 Mike Bostock. Reproduced by permission of Walker Books Ltd.,
London. Published in the U.S. and Canada by Candlewick Press, Inc.,
Cambridge, MA.*

page layouts, and simple captions that give the book
an attractive and inviting look.

Even a book that is sparingly illustrated can be notable for its overall design. Spacious margins and
tastefully ornamented headings can make a long text
seem less forbidding. The format of a nonfiction book
is an asset if it contributes to clarity or if it makes the
book more appealing to its audience.

Guidelines, "Evaluating Nonfiction Books" (see
p. 505) summarizes the key criteria to consider when
evaluating nonfiction books.

# Types of Nonfiction Books

Anyone who chooses nonfiction books for children
soon notices several subgenres or recognizable types
with common characteristics. Knowing about these
types helps the teacher and librarian provide balanced
and rich resources for learning as they choose particular books for particular purposes.

## Concept Books

Concept books explore the characteristics of a class
of objects or of an abstract idea. Most of the nonfiction books intended for very young children are of
this type. Typically they cover such concepts as size,
color, shape, spatial relationships, self, and family.
Concept books for this age are discussed at length in
Chapter 4. For school-age children, concept books
begin with what is already familiar and move toward
the unfamiliar, some by showing new ways to consider well-known materials, others by furnishing new
and different examples or perspectives. Such books
are often useful as idea sources for classroom experiences and discussion.

One good book for discussion is Peter Spier's *People,* an oversize picture book that appeals to many
different ages as it celebrates the possibilities for variation among the several billion human beings who
live on Earth. Spier's drawings include many shapes
and colors of ears, eyes, and noses; costumes, shelters,
and pastimes from around the world; architecture, al-
phabets, and foods. Although the author emphasizes
the uniqueness of individual appearances and preferences, the concept of cultural differences is implicit in
the book. Concept books about culture always raise
the issue of stereotyping. Help children think about
the author's choice of representative images for this
book. Primary-age students might compare Spier's
drawings with the photographs in *Faces* by Shelley
Rotner and Ken Kreisler or *Two Eyes, a Nose and a
Mouth* by Roberta Intrater.

## Nonfiction Picture Books

As earlier sections of this chapter show, more and
more nonfiction books *look* more and more like picture storybooks—that is, they are lavishly illustrated
or published in picture-book format. Books such as
Steve Jenkins's *The Top of the World: Climbing
Mount Everest* or Carol Carrick's *Whaling Days,*
with woodcuts by David Frampton, present information through conventional, well-written expository
text, but the beautiful illustrations and elegant design of these books add to our aesthetic pleasure as
well as to our understanding of the topics they present. Other picture books are anything but conventional in their ways of combining fact with fiction.
Some books, such as *From Pictures to Words: A
Book About Making a Book* by Janet Stevens (see
p. 520), have invented characters and a story that is
imaginative and satisfying in its own right, but such
a narrative framework provides so many facts and
understandings about the wider world (places,
events, processes) that we consider it a natural
choice for sharing information.

One of the first modern picture storybooks,
*Pelle's New Suit* by Elsa Beskow, came to this country from Sweden more than sixty years ago. This
story shows a little boy getting wool from his pet

*Attractive woodcut illustrations by David Frampton evoke the time and place of Carol Carrick's* Whaling Days.

Illustration from *Whaling Days* by Carol Carrick. Illustration copyright © 1993 by David Frampton. Reprinted by permission of Clarion Books/Houghton Mifflin Company. All rights reserved.

lamb, then having it carded, spun, dyed, woven, and finally taken to the tailor to be made into a new suit. Compare this classic with *"Charlie Needs a Cloak"* by Tomie de Paola, which also presents, as a story, basic information about making wool into cloth. The saga of Charlie's cloak is enhanced by humor, and the illustrations serve to emphasize the steps in the cloth-making process. Tomie de Paola was a leader in combining narrative, humor, and attractive pictures to make books that are both good stories and nonfiction resources.

Two beautiful picture books about the medieval period present nonfiction detail and the ambience of the times even more effectively in their illustrations than in the text. Joe Lasker's *Merry Ever After: The Story of Two Medieval Weddings* contrasts the world of the nobility with that of the peasants by focusing on two typical couples betrothed as children and married as teenagers. Readers must consult the pictures as well as the story to get the full description of the two lifestyles. Aliki's *A Medieval Feast* shows the nobility of a manor house and their serfs

preparing for a visit from the king and queen and their large entourage. A flurry of hunting, fishing, and harvesting is followed by scenes in the great kitchen and then the banquet presentation of such foods as a roast peacock reassembled with its feathers and a castle molded of pastry. Both of these picture books are standouts for their glowing, jewel-like colors and the use of decorative symbols and designs from the medieval period.

The most popular nonfiction picture books of recent years, and some of the most innovative, are the Magic School Bus stories by Joanna Cole and Bruce Degen. *The Magic School Bus Inside the Earth* was followed by other popular titles, including *The Magic School Bus in the Time of the Dinosaurs, The Magic School Bus on the Ocean Floor,* and *The Magic School Bus Inside a Hurricane.* All of these fantastic field trips are presided over by Ms. Frizzle, a memorable teacher, and endured by a group of children who develop recognizable personalities. Characterization, humor, and fantasy allow the creators of these books to approach science from a child's point of view, incorporating feelings ("Yuck," says one student participating in the digestive tract tour) as well as facts. Moreover, they bring all the information home, both literally and figuratively, to the classroom as each book ends.

Many nonfiction picture books for older readers tell good stories about places or things, although they might not have the central human characters that bring warmth to fiction. Books like David Macaulay's *Ship* and William Kurelek's *Lumberjack* are examples of this type. Nadia Wheatley and Donna Rawlin's *My Place* visits the same neighborhood in Australia back through many decades to a time before the Europeans arrived. On each double-page spread a new child narrator draws a map of the place and describes life in the neighborhood that is "my place." The book ends in 1788 as a child explains, "My name is Barangaroo. I belong to this place." Cultural, sociological, and environmental concepts in books like these are particularly good springboards for discussion with older children who have some prior knowledge of history and can explore similar issues in their own communities.

## Photographic Essays

With the increased use of photography in children's books today, the photo essay is an increasingly popular form. However, only some of the books that use photographs are photographic essays. Although the books by Dorothy Hinshaw Patent about various animal species (such as *Gray Wolf, Red Wolf*)

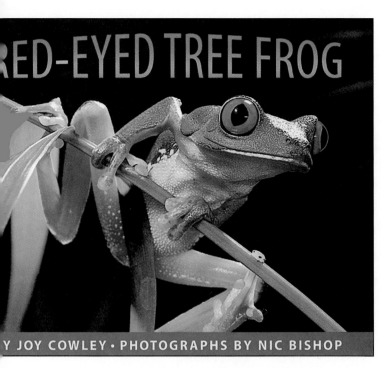

*Nic Bishop has provided amazingly vivid close-up photographs for Joy Cowley's* Red-Eyed Tree Frog.

Photograph by Nic Bishop from *Red-Eyed Tree Frog* by Joy Cowley. Published by the Blue Sky Press, an imprint of Scholastic Inc. Photograph copyright © 1999 by Nic Bishop. Reprinted by permission.

depend on photographs by William Muñoz on almost every page, they are not photographic essays. The essay relies on the camera in different ways: to particularize general information, to document emotion, to assure the reader of truth in an essentially journalistic fashion.

Sensitivity and vitality in the photographs make *Handtalk: An ABC of Finger Spelling and Sign Language* by Remy Charlip and Mary Beth Miller more than a specialized ABC book. Inspired by the language of the deaf, this is a unique volume about communication, made memorable by the expressive photo demonstrations of the language in action. This documentation of life in the language of the deaf is continued in *Handtalk Birthday* and *Handtalk School* by Miller and George Ancona. Ancona is also known for his carefully considered photographic essays in other books such as *Fiesta U.S.A.* and *Let's Dance!*

In Raymond Bial's many books about American cultures and history often gain entry to these cultures through physical structures, as in *Cajun Home* and *One Room School*. By focusing his camera on buildings and the everyday objects within, Bial illuminates much about the people who live or work there. In *One Good Apple: Growing Our Food for the Sake of the Earth* Catherine Paladino provides vivid evidence of the effects of pesticides on the environment and

lucid illustrations of the efforts people around the country are making to counteract those effects.

## Identification Books

In its simplest form, an identification book is a naming book, and this may well be the first sort of book that a very young child sees. *Tool Book* by Gail Gibbons shows simple drawings of common tools in bright colors, with appropriate labels. A phrase or two describes the common function of all the tools displayed on a double spread. This is information for the youngest child. But just as children grow in their ability to discriminate and classify, so do identification books become more detailed, precise, and complex. It is hard to imagine any book more thorough or more technically correct than Helen Roney Sattler's updated volume *The New Illustrated Dinosaur Dictionary*. Students who want to match dinosaur names with further description find plenty of help in this book.

When a child brings a stone or a leaf to school and asks, "What kind is it?" the teacher or librarian has a built-in opportunity to introduce books to help that child discover the answer. Millicent Selsam and Joyce Hunt's First Look At series is useful for teaching younger children how to examine a specimen and pick out the features that will be important in making an identification. The National Audubon Society and Scholastic have created a series of first field guides for children. Among those titles are *Rocks and Minerals* by Edward Riciutti and *Trees* by Brian Cassie.

## Life-Cycle Books

A fascination with animals is one of the most general and durable of children's interests, beginning very early and often continuing through adolescence into adulthood. There is always an audience for factual books that describe how animals live, with an emphasis on the inherent story element. These books cover all or some part of the cycle of life, from the birth of one animal to the birth of its progeny, or the events of one year in the animal's life, or the development of one animal throughout its lifetime. Gail Gibbons has written and illustrated two books that focus on the life cycle of birds, *Penguins!* and *Soaring with the Wind: The Bald Eagle.*

An account of authentic behavior often produces the effect of characterization; thus children frequently read nonfiction books as "stories" rather than as reference books. Holling C. Holling's beautifully illustrated classics *Minn of the Mississippi* and *Pagoo,* which trace the life histories of a turtle and a

*In* From Pictures to Words, *Janet Stevens carries on an imaginary dialogue with animal characters to show children how books are created.*
Copyright © 1995 by Janet Stevens. Reprinted from *From Pictures to Words* by permission of Holiday House.

crawfish, are unique survival stories. The longer life-cycle stories are often stories of survival against the elements and enemies in the environment.

Charles Micucci's attractively designed and thorough books about apples and bees are every bit as intriguing as these life-cycle stories about animals. *The Life and Times of the Apple* details the growth of apples, how they are cross-fertilized and grafted, and how they are harvested and marketed. Micucci also includes information about types of apples, their history, and the legend of Johnny Appleseed. *The Life and Times of the Peanut* and *The Life and Times of the Honeybee* are equally informative.

## Experiment and Activity Books

To some children the word *science* is synonymous with *experiment,* and certainly experience is basic to scientific understandings. Many basic nonfiction books suggest a few activities to clarify concepts; in contrast, experiment books take the activities themselves as content. The appearance of a supplementary experiment or activity, frequently as a final note in a book, is quite common today. For instance, Gail Gibbons includes numbered and illustrated directions for a project on raising bean plants at the end of her *From Seed to Plant,* for primary-age readers.

For very young children, experiments and directions for simple observation are usually presented in a picture-book context with illustrations that show interest and enjoyment as well as proper procedure. Seymour Simon's *Soap Bubble Magic,* illustrated by Stella Ormai, is a book of this kind. Many experiment books for older children also focus on one subject or one material. *The Science Book of Weather* and others by Neil Ardley are appropriate for grades 1 to 4. These books, British imports, are among the first to take advantage of full-color photography and high-artistry layouts in a book of directed experiments. Bernie Zubrowski's books, including *Shadow Play*

*Charles Micucci provides a detailed account in* The Life and Times of the Honeybee.

and *Wheels at Work,* are produced in conjunction with the Boston Children's Museum and emphasize children discovering their own results.

Some of the most engaging books of science experiments are those by Vicki Cobb. An interesting approach to chemistry is found in her *Science Experiments You Can Eat,* a book that is fun for children old enough to handle various cooking procedures safely. *Chemically Active! Experiments You Can Do at Home* is arranged so that one experiment leads directly to the next. All the books by Cobb are designed with a commentary to link the experiments so that they can be read straight through for information as well as used to guide the actual procedures.

Some books that suggest experiments also include experiences of other kinds, along with collections of interesting facts, anecdotes, or other material. These books that encourage children to explore a topic through a broad range of activities have gained popularity in recent years. *Good for Me! All About Food in 32 Bites* by Marilyn Burns is a compilation of facts, learning activities, experiments, and questions that can lead to further investigation. This is one of many titles from the Brown Paper School Books series, which consistently use this format.

Books like these make good browsing and are a source of possible projects for individual study or for activities that might be tried and discussed in class. Teachers as well as students appreciate the variety and creativity of the ideas. However, it is important

to remember that activity books are not designed for reference. There is seldom an index, and headings might have more entertainment value than clarity. For easy access to specific information, other types of books are required.

## Documents and Journals

A small but important contribution to literature for children in recent years has been the publication of books based on original documents and journals. Milton Meltzer uses letters and other primary sources in such fine books as *Voices from the Civil War.* Julius Lester's extraordinary *To Be a Slave,* a Newbery Honor Book in 1969, provides reproductions of primary sources as a background for the study of African American history. The author combines the verbatim testimony of former slaves with his own strong commentary:

> To be a slave was to be a human being under conditions in which that humanity was denied. They were not slaves. They were people. Their condition was slavery. (p. 28)

A more recent work that focuses on a broader sweep of history is *Now Is Your Time! The African American Struggle for Freedom* by Walter Dean Myers. Period photographs and reproductions of lists and documents are an important part of this compelling book.

Firsthand accounts are also the base for Jim Murphy's *The Boys' War: Confederate and Union Soldiers Talk About the Civil War*. On both sides, many soldiers were underage boys who had gone off to war looking for something more adventuresome than routine farm chores. The author quotes a Wisconsin boy who wrote of his experiences at Shiloh:

> I want to say, as we lay there and the shells were flying over us, my thoughts went back to my home, and I thought what a foolish boy I was to run away and get into such a mess as I was in. I would have been glad to have seen my father coming after me. (p. 33)

Books like this lend authenticity to the picture of conflict that students get in historical fiction such as Patricia Beatty's *Charley Skedaddle*.

Russell Freedman frequently uses photographs from archival sources to document his historical books as well as his biographies. *Immigrant Kids* includes reproductions of photos of passengers on the steerage deck of an immigrant liner in 1893, street scenes from New York City's Lower East Side in 1898, and school scenes. In *Kids at Work* he uses photographs by Lewis Hine, who worked to reform child labor laws in the United States in the early part of the twentieth century. *Children of the Wild West* furnishes photographs from a time and place where cameras were scarce. Children interested in the westward movement in the United States can study the pictures as well as the text of this book for information. Photos of families with their covered wagons clearly show modes of dress and meager possessions. Log cabins, sod houses, and schoolrooms can be compared and described. The pictures of Native American children in tribal dress and at government boarding schools are particularly interesting.

Laura Ingalls Wilder fans will be interested in *West from Home: Letters of Laura Ingalls Wilder, San Francisco 1915*. The letters were written to the author's husband while she was visiting her daughter Rose and attending the 1915 Panama Pacific International Exposition. The firsthand detail provides personal insights as well as a measure of the country during that year. There is similar documentary value in Wilder's *The First Four Years*, a journal-like account discovered as a handwritten manuscript among the author's posthumous papers. In this book, which tells of the first years of the Wilders' married life on a claim that had to be made into a farm, the reader can see the problems, the attitudes, and some of the philosophies of another time. Information presented without an intermediary is the unique contribution of documentary literature.

## Survey Books

The purpose of a survey book is to give an overall view of a substantial topic and to furnish a representative sampling of facts, principles, or issues. Such a book emphasizes balance and breadth of coverage, rather than depth.

Seymour Simon's fine books such as *Crocodiles and Alligators* are excellent examples of survey books that will entice children to learn more about animal subjects. Even the end papers are embossed with a pattern that mirrors crocodilian skin. *Raptors* by Bobbie Kalman offers a general introduction to raptors with information about physical characteristics, habitats, nesting habits, and survival techniques. Headings make information easy to find and there are many captioned close-up photographs. A child looking for in-depth information on a specific genus might need to go on to a sources such as Karen Dudley's *Alligators and Crocodiles* or *Bald Eagles*. The survey book furnishes an authoritative introduction to a topic but not necessarily all the information a student could want.

Philip M. Isaacson's *A Short Walk Around the Pyramid and Through the World of Art* is an enter-

*Seymour Simon chooses photographs that never fail to invite the reader's attention in such books as* Crocodiles and Alligators.

Jacket photograph © Tom McHugh/Photo Researchers, Inc. From *Crocodiles & Alligators* by Seymour Simon. Copyright © 1999, used by permission of HarperCollins Publishers.

taining and beautifully written introduction to the visual arts. Included along with painting and sculpture is information about the arts of photography and architecture and such useful things as furniture making and automobile design. This broad survey allows Isaacson to show how the elements of art can convey an emotional impact that enhances our visual experience no matter what the subject or the medium.

A few books attempt to give children a survey of the important people, places, and events in the history of the world. Hendrik Van Loon's *The Story of Mankind* was the first book to interpret world history to children in an interesting and nonfiction fashion. This book, a pioneer in the field and the winner of the first Newbery Medal, in 1922, is now available in a revised edition.

Historical surveys today are more likely to adopt a particular perspective, an "angle" on history that makes wide-ranging content more manageable. In *Food, Houses,* and *Clothing,* Italian artist Piero Ventura looks at history through these familiar lenses that also convey concepts about basic human needs. A similarly successful book for older readers is Suzanne Jurmain's *Once Upon a Horse: A History of Horses—and How They Shaped Our History.* Horse lovers and history browsers alike will find many leads to follow in this lively narrative.

Survey books are available at many different levels of complexity and reading difficulty. A teacher or librarian may need to help children skim to find those that are most appropriate for their use.

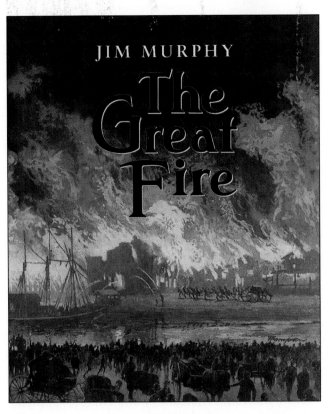

In The Great Fire, *Jim Murphy's exhaustive research and his lively writing style engage the reader in an exciting account of the 1871 Chicago fire.*

Cover illustration by John Thompson from *The Great Fire* by Jim Murphy. Illustration copyright © 1995 by John Thompson. Reprinted by permission of Scholastic Inc.

## Specialized Books

Specialized books are designed to give specific information about a relatively limited topic. These books satisfy particular interests; they are more likely to be used intensively than extensively, on a onetime basis rather than as a frequent reference. James Giblin's many books such as *When Plague Strikes, The Truth About Unicorns,* and *The Mystery of the Mammoth Bones* illustrate how thorough research and good writing can illuminate the most mundane of topics. With their vivid language and highly involving organization, Jim Murphy's books read like suspense novels and are every bit as hard to put down. *Gone A-Whaling* is a history of the whaling industry that focuses on the young boys who signed aboard the whalers. Murphy's other specialized books include *Across America on an Emigrant Train,* the story of Robert Louis Stevenson's trip across the continent in 1879, and *The Great Fire,* about the Chicago fire of 1871.

Many specialized books provide extensions of content areas that are frequently part of the elementary social studies curriculum. Jerry Stanley's *Children of the Dust Bowl* tells how educator Leo Hart started a special school for children of migrant workers who had come to California from drought-stricken Oklahoma in the 1930s. The book also provides information about the climatic and the economic changes that caused this great migration. Howard Greenfeld's *The Hidden Children* details the efforts of the many brave people who risked their lives to hide Jewish children from the Nazis.

Many specialized books are geared to the personal interests of children. There is certainly something about mud that attracts many children. Jennifer Owings Dewey has thoroughly investigated the topic in *Mud Matters.* Dewey's own illustrations and photographs by Stephen Trimble highlight the coverage of such topics as "Ritual Mud," "Building Mud," "Magic Mud," and the "Mud Between Your Toes." *Money Money Money* by Nancy Winslow Parker provides fascinating details about the art and symbols on U.S. currency and will have budding financiers taking a second and third look in their wallets.

Teachers and librarians have noted that specialized books today are more specialized than ever, covering narrow topics and unique interests. These books can be of high quality and of great appeal to children, but they might not be discovered on the library shelf unless they are introduced. Readers do not deliberately seek a book on a topic that they do not know exists. For that reason, an adult might need to make a special effort to point out these special books.

## Craft and How-To Books

A fascinating array of craft and activity books give directions for making and doing. Bobbe Needham's *Ecology Crafts for Kids: 50 Great Ways to Make Friends with Planet Earth* offers directions for more than fifty projects all made from recycled materials and information about environmental issues as well. Janis Herbert's *Leonardo Da Vinci for Kids: His Life and Ideas* is part biography and part activity book. The suggested projects include active ones like making a catapult or a map, and cooking Leonardo's favorite minestrone soup, and more cerebral ones like memory exercises.

Clear directions are usually clearer if appropriately illustrated. *The Children's Book of Yoga* by Thia Luby provides clear photographs demonstrating various yoga positions and includes pictures of animals, plants, and objects that children can imitate in their poses. *Painting Faces* by Suzanne Haldane shows children applying face paint according to different traditions around the globe. Some of the color photographs are sequentially arranged, so that would-be face painters can easily see what areas of paint should be applied first, as well as what the finished product should look like. Line drawings make appropriate pictures to demonstrate the steps in *How to Make Pop-Ups* and *How to Make Super Pop-Ups* by Joan Irvine. This book has a high success rate with students; they are able to make quite complex-looking paper designs in three dimensions with a minimum of adult help. Older readers who have been captivated by the Irvine books will find that *The Elements of Pop-Up* by David A. Carter and James Diaz provides more advanced activities and does this by showing actual pop-up and pull-tab forms.

Some craft books deal so specifically with approaches and techniques common to the activity-centered classroom that it is likely they will be used as much by teachers as by individual children. Helen Roney Sattler's *Recipes for Art and Craft Materials* will prove indispensable to teachers. Included are recipes for a variety of basic substances that children can make for their own use—such as paste, modeling and casting compounds, papier-mâché, inks, and dried-flower preservatives.

Cookbooks for children ought to have sparkling, clear directions and adequate warnings about the safe use of tools and equipment. A popular character who has inspired a cookbook is Peter Rabbit. *The Peter Rabbit and Friends Cookbooks* offers recipes and vi-

gnettes from Beatrix Potter's popular books. Another literature-based recipe collection is Barbara Walker's *The Little House Cookbook: Frontier Foods from Laura Ingalls Wilder's Classic Stories.*

## Using Literature Across the Curriculum

One of the important components of a literature program (see Chapter 13) is using literature across the curriculum. If children are to become real readers, they should meet good books, not only at reading time, but also as they study history, science, the arts—all subject areas. Outstanding nonfiction books, those that might qualify as what author John McPhee calls "the literature of fact," are the most obvious places to begin in choosing titles to use in the content areas.

### Nonfiction Books in the Classroom

Like books of any other genre, the best nonfiction books should be appreciated for their artistry. Good writing, fine illustration, and high-quality bookmaking all have intrinsic aesthetic value. And like fiction, nonfiction books can provide satisfaction and delight for interested readers. Nonfiction books are a bit different, however. They also fulfill special teaching functions that need to be considered in planning classroom materials and activities.

The information in trade books is a major content resource for the curriculum. Elementary school textbooks are frequently overgeneralized or oversimplified in the attempt to keep them reasonably short and readable. A selection of nonfiction books can provide the depth and richness of detail not possible in textbook coverage of the same topic. The latest nonfiction books are also likely to be more up-to-date than textbooks, since the process of producing and choosing textbooks can take many months or even years. The adopted series then might not be revised, or replaced, for quite some time. However, new trade books on popular or timely topics appear every year.

Many teachers would use an up-to-date nonfiction book like Dorothy Hinshaw Patent's *Shaping the Earth* to supplement the science textbook. Others might completely bypass the textbook and assemble many books about space and the solar system (probably including such titles as Seymour Simon's *Comets, Meters, and Asteroids* and Patricia Lauber's *Journey to the Planets*) to provide information much richer than the text could offer.

The availability of several nonfiction books on a single topic is important for teachers to consider because

# *Helping Children Evaluate Nonfiction Books*

**Teaching Feature**

When Rebecca Thomas, a school librarian in Shaker Heights, Ohio, introduced *Storms* by Seymour Simon to a group of fourth graders, she covered up most of the front jacket. With only the title visible, she asked them to think what might be included in a book about storms. Their first response was to name the kinds of storms they knew—thunderstorms, snowstorms, tornadoes, and hurricanes. They also suggested other topics that could be in such a book: winds, thunder and lightning, the damage storms can cause, and how scientists know about storms. They decided that a book about storms should be illustrated with high-quality photographs that really picture storms and their actions.

With the librarian's help, they then began to develop some questions they would use to decide if the book was a good one:

Does the book cover the subject?

How good are the pictures?

Who will be able to understand the book?

How much actual information is included?

Does it set information straight (correct mistaken ideas)?

By the time this brief discussion was finished, the children were eager to see if Seymour Simon's book met their expectations, and of course they registered immediate approval when she showed them the front jacket. As she read aloud, she encouraged students to note whether their questions had been answered. She stopped frequently so they could discuss particular pictures and the clarity of the writing based on their question "Who will be able to understand the book?"

These students used the criteria they had developed in question form to measure the success not only of *Storms* but also of other titles on the same topic as they completed a classroom unit on weather. The librarian's introduction engaged the children's interest in one book as it set the stage for their reading of other nonfiction titles. Helping children focus on the possibilities and strengths of specific books encourages them to develop understandings about genre and the broader world of literature.

*Rebecca Thomas, Librarian*
Fernway School, Shaker Heights, Ohio

---

this presents ready-made opportunities to encourage critical reading. When children's information all comes from one source, they are likely to accept the author's selection and interpretation of facts without question. The use of two or more books provides a built-in comparison. Bruce Brooks's *Making Sense: Animal Perception and Communication* and Margery Facklam's *Bees Dance and Whales Sing: The Mysteries of Animal Communication* are both fine books, with some differences in coverage and emphasis. Encouraging children to ask themselves questions about these differences helps them make practical and critical judgments about what they are reading.

At the prereading level, children can compare books read aloud by the teacher, look critically at the illustrations, and decide which ones give them needed information. A kindergarten teacher who shared several books about tools with her children asked them to decide which book's pictures did the best job of showing how the tools worked. To check their judgment, they took turns at the classroom workbench, and under adult supervision, tried out the tools.

Most teachers or librarians who encourage the critical comparison of books find that helping children construct a chart of similarities and differences is an aid to clear thinking. As older children are introduced to techniques of inquiry, such as using a table of contents, finding information in indexes, and conducting a library search, they can also be encouraged to develop a list of criteria that they would apply to nonfiction books. Such activities help children become more critical readers of nonfiction books and more careful writers of their own materials. The Teaching Feature "Helping Children Evaluate Nonfiction Books" shows how a school librarian and a group of fourth graders developed a list of questions that helped them evaluate nonfiction books.

Authors of fine nonfiction books approach their material in interesting ways that can easily be adapted for the classroom. Although it's more usual to find good books that support a lesson, it's also possible for a good book to suggest a lesson or an entire unit of study. The Web "The World Beneath Your Feet" on pages 526–527, aimed at middle-graders, was developed around the book *Hidden Under the Ground: The World Beneath Your Feet* by Peter Kent. It was planned in keeping with the National Science Education Standards, particularly those

**Buried Beneath Your Feet**
*Graveyards of the Dinosaurs* (Tanaka)
*Mummies Made in Egypt* (Aliki)
*Bodies from the Bog* (Deem)
*Tales Mummies Tell* (Lauber)
*Mummies, Tombs, and Treasure* (Perl)
*Mummy* (Putnam)
*Secrets of the Mummies* (Tanaka)
*Corpses, Coffins and Crypts* (Colman)
*Mummies Unwrapped* (VHS, National
   Geographic)
*At the Tomb of Tutankhamen* (www)
Do all cultures bury their dead?
How are bodies preserved? What natural
   conditions affect the preservation of bodies?

**Under The Ice**
*Discovering the Inca Ice Maiden* (Reinhard)
*Frozen Girl* (Getz)
*Frozen Man* (Getz)
*Secrets of the Ice Man* (Patent)
*Discovering the Ice Man* (Tanaka)
What conditions preserved the bodies in bogs
   and ice? How do scientists study them?
   What can they nd out by studying them?

**Rocks and Fossils**
*Everybody Needs a Rock* (Baylor)
*If You find a Rock* (Christian)
Make up rules for owning a rock.
Find a special rock and sketch it.
Write a description.
Can others nd your rock by reading
   your description?
Find poems about rocks and create a display.
   Write a poem about your rock.

*Stories in Stone: The World of Animal Fossils*
   (Kittinger)
*Fossils and Bones* (Pirotta)
*Digging Up Dinosaurs* (Aliki)
*Fossils Tell of Long Ago* (Aliki)
*Fossil* (Taylor)
Where are fossils found? How are they formed?

*A Look at Rocks: From Coal to Kimberlite*
   (Kittinger)
*A Look at Minerals: From Galena to Gold*
   (Kittinger)
*Rocks and Minerals* (Oldershaw; Parker; Riciutti;
   Symes)
In small groups, study different non ction books
   on the same topic. List your criteria. Meet
   with members of other groups and present
   an award to the best book.

*Smithsonian Gem and Mineral Collection* (www)
Where are the oldest rocks found? What type
   are they?
Study classi cations of rocks.
Make your own collection and create a rock
   museum.

**DIGGING BENEATH THE SURFACE**

**THE WORLD BENEATH YOUR FEET:
A WEB OF POSSIBILITIES**

**What's Under the Surface?**
*Under the Ground* (Delafosse)
*Our Patchwork Planet: The Story of Plate
   Tectonics* (Sattler)
*Planet Earth: Inside Out* (Gibbons)
*Great Archeological Sites* (www)
How is the earth constructed?
Name the earth s layers.

*How to Dig a Hole to the Other Side of the World*
   (McNulty)
*The Magic School Bus Inside the Earth* (Cole)
Read these two books. What is fact and what is
   fantasy in each? How do the authors
   separate the two?

*Great Archeological Sites* (www)
What types of scientists study things beneath
   the surface? Interview an archeologist,
   paleontologist, geologist, etc.

**Movement Beneath Your Feet**
*On Shifting Ground* (Kidd)
*Geysers: When the Earth Roars* (Gallant)
*How Mountains Are Made* (Zoehfeld)
*Earth, Making of a Shifting Planet* (Gallant)
*Earthquakes* (Branley; George; Morris; Pope;
   Simon)
*National Earthquake Information Center* (www)
*Volcanoes* (Branley; Morris; Simon; Sipiera)
*Volcano* (VHS, National Geographic)
*Volcano World* (www)
What different conditions cause earthquakes,
   geysers, and volcanoes? What do they have
   in common?

Make a map of the world showing current
   volcanic and earthquake activity.

526

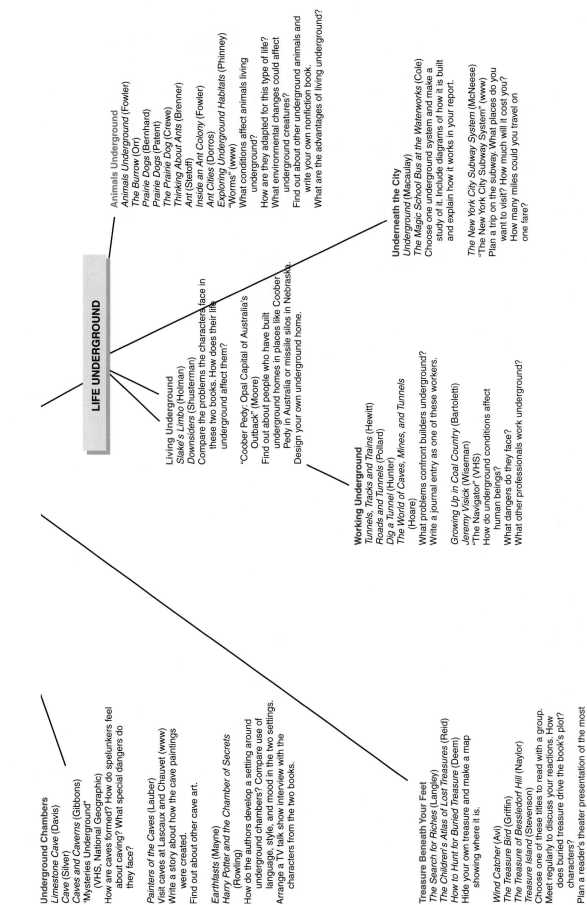

**LIFE UNDERGROUND**

**Animals Underground**
Animals Underground (Fowler)
The Burrow (Orr)
Prairie Dogs (Bernhard)
Prairie Dogs (Patent)
The Prairie Dog (Crewe)
Thinking About Ants (Brenner)
Ant (Stetoff)
Inside an Ant Colony (Fowler)
Ant Cities (Dorros)
Exploring Underground Habitats (Phinney)
"Worms" (www)
What conditions affect animals living underground?
How are they adapted for this type of life?
What environmental changes could affect underground creatures?
Find out about other underground animals and write your own nonfiction book.
What are the advantages of living underground?

**Underneath the City**
Underground (Macaulay)
The Magic School Bus at the Waterworks (Cole)
Choose one underground system and make a study of it. Include diagrams of how it is built and explain how it works in your report.
The New York City Subway System (McNeese)
"The New York City Subway System" (www)
Plan a trip on the subway. What places do you want to visit? How much will it cost you? How many miles could you travel on one fare?

**Living Underground**
Slake's Limbo (Holman)
Downsiders (Shusterman)
Compare the problems the characters face in these two books. How does their life underground affect them?
"Coober Pedy: Opal Capital of Australia's Outback" (Moore)
Find out about people who have built underground homes in places like Coober Pedy in Australia or missile silos in Nebraska. Design your own underground home.

**Working Underground**
Tunnels, Tracks and Trains (Hewitt)
Roads and Tunnels (Pollard)
Dig a Tunnel (Hunter)
The World of Caves, Mines, and Tunnels (Hoare)
What problems confront builders underground? Write a journal entry as one of these workers.
Growing Up in Coal Country (Bartoletti)
Jeremy Visick (Wiseman)
"The Navigator" (VHS)
How do underground conditions affect human beings?
What dangers do they face?
What other professionals work underground?

**Underground Chambers**
Limestone Cave (Davis)
Cave (Silver)
Caves and Caverns (Gibbons)
"Mysteries Underground" (VHS, National Geographic)
How are caves formed? How do spelunkers feel about caving? What special dangers do they face?
Painters of the Caves (Lauber)
Visit caves at Lascaux and Chauvet (www)
Write a story about how the cave paintings were created.
Find out about other cave art.
Earthfasts (Mayne)
Harry Potter and the Chamber of Secrets (Rowling)
How do the authors develop a setting around underground chambers? Compare use of language, style, and mood in the two settings.
Arrange a TV talk show interview with the characters from the two books.

**Treasure Beneath Your Feet**
The Search for Riches (Langley)
The Children's Atlas of Lost Treasures (Reid)
How to Hunt for Buried Treasure (Deem)
Hide your own treasure and make a map showing where it is.
Wind Catcher (Avi)
The Treasure Bird (Griffin)
The Treasure of Bessledorf Hill (Naylor)
Treasure Island (Stevenson)
Choose one of these titles to read with a group. Meet regularly to discuss your reactions. How does buried treasure drive the book's plot? characters?
Plan a reader's theater presentation of the most exciting part.
Buried Blueprints, Maps and Sketches of Lost Worlds and Mysterious Places (Lorenz)
Make a map of one of the settings in the novels.

Tigers swim to get out of the heat.

*Linda Capus Riley's* Elephants Swim, *with collages by Steve Jenkins, introduces young children to concepts about animal behavior.*

Illustration by Steve Jenkins from *Elephants Swim* by Linda Capus Riley. Illustration copyright © 1995 by Steve Jenkins. Reprinted by permission of Houghton Mifflin Company. All rights reserved.

for critical thinking and inquiry. The Web shows how standards might be covered using good nonfiction and also demonstrates how fiction and nonfiction could be connected.

A unit on "Family History" might begin with Lila Perl's *The Great Ancestor Hunt,* which offers good suggestions for collecting family folklore at holiday get-togethers as well as tips for using public records. Investigations begun with Perl's book could be extended through books like David Weitzman's *My Backyard History Book* and lead to a class study of "Immigration" or "Difficult Journeys."

For young children, concept books often lead to ideas for good classification activities. Linda Riley's *Elephants Swim,* with its attractive collages by Steve Jenkins, presents information about animal behavior in water. Children are introduced to words like *paddle, wade, glide, dive,* and *plunge* and to the concept that, unlike humans, many animals take naturally to water. The format of the book invites children to extend their understanding of animal behavior in other environments. Other concept books, such as Hana Machotka's *Outstanding Outsides* or Sandra Markle's *Inside and Outside Spiders,* present excel-

lent opportunities for developing spatial relationships as well as for exploring structures of animal bodies.

Regardless of the topic to be studied, teachers might need to consider common purposes and the functions of nonfiction books so that their choices will represent a wide range of possibilities. The following checklist can be used as a reminder of what to look for:

- Books to attract attention to the topic
- Books for browsing and exploring content
- Books with read-aloud possibilities
- Books for independent reading at varying levels of difficulty
- Basic reference books
- Books with enough information for in-depth study
- Books with a limited focus for very specific interests
- Books to guide activities and experiments
- Books that can be readily compared
- Books that introduce new perspectives or connections
- Books to accommodate new and extended interests

A selection of quality nonfiction books representing these categories supports children's growth in reading and appreciation for good writing as well as their development of understandings within the content area.

## Integrating Fact and Fiction

Using literature across the curriculum can begin with nonfiction books, but it certainly does not have to end there. Many picture books, poems, traditional stories, novels, and biographies are natural choices for extending children's interest or knowledge base in a subject area. However, literature should never be distorted to fulfill the purposes of a lesson. One student participant from a university read Taro Yashima's *Crow Boy* to a class of 9- and 10-year-olds. When she finished the book she told the children that the story took place in Japan and asked them if they knew where Japan was. There was a mad dash for the globe to see who could be the first to locate Japan. Then the participant went on to ask what Japan was, finally eliciting the answer she wanted—"an island." Next she asked what appeared to be a very unrelated question: "Why did Chibi have a rice ball wrapped in a radish leaf for his lunch instead of a hamburger?" The children were baffled. Finally, the participant gave them a brief but erroneous geography lesson in which she told them that because Japan was an island, it was very wet and flat, so the Japanese people could only raise rice, not beef for hamburgers! The student's university supervisor finally stepped in to save the day by helping the children talk about the real strengths of the book, Chibi's loneliness and the artist's use of space and visual symbols.

Scholar Louise Rosenblatt[13] warns against this way of "using" fiction, saying that teachers have a responsibility not to confuse children about the predominant stance or attitude appropriate for a particular reading purpose. The purpose we most want to encourage for works of *fiction* is reading for pleasure and insight (what Rosenblatt calls "aesthetic" reading). The carrying away of factual material ("efferent" reading) is more properly used in reading nonfiction books, although certainly pleasure and insight are also important outcomes of reading nonfiction.

---

[13]Louise Rosenblatt, "Literature—S.O.S.!" *Language Arts* 68 (October 1991): 444–448.

Using literature across the curriculum does not mean forcing connections between fact and fiction, as the student in our example attempted to do. Nor does it mean reading a nature poem for literal information about a bird's habitat or using sentences from a favorite story as the basis for language drill or diagramming sentences. It does mean recognizing that some pieces of literature have a strong background of fact and provide a unique human perspective on historical, scientific, and technological subjects. Works like Jean George's *Julie,* Lois Lowry's *Number the Stars,* and Eve Bunting's *Dandelions* give readers a perspective that allows them to know facts in another way. It is especially important for children to confirm what they are learning from nonfiction sources by meeting similar ideas in the more human frame of fiction.

Pulling together fiction and nonfiction selections that work well together is an ongoing process for most teachers. A record of titles should be kept so that these books can be shelved or displayed together when appropriate. A few sample groupings are shown in the Resources for Teaching box "Fact and Fiction" (see p. 530).

Combining fact and fiction resources on a large scale can lead to the creation of an integrated theme unit encompassing learning in many subjects. As in The World Beneath Your Feet example on pages 526–527 the focus topic might be taken from the sciences, or it might begin with history or social studies (colonial life or houses), or language and the arts (signs and symbols). The topic must be broad enough to allow students to develop in many skill areas as they work through a wide range of interrelated content, using trade books and other materials. Textbooks are used as reference resources, if at all. This challenging but satisfying way of teaching requires a thorough knowledge of children's literature. (See Chapter 13 for more information about planning units of study.)

Fine nonfiction books and related books of fiction are important to the curriculum whether they serve as the major resource or as supplements to formal instructional materials. Enthusiastic teachers who have learned to recognize the best and to choose wisely for a variety of purposes will put children in touch with an exciting and satisfying way to learn.

# RESOURCES FOR TEACHING

## Fact and Fiction: Books to Use Together

### EGGS (GRADES K–2)

*Egg* (Burton) Nonfiction

*A Nestful of Eggs* (Jenkins) Nonfiction

*The Talking Eggs* (San Souci) Traditional

*Chicken Man* (Edwards) Picture Book

*Hilda Hen's Search* (Wormell) Picture Book

*The Extraordinary Egg* (Lionni) Picture Book

*Just Plain Fancy* (Polacco) Picture Book

*When Chickens Grow Teeth* (DeMaupasant) Picture Book

*Cook-a-Doodle-Doo!* (Stevens) Picture Book

*Big Fat Hen* (Baker) Counting Book

### BUGS (GRADES 2–3)

*Bugs* (Parker and Wright) Nonfiction

*Ladybug* (Bernhard) Nonfiction

*Monarch Butterfly* (Gibbons) Nonfiction

*The Big Bug Book* (Facklam) Nonfiction

*Flit, Flutter, Fly* (Hopkins) Poetry

*Joyful Noise* (Fleischman) Poetry

*Little Buggers* (Lewis) Poetry

*Bugs!* (Greenberg) Poetry

*James and the Giant Peach* (Dahl) Fantasy

### WET WEATHER (GRADES 1–3)

*Down Comes the Rain* (Branley) Nonfiction

*The Science Book of Weather* (Ardley) Nonfiction

*A Rainy Day* (Markle) Nonfiction

*Flash, Crash, Rumble and Roll* (Branley) Nonfiction

*Thunderstorms* (Sipiera) Nonfiction

*Storms* (Simon) Nonfiction

*The Tree That Rains* (Bernhard) Traditional

*The Magic Bean Tree* (Van Laan) Traditional

*Come a Tide* (Lyon) Picture Book

*Peter Spier's Rain* (Spier) Picture Book

*Hurricane!* (London) Picture Book

*Twister* (Beard) Picture Book

*In the Rain with Baby Duck* (Hest) Picture Book

*Where Does the Butterfly Go When It Rains?* (Garelick) Picture Book

*Rain Talk* (Serfozo) Picture Book

### NATIVE AMERICANS ON THE PLAINS (GRADES 3–5)

*An Indian Winter* (Freedman) Nonfiction

*Indian Chiefs* (Freedman) Nonfiction

*Children of the Wild West* (Freedman) Nonfiction

*. . . If You Lived with the Sioux Indians* (McGovern) Nonfiction

*Buffalo Hunt* (Freedman) Nonfiction

*Follow the Stars* (Rodanas)Traditional

*Iktomi and the Boulder* (Goble) Traditional

*Shingebiss, An Ojibwe Legend* (Van Laan) Traditional

*Sootface: An Ojibwa Cinderella* (San Souci) Traditional

*Dancing with the Indians* (Medearis) Picture Book

*The Birchbark House* (Erdrich) Historical Fiction

### ONCE UPON THE PRAIRIE (GRADES 3–6)

*Sod Houses on the Prairie* (Rounds) Nonfiction

*Fossil Feud* (Holmes) Nonfiction

*Children of the Wild West* (Freedman) Nonfiction

*Pioneer Girl: Growing Up on the Prairie* (Warren) Biography

*Dandelions* (Bunting) Picture Book

*Dakota Dugout* (Turner) Picture Book

*Three Names* (MacLachlan) Picture Book

*My Prairie Christmas* (Harvey) Picture Book

*Sarah, Plain and Tall* (MacLachlan) Historical Fiction

*Prairie Willow* (Trottier) Picture Book

*Prairie Songs* (Conrad) Historical Fiction

*My Daniel* (Conrad) Historical Fiction

*Calling Me Home* (Hermes) Historical Fiction

# RESOURCES FOR TEACHING

## Fact and Fiction: Books to Use Together con't

### SLAVERY AND FREEDOM (GRADES 4–6)

*Escape from Slavery* (Rappaport) Nonfiction

*To Be a Slave* (Lester) Nonfiction

*Christmas in the Big House, Christmas in the Quarters* (McKissack) Nonfiction

*Amistad Rising: The Story of Freedom* (Chambers) Nonfiction

*From Slave Ship to Freedom Road* (Lester) Nonfiction

*Lincoln: A Photobiography* (Freedman) Biography

*Harriet Beecher Stowe and the Beecher Preachers* (Fritz) Biography

*Anthony Burns: The Defeat and Triumph of a Fugitive Slave* (Hamilton) Biography

*Nettie's Trip South* (Turner) Picture Book

*The Middle Passage* (Feelings) Picture Book

*Sky Sash So Blue* (Hawthorne) Picture Book

*In the Time of the Drums* (Siegelson) Picture Book

*Pink and Say* (Polacco) Picture Book

*The Captive* (Hansen) Historical Fiction

*Steal Away Home* (Ruby) Historical Fiction

*Lessons from a Slave Girl* (Lyons) Historical Fiction

*Jip: His Story* (Paterson) Historical Fiction

*I Thought My Soul Would Rise and Fly* (Hansen) Historical Fiction

*Sarny* (Paulsen) Historical Fiction

*Steal Away Home* (Carbonne) Historical Fiction

*NightJohn* (Paulsen) Historical Fiction

*Silent Thunder* (Pinkney) Historical Fiction

*Jayhawker* (Beatty) Historical Fiction

*With Every Drop of Blood* (Collier and Collier) Historical Fiction

*Forty Acres and Maybe a Mule* (Robinett) Historical Fiction

*North by Night: A Story of the Underground Railroad* (Ayres) Historical Fiction

*Ajeemah and His Son* (Berry) Historical Fiction

*The House of Dies Drear* (Hamilton) Fiction

*I, Too Sing America: Three Centuries of African American Poetry* (Clinton) Poetry

### DIFFICULT JOURNEYS (GRADES 5–8)

**World War II, Asian American**

*I Am an American* (Stanley) Nonfiction

*The Journey* (Hamanaka) Picture Book

*Baseball Saved Us* (Mochizuki) Picture Book

*The Bracelet* (Uchida) Picture Book

*Journey to Topaz* (Uchida) Historical Fiction

*Under the Blood-Red Sun* (Salisbury) Historical Fiction

**World War II, Europe and Asia**

*The Hidden Children* (Greenfeld) Nonfiction

*Rescue* (Meltzer) Nonfiction

*One More Border: The True Story of One Family's Escape from War-Torn Europe* (Kaplan) Nonfiction

*No Pretty Picture: A Child of War* (Lobel) Memoir

*Rose Blanche* (Gallaz and Innocenti) Picture Book

*The Lily Cupboard* (Oppenheim) Picture Book

*Number the Stars* (Lowry) Historical Fiction

*The Man from the Other Side* (Orlev) Historical Fiction

*Greater Than Angels* (Matas) Historical Fiction

*My Freedom Trip* (Park) Historical Fiction

*The Endless Steppe* (Hautzig) Historical Fiction

*Year of Impossible Goodbyes* (Choi) Historical Fiction

*So Far from the Bamboo Grove* (Watkins) Historical Fiction

*War and the Pity of War* (Philip) Poetry

**Modern-Day Refugees**

*A Haitian Family* (Greenberg) Nonfiction

*A Nicaraguan Family* (Malaone) Nonfiction

*The Lost Boys of Natinga: A School for Sudan's Young Refugees* (Walgren) Nonfiction

*On the Wings of Eagles: An Ethiopian Boy's Story* (Schrier) Picture Book

*How Many Days to America?* (Bunting) Picture Book

*My Name Is Marie Isabel* (Ada) Fiction

*Kiss the Dust* (Laird) Fiction

*Tonight, by Sea* (Temple) Fiction

*Grab Hands and Run* (Temple) Fiction

*Goodbye Vietnam* (Whelan) Fiction

*The Frozen Waterfall* (Hiçyilmaz) Fiction

## INTO THE CLASSROOM

### Nonfiction Books

**Room 201**

1. Talk to a group of children to find what special interests or hobbies they have. Make a survey of nonfiction to see what nonfiction books might enrich these interests. Plan a display of some of these books for a classroom or library interest center.
2. Working with one child or a small group of children, select a craft or activity book that seems suited to their age level. Watch carefully as children follow the directions given. What difficulties do they have? What questions do they ask? Could you make the directions clearer, safer, or more imaginative?
3. Work with a group of children in writing a nonfiction book modeled after one of the documentary accounts or a photo essay using their own snapshots. What kinds of research and choices are involved in following the form?

## Personal Explorations

1. Select several nonfiction books on one topic—such as ecology, the solar system, or China. Evaluate them, using the criteria in this chapter. Plan activity cards or questions that would interest children in the books and help them use the books more effectively.
2. Working with a small group of your peers, locate nonfiction books published within a single year. Review and discuss these to select one or more "award winners." What criteria would you use? What categories would you establish? What issues arise as you discuss what makes a high-quality nonfiction book?
3. Choose one nonfiction book with potential for interconnections in many subject areas, such as Aliki's *Mummies Made in Egypt*. Plan questions and activities; choose other literature to help children explore some related topics, such as building the pyramids, writing with hieroglyphics, using preservatives, or the art of ancient Egypt.
4. Develop and use with children a learning activity that will encourage critical reading of nonfiction books. Focus on identifying authors' points of view, comparing authenticity of sources, verifying facts, and the like.
5. Begin a file of book combinations that could be used in science, social studies, the arts, or language study. Consider the different perspectives that children will draw from each.

## Related Readings

Bamford, Rosemary, and Janice Kristo, eds. *Making Facts Come Alive: Choosing Quality Nonfiction for Children.* (Norwood, Mass.: Christopher Gordon, 1998.)

A fine collection of essays about nonfiction books. Chapters provide an overview of types of nonfiction as well as information about integrating nonfiction books across the curriculum.

Freeman, Evelyn B., and Diane Goetz Person. *Using Nonfiction Trade Books in the Elementary Classroom.* Urbana, Ill.: National Council of Teachers of English, 1992.

This collection of essays includes a section by authorities such as Russell Freedman and James Cross Giblin that extends understandings about trends and issues in nonfiction books. Subsequent chapters provide many practical suggestions for integrating nonfiction books throughout the curriculum in primary through middle school classrooms.

Graves, Donald H. *Investigate Nonfiction.* Portsmouth, N.H.: Heinemann, 1989.

Through its insights into children's efforts to create nonfiction, this slim volume provides new ways of thinking about and teaching about the genre.

Harvey, Stephanie. *Nonfiction Matters: Reading, Writing, and Research in Grades 3–8*. York, ME: Stenhouse, 1998.

An excellent book about using nonfiction to develop inquiry projects. In addition to useful information about nonfiction books, the author includes sections on choosing topics, making observations and collecting information, and finding different ways of presenting the results of the inquiry. Appendixes include forms and facsimiles as well as selected nonfiction titles on various topics.

Kobrin, Beverly. *Eyeopeners II: Children's Books to Answer Children's Questions About the World Around Them*. New York: Viking, 1995.

Enthusiastic and practical, this review of more than five hundred nonfiction books offers teaching tips for "parents, grandparents, and other educators." The emphasis on linking specific books and activities and an easy-to-read format combine to make a handy classroom reference.

Pappas, Christine C., Barbara Z. Kiefer, and Linda S. Levstik. *An Integrated Language Perspective in the Elementary School: Theory into Action*. 2nd ed. White Plains, N.Y.: Longman, 1992.

The approaches described in this comprehensive text show literature as one of the aspects of language to be integrated throughout the content areas. The specific examples of teaching strategies and of solving problems of classroom logistics are especially helpful.

http://www.ala.org/parentspage/greatsites/amazing.html
General listing of recommended sites
http://www.culture.gouv.fr/culture/arcnat/en/
Great archeological sites
http://www.nationalgeographic.com/kids/
National Geographic
http://www.nationalgeographic.com/egypt/
At the tomb of Tutankhamen
http://galaxy.einet.net/images/gems/gems-icons.html   Smithsonian
http://volcano.und.nodak.edu/   Volcano World
http://www.primordialsoup.com/   Primordial Soup
http://www.nycsubway.org/   New York City Subway
http://www.nj.com/yucky/worm/   Worm World
http://www.neic.cr.usgs.gov/neis/eqlists/10maps.html
National Earth Quake Information Center

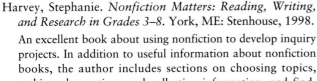

# Children's Literature

## Nonfiction Books

Aliki [Aliki Brandenberg]. *Digging Up Dinosaurs*. Crowell, 1988.
———. *Fossils Tell of Long Ago*. HarperCollins, 1990.
———. *A Medieval Feast*. Crowell, 1983.
———. *Mummies Made in Egypt*. Crowell, 1979.
Ancona, George. *Fiesta U.S.A.* Lodestar, 1995.
———. *Let's Dance!* Morrow, 1998.
Apfel, Necia H. *Orion, the Hunter*. Clarion, 1995.
Ardley, Neil. *The Science Book of Weather*. Gulliver/Harcourt Brace, 1992.
Armstrong, Jennifer. *Shipwreck at the Bottom of the Worlds: The Extraordinary True Story of Shakleton and the Endurance*. Crown, 1988.
Arnold, Caroline. *Dinosaurs Down Under: And Other Fossils from Australia*. Photographs by Richard Hewett. Clarion, 1990.
———. *El Nino: Stormy Weather for People and Wildlife*. Clarion, 1998.
Arnosky, Jim. *All About Owls*. Scholastic, 1995.
———. *All About Turtles*. Scholastic, 2000.
Barton, Byron. *Bones, Bones, Dinosaur Bones*. HarperCollins, 1990.
———. *I Want to Be an Astronaut*. Crowell, 1988.
Bash, Barbara. *Ancient Ones: The World of the Old-Growth Douglas Fir*. Sierra Club, 1994.
Bernhard, Emery. *Prairie Dogs*. Illustrated by Durga Bernhard. Harcourt Brace, 1997.
Bial, Raymond. *Cajun Home*. Houghton Mifflin, 1998.
———. *One Room School*. Houghton Mifflin, 1999.
Blumberg, Rhoda. *Commodore Perry in the Land of the Shogun*. Lothrop, Lee & Shepard, 1985.
———. *What's the Deal? Jefferson, Napoleon and The Louisiana Purchase*. National Geographic, 1998.
Bober, Natalie S. *Abigail Adams: Witness to a Revolution*. Atheneum, 1995.
Brandenburg, Jim. *To the Top of the World: Adventures with Arctic Wolves*. Walker, 1993.
Branley, Franklin. *Down Comes the Rain*. Illustrated by James Graham Hale. HarperCollins, 1997.
———. *Earthquakes*. Illustrated by Richard Rosenblum. HarperCollins, 1994.
———. *Flash, Crash, Rumble and Roll*. Illustrated by Barbara and Ed Emberley. Rev. ed. Crowell, 1985.
———. *Volcanoes*. Illustrated by Marc Simont. HarperCollins, 1985.
———. *What Happened to the Dinosaurs?* Illustrated by Marc Simont. Crowell, 1989.
Brenner, Barbara. *If You Were There in 1492*. Bradbury Press, 1991.
———. *Thinking About Ants*. Illustrated by Carol Schwartz. Mondo, 1997.
Brian, Cassie. *Trees (National Audubon Society First Field Guide)*. Scholastic, 1999.
Brooks, Bruce. *Making Sense: Animal Perception and Communication*. Farrar, Straus & Giroux, 1993.
———. *Predator!* Farrar, Straus & Giroux, 1991.
Burns, Marilyn. *Good for Me! All About Food in 32 Bites*. Little, Brown, 1978.

Burton, Robert. *Egg.* Photographed by Jane Burton and Kim Taylor. Dorling Kindersley, 1994.

Carrick, Carol. *Whaling Days.* Illustrated by David Frampton. Clarion, 1993.

Carter, David A. and James Diaz. *The Elements of Pop-Up.* Simon & Schuster, 1999.

Cassie, Brian. *Trees.* Scholastic, 1999.

Chambers, Veronica. *Amistad Rising: The Story of Freedom.* Illustrated by Paul Lee. Harcourt, 1998.

Charlip, Remy, and Mary Beth Miller. *Handtalk: An ABC of Finger Spelling and Sign Language.* Photographs by George Ancona. Four Winds, 1980.

———. *Handtalk Birthday: A Number and Story Book in Sign Language.* Photographs by George Ancona. Four Winds, 1987.

Cobb, Vicki. *Chemically Active! Experiments You Can Do at Home.* Illustrated by Theo Cobb. Lippincott, 1985.

———. *Science Experiments You Can Eat.* Illustrated by Peter Lippman. Lippincott, 1972.

———. *Why Can't I Live Forever? And Other Not So Dumb Questions About Life.* Illustrated by Mena Bolobowsky. Lodestar, 1997.

Cole, Joanna. *The Magic School Bus at the Waterworks.* Illustrated by Bruce Degen. Scholastic, 1988.

———. *The Magic School Bus Explores the Senses.* Illustrated by Bruce Degen. Scholastic, 1999.

———. *The Magic School Bus Inside the Earth.* Illustrated by Bruce Degen. Scholastic, 1987.

———. *The Magic School Bus Inside a Hurricane.* Illustrated by Bruce Degen. Scholastic, 1995.

———. *The Magic School Bus in the Time of the Dinosaurs.* Illustrated by Bruce Degen. Scholastic, 1994.

———. *The Magic School Bus on the Ocean Floor.* Illustrated by Bruce Degen. Scholastic, 1993.

———. *My Puppy Is Born.* Photographs by Margaret Miller. Mulberry, 1991.

Colman, Penny. *Corpses, Coffins and Crypts: A History of Burial.* Holt, 1997.

———. *Girls: A History of Growing Up Female in America.* Scholastic, 2000.

———. *Rosie the Riveter: Woman Working on the Home Front in World War II.* Crown, 1994.

Cone, Molly. *Come Back Salmon.* Photographs by Sidnee Wheelwright. Sierra Club, 1992.

Conrad, Pam. *Call Me Ahnighito.* Illustrated by Richard Egielski. HarperCollins, 1995.

Cowcher, Helen. *Antarctica.* Farrar, Straus and Giroux, 1990.

Cowley, Joy. *Red-Eyed Tree Frog.* Photographs by Nic Bishop. Scholastic, 1999.

Crewe, Sabrina. *The Prairie Dog.* Illustrated by Graham Allen. Raintree, 1996.

Davis, Wendy. *Limestone Caves.* Children's Press, 1997.

de Bourgoing, Pascale. *Under the Ground.* Illustrated by Danielle Bour. Scholastic, 1995.

Deem, James M. *Bodies from the Bog.* Houghton Mifflin, 1998.

———. *How to Hunt for Buried Treasure.* Illustrated by True Kelley. Houghton Mifflin, 1992.

Delafosse, Claude. *Under the Ground.* Illustrated by Pierre De Hugo. Scholastic, 1999.

de Paola, Tomie. *"Charlie Needs a Cloak."* Simon & Schuster, 1974.

Dewey, Jennifer Owings. *Mud Matters.* Photographs by Stephen Trimble. Cavendish, 1998.

Dorros, Arthur. *Ant Cities.* Crowell, 1987.

———. *Follow the Water from Brook to Ocean.* HarperCollins, 1991.

Dudley, Karen. *Alligators and Crocodiles.* Raintree, 1998.

———. *Bald Eagles.* Raintree, 1997.

Facklam, Margery. *Bees Dance and Whales Sing: The Mysteries of Animal Communication.* Illustrated by Pamela Johnson. Sierra Club, 1992.

———. *The Big Bug Book.* Illustrated by Paul Facklam. Little, Brown, 1994.

Feelings, Tom. *The Middle Passage: White Ships/Black Cargo.* Introduction by Dr. John Henrik Clarke. Dial, 1995.

Fowler, Allan. *Inside an Ant Colony.* Children's Press, 1998.

Freedman, Russell. *Buffalo Hunt.* Holiday House, 1988.

———. *Children of the Wild West.* Clarion, 1983.

———. *Eleanor Roosevelt: A Life of Discovery.* Clarion, 1993.

———. *Indian Chiefs.* Holiday House, 1987.

———. *An Indian Winter.* Holiday House, 1992.

———. *Kids at Work: Lewis Hine and the Crusade Against Child Labor.* Clarion, 1994.

———. *Lincoln: A Photobiography.* Clarion, 1987.

———. *The Wright Brothers.* Holiday House, 1991.

Fritz, Jean. *George Washington's Breakfast.* Illustrated by Tomie dePaola. Paper Star, 1998.

———. *Harriet Beecher Stowe and the Beecher Preachers.* Putnam, 1994.

Gallant, Roy A. *The Dance of the Continents.* Benchmark, 1999.

———. *Earth: The Making of a Planet.* Illustrated by Christopher Schuberth. Cavendish, 1998.

———. *Geysers: When the Earth Roars.* Watts, 1997.

———. *Limestone Caves.* Watts, 1998.

George, Jean Craighead. *Everglades.* Illustrated by Wendell Minor. HarperCollins, 1995.

George, Michael. *Earthquakes.* Creative Education, 1997.

Getz, David. *Frozen Girl.* Illustrated by Peter McCarty. Holt, 1998.

———. *Frozen Man.* Illustrated by Peter McCarty. Holt, 1994.

Gibbons, Gail. *Caves and Caverns.* Harcourt Brace, 1993.

———. *From Seed to Plant.* Holiday House, 1991.

———. *New Road!* Crowell, 1983.

———. *Penguins.* Holiday, 1998.

———. *Planet Earth: Inside Out.* Morrow, 1995.

———. *Soaring with the Wind: The Bald Eagle.* Morrow, 1998.

———. *Tool Book.* Holiday House, 1982.

Giblin, James Cross. *The Mystery of the Mammoth Bones: And How it Was Solved.* HarperCollins, 1999.

———. *The Riddle of the Rosetta Stone: Key to Ancient Egypt.* Crowell, 1990.

———. *The Truth About Unicorns.* HarperCollins, 1991.

———. *When Plague Strikes: The Black Death, Smallpox, AIDS.* Illustrated by David Frampton. HarperCollins, 1995.

Grau, Andrée. *Dance*. Dorling Kindersley, 1998.

Greenaway, Theresa. *Insect*. Dorling Kindersley, 1998.

———. *Jungle*. Photographs by Geoff Dan. Knopf, 1994.

Greenberg, Keith Elliott. *A Haitian Family*. Lerner, 1998.

Greenfeld, Howard. *The Hidden Children*. Ticknor & Fields, 1993.

Guiberson, Brenda Z. *Cactus Hotel*. Illustrated by Megan Lloyd. Holt, 1991.

Haldane, Suzanne. *Painting Faces*. Dutton, 1988.

Hamanaka, Sheila. *The Journey: Japanese Americans, Racism, and Renewal*. Orchard, 1990.

Hamilton, Virginia. *Anthony Burns: The Defeat and Triumph of a Fugitive Slave*. Knopf, 1988.

Harris, Robie H. *It's Perfectly Normal: A Book About Changing Bodies, Growing Up, Sex, and Sexual Health*. Illustrated by Michael Emberley. Candlewick, 1994.

Harris, Robie. *It's So Amazing: A Book About Eggs, Sperm, Birth, Babies, and Families*. Illustrated by Michael Emberley. Candlewick, 1999.

Heller, Ruth. *Many Luscious Lollipops: A Book About Adjectives*. Grosset & Dunlap, 1989.

Herbert, Janis. *Leonardo Da Vinci for Kids: His Life and Ideas*. Chicago Review Press, 1998.

Hewitt, Joan. *Tunnels, Tracks and Trains: Building a Subway*. Lodestar, 1995.

Hirschi, Ron. *Fall*. Photographs by Thomas D. Mangelsen. Cobblehill/Dutton, 1991.

———. *Spring*. Photographs by Thomas D. Mangelsen. Cobblehill/Dutton, 1990.

———. *Summer*. Photographs by Thomas D. Mangelsen. Cobblehill/Dutton, 1991.

———. *Winter*. Photographs by Thomas D. Mangelsen. Cobblehill/Dutton, 1990.

Hoare, Stephen. *The World of Caves, Mines, and Tunnels*. Illustrated by Bruce Hogarth. Peter Bedrick, 1999.

Holling, Holling C. *Minn of the Mississippi*. Houghton Mifflin, 1951.

———. *Pagoo*. Houghton Mifflin, 1957.

Holmes, Thom. *Fossil Feud: The Rivalry of the First American Dinosaur Hunters*. Illustrated by Cameron Clement. Messner, 1998.

Hoyt-Goldsmith, Diane. *Apache Rodeo*. Photographs by Lawrence Migdale. Holiday House, 1995.

———. *Lacrosse: The National Game of the Iroquois* Photographs by Lawrence Migdale. Holiday House, 1998.

———. *Las Posadas: An Hispanic Christmas Celebration*. Photographs by Lawrence Migdale. Holiday House, 1997.

———. *Potlatch: A Tsimshian Celebration*. Photographs by Lawrence Migdale. Holiday House, 1997.

Hunter, Ryan Ann. *Dig a Tunnel*. Illustrated by Edward Miller. Holiday House, 1999.

Intrater, Roberta Grobel. *Two Eyes, a Nose and a Mouth*. Scholastic, 1995.

Irvine, Joan. *How to Make Pop-Ups*. Illustrated by Barbara Reid. Morrow, 1988.

———. *How to Make Super Pop-Ups*. Illustrated by Linda Hendry. Morrow, 1992.

Isaacson, Philip M. *A Short Walk Around the Pyramids and Through the World of Art*. Knopf, 1993.

Jenkins, Priscilla Belz. *A Nestful of Eggs*. Illustrated by Lizzy Rockwell. HarperCollins, 1995.

Jenkins, Steve. *The Top of the World: Climbing Mount Everest*. Houghton Mifflin, 1999.

Jurmain, Suzanne. *Once Upon a Horse: A History of Horses—and How They Shaped Our History*. Lothrop, Lee & Shepard, 1989.

Kalman, Bobbie. *Raptors*. Crabtree, 1998.

Kaplan, William. *One More Border; The True Story of One Family's Escape from War-Torn Europe*. Illustrated by Shelley Tanaka. Groundwood, 1998.

Keates, Colin. *Fossil*. Knopf, 1990.

Kent, Peter. *Hidden Under the Ground: The World Beneath Your Feet*. Dutton, 1998.

Kidd, J. S., and Renee A. Kidd. *On Shifting Ground: The Story of the Continental Drift*. Facts on File, 1997.

Kittinger, Jo S. *A Look at Minerals: From Galena to Gold*. Watts, 1998.

———. *A Look at Rocks: From Coal to Kimberlite*. Watts, 1998.

———. *Stories in Stone: The World Of Animal Fossils*. Watts, 1998.

Knowlton, Jack. *Maps and Globes*. Illustrated by Harriett Barton. Crowell, 1985.

Kuklin, Susan. *From Head to Toe: How a Doll Is Made*. Hyperion, 1994.

Kurelek, William. *Lumberjack*. Houghton Mifflin, 1974.

Langley, Andrew. *The Search for Riches*. Raintree, 1997.

Lasker, Joe. *Merry Ever After: The Story of Two Medieval Weddings*. Viking, 1976.

Lasky, Kathryn. *Traces of Life: The Origins of Humankind*. Illustrated by Whitney Powell. Morrow, 1989.

Lauber, Patricia. *Dinosaurs Walked Here and Other Stories Fossils Tell*. Bradbury Press, 1987.

———. *Journey to the Planets*. Crown, 1993 [1982].

———. *The News About Dinosaurs*. Bradbury Press, 1989.

———. *Painters of the Caves*. National Geographic, 1998.

———. *Seeds: Pop Stick Glide*. Photos by Jerome Wexler. Crown, 1981.

———. *Tales Mummies Tell*. Crowell, 1985.

———. *Volcano: The Eruption and Healing of Mt. St. Helens*. Bradbury Press, 1986.

Lester, Julius. *From Slave Ship to Freedom Road*. Illustrated by Rod Brown. Dial. 1998.

———. *To Be a Slave*. Illustrated by Tom Feelings. Dial, 1968.

Lobel, Anita. *No Pretty Picture: A Child of War*. Greenwillow, 1998.

Locker, Thomas, with Candace Christiansen. *Sky Tree*. HarperCollins, 1995.

Luby, Thia. *The Children's Book of Yoga*. Clear Light, 1998.

Macaulay, David. *Castle*. Houghton Mifflin, 1977.

———. *Cathedral: The Story of Its Construction*. Houghton Mifflin, 1973.

———. *City: The Story of Roman Planning and Construction*. Houghton Mifflin, 1974.

———. *Mill*. Houghton Mifflin, 1983.

———. *Pyramid*. Houghton Mifflin, 1975.

———. *Ship*. Houghton Mifflin, 1993.

———. *Underground*. Houghton Mifflin, 1976.

———. *The Way Things Work.* Houghton Mifflin, 1988.

Machotka, Hana. *Breathtaking Noses.* Morrow, 1992.

Malone, Michael. R. *A Nicaraguan Family.* Lerner, 1998.

Mallory, Kenneth *A Home by the Sea: Protecting Coastal Wildlife.* Gulliver, 1998.

Markle, Sandra. *Earth Alive!* Lothrop, Lee & Shepard, 1991.

———. *Exploring Winter.* Atheneum, 1984.

———. *Inside and Outside Spiders.* Bradbury Press, 1994.

———. *A Rainy Day.* Illustrated by Cathy Johnson. Orchard, 1993.

McClung, Robert. *Possum.* Morrow, 1963.

McGovern, Ann. . . . *If You Lived with the Sioux Indians.* Scholastic, 1976.

McIntosh, Jane. *Pyramid.* Photographs by Geoff Brighting. Knopf, 1994.

McKissack, Patricia C., and Frederick McKissack. *Christmas in the Big House, Christmas in the Quarters.* Illustrated by John Thompson. Scholastic, 1994.

McNulty, Faith. *How to Dig a Hole to the Other Side of the World.* Illustrated by Marc Simont. HarperCollins, 1979.

Meltzer, Milton. *Rescue: The Story of How Gentiles Saved Jews in the Holocaust.* Harper & Row, 1988.

———. *Voices from the Civil War: A Documentary History of the Great American Conflict.* Harper & Row, 1989.

Micucci, Charles. *The Life and Times of the Apple.* Orchard, 1992.

———. *The Life and Times of the Honeybee.* Ticknor & Fields, 1994.

———. *The Life and Times of the Peanut.* Houghton Mifflin, 2000.

Miller, Jonathan. *The Human Body.* Book design by David Pelham. Viking, 1983.

Miller, Margaret. *Guess Who?* Greenwillow, 1994.

Miller, Mary Beth, and George Ancona. *Handtalk School.* Photographs by George Ancona. Four Winds, 1991.

Moore, Kenny. "Coober Pedy: Opal Capital of Australia's Outback." *National Geographic* (November 1976), pp. 560–571.

Morris, Ann. *Shoes Shoes Shoes.* Lothrop, Lee & Shepard, 1995.

———. *Weddings.* Lothrop, Lee & Shepard, 1995.

Morris, Neil. *Volcanoes.* Crabtree, 1995.

Murphy, Jim. *Across America on an Emigrant Train.* Clarion, 1993.

———. *The Boys' War: Confederate and Union Soldiers Talk About the Civil War.* Clarion, 1990.

———. *Gone A-Whaling: The Lure of the Sea and the Hunt for the Great Whale.* Clarion, 1998.

———. *The Great Fire.* Scholastic, 1995.

Myers, Walter Dean. *Now Is Your Time! The African American Struggle for Freedom.* HarperCollins, 1991.

Needham, Bobbe. *Ecology Crafts for Kids: 50 Great Ways to Make Friends with Planet Earth.* Sterling, 1998.

Oldershaw, Cally. *Rocks and Minerals.* Dorling Kindersley, 1999.

Onyefulu, Ifeoma. *Chidi Only Likes Blue: An African Book of Colors.* Dutton, 1997.

———. *Ogbo: Sharing Life in an African Village.* Gulliver Books/Harcourt Brace, 1996.

Orr, Richard. *The Burrow.* Photographs by Shaila Awan. Dorling Kindersley, 1997.

Paladino, Catherine. *One Good Apple: Growing Our Food for the Sake of the Earth.* Houghton Mifflin, 1999.

Parker, Nancy Winslow. *Money, Money, Money: The Meaning of the Art and Symbols on United States Paper Currency.* HarperCollins, 1995.

Parker, Nancy Winslow, and Joan Richards Wright. *Bugs.* Illustrated by Nancy Winslow Parker. Greenwillow, 1987.

———. *Frogs, Toads, Lizards, and Salamanders.* Illustrated by Nancy Winslow Parker. Greenwillow, 1990.

Parker, Steve. *Rocks and Minerals.* Dorling Kindersley, 1997.

Patent, Dorothy Hinshaw. *Prairie Dogs.* Photographs by William Muñoz. Clarion, 1993.

———. *Secrets of the Ice Man (Frozen in Time).* Cavendish, 1998.

———. *Shaping the Earth.* Photographs by William Muñoz. Clarion, 2000.

Pelta, Kathy. *Discovering Christopher Columbus: How History Is Invented.* Lerner, 1991.

Perl, Lila. *The Great Ancestor Hunt: The Fun of Finding Out Who You Are.* Clarion, 1989.

———. *Mummies, Tombs, and Treasure: Secrets of Ancient Egypt.* Illustrated by Erika Weihs. Houghton Mifflin, 1987.

Peters, David. *From the Beginning: The Story of Human Evolution.* Morrow, 1991.

Phinney, Maragaret Y. *Exploring Underground Habitats.* Illustrated by Stephen Petruccio. Mondo, 1999.

Pirotta, Saviour. *Fossils and Bones.* Raintree, 1997.

Platt, Richard. *Stephen Beisty's Cross Sections: Castle.* Illustrated by Stephen Beisty. Dorling Kindersley, 1994.

———. *Stephen Beisty's Cross Sections: Man-of-War.* Illustrated by Stephen Beisty. Dorling Kindersley, 1993.

———. *Stephen Beisty's Incredible Cross Sections.* Illustrated by Stephen Beisty. Dorling Kindersley, 1992.

Pollard, Michael. *Roads and Tunnels.* Raintree, 1996.

Pope, Joyce. *Earthquakes.* Illustrated by Ian Moores. Copper Beech Books, 1998.

Porter, A. P. *Kwanzaa.* Illustrated by Janice Lee Porter. Carolrhoda, 1991.

Potter, Beatrix. *The Peter Rabbit and Friends Cookbook.* Warne, 1994.

Pringle, Laurence. *An Extraordinary Life: The Story of the Monarch Butterfly.* Illustrated by Bob Marstall. Orchard, 1997.

———. *Nuclear Energy: Troubled Past, Uncertain Future.* Macmillan, 1989.

———. *Vanishing Ozone: Protecting Earth from Ultra Violet Radiation.* Morrow, 1995.

Putnam, Jim. *Mummy.* Photographs by Peter Hayman. Knopf, 1993.

Rappaport, Doreen. *Escape from Slavery: Five Journeys to Freedom.* Illustrated by Charles Lilly. HarperCollins, 1991.

Redfern, Martin. *The Kingfisher Young People's Book of Space.* Kingfisher, 1998.

Reid, Struan. *The Children's Atlas of Lost Treasures.* Millbrook, 1997.

Reinhard, Johann. *Discovering the Inca Ice Maiden: My Adventure on Ampato.* National Geographic, 1998.

Riciutti, Edward. *Rocks and Minerals.* Scholastic, 1998.

Riley, Linda Capus. *Elephants Swim.* Illustrated by Steve Jenkins. Houghton Mifflin, 1995.

Robbins, Ken. *Air: The Elements.* Holt, 1996.

———. *A Flower Grows.* Dial, 1990.

Rockwell, Harlow. *My Doctor.* Macmillan, 1973.

Rotner, Shelley, and Ken Kreisler. *Faces.* Photographs by Shelley Rotner. Macmillan, 1994.

Rounds, Glen. *Sod Houses on the Prairie.* Holiday House, 1995.

Royston, Angela. *Insects and Crawly Creatures.* Photographs by Jerry Young. Illustrations by Jane Cradock-Watson and Dave Hopkins. Aladdin, 1992.

Sattler, Helen Roney. *Our Patchwork Planet: The Story of Plate Tectonics.* Illustrated by Guilio Maestro. Lothrop, Lee & Shepard, 1995.

———. *Recipes for Art and Craft Materials.* Lothrop, Lee & Shepard, 1987 [1973].

Schlein, Miriam. *Discovering Dinosaur Babies.* Illustrated by Margaret Colbert. Four Winds, 1991.

Scieszka, Jon. *Math Curse.* Illustrated by Lane Smith. Viking, 1995.

Selsam, Millicent. *Egg to Chick.* Illustrated by Barbara Wolff. Harper Trophy, 1987.

———. *How to Be a Nature Detective.* Illustrated by Marlene Hill Donnelly. HarperCollins, 1995 [1958].

Selsam, Millicent, and Joyce Hunt. *A First Look at Bats.* Illustrated by Harriet Springer. Walker, 1991.

Showers, Paul. *How Many Teeth?* Illustrated by True Kelley. HarperCollins, 1991.

Silver, Donald M. *Cave.* Illustrated by Patricia J. Wynne. McGraw-Hill, 1997.

Simon, Seymour. *Animal Fact Animal Fable.* Illustrated by Diane de Groat. Crown, 1987.

———. *Bones.* Morrow, 1998.

———. *Comets, Meteors, and Asteroids.* Morrow, 1994.

———. *Crocodiles and Alligators.* HarperCollins, 1999.

———. *Earthquakes.* Morrow, 1991.

———. *Earth Words: A Dictionary of the Environment.* Illustrated by Mark Kaplan. HarperCollins, 1995.

———. *Galaxies.* Morrow, 1988.

———. *The Paper Airplane Book.* Illustrated by Byron Barton. Viking, 1971.

———. *Soap Bubble Magic.* Illustrated by Stella Ormai. Lothrop, Lee & Shepard, 1985.

———. *Spring Across America.* Hyperion, 1996.

———. *Storms.* Morrow, 1989.

———. *Volcanoes.* Morrow, 1995.

Sipiera, Paul P., and Diane M. Sipiera. *Thunderstorms.* Children's Press, 1998.

———. *Volcanoes.* Children's Press, 1998.

Skurzynski, Gloria. *Get the Message: Telecommunications in Your High-Tech World.* Bradbury Press, 1993.

Spier, Peter. *People.* Doubleday, 1980.

Stanley, Jerry. *Children of the Dust Bowl: The True Story of the School at Weedpatch Camp.* Crown, 1992.

———. *I Am an American: A True Story of the Japanese Internment.* Crown, 1994.

Stetoff, Rebecca. *Ant.* Benchmark, 1998.

Stevens, Janet. *From Pictures to Words: A Book About Making a Book.* Holiday House, 1995.

Symes, R. F. *Rocks and Minerals.* Photographs by Colin Ketes. Knopf, 1988.

Tanaka, Shelley. *Discovering the Ice Man: What Was It Like to Find a Fifty Three Year Old Mummy.* Illustrated by Laurie McGaw. Hyperion, 1997.

———. *Graveyards of the Dinosaurs.* Illustrated by Alan Barnard. Hyperion, 1998.

———. *Secrets of the Mummies: Uncovering the Bodies of Ancient Egyptians.* Illustrated by Greg Ruhl. Hyperion, 1999.

Taylor, Paul D. *Inside an Ant Colony.* Children's Press, 1998.

Van Loon, Hendrik W. *The Story of Mankind.* Illustrated by John M. Merriam. Rev. ed. Liveright, 1998 [1921].

Ventura, Piero. *Clothing.* Houghton Mifflin, 1994.

———. *Food.* Houghton Mifflin, 1994.

———. *Houses.* Houghton Mifflin, 1994.

Walgren, Judy. *The Lost Boys of Natinga: A School for Sudan's Young Refugees.* Houghton Mifflin, 1998.

Walker, Barbara M. *The Little House Cookbook: Frontier Foods from Laura Ingalls Wilder's Classic Stories.* Illustrated by Garth Williams. Harper & Row, 1979.

Wallace, Karen. *Think of an Eel.* Illustrated by Mike Bostock. Candlewick, 1993.

Warren, Andrea. *Pioneer Girl: Growing Up on the Prairie.* Morrow, 1998.

Waters, Kate. *Samuel Eaton's Day: A Day in the Life of a Pilgrim Boy.* Photographs by Russ Kendall. Scholastic, 1993.

———. *Sarah Morton's Day: A Day in the Life of a Pilgrim Girl.* Photographs by Russ Kendall. Scholastic, 1989.

Weiss, Harvey. *Maps: Getting from Here to There.* Houghton Mifflin, 1991.

Weitzman, David. *My Backyard History Book.* Illustrated by James Robertson. Little, Brown, 1975.

Wheatley, Nadia, and Donna Rawlins. *My Place.* Kane Miller, 1992.

Wick, Walter. *A Drop of Water.* Scholastic, 1997.

Wilder, Laura Ingalls. *The First Four Years.* Illustrated by Garth Williams. Harper & Row, 1971.

———. *West from Home: Letters of Laura Ingalls Wilder, San Francisco 1915.* Edited by Roger McBride. Harper & Row, 1974.

Willard, Nancy. *Gutenberg's Gift: A Book Lover's Pop-up Book.* Illustrated by Bryan Leister. Harcourt Brace, 1995.

Zoehfeld, Kathleen Weidner. *How Mountains Are Made.* Illustrated by James Graham Hale. HarperCollins, 1995.

———. *Wheels at Work.* Illustrated by Roy Doty. Morrow, 1986.

Zubrowski, Bernie. *Shadow Play.* Illustrated by Roy Doty. Morrow, 1995.

## Other References

Ada, Alma Flor. *My Name Is Marie Isabel.* Atheneum, 1993.

Avi. *Wind Catcher.* Simon & Schuster, 1991.

Ayres, Kathryn. *North by Night: A Story of the Underground Railroad.* Delacorte, 1998.

Baker, Keith. *Big Fat Hen*. Harcourt Brace, 1994.

Baylor, Byrd. *Everybody Needs a Rock*. Scribner's, 1987.

Beard, Carleen Bailey. *Twister*. Illustrated by Nancy Carpenter. Farrar, Straus & Giroux, 1999.

Beatty, Patricia. *Charley Skedaddle*. Morrow, 1987.

———. *Jayhawker*. Morrow, 1991.

Bernhard, Emery, and Durga Bernhard. *The Tree That Rains: The Flood Myth of the Huichol Indians of Mexico*. Holiday House, 1994.

Berry, James. *Ajeemah and His Son*. HarperCollins, 1992.

Beskow, Elsa. *Pelle's New Suit*. Harper & Row, 1929.

Bunting, Eve. *Dandelions*. Illustrated by Greg Shed. Harcourt Brace, 1995.

———. *How Many Days to America? A Thanksgiving Story*. Illustrated by Beth Peck. Ticknor & Fields, 1988.

Carbonne, Elisa Lynn. *Steal Away Home*. Knopf, 1999.

Choi, Sook Nyul. *Year of Impossible Goodbyes*. Houghton Mifflin, 1991.

Christian, Peggy. *If You find a Rock*. Illustrated by Barbara Hirsch Lember. Harcourt Brace, 2000.

Clinton, Catherine. *I, Too Sing America: Three Centuries of African American Poetry*. Illustrated by Stephen Alcorn. Houghton Mifflin, 1998.

Collier, James Lincoln, and Christopher Collier. *With Every Drop of Blood*. Delacorte, 1994.

Conrad, Pam. *My Daniel*. Harper & Row, 1989.

———. *Prairie Songs*. Illustrated by Darryl Zudeck. Harper & Row, 1985.

Dahl, Roald. *James and the Giant Peach*. Illustrated by Nancy Burkert. Knopf, 1962.

DeMaupassant, Guy. *When Chickens Grow Teeth*. Illustrated by Wendy Anderson Halperin. Orchard, 1996.

Edwards, Michelle. *Chicken Man*. Lothrop, Lee & Shepard, 1991.

Erdrich, Louise. *The Birchbark House*. Hyperion, 1999.

Fleischman, Paul. *Joyful Noise: Poems for Two Voices*. Illustrated by Eric Beddows. Harper & Row, 1988.

Gallaz, Christophe, and Roberto Innocenti. *Rose Blanche*. Illustrated by Roberto Innocenti. Creative Education, 1985.

Garelick, May. *Where Does the Butterfly Go When It Rains?* Illustrated by Nicholas Wilton. Mondo, 1997.

George, Jean Craighead. *Julie*. HarperCollins, 1995.

Goble, Paul. *Iktomi and the Boulder*. Orchard, 1988.

———. *The Lost Children*. Bradbury Press, 1993.

Greenberg, David. T. *Bugs!* Illustrated by Lynn Munsinger. Little, Brown, 1997.

Griffin, Peni R. *The Treasure Bird*. McElderry, 1992.

Hamilton, Virginia. *The House of Dies Drear*. Illustrated by Eros Keith. Macmillan, 1968.

Hansen, Joyce. *The Captive*. Scholastic, 1994.

———. *I Thought My Soul Would Rise and Fly: The Diary of Patsy a Freed Girl*. Scholastic, 1997.

Harvey, Brett. *My Prairie Christmas*. Illustrated by Deborah Kogan Ray. Holiday House, 1990.

Hautzig, Esther. *The Endless Steppe: Growing Up in Siberia*. Crowell, 1968.

Hawthorn, Libby. *Sky Sash So Blue*. Illustrated by Benny Andrews. Simon & Schuster, 1998.

Hermes, Patricia. *Calling Me Home*. Avon, 1998.

Hesse, Karen. *Come On Rain*. Illustrated by Jon J. Muth. Scholastic, 1999.

Hest, Amy. *In the Rain with Baby Duck*. Illustrated by Jill Barton. Candlewick, 1995.

Hiçyilmaz, Gaye. *The Frozen Waterfall*. Farrar, Straus & Giroux, 1994.

Holman, Felice. *Slake's Limbo*. Atheneum, 1974.

Jacobs, Paul Samuel. *James Printer: A Novel of Rebellion*. Scholastic, 1997.

Laird, Elizabeth. *Kiss the Dust*. Dutton, 1992.

Lewis, J. Patrick. *Little Buggers: Insect and Spider Poems*. Illustrated by Victoria Chess. Dial, 1998.

Lionni, Leo. *The Extraordinary Egg*. Knopf, 1994.

London, Jonathon. *Hurricane!* Illustrated by Henry Sorenson. Lothrop, Lee & Shepard, 1998.

Lorenz, Albert. *Buried Blueprints Maps and Sketches of Lost Worlds and Mysterious Places*. Abrams, 1999.

Lowry, Lois. *Number the Stars*. Houghton Mifflin, 1989.

Luenn, Nancy. *Nessa's Story*. Illustrated by Neil Waldman. Atheneum, 1994.

Lyon, George Ella. *Come a Tide*. Illustrated by Stephen Gammell. Orchard, 1990.

Lyons, Mary E. *Letters from a Slave Girl: The Story of Harriet Jacobs*. Scribner's, 1992.

MacLachlan, Patricia. *Sarah, Plain and Tall*. Harper & Row, 1985.

———. *Three Names*. Illustrated by Alexander Pertzoff. HarperCollins, 1991.

Matas, Carol. *Greater Than Angels*. Simon & Schuster, 1998.

Mayne, William. *Earthfasts*. Peter Smith, 1989.

McCully, Emily Arnold. *The Bobbin Girl*. Dial, 1996.

Medearis, Angela Shelf. *Dancing with the Indians*. Illustrated by Samuel Byrd. Holiday House, 1991.

Mochizuki, Ken. *Baseball Saved Us*. Illustrated by Dom Lee. Lee & Low, 1993.

Naylor, Phyllis Reynolds. *The Treasure of Bessledorf Hill*. Simon & Schuster, 1998.

Oppenheim, Shulamith Levy. *The Lily Cupboard: A Story of the Holocaust*. Illustrated by Ronald Himler. HarperCollins, 1992.

Park, Frances, and Ginger Park. *My Freedom Trip*. Illustrated by Debra Reid Jenkins. Boyds Mills, 1998.

Paterson, Katherine. *Jip: His Story*. Lodestar, 1996.

Paulsen, Gary. *Sarny*. Delacorte, 1997.

Philip, Neil. *War and the Pity of War*. Illustrated by Michael McCurdy. Clarion 1998.

Pinkney, Andrea Davis. *Silent Thunder*. Hyperion, 1999.

Polacco, Patricia. *Just Plain Fancy*. Bantam/Doubleday, 1990.

———. *Pink and Say*. Philomel, 1994.

Reeder, Carolyn. *Shades of Gray*. Macmillan, 1989.

Reiser, Lynn. *The Surprise Family*. Greenwillow, 1994.

Robinett, Harriette Gillem. *Forty Acres and Maybe a Mule*. Atheneum, 1998.

Rockwell, Ann. *The Storm*. Illustrated by Robert Sauber. Hyperion, 1994.

Rodanas, Kristina. *Follow the Stars*. Cavendish, 1998.

Ruby, Lois. *Steal Away Home*. Macmillan, 1994.

Salisbury, Graham. *Under the Blood-Red Sun*. Delacorte, 1994.

San Souci, Robert D. *Sootface: An Ojibwa Cinderella*. Illustrated by Daniel San Souci. Doubleday, 1994.

———. *The Talking Eggs*. Illustrated by Jerry Pinkney. Dial, 1989.

Schrier, Jeffrey. *On the Wings of Eagles: An Ethiopian Boy's Story*. Millbrook, 1998.

Serfozo, Mary. *Rain Talk*. Illustrated by Keiko Narahashi. McElderry, 1990.

Shusterman, Neil. *Downsiders*. Simon & Schuster, 1999.

Siegelson, Kim. *In the Time of the Drums*. Illustrated by Brian Pinkney. Hyperion, 1999.

Spier, Peter. *Peter Spier's Rain*. Doubleday, 1982.

Stevens, Janet, and Susan Crummel Stevens. *Cook-a-Doodle-Doo!* Harcourt Brace, 1999.

Temple, Frances. *Grab Hands and Run*. Orchard, 1993.

———. *Tonight, by Sea*. Orchard, 1995.

Trottier, Maxine. *Prairie Willow*. Illustrated by Laura Fernandez and Rick Jacobson. Stoddart, 1998.

Turner, Ann. *Dakota Dugout*. Illustrated by Ronald Himler. Macmillan, 1985.

———. *Nettie's Trip South*. Illustrated by Ronald Himler. Macmillan, 1987.

Uchida, Yoshiko. *The Bracelet*. Illustrated by Joanna Yardley. Philomel, 1993.

———. *Journey to Topaz*. Illustrated by Donald Carrick. Scribner's, 1971.

Van Laan, Nancy. *The Magic Bean Tree*. Illustrated by Beatriz Vidal. Houghton Mifflin, 1998.

———. *Shingebiss, an Ojibwe Legend*. Illustrated by Betsey Bowen. Houghton Mifflin, 1997.

Watkins, Yoko Kawashima. *So Far from the Bamboo Grove*. Lothrop, Lee & Shepard, 1986.

Whelan, Gloria. *Goodbye Vietnam*. Knopf, 1992.

Wormell, Mary. *Hilda Hen's Search*. Harcourt Brace, 1994.

Yashima, Taro. *Crow Boy*. Viking, 1955.

# Chapter Twelve

## Biography

Barbara Z. Kiefer

*F*ollowing a classroom study of biographies, a fourth-grade teacher asked her students to reflect on their experiences in their response journals. Nicholas, age 10, wrote:

Reading about the lives of other people could be very interesting. Each person has his unique life experiences. You can learn about when and where he was born, how he was raised, what kind of family did he come from. You can also learn about where he went to school and what kind of student he was when he went to school. Most of all, you can learn about his dreams and how he fulfilled his dreams. For example if I happened to be reading a book about Michael Jordan, I would be very interested to know how he trained himself to be a great basketball star. Also why did he all of a sudden switch his career as basketball player to become a baseball player. I would want to know who was his role model when he was young like me. How did he become interested in basketball games? What kind of advice would he give to young people who have the same kind of dream to become a basketball star?

–Nicholas Lee, fourth grade, PS 124, Manhattan, Mary S. Gallivan, teacher

Elementary and middle school students are in the process of becoming themselves, and reading about real people can provide glimpses of the kinds of lives they might choose to live. Biographies can answer questions that are important to young readers like Nicholas and raise questions about how their futures might unfold.

## Biography for Today's Child

In children's literature, biography often bridges the gap between historical fiction and nonfiction books. A life story might read like fiction, but, like other types of nonfiction, it will center on facts and events that can be documented. In the past, writers of biography for children have been allowed more freedom in the use of fictional techniques than those who write for adults. As a result, children's biographies over the years have shown a wide range of factual orientations, from strict authenticity to liberal fictionalization. The trend today, however, is clearly toward authenticity.

*Authentic biography* follows many of the same rules as serious scholarly works written for adults. A book of this type is a well-documented, carefully researched account of a person's life. Only statements that are known to have been made by the subject are included as dialogue. Jean Fritz was one of the first authors to demonstrate that biographies for children could be authentic as well as lively and readable. Her writing helped set a new standard. Her books about famous figures of the American Revolution—including *And Then What Happened, Paul Revere?* and *Will You Sign Here, John Hancock?*—are based on detailed research. The same is true of her more recent, longer books, such as *You Want Women to Vote, Lizzie Stanton?* Natalie S. Bober's *Abigail Adams:*

*Russell Freedman has received many awards for his well-written biographies. This photo from* Eleanor Roosevelt: A Life of Discovery *shows Eleanor with her younger brother*
Franklin D. Roosevelt Library

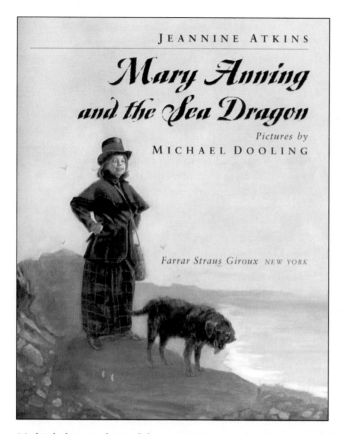

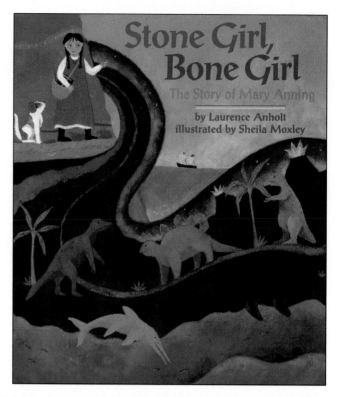

*Multiple biographies of the same person such as Jeannine Atkins's* Mary Anning and the Sea Dragon, *illustrated by Michael Dooling, and Lawrence Anholt's* Stone Girl, Bone Girl, *illustrated by Sheila Moxley, can invite children's critical comparison.*

*Witness to a Revolution,* Russell Freedman's *Babe Didrikson Zaharias,* and Albert Marrin's *Terror of the Spanish Main: Henry Morgan and His Buccaneers* are other excellent examples of authentic biography.

*Fictionalized biography* is grounded in thorough research, but the author dramatizes certain events and personalizes the subject, in contrast to the straight reporting of authentic biography. Fictionalized biography makes use of the narrative rather than the analytical approach. Children come to know the character of the subject as portrayed through actions, deeds, and conversations. In fictionalized biography the author may invent dialogue and even ascribe unspoken thoughts to the subject. These conversations might be based on actual facts taken from diaries, journals, or other period sources.

Several picture books that were published to celebrate the two hundredth anniversary of the birth of Mary Anning use the technique of fictionalized biography. Mary was a young English girl who discovered a dinosaur fossil in Lyme Regis in the late 1700s. *Stone Girl, Bone Girl* by Lawrence Anholt, *Mary Anning and the Sea Dragons* by Jeannine Atkins, *Mary Anning and Her Remarkable Discoveries* by Don Brown, and *The Fossil Girl: Mary Anning's Dinosaur*

*Discovery* by Catherine Brighton all relate incidents from Mary's life. These are fictionalized biographies, however; the factual details are essentially true but their presentation is imagined.

In *At Her Majesty's Request: An African Princess in Victorian England* Walter Dean Myers weaves a fascinating life story around pieces of historical evidence. Sarah Forbes Bonetta was an Egbado Princess, captured by Dahoman raiders and then rescued by British naval Captain Frederick Forbes. Taken to England, she came to the attention of Queen Victoria, who was charmed by the young girl and became Sarah's lifelong patron. Myers tells Sarah's story using her own letters and other primary source materials such as books, newspapers, and Church Mission Society Records, but he fills in many of the details using his imagination. He often does this by supposition. He writes, "Snow! What must she have thought of snow? To see all of London blanketed by soft white flurries?" (p. 33) At other times he must simply base his narrative on the evidence at hand. Myers's engaging story provides an example of fictionalized biography at its best.

Not everyone agrees where to draw the line between fictionalized biography or memoirs and historical fiction. When Jean Fritz wrote about her childhood in China and her much-longed-for trip to the United States in *Homesick: My Own Story,* she found that her "memory came out in lumps," and she finally chose not to worry about exact sequence. She telescoped events of all her childhood into a two-year span:

> but they are all, except in minor details, basically true. The people are real people; the places are dear to me. But most important, the form I have used has given me the freedom to recreate the emotions that I remember so vividly. Strictly speaking, I have to call this book *fiction,* but it does not feel like fiction to me. It is my story, told as truly as I can tell it. (foreword)

The library cataloging information in the front of this book designates it as fiction, but many readers will think of it as the autobiography of Jean Fritz. The inclusion of a section of family photographs from their days in China strengthens the book's claim to authenticity. Fritz's humor, her depth of feeling, and her vivid portrayal of the turmoil in China during the 1920s make *Homesick* worth reading, regardless of the label that is put on it. Older readers and adults might enjoy a sequel, *China Homecoming,* that is clearly nonfiction.

Publishers of biography for children have been quick to capitalize on trends in the social studies curriculum as well as shifts in children's interests. In the mid 1970s, many biographies about leaders in the American Revolution appeared in connection with the Bicentennial. Likewise, dozens of new books about Christopher Columbus came out in time for the quincentennial observation in 1992. As attention to multicultural education has grown, more stories about women, African Americans, and other underrepresented groups have also been written.

In the 1980s, new biographies of popular-culture celebrities and other contemporary figures appeared as publishers recognized children's tremendous interest in sports and entertainment personalities. Although such books tend to be objective and almost journalistic in their approach, many are superficial in scholarship and poorly written. A great number of these and other biographies are published as parts of series, and the result is often life stories that are tailored to fit certain format specifications rather than explored in all their uniqueness. The sales trends at the beginning of the new century seem to be away from media stars toward well-written books about the truly admirable or distinguished.

A rekindled interest in the lives of historical figures, the appearance of many autobiographies by children's authors, and the growing use of photographs and picture-book formats have all had significant impact on the genre of biography. It is true that many mediocre biographies are still being published, but the

*Diane Stanley's picture-book biographies such as* Leonardo da Vinci *include attention to historically accurate visual details as well as to factual information.*

From *Leonardo da Vinci* by Diane Stanley, illustration coyright © 1996 by Diane Stanley. Used by permission of Morrow Junior Books/HarperCollins Publishers.

number of high-quality books has continued to grow. Biographies have received several prestigious awards in recent years. Russell Freedman won the Newbery Medal in 1988 for *Lincoln: A Photobiography* and Newbery Honor designations for *The Wright Brothers: How They Invented the Airplane* in 1992 and *Eleanor Roosevelt: A Life of Discovery* in 1993; Jean Fritz's *The Great Little Madison* was the first-ever winner of the Orbis Pictus Award for nonfiction and Diane Stanley's *Leonardo da Vinci* won in 1997; and *Bill Peet: An Autobiography* was named a Caldecott Honor Book in 1990. Not all good books win awards, of course. Teachers and librarians still need to be able to decide for themselves which biographies are distinctive and deserving of attention. The web "Life Stories" on pages 544–545 shows how a classroom study for middle graders that begins with the genre of biography can be extended to other types of life stories.

## Criteria for Juvenile Biography

The criteria for evaluating biographies for children differ somewhat from those established for juvenile fiction. They also diverge somewhat from generally accepted patterns for adult biography. Children read biography as they read fiction—for the story, or *plot.*

**UNSUNG HEROES AND HEROINES**

*The Way West: Journal of a Pioneer Woman*
  (Knight)
*Yankee Doodle Boy* (Martin)
*Bicycle Rider* (Scioscia)
*Leon's Story* (Tillage)
*Orphan Train Rider: One Boy's True Story*
  (Warren)
*Pioneer Girl: Growing Up on the Prairie*
  (Warren)
What makes a person a hero or heroine?
Find an unsung hero or heroine in your
  own community. Write a biography
  celebrating his or her accomplishments.

**PERSONAL STORIES**

*My Back Yard History Book (Weitzman)*
*Through the Eyes of Your Ancestors* (Taylor)
Visit an oral history website. Collect an oral
  histories of someone in your family.

*Amelia's Notebook* (Moss)
*Scooter* (Williams)
Find other fiction books written in the style of a
  memoir. Use this format to record or write
  about events in your own life.

**FAMOUS CHILDHOODS**

*Eleanor* (Cooney)
*Mozart: Scenes from the Childhood
  of the Great Composer* (Brighton)
*Coming Home: From the Life of
  Langston Hughes* (Cooper)
*Zora Hurston and the Chinaberry Tree* (Miller)
*Escape from Slavery: The Boyhood of
  Frederick Douglass in His Own Words*
  (McCurdy)
*Richard Wright and the Library Card* (Miller)
*Tomas and the Library Lady* (Mora)
What obstacles did each of these people have
  to overcome as children?
How did their childhood experiences influence
  their future lives?
Find out more about them as adults.

**LIFE STORIES:
A WEB OF POSSIBILITIES**

**LIFE CYCLES**

*Penguins* (Gibbons)
*Soaring with the Wind: The Bald Eagle*
  (Gibbons)
*Minn of the Mississippi* (Holling)
*Pagoo* (Holling)
*The Life and Times of the Apple* (Micucci)
*The Life and Times of the Honeybee* (Micucci)
Keep an illustrated notebook of observations
  of one living thing over time.

**LIVING FOR THE SAME CAUSE**

*Sojourner Truth: Ain't I a Woman?* (McKissack)
*Mary McLeod Bethune* (Greenfield)
*Anthony Burns: The Defeat and Triumph of a
  Fugitive Slave* (Hamilton)
*Frederick Douglass: The Last Days of Slavery*
*Harriet Tubman, Conductor on the Underground
  Railroad* (Petry)
How were these people alike and different?
Plan and write a script for a play that depicts
  these characters meeting together and
  sharing experiences.

**ONE LIFE, SEVERAL
POINTS OF VIEW**

*Stone Girl, Bone Girl* (Anholt)
*Mary Anning and the Sea Dragon* (Atkins)
*The Fossil Girl: Mary Anning's Dinosaur
  Discovery* (Brighton)
*Rare Treasure: Mary Anning and Her
  Remarkable Discoveries* (Brown)
How do each of these authors and artists
  represent Mary Anning? Check their
  stories against other sources. How
  accurate are they?
Explore other biographies about a single
  character. Make a comparison chart.

Based on *The Web: Wonderfully Exciting Books.*
Charlotte Huck and Janet Hickman eds.
The Ohio State University. Vol. III 4 (fall 1978).

**AUTOBIOGRAPHIES AND MEMOIRS**

*A Girl from Yamhill: A Memoir* (Cleary)
*Boy: Tales of Childhood* (Dahl)
*Looking Back: A Book of Memories* (Lowry)
*26 Fairmont Avenue* (de Paola)
*The Abracadabra Kid: A Writer s Life*
    (Feischman)
*War Boy: A Country Childhood* (Foreman)
*Bowman s Store: A Journey to Myself*
    (Bruchac)
How has each author  remembered
    their lives?
How have they chosen to present their
    memories?

**PLACES HAVE STORIES**

*William Shakespeare and the Globe* (Aliki)
*Cathedral: The Story of Its Construction*
    (Macaulay)
*City: The Story of Roman Planning and
    Construction* (Macaulay)
*The Story of a Main Street* (Goodall)
*The Story of a Farm (*Goodall)
Categorize the types of changes that have
    occurred in these places over time.
Trace the life story of your own house,
    neighborhood or town.

**HOW DO WE FIND OUT ABOUT
ANCIENT LIVES?**

*Christopher Columbus: The Great Adventure
    and How We Know About It* (West)
*Fossils Tell of Long Ago* (Aliki)
*Archeologists Dig for Clues* (Duke)
Find out how scientists learn about the
    past. If scientists from another planet
    visited your home what might they conclude
    about your life?

**LIVING DURING THE SAME
PERIOD IN HISTORY**

*What's the Big Idea, Ben Franklin?* (Fritz)
*Why Don t You Get a Horse, Sam Adams?* (Fritz)
*Will You Sign Here, John Hancock?* (Fritz)
*Can t You Make Them Behave,
    King George?* (Fritz)
*And Then What Happened, Paul  Revere?* (Fritz)
How does Jean Fritz make her subjects come
    alive? Find out about her research methods.
Choose a period in history. Research and create
    a class book of biographies from that
    time period.

**LIFE IN THE ARTS**

*Sebastian: A Book About Bach* (Winter)
*Duke Ellington: The Piano Prince and His
    Orchestra* (Pinkney)
*Martha Graham: A Dancer's Life* (Freedman)
*Alvin Ailey* (Pinkney)
*In Search of the Spirit: The Loving National
    Treasures of Japan* (Hamanaka)
*Painting Dreams: Minnie Evans, Visionary
    Artist* (Lyons)
*Talking with Tebé: Clementine Hunter Memory
    Artist* (Lyons)
*Starting Home: The Story of Horace Pippin*
    (Lyons)
*My Name is Georgia: A Portrait* (Winter)
*On the Frontier with Mr. Audobon*
*Diego* (Winter)
Choose one artist, musician or dancer to
    research. Present your  ndings in the
    medium that the artist worked in.

**REMARKABLE WOMEN**

*Abigail Adams: Witness to a Revolution* (Bober)
*Cleopatra* (Stanley)
*Charlotte Forten: A Black Teacher in the
    Civil War* (Burchard)
*Babe Didrikson Zaharias* (Freedman)
*Ten Queens: Portraits of Women of Power*
    (Meltzer)
*Eleanor Roosevelt: A Life of Discovery*
    (Freedman)
*You Want Women to Vote, Lizzie Stanton?*
    (Fritz)
What characteristics do these women share?
What dif culties did they face because of their
    gender?
How did they surmount these obstacles?

Children demand a fast-moving narrative. In biography, events and actions become even more exciting because "they really happened." Thus, children like biography written as a story with continuity; they do not want just a collection of facts and dates. An encyclopedia gives them facts in a well-organized fashion. Biography, to do more than this, must help them *know* the person as a living human being.

## Choice of Subject

Formerly, most biographies for children were about familiar figures of the past in the United States, particularly those whose lives offered the readiest action material, such as Daniel Boone or Abraham Lincoln. Now the range of subjects is much broader, including artists and intellectuals as well as soldiers and presidents, plus world figures whose presence suggests the widened concerns of our pluralistic society. Biographies of contemporary figures in the worlds of sports and entertainment continue to reflect the influence of the mass media.

For many years biography for children was limited to subjects whose lives were considered worthy of emulation. This is no longer true. There are books about people remembered for their misdeeds, like *Traitor: The Case of Benedict Arnold* by Jean Fritz. Controversial persons like Fidel Castro, Ho Chi Minh, and Lenin have all been subjects of juvenile biographies. As long as the biographies are objective and recognize the various points of view concerning the subjects, these books can serve a useful purpose in presenting a worldview to boys and girls.

Biographies of less well known figures or subjects whose accomplishments are highly specialized also have value for children. Mary Anning, who was little known a decade ago, had inspired over ten biographies by the end of the twentieth century. Diane Stanley's *The True Adventures of Daniel Hall* is the story of a young New England boy who sailed aboard a whaling ship in 1856. Abused by a cruel captain, he escaped when the boat was off the coast of Siberia. With the help of some local villagers, he managed to survive the awful Siberian winter until he was rescued the following June. Marshall Taylor, a champion cyclist at the end of the nineteenth century when bicycle racing was a popular sport, was the first black person to ride in integrated races. Mary Scioscia's *Bicycle Rider* tells the story of his first victory, focusing on family values and pride of accomplishment. *El Chino* by Allen Say introduces readers to Bong Way "Billy" Wong, a Chinese American who longed to be a great athlete and found his niche as a bullfighter.

A sense of discovery is added to the satisfaction of a good story when children read about intriguing but little-known lives. Children have a right to read biographies about a wide range of subjects—famous persons, great human beings who were not famous, and even antiheroes.

## Accuracy and Authenticity

Accuracy is the hallmark of good biographical writing, whether it is for adults or for children. More and more writers of juvenile biography are acknowledging primary sources for their materials in either an introductory note or an appended bibliography. Conscientious authors of well-written children's biographies frequently travel to the locale of the story in order to get a "feeling" for a place. They visit museums to study actual objects that were used by their subjects; they spend hours poring over original letters and documents. Much of this research might not be used in the actual biography, but its effect will be evident in the author's true insight into the character of the subject and in the accuracy of the historical detail.

The same kind of careful research should be reflected in the accuracy of the illustrations that convey the time, place, and setting. The dress of the period, the interiors of the houses, the very utensils that are used must be authentic representations. Many books, such as Susanna Reich's *Clara Schumann: Piano Virtuoso* and Albert Marrin's *Terror of the Spanish Main: Henry Morgan and His Buccaneers*, make use of reproductions of maps, letters, and artwork of the period to authenticate the subject matter.

But most difficult of all, perhaps, is the actual portrayal of the subject. There are many drawings and paintings of most historical figures, but an accurate likeness is problematical, particularly for subjects who lived before the advent of photography. In their book *Christopher Columbus: The Great Adventure and How We Know About It,* Delno and Jean West point out:

> There are hundreds of paintings, engravings, woodcuts, and statues of Christopher Columbus, but they were all made after he died by people who never saw him. (p. 13)

Several of these competing portraits are reproduced in their book. They also quote Columbus's son, Ferdinand, who described his father's long face, light eyes, big nose, and red hair, so that readers have a basis for reacting to the illustrations.

Photographs provide authentic illustrations for many biographical accounts of recent subjects, such as Russell Freedman's highly acclaimed photobiographies, Elizabeth Partridge's *Restless Spirit: The Life and Work of Dorothea Lange,* Audrey Osofsky's *Free to Dream: The Making of a Poet, Langston*

*Hughes,* and Ruud van der Rol and Rian Verhoeven's *Anne Frank Beyond the Diary.*

An authentic biography must be true in every detail. A fictionalized biography must also be true to the factual record, and any invented dialogue or background detail must be plausible and true to the times. Yet the truth of what is included in a biography does not quite answer the entire question of its accuracy. Sometimes what is left out is just as important as what goes in.

Formerly, authors of biographies for children avoided writing about certain aspects of the lives of their subjects. Serious criticism has been leveled at biographies of Washington and Jefferson that did not include the fact that they owned many slaves. More-recent biographies, even those for younger children, do include this information. In *Thomas Jefferson* James Cross Giblin approaches his subject with the same meticulous research he applies to his many nonfiction books (see Chapter 11). He writes of Jefferson's ambivalence about slavery,

> Thomas also favored the end of the slave trade. Hadn't he written that "all men are created equal"? And didn't he believe that slavery was wrong? Yes, but he also knew that estates like his beloved Monticello could not be run without slave labor. Thomas went back and forth, back and forth about slavery. What could be done about it? He could not make up his mind. (p. 20)

Certain biographers when writing for younger children might present only a portion of a person's life. In planning their picture book *Abraham Lincoln,* the D'Aulaires deliberately omitted his assassination and closed the book with the end of the Civil War. The authors' purpose was to present the greatness of the man as he lived, for too frequently, they believed, children remember only the manner of Lincoln's death. There is a danger, however, that omissions might oversimplify and thereby distort the truth about a person's life. The critic Jo Carr has argued that it is better not to offer biography to young children at all than to present them with unbalanced portraits distorted by flagrant omissions.[1]

For many years it was thought that children were interested only in reading about the childhoods of great men and women and not about the complexities of their adult activities. For this reason many earlier biographies focused primarily on childhood pranks and legends that suggested future accomplishments, but neglected or rushed through the real achievements of later life. The current emphasis on

*Michael Dooling's illustrations for James Giblin's* Thomas Jefferson: A Picture Book Biography *show this American hero in a warm and sympathetic light.*
Illustration by James Cross Giblin from *Thomas Jefferson: A Picture Book Biography* by James Cross Giblin. Illustrations © 1994 by Michael Dooling.

authentic biography has reversed this trend, since it is much more difficult to find primary source material about a subject's childhood than about her or his adult life. Increasingly, the best authors respect children's right to read honest, objective biographies that tell more of the truth and document their writing with source notes or a bibliography. The Teaching Feature "Thinking Critically About Biographies" shows how one teacher asked his students to compare biographies of the same subjects in order to help them think more critically about authors' objectivity and accuracy.

## Style

The author's language is especially important to biography because it bears the burden of making the subject seem alive and sound real. Documented quotes should be woven smoothly into the narrative. When dialogue is invented, it should have the natural rhythms of speech, regardless of the period it represents, because stilted writing makes characters seem wooden.

---

[1]Jo Carr, "What Do We Do About Bad Biographies?" in *Beyond Fact: Nonfiction for Children and Young People* (Chicago: American Library Association, 1982), pp. 119–129.

# Thinking Critically About Biographies

**Teaching Feature**

At Hilltonia Middle School in Columbus, Ohio, Richard Roth put his students in groups of four to consider which of two biographies was the better book. Some groups read about Abraham Lincoln, using *Lincoln: A Photobiography* by Russell Freedman and *True Stories About Abraham Lincoln* by Ruth Belov Gross. Other groups read *Bully for You, Teddy Roosevelt!* by Jean Fritz and a second biography of Roosevelt. Still others read two selections about Leonardo da Vinci.

First, students read the books individually and noted their reactions to the cover, chapter titles, pictures, and content (facts, bias, writing style), and rated their usefulness. Groups needed only two copies of each book, because each student could read one title and then trade with a partner. Sharing copies also encouraged students to take good notes, including page numbers for reference.

When the students had read both books, the teacher gave each student a blank chart with space for rating each book on the same items, with the following directions: "Rate the categories for each book from 1 to 10: 10 is excellent, 5, average, and 1, poor. As a group, decide what score each book deserves for each category. Then total the scores and determine which book the group thought best overall." The final step was to work as a group to compose a recommendation of their top book for other students to read.

Although not all the groups chose the book that the teacher (or critics) would have chosen, the students gained valuable experience in exercising their own judgment. The teacher planned this study because he wanted all his students to have the opportunity to take stock of their own responses and share them with classmates. He also knew that his students would participate more fully in discussion if they first had a chance to formulate their ideas and write them down. In retrospect, he reported that this process really did encourage critical thinking. There were meaningful group discussions with healthy disagreements about which book was superior. Moreover, students were able to rethink their own first impressions and make comparisons in the interest of fairness and accuracy. In the class discussion that followed the completion of small-group work, the teacher gave the students still more to think about by contributing their own perspectives on the books they had read.

Like in most middle schools, this teacher has many students and a limited time with them each day. One of the advantages of this biography study was that it gave him new insight into their responses and the factors that contribute to their reading interests. It also confirmed his thinking that it is important for students to work through their own responses as they develop ways to appreciate literature.

*Richard Roth*
Hilltonia Middle School, Columbus City Schools, Ohio

---

In today's authentic biography, the author's way with words makes all the difference between a dull and a lively book. The opening paragraph of Jean Fritz's *Harriet Beecher Stowe and the Beecher Preachers* shows how the writer can choose and present detail in a way that engages the reader:

> Harriet Beecher had always understood that, along with her sisters, she was second best in her family. On June 14, 1811, when she'd been born, her father had grumbled to a neighbor, "Wisht it had been a boy!" Of course her father was disappointed. He was Lyman Beecher, a minister in Litchfield, Connecticut, and he was collecting boys. (p. 7)

The narrator's tone always pervades the presentation, but a dispassionate point of view usually is used for authentic biography. Whatever the form or viewpoint, the background materials should be integrated into the narrative with smoothness and proportion. The judicious use of quotes from letters or journals may support the authenticity of biography, but it should not detract from the absorbing account of the life of the subject. Children enjoy a style that is clear and vigorous. The research must be there, but it should be a natural part of the presentation. Jean Fritz's *Harriet Beecher Stowe and the Beecher Preachers* provides masterful demonstrations of this kind of clarity.

The choice of narrator, or point of view, is also an important consideration in the style of a biography. Rather than write about the childhood of a famous person, some authors choose to tell the story from the point of view of a child who was close to the adult character. In *Finding Providence: The Story of Roger Williams,* Avi tells the story of Williams through the voice of Williams's daughter, Mary. This childlike perspective is especially appropriate for the book's audience of beginning readers. Mary E. Lyons chose to tell the life story of African American artist Clementine Hunter in the first person. In *Talking with Tebé,* Lyons explains that despite the fact that

*Mary Lyons presents the life of Clementine Hunter through the artist's own words in* Talking with Tebé: Clementine Hunter, Memory Artist.

*Talking with Tebe* by Mary E. Lyons, editor, © 1998. Reprinted by permission of Houghton Mifflin Company.

over eighty articles were written about Hunter, many still did not consider her a real artist.

> These notions convinced me that it was time Hunter spoke for herself. Most of the text in *Talking with Tebé* is written in her own words. I gathered quotations from magazines, newspapers, and twenty-two taped interviews made by Hunter's friend Mildred Bailey, in 1978. A few quotations are from newspaper columns by François Mignon. (p. 6)

Hearing Hunter's story in her own dignified voice lends the book immediacy and impact.

## Characterization

The characterization of the subject of a biography must be true to life, neither adulatory nor demeaning in tone. The reader should have the opportunity to know the person as a real human being with both shortcomings and virtues. To emphasize the worthiness of their subjects, juvenile biographers sometimes portray them as too good to be true.

Jean Fritz is one author who manages to create vivid portraits of great figures without according them pseudosainthood. She has presented Paul Revere as a busy and sometimes forgetful human being in her humorous yet authentic picture-book biography *And Then What Happened, Paul Revere?* He didn't always meet his deadlines, once producing a hymnbook some eighteen months after he had promised it! A dreamer,

he even left one page in his "Day Book" simply for doodling. The author does not debunk her character; she simply makes him come alive by admitting his foibles, as well as describing his accomplishments.

Comparing two or more biographies of the same subject is one way of understanding the importance of characterization. Doris Faber's *Eleanor Roosevelt, First Lady of the World* and Maryann Weidt's *Stateswoman to the World: A Story About Eleanor Roosevelt* are similar in length and coverage. Both are generally suitable for grades 3 to 5. Both books emphasize the young Eleanor's growing desire for independence, but they provide somewhat different views of the childhood experiences that helped shape her determination and sense of duty.

Barbara Cooney's *Eleanor,* a picture-book biography, also focuses on Eleanor's early years. Beginning the story with Eleanor's birth and her mother's disappointment that this ugly little baby was not a boy, Cooney emphasizes Eleanor's lonely and often fearful childhood. Eleanor's admiration for her beautiful mother is continuously rebuffed, and her passionate love for her father is hampered by his frequent absences and his wild ways. By the time she was 9, both of her parents were dead and Eleanor lived year-round with her Grandmother Hall and several aunts and uncles. At 15, Eleanor was sent to boarding school in London where her love for learning and her quiet intelligence were rewarded. Here for the first time she made many friends and became particularly attached to the headmistress, Mlle. Souvestre. When she returned home after three years, Eleanor had gained a confident understanding of her own unique strengths. Cooney's paintings are well suited to her subject and convey a nice sense of the past through muted colors and carefully researched pictorial details. By showing the young Eleanor at the fringes of the pictures on many pages, Cooney emphasizes her isolation and loneliness. Toward the end of the story, however, Eleanor is pictured trying on a new dress, a lovely red gown that Mlle. Souvestre has urged her to purchase in Paris. Here we see Eleanor squarely in the center of the page, her back to the viewer but her familiar face reflected in the full-length mirror to the right. Cooney thus accentuates Eleanor's coming out, her character now fully formed in all its quiet dignity. The book is a masterful example of how far an artist can go in creating authenticity in biography for children.

Biography must not degenerate into mere eulogy; reexamining should not become debunking. The background of subjects' lives, their conversations, their thoughts, and their actions, should be presented as faithfully to the facts as possible. The subject should also be seen in relation to her or his times, for no person can be "read" in isolation.

# GUIDELINES

## Evaluating Juvenile Biography

### CHOICE OF SUBJECT

Does the subject's life offer interest and meaning for today's child?:

Will knowing this historical or contemporary figure help children understand the past or the present?

Can the subject's experiences widen children's views on the possibilities for their own lives?

### ACCURACY AND AUTHENTICITY

Do the text and illustrations reflect careful research and consistency in presentation?

Does the author provide notes about original source material, a bibliography, or other evidence of documentation?

Are there discrepancies of fact in comparison with other books?

Are there significant omissions that result in a distorted picture of the subject's life?

### STYLE

Are quotations or dialogue used in a way that brings the subject to life?

For a fictionalized biography, does the choice of narrator's point of view add to the story?

Is the author's style clear and readable, with background material included naturally?

### CHARACTERIZATION

Is the subject presented as a believable, multidimensional character, with both strengths and weaknesses?

Does the author avoid both eulogizing and debunking?

### THEME

Does the author's interpretation of the subject represent a fair and balanced approach?

Does the author avoid oversimplifying or manipulating the facts to fit the chosen theme?

## Theme

Underlying the characterization in all biography—whether it be authentic or fictionalized—is the author's interpretation of the subject. No matter how impartial an author might be, a life story cannot be written without some interpretation. An author's selection of facts can limit the dimensions of the portraiture or highlight certain features. In this context every author walks a thin line between theme and bias. Time usually lends perspective and objectivity, but contemporary biography might tend more toward bias. Teachers and librarians need to help children realize that all biographies have a point of view determined by their authors. Again, a comparison of several biographies of the same person written in different time periods would help children discover this fact.

Frequently in juvenile biography the theme will be identified in the title, as in *Martin Luther King: The Peaceful Warrior* by Ed Clayton or Milton Meltzer's *Ten Queens: Portraits of Women of Power*. Both of these titles name their subjects and point up the theme of the books. Meltzer explains that his subjects were chosen not because they were heroines or saints but because they were complex women who held power in their hands and used it. His title suggests that these women were not the passive royalty of fairy tales but that they were strong, vigorous, and controlling.

In picture-book biographies, illustrations as well as the story title reveal the theme. Author/illustrator Peter Sis offers an artist's interpretation of Christopher Columbus in *Follow the Dream: The Story of Christo-*

*pher Columbus*. Sis grew up in Czechoslovakia, a country surrounded by a political "wall" known as the Iron Curtain. He relates his background to Columbus's by emphasizing the many forces that walled Columbus in. He describes the ancient maps that showed the known world surrounded by a high wall. One such map is drawn on the book's endpapers; the title page shows a small boy peering out through a small doorway in the wall to the unknown. The wall motif appears consistently throughout the book, always countered by an opening or archway through which Columbus can follow his dream. Although this book ends with the arrival of Columbus in 1492 and says nothing about his character as a leader or his later cruelty to the native people, the theme of breaking down the wall surrounding the old world is a fresh insight. A close examination of the last picture and its border, however, suggests that Sis questions whether civilization was much of a "gift" to the New World.

There is a danger in oversimplifying and forcing all facts to fit a single mold. An author must not recreate and interpret a life history in terms of one fixed picture, particularly in a biography that covers the full scope of a subject's life. The most common people have several facets to their personalities; the great are likely to be multidimensional. The perceptive biographer concentrates on those items from a full life that helped mold and form that personality. It is this selection and focus that create the theme of the biography. The Guidelines "Evaluating Juvenile Biography" summarizes the criteria we have discussed in this section.

# *Types of Presentation and Coverage*

Writers of adult biography are by definition bound to try to re-create the subject's life as fully as possible, with complete detail and careful documentation. Writers of children's biography, however, may use one of several approaches. The resulting types of biography need individual consideration, for each offers to children a different perspective and a different appeal. Keep in mind, however, that a single book might fit into more than one of the following categories.

## Picture-Book Biographies

A biography cast in a picture-book form might span the subject's lifetime or a part of it; it might be directed to a very young audience or to a somewhat older one; it might be authentic or fictionalized. Whatever the case, it remains for the pictures to carry a substantial part of the interpretation, as Leonard Marcus points out:

> Illustrations, then, contribute more to a picture book biography than occasional picture-equivalents of the author's words. They traffic to some degree in unnamable objects, states and feelings. . . . Along with what it tells us about the values, temperament and concerns of a biography's central character, fine illustration also puts us in contact with an individuality—and a form of praise—that is esthetic.[2]

This sense of heightened perception comes with the illustrations by Alice and Martin Provensen for their Caldecott Medal winner *The Glorious Flight: Across the Channel with Louis Blériot, July 25, 1909*. Papa Blériot carries himself with intrepid grace in his unsuccessful attempts to fly, and the pictures that show him above the channel use contrast and perspective to convey the elation and danger of flight. Many historical and background details appear in the illustrations without being mentioned in the text, inviting speculation, inferences, and discussion. Even the hardcover front of this book contains new picture material that will contribute to children's feeling for the time and place.

Ingri d'Aulaire and Edgar Parin d'Aulaire were among the first to create beautifully illustrated picture-book biographies for children. As new citizens of this country, they were fascinated with American heroes, and the biographies they wrote include *George Washington, Abraham Lincoln,* and *Columbus*. Their charming but idealized pictures sometimes made their subjects seem larger than life.

*Malcah Zeldis captures the essence of African American culture and the energy of the civil rights movement in his illustrations for Rosemary Bray's* Martin Luther King.
Illustration from *Martin Luther King* by Rosemary Bray, Illustrated by Malcah Zeldis. Illustration copyright © 1995 by Malcah Zeldis. Used by permission of Greenwillow Books, an imprint of HarperCollins Publishers.

In Jean Fritz's *What's the Big Idea, Ben Franklin?* the droll pictures by Margot Tomes emphasize a particular side of Franklin's character—his ingenuity. Trina Schart Hyman's illustration of Samuel Adams thumbing his nose at the British flag helps set the tone for Fritz's biography *Why Don't You Get a Horse, Sam Adams?* The same illustrator and author highlight their subject's vanity and penchant for flourishes in *Will You Sign Here, John Hancock?* Tomie de Paola's pictures for *Can't You Make Them Behave, King George?* emphasize Fritz's humor as she helps readers think of the unpopular English monarch in a new way.

Other picture-book biographies have established the heroic struggles of many African Americans. David Adler, who has provided many fine biographies for younger readers, tells of the life of an important figure in the fight against slavery and for human rights in *A Picture Book of Sojourner Truth*. In *Dear Benjamin Banneker* Andrea Davis Pinkney and Brian Pinkney have collaborated to tell the story of an African American scientist and inventor who was an important contributor to the development of the United States in its earliest beginnings. Malcah Zeldis's vibrant folk art illustrations for Rosemary L. Bray's *Martin Luther King* are the perfect accompaniment for this story about a

---

[2]Leonard S. Marcus, "Life Drawings: Some Notes on Children's Picture Book Biographies," *The Lion and the Unicorn* 4 (summer 1980): 17.

man of the people, while Floyd Cooper's realistic oil paintings bring the same sense of flowing warmth to *Coming Home: From the Life of Langston Hughes* that this writer's poems brought to his listeners.

The mood or tone of a biography can be quickly established by its pictures. Rocco Baviera's richly textured oil paintings provide a dark and brooding underpinning to Joseph Bruchac's *A Boy Called Slow: The True Story of Sitting Bull*. Brian Pinkney's scratchboard pictures add a sense of vigorous movement to Andrea Davis Pinkney's biographies of Alvin Ailey, Bill Picket, and Duke Ellington. Brian Pinkney's *Duke Ellington: The Piano Prince and His Orchestra* was a Caldecott Honor Book.

Max Ginsburg's paintings capture the high drama of Robert D. San Souci's *Kate Shelley: Bound for Legend*. Kate was a 15-year-old growing up on a farm in Iowa in 1881 when a terrible storm washed away the trestle bridge over Honey Creek. Realizing that the Midnight Express with hundreds of passengers was due, she set off in the storm to give the warning. Ginsburg's vivid paintings convey a sense of mounting tension as the storm builds. The wild fury of the storm and Kate's terrifying struggle to cross the Des Moines River Bridge to reach help is brought to life, and the illustrations underscore the danger and magnify Kate's courage in facing the elements.

A comparison of the impact of the illustrations can be made through four picture-book biographies of fossil discoverer Mary Anning. Michael Dooling's illustrations for *Mary Anning and the Sea Dragon* by Jeannine Atkins are representational oil paintings, whereas Don Brown's impressionistic water color pictures in *Rare Treasure* are lighter in tone and mood. Catherine Brighton's watercolors for *The Fossil Girl* are more solidly realistic but the illustrations are set in comic book format and conversations are carried in speech balloons. Sheila Moxley's bright, flat colors in *Stone Girl, Bone Girl* by Lawrence Anholt give a primitive folk art appeal to the pictures. Children could discuss the effect of the illustrations on their interpretations of Mary's character and her story as well as compare the accuracy of the information conveyed in the four stories.

Diane Stanley is known for biographies in picture-book format with exquisitely detailed paintings. Stanley's *Leonardo da Vinci* was a winner of the Orbis Pictus Award in 1997. Her life of *Joan of Arc* is based on Joan's own words, taken from the transcripts of her trial. The illustrations, which include maps and close-ups of fifteenth-century artifacts, recall the illuminated books of such masters as the Limbourg Brothers. Stanley's *Cleopatra* tells the story of Cleopatra's life from the age of 18 until her death, and shows a woman who was not the siren of movie legend but a bright and intellectually vigorous leader. She had great dreams for

*Max Ginsburg's illustration foretells the tense drama that will unfold in Robert D. San Souci's* Kate Shelley: Bound for Legend, *a picture-book biography of a young American heroine.*

her people and hoped to see these realized through alliances with Julius Caesar and Mark Anthony. The mosaic portrait of Cleopatra on the cover suggests her Greek ancestry, and motifs of Greek art are found throughout the book. No book as brief as this can do full justice to a complex subject, but Stanley does succeed in portraying Cleopatra's strengths as a leader and in providing an intriguing invitation to further study.

Stanley and husband Peter Vennema collaborated in writing *Cleopatra; Shaka: King of the Zulus; Good Queen Bess: The Story of Elizabeth I of England; Charles Dickens: The Man Who Had Great Expectations;* and *Bard of Avon: The Story of William Shakespeare.* Diane Stanley both wrote and illustrated *Peter the Great.* Fay Stanley, Diane Stanley's mother, wrote *The Last Princess: The Story of Princess Ka'iulani of Hawai'i.* Clear, almost primitive paintings by Diane Stanley help to tell the poignant story of the betrayal of Hawaii by Americans and the sad death of Hawaii's last princess at age 23.

In *William Shakespeare and the Globe* Aliki sets the few known facts about Shakespeare in dramatic form and in five acts manages to convey a wealth of information about Shakespeare, his time, and the story of the reconstruction of the Globe theater, which was finished in 1997. The book is a fine example of the integration of pictures and text. The imaginative form, the lively verbal narrative, the quotes from Shakespeare's works, and the pictures, diagrams, maps, and overall visual design convey an understanding of Shakespeare's life that is much more than the sum of anecdotes and facts. Aliki always includes details that intrigue children, but in so doing also provides insight into the way her subjects lived.

The last several years have seen an increased interest in biographies of people in the arts. Jeanette Winter's paintings in her many biographies such as *My Name Is Georgia: A Portrait, Sebastian: A Book About Bach, Cowboy Charlie: The Story of Charles M. Russell,* and *Diego,* written by Jonah Winter, bring rich color and meaning to her brief books. In *Diego* we learn about the life of the famous Mexican artist Diego Rivera. The small pictures construct scenes from his early years, full of a magical sense of celebrations and play, as well as times of turmoil that were reflected in the huge murals Rivera painted as an adult.

Milton Meltzer reminds us that biography is more than the personal history of one person:

> If biography is well done, it is also social history. [As a biographer] I must tell the story of my subject's time and of the people who lived through that time.[3]

This approach usually calls for a complete biography of the subject. In the case of picture-book biographies, it suggests the sharing of several titles with different points of view. Together, they can provide the range of information that sets a subject in context. David Adler's *A Picture Book of Christopher Columbus* portrays a beneficent leader passing out trinkets on the beach at San Salvador and states that he had "found" the New World. Vicki Liestman's *Columbus Day* and Clint Twist's *Christopher Columbus: Discovery of the Americas* present a more balanced picture of Columbus's accomplishments (despite Twist's title). In her note at the beginning of her book, Leistman mentions the A.D. 1000 landing of Leif Eriksson on the coast of North America. She also includes the fact that Columbus forcibly loaded some five hundred natives onto ships bound for Spain.

## Simplified Biographies

Not all children who have an interest in biographical information are in full command of the skills of reading. Some of these children are beginning readers;

some read independently but are not ready for a long or complex text; some are older children with specialized interests but low skill levels. Various kinds of simplified biographies, usually short and with many illustrations, have been published in response to the needs of these children.

Many picture-book biographies, of course, are written in simple language that many primary-grade readers can handle on their own. David Adler's *A Picture Book of Thomas Jefferson* and *A Picture Book of Benjamin Franklin* provide straightforward accounts of highlights from the lives of these two founding fathers. Companion books are available about George Washington, Abraham Lincoln, and John F. Kennedy as well as other well-known figures, such as Sojourner Truth, Martin Luther King, Jackie Robinson, and Rosa Parks. The advantage of these books is their readability and the support provided by their illustrations. The disadvantage is that, to increase readability, the author had to leave out many of the complexities of character and accomplishment that make these subjects memorable.

Aliki also writes and illustrates easy-vocabulary picture biographies. In *The Story of Johnny Appleseed,* she has captured the humor and simplicity of the legendary pioneer. Similar in simplicity is *A Weed Is a Flower: The Life of George Washington Carver.* Again, Aliki has made meaningful for the youngest reader the inspiring story of a man who was born a slave but lived to become one of the greatest research scientists in the United States. Another picture biography by the same author is *The Many Lives of Benjamin Franklin.*

Many simple biographies are not just for beginning readers but are directed toward an 8- or 9-year-old audience. One account that is simply told but difficult to put down is Ann McGovern's *The Secret Soldier: The Story of Deborah Sampson.* Dressed as a man, Deborah Sampson fought in the American Revolution, managing to escape detection for more than a year. Newly proficient readers will appreciate the detail about Deborah's childhood as well as the format that breaks the text into manageable parts.

Several books that are directed at 7- to 10-year-olds emphasize contemporary figures and those from minority populations. These include *Mary McLeod Bethune* by Eloise Greenfield and *Malcolm X* by Arnold Adoff. In *Rosa Parks,* Eloise Greenfield tells the story of the African American woman whose refusal to move to the back of a bus in Montgomery, Alabama, triggered events that grew into the civil rights movement. These books are characterized by brief text enhanced by many pictures.

Laura Driscoll's *Sammy Sosa* and *Slugger Season: McGuire and Sosa* both illustrated by Ken Call are among the simplified biographies that fall into the high-interest/low-reading-level category, where the most popular subjects seem to be from the sports and

[3]Milton Meltzer, "Selective Forgetfulness: Christopher Columbus Reconsidered," *New Advocate* 5 (winter 1992): 1.

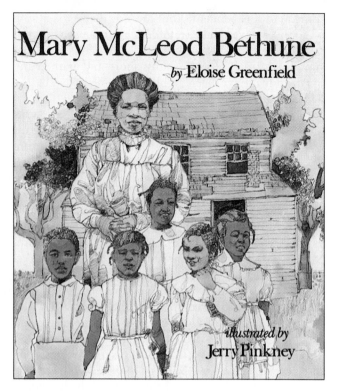

*Younger readers will enjoy simplified biographies such as Eloise Greenfields's* Mary McLeod Bethune *with illustrations by Jerry Pinkney.*

Illustration copyright © 1977 by Jerry Pinkney. Used by permission of HarperCollins Publishers, New York, NY.

entertainment worlds. The text in these books might be very brief, and illustrations or photographs might be used very liberally. In short, the books are designed to catch and keep the eye of the reluctant or less-able older reader. Unfortunately the writing in some of these books is heavily influenced by the tendency to "hype" a subject. Even though children have a great appetite for personal close-ups of celebrities, it is difficult to find books of this type that are written with perspective and produced with care.

Robyn Montana Turner has published well-written, short biographies of artists, including *Frida Kahlo, Dorothea Lange,* and *Georgia O'Keefe.* Illustrated with photographs and many reproductions of each artist's work, these books offer insights into the artist's approach to her work as well as details about her life. In addition to her life of Clementine Hunter discussed earlier, Mary Lyons's fine series on African American artists includes books on painters Minnie Evans, Bill Traylor, and Horace Pippin, quiltmaker Harriet Powers, blacksmith Philip Simmons, and woodworker and carpenter Tom Day. Through words and pictures Lyons gives readers glimpses of social history, fascinating details about the lives of these fine artists, and information about the links each of them had to their African heritage.

## Partial Biographies

One of the liberties allowed writers of biographies for juveniles is the freedom to write about only part of the subject's life. Authors are able to focus, if they wish, on a time of high drama and let the demands of constructing a good story help set the time frame for the book. William Miller has chosen the picture-book format to recount critical moments in the lives of two African Americans. In *Frederick Douglass, The Last Days of Slavery* Miller tells of Douglass's childhood experiences that led to his rebellion against slavery. Miller's *Zora Hurston and the Chinaberry Tree* highlights Zora's important relationship with her mother and her fascination with the folklore and songs of her African American heritage. By highlighting these events, Miller shows how these experiences became influential in the life's work of Douglass and Hurston.

David Kherdian deals with only a portion of the life of Veron Dumehjian, his mother, in *The Road from Home: The Story of an Armenian Girl.* What is central to the story is her family's suffering in the massacre and dispersal of Armenians by the Turks. If those events had been related as only a small part of her life experiences, their impact and historical significance might have been less perceptible. Kherdian chose to assume his mother's first-person point of view, which adds passion and immediacy to this fictionalized biography.

Andrea Warren has focused on the childhood years of two unfamiliar figures. In *Orphan Train Rider: One Boy's True Story,* winner of the 1996 Boston Globe Horn Book Award for nonfiction, Warren relates the story of the Children's Aid Society's efforts to resettle orphaned city children in the Midwest beginning in the 1850s and ending in 1929. This information is grounded in the story of one boy, Lee Nailling, who experienced two difficult placements before he finally found a loving home with his third. His efforts to stay with his younger brother and to find his other siblings are heartbreaking. Lee's story makes the information about the orphan trains all the more poignant and compelling. Warren's *Pioneer Girl: Growing Up on the Prairie* tells the story of Grace McCance Snyder, who grew up in Nebraska in the late 1800s. Warren based the story on Snyder's memoir, and added information on the settlers' life from additional sources. The book makes a wonderful companion to Laura Ingalls Wilder's Little House books and to William Anderson's *Laura Ingall's Wilder: A Biography* and *Laura's Album: A Remembrance Scrapbook of Laura Ingall's Wilder.*

Some partial biographies do furnish information about the subject's entire life but focus on a few incidents that are particularly memorable. Virginia Hamilton has written a complex story in *Anthony*

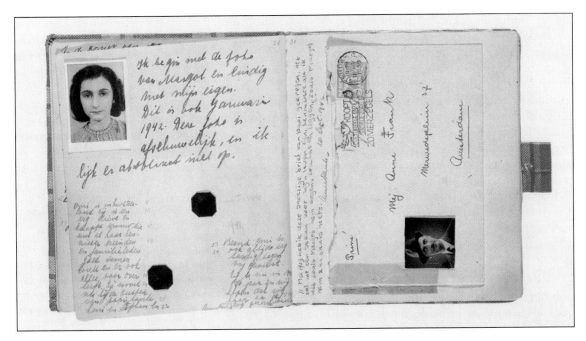

*In* Anne Frank Beyond the Diary *by Ruud van der Rol and Rian Verhoeven, Anne's life is documented by family pictures, maps, letters, and excerpts from her diary.*

From *Beyond the Diary: A Photographic Remembrance* by Ruud van der Rol and Rian Verhoeven: Copyright © AFF/AFS, Amsterdam, The Netherlands.

*Burns: The Defeat and Triumph of a Fugitive Slave.* By creating a fictional narrative about Burns's early life from documents about his later life, she interweaves historical fiction with true biography. Born a slave in Virginia, Anthony Burns was 20 when he escaped to Boston. For a few short months he lived as a free man, until his former owner came to Boston and invoked the Fugitive Slave Act, demanding him back. Thousands of abolitionists rioted and Richard Dana defended him without charge. Yet it was to no avail. Burns was sent back to Virginia, where he was shackled and imprisoned in a tiny room for the next four months. Finally news of his whereabouts reached two ministers in Boston, who raised money to purchase him. He was freed and sent to Canada, where he became a minister. He died when he was only 28 years old, from the dreadful treatment he had received while in jail. Students in middle school interested in pursuing the meaning of the Fugitive Slave Act could do no better than to read this compelling story of the last slave ever seized on Massachusetts soil.

Other biographies are incomplete for the simple reason that a full treatment of the subject's complex life would make a book too long and unwieldy for young readers. There have been several such biographies of Abraham Lincoln, for instance. Carl Sandburg wrote a partial biography for children titled *Abe Lincoln Grows Up.* It was made from the first twenty-seven chapters of the first volume of the longest and most definitive biography of Lincoln for adults, Sandburg's *Abraham Lincoln: The Prairie Years.* For his juvenile biography Sandburg included Lincoln's birth and boyhood until he was 19 and "grown up." In singing prose that begs to be read aloud, the author describes Lincoln's desire for knowledge:

> And some of what he wanted so much, so deep down, seemed to be in books. Maybe in books he would find the answers to dark questions pushing around in the pools of his thoughts, and the drifts of his mind. (p. 135)

Biographical works about real young people in history can provide a limited but interesting view of famous figures who were close to them. Barbara Brenner's *On the Frontier with Mr. Audubon* is technically a partial biography of apprentice painter Joseph Mason. As a young teenager he accompanied John James Audubon on an expedition down the Mississippi River to collect and make life drawings of birds. Mason painted some of the backgrounds for Audubon's *Birds of America*, although his name did not appear on the finished paintings. Brenner used Audubon's diary to reconstruct the activities of their trip, then recreated the story as a journal that the apprentice might have kept, focusing on Audubon's obsession with his work.

Ruud van der Rol and Rian Verhoeven have produced an unusual form of biography in *Anne Frank Beyond the Diary: A Photographic Remembrance.* The authors, both staff members of the Anne Frank House in Amsterdam, have gathered together a variety of materials including photographs from Otto Frank's widow, Elfriede, and Miep Gies, the woman who helped hide the Frank family. In this powerful photo-biography, captioned photographs provide a brief introduction to Anne's childhood before the war and events surrounding Hitler's rise, but the book concentrates mainly on the days following Anne's thirteenth birthday and the gift of her diary. Interspersed with explanatory narrative, the family photographs, maps, diagrams, journal excerpts, and interviews broaden the context for Anne's diary and help readers visualize the setting for her brief life. This documentation helps deepen the power of Anne's words and further strengthens her memory.

## Complete Biographies

Complete biography spans the subject's lifetime. It can be relatively simple or difficult, authentic or fictionalized, but the reader should expect a view that has some depth, some balance, some sense of perspective. Among types of biographies, this category has traditionally been the largest, although in recent years trends have favored other kinds of presentations.

Russell Freedman's *Franklin Delano Roosevelt* is an example of a biography that is complete and authentic. The inherent drama of the subject, the clarity of the writing, and the generous use of photographs all contribute to the book's appeal for readers age 10 and up. His fine biography sketches out Roosevelt's major achievements as a politician and statesman, but its real strength lies in the detailed information it provides about his personal life. Freedman probes the facade of a man who managed to be a very private person in spite of having the very public job of being president of the United States. Students are fascinated by the lengths to which Roosevelt went in order to camouflage his paralysis. He was hardly ever photographed in a wheelchair, but Freedman does provide one such picture. Freedman's *Eleanor Roosevelt* is a wonderful companion book. By highlighting Eleanor's insecurities, as well as her great accomplishments, Freedman presents an inspiring portrait for children awash in modern-day media blitzes that seem to worship glamour and triviality over courage and inner strength.

Barbara Harrison and Daniel Terris's *A Twilight Struggle* is the honest account of the life of another complex American president, John F. Kennedy. The authors describe the contrasts in the man:

> He set highest standards for himself and for his country even while he encouraged the excesses of competition. He sought peace, and he brought the nation to the brink of war. He was full of wit and energy and life, and yet he was preoccupied with tragedy and death. (p. 133)

The authors' candid account of his failings as well as his accomplishments does not diminish Kennedy's place in history but instead broadens our understanding of a man who faced personal and world problems and endured physical and emotional pain to follow his vision for America. Wilborn Hampton's memoir, *Kennedy Assassinated: The World Mourns: A Reporter's Story* makes a compelling companion to this fine biography.

Some of Jean Fritz's picture-book biographies could be classified as complete because they deal with the subject's entire life span, but she has also written longer books about American figures, such as James Madison in *The Great Little Madison*, Theodore Roosevelt in *Bully for You, Teddy Roosevelt!* and General Thomas J. Jackson in *Stonewall*. All three books deal with complex characters in an evenhanded way. In *Stonewall*, for instance, Fritz contrasts the general's heroic Civil War battlefield behavior against his personal idiosyncrasies. The man who kept his line "standing like a stone wall" at Manassas prescribed unusual diets for himself (stale bread and lean meat, or lemons to suck) and lived by arbitrary, self-imposed rules for posture, prayer, and every other form of human conduct. In *Harriet Beecher Stowe and the Beecher Preachers* and *You Want Women to Vote, Lizzie Stanton?* Fritz turns her talents to two important female subjects. Both of these women were born into ages that expected little of them, and both rose above these limitations to contribute to the fight for human rights and women's rights. In all her books Fritz gives us authentic narrative enlivened by personal observations and quotes from contemporaries. Her lists of sources and bibliographies demonstrate her high standards for careful scholarship as well as vivid writing.

The increased interest in biographies of women can be seen in other fine books, such as Patricia and Frederick McKissack's *Sojourner Truth*, Doris Faber's *Calamity Jane*, Polly Schoyer Brooks's *Cleopatra*, and Russell Freedman's *Eleanor Roosevelt, Martha Graham: A Dancer's Life* and *Babe Didrikson Zaharias*. In all these books, through scrupulous research and captivating narration, the authors manage to tackle larger-than-life heroines and turn them into real people without diminishing the significance of their achievements.

Natalie S. Bober's *Abigail Adams: Witness to a Revolution* is as fascinating for its inside look at a critical period of American history as it is for its portrait of an intelligent and independent woman who took very seriously her role as loving wife and mother. Using Adams's letters as her main source (over a thousand of them remain), Bober creates a compelling voice for this extraordinary woman and brings the years of America's beginnings to life.

Becoming immersed in this thorough biography is like being a long-term guest in Abigail's home. Rather than being put off by its length, older children will close the book and return to their own time only with the greatest reluctance. Set in the same time period, *The Ingenious Mr. Peale: Patriot, Painter, and Man of Science* by Janet Wilson is a wonderful companion book. Both volumes paint a vivid portrait of eighteenth-century life and men and women who were actively involved with a wide range of interests and issues.

The story of a twentieth-century contributor to our country's history is told in Elizabeth Partridge's excellent *Restless Spirit: The Life and Work of Dorothea Lange*. The book is made all the more fascinating by the author's personal memories of Lange; her father, Ron Partridge, was Lange's assistant, and Lange was a close family friend until her death. This photobiography is also a history of major social issues of the first half of the twentieth century as we follow Lange from the migrant camps in the depression to the Jim Crow South, to the Japanese internment camps, and to California shipbuilding factories staffed mainly by women during World War II. Lange's commitment to people rather than to pretty pictures is as evident through her moving photographs as through Partridge's words.

Historian Albert Marrin has chosen well-known figures and documents their times as well as their lives. In *The Sea King* Marrin explores the world of Sir Francis Drake. In the compelling prologue Drake has returned to England aboard the *Golden Hind* after sailing around the world. The Spanish Ambassador insists that Drake be executed as "the master thief of the unknown world," and at a court banquet Queen Elizabeth addresses Drake:

> "Master Drake," she said solemnly, a slight frown on her face. "The King of Spain has asked for your head, and we have a weapon here with which to remove it."
>
> One of the court gentleman gave her a gilded sword, which she handed to a visiting French nobleman. "We shall ask Monsieur . . . to be the headsman. (p. 7)

With that command the Frenchman tapped Drake upon his right shoulder and the Queen addressed him, "Arise, Sir Francis Drake." This beginning is indicative of the exciting story that is about to unfold as Marrin provides a highly readable account of a significant historical period and a man who was a central figure in critically important events. Marrin weaves the same attention to detail and good storytelling into other books such as *Unconditional Surrender: U. S. Grant and the Civil War* and *Terror of the Spanish Main: Henry Morgan and His Buccaneers* and *Plains Warrior: Chief Quanah Parker and the Comanches*. These books are illustrated with maps and reproductions of primary source materials and include footnotes and a list of additional readings.

The life of African American poet Langston Hughes is celebrated in Audrey Osofsky's, Free to Dream: The Making of a Poet: Langston Hughes.

From *Free to Dream: The Making of a Poet: Langston Hughes* by Audrey Osofsky, Jacket portrait circa 1925 by Winold Reiss. Courtesy of the National Portrait Gallery, Smithsonian Institution. Used by permission of Lothrop, Lee & Shepard Books, a division of William Morrow Company/HarperCollins Publishers.

Children, particularly those who are avid readers or writers, will enjoy reading about well-known creators of favorite books. Beverly Gherman, who has written fine biographies of Agnes DeMille and Georgia O'Keefe for older readers, uncovers the essence of the gentle and shy creator of *Charlotte's Web* in *E. B. White: Some Writer*. In *Ezra Jack Keats: A Biography with Illustrations*, Dean Engel and Florence B. Freedman have used interviews with Ezra Jack Keats and Keats's essays to form the basis of their loving portrait of this children's author and illustrator, who overcame a variety of obstacles to create a world of pleasure for children. Many of Keats's own drawings are used to illustrate his life and to make the connections between his own experiences and those of his characters.

In Audrey Osofsky's *Free to Dream: The Making of a Poet: Langston Hughes* we come to know this gentle man through excerpts from his poems and wonderful photographs as well as through Osofsky's writing. Older readers familiar with Walt Whitman's poetry will enjoy Catherine Reef's *Walt Whitman*, an honest portrayal of this great American poet. The biography includes mention of his homosexuality and focuses on Whitman's generous spirit and his democratic idealism. Accounts of his life, particularly his involvement in the Civil War as a battlefield nurse, are interspersed with quotes from his poetry and enlivened by photographs of Whitman's times and his works. This same audience will also benefit from the broad perspective presented in Clinton Cox's *Mark Twain*. The subtitle of this book is, appropriately, *America's Humorist, Dreamer, Prophet.* Told in lively prose, Cox's biography is filled with quotes from Twain's writing. In addition we come to see him not merely as a fine storyteller but also as someone haunted by the injustices of racism and committed to the rights of the common people.

The Cherokee leader Sequoyah had unique gifts as a writer and shared these with his people in the form of a whole system of writing, the Cherokee alphabet, which is still used today. Born in the late 1700s, Sequoyah was more than a teacher and author, however. He was a wise and talented leader who strove to unite his people in spite of their betrayal by the United States government. Janet Klausner's fine biography *Sequoyah's Gift* chronicles his life within the context of the broader events surrounding the emerging nation in the early 1800s and the tragedy of the Trail of Tears.

Among the many complete biographies for children are a few that have been awarded the Newbery Medal. One of these is the story of a little-known black pioneer of freedom. *Amos Fortune, Free Man* by Elizabeth Yates is the moving account of a common man who lived simply and greatly. Born free in Africa, he was sold as a slave in North America. In time he purchased his own freedom and that of several others. When he was 80 years old, Amos Fortune purchased twenty-five acres of land in the shadow of his beloved mountain, Monadnock—"the mountain that stands alone." Like Monadnock, Fortune stood alone, a rock of strength and security for all those he loved.

Frequently biographers choose subjects who are credited with unique achievements, whatever the field. Most authors would be dubious about writing an interesting biography for children about a mathematician, but Jean Lee Latham was challenged. She studied mathematics, astronomy, oceanography, and seamanship. Then she went to Boston and Salem to talk with descendants of Nathaniel Bowditch and to do research on the geographical and maritime backgrounds of her story. The result of all this painstaking preparation was the Newbery Medal winner *Carry On, Mr. Bowditch,* the amazing story of Nat Bowditch, who had little chance for schooling but mastered the secrets of navigation and wrote a textbook that was used for more than a hundred years.

A more recent Newbery Medal winner is Russell Freedman's *Lincoln: A Photobiography.* One of the great accomplishments of this book is its groundbreaking use of archival photographs, not just to break up and decorate the text but to seriously extend the reader's understanding of the subject. Yet the text stands as an accomplishment in its own right as a comprehensive, insightful, and readable account of a complex person living in a complicated time. It is very difficult to bring fresh perspective, as Freedman has done, to a story that has been told so often.

## Collective Biographies

Many children looking for biographical information want brief material about specific people or about specific endeavors. Many collective biographies have been published to meet this need. In scope and difficulty they run the gamut—some have one-paragraph sketches of many subjects, others have long essays on just a few. Like other books, collective biographies must be judged on more than title and appearance.

Russell Freedman's *The Wright Brothers: How They Invented the Airplane* is an outstanding biography of two people whose lives and work were so closely intertwined that it would be difficult to choose just one to write about. Using archival photographs as he has done in other books, Freedman reconstructs the engrossing story that led to Kitty Hawk and many years of achievement thereafter. In the process he illuminates the character and commitment of Wilbur and Orville Wright.

Collective biographies are an ideal format for highlighting the contributions of more ordinary people whose lives might not bring with them the documentation that lends itself to the writing of full biographies. *In Search of the Spirit,* by Sheila Hamanaka and Ayano Ohmi, is a beautifully presented photo essay about six Japanese artisans designated as living national treasures for their work. A brief life history is given for each artist, and clear photographs show how each of the men work. The book also provides directions for silk painting, bamboo weaving, Noh movements, and pottery making. Brandon Marie Miller's *Buffalo Gals: Women of the Old West* provides a glimpse of a period in American history when women stepped beyond the usual restraints of their roles. The American West of the 1800s provided the space for women of all races to challenge perceptions of the weaker sex. Joyce Hansen's *Women of Hope: Portraits of African American Women Who Made a Difference* includes stunning photographs of African American women and brief one-page biographies of subjects such as Ruby Dee, Alice Walker, and Fanny Lou Hammer.

Collective biographies seldom deal with subjects whose stories can be woven together as smoothly as *The Wright Brothers* or *Buffalo Gals: Women of the Old West*. Most have many brief entries about individuals whose interests or accomplishments are similar. Women have not been slighted in such collections and books as *Inspirations: Stories About Women Artists* and *Visions: Stories About Women Artists,* both by Leslie Sills, and *Focus: Five Women Photographers* by Sylvia Wolf. Excellent introductions to the stories of women who excelled in the arts, these books feature names that many children will recognize, but they also highlight the achievements of less well known figures from diverse cultures. These include artists Alice Neel and Betye Saar and photographers Flor Garduño and Sandy Skoglund.

Kathleen Krull and Kathryn Hewitt have collaborated on highly entertaining collections of anecdotes about famous politicians, athletes, artists, writers, and musicians. In *Lives of the Artists: Masterpieces, Messes (and What the Neighbors Thought)* Kathe Kollwitz is shown as a passionate antiwar activist who cared little about her appearance. Artist Marcel Duchamp had a wonderful sense of humor, ate spaghetti with butter and cheese for dinner every night, and let his apartment accumulate several inches of dust to use in his paintings. Although these aren't necessarily the facts found in the usual reference books, they help to highlight the uniqueness of the artist. These books also prove to children that heroes and heroines are not always perfect and sometimes are perfectly awful. The visual portraits by Kathryn Hewitt provide summaries of each artist's work and life.

Pat Cummings has provided similar insights into the lives of illustrators of children's books in three volumes of *Talking with Artists*. Illustrators such as Peter Sis, Paul O. Zelinsky, Floyd Cooper, Lois Ehlert, Denise Fleming, Brian Pinkney, and Vera B. Williams respond to Cummings's questions and reflect upon their current work as well as their childhood memories. Each profile is accompanied by examples of the artist's childhood art and current work. In her *Talking with Adventurers,* Cummings interviews such risk takers as ethologist Jane Goodall, underwater photographer David Doubilet and rainforest ecologist Christina Allen.

In *Keeping Secrets: The Girlhood Diaries of Seven Women Writers* Mary Lyons has chosen to examine the childhood diaries of seven women writers of the nineteenth century, and she shapes a narrative of their lives around these private journals. In the musings of

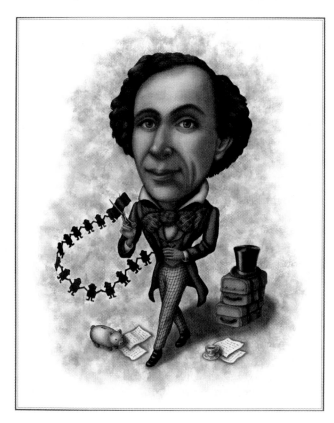

*Kathryn Hewitt's droll caricature of Hans Christian Andersen includes details about his stories in this picture from* Lives of the Writers: Comedies, Tragedies, (and What the Neighbors Thought) *by Kathleen Krull.*

Illustration from *Lives of the Writers: Comedies, Tragedies (and What the Neighbors Thought)* by Kathryn Krull, illustrations copyright ©1994 by Kathryn Hewitt, reprinted with permission of Harcourt, Inc.

Louisa May Alcott, Kate Chopin, Sarah Jane Foster, and others, Lyons identifies the barriers of gender and race that these independent spirits had to face, yet she also reveals that they had the same longings, frustrations, and joys of today's adolescents. Her account of their struggles as young women forges an important link across the centuries. Peter Burchard has also used the diaries of Charlotte Forten, one of Lyons's subjects, as the basis for a longer biography of this courageous teacher and abolitionist.

Sports figures are also included in collective biographies such as *Champions* by Bill Littlefield. Ten well-written portraits of champions like jockey Julie Krone and baseball player Roberto Clemente read like short stories as Littlefield highlights the contributions of men and women athletes, some who have changed the face of their sport. In *Leagues Apart* Lawrence Ritter highlights the lives of twenty-two African Americans who played in the Negro Leagues. This collection not only reveals the important contributions of these men but also portrays the racial bigotry and often humiliating conditions under which they played.

*Take a Walk in Their Shoes* by Glennette Tilley Turner introduces fourteen African Americans who played a part in the struggle for racial equality. An unusual feature is the inclusion of brief dramas that can be performed by children to highlight each subject's contribution. Martin Luther King, Jr., Rosa Parks, Arthur Schomburg, Leontyne Price, Frederick Douglass, and "Satchel" Paige are a few of the prominent African Americans featured in this book.

The Great Lives series offers well-written accounts of achievers in many fields. Doris and Harold Faber are the authors of *Great Lives: Nature and the Environment*, which includes twenty-five biographical sketches spanning almost two centuries. Read individually, each sketch is clear and furnishes the context necessary for understanding its subject. Read as a whole, the book provides excellent perspective on our changing ideas about our relationship to our environment. Some of the other titles in this series are *Great Lives: American Government,* also by Doris and Harold Faber; *Great Lives: Exploration* by Milton Lomask; *Great Lives: Sports* by George Sullivan; *Great Lives: The American Frontier* by Patricia Calvert; and *Great Lives: Human Rights* by William Jay Jacobs.

## Autobiographies and Memoirs

Life stories are often recalled and written down by the subjects themselves, as autobiographies or memoirs. Some children's books based on autobiographical material have been discussed earlier in Chapter 10 as historical fiction. Autobiography has advantages and disadvantages similar to those of nonfiction books of eyewitness history—the warmth and immediacy of personal detail, but a necessarily limited perspective. The criterion of objectivity is reversed here; it is the very subjectivity of this sort of biography that has value. But children do need to be aware of the inherent bias in autobiographies, and they can be encouraged to look to other sources for balance.

Four stories of deprivation and courage are especially powerful for being told in the first person. *Anne Frank: The Diary of a Young Girl* is the classic story of hiding from the Nazis. This is a candid and open account of the changes wrought upon eight people who hid for two years in a secret annex of an office building in Amsterdam and were ultimately found and imprisoned by the Nazis. Anne's diary reveals the thoughts of a sensitive adolescent growing up under extraordinary conditions. No one who lived in the annex survived the war except Anne's father. He returned to their hiding place and found Anne's diary. When it was published, it became an immediate best-seller and was translated into many languages. Its popularity continues today, an appropriate tribute to Anne Frank's amazing spirit.

Anita Lobel's *No Pretty Pictures: A Child of War* is a moving account of the artist's fearful childhood during and after World War II in Poland, where she moved from hiding to concentration camp to refugee camp. *Leon's Story,* by Leon Tillage, is a moving memoir told by an African American man who grew up as a sharecropper's son in the Jim Crow South. Tillage's bravery in the face of lynchings and other horrific occurrences makes this an extraordinary story of courage and endurance. *Red Scarf Girl* is Ji-li Jiang's memoir of growing up in China during the Cultural Revolution. In it she relates the powerful story of her coming of age, as well as her coming of understanding. As the Red Guards gain momentum and members of her family are accused of being reactionaries and worse, we see her change from a fervent believer in the dogma of Chairman Mao to a revolutionary of a different sort. She writes,

> Once my life had been defined by my goals, to be a da-dui-zhang [student chairman of her elementary school], to participate in the exhibition, to be a Red Guard. Now my life was defined by my responsibilities. I had promised to take care of my family, and I would renew that promise everyday. I could not give up or withdraw, no matter how hard life became. I would hide my tears and my fear for Mom and Grandma's sake. It was my turn to take care of them. (p. 263)

These are noble sentiments coming from any young person. They are a remarkable tribute to the human spirit coming from a 14-year-old who had endured three years of a terror campaign.

Autobiographies by creators of children's books provide an easy introduction to this specialized form of writing. The fine photobiographies in the Meet the Author series, published by Richard C. Owen, show each author at home with family and pets; clear maps locate where they live. Each author tells something about his or her childhood and provides personal insights into their writing process. Included in the series are Eve Bunting's *Once Upon a Time,* Lee Bennett Hopkins's *The Writing Bug,* Margaret Mahy's *My Mysterious World,* Rafe Martin's *A Storyteller's Story,* and Cynthia Rylant's *Best Wishes.*

Other popular writers provide longer life stories. In *The Abracadabra Kid: A Writer's Life,* Sid Fleischman recalls his desire to be a magician, his service in World War II, and his successful career as

## RESOURCES FOR TEACHING

### Author Autobiographies

| AUTHOR | TITLE | GRADE LEVEL |
| --- | --- | --- |
| Beverly Cleary | *A Girl from Yamhill: A Memoir* | 5 and up |
| Donald Crews | *Bigmama's* | 1–4 |
| Roald Dahl | *Boy: Tales of Childhood* | 5 and up |
| Tomie de Paola | *26 Fairmont Avenue* | 1–4 |
| Sid Fleischman | *The Abracadabra Kid: A Writer's Life* | 5 and up |
| Michael Foreman | *War Boy: A Country Childhood* | 4–6 |
| Jean Fritz | *Homesick: My Own Story* | 5 and up |
| Helen Lester | *Author: A True Story* | 1–4 |
| Jean Little | *Little by Little: A Writer's Childhood* | 5 and up |
| Phyllis Reynolds Naylor | *How I Came to Be a Writer* | 5 and up |
| Gary Paulsen | *Woodsong* | 5 and up |
| Richard Peck | *Anonymously Yours* | 5 and up |
| Bill Peet | *Bill Peet: An Autobiography* | 3 and up |
| James Stevenson | *Higher on the Door* | 2–5 |
| | *When I Was Nine* | 2–5 |
| Yoshiko Uchida | *The Invisible Thread* | 5 and up |
| Laurence Yep | *The Lost Garden* | 5 and up |

a Hollywood screen writer before he found that his real talent and passion was for writing children's books. In Lois Lowry's *Looking Back: A Book of Memories* the author recalls everyday incidents and important milestones in her life. Each chapter is introduced by a photograph. Reading the book is like having an intimate chat with Lowry over the pages of a photo album. Roald Dahl in *Boy: Tales of Childhood* recounts stories of his early family life and incidents from his boarding school days, including one that became a scene in one of his own novels. Some authors focus on their work, explaining the process of writing a book and adding advice for students who dream of writing for publication. *How I Came to Be a Writer* by Phyllis Reynolds Naylor reveals the same wit as her realistic novels.

Beverly Cleary's memoir *A Girl from Yamhill: A Memoir* speaks to adults who have read her books, as well as to older students. Careful readers will catch many glimpses of her popular character Ramona Quimby in Cleary's own childhood. The portrayal of

her difficult relationship with her mother is particularly good for generating discussion. Cleary's story of her college years and her adult life is told in *My Own Two Feet*.

Resources for Teaching, "Author Autobiographies," lists the titles of a few of the memoirs by authors for children. Most of the books for primary grades are not complete autobiographies but are based on a single incident.

Other memoirs in the form of personal journals and letters can bring the voices of times past vividly to life. Milton Meltzer has based several fine nonfiction books, such as *The American Revolutionaries: A History in Their Own Words*, on such primary sources. In *Lincoln: In His Own Words* and *Frederick Douglass: In His Own Words* Meltzer uses a similar technique, framing selections from the writings and speeches of these two great Americans with commentary that explains the progression of their ideas in the context of their time. Stephen Alcorn's handsome linocut illustrations capture his subjects' lives through

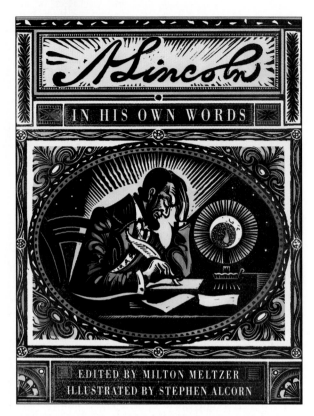

*In* Lincoln: In His Own Words, *Milton Meltzer has used excerpts from Lincoln's writings to tell his life story. Stephen Alcorn's moving linocut illustrations represent critical experiences in Lincoln's life.*

Cover from *Lincoln: In His Own Words* by Milton Meltzer, cover illustration copyright © 1993 by Stephen Alcorn, reprinted by permission of Harcourt, Inc.

compelling visual symbols. Scratchboard illustrations by Michael McCurdy also frame a shorter version of Douglass's words in *Escape from Slavery: The Boyhood of Frederick Douglass in His Own Words.* McCurdy's illustrations lend a similar dignity to Lillian Schisse's adaptation of Amelia Knight's *The Way West: Journal of a Pioneer Woman.* Joseph Plumb Martin's *Yankee Doodle Boy,* edited by George Scheer, is the lively firsthand account of a 15-year-old Connecticut farmer who served with Washington's Continental army. Though the somewhat archaic speech patterns of previous centuries require some editing, these memoirs do not lose their powerful effect for modern audiences under the skillful handling of Meltzer, Schisse, and Scheer.

Biographies of all types give children a glimpse into other lives, other places, other times. The best of them combine accurate information and fine writing in a context that children enjoy—the story that really happened. Good biographies serve to put facts into a frame of human feeling. Children can come to know about historical events or contemporary figures from textbooks, but literature that touches this content will bring them a different quality of knowing—more intimate and more memorable. All children deserve to have such books as part of their experience.

## INTO THE CLASSROOM

### *Biography*

Room 201

1. Gather several picture-book biographies or simplified biographies with many illustrations. What information appears in the pictures but not the text? How do the illustrations help create focus and characterization?
2. Compare picture-book biographies about a historical figure such as Christopher Columbus or Mary Anning. What events and details from the person's life does each author include? How can you evaluate the accuracy of the information given? Do you find any contradictions across books?
3. Select several biographies of one subject, such as Christopher Columbus. Make a chart to compare information, omissions, author's point of view, and the extent of documentation. Consider the ways a broader range of information makes you a more discriminating reader.
4. Choose someone from your own life and write that person's biography. Try to use a variety of sources including interviews, letters and photographs, maps, and newspaper archives.

# Personal Explorations

1. Look at the selection of biographies in a school library. Make a checklist of how many biographies are about men, how many about women. What people have been the subject of many biographies? few biographies? one biography? What contemporary figures are presented in these biographies?

2. Ask children to list the people they would like to read about. How many of their selections are contemporary living figures and how many are historical? How do their preferences match library holdings?

# Related Readings

Fritz, Jean. "The Very Truth." In *Celebrating Children's Books,* ed. Betsy Hearne and Marilyn Kaye, pp. 81–86. New York: Lothrop, Lee & Shepard, 1981.

One of the very best writers of juvenile biography addresses the issue of censorship and discusses the necessity for telling all the truth.

*The Lion and the Unicorn* 4, no. 1 (summer 1980).

This entire issue is devoted to biography for young people. Of special interest are Elizabeth Segel's article about a biography of Beatrix Potter, Leonard Marcus's comments on picture-book biographies for children, and an interview with Milton Meltzer by Geraldine DeLuca and Roni Natov.

Meltzer, Milton. "Selective Forgetfulness: Christopher Columbus Reconsidered." *New Advocate* 5 (winter 1992): 1–9.

A writer of fine complete biographies discusses the dark side of the story of Columbus, namely, his treatment of Indians. He quotes letters and Columbus's own journal as documentation. These are included in his biography *Columbus and the World Around Him* (Franklin Watts, 1990).

Zarnowski, Myra. *Learning About Biographies: A Reading-and-Writing Approach for Children.* Urbana, Ill.: National Council of Teachers of English and the National Council on Social Studies, 1990.

Teachers of upper elementary and middle school students will find many resources here for helping children understand the tasks and responsibilities of a biographer. Discussion of the genre, guides for classroom work, and a bibliography are included.

# Children's Literature

Adler, David A. *A Picture Book of Abraham Lincoln.* Illustrated by John and Alexandra Wallner. Holiday House, 1989.

———. *A Picture Book of Benjamin Franklin.* Illustrated by John and Alexandra Wallner. Holiday House, 1990.

———. *A Picture Book of Christopher Columbus.* Illustrated by John and Alexandra Wallner. Holiday House, 1991.

———. *A Picture Book of George Washington.* Illustrated by John and Alexandra Wallner. Holiday House, 1990.

———. *A Picture Book of Jackie Robinson.* Illustrated by Robert Casilla. Holiday House, 1994.

———. *A Picture Book of John F. Kennedy.* Illustrated by John and Alexandra Wallner. Holiday House, 1990.

———. *A Picture Book of Martin Luther King, Jr.* Illustrated by Robert Casilla. Holiday House, 1989.

———. *A Picture Book of Rosa Parks.* Illustrated by Robert Casilla. Holiday House, 1993.

———. *A Picture Book of Sojourner Truth.* Illustrated by Gershom Griffith. Holiday House, 1994.

———. *A Picture Book of Thomas Jefferson.* Illustrated by John and Alexandra Wallner. Holiday House, 1990.

Adoff, Arnold. *Malcolm X.* Illustrated by John Wilson. Harper Trophy, 1988 [1970].

Aliki [Aliki Brandenberg]. *Fossils Tell of Long Ago.* HarperCollins, 1990.

———. *The Many Lives of Benjamin Franklin.* Aladdin, 1998.

———. *The Story of Johnny Appleseed.* Prentice Hall, 1987 [1963].

———. *A Weed Is a Flower: The Life of George Washington Carver.* Simon & Schuster, 1988 [1965].

———. *William Shakespeare and the Globe.* HarperCollins, 1999.

Anderson, William. *Laura Ingalls Wilder: A Biography.* HarperCollins, 1992.

———. *Laura's Album: A Rembrance Scrapbook of Laura Ingalls Wilder.* HarperCollins, 1998.

Anholt, Lawrence. *Stone Girl, Bone Girl.* Illustrated by Sheila Moxley. Orchard, 1999.

Atkins, Jeannine. *Mary Anning and the Sea Dragon.* Illustrated by Michael Dooling. Farrar, Straus & Giroux, 1999.

Avi. *Finding Providence: The Story of Roger Williams.* Illustrated by James Watling. HarperCollins, 1997.

Bober, Natalie S. *Abigail Adams: Witness to a Revolution.* Atheneum, 1995.

Braun, Barbara. *A Weekend with Diego Rivera.* Rizzoli, 1994.

Bray, Rosemary L. *Martin Luther King.* Illustrated by Malcah Zeldis. Greenwillow, 1995.

Brenner, Barbara. *On the Frontier with Mr. Audubon.* Coward, 1977.

Brighton, Catherine. *The Fossil Girl: Mary Anning's Dinosaur Discovery.* Millbrook, 1999.

———. *Mozart: Scenes from the Childhood of the Great Composer.* Doubleday, 1990.

Brooks, Polly Schoyer. *Cleopatra.* HarperCollins, 1995.

Brown, Don. *Alice Ramsey's Grand Adventure.* Houghton Mifflin, 1997.

———. *Rare Treasure: Mary Anning and Her Remarkable Discoveries.* Houghton Mifflin, 1999.

Bruchac, Joseph. *Bowman's Store: A Journey to Myself.* Dial, 1997.

Bunting, Eve. *Once Upon a Time.* Owen, 1995.

Burchard, Peter. *Charlotte Forten: A Black Teacher in the Civil War.* Crown, 1995.

Calvert, Patricia. *Great Lives: The American Frontier.* Illustrated by Stephen Merchesi. Atheneum, 1997.

Clayton, Ed. *Martin Luther King: The Peaceful Warrior.* Illustrated by David Hodges. Minstrel, 1986 [1968].

Cleary, Beverly. *A Girl from Yamhill: A Memoir.* Morrow, 1988.

———. *My Own Two Feet: A Memoir.* Morrow, 1995.

Conrad, Pam. *Pedro's Journal: A Voyage with Christopher Columbus.* Boyds Mills, 1991.

Cooney, Barbara. *Eleanor.* Viking, 1996.

Cooper, Floyd. *Coming Home: From the Life of Langston Hughes.* Philomel, 1994.

Cox, Clinton. *Mark Twain: America's Humorist, Dreamer, Prophet.* Scholastic, 1995.

Crews, Donald. *Bigmama's.* Greenwillow, 1991.

Cummings, Pat, ed. *Talking with Adventurers.* National Geographic, 1998.

———. *Talking with Artists.* Vol. 1. Bradbury Press, 1992.

———. *Talking with Artists.* Vol. 2. Simon & Schuster, 1995.

———. *Talking with Artists.* Vol. 3. Bradbury Press, 1999.

Dahl, Roald. *Boy: Tales of Childhood.* Farrar, Straus & Giroux, 1984.

d'Aulaire, Ingri, and Edgar Parin d'Aulaire. *Abraham Lincoln.* Rev. ed. Doubleday, 1957.

———. *Columbus.* Zephyr, 1987 [1955].

———. *George Washington.* Doubleday, 1936.

de Paola, Tomie. *26 Fairmont Avenue.* Putnam, 1999.

Driscoll, Laura. *Sammy Sosa: He's the Man.* Illustrated by Ken McCall. Grosset, 1999.

———. *Slugger Season: McGuire and Sosa.* Illustrated by Ken Call. Grosset, 1998.

Duke, Kate. *Archeologists Dig for Clues.* HarperCollins, 1997.

Engel, Dean, and Florence B. Freedman. *Ezra Jack Keats: A Biography with Illustrations.* Silver Moon, 1995.

Faber, Doris. *Calamity Jane: Her Life and Legend.* Houghton Mifflin, 1992.

———. *Eleanor Roosevelt, First Lady of the World.* Illustrated by Donna Ruff. Viking, 1985.

Faber, Doris, and Harold Faber. *Great Lives: American Government.* Scribner's, 1988.

———. *Great Lives: Nature and the Environment.* Scribner's, 1991.

Fleischman, Sid. *The Abracadabra Kid: A Writer's Life,* Greenwillow, 1996.

Foreman, Michael. *War Boy: A Country Childhood.* Arcade, 1990.

Frank, Anne. *Anne Frank: The Diary of a Young Girl.* Rev. ed. Translated by B. M. Mooyart. Introduction by Eleanor Roosevelt. Doubleday, 1967.

Freedman, Russell. *Babe Didrikson Zaharias.* Clarion, 1999.

———. *Eleanor Roosevelt: A Life of Discovery.* Clarion, 1993.

———. *Franklin Delano Roosevelt.* Clarion, 1990.

———. *Lincoln: A Photobiography.* Clarion, 1987.

———. *Martha Graham: A Dancer's Life.* Clarion, 1998.

———. *The Wright Brothers: How They Invented the Airplane.* Holiday House, 1991.

Fritz, Jean. *And Then What Happened, Paul Revere?* Illustrated by Margot Tomes. Coward, 1973.

———. *Bully for You, Teddy Roosevelt!* Illustrated by Mike Wimmer. Putnam, 1991.

———. *Can't You Make Them Behave, King George?* Illustrated by Tomie de Paola. Coward, 1982.

———. *China Homecoming.* Putnam, 1985.

———. *The Great Little Madison.* Putnam, 1989.

———. *Harriet Beecher Stowe and the Beecher Preachers.* Putnam, 1994.

———. *Homesick: My Own Story.* Illustrated by Margot Tomes. Putnam, 1982.

———. *Stonewall.* Illustrated by Stephen Gammell. Putnam, 1979.

———. *Traitor: The Case of Benedict Arnold.* Putnam, 1981.

———. *What's the Big Idea, Ben Franklin?* Illustrated by Margot Tomes. Coward, 1982.

———. *Why Don't You Get a Horse, Sam Adams?* Illustrated by Trina Schart Hyman. Coward, 1982.

———. *Will You Sign Here, John Hancock?* Illustrated by Trina Schart Hyman. Coward, 1982.

———. *You Want Women to Vote, Lizzie Stanton?* Putnam, 1995.

Gherman, Beverly. *Agnes DeMille, Dancing Off the Earth.* Atheneum, 1990.

———. *E. B. White: Some Writer.* Atheneum, 1992.

———. *Georgia O' Keeffe: The "Wideness and Wonder" of Her World.* Atheneum, 1988.

———. *Sandra Day O'Connor: Justice for All.* Illustrated by Robert Masheris. Viking, 1991.

Gibbons, Gail. *Penguins.* Holiday, 1998.

———. *Soaring with the Wind: The Bald Eagle.* Morrow, 1998.

Giblin, James Cross. *George Washington: A Picture Book Biography.* Illustrated by Michael Dooling. Scholastic, 1992.

Goodall, John *The Story of a Farm.* McElderry, 1989.

———. *The Story of a Main Street.* McElderry, 1987.

Greenfield, Eloise. *Mary McLeod Bethune.* Illustrated by Jerry Pinkney. Crowell, 1993 [1977].

———. *Rosa Parks.* Illustrated by Gill Ashby. HarperCollins, 1995 [1973].

Gross, Ruth Belov. *True Stories About Abraham Lincoln.* Illustrated by Jill Kastner. Lothrop, Lee & Shepard, 1989.

Hamanaka, Sheila, and Ayano Ohmi. *In Search of the Spirit: The Loving National Treasures of Japan.* Morrow, 1999.

Hamilton, Virginia. *Anthony Burns: The Defeat and Triumph of a Fugitive Slave.* Knopf, 1988.

Hampton, Wilborn. *Kennedy Assassinated: The World Mourns: A Reporter's Story.* Candlewick, 1997.

Hansen, Joyce. *Women of Hope: Portraits of African American Women Who Made a Difference.* Scholastic, 1998.

Harrison, Barbara, and Daniel Terris. *A Twilight Struggle: The Life of John Fitzgerald Kennedy.* Lothrop, Lee & Shepard, 1992.

Holling, Holling C. *Minn of the Mississippi.* Houghton Mifflin, 1951.

———. *Pagoo.* Houghton Mifflin, 1957.

Hopkins, Lee Bennett. *The Writing Bug.* Owen, 1992.

Jacobs, William Jay. *Great Lives: Human Rights.* Scribner's, 1990.

Jiang, Ji-li. *Red Scarf Girl: A Memoir of the Cultural Revolution.* HarperCollins, 1997.

Kherdian, David. *The Road from Home: The Story of an Armenian Girl.* Greenwillow, 1979.

Klausner, Janet. *Sequoyah's Gift: A Portrait of the Cherokee Leader.* HarperCollins, 1993.

Knight, Amelia. *The Way West: Journal of a Pioneer Woman.* Adapted by Lillian Schisse. Illustrated by Michael McCurdy. Simon & Schuster, 1993.

Krull, Kathleen. *Lives of the Artists: Masterpieces, Messes (and What the Neighbors Thought).* Illustrated by Kathryn Hewitt. Harcourt Brace, 1995.

———. *Lives of the Athletes: Thrills, Spills (and What the Neighbors Thought).* Illustrated by Kathryn Hewitt. Harcourt Brace, 1997.

———. *Lives of the Musicians: Good Times, Bad Times (and What the Neighbors Thought).* Illustrated by Kathryn Hewitt. Harcourt Brace, 1993.

———. *Lives of the Presidents: Fame, Shame (and What the Neighbors Thought).* Illustrated by Kathryn Hewitt. Harcourt Brace, 1998.

———. *Lives of the Writers: Comedies, Tragedies (and What the Neighbors Thought).* Illustrated by Kathryn Hewitt. Harcourt Brace, 1993.

Kuskin, Karla. *Thoughts, Pictures, Words.* Owen, 1995.

Latham, Jean Lee. *Carry On, Mr. Bowditch.* Illustrated by John O'Hara Cosgrave II. Houghton Mifflin, 1955.

Lester, Helen. *Author: A True Story.* Houghton Mifflin, 1998.

Liestman, Vicki. *Columbus Day.* Illustrated by Rick Hanson. Carolrhoda, 1991.

Little, Jean. *Little by Little: A Writer's Beginnings.* Penguin, 1988.

Littlefield, Bill. *Champions: Stories of Ten Remarkable Athletes.* Little, Brown, 1993.

Lobel, Anita. *No Pretty Pictures: A Child of War.* Greenwillow, 1998.

Lomask, William. *Great Lives: Exploration.* Scribner's, 1988.

Lowry, Lois. *Looking Back: A Book of Memories.* Houghton Mifflin, 1998.

Lyons, Mary E. *Catching Fire: Philip Simmons, Blacksmith.* Illustrated by Mannie Garcia. Houghton Mifflin, 1997.

———. *Deep Blues: Bill Traylor, Self-Taught Artist.* Scribner's, 1994.

———. *Keeping Secrets: The Girlhood Diaries of Seven Women Writers.* Holt, 1995.

———. *Letters from a Slave Girl: The Story of Harriet Jacobs.* Scribner's, 1992.

———. *Master of Mahogany: Tom Day, Free Black Cabinetmaker.* Scribner's, 1994.

———. *Painting Dreams: Minnie Evans, Visionary Artist.* Houghton Mifflin, 1996.

———. *Starting Home: The Story of Horace Pippin.* Scribner's, 1993.

———. *Stitching Stars: The Story Quilts of Harriet Jacobs.* Scribner's, 1993.

———. *Talking with Tebé: Clementine Hunter, Memory Artist.* Houghton Mifflin, 1998.

Mahy, Margaret. *My Mysterious World.* Owen, 1995.

Marrin, Albert. *Plains Warrior: Chief Quanah Parker and the Comanches.* Atheneum, 1996.

———. *The Sea King: Sir Francis Drake and His Times.* Atheneum, 1995.

———. *Terror of the Spanish Main: Henry Morgan and His Buccaneers.* Dutton, 1999.

———. *Unconditional Surrender: U. S. Grant and the Civil War.* Atheneum, 1994.

Martin, Joseph Plumb. *Yankee Doodle Boy.* Edited by George Scheer. Illustrated by Victor Mays. Holiday House, 1995 [1964].

Martin, Rafe. *A Storyteller's Story.* Photos by Jill Krementz. Owen, 1992.

McCurdy, Michael, ed. *Escape from Slavery: The Boyhood of Frederick Douglass in His Own Words.* Knopf, 1994.

McGovern, Ann. *The Secret Soldier: The Story of Deborah Sampson.* Illustrated by Ann Grifalconi. Four Winds, 1987 [1975].

McKissack, Patricia C. *Jesse Jackson: A Biography.* Scholastic, 1989.

McKissack, Patricia C., and Frederick McKissack. *Sojourner Truth: Ain't I a Woman?* Scholastic, 1992.

Meltzer, Milton. *The American Revolutionaries: A History in Their Own Words.* Crowell, 1987.

———. *Frederick Douglass: In His Own Words.* Illustrated by Stephen Alcorn. Harcourt Brace, 1995.

———. *Lincoln: In His Own Words.* Illustrated by Stephen Alcorn. Harcourt Brace, 1994.

————. *Ten Queens; Portraits of Women of Power.* Dutton, 1998.

Micucci, Charles. *The Life and Times of the Apple.* Orchard, 1992.

————. *The Life and Times of the Honeybee.* Ticknor & Fields, 1994.

Miller, Brandon Marie. *Buffalo Gals: Women of the Old West.* Lerner, 1995.

Miller, William. *Frederick Douglass: The Last Days of Slavery.* Illustrated by Cedric Lucas. Lee & Low, 1995.

————. *Richard Wright and the Library Card.* Illustrated by Christie Gregory. Lee & Low, 1997.

————. *Richard Wright and the Library Card.* Christie Gregory. Lee & Low, 1997.

————. *Zora Hurston and the Chinaberry Tree.* Illustrated by Cornelius Van Wright and Ying-hwa Hu. Lee & Low, 1994.

Mora, Pat. *Tomas and the Library Lady.* Illustrated by Raul Colon Knopf, 1997.

Moss, Marissa. *Amelia's Notebook.* Pleasant Co. 1999.

Naylor, Phyllis Reynolds. *How I Came to Be a Writer.* Aladdin, 1987 [1978].

Osofsky, Audrey. *Free to Dream: The Making of a Poet, Langston Hughes.* Lothrop, Lee & Shepard, 1996.

Partridge, Elizabeth. *Restless Spirit: The Life and Work of Dorothea Lange.* Viking, 1998.

Paulsen, Gary. *Woodsong.* Bradbury Press, 1990.

Peet, Bill. *Bill Peet: An Autobiography.* Houghton Mifflin, 1989.

Petry, Ann. *Harriet Tubman, Conductor on the Underground Railroad.* Harper Colins, 1996.

Pinkney, Andrea Davis. *Alvin Ailey.* Illustrated by Brian Pinkney. Hyperion, 1993.

————. *Bill Picket: Rodeo Ridin' Cowboy.* Illustrated by Brian Pinkney. Hyperion, 1996.

————. *Dear Benjamin Banneker.* Illustrated by Brian Pinkney. Gulliver, 1994.

————. *Duke Ellington: The Piano Prince and His Orchestra.* Illustrated by Brian Pinkney. Hyperion, 1998.

Provensen, Alice, and Martin Provensen. *The Glorious Flight: Across the Channel with Louis Blériot, July 25, 1909.* Viking, 1983.

Reef, Catherine. *Walt Whitman.* Clarion, 1995.

Reich, Susanna. *Clara Schumann: Piano Virtuoso.* Clarion, 1999.

Ritter, Lawrence S. *Leagues Apart: The Men and Time of the Negro Baseball Leagues.* Morrow, 1995.

Rylant, Cynthia. *Best Wishes.* Photos by Carlo Ontal. Owen, 1992.

San Souci, Robert D. *Kate Shelley: Bound for Legend.* Illustrated by Max Ginsburg. Dial, 1995.

Sandburg, Carl. *Abe Lincoln Grows Up.* Illustrated by James Daugherty. Harcourt Brace, 1975 [1926].

Say, Allen. *El Chino.* Houghton Mifflin, 1990.

Scioscia, Mary. *Bicycle Rider.* Illustrated by Ed Young. Harper & Row, 1983.

Sills, Leslie. *Inspirations: Stories About Women Artists.* Edited by Ann Fay. Albert Whitman, 1989.

————. *Visions: Stories About Women Artists.* Edited by Leslie Sills and Abby Levine. Albert Whitman, 1993.

Sis, Peter. *Follow the Dream: The Story of Christopher Columbus.* Knopf, 1991.

Stanley, Diane. *Joan of Arc.* Morrow, 1998.

————. *Leonardo Da Vinci.* Morrow, 1996.

————. *Peter the Great.* Four Winds, 1986.

————. *The True Adventures of Daniel Hall.* Dial, 1995.

Stanley, Diane, and Peter Vennema. *Bard of Avon: The Story of William Shakespeare.* Illustrated by Diane Stanley. Morrow, 1992.

————. *Charles Dickens: The Man Who Had Great Expectations.* Illustrated by Diane Stanley. Morrow, 1993.

————. *Cleopatra.* Illustrated by Diane Stanley. Morrow, 1994.

————. *Good Queen Bess: The Story of Elizabeth I of England.* Illustrated by Diane Stanley. Four Winds, 1990.

————. *Shaka: King of the Zulus.* Illustrated by Diane Stanley. Morrow, 1988.

Stanley, Fay. *The Last Princess: The Story of Princess Ka'iulani of Hawai'i.* Illustrated by Diane Stanley. Four Winds, 1991.

Stevenson, James. *Higher on the Door.* Greenwillow, 1987.

————. *When I Was Nine.* Greenwillow, 1986.

Sullivan, George. *Great Lives: Sports.* Scribner's, 1988.

Taylor, Maureen. *Through the Eyes of Your Ancestors.* Houghton Mifflin, 1999.

Tillage, Leon. *Leon's Story.* Illustrated by Susan Roth. Farrar, Straus & Giroux, 1997.

Turner, Glennette Tilley. *Take a Walk in Their Shoes.* Illustrated by Elton C. Fax. Cobblehill/Dutton, 1989.

Turner, Robyn Montana. *Dorothea Lange.* Little, Brown, 1994.

————. *Frida Kahlo.* Little, Brown, 1993.

————. *Georgia O'Keefe.* Little, Brown, 1991.

Twist, Clint. *Christopher Columbus: Discovery of the Americas.* Raintree, 1994.

van der Rol, Ruud, and Verhoeven, Rian. *Anne Frank Beyond the Diary: A Photographic Remembrance.* Translated by Tony Langham and Plym Peters. Viking, 1993.

Warren, Andrea. *Orphan Train Rider: One Boy's True Story.* Houghton Mifflin, 1996.

————. *Pioneer Girl: Growing Up on the Prairie.* Morrow, 1998.

Weidt, Maryann N. *Stateswoman to the World: A Story About Eleanor Roosevelt.* Illustrated by Lydia M. Anderson. Carolrhoda, 1991.

Weitzman, David L. *My Back Yard History Book.* Little, Brown, 1975.

West, Delno, and Jean West. *Christopher Columbus: The Great Adventure and How We Know About It.* Atheneum, 1991.

Wilson, Janet. *The Ingenious Mr. Peale: Patriot, Painter, and Man of Science.* Atheneum, 1996.

Williams, Vera B. *Scooter.* Greenwillow, 1993.

Winter, Jeanette. *Cowboy Charlie: The Story of Charles M. Russell.* Harcourt Brace, 1995.

————. *My Name Is Georgia: A Portrait.* Silver Whistle, 1998.

————. *Sebastian: A Book About Bach.* Browndeer, 1999.

Winter, Jonah. *Diego.* Illustrated by Jeannette Winter. Translation by Amy Prince. Knopf, 1991.

Wolf, Sylvia. *Focus: Five Women Photographers.* Albert Whitman, 1994.

Yates, Elizabeth. *Amos Fortune, Free Man.* Illustrated by Nora S. Unwin. Dutton, 1967 [1950].

# Part Three

## Developing a Literature Program

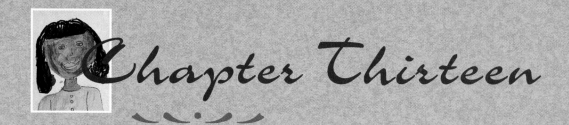

# Chapter Thirteen

# Planning the Literature Program

Students in a fifth- and sixth-grade class unanimously agreed that The Pinballs by Betsy Byars was their favorite book. Their teacher then asked them to discuss the book, telling what it was that made them like it so much. Part of their discussion follows:

Lenny says, "This is the best book I've ever read. I'd like to know Harvey because I'd like to cheer him up." He decides that "he shows real courage because he has two broken legs." Barb adds, "All the kids do because they have to go to a foster home." "So does Thomas J. because the twins are going to die and he has to go to the hospital to see them," says Will.

Jack talks about Carlie, saying, "She's really funny because she's so rude." The teacher suggests that a book that is "basically serious can have funny elements." Tom says, "You know that Carlie is really tough."

Then Tom goes on to explain the title by saying, "Carlie thinks they're pinballs because they are always being thrown around like pinballs."

By April of that year, eighteen of the class had read *The Pinballs*. They also were reading other Betsy Byars books; thirteen had read *The Summer of the Swans*, eight *Good-bye, Chicken Little*.*

Individual children had read many books (from 24 to 122 over the year), yet they singled out *The Pinballs* as their favorite. Though it is still difficult for them to articulate why they like the story, they have moved beyond the usual circular kind of statement, "I liked it because it was good." They are beginning to recognize the importance of character development and readily identify with Carlie and Harvey. Lenny, who was not a particularly good reader and had read few books, empathizes with Harvey to the point of wanting to comfort him. They have extended their horizons to imagine the courage it would require to live in a foster home away from their family and to have to visit people who are dying in the hospital. Tom attempts a rough statement of the meaning of the title without any prompting.

In this class, book discussions occurred every day during the last fifteen minutes of an hour-long period for sustained silent reading. The children readily supported each other in their selection of books and in their evaluations; they exemplify what we have referred to as a "community of readers." It is obvious from their discussion that they were gaining a greater sense of form and were beginning to see more in books than just story.

It takes time for reading and literature to grow in a classroom. The children in this classroom had, for the most part, been exposed to good literature throughout their school attendance. The teacher had been working on a literature-based reading program over a period of several years. Her major goal was to develop children who could read and who loved reading. From this base she added a growing appreciation for and understanding of good literature.

# Purposes of the Literature Program

Each school staff will want to develop its own literature program in terms of the background and abilities of the children it serves. Teachers and librarians need to know both their children and the potential of their material and have an understanding of the structure of literature; then they will be free to make the right match between child and book. This chapter can suggest guidelines and give examples, but it cannot prescribe *the* literature program that would work with all children.

One of the major purposes of any literature program is to provide children with the opportunity to experience literature, to enter into and become involved in a book. The goal of all reading programs should be not only to teach children to learn to read but to help them learn to love reading, to discover joy in reading. Their every activity, every assignment, should pass this test: "Will this increase children's desire to read? Will it make them want to continue

---

*Based on children's comments recorded by Susan Hepler in "Patterns of Response to Literature: A One-Year Study of a Fifth and Sixth Grade Classroom" (Ph.D. dissertation, Ohio State University, 1982).

*Two fourth-grade girls reveal their delight in literature by sharing some "book talk."*
PS 124, New York, New York. Mary S. Gallivan, teacher.

*Two first graders share the reading of a picture book and exchange reading strategies.*
PS 116, New York, New York. Ilana Dubin-Spiegel, teacher.

reading?" A literature program must get children excited about reading, turned on to books, tuned in to literature.

Another important purpose for using real books in a reading program is to help children connect literature with their own lives. As teachers and librarians, we want to encourage children to discover personal meaning in books so that they can better understand their lives and extend their perceptions of others' lives. Kindergarten children listen to *Ira Sleeps Over* by Bernard Waber and talk about their own bears and the decisions they had to make about taking them on vacations or overnights. A fifth grader, when asked why Jean George's *My Side of the Mountain* was his favorite book, replied, "I just always thought I could do what Sam Gribley did." As children search for meaning in books, they naturally connect what they are reading to their own lives.

A school literature program should also help children develop literary awareness and appreciation. We want children to develop an understanding of literary genres, and to recognize the unique qualities and criteria of many types of literature. We want to introduce children to literary classics and to the authors and illustrators who create the books that they love. We expect that over time children will become familiar with the many components of literature, such as the traditional constants of plot, characterization, theme, style,

setting, and author's point of view. However, their knowledge about literature should be secondary to their wide experiencing of literature. Too frequently, we have substituted the study of literary criticism for the experience of literature itself. Attention to content should precede consideration of form.

Teachers need to know something of the structure of literature in order to provide children with a frame of reference to direct their insights. Knowledge of the structure of a discipline frees a teacher in her approach to teaching. Knowing literature, she may tune in to where the children are and extend their thinking and understandings. The teacher does not have to rely on the questions in a teacher's manual; she is free to ask questions directly related to the needs of the children in the class.

A framework for thinking about literature develops gradually as children consider what kinds of stories they particularly like or what kinds of information they need for a particular purpose. When teachers consistently nurture children's enjoyment of literature by reading aloud exciting, well-selected books, and by giving children time to read and discuss books in literature groups, the children's appreciation for quality literature will grow. One major goal of the literature program should be this development of discriminating critical readers.

## Different Plans for Literature Programs

For a good part of this century, reading instruction has been delivered through the medium of basal readers, "a series of sequential, all inclusive instructional

*Children need opportunities to respond to books in a variety of ways. These two first graders are busy creating art following the reading of favorite books.*
PS 116, New York, New York. Ilana Dubin-Spiegel, teacher.

materials."[1] However, in the last twenty-five years we have witnessed an expansion of the role of trade books in the schools. The accumulated weight of evidence of many studies, insights from professional educators, the success of many teachers who are making literature central to the curriculum, and the enthusiastic responses of children to reading real books are some of the reasons behind the growth of literature-based curriculum.

## Literature with a Commercial Reading Program

Commercial reading series, whether they are advertised as "literature-based" or "phonics-based," are in reality very similar to basal readers that have existed for most of the century. They turn up every so often with new content and new names, but they provide the same leveled stories or books, teachers' manuals, ditto sheets, and end-of-the-unit tests as they have always done.[2] The emphasis is still on teaching reading skills and raising reading test scores, and the children spend most of their time filling in the blanks on the worksheets rather than actually reading.

Because the texts are now often drawn from literature (although frequently abridged), the content is more interesting than the "Dick and Jane" type of basal reader. However, children are given no choice of what to read and frequently little time to discuss their responses to the stories. Limiting children's reading to books written at their "reading level" does not encourage them to take risks with more difficult material or to learn how to choose books for different purposes.[3] Nor do the excerpts from real books prepare children to put in the time it may take to get into a full-length book or to experience the joy of being "lost" in a good book for days.

Evaluation of children's progress in a basal reading program is usually determined by the level of book they can read successfully and their performance on the publisher's tests that accompany the basals. Often any direct teaching that takes place is aimed at these criterion tests rather than being planned around the individual needs of students. Grouping children according to reading level also seems to perpetuate the reading problems of the children in the lowest groups. According to the report from the Commission on Reading, these children often "receive less instruction and qualitatively different instruction than the child would in a group designated as high ability."[4]

## Literature Programs Using Real Books

Programs in which trade books are used for all aspects of reading instruction and for integrating traditional areas of the curriculum are an accepted alternative to skills-oriented, textbook-based programs.[5] In a literature-based program, classrooms are flooded with books. Funds usually appropriated for the purchase of basal readers and workbooks are used for obtaining large classroom libraries of 400 to 500 books. There are books in an attractive reading corner, sets of paperback books for in-depth study, and a changing collection of books obtained from the school library and public libraries on whatever unit focus is in progress. Books are displayed along with the children's work. Children's interpretations of books, book surveys, and big books are seen throughout the room. Few commercial charts or pictures are seen, only quantities of children's work with captions, labels, or writing on it.

[1]Kenneth Goodman, Patrick Shannon, Yvonne Freeman, and Sharon Murphy, *Report Card on Basal Readers* (Katonah, N.Y.: Richard C. Owen, 1988), p. 1.

[2]See James V. Hoffman, Sarah J. McCarthy, Bonnie Elliott, Debra L. Bayles, Debra P. Price, Angela Ferree, and Judy A. Abbott, "The Literature-Based Basals in First-Grade Classrooms: Savior, Satan, or Same-old, Same-old?" *Reading Research Quarterly* 33, no. 2 (April/May/June, 1998): 168–197.

[3]See Marilyn Olhausen and Mary Jepson, "Lessons from Goldilocks: 'Somebody's Been Choosing My Books But I Can Make My Own Choices Now!'" *New Advocate 5* (winter, 1992): 31–46, for insights on helping children choose books.

[4]Richard C. Anderson et al., *Becoming a Nation of Readers* (Washington, D.C.: National Institute of Education, 1984).

[5]Sarah J. McCarthy, James V. Hoffman, and Lee Galda, "Readers in Elementary Classrooms: Learning Goals and Instructional Principles That Can Inform Practice," in *Engaged Reading: Processes, Practices, and Policy Implications,* ed. John T. Guthrie and Donna E. Alvermann (New York: Teachers College Press, 1999), pp. 46–80.

*A story map of "The Story of the Three Little Pigs" helped first-grade children to retell the story.*
Columbus Public Schools, Columbus, Ohio. Connie Compton, teacher.

Knowing the research on the importance of reading aloud in developing concepts about print, a sense of story, prediction of plot, and understanding of characters, teachers read aloud to children three and four times a day. They frequently reread favorite stories until children almost know them by heart. Parent aides are encouraged to read aloud to small groups of children. Frequently teachers establish a "buddy system" in which older children read with one or two younger ones.

Rather than work on worksheets or workbook activities, children do a variety of things. Some may be seen reading from the big books, others may be reading individually with the teacher, while still others may be busy reading or writing stories of their own or writing in their literature response journals. Many of the literature extension activities described later in this chapter are done during this work time. Quiet talk about books flows as children create murals or map the action of a story.

An independent reading time is provided every day. Frequently, however, children read quietly in pairs. Time for discussion of books almost always follows these periods.

The in-depth study of the books of one author, a genre of books, or one book begins as early as kindergarten. With older children, sets of paperbacks like *Morning Girl* by Michael Dorris, *Island of the Blue Dolphins* by Scott O'Dell, *Number the Stars* by Lois Lowry, and *Tuck Everlasting* by Natalie Babbitt are used for literature study. All children are involved in groups for in-depth reading, but the groups are not formed on the basis of ability. Rather, children choose to join a reading group based on their interest in the book or a topic, and these groups change as the focus of a study changes.

*A teacher shares her enthusiasm for books with one or two children as well as the class.*
Idyllwild Elementary School, Idyllwild, California. Sharon Schmidt, teacher. Photo by Larry Rose.

Reading and writing across the curriculum are characteristic of this integrated program. Children do research in informational books on the particular class unit. Units and projects that cut across traditional subject-matter areas might be chosen by a class or a small group of children to study. For example, over the period of a year, one second- and third-grade class studied the topics "Fairy Tales," "Plumbing and Water Sources," and "Immigration to the United States." They also had mini-units on "Books by Pat Hutchins," "Grandparents," and "Dinosaurs."

Research skills are learned in the process of using many books and reference books for children's projects along with electronic sources. The library is open all day long for children to use as they research particular topics. Parent assistants may help children in one part of the room to find their materials if the librarian is reading a story or working with others.

Children learn strategies for reading many different types of texts through real reading and inquiry. When teachers do direct teaching of such strategies, the strategies are related to children's needs and not isolated drills. No worksheets or workbooks are used. Rather, children write in their response journals, do purposeful reading, and create their own books and group projects.

Teachers and children keep records of children's reading. Each child has a portfolio containing samples of his or her story writing, artwork, and research reports from the beginning of school. These are shared with parents during individual conference times. Book reports are not required, because children are sharing books in a variety of ways. Teachers know what children are reading because they are reading and reacting in their reading journals each week. All children know what others are reading because they discuss their books every day. Children frequently recommend books to others, as they know each other's reading interests. These children become a community of readers as they discuss and recommend particular titles. Books are an essential part of their lives.

Resources for Teaching, "Approaches to Reading Instruction," contrasts some of the major components of basal reading programs and literature-based reading programs. Literature-based programs that use real books offer a challenge to teachers. They require an in-depth knowledge of children and children's literature. Only when a teacher knows the potential of a child and a book, and is willing to trust the interaction between the two, does learning really occur.

## The Components of a Literature Program

The day-to-day routines in classrooms centered around children's literature may vary greatly according to the age of the students, the needs of the community, and the dictates of local and state curriculum. But children in all literature-based classrooms need to be surrounded by enthusiastic, book-loving adults and many, many good books.

The most important aspect of the classroom environment is the teacher. She or he creates the climate of the classroom and arranges the learning environment. If the teacher loves books, shares them with

children, and provides time for children to read and a place for them to read, children will become enthusiastic readers. The teacher who reads to the children every day, talks about books and characters in books as if they were good friends, and knows poems and stories to tell is serving the class as an adult model of a person who enjoys books. One teacher regularly used to read a new children's book while her class was reading. She would keep the book in an old beat-up briefcase that she delighted in carrying. A kind of game she played with her 7- and 8-year-old students was to keep the book hidden from them. Their delight was to find out what book she was reading, so they could read the same one. Of course they always found out, which was what she had in mind in the first place. Enthusiasm for books is contagious; if the teacher has it, so will the children.

If we want children to become readers, we will want to surround them with books of all kinds. We know that wide reading is directly related to accessibility; the more books available and the more time for reading, the more children will read and the better readers they will become.

Books should be a natural part of the classroom environment. There should be no argument about whether to have a classroom collection of books or a library media center; both are necessary. Children should have immediate access to books whenever they need them. The books in the classroom collection will vary from those in the library media center. Many classrooms have an extensive paperback collection (400 to 500 titles). Frequently, there are five or six copies of the same title, so several children can read the same book and have an in-depth discussion of it.

The classroom teacher will also want to provide for a changing collection of books depending on the themes or units the children are studying. The librarian might provide a rolling cart of materials that will enhance children's study of bugs or folktales or the Civil War or explorers. It is important that teachers be thoroughly acquainted with the content of these books so they can help their students use them. If the library media center does not have particular books that the children or the teacher needs, they might be obtained from local public libraries or from a bookmobile. Some state libraries will send boxes of books to teachers in communities that are not serviced by public libraries. An increasing number of teachers are demanding and receiving their share of monies allocated for instructional materials. Teachers using real books as the heart of their curriculum should receive the same amount of money as those using basal readers, workbooks, social studies, science, and other textbooks. We admire the number of teachers who spend their own money to buy trade books for their

# RESOURCES FOR TEACHING

## Approaches to Reading Instruction

| COMMERCIAL APPROACH | LITERATURE-BASED APPROACH |
|---|---|
| **Medium** | **Medium** |
| A single anthology (usually two per grade level). | Literature of all genres at a variety of ability levels. |
| Or sets of books grouped by ability level. | Multiple copies of key books. |
| **Skills** | **Stategies** |
| The teacher teaches skills to all children at a particular reading level at the same time. | Strategies are taught as needed by teacher or peers. |
| | Strategies are learned in the context of real reading and writing. |
| **Prior to reading** | **Prior to reading** |
| The teacher sets the purpose for reading. | The teacher invites children to read for pleasure and/or links prior experience to the material to be read. |
| Children know they will be asked questions about the selection. | |
| **Follow-up** | **Follow-up** |
| Questions from the teacher. | Book discussions. |
| Workbooks and worksheets. | Response journals. |
| | Authentic responses to books. |
| **Grouping of students** | **Grouping of students** |
| By ability level. | For strategy instruction. |
| | By topic. |
| | By choice. |
| | Social grouping. |
| **Reading silently** | **Reading silently** |
| Brief segments of sustained reading. | Independent reading for a minimum twenty minutes a day and throughout the day as part of authentic learning activities. |
| **Reading aloud** | **Reading aloud** |
| Round-robin reading—children read around a circle. | Readers' theater. |
| | Choral reading. |
| | Book sharing. |
| | Buddy reading. |
| | Teacher conferences. |
| **Assessment** | **Assessment** |
| Basal criterion tests. | Anecdotal records, Checklists. |
| | Miscue or Running records. |
| | Response journals, Response projects. |
| | Retellings. |
| **Goal** | **Goals** |
| High scores on standardized tests. | Lifelong readers. |
| | Strategic readers. |
| | Readers who read with more satisfaction. |

*Every classroom should have an inviting corner where children can choose and read favorite books.*
PS 116, New York, New York. Ilana Dubin-Spiegel, teacher.

*Primary children need to hear many stories read several times a day by an enthusiastic teacher.*
Highland Park Elementary School, South-Western City Schools, Grove City, Ohio. Kristen Kerstetter, teacher.

classrooms, but at the same time we question the practice. Real books are essential to the making of a fluent reader and should be an unquestioned item of every school budget.

# Sharing Literature with Children

From the time of the earliest primitive fire circle to the Middle Ages—when minnesingers and troubadours sang their ballads—to the modern age of television, people have found delight in hearing stories and poems. Because literature serves many educational purposes in addition to entertainment and enjoyment, teachers should place a high priority on sharing literature with children. Boys and girls of all ages should have the opportunity to hear good literature every day.

## Reading to Children

One of the best ways to interest children in books is to read to them frequently from the time they are first able to listen. Preschoolers and kindergartners should have an opportunity to listen to stories three or four times a day. Parent or grandparent volunteers, high school students, college participants—all can be encouraged to read to small groups of children throughout the day. Children should have a chance to hear their favorite stories over and over again at a listening center. A child from a book-loving family might have

heard over a thousand bedtime stories before she ever comes to kindergarten; some children might never have heard one.

Teachers accept the idea of reading at least twice a day to the primary-grade child. The daily story time is advocated by almost all authorities in reading. The research reported in Chapters 1 and 4 emphasizes the importance of reading aloud to all children, not only for enjoyment but also for their growth in reading skills. Reading to children improves children's reading. Rereading favorite stories is as important as the initial reading.

Unfortunately, daily story times are not as common in the middle grades and middle school as in the primary grades, yet we know that they are just as essential there. Reading comprehension is improved as students listen to and discuss events, characters, and motivation. They learn to predict what will happen in exciting tales like Mollie Hunter's *A Stranger Came Ashore* or Louis Sachar's *Holes*. Their vocabulary increases as they hear fine texts such as Donald Hall's *Ox-Cart Man* or Jane Yolen's poetic *Owl Moon*. Older students can discuss homelessness and prejudice as they hear Paula Fox's *Monkey Island* or Leon Tillage's *Leon's Story*. They can add to their knowledge of Abraham Lincoln's presidency by reading Russell Freedman's remarkable photobiography *Lincoln*. Teachers can take advantage of this time to introduce various genres, such as fantasy, biography, or poetry, that students might not be reading on their own.

Primarily, however, the read-aloud time will cause children to want to read. Once children have heard a good book read aloud, they can hardly wait to savor it again. Reading aloud thus generates further interest in books. Good oral reading should develop a taste for fine literature.

## Selecting Books to Read Aloud

Teachers and librarians will want to select read-aloud books in terms of the children's interests and background in literature and the quality of writing. Usually teachers will not select books that children in the group are reading avidly on their own. This is the time to stretch their imaginations, to extend interests, and to develop appreciation of fine writing. If children have not had much experience in listening to stories, begin where they are. Appreciation for literature appears to be developmental and sequential. Six- and 7-year-olds who have had little exposure to literature still need to hear many traditional fairy tales, including "Hansel and Gretel," "Sleeping Beauty," and *The Crane Wife* by Sumiko Yagawa. They delight in such favorite picture storybooks as *Harry the Dirty Dog* by Gene Zion, Patricia C. McKissack's *Flossie & the Fox*, and James Howe's *Horace and Morris but Mostly Dolores*. Other children of the same age who have had much exposure to literature might demand longer chapter books like *Ramona Forever* by Beverly Cleary, *James and the Giant Peach* by Roald Dahl, or Hilary McKay's *Dolphin Luck*.

Picture storybooks are no longer just for "little kids." There is a real place for sharing some of the beautiful picture books with older children as well as younger ones. *Dawn* by Uri Shulevitz creates the same feeling visually as one of Emily Dickinson's clear, rarefied poems. It is a literary experience for all ages, but particularly for anyone who has felt "at-oneness" with the world before the sunrise. Older students particularly enjoy Jon Scieszka's *Squids Will Be Squids* and David Macaulay's puzzling four stories in one in *Black and White*.

The teacher should strive for balance in what is read aloud to children. Children tend to like what they know. Introducing a variety of types of books will broaden their base of appreciation. If 11- and 12-year-olds are all reading contemporary fiction, the teacher might read Brian Jacques's powerful fantasy of the fight to save an ancient stone abbey in *Redwall*, or introduce them to Katherine Paterson's indomitable *Lyddie*, the story of a girl who struggles against the unbearable working conditions of factory girls in the Lowell, Massachusetts, mills of the 1840s. The finely honed writing of Patricia MacLachlan's *Sarah, Plain and Tall*, the story of a mail-order bride and the family who longed for a new mother, could be shared with children as young as third grade and as old as fifth. Most of these books are too good for children to miss and should be read aloud to them.

Primary-grade teachers will read many picture books to their children, certainly a minimum of three to four a day. Middle-grade teachers might present parts of many books to their students during book talks or as teasers to interest children in reading the books. But how many entire books will a teacher read in the course of one school year? An educated guess might be that starting with 8-year-olds—when teachers begin to read longer, continuous stories to boys and girls—an average of some six to ten books are read aloud during the year. This means that for the next four years, when children are reaching the peak of their interest in reading, they might hear no more than forty or so books read by their teachers!

Today when there are thousands of children's books in print, read-aloud choices must be selected with care in terms of their relevance for students and the quality of their writing. A list of suggested books to read aloud is included on the endpapers of this book to serve as a beginning guide. Notice that the overlapping of age groups is deliberate. There is no such thing as a book for 5-year-olds or 10-year-olds. Very popular books, such as those by Dr. Seuss or poems by Shel Silverstein, do not appear on our read-aloud lists because most children will have read them on their own. Only a teacher who knows the children, their interests, and their background of experience can truly select appropriate books for a particular class.

We note with concern the increasing number of teachers who want to read such complex stories as *Tuck Everlasting* by Natalie Babbitt, *A Wrinkle in Time* by Madeleine L'Engle, or *The Giver* by Lois Lowry to 6- and 7-year-olds. Children this age might become involved in the plots of these well-written stories, but they will certainly miss many of the deeper meanings reflected in their themes. Read at the appropriate developmental levels, these books could provide the basis for serious in-depth discussion and study. The number of years when children read literature suited to their age appears to have decreased, as more and more 12- and 13-year-olds begin to read best-sellers and other books written for adults. The inappropriate selection of books for reading aloud by both parents and teachers may contribute to this erosion of childhood.

There is a difference, however, between what parents might choose for family reading and what is appropriate for classroom sharing. Parents have the advantage of knowing all the books that children have enjoyed at home. In a family sharing E. B. White's *Charlotte's Web*, the 5-year-old enjoys the humor of these talking barnyard animals while an 8-year-old might weep at Charlotte's death. The closeness of a family unit helps all members to find enjoyment in a read-aloud story regardless of age level. The teacher, on the other hand, has to consider children's

# RESOURCES FOR TEACHING

## Effective Practices for Reading Aloud

1. Select a story appropriate to the developmental age of the children and their previous exposure to literature.
2. Determine whether you will share the book with the whole class, a small group, or an individual child.
3. Select books that will stretch children's imaginations, extend their interests, and expose them to fine art and writing.
4. Read a variety of types of books to capture the interests of all.
5. Remember that favorite stories should be reread at the primary level.
6. Plan to read aloud several times a day.
7. Select a story that you like so you can communicate your enthusiasm.
8. Choose a story or chapter that can be read in one session.
9. Read the book first so you are familiar with the content.
10. Seat the children close to you so all can see the pictures.
11. Hold the book so children can see the pictures at their eye level.
12. Communicate the mood and meaning of the story and characters with your voice.
13. Introduce books in various ways:
    Through a display
    Through a brief discussion about the author or illustrator
    By asking children to predict what the story will be about through looking at the cover and interpreting the title
    By linking the theme, author, or illustrator to other books children know
14. Encourage older children to discuss the progress of the story or predict the outcome at the end of the chapter.
15. Help children to link the story with their own experiences or other literature.
16. Keep a list of the books read aloud to the whole class that can be passed on to their next teachers.

For further assistance, see Caroline Feller Bauer's *New Handbook for Storytellers* (Chicago: American Library Association, 1993).

backgrounds in literature, or lack of background, as he or she selects appropriate books to capture their attention.

A read-aloud program should be planned. What books are too good to miss? These should be included in the overall plan. Teachers should keep a record of the books that they have shared with the children they teach and a brief notation of the class's reaction to each title. This enables teachers to see what kind of balance is being achieved and what the particular favorites of the class are. Such a record provides the children's future teachers with information on the likes and dislikes of the class and their exposure to literature. It also might prevent the situation that was discovered by a survey of one school in which every teacher in the school, with the exception of the kindergarten and the second-grade teachers, had read *Charlotte's Web* aloud to the class! *Charlotte's Web* is a great book, but not for every class.

Perhaps teachers in a school need to agree on what is the most appropriate time for reading particular favorites. Teachers and librarians should be encouraged to try reading new books to children, instead of always reading the same ones. But some self-indulgence should be allowed every teacher who truly loves a particular book, because that enthusiasm can't help but rub off on children.

Effective oral reading is an important factor in capturing children's interest. Some teachers can make almost any story sound exciting; others plod dully through. The storyteller's voice, timing, and intonation patterns should communicate the meanings and mood of the story. To read effectively, the teacher should be familiar with the story and communicate his or her enthusiasm for the book. Resources for Teaching, "Effective Practices for Reading Aloud," might prove useful. Check the list before selecting and reading a story to a whole class.

## Storytelling

A 5-year-old said to his teacher: "Tell the story from your face." His preference for the story *told* by the teacher or librarian instead of the story read directly from the book is echoed by boys and girls everywhere. The art of storytelling is frequently neglected in the elementary school today. There are so many beautiful books to share with children, we rationalize, and our harried life allows little time for learning stories. Yet children should not be denied the opportunity to hear well-told stories. Through storytelling, the teacher helps transmit the literary heritage.

Storytelling provides for intimate contact and rapport with the children. No book separates the teacher from the audience. The story may be modified to fit group needs. A difficult word or phrase can be explained in context. Stories can be personalized for very young children by substituting their names for those of the characters. Such a phrase as "and, David, if you had been there you would have seen the biggest Billy Goat Gruff . . ." will redirect the child whose interest has wandered. The pace of the story can be adapted to the children's interests and age levels.

Stories that are to be told should be selected with care. Stories worth the telling have special characteristics, including a quick beginning, action, a definite climax, natural dialogue, and a satisfying conclusion. It is best to select stories with only three or four speaking characters so that listeners can keep the characters straight. Finally, stories with rich literary language, such as Rudyard Kipling's *The Elephant's Child*, are best read aloud rather than told. Instead, select stories for telling that provide the immediacy of the storyteller's voice.

Folktales like "The Three Billy Goats Gruff," "The Little Red Hen," and "Cinderella" are particular favorites of younger children. The repetitive pattern of these tales makes them easy to tell. Originally passed down from generation to generation by word of mouth, these tales were polished and embellished with each retelling.

Six-, 7-, and 8-year-olds enjoy hearing longer folktales such as Ashley Bryan's *The Cat's Purr*. They also enjoy some of the tall tales about American folk heroes such as Paul Bunyan, Pecos Bill, and John Henry. Incidents from biographies and chapters from longer books may be told as a way of interesting children in reading them.

## Book Talks

Librarians and teachers frequently use a book talk to introduce books to children. The primary purpose of a book talk is to interest children in reading the book themselves. Rather than reveal the whole story, the book talk tells just enough about the book to entice others to read it. A book talk may be about one title; it may be about several unrelated books that would have wide appeal; or it may revolve around several books with a similar theme, such as "getting along in the family" or "courage" or "survival stories."

The book talk should begin with recounting an amusing episode or with telling about an exciting moment in the book. The narrator might want to assume the role of a character in a book, such as Julie in *Julie of the Wolves* by Jean George, and tell of her experience of being lost without food or a compass on the North Slope of Alaska. The speaker should stop before the crisis is over or the mystery is solved. Details should be specific. It is better to let the story stand on its own than to characterize it as a "terribly funny" story or the "most exciting" book you've ever read. Enthusiasm for the book will convey the speaker's opinion of it. This is one reason why book talks should be given only about stories the speaker genuinely likes. Children will then come to trust this evaluation. It is best if the book is on hand as it is discussed, so that the children can check it out as soon as the book talk is finished.

# Providing Time to Read Books

One of the primary purposes of giving book talks, telling stories, and reading aloud to children is to motivate them to read. A major goal of every school should be to develop children who not only can read but who *do* read—who love reading and will become lifetime readers.

To become fluent readers, children need to practice reading from real books that capture their interest and imagination. No one could become a competent swimmer or tennis player by practicing four minutes a day. Schools have little influence on the out-of-school life of their students, but they do control the curriculum in school. If we want children to become readers, we must reorder our priorities and provide time for children to just read books of their own choosing every day.

Recognizing this need, many teachers have initiated a sustained silent reading (SSR) time. Teachers have used other names, such as "Recreational Reading," "Free Reading," or even the acronym *DEAR* (Drop Everything and Read) used by the teacher in *Ramona Quimby, Age 8* by Beverly Cleary. Whatever the name, however, this is a time when everyone in the class (in some instances, the entire school) reads, including the teacher. SSR times have been successfully established in kindergarten through middle schools. Usually, a reading period is lengthened grad-

*Fourth graders enjoy reading their books during SSR, or independent reading time.*
PS 124, New York, New York. Mary S. Gallivan, teacher.

ually from 10 minutes a day to 20, 30, or, in some upper-grade classes, 45 minutes per day. Recognizing the importance of social interaction among readers, teachers often allow children to read in pairs.

In classrooms that use real books for teaching reading and studying themes that cut across the curriculum, children are reading and writing throughout the day. Teachers still have a special time each day for children to read the books they have chosen to read for pleasure.

## Providing Time to Talk About Books

Equally important as time for wide reading is time to talk about books children are reading. When adults discuss books, we have good conversations about the ones we like, but we seldom quiz each other about character development, themes, or setting of the

story. As teachers, we want to show this same respect for children as they share their thoughts about books.

A good time for informal talk about books is after children have had time to read by themselves. In pairs, small groups, or as a class, children may be invited to tell something about a book, show a picture and tell what is happening, read an interesting or powerful paragraph, and so forth. In such discussions, teachers can learn much about what children are reading and how they talk about books. Margaret Meek observes this about talk in the classroom:

> Left to comment on their own, without the stimulus of a question, children often choose to talk about quite other aspects of a tale than those that preoccupy their elders. . . . They create a tissue of collaborative understandings for each other in a way that no single question from an adult makes possible.[6]

Maryann Eeds and Deborah Wells showed how well fifth and sixth graders explored the meaning of novels they were reading through nondirective response groups.[7] The literature discussion groups met two days a week, thirty minutes a day, for four to five weeks. The leaders were undergraduate education students who were instructed to let meaning emerge from the group rather than solicit it. The results of this study showed that the groups collaborated and built meaning that was deeper and richer than what they attained in their solitary reading. The authors concluded, "Talk helps to confirm, extend, and modify individual interpretations and creates a better understanding of the text."

As teachers listen carefully to children's responses in book discussion groups, they can identify teaching possibilities, plan future conversations, or make use of a teachable moment to make a point. When the teacher is an active participant rather than the director of a group, children more readily collaborate to fill their own gaps in understanding and make meaning together.

More structured discussion may occur with the books a teacher chooses to read aloud or to read with small groups. The teacher can play an important role in engendering fruitful discussions by demonstrating the types of responses she hopes children will make. When the teacher introduces the story, she might invite children to recognize the author or illustrator, to notice the dedication, or to speculate on the book's content as they look at the

---

[6]Margaret Meek, "What Counts as Evidence in Theories of Children's Literature?" *Theory into Practice* 21, no. 4 (1982): 289.

[7]Maryann Eeds and Deborah Wells, "Grand Conversations: An Exploration of Meaning Construction in Literature Study Groups," *Research in the Teaching of English* 23, no. 1 (1989): 4–29.

*Small groups of children need time to discuss books together and time to plan responses to their books.*
PS 124, New York, New York. Mary S. Gallivan, teacher.

cover. As she gives children time to look at the illustrations in picture books, she asks, "How do these pictures make you feel?" "What are you thinking about as you look at these illustrations?" As she reads a chapter book, she asks what might happen next or why a character acts as she does. She might introduce Mollie Hunter's *A Stranger Came Ashore* by reading Mordicai Gerstein's *The Seal Mother* or Jane Yolen's *Greyling* and discussing Selkie lore with the class. She might pause at a chapter's end and ask children how Hunter makes the reader feel that something dreadful is about to happen. She might ask what clues suggest that Finn Learson is not who he pretends to be. She might introduce the term *foreshadowing* and ask them to listen for other examples as she reads. At first the teacher calls attention to aspects such as a well-written passage, an apt chapter heading, or a key moment when a character faces a choice. Later, children will begin noticing the kinds of things the teacher has brought out in these discussions. In this way a teacher models reader behaviors that mature readers practice.[8]

---

[8]See Taffy E. Raphael and Susan I. McMahon, "Book Club: An Alternative Framework for Reading Instruction," *Reading Teacher* 48, no 2 (1994): 102–116, for another approach to discussion groups.

## Providing Time for the In-Depth Study of Books

If children are to have an opportunity to read and discuss widely, this activity should be balanced with a time for studying books deeply. When children work with books in ways that are meaningful to them—through talk, art making, writing, or drama and music—many things happen. Children have greater satisfaction with, and clarify personal meanings about, what they have read. These activities allow many books to be visible in the classroom. One child's work with a book can dramatically influence another child's willingness to read it. Children working on projects use various skills, exercise more choices, develop planning abilities, and experiment with a variety of learning experiences. In addition, these activities can allow children the opportunity to think more deeply about books and to return to them to explore responses in ways that deepen their understandings.

Teachers who know the children in their classes well recognize the diversity of learning styles this sort of active learning accommodates. They plan diverse activities that enhance children's delight in books, make them want to continue reading more and better

A *third- and fourth-grade group heard Byrd Baylor's story* I'm in Charge of Celebrations *and wrote about special days they wanted to remember.*
Mangere Bridge School, Auckland, New Zealand. Colleen Fleming, teacher.

books, and cause them to think both more widely and more specifically about what they have read. They know that many options should be open to children and do not expect all children to choose the same book or have the same type of response to a book. They consult with children about possibilities for projects and do not assign all children to do the same project; neither do they expect children to do an activity for every book that they read. The activities suggested here are planned to increase children's enjoyment and understanding of books. Other suggestions for extending books can be found on the Framework for Webbing feature on page 595.

## Children's Writing and Children's Books

Children's written work should grow out of their own rich experiences, whether with people, places, and things, research and observation, or literature. Children's writing about books can take many forms. Children should have many opportunities to write about the books they are reading. They should also be encouraged to use books as models for their own writing.

Real possibilities for writing are all around us in the classroom; however, it is literature that gives children a sense of how the written word sounds and looks. Frank Smith suggests that the role of literature in the writing program is central:

> Reading seems to me to be the essential fundamental source of knowledge about writing, from the conventions of transcription to the subtle differences of register and discourse structures in various genres.[9]

Literature has made a tremendous impact on reading programs, and so too has the writing process approach. Few teachers would consider teaching reading without including writing, because learning in one area means learning in the other. Literature informs both processes. As children become authors, they look at professional authors to see how a book works and sounds. They borrow and improvise on the language, patterns, and format of published books.[10] Young children rewrite their favorite stories (see Chapter 4), particularly when they can use invented spellings and do not have to produce a "correct" copy. Writing and reading go on all day in a classroom where language arts and reading are intertwined and literature is at the heart of the curriculum.

### *Helping Children Write About Books*

In most schools children are no longer required to write book reports, a particularly inert kind of writing. However, many teachers ask children to write about their reading in other ways. This writing resembles talk, in that a child shares ideas and someone responds to those ideas. Teachers find this is a timesaving idea and can set aside a weekly or biweekly time to react in writing to children's written responses. Some teachers demonstrate supportive responses and let pairs of children react to each other's written work as well. There are various ways a teacher can help children write about their reading.

[9]Frank Smith, *Writing and the Writer* (New York: Holt, 1982), p. 177.

[10]See Frederick R. Burton, "Writing What They Read: Reflections on Literature and Child Writers," in *Stories to Grow On*, ed. Julie M. Jensen (Portsmouth, N.H.: Heinemann, 1989), pp. 97–105.

*After a class study of alphabet books, a fifth grader created "An Occupied Alphabet," showing various occupations.*
Allison Fraser, grade 5. George Mason Elementary School, Alexandria City Public Schools, Alexandria, Virginia. Susan Steinberg, teacher.

A *reading log* is a simple record of the title and author of each book a child has read. Needless to say, this is a burden for young children, but it is a source of pride for second graders and older children who like to recall their reading and measure their progress. Teachers might give children six-by-eight-inch cards and let them fill in one side. Then the teacher and child can use these records for generalizing as they talk together about a child's reading. If a child takes her most recent card to the library, librarians might better help her find a book by seeing what she has enjoyed so far.

In a *response journal* children record their comments as they read a novel. Children respond freely as they think about their reading and write about the things that concern or interest them. A *double-entry draft* is a two-sided journal entry in which the reader copies or paraphrases a quote from the book on the left half of the paper. On the right, the reader comments on the quote. Teachers react to both of these journals and engage in a written dialogue with the reader (thereby creating a *dialogue journal*). Whatever we call it, children's written responses to the books they read provide teachers with another window into understanding how readers teach themselves to read.

Writing about books in the same way every day becomes tedious. Teachers may want to vary the way children can respond. They might invite children to keep a *sketchbook/journal,* where visual art serves as a preface to writing.[11] A single dialogue journal might be kept by a group reading the same book and children can take turns responding. Children might ask their own questions and consider which ones are more interesting to write about.

Teachers might also ask children to address in their journals a particular question about their wide reading or about a class study book. They might write a journal entry from the point of view of a character in the book they are reading, for instance. During the group reading of a novel, a teacher might ask children to write about some issue prior to a class discussion as a way of rehearsing an idea. A small group who have just read the first ten pages of David Almond's *Skellig* might be asked to speculate on the identity of the creature Michael has found. After finishing this novel, children might discuss how and why Michael

---

[11]See Karen Ernst. *Picturing Learning* (Portsmouth, N.H.: Heinemann, 1994).

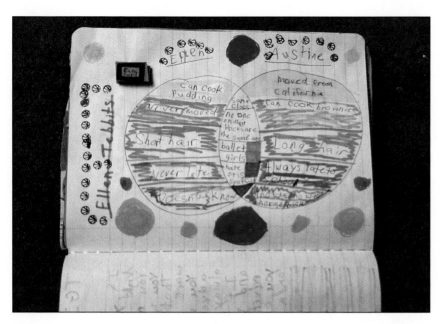

*Fifth graders were invited to record their responses to books in sketchbook journals.*
Beginning with Children School, Brooklyn, New York. Carmen Gordillo, teacher.
Barbara Z. Kiefer

and Mina changed in the story, or what the story made them think about. They might consider how this book is like others they have read, thus making links between books.

What teachers need to avoid, however, is overusing written response, or using a journal as a place in which children answer numbers of questions posed by the teacher. The primary power of journals is that the child owns the ideas, not the teacher. The child is director of the reading, and the child reflects on matters of interest to herself. When children write about their reading, they follow certain patterns, such as retelling, questioning particular words, clarifying meanings, reacting with like or dislike to a particular part of the story, relating a part of the story to their own lives, or otherwise reflecting.

### Books and Children's Writing

When children have a chance to become writers themselves, they begin to notice how other authors work. Literature suggests the many forms that stories, information, or poetry can take; as children experiment with the model, they begin to develop a sensitivity to the conventions of the form. This awareness in turn allows them to bring a wider frame of reference to the reading and writing that follow.

Children in elementary classrooms should have an opportunity to experience a variety of well-written fic-

tion, poetry, and nonfiction. At the same time they can be encouraged to develop an appreciation of language and form through writing. In this way, children develop a sensitivity to language, an increasing control over the power of words, and a diverse writing repertoire.

Ideas for writing can come from the child's own life and from the classroom curriculum. They can also be inspired by books. Teachers can read aloud and then display individual books that serve as springboards or provocative formats for children's writing. Margaret Wise Brown's *The Important Book* or Vera B. Williams's *Three Days on a River in a Red Canoe* could serve as possible models for children to use. Many reading and writing connections have been explored in previous chapters. Resources for Teaching, "Books That Serve as Writing Models," suggest stories that teachers might share as examples and incentives for children's own writing.

### Exploring Literature Through the Visual Arts

Young children communicate through visual symbols as easily as they communicate through language, yet by the middle grades many children feel very insecure about making art. Children of *all* ages who have the opportunity to transform their responses to books through visual means are learning to be confident creators. In addition, their familiarity with art can increase their visual literacy and their aesthetic understanding.

Too often children are given a box of crayons and a small space at the top of some lined newsprint paper and told to "make a picture" of the story. How much better it is to work with children who are "filled to overflowing" with knowledge about a book or theme. How much more lively artwork might be if the teacher provided many materials from which to choose instead of the usual crayons and thin newsprint. Chalk, paints, markers, colored tissue papers, yarn, steel wool, cotton, material scraps, wires—anything that might be useful in depicting characters and scenes should be readily accessible. Teachers might provide more interesting paper such as wallpaper samples, construction paper, hand-painted papers, and remainders from printers. Then when children are asked to make pictures of their favorite part of a story, of a character doing something in the book

## RESOURCES FOR TEACHING

### Books That Serve as Writing Models

| TITLE | AUTHOR | GRADE LEVEL | TYPE OF WRITING |
|---|---|---|---|
| The Jolly Postman or Other People's Letters | Ahlberg and Ahlberg | 1 and up | Letters from one folktale character to another |
| A Gathering of Days: A New England Girl's Journal, 1830–1832 | Blos | 5 and up | Historical fiction in journal form |
| The Burning Questions of Bingo Brown | Byars | 5–8 | Journal of interesting questions |
| Dear Annie | Caseley | 1–4 | Letters between a girl and her grandfather |
| Dear Mr. Henshaw | Cleary | 5–7 | Story told in letters and journal entries |
| Strider | Cleary | 6 and up | Journal entries |
| Catherine Called Birdy | Cushman | 5 and up | Journal entries |
| Anne Frank: The Diary of a Young Girl | Frank | 5 and up | Historical World War II diary |
| My Side of the Mountain | George | 4–7 | Diary |
| Jazmine's Notebook | Grimes | 5–8 | Notebook entries and poems |
| The Private Notebook of Katie Roberts, Age 11 | Hest | 4–6 | Diary and letters |
| George Shrinks | Joyce | 1–3 | Letter |
| Onion Tears | Kidd | 3–6 | Story partially revealed in letters |
| Hey World, Here I Am | Little | 4–7 | Poetry and journal entries from Kate, also a character in Little's books |
| Anastasia Krupnik | Lowry | 3–6 | Lists and poetry |
| Z for Zachariah | O'Brien | 4–6 | Novel in diary form |
| Libby on Wednesday | Snyder | 5–8 | Writing group |
| The Bittersweet Time | Sparks | 4–6 | Diary |
| Cherries and Cherry Pits | Williams | 1 and up | Pictures that serve as prewriting for a child's story |
| Stringbean's Trip to the Shining Sea | Williams | 2 and up | Story in postcard form |
| Three Days on a River in a Red Canoe | Williams | 2–5 | Journal in words and pictures |
| An Island Scrapbook: Dawn to Dusk on a Barrier Island | Wright-Frierson | 1–5 | Naturalist's sketchbook/diary |

they have read, or illustrations for their own stories, the results are more exciting.

Paintings, murals, sculptures, crafts, constructions, assemblages, collages, mobiles and stabiles, stitchery and multimedia creations are among the possibilities for visual expression in the classroom. Children's work should mirror the same range of artistic expression found in the world of visual art outside the classroom. The teacher's role is to design a rich environment for creativity by providing materials, challenging children's thinking, and honoring children's work.

Displays of children's responses can be assembled and mounted carefully. They can be placed alongside a book or books that inspired the work or arranged as a summary of a thematic study. Often a study of a book or genre is extensive enough to warrant a museum exhibit. Explanations written by children help clarify for parents and other classroom observers how the work was created.

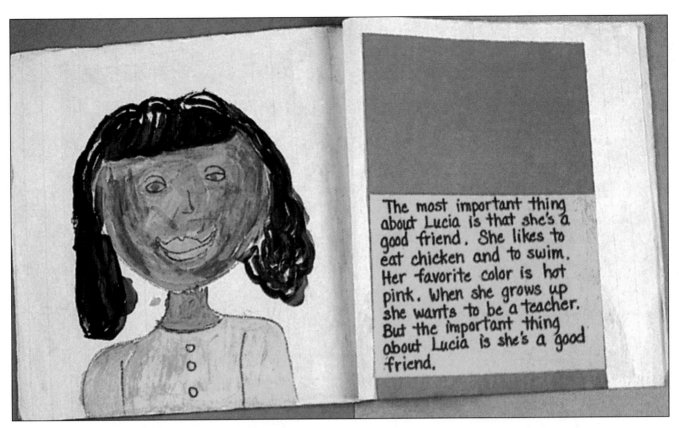

*After interviewing each other, fifth graders painted pictures and wrote biographical sketches following the pattern of* The Important Book *by Margaret Wise Brown, illustrated by Leonard Weisgard.*
Esther L. Walter Elementary School, Anaheim Public Schools, Anaheim, California. Janine Batzle, teacher.

## Media Exploration

A teacher can also make use of a child's desire to replicate an illustrator's way of working by encouraging children to explore various media. Kindergarten children saved their finger-painting pictures, cut them up, and used them to create their own story illustrated in the collage style of three of Eric Carle's stories, *The Very Hungry Caterpillar, The Very Busy Spider,* and *The Very Quiet Cricket*. (See the Teaching Feature "Creating Big Books with Emergent Readers" in Chapter 4). Older children used dampened rice paper, ink, and watercolor to try to capture the look of traditional Japanese artwork used by Anne Buguet in *On Cat Mountain* by Francoise Richard and by Suekichi Akaba in the illustrations for *The Crane Wife* by Sumiko Yagawa. These children were answering for themselves the question "How did the illustrator make the pictures?"

Techniques that easily translate to the elementary classroom include collage, scratchboard, marbleized paper, many varieties of painting and printing, and stencil prints. By making these materials and processes readily available for children, teachers can extend the ways in which they visualize their world as well as their appreciation for illustrators' works. Resources for Teaching, "Exploring Artists Media," provides an overview of illustrators who work in

some of these media and a list of materials that will allow children to explore these techniques.

## Creating Graphic Organizers

A graphic organizer is a visual representation of an idea. Semantic maps, attribute webs, or word webs often are used to help children group similar ideas into categories following a brainstorming session and display them to others. In these graphic organizers, a word or idea is placed at the center of a chart with spokes radiating toward related words, attributes, or other examples. One group listed "Outsiders in Literature" at the center of a semantic map and drew lines out to the various characters from novels who seem different from their peers. At the chart's center were clustered words describing insiders. Word webs or semantic maps are also useful synthesizing aids for children who are organizing material from a variety of books and sources prior to writing a report. The webs that have been used throughout this book are examples of a kind of semantic mapping.

Venn diagrams and comparison charts have been used as tools for organizing talk and thought, too. One teacher asked a group of children who had read many novels by Betsy Byars to discuss how they are similar. Midway through the conversation children had raised such points as "The parents are never around," "The

## Exploring Artists' Media

Try simple art techniques that move children away from pencils and markers.

### MEDIUM Printmaking

| Materials Needed | Books that Use Similar Techniques |
|---|---|
| Styrofoam meat trays | *Stella and Roy Go Camping* by Ashley Wolff |
| Ballpoint pen or other blunt instrument | *My Son Jon* by Jim Aylesworth, illustrated by David Frampton |
| Soft rubber cutting blocks (available from art supply houses) | *Why the Sky Is Far Away* by Mary-Joan Gerson, illustrated by Carla Golembe |
| Linoleum block cutters | *Snowflake Bentley* by Jaqueline Briggs Martin, illustrated by Mary Azarian |
| Potatoes | |
| Water-based printing inks or acrylic paints in tubes | *One Potato A Counting Book of Potato Prints* by Diana Pomeroy |

### MEDIUM Airbrush Technique and Stencils

| Materials Needed | Books Books that Use Similar Techniques |
|---|---|
| Old file folders or stencil paper | *Why Mosquitoes Buzz in People's Ears* by Verna Aardema, illustrated by Leo and Diane Dillon |
| Pastel chalks | |
| Paint | *Sail Away* by Donald Crews |
| Sponges, bristle brush, toothbrush | *All of You was Singing* by Richard Lewis, illustrated by Ed Young |

### MEDIUM Scratchboard and Crayon Resist

| Materials Needed | Books Books that Use Similar Techniques |
|---|---|
| Construction paper or poster board | *In the Time of the Drums* by Kim Siegelson, illustrated by Brian Pinkney |
| Crayons | |
| Black tempera paint or India ink | *Giants in the Land* by Diana Applebaum, illustrated by Michael McCurdy |
| Incising tools or blunt instrument | |
| Commercial scratchboard and tools | *A Creepy Countdown* by Charlotte Huck, illustrated by Jos. A. Smith |

### MEDIUM Collage

| Materials Needed | Books Books that Use Similar Techniques |
|---|---|
| Wallpapers, wrapping papers, string, marbleized papers, construction paper, painted papers, paste papers | *One Horse Waiting for Me* by Patricia Mullins |
| | *The Top of the World: Climbing Mount Everest* by Steve Jenkins |
| | *Angel Hide and Seek* by Ann Turner, illustrated by Lois Ehlert |

main character is usually about our age," and "Some big problem is always there." The teacher then helped children generate a chart with the titles of Byars's books, such as *The Night Swimmers, Cracker Jackson,* and *The Pinballs,* placed top-to-bottom on the left side of a large sheet of paper. Across the top of the chart, the children generated categories, such as "Where the Parents Are," "About the Main Character," "Big Problems," and "Who Helps and How." Now that the conversation was well under way, the graphic organizer helped children focus and continue the discussion while they filled in the grid they had created on the chart. Later, other Byars books were added, such as *The Summer of the Swans* and *The House of Wings,* which children also read to see how they fit the pattern. Children created artwork that represented some of the categories and wrote about how the books were alike and different. These were matted and hung next

*A fourth grader made a stunning collage of McDermott's* Anansi the Spider *using colored tissue paper, yarn, and felt.*
Martin Luther King, Jr., Laboratory School, Evanston Public Schools, Evanston, Illinois. Barbara Friedberg, teacher.

*After reading Kathy Jakobsen's* My New York, *fourth graders created a map of the city that showed their own favorite places in the city.*
PS 124, New York, New York. Mary S. Gallivan, teacher.

*A fourth grader carefully examined Suekichi Akaba illustrations for* The Crane's Wife *by Sumiko Yagawa before trying out his own watercolor response.*
Barrington Elementary School Upper Arlington, OH. Marlene Harbert, teacher.

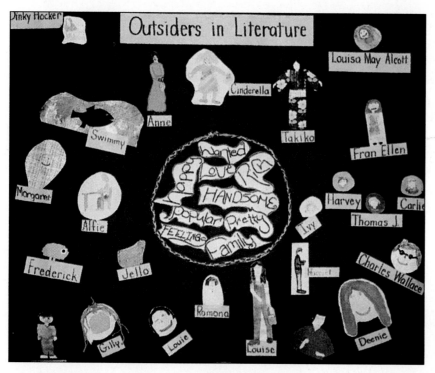

*Fifth and sixth graders made a type of sociogram to identify the "outsiders" in various stories. Personality traits that would make you an "insider" were written in the inner circle.*
Ridgemont Elementary School, Mt. Victory, Ohio. Sheryl Reed and Peggy Harrison, teachers.

## Music and Movement in the Classroom

Children often enjoy singing to picture-book versions of well-known songs. They can also interpret literature by composing music or creating a dance. These activities help them think more carefully about the mood of a story or poem and consider their emotional responses to books more thoroughly.

In recent years, there have been numerous fine picture-book interpretations of well-known songs, including *The Lady with the Alligator Purse,* illustrated by Nadine Bernard Westcott, *The Farmer in the Dell* by Alexandra Wallner, and *A Hunting We Will Go* by Steven Kellogg. To children who already know the song, the text of these books presents easy and enjoyable reading.

Many familiar folksongs have been researched and presented in authentic historic detail by such authors as Peter Spier and Woodie Guthrie. Spier presents *The Star-Spangled Banner* with historical background so that the songs almost become an informational book, too. These various editions are a good way to make American history come alive as children are introduced to many folksongs that are a part of the American folk tradition.

In addition to the classroom extensions suggested, children might enjoy making their own book versions of other traditional songs like "Home on the Range," "Where Have All the Flowers Gone," or "Old Dan Tucker." Scott R. Sanders has invented details and told his own stories for twenty folksongs in *Hear the Wind Blow: American Folk Songs Retold.* Some of these long and often funny stories would inspire fifth and sixth graders' imaginations.

### Matching Music and Literature

The process of identifying appropriate music to accompany prose and poetry selections helps children appreciate mood and tone in both literature and music. Second graders discussed the kind of music that could accompany the action of Maurice Sendak's *Where the Wild Things Are.* They recognized and created music

to the comparison chart. This activity helped the children analyze particular stories, synthesize several stories, and evaluate later readings. From the chart, they were able to generalize about the books by one author, a sophisticated skill for 10- and 11-year-olds.

with increasing tempo and volume, followed by a quiet conclusion of the story. Older children might enjoy reading one of Jack Prelutsky's *Nightmares* poems to music of their own choosing. A teacher might let children listen to Edvard Grieg's "In the Hall of the Mountain King" or Richard Wagner's "Valkyries' Ride" and ask children which of Prelutsky's poems best suit these pieces.

Many themes of subjects featured in literature have counterparts in music. For instance, the quiet awakening of the day in *Dawn* by Uri Shulevitz might be compared to the "Sunrise" movement from the *Grand Canyon Suite* by Ferde Grofé or to Cat Stevens's rendition of Eleanor Farjeon's poem "Morning Has Broken." Teachers can encourage older students to develop their sensitivity to recurring themes in art by juxtaposing literature and music.

### Composing Music

Poetry can be set to music as children create melody and identify the rhythmical elements. One group of talented 7-year-olds composed music to accompany their own sad tale of a princess who was captured during a battle and taken from her palace. Her knight-in-arms wandered the lonely countryside in search of her, while the poor princess grieved for him in her prison tower. The children made up a musical theme for each of the main characters, which they repeated during the various movements of their composition. The story was first told to their classmates and then the song was played on the autoharp and glockenspiel. Older students composed a three-movement rhythmical symphony for Ged in Ursula K. Le Guin's *A Wizard of Earthsea*. A recorder repeated Ged's theme in appropriate places in this percussion piece. When literature provides the inspiration for children's musical compositions, children's appreciation for both literature and music will be enriched.

### Movement and Literature

Increasing attention has been given to children's control of their own body movements. The relationship between thought and movement has received much attention, particularly in England. Basic rhythmical movements might be introduced through Mother Goose rhymes. For example, children could walk to "Tommy Snooks and Bessie Brooks," gallop to "Ride a Cock Horse," jump to "Jack Be Nimble," and run to "Wee Willie Winkie." Nursery rhymes could also motivate dramatic action with such verses as "Hickory Dickory Dock," "Three Blind Mice," and "Jack and Jill."

A favorite poem for young children to move to is "Holding Hands" by Lenore M. Link, which describes the slow ponderous way that elephants walk. By way of contrast, Evelyn Beyer's poem "Jump or

*A group of primary children read five folktales and constructed a comparison chart to show similarities and differences among the stories.*
Wickliffe Alternative School, Upper Arlington, Ohio.
Barbara Z. Kiefer

Jiggle" details the walk of frogs, caterpillars, worms, bugs, rabbits, and horses. It provides a wonderful opportunity for children to develop diverse movements. Both poems can be found in Jack Prelutsky's *Read-Aloud Rhymes for the Very Young*. In Jean Marzollo's *Pretend You're a Cat*, a longer poem that Jerry Pinkney illustrates as a picture book, Pinkney's watercolors portray twelve animals and, on the facing pages, children pretending to walk, wiggle, or jump like those particular animals. Children also enjoy making the hand motions and sounds for *We're Going on a Bear Hunt* by Michael Rosen, as the adventurous family goes through a river, "Splash, splash."

As children learn basic movements, they can use them in different areas of space, at different levels, and at different tempos. Swinging, bending, stretching, twisting, bouncing, and shaking are the kinds of body movements that can be made by standing tall, at a middle position, or by stooping low. For example, "A Swing Song" by William Allingham could be interpreted by swinging, pushing motions that vary in speed according to the words in the poem. Other poetry that suggests movement includes "Stop, Go" by Dorothy Baruch, "The African Dance" by Langston Hughes, and "The Potatoes' Dance" by Vachel Lindsay. All of these poems can be found in *Favorite Poems Old and New* compiled by Helen Ferris.

Children who have had this kind of experience are ready to create rhythmical interpretations of a longer story. *May I Bring a Friend?* by Beatrice Schenk de Regniers, *Where the Wild Things Are* by Maurice Sendak, and *Koala Lou* by Mem Fox are examples of stories that lend themselves to rhythmical interpretations.

*A group of 7-year-olds dance "The Wild Rumpus" after hearing Sendak's* Where the Wild Things Are.
West LaFayette Public Schools, Indiana. Nancy Sawrey, teacher.

## Extending Literature Through Drama

Books become more real to children as they identify with the characters through creative drama. Young children begin this identification with others through *dramatic play*. A 5-year-old engaged in impromptu play might become an airplane zooming to the airport built of blocks; another assumes the role of mother in the playhouse. Sometimes children of this age will play a very familiar story without adult direction. For example, "The Three Billy Goats Gruff" and "The Three Bears" are often favorites. Dramatic play represents this free response of children as they interpret experience.

In schools, this type of natural response can find an outlet in activities that are part of a creative drama program. Creative drama is structured and cooperatively planned playmaking, an approach to learning that focuses on processes rather than production. While occasionally a play developed creatively will be shared with others, the value of creative drama lies in the process of playing and does not require an audience. Creative drama activities exist on a continuum from interpretation to improvisation and can include pantomime, story dramatization, improvisation, reader's theater, and puppetry. All of these activities provide important ways for children to reenter the world of a book, to consider the characters, events, problems, and themes that are central in good literature. Such engagement brings children joy and zest in learning and living while broadening their understandings of both literature and life.

### Dramatizing Stories

Very young children aged 3 through 5 will become involved in dramatic play, but they usually do not have the sustained attention to act out a complete story. They might play a part of a favorite folktale

(for example, crossing the bridge as in "The Three Billy Goats Gruff"), but they seldom will complete a whole story. And no one should expect them to.

Primary-grade children enjoy playing simple stories such as the funny tale *Nine-in-One Grr! Grr!* by Blia Xiong or *The Little Red Hen* by Harriet Ziefert. Folktales are also a rich source of dramatization. They are usually short and have plenty of action, a quick plot, and interesting characters.

Stories from myths, such as "Pandora's Box" or "King Midas' Touch," are fine material for 9- to 11-year-olds to dramatize. Middle-grade children also enjoy presenting parts of books to each other in the form of debates, interviews, or discussions or television talk shows. A group of students played the roles of various characters in Natalie Babbitt's *Tuck Everlasting* and were interviewed by another student who took the role of a television talk-show host. They told about their own roles in the events that had taken place and voiced advantages and disadvantages of Winnie's living forever if she chose to drink water from a magic spring. Teachers can help children focus on important and complex issues that characters face in literature by providing these opportunities to explore ideas. This exploration is often a precursor of children's developing ability to discover themes in literature or factors that influence characters to change.

### Readers' Theater

Teachers who are hesitant to try drama in their classroom might well begin with readers' theater, which involves a group of children in reading a play, a story, or a poem. Children are assigned to read particular

*With the help of their teacher a group of fifth graders create a Reader's Theater performance for their classmates.*
Beginning with Children School, Brooklyn, New York. Carmen Gordillo, teacher.
Barbara Z. Kiefer

parts. After reading through their parts silently, children read the text orally.

Children thoroughly enjoy participating in readers' theater; even though they do not create the dialogue, as they do in improvisation or drama, they do interpret the character's personalities and the mood of the story. They also interact with each other in a kind of play form. The story provides the script, which makes it easy to try in the classroom.

In adapting a story for readers' theater, teachers or students must edit the text to omit phrases like *he said* and *she replied*. A child narrator needs to read the connecting prose between dialogue. Older children can write their own introductions and decide whether to leave out long descriptive passages or summarize them. Many teachers have found it useful to duplicate the parts of the story that children will read. This way, children can highlight their own parts and cross out unnecessary words.

The most effective readers' theater selections contain a lot of dialogue. Folktales are easily adapted for primary children. Some good choices would be Steven Kellogg's *Chicken Little*, Paul Galdone's *The Little Red Hen*, or Joanne Oppenheim's *You Can't Catch Me!*—a tale similar to "The Gingerbread Boy." At first the teacher might read the narrator's part and let children take the different roles. When children become more capable readers and have had practice with readers' theater, they can take over the role of narrator.

A variant of readers' theater best suited to younger children is a form of pantomime called story theater. Here a narrator reads a story aloud while children take the role of characters and act out the unfolding tale. Books that have a lot of action or emotional reaction make the best candidates for story theater. The teacher or librarian might read aloud Alexi Tolstoy's *The Gigantic Turnip* while six children pantomime being the old man, the old woman, the little granddaughter, the dog, the calico cat, and the mouse. As the children gain confidence with this kind of drama, the teacher can stop at appropriate points when the old man calls to his wife and invite the designated child to create the dialogue. Moving from pantomime to extemporaneous dialogue is an easy transition to more complex forms of story reenactment.

### Puppetry

Many children will lose themselves in the characterization of a puppet while hidden behind a puppet stage even though they might hesitate to express ideas and feelings in front of the class. Through puppetry, children learn to project their voices and develop facility in varying their voice quality to portray different characters. For example, a rather quiet, shy child might use a booming voice as he becomes the giant in "Jack and the Beanstalk." Puppetry also facilitates the development of skills in arts and crafts. Problems of stage construction, backdrops for scenery, and the modeling of characters provide opportunities for the development of creative thinking. A well-played puppet show extends children's appreciation and interpretation of stories and makes literature a more memorable experience for them.

Beginning in kindergarten with the construction of paper-bag or simple stick figures, children can gain pleasure from their involvement with puppetry. Materials and types of puppets will range from the simple to the complex, depending on age and the child.

The teaching techniques used in creative drama should be followed, as puppet plays are created cooperatively by children and teachers. It is highly recommended that children "play out" stories before using their puppets. Written scripts are not necessary and can prove very limiting. Playing the story creatively allows the child to identify with the characters before becoming involved with the creation and mechanical manipulation of the puppet.

## Connecting Literature and Life

Children sometimes have difficulty picturing life in other times or places or understanding historical time. They can experience books more completely through making maps and timelines and by compiling special collections. Children who thus ask questions about the details and events in literature are also introduced to methods of inquiry and research.

## Artifacts and Collections

Items or artifacts mentioned in books often seem strange to children, even if explained in context. A child who reads that Ma Ingalls cooked prairie dinners in a spider would be puzzled until she could see this three-legged pan in a reference such as *Colonial Life* by Bobbie Kalman. Hefting a modern-day cast-iron replica would give a child a sense of the endurance of these utensils. This object, although a small part of the story, nonetheless connects reader experience with a part of the real world.

A class collection could involve children in assembling book-related artifacts on a large scale. Second graders studying pioneers, for example, made and collected items that pioneers might have taken west with them: such as a wooden spoon, a corn-husk doll, a flour sack, or a wagon wheel. As the teacher read aloud *Trouble for Lucy* by Carla Stevens, children added to the display their facsimiles of the wagon master's log, a bouquet of wildflowers gathered by those who walked beside the moving wagons, and a "letter" from Marcus Whitman detailing his experiences with the wagon train. Labels were made for each article as it was added to the display.

## Maps and Time Lines

Often authors of books with historical settings include a geographical map to help the reader locate the story setting. In *Araminta's Paint Box* by Karen Ackerman, a map shows two routes—the route a pioneer girl took to California, and the route her paint box took after she lost it. Other stories make sufficient reference to actual places so that children can infer a story location by carefully comparing the story and a contemporary map. One group of fourth graders found on a road map the probable route Ann Hamilton took in the 1780s when she walked across Pennsylvania in Jean Fritz's *The Cabin Faced West*. The movement of the Wilder family in the Little House books by Laura Ingalls Wilder can be followed on a map. Many fictional and biographical accounts of immigrants can be traced on world maps.

As with many of the previous activities or projects in this chapter, maps, too, can help children look across a genre. The sources of folktales might be identified on a world map. The domains of tall-tale heroes and monsters might be located on a U. S. map. African folktales, fiction, and nonfiction might be located on a map of Africa as a way of differentiating features and regions of that continent. Children need many encounters with maps and their working parts (key, symbols, scale, direction) before they become skilled users of all that a map can reveal.

Older children often enjoy making detailed maps of imaginary "countries of the mind," such as that in Lloyd Alexander's *The Remarkable Journey of Prince Jen* or his Prydain in *The Book of Three*, Ursula K. Le Guin's archipelagos in *A Wizard of Earthsea,* or Brian Jacques's Mossflower Woods surrounding *Redwall*. While fantasy provides ample opportunities for children to design their own maps imaginatively, other genres of books can be mapped as well.

The concept of time is difficult for children to grasp until sometime near the end of the concrete operational stage of thinking or the beginning of formal operations (ages 11 to 12). Prior to this period, time lines may help students organize events in a person's life as represented in a book. Time lines also allow children to represent a synthesis of events in several books. A time line from Jean Fritz's *And Then What Happened, Paul Revere?* might include the date of Paul Revere's birth, the date he took over his father's business, the summer he spent in the army, his famous ride, and his death in 1818. Events in the lives of Revere's contemporaries, such as Benjamin Franklin or George Washington, might be more easily compared if they were placed on a time line of the same scale as Revere's.

Placing book events in the world's time challenges even sophisticated readers to select relevant events in both the book and human history. A three-strand time line allows children to separate groups or types of events from others. While *Friedrich*, Hans Peter Richter's story of a Jewish boy caught in pre–World War II Germany, contains a "chronology" of dates in a reference at the back of the book, students might represent selected governmental decrees on one stratum of a time line. A second stratum might represent the number of Jews living in the Third Reich according to yearly censuses. A third stratum might list important events in Friedrich's life. In this way children could see more clearly the political events against which Friedrich's tragic life was played out.

In making time lines, children need to agree on a scale so that events can be clearly shown—by year or by decade, for instance. Time lines can be made of string from which markers for events and years are hung. If children make time lines on a long roll of paper, entries can be written on cards or Post-it notes and placed temporarily along the line. In this way, corrections or realignments can be made easily.

## Jackdaws

The term *jackdaw* comes from the British name for a relative of the crow that picks up brightly colored objects and carries them off to its nest. Commercially prepared jackdaw collections are sometimes available from museums and historical sites. These collections,

## Making a Jackdaw

**Teaching Feature**

Each book will suggest its own specific items or references to collect. Here is a more general list of things that might be included.

- Recipes from the book's time (a typical dinner, a menu for a celebration)
- Price lists of commonly purchased goods then and now (milk, shoes, a dozen eggs, a car)
- A time line of the book's events
- A time line of the period surrounding the book's events

- A map, actual or imagined, of the setting
- A letter, diary, log, or news article that could have been written by or about a book character
- A photocopy of an actual book-related news article or document
- Artwork from the period (painting, architecture, sculpture)
- Songs, music, or dances from the book's setting (sheet music or lyrics, tapes)
- Clothes of characters of the period (paper dolls, catalog format, collage)
- Something about the author of the book
- A list of other fiction or nonfiction references

---

based on an historical event or period, often include facsimile copies of diaries, letters, newspaper articles, advertisements, and other evidence from the time.

Teachers of elementary school children have modified this concept to suit activities and discussion with younger children. These teacher-made collections assemble resource materials that the teacher and children can handle in discussion, in display, or in actual construction and use. A jackdaw for Yoshiko Uchida's *Journey to Topaz*, for example, might include maps of the western United States on which children could locate the camps in which this Japanese American family was imprisoned in World War II. The jackdaw might also include photocopies of newspaper headlines of the time, relevant articles from that period from magazines such as *Time* and *Colliers*, a facsimile copy of one of the exclusion orders families were handed, and information about the author. Articles and documents that could accompany Laurence Yep's *Dragonwings* include reproductions of photographs of turn-of-the-century San Francisco's Chinatown, photographs of contemporary newspaper accounts of Chinese-built airplanes, a kite like the one Moon Shadow flew, and some green tea. Often sources for the factual material on which an historical fiction title is based are given in an author's note. Some jackdaws can then include copies of these actual source materials or "facsimiles" can be created by the children. All materials can be placed in an appropriately decorated portfolio or box. The Teaching Feature "Making a Jackdaw" suggests some of the items that might be included in a jackdaw. Individual book titles will suggest other artifacts that children could include.

Helping children make connections between literature and their own experiences is an important teacher role. However, teachers need to recognize when enough is enough. After a six-week study of Laura Ingalls Wilder's *Farmer Boy*, one fifth grader said, "I hate this book." If teachers' first priority is to foster children's love of reading, they will be less likely to overburden children with factual inquiry. Teachers who appreciate the child's desire to know as a prior condition of learning can appreciate Louise Rosenblatt's criterion for the usefulness of background information: "It will have value only when the student feels the need of it and when it is assimilated into the student's experience of particular literary works."[12]

## Connecting Books Across the Curriculum

The long-term goal of any literature program is the development of a lifetime pattern of preference for reading quality literature. James Britton maintained that in a quality reading/literature program "a student should read *more books* with satisfaction . . . [and] he should read books with *more satisfaction*."[13] This emphasis on both wide reading and in-depth reading

---

[12]Louise Rosenblatt, *Literature as Exploration* (New York: Noble & Noble, 1976), p. 123.

[13]James Britton, "The Nature of the Reader's Satisfaction," in *The Cool Web: The Pattern of Children's Reading*, ed. Margaret Meek, Aidan Warlow, and Griselda Barton (New York: Atheneum, 1978), p. 110.

*A group of fourth graders studying New York City made a display of their responses to the books they had read.*
PS 124, New York, New York. Mary S. Gallivan, teacher.

is characteristic of a literature program that develops fluency and appreciation. It also requires that children make many connections among books and across the curriculum.

Teachers can plan in-depth studies of a single book; books by an author or illustrator; a part of a genre, such as dragon folktales or historical fiction that portrays the colonial period; or a theme that cuts across the curriculum but begins with a subject area such as science.

One way to begin planning curriculum is to make a web of the many possibilities inherent as the class studies a book, a genre, an author, or a theme. Creating a web is a way of brainstorming and outlining over a period of time. The goal is to get as many ideas and books as possible committed to paper before you shape their use in the classroom.

The web "A Framework for Webbing" is really a web on the process of webbing. For this reason, it does not contain any specific titles of books, only general activities for children to do that might help you in your planning. For example, you could place any title of a book, a genre, a topic, or an author/illustrator that the class wants to study in the center of this web and quickly see if there are ideas you could use. Webs are based on the strengths of the books and/or topics and the needs of your students. They present a visual overview of possibilities to be explored, just a beginning plan, rather than a lesson plan set in stone.

Once you have thought of the many possibilities, you need to choose the ones that would be the most useful to try in your class. If your primary students have not done surveys, then you might decide to highlight that particular activity. If you like the idea of putting them in small groups to compare variants of a tale, you might choose that section. Then you can plan a tentative time line: How to begin the unit? What books will you use to introduce the topic? What activities will get the children intrigued to learn more?

Examples of webs that explore a book, a genre, or an author can be found in previous chapters. The webs for Lois Lowry's *The Giver* in Chapter 7 and Elizabeth Speare's *The Sign of the Beaver* in Chapter 10 showed the possibilities inherent in studying a book. The webs "Learning to Read Naturally" in Chapter 4, "Folk and Fairy Tales" in Chapter 6 and "In Praise of Poetry" in Chapter 8 showed the many different ways children could explore a genre; the web "Brian Pinkney" in Chapter 5 pointed out various ways children might study an author or illustrator. The webs "Growing Up is Hard to Do," "The World Beneath Your Feet," and "Life Stories" in chapters 9, 11, and 12, link genres with broader curricular topics. The web "Stewards of the Earth" in this chapter also details a unit designed to integrate many areas of the curriculum. It could be used across grade levels, but it is particularly aimed at fifth and sixth graders.

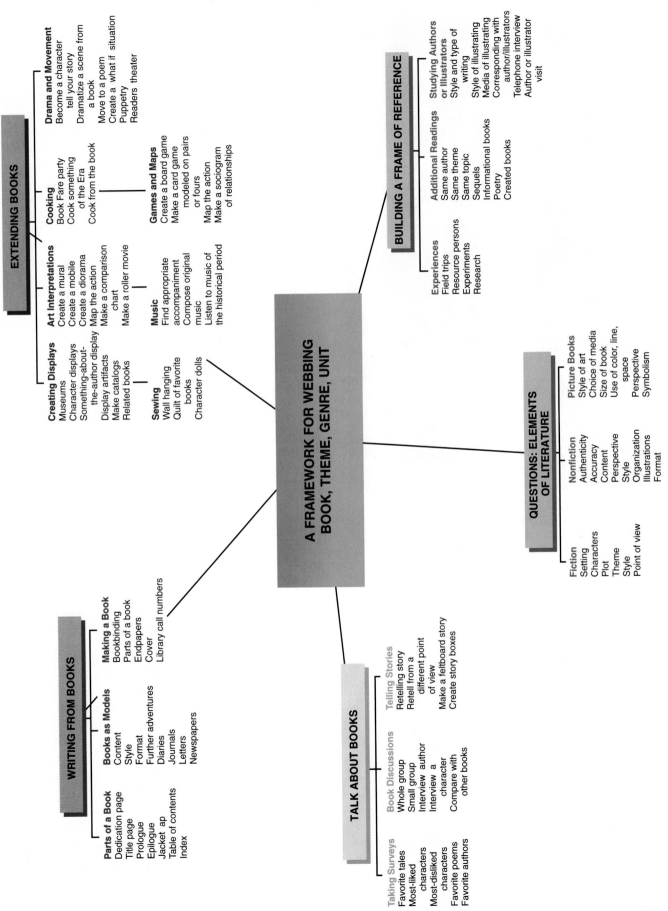

**EXTENDING BOOKS**

**Creating Displays**
Museums
Character displays
Something-about-
    the-author display
Display artifacts
Make catalogs
Related books

**Sewing**
Wall hanging
Quilt of favorite
    books
Character dolls

**Art Interpretations**
Create a mural
Create a mobile
Create a diorama
Make a comparison
    chart
Make a roller movie

**Music**
Find appropriate
    accompaniment
Compose original
    music
Listen to music of
    the historical period

**Cooking**
Book Fare party
Cook something
    of the Era
Cook from the book

**Games and Maps**
Create a board game
Make a card game
    modeled on pairs
    or fours
Map the action
Make a sociogram
    of relationships

**Drama and Movement**
Become a character
    tell your story
Dramatize a scene from
    a book
Move to a poem
Create a what if  situation
Puppetry
Readers theater

**WRITING FROM BOOKS**

**Parts of a Book**
Dedication page
Title page
Prologue
Epilogue
Jacket ap
Table of contents
Index

**Books as Models**
Content
Style
Format
Further adventures
Diaries
Journals
Letters
Newspapers

**Making a Book**
Bookbinding
Parts of a book
Endpapers
Cover
Library call numbers

**A FRAMEWORK FOR WEBBING
BOOK, THEME, GENRE, UNIT**

**TALK ABOUT BOOKS**

**Taking Surveys**
Favorite tales
Most-liked
    characters
Most-disliked
    characters
Favorite poems
Favorite authors

**Book Discussions**
Whole group
Small group
Interview author
Interview a
    character
Compare with
    other books

**Telling Stories**
Retelling story
Retell from a
    different point
    of view
Make a feltboard story
Create story boxes

**QUESTIONS: ELEMENTS
OF LITERATURE**

**Fiction**
Setting
Characters
Plot
Theme
Style
Point of view

**Nonfiction**
Authenticity
Accuracy
Content
Perspective
Style
Organization
Illustrations
Format

**Picture Books**
Style of art
Choice of media
Size of book
Use of color, line,
    space
Perspective
Symbolism

**BUILDING A FRAME OF REFERENCE**

**Experiences**
Field trips
Resource persons
Experiments
Research

**Additional Readings**
Same author
Same theme
Same topic
Sequels
Informational books
Poetry
Created books

**Studying Authors
or Illustrators**
Style and type of
    writing
Style of illustrating
Media of illustrating
Corresponding with
    author/illustrators
Telephone interview
Author or illustrator
    visit

595

*Displaying the results of a thematic studies can invite other students to become interested in the topic.*
Wickliffe Alternative School, Upper Arlington, Ohio.

## Studying a Theme: Stewards of the Earth—Ecology

A thematic unit such as one based on ecology contains many possibilities and provides many opportunities for reflective disciplined inquiry.[14] With a theme as large as "Stewards of the Earth," it is possible for a whole school to embark on a study of ecology. The web "Stewards of the Earth" begins to focus on what aspects of the earth are endangered, why this is so, and what people are doing about it (see pp. 598–599). Some books feature the action of individuals; others show how groups of people form to improve a small part of our ecosystem. Both

---

[14]See Chapter 2, "The Theory Behind Disciplined Inquiry" in Linda Levstik and Keith Barton, *Doing History: Investigating with Children in Elementary and Middle School* (Mahwah, N.J.: Lawrence Erlbaum Associates, 1997), pp. 9–25.

points are worth making in a study of this magnitude: Think globally but act locally; one person can make a difference.

Certain authors are well known for their activist stands on saving the earth. Jean Craighead George, in her novels as well as her nonfiction titles, always addresses interdependence among the living things on the planet. Ron Hirschi, Gail Gibbons, Laurence Pringle, and Helen Roney Sattler are only a few of the many authors of nonfiction who have raised concerns about the environment. Teachers of middle school children might start with futuristic science fiction, such as the titles listed in the web under "Imagine Other Futures," and raise this question: "How did humankind become what it is depicted as being in this imagined future?" Teachers of fifth or sixth graders might anchor this study with a core novel such as Jean George's *The Talking Earth,* Miriam Schlein's narrative of Chinese and American efforts to save the endangered panda in *The Year of the Panda,* Susan Sharpe's fictional account of a boy's discovery of who was dumping toxic waste in the Chesapeake Bay told in *Waterman's Boy,* or Mary Quattlebaum's story of a boy who becomes involved in a community garden in *Jackson Jones and the Puddle of Thorns.* Other classes might start with endangered birds, creatures of the sea, the way places change and why, or observances of nature.

In the "Stewards of the Earth" web, activities that begin a topic are suggested as useful overarching concerns developed within the section that follows. Other activities might follow a particular book or culminate that section's content. There are many community resources that should be tapped in a study such as this, such as classroom visits by park rangers and city planners, field trips to preserves or recycling centers, newspapers and newspaper archives, or interviews with a longtime resident. Books are not the only way to bring the world to the classroom.

Developing a concern for the environment is a lasting topic, and there will always be new problems, new books, and new ways to approach it in the classroom. Even primary children can become interested in the preservation of Earth's natural diversity and the interdependence of all things on Earth.

## Assessment and Evaluation

Assessment and evaluation of children's growth in any area of learning must be consistent with the

*A teacher listens attentively as a first grader reads "The Three Billy Goats Gruff." She is taking a running record of his oral reading.*
Columbus Public Schools, Columbus, Ohio. Connie Compton, teacher.

*Teachers like to have frequent conferences with children about their reading.*
Mission School, Redlands Public Schools, Redlands, California. Myrian Trementozzi, teacher.

goals and purposes of the program. As teachers move toward literature-based curricula that use real books, it makes little sense to evaluate children with tests that are geared to basal readers and hours of workbook practice of fill-in-the-blank, multiple-choice, and short-answer questions. Timed multiple-choice tests following the reading of short paragraphs hardly define what a child has learned as a result of all he or she encounters in the course of reading many books. Information gained by these tests does little to help the classroom teacher plan programs that lead students to become more satisfied, more widely adept readers. Evaluation of children's reading should begin with some knowledge of where individual children are starting; observation and evidence of the child's understandings and abilities as revealed by discussion, classroom interactions, solicited and unsolicited responses to books; and evidence of changes, or growth, in that child's knowledge, appreciation, understandings, and abilities in reading. Informal tests such as Marie Clay's Concepts of Print or Kenneth Goodman's Modified Miscue Analysis give important information about children's reading abilities.[15] These and other methods of assessment demand that teachers constantly sharpen their observational skills, develop some means of record keeping, and be able to recognize important signs of insight and growth in the learners they teach.

Begin where children are. This maxim applies to literature as well as any other area. In planning a literature program, the staff or teacher must first consider what the children's previous experiences with literature have been. Has the child been fortunate enough to have come from a home where reading is valued, where there are many books? Has a child been read to regularly? Or is school the child's first introduction to books? What have previous teachers read aloud to these children? What common experiences, such as author or illustrator studies or thematic groupings in literature, have these children had?

## Record Keeping

As a school year begins, it is important to have some record-keeping systems already in place that are simple and consume as little completion time as possible. In this way, records from the very first days of school can be compared as a child progresses, and the teacher will be better able to plan future curriculum.

One of the best kinds of assessment of children's growth is the notes teachers write as they observe children reading. Many teachers keep a tablet of sticky notes or sheets of gummed labels on their desk or in other parts of the room where reading is likely to occur. As they observe something significant about a child, they can quickly jot it down. Later the piece of paper can be transferred to a

[15]See Marie Clay, *The Early Detection of Reading Difficulties*, 3rd ed. (Portsmouth, N.H.: Heinemann, 1985); and *Reading Miscue Inventory: Alternative Procedures*, ed. Yetta Goodman, et al. (Katonah, N.Y.: Richard C. Owens, 1987).

## CARING FOR THE BIRDS

*Bird* (Burnie)
Find feathers. Determine whether they are wing, pin, down, or some other kind of feather. Mount your collection.

*The After-Christmas Tree* (Tyler)
Make a tree to feed birds, or a feeding station. Observe what comes there.
What birds are endangered? Why?
How can people help birds? Why should we?

*Eagles: Lions of the Sky* (Bernhard)
*Hawk, I'm Your Brother* (Baylor)
*Saving the Peregrine Falcon* (Arnold)
*Where Do Birds Live?* (Hirschi)
Make a tree on which drawings of local birds are placed. Let different people count birds at different sites. How many birds can you count in a half hour?
Which site has the fewest/most birds? Why?

*Pigeons* (Schlein)
How have pigeons helped humankind?
Follow a pigeon. Try to describe its movements.
Debate: Are pigeons "rats with wings"?

## DO ANIMALS COMMUNICATE?

*Bees Dance and Whales Sing: The Mysteries of Animal Communication* (Facklam)
*Koko's Kitten* (Patterson)
*Prairie Dogs Kiss and Lobsters Wave: How Animals Say Hello* (Singer)
How do animals communicate? Make a list of the types of languages animals use.

*Dolphin Adventure* (Grover)
How do people communicate with animals? Why is this exciting?
What good is it to communicate with other species?
Observe a family pet or other animal for several days. Write an informational booklet on how this animal communicates. What do noises mean? Body movements? Expressions?

## DEVELOPING RESPECT AND A SENSE OF WONDER

What kinds of experiences fill us with wonder?
Pretend you are a person in one of these stories.
Tell or write about your moment of wonder:
*Dawn* (Shulevitz)
*Salt Hands* (Aragon)
*The Lady and the Spider* (McNulty)
*The Wonder Thing* (Hathorn)
*Owl Moon* (Yolen)
*The Earth Is Painted Green* (Brenner)
Find examples of language that evoke the senses. Write your own earth poems.

*Heartland; Mojave; Sierra* (Siebert)
*I Wonder If I'll See a Whale* (Weller)
*Whales' Song* (Sheldon)
*The Way to Start a Day* (Baylor)
Make up your own way to greet a day.
Write a story of how your perfect day in nature might begin.

*The Other Way to Listen* (Baylor)
*The Listening Walk* (Showers)
Take a listening walk. What nature sounds can you hear?

## STEWARDS OF THE EARTH: ECOLOGY

## CARING FOR THE ANIMALS

Which animals are endangered? Why?
What animals are now extinct? Why?
*V for Vanishing* (Mullins)
*Aardvarks Disembark* (Jonas)
*And Then There Was One: The Mysteries of Extinction* (Facklam)

*The Year of the Panda* (Schlein)
*The Maze* (Hobbs)
*The Crocodile and the Crane* (Cutchins)
Make a chart of endangered animals; tell why each is endangered; find out what people are doing to help save this animal.

*Lost Wild America: The Story of Our Extinct and Vanishing Wildlife* (McLung)
What are the threats to wildlife? How has this affected conservation policies?

## INTERCONNECTIONS

*Who Really Killed Cock Robin?* (George)
*The Fire Bug Connection* (George)
*The Missing Gator of Gumbo Limbo* (George)
Make a chart of causes and effects for these mysteries.

*Big Friend, Little Friend* (Sussman)
*The Apartment House Tree* (Killion)
What are symbiotic relationships?
Can you name other connected groups?
How do members depend on each other?

What are ecosystems? How are interactions among species vital to the environment?
How are they put out of balance?
*The Talking Earth* (George)
*Everglades* (George)
*The Story of Rosie Dock* (Baker)
*Brother Eagle, Sister Sky* (Jeffers)
What ideas about the earth are expressed?
Do you agree?

*All God's Critters Got a Place in the Choir* (Staines)
*This Land Is Made For You and Me* (Guthrie)
Sing the songs. How do they represent what you've learned?

## IMAGINE OTHER FUTURES, OTHER WORLDS

*Just a Dream* (Van Allsburg)
*Z for Zachariah* (O'Brien)
*The Exchange Student* (Gilmore)
*When the Tripods Came* (Christopher)
*Eva* (Dickinson)
*The Monster Garden* (Alcock)
*The Ear, the Eye and the Arm* (Farmer)
*Time Ghost* (Katz)
How does each author see our future?
What kind of world are humans inhabiting?
    What has disappeared? Why?

*The Lampfish of Twill* (Lisle)
How do authors' imagined worlds encorporate
    environmental messages? How factually
    based are they?

## SAVING THE FORESTS

What kinds of actions damage forests?
List individual actions that might help save trees.
Find out what kinds of paper can be recycled.
Start a recycling spot for school waste paper.

*Giants in the Land* (Applebaum)
*Where Once There Was a Wood* (Fleming)
*The Lorax* (Seuss)

How does nature maintain a balanced ecology?
Should controlled fires be set to keep forests
    in balance?
*Summer of Fire: Yellowstone, 1988* (Lauber)

*Deep Dream of the Rain Forest* (Bosse)
Locate rainforest areas on a map. Make a mural
    of a rain forest from canopy to forest floor.
    Show typical animals found in each zone.

*One Day in the Tropical Rainforest* (George)
*The Great Kapok Tree* (Cherry)
*Rain Forest* (Cowcher)
*Where the Forest Meets the Sea* (Baker)
*Rain Forest Secrets* (Dorros)
Make a collage of articles that come from
    rain forests. What is yet to be discovered
    in rain forests?

## THEN AND NOW: CHANGES

Make a "then and now" chart for one book.
Pretend you are older and looking back on
    a special place. Write about your
    memories and feelings for this place
    that has changed.
Debate: Is change good or bad?
*Grandpa's Mountain* (Reeder)
*Toddlecreek Post Office* (Shulevitz)
*Letting Swift River Go* (Yolen)
*Window* (Baker)
*Heron Street* (Turner)
*My Place* (Wheatley)
Find old photographs of your city or
    neighborhood. Find out what has changed
    since those pictures were taken.
Invite a longtime resident to the classroom to
    talk about changes he or she has seen
    in the place where you live.

## TAKING ACTION

How can individual people help? How do
groups help?
*A River Ran Wild* (Cherry)
*Come Back Salmon* (Cone)
*Miss Rumphius* (Cooney)
*Seedfolks* (Fleischman)
*Jackson Jones and the Puddle of Thorns*
    (Quattlebaum)
*Taking Care of the Earth: Kids in Action*
    (Pringle)
Take a field trip to a trash-burning power
    plant, a recycling center. Report what
    you have found using a "Magic
    School Bus" format.
Interview city council members to find out
    what long-range plans they have for
    areas such as landfills, recycling,
    creation of parks, protection of
    water, etc.
Plant something and watch it grow.
Beautify the grounds and entrance of your
    school. Take care of the plants.

## PROTECTING THE WATER

What endangers our water? How can we help?
*The Magic School Bus at the Waterworks*
    (Cole)
*Waterman's Boy* (Sharpe)
*Everglades* (George)
Write a news account of the capture of the
    polluters.
What are the consequences of water pollution?

## CLEANING UP AFTER OURSELVES

*Waste, Recycling, and Re-use* (Parker)
Form a playground or neighborhood trash
    pickup. Survey the trash to discover patterns.
What is the major source of trash? Who is
    responsible? How might you begin an
    anti-litter campaign?
Make a "life-cycle" map of a piece of trash.
Show where a soda can or cigarette butt starts
    out and where it might end up. Write about
    your map.

*Children's products also reveal understandings and growth. Children created a board game with rules based on the plot of* Big Anthony and the Magic Ring *by Tomie de Paola.*
Highland Park Elementary School, South-Western City Schools, Grove City, Ohio.

notebook under the child's name or into the child's individual folder.

A kindergarten teacher recorded when Jamie wrote his first complete sentence. Another teacher recorded a child's written definition of a story as "a mindfull of life." A fifth-grade teacher recorded one girl's generalizations about the many animal stories she had read during the year. A sixth-grade teacher noted the first time one boy uncharacteristically read for twenty minutes without looking up from his book.

Each day becomes more exciting as the teacher looks for and records typical moments and peak experiences in a child's reading life. These anecdotes make parent conferences rich with positive comments and evidence of growth that the parent recognizes as real. Each observation should be dated so that a teacher can see the ongoing growth of a student over the course of the school year.

Most teachers want children to keep their work together. In a classroom where the room is divided into work areas, generally each child has a writing folder or a work folder, and perhaps a reading log or response journal. Because teachers look at and respond to these, they must be easily accessible to both the children and the teacher. Clearly designated boxes, shelves, or bookcases should be reserved for the classroom's record-keeping folders.

At designated times in the year, teachers may ask children to go through their writing and art folders to select their best examples to include in their assessment portfolio. A portfolio of this sort is a year-long collection of a child's work that may be used in

various ways by the teacher and child. A child can select from a month of writings the one that should go in the file, for instance. A teacher might honor a child's work by suggesting that it would be a fine addition to her special portfolio. If a student has worked cooperatively with another child—for instance, to produce a research report—copies can be made of their project and placed in each child's portfolio. Photographs as well as written work might be included in the collection. As teachers and children confer about the work in the portfolio, the teacher can ask each child why she or he chose this work and record the child's reasons on a sticky note. Together they can build criteria for what constitutes good work. In this way, children know what is expected of them because they have helped to establish the standards.

## Student and Parent Conferences

To help their students become part of a community of readers, teachers will want to plan time to communicate with them regularly about their reading. Parents, too, are an integral part of this community, and they will appreciate being informed about the literacy program and their child's progress. Most schools establish time for parent conferences several times a year, when teachers can share the work the child has accomplished or is presently working on. Emphasis should always be placed on what the child knows and is learning.

Talking with individual children in a conference takes time. Yet in conferences children frequently reveal their growing edges. Teachers will want to have frequent conferences with children about their reading. It helps if a child brings her reading log or response journal and a current book she is reading to such a conference. Teachers can chat with a child about patterns in her reading selections as evidenced by the log. They can recommend another book that fits the pattern, or suggest a sequel or another book by the child's favorite author. They might ask the child to read aloud from his current SSR book or from a title his small group is reading together. It is helpful to remember that a book conversation with a child may be simply a recounting of plot. Teachers can assist children's thinking by asking such questions as "Could there be any other bridges in Katherine Paterson's *Bridge to Terabithia?*" "Now that you've read three books by Gary Paulsen, how could you recognize one he wrote even if you couldn't see the author and title?" "Since you've read so many mysteries, can you say what makes a book a good mystery?"

In many classrooms, children never have a chance to talk alone with the teacher except in disciplinary situations. Conferences can be exceptionally rewarding to both participants.

## Evaluating Children's Literary Understandings

Evaluation of a child's understandings must be seen in light of developmental patterns, as we discussed in Chapter 2. In addition, the teacher must consider a child's understandings as revealed in discussion with the group, in creating products such as murals or imaginary diaries discussed previously, and in some linear sort of way. What did the child start with? What does he know now? What will the child remember long after this moment has passed?

Though the following list of understandings is by no means exhaustive, it suggests how teachers might look at what children know following a study, for example, of the books of Ezra Jack Keats. Do they notice these things:

- Many books feature a character named Peter. Other characters overlap, too.
- Stories are set in the city, in apartment buildings, in the street.
- Illustrations are often collage, using materials, newspaper, wallpaper, marbleized paper, and some paint.
- There are some ideas here. "Giving up things that you've outgrown is part of growing up" from *Peter's Chair;* "There are many things to do outside when it snows, but you can't save snowballs!" from *The Snowy Day.*

In addition, would children be able to pick out a Keats illustration from ones by Vera B. Williams or Pat Hutchins? Would they remember Keats's name? Insights such as these would not be easily revealed in a multiple-choice test. But as children discuss their choices for materials they used in making a picture "like Ezra Jack Keats did," a teacher will see what children had noticed and remembered. When children go to the media center, a teacher might observe whether they ask the librarian for Keats's books by title or by author. Later a teacher might hear a child say about another book, "That's just like *Peter's Chair.* She gave her little sister something she had outgrown."

Third graders who studied folktales might be expected to recognize the following:

- Some common tales
- Typical characters and settings
- Typical traits of characters
- That there are formal beginnings, endings, refrains, and other characteristics of folktale language
- Basic themes such as "Good is always rewarded" or "Little but honest wins over big," although they may not be able to state them succinctly
- That popular tales such as "Cinderella" exist in many versions and variants
- That some commonly recurring patterns, or motifs, such as magical objects, trickery, or wishes, are in many tales

Later, in fourth or fifth grade, when they hear such tales as Susan Cooper's *The Boggart,* Sid Fleischman's *The Whipping Boy,* or Mollie Hunter's *The Mermaid Summer,* can they recognize the folktale elements in these more complex tales?

Children's products also reveal understandings and growth. Did the "story map" of "The Gingerbread Boy" include all the important incidents? Could a child maintain Amos's point of view in his diary from *Amos & Boris* by William Steig? Did the child's version of *The Way to Start a Day* suggest a sensitivity to Byrd Baylor's use and arrangement of words? How did the student's two-part diorama reflect the contrasting settings of seashore and prairies in Patricia MacLachlan's *Sarah, Plain and Tall?* What teachers choose to evaluate depends on what they are hoping to have children understand after reading a book or pursuing a thematic study. It is helpful to list some goals and understandings, based on the evaluative criteria for a particular genre or the particular strengths and content of the theme, before evaluating children's literary understandings.

## Evaluating Children's Growth as Readers

Throughout this text, we have suggested that children's learning accrues, reorganizes, and reformulates based on their own growth both as children and as readers. While observation and evaluation are daily tasks for teachers, the long-range goal of creating enthusiastic, versatile, and skillful readers should be the teacher's focus. By becoming documenters of children's encounters with literature, we become better observers. Observations of change, then, provide us with clues to a child's growth. Guidelines, "Evaluating Children's Growth as Readers," provides a beginning set of questions to guide observations. The most important questions we can ask are often not the easiest to answer: What is a child building? What kind of framework is the child creating based on his or her experiences? How is this sense of literature changing?

## The School and the Community

To be successful, a classroom literature program needs an enthusiastic teacher, a good book collection, and students who are eager to read. However, to create a true community of readers, each teacher must also involve other teachers, students, administrators, librarians, and parents in discovering the delights of good books.

### The Whole-School Program

Children learn what they live. Increasingly, educators are concerned that the quality of living in a school be equal to the quality of learning in that school. The physical environment of the school provides the context of that learning, but it is only one aspect of it. What teachers really believe in and want for their students will usually be taught.

All teachers and librarians must have a strong commitment to literature. Few children discover books by themselves; in most instances, a parent, teacher, or librarian has served as the catalyst for bringing books and children together. As children grow up seeing significant adults as readers, they become readers. Find a teacher who is enthusiastic about children's books, and you will find a class of children who enjoy reading. Invariably, the teacher

who reads, who knows books, and who shares this enthusiasm with students will inspire a love of reading. Many schools have made the development of readers their top priority. As a total school faculty they have met and planned certain activities to promote children's interest in reading.

*Buddy reading* involves students from older grades reading with partners in the kindergarten or first grade. Younger children proudly share a book that they can read with their buddies, and the older children then read a book to their partners. Younger children look forward to their buddy time (which is usually once a week), and the older students take a special interest in the progress of their special child. Buddy reading requires cooperation among teachers to establish schedules. Older students must be taught how to select appropriate books to read aloud and the importance of being supportive of the younger reader's efforts to read or tell a story. Teachers who have tried such programs speak of their value for both sets of readers.

One school planned a whole-school unit on traditional literature. Children from kindergarten through sixth grade studied fairy tales, traditional folktales, fables, and myths. They created a Fairy Tale Museum with such objects as "the very pea that disturbed the princess's sleep" and the golden ball that the Frog Prince retrieved for the spoiled princess. Their *Fairy Tale Newspaper* included interviews with Cinderella and the Pied Piper; classified lost-and-

*Sixth graders enjoy reading with their kindergarten and first-grade buddies.*
Mission School, Redlands Public Schools, Redlands, California. Nancy Anderson, teacher.

*Involving parents in the literature program helps create a sense of community. In this classroom a parent helped children make pasta from the magic pasta pot in Tomie de Paola's* Strega Nona.
Highland Park Elementary School, South-Western City Schools, Grove City, Ohio. Photo by Barbara Peterson.

found ads, including an ad for a found glass slipper; a society column; and a sports page describing the race of the Hare and the Tortoise. Older children created their own mythological characters and stories. Different groups dramatized traditional tales like "The Three Billy Goats Gruff" and "Little Red Riding Hood." This whole-school emphasis created a unity among the children and an appreciation for their traditional literary heritage.

Another school offered many minicourses in literature during Book Week. Children made puppets in one course, created a flannel story in another. Many children wrote their own stories in one course. Then, in another, they were introduced to the use of collage, marbleized papers, and ink prints made from styrofoam. Another course offered bookbinding, and the children ended the week with their own bound and illustrated books. Teachers volunteered to offer the various courses. Some gave minicourses on particular genres of books, like folktales or poetry. Others offered drama and choral speaking. In this particular school, children have an opportunity to do these things frequently. However, the minicourses given near the beginning of school focused attention on bookmaking and provided children with skills they used throughout the year.

## Involving Administrators

No literature program can be successful without the support of the principal. More and more principals and curriculum coordinators are taking time to read aloud to children. One curriculum coordinator makes it a point to read aloud in one of the classrooms in his school district every day.[16] Children look forward to his coming, and he anticipates their response to his choice of books. Another principal has developed a two-tiered reading program called The Principal's Reading Club. Children from kindergarten through second grade make appointments to read with the principal for fifteen minutes from a book of their choice. Students in grades 3 to 6 select a book from a provided list and after three weeks return to discuss it with the principal. The participants receive a reading certificate, button, and pencil that has "I Read to the Principal" on it. More importantly, children see the principal as someone interested in them and their reading, and it's a wonderful way for the principal to get to know children and their reading abilities and preferences.

## The School Library Media Center

Every school needs a trained librarian and a school library media center. While the name has changed over the years to reflect the inclusion of such nonprint materials as films, videos, tapes, slides, computers, and software as well as books, the purpose of the center is to provide the best services and materials to facilitate learning for children.

The library media center should be open all day, every day, to serve students in its unique way. Flexible scheduling of story hours or lessons on library research may be directed by the librarian in a special area, leaving the rest of the resources free for others to use. Children can learn without the constant presence of a teacher or librarian. A trained aide can help children find relevant books, films, videos, and records. Parents have served most effectively as volunteers in the school media center. Children increase in their ability to do independent study by using a variety of sources. An abundance of materials should be readily and freely available.

Increasingly, new school library media centers have become the focal point of many schools, with classrooms radiating out from them. The space should be as flexible and fluid as possible to allow for growth and change. The environment should encourage free access to materials at all times. Children flow in and

out, doing projects, finding resources, making their own books, producing films. As the library media center becomes more closely identified with the total instructional program, it becomes more integrated into the total school environment.

### *The Library Media Specialist*

The library media specialist plays a very important role in the quality of learning and living that takes place in the library media center, the school, and the community.[17] Serving as a full-time contributing faculty member, the librarian works with children, teachers, parents, and volunteer and professional aides. Specialized training provides background knowledge of children's books and all media for instruction, library media procedures, knowledge of children's development and behavior, understanding of various teaching methods, and knowledge of school curriculum needs and organization. Increasingly, the library media specialist is called on to give leadership, not only in providing the materials for instruction, but in shaping the curriculum itself. The library media program should be an integral part of the total school program. Working with teachers, the media specialist needs to be responsive to the curricular and instructional needs of the school. What units of study are the teachers planning to initiate this year? Books, films, and tapes on these subjects should be gathered together for the teachers' and children's use. Bibliographies of print and nonprint materials based on units of work should be developed cooperatively with teachers. Book lists and curriculum resources should be shared. The function of the school library media center is to provide an information-rich environment where teachers and students become effective users of print and nonprint materials.

In one school, the fifth grade was studying the rather abstract theme of famous "crossings." The children and teacher had webbed possibilities, and then the teacher had made an appointment with the librarian. The two of them filled a rolling cart full of books, films, and videos on such subjects as Columbus, the Pilgrims, the slave trade, crossing the Western Divide, and Hannibal crossing the Alps. There were many more topics, but the abstract concept allowed the children to study many time periods and many famous events. Students chose what aspect of the topic they wished to study and then met in their study groups. The librarian worked with each group

---

[16]James Mitchell, "Sound Bytes, Hamburgers and Billy Joel: Celebrating the Year of the Lifetime Reader," *Reading Today* 9 (August/September 1991): 29.

[17]The terms *library media specialist* and *librarian* are used interchangeably to denote the person who is responsible for directing the school library media program. It is assumed that such a director would have had training as a school librarian and as a media specialist and in many instances would also have a teaching certificate.

to find appropriate materials and websites. The children used the library's electronic database and the table of contents and index of each book to see what topics were covered. They checked the dates of publications and looked at the authors' qualifications. All of these research skills were taught in the context of a study in which the children wanted to obtain information, rather than an isolated library skills lesson.

Teachers and library media specialists become partners as they work together to help students learn to use information, to be critical of what they read and see, to make judgments about what is authentic and accurate, and to discover meaning. As students share their findings, they learn to question, compare, and combine information. Only such educated students can become contributing citizens to a democratic society.

*Selecting Materials*

Our children are growing up faster today than twenty years ago. In the limited time children have to be children, we want to give them the very best books available. The adage "The right book at the right time" still holds true. Most children's books have to be read at the appropriate age and developmental stage or they *will never be read.* The 8-year-old does not read *The Tale of Peter Rabbit;* the 12-year-old doesn't want to be seen reading *Ramona Quimby, Age 8;* and the 16-year-old has outgrown *The Sign of the Beaver.* Introduced at the right time, each of these books would have provided a rich, satisfying experience of literature.

The number of books that any one child can read is limited, also. Assuming that a child reads one book every two weeks from the time he is 7 (when independent reading might begin) until he is 13 or 14 (when many young people start reading adult books), he will read about 25 books a year, or some 200 books. Given the number and variety of children's books in print, it is possible that a child could read widely *yet never read a significant book.* Under these circumstances, the need for good book selection becomes even more imperative.

With the increase of both numbers of books published and objections to the selection of certain books, it is essential that schools develop a selection policy. All professional library groups, and other professional organizations like the International Reading Association and the National Council of Teachers of English, strongly recommend that each school district develop a written statement that governs its selection of material. This policy statement should be approved by the school board and subsequently supported by its members if challenged. Factors to be considered in such a policy would include the following: who selects the materials, the quality of materials, appropriate content, needs and interests of special children, school curriculum needs, providing for balance in the collection, and procedures to follow for censorship and challenged material.

Because the subject matter of contemporary children's books is changing, the need for written criteria of selection has increased. Realism in children's books and young-adult novels reflects the same range of topics that can be seen on TV, at the movies, and in current best-sellers. It makes no sense to "protect" children from well-written or well-presented materials on such controversial subjects as abortion, narcotics, or sexual preferences, when they see stories on the same subjects on TV. Increased sensitivity to sexism, racism, and bias in books and nonbook materials is another area of recent concern that points up the need for a clear statement on selection policies. Here are some general guidelines to consider when developing policies for book selection:

1. **Who Selects the Materials?**
   Teachers, students, and parents might recommend particular titles, but the final selection of materials for the school library should be determined by professionally trained personnel. Reliable reviews of children's books play an important part in the selection of books. Four well-known review journals are *Booklist,* the *Bulletin of the Center for Children's Books, Horn Book Magazine,* and the *School Library Journal.* Other sources for reviews are listed in Appendix B.

2. **Quality of Materials**
   Criteria for evaluation and selection of all types of instructional materials should be established and should be available in written form. Books for the collection should meet the criteria of good literature described in preceding chapters. There may need to be a balance between popular demand and quality literature, but this is a decision that must be made by individual librarians, based on their knowledge of the reading abilities and interests of the children they serve and their own basic philosophy of book selection. A written policy statement of the criteria to be used when purchasing books will help solve this dilemma.

3. **Appropriate Content**
   The content of the materials to be selected should be evaluated in terms of the quality of the writing or presentation. Almost any subject can be written about for children, depending on the honesty and sensitivity of its treatment by the author. We should not deliberately shock or frighten children before they have developed the maturity and inner strength to face the tragedies of life. However, literature is one way to experience life, if only vicariously. In the process, a reader can be fortified and educated.

### 4. Children's Needs and Interests

Materials should always be purchased in terms of the children who will be using them. This includes materials for children with special needs and books that represent a wide diversity of multicultural experiences. Children from a particular culture should have opportunities to see themselves reflected in books. In a pluralistic society, however, all children should have an opportunity to read about children of different racial, religious, and ethnic backgrounds. Regardless of a child's background, a good selection policy should give children books that provide insight into their own lives but also take them out of those lives to help them see the world in its many dimensions.

### 5. School Curriculum Needs

Librarians should consider the particular needs of the school curriculum when ordering materials. Particular units in social studies or intensive study of the local region will require additional copies of books about the particular state, industries, and people of the region. The function of the school library media center is to provide a wide range of materials specially chosen to meet the demands of the school curriculum.

### 6. Balance in the Collection

Every school library needs to maintain a balanced collection. Keeping in mind the total needs of the school, the librarian should consider the following balances: book and nonbook material (including videotapes, tapes, records, films, discs, filmstrips, and other materials), hardback and paperback books, reference books, and trade books, fiction and nonfiction, poetry and prose, classics (both old and "new"), realistic and fanciful stories, books for younger and older children, books for poor and superior readers at each grade level, books for teachers to read to students and use for enrichment purposes, and professional books for teachers and parents.

#### Selection Versus Censorship

There is a fine line between careful selection of books for children and censorship. The goal of selection is to *include* a book on the basis of its quality of writing and total impact; the goal of censorship is to *exclude* a book in which the content (or even one part) is considered objectionable. Selection policies recommend a balanced collection representative of the various beliefs held by a pluralistic society; censors would impose their privately held beliefs on all.

The American Library Association's "Library Bill of Rights" was adopted in 1948 and amended in 1967, 1969, and 1980 and reaffirmed in 1996. This statement contains six policies relating to censorship of books and the right of free access to the library for all individuals or groups. This statement has been endorsed by the American Association of School Librarians. To read this statement, see Resources for Teaching, "The Library Bill of Rights."

Almost every school and each children's librarian in a public library has faced some criticism of the books in the children's collection. Criticism is not necessarily censorship, however. Parents, other faculty members, and citizens have a right to discuss the reasons for the selection of a particular book and to make their own feelings known. Only when they seek to have the book banned, removed from the shelves, restricted in use, or altered are they assuming the role of censors.

In the last decade, censorship increased dramatically throughout the country. Individuals and groups from both the right and left, like the Christian Coalition, religious fundamentalists, members of the feminist movement, and the Council on Interracial Books for Children, have all demanded the removal of certain children's books from libraries for various reasons. Targets of the censor generally include profanity of any kind; sex, sexuality, nudity, obscenity; the "isms," including sexism, racism, ageism; and the portrayal of witchcraft, magic, religion, and drugs.

Award books are objects of censorship as readily as other books. The Caldecott Medal book *Sylvester and the Magic Pebble* by William Steig was objected to by law enforcement groups because it portrays police as pigs. It made no difference that all the characters in the book are animals, that Sylvester and his family are donkeys, and that other characters besides police are also shown as pigs.

Madeleine L'Engle's Newbery Medal book *A Wrinkle in Time* has been attacked as being non-Christian because of its references to the Happy Medium and Mrs. Who, Mrs. Whatsit, and Mrs. Which, supernatural beings that some have labeled "witches." Madeleine L'Engle is well known for her adult writings on Christianity; ironically, religious literalists have paid no attention to the total message of good overcoming evil in this well-written fantasy, but have seen only "witches." *The Great Gilly Hopkins,* a National Book Award winner written by Katherine Paterson, a minister's wife and twice the winner of the Newbery Medal for excellence in writing, was criticized because Gilly utters an occasional "damn." Yet surely a foster child who has been in three homes in three years is not likely to be a model of refinement. What is noteworthy about this book is the gradual and believable *change* in Gilly's behavior and character. In Jean Fritz's well-received picture-book biography *And Then What Happened, Paul Revere?* an English Redcoat swears as he apprehends Paul Revere riding to rouse Concord. Fritz was criticized for using *damn,* even though the utterance is a matter of historical record.

# RESOURCES FOR TEACHING

## The Library Bill of Rights

The American Library Association affirms that all libraries are forums for information and ideas, and that the following basic policies should guide their services.

1. Books and other library resources should be provided for the interest, information, and enlightenment of all people of the community the library serves. Materials should not be excluded because of the origin, background, or views of those contributing to their creation.
2. Libraries should provide materials and information presenting all points of view on current and historical issues. Materials should not be proscribed or removed because of partisan or doctrinal disapproval.
3. Libraries should challenge censorship in the fulfillment of their responsibility to provide information and enlightenment.
4. Libraries should cooperate with all persons and groups concerned with resisting abridgment of free expression and free access to ideas.
5. A person's right to use a library should not be denied or abridged because of origin, age, background, or views.
6. Libraries which make exhibit spaces and meeting rooms available to the public they serve should make such facilities available on an equitable basis, regardless of the beliefs or affiliations of individuals or groups requesting their use.

Source: *Information Power: Guidelines for School Library Media Programs* (Chicago: American Library Association, 1998) or http://ala.org/work/freedom/lbr.html.

Contemporary fiction for older children has come under increasing attack as these books have begun to show the influence of the new freedom allowed in books and films for adults. Such titles as Alvin Schwartz's *Scary Stories to Tell in the Dark,* which recounts tales of horror well known in folklore, or Judy Blume's *Deenie,* which includes several references to masturbation, have been targets of criticism and censorship attempts.

A more subtle and frightening kind of censorship is the kind practiced voluntarily by librarians and teachers. If a book has come under negative scrutiny in a nearby town, it might be carefully placed under the librarian's desk until the controversy dies down. Or perhaps the librarians and the teachers just do not order controversial books. "Why stir up trouble when there are so many other good books available?" they falsely reason. In-house censorship or closet censorship is difficult to identify. Selection is a positive process; books are added to a collection for their excellence, to meet a curriculum need, to bring balance to the curriculum. Censorship is negative. Whenever books are rejected for nonliterary reasons, for fear of outside criticism, for example, librarians and teachers need to ask themselves whether they are practicing selection or censorship.

## Dealing with Censorship

If there is a demand for censorship, how should it be handled? The first rule is to recognize that anyone has the right to question specific selections. The second rule is to be prepared—have an accepted response process. A written selection policy statement should contain a standardized procedure to follow when materials are challenged and should be part of district policy. The Guidelines "Dealing with a Demand for Censorship" might be useful.

Several "Reconsideration of Materials" forms are available upon request. The National Council of Teachers of English provides one in their booklet *The Students' Right to Know.*[18] The American Library Association suggests two items to include: (1) "What brought this title to your attention?" (2) "Please comment on the resource as a whole, as well as being specific about those matters that concern you."[19] The major consideration, then, is to have a form available

[18]*The Students' Right to Know* (Urbana, Ill.: National Council of Teachers of English, 1982).

[19]"Statement of Concern About Library/Media Center Resources," in *Intellectual Freedom Manual,* rev. ed. (Chicago: American Library Association, 1996), p. 167.

# GUIDELINES

## Dealing with a Demand for Censorship

1. Do not discuss the issue until you are prepared. Give the person who is seeking to censor a book a form for "reconsideration of a book" and make an appointment to discuss the book.
2. Write out a rationale for choosing and using this book with children if you have not already done so.
3. Make copies of reviews of the questioned book from professional reviewing journals.
4. Notify your principal of the expressed concern. Give her or him copies of the reviews and of your rationale.
5. At your conference, explain the school's selection policy and present copies of the reviews of the book and the rationale explaining your reasons for selecting it.
6. Listen to the stated concern as objectively as possible.
7. Inform the person that the material will be reconsidered by the selection committee if he or she wishes it to be.
8. Submit the reconsideration form to the book selection committee of librarians, teachers, and parent representatives for their discussion and decision.
9. Inform the person expressing the concern what the committee decided and why.

when you need it and to make it specific to the book itself and simple enough to fill out.

Generally, if parents or other citizens feel their voices have been heard and that they have been dealt with fairly, they will abide by the decision of the book selection committee. If, however, they represent a group that is determined to impose its values on the schools, they will continue their pressure. This is why it is essential that every library have a selection policy supported by the board and administration. Librarians and teachers also need to be aware of the support they can obtain from organizations like the Office for Intellectual Freedom of the American Library Association, the Freedom to Read Foundation of ALA, the National Council of Teachers of English, the International Reading Association, the American Civil Liberties Union, and People for the American Way.

Any challenge to a book is a matter to be taken seriously. Ultimately, what is involved is the freedom to learn and freedom of information, both of which are essential to American rights based on our democratic heritage and principles.

## Working with Parents and the Community

Many schools have found that by informing and involving parents in school programs and plans, problems such as censorship are headed off or resolved before they can develop into serious discord. Even more important, parent volunteers can be a particularly rich resource for teachers and librarians. Sometimes these volunteers can be parents of students,

sometimes they might be volunteers from a senior citizen center. One kindergarten/first-grade teacher has "grandmothers" from a senior citizen center who come once a week for the whole morning. They read stories to small groups of children, even individuals. They help make big books that the teacher uses. Whatever is needed, there is an extra pair of hands to do it.

Parents can also serve as resource persons, depending upon their background of experience. One parent who is an Egyptologist became a tremendous resource for third-grade children who were studying mummies. In preparation for this parent's visit, the teacher read aloud *Mummies Made in Egypt* by Aliki, and the children prepared questions to ask him. He brought Egyptian artifacts and pictures to share with them. Another group of first-grade students were studying about families. They wanted to interview the oldest member of their family about his or her childhood. One grandfather was invited to the class, and children learned how to conduct an interview with him. Wherever possible teachers should draw on the expertise of the community.

To help their students become part of a community of readers, teachers will want to plan time to communicate with them regularly about their reading. Parents, too, are an integral part of this community, and they will appreciate being informed about the literacy program and their child's progress.

Students can also reciprocate by contributing to the community themselves. Junior high school students in the Bronx so loved Katherine Paterson's *Bridge to Terabithia* that they wanted to share it with others. A literature group went out to the local senior citizens' residence and read it aloud to these new friends. Those seniors were invited to keep reading logs and join in the book discussions.

In one school the parents and children created the Book Nook, a tiny paperback bookstore literally made from a broom closet. They decorated it with Maurice Sendak posters and a charming hanging lamp and even turned the old sink into a "trading pot" where children could place a "used" paperback and exchange it for another. The whole school takes justifiable pride in this paperback bookstore. In another school the parents made a large wooden case on wheels that can be opened to create a bookstore anywhere in the building. Closed, it can be pushed flat against a wall. Parents will need help in getting such bookstores started and assuming responsibility for their operation. The librarian, a teacher who knows books, parents, and one or two children could serve as the selection committee to order new books. If teachers and parents support the store in the beginning, it will sustain itself once children know its regular hours and can find the books they want to buy and read.

During Book Week one school had someone scheduled to read aloud every hour of the day in the library. The librarian helped the mayor, the police officer, the superintendent, and others select appropriate books for their story time. Different grades were scheduled to hear stories every day that week.

With good planning the community can be a wonderful resource for schools. The more a community participates, the more the people in that community will begin to take ownership and pride in their schools.

## Working with the Public Library

The school librarian should work closely with the children's librarian of the public library. At the beginning of the year, she might send him a list of the possible study units the school will be undertaking. It is not fair to suddenly deluge public librarians with requests for books about building houses when they have had no warning that the entire third grade would study this topic that year.

Most public librarians are very helpful to teachers who want to supplement their classroom library with particular books. In turn, teachers must see to it that these books are handled carefully and returned to the library on time.

Many public libraries are serving their communities in unique ways. Realizing the importance of reading aloud to young children, they might have a story hour three or four times a week. These are scheduled at various times convenient for working parents. Many libraries hold "pajama" story hours at 8 P.M. on nights when they are open. All the children come in their pajamas, hear several stories, and go home to bed.

Increasingly public libraries are giving outreach service to the many children who do not come to the library. Some librarians are holding story hours in soup kitchens for homeless children; others are going to churches and day schools and holding story hours for the unserved children of the community whose parents never bring them to the library.

Some visionary public librarians are sending a welcome kit to each newborn infant in the community. These kits, funded by a local business, include a brief pamphlet on the importance of reading aloud to the young child. A recommended list of books is part of the kit along with the notation that all titles are available in the library. Two books are included, such as *Goodnight Moon* by Margaret Wise Brown and *Clap Hands* by Helen Oxenbury (see Chapter 4). Along with the books are coupons for two more that may be obtained at the library. These forward-looking librarians know how important it is to read to babies and to develop the library habit early. They know that the future of libraries depends on the development of library users; these are apt to be the very youngsters who learned to love the library at an early age.

When teachers, librarians, and parents concentrate on plans to foster a love of reading in each child, communities become caring, literate places to live in. Only when every child has a library card and uses it, when every preschool group hears stories three and four times a day, when all teachers read aloud, when children have substantial time to read books of their own choosing, when all schools have trained librarians and information-rich media centers—only then will we begin to develop a nation of readers.

## Evaluating the Literature Program

It is as easy to identify a school in which literature is an integral part of the curriculum as it is to recognize a home where books are loved and valued. Because we have not recommended any body of content that all children must learn, but rather have suggested that each school should plan its own literature program to include certain categories of experiences with literature, the Guidelines "Evaluating a Literature Program" could serve in two ways. First, it suggests to schools in the planning stages of a literature program what experiences ought to be offered to children. Second, it suggests evaluative criteria for

# Evaluating a Literature Program

## AVAILABILITY OF BOOKS AND OTHER MEDIA

Is there a school library media center in each elementary school building? Does it meet American Library Association standards for books and other media?

Is there a professionally trained librarian and adequate support staff in each building?

Does every classroom contain several hundred paperbacks and a changing collection of hardbacks?

Are reference books easily accessible to each classroom?

May children purchase books in a school-run paperback bookstore?

Do teachers encourage children to order books through various school book clubs?

May children take books home?

Are children made aware of the programs of the public library?

## TIME FOR LITERATURE

Do all children have time to read books of their own choosing every day?

Do all teachers read to the children once or twice a day?

Do children have time to discuss their books with an interested adult or with other children every day?

Are children allowed time to interpret books through art, drama, music, or writing?

Do children seem attentive and involved as they listen to stories? Do they ask to have favorites reread?

Is literature a part of all areas, across the curriculum?

## MOTIVATING INTEREST

Do teachers show their enthusiasm for books by sharing new ones with children, reading parts of their favorite children's books, discussing them, and so on?

Do classroom and library displays call attention to particular books?

Are children encouraged to set up book displays in the media center, the halls, and their classrooms?

Does the media specialist plan special events—such as story hours, book talks, sharing films, working with book clubs?

Do teachers and librarians work with parents to stimulate children's reading?

Are special bibliographies prepared by the librarians or groups of children on topics of special interest— mysteries, animal stories, science fiction, fantasy, and so on?

Are opportunities planned for contacts with authors and illustrators to kindle interest and enthusiasm for reading?

## BALANCE IN THE CURRICULUM

Do teachers and librarians try to introduce children to a wide variety of genres and to different authors when reading aloud?

Do teachers share poetry as frequently as prose?

Do children read both fiction and nonfiction?

Are children exposed to new books and contemporary poems as frequently as some of the old favorites of both prose and poetry?

Do children have a balance of wide reading experiences with small-group, in-depth discussion of books?

## EVALUATING CHILDREN'S GROWTH AS READERS

Do children keep reading logs or records of their free reading?

Do older students (grade 3 and up) keep a response journal of their reading?

Do teachers record examples of children's growth and understanding of literature as revealed in their play, talk, art, or writing?

Do students and teachers together create an assessment portfolio with samples of children's best work?

Are children allowed to respond to books in a variety of ways (art, drama, writing), rather than by required book reports?

Is depth of understanding emphasized, rather than the number of books read?

Are children responding to a greater range and complexity of work?

What percentage of the children can be described as active readers? Has this percentage increased?

Are some children beginning to see literature as a source of lifelong pleasure?

## EVALUATING TEACHERS' PROFESSIONAL GROWTH

Are teachers increasing their knowledge of children's literature?

What percentage of the staff have taken a course in children's literature in the past five years?

Are some staff meetings devoted to ways of improving the use of literature in the curriculum?

Do teachers attend professional meetings that feature programs on children's literature?

Are in-service programs in literature made available on a regular basis?

Are in-service programs, such as administering the running record or the miscue analysis, given regularly?

Are such professional journals as *New Advocate, Horn Book Magazine, Book Links,* and *School Library Journal* available to teachers and librarians?

Are professional books on children's literature available?

Have the teachers and librarians had a share in planning their literature programs?

Do teachers feel responsible not only for teaching children to read but also for helping children find joy in reading?

assessing a literature program already in place in an elementary or middle school.

The first goal of all literature programs should be to develop lifetime readers. Since we know children are reading less and less in their free time at home, the school becomes their last best hope, not only for learning how to read, but also for *becoming readers*. Everything we do with books in schools should be measured against these criteria: Will this help children enjoy books? Will this help children become lifetime readers?

We know that children's reading for pleasure drops off when they are faced with added homework and demands of middle school and high school. But if children have learned to love reading before that time, they will continue to read and increase their reading once they leave college. If they have not discovered the joys of reading before high school, they probably never will.

One 12-year-old wrote to her former fifth-grade teacher two years after moving away to tell her of a wonderful book she had just read. Here is her letter:

> Dear Miss Woolard:
> I just finished the book *A Ring of Endless Light* and I was so excited about it that I just had to write and tell you about it. (It's by Madeleine L'Engle.) She writes with such description that sometimes the book made me smile, and when the characters were hurt or sad, I was also. On page 308 I wanted to scream along with the characters.
>    This is by far the *best* book I have ever read. I discovered it at just the right time; it made me enjoy life more. The book really made me think about life, death, happiness, sadness, self-pity, and what kind of person I want to be. If you have not read this book, I suggest you do. Here are some of my favorite passages from the book [she quotes several]. I have a lot more passages that I like but these two were my favorites. I have no other news, bye, Love, Amber[20]

There is no doubt that Amber will be a lifetime reader, discovering just the right book at "just the right time." And because all readers want to share their love of a fine book, Amber will continue to do this. Here, she chose to share her reactions with her former fifth-grade teacher, who loves books and shared her enthusiasm with her students.

A fourth-grade girl chose to reflect on her reading for a 4-H speech contest. Here is the speech she delivered:

> I know what you're thinking. You're thinking: Uh-oh, another fourth grader about to give another dull

speech about another stupid subject that's so boring that you won't be able to stay awake for another five minutes.

And, ordinarily, that's what happens. And I'm a pretty ordinary kid. I'm in fourth grade; I have blond hair. I weigh about 68 pounds; I'm about four and a half feet tall. I have a hamster and two hermit crabs that I'm crazy about and I have a brother I'm not so crazy about. But am I ordinary? You decide while you listen to some of the experiences I've had.

For instance, one time I moved to the beach because my dad was fired. My sisters and I found out that our cousin had a boyfriend her parents didn't know about. My mom and dad were going through some hard times. I found out that my mom was going to have a baby. But, in the end, it turned out all right. Am I ordinary?

Another experience I had was when I moved into a boxcar with three other kids to hide from our grandfather. We found stuff to cook with and eat on in a junk pile. The oldest kid in our group got a job. After living like this for awhile, we met our grandfather and found out that he was actually very nice. Am I ordinary?

Another time I got a plastic Indian from my best friend and a cupboard from my brother. That night I put my Indian in the cupboard and the next morning I heard rapping sounds coming from the cupboard. It was the Indian! The cupboard had turned the Indian into a real human being! I found out that the cupboard turned any plastic object into the real thing. I turned a few other objects real. Do I still sound ordinary?

How would an ordinary kid like me have these experiences? Easy . . . I read. I love to read. I had these experiences in the books *The Jellyfish Season* [Hahn], *The Boxcar Children* [Warner], and *The Indian in the Cupboard* [Banks]. You're probably thinking, she just read them. But when I'm sitting in front of the fire with my dog on my lap and reading those books, I really am having those experiences. So I guess you were right. I am a pretty ordinary kid, but reading gives me extraordinary experiences. And I suggest it to you, if you are tired of being ordinary.

Susan Komoroske, grade 4
George Mason Elementary School
Alexandria City Public School, Virginia
Susan Steinberg, teacher

It lies within the power of every teacher and librarian to give children a rich experience with literature, to share our enthusiasms for fine books, and to develop readers like Amber and Susan who will find a lifetime of pleasure in the reading of good books.

---

[20]Amber. Letter written to Linda Woolard, Wm. E. Miller Elementary School, by Amber. Reprinted by permission of Linda Woolard, Wm. E. Miller Elementary School, Newark, Ohio.

## INTO THE CLASSROOM

**Room 201**

## Planning the Literature Program

1. Select a book or poem and ask children to extend it through one of the art activities suggested in this chapter. Have them write something to go with their piece. Mount and display their work and writing.
2. Ask at least five children to keep a log of titles and authors of books they have read in a month. What do you observe? What does this suggest to you about these children? about your next steps as a teacher?
3. Give a literature inventory to a group of children and draw some conclusions about their previous exposure to literature. Plan what you think might be a rich literature program for them.
4. Ask small groups of children to plan creative drama activities (interviews, debates, imaginary conversations, and so forth) in response to a book. Which activities required the children to think most deeply about their book?

## Personal Explorations

1. Visit an elementary school and focus on the provisions for a literature program. Does the teacher read to the children? What is read? What are the children reading? What books are available for them to read? How often are these books changed?
2. Spend a day in a school library media center. What does the librarian do? Is she caught up in meeting schedules, or does the center have flexible scheduling? Interview the media specialist and ask to see the current selection policy statement. Ask if the library has had censorship problems and what was done about them.
3. Draw a floor plan of a classroom you would hope to have as a teacher. Plan the reading areas and list what you would have in them.
4. Examine basal readers, sample kits of literature, and published units on literature. Note the purposes, content, plans of organization, and activities. Analyze the types of questions that have been prepared.
5. Using the framework for webbing, choose a book, genre, or unit to web for a particular age level.
6. Working in a small group, choose a chapter book or a picture book and suggest a variety of activities that would extend children's understanding and appreciation of the book. Be prepared to explain how each activity might extend children's thinking or enjoyment.
7. Visit the Banned Books Week website at http://ala.org/bbooks/index.html. Write a rationale for a frequently challenged book.
8. Using the Guidelines "Evaluating a Literature Program" (see p. 610), visit an elementary school and evaluate its program. Certain members of the class could be responsible for finding the answers to different sections of the guide. Combine your findings in a report and make recommendations concerning the literature program of that school.

## Related Readings

Atwell, Nancie. *In the Middle: New Understandings About Writing, Reading, and Learning.* Portsmouth, N.H.: Heinemann, 1998.

This is the revised edition of a breakthrough book on ways to help middle school students find joy in writing and reading. Much attention is given to dialogue journals, both what students write and how the teacher responds.

Bauer, Caroline Feller. *New Handbook for Storytellers.* Chicago: American Library Association, 1993.

This is one of the most thorough resources on storytelling available. It includes suggestions for choosing and telling stories, and ideas for using film, music, crafts, puppetry, and other story media. Information on storytelling festivals throughout the United States is included.

Hancock, Joelie, and Susan Hill, eds. *Literature-Based Reading Programs at Work.* Portsmouth, N.H.: Heinemann, 1988.

Twelve teachers and librarians from Australia and New Zealand describe how they made the change from basal reading programs to literature-based programs. The first section presents articles on setting up a literature-based reading program; the second section deals with special-focus programs such as big books, poetry, and biography.

Johnson, Terry D., and Daphne Louis. *Literacy Through Literature.* Portsmouth, N.H.: Heinemann, 1987.

The first chapter elaborates on underlying assumptions about the importance of literature in literacy; the remainder of the book gives practical suggestions on how to make story maps, literary letters, literary sociograms, and newspapers. Drama, readers' theater, and mime are also included.

McCaslin, Nellie. *Creative Drama in the Classroom.* 5th ed. New York: Longman, 1995.

A well-known drama specialist provides both the theory and the practical help teachers need to initiate a drama program. She includes many suggestions for dramatizing stories and poems, a long section on puppets, and a new one on masks and their importance in drama. A fine revision of a respected book.

Moss, Joy. *Focus Units in Literature: A Context for Literacy Learning.* Katonah, N.Y.: Richard C. Owens.

Moss shows how teachers can help children see patterns among books and relate literature to life. Theory, a narrative of events, and children's dialogue are blended in this helpful book.

Pappas, Christine C., Barbara Z. Kiefer, and Linda S. Levstik. *An Integrated Language Perspective in the Elementary School.* 3rd ed. White Plains, N.Y.: Longman, 1999.

An excellent text that provides integrated language theory and a wealth of examples from the classroom. Eight detailed units for grades K–6 are featured, along with webs to show their development. Chapters on observation and assessment technique are also included. Literature is shown as central to the curriculum.

Peterson, Ralph, and Maryann Eeds. *Grand Conversations: Literature Groups in Action.* New York: Scholastic, 1990.

A fine discussion of teaching with real books. Both theoretical and practical, the book differentiates between *extensive,* or wide, reading where children just read for enjoyment, and *intensive* reading, where students read and study a book in depth. Highly recommended for any teachers involved in a literature-based reading program.

Roser, Nancy L., and Miriam Martinez, eds. *Book Talk and Beyond: Children and Teachers Respond to Literature.* Newark, Del.: International Reading Association, 1995.

A volume of detailed ideas and examples from classrooms where children's talk about literature leads to deepening understanding and appreciation. Sections focus on what teachers need to understand about talk and literature, creating classroom contexts that invite talk, guiding talk, extending talk to dialogue journals, and other responses.

Routman, Regie. *Conversations: Strategies for Teaching, Learning, and Evaluating.* Portsmouth, N.H.: Heinemann, 2000.

An extensive compendium of ways to organize and manage a whole language, literature-based reading and writing program. Journal writing, planning guides, teaching strategies, mini-lessons, evaluation, publishing, and a host of other topics are discussed and illuminated with classroom examples. Helpful bibliographies, both of children's books and of professional references, further extend teachers' thinking.

Short, Kathy Gnagey, and Kathryn Mitchell Pierce, eds. *Talking About Books: Creating Literate Communities.* Portsmouth, N.H.: Heinemann Educational Books, 1998.

Teachers and educators focus on the kinds of learning communities that support readers as they read and interact with others, particularly as they discuss literature. Emphasis is placed on collaborative learning from kindergarten through high school. Practical suggestions are provided about ways to organize the classroom to encourage talk about literature.

Simmons, John S., ed. *Censorship: A Threat to Reading, Thinking, and Learning.* Newark, Del.: International Reading Association, 1994.

Chapters detail examples of censorship in elementary and secondary schools and methods used by censors. Practical information includes how to write rationales for literature selections and ways for teachers, librarians, and administrators to respond to censorship.

Tierney, Robert, Mark A. Carter, and Laura E. Desai. *Portfolio Assessment in the Reading-Writing Classroom.* Norwood, Mass.: Christopher-Gordon, 1991.

A lucid and thorough discussion of the theory and use of portfolios of children's work in the classroom. Examples using elementary and high school students' portfolios, self-assessment by students, and the use of portfolios in parent conferences are included.

Watson-Ellam, Linda. *Start with a Story: Literature and Learning in Your Classroom.* Portsmouth, N.H.: Heinemann, 1991.

Written by a Canadian professor who works extensively with teachers, this useful book contains strategies and activities to help make literature come alive in the classroom with drama, music, art, writing, and bookmaking.

# *Children's Literature*

Aardema, Verna. *Why Mosquitoes Buzz in People's Ears.* Illustrated by Leo and Diane Dillon. Dial, 1975.

Ackerman, Karen. *Araminta's Paint Box.* Illustrated by Betsy Lewin. Atheneum, 1990.

Ahlberg, Janet, and Allan Ahlberg. *The Jolly Postman, or Other People's Letters.* Little, Brown, 1986.

Alcock, Vivien. *The Monster Garden.* Delacorte, 1988.

Alexander, Lloyd. *The Book of Three.* Holt, 1964.

———. *The Remarkable Journey of Prince Jen.* Dutton, 1991.

Aliki [Aliki Brandenberg]. *Mummies Made in Egypt.* Harper & Row, 1985.

Almond, David. *Skellig.* Delacorte, 1999.

Appelbaum, Diana. *Giants in the Land.* Illustrated by Michael McCurdy. Houghton Mifflin, 1993.

Aragon, Jane. *Salt Hands.* Illustrated by Ted Rand. Dutton, 1989.

Arnold, Caroline. *Saving the Peregrine Falcon.* Photographs by Richard R. Hewett. Carolrhoda, 1985.

Aylesworth, Jim. *My Son Jon.* Illustrated by David Frampton. Holt, 1994.

Babbitt, Natalie. *Tuck Everlasting.* Farrar, Straus & Giroux, 1975.

Baker, Jeannie. *The Story of Rosie Dock.* Greenwillow, 1995.

———. *Where the Forest Meets the Sea.* Greenwillow, 1988.

———. *Window.* Greenwillow, 1991.

Banks, Lynne Reid. *The Indian in the Cupboard.* Illustrated by Brock Cole. Doubleday, 1985.

Bauer, Marion Dane. *On My Honor.* Clarion, 1986.

Baylor, Byrd. *Hawk, I'm Your Brother.* Illustrated by Peter Parnall. Macmillan, 1976.

———. *I'm In Charge of Celebrations.* Illustrated by Peter Parnall. Macmillan, 1986.

———. *The Other Way to Listen.* Illustrated by Peter Parnall. Macmillan, 1978.

———. *The Way to Start a Day.* Illustrated by Peter Parnall. Macmillan, 1978.

Bernhard, Emery. *Eagles: Lions of the Sky.* Illustrated by Durga Bernhard. Holiday House, 1994.

Blos, Joan. *A Gathering of Days: A New England Girl's Journal, 1830–1832.* Scribner's, 1979.

Blume, Judy. *Deenie.* Bradbury Press, 1973.

Bosse, Malcolm. *Deep Dream of the Rain Forest.* Farrar, Straus & Giroux, 1993.

Brenner, Barbara, ed. *The Earth Is Painted Green: A Garden of Poems About Our Planet.* Illustrated by S. D. Schindler. Scholastic, 1993.

Brown, Margaret Wise. *Goodnight Moon.* Illustrated by Clement Hurd. Harper & Row, 1947.

———. *The Important Book.* Illustrated by Leonard Weisgard. Harper & Row, 1949.

Bryan, Ashley. *The Cat's Purr.* Atheneum, 1985.

Burnie, David. *Bird.* Knopf, 1988.

Byars, Betsy. *The Burning Questions of Bingo Brown.* Viking Penguin, 1988.

———. *Cracker Jackson.* Viking, 1985.

———. *Goodbye, Chicken Little.* Harper & Row, 1979.

———. *The House of Wings.* Viking, 1972.

———. *The Night Swimmers.* Delacorte, 1980.

———. *The Pinballs.* Harper & Row, 1977.

———. *The Summer of the Swans.* Viking, 1970.

Carle, Eric. *The Very Busy Spider.* Philomel, 1984.

———. *The Very Hungry Caterpillar.* Putnam, 1989 [1969].

———. *The Very Quiet Cricket.* Philomel, 1990.

Caseley, Judith. *Dear Annie.* Greenwillow, 1991.

Cherry, Lynne. *The Great Kapok Tree: A Tale of the Amazon Rain Forest.* Harcourt Brace, 1990.

———. *A River Ran Wild: An Environmental History.* Gulliver, 1992.

Christopher, John. *When the Tripods Came.* Dutton, 1988.

Cleary, Beverly. *Dear Mr. Henshaw.* Morrow, 1983.

———. *Ramona and Her Father.* Illustrated by Alan Tiegreen. Morrow, 1977.

———. *Ramona Quimby, Age 8.* Illustrated by Alan Tiegreen. Morrow, 1981.

———. *Strider.* Illustrated by Paul O. Zelinsky. Morrow, 1991.

Cole, Joanna. *The Magic School Bus at the Waterworks.* Illustrated by Bruce Degen. Scholastic, 1986.

Cone, Molly. *Come Back Salmon.* Photographs by Sidnee Wheelwright. Little, Brown, 1992.

Cooney, Barbara. *Miss Rumphius.* Penguin, 1982.

Cooper, Susan. *The Boggart.* McElderry, 1993.

Cowcher, Helen. *Rain Forest.* Farrar, Straus & Giroux, 1988.

Crews, Donald. *Sail Away.* Greenwillow, 1995.

Cushman, Karen. *Catherine Called Birdy.* Clarion, 1994.

Cutchins, Judy, and Ginny Johnston. *The Crocodile and the Crane.* Morrow, 1986.

Dahl, Roald. *James and the Giant Peach.* Illustrated by Nancy Ekholm Burkert. Knopf, 1961.

de Paola, Tomie. *Big Anthony and the Magic Ring.* Harcourt Brace, 1979.

de Regniers, Beatrice Schenk. *May I Bring a Friend?* Illustrated by Beni Montresor. Atheneum, 1964.

Dickinson, Peter. *Eva.* Delacorte, 1989.

Dorros, Arthur. *Rain Forest Secrets.* Scholastic, 1990.

Ehlert, Lois. *Mole's Hill: A Woodland Tale.* Harcourt Brace, 1994.

Facklam, Margery. *And Then There Was One: The Mysteries of Extinction.* Illustrated by Pamela Johnson. Sierra Club/Little, Brown, 1990.

———. *Bees Dance and Whales Sing: The Mysteries of Animal Communication.* Sierra Club, 1992.

Farmer, Nancy. *The Ear, the Eye and the Arm: A Novel.* Orchard, 1994.

Ferris, Helen, comp. *Favorite Poems Old and New.* Illustrated by Leonard Weisgard. Doubleday, 1957.

Fleischman, Paul. *Seedfolks.* HarperCollins, 1997.

Fleischman, Sid. *The Midnight Horse.* Illustrated by Peter Sis. Greenwillow, 1990.

Fleming, Denise. *Where Once There Was a Wood.* Holt, 1996.

Fox, Mem. *Koala Lou.* Illustrated by Pamela Lofts. Harcourt Brace, 1989.

Fox, Paula. *Monkey Island.* Orchard, 1991.

Frank, Anne. *Anne Frank: The Diary of a Young Girl.* Doubleday, 1952.

Freedman, Russell. *Lincoln: A Photobiography.* Clarion, 1987.

Fritz, Jean. *And Then What Happened, Paul Revere?* Illustrated by Margo Tomes. Coward-McCann, 1973.

———. *The Cabin Faced West.* Putnam, 1958.

Galdone, Paul. *The Little Red Hen.* Houghton Mifflin, 1979 [1973].

George, Jean Craighead. *Everglades.* Illustrated by Wendell Minor. HarperCollins, 1995.

———. *The Fire Bug Connection: An Ecological Mystery.* HarperCollins, 1993.

———. *Julie of the Wolves.* Harper & Row, 1972.

———. *The Missing Gator of Gumbo Limbo: An Ecological Mystery.* HarperCollins, 1992.

———. *My Side of the Mountain.* Dutton, 1988 [1959].

———. *One Day in the Tropical Rainforest.* Illustrated by Gary Allen. HarperCollins, 1990.

———. *The Talking Earth.* Harper & Row, 1983.

———. *Who Really Killed Cock Robin? An Ecological Mystery.* HarperCollins, 1991 [1971].

Gerson, Mary-Joan. *Why the Sky Is Far Away: A Nigerian Folktale.* Illustrated by Carla Golembe. Little, Brown, 1992.

Gerstein, Mordicai. *The Seal Mother.* Dial, 1986.

Gilmore, Kate. *The Exchange Student.* Houghton Mifflin, 1999.

Grimes, Nikki. *Jazmine's Notebook.* Dial, 1998.

Grimm brothers. *Hansel and Gretel.* Illustrated by Anthony Browne. Knopf, 1988 [1981].

Grover, Wayne. *Dolphin Adventure: True Story.* Illustrated by Jim Fowler. Greenwillow, 1990.

Guthrie, Woody. *This Land Is Your Land.* Illustrated by Kathy Jakobsen. Little, Brown, 1998.

Hahn, Mary Downing. *The Jellyfish Season.* Clarion, 1985.

Hall, Donald. *Ox-Cart Man.* Illustrated by Barbara Cooney. Viking, 1979.

Hathorn, Elizabeth. *The Wonder Thing.* Illustrated by Peter Gouldthorpe. Houghton Mifflin, 1996.

Hest, Amy. *The Private Notebooks of Katie Roberts, Age 11.* Candlewick, 1995.

Hirschi, Ron. *Where Do Birds Live?* Photographs by Galen Burrell. Walker, 1987.

Hobbs, Will. *The Maze.* Morrow, 1998.

Huck, Charlotte. *A Creepy Countdown.* Illustrated by Jos. A. Smith. Greenwillow, 1998.

Hunter, Mollie. *The Mermaid Summer.* Harper & Row, 1988.

———. *A Stranger Came Ashore.* Harper & Row, 1975.

Jacques, Brian. *Redwall.* Philomel, 1986.

Jakobsen, Kathy. *My New York.* Little, Brown, 1993.

Jeffers, Susan. *Brother Eagle, Sister Sky: A Message from Chief Seattle.* Dial, 1991.

Jenkins, Steve. *The Top of the World: Climbing Mount Everest.* Houghton Mifflin, 1999.

Jonas, Ann. *Aardvarks Disembark.* Greenwillow, 1990.

Joyce, William. *George Shrinks.* Harper & Row, 1985.

Kalman, Bobbie. *Colonial Life.* Crabtree, 1992.

Katz, Welwyn Wilton. *Time Ghost.* McElderry, 1995.

Keats, Ezra Jack. *Hi Cat!* Macmillan, 1970.

———. *Peter's Chair.* Harper & Row, 1967.

———. *The Snowy Day.* Viking, 1962.

Kellogg, Steven. *A-Hunting We Will Go.* Morrow, 1998.

———. *Chicken Little.* Morrow, 1985.

Kidd, Diana. *Onion Tears.* Illustrated by Lucy Montgomery. Orchard, 1991.

Killion, Bette. *The Apartment House Tree.* Illustrated by Mary Szilagyi. Harper & Row, 1989.

Kipling, Rudyard. *The Elephant's Child.* Illustrated by Lorinda Bryan Cauley. Harcourt Brace, 1983.

Kuskin, Karla. *Dogs & Dragons, Trees & Dreams.* Harper & Row, 1980.

Lauber, Patricia. *Summer of Fire: Yellowstone, 1988.* Orchard, 1990.

Le Guin, Ursula K. *A Wizard of Earthsea.* Illustrated by Ruth Robbins. Parnassus, 1968.

L'Engle, Madeleine. *A Ring of Endless Light.* Farrar, Straus & Giroux, 1980.

———. *A Wrinkle in Time.* Farrar, Straus & Giroux, 1962.

Lewis, Richard. *All of You Was Singing.* Illustrated by Ed Young. Macmillan, 1991.

Lisle, Janet Taylor. *The Lampfish of Twill.* Orchard, 1991.

Little, Jean. *Hey World, Here I Am!* Illustrated by Sue Truesdell. Harper & Row, 1989.

Lowry, Lois. *Anastasia Krupnik.* Houghton Mifflin, 1979.

———. *The Giver.* Houghton Mifflin, 1993.

Macaulay, David. *Black and White.* Houghton Mifflin, 1990.

Martin, Jaqueline Briggs. *Snowfake Bentley.* Illustrated by Mary Azarian. Houghton Mifflin, 1998.

Marzollo, Jean. *Pretend You're a Cat.* Illustrated by Jerry Pinkney. Dial, 1990.

McClung, Robert M. *Lost Wild America: The Story of Our Extinct and Vanishing Wildlife.* Linnet, 1994.

McDermott, Gerald. *Anansi the Spider: A Tale from the Ashanti.* Holt, 1972.

McKay, Hillary. *Dolphin Luck.* McElderry, 1999.

McKissack, Patricia C. *Flossie & the Fox.* Illustrated by Rachel Isadora. Dial, 1986.

McNulty, Faith. *The Lady and the Spider.* Illustrated by Bob Marstall. Harper & Row, 1986.

Mullins, Patricia. *One Horse Waiting for Me.* Simon & Schuster, 1998.

———. *V for Vanishing: An Alphabet of Endangered Animals.* HarperCollins, 1994.

O'Brien, Robert C. *Z for Zachariah.* Macmillan, 1987 [1975].

O'Dell, Scott. *Island of the Blue Dolphins.* Illustrated by Ted Lewin. Houghton Mifflin, 1990 [1960].

Oxenbury, Helen. *Clap Hands.* Macmillan, 1987.

Parker, John. *Waste, Recycling, and Re-use.* Raintree, 1998.

Paterson, Katherine. *Bridge to Terabithia.* Illustrated by Donna Diamond. Crowell, 1977.

———. *The Great Gilly Hopkins.* Crowell, 1978.

———. *Jacob Have I Loved.* Crowell, 1980.

———. *Lyddie.* Lodestar/Dutton, 1991.

Patterson, Francine. *Koko's Kitten*. Photographs by Ronald H. Cohn. Scholastic, 1985.

Pomeroy, Diana. *One Potato: A Counting Book of Potato Prints*. Harcourt Brace, 1996

Prelutsky, Jack. *Nightmares: Poems to Trouble Your Sleep*. Illustrated by Arnold Lobel. Greenwillow, 1976.

———, ed. *Read-Aloud Rhymes for the Very Young*. Illustrated by Marc Simont. Knopf, 1986.

Pringle, Laurence. *Taking Care of the Earth: Kids in Action*. Illustrated by Bobbie Morris. Boyds Mills, 1997.

Quattlebaum, Mary. *Jackson Jones and the Puddle of Thorns*. Delacorte, 1994.

Reeder, Caroline. *Grandpa's Mountain*. Macmillan, 1991.

Richard, Francoise. *On Cat Mountain*. Illustrated by Anne Buguet. Putnam, 1994.

Richter, Hans Peter. *Friedrich*. Holt, 1970.

Rosen, Michael. *We're Going on a Bear Hunt*. Illustrated by Helen Oxenbury. Macmillan, 1989.

Sachar, Louis. *Holes*. Farrar, Straus & Giroux, 1998.

Sattler, Helen Roney. *Recipes for Art and Craft Materials*. Illustrated by Marti Shohet. Lothrop, Lee & Shepard, 1987.

Schlein, Miriam. *Pigeons*. Photographs by Margaret Miller. Crowell, 1989.

———. *The Year of the Panda*. Illustrated by Kam Mak. Crowell, 1990.

Schwartz, Alvin. *Scary Stories to Tell in the Dark*. Illustrated by Stephen Gammell. Harper & Row, 1981.

Scieszka, Jon. *Squids Will Be Squids: Fresh Morals, Beastly Fables*. Illustrated by Lane Smith. Viking, 1992.

Sendak, Maurice. *Where the Wild Things Are*. Harper & Row, 1963.

Seuss, Dr. [Theodore S. Geisel]. *The Lorax*. Random House, 1981.

Sharpe, Susan. *Waterman's Boy*. Bradbury Press, 1990.

Sheldon, Dyan. *Whale's Song*. Ilustrated by Gary Blythe. Dial, 1991.

Showers, Paul. *The Listening Walk*. Illustrated by Aliki. HarperCollins, 1991.

Shulevitz, Uri. *Dawn*. Farrar, Straus & Giroux, 1974.

———. *Toddlecreek Post Office*. Farrar, Straus & Giroux, 1990.

Siebert, Diane. *Heartland*. Illustrated by Wendell Minor. Crowell, 1989.

———. *Mojave*. Illustrated by Wendell Minor. Crowell, 1988.

———. *Sierra*. Illustrated by Wendell Minor. Crowell, 1991.

Siegelson, Kim L. *In the Time of the Drums*. Illustrated by Brian Pinkney. Hyperion, 1999.

Singer, Marilyn. *Prairie Dogs Kiss and Lobsters Wave: How Animals Say Hello*. Illustrated by Normand Chartier. Holt, 1998.

Snyder, Zilpha Keatley. *Libby on Wednesday*. Delacorte, 1990.

Sparks, Ducey Jean. *The Bittersweet Time*. Eerdman's, 1995.

Speare, Elizabeth George. *The Sign of the Beaver*. Houghton Mifflin, 1983.

Spier, Peter. *The Star-Spangled Banner*. Doubleday, 1973.

Staines, Bill. *All God's Critters Got a Place in the Choir*. Illustrated by Margot Zemach. Dutton, 1989.

Steig, William. *Amos & Boris*. Farrar, Straus & Giroux, 1971.

Stevens, Carla. *Trouble for Lucy*, Illustrated by Ronald Himler. Clarion, 1979.

Sussman, Susan, and Robert James. *Big Friend, Little Friend: A Book About Symbiosis*. Houghton Mifflin, 1989.

Tillage, Leon. *Leon's Story*. Illustrated by Barbara Roth. Farrar, Straus & Giroux, 1997.

Tolstoy, Alexei. *The Gigantic Turnip*. Illustrated by Niamh Sharkey. Barefoot Books, 1999.

Turner, Ann. *Angel Hide and Seek*. Illustrated by Lois Ehlert. HarperCollins, 1998.

———. *Heron Street*. Illustrated by Lisa Desimini. Harper & Row, 1989.

Tyler, Linda Wagner. *The After-Christmas Tree*. Illustrated by Susan Davis. Viking, 1990.

Uchida, Yoshiko. *Journey to Topaz*. Illustrated by Donald Carrick. Creative Arts Books, 1985 [1971].

Van Allsburg, Chris. *Just a Dream*. Houghton Mifflin, 1990.

Waber, Bernard. *Ira Sleeps Over*. Houghton Mifflin, 1975.

Wallner, Alexandra. *The Farmer in the Dell*. Holiday House, 1998.

Warner, Gertrude Chandler. *The Boxcar Children #1*. Whitman, 1990 [1924].

Weller, Frances. *I Wonder if I'll See a Whale*. Illustrated by Ted Lewin. Philomel, 1991.

Westcott, Nadine Bernard. *The Lady with the Alligator Purse*. Little, Brown, 1988.

Wheatley, Nadia. *My Place*. Illustrated by Donna Rawlings. Kane Miller, 1993.

White, E. B. *Charlotte's Web*. Harper & Row, 1952.

Wilder, Laura Ingalls. *Farmer Boy*. Illustrated by Garth Williams. Harper & Row, 1973.

Williams, Vera. B. *Cherries and Cherry Pits*. Greenwillow, 1986.

———. *Stringbean's Trip to the Shining Sea*. Illustrated by Vera B. Williams and Jennifer Williams. Greenwillow, 1988.

———. *Three Days on a River in a Red Canoe*. Greenwillow, 1981.

Wolff, Ashley. *Stella and Roy Go Camping*. Dutton, 1999.

Wright-Frierson, Virginia. *An Island Scrapbook: Dawn to Dusk on a Barrier Island*. Simon & Schuster, 1998.

Xiong, Blia. *Nine-in-One Grr! Grr!* Adapted by Cathy Spagnoli. Illustrated by Nancy Hom. Children's Book Press, 1989.

Yagawa, Sumiko. *The Crane Wife*. Translated by Katherine Paterson. Illustrated by Suekichi Akaba. Morrow, 1981.

Yep, Laurence. *Dragonwings*. Harper & Row, 1977.

Yolen, Jane. *Greyling*. Illustrated by David Ray. Philomel, 1991.

———. *Letting Swift River Go*. Illustrated by Barbara Cooney. Little, Brown, 1992.

———. *Owl Moon*. Illustrated by John Schoenherr. Philomel, 1987.

Ziefert, Harriet. *The Little Red Hen*. Illustrated by Emily Bolam. Viking, 1995.

Zion, Gene. *Harry the Dirty Dog*. Illustrated by Margaret Graham. Harper & Row, 1956.

# Appendix A

# Children's Book Awards

The John Newbery Medal is named in honor of John Newbery, a British publisher and bookseller of the eighteenth century. He has frequently been called the father of children's literature, because he was the first to conceive the idea of publishing books expressly for children.

The award is presented each year to "the author of the most distinguished contribution to American literature for children." Only books published in the preceding year are eligible, and the author must be an American citizen or a permanent resident of the United States. The selection of the winner is made by a committee of the Association for Library Service to Children (ALSC) of the American Library Association. There are now fifteen members on this committee. The winning author is presented with a bronze medal designed by René Paul Chambellan and donated by Frederick G. Melcher. The announcement is made in January or early February. Later, at the summer conference of the American Library Association, a banquet is given in honor of the award winners.

In the following list, for each year the Medal winner is listed first (in boldface italic), followed by the Honor Books for that year. The date is the year in which the award was conferred. All books were published the preceding year.

1922 ***The Story of Mankind*** by Hendrik Van Loon. Boni & Liveright.
*The Great Quest* by Charles Boardman Hawes. Little, Brown.
*Cedric the Forester* by Bernard G. Marshall. Appleton.
*The Old Tobacco Shop* by William Bowen. Macmillan.
*The Golden Fleece* by Padraic Colum. Macmillan.
*Windy Hill* by Cornelia Meigs. Macmillan.

1923 ***The Voyages of Doctor Dolittle*** by Hugh Lofting. Stokes.
(No record of the Honor Books.)

1924 ***The Dark Frigate*** by Charles Boardman Hawes. Little, Brown.
(No record of the Honor Books)

1925 ***Tales from Silver Lands*** by Charles J. Finger. Illustrated by Paul Honoré. Doubleday.
*Nicholas* by Anne Carroll Moore. Putnam.
*Dream Coach* by Anne and Dillwyn Parrish. Macmillan.

1926 ***Shen of the Sea*** by Arthur Bowie Chrisman. Illustrated by Else Hasselriis. Dutton.
*The Voyagers* by Padraic Colum. Macmillan.

1927 ***Smoky, the Cowhorse*** by Will James. Scribner's.
(No record of the Honor Books)

1928 ***Gay Neck*** by Dhan Gopal Mukerji. Illustrated by Boris Artzybasheff. Dutton.
*The Wonder-Smith and His Son* by Ella Young. Longmans, Green.
*Downright Dencey* by Caroline Dale Snedeker. Doubleday.

1929 ***Trumpeter of Krakow*** by Eric P. Kelly. Illustrated by Angela Pruszynska. Macmillan.
*The Pigtail of Ah Lee Ben Loo* by John Bennett. Longmans, Green.
*Millions of Cats* by Wanda Gág. Coward-McCann.
*The Boy Who Was* by Grace T. Hallock. Dutton.
*Clearing Weather* by Cornelia Meigs. Little, Brown.
*The Runaway Papoose* by Grace P. Moon. Doubleday.
*Tod of the Fens* by Eleanor Whitney. Macmillan.

1930 ***Hitty, Her First Hundred Years*** by Rachel Field. Illustrated by Dorothy P. Lathrop. Macmillan.
*Pran of Albania* by Elizabeth C. Miller. Doubleday.
*The Jumping-Off Place* by Miran Hurd McNeely. Longmans, Green.
*A Daughter of the Seine* by Jeanette Eaton. Harper & Row.

1931 ***The Cat Who Went to Heaven*** by Elizabeth Coatsworth. Illustrated by Lynd Ward. Macmillan.
*Floating Island* by Anne Parrish. Harper & Row.
*The Dark Star of Itza* by Alida Malkus. Harcourt Brace.
*Queer Person* by Ralph Hubbard. Doubleday.
*Mountains Are Free* by Julia Davis Adams. Dutton.
*Spice and the Devil's Cave* by Agnes D. Hewes. Knopf.
*Meggy McIntosh* by Elizabeth Janet Gray. Doubleday.

1932 ***Waterless Mountain*** by Laura Adams Armer. Illustrated by Sidney Armer and the author. Longmans, Green.
*The Fairy Circus* by Dorothy Lathrop. Macmillan.
*Calico Bush* by Rachel Field. Macmillan.

*Boy of the South Seas* by Eunice Tietjens. Coward-McCann.

*Out of the Flame* by Eloise Lounsbery. Longmans, Green.

*Jane's Island* by Marjorie Hill Alee. Houghton Mifflin.

*Truce of the Wolf* by Mary Gould Davis. Harcourt Brace.

1933 **Young Fu of the Upper Yangtze** by Elizabeth Foreman Lewis. Illustrated by Kurt Wiese. Winston.

*Swift Rivers* by Cornelia Meigs. Little, Brown.

*The Railroad to Freedom* by Hildegarde Swift. Harcourt Brace.

*Children of the Soil* by Nora Burglon. Doubleday.

1934 **Invincible Louisa** by Cornelia Meigs. Little, Brown.

*Forgotten Daughter* by Caroline Dale Snedeker. Doubleday.

*Swords of Steel* by Elsie Singmaster. Houghton Mifflin.

*ABC Bunny* by Wanda Gág. Coward-McCann.

*Winged Girl of Knossos* by Erick Berry. Appleton.

*New Land* by Sarah L. Schmidt. McBride.

*Apprentices of Florence* by Anne Kyle. Houghton Mifflin.

1935 **Dobry** by Monica Shannon. Illustrated by Atanas Katchamakoff. Viking.

*The Pageant of Chinese History* by Elizabeth Seeger. Longmans, Green.

*Davy Crockett* by Constance Rourke. Harcourt Brace.

*A Day on Skates* by Hilda Van Stockum. Harper & Row.

1936 **Caddie Woodlawn** by Carol Ryrie Brink. Illustrated by Kate Seredy. Macmillan.

*Honk the Moose* by Phil Stong. Dodd, Mead.

*The Good Master* by Kate Seredy. Viking.

*Young Walter Scott* by Elizabeth Janet Gray. Viking.

*All Sail Set* by Armstrong Sperry. Winston.

1937 **Roller Skates** by Ruth Sawyer. Illustrated by Valenti Angelo. Viking.

*Phoebe Fairchild: Her Book* by Lois Lenski. Stokes.

*Whistler's Van* by Idwal Jones. Viking.

*The Golden Basket* by Ludwig Bemelmans. Viking.

*Winterbound* by Margery Bianco. Viking.

*Audubon* by Constance Rourke. Harcourt Brace.

*The Codfish Musket* by Agnes D. Hewes. Doubleday.

1938 **The White Stag** by Kate Seredy. Viking.

*Bright Island* by Mabel L. Robinson. Random House.

*Pecos Bill* by James Cloyd Bowman. Whitman.

*On the Banks of Plum Creek* by Laura Ingalls Wilder. Harper & Row.

1939 **Thimble Summer** by Elizabeth Enright. Farrar & Rinehart.

*Leader by Destiny* by Jeanette Eaton. Harcourt Brace.

*Penn* by Elizabeth Janet Gray. Viking.

*Nino* by Valenti Angelo. Viking.

*"Hello, the Boat!"* by Phyllis Crawford. Holt.

*Mr. Popper's Penguins* by Richard and Florence Atwater. Little, Brown.

1940 **Danile Boone** by James H. Daugherty. Viking.

*The Singing Tree* by Kate Seredy. Viking.

*Runner of the Mountain Tops* by Mabel L. Robinson. Random House.

*By the Shores of Silver Lake* by Laura Ingalls Wilder. Harper & Row.

*Boy with a Pack* by Stephen W. Meader. Harcourt Brace.

1941 **Call It Courage** by Armstrong Sperry. Macmillan.

*Blue Willow* by Doris Gates. Viking.

*Young Mac of Fort Vancouver* by Mary Jane Carr. Crowell.

*The Long Winter* by Laura Ingalls Wilder. Harper & Row.

*Nansen* by Anna Gertrude Hall. Viking.

1942 **The Matchlock Gun** by Walter D. Edmonds. Illustrated by Paul Lantz. Dodd, Mead.

*Little Town on the Prairie* by Laura Ingalls Wilder. Harper & Row.

*George Washington's World* by Genevieve Foster. Scribner's.

*Indian Captive* by Lois Lenski. Stokes.

*Down Ryton Water* by E. R. Gaggin. Viking.

1943 **Adam of the Road** by Elizabeth Janet Gray. Illustrated by Robert Lawson. Viking.

*The Middle Moffat* by Eleanor Estes. Harcourt Brace.

*"Have You Seen Tom Thumb?"* by Mabel Leigh Hunt. Stokes.

1944 **Johnny Tremain** by Esther Forbes. Illustrated by Lynd Ward. Houghton Mifflin.

*These Happy Golden Years* by Laura Ingalls Wilder. Harper & Row.

*Fog Magic* by Julia L. Sauer. Viking.

*Rufus M.* by Eleanor Estes. Harcourt Brace.

*Mountain Born* by Elizabeth Yates. Coward-McCann.

1945 **Rabbit Hill** by Robert Lawson. Viking.

*The Hundred Dresses* by Eleanor Estes. Harcourt Brace.

*The Silver Pencil* by Alice Dalgliesh. Scribner's.

*Abraham Lincoln's World* by Genevieve Foster. Scribner's.

*Lone Journey* by Jeanette Eaton. Harcourt Brace.

1946 **Strawberry Girl** by Lois Lenski. Lippincott.

*Justin Morgan Had a Horse* by Marguerite Henry. Wilcox & Follett.

*The Moved-Outers* by Florence Crannell Means. Houghton Mifflin.

*Bhimsa, the Dancing Bear* by Christine Weston. Scribner's.

*New Found World* by Katherine B. Shippen. Viking.

1947 **Miss Hickory** by Carolyn Sherwin Bailey. Illustrated by Ruth Gannett. Viking.

*The Wonderful Year* by Nancy Barnes. Messner.

*Big Tree* by Mary Buff and Conrad Buff. Viking.

*The Heavenly Tenants* by William Maxwell. Harper & Row.

*The Avion My Uncle Flew* by Cyrus Fisher. Appleton.

*The Hidden Treasure of Glaston* by Eleanore M. Jewett. Viking.

1948 **The Twenty-One Balloons** by William Pène DuBois. Viking.

*Pancakes-Paris* by Claire Huchet Bishop. Viking.

*Li Lun, Lad of Courage* by Carolyn Treffinger. Abingdon-Cokesbury.

*The Quaint and Curious Quest of Johnny Longfoot* by Catherine Besterman. Bobbs-Merrill.

*The Cow-Tail Switch* by Harold Courlander and George Herzog. Holt.

*Misty of Chincoteague* by Marguerite Henry. Rand McNally.

1949 *King of the Wind* by Marguerite Henry. Illustrated by Wesley Dennis. Rand McNally.
*Seabird* by Holling Clancy Holling. Houghton Mifflin.
*Daughter of the Mountains* by Louise Rankin. Viking.
*My Father's Dragon* by Ruth S. Gannett. Random House.
*Story of the Negro* by Arna Bontemps. Knopf.

1950 *The Door in the Wall* by Marguerite de Angeli. Doubleday.
*Tree of Freedom* by Rebecca Caudill. Viking.
*Blue Cat of Castle Town* by Catherine Coblentz. Longmans, Green.
*Kildee House* by Rutherford Montgomery. Doubleday.
*George Washington* by Genevieve Foster. Scribner's.
*Song of the Pines* by Walter Havighurst and Marion Havighurst. Winston.

1951 *Amos Fortune, Free Man* by Elizabeth Yates. Illustrated by Nora Unwin. Aladdin.
*Better Known as Johnny Appleseed* by Mabel Leigh Hunt. Lippincott.
*Gandhi, Fighter Without a Sword* by Jeanette Eaton. Morrow.
*Abraham Lincoln, Friend of the People* by Clara I. Judson. Wilcox & Follett.
*The Story of Appleby Capple* by Anne Parrish. Harper & Row.

1952 *Ginger Pye* by Elizabeth Chesley Baity. Viking.
*Minn of the Mississippi* by Holling Clancy Holling. Houghton Mifflin.
*The Defender* by Nicholas Kalashnikoff. Scribner's.
*The Light at Tern Rock* by Julia L. Sauer. Viking.
*The Apple and the Arrow* by Mary Buff. Houghton Mifflin.

1953 *Secret of the Andes* by Ann Nolan Clark. Illustrated by Jean Charlot. Viking.
*Charlotte's Web* by E. B. White. Harper & Row.
*Moccasin Trail* by Eloise J. McGraw. Coward-McCann.
*Red Sails for Capri* by Ann Weil. Viking.
*The Bears on Hemlock Mountain* by Alice Dalgliesh. Scribner's.
*Birthdays of Freedom* by Genevieve Foster. Scribner's.

1954 *And Now Miguel* by Joseph Krumgold. Illustrated by Jean Charlot. Crowell.
*All Alone* by Clarie Huchet Bishop. Viking.
*Shadrach* by Meindert DeJong. Harper & Row.
*Hurry Home, Candy* by Meindert DeJong, Harper & Row.
*Theodore Roosevelt, Fighting Patriot* by Clara I. Judson. Follett.
*Magic Maize* by Buff. Houghton Mifflin.

1955 *The Wheel on the School* by Meindert DeJong. Illustrated by Maurice Sendak. Harper & Row.
*The Courage of Sarah Noble* by Alice Dalgliesh. Scribner's.
*Banner in the Sky* by James Ramsey Ullman. Lippincott.

1956 *Carry On, Mr. Bowditch* by Jean Lee Latham. Houghton Mifflin.
*The Golden Name Day* by Jennie D. Lindquist. Harper & Row.
*The Secret River* by Marjorie Kinnan Rawlings. Scribner's.
*Men, Microscopes and Living Things* by Katherine B. Shippen. Viking.

1957 *Miracles on Maple Hill* by Virginia Sorensen. Illustrated by Beth Krush and Joe Krush. Harcourt Brace.
*Old Yeller* by Fred Gipson. Harper & Row.
*The House of Sixty Fathers* by Meindert DeJong. Harper & Row.
*Mr. Justice Holmes* by Clara I. Judson. Follett.
*The Corn Grows Ripe* by Dorothy Rhoads. Viking.
*The Black Fox of Lorne* by Marguerite de Angeli. Doubleday.

1958 *Rifles for Watie* by Harold Keith. Illustrated by Peter Burchard. Crowell.
*The Horsecatcher* by Mari Sandoz. Westminster.
*Gone-Away Lake* by Elizabeth Enright. Harcourt Brace.
*The Great Wheel* by Robert Lawson. Viking.
*Tom Paine, Freedom's Apostle* by Leo Gurko. Crowell.

1959 *The Witch of Blackbird Pond* by Elizabeth George Speare. Houghton Mifflin.
*The Family Under the Bridge* by Natalie S. Carlson. Harper & Row.
*Along Came a Dog* by Meindert DeJong. Harper & Row.
*Chucaro* by Francis Kalnay. Harcourt Brace.
*The Perilous Road* by William O. Steele. Harcourt Brace.

1960 *Onion John* by Joseph Krumgold. Illustrated by Symeon Shimin. Crowell.
*My Side of the Mountain* by Jean George. Dutton.
*America Is Born* by Gerald Johnson. Morrow.
*The Gammage Cup* by Carol Kendall. Harcourt Brace.

1961 *Island of the Blue Dolphins* by Scott O'Dell. Houghton Mifflin.
*America Moves Forward* by Gerald Johnson. Morrow.
*Old Ramon* by Jack Schaefer. Houghton Mifflin.
*The Cricket in Times Square* by George Selden. Farrar.

1962 *The Bronze Bow* by Elizabeth George Speare. Houghton Mifflin.
*Frontier Living* by Edwin Tunis. World.
*The Golden Goblet* by Eloise J. McGraw. Coward-McCann.
*Belling the Tiger* by Mary Stolz. Harper & Row.

1963 *A Wrinkle in Time* by Madeleine L'Engle. Farrar, Straus.
*Thistle and Thyme* by Sorche Nic Leodhas. Holt, Rinehart & Winston.
*Men of Athens* by Olivia Coolidge. Houghton Mifflin.

1964 *It's Like This, Cat* by Emily Neville. Illustrated by Emil Weiss. Harper & Row.
*Rascal* by Sterling North. Dutton.
*The Loner* by Ester Wier. McKay.

1965 *Shadow of a Bull* by Maia Wojciechowska. Illustrated by Alvin Smith. Atheneum.
*Across Five Aprils* by Irene Hunt. Follett.

1966 *I, Juan de Pareja* by Elizabeth Borten de Treviño. Farrar, Straus.
*The Black Cauldron* by Lloyd Alexander. Holt, Rinehart & Winston.
*The Animal Family* by Randall Jarrell. Pantheon.
*The Noonday Friends* by Mary Stolz. Harper & Row.

1967 *Up a Road Slowly* by Irene Hunt. Follett.
*The King's Fifth* by Scott O'Dell. Houghton Mifflin.
*Zlateh the Goat and Other Stories* by Isaac Bashevis Singer. Harper & Row.
*The Jazz Man* by Mary Hays Weik. Atheneum.

1968 *From the Mixed-Up Files of Mrs. Basil E. Frankweiler* by E. L. Konigsburg. Atheneum.
*Jennifer, Hecate, Macbeth, William McKinley, and Me, Elizabeth* by E. L. Konigsburg. Atheneum.
*The Black Pearl* by Scott O'Dell. Houghton Mifflin.
*The Fearsome Inn* by Isaac Bashevis Singer. Scribner's.
*The Egypt Game* by Zilpha Keatley Snyder. Atheneum.

1969 *The High King* by Lloyd Alexander. Holt, Rinehart & Winston.
*To Be a Slave* by Julius Lester. Dial.
*When Shlemiel Went to Warsaw and Other Stories* by Isaac Bashevis Singer. Farrar, Straus.

1970 *Sounder* by William H. Armstrong. Harper & Row.
*Our Eddie* by Sulamith Isk-Kishor. Pantheon.
*The Many Ways of Seeing: An Introduction to the Pleasures of Art* by Janet Gaylord Moore. World.
*Journey Outside* by Mary Q. Steele. Viking.

1971 *Summer of the Swans* by Betsy Byars. Viking.
*Kneeknock Rise* by Natalie Babbitt. Farrar, Straus.
*Enchantress from the Stars* by Sylvia Louise Engdahl. Atheneum.
*Sing Down the Moon* by Scott O'Dell. Houghton Mifflin.

1972 *Mrs. Frisby and the Rats of NIMH* by Robert C. O'Brien. Atheneum.
*Incident at Hawk's Hill* by Allan W. Eckert. Little, Brown.
*The Planet of Junior Brown* by Virginia Hamilton. Macmillan.
*The Tombs of Atuan* by Ursula K. Le Guin. Atheneum.
*Annie and the Old One* by Miska Miles. Atlantic/Little, Brown.
*The Headless Cupid* by Zilpha Keatley Snyder. Atheneum.

1973 *Julie of the Wolves* by Jean Craighead George. Harper & Row.
*Frog and Toad Together* by Arnold Lobel. Harper & Row.
*The Upstairs Room* by Johanna Reiss. Crowell.
*The Witches of Worm* by Zilpha Keatley Snyder. Atheneum.

1974 *The Slave Dancer* by Paula Fox. Bradbury.
*The Dark Is Rising* by Susan Cooper. Atheneum.

1975 *M. C. Higgins the Great* by Virginia Hamilton. Macmillan.
*My Brother Sam Is Dead* by James Collier and Christopher Collier. Four Winds.
*Philip Hall Likes Me, I Reckon Maybe* by Bette Greene. Dial.
*The Perilous Gard* by Elizabeth Pope. Houghton Mifflin.
*Figgs & Phantoms* by Ellen Raskin. Dutton.

1976 *The Grey King* by Susan Cooper. Atheneum.
*Dragonwings* by Laurence Yep. Harper & Row.
*The Hundred Penny Box* by Sharon Mathis. Viking.

1977 *Roll of Thunder, Hear My Cry* by Mildred D. Taylor. Dial.
*Abel's Island* by William Steig. Farrar, Straus.
*A String in the Harp* by Nancy Bond. Atheneum.

1978 *Bridge to Terabithia* by Katherine Paterson. Crowell.
*Anpao: An American Indian Odyssey* by Jamake Highwater. Lippincott.
*Ramona and Her Father* by Beverly Cleary. Morrow.

1979 *The Westing Game* by Ellen Raskin. Dutton.
*The Great Gilly Hopkins* by Katherine Paterson. Crowell.

1980 *A Gathering of Days: A New England Girl's Journal, 1830–32* by Joan W. Blos. Scribner's.
*The Road from Home: The Story of an Armenian Girl* by David Kherdian. Greenwillow.

1981 *Jacob Have I Loved* by Katherine Paterson. Crowell.
*The Fledgling* by Jane Langton. Harper & Row.
*Ring of Endless Light* by Madeleine L'Engle. Farrar, Straus & Giroux.

1982 *A Visit to William Blake's Inn: Poems for Innocent and Experienced Travelers* by Nancy Willard. Illustrated by Alice and Martin Provensen. Harcourt Brace Jovanovich.
*Ramona Quimbly, Age 8* by Beverly Cleary. Morrow.
*Upon the Head of the Goat: A Childhood in Hungary, 1939–1944* by Aranka Siegal. Farrar, Straus & Giroux.

1983 *Dicey's Song* by Cynthia Voigt. Atheneum.
*The Blue Sword* by Robin McKinley. Greenwillow.
*Doctor De Soto* by William Steig. Farrar, Straus & Giroux.
*Graven Images* by Paul Fleischman. Harper & Row.
*Homesick: My Own Story* by Jean Fritz. Putnam.
*Sweet Whispers, Brother Rush* by Virginia Hamilton. Philomel.

1984 *Dear Mr. Henshaw* by Beverly Cleary. Morrow.
*The Wish-Giver* by Bill Brittain. Harper & Row.
*A Solitary Blue* by Cynthia Voigt. Atheneum.
*The Sign of the Beaver* by Elizabeth George Speare. Houghton Mifflin.
*Sugaring Time* by Kathryn Lasky. Photographs by Christopher Knight. Macmillan.

1985 *The Hero and the Crown* by Robin McKinley. Greenwillow.
*The Moves Make the Man* by Bruce Brooks. Harper & Row.
*One-Eyed Cat* by Paula Fox. Bradbury Press.
*Like Jake and Me* by Marvis Jukes. Illustrated by Lloyd Bloom. Knopf.

1986 *Sarah, Plain and Tall* by Patricia MacLachlan. Harper & Row.
*Commodore Perry in the Land of the Shogun* by Rhoda Blumberg. Lothrop, Lee & Shepard.
*Dogsong* by Gary Paulsen. Bradbury Press.

1987 *The Whipping Boy* by Sid Fleischman. Greenwillow.
*A Fine White Dust* by Cynthia Rylant. Bradbury Press.
*On My Honor* by Marion Dane Bauer. Clarion.
*Volcano* by Patricia Lauber. Bradbury Press.

1988 *Lincoln: A Photobiography* by Russell Freedman. Clarion.
*After the Rain* by Norma Fox Mazer. Morrow.
*Hatchet* by Gary Paulsen. Bradbury Press.

1989 *Joyful Noise: Poems for Two Voices* by Paul Fleischman. Harper & Row.
*In the Beginning: Creation Stories from Around the World* by Virginia Hamilton. Harcourt Brace.
*Scorpions* by Walter Dean Myers. Harper & Row.

1990 *Number the Stars* by Lois Lowry. Houghton Mifflin.
*Afternoon of the Elves* by Janet Taylor Lisle. Orchard.
*Shabanu: Daughter of the Wind* by Suzanne Fisher Staples. Knopf.
*The Winter Room* by Gary Paulsen. Orchard.

1991 *Maniac Magee* by Jerry Spinelli. Little, Brown.
*The True Confessions of Charlotte Doyle* by Avi. Orchard.

1992 *Shiloh* by Phyllis Reynolds Naylor. Atheneum.
*Nothing but the Truth* by Avi. Orchard.
*The Wright Brothers* by Russell Freedman. Holiday House.

1993 *Missing May* by Cynthia Rylant. Jackson/Orchard.
*The Dark-Thirty: Southern Tales of the Supernatural* by Patricia C. McKissack. Knopf.
*Somewhere in the Darkness* by Walter Dean Myers. Scholastic.
*What Hearts* by Bruce Brooks. HarperCollins.

1994 *The Giver* by Lois Lowry. Houghton Mifflin.
*Crazy Lady* by Jane Leslie Conly. HarperCollins.
*Dragon's Gate* by Laurence Yep. HarperCollins.
*Eleanor Roosevelt: A Life of Discovery* by Russell Freedman. Clarion.

1995 *Walk Two Moons* by Sharon Creech. HarperCollins.
*Katherine, Called Birdy* by Karen Cushman. Clarion.
*The Ear, the Eye, and the Arm* by Nancy Farmer. Orchard.

1996 *The Midwife's Apprentice* by Karen Cushman. Clarion.
*What Jamie Saw* by Carolyn Coman. Front Street.
*The Watson's Go to Birmingham—1963* by Christopher Paul Curtis. Delacorte.
*Yolanda's Genius* by Carol Fenner. McElderry.
*The Great Fire* by Jim Murphy. Scholastic.

1997 *The View from Saturday* by E. L. Konigsburg. Atheneum.
*A Girl Named Disaster* by Nancy Farmer. Orchard.
*The Moorchild* by Eloise McGraw. Simon & Schuster.
*The Thief* by Megan Whelan Turner. Greenwillow.
*Belle Prater's Boy* by Ruth White. Farrar, Straus & Giroux.

1998 *Out of the Dust* by Karen Hesse. Scholastic.
*Ella Enchanted* by Gail Carson Levine. HarperCollins.
*Lily's Crossing* by Patricia Reilly Giff. Delacorte.
*Wringer* by Jerry Spinelli. HarperCollins.

1999 *Holes* by Louis Sachar. Delacorte.
*A Long Way from Chicago* by Richard Peck. Dial.

2000 *Bud, Not Buddy* by Christopher Paul Curtis. Delacorte.
*Getting Near to Baby* by Audrey Couloumbis. Putnam.
*Our Only May Amelia* by Jennifer L. Holm. HarperCollins.
*26 Fairmont Avenue* by Tomie de Paola. Putnam

The Caldecott Medal is named in honor of Randolph Caldecott, a prominent English illustrator of children's books during the nineteenth century. This award, presented each year by an awards committee of the Association for Library Service to Children (ALSC) of the American Library Association, is given to "the artist of the most distinguished American picture book for children." In the following list, for each year the Medal winner is listed first (in boldface italic type), followed by the Honor Books for that year. If an illustrator's name is not cited, the author illustrated the book.

1938 *Animals of the Bible, a Picture Book.* Text selected from the King James Bible by Helen Dean Fish. Illustrated by Dorothy O. Lathrop. Stokes.
*Seven Simeons* by Boris Artzybasheff. Viking.
*Four and Twenty Blackbirds* compiled by Helen Dean Fish. Illustrated by Robert Lawson. Stokes.

1939 *Mei Li* by Thomas Handforth. Doubleday.
*The Forest Pool* by Laura Adams Armer. Longmans, Green.
*Wee Gillis* by Munro Leaf. Illustrated by Robert Lawson. Viking.
*Snow White and the Seven Dwarfs.* Translated and illustrated by Wanda Gág. Coward-McCann.
*Barkis* by Clare Turlay Newberry. Harper & Row.
*Andy and the Lion* by James Daugherty. Viking.

1940 *Abraham Lincoln* by Ingri d'Aulaire and Edgar Parin d'Aulaire. Doubleday.
*Cock-a-Doodle-Doo* by Berta Hader and Elmer Hader. Macmillan.
*Madeline* by Ludwig Bemelmans. Simon & Schuster.
*The Ageless Story* by Lauren Ford. Dodd, Mead.

1941 *They Were Strong and Good* by Robert Lawson. Viking.
*April's Kittens* by Clare Turlay Newberry. Harper & Row.

1942 *Make Way for Ducklings* by Robert McCloskey. Viking.
*An American ABC* by Maud Petersham and Miska Petersham. Macmillan.
*In My Mother's House* by Ann Nolan Clark. Illustrated by Velino Herrera. Viking.
*Paddle-to-the-Sea* by Holling Clancy Holling. Houghton Mifflin.
*Nothing at All* by Wanda Gág. Coward-McCann.

1943 *The Little House* by Virginia Lee Burton. Houghton Mifflin.
*Dash and Dart* by Mary Buff and Conrad Buff. Viking.
*Marshmallow* by Clare Turlay Newberry. Harper & Row.

1944 *Many Moons* by James Thurber. Illustrated by Louis Slobodkin. Harcourt Brace.
*Small Rain.* Text arranged from the Bible by Jessie Orton Jones. Illustrated by Elizabeth Orton Jones. Viking.
*Pierre Pidgeon* by Lee Kingman. Illustrated by Arnold Edwin Bare. Houghton Mifflin.
*Good-Luck Horse* by Chih-Yi Chan. Illustrated by Plato Chan. Whittlesey.
*Mighty Hunter* by Berta Hader and Elmer Hader. Macmillan.
*A Child's Good Night Book* by Margaret Wise Brown. Illustrated by Jean Charlot. W. R. Scott.

1945 *Prayer for a Child* by Rachel Field. Pictures by Elizabeth Orton Jones. Macmillan.
*Mother Goose.* Compiled and illustrated by Tasha Tudor. Oxford University Press.
*In the Forest* by Marie Hall Ets. Viking.
*Yonie Wondernose* by Marguerite de Angeli. Doubleday.
*The Christmas Anna Angel* by Ruth Sawyer. Illustrated by Kate Seredy. Viking.

1946 *The Rooster Crows* by Maud Petersham and Miska Petersham. Macmillan.
*Little Lost Lamb* by Margaret Wise Brown. Illustrated by Leonard Weisgard. Doubleday.

*Sing Mother Goose.* Music by Opal Wheeler. Illustrated by Marjorie Torrey. Dutton.

*My Mother Is the Most Beautiful Woman in the World* by Becky Reyher. Illustrated by Ruth C. Gannett. Lothrop.

*You Can Write Chinese* by Kurt Wiese. Viking.

1947 ***The Little Island*** by Golden MacDonald. Illustrated by Leonard Weisgard. Doubleday.

*Rain Drop Splash* by Alvin R. Tesselt. Illustrated by Leonard Weisgard. Lothrop.

*Boats on the River* by Marjorie Flack. Illustrated by Jay Hyde Barnum. Viking.

*Timothy Turtle* by Al Graham. Illustrated by Tony Palazzo. Robert Welch.

*Pedro, Angel of Olvera Street* by Leo Politi. Scribner's.

*Sing in Praise* by Opal Wheeler. Illustrated by Marjorie Torrey. Dutton.

1948 ***White Snow, Bright Snow*** by Alvin Tresselt. Illustrated by Roger Duvoisin. Lothrop.

*Stone Soup.* Told and illustrated by Marcia Brown. Scribner's.

*McElligot's Pool* by Theodor S. Geisel [Dr. Seuss]. Random House.

*Bambino the Clown* by George Schreiber. Viking.

*Roger and the Fox* by Lavinia R. Davis. Illustrated by Hildegard Woodward. Doubleday.

*Song of Robin Hood.* Edited by Anne Malcolmson. Illustrated by Virginia Lee Burton. Houghton Mifflin.

1949 ***The Big Snow*** by Berta Hader and Elmer Hader. Macmillan.

*Blueberries for Sal* by Robert McCloskey. Viking.

*All Around the Town* by Phyllis McGinley. Illustrated by Helen Stone. Lippincott.

*Juanita* by Leo Politi. Scribner's.

*Fish in the Air* by Kurt Wiese. Viking.

1950 ***Song of the Swallows*** by Leo Politi. Scribner's.

*America's Ethan Allen* by Stewart Holbrook. Illustrated by Lynd Ward. Houghton Mifflin.

*The Wild Birthday Cake* by Lavinia R. Davis. Illustrated by Hildegard Woodward. Doubleday.

*Happy Day* by Ruth Krauss. Illustrated by Marc Simont. Harper & Row.

*Henry-Fisherman* by Marcia Brown. Scribner's.

*Bartholomew and the Oobleck* by Theodor S. Geisel [Dr. Seuss]. Random House.

1951 ***The Egg Tree*** by Katherine Milhous. Scribner's.

*Dick Whittington and His Cat.* Told and illustrated by Marcia Brown. Scribner's.

*The Two Reds* by Will [William Lipkind]. Illustrated by Nicolas [Mordvinoff]. Harcourt Brace.

*If I Ran the Zoo* by Theodor S. Geisel [Dr. Seuss]. Random House.

*T-Bone the Baby-Sitter* by Clare Turlay Newberry. Harper & Row.

*The Most Wonderful Doll in the World* by Phyllis McGinley. Illustrated by Helen Stone. Lippincott.

1952 ***Finders Keepers*** by Will [William Lipkind]. Illustrated by Nicolas [Mordvinoff]. Harcourt Brace.

*Mr. T.W. Anthony Woo* by Marie Hall Ets. Viking.

*Skipper John's Cook* by Marcia Brown. Scribner's.

*All Falling Down* by Gene Zion. Illustrated by Margaret Bloy Graham. Harper & Row.

*Bear Party* by William Pène DuBois. Viking.

*Feather Mountain* by Elizabeth Olds. Houghton Mifflin.

1953 ***The Biggest Bear*** by Lynd Ward. Houghton Mifflin.

*Puss in Boots.* Told and illustrated by Marcia Brown. Scribner's.

*One Morning in Maine* by Robert McCloskey. Viking.

*Ape in a Cape* by Fritz Eichenberg. Harcourt Brace.

*The Storm Book* by Charlotte Zolotow. Illustrated by Margaret Bloy Graham. Harper & Row.

*Five Little Monkeys* by Juliet Kepes. Houghton Mifflin.

1954 ***Madeline's Rescue*** by Ludwig Bemelmans. Viking.

*Journey Cake, Ho!* by Ruth Sawyer. Illustrated by Robert McClosky. Viking.

*When Will the World Be Mine?* by Miriam Schlein. Illustrated by Jean Charlot. W. R. Scott.

*The Steadfast Tin Soldier.* Translated by M. R. James. Adapted from Hans Christian Andersen. Illustrated by Marcia Brown. Scribner's.

*A Very Special House* by Ruth Krauss. Illustrated by Maurice Sendak. Harper & Row.

*Green Eyes* by Abe Birnbaum. Capitol.

1955 ***Cinderella*** by Charles Perrault. Illustrated by Marcia Brown. Harper & Row.

*Book of Nursery and Mother Goose Rhymes.* Compiled and illustrated by Marguerite de Angeli. Doubleday.

*Wheel on the Chimney* by Margaret Wise Brown. Illustrated by Tibor Gergely. Lippincott.

1956 ***Frog Went A-Courtin'*** by John Langstaff. Illustrated by Feodor Rojankovsky. Harcourt Brace.

*Play with Me* by Marie Hall Ets. Viking.

*Crow Boy* by Taro Yashima. Viking.

1957 ***A Tree Is Nice*** by Janice May Udry. Illustrated by Marc Simont. Harper & Row.

*Mr. Penny's Race Horse* by Marie Hall Ets. Viking.

*1 Is One* by Tasha Tudor. Oxford University Press.

*Anatole* by Eve Titus. Illustrated by Paul Galdone. Whittlesey.

*Gillespie and the Guards* by Benjamin Elkin. Illustrated by James Daugherty. Viking.

*Lion* by William Pène DuBois, Viking.

1958 ***Time of Wonder*** by Robert McCloskey. Viking.

*Fly High, Fly Low* by Don Freeman. Viking.

*Anatole and the Cat* by Eve Titus. Illustrated by Paul Galdone. Whittlesey.

1959 ***Chanticleer and the Fox.*** Edited and illustrated by Barbara Cooney. Crowell.

*The House That Jack Built* by Antonio Frasconi. Crowell.

*What Do You Say, Dear?* by Sesyle Joslin. Illustrated by Maurice Sendak. W. R. Scott.

*Umbrella* by Taro Yashima. Viking.

1960 ***Nine Days to Christmas*** by Marie Hall Ets and Aurora Labastida. Viking.

*Houses from the Sea* by Alice E. Goudey. Illustrated by Adrienne Adams. Scribner's.

*The Moon Jumpers* by Janice May Udry. Illustrated by Maurice Sendak. Harper & Row.

1961 ***Baboushka and the Three Kings*** by Ruth Robbins. Illustrated by Nicolas Sidjakov. Parnassus.

*Inch by Inch* by Leo Lionni. Obolensky.

1962 *Once a Mouse* by Marcia Brown. Scribner's.
*The Fox Went Out on a Chilly Night* by Peter Spier. Doubleday.
*Little Bear's Visit* by Else Minarik. Illustrated by Maurice Sendak. Harper & Row.
*The Day We Saw the Sun Come Up* by Alice Goudey. Illustrated by Adrienne Adams. Scribner's.

1963 *The Snowy Day* by Ezra Jack Keats. Viking.
*The Sun Is a Golden Earring* by Natalia Belting. Illustrated by Bernarda Bryson. Holt, Rinehart & Winston.
*Mr. Rabbit and the Lovely Present* by Charlotte Zolotow. Illustrated by Maurice Sendak. Harper & Row.

1964 *Where the Wild Things Are* by Maurice Sendak. Harper & Row.
*Swimmy* by Leo Lionni. Pantheon.
*All in the Morning Early* by Sorche Nic Leodhas. Illustrated by Evaline Ness. Holt, Rinehart & Winston.
*Mother Goose and Nursery Rhymes* by Philip Reed. Atheneum.

1965 *May I Bring a Friend?* by Beatrice Schenk de Regniers. Illustrated by Beni Montresor. Atheneum.
*Rain Makes Applesauce* by Julian Scheer. Illustrated by Marvin Bileck. Holiday House.
*The Wave* by Margaret Hodges. Illustrated by Blair Lent. Houghton Mifflin.
*A Pocketful of Cricket* by Rebecca Caudill. Illustrated by Evaline Ness. Holt, Rinehart & Winston.

1966 *Always Room for One More* by Sorche Nic Leodhas. Illustrated by Nonny Hogrogian. Holt, Rinehart & Winston.
*Hide and Seek Fog* by Alvin Tresselt. Illustrated by Roger Duvoisin. Lothrop.
*Just Me* by Marie Hall Ets. Viking.
*Tom Tit Tot.* Edited by Joseph Jacobs. Illustrated by Evaline Ness. Scribner's.

1967 *Sam, Bangs and Moonshine* by Evaline Ness. Holt, Rinehart & Winston.
*One Wide River to Cross* by Barbara Emberley. Illustrated by Ed Emberley. Prentice Hall.

1968 *Drummer Hoff* by Barbara Emberley. Illustrated by Ed Emberley. Prentice Hall.
*Frederick* by Leo Lionni. Pantheon.
*Seashore Story* by Taro Yashima. Viking.
*The Emperor and the Kite* by Jane Yolen. Illustrated by Ed Young. World Publishing.

1969 *The Fool of the World and the Flying Ship* by Arthur Ransome. Illustrated by Uri Shulevitz. Farrar, Straus.
*Why the Sun and the Moon Live in the Sky* by Elphinstone Dayrell. Illustrated by Blair Lent. Houghton Mifflin.

1970 *Sylvester and the Magic Pebble* by William Steig. Windmill/Simon & Schuster.
*Goggles* by Ezra Jack Keats. Macmillan.
*Alexander and the Wind-Up Mouse* by Leo Lionni. Pantheon.
*Pop Corn and Ma Goodness* by Edna Mitchell Preston. Illustrated by Robert Andrew Parker. Viking.
*The Friend, Obadiah* by Brinton Turkle. Viking.
*The Judge* by Harve Zemach. Illustrated by Margot Zemach. Farrar, Straus.

1971 *A Story, A Story* by Gail E. Haley, Atheneum.
*The Angry Moon* by William Sleator. Illustrated by Blair Lent. Atlantic/Little, Brown.
*Frog and Toad Are Friends* by Arnold Lobel. Harper & Row.
*In the Night Kitchen* by Maurice Sendak. Harper & Row.

1972 *One Fine Day* by Nonny Hogrogian. Macmillan.
*If All the Seas Were One Sea* by Janina Domanska. Macmillan.
*Moja Means One: Swahili Counting Book* by Muriel Feelings. Illustrated by Tom Feelings. Dial.
*Hildilid's Night* by Cheli Duran Ryan. Illustrated by Arnold Lobel. Macmillan.

1973 *The Funny Little Woman* by Arlene Mosel. Illustrated by Blair Lent. Dutton.
*Hosie's Alphabet* by Hosea Baskin, Tobias Baskin, and Lisa Baskin. Illustrated by Leonard Baskin. Viking.
*When Clay Sings* by Byrd Baylor. Illustrated by Tom Bahti. Scribner's.
*Snow White and the Seven Dwarfs* by the Brothers Grimm. Translated by Randall Jarrell. Illustrated by Nancy Ekholm Burkert. Farrar, Straus.
*Anansi the Spider* by Gerald McDermott. Holt, Rinehart & Winston.

1974 *Duffy and the Devil* by Harve Zemach. Illustrated by Margot Zemach. Farrar, Straus.
*The Three Jovial Huntsmen* by Susan Jeffers. Bradbury Press.
*Cathedral* by David Macaulay. Houghton Mifflin.

1975 *Arrow to the Sun.* Adapted and illustrated by Gerald McDermott. Viking.
*Jambo Means Hello: Swahili Alphabet Book* by Muriel Feelings. Illustrated by Tom Feelings. Dial.

1976 *Why Mosquitos Buzz in People's Ears* by Verna Aardema. Illustrated by Leo and Diane Dillon. Dial.
*The Desert Is Theirs* by Byrd Baylor. Illustrated by Peter Parnell. Scribner's.
*Strega Nona.* Retold and illustrated by Tomie de Paola. Simon & Schuster

1977 *Ashanti to Zulu: African Traditions* by Margaret Musgrove. Illustrated by Leo and Diane Dillon. Dial.
*The Amazing Bone* by William Steig. Farrar, Straus & Giroux.
*The Contest* by Nonny Hogrogian. Greenwillow.
*Fish for Supper* by M. B. Goffstein. Dial.
*The Golem* by Beverly Brodsky McDermott. Lippincott.
*Hawk, I'm Your Brother* by Byrd Baylor. Illustrated by Peter Parnall. Scribner's.

1978 *Noah's Ark* by Peter Spier. Doubleday.
*Castle* by David Macaulay. Houghton Mifflin.
*It Could Always Be Worse* by Margot Zemach. Farrar, Straus & Giroux.

1979 *The Girl Who Loved Wild Horses* by Paul Goble. Bradbury Press.
*Freight Train* by Donald Crews. Greenwillow.
*The Way to Start a Day* by Byrd Baylor. Illustrated by Peter Parnall. Scribner's.

1980 *Ox-Cart Man* by Donald Hall. Illustrated by Barbara Cooney. Viking.
*Ben's Trumpet* by Rachel Isadora. Greenwillow.

*The Treasure* by Uri Shulevitz. Farrar, Straus & Giroux.
*The Garden of Abdul Gasazi* by Chris Van Allsburg. Houghton Mifflin.

1981 **Fables** by Arnold Lobel. Harper & Row.
*The Bremen-Town Musicians* by Ilse Plume. Doubleday.
*The Grey Lady and the Strawberry Snatcher* by Molly Bang. Four Winds.
*Mice Twice* by Joseph Low. Atheneum.
*Truck* by Donald Crews. Greenwillow.

1982 **Jumanji** by Chris Van Allsburg. Houghton Mifflin.
*A Visit to William Blake's Inn: Poems for Innocent and Experienced Travelers* by Nancy Willard. Illustrated by Alice and Martin Provensen. Harcourt Brace Jovanovich.
*Where the Buffaloes Began* by Olaf Baker. Illustrated by Stephen Gammell. Warne.
*On Market Street* by Arnold Lobel. Illustrated by Anita Lobel. Greenwillow.
*Outside over There* by Maurice Sendak. Harper & Row.

1983 **Shadow** by Blaise Cendrars. Illustrated by Marcia Brown. Scribner's.
*When I Was Young in the Mountains* by Cynthia Rylant. Illustrated by Diane Goode. Dutton.
*A Chair for My Mother* by Vera B. Williams. Morrow.

1984 **The Glorious Flight: Across the Channel with Louis Blériot, July 25, 1909** by Alice and Martin Provensen. Viking.
*Ten, Nine, Eight* by Molly Bang. Greenwillow.
*Little Red Riding Hood* by Trina Schart Hyman. Holiday House.

1985 **Saint George and the Dragon** adapted by Margaret Hodges. Illustrated by Trina Schart Hyman. Little, Brown.
*Hansel and Gretel* by Rika Lesser. Illustrated by Paul O. Zelinsky. Dodd.
*The Story of Jumping Mouse* by John Steptoe. Lothrop, Lee & Shepard.
*Have You Seen My Duckling?* by Nancy Tafuri. Greenwillow.

1986 **Polar Express** by Chris Van Allsburg. Houghton Mifflin.
*The Relatives Came* by Cynthia Rylant. Illustrated by Stephen Gammell. Bradbury Press.
*King Bidgood's in the Bathtub* by Audrey Wood. Illustrated by Don Wood. Harcourt Brace Jovanovich.

1987 **Hey Al** by Arthur Yorinks. Illustrated by Richard Egielski. Farrar, Straus & Giroux.
*Alphabatics* by Suse MacDonald. Bradbury Press.
*Rumpelstiltskin* by Paul O. Zelinsky. Dutton.
*The Village of Round and Square Houses* by Ann Grifalconi. Little, Brown.

1988 **Owl Moon** by Jane Yolen. Illustrated by John Schoenherr. Philomel.
*Mufaro's Beautiful Daughters: An African Story.* Adapted and illustrated by John Steptoe. Lothrop, Lee & Shepard.

1989 **Song and Dance Man** by Karen Ackerman. Illustrated by Stephen Gammell. Knopf.
*The Boy of the Three-Year Nap* by Dianne Stanley. Illustrated by Allen Say. Houghton Mifflin.
*Free Fall* by David Wiesner. Lothrop, Lee & Shepard.
*Goldilocks and the Three Bears.* Adapted and illustrated by James Marshall. Dial.
*Mirandy and Brother Wind* by Patricia McKissack. Illustrated by Jerry Pinkney. Knopf.

1990 **Lon Po Po: A Red Riding Hood Story from China.** Adapted and illustrated by Ed Young. Philomel.
*Bill Peet: An Autobiography* by Bill Peet. Houghton Mifflin.
*Color Zoo* by Lois Ehlert. Lippincott.
*Herschel and the Hanukkah Goblings* by Eric Kimmel. Illustrated by Trina Schart Hyman. Holiday House.
*The Talking Eggs* by Robert D. San Souci. Illustrated by Jerry Pinkney. Dial.

1991 **Black and White** by David Macaulay. Houghton Mifflin.
*Puss in Boots* by Charles Perrault. Translated by Malcolm Arthur. Illustrated by Fred Marcelino. Farrar, Straus & Giroux.
*"More More More," Said the Baby* by Vera B. Williams. Greenwillow.

1992 **Tuesday** by David Wiesner. Clarion.
*Tar Beach* by Faith Ringgold. Crown.

1993 **Mirette on the High Wire** by Emily Arnold McCully. Putnam.
*Seven Blind Mice* by Ed Young. Philomel.
*The Stinky Cheese Man and Other Fairly Stupid Tales* by Jon Scieszka. Illustrated by Lane Smith. Viking.
*Working Cotton* by Sherley Anne Williams. Illustrated by Carole Byard. Harcourt Brace.

1994 **Grandfather's Journey** by Allen Say. Houghton Mifflin.
*Peppe the Lamplighter* by Elisa Bartone. Illustrated by Ted Lewin. Lothrop, Lee & Shepard.
*In the Small, Small Pond* by Denise Fleming. Holt.
*Owen* by Kevin Henkes. Greenwillow.
*Raven: A Trickster Tale from the Pacific Northwest* by Gerald McDermott. Harcourt Brace.
*Yo! Yes?* by Chris Raschka. Orchard.

1995 **Smoky Night** by Eve Bunting. Illustrated by David Diaz. Harcourt Brace.
*Swamp Angel* by Paul O. Zelinsky. Dutton.
*John Henry* by Jerry Pinkney. Dial.
*Time Flies* by Eric Rohmann. Crown.

1996 **Officer Buckle and Gloria** by Peggy Rathman. Putnam.
*Alphabet City* by Stephen T. Johnson. Viking.
*Zin! Zin! Zin! A Violin* by Lloyd Moss. Illustrated by Marjorie Priceman. Simon & Schuster.
*The Faithful Friend* by Robert D. San Souci. Illustrated by Brian Pinkney. Simon & Schuster.
*Tops and Bottoms* by Janet Stephens. Harcourt Brace.

1997 **Golem** by David Wisniewski. Clarion.
*The Gardener* by Sarah Stewart. Illustrated by David Small. Farrar, Straus & Giroux.
*The Graphic Alphabet* by David Pelletier. Orchard.
*The Paperboy* by Dav Pilkey. Orchard.
*Starry Messenger* by Peter Sis. Farrar, Straus & Giroux.

1998 **Rapunzel** by Paul O. Zelinsky. Dutton.
*Duke Ellington: The Piano Prince and His Orchestra* by Andrea Pinkney. Illustrated by Brian Pinkney. Hyperion.
*Harlem* by Walter Dean Myers. Illustrated by Christopher Myers. Scholastic.
*There Was an Old Lady Who Swallowed a Fly* by Simms Taback. Viking.

1999 **Snowflake Bentley** by Jacqueline Briggs Martin. Illustrated by Mary Azarian. Houghton Mifflin.
*No, David!* by David Shannon. Scholastic.
*Snow* by Uri Shulevitz. Farrar, Straus & Giroux.
*Tibet: Through the Red Box* by Peter Sis. Farrar, Straus & Giroux.

2000 *Joseph Had a Little Overcoat* by Sims Taback. Viking.
*A Child's Calendar* by John Updike. Illustrated by Trina Schart Hyman. Holiday House.
*Sector 7* by David Weisner. Clarion.
*The Ugly Duckling* by Hans Christian Andersen. Morrow.
*When Sophie Gets Angry—Really, Really Angry* by Molly Bang. Scholastic.

The Batchelder Award, established in 1966, is given by the Association of Library Service to Children (ALSC) of the American Library Association to the publisher of the most outstanding book of the year that is a translation, published in the United States, of a book that was first published in another country. In 1990, honor books were added to this award. The original country of publication is given in parentheses.

1968 *The Little Man* by Erich Kastner, translated by James Kirkup. Illustrated by Rick Schreiter. Knopf. (Germany)

1969 *Don't Take Teddy* by Babbis Friis-Baastad, translated by Lise Somme McKinnon. Scribner's. (Norway)

1970 *Wildcat Under Glass* by Alki Zei, translated by Edward Fenton. Holt. (Greece)

1971 *In the Land of Ur* by Hans Baumann, translated by Stella Humphries. Pantheon. (Germany)

1972 *Friedrich* by Hans Peter Richter, translated by Edite Kroll. Holt. (Germany)

1973 *Pulga* by S. R. Van Iterson, translated by Alison and Alexander Gode. Morrow. (Netherlands)

1974 *Petro's War* by Aldi Zei, translated by Edward Fenton. Dutton. (Greece)

1975 *An Old Tale Carved out of Stone* by A. Linevsky, translated by Maria Polushkin. Crown. (Russia)

1976 *The Cat and Mouse Who Shared a House* by Ruth Hurlimann, translated by Anthea Bell. Illustrated by the author. Walck. (Germany)

1977 *The Leopard* by Cecil Bødker, translated by Gunnar Poulsen. Atheneum. (Denmark)

1978 No Award

1979 Two awards given

*Konrad* by Christine Nostlinger, translated by Anthea Bell. Illustrated by Carol Nicklaus. Watts. (Germany)

*Rabbit Island* by Jörg Steiner, translated by Ann Conrad Lammers. Illustrated by Jörg Müller. Harcourt Brace. (Germany)

1980 *The Sound of the Dragon's Feet* by Alki Zei, translated by Edward Fenton. Dutton. (Greece)

1981 *The Winter When Time Was Frozen* by Els Pelgrom, translated by Maryka and Rafael Rudnik. Morrow. (Netherlands)

1982 *The Battle Horse* by Harry Kullman, translated by George Blecher and Lone Thygesen-Blecher. Bradbury. (Sweden)

1983 *Hiroshima No Pika* by Toshi Maruki, translated by the Kurita Bando Agency. Lothrop, Lee & Shepard. (Japan)

1984 *Ronia the Robber's Daughter* by Astrid Lindgren, translated by Patricia Crampton. Viking. (Sweden)

1985 *The Island on Bird Street* by Uri Orlev, translated by Hillel Halkin. Houghton Mifflin. (Israel)

1986 *Rose Blanche* by Christophe Gallaz and Roberto Innocenti, translated by Martha Coventry and Richard Graglia. Creative Education. (Italy)

1987 *No Hero for the Kaiser* by Rudolf Frank, translated by Patricia Crampton. Lothrop, Lee & Shepard. (Germany)

1988 *If You Didn't Have Me* by Ulf Nilsson, translated by Lone Tygesen-Blecher and George Blecher. Illustrated by Eva Eriksson. McElderry. (Sweden)

1989 *Crutches* by Peter Hätling, translated by Elizabeth D. Crawford. Lothrop, Lee & Shepard. (Germany)

1990 *Buster's World* by Bjarne Reuter, translated by Anthea Bell. Dutton. (Denmark)

1991 *Two Long and One Short* by Nina Ring Aamundsen. Houghton Mifflin. (Norway)

1992 *The Man From the Other Side* by Uri Orlev, translated by Hillel Halkin. Houghton Mifflin. (Israel)

1993 No Award

1994 *The Apprentice* by Molina Llorente, translated by Robin Longshaw. Farrar, Straus & Giroux. (Spain)

1995 *The Boys from St. Petri* by Bjarne Reuter, translated by Anthea Bell. Dutton. (Denmark)

1996 *The Lady with the Hat* by Uri Orlev, translated by Hillel Halkin. Houghton Mifflin. (Israel)

1997 *The Friends* by Kazumi Yumoto, translated by Cathy Hirano. Farrar, Straus & Giroux. (Japan)

1998 *The Robber and Me* by Josef Holub, translated by Elizabeth C. Crawford. Holt. (Germany)

1999 *Thanks to My Mother* by Schoschana Rabinovici, translated by James Skofield. Dial. (Germany)

2000 *The Baboon King* by Anton Quintana, translated by John Nieuwenhuizen. Walker. (The Netherlands)

The Laura Ingalls Wilder Award is given to an author or illustrator whose books (published in the United States) have made a substantial and lasting contribution to literature for children. Established in 1954, this medal was given every five years through 1980. As of 1983, it is given every three years by the Association of Library Service to Children (ALSC) of the American Library Association. The following are the award winners thus far.

1954 Laura Ingalls Wilder
1960 Clara Ingram Judson
1965 Ruth Sawyer
1970 E. B. White
1975 Beverly Cleary
1980 Theodor S. Geisel [Dr. Seuss]
1983 Maurice Sendak
1986 Jean Fritz
1989 Elizabeth George Speare
1992 Marcia Brown
1995 Virginia Hamilton
1998 Russell Freedman

The Hans Christian Andersen prize, the first international children's book award, was established in 1956 by the International Board on Books for Young People. Given every two years, the award was expanded in 1966 to honor an illustrator as well as an author. A committee composed of members from different countries judges the selections recommended by the board or library associations in each country. The following have won the Hans Christian Andersen Prize.

1956 Eleanor Farjeon. Great Britian.

1958 Astrid Lindgren. Sweden.

1960 Eric Kästner. Germany.

1962 Meindert DeJong. United States.

1964 René Guillot. France.

1966 Tove Jansson (author). Finland.
Alois Carigiet (illustrator). Switzerland.

1968 James Krüss (author). Germany.
Jose Maria Sanchez-Silva (author). Spain.
Jiri Trnka (illustrator). Czechoslovakia.

1970 Gianni Rodari (author). Italy.
Maurice Sendak (illustrator). United States.

1972 Scott O'Dell (author). United States.
Ib Spang Olsen (illustrator). Denmark.

1974 Maria Gripe (author). Sweden.
Farshid Mesghali (illustrator). Iran.

1976 Cecil Bødker (author). Denmark.
Tatjana Mawrina (illustrator). U.S.S.R.

1978 Paula Fox (author). United States.
Svend Otto (illustrator). Denmark.

1980 Bohumil Riha (author). Czechoslovakia.
Suekichi Akaba (illustrator). Japan.

1982 Lygia Bojunga Nunes (author). Brazil.
Zibigniew Rychlicki (illustrator). Poland.

1984 Christine Nostlinger (author). Austria.
Mitsumasa Anno (illustrator). Japan.

1986 Patricia Wrightson (author). Australia.
Robert Ingpen (illustrator). Australia.

1988 Annie M. G. Schmidt (author). Netherlands.
Dusan Kallay (illustrator). Yugoslavia.

1990 Tormod Haugen (author). Norway.
Lisbeth Zwerger (illustrator). Austria.

1992 Virginia Hamilton (author). United States.
Kveta Pacovská (illustrator). Czechoslovakia.

1994 Michio Mado (author). Japan.
Jorg Muller (illustrator). Switzerland.

1996 Uri Orlev (author). Israel.
Klaus Ensikat (illustrator). Germany.

1998 Katherine Paterson (author). United States.
Tomi Ungerer (illustrator). France.

2000 Anna Maria Machado (author). Brazil.
Anthony Browne (illustrator). United Kingdom.

## GENERAL AWARDS

### Boston Globe–Horn Book Awards

The Horn Book Magazine, 11 Beacon St., Boston, MA 02108. Currently given for outstanding fiction or poetry, outstanding nonfiction, and outstanding illustration.

### Golden Kite Award

Presented annually by the Society of Children's Book Writers to members whose books of fiction, nonfiction, and picture illustration best exhibit excellence and genuinely appeal to interests and concerns of children.

### International Reading Association Children's Book Award

International Reading Association, 800 Barksdale Rd., Newark, DE 19711. An annual award for first or second book to an author from any country who shows unusual promise in the children's book field. Since 1987, the award has been presented to both a picture book and a novel.

### New York Times Choice of Best Illustrated Children's Books of the Year

The New York Times, 229 W. 43rd St., New York, NY 10036. Books are selected for excellence in illustration by a panel of judges.

## AWARDS BASED ON SPECIAL CONTENT

### Jane Addams Book Award

Jane Addams Peace Association, 777 United Nations Plaza, New York, NY 10017. For a book with literary merit stressing themes of dignity, equality, peace, and social justice.

### Association of Jewish Libraries Awards

National Foundation for Jewish Culture, 122 E. 42nd St., Room 1512, New York, NY 10168. Given to one or two titles that have made the most outstanding contribution to the field of Jewish literature for children and young people. The Sydney Taylor Body of Work Award, established in 1981, is given for an author's body of work.

### Catholic Book Awards

Catholic Press Association of the United States and Canada, 119 N. Park Ave., Rockville Centre, NY 11570. Honors selected in five categories and awarded to books with sound Christian and psychological values.

### Child Study Children's Book Committee at Bank Street College Award

Bank Street College of Education, 610 W. 112th St., New York, NY 10025. For a distinguished book for children or young people that deals honestly and courageously with problems in the world.

### Christopher Awards

The Christophers, 12 E. 48th St., New York, NY 10017. Given to works of artistic excellence affirming the highest values of the human spirit.

### Eva L. Gordon Award for Children's Science Literature

Helen Ross Russell, Chairman of Publications Committee, ANNS, 44 College Dr., Jersey City, NJ 07305. Given by the American Nature Study Society to an author or illustrator whose body of work in science trade books is accurate, inviting, and timely.

### Jefferson Cup Award

Children's and Young Adult Roundtable of the Virginia Library Association, P.O. Box 298, Alexandria, VA 22313. Presented for a distinguished book in American history, historical fiction, or biography.

### Ezra Jack Keats Awards

Given biennially to a promising new artist and a promising writer. The recipients receive a monetary award and a medallion from the Ezra Jack Keats Foundation.

**Coretta Scott King Awards**

Social Responsibilities Round Table of the American Library Association, 50 E. Huron St., Chicago, IL 60611. Given to an African American author and an African American illustrator for outstanding inspirational and educational contributions to literature for children.

**National Council of Teachers of English Award for Excellence in Poetry for Children**

National Council of Teachers of English, 1111 Kenyon Rd., Urbana, IL 61801. Given formerly annually and presently every three years to a living American poet for total body of work for children ages 3 to 13.

**National Jewish Book Awards**

JWB Jewish Book Council, 15 E. 26th St. New York, NY 10010. Various awards are given for work or body of work that makes a contribution to Jewish juvenile literature.

**New York Academy of Sciences Children's Science Books Awards**

The New York Academy of Sciences, 2 E. 63rd St., New York, NY 10021. For books of high quality in the field of science for children; three awards are given: Younger Children, Older Children, and the Montroll Award for a book that provides unusual historical data or background on a scientific subject.

**Scott O'Dell Award for Historical Fiction**

Zena Sutherland, 1418 E. 57th St., Chicago, IL 60637. Honors a distinguished work of historical fiction set in the New World.

**Orbis Pictus Award for Outstanding Nonfiction for Children**

Presented annually by the National Council of Teachers of English to the outstanding nonfiction book of the previous year.

**Phoenix Award**

Given to the author of a book published for children twenty years before that has not received a major children's book award. Sponsored by the Children's Literature Association.

**Edgar Allan Poe Awards**

Mystery Writers of America, 1950 Fifth Ave., New York, NY 10011. For best juvenile mystery.

**Michael J. Prinz Award**

Given to a book that exemplifies literary excellence in young adult literature. Sponsored by the Young Adult Library Services Association of the American Library Association.

**Robert F. Sibert Informational Book Award**

Honors the author whose work of nonfiction has made a significant contribution to the field of children's literature in a given year. Sponsored by Association of Library Services to Children.

**Washington Post/Children's Book Guild Nonfiction Award**

Washington Post, 1150 15th St., NW, Washington, DC 20071. Given to an author or illustrator for a body of work in juvenile informational books.

**Western Writers of America Spur Award**

Western Writers of America, Inc., 508 Senter Pl., Selah, WA 98942. For the best western juvenile in two categories, fiction and nonfiction.

**Carter G. Woodson Book Award**

National Council for the Social Studies, 3501 Newark St., NW, Washington, DC 20016. Presented to outstanding social science books for young readers that treat sensitively and accurately topics related to ethnic minorities.

## AWARDS FOR LASTING CONTRIBUTIONS OR SERVICE TO CHILDREN'S LITERATURE

**Arbuthnot Award**

International Reading Association, 800 Barksdale Rd., Newark, DE 19714. Named after May Hill Arbuthnot, an authority on literature for children, this award is given annually to an outstanding teacher of children's literature.

**Arbuthnot Honor Lecture**

The Association of Library Service to Children (ALSC) of the American Library Association, 50 E. Huron St., Chicago, IL 60611. This free public lecture is presented annually by a distinguished author, critic, librarian, historian, or teacher of children's literature. Both the lecturer and the site for the lecture are chosen by an ALSC committee.

**Grolier Foundation Award**

American Library Association Awards Committee, 50 E. Huron St., Chicago, IL 60611. Given to a community librarian or a school librarian who has made an unusual contribution to the stimulation and guidance of reading by children and young people.

**Landau Award**

Salt Lake County Library System, 2197 E. 7000 S., Salt Lake City, UT 84121. Cosponsored by the Department of Education of the University of Utah and Salt Lake County Library System. The award is given biennially to a teacher of children's literature who has most inspired students to pursue a knowledge of the field.

**Lucile Micheels Pannell Award**

Awards in the "general store" category and in the "children's specialty bookstore" category are presented annually by the Women's National Book Association to the owners of two bookstores whose innovative programs encourage children's reading.

**Regina Medal**

Catholic Library Association, 461 West Lancaster Ave., Haverford, PA 19041. For "continued distinguished contribution to children's literature."

**University of Southern Mississippi Children's Collection Medallion**

University of Southern Mississippi Book Festival, USM Library, Hattiesburg, MS 39401. For a writer or an illustrator who has made an "outstanding contribution to the field of children's literature."

For more information about these and other awards, including complete lists of the prizewinners, see *Children's Books: Awards & Prizes*, published and revised periodically by the Children's Book Council, 568 Broadway, New York, NY 10012. Beginning in 1990, each year's *Books in Print* also publishes a listing of the current winners of various prizes.

# Appendix B

## Book Selection Aids

Note: Publishers' addresses may change. For complete and up-to-date information, see the current edition of *Literary Market Place* or *Children's Books in Print.*

### COMPREHENSIVE LISTS AND DIRECTORIES

*Children's Books in Print.* R. R. Bowker, 121 Chanlon Rd., New Providence, NJ 07974. Annual. $149.95.

A comprehensive listing of children's books currently in print. Includes titles for grades K–12. Titles are arranged alphabetically by author, title, and illustrator. A list of publisher addresses is provided. Also includes children's book awards for the previous ten years.

*Children's Media Market Place,* 4th ed. Barbara Stein. Neal-Schuman Publishers, 23 Leonard St., New York, NY 10013. 1988. 397 pp. $45.00, paper.

Annotated list of publishers of books and producers and distributors of nonprint materials, indexed by format, subject, and special interest. Includes a directory of wholesalers, bookstores, book clubs, and children's television sources.

*Educational Media and Technology Yearbook.* Libraries Unlimited, P.O. Box 263, Littleton, CO 80160. Annual. $60.00.

Includes articles, surveys, and research on various aspects of media administration, creation, and use. Lists organizations, foundations, and funding agencies for media as well as information on graduate programs. Includes an annotated mediography of basic resources for library media specialists.

*Guide to Reference Books for School Media Centers,* 5th ed. Barbara Ripp Stanford. Libraries Unlimited, P.O. Box 263, Littleton, CO 80160. 1998, 407 pp. $36.00.

Includes annotations and evaluations for 2,000 useful reference tools for school media centers. Materials are arranged in order by subject. Also includes a list of sources and selection aids for print and nonprint materials.

*Magazines for Children: A Guide for Parents, Teachers, and Librarians,* 2nd ed. Selma K. Richardson. American Library Association, 50 E. Huron St., Chicago, IL 60611. 1991. 139 pp. $22.50, paper.

An annotated list of magazines designed especially for children ages 2 to 14; includes descriptions of the publications, age levels of users, and evaluative comments.

*Magazines for Young People,* 2nd ed. Bill Katz and Kinda Sternberg Katx. R. R. Bowker, 121 Chanlon Rd., New Providence, NJ 07974. 1991. 250 pp. $49.95.

Evaluates over 1,000 magazines, journals, and newsletters for children and teachers in 60 subject areas.

*Reference Books for Children.* Carolyn Sue Peterson and Ann D. Fenton. Scarecrow Press, 52 Liberty St., Box 4167, Metuchen, NJ 08840. 1992. 414 pp. $47.50.

Contains annotated entries over a broad range of curriculum areas, collection needs, interests, and reading levels of children. Books are classified by subject. Annotations provide some guidance in making selections for school collections.

*Subject Guide to Children's Books in Print.* R. R. Bowker, 121 Chanlon Rd., New Providence, NJ 07974. Annual. $149.95.

A companion volume to *Children's Books in Print.* Arranges all children's titles currently in print using over 6,000 subject headings. Particularly useful for finding and ordering titles on specific subjects; however, titles are not annotated.

### GENERAL SELECTION AIDS

*Adventuring with Books: A Booklist for Pre-K–Grade 6,* 11th ed. Wendy Sutton, ed. National Council of Teachers of English, 1111 Kenyon Rd., Urbana, IL 61601. 1997. 401 pp. $22.95, paper.

Annotates about 1,800 children's titles published from 1992 to 1995. Annotations include summary, age, and interest levels. Contents are arranged by genre, broad subject, and theme. Author, title, and subject indexes.

*Award-Winning Books for Children and Young Adults.* Betty L. Criscoe. Scarecrow Press, 52 Liberty St., Box 4167, Metuchen, NJ 08840. Annual. $37.50.

Lists books that won awards during the previous year. Includes descriptions of the awards, criteria used for selection, plot synopses of winners, grade levels, and genres.

*Best Books for Children: Pre-school Through Grade 6,* 6th ed. John T. Gillespie. R. R. Bowker, 121 Chanlon Rd., New Providence, NJ 07974. 1998. 1,537 pp. $65.00.

*Best Books for Young Teen Readers: Grades 7–10*, 6th ed. John T. Gillespie and Corinne J. Naden. R. R. Bowker, 121 Chanlon Rd., New Providence, NJ 07974. 2000. 850 pp. $65.00.

Annotated listing of books that are selected to satisfy recreational needs, curricular needs, and interests of elementary schoolchildren. Books are arranged by broad age groups, subdivided by types of books. Contains author, title, illustrator, and subject indexes.

*Children's Catalog*, 17th ed. H. W. Wilson Co., 950 University Ave., Bronx, NY 10452. 1996. 1,346 pp. $105.00.

A classified (Dewey Decimal System) catalog of about 6,000 recent "best" children's books, including publishing affirmation, grade level, and a brief summary of each title. Also includes alphabetical author, title, subject, and analytical indexes. Contains a list of publishers with addresses. A new edition is issued every five years, with annual supplements in other years.

*Choosing Books for Children*. Betsy Hearne. University of Illinois Press, 1325 S. Oak St., Champaign, IL 61820. 1999. 250 pp. $27.05.

Contains general selection advice for parents, teachers, and librarians, combined with bibliographies.

*The Elementary School Library Collection: A Guide to Books and Other Media*, 21st ed. Linda L. Holms, ed. Brodart Co., 500 Arch St., Williamsport, PA 17705. 1998. 1,150 pp. $99.95.

A basic bibliography of materials, both print and nonprint, for elementary school media center collections. Materials are interfiled and arranged by subject classification (Dewey Decimal System). All entries include bibliographic information, age level, and a brief annotation. Contains author, title, and subject indexes.

*Eyeopeners II*. Beverly Kobrin. Scholastic, 555 Broadway, New York, NY 10012. 1995. 305 pp. $6.95, paper.

Over 500 nonfiction titles are arranged in subject categories and annotated with brief summaries and ideas for classroom use. Indexed by author, illustrator, title, and subject.

*Fiction for Youth: A Guide to Recommended Books*. Lillian L. Shapiro. Neal-Schuman Publishers, 23 Leonard St., New York, NY 10013. 1992. 300 pp. $35.00.

Provides a core collection of titles designed to encourage reading by young people who can read but don't choose to do so.

*The Horn Book Guide to Children's and Young Adult Books*. Horn Book, Inc., 11 Beacon St., Boston, MA 02108. Semiannual. $50 per annum.

Provides short reviews of children's and young-adult books published in the United States during the prior publishing season with references to longer reviews in *Horn Book Magazine*. Books are given a numerical evaluation from 1 to 6.

*More Exciting, Funny, Scary, Short, Different, and Sad Books Kids Like About Animals, Science, Sports, Families, Songs, and Other Things*. Frances Laverne Carroll and Mary Meacham. American Library Association, 50 E. Huron St., Chicago, IL 60611. 1992. 192 pp. $18.00, paper.

An annotated bibliography of titles that focuses on subjects and books that have been popular with children in second through fifth grades.

*New York Times Parents' Guide to the Best Books for Children*. Eden Ross Lipson. Times Books/Random House, 201 E. 50th St., New York, NY 10022. 1988. 421 pp. $12.95.

Indexes books by age appropriateness, listening level, author, title, illustrator, and subject. Books are arranged in broad categories, such as wordless books and picture storybooks.

*Your Reading: A Booklist for Junior High and Middle School Students*, Barbara Samuels, ed. National Council of Teachers of English, 1111 Kenyon Rd., Urbana, IL 61801. 1997. 381 pp. $21.95.

An annotated list of over 2,000 books for grades 5 to 9, arranged in broad subject categories. Includes author and title indexes.

## BOOKLISTS FOR VARIOUS LEVELS OF READERS

*Beyond Picture Books: A Guide to First Readers*. Barbara Barstow and Judith Riggle. R. R. Bowker, 121 Chanlon Rd., New Providence, NJ 07974. 1995. 501 pp. $49.95.

Annotates over 1,600 first readers for ages 4 to 7, with a plot summary, brief evaluation, and bibliographic information. Indexes by title, illustrator, readability, series, and subject.

*Books for the Gifted Child*. Volume 1: Barbara Holland Baskin and Karen H. Harris. 1980. 263 pp. $29.95. Volume 2: Paula Hauser and Gail Nelson. 1988. 244 pp. $39.95. R. R. Bowker, 121 Chanlon Rd., New Providence, NJ 07974.

Each volume critically annotates about 150 titles that would be useful in working with gifted children, ages preschool through 12. They are arranged in alphabetical order with bibliographic information and reading level included. Several chapters on the gifted are included in the book.

*Choices: A Core Collection for Young Reluctant Readers*, Vol. 4. Beverley Fahey and Maureen Whalen, eds. John Gordon Burke, Publisher. P.O. Box 1492, Evanston, IL 60204-1492. 1998. 272 pp. $45.00.

Annotates books for second through sixth graders reading below grade level, published between 1983 and 1988, with plot summary, interest level, and reading level. Contains author and subject indexes.

*Gifted Books, Gifted Readers*. Nancy Polette. Libraries Unlimited, P.O. Box 263, Littleton, CO 80160. 2000. 250 pp. $19.00.

Provides suggested units with activities and lists of books for four primary elements of literature (style, theme, character, setting). Books that stress these elements, or can be used to motivate thinking about them, are included in the lists.

*More Rip-Roaring Reads for Reluctant Teen Readers*. Bette D. Ammon and Gale W. Sherman. Libraries Unlimited, P. O. Box 263, Littleton, CO 80160. 1998. 161 pp. $26.50, paper.

Lists books of high literary quality for reluctant readers in grades 3 to 12. Has brief annotations, reading and interest levels, and popular subject headings.

# BOOKLISTS AND INDEXES FOR PARTICULAR SUBJECTS

## PICTURE BOOKS AND CONCEPT BOOKS

*A to Zoo: Subject Access to Children's Picture Books,* 5th ed. Carolyn W. Lima. R. R. Bowker, 121 Chanlon Rd., New Providence, NJ 07974. 1993. 1,398 pp. $65.00.

Provides subject access to over 8,000 picture books through 600 subject headings with cross-references and full bibliographic citations. Most titles are useful for children from preschool through second grade. Includes author, illustrator, and title lists.

*Alphabet: A Handbook of ABC Books and Activities for the Elementary Classroom,* 2nd ed. Patricia L. Roberts. Scarecrow Press, 52 Liberty St., Box 4167, Metuchen, NJ 08840. 1994. 220 pp. $34.50.

Reviews over 200 alphabet books and provides about 80 activities to use with children from preschool to grade 6.

*Alphabet Books as a Key to Language Patterns: An Annotated Action Bibliography.* Patricia L. Roberts. Shoe String Press, P. O. Box 4327, 925 Sherman Ave., Hamden, CT 06514. 1987. 263 pp. $27.50.

Lists over 500 alphabet books that can be used in aiding language development under categories such as alliteration, rhymes and verses, and wordless books.

*Counting Books Are More Than Numbers: An Annotated Action Bibliography.* Patricia L. Roberts. Shoe String Press, P. O. Box 4327, 925 Sherman Ave., Hamden, CT 06514. 1990. 264 pp. $32.50.

Describes 350 books for preschool through second grades that can be used to encourage early understanding of mathematical concepts.

*Information Picture Books for Children.* Patricia Jean Cianciolo. American Library Association, 50 E. Huron St., Chicago, IL 60611. 1997. 192 pp. $34.00, paper.

An annotated listing of nonfiction books, divided into major subject areas such as "The Natural World" or "Numbers and Arithmetic." Annotations include age levels, and brief synopses.

*Picture Books for Children,* 4th ed. Patricia Jean Cianciolo. American Library Association, 50 E. Huron St., Chicago, IL 60611. 1997. 243 pp. $40.00, paper.

An annotated listing of picture books, divided into major subject areas such as "Me and My Family" or "The Imaginative World." Annotations include descriptions of media, age levels, and brief synopses of plot. Material is largely new to this edition, so older editions remain useful.

*Reading in a Series: A Selection Guide to Books for Children.* Catherine Barr. R. R. Bowker, 121 Chanlon Rd., New Providence, NJ 07974. 1999. 596 pp. $65.00.

This annotated guide is organized alphabetically by series titles and includes information about the author, genre, and appropriate audience. Appendices include series books for reluctant readers and ESL students.

## FOLKLORE AND STORYTELLING AND READING ALOUD

*Caroline Feller Bauer's New Handbook for Storytellers.* Caroline Feller Bauer. American Library Association, 50 E. Huron St., Chicago, IL 60611. 1993. 550 pp. $30.00, paper.

A thorough guide to telling stories, this book includes ideas for creating puppets, story media, and using music and film in storytelling.

*For Reading Out Loud! A Guide to Sharing Books with Children.* Margaret Mary Kimmel and Elizabeth Segel. Dell Publishing, 666 Fifth Ave., New York, NY 10103. 1988. 240 pp. $16.95, paper.

Contains suggestions for reading aloud effectively to elementary and middle school students and an annotated list of good titles.

*Index to Fairy Tales, 1987–1992: Including 310 Collections of Fairytales, Folklore, Legends and Myths,* 6th supp. Joseph W. Sprug, comp. Scarecrow Press, 52 Liberty St., Box 4167, Metuchen, NJ 08840. 1994. 602 pp. $62.50.

Indexes a broad range of collections of folktales and other folk literature by author, compiler, subject of tale (including characters, countries, and so on), and titles of tale. Various editions cover different collections, so the total coverage is quite broad.

*More Books Kids Will Sit Still For: The Complete Read-Aloud Guide,* 2nd ed. Judy Freeman. R. R. Bowker, 121 Chanlon Rd., New Providence, NJ 07974. 1995. 869 pp. $49.95.

Lists over 2,000 titles recommended for reading aloud, and includes plot summaries, extension ideas, and related titles.

*The Read-Aloud Handbook,* 4th. ed. Jim Trelease. Penguin Books, 375 Hudson St., New York, NY 10014. 1995. 387 pp. $12.95, paper.

Contains a rationale for reading aloud, tips for good presentations, and an annotated list of books recommended for reading aloud.

*Stories: A List of Stories to Tell and Read Aloud,* 3rd ed. Marilyn B. Iarusso, ed. New York Public Library Publications Office, Fifth Ave. & 42nd St., New York, NY 10018. 1990. 104 pp. $6.00.

Suggests proven stories to tell and read aloud to children. Includes poetry. Entries are briefly annotated.

*Storyteller's Sourcebook.* Margaret Read MacDonald, ed. Gale Research, 835 Penobscot Bldg., Detroit, MI 48226-4094. 1982. 840 pp. $95.00.

Provides access to folktales and folk literature in 700 collections. Tales are indexed by subject, motif, and title. Index is particularly useful in locating variants of tales.

*Storytelling with Puppets,* 2nd ed. Connie Champlin. American Library Association, 50 E. Huron St., Chicago, IL 60611. 264 pp. $35.00.

Techniques for storytelling to younger audiences include open box theatre, sound and action stories, and story aprons. Attention is given to multicultural themes and literature-based instruction.

*The Storytime Sourcebook: A Compendium of Ideas and Resources for Storytellers.* Carolyn M. Cullum. Neal-Schuman Publishers, 23 Leonard St., New York, NY 10013, 1990. 175 pp. $24.95.

Arranged by themes, lists plans for story hour programs including books, films, filmstrips, videocassettes, and toys. Includes activities for 3- to 7-year-olds. Print and nonprint indexes.

## HISTORICAL FICTION, HISTORY, AND BIOGRAPHY

*American History for Children and Young Adults: An Annotated Bibliographic Index.* Vandelia VanMeter. Libraries Unlimited, P. O. Box 263, Littleton, CO 80160. 1997. 280 pp. $38.50.

Books reviewed between 1980 and 1988 are arranged by time periods, subdivided by subject. Indexed by grade level.

*From Biography to History: Best Books for Children's Entertainment and Education.* R. R. Bowker, 121 Chanlon R. New Providence NJ 07974. 1998. 550 pp. $59.95.

Indexes biographies in collections by individuals' names and by subject. Biographies are suitable for elementary school through junior high school.

*Literature Connections to World History: K–6 Resources to Enhance and Entice.* Lynda G. Adamson. Libraries Unlimited, P. O. Box 263, Littleton, CO 80160. 1998. 326 pp. $30.00.

Lists and annotates books and media for younger readers about world history by time period and subject. Includes fiction and nonfiction.

*Literature Connections to World History: 7–12 Resources to Enhance and Entice.* Lynda G. Adamson. Libraries Unlimited, P. O. Box 263, Littleton, CO 80160. 1998. 326 pp. $32.50.

Lists and annotates books and media for adolescents about world history by time period and subject. Includes fiction and nonfiction.

*Peoples of the American West: Historical Perspectives Through Children's Literature.* Mary Hurlbut Cordier. Scarecrow, 52 Liberty St., Box 4167, Metuchen, NJ 08840. 1989. 230 pp. $22.50.

Contains an analysis of historical fiction of the West as a genre and an annotated list of 100 books separated into grades K–3 and 4–9.

*Reference Guide to Historical Fiction for Children and Young Adults.* Lynda G. Adamson. Greenwood Publishing Group. Greenwood Dr., 88 Post Rd., W., P. O. Box 5007, Westport, CT 06881. 1987. 401 pp. $49.95.

Authors, titles, main characters, and historical events are listed in dictionary format with longer entries under authors that describe their works. Appendixes list books by periods and events and by readability level.

## CULTURAL AND SEXUAL IDENTITY

*Against Borders: Promoting Books for a Multicultural World.* Hazel Rochman. American Library Association, 50 E. Huron St., Chicago, IL 60611. 1993. 288 pp. $25.00, paper.

Essays and annotated book lists focus on specific ethnic groups and issues that tie world cultures together through themes.

*American Indian Reference Books for Children and Young Adults.* Barbara J. Kuipers. Libraries Unlimited, P. O. Box 263, Littleton, CO 80160. 1995. 260 pp. $27.50.

Lists over 200 nonfiction sources of material on Native Americans for grades 3 to 12. Includes strengths and weaknesses of each book as well as curriculum uses. A section of the book deals with general selection criteria to use for these subjects.

*Basic Collection of Children's Books in Spanish.* Isabel Schon. Scarecrow Press, 52 Liberty St., Box 4167, Metuchen, NJ 08840. 1986. 230 pp. $17.50.

More than 500 titles for preschool through grade 6 are arranged in Dewey order, with access through author, title, and subject indexes. A list of Spanish language distributors is included.

*The Black American in Books for Children: Readings in Racism,* 2nd ed. Donnarae MacCann and Gloria Woodward. Scarecrow Press, 52 Liberty St., Box 4167, Metuchen, NJ 08840. 1985. 310 pp. $31.00.

Collections of articles in which the issue of racism in children's books is considered from a variety of points of view. Includes many citations to books of both good and poor quality that reflect positive and negative values.

*The Black Experience in Children's Books.* Barbara Rollock, selector. New York Public Library Publications Office, Fifth Ave. & 42nd St., New York, NY 10018. 1989. 112 pp. $6.00.

An annotated list that presents titles about the black experience in the United States as well as in other areas of the world. Criteria for selection and inclusion in the list are described.

*Books in Spanish for Children and Young Adults: An Annotated Guide,* series 3. Isabel Schon. Scarecrow Press, 52 Liberty St., Box 4167, Metuchen, NJ 08840. 1989. 180 pp. $20.00.

Contains listings of books for preschool through high school that have been published since 1982. The listed books represent diverse Hispanic cultures, including Mexico and Central and South America.

*Connecting Cultures: A Guide to Multicultural Literature for Children.* Rebecca L. Thomas. R. R. Bowker, 121 Chanlon Rd., New Providence, NJ 07974. 1996. 689 pp. $40.00.

Annotated lists for grades K–6 includes fiction folktales, poetry, and songbooks about diverse cultural groups

*A Guide to Non-Sexist Children's Books: Volume 2, 1976–1985.* Denise Wilms and Ilene Cooper, eds. Academy Publisher, 213 W. Institute Pl., Chicago, IL 60610. 1987. 240 pp. $17.95; $8.95, paper.

Lists over 600 books in sections by grade level, through twelfth grade, subdivided into fiction and nonfiction. Indexes by author, title, fiction, and nonfiction subjects. Volume 1, which covered books up to 1976, is also available.

*A Latino Heritage: A Guide to Juvenile Books About Latino Peoples and Cultures,* series 5. Isabel Schon. Scarecrow Press, 52 Liberty St., Box 4167, Metuchen, NJ 08840. 1995. 210 pp. $34.50.

An annotated subject bibliography of works about the people, history, culture, and politics in the Latino countries as well as works about Latino people in the United States. The author indicates in the annotations the passages in which cultural bias and stereotyping might appear. Covers grades K–12. Volumes 2 (1985) and 3 (1988) are also available.

*Kaleidoscope—A Multicultural Booklist for Grades K–8,* 2nd ed. Rosalinda Benavides Barrer and Verlinda D. Thompson, eds. National Council of Teachers of English, 1111 W. Kenyon Road, Urbana, IL 61801-1096. 1997. 220 pp. $16.95.

Celebrating cultural diversity with annotations of nearly 400 books, covers a range from poetry to arts to biographies, folktales, and picture books, focusing especially on people of color.

*Our Family, Our Friends, Our World: An Annotated Guide to Significant Multicultural Books for Children and Teenagers.* Lyn Miller-Lachman. R. R. Bowker, 121 Chanlon Rd., New Providence, NJ 07974. 1992. 400 pp. $39.95.

Annotated lists of fiction and nonfiction about ethnic and cultural minority groups in the United States and Canada, and about cultures in various parts of the world.

## OTHER SOCIAL ISSUES

*The Bookfinder, Volume 5: When Kids Need Books.* Sharon Spredemann Dreyer. American Guidance Service. Publishers' Building, Circle Pines, MN 55014-1796. 1994. 519 pp. $64.95; $29.95, paper.

Subject, author, and title indexes are provided on the top half of the publication, and lengthy reviews that include subject cross-references, age levels, and specific information about the content of the book are on the bottom half. Both fiction and nonfiction are included. The books focus on problems children may experience, feelings, and relationships.

*Books to Help Children to Cope with Separation and Loss,* 4th ed. Masha K. Rudman, comp. R. R. Bowker, 121 Chanlon Rd., New Providence, NJ 07974. 1994. 514 pp. $55.00.

Includes several chapters on bibliotherapy plus annotated lists of titles in such categories as death, divorce, adoption, and foster children, and loss of mental or physical functions. About 600 books are arranged by topic with an annotation evaluation and recommendations for use with children. Age levels from 3 to 16; interest, and reading level are included in each annotation.

*Portraying Persons with Disabilities: An Annotated Bibliography of Fiction for Children.* Debra Robertson. R. R. Bowker, 121 Chanlon Rd., New Providence, NJ 07974. 1992. 482 pp. $39.95.

Updates *Notes from a Different Drummer* and *More Notes from a Different Drummer,* books that provide annotated lists of titles that portray the disabled in fiction. Includes titles that promote better understanding and acceptance of the disabled.

*Portraying Persons with Disabilities: An Annotated Bibliography of Nonfiction for Children.* Joan Brest Friedberg, June B. Mullins, and Adelaide Weir Sukiennik. R. R. Bowker, 121 Chanlon Rd., New Providence, NJ 07974. 1992. 400 pp. $39.50.

Updates *Accept Me as I Am,* listing over 350 nonfiction titles about the disabled. Includes introductory essays about the portrayal of disabilities in literature for children.

## CURRICULUM AREAS AND GENRES OF LITERATURE

*Anatomy of Wonder: A Critical Guide to Science Fiction.* Neil Barron, ed. R. R. Bowker, 121 Chanlon Rd., New Providence, NJ 07974. 1995. 1,000 pp. $52.00.

Includes a chapter that annotates titles for children and young adults, as well as 3,000 additional titles that would appeal to readers of the genre. Includes discussion of sci-fi poetry, film connections, and a chapter on classroom aids.

*Celebrations: Read-Aloud Holiday and Theme Book Programs.* Caroline Feller Bauer. H. W. Wilson, 950 University Ave., Bronx, NY 10452. 1985. 301 pp. $35.00.

Includes readings and plans for holiday activities for both well-known and Bauer's invented holiday occasions.

*Fantasy Literature for Children and Young Adults: An Annotated Bibliography,* 3rd. ed. Ruth Nadelman Lyn. R. R. Bowker, 121 Chanlon Rd., New Providence, NJ 07974. 1995. 1,150 pp. $52.00.

Annotates about 4,800 fantasy novels for 8- to 17-year-olds in ten chapters arranged by topics. Includes specific subject indexes.

*Index to Children's Songs: A Title, First Line, and Subject Index.* Carolyn Sue Peterson and Ann D. Fento. H. W. Wilson Company, 950 University Ave., Bronx, NY 10452. 1979. 318 pp. $33.00.

Indexes over 5,000 songs in 298 children's songbooks, both single titles and collections. Songs are indexed by title and first line as well as by 1,000 subject headings and cross-references.

*Index to Poetry for Children and Young People, 1993–1997.* G. Meredith Blackburn, et al. H. W. Wilson Co., 950 University Ave., New York, NY 10452. 1999. 358 pp. $70.00.

The latest in a series of volumes that index collections of poetry by author, title, first line, and subject. Different collections are indexed in each volume. Classifies poems under a wide variety of subjects, making for easy access to poems by their topics.

*It's the Story That Counts: More Children's Books for Mathematical Learning, K–6.* David J. Whitin and Sandra Wilde. 1995. 224 pp. $21.50, paper. Both published by Heinemann Books, 361 Hanover St., Portsmouth, NH 03801.

The first book discusses basic concepts in mathematics, such as place value, classification, and geometry, and suggests ways to explore these concepts with children's books. The second title highlights children's responses to many of these books and suggests additional titles and ideas, including multicultural perspectives, for exploring mathematics.

*The Literature of Delight: A Critical Guide to Humorous Books for Children.* Kimberly Olson Fakih. R. R. Bowker, 121 Chanlon Rd., New Providence, NJ 07974. 1993. 269 pp. $40.00.

Lists 1,000 fiction and nonfiction books with humorous presentations. Chapters include books of nonsense, books of satire and parody, poetry, and so on.

*Read Any Good Math Lately? Children's Books for Mathematical Learning, K–6.*

David J. Whitin and Sandra Wilde. 1992. 206 pp. $20.00, paper.

## INFORMATION ABOUT AUTHORS AND ILLUSTRATORS

*Bookpeople: A Second Album.* 1990. 200 pp. $20.00, paper.

*Bookpeople: A Multicultural Album.* 1992. 170 pp. $23.50, paper.

Both by Sharon L. McElmeel. Libraries Unlimited, P. O. Box 263, Littleton, CO 80160.

Each volume introduces authors and illustrators of picture books for grades 3 to 9. Brief biographies include highlights of life and career and selected bibliographies of their work.

*Children's Book Illustration and Design II.* Julie Cummins ed. PBC International, One School St., Glen Cove NY, 11542. 1997. 240 pp. $55.00, hardcover.

This beautifully designed and printed volume includes a sample of picture book illustrators, brief biographies and information about the illustrators medium and technique.

*Children's Books and Their Creators.* Anita Silvey, ed. Houghton Mifflin, 222 Berkeley St., Boston, MA 02116. 1995. 800 pp. $40.00.

This handsomely designed book includes biographical descriptions of and first-person reflections by important twentieth-century authors and illustrators and critical essays on a range of topics central to the study of children's literature.

*The Illustrator's Notebook.* Lee Kingman, ed. Horn Book, 11 Beacon St., Boston, MA 02108. 1978. 168 pp. $28.95.

Contains excerpts from articles by artists and illustrators that have appeared in the *Horn Book Magazine.* Articles discuss philosophy of illustration, history, illustration's place in the arts, and their experiences with various techniques of illustration.

*Illustrators of Children's Books 1744–1945.* Bertha E. Mahony, Louise Payson Latimer, and Beulah Formsbee, eds. 1947. 527 pp. $35.95.

*Illustrators of Children's Books 1946–1956.* Bertha Mahony Miller, RuthHill Viguers, and Marcia Dalphin, eds. 1958. 229 pp. $30.95.

*Illustrators of Children's Books 1957–1966.* Lee Kingman, Joanna Foster, and Ruth Giles Lontoft, eds. 1968. 295 pp. $30.95.

*Illustrators of Children's Books 1967–1976.* Lee Kingman, Grace Allen Hogarth, and Harriet Quimbly, eds. 1978. 290 pp. $35.95.

All published by Horn Book, 11 Beacon St., Boston, MA 02108.

All four volumes contain brief biographical and career sketches of artists and illustrators for children who were actively at work in this field during the period covered by the volume. Articles discuss techniques, philosophy, and trends in illustration during the period. Bibliographies are included for each illustrator as well as selected bibliographies covering art and illustration of the period. Volume 4 contains a cumulative index.

*The Marble in the Water: Essays on Contemporary Writers of Fiction for Children and Young Adults.* David Rees. Horn Book, 11 Beacon St., Boston, MA 02108. 1980. 224 pp. $9.95, paper.

Essays on 18 British and American authors, including Beverly Cleary, Paula Fox, Judy Blume, and Paul Zindel.

*Meet the Authors and Illustrators: 60 Creators of Favorite Children's Books Talk About Their Work.* Vol. 2. Deborah Kovacs and James Preller. Scholastic Inc., 730 Broadway, New York, NY 10003. 1993. 142 pp. $19.95.

Two children's book authors have collected information on favorite authors and illustrators from around the world. Each two-page highlight includes information about the author or illustrator, selected titles, pictures, and a "do-it-yourself" activity suggested for children.

*Newbery Medal Books: 1922–1955.* Bertha Mahoney Miller and Elinor Whiteney Field, eds. 1955. 458 pp. $22.95.

*Caldecott Medal Books: 1938–1957.* Bertha Mahony Miller and Elinor Whitney Fields, eds. 1957. 239 pp. $22.95.

*Newbery and Caldecott Medal Books: 1956–1965.* Lee Kingman, ed. 1965. 300 pp. $22.95.

*Newbery and Caldecott Medal Books: 1966–1975.* Lee Kingman, ed. 1975. 321 pp. $22.95.

*Newbery and Caldecott Medal Books: 1976–1985.* Lee Kingman, ed. 1986. 321 pp. $24.95.

All published by Horn Book, 11 Beacon St., Boston, MA 02108.

Each volume contains biographical sketches and texts of the award winners' acceptance speeches as well as general observations of trends in the awards.

*Pauses: Autobiographical Reflections of 101 Creators of Children's Books.* Lee Bennett Hopkins. HarperCollins, 10 E. 53rd St., New York, NY 10022. 1995. 233 pp. $23.00.

A collection of personal reflections taken from interviews with noted authors and illustrators.

*A Sense of Story: Essays on Contemporary Writers for Children.* John Rowe Townsend. Horn Book, 56 Roland St Ste. 200 Beacon St., Boston, MA 02129. 1973. 216 pp. $6.95.

Includes essays on 19 English-language authors for children, including brief biographies, notes on their books, critical remarks, and lists of their books. Essays reflect the critical position of the author.

*Seventh Book of Junior Authors and Illustrators.* Sally Holmes Holtze, ed. 1983. 375 pp. $55.00.

Latest in a series published by H. W. Wilson Co., 950 University Ave., Bronx, NY 10452.

These volumes provide readable biographies of popular authors for young people that include, generally, a biographical statement by the author or illustrator, a photograph, a brief biography, and a list of that person's works.

*Something About the Author.* Anne Commaire. Gale Research, 835 Penobscot Bldg., Detroit, MI 48226-4094. There are over 108 volumes in print, added to periodically. $137.00.

Clear and sizable essays on contemporary authors and illustrators. Updating allows more-recent authors to be included. Contains photographs as well as reproductions from works of the illustrators. Suitable for middle-grade children to use for gathering biographical information.

*A Sounding of Storytellers: New and Revised Essays on Contemporary Writers for Children.* John Rowe Townsend. Harper & Row, 10 E. 53rd St., New York, NY 10022. 1979. 218 pp. $15.25.

Townsend reevaluates seven of the authors included in his earlier *A Sense of Story,* including the new ground they have covered in more-recent works. Several American authors are included in the new selections, including Vera and Bill Cleaver, Virginia Hamilton, and E. L. Konigsburg.

## PERIODICALS

*Appraisal: Science Books for Young People.* Children's Science Book Review Committee, North Eastern University, 54 Lake Hall, Boston, MA 02115. Quarterly. $46.00.

Each issue contains reviews of about 75 children's and young-adult science and technology books. Gives age levels and ratings of quality.

*Bookbird.* IBBY, The International Board on Books for Young People, P. O. Box 3156, West Lafayette, IN 47906. Quarterly. $30.00.

This excellent journal reflects the international character of children's literature through articles and profiles of authors and illustrators from member countries. Themed issues have included "Children's Poetry," "Southeast Asia," "Girls and Women," and "Philosophy for Children."

*Book Links.* American Library Association, 50 E. Huron St., Chicago, IL 60611. Six times/year. $20.00.

This publication connects books, libraries, and classrooms. Special features include "book strategies" or guides for teaching a particular book, interviews with authors and illustrators to discover their personal story behind the book, book themes, poetry, and "just for fun," books for children to read and enjoy.

*Booklist.* American Library Association, 50 E. Huron St., Chicago, IL 60611. Twice/month. $69.50.

Reviews both adult and children's titles, including both print and nonprint materials. Reviews are annotated and graded by age levels and grades. Includes reviews of new selection tools. Often contains subject lists of good books in particular fields. Lists prizewinning books annually.

*Book Review Digest.* H. W. Wilson Co., 950 University Ave., Bronx, NY 10452. Ten times/year. Service basis rates quoted on request.

Evaluates about 4,000 adult and children's books per year. For those books included, provides citations from several reviews that have appeared in other review periodicals.

*Book World.* c/o Washington Post, 1150 15th St. NW, Washington, DC 20071. Weekly. $26.00.

A weekly supplement to the *Post* and several other newspapers. Reviews children's books regularly. Issues large special children's book editions in fall and spring.

*The Bulletin of the Center for Children's Books.* University of Illinois Press, 54 E. Gregory Dr., Champaign, IL 61820. 11 issues. $35.00.

Reviews about 75 current children's books in each issue with negative as well as favorable reviews. Each entry is graded. Annotations stress curricular use, values, and literary merit.

*Canadian Children's Literature.* CC Press, P. O. Box 335, Guelph, Ontario, NIH 6K5, Canada. Quarterly. US $39.00.

Literary analysis, criticism, and reviews of Canadian children's literature. A thematic approach for each issue. Predominantly written in English, but some articles are in French or in French and English.

*CBC Features.* Children's Book Council, 568 Broadway, New York, NY 10012. A one-time $35.00 charge for placement on a mailing list. Twice/year.

A newsletter about children's books, including information about special events, free and inexpensive materials from publishers, and lists of prizewinners, as well as discussion of new books.

*Childhood Education.* Association for Childhood Education International, 11501 Georgia Ave., Ste. 312, Wheaton, MD 20902. Five times/year. $57.00.

Includes a column on children's books that contains annotated reviews on about 25 books.

*Children's Literature in Education.* c/o Agathon Press, 233 Spring St., New York, NY 10013. Quarterly. $29.00.

Publishes longer articles on English and American children's literature, including criticism, history, and biographical essays.

*Cricket Magazine.* Marianne Carus, ed. Carus Corp., 315 Fifth St., Box 300, Peru, IL 61354. Monthly. $32.95.

A literary magazine for children of elementary school age. Includes new stories and poems by well-known children's authors as well as excerpts and serializations of older pieces of literature. Includes children's reviews of books, interviews with authors, and children's writing.

*Five Owls.* Five Owls, 2004 Sheridan Ave., S., Minneapolis, MN 55405. Bimonthly. $35.00.

Each issue provides an article on a theme or topic and bibliographies that enhance or support it. Includes a signed review section.

*Horn Book Magazine.* Horn Book, Inc., 56 Roland St., Ste, 200, Boston, MA 02129. Bimonthly. $24.95. *http://www.hbook.com/*

Includes detailed reviews of children's books judged by the editorial staff to be the best in children's literature. Contains articles about the literature, interviews with authors, and text of important speeches in the field of literature (Newbery and Caldecott acceptance speeches are published in the August issue each year). October issue lists the outstanding books of the previous year.

*Journal of Youth Services in Libraries.* Association for Library Services to Children and Young Adult Services Division, American Library Association, 50 E. Huron St., Chicago, IL 60611. Quarterly. $40.00.

Formerly *Top of the News.* Provides articles on issues in children's literature and children's librarianship, international news, texts of speeches, and lists of upcoming events of interest in the field. Articles are often annotated bibliographies on subjects of current interest.

*Knowledge Quest.* (formerly *School Library Media Quarterly.*) American Association of School Librarians, American Library Association, 50 E. Huron St., Chicago, IL 60611. Quarterly. $40.00.

Official journal of the AASL. Includes articles on book evaluations, censorship, library services, standards of service, and so on.

*Language Arts.* National Council of Teachers of English, 1111 Kenyon Rd., Urbana, IL 61801. Monthly September to May. $50.00.

"Books for Children" section features regular reviews of new books. Several issues focus on literature and reading, containing articles on authors, using literature in the classroom, and so on.

*The Lion and the Unicorn.* Johns Hopkins University Press, 2715 N. Charles St., Baltimore, MD 21218. Annual. $26.50.

Literary criticism, book reviews, and interviews with authors of children's literature. Each issue presents a particular theme or genre around which articles are centered.

*The New Advocate.* Christopher-Gordon, 1502 Peovidence Hwy. Ste. 12., Norwood, MA 02062. Quarterly. $45.00.

Includes articles about authors and illustrators, literary qualities, and classroom uses of children's literature as well as selected book reviews.

*The New York Times Book Review.* New York Times Co., 229 W. 43rd St., New York, NY 10036. Weekly. $52.00.

Weekly column entitled "For Younger Readers" reviews a few children's books. Two issues in fall and spring are devoted to children's books exclusively. Before Christmas, a list of outstanding books is included.

*Publisher's Weekly.* R. R. Bowker, 121 Chanlon R. New Providence NJ 07974. Weekly. $189.00.

Twice a year, in spring and fall, a "Children's Book Number" is published that includes new titles from all major publishers, as well as reviews. Negative reviews are included. Occasionally includes feature articles on children's books and publishing for children.

*School Library Journal.* P. O. Box 57559, Boulder, CO 80322. Monthly. $97.50.

Reviews most children's books, using librarians, teachers, and critics from around the country as reviewers. Includes both positive and negative reviews. Categorizes reviews by age levels. Also includes feature articles on children's literature, children's library services, technology, and nonprint materials. December issue includes a "Best Books" section.

*Science Books and Films.* American Association for the Advancement of Science, Dept. SBF. Box 3000, Denville, NJ. 07834. Quarterly. $40.00.

Reviews trade, test, and reference books for students in all grades in both pure and applied sciences. Includes nonprint materials. Indicates level of expertise required to use a piece of material. Books are reviewed by specialists in the field.

*Science and Children.* National Science Teachers Association, 1840 Wilson Blvd. Arlington VA 22201 Eight times/year. $72.00.

Includes a monthly column that reviews books and nonprint materials.

*Signal: Approaches to Children's Books.* Thimble Press, Lockwood Station Rd., South Woodchester, Glos. GL5 5EQ England. Three times/year. $27.00.

Articles of criticism on history of children's literature and on theory and practice of classroom usage. The literature considered is largely British.

*Teaching and Learning Literature with Children and Young Adults.* Essmont Publishing, P. O. Box 186, Brandon, VT 05733. Five times/year. $34.95.

This journal includes thoughtful essays and critiques on a range of topics and genres in children's literature. Each issue includes a "Workshop" feature, ideas for deepening children's responses and understandings to books.

*The WEB: Wonderfully Exciting Books.* Ohio State University, The Reading Center, 200 Ramseyer Hall, Columbus, OH 43210. Three times/year. $10.00.

Devoted to helping teachers incorporate children's literature into the curriculum through reviews that emphasize classroom use and through a "web of possibilities" for a major thematic area that is included in each issue. Reviews are written by practicing teachers and librarians.

*Wilson Library Bulletin.* The H. W. Wilson Co., 950 University Ave., Bronx, NY 10452. Monthly September to June. $52.00.

Includes discussions and reviews of all types of books and materials. Features a monthly column of reviews of children's books, plus articles about authors, a list of awards, and so on. The October issue is devoted to children's books.

## SELECTED PROFESSIONAL WEBSITES

American Association of School Librarians

*http://www.ala.org/aasl/index.html*

This is a division of the American Library Association responsible for planning, improving and extending library media services for children and young people. Their website offers Kids connect, a question answering and referral service to help to K-12 students with research or personal interests.

The Association of Library Services to Children

*http://www.ala.org/alsc/*

The Association of Library Services to Children of. This is the division of the American Library Association that oversees the Caldecott and Newbery awards and provides many other activities relating to children and books.

The Cooperative Children's Book Center (CCBC)

*http://www.soemadison.wisc.edu/ccbc/index.htm*

The Cooperative Children's Book Center at The University of Wisconsin is a non-circulating examination study and research library for adults with an interest in children and young adult literature. CCBC-Net is an electronic forum to discuss books for children and young adults.

The Children's Book Council

*http://www.cbcbooks.org/*

The Children's Book Council is the trade association of US publishers of children's books. The Council promotes the use and enjoyment of trade books and related materials for young people and disseminates information about children's trade book publishing. This site provides links to author websites and provides bibliographies such as Notable Social Studies Trade Books for Children and Outstanding Science Books for Children.

The International Reading Association.

*http://www.reading.org/*

The organization seeks to promote literacy by improving the quality of reading instruction, serving as a clearing house for reading research, and promoting life-long reading habits.

The National Council of Teachers of English

*http://www.ncte.org/*

NCTE is a professional organization of educators in English Studies, Literacy and the Language Arts. NCTE-talk provides a monthly forum on special interests such as assessment.

The Young Adult Services Association of the American Library Association

*http://www.ala.org/yalsa/*

This is the division of the Association that oversees the Printz Award and provides many other activities relating to young adults.

# Appendix C

## Publishers' Addresses

Note: Publishers' addresses may change. For complete and up-to-date information, see the current edition of *Literary Market Place* or *Children's Books in Print*.

Abrams, 100 Fifth Ave., New York, NY 10010.
  *http://www.abramsbooks.com*
Addison-Wesley, 1 Jacob Way, Reading, MA 01867.
Aladdin Books, see Simon & Schuster.
Apple Soup, see Random House, Inc.
Arcade Publishing, 141 Fifth Ave., New York, NY 10010.
Astor-Honor, 530 Fifth Ave., New York, NY 10036.
Atheneum Publishers, see Simon & Schuster.
Atlantic Monthly Press, 19 Union Square West, New York, NY 10013.
Avon Books, 1350 Avenue of the Americas, New York, NY 10019.
Bantam Doubleday Dell, see Random House
Barefoot Books, 37 W. 17th St., 4th flr. East, New York 10011.
  *http://www.barefoot-books.com*
Black Butterfly Children's Books, see Writers and Readers Publishing.
Blue Sky, see Scholastic.
Boyds Mills Press, 910 Church St., Honesdale, PA 18431.
Bradbury Press, see Simon & Schuster.
Browndeer Press, see Harcourt Brace.
Camelot, see Avon.
Candlewick Press, 2067 Massachusetts Ave., Cambridge, MA 02140.
Carolrhoda Books, Inc., 241 First Avenue North, Minneapolis, MN 55401.
Charlesbridge Publishing, 85 Main St. Watertown MA, 02472.
  *http://www.charlesbridge.com*
Children's Book Press, 246 First St., Ste. 101, San Francisco, CA 94105.
Clarion Books, 215 Park Ave., New York, NY 10003.
Cobblehill Books, see Penguin Putnam Inc.
Collier, see Simon & Schuster.
Creative Arts Books, 833 Bancroft Way, Berkeley, CA 94710.
Creative Education Inc., 123 S. Broad, Mankato, MN 56001.
Crestwood House, 1633 Broadway New York, NY 10019.
Thomas Y. Crowell, see HarperCollins.
Crown Publishers, see Random House, Inc.
Delacorte Press, see Random House, Inc.
Dell Publishing, see Random House, Inc.

Dial, see Penguin Putnam Inc.
Disney Press, 114 Fifth Ave., 12th Floor, New York, NY 10011.
DK Publishing, Inc. (formerly Dorling Kindersley Publishing, Inc.), 95 Madison Ave., 10th Floor, New York, NY 10016.
Doubleday, see Random House, Inc.
Dover Publications, Inc., 180 Varick St., New York, NY 10014.
Dutton Children's Books, see Penguin Putnam Inc.
Farrar, Straus & Giroux, Inc., 19 Union Square West, New York, NY 10003.
Four Winds Press, see Simon & Schuster.
Franklin Watts, see Grolier Children's Publishing.
David R. Godine, Publishers, Inc., 300 Massachusetts Ave., Boston, MA 02115.
Golden Books, 888 7th Ave., New York, NY 10106.
Green Tiger Press, 435 E. Carmel St., San Marcos, CA 92069.
Greenwillow Books, see HarperCollins.
Grolier Children's Publishing, 90 Sherman Turnpike, Danbury CT 06816.
Grosset & Dunlap, Inc., see Penguin Putnam Inc.
Gulliver Books, see Harcourt Brace.
Harcourt Brace Children's Books, 525 B St., Suite 1900, San Diego, CA 92101-4495. *http://www.harcourtbooks.com*
HarperCollins Children's Books, 1350 Avenue of the Americas, New York, NY 10019. *http://www.harperchildrens.com*
Harper Trophy Paperbacks, see HarperCollins.
Henry Holt and Company, Inc., 115 West 18th St., New York, NY 10011.
Holiday House, 425 Madison Ave., New York, NY 10017.
Houghton Mifflin, 222 Berkley St., Boston, MA 02116.
Hyperion Books, see Disney Press.
Jewish Publication Society, 60 East 42nd St., Suite 1339, New York, NY 10165.
Joy Street Books, see Little, Brown.
Jump at the Sun, see Disney Press.
Kane/Miller Book Publishers, P. O. Box 310529, Brooklyn, NY 11231.
Alfred A. Knopf, see Random House, Inc.
Lee & Low Books Inc., 95 Madison Ave., New York, NY 10016. *http://www.leeandlow.com/home/index.html*
Lerner Publications Company, 241 First Ave., North, Minneapolis, MN 55401.
Lippincott Junior Books, see HarperCollins.
Little, Brown & Co., 3 Center Plaza, Boston, MA 02108.

**Little Simon,** see Simon & Schuster.

**Lodestar Books,** see Penguin Putnam Inc.

**Lothrop, Lee & Shepard Books,** see HarperCollins.

**Margaret K. McElderry Books,** see Simon & Schuster.

**Macmillan Publishing Co.,** see Simon & Schuster.

**The Millbrook Press, Inc.,** 2 Old New Milford Rd., Brookfield, CT 06804. *http://www.millbrookpress.com*

**Morrow Junior Books,** see HarperCollins.

**Mulberry Books,** see HarperCollins.

**National Geographic Press,** 1147 17th St. NW, Washington, DC 20036. *http://www.nationalgeographic.com*

**North-South Books,** 1123 Broadway, Suite 1016, New York, NY 10010.

**Orchard Books,** see Grolier Children's Publishing.

**Random House, Inc.,** 1540 Broadway, New York, NY, 10036 *http://www.randomhouse.com*

**Richard C. Owen, Publishers, Inc.,** P. O. Box 585, Katonah, NY 10536.

**Oxford University Press,** 198 Madison Ave., New York, NY 10016. *http://www.oup-usa.org*

**Pantheon,** see Random House Inc.

**Paper Star,** see Penguin Putnam Inc.

**Parents Magazine Press,** 685 Third Ave., New York, NY 10017.

**Parnassus Press,** see Houghton Mifflin.

**Penguin Putnam Inc.,** 375 Hudson St., New York, NY 10014. *http://www.penguinputnam.com/yreaders*

**Philomel Books,** see Penguin Putnam Inc.

**Phyllis Fogelman Books,** see Penguin Putnam Inc.

**Picture Book Studio,** 2 Center Plaza, Boston, MA 02108.

**Pleasant Company,** 8400 Fairway Place, P. O. Box 998, Middleton, WI 53562.

**Prentice Hall,** 115 Columbus Circle, New York, NY 10023.

**Puffin Books,** see Penguin Putnam Inc.

**G. P. Putnam's Sons,** see Penguin Putnam Inc.

**Rand McNally,** P. O. Box 7600, Chicago, IL 60680.

**Random House Inc.,** 201 E. 50th St., New York, NY 10022. *http://www.randomhouse.com*

**Rizzoli International Publications, Inc.,** 300 Park Ave., South, New York, NY 10010.

**Scholastic Inc.,** 555 Broadway, New York, NY 10012. *http://www.scholastic.com*

**Charles Scribner's Sons,** see Simon & Schuster.

**Sierra Club Books for Children,** 100 Bush St., San Francisco, CA 94104.

**Silver Moon Press,** 126 Fifth Ave., Suite 803, New York, NY 10011.

**Silver Whistle,** see Harcourt Brace.

**Simon & Schuster Books for Young Readers,** 1230 Avenue of the Americas, New York, NY 10020. *http://www.SimonSaysKids.com*

**St. Martins' Press,** 175 5th Ave., S., New York, NY 10010.

**Steward, Tabori & Chang, Inc.,** 575 Broadway, New York, NY 10012.

**Tambourine Books,** see HarperCollins.

**Ticknor & Fields,** see Clarion.

**Tricycle Press,** P. O. Box 7123, Berkeley, CA 94707.

**Troll Associates,** 100 Corporate Dr., Mahwah, NJ 07430.

**Tundra Books,** 481 University Ave., #802, Toronto, Ontario M5G 2E9, Canada.

**Viking,** see Penguin Putnam Inc.

**Waldman,** 525 N. Third St., Minneapolis, MN 55401.

**Walker & Co.,** 435 Hudson St., New York, NY 10014.

**Frederick Warne & Co., Inc.,** see Penguin Putnam Inc.

**Franklin Watts, Inc.,** see Grolier Children's Publishing.

**Western,** see Golden Books.

**Winslow Press,** 770 E. Atlantic Ave., Ste. 201, Delray Beach, FL 33483. *http://www.winslowpress.com*

**Albert Whitman & Co.,** 6340 Oakton St., Morton Grove, IL 60053.

**Writers and Readers Publishing, Inc.,** 625 Broadway, New York, NY 10012.

## PAPERBACK BOOK CLUB ADDRESSES

**The Scholastic Book Clubs** [Firefly: Preschool–K; See Saw: K–1; Lucky: 2–3; Arrow: 4–6]: Scholastic, Inc., 730 Broadway, New York, NY 10003. *http://teacher.scholastic.com/bookclubs/catalog/catalogs.htm*

**The Troll Book Clubs:** Troll Associates, Inc., 100 Corporate Dr., Mahwah, NJ 07430. *http://www.troll.com/index.shtml*

# Name Index

# Subject Index